EQUITY AND THE LAW OF TRUSTS

EQUITY AND THE LAW OF TRUSTS

Tenth Edition

PHILIP H PETTIT MA

of the Middle Temple, Barrister

Emeritus Professor of Equity, Universities of Bristol and Buckingham

OXFORD

UNIVERSITY PRESS

OXFORD

UNIVERSITY PRESS

Great Clarendon Street, Oxford OX2 6DP

Oxford University Press is a department of the University of Oxford.
It furthers the University's objective of excellence in research, scholarship,
and education by publishing worldwide in

Oxford New York

Auckland Cape Town Dar es Salaam Hong Kong Karachi
Kuala Lumpur Madrid Melbourne Mexico City Nairobi
New Delhi Shanghai Taipei Toronto

With offices in

Argentina Austria Brazil Chile Czech Republic France Greece
Guatemala Hungary Italy Japan Poland Portugal Singapore
South Korea Switzerland Thailand Turkey Ukraine Vietnam

Oxford is a registered trade mark of Oxford University Press
in the UK and in certain other countries

Published in the United States
by Oxford University Press Inc., New York

British Library Cataloguing in Publication Data

Data available

Library of Congress Cataloging in Publication Data

Data available

Typeset in Minion
by RefineCatch Limited, Bungay, Suffolk
Printed in Great Britain
on acid-free paper by
Antony Rowe Limited, Chippenham, Wiltshire
ISBN 0–19–928534–9   978–0–19–928534–1

3 5 7 9 10 8 6 4

To Charles and Marguerite,
Richard and Claire

PREFACE

The publication of a tenth edition seems to be some sort of a milestone, and it is tempting to reflect on the changes in equity and the law of trusts since the first edition came out in 1966, and to consider how far these changes have kept up with the very considerable social and economic changes that have taken place during the last forty years. This would, however, demand more pages than would be appropriate in a preface and I shall accordingly restrict myself to drawing attention to the main developments which have occurred since the previous edition.

There has been no major legislation, such as the Trustee Act 2000 introduced in the previous edition, affecting the area of law covered in this book. Same sex marriages remain impossible in English law, but the Civil Partnership Act 2004, when brought into force, will in many respects assimilate the rights of same sex couples to those of married couples: it incorporates corresponding provisions to those in s 17 of the Married Women's Property Act 1882 (resolution of property disputes between husband and wife); s 37 of the Matrimonial Proceedings and Property Act 1970 (contributions to improvements to property); and Part 2 of the Matrimonial Causes Act 1973 (financial provision and property adjustment orders). It is thought that the 2004 Act will be brought into force on 5th December 2005.

The Mental Capacity Act 2005 was one of the last Acts to receive the Royal Assent before the prorogation of Parliament prior to the May 2005 election. When brought into force it will, inter alia, repeal the Enduring Powers of Attorney Act 1985 and introduce a lasting power of attorney to replace an enduring power of attorney. It is thought unlikely that it will be brought into force before 2007.

In relation to land, account has been taken of the Land Registration Act 2002 which repealed and replaced most of the earlier land registration legislation.

Had the Charities Bill reached the statute book it would have necessitated extensive amendments to the chapters on *Charitable Trusts* and *The Administration of Charities*, but it was lost on the prorogation of Parliament in April 2005. It would have provided a general statutory definition of charity for the purposes of the law for the first time, and would have made many significant changes in charity administration, including the creation of a Charity Appeal Tribunal to hear many appeals from decisions of the Charity Commission, now to be a body corporate replacing the Charity Commissioners, and the provision of a new legal form, the Charitable Incorporated Organisation, specifically to meet the needs of charities. The Bill resurfaced in the Queen's Speech in May and is almost certain to become law in the new session of Parliament.

Important cases reported since the last edition include the House of Lords decisions in *Twinsectra Ltd v Yardley* (the meaning of dishonesty in accessory liability, and *Quistclose* trusts) and *Royal Bank of Scotland v Etridge (No 2)* (undue influence); the Privy Council advice in *Schmidt v Rosewood Trust Ltd* (right of beneficiaries to trust information); and the Court of Appeal decisions in *Great Peace Shipping Ltd v*

Tsavliris Salvage (International) Ltd (disapproving *Solle v Butcher* in relation to rescission of a contract on the ground of mistake where that contract is valid and
enforceable on ordinary principles of contract law); *Pennington v Waine* (further
relaxation of the principles established in *Milroy v Lord*); *Customs and Excise Commissioners v Barclays Bank plc* (remedies where a bank mistakenly releases assets in breach
of an injunction); *Oxley v Hiscock* and *Jennings v Rice* (common intention constructive trusts and proprietary estoppel) and the *Douglas v Hello! Ltd* litigation, where the
Court of Appeal decision in May 2005 may well go to the House of Lords. Though
primarily concerned with breach of confidence and the right of privacy it has
importance in connection with the grant of injunctions.

I have endeavoured to state the law as mid-May 2005. It has been possible to
introduce a few minor additions at proof stage. I have continued with my policy of
citing selected cases from, and referring to periodicals published in, other common
law jurisdictions.

Those familiar with previous editions of this work may have observed that it is no
longer published under the Butterworths imprint and that it is now published by
Oxford University Press, which acquired Butterworths' academic law list in 2004.
There is no publisher to whom I would have preferred to be transferred. I enjoyed a
happy relationship with Butterworths for over 40 years. Clearly I cannot have so long
a relationship with the OUP (though hopefully the book will), but it has had an
equally happy start, and I would like to thank the OUP editorial staff for their efficiency in dealing with the project.

Philip H Pettit
July 2005

CONTENTS

TABLE OF STATUTES

TABLE OF CASES

ABBREVIATIONS

The following abbreviations have been used in relation to legal periodicals

AALR	Anglo American Law Review
Adel LR	Adelaide Law Review
Alberta LR	Alberta Law Review
ALJ	Australian Law Journal
All ER Rev	All England Law Reports Annual Review
Am JLH	American Journal of Legal History
ASCL	Annual Survey of Commonwealth Law
Auck ULR	Auckland University Law Review
Bond LR	Bond Law Review
BTR	British Tax Review
CBR	Canadian Bar Review
CC	Charity Commission leaflet
CJQ	Civil Justice Quarterly
CLJ	Cambridge Law Journal
CLP	Current Legal Problems
CLPR	Charity Law and Practice Review
CLY	Current Law Yearbook
Calif LR	California Law Review
Cambrian LR	Cambrian Law Review
Cant LR	Canterbury Law Review
CLWR	Common Law World Review
Co Law	Company Lawyer
Col LR	Columbian Law Review
Conv	Conveyancer and Property Lawyer (New Series)
Crim LR	Criminal Law Review
Dal LJ	Dalhousie Law Journal
Deak LR	Deakin Law Review
Dec Ch Com	Decisions of the Charity Commissioners
Denning LJ	Denning Law Journal
E & L	Education & the Law
EG	Estates Gazette
EHR	English Historical Review

ELJ	Education Law Journal
ET & PJ	Estates Trusts & Pensions Journal
Fam Law	Family Law
GLR	Griffiths Law Review
HLR	Harvard Law Review
ICLQ	International and Comparative Law Quarterly
Ind LJ	Industrial Law Journal
Ir Jur NS	Irish Jurist (New Series)
JBL	Journal of Business Law
JLH	Journal of Legal History
JMCL	Journal of Malaysian and Comparative Law
JPEL	Journal of Planning and Environmental Law
JSW & FL	Journal of Social Welfare and Family Law
Jur R	Juridical Review
KCLJ	Kings College Law Journal
Law Com CP	Law Commission Consultation Paper
Law Com No	Law Commission Report Number
LJ	Law and Justice
LMCLQ	Lloyd's Maritime and Commercial Law Quarterly
Lpool LR	Liverpool Law Review
LQR	Law Quarterly Review
LS	Legal Studies
LSG	Law Society's Gazette
L Teach	Law Teacher
McGill LJ	McGill Law Journal
Mal LR	Malaya Law Review
Man LJ	Manitoba Law Journal
Mich LR	Michigan Law Review
MLJ	Malaya Law Journal
MLR	Modern Law Review
Mon LR	Monash University Law Review
MULR	Melbourne University Law Review
New LR	Newcastle Law Review
NILQ	Northern Ireland Law Quarterly
Nott LJ	Nottingham Law Journal
NLJ	New Law Journal
NYULR	New York University Law Review

NZLJ	New Zealand Law Journal
NZULR	New Zealand Universities Law Review
OLR	Ottawa Law Review
Osg Hall LJ	Osgoode Hall Law Journal
Otago LR	Otago Law Review
Ox JLS	Oxford Journal of Legal Studies
PCB	Private Client Business
PLJ	Property Law Journal
Pub L	Public Law
QITLJ	Queensland Institute of Technology Law Journal
QLSJ	Queensland Law Society Journal
RLR	Restitution Law Review
RR	Review of the Register leaflet issued by the Charity Commission
S Ac LJ	Singapore Academy of Law Journal
SCLR	Supreme Court Law Review (Canada)
SJLS	Singapore Journal of Legal Studies
Sol Jo	Solicitor's Journal
Stat LR	Statute Law Review
Sydney LR	Sydney Law Review
T & ELJ	Trusts & Estates Law Journal
T & ELTJ	Trusts & Estates Law & Tax Journal
TL & P	Trust Law and Practice
Tru LI	Trust Law International
Tulane LR	Tulane Law Review
UBCLR	University of British Columbia Law Review
UNSWLJ	University of New South Wales Law Journal
U Penn LR	University of Pennsylvania Law Review
UQLJ	University of Queensland Law Journal
UT Fac L Rev	University of Toronto Faculty Law Review
U Tas LR	University of Tasmania Law Review
UTLJ	University of Toronto Law Journal
UWALR	University of Western Australia Law Review
VUWLR	Victoria University of Wellington Law Review
WILJ	West Indies Law Journal
Yale LJ	Yale Law Journal

Case references: Where footnote references to English cases decided since the Judicature Acts are not followed by an indication of the court in which they were decided, it can be assumed that the decision was at first instance in the High Court.

Reports: In Chapters 13 and 14 the 'Reports' referred to are the annual reports of the Charity Commissioners for England and Wales, presented in pursuance of s 1(5) of the Charities Act 1993 replacing identical provisions in the Charities Act 1960.

1

HISTORY OF THE COURT OF CHANCERY AND INTRODUCTION TO EQUITY

1 HISTORY OF THE COURT OF CHANCERY[1]

If law be regarded in general terms as the rules enforced in the courts for the promotion of justice,[2] equity may be described as that part of the law which immediately[3] prior to the coming into force of the Supreme Court of Judicature Acts 1873 and 1875[4] on 1 November 1875 was enforced exclusively in the Court of Chancery, and not at all in the Courts of Common Law—Common Pleas, Exchequer and King's Bench. Although in origin the jurisdiction of the Court of Chancery was undoubtedly based on moral principles designed to remove injustices incapable of being dealt with in the common law courts, equity was always, at least until the Judicature Acts, essentially a supplementary jurisdiction, an appendix or gloss on the common law.[5] In some sense this remains the case although developments in equitable doctrine since that date have been said to render the description of equity as an appendix to the common law 'an utterly misleading statement of equity's place in the scheme of things today'.[6] It is accordingly not really possible to define it successfully; it can only be described by giving an inventory of its contents or in the historical terms set out above.

The position at the end of the thirteenth century, even after the last of the three common law courts to evolve out of the Curia Regis had become separate, was that a

---

[1] For a fuller account see Holdsworth, *History of English Law*, vol 1, p 395 et seq; Potter's *Historical Introduction to English Law*, 4th edn, p 152 et seq; Kerly, *History of Equity*, and also Milson, *Historical Foundations of the Common Law*, 2nd edn, p 82 et seq.

[2] This begs the real question, what is justice? which is, however, outside the scope of this book, being a question for jurisprudence and philosophy. Of course, in practice, many matters that justice would demand are not enforced in the courts for various reasons, many being unsuitable for judicial enforcement, and some of the rules enforced fail to achieve justice either generally or in a particular case.

[3] Before 1842 the Court of Exchequer had an equity jurisdiction. The statement following in the text relates to the central courts and disregards the Palatine Courts (abolished by the Courts Act 1971) and the County Courts.

[4] Now replaced by the Supreme Court Act 1981.

[5] Maitland, *Equity*, 2nd (Brunyate) edn, p 18. See also (1997) 113 LQR 601 (A J Duggan).

[6] See (1994) 110 LQR 238 (A Mason).

residuum of justice was still thought to reside in the King. If, therefore, the common
law courts for any reason failed to do justice, an aggrieved person might petition the
King or the King's Council. From early times these petitions seeking the King's extraordinary justice seem to have been referred to the Chancellor, and as early as the reign
of Edward I petitions are to be found addressed to the 'Chancellor and the Council'.
This procedure steadily became more frequent, and by the end of the fourteenth
century petitions began to be addressed to the Chancellor alone. However they were
addressed, the petitions were in fact dealt with by the Chancellor, though at first
purely as a delegate of the Council. As the practice became habitual and references
frequent, the Chancellor and his office the Chancery, acquired the characteristics of a
court, though so far as is known it was not until 1474 that the Chancellor made a
decree upon his own authority.[7]

The cases referred to the Chancellor and the Chancery fall into two main groups,
first, cases where the law was defective, and secondly, those where there was theoretic-
ally a remedy at common law, but the petitioner was unable to obtain it because of the
disturbed state of the country, or the power and wealth of the other party, who might
be able to put improper pressure on the jury or even the court. For a long time[8] the
latter was the most important and frequent type of case to be dealt with. In exercising
jurisdiction in cases of this kind it is unlikely that the Chancellor regarded himself as
administering a separate system of law—indeed he was not. It was a jurisdiction which
was a cause of considerable complaint and it may well be that the Chancellor's powers
would have disappeared at about the end of the fourteenth century if it had not been
for the other head of jurisdiction, which must now be considered.

During the early period of growth of the common law, there was rapid development as new writs were created to meet new cases, and, moreover, the common law
judges had a wide discretion to do justice, particularly in the informal procedure by
plaint or bill (as opposed to actions begun by writ), and in proceedings in the General
Eyre. At first, therefore, there was little scope for a jurisdiction to remedy the defects of
the common law. However, this early rapid development ceased with the Provisions of
Oxford in 1258, and only proceeded slowly after the controversial[9] *in consimili casu*
clause of the Statute of Westminster the Second in 1285, so that it is fair to say that by
the end of the thirteenth century the common law formed a rigid system which was
unadaptable, or at least could only be slowly adapted, to meet new types of case.
Moreover plaints without writ, for reasons which are not fully explained, apparently

---

[7] Though he seems to have dismissed a petition without consulting the Council nearly a century before.
For a discussion of an early Tudor debate on the relation between law and equity see (1998) 19 JLH 143
(G Behrens).

[8] The change seems to have taken place during the reign of Henry VI. The business of the Court
of Chancery multiplied three times between 1420 and 1450, by which time nine-tenths of its work was
concerned with uses—see (1970) 86 LQR 84 (Margaret E Avery).

[9] See (1931) 31 Col LR 778 (T F T Plucknett); (1931) 47 LQR 334 (W S Holdsworth); (1936) 52 LQR 68
(P A Landon); (1936) 52 LQR 220 (T F T Plucknett); (1937) 46 Yale LJ 1142 (Elizabeth Dix); Fifoot, *History
and Sources of the Common Law*, p 66 et seq; Kiralfy, *The Action on the Case*, p 19 et seq; J H Baker, *An
Introduction to English Legal History*, 4th edn, p 61 et seq.

ceased to be available in the fourteenth century, and at about the same time General Eyres virtually ceased to be held. Consequently hardship increasingly often arose because of defects in the law, and petitions began to be brought on this ground. In giving relief in these cases new law was being created, and it was this new law which became known as 'equity' in contrast to the 'common law' dispensed in the common law courts.[10]

For a long time there was close consultation between the Chancellor and the common law judges as to the types of case in which relief should be granted. This reduced the risk of conflict from the point of view of personalities; and from the point of view of principle, conflict between the jurisdictions was reduced by the fact that it was a cardinal rule of the Court of Chancery that equity acts in personam. Thus in the central institution of equity jurisdiction, the trust, the Chancellor never denied that the trustee was the legal owner of the trust property, but merely insisted that the trustee should deal with it in accordance with the trust for the benefit of the beneficiaries. This remains the law today. Thus Scott J recently observed:[11] 'The jurisdiction of the court to administer trusts . . . is an in personam jurisdiction.' Failure to comply with the Chancellor's order would be a contempt of court, which was punishable by imprisonment until the trustee was prepared to comply with the order. Originally this procedure in personam, against the person of the defendant, was the only process of the Court of Chancery for enforcing its decrees.[12]

None the less conflict did arise in the sixteenth century as the Chancellor extended and consolidated his jurisdiction, and the dispute centred on what became known as 'common injunctions' issued by the Chancellor restraining parties to an action at common law either from proceeding with their action at law, or, having obtained judgment, from enforcing it. The dispute finally came to a head under James I, when Coke was Chief Justice and Ellesmere Lord Chancellor. The validity or invalidity of these injunctions would, it was recognized, determine the question whether legal supremacy was vested in the common law courts or the Chancery. The matter was referred by the King to Bacon, the Attorney-General, and other counsel, and in due course he accepted their advice that the injunctions were valid and in 1616 accordingly issued an order in favour of the Chancery. This proved to be a final settlement of the dispute, although it was not fully accepted by the common lawyers until the end of the century.

From a broad point of view the settlement did not prove altogether satisfactory by reason of the defects which grew up in the Court of Chancery during the latter part of

---

[10] In addition to the equitable jurisdiction known as the 'English side' simply because the pleadings were in the native language, there was the relatively unimportant and largely separate 'Latin side' of the jurisdiction, so called because the records were kept in Latin. This comprised certain specialized matters such as questions relating to royal grants and inquisitions relating to the Crown's property rights, and the ordinary common law jurisdiction in personal actions brought by or against officers of the court.

[11] *Chellaram v Chellaram* [1985] 1 All ER 1043 at 1053.

[12] Sequestration was introduced towards the end of the sixteenth century and now there are various powers for the court to make vesting orders, etc, see eg Trustee Act 1925, ss 44 et seq; Supreme Court Act 1981, s 39.

the seventeenth and the eighteenth century. There was corruption and abuse of the process of the court,[13] an inadequate number of judicial staff, too many and incompetent officials, an over-elaborate system of rehearing and appeals and a generally unsatisfactory organization which led to such expense, delays and injustice that the business of the court declined. After piecemeal reforms beginning with the appointment of a Vice-Chancellor in 1813, and becoming much more numerous after the Whig victory in 1830, the Court of Chancery finally ceased to exist as a separate court as a result of the major reorganization of the whole judicial system by the Judicature Acts 1873 and 1875. Its jurisdiction was transferred to the Supreme Court of Judicature, most of the jurisdiction at first instance being assigned to the Chancery Division of the High Court.

It should be added in conclusion that limited jurisdiction in equity matters is given to the county courts, the relevant statute now being the County Courts Act 1984.[14]

2 JURISDICTION OF THE COURT OF CHANCERY

Originally, as we have seen, the Chancellor did not have any clearly defined jurisdiction, but dispensed an extraordinary justice remedying the defects of the common law on grounds of conscience[15] and natural justice, a function for which he was well qualified as he was commonly an ecclesiastic, well versed in both the civil and canon law. He was indeed sometimes called the 'Keeper of the King's Conscience'. In the absence of fixed principles the decision at first depended to a large degree upon the Chancellor's personal ideas of right and wrong; thus Selden,[16] in the mid-seventeenth century, observed that equity varied according to the conscience of the individual Chancellor in the same way as if the standard measure were a Chancellor's foot. This state of affairs began to be less true in the later seventeenth century as the principles of equity began to become more fixed. Cases in the Chancery began to be reported around the middle of the century and were increasingly cited, relied on and followed in subsequent cases. The Chancellors began to say that although they had a discretion it should be exercised not according to conscience but in accordance with precedent.[17]

---

[13] The Chancery became very ready to issue injunctions by reason of the profits which thereby accrued, and litigants were able to use them purely as delaying tactics. See (1988) 11 UNSWLJ 11 (C J Rossiter & Margaret Stone).

[14] Section 23 and SI 1981/1123. So far as the estates of deceased persons and trusts are concerned, there is jurisdiction where the estate or fund subject to the trust does not exceed in amount or value the sum of £30,000. There is unlimited jurisdiction in certain equity proceedings (but excluding proceedings under the Variation of Trusts Act 1958) by written consent of the parties under s 24, as amended by the Courts and Legal Services Act 1990, s 125(3), Sch 18, para 49(3).

[15] See (2001) 46 McGill LJ 573 (D R Klinck) for an interesting account of the meaning of conscience in early equity, its development from the fifteenth to the nineteenth century and its position in current Canadian equity.

[16] *Table Talk of John Selden* (ed Pollock 1927), p 43.

[17] See an article entitled 'Precedent in Equity' in (1941) 57 LQR 245 (W H D Winder).

Lawyers rather than ecclesiastics became appointed Chancellors, the last of the non-legal Chancellors being Lord Shaftesbury, who held office during 1672–73. With his successor, Lord Nottingham (1673–82), often called the father of modern equity, the development of a settled system of equity really began, to be continued under succeeding Chancellors, notably Lord Hardwicke (1736–56), and completed in the early nineteenth century by Lord Eldon (1801–06 and 1807–27). The result of their work was to transform equity into a system of law almost as fixed and rigid as the rules of the common law. Accordingly Lord Eldon could observe[18] 'Nothing would inflict on me greater pain, in quitting this place,[19] than the recollection that I had done anything to justify the reproach that the equity of this court varies like the Chancellor's foot', and it has since been bluntly stated[20] that 'This Court is not a Court of conscience'. By the early nineteenth century, equity, as stated in the opening sentence of this book, had become simply that part of the law enforced in the Court of Chancery.

A related matter is whether it is any longer open to equity to invent new equitable interests. Though there is no fiction in equity as there has been said to be at common law that the rules have existed from time immemorial,[21] and though 'it is perfectly well known that they have been established from time to time—altered, improved and refined from time to time. In many cases we know the names of the Chancellors who invented them',[22] yet it is in principle doubtful whether a new right can now be created. Extra-judicially Lord Evershed observed[23] that s 25(11)[24] of the Judicature Act 1873 put a stop to, or at least a very severe limitation on, the inventive faculties of future Chancery judges, and Lord Denning said, again extra-judicially,[25] that 'the Courts of Chancery are no longer courts of equity. . . . They are as fixed and immutable as the courts of law ever were.' The Court of Appeal, moreover, has observed[26] that if a 'claim in equity exists, it must be shown to have an ancestry founded in history and in the practice and precedents of the courts administering equity jurisdiction. It is not sufficient that because we may think that the "justice" of the present case requires it, we should invent such a jurisdiction for the first time', and again, more recently, that 'the creation of new rights and remedies is a matter for Parliament, not

---

[18] In *Gee v Pritchard* (1818) 2 Swans 402 at 414.   [19] Ie the Court of Chancery.

[20] Per Buckley J in *Re Telescriptor Syndicate Ltd* [1903] 2 Ch 174 at 195, 196.

[21] This has been said to be a fairy tale in which no one any longer believes. In truth, judges make and change the law. The whole of the common law is judge-made and only by judicial change in the law is the common law kept relevant in a changing world. See *Kleinwort Benson Ltd v Lincoln City Council* [1998] 4 All ER 513, HL, esp per Lord Browne-Wilkinson at 518, and Lord Goff at 534, 535.

[22] Per Jessel MR in *Re Hallett's Estate* (1880) 13 Ch D 696 at 710, CA—said, however, to be 'rather an overstatement' by Lord Evershed in the 1954 Lionel Cohen Lectures entitled 'Aspects of English Equity', p 13.

[23] (1953) 6 CLP 11, 12.

[24] This sub-section is discussed at p 8, post. Lord Evershed's point is that the sub-section necessarily proceeded upon the view that the rules of equity were then a known body of established doctrine.

[25] (1952) 5 CLP 8.

[26] *Re Diplock* [1948] Ch 465 at 481, 482, [1948] 2 All ER 318 at 326. CA; affd sub nom *Ministry of Health v Simpson* [1951] AC 251, [1950] 2 All ER 1137, HL; *Thompson v Earthy* [1951] 2 KB 596, [1951] 2 All ER 235.

the judges'.[27] Further, so far as an equitable interest in land is concerned, s 4(1) of the Law of Property Act 1925 provides that after 1925 such an interest is only capable of being validly created in any case in which an equivalent equitable interest in property real or personal could have been created before 1926.[28] In principle, it is very doubtful, therefore, whether new equitable interests can any longer be created, except through the extension and development of existing equitable interests by exactly the same process as extension and development may take place at law. As to that process an Australian judge has observed,[29] 'It is inevitable that judge made law will alter to meet the changing conditions of society. That is the way it has always evolved. But it is essential that new rules should be related to fundamental doctrine. If the foundations of accepted doctrine be submerged under new principles, without regard to the inter-action between the two, there will be high uncertainty as to the state of the law, both old and new.'

The proper approach is, it is submitted, that stated by Bagnall J in *Cowcher v Cowcher*,[30] who said:

I am convinced that in determining rights, particularly property rights, the only justice that can be attained by mortals, who are fallible and are not omniscient, is justice according to law; the justice which flows from the application of sure and settled principles to proved or admitted facts. So in the field of equity the length of the Chancellor's foot has been meas-ured or is capable of measurement. This does not mean that equity is past child-bearing;[31] simply that its progeny must be legitimate—by precedent out of principle. It is well that this should be so; otherwise no lawyer could safely advise on his client's title and every quarrel would lead to a law suit.

Of recent years some common law lawyers have sought to give equity a much wider and less precise jurisdiction. Such a development is, it is submitted, not only contrary to precedent and the historical development of equity, but is undesirable for the reasons given by Bagnall J, and unnecessary by reason of the improvements in the machinery for law reform[32] which enable defects in the law to be corrected by legisla-tion more rapidly than in the past.

It is convenient to mention briefly at this point that one distinction between the common law and equity lay in the remedies available. In general the only remedy available at common law, apart from a real action for the specific recovery of certain interests in land,[33] was damages, and a plaintiff who established his right and the

---

[27] Per Megaw LJ giving the judgment of the court in *Western Fish Products Ltd v Penwith District Council* [1981] 2 All ER 204 at 218, CA.

[28] See (1952) 16 Conv 323 (F R Crane).

[29] *Allen v Snyder* [1977] 2 NSWLR 685 at 689, per Glass J A. See also *Lonrho plc v Fayed (No 2)* [1991] 4 All ER 961, [1992] 1 WLR 1 at 969, 9, per Millett J; *Kleinwort Benson Ltd v Lincoln City Council*, supra, HL.

[30] [1972] 1 All ER 943 at 948; *Harris v Digital Pulse Property Ltd* (2003) 197 ALR 626.

[31] But in [1982] Cambrian LR 24, Goulding J said extrajudicially that whether or not equity is past child-bearing, she ought to be!

[32] In particular the establishment of the Law Commission.

[33] See Cheshire and Burn, *Modern Law of Real Property*, 16th edn, p 26; Holdsworth, *History of English Law*, vol 3, p 3 et seq.

breach of it by the defendant was entitled to this remedy as a matter of right, no matter how little merit there might seem to be in his claim. Equity, on the other hand, had no power,[34] until Statute intervened,[35] to award damages at all, though in some circumstances it might award monetary compensation for breach of trust or the infraction of a fiduciary duty.[36] However it invented a variety of remedies, the grant of which is always in the discretion of the court; the most important are specific performance and injunction. As we shall see, these are orders in personam directing a person to do or not to do some specified thing, and disobedience of such an order is a contempt of court. An equitable remedy may be awarded both to enforce a right recognized only in equity, and also to enforce a legal right, though this will only be done where the common law remedy of damages is regarded as inadequate.

3   FUSION OF THE ADMINISTRATION OF LAW AND EQUITY

The reorganization of the courts carried out by the Judicature Acts 1873 and 1875 produced one Supreme Court administering both law and equity. Though for the sake of convenience the High Court, dealing with cases at first instance, was divided into divisions,[37] every judge of each division was, by s 24[38] of the 1873 Act, given the power and duty to recognize and give effect to both legal and equitable rights, claims, defences and remedies. Further, by s 25, provision was made for situations where the rules of law and equity were in conflict. After dealing specifically with a number of particular cases, it was provided[39] in general terms that in all other cases in which there was a conflict or variance between the rules of equity and the rules of common law with reference to the same matter, the rules of equity should prevail.

---

[34] Or, if it had, which is, perhaps, the better view, from a very early time considered it to be ordinarily undesirable to exercise it. See (1992) 109 LQR 652 (P M McDermott), a revised version of which appears in his book *Equitable Damages*, ch 1, and p 522 infra. Extrajudicially Lord Millett has said that 'damages for breach of trust' (or fiduciary duty) is a misleading expression the use of which should be stamped out: (1998) 114 LQR 214. See also (1999) 37 Alberta LR 95 (J Berryman); (1999) 37 Alberta LR 114 (P M Perell).

[35] Lord Cairns' Act (Chancery Amendment Act 1858). Note that the remedy of damages is available in cases of breach of confidence, 'despite the equitable nature of the wrong, through a beneficent interpretation of Lord Cairns' Act' (as to which see p 580 et seq, post): *A-G v Guardian Newspapers Ltd (No 2)* [1990] 1 AC 109 at 286, [1988] 3 All ER 545 at 662, per Lord Goff, HL. See *Seager v Copydex Ltd* [1967] 2 All ER 415, [1967] 1 WLR 923, CA.

[36] In Australia it has been said to be 'an equitable monetary remedy which is available when the equitable remedies of restitution and account are not appropriate': *O'Halloran v R T Thomas and Family Property Ltd* (1998) 45 NSWLR 262; and see *Duke Group Ltd (in liq) v Pilmer* (1999) 153 Fed LR 1 at p 165 et seq and on appeal sub nom *Pilmer v Duke Group (in liq)* (2001) 180 ALR 249: See (1982) 13 MULR 349 (I E Davidson); *Day v Mead* [1987] 2 NZLR 443, noted (1989) 105 LQR 32 (Margaret Vennell); (1993) 67 ALJ 596 (L Aitken); (1994) 24 VUWLR 19 (C Rickett and T Gardner). See p 522 infra.

[37] Originally five, now three, namely, Chancery, Queen's Bench, and Family Divisions.

[38] Now replaced by s 49 of the Supreme Court Act 1981.

[39] Judicature Act 1873, s 25(11), now replaced by s 49 of the Supreme Court Act 1981.

(a) THE EFFECT OF SS 24 AND 25[40]

Before the Judicature Acts there were cases where common law and equity had different rules which might give rise to inconsistent remedies. In such cases the equitable rule would ultimately prevail by means of the grant of a common injunction.[41] Section 24(5) abolished the common injunction, but even without this the result in any particular case would have been the same as before the Act in litigation in the High Court, because, as we have seen, every judge was bound to have regard to all equitable rights, claims, defences and remedies.

Curious as it was that prior to the Acts there should have been different rules relating to the same subject matter in different courts, it would have been even more strange if these conflicting rules had continued to exist when both were being administered in the same court, notwithstanding provisions as to which rule should prevail. What s 25(11) does, after dealing with particular cases, is to provide that in all courts where there are conflicting rules, in the sense referred to above, the legal rule is abolished and the equitable rule is to replace it for all purposes. The court in such cases has henceforward only one rule to enforce.

It should be stressed that in many cases there were differences between the rules of common law and equity which did not result in conflict and to which ss 24 and 25 had no application. Thus, for example:

(i)   The common law would award damages for breach of a voluntary contract made by deed, or for breach of a contract of personal service,[42] but in neither case was a remedy available in equity. Equity would not however restrain a plaintiff from obtaining his common law remedy.

(ii) In some cases common law and equity might give different but compatible remedies. For instance, in a case of nuisance common law would give damages for the injury suffered by the plaintiff, while equity would grant an injunction restraining further commission of the tort.

(iii) In relation to the tort of conversion, this was a common law cause of action and the common law did not recognize the equitable title of the beneficiary under a trust. It recognized only the title of the trustee, as the person normally entitled to immediate possession of the trust property. An equitable owner had no title at common law to sue in conversion, unless he could also show that he had actual possession or an immediate right to possession of the goods claimed.[43] Again, the House of Lords has rejected as insupportable the proposition that 'a person who has the equitable ownership of goods is entitled to

---

[40] See, generally, Maitland, *Equity*, 2nd (Brunyate) edn, p 16–20, 149–159; Meagher, Gummow and Lehane, *Equity—Doctrines and Remedies*, 3rd edn, p 36 et seq; (1975) 39 Cony 1 & 236 (J T Farrand and P Jackson); (1982) 26 Am JLH 227 (D O'Keefe).

[41] See p 3 supra and p 626, infra.   [42] See chapter 29, section 2(c) infra.

[43] *MCC Proceeds Inc v Lehman Bros International (Europe)* [1998] 4 All ER 675, CA.

sue in tort for negligence anyone who for want of care causes them to be lost or damaged without joining the legal owner as a party to the action'.[44]

Such cases remain unaffected by the Judicature Acts.

Reverting to s 25(11), this provision was applied in *Berry v Berry*[45] to prevent a wife succeeding in an action on a separation deed. The deed had been varied by a simple contract, which was no defence to an action at law, but the equitable rule was that such a variation is effective, and that rule prevailed. Again in *Walsh v Lonsdale*[46] there was an agreement for a lease of a mill for seven years at a rent payable quarterly in arrears, with a provision entitling the landlord to demand a year's rent in advance. No formal lease was ever executed and the lease as such was accordingly void at law.[47] The tenant entered into possession and paid rent quarterly in arrears for some 18 months, when a year's rent was demanded in advance. On failure to pay, the landlord dis-trained and the action was for damages for illegal distress. The tenant contended that having gone into possession and paid by reference to a year he was a yearly tenant upon such of the terms of the agreement as were not inconsistent with the yearly tenancy, that the provision for payment of a year's rent was inconsistent, that the landlord accordingly was not entitled to make the demand and the distress was unlawful. This argument represented the common law view before 1875. The court, however, held that the equitable view must prevail, namely that this being an agree-ment of which specific performance would be granted, the rights and liabilities of the parties must be ascertained as if the lease had actually been executed containing all the agreed terms.[48]

(b) FUSION OF LAW AND EQUITY OR MERELY FUSION OF THEIR ADMINISTRATION

The orthodox view is that there has merely been a fusion of administration, 'the two streams of jurisdiction, though they run in the same channel, run side by side and do

---

[44] *Leigh and Sillivan Ltd v Aliakmon Shipping Co Ltd* [1986] 1 AC 1, 14.

[45] [1929] 2 KB 316, DC. For other examples see *Job v Job* (1877) 6 Ch D 562; *Lowe v Dixon* (1885) 16 QBD 455. See also *Raineri v Miles* [1981] AC 1050 [1980] 2 All ER 145, HL.

[46] (1882) 21 Ch D 9, CA. Dicta of Jessel MR in this case which appear to suggest that the distinction between legal and equitable interests has been abolished are misleading. See Megarry and Wade, *Law of Real Property*, 6th edn, p 773 et seq stressing that the doctrine of *Walsh v Lonsdale* depends upon the availability of specific performance, and contrast the same judge's orthodox statement of the position in *Salt v Cooper* (1880) 16 Ch D 544 at 549, CA. His decision was affirmed on appeal without comment on his remarks on this point. See also (1987) 7 Ox JLS 60 (S Gardner); *Chan v Cresdon Pty Ltd* (1989) 168 CLR 242, 89 ALR 522.

[47] Section 3 of the Real Property Act 1845, now replaced by s 52(1) of the Law of Property Act 1925.

[48] The principle of *Walsh v Lonsdale*, supra, has been held to be applicable twice, eg where V agrees to sell the fee simple to P, who agrees to grant a lease thereof to T—*Industrial Properties (Barton Hill) Ltd v Associated Electrical Industries Ltd* [1977] QB 580, [1977] 2 All ER 293, CA. See Maitland, *Equity*, 2nd (Brunyate) edn, p 16–18, and contrast Hohfeld, *Fundamental Legal Conceptions*, p 121 et seq.

not mingle their waters'.[49] More recently the view has been expressed that law and
equity themselves are fused.[50] This view has been put most clearly and most authori-
tatively by Lord Diplock in *United Scientific Holdings Ltd v Burnley Borough Council.*[51]
He said:

My Lords, if by 'rules of equity' is meant that body of substantive and adjectival law, that
prior to 1875, was administered by the Court of Chancery but not by courts of common law,
to speak of the rules of equity as being part of the law of England in 1977 is about as
meaningful as to speak similarly of the statutes of Uses or of Quia Emptores. Historically all
three have in their time played an important part in the development of the corpus juris into
what it is today; but to perpetuate a dichotomy between rules of equity and rules of common law which it was a major purpose of the Supreme Court of Judicature Act 1873 to do
away with, is, in my view, conducive to erroneous conclusions as to the ways in which the
law of England has developed in the last 100 years.

It is respectfully submitted that these propositions cannot be accepted. Baker has
pointed out[52] that no one thinks that the rules of equity have remained unchanged
since 1875—they have developed in the same way as rules of common law. As to the
comparison with Quia Emptores, Baker observes that this is still in force today and is
said to be 'one of the pillars of the law of real property'.[53] Most importantly it is a
complete misapprehension to think that it was a purpose of the Judicature Acts to do
away with the dichotomy between rules of equity and rules of common law. Introducing the second reading the Attorney-General said[54] in terms that 'The Bill was not
one for the fusion of law and equity' and he went on to explain what the purpose of
the Bill was:

The defect of our legal system was, not that Law and Equity existed, but that if a man went
for relief to a Court of Law, and an equitable claim or an equitable defence arose, he must go
to some other Court and begin afresh. Law and Equity therefore, would remain if the Bill
passed, but they would be administered concurrently, and no one would be sent to get in one
Court the relief which another Court had refused to give. . . . Great authorities had no doubt
declared that law and Equity might be fused by enactment; but in his opinion, to do so
would be to decline to grapple with the real difficulty of the case. If an Act were passed doing
no more than fuse law and Equity, it would take 20 years of decisions and hecatombs of
suitors to make out what Parliament meant and had not taken the trouble to define. It was
more philosophical to admit the innate distinction between Law and Equity, which you

---

[49] Ashburner's *Principles of Equity*, 2nd edn, p 18; (1954) 70 LQR 326 (Lord Evershed); (1961) 24 MLR
116 (V T H Delaney); Snell's *Principles of Equity*, 30th edn, p 11; Megarry and Wade, *Law of Real Property*,
6th edn, p 103; (1977) 93 LQR 529 (P V Baker); (1977) 6 AALR 119 (T G Watkin). See (1993) 5 Cant LR 299
(Julie Maxton); (2003) 26 UNSWLJ 357 (M Tilbury).
[50] Per Lord Denning in *Errington v Errington* [1952] 1 KB 290 at 298, [1952] 1 All ER 149 at 155, CA.
A case for integration is made in [2002] CLP 223 (Sarah Worthington).
[51] [1977] 2 All ER 62 at 68, HL. See also Lord Simon at 83, 84 and *Canson Enterprises Ltd v Boughton & Co*
(1991) 85 DLR (4th) 129.
[52] (1977) 93 LQR 529.   [53] Megarry and Wade, *Law of Real Property*, 6th edn, p 29.
[54] Hansard 3rd Series vol 216, 644, 645. See to the same effect *Salt v Cooper* (1880) 16 Ch D 544 at 549, per
Jessel MR; (1995) 9 Tru LI 35, 37 (Lord Millett).

could not get rid of by Act of Parliament, and to say not that the distinction should not exist, but that the Courts should administer relief according to legal principles when these applied, or else according to equitable principles. That was what the Bill proposed, with the addition that, whenever the principles of Law and Equity conflicted, equitable principles should prevail.

The orthodox view was recently reasserted by Mummery LJ[55] who observed that the Judicature Acts 'were intended to achieve procedural improvements in the administration of law and equity in all courts, not to transform equitable interests into legal titles or to sweep away altogether the rules of the common law, such as the rule that a plaintiff in an action for conversion must have possession or a right to immediate possession of the goods'.

Though it is clear that the decision in a case may well depend upon an amalgam of rules from both common law and equity, as in *Walsh v Lonsdale*,[56] and though on a broader canvas one may regard the law of real property, for instance, as an amalgam of statute, common law and equity, it is accordingly submitted that to talk of the fusion of law and equity is misleading. The facts, inter alia, that the trust has been unaffected and there is still duality of legal and equitable ownership,[57] that in the law of property legal rights and equitable rights, even though for some purposes equivalent as in *Walsh v Lonsdale*, may have different effects, for instance as regards third parties, that purely equitable rights can still only be enforced by equitable remedies,[58] and that the writ ne exeat regno is only available in relation to an equitable debt,[59] are inconsistent with the idea conveyed by the phrase 'fusion of law and equity'. Also the language of s 49 of the Supreme Court Act 1981, which replaces s 25(11) of the Judicature Act 1873, appears to assume the continued separate existence of rules of equity and rules of the common law.

Those who refer to the fusion of law and equity commonly make little effort to explain precisely what they mean by the phrase, nor do they deal with the arguments set out above. Recently, moreover, Lord Browne-Wilkinson was careful to refer to the fusion of the administration of law and equity,[60] and Lord Millett, writing

---

[55] In *MCC Proceeds Inc v Lehman Bros International (Europe)* [1998] 4 All ER 675, CA, at 691.

[56] (1882) 21 Ch D 9, CA.

[57] See *Joseph v Lyons* (1884) 15 QBD 280, 287, per Lindley LJ cited by Mummery LJ in *MCC Proceeds Inc v Lehman Bros International (Europe)*, supra, CA, at 691.

[58] Thus an equitable owner cannot purely as such sue in conversion: *MCC Proceeds Inc v Lehman Bros International (Europe)*, CA, supra. Now, however, there is statutory power for the court to award damages in lieu of or in addition to an injunction or specific performance—Supreme Court Act 1981, s 50. See [1996] CLJ 36 (A Tettenborn).

[59] See p 729, post.

[60] In *Tinsley v Milligan* [1993] 3 All ER 65 at 86, 90, HL: his reference to 'the fusion of law and equity' in *Lord Napier and Ettrick v Hunter* [1993] 1 All ER 385, [1993] 2 WLR 42, HL, at 406, 408; 65, 66, can, perhaps, be regarded as a loose shorthand. See, generally, (1993) 5 Bond LR 152 (Fiona Burns); (1994) 110 LQR 260 (A Mason); [1994] Conv 13 (Jill Martin); (2002) 22 Ox JLS 1 (A Burrows).

extrajudicially,[61] has observed that the opinion that the Judicature Acts had the effect of fusing law and equity to the extent that they have become a single body of law rather than two separate systems of law administered together is now widely discredited. He referred with approval to the view of a New Zealand judge[62] that: 'Neither law nor equity is now stifled by its origin and the fact that both are administered by one court has inevitably meant that each has borrowed from the other in furthering the harmonious development of the law as a whole.'

4 USES AND TRUSTS

(a) HISTORY OF THE TRUST

Maitland called[63] the trust 'the greatest and most distinctive achievement performed by Englishmen in the field of jurisprudence'. It is the outstanding creation of equity. Under a trust, in the most general terms, trustees, who get no benefit therefrom, are required to hold property of which they are the legal owners for the benefit of other persons, the cestuis que trust or beneficiaries.

Even before the Conquest cases have been found of land being conveyed to one man to be held by him on behalf of or 'to the use of[64] another, but for a considerable time this only seems to have been done for a limited time and a limited purpose, such as for the grantor's family while he went on a crusade. From the early thirteenth century the practice grew up of conveying land in a general way for more permanent purposes. For various reasons a landowner might convey land by an ordinary common law conveyance to persons called 'feoffees[65] to uses' directing them to hold the land for the benefit of other persons, the cestuis que use, who might indeed be or include the feoffor himself. After early doubts the common law refused to take any account of the uses, that is, the directions given to the feoffees to uses, who, though they were bound in honour, could not be sued either by the feoffor or the cestuis que use. The common law in fact treated the feoffees to uses as the unfettered owners of the property, and completely disregarded the claims of the cestuis que use.

It was clearly highly unsatisfactory that feoffees to uses should be able to disregard

---

[61] (1995/96) 6 KCLJ 1, reprinted (1995) 9 Tru LI 35. Hayton & Marshall, *Law of Trusts and Equitable Remedies*, 11th edn, p 14, say that it is a fallacy to assume that law and equity have been fused into a new body of principles.

[62] Somers J in *Elders Pastoral Ltd v Bank of New Zealand* [1989] 2 NZLR 180, 193.

[63] *Selected Historical Essays* 129 (1936). There is no institution quite like the trust in civil law systems based on Roman law—see (1974) 48 Tulane LR 917 (J H Merryman). See also (1980) 25 McGill LJ 42 (Yves Caron) on the trust in Quebec, and W A Wilson (ed), *Trusts and Trust-like Devices*, [1997] CLJ 175 (N G Jones).

[64] From the Latin ad opus—Pollock and Maitland, *History of English Law*, 2nd edn, vol 2, p 228.

[65] The mode of conveyance was normally feoffment with livery of seisin, and the person conveying the land was accordingly the feoffor, the person receiving it the feoffee.

the dictates of good faith, honour and justice with impunity,[66] and from the end of the fourteenth or the early fifteenth century[67] the Chancellor began to intervene and compel the feoffees to uses to carry out the directions given to them as to how they should deal with the land. The Chancellor never, however, denied that the feoffees to uses were the legal owners of the land. He merely ordered the feoffees to uses to carry out the directions given to them, and failure to carry out the order would be a contempt of court which would render the feoffees liable to imprisonment until they were prepared to comply.

The device of the use was adopted for various purposes. It enabled a landowner, for example, to evade some of the feudal dues which fell on the person seised of land; to dispose of his land by his will; to evade mortmain statutes; and more effectively to settle his land. The use developed considerably during the fifteenth and early sixteenth centuries, so much so that it was said in 1500 that the greater part of the land in England was held in use,[68] and the rights of the cestui que use were so extensive that it became recognized that there was duality of ownership. One person, the feoffee to uses, was the legal owner according to the common law—a title not disputed by the Chancellor. But the feoffee to uses had only the bare legal title; beneficial ownership was in the equitable owner, the cestui que use. A stop was put to the development of the use in 1535, however, when, largely because the King was losing so many feudal dues by the device of the use, the Statute of Uses[69] was passed to put an end to uses, or at least severely to limit them. In cases where the Act applied the use was 'executed', that is to say, on the one hand the feoffees to uses were deprived of their seisin of the land—indeed they commonly dropped out of the picture altogether—and on the other hand the equitable estates of the cestuis que use were turned into equivalent legal estates carrying seisin. Though the Act executed the vast majority of uses there were cases to which it did not apply—where, for instance, the feoffees to uses had active duties to perform—and thus the use never became completely obsolete.

One special case which should be mentioned was the use upon a use, as where land is limited to A and his heirs to the use of B and his heirs to the use of C and his heirs. It was decided before 1535 that C took nothing in such a case: A had the legal fee simple, B the equitable fee simple, but the limitation to C was repugnant to B's interest and accordingly void. After the Statute of Uses the second use was still held to be void,[70] though the first use was executed so as to give B the legal fee simple and leave A, like C, with nothing at all. Eventually, however, by steps which are not very clear[71] the

---

[66] There may have been a remedy in the ecclesiastical courts, at least after the death of the feoffor, see (1979) 70 Col LR 1503 (R H Helmholz).

[67] See J H Baker, *An Introduction to Legal History*, 4th edn, p 251, n 12, and (1982) 98 LQR 26 (John Barton).

[68] Y B Mich 15 Hen VII 13 pl 1, per Frowike C J.

[69] For background see (1967) 82 EHR 676 (E W Ives).

[70] *Tyrrel's Case* (1557) 2 Dyer 155a. But see (1966) 82 LQR 215 (J L Barton); (1993) 14 JLH 75 (I N G Jones).

[71] The political background was that after the abolition of military tenure in 1660 the King ceased to have any substantial interest in the maintenance of feudal dues.

Chancellor, at about the middle of the seventeenth century,[72] or perhaps earlier,[73] began to enforce this second use and it had become a well-established practice by the end of the century. As a matter of terminology the second use thus enforced became called a trust, and as a matter of drafting the basic formula was 'unto and to the use of B and his heirs in trust for C and his heirs'. B took the legal fee simple at common law, but the use in his favour prevented the second use being executed by the Statute of Uses, leaving it to be enforced in equity as a trust. The result was to restore duality of ownership, B being the legal and C the equitable owner. The use was in effect resuscitated under the name of trust.

In the opinion of Lord Browne-Wilkinson[74] it remains a fundamental principle that equity operates on the conscience of the owner of the legal interest. So, in the case of a trust, the conscience of the legal owner requires him to carry out the purposes for which the property was vested in him (express or implied trust) or which the law imposes on him by reason of his unconscionable conduct (constructive trust). Accordingly he cannot be a trustee if and so long as he is ignorant of the facts alleged to affect his conscience, that is, until he is aware that he is intended to hold the property for the benefit of others in the case of an express or implied trust, or, in the case of a constructive trust, of the factors which are alleged to affect his conscience. Extrajudicially Lord Millett has expressed a different view[75] observing that a resulting trust can arise even if the recipient is unaware of the transfer or of the circumstances in which it was made, and he is unpersuaded by the explanation given by Lord Browne-Wilkinson of the cases[76] where this has occurred. Lord Browne-Wilkinson, it has been contended, exaggerates the role that conscience plays in the law of property.[77] Maybe the better view is that a resulting trust arises as soon as the property is transferred, but the transferee does not become subject to a fiduciary duty, or liable for breach of trust, until he is aware of his position.[78]

Once a trust is established, as from the date of its establishment the beneficiary has, in equity, a proprietary interest in the trust property,[79] which proprietary interest will be enforceable in equity against any subsequent holder of the property (whether the original property or substituted property into which it can be traced) other than a purchaser for value of the legal interest without notice. Moreover if the trustee

---

[72] But later than *Sambach v Dalston (or Daston)* (1635) Toth 188, sub nom *Morris v Darston* Nels 30, according to the orthodox view. See (1958) 74 LQR 550 (J E Strathdene); (1957) 15 CLJ 72 (D E C Yale); A W B Simpson, *A History of the Land Law*, 2nd edn, p 201 et seq.

[73] At least 10 years before *Sambach v Dalston*, supra, and perhaps as early as 1560 if not before: see (1977) 93 LQR 33 (J H Baker); [2002] Cambrian LR 67 (N G Jones).

[74] See *Westdeutsche Landesbank Girozentrale v Islington London Borough Council* [1996] 2 All ER 961, HL, at 988.

[75] In Cornish et al (eds) *Restitution: Past, Present and Future*, p 201.

[76] Including *Re Vinogradoff* [1935] WN 68, discussed infra, p 178.

[77] (1988) 12 Tru LI 226 (W Swadling).

[78] See (1998) 114 LQR 399 (Millett LJ); Hanbury and Martin *Modern Equity*, 16th edn, p 239; *Port of Brisbane Corporation v ANZ Securities Ltd (No 2)* [2002] QCA 158, [2003] 2 Qd R 661.

[79] See (2004) 120 LQR 108 (R C Nolan).

becomes bankrupt the trust property is not available to the trustee's creditors, but remains subject to the trust and unaffected by the bankruptcy.

The trust has become a much more highly developed institution than the use had ever been, and has since been, and now is, used for a wide variety of purposes. In developing the trust equity in general followed the law, and permitted equitable estates to be created corresponding to the legal estates recognized in the common law courts, and these equitable estates were commonly made subject to incidents and rules corresponding to those applying to the equivalent legal estates. Exceptionally, however, the Chancellor regarded himself as entitled to depart from the legal rule where he considered it to be unduly technical or inequitable.

(b) PURPOSE FOR WHICH A TRUST IS SET UP

(i) Introduction

Although cases do arise where the whole legal estate is vested in a trustee and the whole equitable interest in a sole beneficiary, it is seldom that such a simple trust is deliberately created. Much more common is some species of settlement constituted by a will, or inter vivos upon marriage or on some other occasion, whereby provision is made for a family. The avoidance of taxes may well dictate the form which a family settlement shall take and, indeed, may be a primary reason why any settlement is made, just as landowners took advantage of the use before 1535 in order to evade the payment of feudal dues. In addition to or as part of tax saving the objects of a family settlement may include the more equal distribution of funds among the members of the family, the passing of wealth to future generations, born or unborn, and making provision for minors, spendthrifts, or those members of the family who by reason of mental or physical disability are unable to provide for themselves. And the 'family' provided for may be a mistress and illegitimate children.

(ii) Forms of family trust

The forms of trust that may be used include the following:

(a) The life interest trust. In its classic form this entitled the life tenant to the income and use of the trust assets, but he had no recourse to capital which had to be retained for the beneficiaries in remainder. In the modern life interest trust the trustees are commonly given wide powers, on the one hand to advance capital to the life tenant, and on the other hand to revoke his life interest in whole or in part.

(b) Discretionary trusts.[80] These may be useful to enable trustees to take account, inter alia, of the changing circumstances and needs of the beneficiaries, who may not even be in existence when the trust was created.

---

[80] See p 76 et seq, infra.

(c) Protective trusts.[81] These may be used to protect assets against both spendthrift beneficiaries and outside claimants.

(d) Accumulation and maintenance settlements. These exist because of the tax advantages they enjoy under inheritance tax legislation. They are commonly created for the benefit of grandchildren, and to qualify for privileged inheritance tax treatment must satisfy the three requirements set out in the Inheritance Tax Act 1984.[82]

(iii) Use of tax havens

Lord Walker recently observed[83] that it:

has become common for wealthy individuals in many parts of the world (including countries which have no indigenous law of trusts) to place funds at their disposition into trusts (often with a network of underlying companies) regulated by the law of, and managed by trustees resident in, territories with which the settlor (who may be also a beneficiary) has no substantial connection. These territories (sometimes called tax havens) are chosen not for their geographical convenience . . . but because they are supposed to offer special advantages in terms of confidentiality and protection from fiscal demands (and, sometimes, from problems under the insolvency laws, or laws restricting freedom of testamentary disposition, in the country of the settlor's domicil). The trusts and powers contained in a settlement established in such circumstances may give no reliable indication of who will in the event benefit from the settlement. Typically it will contain very wide discretions exercisable by the trustees . . . in favour of a widely-defined class of beneficiaries. The exercise of those discretions may depend on the settlor's wishes as confidentially imparted to the trustees . . . As a further cloak against transparency, the identity of the true settlor may be concealed behind some corporate figurehead.

(iv) Blind trusts

A blind trust arises where the settlor transfers property to a trustee, commonly on a resulting trust for himself, giving the trustee full power to deal with the trust property without reference to him and restricting the right of the settlor to information about the trust property and the dealings of the trustee with it. A blind trust may be set up, for example by a politician, to make it impossible for him to be attacked on the ground of conflict of interest.[84]

(v) Unit trusts[85]

These provide a simple way for an investor to have a varied portfolio, thereby spreading his risk. A unit trust is set up under a trust deed made between parties known as

---

[81] See p 79 et seq, infra.   [82] Section 71.

[83] In *Schmidt v Rosewood Trust Ltd* [2003] UKPC 26, [2003] 3 All ER 76 at 1.

[84] See [1999] PCB 29 (Judith Morris); [1999] PCB 292 (D Hochberg and W Norris).

[85] See (2002) 36 T & ELJ 13 (E Nugee). Note that the so-called investment trust is not a trust at all, but a company formed to acquire and hold property by way of investment. In accordance with the principles of company law the shareholders have no direct beneficial interest in the property so acquired.

the trustee and the manager. It is in essence the same institution as a particular kind of deed of settlement company known as a management trust which became familiar in about the middle of the nineteenth century. Following the Companies Act 1862 the management trust was held to be illegal in *Sykes v Beadon*[86] and all but one were wound up or registered as companies under the Companies Act. That one, however, the Submarine Cables' Trust, continued in existence and successfully contended[87] before the Court of Appeal in the following year that *Sykes v Beadon*[88] had been wrongly decided. Nevertheless no more management trusts appear to have been created until the early nineteen thirties, when the institution was reintroduced and became known as the unit trust.[89] Unit trust deeds vary widely in their terms, but the general principle is that securities are vested in the trustee under the trust deed, initially on trust for the manager. The beneficial interest thus held by the manager is divided up into a large number of units, sub-units or shares which are offered to the public at a price based on the market value of the securities plus an initial service charge. The investor who purchases units accordingly becomes the beneficial owner of an undivided share of the securities in proportion to the number of units he holds.[90] Many matters are dealt with in the trust deed: provision is made, inter alia, for the remuneration of the trustee and the manager out of income; for the manager to repurchase shares from unit holders who wish to dispose of their investment, and for resale by the manager to new investors, though units may be dealt with on the market in the usual way; and for the duration of the trust which has usually been fixed, with perhaps unnecessary caution,[91] at less than 21 years to avoid the possible infringement of the rule against perpetuities. Even so, however, the trust deed commonly provides for an extension of the trust if the unit holders so desire. Unit trusts may be either fixed or flexible. The fixed trust under which the portfolio of investments is normally bound to remain unaltered has become unpopular,[92] and the flexible trust which gives the manager power to switch securities is much more common. It gives the unit holder the benefit of the manager's financial skill and acumen, but correspondingly makes him dependent upon the manager's ability, or lack of it, and integrity.[93] The trustee has considerable control over the manager by reason of the fact that the trust deed must provide for requiring the manager to retire from the trust if the trustee certifies that it is in the interest of the beneficiaries under the trust that he should do so. Further, an investigating authority may appoint inspectors to investigate and report on the administration of any authorized unit trust scheme, if it appears that it is in the

---

[86] (1879) 11 Ch D 170.　　[87] In *Smith v Anderson* (1880) 15 Ch D 247, CA.　　[88] Supra.

[89] The longest surviving unit trust is thought to be the M & G General Trust launched as the First British Fixed Trust on 22 April 1931.

[90] See *Costa & Duppe Properties Pty Ltd v Duppe* [1986] VR 90.

[91] Cf *Re AEG Unit Trust (Managers) Ltd's Deed* [1957] Ch 415, [1957] 2 All ER 506.

[92] The court had to consider a fixed unit trust in *Re Municipal and General Securities Co Ltd's Trust, Municipal and General Securities Co Ltd v Lloyds Bank Ltd* [1950] Ch 212, [1949] 2 All ER 937.

[93] It is understood that there has been no case involving an authorized unit trust in which investors have suffered a loss through dishonesty of the managers of the trust. Statutory protection is given to the investor by the Financial Services Act 1986.

interests of unit holders to do so or the matter is one of public concern.[94] No inspector has yet been appointed under this provision.

(vi) Pension scheme trusts[95]

These are of great importance, but they are of quite a different nature from traditional trusts. The traditional trust is one under which the settlor, by way of bounty, transfers property to trustees to be administered for the beneficiaries as objects of his bounty. Normally, there is no legal relationship between the parties apart from the trust. The beneficiaries have given no consideration for what they receive. The settlor, as donor, can impose such limits on his bounty as he chooses. In a pension scheme by contrast the benefits are part of the consideration which an employee receives in return for the rendering of his services. In many cases membership of the pension scheme is a requirement of employment. Beneficiaries of the scheme, the members, far from being volunteers have given valuable consideration. The company employer is not conferring a bounty.[96]

Though, on the one hand, it is clear that in general the principles applicable to private trusts as a matter of trust law apply equally to pension schemes,[97] on the other hand, in view of the differences referred to, it is dangerous to apply uncritically in the field of pension funds concepts which have been developed in the field of private trusts. Thus while in a private trust it is axiomatic that a trustee should not be asked to exercise a discretion as to the application of a fund amongst a class of which he is a member, if under a pension scheme an employer has a power of amendment in relation to a pension fund which has not been wound up, he is entitled to exercise it in any way which will further the purposes of the scheme, and his exercise of the power will not necessarily be invalid because the employer may benefit directly or

---

[94] Financial Services and Markets Act 2000, s 284, which in sub-s (11) defines 'investigating authority' as the Financial Services Authority or the Secretary of State.

[95] See Nobles, *Pensions Employment & the Law*; (1992) 6 Tru LI 119 (Lord Browne-Wilkinson); (1996) 75 CBR 221 (Eileen Gillese); [1997] Conv 89 (Marina Milner), arguing that a new form of trust is evolving; [2005] Conv 229 (D Hayton). See also (2000) 14 Tru LI 130 (S E K Hulme); (2002) 16 Tru LI 74 (D Pollard); (2002) 16 Tru LI 214 (Lord Scott).

[96] *Mettoy Pension Trustees Ltd v Evans* [1991] 2 All ER 513, [1990] 1 WLR 1587 at 537, 549, 1610, 1618, per Warner J; *Stannard v Fisons Pension Trust Ltd* [1992] IRLR 27, CA; *Air Jamaica Ltd v Joy Charlton* [1999] 1 WLR 1399, PC, noted [2000] Conv 170 (C Harpum); (2000) 116 LQR 15 (CEF Rickett and Ross Grantham) *Re UEB Industries Ltd Pension Plan* [1992] 1 NZLR 294. See (1990) 4 TL & P 94 (D Higgins); (1990) 4 TL & P 156 (I Pittaway); (1990) 53 MLR 377 (R Nobles); (1991) 5 TL & P 56 (P Docking); [1992] 1 GLR 210 (Samantha Travers); (1993) 56 MLR 471 (G Moffat); [1993] Conv 283 (D Hayton); (1994) 14 LS 345 (R Nobles).

[97] *Cowan v Scargill* [1985] Ch 270, 292, [1984] 2 All ER 750, 764, per Megarry V-C; *Wilson v Law Debenture Trust Corpn plc* [1995] 2 All ER 337, 347, per Rattee J. Although there are no special rules of construction applicable to pension schemes, the courts' approach to the construction of the relevant documents should be practical and purposive, rather than detached and literal, so as to give reasonable and practical effect to the scheme: see *National Grid Co plc v Mayes* [2000] ICR 174, CA, revsd [2001] UKHL 20, [2001] 2 All ER 417, HL, without comment on this point. In Canada a pension trust has been said to be a classic trust: *Schmidt v Air Products of Canada Ltd* [1994] 2 SCR 611; *Bathgate v National Hockey League Pension Society* (1994) 16 OR (3d) 761, 776. Similarly in New Zealand: *Stuart v Armourguard Security Ltd* [1996] 1 NZLR 484. See (2003) 17 Tru LI 129 (K Rowley).

indirectly.[98] The Goode Committee report[99] concluded that criticism of trust law as the basis for pension schemes following the Maxwell affair was largely misplaced. It endorsed the view which had been expressed in the great weight of evidence submitted to the Committee that trust law in itself is broadly satisfactory and should continue to provide the foundation for interests, rights and duties arising in relation to pension schemes, though some of its principles required modifications in their application to pensions.

(vii) Other trust situations

Under the 1925 property legislation a trust arises in all cases of beneficial co-ownership of land.[100] One result of this is that where the matrimonial home is owned, it is usually subject to a trust. Again under the 1925 legislation a trust arises when a person dies intestate. Clubs and societies, unincorporated bodies of all kinds, and most charities commonly have their funds and property vested in trustees, and under time sharing schemes the villas or apartments to be time-shared are usually vested in a trustee.[101]

A trust may also come into being as part of commercial arrangements. An example of this is *Barclays Bank Ltd v Quistclose Investments Ltd.*[102]

(c) CONCLUSION

One might sum up the present position by saying that in the complexity of modern society there are few aspects of human activity which do not run more smoothly through the assistance of the trust concept.[103] However after observing that the trust has become a valuable device in commercial and financial dealings in the modern world, Lord Browne-Wilkinson issued a valuable warning.[104] The fundamental principles of equity, he said, apply as much to such trusts as they do to the traditional

---

[98] *British Coal Corpn v British Coal Staff Superannuation Scheme Trustees Ltd* [1995] 1 All ER 912, said to have been wrongly decided on another point by Lord Hoffman and Lord Scott in *National Grid Co plc v Mayes*, supra, HL. See also *Jefferies v Mayes* (1997) *Times*, 30 June.

[99] Report of the Pension Law Review Committee, 1993, Cm 2342, paras 4.1.12 and 4.1.14. The Report includes an extensive (though not exhaustive) bibliography. See (1993) 7 Tru LI 191 (D A Chatterton); (1994) 8 Tru LI 35 (Vinelott J).

[100] The amendments to the law made by the Trusts of Land and Appointment of Trustees Act 1996 do not affect the validity of this proposition.

[101] See (1987) 84 LSG 19 (J Edmonds). The rules of the European Holiday Timeshare Association are partly based on the Public Trustee Rules 1911 (as amended).

[102] [1970] AC 567. [1968] 3 All ER 651, HL, and see p 169, infra. As to trusts in business and commerce, see Underhill and Hayton, *Law of Trusts and Trustees*, 16th edn, p 39–48. See also (1981) 13 MULR 1 (H A J Ford); (1983) 21 Alberta LR 395 (D W M Waters); [1987] JMCL 1 (D W M Waters); (1987) 3 QITLJ 17 (D G Gardiner); [1993] JBL 24 (G M D Bean); (1992) 15 UNSWLJ 256 (Sarah Worthington); (1997) 107 Yale LJ 105 (J H Langbein)

[103] See per Roxburgh J in *Re a Solicitor* [1952] Ch 328 at 332, [1952] 1 All ER 133 at 136. See also (1986) 36 UTLJ 186 (A I Ogus). For speculation as to the future see [2000] PCB 94, 163, 244 (D Hayton).

[104] In *Target Holdings Ltd v Redferns (a firm)* [1996] AC 421, [1995] 3 All ER 785, HL, at 435, 795. See pp 522, 523 infra.

trusts in relation to which those principles were originally formulated. But if the trust is not to be rendered commercially useless it is important to distinguish between the basic principles of trust law and those specialist rules developed in relation to traditional trusts which are applicable only to such trusts and the rationale of which has no application to trusts of quite a different kind.

5 EQUITABLE INTERESTS AND EQUITIES

(a) DEFINITION AND DISTINCTION

It would no doubt be as satisfying to the reader as to the author to have clear definitions of these terms and certainty as to what rights come within each category and the consequences that thereby attach to them. This, however, is by no means the position, nor perhaps is it surprising since equity has grown by filling in gaps in the common law and is still in the process of development. Before discussing the matter something should be said about the distinction between property rights and personal rights. Lord Wilberforce[105] has stated that before an interest can be admitted into the category of property 'it must be definable, identifiable by third parties, capable in its nature of assumption by third parties, and have some degree of permanence and stability'. All the Law Lords in that case agreed that the right in question, that of a deserted wife to remain in the former matrimonial home, was a personal and not a property right. The owner of a property right can normally (i) in case of dispute recover the property itself as opposed to merely recovering damages payable out of no specific fund; (ii) transfer his right to another; and (iii) enforce his right against at least some third parties. But a property right can exist without all of these elements being present.

With this in mind let us first turn to consider equitable interests of which the interest of a beneficiary under a trust is the earliest and prime example. This is a proprietary interest which can be assigned inter vivos or disposed of by will, and is normally binding on third parties—unless a third party can establish that he is a bona fide purchaser for value of a legal estate, without notice, actual or constructive, of the equitable interest. In course of time the Court of Chancery came to protect other rights unrecognized by the common law and in 1965[106] Lord Upjohn regarded the list set out by Professor Crane[107] as being complete. It comprised, in addition to beneficial

---

[105] *National Provincial Bank Ltd v Ainsworth* [1965] AC 1175 at 1248, [1965] 2 All ER 472 at 494, HL. See, generally, Meagher, Gummow and Lehane, *Equity: Doctrine and Remedies*, 3rd edn, p 103 et seq; (1996) 16 LS 200 (J Hill). See also [2002] CLJ 423 (Christine Davis).

[106] In *National Provincial Bank Ltd v Ainsworth* [1965] HL supra at 1238, 488.

[107] (1955) 19 Conv 343. It is submitted that at least equitable easements and profits should be added to the list. Note that an equitable charge, unlike an equitable mortgage, does not give the chargee an equitable interest in the land: *Bland v Ingram's Estates Ltd* [2002] 1 All ER 221, CA.

interests under trusts, equitable mortgages, vendor's liens, restrictive covenants and estate contracts.

In other cases where equity intervened to protect a plaintiff the effect was not to confer on him an equitable interest, and he would be said to have an equity or a mere equity. Unfortunately the picture is far from clear. In the widest sense an equity includes the right of the plaintiff in every case where he can call upon equity to mitigate the rigours of the common law. However, when used in contradistinction to an equitable interest as denoting a right which in some circumstances may bind successors it was said by Lord Upjohn[108] to be a word of limited application: the term includes the right of a grantor to have a conveyance he has made set aside on the ground of the grantee's fraud or undue influence,[109] the right to rectification of a document which incorrectly embodies the agreement between the parties,[110] and the right of consolidation of mortgages. Lord Upjohn went on to say that it was not possible for a mere equity to bind a purchaser unless such an equity is ancillary to or dependent upon an equitable estate or interest in land, and summed up the position thus: 'A mere "equity" naked and alone is, in my opinion, incapable of binding successors in title even with notice; it is personal to the parties.' The deserted wife in the case before him had only a personal equity which did not bind the purchasers. But if a tenant has a lease which does not accurately set out the agreed terms of the tenancy and a right to have the lease rectified, a purchaser of the reversion with notice will be bound by the equity which is ancillary to the tenant's property interest.

According to Neave and Weinberg[111] 'the expression "an equity" has come to be used in the sense of a proprietary interest ranking at the bottom of a hierarchy of proprietary interests consisting of legal interests, equitable interests and equities'. Neave and Weinberg argue that equities fall into two groups which they call 'defined equities' and 'undefined equities'. By 'defined equities' they mean those where there is no doubt about the plaintiff's entitlement to a remedy against the other party to the transaction, such as the right to have a conveyance set aside for fraud or a contract rectified where it does not represent the true agreement of the parties. In these cases the enforcement of the plaintiff's right is no more discretionary than where he seeks to assert an estate contract against the vendor. A defined equity is a proprietary interest. 'Undefined equities' are at a different stage of development. Where the facts do not fall into any established category the court has first to be persuaded to give a remedy against the other party to the transaction. The court has a wide discretion whether to accept that there is a personal equity. If it does the next question is whether

---

[108] [1965] AC 1175, [1965] 2 All ER 472, HL.

[109] Contrast *Gross v Lewis Hillman Ltd* [1970] Ch 445, [1969] 3 All ER 1476, CA (right of purchaser to rescind a purchase of land for misrepresentation).

[110] See *Blacklocks v J B Developments (Godalming) Ltd* [1982] Ch 183, [1981] 3 All ER 392; *Boots the Chemist Ltd v Street* (1983) 268 EG 817; *Nurdin & Peacock plc v D B Ramsden & Co Ltd* [1999] 1 EGLR 119. See also *Itco Properties Ltd v Mohawk Oil Co* (1988) 62 Alta LR (2d) 42, 91 AR 76, where a right to rectification was held to be assignable.

[111] (1978–80) 6 U Tas LR 24, 115.

it is enforceable against third parties so as to become an equity in the proprietary sense. If the court provides the remedy sufficiently often, the equity may be converted into a defined equity and ultimately both defined and undefined equities may become equitable interests. Neave and Weinberg's view stresses flexibility: they consider that the use of the equity device enables the court to modify the rigid structure of legal and equitable interests.

It is indeed difficult to find two writers who share the same view. Wade[112] suggested that the dividing line between equitable interests and mere equities is the discretionary character of the latter, but nevertheless admitted that this puts the right of a purchaser under an estate contract in the wrong category since he relies on the discretionary remedy of specific performance. Maudsley[113] submitted the test should be whether the 'interest' is capable of being bought and sold in the market place, but accepted that this test would put at least restrictive covenants in the wrong group.

Though the distinction is far from clear it may yet be of importance where a question arises as to the priority of competing interests. Moreover in relation to registered land the Land Registration Act 2002[114] now provides that both an equity by estoppel[115] and a mere equity have effect from the time the equity arises as an interest capable of binding successors in title.

(b) EQUITABLE RULES AS TO PRIORITIES

The rules relating to priorities are complex: they depend in the first instance on the kind of property that is being dealt with, and have since 1925 been much affected by statutory provisions as to registration and in relation to overreaching. For present purposes it will suffice to mention the bare essentials of the basic equitable rules.[116] These are:

i   estates and interests rank in order of their creation. This is the primary rule because it is always applied in the absence of special circumstances and it establishes the burden of proof;[117]

ii   the superiority of the legal estate. Someone with a legal estate or interest may gain priority over an earlier equitable interest. In order to do this he must establish that

---

112 [1955] CLJ 160–161. See also (1955) 71 LQR 482 (R E Megarry).
113 Hanbury & Maudsley's *Modern Equity*, 13th edn, p 873.   114 Section 116.
115 See p 201 et seq, infra.
116 These rules were not relevant in *Bristol and West Building Society v Henning* [1985] 2 All ER 606, [1985] 1 WLR 778, CA, or in *Equity and Law Home Loans Ltd v Prestidge* [1992] 1 All ER 909, [1992] 1 WLR 137, CA, where the owner of the equitable interest had consented, or was deemed to have consented, to the creation of the mortgage, which accordingly had priority. See (1996) 3 Deak LR 147 (H Long).
117 *A-G v Biphosphated Guano Co* (1879) 11 Ch D 327, CA.

he is a bona fide purchaser for value[118] of a legal estate without notice, actual or constructive, of the prior equitable interest;[119]

iii   the rule giving priority to the owner of a legal interest only applies where, as it is said, the equities are equal. 'Equity' is here used in yet another sense: what is meant is that the owner of a legal interest may be postponed if there is fraud, misrepresentation or gross negligence on his part;

iv   where there are two competing equitable interests the primary rule again applies that they rank in order of their creation, again subject to the proviso that the equities are equal.[120] Thus the primary rule applied to the equitable interests in *Cave v Cave*[121] where a sole trustee purchased land out of trust moneys in breach of trust, the conveyance being taken in the name of his brother. The brother created first a legal mortgage and then an equitable mortgage. It was held that the legal mortgagee had priority by virtue of his legal estate, but that, the equities being equal, the primary rule applied to give the beneficiaries under the trust priority to the equitable mortgagee. The equities were not, however, equal in *Rice v Rice*[122] where a vendor indorsed a receipt on, and handed the title deeds over to, a purchaser without having received the purchase money. Though the vendor still retained an equitable interest, his vendor's lien for the purchase price, it was held that a subsequent equitable mortgagee of the property without notice of the lien had priority though later in point of time, because the vendor's conduct had led him to assume there was no competing equitable interest;

v   where, however, the competition is between an equitable interest and a mere equity, the position is analogous to that between a legal estate and an equitable interest, ie the bona fide purchaser of an equitable interest takes free from a prior equity of which he has no notice.[123] The fullest judicial discussion of the matter is in the Australian case of *Latec Investments Ltd v Hotel Terrigal Pty Ltd*.[124] In that case a

---

[118] Note that the common law rule that the court does not inquire into the adequacy of consideration is not relevant here. The concept of 'purchaser for value' is based on equity which looks at the substance not the form. Thus on the assignment of a lease the liability of the assignee for rent and the tenant's obligations and the indemnity to the assignor suffices to render him a purchaser for value: *Nurdin & Peacock plc v D B Ramsden & Co Ltd* [1999] 1 EGLR 119.

[119] See *Macmillan Inc v Bishopsgate Investment Trust plc (No 3)* [1995] 3 All ER 747, noted (1996) 10 Tru LI 20 (G Virgo); *MCC Proceeds Inc v Lehman Bros International (Europe)* [1998] 4 All ER 675, CA; *State Bank of India v Sood* [1997] Ch 276, [1997] 1 All ER 169, CA. See also [1997] Conv 431 (J Howell).

[120] See Snell's *Principles of Equity*, 30th edn, p 63; *Lloyds Bank v Bullock* [1896] 2 Ch 192; *Capell v Winter* [1907] 2 Ch 376 at 382; *Jacobs v Platt Nominees Pty Ltd* [1990] VR 146; *Secureland Mortgage Investments Nominees Ltd v Harmore & Co Solicitor Nominee Co Ltd* [1991] 2 NZLR 399.

[121] (1880) 15 Ch D 639; *Wu v Glaros* (1991) 55 SASR 408.

[122] (1854) 2 Drew 73; *Re King's Settlement* [1931] 2 Ch 294; *Abigail v Lapin* [1934] AC 491, [1934] All ER Rep 720, PC; *Heid v Reliance Finance Corpn Pty Ltd* (1984) 154 CLR 326. Contrast *Capell v Winter* [1907] 2 Ch 376.

[123] *Cave v Cave* supra; *Westminster Bank Ltd v Lee* [1956] Ch 7, [1955] 2 All ER 833; *National Provincial Bank Ltd v Ainsworth* [1965] AC 1175, [1965] 2 All ER 472, HL; *Taylor Barnard Ltd v Tozer* [1984] 1 EGLR 21; *Mid-Glamorgan County Council v Ogwr Borough Council* (1993) 68 P & CR 1, CA. But see (2002) 118 LQR 296 (D O'Sullivan).

[124] (1965) 113 CLR 265, [1966] ALR 775, Taylor J, though he agreed with Kitto and Menzies JJ in the result, considered that the plaintiff had an equitable interest but there was an impediment to his title which a Court of Equity would not remove. See also *Blacklocks v J B Developments (Godalming) Ltd* [1982] Ch 183, [1981] 3 All ER 392; [1995] Denning LJ 153 (J Reeder and G Kinley).

mortgagee purported to exercise its power of sale in favour of a wholly owned subsidiary. The circumstances were such that the exercise of the power of sale was fraudulent. The purchaser created an equitable charge on the land in favour of a third party who had no notice of the circumstances of the sale. Five years later the mortgagor sought to have the sale set aside, and he succeeded against the mortgagee and the purchaser. It was unanimously held, however, that he was bound by the equitable charge of the third party, by the majority on the ground that the mortgagor's right to have the sale set aside was a mere equity,[125] and against that the plea of the bona fide purchaser for value without notice, even of an equitable interest, could successfully be put forward. Accordingly as against the third party the mortgagor could not establish his equity of redemption and there was therefore no prior equitable interest to which his conveyance could be held subject.

It is submitted that the courts retain considerable flexibility because of the proviso that the rules only apply 'where the equities are equal'. Even the purchaser of a legal estate will be bound if he takes with notice of a prior equitable interest, and the existence of the proviso may enable the courts to avoid grappling with the difficulties raised by the uncertainties as to the distinction between equitable interests and mere equities.

6 TRUSTS AND TAXATION

As we have noted, in many cases the stimulus to create a settlement may not be so much a wish to provide for the family as a desire to reduce the incidence of taxation. It is clear, however, that there are very real limits as to what can be done. Basically, a settlor cannot both eat his cake and have it, and if he wishes to reduce the incidence of tax it can only be by, in effect, giving his property to other persons, though the gift may be by way of trust or settlement under which the interests of individual beneficiaries are restricted. Tax considerations may not only be the reason why a trust or settlement is made or why it is made in a particular way, but may also be the reason why the provisions of a trust may be sought to be varied, perhaps with the assistance of the court under the Variation of Trusts Act 1958.

It will be realized that the various taxes have their own textbooks and there are also specialized books dealing with the taxation of trusts and settlements, and even with what is called tax planning. A vital distinction exists between 'tax evasion', that is, non-payment of taxes which one is under a legal duty to pay, which is clearly illegal and may result in criminal proceedings, and 'tax avoidance' which is the arrangement

---

[125] It makes no difference that, where the question is whether the plaintiff can assign it in his lifetime or leave it by his will, the right to have a conveyance set aside for fraud may be regarded as an equitable interest: *Stump v Gaby* (1852) 2 De GM & G 623; *Gresley v Mousley* (1859) 4 De G & J 78; *Dickinson v Burrell* (1866) LR 1 Eq 337.

of one's financial affairs so that no liability or a reduced liability to tax accrues, which is perfectly legal. Though there are judicial dicta which disapprove of schemes which have been entered into to avoid tax, there are many more judgments recognizing the right of individuals to dispose of their capital and income so as to attract the least amount of tax.[126]

The courts themselves have, indeed, been prepared to give their assistance in the creation of tax avoidance schemes, in particular under the Variation of Trusts Act 1958, though Lord Denning MR has observed:[127] 'The avoidance of tax may be lawful, but it is not yet a virtue'. More recent cases, however, indicate an increasingly critical approach by the courts to the manipulation of financial transactions to the advantage of the taxpayer.[128]

It is not proposed to attempt to deal with any of the above-mentioned taxes even in outline, but it seems desirable at this early stage to stress the practical importance of tax considerations. Fortunately, however, an understanding of equity and trusts does not demand a knowledge of tax law, though it will be found that numerous points of trust law have been decided in litigation with the Inland Revenue. It should be noted, however, that in a tax statute a word may have a different meaning from the one it has in ordinary trust law.[129]

7 TRUSTS AND THE CONFLICT OF LAWS

The Recognition of Trusts Act 1987 brings into force for the United Kingdom the main provisions of the Hague Convention on the Law Applicable to Trusts and on their Recognition,[130] the purpose of which is to establish common principles between states on the law of trusts and to deal with the most important issues concerning their recognition. It is intended in particular to assist civil law countries which are not generally familiar with the trust concept to deal fairly, expeditiously and effectively with trust issues arising within their jurisdiction. It does not make much change of substance to the existing law in the United Kingdom, though some points are clarified. The Convention only applies to trusts created voluntarily and evidenced in writing, but so far as the United Kingdom is concerned it is extended by s 1(2) to any other trusts of property arising under the law of any part of the United Kingdom or by virtue of a judicial decision whether in the United Kingdom or elsewhere.

---

[126] See per Viscount Sumner in *Levene v IRC* [1928] AC 217 at 227, [1928] All ER Rep 746 at 751.

[127] *Re Weston's Settlements* [1969] 1 Ch 223 at 245, [1968] 3 All ER 338 at 342.

[128] *W T Ramsay Ltd v IRC* [1982] AC 300, [1981] 1 All ER 865, HL; *Furniss v Dawson* [1984] AC 474, [1984] 1 All ER 530, HL; *Craven v White* [1989] AC 398, [1988] 3 All ER 495, HL; *Fitzwilliam v IRC* [1993] 3 All ER 184, [1993] 1 WLR 1189, HL; and see (1984) 43 CLJ 259 (D Hayton).

[129] See *J Sainsbury plc v O'Connor* [1991] 1 WLR 963, CA.

[130] Cmnd 9494. See (1987) 131 Sol Jo 827 (T Prime); (1987) 36 ICLQ 260 (D J Hayton); (1987) 36 ICLQ 454 (Ann Wallace). See also Dicey and Morris, *Conflict of Laws*, 13th edn, p 1087 et seq.

Article 6 provides that a trust shall be governed by the law chosen by the settlor. The choice must be express or be implied in the terms of the instrument creating or the writing evidencing the trust, interpreted, if necessary, in the light of the circumstances of the case. Where no applicable law has been chosen, Article 7 provides that a trust shall be governed by the law with which it is most closely connected.

In ascertaining the law with which a trust is most closely connected reference shall be made in particular to:

i   the place of administration of the trust designated by the settlor;

ii   the situs of the assets of the trust;

iii   the place of residence or business of the trustee;

iv   the objects of the trust and the places where they are to be fulfilled.

The law specified by Article 6 or 7 governs the validity of the trust, its construction, its effects and the administration of the trust.

2

THE TRUST CONCEPT

1 DEFINITION OF A TRUST

It is commonly observed that no one has succeeded in producing a wholly satisfactory definition of a trust, although the general idea is not difficult to grasp. The general idea is expressed by saying that the trustee is the nominal owner of the trust property, but that the real or beneficial owner is the cestui que trust, or, alternatively, that the trustee is the legal owner, the cestui que trust the equitable owner. Though adequate to give the general idea, neither statement is altogether satisfactory as a definition, for neither covers, for instance, cases where a sub-trust has been created, such as where trustees hold a fund on trust for X and Y in equal shares, and X and Y both declare themselves trustees of their respective shares for their children. In such a case under the head trust, the trustees are nominal owners, but X and Y can hardly be regarded as the real or beneficial owners; and under the sub-trust it is clear that X and Y are not the legal owners at all, but are trustees of the respective equitable half shares.

Having regard to the above considerations, a trust can be said to exist whenever equity imposes on a person (the trustee) a duty to deal with property[1] under his control,[2] either for the benefit of other persons[3] (the beneficiaries or cestuis que trust),[4] any one of whom may enforce the obligation, or for a charitable purpose, which may be enforced at the instance of the Attorney-General, or for some other purpose permitted by law though unenforceable.[5]

According to Lord Browne-Wilkinson[6] it would be wrong to say that if the legal title

---

[1] This may comprise any proprietary interest which a person can, at law or in equity, transfer or assign. See p 47, infra.

[2] The control may be nominal: see *Re Marshall's Will Trusts* [1945] Ch 217, [1945] 1 All ER 550.

[3] A trustee (except, it seems, a trustee under a half-secret trust—see pp 132–133, infra) can himself be a beneficiary, but a sole trustee cannot be the sole beneficiary: *Re Cook* [1948] Ch 212, [1948] 1 All ER 231.

[4] This seems to be the correct plural of cestui que trust, not cestui que trusts or cestuis que trustent: (1910) 26 LQR 196 (C Sweet).

[5] See, generally, (1899) 15 LQR 294 (W G Hart); [2002] 61 CLJ 657 (P Parkinson). As to unenforceable trusts see p 58 et seq, infra.

[6] In *Westdeutsche Landesbank Girozentrale v Islington London Borough Council* [1996] AC 669, [1996] 2 All ER 961, HL, at 707, 989, where mortgagor is misprinted as mortgagee in both reports. *Don King Productions Inc v Warren*, per Lightman J at first instance [1998] 2 All ER 608, 630; affd [2000] Ch 291, [1999] 2 All ER 218, CA. See also *R v Chester and North Wales Legal Aid Area Office (No 12), ex p Floods of Queensferry Ltd* [1998] 1 WLR 1496, CA.

is in A but the equitable interest in B, A necessarily holds as trustee for B; there are many cases where B enjoys rights which, in equity, are enforceable against the legal owner, A, without A being a trustee, for example, an equitable right to redeem a mortgage, equitable easements, restrictive covenants and the right to rectification. Even in cases where the whole beneficial interest is vested in B and the bare legal interest is in A, A is not necessarily a trustee, for example, where title to land is acquired by estoppel as against the legal owner; and a mortgagor who has fully discharged his indebtedness enforces his right to recover the mortgaged property in a redemption action, not an action for breach of trust. Lord Millett, writing extra-judicially,[7] is not, however, convinced, and considers that a trust exists whenever the legal title is in one party and the equitable title in another.

2   COMPARISON WITH OTHER LEGAL CONCEPTS

(a)   TRUST AND BAILMENT

Blackstone[8] has caused some confusion by defining bailment as 'a delivery of goods in trust, upon a contract expressed or implied, that the trust shall be faithfully executed on the part of the bailee'. It may well be that the bailee is, in a popular sense, entrusted with the goods lent, hired out, deposited for safe custody, or whatever it may be; there is, however, no trust in the technical sense and the concepts are distinct. It is indeed better to define bailment as a delivery of personal chattels upon a condition, express or implied, that they shall be redelivered to the bailor, or according to his directions, when the purpose of the bailment has been carried out. Bailment was a recognized common law institution, while trusts, of course, were only recognized by courts of equity. Apart from historical and procedural differences, bailment only applies to personal property, while the trust concept applies to all kinds of property. The essential difference is, perhaps, that the bailee has, as it is said, only a special property in or special ownership of the goods bailed, the general property or general ownership remaining in the bailor, while the trustee is the full owner. Consequently the bailee cannot, as a rule,[9] pass a title to the goods which will be valid as against the bailor, but a trustee can pass a good title to someone who acquires legal ownership bona fide for value without notice of the trust.

(b)   TRUST AND CONTRACT

Again there is the historical distinction that contract was developed by the common law courts while the trust was a creature of equity. In general the purposes are different:

---

[7] In Cornish et al (eds) *Restitution: Past, Present and Future*, p 204.

[8] *Commentaries*, Book II, p 451; see Maitland's *Equity*, 2nd (Brunyate) edn, Lecture IV.

[9] There are important exceptions, eg under the Factors Act 1889; estoppel.

a contract usually represents a bargain between the contracting parties giving each some advantage, while the beneficiary under a trust is commonly a volunteer, and the trustee himself usually obtains no benefit from the trust at all.[10] It is of the essence of a contract that the agreement is supported by consideration, but in the case of a trust[11] there is no need for consideration to have been given in order for it to be enforceable. This distinction is blurred by the fact that a contract by deed is enforceable at law without value having been given.

(c) TRUST AND AGENCY

It is sometimes said that an agent is a trustee for his principal of property belonging to the principal committed to his charge, either generally,[12] or, according to Keeton and Sheridan,[13] only where there is some special, confidential relationship. There is no doubt that a principal can commonly exercise the same remedies against his agent as a cestui que trust can against his trustee, but Professor Powell has pointed out[14] that this 'does not necessarily mean that an agent is a trustee or that a trustee is an agent. It means simply that agents and trustees have something in common—and that "something in common" is that they both hold a fiduciary position which imposes on them certain obligations.' Thus both agents and trustees are under a duty not to let their interests conflict with their duties, not to make any unauthorized profits and to keep proper accounts.

There are, however, considerable differences. Thus the relationship of principal and agent is created by their agreement, but this is not so in the case of trustee and beneficiary. The trustee does not represent the beneficiaries, though he performs his duties for their benefit, as the agent represents his principal. Further the trustee does not bring his beneficiaries into any contractual relationship with third parties, while it is the normal function of an agent to do so. Again the concept of a trust necessarily involves the concept of trust property over which the trustee has at least nominal control, but an agent need never have any control over any property belonging to his principal. An agent is subject to the control of his principal, but a trustee is not subject to control by the beneficiaries except in the sense that the beneficiaries can take steps to compel him to carry out the terms of the trust. Further it may be observed that the statutory provisions relating to trustees do not in general apply to agents. It may, however, be a matter of some difficulty to decide on the facts whether

---

[10] See chapter 20, infra.

[11] Provided it is completely constituted—see chapter 6, p 98 et seq, infra.

[12] See (1898) 14 LQR 272 (Spencer Brodhurst); (1933) 49 LQR 578 (W S Holdsworth); (1954) 17 MLR 24 (F E Dowrick); [1975] CLP 39 (J D Stephens); *Neste Oy u Lloyds Bank plc* [1983] 2 Lloyd's Rep 658.

[13] *Law of Trusts*, 12th edn, p 246.

[14] *Law of Agency*, 2nd edn, p 25; F E Dowrick, loc cit. *Ian Scott & Co v Medical Installations Co Ltd* (1981) 258 EG 556 illustrates the fiduciary nature of an agent's position. See also *Brandeis (Brokers) Ltd v Black* [2001] 2 All ER (Comm) 980.

a particular transaction sets up a trust or agency, nor are the institutions mutually exclusive.[15]

An agent may become a constructive trustee. If, for instance, his principal directs him to buy Blackacre, and he purports to buy it for himself, he will be held to be a constructive trustee of it for his principal.[16] Likewise if his principal transfers property to him for sale, investment or safe custody.[17] Also where he receives property on behalf of his principal, provided he is under a duty to keep it separate from his own property.[18]

(d) TRUSTS AND POWERS[19]

(i) Basic distinction

A power can be sufficiently defined for present purposes as an authority vested in a person to deal with or dispose of property not his own.[20] It can be distinguished from a trust succinctly—a trust is imperative, a power discretionary. One type of power in particular which is liable to be confused with a trust is a special[21] power of appointment. This is a power given to someone (called the donee of the power) under a trust or settlement authorizing him to appoint some or all of the trust property among a limited class of persons (called the objects of the power). The donee of the power can choose whether to make an appointment or not, and if by the end of the period during which the power can be exercised he has failed to make a valid appointment whether intentionally or unintentionally, the objects of the power can do nothing about it and the court has no jurisdiction to intervene.[22] If there is a gift over in

---

[15] See (1892) 8 LQR 220 (C Sweet); Scott, *Law of Trusts*, 4th edn, vol 1, p 95.

[16] *Longfield Parish Council v Robson* (1913) 29 TLR 357.

[17] See *Re Hallett's Estate* (1880) 13 Ch D 696; *Burdick v Garrick* (1870) 5 Ch App 233.

[18] *Lyell v Kennedy* (1889) 14 App Cas 437; *Foley v Hill* (1848) 2 HL Cas 28; *Aluminium Industrie Vaassen BV v Romalpa Aluminium Ltd* [1976] 2 All ER 552, [1976] 1 WLR 676; *Clough Mill Ltd v Martin* [1984] 3 All ER 982, [1985] 1 WLR 111, CA. As to bribes received by an agent see *A-G of Hong Kong v Reid* [1994] 1 AC 324, [1994] 1 All ER 1, PC.

[19] See generally [1970] ASCL 187 (J D Davies); (1971) 29 CLJ 68 (J Hopkins); (1971) 87 LQR 31 (J W Harris); (1974) 37 MLR 643 (Y Grbich); (1976) 54 CBR 229 (M C Cullity); (1977) 3 Mon LR 210 (Y Brbich); (1992) 5 Cant LR 67 (N P Gravells).

[20] *Freme v Clement* (1881) 18 Ch D 499; *Re Armstrong* (1866) 17 QBD 521.

[21] Contrast a general power of appointment, where the person to whom it is given may appoint to himself and make himself owner. In addition to general and special powers there are powers in a hybrid category. See (1949) 13 Conv 20 (J G Fleming); (1954) 18 Conv 565 (F R Crane). These 'hybrid' or 'intermediate powers', ie powers exercisable in favour of anyone, with certain exceptions, may be validly conferred upon trustees. They enable trustees to deal with virtually all eventualities, and at the same time make the maximum tax savings. See *Re Manisty's Settlement, Manisty v Manisty* [1974] Ch 17, [1973] 2 All ER 1203; *Re Hay's Settlement Trusts* [1981] 3 All ER 786; (1974) 33 CLJ 66 (John Hopkins). In the following discussion 'power' means a special or intermediate power of appointment. There is no rule of law against testamentary delegation which prevents the use of wide powers of appointment in wills: *Re Beatty's Will Trusts* [1990] 3 All ER 844, [1990] 1 WLR 1503; noted (1991) 107 LQR 211 (J D Davies); *Gregory v Hudson* (1998) 45 NSWLR 301.

[22] The court does, of course, have jurisdiction to see that a person does not exceed the power given to him. Thus an appointment which goes beyond the limits set to the power by the terms of the power itself or by law

default of appointment it will take effect: if not, there will be a resulting trust for the testator's[23] estate. Suppose, however, that instead of a person being given a mere power of appointment, a fund is given to trustees on trust to divide it among an ascertainable class of persons: in such case even though the trustees have been directed to divide it in such shares as they in their absolute discretion should think fit,[24] they would be under a duty to make the division, and in case of a failure to distribute any potential beneficiary could apply to the court which would see to it that the division took place.

It will have been observed that in the illustration of a power just given reference was made to a power of appointment arising under a trust. Since 1925 most powers, including all powers of appointment, are equitable only and can therefore only subsist behind a trust or settlement. Accordingly the real question is whether a particular provision in a trust instrument confers a power or imposes a trust. The fact that the provision is contained in a trust instrument does not mean, on the one hand, that an individual who, under a trust, is given a power of appointment is thereby necessarily constituted a trustee; nor, on the other hand, does it prevent a trustee being given a mere power of appointment, though where a power is given to a trustee ex officio he is not in the same position as an individual.

At one extreme, if a mere power is given to an individual he is under no duty to exercise it or even to consider whether he should exercise it. He owes no duty at all to the objects of the power. He is free to release the power even if he does so because as a consequence he will receive some benefit from one or other of the persons who take in default of appointment.[25] The objects can only complain if there is an excessive execution of the power, or if the appointment made constitutes a fraud on the power. At the other extreme if property is given to trustees on discretionary trusts the court will see to it that the trust is carried out.

In between these two extremes is the case where a power is given to a trustee ex officio.[26] In this case by reason of his fiduciary position the trustee, unlike an individual, is under a duty to consider[27] whether and in what way he should exercise the

---

is known as an excessive execution of the power and is void, eg appointment to grandchildren under a power to appoint to children. Again an appointment is void if it is 'a fraud on the power', or in more modern parlance an improper use of the power for a collateral purpose.

[23] Or for the settlor (or his estate) if the trust is created inter vivos.

[24] Ie a discretionary trust, see p 76, infra.

[25] *Re Greaves' Will Trusts* [1954] Ch 434, [1954] 1 All ER 771, CA; *Re Gulbenkian's Settlement Trusts* [1970] AC 508 at 518, [1968] 3 All ER 785 at 787, HL, per Lord Reid.

[26] A power given to trustees ex officio is not capable of being released, *Re Wills's Trust Deeds* [1964] Ch 219, [1963] 1 All ER 390; *Re Manisty's Settlement* [1974] Ch 17, [1973] 2 All ER 1203, in the absence of words in the trust deed authorizing them to do so, *Muir v IRC* [1966] 3 All ER 38, [1996] 1 WLR 1269, CA. Note that although an employer is not to be treated as a fiduciary when he exercises powers vested in him under a pension scheme, he owes an implied obligation of good faith to his employees: *National Grid Co plc v Mayes* [2001] UKHL 20, [2001] 2 All ER 417, HL.

[27] The duty of the trustees is to give properly informed consideration to the exercise of their powers—see *Stannard v Fisons Pension Trust Ltd* [1992] IRLR 27, CA.

power and cannot refuse to consider whether it ought to be exercised. As explained by
Megarry VC in *Re Hay's Settlement Trusts*:[28]

Normally the trustee is not bound to exercise [a mere power], and the court will not compel
him to do so. That, however, does not mean that he can simply fold his hands and ignore it,
for normally he must from time to time consider whether or not to exercise the power, and
the court may direct him to do this.

The decision of the trustees in the exercise of their discretion will not normally be
interfered with by the court. If for some reason the trustees cannot exercise the power,
the remedies available in discretionary trusts[29] have been held to be equally available.[30]

It is not always easy in practice to decide whether on its true construction a particular provision constitutes a power or a trust, as appears from a series of cases culminat-
ing in *McPhail v Doulton*.[31] In that case the judge at first instance and a majority in
the Court of Appeal held that the trustees had a mere power, while the House of Lords
unanimously agreed that the relevant provision constituted a trust. In the House of
Lords, Lord Wilberforce observed[32] how narrow and artificial the distinction could be:

what to one mind may appear as a power of distribution coupled with a trust to dispose of
the undistributed surplus, by accumulation or otherwise, may to another appear as a trust
for distribution coupled with a power to withhold a portion and accumulate or otherwise
dispose of it.

(ii) Special power of appointment—mere power or trust power

The inherent difficulty in understanding the relationship between trust and power is
not helped by the terminology used. In this context a power is commonly referred to
as a mere power, bare power or power collateral—these terms appear to be synonymous—in order to distinguish it from what is variously called a trust power, a power in
the nature of a trust, or a power coupled with a duty. A power will be a trust power
where, although at first sight it may appear to be a mere power, it is held that on the
true construction of the instrument there is an element of trust. It will later be
submitted that the term 'trust power' is used in two quite different senses.

The question whether a power is a mere power or a trust power has often arisen in
family trusts where the person to whom a power of appointment has been given has
died without exercising it, and where there is no gift over in default of appointment.
In such a case, if the court holds that the power is a mere power then, as we have seen,
the objects have no claim, and there will be a resulting trust: if, however, the court

---

[28] [1981] 3 All ER 786 at 792. No hint is given to the significance of the word 'normally' on either occasion
when it is used: *Re Gulbenkian's Settlement Trusts*, supra, HL at 518, 787 per Lord Reid; *McPhail v Doulton*
[1971] AC 424 at 449, [1970] 2 All ER 228 at 240, per Lord Wilberforce. See *Vestey v IRC (No 2)* [1979] 2 All
ER 225, esp at 235; affd [1980] AC 1148, [1979] 3 All ER 976, HL.

[29] See *McPhail v Doulton*, supra, HL at 457, 247, per Lord Wilberforce, and p 78, post.

[30] *Mettoy Pension Trustees Ltd v Evans*, supra (pension fund surplus: trustee, the company, in liquidation),
noted (1991) 107 LQR 214 (S Gardner); [1991] Conv 364 (Jill Martin). See also [1992] JBL 261 (R Nobles).

[31] Supra, HL. See *Pearson v IRC* [1981] AC 753, [1980] 2 All ER 479, HL.

[32] Supra, at 448, 240, HL.

holds that the power is a trust power, in default of appointment there will be held to be a trust in favour of the objects of the power. A leading case is *Burrough v Philcox*,[33] where a testator gave his surviving child, in the events which happened, power 'to dispose of all my real and personal estates amongst my nephews and nieces or their children, either all to one of them, or to as many of them as my surviving child shall think proper'. No appointment was made and the court held that the effect of this provision was to create a trust in favour of the nephews and nieces, and their children, subject to a power of selection in the surviving child, and that since the power had not been exercised the nephews and nieces and their children took equally. As Lord Cottenham explained,[34] 'when there appears a general intention in favour of a class, and a particular intention in favour of individuals of a class to be selected by another person, and the particular intention fails, from that selection not being made, the court will carry into effect the general intention in favour of the class'. In such a case it is the duty of the donee of the power to execute it and 'the court will not permit the objects of the power to suffer by the negligence or conduct of the donee, but fastens upon the property a trust for their benefit'.

Whether a power is a mere power or a trust power is a question of 'intention or presumed intention to be derived from the language of the instrument'.[35] It is clear, however, that a gift over in default of appointment, though not upon some other event,[36] is conclusive against the power being a trust power for it is inconsistent with an intention to benefit the objects of the power if the donee fails to exercise it.[37] This is so even though the gift over is itself void for some reason.[38] An ordinary residuary gift is not, however, a gift over for this purpose.[39]

Where there is no gift over, there is no 'inflexible and artificial rule of construction'[40] to the effect that a trust must be implied.

Although Evershed MR thought it 'clear that, where there is a power to appoint among a class, there will prima facie be implied a gift over in default of appointment to all the members of the class in equal shares',[41] it is submitted that the better view is that the court will be unwilling to infer a trust from a power in the absence of some other indication of an intention to benefit the class. Thus it was held that there was a mere power and no trust in *Re Weekes' Settlement*,[42] where a testatrix, having given her husband a life interest in certain property, gave him 'power to dispose of all such property by will amongst our children'; in *Re Combe*[43] where, following life interests to his wife and son, a testator directed his trustees to hold the property 'in trust for

---

[33] (1840) 5 My & Cr 72; *Brown v Higgs* (1803) 8 Ves 561 (affd (1813) 18 Ves 192, HL).

[34] *Burrough v Philcox* (1840) 5 My & Cr 72 at 92.

[35] Per Evershed MR in *Re Scarisbrick's Will Trusts* [1951] Ch 622 at 635, [1951] 1 All ER 822 at 828, CA.

[36] *Re Llewellyn's Settlement* [1921] 2 Ch 281.

[37] *Re Mills* [1930] 1 Ch 654, [1930] All ER Rep 355, CA.   [38] *Re Sprague* (1880) 43 LT 236.

[39] *Re Brierley* (1894) 43 WR 36, CA.

[40] Per Tomlin J in *Re Combe* [1925] Ch 210 at 216, [1925] All ER Rep 159 at 162.

[41] *Re Scarisbrick's Will Trusts* [1951] Ch 622 at 635, [1951] 1 All ER 822 at 828, CA.

[42] [1897] 1 Ch 289.   [43] [1925] Ch 210, [1925] All ER Rep 159.

such person or persons as my said son . . . shall by will appoint, but I direct that such appointment must be confined to any relation or relations of mine of the whole blood'; and in *Re Perowne*,[44] where a testatrix gave her husband a life interest in her estate and continued, 'knowing that he will make arrangements for the disposal of my estate, according to my wishes, for the benefit of my family'.

In most of the family trust cases where the court has decided that the power is a trust power, the court has held that the power remains a power, but, finding an intention on the part of the testator to benefit the objects of the power in any event, has implied a trust in their favour in default of appointment. Thus in *Re Wills' Trust Deeds*[45] Buckley J said that it really turns on 'the question whether on the particular facts of each case it was proper to infer a trust in default of appointment for the objects of the power. The court did not, and, I think, could not compel the donee personally to exercise the power but carried what it conceived to be the settlor's intention into effect by executing an implied trust in default of appointment.' Where the court holds that a trust is to be implied in default of appointment, it determines logically who the beneficiaries under the trust should be. A typical case is *Walsh v Wallinger*[46] where a husband left property to his wife 'trusting that she will, at her decease, give and bequeath the same to our children in such a manner as she shall appoint'. Since the wife's power of appointment could only be exercised by will, an appointment by the wife could only be made to children living at her death. No appointment having been made the court held that there was an implied trust in default of appointment for those children only who survived the wife,[47] as being those whom the testator presumably intended to benefit. It is always a question of the construction of the particular instrument and some cases cited in this context do not really involve an implied trust at all. An example is *Lambert v Thwaites*[48] where the trust was, in effect, to sell real estate and divide the proceeds 'amongst all and every the children [of RW] in such shares and proportions, manner and form' as RW should by will appoint. It was held that on its true construction this was a trust for all the children of RW, subject, however, to the power of appointment. The children accordingly obtained vested interests liable to be divested if the power of appointment was exercised. RW having died without exercising the power, all his children, including the estate of his deceased son Alfred, took equal shares.

It may be added that where the court holds there is an implied trust in default of appointment, it applies the maxim 'equality is equity' and divides the property among the beneficiaries equally.[49]

---

[44] [1951] Ch 785, [1951] 2 All ER 201.   [45] [1964] Ch 219, [1963] 1 All ER 390.

[46] (1830) 2 Russ & M 78; *Re Arnold's Trusts* [1947] Ch 131, [1946] 2 All ER 579. For the special position where there is a trust power in favour of relations or members of the donee's family see *IRC v Broadway Cottages Trust* [1955] Ch 20, [1954] 3 All ER 120, CA, and cases there cited; *Re Poulton's Will Trusts* [1987] 1 All ER 1068, [1987] 1 WLR 795.

[47] Ie the estates of children who had predeceased their mother got nothing.

[48] (1866) LR 2 Eq 151, Kindersley VC observed at 157: 'In the case now before the Court there is in express terms a direct gift to the children.'

[49] *Wilson v Duguid* (1883) 24 Ch D 244; *Re Llewellyn's Settlement* [1921] 2 Ch 281; *Re Arnold's Trusts*, supra.

(iii) Trust in default of appointment or discretionary trust

As has just been seen, in most of the family trust cases where a power has been held to be a trust power, the court has implied a trust in default of appointment. In other cases,[50] however, it has also been called a trust power where the court has held that the power was of a fiduciary character which the donee of the power was under a duty to exercise, and that if he should fail to exercise the power, the court would in some way see to it that the duty was carried out. As Lord Eldon said in *Brown v Higgs*,[51] 'the court adopts the principle as to trusts and will not permit his [ie the donee of the power] negligence, accident or other circumstances to disappoint the interests of those for whose benefit he is called upon to execute it' but will 'discharge the duty in his room and place'.

This second construction has been adopted in a number of cases concerning large benevolent funds, such as *McPhail v Doulton*[52] where the trustees were directed to make grants out of income 'at their absolute discretion . . . to . . . any of the officers and employees or ex-officers or ex-employees of the Company or to any relatives or dependants of any such persons'. As already mentioned, in that case all the Law Lords agreed that it was a case of a trust, not a mere power. Though they differed on other points going to the very validity of the trust, they also agreed that, if the trust was valid, the trustees would be under a fiduciary duty to exercise the power, and that if the trustees failed to exercise it, then the court would do so.[53]

It is unfortunate that the term 'trust power' has been used in these two different senses, viz (i) where the court implies a trust in default of appointment, and (ii) where it holds the power to be of a fiduciary nature, which it will itself exercise if necessary. It is, indeed, somewhat curious as well as unfortunate, for a trust power in the second sense is indistinguishable from what is usually referred to as a 'discretionary trust', that is, a trust under which the trustees are given a discretionary and fiduciary power to decide which of the class of potential beneficiaries shall take.[54] Indeed in further proceedings in *McPhail v Doulton*,[55] the term used is discretionary trust and not trust power. It is to be hoped this will become the accepted terminology, and that the term 'trust power' will be restricted to the case where a trust is implied in default of appointment.

A trust power in the sense of a discretionary trust has been described as intermediate between trusts and powers: it is, it is submitted, essentially a trust and is in most

---

[50] Eg *Brown v Higgs* (1803) 8 Ves 561; affd (1813) 18 Ves 192, HL, though it has not by any means always been so regarded, and was one of the few cases cited in *Re Wills' Trust Deeds*, supra; *Burrough v Philcox* (1840) 5 My & Cr 72, where dicta can be found to support both views; *Re Leek* [1967] Ch 1061, [1967] 2 All ER 1160; (affd [1969] 1 Ch 563, [1968] 1 All ER 793, CA). See (1971) 29 CLJ 68 (J Hopkins).

[51] Supra.   [52] [1971] AC 424, [1970] 2 All ER 228, HL.

[53] As to how the court would exercise the power, see p 78 infra.

[54] See p 76, infra. See also [1984] Conv 227 (R Bartlett and C Stebbings).

[55] *Re Baden's Deed Trusts (No 2)* [1972] Ch 607, [1971] 3 All ER 985; affd [1973] Ch 9, [1972] 2 All ER 1304, CA.

respects treated as such, but in one important respect, as will be seen shortly, it has been virtually assimilated to a mere power.

It should be added that the courts have in fact seldom discussed,[56] and often do not seem to have recognized the existence of, the two different senses in which the term, 'trust power' is used. What has usually happened in practice is that the court has in substance discussed either the question 'is it a mere power or is there an implied trust in default of appointment?' or, alternatively, the question 'is it a mere power or a discretionary trust?' Assuming that the courts in future distinguish between the two senses of trust power, it seems a clear inference from *McPhail v Doulton*[57] that in the case of a 'trust power' for a large class or classes of beneficiaries, the second sense, that of discretionary trust, is likely to be thought more appropriate, though it may well be that where the trust power is in favour of a small defined class of persons the court will prefer to imply a trust in default of appointment.

(iv) Mere powers and discretionary trusts

As we shall see,[58] the assimilation of the rules as to certainty for powers and discretionary trusts has removed the main practical reason for having to distinguish between them. Certain differences remain, however, and in appropriate circumstances may be of considerable importance. There is still a vital distinction where the power or trust is not exercised. In the case of a mere power the property goes to the persons entitled in default of appointment, either by express or implied gift over or by way of resulting trust, while in the case of a discretionary trust the beneficiaries will not be allowed to suffer by reason of the default of the trustees and the court will in some way ensure that the trust is executed.

Another distinction was suggested by Lord Wilberforce in *McPhail v Doulton.*[59] 'As to the trustees' duty of enquiry or ascertainment,' he said, 'in each case the trustees ought to make such a survey of the range of objects or possible beneficiaries as will enable them to carry out their fiduciary duty. A wider and more comprehensive range of enquiry is called for in the case of [discretionary trusts][60] than in the case of powers.' In so far as it relates to powers, this rather vague dictum is dealing with, and is restricted to, powers given to trustees. An individual to whom a mere power is given is normally under no fiduciary duty to survey the range of objects at all. Where trustees have a power which they have decided to exercise it has been cogently argued[61] that the distinction drawn by Lord Wilberforce is invalid, and that the duty of the enquiry should be the same as in a discretionary trust. The fiduciary obligation at this stage should be the same. There is no justification for allowing one fiduciary to

---

[56] Chitty J noted the distinction in *Wilson v Duguid* (1883) 24 Ch D 244 at 249, but said that in that case there was a plain implication of a trust in default of appointment, and no need to refer to the concept of a duty to be exercised by the trustees. See (1962) 26 Conv 92 (M G Unwin); (1967) 31 Conv 364 (F R Crane).

[57] Supra, HL.   [58] See p 51 et seq, infra.

[59] [1971] AC 424 at 457, [1970] 2 All ER 228 at 247, HL. See generally (1990) 4 TL & P 117 (Fiona Spearing).

[60] Lord Wilberforce actually used the term 'trust powers'.   [61] (1974) 38 Conv 269 (L McKay).

discharge his duty by a lower, or higher, standard than another. The difference appears at the earlier stage previously discussed.[62]

In *Re Hay's Settlement Trusts*,[63] Megarry VC considered how in the case of a power given to trustees the duty of making a responsible survey and selection should be carried out in the absence of any complete list of objects. The trustee, he said, 'must not simply proceed to exercise the power in favour of such of the objects as happen to be at hand or claim his attention. He must first consider what persons or class of persons are objects of the power. ... In doing this, there is no need to compile a complete list of the objects, or even to make an accurate assessment of the number of them: what is needed is an appreciation of the width of the field.' Having applied his mind to the 'size of the problem' he can then consider in individual cases whether, in relation to other possible claimants, a particular grant is appropriate, though he is not required to make an exact calculation whether, as between deserving claimants, A is more deserving than B.

(v) Unenforceable trusts or trusts of imperfect obligation

These trusts, as the alternative names imply, constitute an exception to the principle that trusts are imperative, powers discretionary. In these trusts the trustees cannot be compelled to carry out their duties; they are, in substance, powers rather than trusts and are admittedly anomalous and exceptional. They are discussed later.[64]

(e) TRUSTS AND THE ADMINISTRATION OF ESTATES OF DECEASED PERSONS

Though different in origin, trusts having been developed by the Lord Chancellor and the jurisdiction over personal representatives having been at first exercised only in the ecclesiastical courts, it is not now possible to draw a clear line between trustees and personal representatives. In fact a person may well be at the same time both trustee and personal representative, though for particular purposes one office may be pre-dominant. The main principles which produce this somewhat confusing situation are as follows.

(i) Until the coming into force of s 50 of the Administration of Justice Act 1985, the rule was that a personal representative retained his office for the whole of his life,[65] unless that grant was originally of a limited duration, or was subsequently revoked by the court. An example of a limited grant is where a minor is appointed sole executor. In this case a grant of administration is made to his parents or guardians for his use and benefit until he attains the age of 18 years. Such a grant automatically determines

---

[62] See p 31, supra.   [63] [1981] 3 All ER 786, [1982] 1 WLR 202. See [1982] Conv 432 (A Grubb).
[64] See p 58 at seq, infra.
[65] *Re Timmis* [1902] 1 Ch 176 at 183 per Kekewich J; *George Attenborough & Son v Solomon* [1913] AC 76 at 83, HL, per Haldane LC; *Harvell v Foster* [1954] 2 QB 367, [1954] 2 All ER 736, CA, per Evershed MR; *Re Aldhous* [1955] 2 All ER 80, [1955] 1 WLR 459.

on his attaining that age or earlier death. As to revocation, this may occur for various reasons, for example, if it appears that the presumed deceased is still alive. The 1985 Act now empowers the court to appoint a substituted personal representative in place of the existing personal representative or representatives or any of them, or to remove one or more, but not all, of the existing personal representatives.

(ii) In a number of cases of which *Re Ponder*[66] is perhaps the best known, it has been held that a personal representative who has paid all expenses and debts, cleared the estate and completed his duties in a proper way, becomes functus officio[67] as such, and holds the residue not as a personal representative, but as a trustee, and can accordingly exercise the statutory power to appoint new trustees. Some doubt was cast upon this view by a reserved judgment of a strong Court of Appeal in *Harvell v Foster*,[68] where an administrator was held liable as such[69] when all the duties of his office had been performed save the distribution of the net residue, which was impossible by reason of the minority of the residuary legatee. Danckwerts J criticized dicta in this case in *Re Cockburn*[70] and had no doubt that a personal representative who has completed his duties in a proper way can appoint new trustees. There seems in fact to be no necessary conflict between *Re Cockburn* and *Re Ponder* on the one hand, and *Harvell v Foster* on the other, if it is accepted, as it was by the Court of Appeal in the last mentioned case, disapproving on this point Sargant J's view in *Re Ponder*, that the offices of personal representative and trustee are not mutually exclusive. On this basis he can, qua trustee, exercise the statutory power to appoint new trustees,[71] while, qua personal representative, he remains liable for any failure to carry out his duties as such.

It should be observed that until the estate, whether of a testator[72] or an intestate,[73] is fully administered, the residuary legatees, or the next of kin of an intestate, are not to be regarded as the beneficial owners of the unadministered assets. The personal representatives hold the assets in full ownership without distinction between legal and equitable interests. It is also true, however, that they hold them for the purpose of carrying out the functions and duties of administration, not for their own benefit, and that these functions and duties may be enforced by creditors and beneficiaries. The result therefore is that a personal representative is in a fiduciary position with regard to the assets that come to him in the right of his office and for certain purposes and in

---

[66] [1921] 2 Ch 59; *Re Yerburgh* [1928] WN 208; *Re Cockburn's Will Trusts* [1957] Ch 438, [1957] 2 All ER 522. See (1991) 11 Ox JLS 609 (Chantal Stebbings).

[67] As to this term see [1990] Conv 427 (Chantal Stebbings).

[68] Supra. See (1955) 19 Conv 199 (B S Ker).

[69] The action was actually against the sureties in the administration bond. As to sureties, see now the Supreme Court Act 1981, s 120.

[70] Supra.

[71] But where land is concerned see *Re King's Will Trusts* [1964] Ch 542, [1964] 1 All ER 833; [1976] CLP 60 (E C Ryder) and p 40 n 81, infra.

[72] *Stamp Duties Comr (Queensland) v Livingston* [1965] AC 694, [1964] 3 All ER 692, PC. See [1992] Conv 92 (Julie Maxton).

[73] *Eastbourne Mutual Building Society v Hastings Corpn* [1965] 1 All ER 779.

some aspects he is treated by the court as a trustee. But equity has never recognized or created for residuary legatees, or the next of kin of an intestate, a beneficial interest in the assets in the hands of the personal representatives during the course of administration.[74] One consequence of this is that personal representatives are not under the same duty as trustees to hold the balance evenly between the beneficiaries.[75] And the memoranda in *Crowden v Aldridge*[76] could not operate as assignments because when they were signed none of the residuary legatees had any beneficial interest in the estate. They constituted a direction to the executors varying their obligations in the administration and distribution of the estate.

(iii) The same persons are commonly appointed as executors and trustees by a testator. In the absence of an express assent, an implied assent to themselves as trustees will readily be inferred from their conduct where executors have completed their duties as such. This was of vital importance in *Attenborough v Solomon*[77] by reason of an important difference between the power of one of two or more trustees, and that of one of two or more personal representatives. Trustees can only act unanimously,[78] and accordingly one of two or more trustees has no power to deal with or dispose of the trust property. By contrast one of two or more personal representatives has full power to deal with or dispose of pure personalty, and it seems to make no difference whether he is an executor or an administrator. So far as land is concerned, whether freehold or leasehold, where there are two or more personal representatives they must all concur in any contract or conveyance in respect thereof.[79]

In *Attenborough & Son v Solomon*[80] the property involved was pure personalty, and what had happened was that long after the debts and pecuniary legacies had been paid and the residuary account passed, one of two persons appointed as executors and trustees pledged certain plate forming part of the residuary estate with pawnbrokers and misapplied the money so raised. After the death of the pledgor, the transaction was discovered and an action was brought by the surviving coexecutor and a new trustee against the pawnbroker to recover the plate. They were held entitled to succeed on the ground that the proper inference to be drawn was that before the date of the pledge the executors had assented to the trust disposition taking effect and held the

---

[74] *Stamp Duties Comr (Queensland) v Livingston*, supra; *Re Leigh's Will Trusts* [1970] Ch 277, [1969] 3 All ER 432; *Marshall v Kerr* [1995] 1 AC 148, [1994] 3 All ER 106, HL. But note that, subject to the right of the personal representatives to resort to it for the purposes of administration, a specific bequest or devise belongs to the legatee or devisee as soon as the testator dies—*Re K* [1986] Ch 180, [1985] 2 All ER 833, CA. See (1965) 23 CLJ 44 (S J Bailey); Meagher, Gummow and Lehane, *Equity—Doctrine and Remedies*, 3rd edn, p 96 et seq.

[75] *Re Hayes's Will Trusts* [1971] 2 All ER 341, [1971] 1 WLR 758 (power to sell to a beneficiary at estate duty valuation. Executors bound to consider interest of estate as a whole, but under no duty to consider effect between trust beneficiaries). See p 428 et seq as to duty of trustees.

[76] [1993] 3 All ER 603, [1993] 1 WLR 433, criticized [1994] Conv 446 (J G Ross and Martyn).

[77] [1913] AC 76, HL; *Phillipo v Munnings* (1837) 2 My & Cr 309; *Re Claremont* [1923] 2 KB 718.

[78] For discussion of this rule see chapter 17, section 3, p 395 et seq, infra.

[79] Administration of Estates Act 1925, ss 2(2) as amended by the Law of Property (Miscellaneous Provisions) Act 1994, s 16.

[80] Supra, HL. See [1984] Conv 423 (Chantal Stebbings).

plate not as executors but as trustees. Since 1925 it should be noted that an assent to land must be in writing, even in the case of a personal representative assenting to himself as a trustee.[81]

(iv) The amount of overlapping has been increased by the definition in the Trustee Act 1925[82] of a trustee as including a personal representative, where the context admits, and by the provisions of the Administration of Estates Act 1925[83] which constitute an administrator and express trustee both on a total and partial[84] intestacy. Further ss 1–9, 12, 13 and 15–18 of the Trusts of Land and Appointment of Trustees Act 1996[85] apply to personal representatives, but with appropriate modifications and without prejudice to the functions of personal representatives for the purposes of administration,[86] and the Trustee Act 2000 likewise applies to personal representatives with appropriate modifications.[87]

(v) The distinction between personal representative and trustee may also be relevant with regard to the Statutes of Limitation,[88] and by reason of the rule that a sole personal representative, whether or not a trust corporation, can give a valid receipt for capital money arising on a sale of the deceased's land, while there must be at least two trustees of a trust of land for this purpose, unless the sole trustee happens to be a trust corporation.[89] For most purposes, however, Jessel MR correctly summarized the position when he observed in *Re Speight*:[90]

In modern times the Courts have not distinguished between . . . executors and trustees but they have put them all together and considered that they are all liable under the same principles.

---

[81] Administration of Estates Act 1925, s 36; *Re King's Will Trusts* [1964] Ch 542, [1964] 1 All ER 833, criticized in (1964) 28 Conv 298 (J F Garner), and not followed in Ireland: *Mohan v Roche* [1991] 1 IR 560, noted [1992] Conv 383 (J A Dowling). According to this not altogether convincing decision, without a written assent a personal representative who has become a trustee cannot, as regards land, take advantage of s 40 of the Trustee Act 1925 (discussed in chapter 15, section 2) on the appointment of new trustees. Cf *Re Cockburn's Will Trusts* [1957] Ch 438, [1957] 2 All ER 522, apparently not cited in *Re King's Will Trusts* supra. The most valuable discussion is in [1976] CLP 60 (E C Ryder). The Court of Appeal proceeded on the basis that *Re King's Will Trusts* was correctly decided in *Re Edward's Will Trusts* [1982] Ch 30, [1981] 2 All ER 941, CA, discussed [1981] Conv 450 (G Shindler) and [1982] Conv 4 (P W Smith). It seems that the rule is now so well understood and established in practice that its advantages in certainty outweigh the occasional practice difficulties, and Law Com No 184 accordingly does not recommend a change in the law. As to assents over personal property see [1990] Conv 257 (Chantal Stebbings).

[82] Section 68(17).

[83] Section 33, as amended by the Trusts of Land and Appointment of Trustees Act 1996 and the Trustee Act 2000. Cf Land Transfer Act 1897, s 2, and *Toates v Toates* [1926] 2 KB 30, DC.

[84] Section 9 is prospectively amended by the Mental Capacity Act 2005, Sch 6, para 41.

[85] Administration of Estates Act 1925, s 49, as amended.

[86] Trusts of Land and Appointment of Trustees Act 1996, s 18.   [87] Trustee Act 2000, s 35.

[88] See chapter 24, section 3(d), p 538 infra.

[89] Law of Property Act 1925, s 27(2), as substituted by the Law of Property (Amendment) Act 1926, s 7, and Schedule and amended by the Trusts of Land and Appointment of Trustees Act 1996.

[90] (1883) 22 Ch D 727 at 742, CA; affd sub nom *Speight v Gaunt* (1883) 9 App Cas 1, HL.

(f) TRUST AND RESTITUTION

Restitution, which may be described as 'the law concerned with reversing a defendant's unjust enrichment at the claimant's expense'[91] has now been recognized by the
House of Lords as a part of English law.[92] Burrows[93] states that it 'is most akin to, and
belongs aside, contract and tort', but there is an overlap with the law of trusts. Thus
both the works cited include sections dealing with restitution in respect of benefits
acquired in breach of fiduciary relationships, such as profits made by a trustee out of
his trust.

In *Westdeutsche Landesbank Girozentale v Islington London Borough Council*[94] Lord
Goff observed that in recent years restitution lawyers, since certain equitable institutions, notably the constructive trust and the resulting trust, have been perceived to
have the function of reversing unjust enrichment, had sought to embrace those
institutions within the law of restitution, if necessary moulding them to make them
fit for that purpose. Equity lawyers, on the other hand, were concerned that the trust
concept should not be distorted, and also that the practical consequences of the
imposition of a trust should be fully appreciated. In the same case Lord Browne-
Wilkinson said that the resulting trust is an unsuitable basis for developing proprietary restitutionary remedies. However, he added, the remedial constructive trust, if
introduced into English law, might provide a more satisfactory road forward.[95]

---

[91] Burrows, *The Law of Restitution* (2nd edn), 1. See also Goff & Jones, *The Law of Restitution*, 6th edn,
chap. 1. S Headley in [1995] CLJ 578 argues that emphasis on the theory of unjust enrichment has gone
much too far.

[92] *Lipkin Gorman (a firm) v Karpnale Ltd* [1991] 2 AC 548, [1992] 4 All ER 512, HL; *Woolwich Equitable
Building Society v IRC* [1993] AC 70, sub nom *Woolwich Building Society v IRC (No 2)* [1992] 3 All ER 727, HL.

[93] Loc cit.   [94] [1996] AC 669, [1996] 2 All ER 961, HL, noted [1997] Conv 1 (AJ Oakley).

[95] At 999. But see *Re Polly Peck International plc (in administration) (No 2)* [1998] 3 All ER 812, CA, p 66 et
seq, infra.

3

THE ESSENTIALS OF A TRUST

1 CAPACITY OF SETTLOR AND BENEFICIARIES

(a) CAPACITY OF SETTLOR

Capacity to create a trust is, in general, the same as capacity to hold and dispose of any legal or equitable estate or interest in property.

A minor cannot, since 1925, hold a legal estate in land[1] and accordingly cannot settle it.[2] As regards other property, the position is similar to the rule in relation to contracts involving the acquisition of an interest in property of a permanent nature;[3] accordingly an inter vivos settlement by a minor is voidable in the sense that it will be binding upon the minor after he comes of age unless he repudiates it on, or shortly after, attaining his majority.[4] So far as a settlement by will is concerned, a minor cannot make a valid will,[5] unless he is a soldier[6] being in actual military service or a mariner or seaman being at sea.[7]

Where a person, referred to in the Mental Health Act 1983 as a patient, is incapable, by reason of mental disorder, of managing and administering his property and affairs, and a receiver has been appointed,[8] any purported inter vivos disposition, including a settlement, executed by him will, it is thought, he void under the 1983 Act for the same reasons as it was held void under the old law, namely that by the appointment the right of the patient to manage his affairs is suspended, and the sole management thereof in the meantime is committed to the receiver.[9] He may, however, make a will during a lucid interval because a will does not take effect until death, at which time

---

[1] Law of Property Act 1925, s 1(6).   [2] He can however have an equitable interest.

[3] See Cheshire, Fifoot and Furmston, *Law of Contract*, 14th edn, p 483 et seq.

[4] *Edwards v Carter* [1893] AC 360, HL. The position is unaffected by the Minors' Contracts Act 1987.

[5] Wills Act 1837, s 7, as amended by s 3 Family Law Reform Act 1969.

[6] Including a member of the Royal Air Force: Wills (Soldiers and Sailors) Act 1918, s 5(2).

[7] Wills Act 1837, s 11, as amended by the Wills (Soldiers and Sailors) Act 1918. The privilege also extends to a member of the Royal Naval and Marine Forces when so circumstanced that if he were a soldier he would be in actual military service.

[8] Mental Health Act 1983, ss 94, 99.

[9] *Re Walker* [1905] 1 Ch 160, CA (lunatic so found by inquisition); *Re Marshall* [1920] 1 Ch 284, [1920] All ER Rep 190 (receiver appointed under Lunacy Act 1890).

the Court of Protection has no further concern for his affairs. There is therefore no conflict of control.[10]

Where a receiver has not been appointed the question is whether the person concerned is capable of understanding what he does by executing the deed in question when its general purport has been fully explained to him. For the making of a valid will a high degree of understanding is required, including an understanding of the claims of all potential beneficiaries and the extent of the property to be disposed of. The same degree of understanding may be required in the case of an inter vivos gift or settlement, though here it varies with the circumstances of the transaction, and a much lower degree of understanding would suffice if the subject matter and value of a gift are trivial in relation to the donor's other assets.[11]

By the Mental Health Act 1983[12] jurisdiction is given to the judge[13] to make orders or give directions for the settlement of any property of a patient as defined above; and to make a will for him,[14] provided the patient is of full age.[15] This involves power to make such consequential vesting or other orders as may be required;[16] and to vary the settlement, at any time before the death of the patient, if it appears that some material fact was not disclosed when the settlement was made, or that there had been some substantial change in circumstances.[17] In exercising the jurisdiction the judge will be guided by what it is thought likely the patient would himself do if he were not under disability, but on the assumption that his circumstances in other respects are what they are in fact.[18] Thus in *Re TB*[19] the court approved a revocable settlement of the whole of a patient's property in favour of the patient's illegitimate son and his family. The effect of this was to benefit the son and his family, who otherwise[20] would get nothing at all, to the exclusion of the patient's collateral next-of-kin, if, as was expected, the patient were to die without recovering his testamentary capacity.

Part 7 (ss 93–113) of the Mental Health Act 1983 will be repealed and replaced by provisions in the Mental Capacity Act 2005 when that Act is brought into force. The

---

[10] *Re Beaney* [1978] 2 All ER 595, [1978] 1 WLR 770.

[11] *Re Beaney*, supra. See [1984] Conv 32 and [1986] Conv 78 (A H Hudson). As to the burden of proof see *Williams v Williams* [2003] EWHC 742 (Ch), [2003] All ER(D) 403 (Feb).

[12] Sections 95, 96 and 97.

[13] Defined for this purpose by s 94 (as amended by the Public Trustee and Administration of Funds Act 1986).

[14] See (1985) 82 LSG 1617 (J M R Thurston). For instances of the exercise of the power see *Re Davey* [1980] 3 All ER 342, [1981] 1 WLR 164; *Re C*, [1991] 3 All ER 866 (Ct of Protection); *Re D (J)* [1982] Ch 237, [1982] 2 All ER 37.

[15] Ibid, s 96(4)(a).   [16] Ibid, s 96(2).   [17] Ibid, s 96(3).

[18] *Re C* supra (Ct of Protection) noted [1991] JSW & FL 494 (Carol Brennan). Cf *Re S* [1997] 1 FLR 96 (Ct of Protection).

[19] [1967] Ch 247, [1966] 3 All ER 509 (Ct of Protection).

[20] But see now Family Law Reform Act 1987, s 1.

2005 Act provides that if a person lacks capacity[21] in relation to a matter concerning his property and affairs the court may by making a order, make the decision on his behalf.[22] The powers of the court are subject to the principles set out in s 1, which require that the decision be made in his best interests.[23] In particular the powers extend to the settlement of that person's property, whether for his benefit or for the benefit of others, and the execution for him of a will.[24] It is thought that the approach of the courts to the new provisions will be the same as that to the 1983 Act.

(b) CAPACITY OF BENEFICIARY

In general, anyone who can hold an interest in property can be a beneficiary under a trust. A minor can have an equitable interest in land, although he cannot hold a legal estate.[25] It should be added that a beneficiary may be a trustee, even a sole trustee, though a sole trustee cannot hold on trust for himself as sole beneficiary. No trust can exist where the entire estate, both legal and equitable, is vested in one person.[26] The legal title carries with it all rights. Accordingly where the absolute owner at law and in equity pays money or transfers property to another under what turns out to be a void contract, it cannot successfully be contended that the transferor retains the equitable interest in the money or property transferred. The only question could be whether the circumstances were such as to impose a trust on the transferee.[27]

2 THE THREE CERTAINTIES

Lord Langdale's judgment in *Knight v Knight*[28] is frequently referred to as setting out the proposition that in order for a trust to be valid the 'three certainties' must be present—certainty of words, certainty of subject, and certainty of object. There was, however, nothing novel in this statement. Lord Eldon, for instance,[29] said that in order

---

[21] A person lacks capacity in relation to a matter if, on the balance of probabilities, at the material time he is unable to make a decision for himself in relation to the matter because of an impairment of, or a disturbance in the functioning of the mind or brain, whether permanent or temporary: s 2(1),(2),(4). As to establishing lack of capacity note s 2(3), and in the case of persons under the age of 16 there are limitations on the exercise of powers under the Act: ss 2(5),(6), 18(3).

[22] Section 16(1)(2)(a). Alternatively the court may appoint a person ('a deputy') to make decisions on his behalf; s 16(2)(b).

[23] What is required in determining a person's best interests is explained in s 4.

[24] Section 18(1)(h),(i).   [25] Law of Property Act 1925, s 1(6).

[26] *Re Cook* [1948] Ch 212, [1948] 1 All ER 231.

[27] *Westdeutsche Landesbank Girozentrale v Islington London Borough Council* [1996] 2 All ER 961, HL, per Lord Browne-Wilkinson at 989, 991, 992.

[28] (1840) 3 Beav 148. For a case where the question of uncertainty arose in an unusual form, see *Muir v IRC* [1966] 3 All ER 38, [1966] 1 WLR 1269, CA. See (1979) 8 AALR 123 (T G Watkin); (1986) 8 U Tas LR 209 (J D Davies). Text above cited *Creaglean v Hazen* (1999) 551 APR 240.

[29] In *Wright v Aykyns* (1823) Turn & R 143 at 157.

for a trust to be valid, 'first, that the words must be imperative . . .; secondly, that the subject must be certain . . .; and thirdly, that the object must be as certain as the subject'. Each of these three certainties will now be considered in turn.

(a) CERTAINTY OF WORDS

Since 'equity looks to the intent rather than the form' there is no need for any technical expression to be used in order to constitute a trust.[30] It is a question in every case of construction of the words used to ascertain whether they (together with any admissible extrinsic evidence[31]) establish an intention to set up a trust. Thus in *Re Kayford Ltd*[32] members of the public paid money to the company for the future supply of goods. The company having doubts as to its ability to deliver the goods paid the money into a separate account on trust for the customers pending delivery. A trust was established. In contrast in *Re B (Child: Property Transfer)*[33] it was held that an order under the Guardianship of Minors Act 1971 transferring property from the father to the mother 'for the benefit of the child' did not create a trust in favour of the child.

The question has often arisen under wills whether a trust is created where the testator has in terms expressed his confidence, wish, belief, desire, hope or recommendation that the legatee or devisee will use the gift in a certain way, or whether in such a case the legatee or devisee takes beneficially with at most a moral obligation to use the gift in the way indicated. In the earlier cases[34] the courts were very ready to hold that such precatory words set up what is commonly called a 'precatory trust'. Rigby LJ[35] has however, castigated this phrase as 'a misleading nickname', pointing out that if, as a matter of construction, precatory words are held to set up a

---

[30] Conversely it has been held in New Zealand that the use of the word 'trust' in a statute does not necessarily give rise to a trust in the equity sense, and it is thought that the same would be true in England: *Wellington Harness Racing Club v Hutt City Council* [2004] 1 NZLR 82.

[31] The Administration of Justice Act 1982, s 21 provides that extrinsic evidence, including evidence of the testator's intention, may be admitted to assist in the interpretation of a will in so far as any part is meaningless or ambiguous on its face or in the light of surrounding circumstances.

[32] [1975] 1 All ER 604, [1975] 1 WLR 279, criticized (1983) 21 Alberta LR 295 (D W M Waters) and discussed [1985] JBL 456 (P Richardson). Likewise in *Re Chelsea Cloisters Ltd* (1980) 41 P & CR 98, CA (tenants' deposits—landlord company in liquidation); *Re Eastern Capital Futures Ltd* [1989] BCLC 371; *Re Lewis's of Leicester Ltd* [1995] 1 BCLC 428; *Re Branston & Gothard Ltd* [1999] BPIR 466; *Re Japan Leasing (Europe) plc* [2000] 2 WTLR 301. See the discussion in (1980) 43 MLR 489 (W Goodhart & G Jones); [1994] Denning LJ 93 (G McCormack).

[33] [1999] 2 FLR 418, CA, noted (1999) 11 T & ELJ 10 (S Webster). See also *Re H B Haina & Associates Inc* (1978) 86 DLR (3d) 262 (advance payments received by travel agent and deposited in so-called 'trust account': trust not established); *Re Multi Guarantee Co Ltd* [1987] BCLC 257, CA, discussed (1988) 85 LSG 36/14 (I M Hardcastle); *Customs and Excise Commissioners v Richmond Theatre Management Ltd* [1995] STC 257; *Re Holiday Promotions (Europe) Ltd* [1996] 2 BCLC 618. For a novel approach see (1983) 33 UTLJ 381 (M Pickard).

[34] Eg *Palmer v Simmonds* (1854) 2 Drew 221; *Gully v Cregoe* (1857) 24 Beav 185.

[35] In *Re Williams* [1897] 2 Ch 12 at 27, CA.

trust, the trust so constituted is a perfectly ordinary trust with no special or unusual characteristics.

It is generally agreed that there was a change of approach by the courts during the nineteenth century. *Lambe v Eames*,[36] in 1871, is sometimes said to be the turning point,[37] but Lord St Leonards had pointed out the change of attitude more than 20 years before.[38] There is in fact, no clear dividing line and even after *Lambe v Eames*[39] there are cases[40] where the older approach is still adopted.

The proper attitude to precatory words is stated in the judgment of Cotton LJ in *Re Adams and the Kensington Vestry*,[41] where it was held that there was no trust created by a testator who gave all his property to his wife 'in full confidence that she will do what is right as to the disposal thereof between my children, either in her lifetime, or by will after her decease'. He said:

> ... some of the older authorities went a great deal too far in holding that some particular words appearing in a will were sufficient to create a trust. Undoubtedly confidence, if the rest of the context shows that a trust is intended, may make a trust,[42] but what we have to look at is the whole of the will which we have to construe, and if the confidence is that she will do what is right as regards the disposal of property, I cannot say that that is, on the true construction of the will, a trust imposed upon her. Having regard to the later decisions, we must not extend the old cases in any way, or rely upon the mere use of any particular words, but, considering all the words which are used, we have to see what is their true effect, and what was the intention of the testator as expressed in his will.

Again, there was held to be no trust created in *Re Hamilton*,[43] and the legatees took beneficially where, after giving legacies to two nieces, a testator continued 'I wish them to bequeath them equally between the families of [O] and [P] in such mode as they shall consider right.'

Other cases illustrating the modern approach, and in which it was held that no trust was constituted, include *Mussoorie Bank Ltd v Raynor*,[44] where a testator gave all his estate to his wife 'feeling confident that she will act justly to our children in dividing the same when no longer required by her', *Re Diggles*,[45] where the relevant words were 'it is my desire that she allows X an annuity of £25', and *Re Johnson*,[46]

---

[36] (1871) 6 Ch App 597.   [37] Eg Cozens-Hardy MR in *Re Atkinson* (1911) 103 LT 860 at 862, CA.

[38] *A Treatise of the Law of Property*, p 375 et seq, published in 1849. See also the argument of Mr Richards in *Knight v Knight* (1840) 3 Beav 148 at 165 et seq.

[39] (1871) 6 Ch App 597.

[40] Eg *Curnick v Tucker* (1874) LR 17 Eq 320; *Le Marchant v Le Marchant* (1874) LR 18 Eq 414.

[41] (1884) 27 Ch D 394 at 410, CA. A similar case is *Re Hutchinson and Tenant* (1878) 8 Ch D 540. See, now the Administration of Justice Act 1982, s 22 which provides that, except where a contrary intention is shown, it is to be presumed that if a testator leaves property to his spouse in terms which in themselves would give an absolute interest to the spouse, but by the same instrument purports to give his issue an interest in the same property, the gift to the spouse is nevertheless absolute.

[42] Cf *Comiskey v Bowring-Hanbury* [1905] AC 84, HL.

[43] [1895] 2 Ch 370, CA. See esp. per Lopes LJ at 374.   [44] (1882) 7 App Cas 321, PC.

[45] (1888) 39 Ch D 253, CA. Cf *Re Oldfield* [1904] 1 Ch 549, CA, where at first instance, Kekewich J said, 'a desire carries no obligation except a moral one'.

[46] [1939] 2 All ER 458, applied *Re the Will of Logan* [1993] 1 Qd R 395; *Re Atkinson* (1911) 103 LT 860, CA.

where, after leaving half of his estate to his mother, the testator provided 'I request that my mother will on her death leave the property or what remains of it . . . to my four sisters.'

The modern attitude does not, of course, prevent the court from holding that a trust is created by precatory words where, as a matter of construction, this appears to be the intention of the testator;[47] and, at any rate according to Wynn-Parry J in *Re Steele's Will Trusts*,[48] if a testator uses language which is the same, mutatis mutandis, as that used in an earlier case in which it was held that a trust was constituted, he thereby shows an intention in like manner to set up a trust. If rightly decided, it is submitted that the principle of *Re Steele's Will Trusts*[49] should be restricted to cases where the older authority comprises a more or less complex limitation which might reasonably be regarded as having been used as a precedent for the later will.

It may be added that the normal rules of construction apply to trust documents. However a benignant construction may be given so as to save a gift for charity,[50] and in non-charity cases a purposive construction may be given where appropriate. In two related unreported cases[51] there was a discretionary trust for the settlor's children and remoter issue *born* 'during the Trust Period', which was defined as 80 years commencing at the date of the settlement. For many years the trust was administered on the assumption that the settlor's children in being at the date of the settlement were included as potential beneficiaries. When this was challenged, it was held that 'born' should be construed as more or less equivalent to 'living', and accordingly the trust had been correctly administered.

(b) CERTAINTY OF SUBJECT

The scope of trusts recognized in equity is virtually unlimited. There can be a trust of a chattel or of a chose in action, or of a right or obligation under an ordinary legal contract, just as much as a trust of land or money.[52] It even seems that there is no objection to a party to a contract involving skill and confidence or containing non-assignment provisions becoming trustee of the benefit of being the contracting party as well as of the benefit of the rights conferred.[53] In *Abrahams v Trustee in Bankruptcy of Abrahams*[54] it was held that where a person paid money to a lottery syndicate she gained the right to have any winnings received duly administered in accordance with

---

[47] *Comiskey v Bowring-Hanbury* [1905] AC 84, HL: *Re Burley* [1910] 1 Ch 215.

[48] [1948] Ch 603, [1948] 2 All ER 193. The earlier case here was *Shelley v Shelley* (1868) LR 6 Eq 540.

[49] Supra.   [50] See p 252, infra.

[51] *I Johnson v Rhodes* (1994) and *E Johnson v Rhodes* (1995) discussed by J Child in [2000] PCB 230.

[52] See *Lord Strathcona Steamship Co Ltd v Dominion Coal Co Ltd* [1926] AC 108, 124, [1925] All ER Rep 87, 95, per Lord Shaw, cited by Lightman J in *Don King Productions Inc v Warren* [1998] 2 All ER 608; affd [2000] Ch 291, [1999] 2 All ER 218, CA.

[53] *Don King Productions Inc v Warren* [1998] 2 All ER 608, per Lightman J at 634; affd [2000] Ch 291, [1999] 2 All ER 218, CA. But a provision in the contract prohibiting a party from declaring himself a trustee would be effective.

[54] [1999] BPIR 637, noted (2000) 18 T & ELJ 21 (D Unwin).

whatever rules of the syndicate then applied. That right was property which was capable of being held on a resulting trust. And in *Swift v Dairywise Farms Ltd*[55] it was held that a milk quota, which must be attached to a holding of appropriate land, known as a euroholding, could be the subject of a trust. If T held a quota on trust for B, then where B had no euroholding he could not, therefore, require T to transfer the quota to him. He could, however, require T to realize the quota and transfer the proceeds to him.

This requirement of certainty of subject is somewhat ambiguous,[56] for the phrase may mean that the property subject to the trust must be certain, or that the beneficial interests of the cestuis que trust must be certain.

(i) Certainty of subject matter[57]

It is abundantly clear that in order to establish a trust the trust property must be identifiable.[58] Where it cannot be clearly identified, the purported trust is altogether void as, for instance, in *Palmer v Simmonds*,[59] where the subject of the alleged trust was 'the bulk of my said residuary estate'. Nor was a trust established in *Re London Wine Co (Shippers) Ltd*[60] where a company had stocks of wine in various warehouses which it sold to various customers, the intention being that the wine purchased should become the property of the customers but stored by the company at the customers' expense. It was argued that if the legal title had not passed to the customers, there was a trust in their favour. The court seems to have accepted that there was an intention to create a trust, but held that it nevertheless failed on the ground of uncertainty of subject matter, for there was never any segregation or appropriation of the wine within the warehouse until actual delivery of the wine to a purchaser. This last decision seems right in principle, but the subsequent Court of Appeal decision in *Hunter v Moss*[61] causes difficulties. There it was held at first instance that the requirement of certainty does not apply in the same way to trusts of intangible assets such as, in the case before the court, 50 out of 950 indistinguishable shares. In such cases, it was held, the question of certainty depends not on the application of any immutable principle based on the requirements of a need for segregation or appropriation, but rather on whether, immediately after the purported declaration of trust, the court

---

[55] [2000] 1 All ER 320, noted [2000] All ER Rev 247 (PJ Clark), affd [2001] BCLC 672, CA on different grounds.

[56] See (1940) 4 MLR 20 (Glanville Williams).

[57] See (1986) 61 Tulane LR 45 (Jane Baron), [2002] 61 CLJ 657 (P Parkinson).

[58] See *Westdeutsche Landesbank Girozentrale v Islington London Borough Council* [1996] 2 All ER 961, HL, per Lord Browne-Wilkinson at 988.

[59] (1854) 2 Drew 221; cp *Bromley v Tryon* [1952] AC 265, [1951] 2 All ER 1058, HL, and on another point, *Richardson v Watson* (1833) 4 B & Ad 787.

[60] (1975) 126 NLJ 977. See *Re Goldcorp Exchange Ltd (in receivership)* [1995] 1 AC 74, [1994] 2 All ER 806, PC, discussed [1995] RLR 83 (P Birks); *Re Stapylton Fletcher Ltd* [1995] 1 All ER 192, [1994] 1 WLR 1181, noted (1995) 16 Co Law 111 (J Breslin); [1995] 48(1) CLP 113 (Alison Clarke).

[61] [1994] 3 All ER 215, [1994] 1 WLR 452, CA. The decision was followed by Neuberger J in *Re Harvard Securities Ltd* [1997] 2 BCLC 369, noted (1998–99) 9 KCLJ 112 (Theresa Villiers). Cf *Re CA Pacific Finance Ltd (in liq)* [2000] 1 BCLC 494 (Hong Kong CFI).

could, if asked, make an order for the execution of the purported trust. On this basis the trust was upheld. The Court of Appeal expressly agreed with the conclusion of the judge below on the uncertainty point, and should, perhaps, be treated as accepting his reasoning, though it has been much criticized, it is thought rightly, by most of the commentators,[62] arguing that intangible assets are not in a different position from tangible. Nor is the analogy drawn by the court with a demonstrative legacy of shares valid, for a trust of such shares will become completely constituted only when the particular shares have been vested in the trustee.

It may be added, as to the segregation of funds, that Watkins LJ, giving the judgment of the court, said in *R v Clowes (No 2)*[63] that the effect of the authorities seemed to be 'that a requirement to keep moneys separate is normally an indicator that they are impressed with a trust, and that the absence of such a requirement, *if there are no other indicators of a trust*, normally negatives it. The fact', he continued, 'that a transaction contemplates the mingling of funds is, therefore, not necessarily fatal to a trust.' Further the courts are slow to introduce trusts into everyday commercial transactions.[64]

Sprange v Barnard[65] illustrates the way in which the question has arisen in a number of cases. There a testatrix gave property to her husband 'for his sole use' and continued 'at his death, the remaining part of what is left, that he does not want for his own wants and use, to be divided between' a brother and sisters. It was held that there was no trust since it was uncertain what would be left at the death of the husband. The husband accordingly took absolutely. In practice, the question of certainty of subject is often associated with that of certainty of words. In giving the advice of the Privy Council in *Mussoorie Bank Ltd v Raynor*,[66] Sir Arthur Hobhouse observed, 'uncertainty in the subject of the gift has a reflex action upon the previous words, and throws doubt upon the intention of the testator, and seems to shew that he could not possibly have intended his words of confidence, hope, or whatever they may be—his appeal to the conscience of the first taker—to be imperative words'.

(ii) Certainty of beneficial interests

If there is certainty of words, and the property subject to the trust is clearly identified, the trust will be valid. If, however, the beneficial interests to be taken are not certain, those interests will fail for uncertainty, and the trustees will hold on a resulting trust

---

[62] See [1993] Conv 466 (Alison Jones); (1994) 28 L Teach 312 (P Luxton); [1994] CLJ 448 (M Ockleton); All ER Rev 1994 250 (P J Clarke); (1995) 110 LQR 335 (D Hayton). Contra Jill Martin in [1996] Conv 223. See also [1999] JBL 1 (Sarah Worthington).

[63] [1994] 2 All ER 316, CA at 325; *Bank of Montreal v British Columbia (Milk Marketing Board)* (1994) 94 BCLR (2d) 281; *Air Canada v M & L Travel Ltd* (1994) 108 DLR (4th) 592.

[64] See *Neste Oy v Lloyds Bank plc* [1983] 2 Lloyd's Rep 658 per Bingham J at 665, cited with approval in *R v Clowes (No 2)*, supra, CA. See also *Re ILG Travel Ltd* [1995] 2 BCLC 128, where the agreement was held to take effect as an equitable charge.

[65] (1789) 2 Bro CC 585. Principle of case valid though decision perhaps doubtful—contrast *Re Last* [1958] P 137, [1958] 1 All ER 316. Cf *Re Jones* [1898] 1 Ch 438 (absolute gift—gift over of what remains void for repugnancy).

[66] (1882) 7 App Cas 321 at 331, PC.

for the settlor, as in *Boyce v Boyce*,[67] where a testator devised two houses to trustees on trust to convey one to Maria 'whichever she may think proper to choose or select' and the other to Charlotte. Maria predeceased the testator and it was accordingly held that Charlotte had no claim. There is no uncertainty, however, where there is a discretion given to the trustees to determine the exact quantum of the beneficial interests, or where the words used by the testator are a sufficient indication of his intention to provide an effective determinant of what he intends. Thus in *Re Golay*[68] the testator directed his executors to let T 'enjoy one of my flats during her lifetime and to receive a reasonable income from my other properties'. It was held, a little surprisingly, perhaps, that the words 'reasonable income' directed an objective determinant of amount which the court could if necessary apply, and accordingly the gift did not fail for uncertainty. Again, in other circumstances the court may cure an apparent uncertainty by applying the maxim that equality is equity. Further, if there is an absolute gift in the first instance, and trusts are engrafted or imposed on that absolute interest which fail for uncertainty, or indeed any other reason, then the absolute gift takes effect so far as the trusts have failed.[69]

(c) CERTAINTY OF OBJECTS[70]

(i) Need for ascertainable beneficiaries

For reasons that will appear, in considering what test for certainty of objects has to be applied in order that a disposition shall be valid it is sensible to consider not only the rules that apply to trusts, but also those that apply to powers. Moreover, it will be convenient to discuss first a mere power, then a fixed trust, that is, where the interest of the beneficiaries is determined by the settlor and is not dependent upon the discretion of the trustees, and finally a discretionary trust. There is no need to consider separately a trust power in the first sense,[71] that is, where the court implies a trust in default of appointment, for this simply comprises a mere power followed by a fixed trust, to each of which the appropriate test must be applied separately. In this last case it could happen that the power would be valid, but the trust in default void for uncertainty.[72] It should be noted that we are not here concerned with cases where there is a condition or description attached to one or more individual gifts; in such cases uncertainty as to some other persons who may have been intended to take does

---

[67] (1849) 16 Sim 476; *Re Double Happiness Trust* [2003] WTLR 367 (Jersey Royal Court). Cf *Guild v Mallory* (1983) 41 OR (2d) 21.

[68] [1965] 2 All ER 660, [1995] 1 WLR 969. See (1965) 81 LQR 481 (R E Megarry).

[69] *Lassence v Tierney* (1849) 1 Mac & G 551; *Hancock v Watson* [1902] AC 14, HL.

[70] See, generally 1971 CLP 133 (Harvey Cohen); (1971) 87 LQR 31 (J W Harris); (1971) 29 CLJ 68 (J Hopkins); (1973) 5 NZULR 348 (Y F R Grbich); (1980) 9 Sydney LR 58 (R P Austin); (1988) 20 OLR 377 (D R Klinck).

[71] See p 35, supra.   [72] Cf *Re Sayer* [1957] Ch 423, [1956] 3 All ER 600.

not in any way affect the quantum of the gift to persons who undoubtedly possess the qualification.[73]

(ii) Test for a mere power

So far as a mere power is concerned the law is 'that the power is valid if it can be said with certainty whether any given individual is or is not a member of the class and does not fail simply because it is impossible to ascertain every member of the class'.[74] Thus in *Re Coates*[75] it was held that the following provisions in a will conferred a valid power on the wife; 'if my wife feels that I have forgotten any friend I direct my executors to pay to such friend or friends as are nominated by my wife a sum not exceeding £25 per friend with a maximum aggregate payment of £250 so that such friends may buy a small memento of our friendship.' In this case Roxburgh J applied the dictum of Lord Tomlin in *Re Ogden*:[76] 'The question is one of degree in each case, whether having regard to the language of the will, and the circumstances of the case, there is such uncertainty as to justify the court in coming to the conclusion that the gift is bad.' In this sort of case, as Harman J said in *Re Gestetner Settlement*[77] 'there is no duty to distribute, but only a duty to consider', and it is not necessary that all the possible members of the class should be considered, provided it can be ascertained whether any given postulant is a member of the class or not.

Shortly before the House of Lords decision in *Re Gulbenkian's Settlement Trusts*,[78] there had been cases[79] proposing a less stringent test, namely that if you could find a person clearly within the description of the class intended to be benefited, the power would be good even though you might be able to envisage cases where it would be difficult or impossible to say whether a person was within the description or not. This test was decisively rejected in *Re Gulbenkian's Settlement Trusts*[80] which was followed in *McPhail v Doulton*,[81] but the judgments in the subsequent proceedings in the latter case, reported as *Re Baden's Deed Trusts (No 2)*,[82] have somewhat confused the position. The test laid down in the two House of Lords decisions was, it will be recalled, whether 'it can be said with certainty that *any* given individual is or is *not* a member of that class'.[83]

The majority of the Court of Appeal in *Re Baden's Deed Trusts (No 2)*[84] held in effect that a power[85] may be valid even though there may be a substantial number of

---

[73] *Re Barlow's Will Trusts* [1979] 1 All ER 296, [1979] 1 WLR 278, discussed [1980] Conv 263 (Lindsay McKay); (1979) 30 NILQ 24 (R Burgess); (1983) 98 LQR 551 (C T Emery).

[74] Per Lord Wilberforce in *McPhail v Doulton* [1971] AC 424, [1970] 2 All ER 228, HL.

[75] [1955] Ch 495, [1955] 1 All ER 26; *Re Sayer Trust*, supra.

[76] [1933] Ch 678 at 682, [1933] All ER Rep 720 at 722.

[77] [1953] Ch 672 at 688, [1953] 1 All ER 1150 at 1155.   [78] [1970] AC 508, [1968] 3 All ER 785, HL.

[79] *Re Gibbard* [1966] 1 All ER 273, [1967] 1 WLR 42; *Re Leek*, at first instance [1967] Ch 1061, [1967] 2 All ER 1160; *Re Gulbenkian's Settlement Trusts*, in the Court of Appeal [1968] Ch 126, [1967] 3 All ER 15.

[80] Supra, HL.   [81] Supra, HL.   [82] [1973] Ch 9, [1972] 2 All ER 1304, CA.

[83] Italics supplied.   [84] Supra.

[85] Technically the case concerned a discretionary trust to which, as we shall see, the same principles now apply.

persons as to whom it is impossible to say whether they are within the class or not, provided, according to Megaw LJ, that as regards at least a substantial number of objects, it can be said with certainty that they fall within it. Sachs LJ said that so long as the class of persons to be benefited is conceptually certain,[86] evidential uncertainty as to whether or not a given individual is within the class does not matter. The power can only be exercised in favour of persons who are proved to be within it. 'Conceptual certainty' refers to the precision of language used by the settlor to define the class of person whom he intends to benefit: 'evidential certainty' refers to the extent to which the evidence in a particular case enables specific persons to be identified as members of those classes. The latter is sometimes confused with 'ascertainability', which refers to the extent to which the whereabouts or continued existence of persons identified as beneficiaries or potential beneficiaries can be ascertained.[87] Stamp LJ, however, gave a forceful dissenting opinion, arguing in substance that this would be to bring in by the back door the test decisively rejected by the House of Lords in *Re Gulbenkian's Settlement Trusts*,[88] namely that the trust is good if there are individuals—or even one —of whom you can say with certainty that he is a member of the class, notwithstanding there may be others whose status is uncertain. The House of Lords test in his view requires it to be possible to say positively of any individual that he either is, or alternatively is not, within the class.

Lastly, reference should be made to a point made by Templeman J in *Re Manisty's Settlement*.[89] After holding that a power cannot be uncertain merely because it is wide in ambit, and that it does not matter that the power does not attempt to classify the beneficiaries, but only to specify or classify excepted persons, he went on to say that in his view a capricious power could not be validly created, 'A power to benefit "residents of Greater London",' he said, 'is capricious because the terms of the power negative any sensible intention on the part of the settlor. If the settlor intended and expected the trustees would have regard to persons with some claim on his bounty or some interest in an institution favoured by the settlor, or if the settlor had any other sensible intention or expectation, he would not have required the trustees to consider only an accidental conglomeration of persons who have no discernible link with the settlor or with any institution. A capricious power negatives a sensible consideration by the trustees of the exercise of the power.' Megarry VC in *Re Hay's Settlement Trusts*[90] sounded somewhat unenthusiastic about these dicta, observing that he did not think that Templeman J had in mind a case in which the settlor was, for instance, a former chairman of the Greater London Council. In any case, he said, an intermediate power cannot be void on this ground.

---

[86] Eg 'first cousins' as contrasted with 'someone under a moral obligation'.
[87] This last point is made by C T Emery (1982) 98 LQR 551, to whom I am indebted for the above definitions. See *McCracken v A-G for Victoria* [1995] 1 VR 67, where the judge thought it not always easy to discern the boundary between the two kinds of uncertainty.
[88] Supra, HL.
[89] [1974] Ch 17 at 27, [1973] 2 All ER 1203 at 1211; criticized (1974) 38 Conv 269 (L McKay).
[90] [1981] 3 All ER 786, [1982] 1 WLR 202.

(iii) Test for a fixed trust

As regards fixed trusts, Lord Evershed MR observed, in *Re Endacott*,[91] that 'No principle perhaps has greater sanction or authority behind it than the general proposition that a trust by English law, not being a charitable trust, in order to be effective, must have ascertained or ascertainable beneficiaries.' In the present context there is some danger of confusion by reason of the fact that the most elaborate consideration of what is meant by certainty of beneficiaries has been in relation to discretionary trusts at a time when it was thought that they were to be treated for this purpose in the same way as fixed trusts. Until the House of Lords decision in *McPhail v Doulton*[92] the law in relation to discretionary trusts was that where there was a trust for such of a given class of objects as the trustees should select, it was essential that the trustees should know, or be able to ascertain, all the objects from which they were enjoined to select by the terms of the trust. The duty of selection being a fiduciary one, it was considered that trustees could not properly exercise their discretion unless and until they knew of what persons exactly the class consisted among whom they were called on to make their selection. Likewise, if the trustees failed to act, and the court was called upon to do so, it was thought, prior to *McPhail v Doulton*,[93] that the court could only act by way of equal division, which would be impossible unless there was a complete list of potential beneficiaries.[94]

The relevant date for deciding whether the membership of the class was ascertainable or not was the date when the trust came into existence.[95] The fact that it might be difficult or expensive to ascertain the membership of the class did not matter. Thus in *Re Eden*,[96] Wynn-Parry J stated: 'it may well be that a large part, even the whole of the funds available, would be consumed in the inquiry. To say the least of it, that would be very unfortunate, but that cannot of itself constitute any reason why such an inquiry, whether by the trustees or by the court, should not be undertaken.' In order to hold the trust valid the court had to be satisfied affirmatively that there was at least a probability of the objects being completely ascertained.[97]

So far as concerns the ascertainment of the objects of a fixed trust, the above propositions still seem to represent the law.[98] Suppose, for instance, that a whimsical

---

[91] [1960] Ch 232 at 246, [1959] 3 All ER 562 at 568, CA.

[92] [1971] AC 424, [1970] 2 All ER 228, HL.

[93] Supra, HL. For the present position see pp 78–79, infra.

[94] See *IRC v Broadway Cottages Trust* [1955] Ch 20, [1954] 3 All ER 120, CA, per Jenkins LJ; *Re Gulbenkian's Settlement Trusts* [1970] AC 508, [1968] 3 All ER 785, HL. See also *Re Ogden* [1933] Ch 678, [1933] All ER Rep 720, where a gift of residue, to be distributed among such political bodies having as their object the promotion of Liberal principles as the residuary legatee should select, was held to be a valid trust on evidence that the class benefited was capable of ascertainment.

[95] *Re Hain's Settlement* [1961] 1 All ER 848, CA; *Re Culbenkian's Settlement Trusts*, supra, HL.

[96] [1957] 2 All ER 430 at 435.

[97] *Re Saxone Shoe Co Ltd's Trust Deed* [1962] 2 All ER 904, [1962] 1 WLR 943, per Cross J, who also referred to a qualification applying to discretionary trusts which cannot apply to fixed trusts, namely that there is no need to trace persons in whose favour the trustees can say in advance that they will not exercise their discretion. In a fixed trust ex hypothesi all the members of the class must take.

[98] See *Re Beckbessinger* [1993] 2 NZLR 362. See also [1984] Conv 22 (P Matthews) whose views are, it is submitted, effectively refuted by Jill Martin [1984] Conv 304 and D J Hayton [1984] Conv 307. In Australia, in

testator were to direct trustees to divide a fund equally between a class of persons such as the objects of the trust in *McPhail v Doulton*.[99] In such a case the trust would seem to be void for uncertainty unless the test of certainty set out above could be satisfied.

(iv) Test for a discretionary trust

Turning to discretionary trusts, as already mentioned, prior to the House of Lords decision in *McPhail v Doulton*[100] a discretionary trust was treated in the same way as a fixed trust and the consequence was that the validity of a disposition might have depended upon the technical question whether it fell on one side or other of the narrow dividing line between trust and power. The result met with judicial criticism. For instance Harman LJ referring to what he called this 'most unfortunate doctrine', said:[101] 'it ought to make no difference to the validity of the provisions of the deed whether, on a minute analysis of the language used in this clause, it should be construed as creating a trust or a power ... the fact that it does is an absurd and embarrassing result.' The House of Lords has now decided, by a bare majority, that 'the test for the validity of [a discretionary trust][102] ought to be similar to that accepted by this House in *Re Gulbenkian's Settlement*[103] for powers, namely that the trust is valid if it can be said with certainty that any given individual is or is not a member of the class.'[104] The doubts as to whether the word 'similar' meant resemblance rather than identity have been silenced by *Re Baden's Deed Trusts (No 2)*,[105] which makes it clear that the test to be applied to mere powers and discretionary trusts is precisely the same.

In relation to trusts Lord Wilberforce in *McPhail v Doulton*[106] further observed that even where the meaning of the words used is clear, the definition of beneficiaries may be so hopelessly wide as not to form 'anything like a class', so that the trust is administratively unworkable. This proposition does not apply to powers. The courts have a much more limited function[107] in respect of powers and cannot be called upon

---

West v Weston (1997–98) 44 NSWLR 657, the rule was modified in a case where there was a gift to the issue of the testator's four grandparents equally per capita. Some three years after the testator's death in 1975 issue had been ascertained and it was possible more might come to light. The rule, it was held, will be satisfied if, within a reasonable time after the gift comes into effect, the court can be satisfied on the balance of probabilities that the substantial majority of the beneficiaries have been ascertained and that no reasonable inquiries could be made which would improve the situation.

99   [1971] AC 424, [1970] 2 All ER 228, HL. The objects are set out above at p 35.   100   Ibid.

101   *Re Baden's Deed Trusts* [1969] 2 Ch 388 at 397, [1969], 1 All ER 1016 at 1019, CA; revsd sub nom *McPhail v Doulton*, HL, supra.

102   Lord Wilberforce actually used the phrase 'trust powers'.

103   Supra, HL. See also *Re Beckbessinger* [1993] 2 NZLR 362.

104   Per Lord Wilberforce in *McPhail v Doulton* [1971] AC 424, [1970] 2 All ER 228, HL. Hopkins in (1971) 29 CLJ at 101 raises the question as to the application of the new rule to discretionary trusts of capital as opposed to income. It is submitted that it should apply equally to both.

105   Supra, CA, and per Brightman J at first instance, [1972] Ch 607, [1971] 3 All ER 985.

106   [1971] AC 424 at 457, [1970] 2 All ER 288 at 247, HL discussed in *Re Manisty's Settlement* [1974] Ch 17, [1973] 2 All ER 1203; *Re Hay's Settlement Trusts* [1981] 3 All ER 786, [1982] 1 WLR 202.

107   Primarily to determine whether a power is valid and, if so, whether a particular exercise of the power is within its scope.

to administer them.[108] It should be added that it has been strongly contended[109] that the proposition rests upon no satisfactory basis and should be discarded. The possible bases examined and rejected were the need for common attributes among the beneficiaries; mere size; inability of the trustees to perform the administrative duties; and inability of the court to execute the trust. However, Megarry VC in *Re Hay's Settlement Trusts*[110] indicated that had he not already held the discretionary trust void on other grounds, he would have held it void as being administratively unworkable. Further, Lord Wilberforce's dictum was applied and the trust held void in *R v District Auditor, ex p West Yorkshire Metropolitan County Council*,[111] where Lloyd LJ said that there was a fundamental difficulty in that a trust with as many as two and a half million potential beneficiaries would be quite simply unworkable. The class was far too large.

(v) Trusts for purposes

The fundamental rule that the object of a trust must be certain applies equally to trusts for purposes. Thus trusts for philanthropic,[112] or patriotic,[113] or public,[114] or benevolent[115] purposes are all void, for these words have no technical legal meaning and the court would accordingly be unable to determine whether the trustees had or had not carried out their trust by applying the trust funds in any particular way. Similarly trusts for 'the formation of an informed international public opinion' and 'the promotion of greater co-operation in Europe and the West in general' are void as being too vague and uncertain,[116] and a trust to apply the subject-matter for such purposes as the donee may think fit, is also void for uncertainty.[117] Again in *Re Challoner Club Ltd (in liquidation)*,[118] where the officers of a club deposited donations received from members as a rescue fund in a separate bank account not to be used until the future of the club was known, no trust was created since the terms of the intended trust were not certain. The money in the account was therefore part of the club assets for the purposes of the liquidation despite the assurances to the contrary which the officers had given to the members. Charity, however, is a term of art and, even though there may be uncertainty in the sense that no particular charitable purpose is specified, or only referred to in vague terms, this does not matter, provided the gift is exclusively for charitable purposes. In another sense charity is one and

---

[108] *Re Hay's Settlement Trusts*, supra. But see (1991) 107 LQR 214 (S Gardner) suggesting that the question may need to be reconsidered in the light of *Mettoy Pension Trustees Ltd v Evans* [1991] 2 All ER 513, [1990] 1 WLR 1587—see p 32 ante.

[109] (1974) 38 Conv 269 (L McKay).

[110] Supra. See [1982] Conv 432 (A Grubb); (1986) 8 U Tas LR 209 (J D Davies); [1990] Conv 24 (I Hardcastle).

[111] [1986] RVR 24, DC noted (1986) 45 CLJ 391 (C Harpum).

[112] *Re Macduff* [1896] 2 Ch 451, CA.

[113] *A-G v National Provincial and Union Bank of England* [1924] AC 262, HL.

[114] *Houston v Burns* [1918] AC 337, HL.

[115] *Chichester Diocesan Fund v Simpson* [1944] AC 341, HL.

[116] *Re Koeppler's Will Trusts* [1984] Ch 243, [1984] 2 All ER 111; revsd [1986] Ch 423, [1985] 2 All ER 869, CA, but approved on this point.

[117] *Re Pugh's Will Trusts* [1967] 3 All ER 337, [1967] 1 WLR 1262.   [118] (1997) Times, 4 November.

indivisible, and if necessary a scheme will be made to specify the particular charity which is to benefit.[119]

(vi) Consequences of failure of trust for uncertainty

In any case where there is uncertainty of objects, assuming the other two certainties are present, the trustee cannot take beneficially, but will hold the trust property on a resulting trust for the settlor, or, where the trust arises under a will, for the persons entitled to the residue, or on intestacy, as the case may be.

3 THE BENEFICIARY PRINCIPLE

Even where the purpose of a trust is clearly defined so that the trust cannot be said to be void for uncertainty, further difficult problems may arise where the object of a trust is a non-human beneficiary, such as a dog, an unincorporated association or a non-charitable purpose.[120] The basic principle, subject perhaps to the possibility of review of the decisions by the House of Lords, and with the exception of charitable trusts, is that 'a trust to be valid must be for the benefit of individuals'.[121] This is the principle stated by Grant MR in *Morice v Bishop of Durham*,[122] that 'there must be somebody in whose favour the court can decree performance', restated by Harman J in *Re Wood*,[123] who observed 'that a gift on trust must have a cestui que trust', and since affirmed by Roxburgh J in *Re Astor's Settlement Trusts*[124] and the Court of Appeal in *Re Endacott*.[125] Accordingly it has been said:[126] 'A gift can be made to persons (including a corporation) but it cannot be made to a purpose or to an object; so, also, a trust may be created for the benefit of persons as cestuis que trust, but not for a purpose or object unless the purpose or object be charitable.' The idea behind this seems to be that otherwise the validity of the trust would depend upon the whim of

---

[119] See chapter 14, section 5, p 321 et seq, infra.

[120] For a full and penetrating discussion see Morris and Leach, *The Rule Against Perpetuities*, 2nd edn, p 307 et seq. See also (1977) 40 MLR 397 (N P Gravells), where the case for the validation of public purpose trusts is argued; 'Equity and Contemporary Legal Developments' (ed S Goldstein) 302 (R B M Cotterrell). Cf *R v District Auditor, ex p West Yorkshire Metropolitan County Council* [1986] RVR 24, DC; *Rowland v Vancouver College Ltd* (2001) 205 DLR (4th) 193.

[121] Per Lord Parker, in *Bowman v Secular Society Ltd* [1917] AC 406 at 441, HL.

[122] (1805) 10 Ves 522; affg (1804) 9 Ves 399 at 405.

[123] [1949] Ch 498 at 501, [1949] 1 All ER 1100 at 1101.

[124] [1952] Ch 534, [1952] 1 All ER 1067; *Re Shaw* [1957] 1 All ER 745, [1957] 1 WLR 729; compromised, [1958] 1 All ER 245n, CA.

[125] [1960] Ch 232, [1959] 3 All ER 562, CA. Yet two years later in *Re Harpur's Will Trusts* [1962] Ch 78, [1961] 3 All ER 588, CA, Evershed MR, who was a member of the court in *Re Endacott*, observed, at 91, 592, that a trust to apply income, restricted to the perpetuity period, 'for certain named purposes such as the trustees think fit, some of the purposes being charitable and some not charitable' would be valid.

[126] *Leahy v A-G of New South Wales* [1959] AC 457 at 478, [1959] 2 All ER 300 at 307, PC, per Viscount Simonds; *Re Recher's Will Trusts* [1972] Ch 526, [1971] 3 All ER 401.

the trustee, and 'a court of equity does not recognize as valid a trust which it cannot both enforce and control'.[127] This 'beneficiary principle', which operates to invalidate non-charitable purpose trusts, may, however, be held to be inapplicable in certain situations, and is also subject to exceptions.

Before considering the situations where the beneficiary principle does not operate, one should note that it has recently been argued that the principle is unduly restrictive and that a settlor should be able to confer enforcement rights on persons other than the beneficiaries (including himself) so that non-charitable purpose trusts would be valid, so long as they are administratively workable and are limited to a valid perpetuity period.[128]

(a) SITUATIONS OUTSIDE THE SCOPE OF THE BENEFICIARY PRINCIPLE

(i) *Re Denley's Trust Deed*[129]

It was held in this case that a distinction must be drawn between 'purpose or object trusts which are abstract or impersonal' and which are void on the principle set out above, and a trust which 'though expressed as a purpose, is directly or indirectly for the benefit of an individual or individuals'. Such a trust, Goff J said, is in general outside the mischief of the principle that every trust must have a certain cestui que trust. He accordingly held valid a trust for the provision of a recreation or sports ground, during a period limited within the perpetuity period, for the benefit of what he held to be an ascertainable class. One interpretation of this decision is that in this sort of case the need for enforceability is met by the existence of *factual* beneficiaries, that is, persons who, though not actually cestuis que trust, are interested in the disposal of the property.[130] Vinelott J in *Re Grant's Will Trust*,[131] however, considered that *Re Denley's Trust Deed*[132] fell altogether outside the categories of gifts to unincorporated associations and purpose trusts. He could:

see no distinction in principle between a trust to permit a class defined by reference to employment to use and enjoy land in accordance with rules to be made at the discretion of trustees on the one hand, and, on the other hand, a trust to distribute income at the discretion of trustees amongst a class, defined by reference to, for example, relationship to

---

[127] Per Roxburgh J in *Re Astor's Settlement Trusts*, supra, at 549, 1075.

[128] (2001) 117 LQR 96 (D Hayton), (2003) 17 Tru LI 144 (J Hilliard).

[129] [1969] 1 Ch 373, [1968] 3 All ER 65, applied in *Re Lipinski's Will Trusts* [1976] Ch 235, [1977] 1 All ER 33. There are difficulties in reconciling this decision with *dicta* in *Leahy v A-G of New South Wales*, supra. See [1968] ASCL, p 437 et seq (J D Davies); (1969) 32 MLR 96 (J M Evans); (1970) 34 Conv 77 (P A Lovell); (1973) 37 Conv 420 (L McKay). See also *Strathalbyn Show Jumping Club Inc v Mayes* (2001) 79 SASR 54.

[130] See (1980) 39 CLJ 88 (C E F Rickett); [1982] Conv 118, 177 (Ann R Everton).

[131] [1979] 3 All ER 359. See (1980) 43 MLR 459 (B Green). Cf *Re Bowes* [1896] 1 Ch 507 (trust to lay out £5000 on planting trees on settled estates; held persons entitled to estate entitled to have the money whether actually so laid out or not).

[132] Supra.

the settlor. In both cases the benefit to be taken by any member of the class is at the discretion of the trustees, but any member of the class can apply to the court to compel the trustees to administer the trust in accordance with its terms.

(ii) Contractual situations

In some circumstances it may be held that on a true analysis of the facts there is no trust and the matter is one of contract. Thus it was held in *Conservative and Unionist Central Office v Burrell*,[133] where funds were contributed to a treasurer of the party, that he held them subject to a mandate to use them in a particular way. No trust arose, except the fiduciary relationship inherent in the relationship of principal and agent.[134]

(b) EXCEPTIONS TO THE BENEFICIARY PRINCIPLE

There are admitted exceptions to the beneficiary principle. These have been said 'properly [to] be regarded as anomalous and exceptional'[135] perhaps 'concessions to human weakness or sentiment',[136] or 'merely occasions when Homer has nodded'.[137] They are known as 'unenforceable trusts' or 'trusts of imperfect obligation', and seem to be restricted to trusts arising under wills where the legacy will fall into a residuary gift if the unenforceable trust is not carried out.[138] The court can indirectly enforce the trust in such a case by obtaining an undertaking from the trustee to apply the legacy towards the unenforceable purpose, and giving the residuary legatees liberty to apply if the undertaking is not carried out. Evershed MR in *Re Endacott*[139] referred with apparent approval to the classification of these exceptions put forward by Morris and Leach[140] into five groups, namely:

(i) Trusts for the erection or maintenance of monuments or graves. If the tomb can be regarded as part of the fabric of a church,[141] or the trust is for the maintenance of a churchyard in general,[142] the trust is charitable and clearly valid. Equally clearly a trust for the maintenance of a tomb or a monument not in a church for ever or for an

---

133 [1982] 2 All ER 1, [1982] 1 WLR 522, CA.

134 See [1982] NZLJ 335 (C E F Rickett); [1983] Conv 150 (P Creighton); [1983] 133 NLJ 87 (C T Emery).

135 Per Roxburgh J in *Re Astor's Settlement Trusts*, supra, at 1074, 547, and per Evershed MR in *Re Endacott*, supra, CA.

136 Ibid.   137 Per Harman LJ in *Re Endacott* supra, at 250, 571, CA.

138 *Re Astor's Settlement Trusts*, supra. Sed quaere—there will always be someone entitled to the fund if the unenforceable trust is not carried out, either under the intestacy rules, or by way of resulting trust or otherwise, who could be given liberty to apply.

139 Supra.

140 Morris and Leach, *The Rule Against Perpetuities*, 2nd edn, p 301. For an Australian view see (1987) 14 UQLJ 175 (P Jamieson).

141 *Hoare v Osborne* (1866) LR 1 Eq 585; *Re King* [1923] 1 Ch 243.

142 *Re Vaughan* (1886) 33 Ch D 187 (per North J at 192), 'I do not see any difference between a gift to keep in repair what is called "God's House" and a gift to keep in repair the churchyard round it which is often called "God's Acre")'; *Re Manser* [1905] 1 Ch 68; *Re Eighmie* [1935] Ch 524.

indefinite period is void as offending against the rule against perpetual trusts.[143] A trust for the erection of a monument to the testator or some member of his family, or for the maintenance of a tomb has, however, been held valid, where it would not continue beyond the perpetuity period.[144] Though valid, such a trust is unenforceable in that no one can compel the trustee to carry it out; but if he wishes to perform it, no one can prevent him from doing so, and only if and in so far as he chooses not to do so will there be a resulting trust for the residuary legatees. The rule that the trust must not continue beyond the perpetuity period,[145] sometimes called the rule against perpetual trusts, is generally thought to have been entirely unaffected by the Perpetuities and Accumulations Act 1964.[146]

(ii) Trusts for the saying of masses, if these are not charitable. Trusts for the saying of masses in public have been held to be charitable.[147] Where masses are to be said privately such trusts are not charitable. They might, perhaps, be valid unenforceable trusts[148] provided they are restricted to the perpetuity period, with like effects to those referred to under (i) above.

(iii) Trusts for the maintenance or benefit of animals in general, or of a class of animals are charitable.[149] A trust for the benefit of specific animals is however, not charitable, but in several cases[150] such a trust has been held to be a valid unenforceable trust, if restricted to the perpetuity period, again with like effects to those referred to under (i) above. It may be observed that in the only case in which this point was discussed,[151] the judge, North J, did not treat animal cases as exceptions to a rule, but dissented from the view that the court will not recognize a trust unless it is capable of being enforced by someone.

(iv) Trusts for the benefit of unincorporated associations. There is no difficulty where the purposes of the association are charitable—the trust will not then be void either for uncertainty, perpetuity or unenforceability. Cases of non-charitable associations were said to form a more doubtful group by Morris and Leach,[152] and recent

---

[143] *Hoare v Osborne*, supra; *Re Vaughan*, supra; *Re Elliot* [1952] Ch 217, [1952] 1 All ER 145; *Pedulla v Nasti* (1990) 20 NSWLR 720 (trust for the 'erection and maintenance of a vault or chapel in which to house my ashes' held void for perpetuity). See chapter 11, section 2, p 218, infra.

[144] *Trimmer v Danby* (1856) 25 LJ Ch 424 (legacy to his executors in the will of the artist J M W Turner 'to erect a monument to my memory in St Paul's Cathedral, among those of my brothers in art' held valid but unenforceable. The executors chose to carry it out); *Pirbright v Salwey* [1896] WN 86; *Re Hooper* [1932] 1 Ch 38. In *Mussett v Bingle* [1876] WN 170 it was either assumed the monument must be erected within 21 years or the point was not taken, though the trust for the maintenance of the monument was held void for perpetuity.

[145] As to what is meant by the perpetuity period, see p 218, infra.   [146] The relevant section is 15(4).

[147] *Re Hetherington* [1990] Ch 1, [1989] 2 All ER 129. See pp 261 and 280, infra. The law in Australia is similar: *Crowther v Brophy* [1992] 2 VR 97.

[148] *Bourne v Keane* [1919] AC 815, HL.   [149] See chapter 13, section 2(e), infra, p 264.

[150] *Pettingall v Pettingall* (1842) 11 LJ Ch 176; *Mitford v Reynolds* (1848) 16 Sim 105; *Re Dean* (1889) 41 Ch D 552; *Re Haines* (1952) Times, 7 November. See (1983) 80 LSG 2451 (P Matthews).

[151] *Re Dean*, supra.   [152] Op cit, p 310.

decisions indicate that this group should be deleted as an exception. Other difficulties in connection with unincorporated associations are discussed below.

(v) *Miscellaneous cases.* The most important case is *Re Thompson*,[153] where a testator gave a legacy of £1,000 to his friend G W L to be applied to him in such manner as in his discretion he might think fit towards the promotion and furtherance of fox-hunting. Clauson J refused to accept the argument based on *Morice v Bishop of Durham*[154] that the trust was invalid, and indirectly enforced the trust in the usual way by requiring an undertaking from the trustee to apply the legacy towards the object expressed in the will, and giving the residuary legatees liberty to apply to the court in case the trustee failed to carry out his undertaking.

Finally, it should be mentioned that in the present state of the authorities it seems impossible to accept the attractive proposition that an unenforceable trust should be allowed to take effect as a power.[155] In two cases[156] the Court of Appeal has made clear statements to the contrary observing, for instance, in *IRC v Broadway Cottages Trust*:[157] 'We do not think a valid power is to be spelt out of an invalid trust.' If, however, a provision is drafted as a mere power to appoint for a specific non-charitable purpose limited in its exercise to the perpetuity period, it seems it may well be valid.[158] The donee of the power may exercise it if he wishes to do so, and if he does not the property will pass to the persons entitled in default of appointment, or be held on a resulting trust for the settlor or his estate.

4 TRUSTS FOR THE BENEFIT OF UNINCORPORATED ASSOCIATIONS

Viscount Simonds has referred to the difficulties arising out of 'the artificial and anomalous conception of an unincorporated society which, though it is not a separate entity in law, is yet for many purposes regarded as a continuing entity and, however inaccurately, as something other than an aggregate of its members'.[159] It is now clear

---

[153] [1934] Ch 342, [1933] All ER Rep 805.   [154] *Supra.*

[155] Morris and Leach, *The Rule Against Perpetuities*, 2nd edn, p 391 et seq. See the American Law Institute's Restatement of Trusts, 2d (1959), para 124.

[156] *IRC v Broadway Cottages Trust* [1955] Ch 20, [1954] 3 All ER 120, CA; *Re Endacott* [1960] Ch 232, [1959] 3 All ER 562, CA.

[157] [1955] Ch 20 at 36, [1954] 3 All ER 120 at 128, CA. See *Daniels v Daniels' Estate* [1992] 2 WWR 697 where a gift of residue to his executors 'to distribute as they see fit' failed for uncertainty of object, reversing the decision at first instance that the clause conferred a valid general power of appointment.

[158] *Re Douglas* (1887) 35 Ch D 472, CA.

[159] *Leahy v A-G of New South Wales* [1959] AC 457 at 477, [1959] 2 All ER 300 at 306, PC. There are three essential characteristics of an unincorporated association, namely: (i) there must be members of the association; (ii) there must be a contract binding the members inter se; (iii) there must by a matter of history have been a moment in time when a number of persons combined or banded together to form the association.

that in the case of a gift to an unincorporated non-charitable association one must first construe the gift, and then decide what results flow from that construction. It appears from *Re Recher's Will Trusts*[160] that there are four possible interpretations of such a gift.

(i) As a gift to the individual members of the association at the date of the gift for their own benefit as joint tenants or tenants in common, so that they could at once, if they pleased, agree to divide it amongst themselves, each putting his share into his own pocket. The association on this construction is used in effect as a convenient label or definition of the class which is intended to take. On the basis that the gift is to the individual members it follows that any member, after severance if he took as a joint tenant, can claim an *aliquot* share whether or not he continues to be a member of the association and irrespective of the wishes of the other members. In *Leahy v A-G of New South Wales*,[161] it was observed that it is by reason of this construction:

that the prudent conveyancer provides that a receipt by the treasurer or other proper officer of the recipient society for a legacy to the society shall be a sufficient discharge to executors.[162] If it were not so, the executors could only get a valid discharge by obtaining a receipt from every member. This must be qualified by saying that, by their rules, the members might have authorized one of themselves to receive a gift on behalf of them all.

This first construction may even be given to a gift for the general purposes of the association,[163] although it may clearly not be contemplated that the individual members shall divide it amongst themselves, provided there is nothing in the constitution of the society to prohibit it.[164] It would, however, be very difficult to give this construction to a gift by name to a society engaged in philanthropic work.[165]

(ii) As a gift not only to present members, but also to future members for ever or for an indefinite period. On this construction, unless the duration was limited to the perpetuity period, it would, prior to the Perpetuities and Accumulations Act 1964, have failed for perpetuity. Since that Act it is submitted it will not fail for perpetuity,

---

Three further normal but not essential characteristics are: (iv) there will normally be some constitutional arrangement for meetings of members and for the appointment of committees and officers; (v) a member will normally be free to join or leave the association at will; (vi) the association will normally continue in existence independently of any change that may occur in the composition of the association.

[160] [1972] Ch 526, [1971] 3 All ER 401, following *Leahy v A-G of New South Wales*, supra, PC and *Neville Estates Ltd v Madden* [1962] Ch 832, [1961] 3 All ER 769. See (1965) 29 Conv 165 (J A Andrews); (1971) 8 MULR 1 (P W Hogg); (1973) 47 ALJ 305 (R Baxt); [1985] Conv 318 (Jean Warburton). Cf *Artistic Upholstery Ltd v Art Firma (Furniture) Ltd* [1999] 4 All ER 277, [2000] FSR 311.

[161] [1959] AC 457 at 477, [1959] 2 All ER 300 at 306, PC.

[162] But even this will not save the gift where there is in fact no association. Thus the gift to the Oxford Group failed in *Re Thackrah* [1939] 2 All ER 4. See E O Walford, loc cit.

[163] *Bowman v Secular Society Ltd* [1917] AC 406, HL: *Re Ogden* [1933] Ch 678, [1933] All ER Rep 720.

[164] *Re Clarke* [1901] 2 Ch 110. Cf *Re Drummond* [1914] 2 Ch 90, [1914–15] All ER Rep 223; disapproved *Leahy v A-G of New South Wales*, supra.

[165] *Re Haks* [1972] Qd R 59.

but will operate in favour of those members ascertained within the perpetuity period.[166]

(iii) As a gift to the trustees or other proper officers of the association on trust to carry into effect the purposes of the association. On this construction the rule in *Morice v Bishop of Durham*[167] applies and the gift will fail for the want of a beneficiary. It is only if on this construction the gift were to be held valid—which, it is submitted, is not the case—that unincorporated associations would constitute an exception to the beneficiary principle, for each other construction is based on a gift to individuals.

(iv) As a gift to the existing members of the association beneficially, but on the basis that the subject matter of the gift is given as an accretion to the funds of the association and falls to be dealt with in accordance with the rules of the association by which the members are contractually bound inter se.[168] On this construction the gift will be valid. Though beneficially entitled an individual member cannot claim to be paid out his share. His share will accrue to the other members on his death or resignation, even though such members include persons who become members after the gift took effect.[169] This fourth construction was held to be the proper way to construe the gift to the Anti-Vivisection Society in *Re Recher's Will Trusts*[170] itself. The gift would accordingly have been held good had the society still been in existence, but on the facts it was held to fail because it had been dissolved before the testatrix died.

In *Re Lipinski's Will Trusts*[171] the matter was more complicated in that there was a gift by will to an association for a specific purpose. This purpose was within the powers of the association and was one of which the members were beneficiaries. Oliver J held that the gift was valid. 'Where the donee association is itself the beneficiary of the

---

[166] Perpetuities and Accumulation Act 1964, ss 4(4) and 3(1) and (4) and see [1976] ASCL 421 (J Hackney). The effect of the Act is not considered by Vinelott J in *Re Grant's Will Trusts* [1979] 3 All ER 359, [1980] 1 WLR 360, nor by Brightman J in *Re Recher's Will Trusts* [1972] Ch 526, [1971] 3 All ER 401, who restated the old rule that if construed as a gift to all members, present and future, beneficially it would be void for perpetuity.

[167] (1805) 10 Ves 522; affg (1804) 9 Ves 399; *Re Grant's Will Trusts*, supra.

[168] In [1995] Conv 302 (P Matthews) it is argued that whether a gift falls within (i) or (iv) is 'a matter of construction *of the rules themselves* and has nothing to do with the donor's intentions'. Simon Gardner, however, in [1998] Conv 8, persuasively contends that the donor's intention is significant in determining whether the gift is to the members 'on account of the club', or in their personal capacity.

[169] This is not easily reconciled with the Law of Property Act 1925, s 53(1)(c), which requires the disposition of an equitable interest to be in writing, and there are also difficulties in regard to infant members. See [1971] ASCL 379 (J Hackney).

[170] [1972] Ch 526, [1971] 3 All ER 401. See *Universe Tankships Inc of Monrovia v International Transport Workers' Federation* [1983] 1 AC 366, [1982] 2 All ER 67, HL, discussed (1983) 133 NLJ 515 (J McMullen & A Grubb); (1982) 45 MLR 561, (1983) 46 MLR 361 (B Green). The same construction was applied to the local branch of a trade union in *News Group Newspapers Ltd v SOGAT 1982* [1986] ICR 716, CA. The funds of the local branch, an unincorporated association, were accordingly not subject to the writ of sequestration of the funds of SOGAT 1982.

[171] [1976] Ch 235, [1977] 1 All ER 33. See [1976] ASCL 419 (J Hackney); (1977) 40 MLR 231 (N P Gravells); (1977) 41 Conv 179 (K Widdows); (1980) 39 CLJ 88 (C E F Rickett); (1977) 9 VUWLR 1 (I McKay).

prescribed purpose,' he said '. . . the gift should be construed as an absolute one [on the fourth construction] the more so where, if the purpose is carried out, the members can by appropriate action vest the resulting property in themselves, for here the trustees and the beneficiaries are the same persons.' Alternatively, he continued, the same result is reached by applying the principle of *Re Denley's Trust Deed*[172] and treating the gift as one of the specification of a particular purpose for the benefit of ascertained beneficiaries, the members of the association for the time being. It was, he thought, significant that the members could by an appropriate majority alter their constitution so as to divide the association's assets among themselves. This last point was stressed by Vinelott J in *Re Grant's Will Trusts*,[173] who said:

It must, as I see it, be a necessary characteristic of any gift within [this] category that the members of the association can by an appropriate majority (if the rules so provide), or acting unanimously if they do not, alter their rules so as to provide that the funds, or part of them, shall be applied for some new purpose, or even distributed amongst the members for their own benefit. For the validity of a gift within this category rests essentially on the fact that the testator has set out to further a purpose by making a gift to the members of an association formed for the furtherance of that purpose in the expectation that, although the members at the date when the gift takes effect will be free, by a majority if the rules so provide or acting unanimously if they do not, to dispose of the fund in any way they may think fit, they and any future members of the association will not in fact do so but will employ the property in the furtherance of the purpose of the association and will honour any special condition attached to the gift.

[172] [1969] 1 Ch 373, [1968] 3 All ER 65, discussed p 57, supra.
[173] [1979] 3 All ER 359, [1980] 1 WLR 360, where the members did not fully control the funds and the gift failed. See (1980) 130 NLJ 532 (A M Tettenborn).

4

CLASSIFICATION AND JURISTIC NATURE OF TRUSTS

1 CLASSIFICATION

(a) EXPRESS, RESULTING, IMPLIED AND CONSTRUCTIVE TRUSTS

There is no generally agreed classification, and it has even been judicially suggested[1] that the boundaries of constructive trust may have been left deliberately vague, so as not to restrict the court by technicalities in deciding what the justice of a particular case may demand. Nevertheless it may be important in particular contexts to be able to put a trust in one category or another. Thus as a general rule a declaration of trust of land must be evidenced by writing, but this rule does not apply to resulting, implied and constructive trusts;[2] and although the appointment of a minor as an express trustee is void,[3] he can hold property as a trustee upon a resulting trust.[4]

(i) Express trust

'An express trust is one which is deliberately established and which the trustee deliberately accepts.'[5]

(ii) Implied trust

The term implied trust is used in more than one sense, though it is doubtful whether it is really a distinct category.[6] In one sense an implied trust may be said to arise where the intention of the settlor to set up a trust is inferred from his words or actions, for example precatory trusts.[7] Implied trusts in this sense are probably best regarded as express trusts, in that the trust is expressed, albeit in ambiguous and uncertain language. Again, as mentioned below, many, perhaps all, resulting trusts depend upon the implied intention of the grantor. Some accordingly treat resulting and implied trusts as synonymous though others consider implied trust as synonymous with constructive trust.

---

[1] Per Edmund Davies LJ in *Carl-Zeiss-Stiftung v Herbert Smith & Co (No 2)* [1969] 2 All ER 367 at 381, CA. See, generally, (1998) 114 LQR 399 (P J Millett); (1999) 18 NZULR 305 (C E F Rickett).
[2] Law of Property Act 1925, s 53(2). [3] Law of Property Act 1925, s 20.
[4] *Re Vinogradoff* [1935] WN 68.
[5] Per Tipping J in *Fortex Group Ltd v MacIntosh* [1998] 3 NZLR 171.
[6] See [2002] NZLJ 176 (Nicky Richardson). [7] See pp 45–47, supra.

(iii) Resulting trust

The term resulting trust seems to be limited to three[8] fairly well defined categories, first, where a man purchases property and has it conveyed or transferred into the name of another or the joint names of himself and another when the beneficial interest will normally, as it is said, result to the man who put up the purchase money; secondly, where there is a voluntary conveyance or transfer into the name of another or into the joint names of the grantor and another where likewise there is prima facia a resulting trust for the grantor; and thirdly, where there is a transfer of property to another on trusts which leave some or all of the equitable interest undisposed of. Again there is a resulting trust, whether the reason is that there is no attempt to dispose of part of the equitable interest, as where property is given to trustees on trust for X for life, and nothing is said as to what is to happen after X's death, or that a purported disposition fails, as where a declared trust is void for uncertainty.

In *Re Vandervell's Trusts (No 2)*[9] Megarry J classified the first two categories as 'presumed resulting trusts', because they depend upon the presumed intention of the grantor, while the third category he called an 'automatic resulting trust', because it does not depend on any intentions or presumptions, but is the automatic consequence of the transferor's failure to dispose of what is vested in him. In *Westdeutsche Landesbank Girozentrale v Islington London Borough Council*[10] Lord Browne-Wilkinson doubted Megarry J's analysis of the third category, stating that in his view if the settlor has expressly, or by necessary implication, abandoned any beneficial interest in the trust property there would be no resulting trust but the undisposed-of equitable interest would vest in the Crown as bona vacantia.

Chambers[11] has suggested that all cases of resulting trust arise by operation of law when property has been transferred to another and the provider of that property did not intend to benefit the recipient: it depends on lack of an intention to benefit the recipient. The resulting trust, he contends, is an equitable response to this lack of intention and actively reverses unjust enrichment. Although this view has powerful extrajudicial support,[12] it has also met with severe criticism.[13] In *Carlton v Goodman*[14] the alternative theories were considered but since, on the facts, they both led to the same result, it was not necessary to decide between them.

---

[8] The first two categories were treated as one by Lord Browne-Wilkinson in *Westdeutsche Landesbank Girozentrale v Islington London Borough Council* [1996] AC 669, [1996] 2 All ER 961, HL.

[9] [1974] Ch 269, [1974] 1 All ER 47; revsd [1974] Ch 269, [1974] 3 All ER 205, CA, without discussing this classification. See *Allen v Rochdale Borough Council* [2000] Ch 221, [1999] 3 All ER 443, CA.

[10] [1996] 2 All ER 961, HL, at 991.

[11] *Resulting Trusts*. See also *Equity and Contemporary Legal Developments* (ed S Goldstein) 335 (P Birks) and [2002] 16 Tru LI 104, 138 (R Chambers) on resulting trusts in Canada.

[12] See Lord Millett in (1998) 114 LQR 399.   [13] (1996) 16 LS 110 (W Swadling).

[14] [2002] EWCA Civ 545, [2002] 2 FLR 259.

(iv) Constructive trust[15]

There are two distinct types of constructive trust, namely, (1) the institutional constructive trust and, (2) the remedial constructive trust. Only the first of these is presently recognized as valid in English law.[16]

(a) *The institutional constructive trust.* Under such a trust, 'the trust arises by operation of law as from the date of the circumstances which give rise to it: the function of the court is merely to declare that such a trust has arisen in the past. The consequences that flow from such a trust having arisen (including the possibly unfair consequences to third parties who in the interim have received the trust property) are also determined by rules of law, not under a discretion.'[17] In English law the constructive trust is a substantive institution, in principle like any other trust. Express trusts and constructive trusts are two species of the same genus.

Common situations in which a constructive trust will be imposed are (i) where a stranger to the trust, not being a bona fide purchaser for value without notice, is found in possession of trust property. He will be compelled to hold it on trust for the beneficiaries as a constructive trustee, (ii) where a trustee makes some profit out of his trust. He will be compelled to hold it as a part of the trust property, (iii) under a contract for the sale of land when the vendor is a constructive trustee for the purchaser until completion. It should be remembered, however, that 'where there is an express declaration of trust, the doctrine of constructive trusts cannot be used so as to contradict the expressly declared trust. The doctrine of constructive trusts is one which applies in circumstances in which there is no declared trust.'[18]

---

[15] See [1999] CLJ 294 (L Smith); (1999) 37 Alberta LR 133 (L I Rotman). Ormiston JA recently observed, 'The subject of constructive trusts has over the years become contentious and differences in analysis have tended to confuse rather than inform': *Nolan v Nolan* [2004] VSCA 109, [2004] WTLR 1261 (Australia).

[16] See *Re Sharpe (a bankrupt)* [1980] 1 All ER 198 at 203, per Browne-Wilkinson J; *Halifax Building Society v Thomas* [1995] 4 All ER 673, 682, [1996] 2 WLR 63, 72, CA, per Peter Gibson LJ; *Westdeutsche Landesbank Girozentrale v Islington London Borough Council* [1996] AC 669 at 714–715, [1996] 2 All ER 961 at 997, HL, per Lord Browne-Wilkinson; *Re Polly Peck International plc (in administration) (No 2)* [1998] 3 All ER 812, CA; [1980] Conv 207 (Jill Martin); (1998) 114 LQR 399 (P J Millett). Note, however, *Ocular Sciences Ltd v Aspect Vision Care Ltd* [1997] RPC 289 where Daddie J, at 411–416, appears to regard constructive trust as a remedy, though on the facts no trust was imposed. He said, at 416, 'the imposition of a constructive trust is part of the equitable armoury of the court'.

[17] *Westdeutsche Landesbank Girozentrale v Islington London Borough Council*, supra, HL, per Lord Browne-Wilkinson. But in the Australian case of *Muschinski v Dodds* (1985) 160 CLR 583 a constructive trust was expressly imposed only from the date of publication of reasons for the judgment so as to safeguard the legitimate interests of third parties. This would seem only to be appropriate in the case of a remedial constructive trust, and it is to be noted that in *Muschinski v Dodds* Deane J saw the constructive trust both as 'remedy' and 'institution', but having a predominantly remedial character. See also *Parsons v McBain* (2001) 109 FCR (Aust) 120.

[18] *Pink v Lawrence* (1977) 36 P & CR 98 at 101, CA, per Buckley LJ; *Goodman v Gallant,* [1986] Fam 106, [1986] 1 All ER 311, CA. See also *Pettitt v Pettitt* [1970] AC 777, [1969]. 2 All ER 385, HL, esp, per Lord Upjohn at 813, 405, cited pp 182, 183 infra.

In *Paragon Finance plc v D B Thakerar & Co (a firm)*[19] Millett LJ explained that the term 'constructive trust' is used to describe two entirely different situations. First, it covers cases:

where the defendant though not expressly appointed as trustee, has assumed the duties of a trustee by a lawful transaction which was independent of and preceded the breach of trust and is not impeached by the plaintiff. The second covers those cases where the trust obligation arises as a direct consequence of the unlawful transaction which is impeached by the plaintiff.

A constructive trust arises by operation of law whenever the circumstances are such that it would be unconscionable for the owner of property . . . to assert his own beneficial interest in the property and deny the beneficial interest of another. In the first class of case . . . the constructive trustee really is a trustee. He does not receive the trust property in his own right but by a transaction by which both parties intend to create a trust from the outset and which is not impugned by the plaintiff. His possession of the property is coloured from the first by the trust and confidence by means of which he obtained it, and his subsequent appropriation of the property to his own use is a breach of that trust . . . In these cases the plaintiff does not impugn the transaction by which the defendant obtained control of the property. He alleges that the circumstances in which the defendant obtained control make it unconscionable for him thereafter to assert a beneficial interest in the property.

The second class of case . . . arises when the defendant is implicated in a fraud. Equity has always given relief against fraud by making any person sufficiently implicated in the fraud accountable in equity. In such a case he is traditionally though I think unfortunately described as a constructive trustee and said to be 'liable to account as constructive trustee'. Such a person is not in fact a trustee at all, even though he may be liable to account as if he were. He never assumes the position of a trustee, and if he receives the trust property at all it is adversely to the plaintiff by an unlawful transaction which is impugned by the plaintiff. In such a case the expressions 'constructive trust' and 'constructive trustee' are misleading, for there is no trust and usually no possibility of a proprietary remedy; they are 'nothing more than a formula for equitable relief'.[20]

(b) *The remedial constructive trust.* In some other jurisdictions the view is taken that express and constructive trusts are distinct concepts and not two species of a single genus.[21] Canada has been a pioneering jurisdiction in this respect, and has developed

---

[19] [1999] 1 All ER 400, CA, at 408–409 and as Lord Millett in *Dubai Aluminium Co Ltd v Salaam* [2002] UKHL 48, [2003] 1 All ER 97, at 130–131, and extrajudicially in (1998) 114 LQR 399.

[20] Per Ungoed-Thomas J in *Selangor United Rubber Estates Ltd v Cradock (No 3)* [1968] 2 All ER 1073, [1968] 1 WLR 1555 at 1097, 1582; see *Governor and Company of the Bank of Scotland v A Ltd* [2001] 3 All ER 58, CA. But see (2004) 67 MLR 16 (S B Elliott and C Mitchell).

[21] See *Scott on Trusts*, 4th edn, vol v, sections 461, 462; American Restatement of the Law of Restitution, Section 160.

the remedial constructive trust as a remedy for unjust enrichment.[22] A Canadian judge has explained the distinction thus:[23]

In a substantive constructive trust, the acts of the parties in relation to some property are such that those acts are later declared by a court to have given rise to a substantive constructive trust and to have done so at the time when the acts of the parties brought the trust into being . . . In a remedial constructive trust . . . the acts of the parties are such that a wrong is done by one of them to another so that, while no substantive trust relationship is then and there brought into being by those acts, none the less a remedy is required in relation to property and the court grants that remedy in the form of declaration which when the order is made creates a constructive trust by one of the parties in favour of another party.

Lord Browne-Wilkinson has described a remedial constructive trust succinctly[24] as a 'judicial remedy giving rise to an enforceable obligation: the extent to which it operates retrospectively to the prejudice of third parties lies in the discretion of the court'. It 'depends for its very existence on an Order of the Court; such Order being creative rather than simply confirmatory'.[25]

The Canadian development, which originated as a remedy in property disputes between married and unmarried couples,[26] has been extended beyond family property cases.[27] It has been said[28] not to expunge the constructive trust in situations in which English courts of equity traditionally find a constructive trust, but it is applied

---

[22] As to Australia see *Baumgartner v Baumgartner* (1988) 62 ALJR 29; *Bryson v Bryant* (1992) 29 NSWLR 188, noted (1994) 16 Sydney LR 412 (Joellen Riley); (1997) 113 LQR 227 (Rebecca Bailey-Harris); *Parij v Parij* (1998) 72 SASR 153; *Lloyd v Tedesco* [2002] 25 WAR 360, noted (2002) 16 Tru LI 182 (J Edelman). In Australia and New Zealand the preferred basis seems to be unconscionability (1994) 8 Tru LI 74 (M Bryan). As to New Zealand see *Gillies v Keogh* [1989] 2 NZLR 327, where Cooke P said, at 331, that 'reasonable expectations in the light of the conduct of the parties are at the root of the matter'; *Phillips v Phillips* [1993] 3 NZLR 159 (referring to 'the reasonable expectation test'); *Commonwealth Reserve I v Chodar* [2001] 2 NZLR 374, (1996) 6 Cant LR 369 (Nicky Richardson); [1999] NZLJ 175 (S Trew). The extensive recent literature includes; (1991) 14 NZULR 375 (I S R Scott); [1991] Conv 125 (C Rickett); (1993) 43 UTLJ 217 (P Parkinson); [1991] NZLJ 90 (R Fardell and K Fulton); (1992) 7 Auck ULR 147 (J Dixon); (1993) 109 LQR 263 (S Gardner); *The Frontiers of Liability* (ed P Birks) vol 2, 165 (D W M Waters); ibid 186 (S Gardner); 204 (J Eekelaar); 214 (P Birks); 224 (J D Davies); (2000) Deak LR 31 (S Evans).

[23] Lambert JA in *Atlas Cabinets and Furniture Ltd v National Trust Co Ltd* (1990) 68 DLR (4th) 161.

[24] In *Westdeutsche Landesbank Girozentrale v Islington London Borough Council* [1996] AC 669, [1996] 2 All ER 961, HL, at 714, 715, 997.

[25] Per Tipping J in *Fortex Group Ltd v MacIntosh* [1998] 3 NZLR 171; *Commonwealth Reserve I v Chodar* [2001] NZLR 374. See [1999] LMCLQ 111 (C Rickett and R Grantham); [2001] 5 Deak LR 31 (S Evans).

[26] See *Pettkus v Becker* (1980) 117 DLR (3d) 257; *Sorochan v Sorochan* (1986) 29 DLR (4th) 213; *Rawluk v Rawluk* (1990) 65 DLR (4th) 161; *Peter v Beblow* (1993) 101 DLR (4th) 621; *LeClair v LeClair Estate* [1998] 9 WWR 182. See also (1999) 37 Alberta LR 1 (Mitchell McInnes); (1999) 37 Alberta LR 173 (R Chambers).

[27] See *LAC Minerals Ltd v International Corona Resources Ltd* (1989) 61 DLR (4th) 14; *Soulos v Korkontzilas* (1997) 146 DLR (4th) 214, noted (1997) 31 UBCLR 341 (K B Farquhar); (1997) 76 CBR 539 (L D Smith); (1998) 114 LQR 14 (L Smith); (1999) 10 SCLR 461 (L I Rotman).

[28] In *Soulos v Korkontzilas*, supra, at 222, 223. See (1997) 42 McGill LJ 437 (S Hoegner); (1998) 25 Man LJ 513 (M McInnes).

in circumstances in which the familiar principles of English Law would lead to the same result.[29]

Lord Denning sought to introduce a similar approach in several cases in the 1970s. Thus in *Hussey v Palmer*[30] he defined a constructive trust as 'a trust imposed by law whenever justice and good conscience require it . . . It is an equitable remedy by which the court can enable an aggrieved party to obtain restitution.' Lord Denning's view may well have influenced the Canadian development, but they have not prevailed in English law.[31] However, in *Re Polly Peck International plc (in administration) (No 2)*[32] Nourse LJ referred to several cases[33] where judges have accepted the possibility that the remedial constructive trust may become part of English law. But, he pointed out, the judicial observations in those cases were both obiter and tentative. A remedial constructive trust, he continued, gives the court a discretion to vary proprietary rights, which is something no court has power to do without the authority of Parliament. Statutory authority, such as the Variation of Trusts Act 1958 and the Matrimonial Causes Act 1973, is required to give the court jurisdiction to vary proprietary rights. Extrajudicially Lord Millett has said that the remedial constructive trust is unlikely to take root in England.[34]

(b) TRUSTS OF LAND

Prior to 1997 when land was settled on trust in nearly every case the land would be either settled land under the Settled Land Act 1925, or held upon trust for sale under the Law of Property Act 1925.[35]

If the land was settled land as defined in the Settled Land Act 1925,[36] the beneficiaries were treated as having equitable interests in the land, even if the land was in fact sold and was represented by capital money in the hands of the trustees of the settlement.[37] The powers of management were normally vested in the tenant for life.[38]

---

[29] See *Re Polly Peck International plc (in administration) (No 2)* [1998] 3 All ER 812, CA, per Nourse LJ at 831.

[30] [1972] 3 All ER 744, [1972] 1 WLR 1286, CA. See also *Cooke v Head* [1972] 2 All ER 38, [1972] 1 WLR 518, CA; *Eves v Eves* [1975] 3 All ER 768, [1975] 1 WLR 1388, CA.

[31] See *Burns v Burns* [1984] Ch 317, [1984] 1 All ER 244, CA; *Grant v Edwards* [1986] Ch 638, [1986] 2 All ER 426, CA.

[32] [1998] 3 All ER 312, CA.

[33] *Metall und Rohstoff AG v Donaldson Lufkin & Jenrette Inc* [1990] 1 QB 391, [1989] 3 All ER 14, CA; *Re Goldcorp Exchange Ltd (in receivership)* [1995] 1 AC 74, [1994] 2 All ER 806, PC; *Westdeutsche Landesbank Girozentrale v Islington London Borough Council*, supra, HL. See the valuable article by Birks in (1998) 12 Tru LI 202. See also *Re Esteem Settlement* [2003] JLR 188 (Jersey Royal Court), noted PCB 153 (Zillah Howard).

[34] Cornish et al (eds) *Restitution: Past, Present and Future*, p 199.

[35] An exceptional case was where a trustee held land on a bare trust for a beneficiary absolutely entitled. Note, however, *Wilson v Wilson* [1969] 3 All ER 945, [1969] 1 WLR 1470, where Buckley J held that the trustees in that case held on a statutory trust for sale for one of them alone. Harpum in [1990] CLJ 277 says that it is quite impossible to find a trust for sale in such circumstances.

[36] Section 1. The primary case is where land is limited in trust for any persons by way of succession. By s 1(7) it cannot be settled land if it is held on trust for sale.

[37] Ibid, s 75(5).   [38] Ibid, ss 19, 20, 23, 108(2).

Social changes, the effects of taxation and the complexity of the provisions of the Settled Land Act 1925 had the result that few new settlements were being created. Provisions in the Trusts of Land and Appointment of Trustees Act 1996[39] have taken account of this and made it impossible to create a new settlement under the 1925 Act,[39] though existing settlements continue so long as there is relevant property subject to the settlement.[40] Land vested in trustees on charitable, ecclesiastical or public trusts was before 1997 deemed to be settled land,[41] but since 1996 no land held on such trusts is or is deemed to be settled land even if it was or was deemed to be, settled land before 1997.[42]

Where, before 1997, land was conveyed to trustees in fee simple upon trust to sell it and to hold the proceeds of sale on trust for X for life with remainder to Y absolutely, a trust for sale governed by the Law of Property Act 1925 would have been created. The trustees would have been under a duty to sell the land[43] and the powers of management were vested in them.[44] Moreover under the doctrine of conversion the beneficiaries were treated as having interests in personalty, not in the land, even while the land remained unsold. Trusts for sale were also created by statute, as noted below.

Very considerable changes were made by the Trusts of Land and Appointment of Trustees Act 1996. The trust for sale is now subsumed within the definition of a 'trust of land' in the 1996 Act, as meaning any trust of property which consists of or includes land. It includes any description of trust (whether express, implied, resulting or constructive), including a trust for sale and a bare trust.[45] Though it is still possible to create a trust for sale, the doctrine of conversion no longer applies, whenever the trust came into being.[46] Beneficiaries under a trust of land have equitable interests in the land itself. Moreover, in the case of every trust for sale of land created by a disposition there is to be implied, despite any provision to the contrary made by the disposition, a power for the trustees to postpone sale of the land; and the trustees are not liable in any way for postponing sale of the land, in the exercise of their discretion, for an indefinite period.[47] The practical consequence would seem to be that the land will be retained unless the trustees agree to sell it.

It may be added that for the purpose of exercising their functions as trustees, the trustees of land have in relation to the land subject to the trust all the powers of an absolute owner.[48]

---

[39] Section 2(1) slightly qualified by sub-ss (2), (3). The Act came into force on 1 January 1997.

[40] Ibid, s 2(4).   [41] Settled Land Act 1925, s 29.

[42] Trusts of Land and Appointment of Trustees Act 1996, s 1(5).

[43] But with power to postpone the sale indefinitely: Law of Property Act 1925, s 25.

[44] Though these could often be delegated under s 29 of the Law of Property Act 1925.

[45] Trusts of Land and Appointment of Trustees Act 1996, s 1(1), (2). The definition includes a trust created, or arising, before 1997. It does not include settled land or land to which the Universities and College Estates Act 1925 applies: s 1(3).

[46] Ibid, s 3(1), (3). There is an exception in relation to wills of testators who have died before 1997: ibid, s 3(2).

[47] Ibid, s 4.   [48] Ibid, s 6(1). See p 465, infra.

(c) STATUTORY TRUSTS

In contrast to the trusts considered above, which were either set up by act of parties or imposed by a court of equity, a trust may be created by statute in specified circumstances. Among the most important are the trust arising on intestacy under s 33 of the Administration of Estates Act 1925 as amended by the Trusts of Land and Appointment of Trustees Act 1996 and the Trustee Act 2000, and the trust imposed by ss 34 and 36 of the Law of Property Act 1925 as likewise amended in cases of undivided shares and joint tenancy of land. Prior to the 1996 Act these provisions imposed a trust for sale, but since that Act they impose a trust without a duty to sell.[49]

A limited special case is a trust of service charge money set up under s 42 of the Landlord and Tenant Act 1987.[50]

(d) EXECUTORY AND EXECUTED TRUSTS

This is a division of express trusts. Although as Lord St Leonards pointed out in *Egerton v Earl Brownlow*,[51] in one sense all trusts are executory in that there is always something to be done, the terms 'executory' and 'executed' are used, he continued, with a technical meaning.

An executed trust is where the settlor has been his own conveyancer, that is, where he has defined exactly the interests to be taken by the beneficiaries or, in other words, has set out the limitations of the equitable interests in complete and final form.

An executory trust is where he has merely expressed his general intention as to the way in which the property shall go, the limitations really only being intended as instructions as to the mode in which a formal settlement should ultimately be made.[52] The doctrine of executory trusts, however, has its limits. Before it can be applied, it must be possible to ascertain from the language of the document directing the setting-up of the trust, at least in general terms, the trusts which one is to impose on the property to be settled. It was held that this could not be done, and the trust accordingly failed, in *Re Flavel's Will Trusts*,[53] where a testator left a share of residue to trustees 'for formation of a superannuation bonus fund for the employees' of a named company.

The importance of the distinction between executory and executed trusts lies in their construction. In the case of an executed trust equity will follow the law and give a strict construction to technical words; if strict conveyancing language with a definite legal meaning is used in the creation of a trust of an equitable estate, it is not competent to a court to disregard that legal meaning even though a contrary intention may

---

[49] Trusts of Land and Appointment of Trustees Act 1996, s 5; Sch 2 paras 3, 4, 5; Sch 4.
[50] Discussed (1990) 140 NLJ 785 (R Dickson).   [51] (1853) 4 HL Cas 1, 210.
[52] See *Stanley v Lennard* (1758) 1 Eden 87; *Jervoise v Duke of Northumberland* (1820) 1 Jac & W 559, and see *Davis v Richards and Wallington Industries Ltd* [1991] 2 All ER 563, [1990] 1 WLR 1511. See also per Lord Colonsay in *Sackville-West v Viscount Holmesdale* (1870) LR 4 HL 543 at 570.
[53] [1969] 2 All ER 232, [1969] 1 WLR 444.

appear from the rest of the deed.[54] However, even in an executed trust the use of untechnical expressions may enable the court to give effect to the settlor's intentions.[55] By contrast in the case of an executory trust the court is not bound to construe technical expressions in a technical way, but can look at the whole instrument in order to discover what is the real intention of the settlor, or testator, and order the formal settlement to be drafted so as to fulfil, so far as possible, these real intentions.[56]

Most cases on executory trusts have been cases on marriage articles, where the articles direct a more formal conveyance to be made, and themselves express the limitations in an informal manner, but executory trusts may arise under wills,[57] or indeed under inter vivos dispositions other than marriage articles.[58] It may be added that the practical importance of the distinction between executed and executory trusts has been considerably reduced as a result of the abolition[59] of the rule in *Shelley's Case*,[60] and the provisions of ss 60 and 130 of the Law of Property Act 1925.

(e) PRIVATE AND CHARITABLE TRUSTS

A private trust is for the benefit of an individual, or a number or class of specified persons, all of whom must be definitely ascertained within the perpetuity period; a public or charitable trust has as its object charity in a technical sense and usually requires an element of public benefit. The definition of charity, and the advantages and disadvantages of charitable trusts, are discussed in chapter 13.

(f) COMPLETELY AND INCOMPLETELY CONSTITUTED TRUSTS

This distinction is discussed in chapter 6, infra.

(g) SIMPLE AND SPECIAL TRUSTS

The distinction has not been fully worked out by the courts. The term 'bare trust', which seems to be synonymous with 'simple trust' or 'naked trust', has been the subject of conflicting views in several cases where the point has arisen on the construction of that term in a statute. Hall VC in *Christie v Ovington*[61] took the view, in connection with s 5 of the Vendor and Purchaser Act 1874, that a bare trustee was 'a trustee to whose office no duties were originally attached, or who, although such duties were originally attached to his office, would, on the requisition of his cestuis que trust, be compellable in equity to convey the estate to them, or by their direction'.

---

[54] *Re Bostock's Settlement* [1921] 2 Ch 469, CA.   [55] *Re Arden* [1935] Ch 326.

[56] See per Lord Westbury in *Sackville-West v Viscount Holmesdale* (1870) LR 4 HL 543 at 565; *Re Bostock's Settlement* [1921] 2 Ch 469, CA.

[57] *Re Spicer* (1901) 84 LT 195.   [58] *Mayn v Mayn* (1867) LR 5 Eq 150.

[59] By the Law of Property Act 1925, s 131, as amended by the Trusts of Land and Appointment of Trustees Act 1996.

[60] (1581) 1 Co Rep 93b.   [61] (1875) 1 Ch D 279.

Jessel MR in *Morgan v Swansea Urban Sanitary Authority*[62] criticized this definition on two grounds: first, he said the concept of a trustee necessarily connotes duties, and the definition would be meaningless unless 'duties' means active duties in the sense of trusts to sell or lease or something of that sort. Secondly, he said that as it stands the second part of the definition is totally unhelpful, since in any trust all the cestuis que trust, if sui iuris, can together compel the trustees to convey the estate. It would, he said, have a meaning, if it continued 'and has been requested by them so to convey it' for after such request it would be wrong of the trustee to continue to hold the estate. However, Jessel MR's own view was that a bare trustee meant a trustee without any beneficial interest.

Jessel MR's view is supported by *Re Blandy Jenkins' Estate*,[63] where the point arose under the Fines and Recoveries Act 1833,[64] and by the opinion of Kenyon CJ in the older case of *Roe d Reade v Reade*.[65] On the other side the view that the test is whether the trustee has active duties to perform was applied in *Re Docwra*,[66] *Re Cunningham and Frayling*[67] and *Schalit v Joseph Nadler Ltd*,[68] though in the last case the earlier cases were not referred to. This view or a variant of it also seems to be the one preferred by textbook writers.[69] The matter was discussed by Gummow J in the Australian case of *Herdegen v Federal Comr of Taxation*,[70] who pointed out that the meaning may very from statute to statute. In construing the statute before him he combined the two views referred to above and said that 'bare trustees' meant 'those trustees who have no interest in the trust assets other than that existing by reason of the office and the legal title as trustee and who never have had active duties to perform or who have ceased to have those duties, such that in either case the property awaits transfer to the beneficiaries or at their direction.' A bare trust of land is a 'trust of land' within the Trusts of Land and Appointment of Trustees Act 1996[71] and the trustees of such a trust accordingly have in relation to the land subject to the trust all the powers of an absolute owner.[72]

If a trust is not a simple one, it is a special one. On the basis that under a special trust the trustee has active duties to perform, a further subdivision can be made into ministerial and discretionary, according to the degree of judgment and discretion that the trustee is required to exercise.

(h) FIXED AND DISCRETIONARY TRUSTS

In a fixed trust the trust instrument sets out the share or interest that each beneficiary is to take, and accordingly each beneficiary is the owner of the specified interest that he has been given.

---

[62] (1878) 9 Ch D 582. The view of Jessel MR was preferred by Mason P in *Chief Comr of Stamp Duties v ISPT Pty Ltd* (1997) 45 NSWLR 639.

[63] [1917] 1 Ch 46.   [64] Sections 27 and 22.   [65] (1799) 8 Term Rep 118.

[66] (1885) 29 Ch D 693.   [67] [1891] 2 Ch 567.   [68] [1933] 2 KB 79, [1933] All ER Rep 708, DC.

[69] Underhill and Hayton, *Law of Trusts and Trustees* 16th edn, pp 57–59; Lewin on *Trusts*, 17th edn, p 13. Cf *Worthing Rugby Football Club Trustees v IRC* [1985] 1 WLR 409.

[70] (1988) 84 ALR 271.   [71] Section 1(1), (2a).   [72] Ibid, s 6. See chapter 22, section 9, infra.

Trustees are often given discretions of varying kinds, for example, as to how the trust funds should be invested, but the phrase discretionary trust means a trust under which the trustees are given a discretion to pay or apply income or capital, or both, to or for the benefit of all, or any one or more exclusively of the others, of a specified class or group of persons, no beneficiary being able to claim as of right that all or any part of the income or capital is to be paid to him or applied for his benefit. They may even be given power to include or exclude any person (or charity) from the class of potential beneficiaries,[73] either permanently or for a specified period.

The trustees may thus have power to decide both who shall benefit and what the benefits shall be. A potential beneficiary cannot be said to be the owner of an equitable interest unless and until the trustees exercise their discretion in his favour. Discretionary trusts are further discussed below.[74]

(i) TRUSTS IN THE HIGHER SENSE AND TRUSTS IN THE LOWER SENSE

Where it alleged that the Crown is a trustee, the real position may be that there is a governmental obligation or 'trust in the higher sense'. Although this is no mere moral obligation it is not enforceable in the courts and is outside the scope of this book. A 'trust in the lower sense' or true trust is an equitable obligation originally created by the Court of Chancery and fully enforceable in the courts.[75] Whether an instrument has created a true trust or a trust in the higher sense is a matter of construction, looking at the whole of the instrument in question, its nature and effect, and its context.

2 DISCRETIONARY AND PROTECTIVE TRUSTS

(a) LIMITATIONS UPON CONDITION AND DETERMINABLE INTERESTS

One might think that a gift to X for life or until he becomes bankrupt would have the same effect as a gift to X for life on condition that if he becomes bankrupt his interest shall determine. In law, however, a distinction must be drawn between a determinable interest, where the determining event is incorporated in the limitation so that the

---

[73] *Re Manisty's Settlement* [1974] Ch 17, [1973] 2 All ER 1203.   [74] Infra, p 76.

[75] *Tito v Waddell (No 2)* [1977] Ch 106, [1977] 3 All ER 129. See also *Guerin v R* (1984) 13 DLR (4th) 321, discussed (1985) 30 McGill LJ 559 (J Hurley), (1986) 18 OLR 307 (Darlene M Johnston); *Aboriginal Development Commission v Treka Aboriginal Arts and Crafts Ltd* [1984] 3 NSWLR 502; *Principal Savings & Trust Co v British Columbia* (1994) 20 Alta LR (3d) 388. Note *Philipp Bros v Republic of Sierra Leone* [1995] 1 Lloyd's Rep 289, CA, where it was held that the payment of aid by the European Commission to the Republic of Sierra Leone did not give rise to a claim that the money was held on trust. Nor is cash belonging to a prisoner paid into an account under the control of the governor held by him as a trustee: *Duggan v Governor of Full Sutton Prison* [2004] EWCA Civ 78, [2004] 2 All ER 966.

interest automatically and naturally determines if and when the event happens, and a grant upon a condition subsequent, where an interest is granted subject to an independent proviso that the interest may be brought to a premature end if the condition is fulfilled.[76] In the latter case, if for any reason the condition is void, the grant becomes absolute and the interest will not be liable to premature determination.[77] These principles apply in general to all estates and interests in property, but for present purposes we are concerned with their effect upon life interests.

Conditions which have been held void include conditions intended to secure the premature determination of the interest granted on alienation[78] or bankruptcy.[79] There is no doubt, however, that the corresponding determinable limitation, that is a grant of a life interest to X until he attempts to alienate the same or becomes bankrupt, is perfectly valid,[80] and in dealing with life interests the courts, it seems, will not be astute to construe a provision as a condition if it can be constructed as a determinable limitation.

An important restriction on the validity of such a determinable limitation is that a man cannot settle his own property on himself until his bankruptcy, so as to defeat the claim of his trustee in bankruptcy,[81] though there is no objection to a limitation which takes effect so as to defeat a particular alienee.[82] Where a man does settle property on himself, and, as is usually the case, the life interest is determinable not only on bankruptcy but also upon other events such as an attempted alienation or charge, then, on the one hand, if bankruptcy is the first determining event to happen, the life interest will vest indefeasibly in the trustee in bankruptcy and will no longer be capable of being determined by the happening of any subsequent specified determining event;[83] on the other hand, if one of the other determining events is the first to happen, the life interest will automatically come to an end and if the life tenant subsequently becomes bankrupt the bankrupt will have no interest in the property to pass to his trustee in bankruptcy.[84]

---

[76] For a discussion of the distinction see Cheshire and Burn, *Modern Real Property*, 16th edn, pp 359 et seq; Megarry and Wade, *The Law of Real Property*, 6th edn, p 64 et seq.

[77] *Sifton v Sifton* [1938] AC 656 at 677, PC.

[78] *Brandon v Robinson* (1811) 18 Ves 429; *Rochford v Hackman* (1852) 9 Hare 475; *Re Trusts of the Scientific Investment Pension Plan* [1999] Ch 53, [1998] 3 All ER 154 where the distinction was said to be 'not a particularly attractive one, being based on form rather than substance'. See, generally, *Re Brown* [1954] Ch 39, [1953] 2 All ER 1342; (1943) 59 LQR 343 (Glanville Williams). As to bankrupts and their rights under an annuity contract or pensions scheme containing a restriction against alienation see *Krasner v Dennison* [2001] Ch 76, [2000] 3 All ER 234, CA; *Rowe v Sanders* [2002] 2 All ER 800, CA.

[79] *Re Dugdale* (1888) 38 Ch D 176. See *Money Markets International Stockbrokers Ltd (in liquidation) v London Stock Exchange Ltd* [2001] 4 All ER 223.

[80] See eg *Brandon v Robinson* (1811) 18 Ves 429.

[81] *Wilson v Greenwood* (1818) 1 Swan 471 at 481, footnote; *Mackintosh v Pogose* [1895] 1 Ch 505; *Re Wombwell* (1921) 125 LT 437.

[82] *Re Johnson, ex p Matthews* [1904] 1 KB 134, DC.   [83] *Re Burroughs-Fowler* [1916] 2 Ch 251.

[84] *Re Richardson's Will Trusts* [1958] Ch 504, [1958] 1 All ER 538; *Re Detmold* (1889) 40 Ch D 585; *Re Brewer's Settlement* [1896] 2 Ch 503.

(b) DISCRETIONARY TRUSTS[85]

A discretionary trust may be exhaustive, that is where the trustees are bound to distribute the whole income, but have a discretion as to how the distribution is to be made between the objects. Alternatively according to the cases cited below a discretionary trust may be non-exhaustive, in which case the trustees have a discretion not only as to how the distribution is to be made, but also as to whether and to what extent it is to be made at all. It is submitted that the term 'non-exhaustive discretionary trust' in fact conceals the two alternatives referred to by Lord Wilberforce in *McPhail v Doulton*[86] viz a power of distribution coupled with a trust to dispose of the undistributed surplus, by accumulation or otherwise, and a trust for distribution coupled with a power to withhold a portion and accumulate or otherwise dispose of it. The distinction between these alternatives does not appear to have been raised in *Gartside v IRC*[87] and it is submitted that it is only if the provision there in question was construed in the latter sense that it should properly have been called a discretionary trust. It was in fact consistently so called by their Lordships, though the language of the will is similar to that given as a typical example of a mere power by Russell LJ in *Re Baden's Deed Trusts*.[88]

The nature of the interest of a discretionary beneficiary has been discussed in relation to statutory provisions relating to estate duty, a tax which has now been abolished. In *Gartside v IRC*,[89] which involved a non-exhaustive trust, Lord Reid made it clear that the objects of a discretionary trust do not have concurrent interests in the income, nor do they have a group interest. They all have individual rights: they are in competition with each other and what the trustees give to one is his alone. The reference to a class or group of objects under a discretionary trust is merely a convenient form of reference to indicate individuals who satisfy requirements to qualify as objects who may separately receive benefits under the exercise of the discretion. Subsequently Cross J in *Re Weir's Settlement*[90] and Ungoed-Thomas J in *Sainsbury v IRC*[91] have taken the same view in the case of an exhaustive trust. The cases cited also lay down that the separate 'interest' of each separate object is unquantifiable, and of a

---

[85] See (1957) 21 Conv 55 (L A Sheridan); (1967) 31 Conv 117 and [1968] BTR 351 (A J Hawkins); [1977] Mon LR 210 (Y Grbich); [1982] Conv 118, 177 (Ann R Everton).

[86] [1971] AC 424 at 448, [1970] 2 All ER 228 at 240, HL.

[87] [1968] AC 553, [1968] 1 All ER 121, HL. Cf *Pearson v IRC* [1981] AC 753, [1980] 2 All ER 479, HL, (decided by a bare majority in the House of Lords, which disagreed with all the judges below). There seems much to be said for the dissenting speech of Lord Russell of Killowen. The analysis of trust law by Fox J at first instance in [1980] Ch 1 at 14–15, [1979] 1 All ER 273 at 281–282, repays study. As pointed out by Vinelott J in *IRC v Berrill* [1982] 1 All ER 867, [1981] 1 WLR 1449, there is nothing in the speeches in the House of Lords casting any doubt on its accuracy or completeness.

[88] [1969] 1 All ER 1016 at 1022, CA. In *Re Weir's Settlement* [1971] Ch 145 at 164, [1970] 1 All ER 297 at 300, CA, Russell LJ referred to *Gartside v IRC*, supra, HL as 'a case of a non-exhaustive discretionary power or trust'.

[89] [1968] AC 553, [1968] 1 All ER 121, HL.

[90] [1969] 1 Ch 657, [1968] 2 All ER 1241; revsd [1971] Ch 145, [1970] 1 All ER 297, CA, without casting doubt on relevant dicta in court below.

[91] [1970] Ch 712, [1969] 3 All ER 919.

limited kind. What he has is a right to be considered as a potential beneficiary, a right to have his interest protected by a court of equity and a right to take and enjoy whatever part of the income the trustees choose to give him. He could accordingly go to the court if the trustees refused to exercise their discretion at all, or exercised it improperly.[92] He has also, it has been said,[93] a right to have the trust property properly managed and to have the trustee account for his management. It follows from what has been said that it is very difficult to explain where the equitable interest lies in the case of discretionary trusts. Perhaps the true view is that the beneficial interest is in suspense until the trustees exercise their discretion.[94]

The rights of a potential beneficiary under a discretionary trust are in fact similar to those of the object of a mere power given to trustees in their fiduciary capacity.[95] He has merely a hope not an entitlement that it will be exercised in his favour.[96] The main difference lies in the fact that the object of a mere power has no ground of complaint if, after due consideration, the trustees decide not to exercise the power at all. Further although 'the discretion of the trustees ought to be exercised promptly in every case where its exercise is obligatory',[97] with such necessary limitations on absolute obligations as the necessities of the case demand,[98] the consequences of non-exercise are quite different in the two situations. If a merely permissive power is not exercised by the trustees within a reasonable time, it ceases to be exercisable and the trusts in default operate. But in the case of a trust, where the trustees are under a duty to distribute, but neglect to do so within a reasonable time, the court has allowed trustees, willing and competent to do so, to repair their own inaction.[99] It should be added that an object of a discretionary trust may renounce his right to be considered as a potential beneficiary and, at any rate if he does so for valuable consideration, he thereupon ceases to be an object of the trust.[100]

If an object of a discretionary trust assigns his interest or becomes bankrupt, it is

---

[92] *Tempest v Lord Camoys* (1882) 21 Ch D 571, CA; *Martin v Martin* [1919] P 283, CA; *Gartside v IRC*, supra, HL. See p 496 et seq, infra. The preceding six lines of the text were quoted with implicit approval in *Quinn v Executive Director and Director (Westman Region) of Social Services* [1981] 5 WWR 565.

[93] Per Powell J in *Spellson v George* (1987) 11 NSWLR 300 at 316, cited with approval in *Schmidt v Rosewood Trust Ltd* [2003] UKPC 26, [2003] 3 All ER 76. See p 396, infra.

[94] See *Barclays Bank Ltd v Quistclose Investments Ltd* [1970] AC 567, [1968] 3 All ER 651, HL; *Re Northern Developments (Holdings) Ltd* (6 October 1978, unreported) but discussed in *Carreras Rothmans Ltd v Freeman Mathews Treasure Ltd* [1985] Ch 207, [1985] 1 All ER 155 esp per Peter Gibson J at 166. But see *Twinsectra Ltd v Yardley* [2002] 2 All ER 377, HL, per Lord Millett at 400, 401. Note, however, that Lord Millett did not refer to the discretionary trust.

[95] See *Vestey v IRC (No 2)* [1979] Ch 198, [1979] 2 All ER 225; affd [1980] AC 1148, [1979] 3 All ER 976, HL.

[96] *Re Smith* [1928] Ch 915.

[97] *Re Locker's Settlement Trusts* [1978] 1 All ER 216 at 219, per Goulding J.

[98] *Re Gourju's Will Trusts* [1943] Ch 24 at 34, per Simmonds J. But they cannot validly exercise their discretion in advance— *Re Vestey's Settlement* [1950] 2 All ER 891 at 895, CA, per Evershed MR (not reported on this point in [1951] Ch 209). See also *Re Allen-Meyrick's Will Trusts* [1966] 1 All ER 740, [1966] 1 WLR 499; *Re Gulbenkian's Settlement Trusts (No 2)* [1970] Ch 408, [1969] 2 All ER 1173.

[99] *Re Locker's Settlement Trusts*, supra; *Breadner v Granville-Grossman* [2000] 4 All ER 205. As to the position if they are not willing, see p 79 infra.

[100] *Re Gulbenkian's Settlement Trusts (No 2)* [1970] Ch 408, [1969] 2 All ER 1173.

clear that the assignee or trustee in bankruptcy cannot, any more than the discretionary beneficiary could have done, demand payment of any part of the fund.[101] If the trustees exercise their discretion in favour of a discretionary beneficiary by paying or delivering money or goods to him, or even, it seems, by appropriating money or goods to be paid or delivered to him, the title to the money or goods passes to the assignee or trustee in bankruptcy.[102] And, where the trustees have actually paid the discretionary beneficiary after notice of an assignment or bankruptcy, they have been held liable to the assignee or trustee in bankruptcy for all the money paid.[103] It seems, however, that the trustees can validly expend the whole or any part of the fund for his maintenance, for instance, in paying a hotel keeper to give him a dinner, or in paying the rent of the house in which he is living,[104] and in respect of any such payment an assignee or trustee in bankruptcy will have no claim.[105]

The position is quite different where the trustees are bound to apply the whole fund for the benefit of a particular person, even though they may be given a discretion as to the method in which the fund is to be applied for his benefit. In this case the beneficiary, if sui iuris, is entitled to demand payment of the whole fund, which will pass to an assignee or trustee in bankruptcy.[106] Similarly where two or more persons together (constituting a closed class) are the sole objects of an exhaustive discretionary trust and between them entitled to have the whole fund applied to them or for their benefit, though no one by himself may be able to demand any payment, they can, if sui iuris, all join together and require the trustees to pay over the fund to them.[107] Similarly they may agree and assign to a third party all the capital or income as the case may be of the trust fund, when the trustees will become obliged to pay it to the third party.[108] But where the class is not a closed class, even a sole member of the class for the time being cannot claim an immediate entitlement to the income so long as there exists a possibility that another member of the class could come into existence before a reasonable time for the distribution of the accrued income has elapsed.[109]

A quite separate problem is as to what should happen if trustees fail to execute a discretionary trust. Being a trust, the court will see to it that it does not fail, and before

---

[101] *Re Smith* [1928] Ch 915; *R v Barnet Magistrates' Court, ex p Cantor* [1998] 2 All ER 333, [1999] 1 WLR 335, QBD.

[102] *Re Coleman* (1888) 39 Ch D 443, CA.

[103] *Re Neil* (1890) 62 LT 649; *Re Bullock* (1891) 60 LJ Ch 341. According to *Re Ashby* [1892] 1 QB 872, however, the trustee in bankruptcy or assignee can only claim to the extent to which sums are paid in excess of the amount necessary for the mere support of the object of the trust.

[104] *Re Allen-Meyrick's Will Trusts* [1966] 1 All ER 740, [1966] 1 WLR 499.

[105] *Re Coleman*, supra; *Re Bullock*, supra.

[106] *Green v Spicer* (1830) 1 Russ & M 395; *Younghusband v Gisborne* (1844) 1 Coll 400; *Re Smith* [1928] Ch 915. See chapter 17, section 6, p 405, post.

[107] *Re Smith*, supra; *Re Nelson* [1928] Ch 920n, CA; *Sir Moses Montefiore Jewish Home v Howell & Co (No 7) Pty Ltd* [1984] 2 NSWLR 406.

[108] See *Re Weir's Settlement* [1969] 1 Ch 657, [1968] 2 All ER 1241, at first instance at 683, 1248; *Sainsbury v IRC* supra at 725, 927; *Thorn v IRC* [1976] 2 All ER 622, [1976] 1 WLR 915.

[109] *Re Trafford's Settlement* [1985] Ch 32, [1984] 1 All ER 1108.

McPhail v Doulton[110] it was thought that all that the court could do was to order equal division. This, it will be recalled, is the reason why before that decision it was thought that a discretionary trust would only be valid if you could get a complete list of potential beneficiaries. In that case, however, it was held that the court was not so restricted but may execute a trust power by appointing new trustees, or by authorizing or directing representative persons of the classes of beneficiaries to prepare a scheme of distribution, or even, should the proper basis for distribution appear, by itself directing the trustees so to distribute.[111]

(c) PROTECTIVE TRUSTS [112]

Protective trusts may be set out expressly,[113] or the instrument may incorporate the statutory provisions in s 33 of the Trustee Act 1925, which take effect subject to any modifications contained in the instrument creating the trust. Section 33(1) provides as follows:

Where any income, including an annuity or other periodical income payment, is directed to be held on protective trusts for the benefit of any person (in this section called 'the principal beneficiary') for the period of his life or for any less period, then, during that period (in this section called 'the trust period'), the said income shall, without prejudice to any prior interest, be held on the following trusts, namely:

(i)   Upon trust for the principal beneficiary during the trust period or until he, whether before or after the termination of any prior interest, does or attempts to do or suffers any act or thing, or until any event happens, other than an advance under any statutory or express power,[114] whereby if the said income were payable during the trust period to the principal beneficiary absolutely during that period, he would be deprived of the right to receive the same or any part thereof . . . [and thereafter] . . .

(ii)   . . . upon trust for the application thereof for the maintenance or support,[115] or otherwise for the benefit, of all or any one or more exclusively of the other or others of the following persons (that is to say)—

---

[110] [1971] AC 424, [1970] 2 All ER 228, HL.

[111] See per Lord Wilberforce in *McPhail v Doulton*, supra at 457, 247; applied *Mettoy Pension Trustees Ltd v Evans* [1991] 2 All ER 513, [1990] 1 WLR 1587. See (1967) 31 Conv 117 (A J Hawkins); (1971) 29 CLJ 68 (J Hopkins).

[112] Sometimes called 'spendthrift trusts'. See (1957) 21 Conv 110 (L A Sheridan).

[113] See eg *Re Munro's Settlement Trusts* [1963] 1 All ER 209, [1963] 1 WLR 145, where it is pointed out that a beneficiary under a discretionary trust is in a somewhat different, and perhaps stronger, position than a mere expectant heir.

[114] Even if this clause is omitted in an express protective trust, a consent to an advancement will not normally cause forfeiture of the determinable life interest—*Re Rees' Will Trusts* [1954] Ch 202, [1954] 1 All ER 7.

[115] The trustees may apply the income to the maintenance and support of the principal beneficiary without regard to any debt he may owe to the trust estate—*Re Eiser's Will Trusts* [1937] 1 All ER 244.

(a) the principal beneficiary and his or her wife or husband, if any, and his or her children or more remote issue,[116] if any; or

(b) if there is no wife or husband or issue of the principal beneficiary in existence, the principal beneficiary and the person who would, if he were actually dead, be entitled to the trust property or the income thereof or to the annuity fund, if any, or arrears of the annuity, as the case may be:

as the trustees in their absolute discretion, without being liable to account for the exercise of such discretion, think fit.

When the Civil Partnership Act 2004 is brought into force, subsection (1)(ii)(a),(b) will be amended by substituting 'spouse or civil partner' for 'wife or husband'.

Subsection (3) specifically provides that nothing in the section shall validate any trust which would otherwise be invalid,[117] such as a settlement by a man of his own property on himself until bankruptcy.[118]

It is not necessary in order to invoke the section to use the actual words mentioned therein, provided the reference is sufficiently clear. In *Re Platt*[119] a gift to be held 'for a protective life interest' was held to be effective, and in *Re Wittke*[120] a gift of income 'upon protective trusts for the benefit of my sister' was also held to be adequate, consequent upon the decision as a question of construction that the sister was intended to take a life interest.

It is, of course, a question of construction of the particular terms of the relevant clause in s 33 or the express limitation as the case may be, whether a particular event determines the interest of the principal beneficiary. Where the protective trusts under s 33 have applied, events which have been held to have this effect have included the Trading with the Enemy Act 1939 and Orders[121] made thereunder, whereby money payable to a person resident in enemy territory was directed to be paid to the Custodian of Enemy Property,[122] and an order made in the Probate Divorce and Admiralty Division of the High Court that the principal beneficiary should charge his interest with the payment of £50 per annum,[123] but not an order diverting a part of the income from a husband to a wife in priority to the protective trust.[124] Decisions on express provisions, differing to a greater or lesser extent from the provisions of s 33,

---

[116] Including, in relation to any disposition made after 31 December 1969, illegitimate children on issue: the Family Law Reform Act 1987, s 19, as amended by the Trusts of Land and Appointment of Trustees Act 1996.

[117] Trustee Act 1925, s 33(3).   [118] See p 75, supra.

[119] [1950] CLY 4386. Contrast *Re Trafford's Settlement* [1985] Ch 32, [1984] 1 All ER 1108.

[120] [1944] Ch 166, [1944] 1 All ER 383.

[121] Trading with the Enemy (Custodian) Order 1939 (SR & O 1939 No 1198). Later orders of this kind contained a proviso that vesting in the Custodian of Enemy Property should not take place if it would cause a forfeiture, eg The Trading with the Enemy (Custodian) (No 2) Order 1946 (SR & O 1946, No 2141).

[122] *Re Gourju's Will Trusts* [1943] Ch 24, [1942] 2 All ER 605; *Re Wittke* [1944] Ch 166, [1944] 1 All ER 383; contrast *Re Harris* [1945] Ch 316, [1945] 1 All ER 702; *Re Pozot's Settlement Trusts* [1952] Ch 427, [1952] 1 All ER 1107, CA, where the protective trusts were not in the statutory form.

[123] *Re Richardson's Will Trusts* [1958] Ch 504, [1958] 1 All ER 538; *Edmonds v Edmonds* [1965] 1 All ER 379n, [1965] 1 WLR 58.

[124] *General Accident Fire and Life Assurance Corpn Ltd v IRC* [1963] 3 All ER 259, [1963] 1 WLR 1207, CA.

suggest that the interest of the principal beneficiary under s 33 would be determined, inter alia, by the trustee impounding part of the income of the principal beneficiary in order to repair a breach of trust by the trustee in paying part of the trust fund to the principal beneficiary at his own instigation,[125] or an order of sequestration of the income;[126] but not by an order of the court under s 57 of the Trustee Act 1925 varying the effect of the trusts,[127] nor by a garnishee order,[128] nor by an authority to the trustees to pay dividends from trust shares to creditors, if no dividend is in fact declared.[129]

There is no reason why there should not be a series of two or more protective trusts in favour of the same beneficiary, for example, the first trust until he attains the age of 30, the second for the remainder of his life thereafter. This would give the principal beneficiary a second chance to enjoy the income as of right, and thus prevent a youthful indiscretion from making him dependent on the discretion of the trustees for the rest of his life.[130]

3 NATURE OF A TRUST[131]

It may seem strange, though it is perhaps not untypical of English law, that although the trust is so highly developed an institution, it is impossible to say with assurance what is the juristic nature of the interest of a cestui que trust.[132] If one considers the traditional classification of rights into rights in rem which are good against persons generally and rights in personam which are rights against a specified person or persons, the right of a cestui que trust seems to be rather less than one and rather more than the other. The traditional view which was insisted upon by Maitland[133] is that the interest of the cestui que trust is necessarily a right in personam. The main reason why Maitland thought the contrary view untenable was the undoubted rule[134] that an equitable interest will not avail against a subsequent bona fide purchaser for value of a legal estate without notice of the trust–'such a purchaser's plea of a purchase for

---

[125] *Re Balfour's Settlement* [1938] Ch 928, [1938] 3 All ER 259; Contrast *Re Brewer's Settlement* [1896] 2 Ch 503. As to impounding a beneficiary's income see chapter 24, section 3(c), p 537, infra.

[126] *Re Baring's Settlement Trusts* [1940] Ch 737, [1940] 3 All ER 20.

[127] *Re Mair* [1935] Ch 562, [1935] All ER Rep 736. Contrast *Re Salting* [1932] 2 Ch 57. As to the effect of s 57 of the Trustees Act 1925, see chapter 23, section 2(b), infra.

[128] *Re Greenwood* [1901] 1 Ch 887; *Permanent Trustee Co Ltd v University of Sydney* [1983] 1 NSWLR 578.

[129] *Re Longman* [1955] 1 All ER 455, [1955] 1 WLR 197.

[130] See (1958) 74 LQR 182 (R E Megarry), and *Re Richardson's Will Trusts* [1958] Ch 504, [1958] 1 All ER 538.

[131] See (1967) 45 CBR 219 (D W M Waters); *Burns Philp Trustee Co Ltd v Viney* [1981] 2 NSWLR 216; *Connel v Bond Corpn Pty* (1992) 8 WAR 352.

[132] As to the interest of persons entitled to the estate of a deceased person, see p 38, supra.

[133] *Equity*, 2nd (Brunyate) edn p 106 et seq; (1917) 17 Col LR 467 (H F Stone). See generally Winfield, *Province of the Law of Tort*, p 108 et seq; (1954) 32 CBR 520 (V Latham).

[134] Now considerably affected by the provisions as to registration under the Land Charges Act 1972, which do not, however, apply to the ordinary trust interest.

valuable consideration without notice is an absolute, unqualified, unanswerable defence, and an unanswerable plea to the jurisdiction of this court'.[135] This view is also consistent with the historical development of the trust under which the beneficiary could originally only sue the original feoffee to uses, then a rapidly increasing number of classes of persons until ultimately it became convenient and possible, instead of listing the persons against whom the right could be enforced, to say it was enforceable against everyone except the bona fide purchaser for value of a legal estate without notice.

This traditional view has met with some criticism. Scott[136] has argued that the right of the cestui que trust is a right in rem because it is available against persons generally, although there are some exceptions, in the same way as the owner of a cheque is regarded as having a right in rem to it, although he may be defeated by a holder in due course. Further it has been suggested that the traditional view is not adequate to explain the rules as to following the trust property.[137] In so far as a cestui que trust can do this he is, it is said, exercising a right in rem, a proprietary right which is clearly greater than a right in personam. Moreover the House of Lords, in *Baker v Archer-Shee*,[138] which depended upon the nature of a life interest in a settled fund, seems to have committed English law[139] to what is sometimes called the 'realist' view, which can hardly be reconciled with traditional theory. The majority of their Lordships[140] took the view that a beneficiary 'was sole beneficial owner of the interest and dividends of all the securities, stocks and shares forming part of the trust fund',[141] and in a subsequent case[142] the House unanimously agreed that this constituted the binding ratio decidendi of the former case. Thus Viscount Dunedin observed[143] that Viscount Sumner's opinion had been 'rejected by the majority on the view that there was in the beneficiary a specific equitable interest in each and every one of the stocks, shares, etc, which formed the trust fund', and Lord Tomlin said,[144] 'I do not think that it can be doubted that the majority of your Lordships' House in the former case founded themselves upon the view that according to English law . . . [the beneficiary] had a property interest in the income arising from the securities, stocks and shares constituting the American trust, and that but for the existence of that supposed property interest the decision would have been different.' Most recently Lord Browne-Wilkinson has said[145] in terms that the owner of an equitable estate has a right in rem not merely a right in personam. It may be added that the traditional view was

---

[135] *Pilcher v Rawlins* (1872) 7 Ch App 259 at 268, 269, per James LJ.

[136] (1917) 17 Col LR 269.   [137] See chapter 25, section 2, infra.

[138] [1927] AC 844, HL; (1928) 44 LQR 468 (H G Hanbury).

[139] Contrast the law of New York—*Archer Shee v Garland* [1931] AC 212, HL.

[140] Lords Atkinson, Carson and Wrenbury.

[141] Supra, at 870, per Lord Carson. Cf *O'Rourke v Darbishire* [1920] AC 581, [1920] All ER Rep 1, HL.

[142] *Archer-Shee v Garland* [1931] AC 212, HL; *IRC v Berrill* [1982] 1 All ER 867, [1981] 1 WLR 1449, and see *Pritchard v M H Builders (Wilmslow) Ltd* [1969] 2 All ER 670, [1969] 1 WLR 409; *Re Cuff Knox* [1963] IR 263; *Costa & Duppe Properties Ltd v Duppe* [1986] VR 90.

[143] *Archer-Shee v Garland*, supra, at 221.

[144] Ibid, at 222.   [145] In *Tinsley v Milligan* [1993] 3 All ER 65 at 86, HL.

repeated by the Divisional Court in *Schalit v Joseph Nadler Ltd*[146] but it can carry little weight as *Baker v Archer-Shee*[147] does not even appear to have been cited.[148]

In the light of the considerations discussed, some modern writers have attempted to find a compromise solution. Thus Hanbury[149] regarded equitable interests as hybrids, not quite rights in rem because of the doctrine of the bona fide purchaser, and not quite rights in personam because of the doctrine of following trust funds, while Marshall[150] said that a cestui que trust always has a personal right, and in some cases he has a real right also. There seems much to be said for treating the interest of a cestui que trust as sui generis, instead of trying to force it into a classification which is really inadequate. It may be added that the position is further complicated by the possibility of the registration of certain equitable interests under the Land Charges Act 1972. Whatever the nature of an equitable interest may be before registration, it would seem to become a right in rem by virtue thereof, since registration is deemed to constitute actual notice to all persons and for all purposes connected with the land affected.[151] An equitable interest under a trust, however, is not in general capable of registration but one exception is under a contract for the sale of land where, on the one hand, the vendor is regarded as a constructive trustee for the purchaser,[152] and, on the other hand, the equitable interest of the purchaser is registrable as a land charge class C(iv) under s 2(4) of the Land Charges Act 1972. In such case, after registration, the purchaser would clearly seem to be properly referred to as the equitable owner of the subject matter of the contract.

None of the above cases was referred to in *Webb v Webb*[153] where the question was one of the construction of Article 16(1) of the Brussels Convention,[154] which provides that the courts of the contracting state in which the property is situated have exclusive jurisdiction, regardless of domicile, in proceedings which have as their object rights in rem in immovable property. On a reference from the Court of Appeal the Court of Justice of the European Communities held that an action for a declaration that a person holds immovable property as trustee and for an order requiring that person to execute such documents as should be required to vest the legal ownership in the plaintiff does not constitute an action in rem for the purpose of Article 16(1) of the convention but an action in personam. The plaintiff is not claiming that he already

---

[146] [1933] 2 KB 79, [1933] All ER Rep 708, DC.   [147] Supra.

[148] But see (1954) 32 CBR 520 at 537 (V Latham) for a contrary view.

[149] *Modern Equity*, 8th edn, p 446. See also Holdsworth, *History of English Law*, vol IV, p 432 et seq and, in relation to constructive trusts, (1985) 17 OLR 72 (Debra Rankin).

[150] Nathan & Marshall, *A Casebook on Trusts*, 5th edn, p 9, and see 11th edn by D Hayton at p 24 et seq.

[151] Law of Property Act 1925, s 198, as amended by the Local Land Charges Act 1975, s 17(2) and Sch 1. See also the Land Registration Act 2002, s 116.

[152] See p 163, infra.

[153] [1994] QB 696, [1994] 3 All ER 911, ECJ, noted (1994) 110 LQR 526 (A Briggs); (1994) 8 Tru LI 99. (P Birks); [1996] Conv 125 (Catherine MacMillian); *Ashurst v Pollard* [2001] Ch 595, [2001] 2 All ER 75, CA. Contrast *Re Hayward (decd)* [1997] Ch 45, [1997] 1 All ER 32.

[154] The Convention on Jurisdiction and the Enforcement of Judgments in Civil and Commercial Matters 1968, set out in Sch 1 to the Civil Jurisdiction and Judgments Act 1982.

enjoys rights directly relating to the property which are enforceable against the whole world, but is seeking only to assert rights against the alleged trustee. In the opinion of the Advocate General the dividing line lies between actions whose principal subject matter is a dispute over ownership between persons who do not claim inter se any fiduciary relationship and actions concerning a breach of fiduciary duty which, if found to have been committed, will have effects in rem. In the latter case the personal nature of the relations is the overriding factor.

5

FORMAL REQUIREMENTS OF EXPRESS TRUSTS

Apart from statute, there are no requirements as to writing or other formalities in connection with the creation of trusts or dealings with equitable interests, whether inter vivos or testamentary, and whether relating to real or personal property. The statutory provisions, however, are of wide ambit and must now be considered. Resulting, implied and constructive trusts are not within the scope of this chapter, but for the avoidance of doubt it may be mentioned that the Law of Property Act 1925, s 53(2), expressly provides that s 53 does not affect the creation or operation of resulting, implied or constructive trusts, and the Law of Property (Miscellaneous Provisions) Act 1989, s 2(5) provides likewise in relation to s 2 of that Act.

1 INTER VIVOS TRANSACTIONS

(a) CONTRACTS TO CREATE A TRUST OR DISPOSE OF A SUBSISTING EQUITABLE INTEREST

(i) Land

Such contracts if relating to land or any interest therein come within the scope of s 2 of the Law of Property (Miscellaneous Provisions) Act 1989.[1] It provides as follows:

(1) A contract for the sale or other disposition[2] of an interest in land[3] can only be made in writing and only by incorporating all the terms which the parties have expressly agreed in one document or, where contracts are exchanged, in each.

(2) The terms may be incorporated in a document either by being set out in it or by reference to some other document.

---

[1] Replacing the Law of Property Act 1925, s 40(1). See [1989] Conv 431 (P H Pettit); [1989] LSG 86/39/15 (P Kenny and Ann Kenny); (1990) 106 LQR 396 (G Hill); (1990) 140 NLJ 105 (C J Davis, N P Gravells, A M Pritchard); [1990] Conv 441 (Jean Howell); [1990] LS 325 (L Bently and P Coughlan); (1993) 22 AALR 499 (M Haley).

[2] 'Disposition' has the same meaning as in the Law of Property Act 1925—see p 89 et seq, infra.

[3] By s 2(6), as amended by the Trusts of Land and Appointment of Trustees Act 1996, 'interest in land' is defined as meaning any estate, interest or charge in or over land.

(3) The document incorporating the terms or, where contracts are exchanged, one of the documents incorporating them (but not necessarily the same one) must be signed by or on behalf of each party to the contract.[4]

Signature is required by both parties and the effect of non-compliance is to make the contract a complete nullity.

(ii) Pure personalty

There are no requirements of writing in connection with contracts to create a trust or to dispose of equitable interests in pure personalty.

(iii) Equitable interests in pure personalty and, semble, land

By way of qualification to what has been said in (i) and (ii) above, it should be said that a contract to assign an equitable interest may come within the scope of s 53(1)(c) of the Law of Property Act 1925 as being a 'disposition' of a subsisting equitable interest. This is discussed later.[5]

(b) DECLARATIONS OF TRUST INTER VIVOS

The more obvious use of the phrase 'declaration of trust' is to describe the case where the owner of property declares that henceforth he will hold it on certain trusts. There are two cases. First, where the settlor was owner of the property both at law and in equity, when the result is that he remains the legal owner while the equitable title is vested in the beneficiaries under the trust. Secondly, where the settlor was merely the equitable owner before the declaration of trust, when the effect seems to depend upon whether the trust declared is a bare or simple trust, or whether it is a special trust under which the trustee has some active duties to perform. If the trust is or becomes a bare trust, imposing no active duties on the settlor-trustee, it seems that the settlor-trustee 'disappears from the picture'[6] and the legal owner becomes a trustee for the ultimate beneficiary. Thus in *Grainge v Wilberforce*,[7] Chitty J is reported as holding that the case before him 'fell within the principle that where A was trustee for B, who was trustee for C, A held in trust for C, and must convey as C directed'. If, however, the trust declared imposes any duties on the trustee it would, it is submitted, be

---

[4] For the effect of a court order for rectification of one or more of the relevant documents see s 2(4). Where one document incorporates another document it is the first document that must be signed; and it is no signature within the Act where the party whose signature is said to appear on a contract is only named as the addressee of a letter prepared by him: *Firstpost Homes Ltd v Johnson* [1995] 4 all ER 355, [1995] 1 WLR 1567, CA, noted [1996] CLJ 192 (A J Oakley). The Act applies equally to the variation of a contract within the Act: *McCausland v Duncan Lawrie Ltd* [1996] 4 All ER 995, [1997] 1 WLR 38, CA.

[5] Infra p 89 et seq.

[6] Per Upjohn J in *Grey v IRC* [1958] Ch 375 at 382, [1958] 1 All ER 246 at 251; revsd on appeal [1958] Ch 690, [1958] 2 All ER 428. The CA decision was affirmed by HL on different grounds [1960] AC 1, [1959] 3 All ER 603.

[7] (1889) 5 TLR 436; *Corin v Patton* (1990) 92 ALR 1. Cf *BS Lyle Ltd v Rosher* [1958] 3 All ER 597, [1959] 1 WLR 8, HL.

impossible for the settlor-trustee to drop out of the picture, and the effect would be to create a sub-trust[8] under which the settlor would henceforth hold the equitable property as a trustee for the beneficiaries who would have subsidiary equitable interests.

The perhaps less obvious use of the phrase 'declaration of trust' is to describe an alternative mode in which a trust may be created, namely, by a transfer of the property to trustees and a direction to the trustees to hold the property on specified trusts, the direction to the trustees by the equitable owner really constituting the declaration of trust.[9]

(i) Land

As regards land or any interest therein,[10] s 53(1)(b)[11] of the Law of Property Act 1925 provides:

A declaration of trust respecting any land or any interest therein must be manifested and proved by some writing signed by some person who is able to declare such trust or by his will.

Although the wording is somewhat different, the requirement of writing in s 53(1)(b) is generally thought to be the same as was required under s 40(1), now repealed, and reliance can accordingly be placed on decisions on the latter section. Thus the writing is only required as evidence of the declaration of trust,[12] and need not therefore be contemporaneous with it.[13] The writing need not be in any particular form,[14] but must contain all the material terms of the trust,[15] and joinder of documents is permitted.[16] Under s 53(1)(b) signature by an agent is not permitted; the signature must be by

---

[8] In *Re Lashmar* [1891] 1 Ch 258, CA, where it was held that the trustee disappeared from the picture, Lindley LJ expressly pointed out that *Onslow v Wallis* (1849) 1 Mac & G 506, was to be distinguished on the ground that there the trustee had duties to perform, and said that had there been any duties to perform in the case before them, the decision of the court would have been the other way. But see (1984) 47 MLR 385 (B Green).

[9] But see (1975) 7 OLR 483 (G Battersby).

[10] 'Land' is widely defined in the Law of Property Act 1925, s 205(1)(ix) as amended by the Trusts of Land and Appointment of Trustees Act 1996 as including inter alia, land of any tenure (this includes leaseholds: *Re Brooker* [1926] WN 93; *Re Berton* [1939] Ch 200, [1938] 4 All ER 285), mines and minerals, buildings or parts of buildings, and other corporeal hereditaments, and also incorporeal hereditaments.

[11] Replacing s 7 of the Statute of Frauds (1677). Care must be taken in applying decisions on the old Act where there have been changes in the wording—see *Grey v IRC* [1960] AC 1, [1959] 3 All ER 603, HL.

[12] *Forster v Hale* (1798) 3 Ves 696; affd (1800) 5 Ves 308; *Re Holland* [1902] 2 Ch 360, CA. If it has been destroyed secondary evidence may be admissible: *Barber v Rowe* [1948] 2 All ER 1050, CA.

[13] *Rochefoucauld v Boustead* [1897] 1 Ch 196, CA.

[14] See eg *Deg v Deg* (1727) 2 P Wms 412—recital in deed; *Forster v Hale* (1798) 3 Ves 696; affd (1800) 5 Ves 308—correspondence; *Cohen v Roche* [1927] 1 KB 169; *Hill v Hill* [1947] Ch 231, [1947] 1 All ER 54, CA.

[15] *Hawkins v Price* [1947] Ch 645, [1947] 1 All ER 689; *Tweddell v Henderson* [1975] 2 All ER 1096, [1975] 1 WLR 1496; *Ram Narayan v Rishad Hussain Shah* [1979] 1 WLR 1349, PC (writing insufficient where it omitted reference to chattels included in one indivisible contract for land and chattels) discussed [1980] Conv 92.

[16] *Timmins v Moreland Street Property Co Ltd* [1958] Ch 110, [1957] 3 All ER 265, CA; *Elias v George Sahely & Co (Barbados) Ltd* [1983] 1 AC 646, [1982] 3 All ER 801, PC, discussed (1983) 133 NLJ 841 (H W Wilkinson), and see (1958) 22 Conv 275 (G H L Fridman).

'some person who is able to declare such trust'.[17] In the first type of declaration of trust, where the owner of property declares himself to be a trustee thereof, he is clearly the person who must sign the writing. In the second type of declaration of trust, where there is separation of the legal and equitable interests and the declaration of trust takes the form of a direction to the trustees by the equitable owner, it has been settled that it is the equitable owner who must sign the writing if it is to be effective.[18]

Section 53(1)(b) does not contain any express sanction for failure to comply with its provisions. The assumption of most textbook writers[19] is probably right, that since s 53(1)(b) merely requires writing as evidence, absence of writing does not make the declaration of trust void,[20] but merely unenforceable as was previously the case under s 40(1).[21]

(ii) Pure personalty

There is no requirement of writing and a trust may accordingly be declared by unsigned writing, by word of mouth, and even by conduct.[22]

(iii) Equitable interests in real or personal property

By way of qualification to what has been said above, writing may be required in some cases under s 53(1)(c)[23] as a declaration of trust may also be a disposition within that section. The distinction between the two types of declaration of trust must be borne in mind.

Where the declaration of trust consists of a direction to the trustees by the equitable owner, it is now settled beyond dispute that, at any rate where an equitable interest in pure personalty is concerned, such a declaration is a disposition within s 53(1)(c), though it does not, of course, fall within s 53(1)(b). The point arose in *Grey v IRC*[24] where on 1 February 1955 a settlor transferred 18,000 shares to trustees to be held by them as nominees for himself. On 18 February 1955 he orally directed the trustees to hold the shares on specified trusts and on 25 March 1955 the trustees executed a deed of declaration of trust reciting the directions given to them on 18 February and declaring that they had been holding the shares on the specified trusts since that date.

---

[17] See (1984) 54 CLJ 306 (T G Youdan). Contrast s 53(1)(c) discussed p 89 et seq, post, and s 2 of the Law of Property (Miscellaneous Provisions) Act 1989, discussed p 85, ante.

[18] *Tierney v Wood* (1854) 19 Beav 330; *Kronheim v Johnson* (1877) 7 Ch D 60; *Grey v IRC* [1958] Ch 690 at 709, [1958] 2 All ER 428 at 433, CA; affd [1960] AC 1, [1959] 3 All ER 603, HL.

[19] See eg Underhill and Hayton, *Law of Trusts and Trustees*, 16th edn, p 236; (1984) 43 CLJ 306 (T G Youdan).

[20] Contrast the effect of s 53(1)(c) replacing s 9 of the Statute of Frauds, p 89, infra.

[21] *Leroux v Brown* (1852) 12 CB 801; *Britain v Rossiter* (1879) 11 QBD 123, CA; *Maddison v Alderson* (1883) 8 App Cas 467, HL; *Rochefoucauld v Boustead* [1897] 1 Ch 196, CA.

[22] *Kilpin v Kilpin* (1834) 1 My & K 520; *M'Fadden v Jenkyns* (1842) 1 Ph 153; *Jones v Lock* (1865) 1 Ch App 25; *Grey v IRC*, supra, CA, per Evershed MR at 708, 432, per Morris LJ at 719, 440. Both judges refer to 'personal property', but it is thought that they cannot have meant to include leaseholds.

[23] The nature of the requirement of writing under s 53(1)(c) and the effect of failure to observe it are dealt with at p 89 et seq, infra.

[24] [1960] AC 1, [1959] 3 All ER 603, HL. Cf *Parker v Parker and Ledsham* [1988] WAR 32.

This deed was also executed by the settlor to testify the giving of the directions and their nature.[25] The object of dealing with the matter in this way was to avoid liability to stamp duty.[26] If the directions of 18 February were valid they would, being oral, attract no duty themselves, and the deed of 25 March would likewise attract no duty as it would not be a 'disposition'. The House of Lords, however, held that the oral direction given by the settlor on 18 February was a purported disposition of an equitable interest within s 53(1)(c) and was thereby rendered invalid as it was not in writing. Therefore the deed of 25 March was an effective disposition attracting ad valorem stamp duty.

Where the declaration of trust is in respect of an equitable interest in land, writing is already required by s 53(1)(b).[27] It may, however, be important to know whether s 53(1)(c) also applies, as the requirement of writing, and probably the effects of absence of writing, differ[28] under the two provisions. Though the point is not referred to, the reasoning in *Grey v IRC*[29] would seem to apply equally to interests in land and interests in pure personalty.

Where the equitable owner of pure personalty[30] declares a trust not by giving a direction to the trustees but by declaring himself a trustee thereof s 53(1)(c) applies where the trust declared is a bare or simple trust under which the trustee has no active duties to perform, when the settlor disappears from the picture and the equitable interest is in effect transferred to the ultimate beneficiary.[31] Otherwise, where the settlor-trustee has some active duties to perform, it is submitted that he does not disappear from the picture, but remains the owner of the original equitable interest, while under the sub-trust thus created a new subsidiary equitable interest becomes vested in the ultimate beneficiary. In this case there would seem to be no disposition of the original equitable interest and accordingly s 53(1)(c) would appear not to apply.

(c) DISPOSITIONS OF EQUITABLE INTERESTS INTER VIVOS

Section 53(1)(c) of the Law of Property Act 1925 provides:

A disposition of an equitable interest or trust subsisting at the time of the disposition, must be in writing signed by the person disposing of the same, or by his agent thereunto lawfully authorised in writing or by will.

---

[25] See *Grey v IRC* per Evershed MR in CA [1958] 2 All ER 428 at 432.

[26] In (1984) 47 MLR 385 (B Green) it is pointed out that an effective scheme might have been for (i) the settlor to declare himself a trustee on the specified trusts, (ii) the settlor to appoint the trustees as new trustee in his place, and to transfer the shares to them, and (iii) for the trustee to execute a deed of declaration of trust.

[27] *Tierney v Wood* (1854) 19 Beav 330.   [28] For the requirements and effect of s 53(1)(c) see below.

[29] Supra.   [30] The reasoning would seem equally to apply to land.

[31] See the discussion at p 86, supra. As was pointed out in *Crowden v Aldridge* [1993] 3 All ER 603, [1993] 1 WLR 433, Upjohn J at first instance and all three members of the Court of Appeal in *Grey v IRC*, supra, analysed the transaction in that case as one of declaration of trust rather than assignment, and the Court of Appeal held that it was nevertheless a disposition. The Court of Appeal decision was affirmed by the House of Lords without finding it necessary to determine the quality of the transaction. Contra (1984) 47 MLR 385 (B Green); Riddall, *Law of Trusts*, 6th edn, p 56.

Unlike s 53(1)(*b*), but like s 2 of the Law of Property (Miscellaneous Provisions) Act 1989, s 53(1)(*c*) requires that the disposition shall actually be in writing, and not merely evidenced in writing; signature must be by the person making the disposition, or, like s 2 but unlike s 53(1)(*b*), by his duly authorized agent. The requirement that the disposition must actually be in writing, if not complied with at the time, clearly cannot be rectified subsequently,[32] and accordingly it always seems to have been assumed that absence of writing makes the purported disposition void. This view seems to be implicit in two important decisions of the House of Lords, *Grey v IRC*[33] and *Oughtred v IRC*.[34] The disposition may be contained in more than one document, provided there is sufficient reference in the signed document to the other or others.[35]

The meaning of the phrase 'disposition of an equitable interest or trust' has given rise to difficulties. Some points have been clarified by the courts, while others remain more or less uncertain.

(i) Direct assignment

The phrase clearly includes a direct assignment or transfer by a beneficiary of his equitable interest to another. It will accordingly be void if not in writing.

(ii) Direction to trustee

As was explained in the previous sub-section, *Grey v IRC*[36] establishes that the term disposition includes the case where the equitable owner directs the trustee to hold the property in trust for a third party.[37]

(iii) Disposition to fiduciary

It was held in *Re Tyler's Fund Trusts*,[38] that there is no need, where the assignee is to take in a fiduciary capacity, for the writing to contain particulars of the trust. In that case a written direction by the equitable owner to the trustee telling him to hold the trust property on trusts previously communicated orally was held to be valid, the judge treating the equitable owner as having assigned his equitable interest to the trustee as a fiduciary. There is no necessary conflict between this decision and *Grey v IRC*,[39] but it is unfortunate that the earlier decision was not referred to.

(iv) Declaration of trust by equitable owner

As was explained above this would seem to constitute a disposition in the case where the equitable owner 'disappears from the picture'.[40]

---

[32] Except, of course, by a fresh independent disposition in writing.
[33] [1960] AC 1, [1959] 3 All ER 603. Cf (1959) 17 CLJ 99 (J C Hall).
[34] [1960] AC 206, [1959] 3 All ER 623, HL.
[35] *Re Danish Bacon Co Ltd Staff Pension Fund* [1971] 1 All ER 486, [1971] 1 WLR 248.
[36] Supra, HL.   [37] See pp 88–89 supra.   [38] [1967] 3 All ER 389, [1967] 1 WLR 1269.
[39] Supra, HL.   [40] See p 86, supra.

(v) Contract to assign an equitable interest

In *Oughtred v IRC*[41] there was a settlement under which shares were limited to O for life with remainder to her son P absolutely. By an oral agreement on 18 June 1956 made between O and P it was agreed that on 26 June 1956 they would effect an exchange: P would make over to his mother his reversionary interest in the settled shares, and she, in exchange, would make over to him absolutely a separate block of shares in the same company which were her absolute property. In an attempt to save liability to stamp duty, the agreement was carried into effect on 26 June by the execution of three documents (i) a transfer of her own shares by O to P; (ii) a deed of release whereby O and P gave a release to the trustees in respect of anything done by the trustees in the execution of the trusts of the settlement and (iii) a transfer (referred to as 'the disputed transfer') of the previously settled shares by the trustees to O. Stamp duty was claimed on the disputed transfer.

One contention by the Inland Revenue was that the oral agreement of 18 June could not, because of s 53(1)(*c*), effect a disposition of P's reversionary interest, which remained vested in him until the execution of the disputed transfer. The contrary argument was that the effect of the oral contract was to make P a constructive trustee of the reversionary interest in favour of O, under a well-settled principle discussed later,[42] so that the entire beneficial interest had already passed to her before the disputed transfer was executed, and, as we have seen, a constructive trust is exempted from the requirement of writing by s 53(2). The transfer on this basis, it was said, would only operate on the bare legal estate and would not attract stamp duty.

The basis of decision adopted by the majority was that, even if the oral agreement was effective to pass the equitable interest in the settled shares to the mother, the transfer, as the instrument by which the transaction was completed, was nonetheless a conveyance on sale within s 54 of the Stamp Act 1891, but different views were expressed as to whether s 53(2) applied. In *Neville v Wilson*[43] the Court of Appeal applied what they described as the 'unquestionably correct' view of Lord Radcliffe that a specifically enforceable agreement to assign an interest in property creates an equitable interest in the assignee under a constructive trust, and that s 53(2) operates to exclude the requirement of writing under s 53(1)(*c*) in such a case.

(vi) Disclaimer

This arose in *Re Paradise Motor Co Ltd*,[44] where 350 shares had been transferred into the name of J by way of gift. By the time of the action 300 shares had been re-transferred into the name of the donor, W, and the remaining shares were still in the

---

[41] Supra; *Bishop Square Ltd v IRC* (1997) 78 P & CR 169, CA. See (1984) 47 MLR 385 (B Green).

[42] See p 163, infra.

[43] [1997] Ch 144, [1996] 3 All ER 171, CA, noted [1996] Conv 368 (M P Thompson); [1996] CLJ 436 (R Nolan); (1997) 113 LQR 213 (P Milne); (1997) 6 Nott LJ 86 (G Watt).

[44] [1968] 2 All ER 625, [1968] 1 WLR 1125, CA; *Sembaliuk v Sembaliuk* (1985) 15 DLR (4th) 303; *Re Smith (decd)* [2001] 3 All ER 552. See Meagher, Gummow and Lehane, *Equity—Doctrine and Remedies*, 3rd edn, p 223; [1979] Conv 17 (G Battersby).

name of J. The evidence established an attempted disclaimer by J of the gift, and it was held that this was effective, though merely oral, notwithstanding s 53(1)(c). The short answer, it was said, 'is that a disclaimer operates by way of avoidance and not by way of disposition'. It is unfortunate that this was not further explained particularly since in s 205(1)(ii) 'disposition' is defined as including a conveyance, which is in turn defined as including a disclaimer. This definition, of course, applies only where the context does not otherwise require, which does not seem to be the case here.

(vii) Transfer by bare trustee of the legal estate

Section 53(1)(c) does not apply to the case where the equitable owner directs the trustee to transfer the legal estate to a third party and the transfer duly takes place. The point arose in *Vandervell v IRC*[45] where a bank holding shares as a bare trustee transferred them on the directions of the equitable owner to a charity. In dismissing the argument that no beneficial interest passed to the charity in the absence of a writing signed by the equitable owner, Lord Upjohn pointed out[46] that the object of the section is 'to prevent hidden oral transactions in equitable interests in fraud of those truly entitled, and making it difficult, if not impossible, for the trustees to ascertain who are in truth his (sic) beneficiaries'. However, he continued, when the beneficial owner 'owns the whole beneficial estate and is in a position to give directions to his bare trustee with regard to the legal as well as the equitable estate there can be no possible ground for invoking the section where the beneficial owner wants to deal with the legal estate as well as the equitable estate'. Accordingly if the bare trustee, on the directions of the beneficial owner who intends the beneficial interest to pass, transfers the legal estate to a third party, that third party will also acquire the beneficial interest without any need for any further document. Though a convenient decision, its reasoning is not altogether convincing.

(viii) Declaration of new trusts by trustee with assent of beneficiary

In *Re Vandervell's Trusts (No 2)*[47] a trustee company held an option to purchase shares in a company controlled by V on such trusts as might be declared by the trustee company or V and pending such declaration of trust on a resulting trust for V. It exercised the option by using moneys held on trust for V's children, and informed the Revenue authorities that the shares would henceforth be held by them on the trusts of

---

[45] [1967] 2 AC 291, [1967] 1 All ER 1, HL; (1966) 24 CLJ 19 (G Jones); (1967) 31 Conv 175 (S M Spencer); (1967) 30 MLR 461 (N Strauss); [1979] Conv 17 (G Battersby); (1984) 47 MLR 385 (B Green); [2002] 61 CLJ 169 (R C Nolan).

[46] At 311. There seems to be much to be said for Harman LJ's succinct statement in CA that 's 53(1)(c) in dealing with dispositions of an equitable interest, only applies where the disponer is not also the controller of the legal interest'; [1965] 2 All ER 37, 49.

[47] [1974] Ch 269, [1974] 1 All ER 47; revsd [1974] Ch 308, [1974] 3 All ER 205, CA. This difficult decision is discussed in (1974) 38 Conv 405 (P J Clarke); [1974] ASCL 528 (J Hackney); (1985) 38 MLR 557 (J W Harris); (1975) 7 OLR 483; [1979] Conv 17 (G Battersby) and (1984) 47 MLR 385 (B Green). For an interesting comparison of the judgment of Megarry J at first instance, and Denning MR in the Court of Appeal, see (1987) 37 UTLJ 358 (D R Klinck).

the children's settlement. Dividends on the shares received by the trustee company were paid to the children's settlement. At first instance Megarry J had held that there was nothing to negative the resulting trust for V, which applied to the shares themselves when the option had been exercised, and there seems much to be said for his view. The Court of Appeal, however, reversed his decision, though the ratio decidendi is not altogether clear. It is, perhaps, that the acts of the trustee company were sufficient evidence of a declaration of trust which, made with V's consent, without any need for writing, operated to create new equitable interests in the children which automatically put an end to V's equitable interest, and not by way of disposition of V's equitable interest. It would presumably have been different if V had declared the new trusts. It seems to have been regarded as significant that the trust for V was a resulting trust. The comment has been made[48] that 'a "hard-case" may have been avoided; but as to what law the decision may have had, only clarification in future decisions will reveal'.

(ix) Surrender up of equitable interest

There seems little doubt but that a surrender is a disposition,[49] though it has been diffidently suggested that it may not be because it involves the extinguishment of a subsisting equitable interest, and extinction is not disposition.[50]

(x) Nominations under staff pension fund

Megarry J thought[51] it very doubtful whether the section would apply to a nomination made under a staff pension fund, where a member had power to appoint a nominee to receive the moneys otherwise due to his personal representatives in the event of his death, and this view was accepted by counsel for the defendant in *Gold v Hill.*[52]

(xi) Variation of Trusts Act 1958

The relationship between this Act and s 53(1)(c) is dealt with in chapter 23, section 3(d), infra.

(xii) Statutory definition of 'disposition' and 'equitable interest'

The House of Lords, in *Rye v Rye*,[53] held that 'conveyance' in s 205(1)(ii) of the Law of Property Act 1925, the definition section, applies only to an instrument in writing as

---

[48] J W Harris, loc cit.

[49] See per Lord Hoffman in *Newlon Housing Trust v Alsulaimen* [1999] 1 AC 313, [1998] 4 All ER 1, HL (actual decision on meaning of 'disposition' in s 37(2) of the Matrimonial Causes Act 1973).

[50] (1960) BTR 20 (J G Monroe). The suggestion is not accepted by Meagher, Gummow and Lehane, op cit, p 214.

[51] In *Re Danish Bacon Co Ltd Staff Pension Fund Trusts* [1971] 1 All ER 486, [1971] 1 WLR 248. The decision in that case that it was not a testamentary paper within the Wills Act 1837 was applied by the Privy Council in *Baird v Baird* [1990] 2 AC 548, [1990] 2 All ER 300, PC, noted [1990] Conv 458 (G Kodilinye); (1990) 4 TL & P 103 (Meryl Thomas).

[52] [1999] 1 FLR 54 (no difference where nomination expressed in the form of a trust).

[53] [1962] AC 496, [1962] 1 All ER 146, HL.

distinct from an oral disposition. In the same sub-section 'disposition' is defined as including 'a conveyance and also a devise, bequest or an appointment of property contained in a will'. On the basis of the decision in *Rye v Rye*[54] 'disposition' would likewise appear to be restricted to an instrument in writing. If this were to be so, an oral disposition would not be a 'disposition' within the meaning of the Act and would not be caught by s 53(1)(*c*). This would be a strange result. The point has not yet come before the courts, who might get over the difficulty by making use of the phrase 'unless the context otherwise requires' which governs all the definitions in s 205.

Further, the definition of 'equitable interest' in s 205(1)(*x*)[55] is in terms of interests in or over land. It always seems to have been assumed, however, though the point has not been taken in the cases, that s 53(1)(*c*) applies equally to equitable interests in personalty, and it is now probably too late to argue to the contrary.[56]

(d) EQUITY WILL NOT PERMIT A STATUTE TO BE USED AS AN INSTRUMENT OF FRAUD

All the statutory provisions that have been discussed have their origin in the Statute of Frauds (1677) the purpose of which appears from its title, namely, to prevent the injustice that was thought likely to occur from perjury or fraud when oral evidence was admitted.[57] Although the Court of Chancery was bound by statute, it nevertheless regarded itself as having power to intervene where the strict application of the statute would actually promote the fraud it was intended to prevent. Until the Law of Property (Miscellaneous Provisions) Act 1989 the leading example of the maxim heading this section was the equitable doctrine of part performance.[58] Since that Act however this doctrine has had no part to play in contracts concerning land.

In the leading case of *Rochefoucauld v Boustead*[59] it was said:

> It is further established . . . that the Statute of Frauds does not prevent the proof of a fraud; and that it is fraud on the part of a person to whom land is conveyed as a trustee, and who knows it was so conveyed, to deny the trust and claim the land himself. Consequently, notwithstanding the statute, it is competent for a person claiming land conveyed to another to prove by parol evidence that it was so conveyed upon trust for the claimant, and that the grantee, knowing the facts, is denying the trust and relying upon the form of conveyance and the statute, in order to keep the land himself.

It is not necessary that the actual conveyance shall have been fraudulently obtained, nor is there any need for the conveyance to include any express stipulation that the grantee is in so many words to hold as trustee. 'The fraud which brings the principle

---

[54] Supra, HL.   [55] As amended by the Trusts of Land and Appointment of Trustees Act 1996.

[56] See (1984) 47 MLR 385 (B Green).

[57] See (1947) 63 LQR (E Robel); [1983] Am JLH 354 (P Hamburger); (1984) 43 CLJ 306 (T G Youdan).

[58] See *Steadman v Steadman* [1976] AC 536, [1974] 2 All ER 977, HL.

[59] [1897] 1 Ch 196 at 206, CA. Cf *Wratten v Hunter* [1978] 2 NSWLR 367.

into play arises as soon as the absolute character of the conveyance is set up for the purpose of defeating the beneficial interest.'[60]

It is clear that the Court of Appeal in *Rochefoucauld v Boustead*[61] were actually enforcing the express trust notwithstanding the absence of writing and the provisions of the statute. Lindley LJ giving the judgment of the court, said in terms:

The trust which the plaintiff has established is clearly an express trust ... which both plaintiff and defendant intended to create. This case is not one in which an equitable obligation arises although there may have been no intention to create a trust. The intention to create a trust existed from the first.

This is how the decision was understood and applied by Ungoed-Thomas J at first instance in *Hodgson v Marks*,[62] where the plaintiff had transferred a house to one Evans, it being orally agreed between her and Evans that the house was to remain hers though in Evans' name. At first instance no attempt was made to rely on s 53(2), which excludes from the operation of s 53(1) resulting, implied and constructive trusts. In the Court of Appeal,[63] the actual decision was on the basis of s 53(2), but the court seems to have taken the same view as Ungoed-Thomas J on the point being discussed for it was observed: 'Quite plainly Mr Evans could not have placed any reliance on s 53, for that would have been to use the section as an instrument of fraud.'[64]

Unfortunately the Court of Appeal in *Bannister v Bannister*,[65] though apparently intending to apply *Rochefoucauld v Boustead*,[66] treated it as a case of constructive trust, and for this reason excluded from s 53(1), and this view has been followed without discussion in subsequent decisions. For example, in *Re Densham*[67] Goff J said: 'To hold such an agreement unenforceable unless in writing ... is in my opinion contrary to

---

[60] *Bannister v Bannister* [1948] 2 All ER 133, CA, at 136.

[61] Supra, CA. See also *Davies v Otty (No 2)* (1865) 35 Beav 208, where Romilly MR said 'I am of opinion that it is not honest to keep the land. If so, this is a case in which, in my opinion, the Statute of Frauds does not apply.' However he then went on to say the plaintiff must succeed on the basis of resulting trust. The two grounds are inconsistent alternatives.

[62] [1971] Ch 892, [1970] 3 All ER 513.

[63] [1971] Ch 892, [1971] 2 All ER 684. The main point of the decision was whether the plaintiff had an overriding interest under s 70(1)(g) of the Land Registration Act 1925. See (1971) 35 Conv 255 (I Leeming); (1973) 36 MLR 25 (R H Maudsley). See the much criticized decision in *Peffer v Rigg* [1978] 3 All ER 745, [1977] 1 WLR 285 and comment in (1977) 93 LQR 341 (R J Smith); (1977) 36 CLJ 227 (D Hayton); (1977) 41 Conv 207 (F R Crane); [1985] CLJ 280 (M P Thompson). In Law Com No 254, para 3.44, it is said that it is generally assumed that the reasoning in that case cannot be supported.

[64] Ungoed-Thomas J thought the defendant, a purchaser for value without notice from Evans, would likewise be unable to rely on s 53(1), but this point was left open in the Court of Appeal.

[65] [1948] 2 All ER 133, CA. On the plaintiff's oral undertaking that the defendant would be allowed to live in a cottage rent free for as long as she desired, the defendant agreed to sell to him, at a price well below the contemporary value of the two cottages, that and an adjacent cottage. The conveyance executed in due course contained no reference to the plaintiff's undertaking. Subsequently the plaintiff claimed possession of the premises occupied by the defendant, and claimed that the alleged trust contained in the oral understanding was defeated by the absence of writing.

[66] Supra, CA.

[67] [1975] 3 All ER 726 at 732. See also *Neale v Willis* (1968) 19 P & CR 836; *Binions v Evans* [1972] Ch 359, [1972] 2 All ER 70, CA; *Allen v Snyder* [1977] 2 NSWLR 685.

equitable principles, because once the agreement is formed it would be unconscionable for a party to set up the statute and repudiate the agreement. Accordingly, in my judgment he or she becomes a constructive trustee of the property so far as necessary to give effect to the agreement. That, in my judgment, was established long ago in *Rochefoucauld v Boustead*[68] . . .' As previously indicated, the court in *Rochefoucauld v Boustead* did not impose a constructive trust, and it is respectfully suggested that it is at least a little curious to say, in effect, that the express trust being unenforceable because it is not in writing, the court will impose a constructive trust to carry out the terms of the express trust. It is submitted that it would be much better in these cases to reach the same result by a straightforward application of the principle in fact laid down in *Rochefoucauld v Boustead*, namely that in a case of fraud equity will allow an express trust to be established by parol evidence notwithstanding the statute. But it would be wrong to deny that the trend in recent cases[69] is in favour of constructive trust.

It has been pointed out that both *Rouchefoucauld v Boustead*[70] and *Bannister v Bannister*[71] were cases where A had, in effect, transferred land to B subject to an oral arrangement under which B was to hold it for the benefit of A. Different views have been put forward as to whether the principle of these cases would apply where B had agreed to hold for a third party, C. Feltham argues[72] that neither precedent nor policy support a further erosion of s 53, while Youdan[73] asserts the contrary view.

Finally it should be observed that it is doubtful whether the maxim would be applied to a modern statute. 'It is no "fraud" to rely on legal rights conferred by Act of Parliament.'[74]

2 THE CREATION OF TRUSTS AND THE DISPOSITION OF EQUITABLE INTERESTS BY WILL

The provisions of the Law of Property Act 1925 do not affect wills,[75] but the requirements of the Wills Act 1837, which apply to both legal estates and equitable interests in all forms of property, both land and pure personalty, are even more stringent. Section 9 of the Act as substituted by s 17 of the Administration of Justice Act 1982 provides as follows:

---

[68] Supra, CA. A similar view to that in the text is taken by Hayton and Marshall, *Cases and Commentary on the Law of Trusts*, 11th edn, p 75 et seq.

[69] Most recently *Ashburn Anstalt v Arnold* [1989] Ch 1, [1988] 2 All ER 147, CA.   [70] Supra, CA.

[71] Supra, CA.   [72] [1987] Conv 246.   [73] [1984] CLJ 306 and [1988] Conv 267.

[74] *Midland Bank Trust Co Ltd v Green* [1981] AC 513 at 530, [1981] 1 All ER 153, HL, per Lord Wilberforce at 530.

[75] Law of Property Act 1925, s 55(a).

No will shall be valid unless—

(a) it is in writing, and signed by the testator, or by some other person in his presence and by his direction; and

(b) it appears that the testator intended by his signature to give effect to the will; and

(c) the signature is made or acknowledged by the testator in the presence of two or more witnesses present at the same time; and

(d) each witness either—

    (i)   attests and signs the will; or

    (ii) acknowledges his signature,

in the presence of the testator (but not necessarily in the presence of any other witness),

but no form of attestation shall be necessary.

Failure to comply with the statutory requirements makes the purported will absolutely void.

It was at one time thought that the cases on fully-secret and half-secret trusts[76] represented an exception to the operation of s 9, being a further application of the maxim that equity will not permit a statute to be used as an instrument of fraud.[77] As will be explained later,[78] it can now be regarded as settled that there is no conflict between the rules relating to fully-secret and half-secret trusts and the provisions of the Wills Act 1837 and accordingly it would be inappropriate and indeed misleading to discuss the former in this section.

---

[76] Discussed in chapter 7, p 127, infra.

[77] This was undoubtedly the principle upon which the doctrine of secret trusts was originally based, but in course of time the basis of the doctrine has changed.

[78] See p 128, infra.

6

COMPLETELY AND INCOMPLETELY CONSTITUTED TRUSTS

1 THE PERFECT CREATION OF A TRUST

The classic statement of the law as to what is meant by the perfect creation, or complete constitution, of an inter vivos trust is to be found in the judgment of Turner LJ in the leading case of *Milroy v Lord*:[1]

... in order to render a voluntary settlement valid and effectual, the settlor must have done everything which, according to the nature of the property comprised in the settlement, was necessary to be done in order to transfer the property and render the settlement binding upon him. He may, of course, do this by actually transferring the property to the persons for whom he intends to provide, and the provision will then be effectual, and it will be equally effectual if he transfers the property to a trustee for the purposes of the settlement, or declares that he himself holds in trust for those purposes; ... but, in order to render the settlement binding, one or other of these modes must ... be resorted to, for there is no equity in this court to perfect an imperfect gift. The cases I think go further to this extent, that if the settlement is intended to be effectuated by one of the modes to which I have referred, the court will not give effect to it by applying another of those modes. If it is intended to take effect by transfer; the court will not hold the intended transfer to operate as a declaration of trust, for then every imperfect instrument would be made effectual by being converted into a perfect trust.

Each of the two alternative modes of constituting an inter vivos trust—the effective transfer of the trust property to trustees, or the declaration by the settlor that he is a trustee thereof—requires further consideration.[2]

It should be observed that a trust created by will cannot fail on the ground that it is incompletely constituted. On the death of the testator the trust property will vest in

---

[1] (1862) 4 De GF & J 264 at pp 274–275. Hayton and Marshall, *Cases and Commentary on the Law of Trusts*, 11th edn, p 239, point out that, though treated as a voluntary settlement, the deed was in fact expressed to be made in consideration of one dollar. In *Mountford v Scott* [1975] Ch 258, [1975] 1 All ER 198, CA, payment of £1 was treated as valuable consideration enabling a decree of specific performance to be granted. See [1982] Conv 352 (Sophie Smith); *Dean and Westham Holdings Pty Ltd v Lloyd* [1990] 3 WAR 235.

[2] See *Caroyo Property Ltd v Total Australia Ltd* [1987] 2 Qd R 11 where Connolly J cited the text above.

his personal representatives who[3] will be under a duty to vest it in the trustees appointed by the testator. As we shall see,[4] the trust will be enforceable even if, for example, all the trustees appointed predecease the testator, or all disclaim the trust. The personal representatives in whom the trust property must in every case vest initially would in such circumstances themselves hold as trustees until other trustees were appointed.

(a) THE EFFECTIVE TRANSFER OF THE TRUST PROPERTY TO TRUSTEES

(i) Settlor the owner of the property both at law and in equity

Here he must normally, if he intends to constitute the trust by transfer, vest the legal interest in the property in the trustee: exceptionally, if he cannot do this, the trust may nevertheless be effective if it can be established that the settlor has done everything in his power, according to the nature of the property given, to give the trustee a complete legal title. What is necessary to pass the legal title depends on the nature of the property: thus (a) in the case of land, whether freehold or leasehold, there must be a deed,[5] (b) in the case of personal chattels capable of passing by delivery, there must be either delivery or a deed of gift,[6] and (c) in the case of registered shares there must be an appropriate entry in the company's register made in pursuance of a proper instrument of transfer.[7]

In *Milroy v Lord*[8] the attempt to create a trust failed, the legal title not having been vested in the trustee due to the fact that the wrong form of transfer was used for the purpose of transferring the bank shares which were intended to constitute the trust property. This was distinguished in *Jaffa v Taylor Gallery Ltd*[9] where a physical transfer of the trust property to the trustees was held not to be required. The trust property, a

---

[3] Subject to their rights and duties for the purposes of administration of the estate, for instance to pay the deceased's debts.

[4] Page 347, infra.

[5] Law of Property Act 1925, s 52(1). When electronic conveyancing is introduced an appropriate document in electronic form will be regarded as a deed: Land Registration Act 2002, s 91(5).

[6] *Cochrane v Moore* (1890) 25 QBD 57, CA; *Re Cole* [1964] Ch 175, [1963] 3 All ER 433, CA; *Thomas v Times Book Co Ltd* [1966] 2 All ER 241, [1966] 1 WLR 911 (this concerned the original manuscript of *Under Milk Wood*); *Balding v Ashley* (1991) unreported, CA (registration of car in name of alleged donee ineffective, but handing over keys could constitute constructive delivery); and see [1953] CLJ 355 (J W A Thornely); (1964) 27 MLR 357 (A L Diamond). See *Richert v Stewards' Charitable Foundation* [2005] BCSC 211, [2005] WTLR 371.

[7] Including the statutory stock transfer form under the Stock Transfer Act 1963 as amended by the Stock Exchange (Completion of Bargains) Act 1976. Note, however, that neglect of inessential matters on a transfer is not necessarily fatal to a transfer's validity, but may be treated as a mere irregularity and disregarded—*Re Paradise Motor Co Ltd* [1968] 2 All ER 625, [1968] 1 WLR 1125, CA. As to electronic transfer under the CREST system, see (1996) 146 NLJ 964 (R Pinner).

[8] (1862) 4 De GF & J 264, See also *Re Wale* [1956] 3 All ER 280, [1956] 1 WLR 1346; *Spellman v Spellman* [1961] 2 All ER 498, [1961] 1 WLR 921, CA; (1992) 13 QL 86 (Suzanne Rigney).

[9] (1990) *Times*, 21 March.

painting, was in the hands of a third party as agent of the settlor. By a document the settlor purported to give the painting to his three children. As two of the children were minors the settlor 'placed their interests in the hands of trustees'. This last statement was not further explained, nor was it stated whether or not the document was under seal which, as the law then stood, was needed for a valid deed. Each trustee agreed to act and was given a copy of the document. It was held that the declaration of trust constituted a transfer of property in the painting to the trustees, the judge observing that he 'could not conceive that a physical transfer had to take place and indeed it would be absurd so to find when one trustee was in Northern Ireland, another in England and when the third owner was the adult third plaintiff'.

Milroy v Lord[10] is also a leading authority for the rule that if a prospective settlor attempts to set up a trust by transferring property to a trustee, and the attempted transfer is for any reason ineffective, it is impossible to construe it as a declaration of trust. Exactly the same principle applies where a prospective donor attempts to transfer property to a person beneficially, and the transfer is ineffective. In neither case is there an equity to complete the imperfect gift by construing it as a declaration of trust, whether the imperfect gift was direct or through the intervention of trustees. There is a vital distinction between an intention to transfer property and an intention to retain it albeit in an altered capacity as trustee. An intention to do the former, even though the execution is ineffective, cannot be construed as the latter quite different intention.[11] An illustration is to be found in *Richards v Delbridge*[12] where JD, who was possessed of certain leasehold business premises, indorsed and signed on the lease a memorandum in these terms: 'This deed and all thereto belonging I give to EBR from this time forth, with all the stock-in-trade', EBR was JD's infant grandson. JD shortly afterwards delivered the lease to EBR's mother on his behalf. Subsequently, after JD's death, it was claimed that there was a trust in favour of EBR. It was held, however that there was no effective transfer of the lease,[13] and, further, that the ineffective attempt to transfer could not be construed as a declaration of trust.

More recent cases have modified the strictness of the rule. Thus although the legal title may remain vested in the settlor, an attempted transfer by him to a trustee may nevertheless be effective in equity and may enable an enforceable trust to be established where the settlor has done everything in his power to divest himself of the property in favour of the trustee.[14] Where this is the position the property is regarded as effectively transferred in equity, the settlor retaining the bare legal title on trust for the transferee.[15] Thus in *Re Rose*[16] the deceased executed two transfers in proper form

---

[10] Supra.   [11] See Maitland, *Equity*, 2nd (Brunyate) edn, p 72.

[12] (1874) LR 18 Eq 11. See also the cases cited in note 8, supra.

[13] This would have required an assignment under seal; Real Property Act 1845, s 3; now replaced by Law of Property Act 1925, s 52(1).

[14] The same principle applies to the case of a gift to a donee beneficially.

[15] The transferee may himself be a trustee, or may take beneficially.

[16] [1952] Ch 499, [1951] 1 All ER 1217, CA. It is submitted that this decision is unlikely to be upset notwithstanding the criticisms in (1976) 40 Conv 139 (L McKay). See also [1998] CLJ (Sarah Lawrie and P Todd). It was applied in *Mascall v Mascall* (1984) 50 P & CR 119, CA (gift of land complete when father

dated March 1943, each in respect of 10,000 shares in an unlimited company, one transfer being in favour of his wife beneficially and the other in favour of his wife and X as trustees. At the date of their execution the transfers and the related share certificates were handed to the transferees. The legal title to the shares could, of course, only pass by an appropriate entry in the register of the company, whose articles of association authorized the directors to refuse to register any transfer. The transfers were in fact registered on 30 June 1943. The deceased died on 16 February 1947, and whether or not estate duty was payable on the shares transferred by the two transfers of 30 March 1943, depended upon whether the transfers were effective before 10 April 1943. Although the legal title clearly did not vest in the respective transferees until 30 June 1943, the principle set out above was laid down. It was accordingly held that, the deceased having 'done all in his power to divest himself of and to transfer to the transferees the whole of the right, title and interest, legal and equitable, in the shares in question',[17] the gift of the beneficial interest in the shares had been made and completed on 30 March 1943. Between that date and 30 June 1943, the deceased was a trustee of the bare legal title for the transferees.[18] Most recently, in *Pennington v Waine*,[19] it was held that the delivery of the share transfers required in *Re Rose*[20] may be dispensed with in circumstances in which it would be unconscionable to recall the gift. This further modification of the principle established by *Re Rose* arguably goes too far.[21]

(ii) Settlor possessing merely an equitable interest in the property

Here a trust[22] of that equitable interest can be completely constituted by an assignment[23] of that interest to trustees: there is no need for him to compel a transfer of the legal title, even if he can do so. As we have already seen, a disposition of an equitable

---

handed over transfer and land certificate to son, who was left to have transfer stamped and title in land register altered), discussed (1985) 82 LSG 1629 (H W Wilkinson), and see (1999) 50 NILQ 90 (A Dowling). See also *Re Fry* [1946] Ch 312, [1946] 2 All ER 106; *Re Rose* [1949] Ch 78, [1948] 2 All ER 971; *Vandervell v IRC* [1967] 2 AC 291 at 330, [1967] 1 All ER 1 at 18, HL, per Lord Wilberforce; *Corin v Patton* (1990) 92 ALR 1.

[17] *Re Rose* [1952] Ch 499 at 515, [1952] 1 All ER 1217 at 1225, per Jenkins LJ.

[18] The Court of Appeal actually considered the case of the transfer to the wife beneficially, saying that the same principle would apply in the case of the transfer to trustees, where there would be a sub-trust in favour of the ultimate beneficiaries. See *Macmillan Inc v Bishopsgate Investment Trust plc (No 3)* [1995] 3 All ER 747, noted [1995] LMCLQ 308 (Joanna Bird).

[19] [2002] EWCA Civ 227, [2002] 4 All ER 215, noted [2002] LMCLQ 296 (H Tjio and T M Yeo); (2003) 17 Tru LI 35 (D Ladds); [2003] PCB 393 (Judith Morris); [2003] CLJ 263 (Abigail Doggett); [2003] Conv 364 (J Garton). The statement in the text represents the opinion of Arden and Schiemann LJJ. Clarke LJ went even further. His view was that signing a share transfer form without delivery would constitute a valid equitable assignment where there was no intention of revoking it.

[20] Supra, CA.   [21] See (2002) 38 T & ELJ 4 (J N McGhee); [2003] Conv 192 (Margaret Halliwell).

[22] Strictly a sub-trust.

[23] In *Re McArdle* [1951] Ch 669, [1951] 1 All ER 905, CA. Jenkins LJ observed that 'A voluntary equitable assignment, to be valid, must be in all respects complete and perfect so that the assignee is entitled to demand payment from the trustee or holder of the fund, and that the trustee is bound to make payment to the assignee, with no further act on the part of the assignor remaining to be done to perfect the assignee's title.' Cf *Re Wale* [1956] 3 All ER 280, [1956] 1 WLR 1346; *Letts v IRC* [1956] 3 All ER 588, [1957] 1 WLR 201.

interest must be in writing.[24] Thus in *Kekewich v Manning*[25] trustees held certain shares on trust for A for life with remainder to B absolutely. B in effect executed a voluntary assignment of his equitable revisionary interest to C upon trust for D. It was held, even on the assumption that the assignment was purely voluntary, that a valid trust was effectively created of the equitable interest, though the legal title, of course, remained vested in the original trustees. Note, however, that if C were a bare trustee no new trust would seem to be created, for C would presumably drop out of the picture leaving D as a direct beneficiary under the head trust.[26] In such case B could deal with his equitable interest so as to achieve substantially the same result either by assigning his equitable interest directly to D beneficially, or by directing the original trustees henceforth to hold that interest for the benefit of D. Such methods are commonly included within the meaning of the phrase 'declaration of trust', in addition to the meaning of the phrase now to be discussed.

(b) A DECLARATION OF TRUST

Whether the settlor has a legal or merely an equitable interest in property, he can completely constitute a trust by declaring[27] that he holds it on trust for the intended beneficiary. 'Where a declaration of trust is relied on the Court', it has been said,[28] 'must be satisfied that a present irrevocable declaration of trust has been made.' A settlor, however, 'need not use the words, "I declare myself a trustee", but he must do something which is equivalent to it and use expressions which have that meaning'.[29] It is even possible for a declaration of trust to be implied from conduct.[30]

It may be added that although equity will not assist a volunteer and thus will not perfect an imperfect gift or an incompletely constituted trust, it will not strive officiously to defeat a gift. Accordingly the principle that, where a gift is incompletely constituted, the court will not hold it to operate as a declaration of trust, does not prevent the court from construing it to be a trust if that interpretation is permissible as a matter of construction, which may be a benevolent construction.[31]

The evidence was held to establish a trust in *Paul v Constance*,[32] where C, separated from his wife, the defendant, began living with the plaintiff as man and wife in 1967. C received £950 as damages for personal injuries in 1973, and he and the plaintiff

---

[24] Law of Property Act 1925, s 53(1)(c).

[25] (1851) 1 De GM & G 176, and see *Gilbert v Overton* (1864) 2 Hem & M 110; *Ellison v Ellison* (1802) 6 Ves 656; *Chief Comr of Stamp Duties v ISPT Pty Ltd* (1997) 45 NSWLR 639.

[26] See p 86, supra.   [27] The formal requirements were discussed in chapter 5.

[28] *Re Cozens* [1913] 2 Ch 478 at 486, per Neville J.

[29] *Richards v Delbridge* (1874) LR 18 Eq 11 at 14, per Jessel MR.

[30] See eg *Gray v Gray* (1852) 2 Sim NS 273; *Gee v Liddell* (1866) 35 Beav 621; and contrast *Re Cozens* [1913] 2 Ch 478. See also *Secretary, Department of Social Security v James* (1990) 95 ALR 615.

[31] *Pennington v Waine* [2002] EWCA Civ 227, [2002] 4 All ER 215 per Arden LJ at 61.

[32] [1977] 1 All ER 195, CA, applied *Rowe v Prance* [1999] 2 FLR 787, noted [1999] Fam Law 721 (M Pawlowski and K Everett); (1999) 10 T & ELJ (R Leonard); [2000] Conv 58 (S Baughan). Contrast *Arthur v Public Trustee* (1988) 90 FedLR 203 (Aust).

decided to use it to open a deposit account which, because they were not married, was put in the name of C alone. On many occasions, both before and after the deposit, C told the plaintiff that the money was as much hers as his. After C's death, it was held that in the context of their relationship these words could properly be construed as equivalent to a declaration of trust by C of the moneys in the account for C and the plaintiff in equal shares. There was, however, held to be no declaration of trust in *Jones v Lock*[33] where a father died shortly after putting a cheque for £900 (received by the father in payment of a mortgage) into the hand of his nine-month old baby saying 'I give this to baby; it is for himself', and then taking back the cheque and putting it away. And it seems that payments added to a cheque or credit card voucher in settlement of a restaurant bill by way of a tip are not held by the restaurateur on trust.[34] It should, however, be added that there is no need for the declaration of trust to be communicated to the cestui que trust.[35]

(c) THE INTERMEDIATE CASE

Until very recently it had been thought that *Milroy v Lord*[36] laid down the methods discussed above as two discrete alternative ways to create a trust. In the novel case of *T Choithram International SA v Pagarani*[37] the facts did not fall squarely within either of the two methods. The facts, slightly simplified, were that the settlor (now deceased) executed a trust deed, of which he was one of the trustees, establishing a charitable foundation, and immediately afterwards orally purported to give all his wealth to the foundation. His family had already been provided for. No transfers of his assets took place in his lifetime, though they were registered in the names of the surviving trustees of the foundation after his death. The Privy Council held that the gift 'to the foundation' could only mean 'I give to the trustees of the foundation trust deed to be held by them on the trusts of the foundation trust deed'. Although his words were apparently words of outright gift they were essentially words of gift on trust. In one composite transaction on the same day the settlor had declared that he was giving property to a trust which he himself had established and of which he had appointed himself one of the trustees. His conscience was affected and it would be unconscionable and contrary to the principles of equity to allow him to resile from his gift. In the absence of special factors where one of a larger body of trustees has the trust property vested in him he is bound by the trust and must give effect to it by transferring the trust property into the names of all the trustees. The trustees of the foundation accordingly held the assets on the trusts of the foundation trust deed.

---

[33] (1865) 1 Ch App 25. Nor could it have been a gift, as the title to the non-bearer cheque could only have passed by endorsement.

[34] *Nerva v R L & G Ltd* [1995] IRLR 200. Contrast *Shabinsky v Horwitz* (1973) 32 DLR (3d) 318.

[35] *Tate v Leithead* (1854) Kay 658; *Middleton v Pollock* (1876) 2 Ch D 104; *Standing v Bowring* (1885) 31 Ch D 282, CA.

[36] (1862) 4 De G F & J 264.

[37] [2001] 2 All ER 492, [2001] 1 WLR 1, PC, noted [2001] CLJ 483 (J Hopkins); [2001] Conv 515 (C Rickett).

2 THE POSITION OF A VOLUNTEER

(a) MEANING OF THE TERM VOLUNTEER

A beneficiary under a trust is a volunteer unless either he has provided valuable consideration in a common law sense, or he is, as it is said, within the scope of the marriage consideration. So far as value in the common law sense is concerned, reference may be made to the discussion of consideration in works on the law of contract,[38] but some explanation must be given of what is meant by marriage consideration.

Marriage has been said to be 'the most valuable consideration imaginable'[39] and a settlement or trust made or agreed to be made before[40] and in consideration of marriage is accordingly regarded as made for value. The question is who can take advantage of this, or, in other words, who is within the scope of the marriage consideration.[41] It is now clear that only the husband, wife and issue[42] of the marriage are within the scope of the marriage consideration.[43] Some other cases[44] which held, or suggested, that other persons such as illegitimate children or children by a former or possible second marriage were within the marriage consideration, can now, it seems only be supported on the ground that the interest of such persons, on the special facts of the cases, were so intermingled with the interests of issue of the marriage, that they could not be separated, and the latter could only be enforced if the former were also admitted.

---

[38] See eg Cheshire, Fifoot and Furmston, *The Law of Contract*, 14th edn, p 79 et seq. Note that a beneficiary under a pension scheme is not a volunteer—see p 18, supra.

[39] *A-G v Jacobs-Smith* [1895] 2 QB 341 at 354, CA, per Kay LJ. Note, however the provisions of s 4(6) of the Land Charges Act 1972, which put a purchaser for money or money's worth in a better position than one who can only rely on the consideration of marriage. See also *A-G for Ontario v Perry* [1934] AC 477, [1934] All ER Rep 422, PC.

[40] A post-nuptial settlement executed in pursuance of an ante-nuptial agreement would be regarded as made for value (*Re Holland* [1902] 2 Ch 360, CA); but neither a post-nuptial settlement made otherwise than in pursuance of an ante-nuptial agreement nor a mere post-nuptial agreement.

[41] It is not clear whether the formation of a civil partnership would be treated as equivalent to marriage in this context when the Civil Partnership Act 2004 is brought into force. The Law of Property Act 1925, s 205(1)(xxi), provides that ' "valuable consideration" includes marriage' and the 2004 Act, s 261(1), Sch 27 para 7, when brought into force will add the words 'and formation of a civil partnership', but this definition is only for the purposes of the Act.

[42] Whether children or more remote issue—*Macdonald v Scott* [1893] AC 642 at 650, HL, per Lord Herschell.

[43] *De Mestre v West* [1891] AC 264, PC; *A-G v Jacobs-Smith* [1895] 2 QB 341, CA; *Re Cook's Settlement's Trusts* [1965] Ch 902, [1964] 3 All ER 898. It is submitted that the position is unaffected by the Family Law Reform Act 1969.

[44] *Newstead v Searles* (1737) 1 Atk 264; *Clarke v Wright* (1861) 6 H & N 849, Ex Ch.

(b) THE POSITION BEFORE THE CONTRACTS (RIGHTS OF THIRD PARTIES) ACT 1999

The main importance of knowing whether or not a trust had been completely constituted arose in connection with the enforcement of the trust by a beneficiary thereunder who was a volunteer. If a beneficiary had provided valuable consideration, then he could have the trust enforced even though it had not been completely constituted; that is to say, he could enforce a contract or covenant to create a trust; but if he was a volunteer, even though he might be specially an object of the intended trust,[45] he would only succeed if the trust had been completely constituted.[46]

(i) Beneficiary not a volunteer

Here the law is unaffected by the 1999 Act. The beneficiary can enforce not only a completely but also an incompletely constituted trust. He can, if need be, compel his trustee to bring an action at law for damages for breach of the contract or covenant to create a trust; to such an action the settlor, in appropriate circumstances, might plead the Limitation Act 1980. In most cases, however, the beneficiary would choose to assert his equitable rights based on the availability of the equitable remedy of specific performance, as a result of which the property contracted or covenanted to be settled would be regarded as subject to a trust. Thus in *Pullan v Koe*[47] there was a marriage settlement in 1859 which contained a covenant by the husband and wife with the trustees to settle the wife's after acquired property of the value of £100 or upwards. In 1879 the wife had received £285 which she had paid into her husband's banking account, on which she had power to draw. Shortly afterwards, part of this sum was invested in two bearer bonds which remained at the bank until the death of the husband in 1909 and at the time of the action were in the possession of the executors. The trustees of the marriage settlement, with the object of benefiting the widow and nine surviving children of the marriage, brought an action against the husband's executors. Any claim by the trustees at law for damages for breach of the covenant would long since have been barred by the Statute of Limitation since the cause of action had arisen when the covenant was broken in 1879; the court, however, held that the moment the wife received the £285 it was specifically bound by the covenant and was consequently subject to a trust enforceable[48] in favour of the wife and children being persons within the marriage consideration. It seems clear that the beneficiaries, not being volunteers, would have had their interests equally protected, even if the trustees had been unwilling to bring proceedings to enforce the covenant.

---

[45] *Re Cook's Settlement Trusts* [1965] Ch 902, [1964] 3 All ER 898.

[46] Note also that if an incompletely constituted trust is enforced by a beneficiary who has given valuable consideration it enures for the benefit of a volunteer—*Davenport v Bishopp* (1843) 2 Y & C Ch Cas 451; affd (1846) 1 Ph 698.

[47] [1913] 1 Ch 9; *Sonenco (No 77) Pty Ltd v Silvia* (1989) 89 ALR 437.

[48] The claim could, of course, have been defeated by a bona fide purchaser for value without notice who acquired the legal title, but neither the husband, nor his executors claiming through him, were in this position.

It should be noted, however, that even a beneficiary who has provided consideration will be unable to do more than compel his trustee to exercise his remedy at law, where the contract or covenant is one to which the remedy of specific performance is not appropriate so that there is never any property subject to a trust. This is commonly the position where there is a covenant merely to pay money, as in *Stone v Stone*,[49] in which case it was held that an action at law on the covenant to settle £1,000 being barred by the Statute of Limitation, the beneficiaries, though purchasers, were without remedy.

(ii) Beneficiary a volunteer – the equitable rules

If the trust is completely constituted the fact that a beneficiary is a volunteer is irrelevant: he is just as much entitled to enforce the trust as a cestui que trust who has provided consideration. If, however, the trust is not completely constituted, a volunteer beneficiary will gain no assistance from a court of equity. This can be illustrated by *Re Plumptre's Marriage Settlement*.[50] There, under a marriage settlement made in 1878, certain funds coming from the wife's father were settled upon the usual trusts of a wife's fund, with an ultimate remainder, in the events which happened, for the wife's statutory next-of-kin. The settlement contained an after-acquired property clause, which was held to cover a sum of stock given by the husband to the wife, which she subsequently sold and reinvested and which remained registered in her name on her death in 1909. The facts of this case, it will have been observed, are very similar to those in *Pullan v Koe*[51] and it was likewise held that any action at law would be barred by the Statute of Limitation. By contrast with *Pullan v Koe*, however, the beneficiaries under the settlement who were seeking to enforce the covenant, that is the next-of-kin, were not within the marriage consideration but were mere volunteers. It was accordingly held that they could not enforce the covenant against the husband, as administrator of his wife's estate.

As appears from the above cases, the fact that the obligation is contained in a deed makes no difference in equity which has no special regard to form.[52] It may well be asked, however, whether the trustees with whom the covenant is made can, or should, bring an action at law for damages since the common law regards consideration and the formality of a deed as alternative requirements. On this question it has been held that volunteers cannot compel trustees to take proceedings for damages, and further, that if the trustees ask the court for directions as to what they should do, they will be directed not to take any steps either to compel performance of the covenant or to recover damages through the failure to implement it. Thus in the leading case of *Re Pryce*,[53] there was a marriage settlement under which the wife covenanted to settle

---

[49] (1869) 5 Ch App 74. In *Pullan v Koe*, supra, a specific fund of money was impressed with a trust. Cf *Beswick v Beswick* [1968] AC 58, [1967] 2 All ER 1197, HL, discussed p 110, infra.

[50] [1910] 1 Ch 609; *Jefferys v Jefferys* (1841) Cr & Ph 138; *Re D'Angibau* (1879) 15 Ch D 228, CA.

[51] [1913] 1 Ch 9, discussed supra, p 105.

[52] See eg *Jefferys v Jefferys*, supra; *Kekewich v Manning* (1851) 1 De GM & G 176.

[53] [1917] 1 Ch 234; *Re Kay's Settlement* [1939] Ch 329, [1939] 1 All ER 245. See 'Incompletely Constituted Trusts' by R H Maudsley in *Perspectives of Law* (ed R Pound), p 240.

after-acquired property. The beneficial limitations of funds brought into the settlement by the wife (including any after-acquired property) were successive life interests to the wife and the husband, remainder to the children of the marriage (of whom there were never in fact any), and an ultimate remainder to the wife's next-of-kin, who were of course volunteers. The husband was dead and the wife did not wish the covenant to be enforced. The court held that the trustees *ought* not to take any steps to compel the transfer or payment to them of the after-acquired property. Notwithstanding powerful academic criticism,[54] *Re Pryce*[55] and *Re Kay's Settlement*[56] were followed in *Re Cook's Settlement Trusts*.[57]

(iii) Beneficiary a covenantee

Even where the cestui que trust is a volunteer, there is a clear decision at first instance,[58] that if the covenant is made with him, there is no answer to an action by him at common law on the covenant, and substantial damages for breach thereof will be awarded. But, as a volunteer, he will not be able to obtain the equitable remedy of specific performance.

(iv) Performance of unenforceable covenant

It is clear that if the settlor has in fact transferred property to trustees in compliance with an unenforceable covenant to settle the same in favour of volunteers, he thereby completely constitutes the trust, and cannot thereafter claim to recover the property, which must be held by the trustees on the declared trusts.[59]

(v) *Re Ralli's Will Trusts*[60]

In this case the testator, who died in 1892, left a half share of his residue to his widow for life with remainder to his daughter Helen absolutely. By her marriage settlement in 1924 Helen covenanted to assign her revisionary interest in the testator's estate to the trustees on trust after her death, in the events which happened, for persons who were mere volunteers. The widow died in 1961, Helen having predeceased her without having executed an assignment of revisionary interest to the trustees. The plaintiff became the sole surviving trustee of both the will of the testator and Helen's marriage settlement. Helen's personal representatives claimed that her share of residue should be paid over to them, and that they would not then be compelled to pay it over to the plaintiff as trustee of the marriage settlement, as equity would not assist the beneficiaries thereunder being mere volunteers. The court held for the plaintiff on two

---

[54] (1960) 76 LQR 100 (D W Elliott); (1962) 76 LQR 228 (J A Hornby). As to the position if trustees do not ask the court for directions, but choose to bring an action see D W Elliott, loc cit; [1988] Conv 19 (D Goddard); R H Maudsley, op cit, p 244; [1967] ASCL p 392 (J D Davies).

[55] Supra.   [56] Supra.   [57] [1965] Ch 902, [1964] 3 All ER 898. See p 116, infra.

[58] *Cannon v Hartley* [1949] Ch 213, [1949] 1 All ER 50.

[59] *Paul v Paul* (1882) 20 Ch D 742, CA; *Re Adlard* [1954] Ch 29, [1953] 2 All ER 1437; *Re Ralli's Will Trusts* [1964] Ch 288, [1963] 3 All ER 940.

[60] [1964] Ch 288, [1963] 3 All ER 940. An analogy may be drawn with the rule in *Strong v Bird* (1874) LR 18 Eq 315, discussed infra, p 118 et seq.

grounds. The first ground was that on the true construction of the settlement Helen had effectively declared herself a trustee of her equitable reversionary interest. Secondly Buckley J held that it was irrelevant that the plaintiff, the settlement trustee, had acquired the legal title as trustee of the will. The question was, who was entitled in equity? Helen, having covenanted to assign her share to the plaintiff would not be allowed to assert a claim in equity against him, and her personal representatives could be in no better position. The inability of the volunteers under the settlement to enforce their rights against Helen was irrelevant: it was sufficient for them to rely on their claim against the plaintiff as settlement trustee. The trust became completely constituted by the chance acquisition by the sole surviving trustee of the legal estate in a different capacity. If, as might easily have happened, the will trustee and the settlement trustee had been different persons, the result, disregarding the first ground, would have been quite different. Helen's personal representatives would then have been able to claim her share from the will trustee, and the volunteers under the marriage settlement would have been unable to compel the enforcement of the covenant. Buckley J's reasoning is not entirely convincing, and it is difficult to distinguish *Re Brooks' Settlement Trusts*[61] which, if it had been cited to the judge, might well have persuaded him to a different conclusion, in favour of the argument put forward by Helen's personal representatives.

(c) CONTRACTS (RIGHTS OF THIRD PARTIES) ACT 1999

The law as stated above has been considerably modified by the Contracts (Rights of Third Parties) Act 1999, though never to the disadvantage of beneficiaries. The Act, which does not apply to contracts entered into before 11 May 2000,[62] provides that a person who is not a party to a contract[63] may in his own right enforce a term of the contract where the term purports to confer a benefit on him.[64] This includes a beneficiary under a contract or covenant[65] to create a trust. The third party must be expressly identified in the contract by name, as a member of a class or as answering a particular description but need not be in existence when the contract is entered into.[66] It is provided, however, that these provisions do not apply if on a proper construction of the contract it appears that the parties did not intend the term to be enforceable by the third party.[67] There is available to the third party any remedy that would have been

---

[61] [1939] Ch 993, [1939] 3 All ER 920.

[62] Contracts (Rights of Third Parties) Act 1999, s 10(2). By s 10(3) a contract made on or after 11 November 1999 may expressly provide that the Act is to apply.

[63] As to the rights of a beneficiary who is a party to the deed, see *Cannon v Hartley* [1949] Ch 213, [1949] 1 All ER 50, and p 107, supra.

[64] Contracts (Rights of Third Parties) Act 1999, s 1(1)(b). On the Act generally see (2001) 60 CLJ 353 (N Andrews); (2004) 120 LQR 292 (R Stevens).

[65] It is clear from the Contracts (Rights of Third Parties) Act 1999, s 7(3) that s 1 of that Act applies both to a simple contract and a specialty.

[66] Ibid, s 1(3).

[67] Ibid, s 1(2). This would seem to leave scope for the same arguments as those considered infra, pp 115–117, as to whether there was a trust of the benefit of the covenant.

available to him in an action for breach of contract if he had been a party to the contract: this enables him to sue for damages and obtain substantial damages, but it is thought that a third party volunteer will still be unable to obtain specific performance, for the Act does not appear to affect the rule that equity will not assist a volunteer.[68]

The Act would not appear to affect the result in cases such as *Re Plumptre's Marriage Settlement*[69] for the Limitation Act would defeat the claim at law as much at the instance of the next-of-kin as of the trustee.[70] Further, as noted above, the position in equity is unchanged by the Act. However in a case such as *Re Pryce,*[71] where there is no case for the application of the Limitation Act, the next-of-kin should be able to sue for damages unless the defendant could establish that the parties did not intend the term to be enforceable by a third party, though as volunteers they would still be unable to claim specific performance.[72]

Any right or remedy of the third party that exists or is available apart from the Act is unaffected by it,[73] and the right, if any, of the trustees to sue the settlor is likewise unaffected.[74] We will, therefore, go on to consider how equity sometimes enabled the volunteer to protect his interest, though the volunteer beneficiary is likely to prefer to proceed under the Act.

3 TRUSTS OF A CHOSE IN ACTION

(a) THIRD PARTY CONTRACT — ACTION FOR DAMAGES BY CONTRACTING PARTY

There is no difficulty over the concept of a chose in action constituting the trust property: to give a simple illustration, if A owes B £250, B may assign the debt to trustees on trust for X and Y equally so as to create an effective trust. Suppose, however, A enters into a contract with B under which A is to confer some benefit upon C. At common law the rule was that only a person who is a party to a contract can sue on it:[75] this meant that C would be unable to sue either directly or indirectly for the benefit which A had agreed with B to give him. As we have just seen, this rule has been reversed by the Contracts (Rights of Third Parties) Act 1999. This does not affect the rule that if A fails to confer the benefit on C, B, the promisee, can sue A, the promisor, although the nature of the remedy which the court will grant will depend on the

---

[68] See *Cannon v Hartley* [1949] Ch 213, [1949] 1 All ER 50. Of course a mere promise without consideration and not by deed remains unenforceable.

[69] Supra.   [70] Ibid, s 3(2)(*b*).

[71] Supra. If the trustees were asked to sue by the beneficiaries, it is thought that they would be wise to seek the directions of the court rather than rely on *Re Pryce*.

[72] Lewin, *The Law of Trusts* (17th edn), p 269 suggests that in the case of a marriage contract beneficiaries outside the marriage consideration could obtain specific performance.

[73] Ibid, s 7(1).   [74] [1939] Ch 993, [1939] 3 All ER 920.

[75] *Tweddle v Atkinson* (1861) 1 B & S 393. See *Darlington Borough Council v Wiltshier Northern Ltd* [1995] 3 All ER 895, CA and authorities therein cited.

circumstances of each case.[76] It is expressly provided that the 1999 Act does not affect any right of the promisee to enforce any term of the contract.[77]

B has always been able to bring an action for damages for breach of contract. The general principle is that a claimant may only recover damages for a loss which he has himself suffered.[78] One exception as we shall see,[79] is where he entered into the contract as trustee for C, when he can obtain substantial damages measured by the loss to C but which he must hold for C's benefit. The 1999 Act[80] provides that where B has recovered in respect of C's loss, in any proceedings brought by the third party under the Act the court must reduce any award to him to the extent appropriate to take into account of the sum recovered by B.

(b) EQUITABLE REMEDIES FOR CONTRACTING PARTY

As an alternative to damages, according to the circumstances, some equitable remedy may be available. Thus all the Law Lords agreed in *Beswick v Beswick*,[81] as indeed had the judges in the Court of Appeal, that in an appropriate case B could obtain a decree of specific performance against A, compelling him to confer the agreed benefit on C, even though the obligation of A may merely be to make a money payment. If damages would be nominal, this has been said to be an argument in favour of, rather than against, the availability of specific peformance.[82] In other circumstances some other remedy such as an injunction may be appropriate.[83]

It will be useful to consider the application of these principles to the facts of *Beswick v Beswick*.[84] In this case one Peter Beswick agreed with his nephew, the defendant, to assign to him the goodwill and assets of the business of a coal merchant carried on by him in consideration of the defendant employing him as consultant to the business for the remainder of his life at a weekly rate of £6 10s 0d; and for the like consideration the defendant agreed to pay, after Peter Beswick's death, an annuity of £5 per week to his widow. Peter Beswick died intestate, having been duly paid £6 10s 0d per week during his lifetime. Having made one payment of £5 to his widow, the defendant repudiated his liability. The widow took out letters of administration to Peter Beswick's estate and brought an action suing both personally and as administratrix. The claim in the personal capacity failed, but as administratrix it was held that, the legal remedy of damages being inadequate, she was entitled to a decree of specific performance.[85] Under the Contracts (Rights of Third Parties) Act 1999 she would on

---

[76] *Snelling v John G Snelling Ltd* [1973] QB 87, [1972] 1 All ER 79.   [77] Section 4.

[78] See eg *Panatown Ltd v Alfred McAlpine Construction Ltd* [2000] 4 All ER 97, HL, per Lord Clyde at 100, but see also per Lord Goff at 120.

[79] See p 112, infra.   [80] In s 5.

[81] [1968] AC 58, [1967] 2 All ER 1197, HL. See also *Gurtner v Circuit* [1968] 2 QB 587, [1968] 1 All ER 328, CA.

[82] But see p 664, infra.

[83] See *Snelling v John G Snelling Ltd*, supra, and (1973) 36 MLR 214 (Alan Wilkie).

[84] Supra, HL.

[85] Note that as administratrix the widow stood in the shoes of Peter Beswick and was not a volunteer; nor was she a trustee.

similar facts now be able to bring an action in her personal capacity for damages, but still not, it is thought, for specific performance.

It should be added that Lord Denning MR appears to have taken the view that in the sort of third party contract under discussion, if the contracting party B can obtain specific performance, the same remedy is directly available to the third party, C. In *Neale v Willis*[86] a husband borrowed £50 from his mother-in-law to assist in buying a house, on the express undertaking that the house would be in the joint names of his wife and himself. He broke the undertaking and had the house conveyed into his name alone. Lord Denning observed correctly that, following *Beswick v Beswick*,[87] the mother-in-law could have obtained specific performance. Counsel had, however, pointed out that this was an action by the wife—the third party—and that the mother-in-law was not even a party to the action. Lord Denning expressed himself unimpressed by this distinction and was prepared to enforce the agreement at the instance of the wife. It is respectfully submitted that *Beswick v Beswick*[88] cannot be called in aid in this way to support an action by a third party. Their Lordships in that case, as we have seen, drew a clear distinction between the widow qua third party suing personally and the widow qua administratrix suing in her representative capacity. It was only in the latter capacity that her claim succeeded. Lord Hodson[89] made explicit what is implicit in the speeches of the other Law Lords when he said: 'although the widow cannot claim specific performance in her personal capacity . . .' It is accordingly respectfully submitted that the opinion of Lord Denning in *Neale v Willis*[90] is wrong on this point, though it may well be that the case itself is rightly decided on the other ground[91] supported by the other members of the court.

(c) OTHER RELEVANT COMMON LAW PRINCIPLES

A further rule at common law is that B cannot require A to confer the benefit on him instead of C: A is fully entitled to insist on carrying out the contract according to its terms by conferring the benefit on C.[92] If he does so, B cannot sue C at common law in an action for money had and received.[93] It may be, however, that prima facie C could be called on to account to B in equity, on the basis that he holds on a resulting trust for B who has furnished the consideration.[94] The presumption of a resulting trust, if it

---

[86] (1968) 19 P & CR 836, CA.   [87] Supra, HL.   [88] Supra, HL.

[89] Supra, at 81, 1207. The distinction is also clearly drawn by Ormrod J in *Snelling v John G Snelling Ltd* [1973] QB 87, [1972] 1 All ER 79.

[90] Supra.

[91] The principle applied in *Bannister v Bannister* [1948] 2 All ER 133, CA, discussed supra, p 95.

[92] *Re Stapleton-Bretherton* [1941] Ch 482, [1941] 3 All ER 5; *Re Schebsman* [1944] Ch 83, [1943] 2 All ER 768, CA; *Re Miller's Agreement* [1947] Ch 615, [1947] 2 All ER 78.

[93] *Re Schebsman*, supra.

[94] *Re Policy No 6402 of the Scottish Equitable Life Assurance Society* [1902] 1 Ch 282; and see the cases cited in n 11, supra. See also (1944) 7 MLR 123 (Glanville Williams).

exists, will often in practice be rebutted by the presumption of advancement,[95] or proof of an intent that C should take the property for his own use and benefit. Apart from presumptions, whether the parties intended C to be a mere nominee, or to take for his own use and benefit, is a question of construction of the agreement read in the light of all the circumstances which were known to the parties.[96]

Previously A and B could freely come to a fresh agreement, releasing the old one, or varying it as they wished,[97] or B could simply release A from his obligation. The Contracts (Rights of Third Parties) Act 1999, however, now limits their powers where a third party has a right under the Act to enforce a term of the contract.[98] Section 2(1) provides[99] that in such a case A and B cannot, by agreement, rescind the contract, or vary it in such a way as to extinguish or alter C's entitlement under that right without his consent.[100] The section applies if either—

(a) C has communicated his assent[101] to the term to A,

(b) A is aware that C has relied on the term, or

(c) A can reasonably be expected to have foreseen that the third party would rely on the term and C has in fact relied on it.

(d) INTERVENTION BY EQUITY

In some circumstances the above rules may be qualified by the intervention of equity:[102] this will be so if it can be established that B has constituted himself a trustee for C of the benefit of the contract. If this can be shown, B, as trustee for C, can sue A and recover substantial damages, the measure of damages being the loss suffered by C.[103] If B refuses to sue, C, the beneficiary, can himself bring proceedings, but he must join B in the action as co-plaintiff, if he consents, or as defendant, if he refuses.[104] It is important to observe that if a trust is established, it is not open to A and B to release A

---

[95] See chapter 9, section 2(d), p 180, infra.

[96] *Beswick v Beswick* [1968] AC 58, [1967] 2 All ER 1197, HL.

[97] *Re Schebsman,* supra, CA; *Green v Russell* [1959] 2 QB 226, [1959] 2 All ER 525, CA.

[98] Ie under s 1.   [99] Subject to any express term of the contract: ibid, s 2(3).

[100] As to the power of the court to dispense with consent see ibid, s 2(4)–(6).

[101] The assent may be by words or conduct, but must have been received by A: ibid, s 2(2).

[102] In other cases by the intervention of the legislature, eg Road Traffic Act 1988, s 148(7). There are also some exceptions at common law—see *Alfred McAlpine Construction Ltd v Panatown Ltd* [2001] 1 AC 518; sub nom *Panatown Ltd v Alfred McAlpine Construction Ltd* [2000] 4 All ER 97, HL.

[103] *Lamb v Vice* (1840) 6 M & W 467; *Robertson v Wait* (1853) 8 Exch 299; *Lloyds v Harper* (1880) 16 Ch D 290, CA.

[104] *Gandy v Gandy* (1885) 30 Ch D 57, CA; *Vandepitte v Preferred Accident Insurance Corpn of New York* [1933] AC 70, PC; *Harmer v Armstrong* [1934] Ch 65, [1933] All ER Rep 778, CA. But the courts will be astute to disallow use of this 'procedural shortcut' in a commercial context where it has no proper place: see per Lightman J in *Don King Productions Inc v Warren* [1998] 2 All ER 608, 634; affd [2000] Ch 291, [1999] 2 All ER 218, CA. Cf *Bradstock Trustee Services Ltd v Nabarro Nathanson (a firm)* [1995] 4 All ER 888, [1995] 1 WLR 1405; *Baxter International Inc v Nederlands Produktielaboratorium voor Blaedtrans-fiesapparatour BV* [1998] RPC 250.

from his obligation to benefit C or in any way to vary it.[105] It may also be noted that it is not essential for C to be ascertained at the date of the contract.[106]

The problem is to know in what circumstances B will be regarded as a trustee: no satisfactory test can be suggested, and it has been said that 'the way in which the court will decide a novel case is almost completely unpredictable'.[107] What can be said with a fair degree of confidence is that the onus of establishing a trust is a heavy one—'the intention to constitute the trust must be affirmatively proved',[108] or, as was said in another case,[109] 'It is not legitimate to import into the contract the idea of a trust when the parties have given no indication that such was their intention.' Though this seems to represent the present state of the law in England, one sympathizes with the difficulty felt by Fullager J in *Wilson v Darling Island Stevedoring and Lighterage Co Ltd*[110] in understanding the reluctance of the courts to infer a trust in some of the cases, particularly perhaps in the insurance cases.

Fletcher v Fletcher[111] is an interesting and important case. Here the settlor, by a voluntary deed, covenanted with trustees that if A and B (his natural sons, at that time infants) or either of them should survive him and attain full age, his personal representatives should within twelve months of his death pay £60,000 to the trustees on trust for A and B or such one of them as should attain the age of 21. A and B both survived the settlor, but B died without attaining full age. The trustees refused to sue, but the court held that this fact did not prejudice the right of A to recover payment of the debt out of the assets of the convenantor. In the course of the judgment Wigram VC said[112] 'One question made in argument has been, whether there can be a trust of

---

[105] *Re Schebsman* [1944] Ch 83, [1943] 2 All ER 768, CA; but see *Hill v Gomme* (1839) 5 My & Cr 250, where the contrary is suggested, *Re Empress Engineering Co* (1880) 16 Ch D 125 at 129, CA; *Re Flavell* (1883) 25 Ch D 89 at 102, CA.

[106] *Swain v Law Society* [1980] 3 All ER 615 per Slade J at 624. The decision was reversed [1981] 3 All ER 797, [1981] 1 WLR 17, CA without casting any doubt on this dictum, and eventually restored by the House of Lords on different grounds [1983] 1 AC 598, [1982] 2 All ER 827.

[107] (1944) 7 MLR 123 (G L Williams) and see (1948) 21 ALJ 455 and 22 ALJ 67 (J G Starke). Barrington J said in an Irish case, *Cadbury Ireland Ltd v Kerry Co-operative Creamery Ltd* [1982] ILRM 77, that the courts were more ready to infer that the promisee in a contract is a trustee for the third party where the promisee has some contractual or fiduciary duty to the third party. The Australian courts have recently shown a greater willingness to infer a trust—see (1995) 14 U Tas LR 143 (D M Dwyer).

[108] *Vandepitte v Preferred Accident Insurance Corpn of New York* [1933] AC 70 at 79–80, PC; *Burton v FX Music Ltd* [1999] EMLR 826.

[109] *Re Schebsman supra*, CA at 89, per Lord Greene, MR. Moreover it has been said that 'the concept of constructive trusteeship of promises which confer a benefit on a cestui que trust is not capable in private law of extension to promises which impose a burden on a cestui que trust': *Swain v Law Society supra*, HL, at 612, 833, per Lord Diplock.

[110] (1956) 95 CLR 43, and see the valuable judgments in *Trident General Insurance Co Ltd v McNiece Bros Pty Ltd* (1988) 80 ALR 574.

[111] (1844) 4 Hare 67. *Re Cavendish Browne's Settlement Trusts* [1916] WN 341, may also be explained on the same basis. Contrast *Colyear v Lady Mulgrave* (1836) 2 Keen 81, where the covenantee was not intended to be a trustee. For a full discussion of the cases up to 1930 see (1930) 46 LQR 12 (Corbin).

[112] (1844) 4 Hare 67, 74.

a covenant the benefit of which shall belong to a third party; but I cannot think there is any difficulty in that . . .' There was held to be a completely constituted trust of the chose in action, the benefit of the covenant, which the beneficiary could enforce if the trustee failed or refused to act. In the light of the attitude shown by the courts in subsequent cases it has been doubted whether on similar facts a court today would find an intention to create a trust.[113]

Numerous cases have arisen in connection with policies of insurance. Two points emerge from the cases:[114] (i) the mere fact that A takes out a policy which is expressed to be for the benefit of B or on behalf of B does not constitute a trust for B; and (ii) the mere fact that the policy provides that the policy moneys are to be payable to B does not create a trust in favour of B. The more recent decisions in the higher courts suggest that the burden of establishing a trust is not easy to discharge.[115] In particular it has recently been said that trusts should not lightly be implied in commercial affairs.[116] However, if the policy moneys are actually paid over to the third party, the third party will, even in the absence of a trust, be entitled to retain them as against the assured's estate, provided that under the contract the policy moneys were to be paid out for his own use and benefit.[117]

The same problem has arisen in cases where a partnership deed, or a deed of dissolution of partnership, contains a covenant by the surviving partner. Again, the latest cases suggest that it is far from easy to establish a trust,[118] though in an earlier case[119] a covenant in a partnership deed was held, in the events which happened, to constitute the personal representative of the deceased partner a trustee, notwithstanding the fact that the existence of the trust would have disabled the partners from cancelling or varying the partnership deed in so far as doing so might affect the trust.

The above rules are unaffected by the Contracts (Rights of Third Parties) Act

---

[113] [1979] CLP 1 (C E F Rickett); Hanbury and Martin, *Modern Equity*, 16th edn, at pp 136, 137, point out two difficulties of this decision. First, that positive evidence of the intention to create a trust of the benefit of the covenant is lacking. Secondly, that a trust of such a chose in action should be created by the covenantee and not the covenantor, and on the facts the covenantee did not originally know of the arrangement, and as soon as he did, wished to decline the trust. J D Feltham, however, in (1982) 98 LQR 17, thinks that in the case of a voluntary covenant one should look to the intention of the settlor who, in the absence of evidence to the contrary, should be presumed to intend a trust for the volunteer beneficiary.

[114] *Re Webb* [1941] Ch 225, [1941] 1 All ER 321, where the earlier cases are reviewed; *Re Foster's Policy* [1966] 1 All ER 432; *Swain v Law Society*, supra, HL. Cf (1993) 22 AALR 221 (W Anderson).

[115] *Vandepitte v Preferred Accident Insurance Corpn of New York* [1933] AC 70, PC; *Re Schebsman* [1944] Ch 83, [1943] 2 All ER 768, CA; *Green v Russell* [1959] 2 QB 226, [1959] 2 All ER 525, CA. A trust was established in *Royal Exchange Assurance v Hope* [1928] Ch 179, CA: *Re Gordon* [1940] Ch 851; *Re Foster's Policy*, supra.

[116] See *E D & F Man (Sugar) Ltd v Evalend Shipping Co SA* [1989] 2 Lloyd's Rep 192 at 202.

[117] *Beswick v Beswick* [1968] AC 58, [1967] 2 All ER 1197, HL.

[118] *Re Miller's Agreement* [1947] Ch 615, [1947] 2 All ER 78.

[119] *Re Flavell* (1883) 25 Ch D 89, CA not cited in either of the cases in the two previous notes.

1999,[120] but may well cease to be called on in practice in view of the direct rights given to third parties by s 1.[121]

4 TRUSTS OF THE BENEFIT OF A CONTRACT AND VOLUNTEERS

Some of the cases just considered seem to offend against the maxim previously discussed[122] that equity will not assist a volunteer. Assuming that the intention to create a trust has been established, the difficulty is to establish that the trust has been completely constituted by the vesting of the trust property in the trustee, and, indeed, of what the trust property consists.

One answer to the difficulty is said to be that the maxim does not apply to a completely constituted trust, and that in such cases the trust property, that is, a chose in action, the benefit of the contract, is fully vested in the trustee. This view explains cases such as *Fletcher v Fletcher*,[123] but should it seems have produced a different result in *Re Pryce*[124] and *Re Kay's Settlement*[125] and at first sight seems inconsistent with the principle frequently laid down by Lord Eldon, which has been repeated in and formed the basis of subsequent decisions, that there is a vital distinction between the case where the trust has been completely constituted by the transfer of the property, and the case where the matter 'rests in covenant, and is purely voluntary',[126] when equity will refuse to give any assistance towards the constitution of the trust. As to *Re Pryce*[127] and *Re Kay's Settlement*,[128] the answer, it has been contended,[129] is that these cases were wrongly decided, while as to Lord Eldon's rule the point is said to be that the trust of the benefit of the contract or covenant is completely constituted. Lord Eldon's rule prevents the volunteer from claiming specific performance of a covenant to settle specific property, and disables him from claiming that such specified property is subject to the trusts of the settlement unless and until it is conveyed to the trustees, but, according to this argument, even a volunteer should be able to compel the trustees to sue for damages for breach of the covenant, for the right to sue, that is, the benefit of the contract, is held by the trustee on a completely constituted trust.

---

[120] Section 7(1).   [121] See p 108, supra.   [122] See p 104 et seq, supra.

[123] (1844) 4 Hare 67, discussed at 110, supra; *Williamson v Codrington* (1750) 1 Ves Sen 511; *Cox v Barnard* (1850) 8 Hare 310; *Gandy v Gandy* (1885) 30 Ch D 57, CA.

[124] [1917] 1 Ch 234, and see p 106, supra.

[125] [1939] Ch 329, [1939] 1 All ER 245, and see p 107, supra.

[126] *Ellison v Ellison* (1802) 6 Ves 656 at 662, per Lord Eldon. See also *Re D'Angibau* (1879) 15 Ch D 228, CA; *Re Plumptre's Marriage Settlement* [1910] 1 Ch 609; *Re Kay's Settlement* supra. See (1988) 8 LS 172 (M R T MacNair).

[127] [1917] 1 Ch 234.   [128] [1939] Ch 329, [1939] 1 All ER 245.

[129] See (1960) 76 LQR 100 (D W Elliott); (1961) 78 LQR 228 (J A Hornby); (1965) 23 CLJ 46 (Gareth Jones); (1966) 29 MLR 397 (Duncan Matheson); (1996) 70 ALJ 911 (D Wright).

These arguments were not accepted by Buckley J in *Re Cook's Settlement Trusts*,[130] who followed *Re Pryce* and *Re Kay's Settlement* without disapproval. The judge said that a covenant to settle future property was not a property right and accordingly was not capable of being made the subject of an immediate trust. The covenant before him was, he said, 'an executory contract to settle a particular fund or particular funds of money which at the date of the covenant did not exist and might never come into existence . . . The case . . . involves the law of contract, not the law of trusts.' It is not clear why the benefit of the covenant did not constitute a property right, though the actual decision may be right on the ground that there was no intention to create a trust of the promise. The benefit of a contract is equally a chose in action whether it relates to present or future property.

Though there has been some academic support[131] for *Re Pryce* and the cases that follow it, there has been further forceful criticism.[132] It is suggested notwithstanding the closely reasoned and persuasive arguments of the critics, that *Re Pryce*, *Re Kay's Settlement* and *Re Cook's Settlement Trust* are not likely to be overruled. There is after all somewhat of a paradox in the proposition that a contract to create a trust which equity would not permit trustees to enforce in the Court of Chancery should give rise to a remedy at common law. Even on the basis that there is a trust of the benefit of the contract or covenant, an argument could be put forward not only to deprive the volunteers of any right to compel the trustees to sue, but also to deprive the trustees of power to choose whether to sue or not, namely that the trusts attaching to the benefit of the contract or covenant are not necessarily the same as those which will attach to any property actually transferred thereunder. The reluctance of equity to assist volunteers might lead the court to hold that the volunteer has no equitable interest in the benefit of the contract, and on this basis if all the beneficiaries under the settlement are volunteers the whole equitable interest in the benefit of the con-tract would result to the settlor, on which basis the court would surely, and rightly, direct the trustees not to sue, even if an application of the *Saunders v Vautier*[133] principle does not enable the settlor himself to do so. But if, as in *Davenport v Bishopp*,[134] someone who has or is deemed to have furnished consideration enforces the covenant as he may, the trusts of the settlement, including the interests of volun-teers, will naturally attach to the property which actually comes into the hands of the trustees.

On this last view the main difficulty is to discover the intention of the settlor. If as in *Fletcher v Fletcher*,[135] the intention is to create an immediate trust of the benefit of the covenant at law in favour of volunteers, the trust is completely constituted as from

[130] [1965] Ch 902, [1964] 3 All ER 898; [1966] 30 Conv 286 (M C Cullity and H A J Ford); [1982] Conv 280 (M W Friend); (1986) 60 ALJ 387 (S Lindsay and P Ziegler).

[131] ASCL [1967] pp 387 et seq (J D Davies); (1969) 85 LQR 213 (W A Lee).

[132] (1975) 91 LQR 236 (J L Barton); (1976) 92 LQR 427 (R P Meagher and J R F Lehane); [1988] Conv 19 (D Goddard).

[133] See chapter 17, section 6, p 405.   [134] (1843) 2 Y & C Ch Cas 451.

[135] (1844) 4 Hare 67.

the moment the covenant is executed and the volunteer beneficiaries have immediate equitable rights which they can enforce by compelling the trustees to sue on the covenant. If, however, the intention is not to give volunteers any equitable rights in the benefit of the covenant, they have no rights which they can enforce either directly or indirectly, unless and until property is actually transferred to the trustees under the covenant. And in construing the settlement to ascertain the intention one would have to bear in mind that, as we have seen,[136] the intention to create a trust must be affirmatively proved.

The difficulties discussed above are now increasingly unlikely to arise for, as we have seen,[137] the Contracts (Rights of Third Parties) Act 1999 enables a third party to sue directly in relation to contracts entered into after 10 May 2000.[138]

5 TRUSTS OF FUTURE PROPERTY

Future property, for example the hope a person may have that he will take under the will or on the intestacy of a living person,[139] or under the exercise of a special power of appointment,[140] future royalties,[141] and the proceeds of any future sale of specific property,[142] cannot be owned for the simple reason that they do not exist, and for the same reason cannot be assigned either at law or in equity[143] or held on trust. So far as trust is concerned it makes no difference whether the alleged settlor has (a) purported to make a voluntary assignment to trustees on declared trusts, or (b) declared himself a trustee of the future property for specified beneficiaries.

Suppose, however, that the future property materializes, for example, the hope of the settlor that he will receive a legacy is fulfilled on the death of the testator. In principle in neither situation will the beneficiaries have an enforceable claim, for equity will not assist a volunteer. An illustration of situation (a) is *Re Ellenborough*[144] where by a voluntary settlement X purported to assign to trustees property to which she might

---

[136] See p 113, supra.

[137] See p 109, supra, and in particular n 67 on that page.

[138] See the Contracts (Rights of Third Parties) Act 1999, s 10(2), and note the qualified extension in s 10(3).

[139] *Re Lind* [1915] 2 Ch 345, CA; *Wu Koon Tai v Wu Yau Loi* [1997] AC 179, PC.

[140] *Re Brooks' Settlement Trusts* [1939] Ch 993, [1939] 3 All ER 920. Note that in this case he had a mere expectancy: if, however, a person is entitled to property in default of appointment he has a vested interest liable to be divested by the exercise of the power of appointment, and this interest can be owned, assigned and held on trust.

[141] *Re Trytel* [1952] 2 TLR 32. See *Performing Right Society Ltd v Rowland* [1997] 3 All ER 336.

[142] *Re Cook's Settlement Trusts* [1965] Ch 902, [1964] 3 All ER 898.

[143] *Meek v Kettlewell* (1842) 1 Hare 464; affd (1843) 1 Ph 342; *Re Ellenborough* [1903] 1 Ch 697.

[144] Supra. X had by the settlement likewise covenanted to assign property to which she might become entitled under her sister's will. This property had been transferred to the trustees and it was not suggested that it was not held by them on the trusts of the voluntary settlement. The transfer can be regarded as a confirmation of the declaration of trust: *Re Bowden* [1936] Ch 71; *Re Adlard* [1954] Ch 29, [1953] 2 All ER 1437. See *Re Plumptre's Marriage Settlement* [1910] 1 Ch 609 and p 106, supra.

become entitled under her brother's will. On the death of her brother she received property under his will but was unwilling to transfer it to the trustees. It was held that she was entitled to refuse to do so. If, however, the second ground of the decision in *Re Ralli's Will Trusts*[145] is valid, it would seem that if the brother's executors had happened to be the same persons as the trustees of the voluntary settlement X would not have been able to call for the transfer of the property but it would have been held upon the trusts of the settlement. In situation (b) the trust will be enforceable if the declaration is confirmed after the property has been received by the settlor.[146]

The position is quite different if the settlor has received valuable consideration for creating the trust. Just as an assignment of future property for valuable consideration is effective in equity which construes the assignment as a contract binding the conscience of the assignor and binding the subject matter of the contract when it comes into existence,[147] so in the case of a trust of future property created for valuable consideration, once it materializes into existing property it is treated in equity as being held on trust for the beneficiaries.[148] The settlor's conscience is bound so that he cannot keep it for himself.[149]

6 EXCEPTIONS TO THE MAXIM THAT EQUITY WILL NOT ASSIST A VOLUNTEER

(a) THE RULE IN *STRONG V BIRD* [150]

Where a donor has attempted to make an immediate gift inter vivos of either real[151] or personal[152] property to a donee, which gift has failed by reason of the fact that the legal formalities necessary for the proper transfer of title to the particular property in question have not been complied with, then if the donee has subsequently become the executor or administrator[153] of the donor, the gift is considered to have been perfected

---

[145] [1964] Ch 288, [1963] 3 All ER 940. See p 107 supra.   [146] *Re Northcliffe* [1925] Ch 651.

[147] *Tailby v Official Receiver* (1888) 13 App Cas 523, HL; *Re Ellenborough*, supra. A devisee of land comprised in an unadministered estate can enter into a binding contract to sell it in the same way as he can contract to assign a future chose in action: *Wu Koon Tai v Wu Yau Loi* [1997] AC 179, PC.

[148] *Holroyd v Marshall* (1862) 10 HL Cas 191; *Tailby v Official Receiver* supra, HL; *Re Lind* [1915] 2 Ch 345, CA. See *Pullan v Koe* [1913] 1 Ch 9, and p 105, supra.

[149] *Re Ellenborough*, supra.

[150] (1874) LR 18 Eq 315. Meagher, Gummow and Lehane, *Equity—Doctrine and Remedies*, 3rd edn, pp 735 et seq, point out that *Strong v Bird* did not in fact lay down the rule attributed to it, and that the rule is based on a misconstruction of the decision. See [1982] Conv 14 (G Kodilinye).

[151] *Re James* [1935] Ch 449, [1935] All ER Rep 235.

[152] The rule applies to the release of a debt, as in *Strong v Bird*, supra, itself.

[153] *Re James*, supra, followed in *Re Gonin* [1979] Ch 16, [1977] 2 All ER 720, where, however, Walton J expressed doubt as to whether it was right in principle. It seemed wrong to him that it should depend on the chance of who should manage to obtain a grant of letters of administration. The editorial note to this case in (1977) 93 LQR 485 is to the effect that these doubts are unjustifiable in the light of the reasons given in *Re Stewart* [1908] 2 Ch 251, which are set out below, but Ford & Lee, *Principles of the Law of Trusts*, 3rd edn,

by the vesting of the legal title in the donee. For the rule to apply it is necessary to show that the testator had up to the moment of his death a continuing intention that the gift should have been given at the time when it was given,[154] and, where the donor has appointed the donee his executor, that the testator had not any intention inconsistent with an intention to bring about the result flowing from the appointment.[155] The rule does not apply where there is a mere promise to make a gift in the future,[156] or where there is an intention to give, and the gift is not completed because the intending donor desires first to apply the subject matter of the contemplated gift to some other purpose.[157] The rule in *Strong v Bird* has been said[158] to rest on two grounds, first, that the vesting of the property in the personal representative at the donor's death completes the imperfect gift made in the lifetime, and, secondly, that the intention of the donor to give the benefit to the donee is sufficient to countervail the equity of the beneficiaries under the will.

(b) DONATIO MORTIS CAUSA[159]

'The principle of not assisting a volunteer to prefect an incomplete gift does not apply to a donatio mortis causa',[160] though it is not in every case that the assistance of equity is required. A donatio mortis causa has been described as:

a singular form of gift. It may be said to be of an amphibious nature, being a gift which is neither entirely inter vivos nor testamentary. It is an act inter vivos by which the donee is to have the absolute title to the subject of the gift not at once but if the donor dies. If the donor dies the title becomes absolute not under but as against his executor. In order to make the gift valid it must be made so as to take complete effect on the donor's death.[161]

para 3340 regard it as a 'questionable extension'. It makes no difference that the donee is merely one of several executors or administrators, for in the eye of the law the whole of the property vests in each personal representative: *Re Stewart* [1908] 2 Ch 251; *Re James* [1935] Ch 449, [1935] All ER Rep 235.

[154] *Re Pink* [1912] 2 Ch 528, CA; *Re Freeland* [1952] Ch 110, sub nom *Jackson v Rodger* [1952] 1 All ER 16, CA; *Re Gonin*, supra; *Benjamin v Leicher* (1998) 45 NSWLR 389.

[155] *Re Pink*, supra.

[156] *Re Innes* [1910] 1 Ch 188, though it was held to apply in *Re Goff* (1914) 111 LT 34, where there was an intention to give only if the donor predeceased the donee. See Waters, *The Law of Trusts in Canada*, 2nd edn, pp 168, 169; [1982] Conv 14 (G Kodilinye).

[157] *Re Freeland*, supra, CA.   [158] See eg *Re Stewart* [1908] 2 Ch 251 at 254–255, per Neville J.

[159] See, generally, Borkowski, *Deathbed Gifts*. The pages in a previous edition corresponding to pp 119 and 120 were cited by Glennie J in *Armstrong v Hachen Estate* (2000) 598 APR 110 at 151–154.

[160] Per Lindley LJ in *Re Dillon* (1890) 44 Ch D 76 at 83, CA, citing *Duffield v Elwes* (1827) 1 Bli NS 497.

[161] *Re Beaumont* [1902] 1 Ch 889 at 892, per Buckley J. A donatio, like a testamentary gift, is liable to inheritance tax. As to whether the subject-matter of a valid donatio is liable for the deceased's debts see [1978] Conv 130 (Shân Warnock-Smith). As to the degree of mental competence required see *Re Beaney* [1978] 2 All ER 595, [1978] 1 WLR 770, and p 42, supra.

The title of the donee can never be complete until the donor is dead,[162] and, accordingly, the donatio will fail if the donee predeceases the donor.[163]

If there has been a delivery of the subject matter of the donatio such as would suffice to constitute an effective inter vivos gift, death makes the conditional gift unconditional and the donatio becomes effective and complete without any further act being necessary. Where, however, delivery would be ineffective to transfer the title in the case of an inter vivos gift, as in the case of land or many choses in action, it may nevertheless suffice to constitute a valid donatio mortis causa.[164]

In such case the legal title will be held by the personal representatives on trust for the donee, and the donee will, if need be, be able to compel the personal representatives to lend their names to any necessary action, on receiving an appropriate indemnity.[165] It is where the transfer has been inchoate or incomplete that equity allows an exception to the rule that it will not complete an imperfect gift.

In order for a donatio mortis causa to be effective, there are three conditions which must be complied with,[166] namely—

(i) The gift must be made in contemplation, although not necessarily in expectation, of impending death.[167] This requirement will readily be treated as satisfied where it was made during the donor's last illness, but it is not necessary that the donor should be 'in extremis' when the gift is made.[168] The reported cases all contemplate death through illness, but on principle there seems no reason why the contemplation of death from some other source should not be equally effective.[169] But, of course, a merely general contemplation of death, on the ground that everyone must die at some time or other, is inadequate. Prior to the Suicide Act 1961, which provided that suicide should no longer be a crime, it had been held[170] that a purported donatio mortis causa in contemplation of suicide was not valid, as it would otherwise allow the donor to give effect to his gift by means of committing a crime. By virtue of the Act this reason is no longer applicable, though it is arguable that such a donatio mortis causa should not be recognized on grounds of public policy. It does not matter that death actually occurs from a disease[171] other than that contemplated.[172]

---

[162] *Duffield v Elwes*, supra; *Delgoffe v Fader* [1939] Ch 922, [1939] 3 All ER 682.

[163] *Tate v Hilbert* (1793) 2 Ves 111 at 120; *Walter v Hodge* (1818) 2 Swan 92 at 99.

[164] *Ward v Turner* (1752) 2 Ves Sen 431; *Re Wasserberg* [1915] 1 Ch 195, [1914–15] All ER Rep 217.

[165] *Duffield and Elwes*, supra; *Delgoffe v Fader*, supra; *Re Lillingston* [1952] 2 All ER 184.

[166] *Sen v Headley* [1991] 2 All ER 636, CA, per Nourse LJ at 639.

[167] It is thought that the test is subjective. Some support for this view can, perhaps, be drawn from *Re Miller* (1961) 105 Sol Jo 207, though the point was not taken and the donatio failed on other grounds. But see the Canadian case of *Thompson v Mechan* [1958] OR 357 where the alleged donatio failed because, inter alia, the donor could not properly be said to have contemplated dying from 'a cause that exists only in his fancy or imagination'—air travel.

[168] *Walter v Hodge* (1818) 2 Swans 92 per Plumer MR at 100; *Saulnier v Anderson* (1987) 43 DLR (4th) 19.

[169] See the discussion in *Agnew v Belfast Banking Co* [1896] 2 IR 204.

[170] *Re Dudman* [1925] Ch 553.

[171] Or, probably, from any other source, including suicide not contemplated at the date of the gift: *Mills v Shields* [1948] IR 367.

[172] *Wilkes v Allington* [1931] 2 Ch 104.

(ii) The gift must be made on the condition that it is to be absolute and perfected only on the donor's death, being revocable until that event occurs. It must be distinguished on the one hand from an intention to make an immediate or irrevocable gift,[173] and on the other hand from an attempted nuncupative will.[174] It may be revoked by the donor in his lifetime and will automatically be revoked by his recovery from a possibly terminal illness.[175] If it is revoked, the donee will thereafter hold any property that has been transferred as trustee for the donor.[176] The condition need not be express, and will readily be implied where the gift is made in expectation of death.[177] Probably, somewhat illogically, the better view is that the necessary condition may be implied notwithstanding the fact that the donor knows that there cannot be any recovery.[178] In his lifetime the donatio will be revoked by the donor recovering dominion over the subject-matter of the gift,[179] but not by the mere fact of the donor taking the property back for safe custody.[180] It is said to be impossible, however, to revoke a donatio mortis causa by will, for death makes the gift complete,[181] though a donatio may be satisfied by a legacy contained in a subsequent testamentary instrument.[182]

(iii) There must be a delivery of the subject matter of the gift, or the essential indicia of title thereto, which amounts to a parting with dominion. This means, primarily, physical delivery of the subject matter of the donatio with intent to part with the dominion and not merely, for instance, with intent to ensure its safe custody.[183] Failure to part with the dominion inevitably means failure of the donatio mortis causa, as, for instance, in *Bunn v Markham*,[184] where the property was, by the deceased's directions, sealed in three parcels and the names of the intended donees written thereon. The deceased declared that they were intended for the named donees and directed that they should be given to them after his death. The parcels were then replaced in the chest to which the deceased retained the key, and it was held that there was no sufficient delivery and accordingly no effective donatio mortis causa. Again there is no delivery if the donee refuses to accept it.[185]

Delivery, however, need not be by the donor personally into the hands of the donee. It may be made by a duly authorized agent of the donor,[186] though it must, of course,

---

[173] If the intention is to make an inter vivos gift, which is incomplete and accordingly fails, it cannot be treated as a donatio mortis causa even though this might validate it: *Edwards v Jones* (1836) 1 My & Cr 226.

[174] *Solicitor to the Treasury v Lewis* [1900] 2 Ch 812.

[175] Or the cessation of the possibility of death from the other contemplated source, as the case may be.

[176] *Staniland v Willott* (1852) 3 Mac & G 664; *Re Wasserberg* [1915] 1 Ch 195.

[177] *Gardner v Parker* (1818) 3 Madd 184; *Re Lillingston* [1952] 2 All ER 184.

[178] *Wilkes v Allington* [1931] 2 Ch 104 at 111, per Lord Tomlin; *Re Lillingston*, supra; *Re Mustapha* (1891) 8 TLR 160.

[179] *Bunn v Markham* (1816) 7 Taunt 224.   [180] *Re Hawkins* [1924] 2 Ch 47, [1924] All ER Rep 430.

[181] See eg White and Tudor's *Leading Cases in Equity*, 9th edn, vol 1, p 355.

[182] *Jones v Selby* (1710) Prec Ch 300, where satisfaction was said to be equivalent to a revocation: *Hudson v Spencer* [1910] 2 Ch 285.

[183] *Hawkins v Blewitt* (1798) 2 Esp 663.   [184] (1816) 7 Taunt 224.

[185] *Cant v Gregory* (1894) 10 TLR 584, CA.

[186] *Re Craven's Estate* [1937] Ch 423, [1937] 3 All ER 33.

be made before the donor dies;[187] or likewise to an agent for the donee,[188] but mere delivery to an agent of the donor is ineffective,[189] unless he can be regarded as a fiduciary agent holding on trust for the donee.[190] Again, an antecedent delivery of the chattel, that is, anterior to the date of the actual gift, is adequate, even though made alio intuitu,[191] for example, for safe custody only, and it seems that words of gift subsequently followed by delivery may suffice.[192] Further, a donatio mortis causa is not invalidated by the fact that it is expressed to be subject to an express charge or trust, even to an indefinite extent, for example, to pay funeral expenses.[193]

It is settled, however, that delivery of the key to the box or other receptacle or place in which the subject matter of the alleged donatio is contained may be a sufficient delivery of such subject matter if the requisite intent appears.[194] The better view, it is submitted, is that this is not to be regarded as a symbolic delivery, but as giving to the donee the means of getting at the subject matter, and correspondingly depriving the donor of his power of dealing with it;[195] and, further, that it applies not only to bulky articles, but also to things which are incapable of actual manual delivery.[196] Even where delivery of the key only transfers a partial dominion over the subject of the donation, as where the key to a safe deposit at Harrod's Ltd, was handed over, but under the terms of the contract of deposit the contents would only be handed over to anyone other than the actual depositor on production, in addition to the key, of a signed authority and the giving of a password, this may be sufficient delivery and equity will complete the imperfect gift.[197] Delivery of a key will be equally effective if it merely gives the donee the means of getting at another key which in turn gives access to the place in which the subject matter of the donatio is contained.[198] But if the

---

[187] *Hardy v Baker* (1738) West temp Hard 519; *Re Miller* (1961) 105 Sol Jo 207. Mellows: *The Law of Succession*, 5th edn, p 526, suggests that the Post Office could be treated as a fiduciary agent with a duty to deliver the insurance policy to the addressee so that there was sufficient delivery. See also Borkowski: *Deathbed Gifts*, p 66.

[188] *Moore v Darton* (1851) 4 De G & Sm 517. Perhaps a doubtful decision on the facts.

[189] *Powell v Hellicar* (1858) 26 Beav 261; *Farquharson v Cave* (1846) 2 Coll 356.

[190] *Mills v Shields* [1948] IR 367. There seems to be no English authority to support this qualification, but see n 185 supra.

[191] *Cain v Moon* [1896] 2 QB 283, DC; *Birch v Treasury Solicitor* [1951] Ch 298, [1950] 2 All ER 1198, CA.

[192] *Re Weston* [1902] 1 Ch 680.

[193] *Hills v Hills* (1841) 8 M & W 401; *Re Ward* [1946] 2 All ER 206; *Birch v Treasury Solicitor*, supra.

[194] *Jones v Selby* (1710) Prec Ch 300; *Re Mustapha* (1891) 8 TLR 160. In *Trimmer v Danby* (1856) 25 LJ Ch 424 the artist J M W Turner had delivered the key to a box containing certain bonds to his housekeeper of some 40 years. Despite evidence of an intention of gift, the alleged donatio failed on the ground that the delivery of the key was in her capacity as a housekeeper for the purpose of safekeeping. Cf (1956) 19 MLR 394 (A C H Barlow).

[195] *Birch v Treasury Solicitor*, supra; contra, *Jarman on Wills*, 8th edn, vol 1, p 47.

[196] It is submitted that decisions such as *Jones v Selby*, supra, and *Re Mustapha*, supra, are to be preferred on this point to dicta in other cases, eg *Re Wasserberg* [1915] 1 Ch 195, [1914–15] All ER Rep 217.

[197] *Re Lillingston* [1952] 2 All ER 184; *Re Wasserberg*, supra.

[198] *Re Lillingston*, supra 'it does not matter in how many boxes the subject of a gift may be contained or that each, except the last, contains a key which opens the next, so long as the scope of the gift is made clear', per Wynn-Parry LJ [1952] 2 All ER 184 at 191.

donor retains a duplicate key, it seems there is no effective delivery, for the donor is still able to deal with the subject matter and cannot be said to have parted with dominion.[199] For the same reason there can be no donatio mortis causa if the alleged donor parts with possession of a locked box or other receptacle, but retains possession of the key.[200]

There may be more difficulty where the subject matter of the alleged donatio mortis causa is not a chattel capable of actual delivery as explained in the preceding paragraphs, but is a chose in action. There will be no problem where there has been such delivery of a banknote,[201] or a negotiable instrument, other than one drawn by the donor,[202] in such a condition that mere delivery of the document will effect a transfer of the chose in action which it represents; nor in any other case where the formalities of transfer have been carried out so as to pass the legal title.[203] Where, however, the title to the chose in action does not pass by mere delivery of any document, and where there has been no formal transfer of the legal title, it is the law that for the purposes of a donatio mortis causa delivery of the appropriate document may be regarded as equivalent to a transfer and equity will complete the imperfect gift. The question what are the appropriate documents which must be delivered is to be answered by applying the test propounded by the Court of Appeal in *Birch v Treasury Solicitor*,[204] namely, 'that the real test is whether the instrument "amounts to a transfer"[205] as being the essential indicia or evidence of title, possession or production of which entitles the possessor to the money or property purported to be given'.[206] In that case it was held that the choses in action respectively represented by a Post Office Savings Bankbook, a London Trustee Savings Bankbook, a Barclays Bank deposit book and a Westminster Bank deposit account book were each the subject of a valid donatio mortis causa by delivery of the appropriate book. Other cases have held valid the donatio mortis causa of a bond,[207] bills of exchange, cheques and promissory notes payable to the donor, even though unendorsed and therefore not transferable by delivery,[208] a banker's deposit note,[209] national savings certificates,[210] an insurance

[199] *Re Craven's Estate* [1937] Ch 423 at 428, [1937] 3 All ER 33 at 38, per Farwell J. This was distinguished in relation to an alleged donatio mortis causa of a car in *Woodard v Woodard* [1995] 3 All ER 980, CA, noted (1991) 5 Tru LI 124 (Debra Morris) [1992] Conv 53 (Jill Martin) and [1994] 144 NLJ 48 (M Pawlowski). Here the donee already had possession of the car and one set of keys, but the vehicle registration document and a second set of keys (the existence of which was doubtful) were not handed over. Note that the question was said not to be so much one of dominion as one of intention.

[200] *Re Johnson* (1905) 92 LT 357; *Reddel v Dobree* (1839) 10 Sim 244.

[201] *Miller v Miller* (1735) 3 P Wms 356; *Re Hawkins* [1924] 2 Ch 47, [1924] All ER Rep 430.

[202] See p 125, infra.   [203] *Staniland v Willott* (1852) 3 Mac & G 664.

[204] [1951] Ch 298 at 311, [1950] 2 All ER 1198 at 1207, CA.

[205] Adopting the phrase uttered by Lord Hardwicke LC in *Ward v Turner* (1752) 2 Ves Sen 431 at 444.

[206] It is no longer regarded as necessary that the document handed over contain a record of all the essential terms of the contract. Cf *Re Weston* [1902] 1 Ch 680; *Delgoffe v Fader* [1939] Ch 922, [1939] 3 All ER 682.

[207] *Gardner v Parker*, supra; *Re Wasserberg* [1915] 1 Ch 195, [1914–15] All ER Rep 217.

[208] *Re Mead* (1880) 15 Ch D 651; *Clement v Cheesman* (1884) 27 Ch D 631.

[209] *Re Dillon* (1890) 44 Ch D 76, CA.   [210] *Darlow v Sparks* [1938] 2 All ER 235.

policy,[211] guaranteed investment certificates[212] and even a mortgage.[213] In the case of an intangible thing such as a chose in action parting with dominion over the essential indicia of title will usually suffice for the parting with dominion over the subject matter of the gift.[214] The unfortunate plaintiff failed, however, in the New Zealand case of *Wilson v Paniani*,[215] where there was no doubt but that the deceased donor intended to make a gift of the sum represented by the cheque which she had received from her pension fund and handed over to the plaintiff. The plaintiff paid the cheque into her bank account, but the pension fund, which had discovered that it was only about half the sum to which the donor was entitled, stopped it prior to issuing a new cheque for the larger sum. The donor, on being informed of this, reaffirmed her intention that the plaintiff should have the sum represented by the original cheque, and indicated that the balance should go to children and grandchildren. The donor died shortly afterwards, and two days later a cheque for the increased amount was paid into her estate account. The plaintiff failed because all that she had been given was the right to recover such funds as the cheque given to her would produce, which was nil; and there was no dealing with the second cheque or its proceeds to give rise to a donatio mortis causa in respect of it or any part of it.

Dicta of Lord Eldon in *Duffield v Elwes*[216] led to the common assumption that these cannot be a donatio mortis causa of land. In *Sen v Headley*[217] it was held that, admitting the doctrine of donatio mortis causa to be anomalous, there was no justification for an anomalous exception. A donatio mortis causa of land is neither more or less anomalous than any other and is capable of being made provided, of course, that the general requirements for such a gift are satisfied. The facts of that case were that the deceased had uttered words of gift, without reservation, when in hospital knowing he did not have long to live and when there could have been no practical possibility of his ever returning home. He had parted with dominion over the title deeds by delivering to the plaintiff the only key to the steel box in which they were kept. The plaintiff had her own set of keys to the house and was in effective control of it. This was held to constitute parting with dominion over the house.

(iv) It is commonly stated that some things cannot form the subject matter of a donatio mortis causa. These seem to fall into two categories:

First,[218] it was stated in *Moore v Moore*[219] that railway stock, and in *Re Weston*[220] that

---

[211] *Witt v Amis* (1861) 1 B & S 109; *Amis v Witt* (1863) 33 Beav 619.

[212] *Saulnier v Anderson* (1987) 43 DLR (4th) 19.

[213] *Duffield v Elwes* (1827) 1 Bli NS 497, followed without comment in *Wilkes v Allington* [1931] 2 Ch 104.

[214] *Sen v Headley* [1991] 2 All ER 636 at 645, CA per Nourse LJ giving the judgment of the court.

[215] [1996] 3 NZLR 378.   [216] Supra.

[217] Supra, CA, noted [1991] Conv 307 (Margaret Halliwell); [1991] CLJ 404 (J W A Thornely); (1993) 109 LQR 19 (P V Baker).

[218] See generally (1966) 30 Conv 189 (Alec Samuels). In Australia it has been held, in *Public Trustee v Bussell* (1993) 30 NSWLR 111, that a delivery of share certificates can be a valid donatio mortis causa: they constitute indicia of title and handing them over is a delivery of part of the means of getting at the property.

[219] (1874) LR 18 Eq 474.   [220] [1902] 1 Ch 680, but see (1947) 204 LTJo 142.

building society shares are not a proper subject of a donatio mortis causa. In *Re Weston* the court held that the building society shares were not distinguishable from the railway stock in *Moore v Moore*,[221] which in its turn merely followed *Ward v Turner*,[222] which was treated as deciding that the South Seas annuities, the subject of the case, could not be the subject of a donatio mortis causa. It is submitted that *Ward v Turner* should be regarded as deciding not that South Sea annuities could never be the subject of a donatio mortis causa, but that the delivery of the receipts in that case did not 'amount to a transfer'. It is noteworthy that Lord Hardwicke in his judgment said that, after acceptance of the stock, the receipts 'are nothing but waste paper, and are seldom taken care of afterwards'. If *Ward v Turner*[223] is properly to be explained on this ground, it would undermine the authority of *Moore v Moore*[224] and *Re Weston*[225] on this point. These latter cases, moreover, are not easy to reconcile with *Staniland v Willott*,[226] where it was held that a valid donatio mortis causa was constituted by a complete transfer of shares in a public company. On the view now being suggested this second category altogether disappears. Support for this view from a different angle may be found in the unwillingness of the court in *Sen v Headley*[227] to accept anomalous exceptions to the rule, as already noted in connection with a donatio mortis causa of land.

Secondly, it is clear that there cannot be a valid donatio mortis causa of the donor's own cheque or promissory note.[228] The point here is that a man's own cheque or promissory note is not property when given by the donor to the donee; a cheque is merely a revocable order to the banker to make the payment to the person in whose favour the cheque is drawn and the gift of a promissory note is merely a gratuitous promise. It may be otherwise if a cheque has actually been paid during the donor's lifetime,[229] or immediately after the death before the banker has been apprised of it,[230] or negotiated for value.[231]

(v) The onus is on the donee to prove the alleged donatio mortis causa, and where a claimant's case depends entirely on his own evidence the court must scrutinize it very carefully. However the uncorroborated evidence of the claimant may suffice if the court is satisfied as to its truthfulness.[232]

---

[221] (1874) LR 18 Eq 474.   [222] (1752) 2 Ves Sen 431.
[223] Supra. See per Lord Harwicke LC at 444.   [224] Supra.   [225] Supra.
[226] (1852) 3 Mac & G 664. See also *Re Craven's Estate* [1937] Ch 423, [1937] 3 All ER 33.
[227] [1991] Ch 425, [1991] 2 All ER 636, CA.
[228] *Re Beaumont* [1902] 1 Ch 889; *Re Leaper* [1916] 1 Ch 579; *Re Swinburne* [1926] Ch 38, [1925] All ER Rep 313, CA (actually a decision on an inter vivos gift); *Curnock v CIR* [2003] WTLR 955.
[229] *Bouts v Ellis* (1853) 17 Beav 121; affd (1853) 4 De G M & G 249. It is enough if it has been accepted by the banker during the donor's lifetime; *Re While* [1928] WN 182; *Re Beaumont* [1902] 1 Ch 889.
[230] *Tate v Hilbert* (1793) 2 Ves 111; *Lumsden v Miller* (1980) 110 DLR (3d) 226.
[231] *Tate v Hilbert*, supra; *Rolls v Pearce* (1877) 5 Ch D 730.
[232] *Re Dillon* (1890) 44 Ch D 76, CA; *Birch v Treasury Solicitor* [1951] Ch 298, [1950] 2 All ER 1198, CA.

(c) STATUTORY PROVISIONS

Occasionally statute will complete an imperfect gift. A legal estate in land is not capable of being held by a minor.[233] A purported conveyance of a legal estate in land to a minor or minors is accordingly not effective to pass the legal estate. However the Trusts of Land and Appointment of Trustees Act 1996 provides[234] that it is to operate as a declaration that the land is held in trust for the minor or minors.

(d) PROPRIETARY ESTOPPEL

The effect of this principle,[235] which is discussed later, may sometimes be to complete an imperfect gift.

---

[233] Law of Property Act 1925, s 1(6).

[234] Section 52, Sch 1, para 1. This paragraph also deals with a conveyance to a minor and a person of full age, and cases previously coming within s 27 of the Settled Land Act 1925 (repealed by the 1996 Act).

[235] Infra, p 201, et seq.

7

SECRET TRUSTS AND MUTUAL WILLS

1 FULLY-SECRET AND HALF-SECRET TRUSTS[1]

(a) THE PRINCIPLE UPON WHICH SECRET TRUSTS ARE ENFORCED

A typical case of a fully-secret trust would be where a testator had left property by his will to X absolutely, on the face of the will for his own benefit, but where in fact during his lifetime the testator had informed X that the property left to him by will was not for his own benefit but for certain persons or charitable purposes, and where X had promised to carry the testator's intention into effect. From early times the Court of Chancery would, in such cases, compel X to carry out the trusts, though difficulty was felt in reconciling the result with the provisions of s 9 of the Wills Act 1837,[2] which require a testamentary disposition to be made in a specified form. At first the accepted explanation was that this was an application of the maxim we have already met, that 'equity will not permit a statute to be used as an instrument of fraud';[3] it would be fraud on the part of the secret trustee to rely on the absence of the statutory formalities in order to deny the trust and keep for himself property which he well knew the testator did not intend him to enjoy beneficially. More recent cases, however, appear to establish that there is no conflict with the Wills Act 1837, since the trust operates outside or, as it is said, dehors the will. Where the will is executed in proper form, X will be able to establish his legal title to the property: but if the intention of the testator had been communicated to X by the testator in his lifetime, and X has acquiesced, his conscience will be bound in equity and he will be compelled to hold the property on trust for the persons or purposes indicated by the testator.[4] This trust is not regarded as a testamentary disposition coming within the Wills Act, but as a

---

[1] See generally (1947) 12 Conv 28 (J G Fleming); (1963) 27 Conv 92 (J A Andrews); [2000] Conv 40 (Diana Kincaid). A survey of the use of secret trusts in reported in [2003] Conv 203 (Rowena Meager). For the position in New Zealand see (1995) 6 Cant LR 108 (Nicky Richardson); *Brown v Pourau* [1995] 1 NZLR 352, noted [1996] Conv 302 (C E F Rickett).

[2] Prior to this Act, the Statute of Frauds (1677), and see p 96, supra.

[3] See eg *Jones v Badley* (1868) 3 Ch App 362, per Lord Cairns; *McCormick v Grogan* (1869) LR 4 HL 82, per Lord Hatherley. D R Hodge in [1980] Conv 34 argues in favour of this maxim as the basis of secret trusts, and does not think it inconsistent with the secret trust being outside the will.

[4] See eg *Cullen v A-G for Ireland* (1866) LR 1 HL 190, per Lord Westbury; *Re Blackwell, Blackwell v Blackwell* [1929] AC 318, HL.

trust within the ordinary equity jurisdiction. There will, of course, be no secret trust if the evidence shows that the testator intended to impose, not a binding obligation, but a mere moral obligation, on the alleged secret trustee.[5]

A half-secret trust differs from a fully-secret trust in that the will declares that the property is given to X on trust, though the trusts are not expressed in the will, but have likewise been communicated to X by the testator during his lifetime.[6] Though there are authorities going back as far as the seventeenth century, there was greater difficulty in establishing their validity. So long as the basis was thought to be fraud, the difficulty was that even if the intended beneficiaries did not take, it was clear that the secret trustee could not keep the property for himself as he was expressed to be a mere trustee in the will. If the Wills Act applied to invalidate the secret trust there would be a resulting trust to the estate. In *Blackwell v Blackwell*[7] however, it was finally established that half-secret and fully-secret trusts are enforced on the same principles.

The modern view was well expressed by Megarry VC in *Re Snowden (decd)*,[8] who said:

the whole basis of secret trusts . . . is that they operate outside the will, changing nothing that is written in it, and allowing it to operate according to its tenor, but then fastening a trust on to the property in the hands of the recipient.

Two cases may be mentioned as illustrations. In *Re Gardner*[9] there was a secret trust and one of the beneficiaries thereunder had predeceased the testatrix. Although a gift by will lapses if the beneficiary predeceases the testator it was held that the share of the deceased beneficiary did not lapse, but passed to her personal representative, since her title arose not under the will, but by the trust created[10] during her lifetime by communication and acceptance thereof by the secret trustee. In *Re Young*[11] the problem arose in an acute form. Section 15 of the Wills Act 1837[12] provides that a legacy to an attesting witness is ineffective; the facts were that one of the attesting witnesses was a beneficiary under a secret trust. It was held that he did not take under the will and that

---

[5] *Kasperbauer v Griffith* [2000] 2 WTLR 333, CA, noted [1998] 1 T & ELJ 20 (Elizabeth Hailstone), where it was doubted whether a secret trust could be created over the death benefit in a pension scheme, which the testator did not own or control and which he could never bring into his own ownership or dispose of as he willed.

[6] See p 133, infra, for the position as to the time of communication in the case of half-secret trust. In *Jankowski v Pelek Estate* [1996] 2 WWR 457 the court was divided as to whether the trust was fully secret or half secret.

[7] Supra, approving *Re Fleetwood* (1880) 15 Ch D 594; *Re Huxtable* [1902] 2 Ch 793, CA.

[8] [1979] 2 All ER 172 at 177. But see (1999) 115 LQR 631 (Patricia Critchley).

[9] [1923] 2 Ch 230. See [2004] Conv 388 (M Pawlowski and J Brown).

[10] Though it illustrates the present point well, it is difficult to see how the beneficiary could have obtained a transmissible interest before the trust was completely constituted by the trust property vesting in the secret trustee on the death of the testatrix.

[11] [1951] Ch 344, [1950] 2 All ER 1245.

[12] Now modified by the Wills Act 1968, which allows the attesting witness-legatee to take if the will is duly executed without his attestation. Section 15 invalidates only beneficial gifts. Accordingly attestation by the trustee under a half-secret trust would not affect the validity of the half-secret trust, and this may well also be the position in the case of a fully-secret trust.

he was therefore unaffected by the statutory provisions. 'The whole theory', it was said,[13] 'of the formation of a secret trust is that the Wills Act 1837 has nothing to do with the matter.' It may be added that where it is the secret trustee, and not the beneficiary thereunder, who predeceases the testator, or where the secret trustee disclaims the devise or legacy, the better view is, perhaps, that the secret trust fails in the case of a fully-secret trust, on the ground that it only affects the property by reason of the personal obligation binding the individual devisee or legatee.[14] In the case of a half-secret trust, however, the trust may well be good, on the principle that equity will not allow a trust to fail for want of a trustee.[15]

There is no general agreement as to whether secret trusts are express or constructive. Snell,[16] for example, deals with secret trusts under the head of express trusts. Underhill and Hayton[17] treat secret trusts within the Division dealing with express trusts 'because of their affinity with express trusts', but nevertheless say they should be categorized as constructive trusts. Sheridan[18] considers that although half-secret trusts are express, fully-secret trusts are constructive. But, it may be asked, as the trust operates outside the will, why should the fact that the existence of the trust is disclosed in the will alter the character of the trust? It is submitted that secret trusts are express trusts, being based on the expressed intention of the testator communicated to and acquiesced in by the secret trustee.[19] On this basis one runs into the difficulty that s 53(1)(b) of the Law of Property Act 1925[20] would seem to require writing where the subject of the secret trust is land. This was in fact held to be the case in *Re Baillie*,[21] which concerned a half-secret trust, but more recently, in *Ottaway v Norman*,[22] a fully-secret trust of land was held valid on parol evidence. In this case the trust seems to have been treated as constructive rather than express, but there was no discussion of this point, and no reference was made to any possible requirement of writing. However, even if a secret trust is express, it is arguable that it should be enforced notwithstanding the absence of writing by an application of the maxim that equity will not permit a statute to be used as an instrument of fraud.[23]

It should be added that in *Nichols v IRC*[24] it was conceded by counsel that the

---

[13] Per Danckwerts J at 350, 1250.

[14] *Re Maddock* [1902] 2 Ch 220 at 231, CA, per Cozens Hardy LJ; contra *Re Blackwell, Blackwell v Blackwell* [1929] AC 318 at 328, HL, per Lord Buckmaster.

[15] See infra, p 347.   [16] *Principles of Equity*, 30th edn, p 132 et seq.

[17] *Law of Trusts and Trustees*, 16th edn, p 257 et seq. Hayton and Marshall, *Cases and Commentary on the Law of Trusts*, 11th edn, p 121, not surprisingly, take a similar view. See also (1972) 23 NILQ 263 (R Burgess).

[18] (1951) 67 LQR 314 (L A Sheridan).

[19] See (1991) 5 Tru LI 69 (P Coughlon) citing the Irish case of *Re Prendiville* (5 December 1990, unreported), a half-secret trust case.

[20] See p 87, supra.

[21] (1886) 2 TLR 660. In *Re Young* [1951] Ch 344, [1950] 2 All ER 1245 (trust held to have been validly established by parol evidence; no point was taken on s 53(1)(b)).

[22] [1972] Ch 698, [1971] 3 All ER 1325 but the evidence did not establish a secret trust in the residuary estate.

[23] See p 94, supra. See Hanbury and Martin, *Modern Equity*, 16th edn, pp 168, 169.

[24] [1973] 3 All ER 632; affd on different grounds [1975] 2 All ER 120, CA.

doctrine of secret trusts applies to inter vivos gifts, and reference was made to
Bannister v Bannister,[25] which has already been discussed. It is suggested, however,
that the better view is that of Pennycuick J who observed, in *Re Tyler's Fund Trusts:*[26]
'It is probably true to say that the particular principles of law applicable to secret
trusts are really concerned only with trusts created by will.'

(b) EVIDENCE

The alleged secret trust must, of course, be established by evidence. It was not established in *Re Snowden*[27] where it appeared that the testatrix had simply left the residue
to her brother,[28] as a matter of family confidence and probity, to do what he thought
she would have done if she had ever finally made up her mind. There was no real
evidence that she intended the sanction to be the authority of a court of justice and
not merely the conscience of her brother.

As to the standard of proof, there are no special rules as to the evidence required to
establish a secret trust. Where no question of fraud arises, the standard of proof is the
ordinary civil standard of proof that is required to establish an ordinary trust. According to Megarry VC, if a secret trust can be held to exist in a particular case only by
holding the legatee guilty of fraud, then no secret trust should be found unless the
standard of proof suffices for fraud.[29] It is, however, submitted that the principles on
which secret trusts are enforced today never make it necessary to establish fraud on
the part of the legatee and that accordingly the ordinary civil standard of proof is
always appropriate.[30]

(c) FULLY-SECRET TRUSTS

As already indicated, the essential factors that must be present in order to raise a trust
are the communication of the intention of the testator to the secret trustee, and his
express or tacit[31] promise to carry out the testator's intention on the faith of which the

---

[25] [1948] 2 All ER 133, CA, discussed supra, p 95.

[26] [1967] 3 All ER 389 at 392. The dictum of Pennycuick J requires slight modification to cover the
analogous cases referred to in the next following paragraph infra. The phrase 'created by will' is not a very
happy one but the meaning seems clear.

[27] [1979] Ch 528, [1979] 2 All ER 172. There seems much to be said for the suggestion that the evidence
pointed to a secret trust in favour of the testatrix's relatives, subject to a power of selection in her brother—see
[1980] Conv 341 (D R Hodge).

[28] Who died six days after the testatrix.

[29] *Re Snowden* [1979] Ch 528, [1979] 2 All ER 271; *Re Riffel Estate* (1988) 64 Sask R 190; *Glasspool v
Glasspool* (1999) 53 BCLR (3d) 371. Contra *Ottaway v Norman* [1972] Ch 698 at 712, [1971] 3 All ER 1325 at
1333, per Brightman J.

[30] As argued by C E F Rickett in (1979) 38 CLJ 260; (1979) 43 Conv 448 (F R Crane).

[31] If the intention is communicated to the secret trustee, it seems that silence on his part will normally be
treated as consent to act—*Moss v Cooper* (1861) 1 John & H 352. But mere knowledge of the testator's
intention has been held, in Singapore, not to suffice: *Kamla Lal Hiranand v Harilela Padma Hari* [2000] 3 SLR
696, citing text above (in earlier edn).

testator either makes a disposition in favour of the secret trustee,[32] or leaves an existing disposition unrevoked.[33] A trust is raised in exactly the same way if on the strength of such a promise by an intestate successor, a man fails to make a will,[34] or if he destroys a codicil so as to revive the effect of prior testamentary provisions in favour of the secret trustee.[35] In most of the cases the obligation imposed on the secret trustee is to make some form of inter vivos transfer, but in *Ottaway v Norman*[36] the doctrine was held to apply equally where the obligation was to make a will in favour of the beneficiary under the secret trust.

The communication to the secret trustee, which may be through an authorized agent,[37] must take place during the testator's lifetime, though it matters not whether it is before or after the date of the will. If, however, the alleged secret trustee only learns of the alleged trust after the death of the testator, the trust will be ineffective. On the death the property passes under the will to a beneficiary whose conscience is perfectly clear, and his absolute title will not be affected by anything he may subsequently learn about the testator's intentions, which have not been expressed in compliance with the Wills Act 1837. Thus in *Wallgrave v Tebbs*[38] the testator bequeathed £12,000 and devised certain lands to T and M as joint tenants. Neither T nor M had ever had any communication with the testator about his will, or about any of his intentions or wishes with respect to the disposition of his property. The evidence showed that the testator wished certain charitable purposes to be carried out and felt confident that T and M would carry them out. T and M claimed to take the property absolutely free from the trust, though they admitted that they would, if they succeeded, apply the property substantially as the testator wished. It was held that in the absence of any communication in the testator's lifetime, T and M took absolutely.

It is not sufficient to communicate merely the fact of the trust to the secret trustee: the details of the trust must also be communicated to and accepted by him. If there is merely communication and acceptance of the fact of the trust, the secret trustee will hold on trust for the residuary devisees or legatees, or the persons entitled on intestacy if there is no residuary gift, or if residue is given on a secret trust.[39] He cannot take beneficially, as he has accepted the position of trustee, but communication of the particular trusts after the death by an unattested paper is not permitted, as this would

---

[32] *Drakeford v Wilks* (1747) 3 Atk 539.   [33] *Moss v Cooper* (1861) 1 John & H 352.

[34] *Stickland v Aldridge* (1804) 9 Ves 516; *Re Gardner* [1920] 2 Ch 523, CA.

[35] *Tharp v Tharp* [1916] 1 Ch 142; compromised on appeal [1916] 2 Ch 205, CA.

[36] [1972] Ch 698, [1971] 3 All ER 1325—the secret trustee was beneficially entitled for life. It was observed in this case that if a will contains a gift which is in terms absolute, clear evidence is needed before the court will assume that the testator did not mean what he said. The decision is not without its difficulties—see (1973) 36 MLR 210 (S M Bandali); [1971] ASCL 382 (J Hackney).

[37] *Moss v Cooper*, supra, where the question of communication through an unauthorized agent was raised but not answered.

[38] (1855) 2 K & J 313. See *Jones v Badley* (1868) 3 Ch App 362. See also (1997) 18 JLH 1 (Chantel Stebbings).

[39] The same result would follow if the trusts were communicated but were void for uncertainty, illegality, or other cause.

be a means by which a testator could evade the provisions of the Wills Act 1837.[40] It would, however, probably be a sufficient communication if the details of the trust were handed over to the secret trustee by the testator during his lifetime in a sealed envelope, even though this was marked 'Not to be opened until after my death'.[41]

Difficulties have arisen where there has been communication to one, or some only, of two or more secret trustees.[42] If the gift in the will is to two or more persons as tenants in common, then only the person, or persons, to whom the secret trust was communicated in the testator's lifetime are bound by it; the other person or persons take their respective shares beneficially.[43] Where the gift is to persons as joint tenants a curious distinction is drawn between the cases where one, or more, of the secret trustees have accepted the trust prior to the execution of the will, and the case where the acceptance was subsequent to the will (though, of course, during the testator's lifetime). In the first case all the joint tenants are bound by the trust,[44] on the ground that no one can take a benefit which has been procured by fraud. For no satisfactory reason this principle does not apparently apply in the latter case, where only the person or persons who have accepted the trust are bound by it.[45]

(d) HALF-SECRET TRUSTS

Here, as we have seen, the will expressly states that the gift is on trust, so there is no possibility of the secret trustee claiming beneficially. The problem accordingly is whether he holds on trust for the residuary devisees or legatees, or the persons entitled on intestacy, if there is no residuary gift or if residue is given, or whether the secret trusts communicated to and accepted by him can be enforced. There are, however, rather more difficulties and uncertainties in the relevant law than in the case of fully-secret trusts.

What may, perhaps, be called the primary rule is the rule that evidence as to the alleged half-secret trust is inadmissible if it contradicts the terms of the will. Thus in *Re Keen*[46] the testator bequeathed £10,000 to X and Y 'to be held upon trust and disposed of by them among such person, persons or charities as may be notified by me to them or either of them during my lifetime'. As a matter of construction it was held that the will referred to a future notification, and the court held that evidence of

---

[40] *Re Boyes* (1884) 26 Ch D 531.

[41] *Re Boyes*, supra; *Re Keen* [1937] Ch 236, [1937] 1 All ER 452, CA, where arguing by analogy Lord Wright MR said 'a ship which sails under sealed orders is sailing under orders though the exact terms are not ascertained by the captain till later'.

[42] The propositions below are disputed in (1972) 88 LQR 225 (B Perrins) where it is argued that in every case where there has been a communication to X (one of two secret trustees X and Y) only, yet it is alleged that X and Y are both bound by the secret trust, the question is whether the gift to Y in the will was induced by the promise made by X to the testator.

[43] *Tee v Ferris* (1856) 2 K & J 357; *Re Stead* [1900] 1 Ch 237.

[44] *Russell v Jackson* (1852) 10 Hare 204; *Re Stead*, supra.

[45] *Moss v Cooper* (1861) 1 John & H 352; *Re Stead*, supra.

[46] [1937] Ch 236, [1937] 1 All ER 452, CA. See also *Re Spence* [1949] WN 237.

a prior notification was inadmissible as it would be inconsistent with the express terms of the will. Another aspect of this rule is that a person named as trustee in the will is not permitted to set up any beneficial interest in himself,[47] though it is a different matter if on its true construction the will gives property to a person conditionally on his discharging the testator's wishes communicated to him.[48]

A further problem arises in connection with this rule where the will gives property to persons in some such terms as in *Re Spencer's Will*[49] 'relying, but not by way of trust, upon their applying the sum in or towards the object privately communicated to them' by the testator. In that case the Court of Appeal held that evidence would be admissible to show that the legatees had in fact accepted a secret trust,[50] though it is not made clear how this is to be reconciled with the rule, as such evidence would contradict the terms of the will. Indeed, it seems doubtful whether the point was argued. This decision was distinguished in *Re Falkiner*,[51] where it was held that the true inference was that the alleged secret trustee, knowing the contents of the will, had agreed to give effect to the testatrix's wishes in accordance with the scheme of the will, which included a provision that there should be no trust or legal obligation.

Turning to another matter, the most important distinction between fully-secret and half-secret trusts is that in the latter case the communication to and acceptance of the trusts will not merely be ineffective if it takes place after the testator's death, but even if it takes place during his lifetime but after the execution of his will. 'A testator', it has been said,[52] 'cannot reserve to himself a power of making future unwitnessed dispositions by merely naming a trustee and leaving the purposes of the trust to be supplied afterwards nor can a legatee give testamentary validity to an unexecuted codicil by accepting an indefinite trust, never communicated to him in the testator's lifetime', and on this basis it has been stated that in the case of a half-secret trust communication cannot be effective if made after the date of the will. This argument, which, if valid, would apply equally to fully-secret trusts, is, it is submitted, invalid as it fails to take into account the basis of the secret trusts, that is, that they operate entirely outside the will. The secret trustee, whether it is a fully-secret or half-secret trust, should, on principle, take the property bound by an equitable obligation if he has accepted the trust at any time during the testator's lifetime, whether before or after the date of the will being irrelevant. However, although not finally settled, the weight of dicta favours the view that in the case of half-secret trusts the communication and acceptance of the trust

---

[47] *Re Rees' Will Trusts* [1950] Ch 204, [1949] 2 All ER 1003, CA; *Re Huxtable*, supra; *Re Pugh's Will Trusts* [1967] 3 All ER 337. Cp *Re Tyler's Fund Trusts* [1967] 3 All ER 389.

[48] See eg *Irvine v Sullivan* (1869) LR 8 Eq 673.

[49] (1887) 3 TLR 822, CA.

[50] This, of course, would be a fully-secret trust, not a half-secret trust.

[51] [1924] 1 Ch 88, applied in *Re Stirling* [1954] 2 All ER 113. The distinction lacks plausibility, according to Waters, *The Law of Trusts in Canada*, 2nd edn, p 230.

[52] Per Viscount Sumner in *Re Blackwell, Blackwell v Blackwell* [1929] AC 318 at 339, HL.

must be prior to, or contemporaneously with, the execution of the will,[53] and the contrary view seems to have been considered unarguable in *Re Bateman's Will Trusts*,[54] the most recent case. In Australia, however, the courts have refused to apply the English rule and have held that a half-secret trust can be communicated at any time before the testator's death, as in the case of a fully-secret trust.[55]

Where a testator makes a gift to two or more persons who on the face of the will are trustees, who always hold as joint tenants, it is clear, assuming that the law as stated in the preceding paragraph is correct, that if there had been no communication of the trusts by the time that the will was executed, the trustees would hold the property on trust for the residuary devisees or residuary legatees, or the persons entitled on intestacy if there is no residuary gift or if it is a gift of residue.[56] Where the trust has been communicated to and accepted before the date of the will by one, or some only, of the trustees the position seems to be the same as in fully-secret trusts, that is, the gift being to them as joint tenants, acceptance by one binds all.[57] What has been said is subject to the qualification that, as we have already seen, if the evidence as to communication contradicts the terms of the will it is inadmissible; so if the will states that the trusts have been communicated to all the trustees, evidence of communication to one only would seem to be inadmissible.[58]

The last point to be mentioned was decided in *Re Cooper*.[59] There the testator bequeathed £5,000 to two persons as trustees on the face of the will, and the trusts were duly communicated to them by the testator and accepted prior to the execution of the will. Subsequently the testator executed a codicil whereby he in effect increased the legacy to £10,000, the trustees 'knowing my wishes regarding the sum'. The

---

[53] *Johnson v Ball* (1851) 5 De G & Sm 85; *Blackwell v Blackwell*, supra; *Re Keen* [1937] Ch 236, [1937] 1 All ER 452, CA. The apparent rule is criticized by Holdsworth (1937) 63 LQR 501 and by Parker and Mellows, *The Modern Law of Trusts*, 8th edn p 127, but approved (1972) 23 NILQ 263 (R Burgess) and [1981] Conv 335 (T G Watkin), who would like to see the rule extended by statute to fully secret trusts. See also [1992] Conv 202 (J Mee) discussing the different rule in Irish law. The unsatisfactory position is, perhaps, due to confusion with the probate doctrine of incorporation by reference, under which a document not properly executed in accordance with the provisions of the Wills Act 1837 may be incorporated in the will and granted probate. In order for this to happen the document sought to be incorporated must already be in existence when the will is executed and referred to therein as an existing document in terms enabling it to be clearly identified. See *Re Schintz's Will Trusts* [1951] Ch 870, [1951] 1 All ER 1095. It has recently been argued, contrary to what is said above, that the incorporation doctrine is the basis of the half-secret trust—[1979] Conv 360 (Paul Matthews). Counter arguments are put in [1980] Conv 341 (D R Hodge). An alternative view accepts the distinction between fully secret and half-secret trusts, and explains it in terms of the extrinsic evidence rule—[1985] Conv 248 (B Perrins), and D Wilde seeks to justify it, in [1995] Conv 366, on the ground that a fully secret trust is commonly set up without legal advice, while a half-secret trust almost always involves a solicitor.

[54] [1970] 3 All ER 817, [1970] 1 WLR 1463.

[55] *Legerwood v Perpetual Trustee Co Ltd* (1997) 41 NSWLR 532. Moreover the English courts have refused to apply the rule to the analogous case of nomination under a life insurance policy: *Gold v Hill* [1999] 1 FLR 54.

[56] The same result would follow if the trusts were duly communicated in time, but were void for uncertainty, illegality or other cause. See eg *Re Hawksley's Settlement* [1934] Ch 384, [1934] All ER Rep 94.

[57] *Re Young* [1951] Ch 344, [1950] 2 All ER 1245.

[58] *Re Spence* [1949] WN 237. Contrast *Re Keen* [1937] Ch 236, [1937] 1 All ER 452, CA, where the will referred to communication to the trustees 'or one of them'.

[59] [1939] Ch 811, [1939] 3 All ER 586, CA.

increase of the legacy was never communicated to the trustees by the testator. It was held that the secret trusts were effective as to the first £5,000 but failed as to the additional £5,000 given by the codicil.

2 MUTUAL WILLS[60]

Mutual wills are generally regarded as a case of constructive trust.[61] They arise where two persons, usually, but not essentially,[62] husband and wife, have made an agreement as to the disposal of their property, and each has in accordance with the agreement executed a will, the two wills containing, mutatis mutandis, similar provisions. The mutual wills may give the survivor only a life interest,[63] or, it seems, after some hesitation, an absolute interest.[64] In either case it may well be a term of the agreement that the wills shall not be revoked,[65] and if one or the other nevertheless purports to revoke his mutual will, various problems may arise.

In the first place, it is quite clear that a will cannot be made irrevocable.[66] In *Re Hey's Estate*[67] a husband and wife made mutual wills in 1907. The husband died in 1911 and his will was duly proved, under which the wife took certain benefits. Subsequently the wife executed a codicil in 1912 and a fresh will in 1913. These later instruments were made in breach of a definite agreement between the husband and wife in 1907 when the mutual wills were executed that they should be irrevocable. It was held that the will of 1907 was none the less revocable, for our testamentary law regards revocability as an essential characteristic of a will, and probate was accordingly ordered of the will of 1913.

It by no means follows, however, that an agreement such as that entered into by the husband and wife above in 1907 is worthless. At law, an action for damages will lie for breach of a covenant or contract not to revoke a will at the suit of the other party, and it is arguable that an intended beneficiary under the mutual will may now sue directly under the Contracts (Rights of Third Parties) Act 1999.[68] Further, in equity, a mutual will of which probate will not be granted may be enforced under a trust. Equity takes the view, where two persons have agreed to make and have in fact executed mutual wills, and where it was a term of the agreement that such wills should not be revoked, that the first of them to die dies with the implied promise of the survivor that the

---

[60] See, generally (1951) 15 Conv 28 (G Boughen Graham); (1970) 34 Conv 230 (R Burgess); [1982] Conv 228 (Keith Hodkinson); (1982) 79 LSG 1305 (T Prime); (1988) 138 NLJ 351 (F H G Sunnocks); [1997] Conv 182 (A Harper). See also (1989) 105 LQR 534 (C E F Rickett).

[61] See *Re Cleaver* [1981] 2 All ER 1018 and C E F Rickett in (1982) 8 Adel LR 178.

[62] *Lord Walpole v Lord Orford* (1797) 3 Ves 402.

[63] Eg *Dufour v Pereira* (1769) 1 Dick 419—the earliest and leading case on mutual wills.

[64] *Re Green* [1951] Ch 148, [1950] 2 All ER 913; disregarding doubts suggested by *Re Oldham* [1925] Ch 75.

[65] Except, of course, as a result of a subsequent agreement.

[66] *Vynior's Case* (1609) 8 Co Rep 81b.   [67] [1914] P 192.   [68] See p 108 et seq, supra.

agreement shall hold good. Accordingly, if the survivor revokes[69] or alters his will, as we have seen he can, his personal representatives will take his property upon trust to perform the agreement, for the will of the one who has died first has, by his death, become irrevocable.[70] The principle has been held to apply equally whether or not the survivor takes any benefit under the will of the first to die.[71]

Similar principles[72] apply in the case of a joint will, as is illustrated by *Re Hagger*.[73] There under the joint will the survivor was to have a life interest in certain joint property with remainders over. The husband and wife agreed not to revoke the joint will. The wife was the first to die, and subsequently, but before the death of the husband, one of the remaindermen died. The husband subsequently made a fresh will inconsistent with the joint will. It was held that from the death of the wife the husband held the property upon the trusts of the joint will, and accordingly there was no lapse of the share of the beneficiary who survived the wife but predeceased the husband, and his share was payable to his personal representatives as part of his estate.

In order to establish the trust it is not sufficient to establish an agreement to make mutual wills followed by their due execution: it is essential that an agreement not to revoke them be proved. This agreement, although it does not restrain the legal right to revoke, is the foundation of the right in equity.[74] Such an agreement will not be implied from the mere making of mutual wills. In *Re Oldham*[75] it was pointed out that 'the fact that those two wills were made in identical terms connotes no more than an agreement of so making them'; other evidence, which may consist of recitals in the mutual wills,[76] or of evidence outside them[77] must be brought to establish the agreement not to revoke them. The agreement, if it relates to land, is deprived of any legal effect as a contract by s 2(1) of the Law of Property (Miscellaneous Provisions) Act 1989. However it was held in *Healey v Brown*,[78] in the absence of writing, that there was a constructive trust of the share in what had been the matrimonial home of the first to die, but a dictum of Morritt LJ in *Re Goodchild (decd)*[79] was held to inhibit a constructive trust of the survivor's share.

Even assuming that an agreement not to revoke the mutual wills is established, a

---

[69] This includes revocation by a subsequent marriage: *Re Goodchild (decd)* [1997] 3 All ER 63, [1997] 1 WLR 1216, CA.

[70] *Dufour v Pereira* (1769) 1 Dick 419; *Stone v Hoskins* [1905] P 194. Cf *Staib v Powell* [1979] Qd R 151.

[71] *Re Dale* [1994] Ch 31, [1993] 4 All ER 129, discussed [1994] NLJ Charities Supp 34 (D Brown); (1994) 144 NLJ 1272 (P O'Hagan); (1995) 58 MLR 95 (A H R Brierly).

[72] The Canadian courts have held that it is easier to infer an intention not to revoke from the terms of the will alone in the case of a joint will as opposed to mutual wills—*Re Grisor* (1980) 101 DLR (3d) 728.

[73] [1930] 2 Ch 190.

[74] *Gray v Perpetual Trustee Co Ltd* [1928] AC 391, PC; *Re Cleaver* [1981] 2 All ER 1018; *Re Goodchild (decd)*, supra, CA; *Lewis v Cotton* [2001] 2 NZLR 21, noted 36 T & ELJ 1 (Zandra Houston); *Birch v Curtis* [2002] EWHC 1158 (Ch), [2002] 2 FLR 847, noted (2002) 43 T & ELJ 14 (D Rowell). But see (2003) 27 MULR 217 (Julie Cassidy).

[75] [1925] Ch 75.   [76] *Re Green* [1951] Ch 148, [1950] 2 All ER 913.

[77] *Re Heys' Estate* [1914] P 192.

[78] [2002] WTLR 849, noted (2002) 41 T & ELJ 7 (D Jackson); [2003] Conv 239 (Christine Davis).

[79] Supra, CA, at 76. See also *Humphreys v Green* (1882) 10 QBD 148, CA.

trust is not created at once, and, indeed, may never arise at all. Clearly the parties may release each other from their bargain by mutual agreement, and it seems that during their joint lifetimes either may revoke his will separately, provided he gives notice of the revocation to the other party.[80] Such other party thereby acquires an opportunity to alter his own will, and the ground upon which a trust is raised ceases to exist. Further, even though no notice be given during their joint lives, where the one who dies first has departed from the bargain by executing a fresh will revoking the former one, the survivor, who has, on the death of the other party to the agreement, notice of the alteration, cannot, on the one hand, claim to have the later will of the deceased set aside or modified, or indirectly enforced by way of declaration of trust or otherwise.[81] On the other hand, the survivor will no longer be bound by the agreement and can leave his entire estate uninhibited by the terms of the mutual will, and this is so even where the will of the first to die has not been revoked but merely varied by a codicil, at least where the alteration is 'not insignificant'.[82] In such cases, therefore, no trust will ever come into being. However the principles giving rise to a trust have been held to be applicable in a case where a party, not being the first to die, has, by reason of senile dementia, lost the capacity to revoke his will and make a new will. The wife was in this position in *Low v Perpetual Trustees WA Ltd*,[83] and the personal representatives of the husband, who was the first to die and who had made a fresh will, were held to hold his estate upon trust to perform the terms of the mutual wills.

In practice, the most difficult problem may well be to ascertain exactly what property is subject to the trusts: this is strictly a question of the construction of the mutual wills. In *Re Hagger*,[84] the facts of which have already been mentioned, it was held that the joint will effected a severance of the joint interest of the husband and wife, and the trust operated as from the wife's death, not only on her interest in the property, but also on the interest of the surviving husband. In *Re Green*,[85] the mutual wills of husband and wife were in identical form, mutatis mutandis. Apart from certain specific real property, the husband divided his residue into two equal shares, one moiety being considered as his own personal estate and the other moiety as the equivalent to

---

[80] *Dufour v Pereira*, supra.

[81] *Stone v Hoskins* [1905] P 194. But there may be a claim for damages where there has been unilateral revocation in breach of contract. The decision in *Stone v Hoskins* was doubted in the Australian case of *Bigg v Queensland Trustees Ltd* [1990] 2 Qd R 11 where the plaintiff and the deceased (his wife) had executed mutual wills leaving their property to each other and on the death of the survivor to their respective children by previous marriages. By later wills the deceased revoked her mutual will, appointed the defendant as executor and altered the disposition of her property. The plaintiff made and continued to make investments in the deceased's name in the belief that the mutual will still stood. It was held that the defendant held all the deceased's estate on trust for the plaintiff. However in (1991) 54 MLR 581 C E F Rickett points out that this was not an action against a survivor and in his opinion was not a mutual wills case at all. In his view the primary remedy was in contract, with the possibility of claims in restitution or reliance on promissory estoppel. See (1991) 21 QLSJ 121 (M Weir).

[82] *Re Hobley, deceased* (1997) *Times*, 16 June. See [1998] PCB 332 (A Norris and H Legge).

[83] (1995) 14 WAR 35. An Australian case, but it is thought the English courts would come to the same conclusion.

[84] Supra.   [85] [1951] Ch 148, [1950] 2 All ER 913.

any benefit which he had received from his wife by reason of her predeceasing him, as in fact happened. The husband subsequently revoked his first, mutual, will and after the husband's death the court held that the trust operated only on one-half of the husband's residuary estate, that is, the moiety which he had notionally received from his wife. The other moiety passed under his fresh will. The questions as to how far in such circumstances the survivor is entitled to dispose of his own property in his lifetime,[86] and as to what extent after-acquired property is subject to the trust have not yet been judicially explored.[87]

As has been mentioned in connection with *Re Hagger*,[88] the same principles apply where two persons have executed a joint will.[89] In such cases on the death of one of the joint testators probate will be granted of so much of the joint will as becomes operative on his death.[90] The survivor of joint testators will be bound by a trust in the same way and to the same extent as if they had executed mutual wills.

It is thought that similar principles would be applied in analogous situations. There do not seem to be any English cases, but in Canada they have been applied where the agreement is subsequent to the making of the wills; and where the agreement is that if one party makes a change in a particular part of his will (having a right under the agreement to do so) the other party will make a corresponding change. In this last case if the survivor does not make the change, equity will treat the case as if he had done so, and compel the personal representatives to distribute the estate on that basis.[91]

---

[86] The judge in *Healey v Brown* [2002] WTLR 849 had no doubt that, where the subject was the matrimonial home, the survivor could sell it and use the proceeds to fund a place in a nursing home.

[87] See the discussion in (1951) 14 MLR 136 (J D B Mitchell).   [88] Supra.

[89] It was at one time thought that a joint will was impossible but there is now no doubt that it can be valid (see eg *Re Duddell* [1932] 1 Ch 585, [1932] All ER Rep 714). Joint wills are rare in practice and Underhill and Hayton *Law of Trusts and Trustees*, 16th edn, p 427 states that they are to be deprecated and that practitioners should do their utmost to ensure that separate wills are drafted. See (1996) 139 Sol Jo (R Shah). See also *Re Ohorodynk* (1979) 97 DLR (3d) 502, appeal dismissed (1980) 102 DLR (3d) 576—criticized (1979) 29 UTLJ 390 (T G Youdan).

[90] *Re Piazzi-Smyth's Goods* [1898] P 7.

[91] *Re Fox* [1951] OR 378. See (1979) 29 UTLJ 390 (T G Youdan).

8

CONSTRUCTIVE TRUSTS

As will be realized it is impossible to make an exhaustive list of constructive trust situations, but a discussion of some of the more common and important circumstances which have been held to give rise to a constructive trust follows. As a general principle it may be said that property subject to a constructive trust must have come into the hands of the alleged trustee as a result of unconscionable dealing or in breach of a fiduciary obligation.[1] In addition, as we have seen, some take the view that secret trusts and mutual wills are enforced on the basis of constructive trust, and also cases such as *Rochefoucauld v Boustead*[2] and *Bannister v Bannister*.[3]

1 THE RULE IN *KEECH V SANDFORD*[4]

Where a trustee who held a lease for the benefit of a cestui que trust has made use of the influence which his situation has enabled him to exercise to obtain a new lease, he will be compelled in equity to hold the new lease thus acquired as a constructive trustee for the benefit of the cestui que trust. The length to which the doctrine has been carried is exemplified by *Keech v Sandford*[5] itself. There the rule was still adhered to despite express proof of the lessor's refusal to renew the lease for the benefit of the cestui que trust, the court apparently taking the view that to relax the rule would give the trustees too great an opportunity to defraud the beneficiaries. The renewed lease is regarded in equity as an accretion to or graft upon the original term and subject accordingly to the same trusts. The doctrine is not restricted to cases where the old lease was renewable by custom or agreement: it applies also where there is no obligation to grant a new lease, and notwithstanding the fact that the old lease has expired.[6]

The principle that a trustee who renews a lease will be treated as a constructive

---

[1] *French v Mason* (1998) *Times*, 13 November.   [2] [1897] 1 Ch 196, CA. See p 94 et seq, supra.
[3] [1948] 2 All ER 133, CA.
[4] (1726) Sel Cas Ch 61 See (1972) 36 Conv 159 (D R Paling) where the pleadings are transcribed. Many of the relevant cases are reviewed in *Re Biss* [1903] 2 Ch 40, CA. See also (1969) 33 Conv 161 (S Cretney); (1974) 38 Conv 330 (D Paling); (1987) 1 TL & P 171 (Fiona Spearing).
[5] Supra, applied *Warman International Ltd v Dwyer* (1995) 128 ALR 201, noted [1995] LMCLQ 462 (P Jaffey). See *A-G for Hong Kong v Reid* [1994] 1 AC 324, [1994] 1 All ER 1, PC.
[6] *Pickering v Vowles* (1783) 1 Bro CC 197.

trustee of the renewed lease or, to put it another way, the presumption of personal incapacity to retain the benefit, has been extended to other cases where there is a fiduciary relationship. Apart from the case of the trustee, there are other persons in connection with whom the presumption cannot be rebutted,[7] namely, personal representatives,[8] agents, tenants for life[9] and presumably in most cases as a result of the Law of Property Act 1925[10] joint tenants and tenants in common. In some other cases, namely, mortgagors,[11] mortgagees,[12] and partners,[13] the presumption of personal incapacity has been said to be 'at most a rebuttable presumption of fact'.[14] These seem to be the only cases in which any such presumption arises, and the Court of Appeal in *Re Biss*[15] expressly disapproved of dicta[16] suggesting that if any person, only partly interested in an old lease, obtained from the lessor a renewal, he must be held a constructive trustee of the new lease, whatever might be the nature of his interest or the circumstances under which he obtained the new lease.

In *Re Biss*[17] itself it was held that the principle in *Keech v Sandford*[18] did not apply. There a lessor granted a lease for seven years of a house in which the lessee carried on a profitable business. On the expiration of the term the lessor refused to renew, but allowed the lessee to remain as tenant from year to year at an increased rent. During that tenancy the lessee died intestate, leaving a widow and three children, one being an infant. The widow alone took out administration to her husband's estate, and she and the two adult children, one of whom was a son, continued to carry on the business under the existing yearly tenancy. The widow and son each applied to the lessor for a new lease for the benefit of the estate, which he refused to grant but, having determined the yearly tenancy by notice, he granted to the son, who had never become an administrator of his father's estate, 'personally' a new lease for three years at a still further increased rent. The widow, as sole administratrix, applied to have the new lease treated as taken by the son for the benefit of the estate. The court, however, in the absence of a fiduciary relationship, held the son entitled to keep the lease for his own benefit.

---

   7 *Re Biss* [1903] 2 Ch 40, CA; *Re Knowles' Will Trusts* [1948] 1 All ER 866, CA.
   8 Including an executor de son tort *Mulvany v Dillon* (1810) 1 Ball & B 409.
   9 *James v Dean* (1808) 15 Ves 236; *Lloyd-Jones v Clark-Lloyd* [1919] 1 Ch 424, CA and now see ss 16(1) and 107, Settled Land Act 1925.
   10 Sections 34, 36, as amended by the Trusts of Land and Appointment of Trustees Act 1996. But not if the legal estate is vested in outside trustees. In such case there is no fiduciary relationship, either in the case of tenants in common—*Kennedy v de Trafford* [1897] AC 180, HL, or of joint tenants—*Re Biss*, supra.
   11 *Leigh v Burnett* (1885) 29 Ch D 231.
   12 *Nelson v Hannam and Smith* [1943] Ch 59, [1942] 2 All ER 680, CA.
   13 *Clegg v Edmondson* (1857) 8 De GM & G 787; *Chan v Zacharia* (1983) 53 ALR 417. But see *Thompson's Trustee v Heaton* [1974] 1 All ER 1239, the note in (1975) 38 MLR 226 (Paul Jackson) and Oakley, *Constructive Trusts* 3rd edn, p 159, suggesting that the presumption should be irrebuttable in the case of partners.
   14 *Re Biss*, supra, at 56, per Collins MR; *Harris v Black* (1983) 46 P & CR 366, CA (not applied where two trustees were joint beneficiaries and one of them did not wish to apply for a new tenancy under the Landlord & Tenant Act 1954, Part II). Cf *Glennon v Taxation Comr of Commonwealth of Australia* (1972) 127 CLR 503.
   15 Supra.   16 Per Lord Bathurst LC in *Rowe v Chichester* (1773) Amb 715.
   17 Supra.   18 Supra.

Another way in which the rule in *Keech v Sandford*[19] has been extended is by its application to the acquisition by a trustee of the reversion expectant on a lease. The earlier cases, however, laid down a distinction for which no really satisfactory justification can be put forward.[20] This was that the rule applied to the purchase of reversions on leases when the leases were renewable by custom or agreement,[21] on the ground that it deprived the beneficiaries of the chance of renewal for their benefit, but not where there was no right or custom of renewal.[22] This distinction does not appear to have been mentioned to the Court of Appeal in *Protheroe v Protheroe*,[23] where it was held that the purchased reversion was held on trust although there was presumably no right or custom of renewal. It was a case where the husband held the lease of what had been the matrimonial home as trustee for himself and his wife in equal shares, and after the parties had separated and the wife had filed a petition for divorce, he purchased the freehold reversion. It was held that the freehold reversion must be regarded in equity as acquired on the same trusts as the lease.

It should be observed that where a man is held to be a constructive trustee under the rule in *Keech v Sandford*,[24] he is entitled to a lien on the property for the expenses of renewal,[25] and the costs of permanent improvements,[26] and he is entitled to be indemnified against the covenants in the new lease.[27] If the lease comprises business premises upon which the trustee carries on a business he will be accountable for the whole of the profits though allowances may be made for his time, energy and skill.[28]

2 OBLIGATION TO ACCOUNT AS A CONSTRUCTIVE TRUSTEE FOR PROFITS RECEIVED BY VIRTUE OF HIS POSITION AS TRUSTEE

Various cases may be mentioned to illustrate the wide principle, continually re-stated, that 'whenever a trustee, being the ostensible owner of property, acquires any benefit as the owner of that property, that benefit cannot be retained by himself, but must be

---

[19] Supra. See *Owen v Williams* (1773) Amb 734: *Giddings v Giddings* (1827) 3 Russ 241.

[20] See (1969) 33 Conv 161 (S Cretney) for an historical explanation coupled with the opinion that the distinction is now irrelevant.

[21] *Re Lord Ranelagh's Will* (1884) 26 Ch D 590; *Phillips v Phillips* (1885) 29 Ch D 673, CA. Cf *Griffith v Owen* [1907] 1 Ch 195.

[22] *Longton v Wilsby* (1897) 76 LT 770; *Bevan v Webb* [1905] 1 Ch 620. And see per Wilberforce J at first instance in *Phipps v Boardman* [1964] 2 All ER 187 at 202.

[23] [1968] 1 All ER 1111, CA. See (1968) 32 Conv 220 (F R Crane) and (1968) 31 MLR 707 (P Jackson). See also *Thompson's Trustee v Heaton* [1974] 1 All ER 1239; *Metlej v Kavanagh* [1981] 2 NSWLR 339 and note in (1975) 38 MLR 226 (Paul Jackson).

[24] Supra.   [25] *Isaac v Wall* (1877) 6 Ch D 706; *Re Lord Ranelagh's Will* (1884) 26 Ch D 590.

[26] *Mill v Hill* (1852) 3 HL Cas 828; *Rowley v Ginnever* [1897] 2 Ch 503.

[27] *Mill v Hill* (1852) 3 HL Cas 828.   [28] *Re Jarvis* [1958] 2 All ER 336.

surrendered for the advantage of those who are beneficially interested'.[29] The object of the equitable remedies of account or the imposition of a constructive trust is to ensure that the defaulting fiduciary does not retain the profit: it is not to compensate the beneficiary for any loss.[30] The principle applies equally to a custodian trustee,[31] and to other persons in a fiduciary position[32] including agents,[33] solicitors,[34] company directors,[35] company promoters[36] and partners[37] though its application and precise scope must be moulded according to the nature of the relationship.[38] In *Reading v A-G*[39] there was held to be a fiduciary relationship between the Crown and an army sergeant stationed in Cairo who, on several occasions, while in uniform, boarded a private lorry and escorted it through Cairo, thus enabling it to pass the civilian police without being inspected. The Crown was held to be entitled to the money he received for the misuse of his uniform and position. In the Court of Appeal in that case it was said[40] that in this context 'a fiduciary relation exists (a) whenever the plaintiff entrusts to the defendant property tangible or intangible (as, for instance, confidential information) and relies on the defendant to deal with such property for the benefit of the plaintiff or for purposes authorized by him and not otherwise; and (b) whenever the plaintiff entrusts to the defendant a job to be performed, for instance, the negotiation of a

---

29 Per Lord Cairns LC in *Aberdeen Town Council v Aberdeen University* (1877) 2 App Cas 544 at 549, HL; *A-G for Hong Kong v Reid* [1994] 1 AC 324, [1994] 1 All ER 1, PC. See *Re Edwards' Will Trusts* [1982] Ch 30, [1981] 2 All ER 941, CA (access strip conveyed to trustee in consequence of his occupation of property as trustee). See also (1989) 48 CLJ 302 (I M Jackman).

30 *United Pan-Europe Communications NV v Deutsche Bank AG* [2002] 2 BCLC 461, CA, per Morritt LJ at 484.

31 *Re Brooke Bond & Co Ltd's Trust Deed* [1963] Ch 357, [1963] 1 All ER 454, where, however, the court authorized the custodian trustee to retain the profits.

32 As to what is meant by a 'fiduciary' obligation or relationship see Finn, *Fiduciary Obligations,* (1989) 68 CBR 1 (J R M Gautreau); (1989) 9 Ox JLS 285 (R Flannigan); *Hospital Products Ltd v United States Surgical Corpn* (1984) 55 ALR 417, discussed (1986) 6 Ox JLS 444 (R P Austin); (1986) 8 U Tas LR 311 (D S K Ong); *News Ltd v Australian Rugby Football League Ltd* (1996) 139 ALR 193, at 310–314; *LAC Minerals Ltd v International Corona Resources Ltd* (1989) 61 DLR (4th) 14; *Estate Realties Ltd v Wignall* [1991] 3 NZLR 482; *Hodgkinson v Simms* (1994) 117 DLR (4th) 151; *Pilmer v Duke Group Ltd (in liq)* (2001) 180 ALR 249 (held there was no fiduciary duty), noted [2001] CLJ 480 (M D J Conaglen); (1990) 69 CBR 455 (D W M Waters); [1990] LMCLQ 4 (J D Davies); [1990] LMCLQ 460 (P Birks); (1991) 108/109 LJ 4 (G Jones).

33 See eg *Parker v McKenna* (1874) 10 Ch App 96 per Lord Cairns at 118.

34 *Brown v IRC* [1965] AC 244, [1964] 3 All ER 119, HL. See also *Alimand Computer Systems v Radcliffes & Co* (1991) *Times,* 6 November (solicitors trustees of funds paid to them by clients as stakeholders).

35 *Regal (Hastings) Ltd v Gulliver* [1942] 1 All ER 378, HL; *Selangor United Rubber Estates Ltd v Craddock (No 3)* [1968] 2 All ER 1073; *Guinness plc v Saunders* [1990] 2 AC 663, [1990] 1 All ER 652, HL. See [1986] JBL 23 (D W Fox); (1985) 23 Osg Hall LJ 203 (Lord Wedderburn); (1994) 45 NILQ 1 (J P Lowry) (arguing for greater flexibility in the application of the principle to company directors).

36 *Jubilee Cotton Mills Ltd v Lewis* [1924] AC 958, HL.

37 *Aas v Benham* [1891] 2 Ch 244, CA; *Thompson's Trustee v Heaton* [1974] 1 All ER 1239. In *Fraser Edmiston Pty Ltd v AGT (Qld) Pty Ltd* [1988] 2 Qd R 1, it was held that a fiduciary relationship existed although the partnership negotiations never matured into an agreement.

38 *New Zealand Netherlands Society Oranje Inc v Kuys* [1973] 2 All ER 1222, PC (officer of an unincorporated non-profit making society). See (1975) UTLJ 1 (E J Weinrib).

39 [1951] AC 507, [1951] 1 All ER 617, HL. See (1968) 84 LQR 472 (Gareth Jones).

40 [1949] 2 KB 232 at 236, [1949] 2 All ER 68 at 70, CA.

contract on his behalf or for his benefit, and relies on the defendant to procure for the plaintiff the best terms available.'

A claimant may have alternative remedies. In *Tang Man Sit (personal representative) v Capacious Investments Ltd*[41] the classic example was said to be (1) an account of the profits made by a defendant in breach of his fiduciary obligations and (2) compensation for the loss suffered by the claimant by reason of the same breach. The former is measured by the wrongdoer's gain, the latter by the injured party's loss. The claimant must choose between them when, but not before, judgment is given in his favour and the judge is asked to make orders against the defendant.

The cases can be loosely grouped as follows.

(a) FEES PAID TO TRUSTEE DIRECTORS

On one side of the line are *Re Francis*,[42] where trustees were required to account for remuneration which they voted to themselves as directors by virtue of their holding of the trust shares; and *Re Macadam*[43] where trustees had power as such, and by virtue of the articles of the company, to appoint two directors of it. By the exercise of this power they appointed themselves, and were held liable to account for the remuneration they received for their services as directors,[44] because they had acquired it by the direct use of their trust powers. Cohen J observed[45] '. . . the root of the matter . . . is: Did the trustee acquire the position in respect of which he drew the remuneration by virtue of his position as trustee?'

On the other side of the line is *Re Dover Coalfield Extension Ltd*,[46] where it was held that the directors were not liable to account for their remuneration. They had become directors before they held any trust shares, and although the trust shares were subsequently registered in their names in order to qualify them to continue as directors, it was not by virtue of the use of those shares that they either became entitled or continued to earn their fees. And from *Re Gee*,[47] where the earlier cases were reviewed, it appears that if the use of, or failure to use, the trust votes could not prevent the appointment of the trustee to a remunerative position in the company, he will not be called upon to account; further, there is no reason why a trustee should not use the votes attached to his own shares, as opposed to those attached to the trust shares, in

---

[41] [1996] AC 514, [1996] 1 All ER 193, PC. Lord Nicholls, delivering the judgment of the Board, said it was more accurate to refer to compensation rather than damages. In the case before them nothing turned on the historic distinction between damages, awarded by common law courts, and compensation, a monetary remedy awarded by the Court of Chancery for breach of equitable obligation. He found it convenient therefore to use the nomenclature of damages which had been adopted throughout the case.

[42] (1905) 92 LT 77.   [43] [1946] Ch 73, [1945] 2 All ER 664.

[44] The court, however, allowed remuneration under the inherent jurisdiction—see *Re Masters* [1953] 1 All ER 19; *Re Keeler's Settlement Trusts* [1981] Ch 156, [1981] 1 All ER 888.

[45] [1946] Ch at 82, [1945] 2 All ER at 672.

[46] [1908] 1 Ch 65, CA. Also *Re Lewis* (1910) 103 LT 495, [1908–10] All ER Rep 281.

[47] [1948] Ch 284, [1948] 1 All ER 498; *Re Northcote's Will Trust*, [1949] 1 All ER 442. *Re Gee* was distinguished in *Re Orwell's Will Trusts* [1982] 3 All ER 177.

favour of his own appointment.[48] It may be added that there is, of course, no reason why, as in *Re Llewellin's Will Trusts*,[49] a testator holding a majority of shares should not effectively empower his trustees to appoint themselves as directors and arrange for their remuneration without being liable to account therefor.

(b) OTHER CASES IN WHICH TRUSTEES ACCOUNTABLE FOR PAYMENTS RECEIVED

In *Williams v Barton*,[50] the defendant, one of two trustees of a will, was clerk to stockbrokers on the terms that he should get a half commission on business introduced by him. He persuaded his co-trustee to employ his firm, and was held accountable as a constructive trustee for the half commission received by him. On principle any payment made to a trustee to induce him to act in any particular way in connection with the trust business must be held by him as a part of the trust funds. Thus in *Sugden v Crossland*,[51] a payment of £75 made to a trustee in consideration of his retiring from the trust and appointing the person making the payment as a new trustee was directed to be held as a part of the trust funds. A very curious case was *Re Payne's Settlement*,[52] where an eccentric mortgagor devised the equity of redemption to the mortgagee, with whom he had no other relationship. The mortgagee happened to be a trustee, and it was held he took the equity of redemption as a part of the trust estate.

(c) COURT ACTING TO PREVENT TRUSTEE PROFITING

The same fundamental principle may call for somewhat different action in different circumstances. Thus in *Wright v Morgan*[53] it was held that an option to purchase trust property could not be validly assigned to a trustee as it would involve him in a conflict of duty and interest[54] and for the same reason the court granted an injunction in *Re Thompson*,[55] to restrain an executor carrying on the testator's business as yacht agent from setting up in competition.

---

[48] It is not possible to split one's vote on a show of hands. A trustee shareholder, even though he had a larger personal shareholding, was accordingly held to be in breach of trust in voting for a resolution detrimental to the interests of his beneficiary—*McGratton v McGratton* [1985] NI 18, CA.

[49] [1949] Ch 225, [1949] 1 All ER 487. Similarly in *Re Sykes* [1909] 2 Ch 241, CA, a trustee was held entitled to retain profits made in supplying goods to the estate in connection with a business by virtue of a clause in the will. And see *Re Waterman's Will Trusts* [1952] 2 All ER 1054.

[50] [1927] 2 Ch 9.   [51] (1856) 3 Sm & G 192.   [52] (1886) 54 LT 840.

[53] [1926] AC 788, [1926] All ER Rep 201, PC. Contrast *Patel v Patel* [1982] 1 All ER 68, CA, a Rent Act case, where it was held that trustees were not acting in breach of trust in seeking to live in a house subject to the trust of which the beneficial owners were young children who the trustees had adopted on the death of their parents.

[54] Even though the price was to be fixed by valuation there would be a conflict in relation to the time of sale; the trustee, qua trustee, would want to sell when prices were high, but qua individual would want the sale to take place when they were low.

[55] [1930] 1 Ch 203. Whether or not an injunction is granted may depend on the nature of the business. Cf *Moore v M'Glynn* [1894] 1 IR 74.

An Australian case which it is difficult to categorize is *Malsbury v Malsbury*,[56] where the court, relying on the *Keech v Sandford*[57] principle, held there was a constructive trust. The property was held by the defendants, the plaintiff's son and daughter-in-law, under an express trust to allow him to live there for life as part of a family unit in which his son would be an integral part and in which he would be cared for as a member of the family. The son having divorced and left the property the express trust was impossible of performance. It was held that the defendants could not withdraw from the plaintiff the essential rights reserved for him and yet require him to accept as fulfilment of the terms of the trust an arid right of residence. The defendants were constructive trustees of the property for themselves and the plaintiff in shares proportionate to their respective contributions towards its purchase.

(d) CASES INVOLVING OTHER FIDUCIARY RELATIONSHIPS

In *Regal (Hastings) Ltd v Gulliver*,[58] the essence of the matter, simplifying the facts slightly, was that the appellant company (Regal) formed a subsidiary company, A Ltd, which had an authorized share capital of £5,000, to acquire the leases of two cinemas. The prospective landlord required a guarantee of the rent by the directors unless the paid up capital of A Ltd was fully subscribed. The directors were unwilling to give the guarantees and Regal could only put £2,000 into A Ltd. The directors, acting honestly and in the best interests of Regal, provided the remaining £3,000. In the events which happened a purchaser bought the shares both in the Regal and in A Ltd, paying for the latter the price of £3 16s 1d per share: the directors had subscribed for these shares at the price of £1 per share. The action was brought by the Regal, now under the control of the purchaser, against the now ex-directors to recover the profits they had made. The directors were held to be in a fiduciary relationship to the appellants, and liable to account.[59] The strict principle to be applied was thus stated by Lord Russell of Killowen:[60]

The rule of equity which insists on those, who by use of a fiduciary position make a profit, being liable to account for that profit, in no way depends on fraud, or absence of bona fides, or upon such questions or considerations as whether the profit would or should otherwise have gone to the plaintiff, or whether the profiteer was under a duty to obtain the source of

---

[56] [1982] 1 NSWLR 226.   [57] (1726) Sel Cas Ch 61.

[58] [1942] 1 All ER 378, subsequently reported in [1967] 2 AC 134n. The effect of the decision was a windfall for the purchaser, who in substance recouped much of the price he had paid for A Ltd. The principle was extended in *CMS Dolphin Ltd v Simonet* [2001] 2 BCLC 704, noted (2002) 37 T & ELJ 9 (G Bennett), to a director who resigned to take advantage of a business opportunity of which he had knowledge as a result of his having been a director. The extent of the fiduciary obligation of an ex-director is considered by Perlie Koh in [2003] CLJ 403. See also (2003) 66 MLR 852 (S Scott).

[59] The case was pleaded as a personal claim to account. Since the directors had the means to meet any judgment it was not necessary to decide whether they were constructive trustees of the profits received: in principle it is submitted they were.

[60] At pp 386, 144–145, applied *Patel v London Borough of Brent* [2003] EWHC 3081 (Ch), [2004] WTLR 577, discussed (2004) 60 T & ELJ 4 (J Small and D Radley-Gardner).

the profit for the plaintiff, or whether he took a risk or acted as he did for the benefit of the plaintiff, or whether the plaintiff has in fact been damaged or benefited by his action. The liability arises from the mere fact of a profit having, in the stated circumstances, been made. The profiteer, however honest and well-intentioned, cannot escape the risk of being called upon to account.

The same principles were applied in the leading case of *Boardman v Phipps*,[61] where the facts, somewhat simplified, were that B at all material times acted as solicitor to the trustees, and for the co-appellant P, one of the beneficiaries. The trust property included shares in a private company. In 1956, B and F, the active trustee, a chartered accountant, considered that the position of the company was unsatisfactory and that something must be done to improve it. Following the 1956 annual general meeting of the company, B and P decided, with the knowledge of two of the three trustees, including F, that they should try to obtain control of the company by purchasing shares. The trustees had no power to invest trust moneys in shares of the company. B, purporting to act on behalf of the trustees as shareholders, obtained much information from the company, and after long and difficult negotiations B and P, in July 1959, purchased more than two-thirds of the shares, virtually all the remainder being still held by the trustees. A considerable profit subsequently arose from capital distribution on the shares. It was accepted that B had acted with complete honesty throughout.[62] At the time of the purchase of the shares, the beneficiaries were absolutely entitled in possession to their respective shares (following the death of an annuitant in November 1958), which were in fact distributed in 1960. The action was brought by one of the beneficiaries, having an interest in five eighteenths of the trust fund claiming that B and P were constructive trustees of a corresponding five eighteenths of the shares purchased, and were liable to account to him for the profit thereon. The claim succeeded, and was affirmed by the Court of Appeal and ultimately by the House of Lords (though here only by a bare majority), on the ground that both the information which satisfied B and P that the purchase of the shares would be a good investment and the opportunity to bid for them came to them as a result of B's acting or purporting to act on behalf of the trustees for certain purposes.[63] In so holding the majority took the view that the claimant beneficiary was 'a fortunate man in that the rigour of equity enabled him to participate in the profits' and directed that payment should be allowed on the liberal scale to B and P in respect of their work and skill in

---

[61] [1967] 2 AC 46, [1966] 3 All ER 271, HL; *Swain v Law Society* [1981] 3 All ER 797, CA; reversed on different grounds [1983] 1 AC 598, [1982] 2 All ER 827, HL. See (1968), 84 LQR 472 (Gareth Jones); [1978] Conv 114 (B A K Rider); (1979) 95 LQR 68 (A M Tettenborn); (1984) 134 NLJ 891 (E Leigh Sagar). See also *Hanson v Lorenz and Jones* [1986] NLJ Rep 1088, CA, where it was held that a solicitor is under no duty to account to his client for profit made from a joint venture in circumstances where the client understood the terms and effect of the agreement and those terms were fair.

[62] Note *Badfinger Music v Evans* [2001] WTLR 1 where it was held that though honesty is an important factor it is not necessarily determinative. Remuneration was awarded to a party whose conduct was open to serious criticism, though the allegation of outright dishonesty was rejected.

[63] It is not entirely clear whether the House of Lords held that B and P were constructive trustees or merely personally liable: see [1994] RLR 56 (D Crilley).

obtaining the shares and the profits in respect thereof.[64] However, as Lord Goff pointed out in *Guinness plc v Saunders*,[65] strictly speaking any payment is irreconcilable with the fundamental principle that a trustee is not entitled to remuneration for services rendered by him to the trust.[66] It can, he said, only be reconciled with it to the extent that any such payment does not conflict with the policy underlying the rule. In his view, adopted in *Quarter Masters UK Ltd (in liquidation) v Pyke*,[67] such a conflict will only be avoided if the exercise of the jurisdiction is restricted to those cases where it cannot have the effect of encouraging trustees in any way to put themselves in a position where their interest conflicts with their duties as trustees. Lord Upjohn, dissenting, in the House of Lords fully accepted 'the fundamental rule of equity that a person in a fiduciary capacity must not make a profit out of his trust, which is part of the wider rule that a trustee must not place himself in a position where his duty and his interest may conflict'. There seems, however, something to be said for his opinion that it was an over-rigid application of the rule to apply it to the facts of *Boardman v Phipps*,[68] and that the dictum of Lord Selborne LJ in *Barnes v Addy*[69] should have been applied: 'It is equally important to maintain the doctrine of trusts which is established in this court, and not to strain it by unreasonable construction beyond its due and proper limits.' If a defendant has breached his fiduciary duty of loyalty he is liable in respect of any profits he has received: there is no requirement that the profit was obtained 'by virtue of his position'. The purpose of imposing a proprietary remedy is not to compensate the beneficiary but to ensure that the fiduciary does not profit from his breach of duty.[70]

Another case is *Industrial Development Consultants Ltd v Cooley*[71] where the defendant was managing director of the plaintiff company. The defendant was

---

[64] Account would, of course, also be taken of their expenditure. See also *O'Sullivan v Management Agency and Music Ltd* [1985] QB 428, [1985] 3 All ER 351, CA, noted (1986) 49 MLR 118 (W Bishop and D D Prentice), where an appropriate allowance was made even though there was moral blameworthiness on the part of the fiduciary; *Estate Realties Ltd v Wignall* [1992] 2 NZLR 615 (likewise moral blameworthiness); *Re Berkeley Applegate (Investment Consultants) Ltd* [1989] Ch 32, [1988] 3 All ER 71; *John v James* [1991] FSR 397, at 434. It has been suggested that it is unlikely that such an allowance will ever be granted again and that *Boardman* must be considered a mere aberration: [1995] Newc LR Vol 1 No 1 p 73 (D Cowan, L Griggs, J Lawry). See also (2004) 21 NZULR 146 (Jessica Palmer).

[65] [1990] 2 AC 663, [1990] 1 All ER 652, HL.

[66] For the principle and the qualifications to it see p 443 et seq, infra.

[67] [2004] EWHC 1815 (Ch), [2005] 1 BCLC 245.　　[68] Supra.

[69] (1874) 9 Ch App 244 at 251, CA.

[70] *United Pan-European Communications NV v Deutsche Bank AG* [2000] 2 BCLC 461, CA.

[71] [1972] 2 All ER 162, doubted by J D Davies in [1998] SJLS 1 in a useful article on fiduciary liability. Contrast *Plus Group Ltd v Pyke* [2002] EWCA Civ 370 noted [2003] CLJ 42 (Pearlie Koh); *Warman International Ltd v Dwyer* (1995) 128 ALR 201, where the High Court of Australia held that the liability of a fiduciary to account does not depend upon detriment to the plaintiff or the dishonesty and lack of bona fides of the fiduciary; *Nottingham University v Fishel* [2000] IRLR 471 (mere fact person is an employee does not mean he owes fiduciary duties) noted (2001) 30 Ind LJ 100 (Vanessa Sims); *Bhullar v Bhullar* [2003] EWCA Civ 424, [2003] 2 BCLC 241, noted (2004) 120 LQR 198 (D D Prentice and Jenny Payne). See also *Item Software (UK) Ltd v Fassihi* [2004] EWCA 1244, [2004] IRLR 928, noted (2005) 121 LQR 213 (A Berg).

privately offered a contract by a third party, who made it clear that he was not willing to contract with the plaintiffs. The defendant concealed the offer from the plaintiffs and obtained his release from his employment with them. About a week later he entered into a contract with the third party. He was held liable to account to the plaintiffs for all the benefit he had received or would receive under the contract with the third party. He had been in a fiduciary relationship with the plaintiffs, and in breach of his fiduciary duty had failed to disclose information of concern to the plaintiffs, and had indeed embarked on a deliberate course of conduct which had put his personal interest as a potential contracting party in direct conflict with his fiduciary duty as managing director of the plaintiffs. Whether the benefit of the contract would have been obtained for the plaintiffs but for the defendant's breach of fiduciary duty was held to be irrelevant.

The Privy Council took a much less strict view in *Queensland Mines Ltd v Hudson*.[72] Hudson was the managing director of Queensland which was interested in obtaining mining exploration licences. At a late stage Queensland ran into financial difficulties and could not proceed. Hudson resigned as managing director (though he remained on the board for 10 years) and took the licences in his own name, though initially for and on behalf of Queensland. At a board meeting in 1962 Hudson gave his assessment of the likely risks and benefits of exploiting the licences, whereupon the Board resolved not to pursue the matter further. Hudson went ahead on his own and from 1966 onwards received substantial royalties. The Privy Council held that Hudson was not accountable for the profit on two grounds, (i) the rejection of the opportunity to exploit the licences took the project outside the scope of Hudson's fiduciary duties to the company: this is difficult to reconcile with *Regal (Hastings) Ltd v Gulliver*.[73] It is, however, difficult to deny a conflict of interest where directors acquire for themselves an opportunity which they have rejected on behalf of the company; and (ii) that at the 1962 Board meeting, the Board had given its fully informed consent to Hudson exploiting the licences in his own name, for his own gain, and at his own risk and expense. In order to be effective however, consent should be given not by the Board but by the shareholders in general meeting.[74]

The last case to mention is *Guinness plc v Saunders*[75] where it was held that money paid to W, a director of Guinness, by that company under a void contract was received by him as a constructive trustee notwithstanding that, for the purposes of the action, it was assumed that he acted in good faith, believing that his services were rendered under a contract binding on the company.

Where property is acquired, in breach of fiduciary duty, with mixed trust money and personal money it may be appropriate to restrict the profit or gain to be accounted for to a proportionate part of the total profit or gain. Relevant circumstances include

---

72 [1978] 18 ALR 1, PC; *Island Export Finance Ltd v Umunna* [1986] BCLC 460.

73 [1942] 1 All ER 378 subsequently reported in [1967] 2 AC 134n.

74 See (1979) 42 MLR 711 (G R Sullivan); [1980] Conv 200 (W J Braithwaite).

75 [1990] 2 AC 663, [1990] 1 All ER 652, HL, noted [1990] Conv 296 (S Goulding); [1990] CLJ 220 (J Hopkins); (1990) 106 LQR 365 (J Beatson and D D Prentice).

the source from which and the time at which the personal contribution is made and the nature of the profit gained by the acquisition. It has been held in Australia[76] that a fiduciary is liable for the whole and not merely a proportion of the profit where trust moneys contributed to the purchase price, but the 'personal money' allegedly contributed by the fiduciary comprised only his personal liability on a mortgage on the security of the property acquired.

It seems that where a third party, having received confidential information, with knowledge or notice that the information has been imparted in breach of fiduciary duty, uses that information to acquire property, he will not be liable unless it would be unconscionable for him to retain the benefit thus obtained.[77]

(e) BRIBES

The general principle of the cases discussed above is that the fiduciary is not merely personally liable to account, as is clearly the case, but is also a constructive trustee of profits that he receives by virtue of his position. An Australian judge, Deane J, explained the position as follows:[78]

Stated comprehensively in terms of the liability to account, the principle of equity is that a person who is under a fiduciary obligation must account to the person to whom the obligation is owed for any benefit or gain (i) which has been obtained or received in circumstances where a conflict or a significant possibility of conflict existed between his fiduciary duty and his personal interest in the pursuit or possible receipt of such a benefit or gain or (ii) which was obtained or received by use or by reason of his fiduciary position or of opportunity or knowledge resulting from it. Any such benefit or gain is held by the fiduciary as a constructive trustee.

Thus it was held in terms in *Guinness plc v Saunders*,[79] referred to above, that the director was, and always had been, a constructive trustee for Guinness of the £5.2m received by him in breach of his fiduciary duty.

In relation to bribes Lord Templeman said in *A-G for Hong Kong v Reid*[80] that it had always been assumed that the law had been definitively settled by the Court of Appeal

---

[76] *Paul A Davies (Australia) Pty Ltd v Davies* [1983] 1 NSWLR 440; *Australian Postal Corpn v Lutak* (1991) 21 NSWLR 584. See (1993) 13 LS 271 (L Aitken).

[77] *Satnam Investments Ltd v Dunlop Heywood & Co Ltd* [1999] 3 All ER 652, CA, noted (1999) 143 Sol Jo 984 (M Draper), applied *Crown Dilmun plc v Sutton* [2004] EWHC 52 (Ch), [2004] WTLR 497, noted (2004) 61 TELTJ 16 (Rachel Nelson), where Peter Smith J agreed with the criticism of the rule in Goff & Jones, *Law of Restitution* (6th edn) chapter 33, paras 019–020.

[78] In *Chan v Zacharia* (1984) 53 ALR 417 at 433, cited with evident approval by Walters J in *Jurley v BGH Nominees Pty Ltd (No 2)* (1984) 37 SASR 499, and by Morritt LJ in *Don King Productions Inc v Warren* [2000] Ch 291, [1999] 2 All ER 218, CA.

[79] Supra.

[80] [1994] 1 All ER 1, PC, noted [1994] CLJ 31 (A J Oakley); [1994] Conv 156 (Alison Jones); [1994] LMCLQ 189 (R A Pearce); [1994] Co Law 3 (R C Nolan); [1994] 5 Cant LR 374 (P Devonshire); (1995) 58 MLR 87 (T Allen); [1996] JBL 22 (D Cowan, R Edmunds, J Lowry); [1996] 19 UNSWLJ 378 (C Rotherman); [1995] CLJ 60 (S Gardner). See also [1993] RLR 7 (Sir Peter Millett).

decision in *Lister & Co v Stubbs*,[81] where it was held that if a fiduciary accepts a bribe, his only obligation is to account for the sum he receives and he is not regarded as a constructive trustee of it. In *A-G for Hong Kong v Reid*[82] the Privy Council refused to apply *Lister & Co v Stubbs*[83] saying that it was not consistent with the principles that a fiduciary must not be allowed to benefit from his own breach of duty, that the fiduciary should account for the bribe as soon as he receives it and that equity regards as done that which ought to be done. From these principles it follows that the bribe and the property from time to time representing it are held on a constructive trust for the person injured. A fiduciary, of course, remains personally liable for the amount of the bribe if, in the event, the value of the property then recovered by the injured person proves to be less than that amount. The advice of the Privy Council is, of course, technically not binding on the English courts. It seems not unreasonable to assume, however, that if the point were to come to the House of Lords their Lordships would take the same view as the Privy Council and would overrule *Lister & Co v Stubbs*.[84] In *Daraydan Holdings Ltd v Solland International Ltd*[85] Lawrence Collins J said that, if he had not been able to distinguish *Lister & Co v Stubbs*, it would have been proper for him to apply the view of the Privy Council.

It may be added that not only is the bribed fiduciary liable but an account of profits is available against the briber.[86]

3 STRANGERS TO THE TRUST

(a) INTRODUCTION

Where trustees improperly allow trust property to come into the hands of strangers to the trust, the trustees will, of course, be personally liable for breach of trust. This, however, will not be an adequate remedy for the beneficiaries if the trustees have not the means to repair the breach of trust, and the beneficiaries in that case will want to know whether, and to what extent, a stranger to the trust may be liable. There are three situations.

First, the stranger may be under no liability at all. On general principles this will be

---

81 (1890) 45 Ch D 1, CA, a much criticized decision.

82 Supra, PC. See *Secretary for Justice v Hon Kam Wing* [2003] 1 HK LRD 524.

83 Supra, CA.

84 Supra, CA. See *Worcester Works Finance Ltd v Cooden Engineering Ltd* [1972] 1 QB 210, [1971] 3 All ER 708, CA, per Denning MR at 217, 711. For a contrary view see [1994] RLR 57 (Darrall Crilley); All ER Rev 1994, 366 (W J Swadling). Note moreover *A-G's Reference (No 1 of 1985)* [1986] QB 491, [1986] 2 All ER 219, CA, discussed p 549, infra, but not referred to in *A-G for Hong Kong v Reid*, PC, supra, and see (1994) 110 LQR 180 (J C Smith) on the possible effect of this last decision on the criminal law.

85 [2004] EWHC 622 (Ch), [2004] WTLR 815, noted [2005] Conv 88 (Margaret Halliwell). See (2005) 121 LQR 23 (H N Bennett).

86 *Fyffes Group Ltd v Templeman* [2000] 2 Lloyd's Rep 643.

the case if he can establish that he is a bona fide purchaser for value of a legal estate without notice.[87]

Secondly, as we shall see,[88] a beneficiary may have a proprietary remedy where he is able to trace the trust property into the hands of a third party who is what is known as an 'innocent volunteer', that is, one who has acquired the trust property bona fide without notice of the breach of trust, but who has not given value. Where tracing is possible, the third party will be required to restore an unmixed fund to the trust (whether or not it retains its original form), or, where it has been mixed with property belonging to the innocent volunteer, there will be a declaration of charge. The innocent volunteer will not, however, be liable as a constructive trustee so as to be personally accountable if he has parted with the trust property without having previously acquired some knowledge of the existence of the trust.[89] Such accountability may arise if he loses his innocence and becomes liable in the third situation about to be considered.

Thirdly, as will now be discussed, the stranger may be liable as a constructive trustee, that is, he will not only hold any trust property in his hands as a trustee, but will also be personally accountable for any loss to the trust estate even though he may no longer have any of the trust funds in his possession or under his control. The cases can be put under three heads:

(i) trustee de son tort,

(ii) recipient liability, or knowing receipt or dealing,[90]

(iii) accessory liability[91] or knowing assistance.

(b) TRUSTEE DE SON TORT

The phrase 'trustee de son tort' describes a person who, not being a trustee and not having authority from a trustee, takes upon himself to intermeddle with trust matters

---

[87] *Pilcher v Rawlins* (1872) 7 Ch App 259.

[88] See chapter 25, pp 550 infra. See also (1986) 13 Co Law 44 (Ben Strong) (1987) 46 CLJ (D J Hayton).

[89] *Re Diplock* [1948] 2 All ER 318 at 324–325, 347, CA; affd sub nom *Ministry of Health v Simpson* [1951] AC 251, [1959] 2 All ER 1137, HL; *Re Montagu's Settlement Trusts* (1985) [1987] Ch 264, [1992] 4 All ER 308; *Agip (Africa) Ltd v Jackson* [1992] 4 All ER 385 at 403; affd [1991] Ch 547, [1992] 4 All ER 451, CA; *Westdeutsche Landesbank Girozentrale v Islington London Borough Council* [1996] AC 669, [1996] 2 All ER 961, HL, per Lord Browne-Wilkinson at 705–706, 988; *Bristol and West Building Society v Mothew (t/a Stapley & Co)* [1996] 4 All ER 698, CA, per Millett LJ at 716–717.

[90] In relation to the classification into heads (ii) and (iii) reference is often made to the dictum of Lord Selborne in *Barnes v Addy* (1874) 9 Ch App 244, at 251–252: '. . . strangers are not to be made constructive trustees . . . [unless they] receive and become chargeable with some part of the trust property, or unless they assist with knowledge in a dishonest and fraudulent design on the part of the trustees.'

[91] The preferred phase in *Royal Brunei Airlines Sdn Bhd v Tan* [1995] 2 AC 378, [1995] 3 All ER 97, PC. See generally, (1987) 61 ALJ 281 (M J Bridle and J A Hooley); (1991) 135 Sol Jo 502 (Margaret Halliwell); *Equity and Contemporary Legal Developments* (ed S Goldstein) 374 (G H Jones); (1991) 5 SJLS 26 (T Hans).

or to do acts characteristic of the office of trustee.[92] The expression seems to have been adopted by analogy with the expression executor de son tort in the law relating to the administration of assets to cover the situation where a stranger has positively assumed to act as trustee. This is consistent with the opinion of Ungoed-Thomas J in *Selangor United Rubber Estates v Cradock (No 3)*,[93] where he distinguished between what he called:

two very different kinds of so-called constructive trustees.

(i)   Those who, though not appointed trustees, take on themselves to act as such and to possess and administer trust property for the beneficiaries, such as trustees de son tort. Distinguishing features [include] (a) they do not claim to act in their own right but for the beneficiaries, and (b) their assumption to act is not of itself a ground of liability (save in the sense of course of liability to account and for any failure in the duty so assumed), and so their status as trustees precedes the occurrence which may be the subject of claim against them.

(ii)   Those whom a court of equity will treat as trustees by reason of their action, of which complaint is made. Distinguishing features are (a) that such trustees claim to act in their own right and not for beneficiaries, and (b) no trusteeship arises before, but only by reason of, the action complained of.

Trustees de son tort are perhaps better described as de facto trustees. In their relation with the beneficiaries they are treated in every respect as if they had been duly appointed. They are true trustees and are fully subject to fiduciary obligations. Their liability is strict; it does not depend on dishonesty. Like express trustees they cannot plead the Limitation Acts as a defence to a claim for breach of trust.[94]

(c) KNOWING RECEIPT OR DEALING: RECIPIENT LIABILITY

These are situations where a person:

(1) knowingly receives trust property in breach of trust ('receipt of property constructive trust');[95] or

(2) receives trust property without notice of the trust and subsequently deals with it in a manner inconsistent with the trusts of which he has become cognisant ('wrongful dealing constructive trust'); or

---

[92] See *Mara v Browne* [1896] 1 Ch 199, CA; *Taylor v Davies* [1920] AC 636, PC, per Viscount Cave at 651; *Dubai Aluminium Co Ltd v Salaam* [2002] UKHL 48, [2003] 1 All ER 97 per Lord Millett at128–131. There is a useful discussion in *Nolan v Nolan* [2004] VSCA 109, [2004] WTLR 1261 (Australia), noted (2004) 62 TELTJ 18. Note *Re Barney* [1892] 2 Ch 265 where Kekewich J said that in order to be a trustee de son tort a person must have the trust property vested in him or at least have the right to call for a transfer.

[93] [1968] 2 All ER 1073 at 1095.

[94] See *Dubai Aluminium Co Ltd v Salaam*, supra, HL, per Lord Millett at 130.

[95] The directors of a limited company are treated as if they were trustees of those funds of the company which are in their hands or under their control, and if they misapply them they commit a breach of trust: *Belmont Finance Corpn v Williams Furniture Ltd (No 2)* [1980] 1 All ER 393, CA; *J J Harrison (Properties) Ltd v Harrison* [2001] EWCA Civ 1467, [2002] 1 BCLC 162, noted [2002] 152 NLJ 304 (S Bhandari).

(3) receives trust property knowing it to be such but without breach of trust and subsequently deals with it in a manner inconsistent with the trusts.[96]

In *Agip (Africa) Ltd v Jackson*[97] these three cases were put into two separate categories, in each of which it is immaterial whether the breach of trust was fraudulent or not.

Head (3) is that of a person, usually an agent of the trustees, who receives the trust property lawfully and not for his own benefit but who then either misappropriates it or otherwise deals with it in a manner which is inconsistent with the trust. He is liable to account as a constructive trustee if he received the trust property knowing it to be such, though he will not necessarily be required in all circumstances to have known the exact terms of the trust.

Heads (1) and (2) above relate to a person who receives for his own benefit trust property transferred to him in breach of trust. The claimant in these situations must show, firstly, a disposal of his assets in breach of fiduciary duty; secondly, the beneficial receipt by the defendant of assets which are traceable as representing the assets of the claimant; and, thirdly, knowledge on the part of the defendant that the assets he received are traceable to a breach of trust or fiduciary duty.[98] The receipt must be the direct consequence of the alleged breach of trust or fiduciary duty of which the recipient is said to have knowledge.[99]

Where there is a company intermediary the court is entitled to pierce the corporate veil and recognize the receipt of a company as that of the individual in control of it if the company had been used as a device or façade to conceal the true facts, thereby avoiding or concealing any liability of that individual. It is, however, insufficient that the company had been involved in some impropriety, not linked to the use of the corporate structure to avoid or conceal that liability. Nor can the court pierce the corporate veil merely on the grounds that it was necessary to do so in the interests of justice and no unconnected third party was involved.[100]

The Court of Appeal reaffirmed, in *Bank of Credit and Commerce International*

---

[96] *Re Montagu's Settlement Trusts* [1987] Ch 264, *Lipkin Gorman v Karpnale Ltd* [1987] 1 WLR 987; affd in part, reversed in part [1989] 1 WLR 1340, CA; reversed in part [1991] 2 AC 548, HL, relying on the law of restitution; *Baden v Société Générale pour Favoriser le Développment du Commerce et de l'Industrie en France SA* [1983] BCLC 325 (appeal dismissed [1985] BCLC, 258n, CA). As to the position in Canada see *Banton v CIBC Trust Corporation* (2001) 197 DLR 212 and (2002) 81 CBR 171 (M McInnes). See [1996] JBL 165 (M Bryan).

[97] [1990] Ch 265, [1992] 4 All ER 385; affd [1991] Ch 547, [1992] 4 All ER 451, CA, per Millett J at first instance at 403, 404. For the judge's extra-judicial views see *Equity and Contemporary Legal Developments* (ed S Goldstein) 407 and (1991) 107 LQR 71. See also [1991] LMCLQ 378 (E McKendrick); (1994) 57 MLR 38 (S Fennell); (1995) 16 Co Law 35 (C E F Rickett); [1999] NZLJ 40 (C E F Rickett).

[98] *El Ajou v Dollar Holdings plc* [1994] 2 All ER 685, CA, per Hoffman LJ at 700; *Bank of Credit and Commerce International (Overseas) Ltd (in liquidation) v Akindele* [2000] 4 All ER 221, CA, noted (2000) 59 CLJ 447 (R Nolan); (2000) 14 Tru LI 224 (J E Penner); (2001) 15 Tru LI 151 (P Jaffrey); (2001) 21 Ox JLS 239 (Susan Thomas); [2001] RLR 99 (J Stevens). As to attribution of knowledge to a company see *El Ajou v Dollar Holdings plc,* supra, CA; *K & S Corporation Ltd v Sportingbet Australia* (2003) 86 SASR 312 (first four categories of knowledge sufficient: on facts no need to decide on fifth).

[99] See *Brown v Bennett,* [1999] 1 BCLC 649, CA, per Morritt LJ at 655.

[100] *Trustor AB v Smallbone (No 2)* [2001] 3 All ER 987, [2001] 1 WLR 1177, noted (2003) 119 LQR 13 (Susan Watson).

(Overseas) Ltd (in liquidation) v Akindele,[101] the 'clear authority' of *Belmont Finance Corpn v Williams Furniture Ltd (No 2)*[102] that although a knowing recipient will often be found to have acted dishonestly, it has never been a prerequisite of liability that he should. As Vinelott J stated in *Eagle Trust plc v SBC Securities Ltd*:[103]

... in a 'knowing receipt' case it is only necessary to show that the defendant knew that the moneys paid to him were trust moneys and of circumstances which made the payment a misapplication of them. Unlike a 'knowing assistance' case it is not necessary, and never has been necessary, to show that the defendant was in any sense a participator in a fraud.

Citing this dictum with approval Nourse LJ in *Akindele*[104] went on to say that while in theory it is possible for a misapplication not to be fraudulent and the recipient to be dishonest, in practice such a combination must be rare.

Turning to the question of knowledge, Nourse LJ said that with the proliferation in the last 20 years or so of cases in which the misapplied assets of companies had come into the hands of third parties, there had been a sustained judicial and extra-judicial debate as to the knowledge on the part of the recipient which is required in order to found liability in knowing receipt. Expressed in the simplest terms, he continued, the question is whether the recipient must have actual knowledge (or the equivalent) that the assets received are traceable to a breach of trust or whether constructive knowledge is enough. He referred to dicta in a series of cases[105] which might be thought to provide strong support for the view that constructive knowledge is enough. However, as he went on to point out, in each of the Court of Appeal cases referred to actual knowledge was found and, moreover, the decisions in the *Karak* case and the *Agip* case were based on knowing assistance, not knowing receipt. The seminal judgment, he said, was that of Megarry V-C in *Re Montagu's Settlement Trusts*.[106] The facts of that case were that by a family re-settlement in 1923 the future tenth Duke of Manchester assigned certain chattels to which he was entitled in remainder on the death of the ninth Duke to trustees upon trust, on the death of the ninth Duke, to select such chattels as they thought fit for inclusion in the settlement and to hold the remainder (if any) in trust for the tenth Duke absolutely. The ninth Duke died in 1947. No selection was ever made and the chattels were released to the tenth Duke in 1948 and 1949. This was a breach of trust because he was only entitled to receive what was left

---

101   Supra, CA. Also in *Houghton v Fayers*, supra, CA.

102   [1980] 1 All ER 393, CA (a decision said sometimes to have been overlooked in this context).

103   [1992] 4 All ER 488 at 501. See also *Polly Peck International plc v Nadir (No 2)* [1992] 4 All ER 769, CA, per Scott LJ at 777; *Agip (Africa) Ltd v Jackson*, [1990] Ch 265, [1992] 4 All ER 385, per Millet J at 292, 404, affd [1991] Ch 547, [1992] 4 All ER 451, CA.

104   Supra, CA. Also in *Houghton v Fayers*, supra, CA.

105   Including *Karak Rubber Co Ltd v Burden (No 2)* [1972] 1 All ER 1210 per Brightman J at 1234; *Agip (Africa) Ltd v Jackson*, supra at first instance per Millet J at 291, 403; *Houghton v Fayers* [2000] 1 BCLC 511 per Nourse LJ himself at 516.

106   [1987] Ch 264, [1992] 4 All ER 308, adopted by Steyn J in *Barclays Bank plc v Quincecare Ltd* [1992] 4 All ER 363 and by Alliott J at first instance in *Lipkin Gorman (a firm) v Karpnale Ltd* [1992] 4 All ER 331, [1987] 1 WLR 987; reversed in part [1992] 4 All ER 409, [1989] 1 WLR 1340, CA; in turn reversed in part [1991] 2 AC 548, [1992] 4 All ER 512, HL. See (1992) 12 LS 332 (Helen Norman); *Equity and Contemporary Legal Developments* (ed S Goldstein) 46 (J D Davies).

of the settled chattels after the selection had been made. The Duke's solicitor, who knew of the settlement and at an earlier stage had known of the effect of the clause relating to the chattels, informed the Duke in writing in 1948 that he was free to sell the chattels released. The tenth Duke died in 1977, having sold some of the chattels in his lifetime. One of the claims made in an action by the eleventh Duke was that the tenth Duke had become a constructive trustee of the chattels.

Megarry V-C drew a distinction between the equitable doctrine of tracing and the imposition of a constructive trust by reason of the knowing receipt of trust property. Tracing, he said, is primarily a means of determining rights of property, in relation to which the doctrine of the purchaser without notice is appropriate. Where chattels are traced into the hands of a volunteer he may be liable to yield up any chattels that remain, or the traceable proceeds of any that have gone, but unless he is a constructive trustee he will not be liable if the chattels have gone and there are no traceable proceeds. The imposition of a constructive trust, however, creates personal obligations that go beyond mere property rights. In considering whether a constructive trust has arisen in a case of knowing receipt of trust property, the basic question is whether the conscience of the recipient is sufficiently affected to justify the imposition of such a trust. This primarily depends on the knowledge of the recipient, and not on notice to him. 'The cold calculus of constructive and imputed notice does not seem to me to be an appropriate instrument for deciding whether a [person's] conscience is sufficiently affected for it to be right to bind him by the obligations of a constructive trustee.'[107] It must be admitted that judges and academics have not always been careful to maintain the distinction in their use of the words 'knowledge' and 'notice'.

The effect of Megarry V-C's decision, according to Nourse LJ in *Akindele*[108] is that in order to establish liability in knowing receipt, the recipient must have actual knowledge (or its equivalent) that the assets received are traceable to a breach of trust and that constructive knowledge is not enough. Hitherto reference has often been made to *Baden v Société Générale pour Favouriser le Développment du Commerce et de l'Industrie en France SA*[109] where Peter Gibson J said that there were five categories of knowledge, namely:

(i)   actual knowledge;
(ii)   wilfully shutting one's eyes to the obvious—'Nelsonian knowledge';[110]

---

[107] Per Megarry VC in *Re Montagu's Settlement Trusts* supra, at pp 273, 320. But see (1987) 50 MLR 217 (C Harpum).

[108] *Bank of Credit and Commerce International (Overseas) Ltd (in liquidation) v Akindele* [2000] 4 All ER 221, CA, at 234. There was already a line of cases holding that in commercial cases constructive notice was not enough: *Eagle Trust plc v SBC Securities Ltd* [1992] 4 All ER 488; *Cowan de Groot Properties Ltd v Eagle Trust plc* [1992] 4 All ER 700; *Eagle Trust plc v SBC Securities (No 2)* [1996] 1 BCLC 121. In other jurisdictions constructive notice has been held sufficient even in the case of commercial transactions: *Equiticorp Industries Group Ltd v Hawkins* [1991] 3 NZLR 700; *Citadel General Assurance Co v Lloyds Bank Canada* (1997) 152 DLR (4th) 411, noted (1998) 114 LQR 394 (L Smith); (1999) 10 SCLR 461 (L I Rotman).

[109] [1983] BCLC 325 (appeal dismissed [1985] BCLC 258n, CA).

[110] As to blind-eye knowledge see *Bank of Credit & Commerce International SA (in liquidation) (No 15)* [2004] EWHC 528 (Ch), [2004] 2 BCLC 279.

(iii)   wilfully and recklessly failing to make such inquiries as an honest and reasonable man would make;

(iv)   knowledge of circumstances which would indicate the facts to an honest and reasonable man;

(v)   knowledge of circumstances which would put an honest and reasonable man on inquiry.

The essential difference between (ii) and (iii) on the one hand and (iv) and (v) on the other hand is that the former are governed by the words 'wilfully' or 'wilfully and recklessly'; (ii) and (iii) seem to be equivalent to actual notice, (iv) and (v), however, have no such adverbs and seem to be cases of constructive notice. They are cases of carelessness or negligence being tested by what an honest and reasonable man would have realized or would have inquired about, even if the person concerned was, for instance, not at all reasonable. Megarry V-C in *Re Montagu's Settlement Trusts*[111] accepted the five categories of knowledge set out in the *Baden* case[112] as useful guides, but thought that the modern tendency in equity was to put less emphasis on the detailed rules that have emerged from the cases, and to give more weight to the underlying principles that engendered them. Nourse LJ in *Akindele*,[113] however, had grave doubts about its utility in cases of knowing receipt. He observed that the fivefold categorization had been put to the judge on an agreed basis, and that both counsel accepted that all five categories of knowledge were relevant and neither sought to submit that there was any distinction for that purpose between knowing receipt and knowing assistance: the claim in constructive trust was based squarely on knowing assistance and not on knowing receipt. The purpose, he said, to be served by a categorization of knowledge could only be to enable the court to determine whether, in the words of Buckley LJ in *Belmont (No 2)*,[114] the recipient can 'conscientiously retain [the] funds against the company' or, in the words of Megarry V-C in *Re Montagu's Settlement Trusts*,[115] '[the recipient's] conscience is sufficiently affected for it to be right to bind him by the obligations of a constructive trustee'. But if that is the purpose, Nourse LJ continued, there is no need for categorization. All that is necessary is that the recipient's state of knowledge should be such as to make it unconscionable for him to retain the benefit of the receipt. This he propounded as a single test of knowledge for knowing receipt. He accepted that difficulties of application could not be avoided, but it would enable the courts to give commonsense decisions in the commercial context in which claims in knowing receipt are frequently made. One of the difficulties will be to draw the line between dishonesty, which is not required for liability, and unconscionability, which is.

In *Re Montague's Settlement Trusts*[116] Megarry V-C further agreed with the

---

[111] Supra.   [112] Supra.

[113] *Bank of Credit and Commerce International (Overseas) Ltd (in liquidation) v Akindele* [2001] Ch 437, [2000] 4 All ER 221, CA.

[114] *Belmont Finance Corpn v Williams Furniture Ltd (No 2)* [1980] 1 All ER 393 CA, at 405.

[115] Supra.   [116] Supra.

observation of Peter Gibson J in the *Baden* case[117] that 'the court should not be astute to impute knowledge where no actual knowledge exists'. And in *Re Clasper Group Services Ltd*[118] Warner J said that 'in considering whether a particular person may be treated as having had knowledge of any of those kinds, the court must have regard to what Lawson J in *International Sales and Agencies Ltd v Marcus*[119] called the "attributes" of that person'. Thus in the *Clasper Group* case,[120] on the facts, the person in question was young, inexperienced, and in a lowly position, and because of this his conscience was not affected in such a way as to constitute him a constructive trustee.

Megarry V-C further observed that a person is not to be taken to have knowledge of a fact he once knew but has genuinely forgotten: the test is whether the knowledge continues to operate on that person's mind at the time in question. Finally Megarry V-C thought it at least doubtful whether there is a general doctrine of 'imputed knowledge' corresponding to 'imputed notice'.

In the light of his views as to the law Megarry V-C held, on the facts, that the tenth Duke did not have any knowledge at any material time that the chattels that he was receiving or dealing with were chattels that were still subject to any trust. There was no reason why the solicitor's knowledge of the settlement at some earlier time should be imputed to the Duke so as to affect his conscience. Nor did his failure to inquire impose a constructive trust. Even if he had once known the relevant terms of the settlement, there was nothing to suggest that he remembered them when he received the trust property. Though the assignment of the chattels to him was a breach of trust, he did not become a constructive trustee of them.

Extrajudicially[121] Lord Nicholls has suggested that it would be better if cases of misapplied property gave rise to restitutionary liability regardless of fault but subject to a defence of change of position. This is clearly not the law as it stands, and in *Akindele*[122] Nourse LJ doubted whether it would in fact be preferable to fault-based liability in many commercial transactions. He did not think that, simply on proof of an internal misapplication of a company's funds, the burden should shift to the recipient to defend the receipt either by a change of position or perhaps in some other way. Moreover, he said, if the circumstances of the receipt were such as to make it unconscionable for the recipient to retain the benefit of it, there would be an obvious difficulty in saying that it is equitable for a change of position to afford him a defence.

---

[117] Supra.   [118] [1989] BCLC 143.

[119] [1982] 3 All ER 551 at 558.   [120] Supra.

[121] Cornish, Nolan, O'Sullivan and Virgo (eds) *Restitution Past, Present and Future: Essays in Honour of Gareth Jones*, pp 238–239.

[122] Supra, CA.

(d) THE ACCESSORY LIABILITY PRINCIPLE—KNOWING ASSISTANCE

In a much quoted dictum in *Barnes v Addy*[123] Lord Selborne said that a person would be liable as a constructive trustee if he had knowingly assisted in a dishonest and fraudulent design on the part of the trustees, even though no part of the trust property may ever come into his hands. In *Royal Brunei Airlines Sdn Bhd v Tan*[124] the Privy Council said that something had gone wrong in the subsequent cases because of a tendency to cite, interpret and apply Lord Selborne's dictum as if it were a statute, as a result of which the courts found themselves wrestling with the interpretation of the individual ingredients, especially 'knowingly', but also 'dishonest and fraudulent design on the part of the trustees', without examining the underlying reason why a third party who has received no trust property is being made liable at all. Moreover the approach exemplified by *Belmont Finance Corpn Ltd v Williams Furniture Ltd*[125] leads to the conclusion that a third party who dishonestly procures or assists in a breach of trust, the trustee himself being perfectly innocent,[126] is not liable under the accessory liability principle—a conclusion which the Privy Council considered could not be right. What matters is the state of mind of the third party sought to be made liable, not the state of mind of the trustee.

In *Royal Brunei Airlines Sdn Bhd v Tan*[127] the Privy Council took the opportunity to review the law on what it preferred to call the accessory liability principle, and the judgment of the Board delivered by Lord Nicholls was treated by the House of Lords in *Twinsectra Ltd v Yardley*[128] as correctly stating the law. It may be noted that in so far as a stranger who does not receive the trust property is made liable as a constructive trustee there is an anomaly, for on general principles in order for a person to be a trustee there must be trust property vested in him.[129] As previously explained[130]

---

[123] (1874) 9 Ch App 244, CA.

[124] [1995] 2 AC 378, [1995] 3 All ER 97, PC (where the relevant New Zealand cases are referred to); *Balfron Trustees Ltd v Peterson* [2002] Lloyd's PN 1. See also *Barlow Clowes International Ltd v Eurotrust International Ltd* [2004] WTLR 1365 (Isle of Man HC). For the Canadian approach see *Air Canada v M & L Travel Ltd* (1994) 108 DLR (4th) 592, and (1995) 74 CBR 29 (T Allen).

[125] [1979] Ch 250, [1979] 1 All ER 118, CA.

[126] The trustee himself is, of course, liable for a breach of trust, even though innocent—see chapter 24, section 1(a), infra, p 520.

[127] Supra, PC, noted [1995] CLJ 305 (R Nolan); (1995) 111 LQR 545 (C Harpum); (1995) 92/28 LSG 20 (J Snape and G Watt); (1995) 9 Tru LI 102 (G McCormack); 1996 LMCLQ 1 (P Birks); (1996) 112 LQR 56 (S Gardner); (1996) 140 Sol Jo 156 (Jill Martin); All ER Rev 1995, 323 (P J Clarke); (1996) 30 L Teach 111 (G Ferris); (1996) 59 MLR 443 (A Berg); 1995 RLR 105 (J Stevens). See, generally, (2004) 67 MLR 16 (S B Elliott and C Mitchell), who argue that dishonest assistance yields a duplicative secondary liability comparable to secondary criminal liability.

[128] [2002] 2 All ER 377, HL (though Lord Millett differed from the majority as to its interpretation), noted (2002) 118 LQR 502 (T M Yeo and H Tjio). See (2003) 44 T & ELJ 3 (J McDonnell).

[129] This was said by Lord Browne-Wilkinson in *Westdeutsche Landesbank Girozentrale v Islington London Borough Council* [1996] 2 All ER 961, HL, at 988 to be the only apparent exception to the general principle. See (1977) 28 NILQ 123 (R H Maudsley).

[130] See p 67, supra.

though traditionally referred to as constructive trust it is not really a case of trust at all but one of personal accountability.

Lord Nicholls said that different considerations apply to cases of knowing receipt and accessory liability: the former is restitution based while the latter is not. In relation to accessory liability, with which alone the case was concerned, he dismissed out of hand on the one hand the possibility that a third party who does not receive trust property ought never to be liable directly to the beneficiaries merely because he assisted the trustee to commit a breach of trust or procured him to do so, and, on the other hand, that there is liability where a third party deals with a trustee without knowing, or having any reason to suspect, that he is a trustee, or, being aware that he is a trustee, has no reason to know or suspect that the transaction in question is inconsistent with the terms of the trust. Accepting, therefore, that in some circumstances a third party may be liable directly to a beneficiary Lord Nicholls went on to identify the touchstone of liability which, he said, was dishonesty or lack of probity, which is synonymous. The term 'unconscionable' is, he added, better avoided in this context. Dishonesty means simply not acting as an honest person would in the circumstances, which is an objective standard, even though there is a subjective element in that conduct is assessed in the light of what a person actually knew at the time, as distinct from what a reasonable person would have known or appreciated. For the most part it is to be equated with conscious impropriety.[131] 'Nelsonian blindness' to the facts can also found liability, because honest people do not close their minds to obvious indications of improper conduct which come to their attention. Nor do they refrain from asking pertinent questions for fear of gaining actual knowledge of the suspected unpalatable truth. When called upon to decide whether a person was acting honestly, a court will look at all the circumstances known to the third party at the time. The court will also have regard to personal attributes of the third party such as his experience and intelligence, and the reason why he acted as he did. Acting in reckless disregard of others' rights or possible rights can be a tell-tale sign of dishonesty. The standard of proof of dishonesty, although not so high as the criminal standard, involves a high level of probability. An objective test of whether the defendant ought, as a reasonable businessman, to have appreciated the presence of fraud is not sufficient.[132]

Lord Nicholls summarized the overall conclusion of the Board as follows:

. . . dishonesty is a necessary ingredient of accessory liability. It is also a sufficient ingredient. A liability in equity to make good resulting loss attaches to a person who dishonestly procures or assists in a breach of trust or fiduciary obligation.[133] It is not necessary that, in

---

[131] See *Cowan de Groot Properties Ltd v Eagle Trust plc* [1992] 4 All ER 700 at 761.

[132] *Heinl v Jyske Bank (Gibraltar) Ltd* [1999] 34 LS Gaz R 33, CA.

[133] Note, however, that in *Brown v Bennett* [1998] 2 BCLC 97, noted (1998) 114 LQR 357 (R B Grantham and C E F Rickett), Rattee J seemed to think that this head of liability was restricted to a breach of trust in relation to property, a breach of duty in relation to management not being sufficient. On appeal, [1999] 1 BCLC 649, CA, it was not necessary to decide the matter, which was said to be an arguable point. The Court of Appeal left it open in *Goose v Wilson Sandford & Co (a firm)* (2000), unreported, but cited in *Gencor ACP Ltd v Dalby* [2000] 2 BCLC 734. See also (2001) 117 LQR (C Mitchell).

addition, the trustee or fiduciary was acting dishonestly, although this will usually be so where the third party who is assisting him is acting dishonestly. 'Knowingly' is better avoided as a defining ingredient of the principle, and in the context of this principle the *Baden*[134] scale of knowledge is best forgotten.[135]

It is not necessary, however, to show a precise causal link between the assistance and the loss.[136]

In *Twinsectra Ltd v Yardley*[137] the House of Lords had to examine the meaning of the term 'dishonesty'. The majority view was most fully explained by Lord Hutton, who observed that the courts often draw a distinction between subjective dishonesty and objective dishonesty. There are, he said, three possible standards which can be applied. There is the purely subjective standard, whereby a person is only regarded as dishonest if he transgresses his own standard of honesty, even if that standard is contrary to that of reasonable and honest people. This standard has been rejected by the courts. Secondly, there is a purely objective standard whereby a person acts dishonestly if his conduct is dishonest by the ordinary standards of reasonable and honest people, even if he does not realize this. Thirdly, there is a standard which combines an objective and a subjective test, and which requires that before there can be a finding of dishonesty it must be established that the defendant's conduct was dishonest by the ordinary standards of reasonable and honest people and that he himself realized that by those standards his conduct was dishonest. This 'combined test' was held to be the correct one. It was thought to be less than just for the law to permit a finding that a defendant had been 'dishonest' in assisting in a breach of trust where he knew of the facts which created the trust and its breach but had not been aware that what he was doing would be regarded by honest men as being dishonest.

In a powerful speech dissenting on this issue Lord Millett said that the question was not whether Lord Nicholls had used the word 'dishonesty' in a subjective or objective sense in the *Royal Brunei* case, but whether a plaintiff should be required to establish

---

134 *Baden v Société Générale pour Favouriser le Développment du Commerce et de l'Industrie en France SA* [1992] 4 All ER 161: see pp 155, 156, supra.

135 But this, S Gardner says ((1996) 112 LQR 56) cannot be right. An assessment of whether a certain action is dishonest requires reference to what the defendant knew as he performed it. And in *Bank of Credit and Commerce International (Overseas) Ltd (in liquidation) v Akindele* [2000] 4 All ER 221, CA at 235 Nourse LJ expressed the view that the categorization in *Baden* is often helpful in identifying different states of knowledge which may or may not result in a finding of dishonesty for the purposes of knowing assistance.

136 *Casio Computer Ltd v Sayo* [2001] EWCA Civ 661, unrep, at [15]; (2004) 67 MLR 16 (S B Elliott and C Mitchell).

137 [2002] 2 All ER 377, HL, noted [2002] Conv 387 (M P Thompson); (2002) 146 Sol Jo 472 (M Pooles and S Charlwood); [2002] CLJ 524 (Rosy Thornton); (2002) 36 T & ELJ 4 (J R Martyn); (2002) 16 Tru LI 223 (J Glister); [2002] RLR 112 (C Rickett); [2003] Conv 398 (Georgina Andrews). See also *Bank of Scotland v A Ltd* [2001] EWCA Civ 52, [2001] 3 All ER 58; US *International Marketing Ltd v National Bank of New Zealand*, 28 Oct 2003, unrep, discussed (2004) 120 LQR 208 (T M Yeo). In New Zealand opposing views have been expressed as to bringing back a subjective knowledge requirement: see [2004] NZLJ 454 (J V Ormsby, Wynn Williams & Co) and 456 (C Cato).

that an accessory to a breach of trust had a dishonest state of mind;[138] or whether it should be sufficient to establish that he acted with the requisite knowledge (so that his conduct was objectively dishonest). Lord Millett preferred the objective approach which, he said, accords with traditional doctrine. Consciousness of wrongdoing is an aspect of mens rea and an appropriate condition of criminal liability, but not of civil liability. For the purpose of civil liability it should not be necessary that the defendant realized that his conduct was dishonest; it should be sufficient that it constituted intentional wrongdoing. As to the knowledge required, in his opinion knowledge of the arrangements which constitute the trust is sufficient; it is not necessary that the defendant should appreciate that they do. The gravamen of the charge against the accessory is that he is assisting a person who has been entrusted with the control of a fund to dispose of the fund in an unauthorized manner. He should be liable if he knows of the arrangements by which that person obtained control of the money and that his authority to deal with the money was limited, and participates in a dealing with the money in a manner which he knows to be unauthorized. 'Knowing assistance', as he would prefer to call it, is the equitable counterpoint of the tort of wrongful interference with the performance of a contract, where liability depends on knowledge and dishonesty is not required.

It may be added that it may not be a prerequisite of liability for 'knowing assistance' that any property should have been received or handled by the defendant. Without deciding, the Court of Appeal referred to the issue whether the dishonest breach of trust in which the defendant assisted must have involved the misapplication of trust property or its proceeds of sale, and did not rule out the possibility of a claim in its absence.[139]

(e) POSSESSION BY AN AGENT OF TRUSTEES

The question has often arisen as to whether an agent of trustees, such as a solicitor, banker or broker, has himself become a constructive trustee of trust property which has come into his hands. It is clear that in this context such an agent is a stranger to the trust, and the principles applicable to cases of knowing receipt and dealing[140] have been formulated in terms to cover the special case. In *Lee v Sankey*,[141] Bacon VC said:

It is well established by many decisions, that a mere agent of trustees is answerable only to

---

[138] Ie so that he was subjectively dishonest in the sense used in *R v Ghosh* [1982] QB 1053, [1982] 2 All ER 689, CA. Note that in the *Royal Brunei* case, supra, PC, Lord Nicholls said, at 389, 106, 'If a person knowingly appropriates another's property, he will not escape a finding of dishonesty simply because he sees nothing wrong in such behaviour.'

[139] *Goose v Wilson Sandford & Co* [2001] Lloyd's Rep PN 189, CA.

[140] See [1991] LMCLQ 356 (Y C Tan). It is perhaps arguable that an agent in some respects may be in a different position from other strangers—*Carl Zeiss-Stiftung v Herbert Smith & Co (No 2)* [1969] 2 Ch 276 at 299, [1969] 2 All ER 367 at 380 per Sachs LJ, CA.

[141] (1872) LR 15 Eq 204; *Lord Napier and Ettrick v R F Kershaw Ltd* [1993] 1 Lloyd's Rep 10, CA, noted [1993] Conv 391 (Alison Jones); [1993] 143 NLJ 1061 (Jill Martin). This point was not discussed on appeal [1993] AC 713, [1993] 1 All ER 385, HL.

his principal and not to cestuis que trust in respect of trust moneys coming to his hands merely in his character of agent, But it is also not less clearly established that a person who received into his hands trust moneys, and who deals with them in a manner inconsistent with the performance of trusts of which he is cognisant, is personally liable for the consequences which may ensue upon his so dealing.

In other words[142] 'an agent in possession of money which he knows to be trust money, so long as he acts honestly, is not accountable to the beneficiaries interested in the trust money unless he intermeddles in the trust by doing acts characteristic of a trustee and outside the duties of an agent.' On the one hand, in *Mara v Browne*[143] trustees employed a solicitor who advised improper investments, which were actually carried through by him on being paid trust moneys for the purpose. It was held that the solicitor had acted only in his character of solicitor to the trustees and that consequently he was not liable as a constructive trustee in the sense of a trustee de son tort.[144] Of course if he had acted dishonestly he would have become accountable as a constructive trustee, or, in Lord Millett's preferred phrase,[145] 'accountable in equity', and his firm would have been vicariously liable. And even in the absence of dishonesty a claim brought in due time against the solicitor for negligence in advising an improper investment would probably have succeeded, but at the time of the action such a claim, unlike a claim for breach of trust, would have been statute barred.

On the other hand, in *Lee v Sankey*[146] trustees of a will employed solicitors to receive the proceeds of the sale of their testator's real estate. The solicitors improperly paid over the proceeds of sale to one only of the trustees, who subsequently became bankrupt, without the receipt or authority of the other. It was held that the solicitors were liable to make good the loss to the trust estate which accrued.

The law is reluctant to make a mere agent a constructive trustee. There must be a want of probity. As Sachs LJ said in *Carl-Zeiss-Stiftung v Herbert Smith (No 2)*,[147] 'professional men and agents who have received moneys as such and have acted bona fide are accountable only to their principals unless dishonesty as well as cognisance of trusts is established against them'. Accordingly mere notice of a claim asserted by a third party is insufficient to render the agent guilty of a wrongful act in dealing with property derived from his principal in accordance with the latter's instructions unless the agent knows that the third party's claim is well founded and that the principal

---

[142] In *Williams-Ashman v Price* [1942] Ch 219 at 228, [1942] 1 All ER 310 per Bennett J at 313, citing *Mara v Browne* [1896] 1 Ch 199, CA.

[143] Supra. See also *Barnes v Addy* (1874) 9 Ch App 244; *Re Blundell* (1888) 40 Ch D 370; *Goddard v DFC New Zealand Ltd* [1991] 3 NZLR 580. Also contrast *Bridgman v Gill* (1857) 24 Beav 302, with *Thomson v Clydesdale Bank Ltd* [1893] AC 282, HL, and *Coleman v Bucks and Oxon Union Bank* [1897] 2 Ch 243, a rather surprising decision on the facts.

[144] See pp 151, 152, supra.

[145] *Dubai Aluminium Co Ltd v Salaam* [2002] UKHL 48, [2003] 1 All ER 97 at 131, where he also said that *Re Bell's Indenture* [1980] 3 All ER 425 should be overruled. See (2002) 153 NLJ 405 (J Mitchell).

[146] (1873) LR 15 Eq 204.

[147] Supra, CA, at 380. See also *Eagle Trust plc v SBC Securities Ltd* [1992] 4 All ER 488, [1993] 1 WLR 484 (the order was set aside in the Court of Appeal and the plaintiff was given liberty to amend the writ and statement of claim: [1993] 1 WLR 508); *Winslow v Richter* (1989) 61 DLR (4th) 549.

accordingly had no authority to give such instructions.[148] And it has been held that banks do not become constructive trustees merely because they entertain suspicions as to the provenance of money deposited with them.[149]

4 THE VENDOR UNDER A CONTRACT FOR THE SALE OF LAND

Numerous cases[150] from the middle of the seventeenth century onwards establish[151] the general proposition that where there is a contract for the sale of land[152] the purchaser becomes the owner in equity of the land or, as Lord Hardwicke put it,[153] the rule is 'that the vendor of the estate is from the time of his contract, considered as a trustee for the purchasers'.[154] There are, however, difficulties, some of which are due to the fact that the nature of the trust and the duties of the vendor as trustee may undergo important changes. When the purchaser has paid the purchase price in full and has no other obligation to perform under the contract, the vendor is a trustee without qualification, a naked, bare, or mere trustee,[155] but until that state has been reached, he 'is only a trustee in a modified sense',[156] a 'quasi-trustee',[157] or as Jessel MR put it,[158] 'He is certainly a trustee for the purchaser, a trustee, no doubt, with peculiar duties and liabilities, for it is a fallacy to suppose that every trustee has the same duties and liabilities; but he is a trustee.'

[148] *Carl-Zeiss-Stiftung v Herbert Smith (No 2)*, supra, CA.

[149] *A Bank v A Ltd* (2000) *Times*, 18 July.

[150] See (1960) 24 Conv 47 (P H Pettit); [1984] Conv 43 (M P Thompson); [1987] Ox JLS 60 (S Gardner).

[151] The only dissenting voice seems to be that of Brett LJ in *Rayner v Preston* (1881) 18 Ch D 1, CA.

[152] Or other property where the contract is specifically enforceable—see *Neville v Wilson* [1997] Ch 144, [1996] 3 All ER 171, CA; *Michaels v Harley House (Marylebone) Ltd* [2000] Ch 404, [1999] 1 All ER 356, CA.

[153] *Green v Smith* (1738) 1 Atk 572 at 573. The purchaser's equitable interest is not destroyed if the vendor is a company which is placed in receivership by a debenture holder: *Freevale Ltd v Metrostore (Holdings) Ltd* [1984] Ch 199, [1984] 1 All ER 495, discussed [1984] Conv 446 (D Milman and S Coneys). See *Property Discount Corpn Ltd v Lyon Group Ltd* [1980] 1 All ER 334 at 330, per Goulding J; affd [1981] 1 All ER 379, [1981] 1 WLR 300, CA.

[154] See chapter 31, section 2(b), p 733. The proposition seems not to apply to the grantor of an option: see (1984) 43 CLJ 55 (S Tromans).

[155] Such a trust has no existence except as the equitable consequence of the contract, with potentially fatal results if the contract was registrable under s 4(6) of the Land Charges Act 1972: *Lloyds Bank plc v Carrick* [1996] 4 All ER 630, CA, noted [1996–97] KCLJ 117 (Theresa Villiers); [1997] CLJ 32 (Nika Oldham); (1998) 61 MLR 486 (N Hopkins).

[156] *Royal Bristol Permanent Building Society v Bomash* (1887) 35 Ch D 390 at 397 per Kekewich J.

[157] *Cumberland Consolidated Holdings Ltd v Ireland* [1946] KB 264 at 269, [1946] 1 All ER 284 at 286, per Lord Greene MR giving the judgment of the Court of Appeal.

[158] In *Earl of Egmont v Smith* (1877) 6 Ch D 469 at 475; *Berkley v Poulett* [1977] 1 EGLR 86, CA, per Stamp LJ at 93.

The reason for the special position of the vendor-trustee is given by Lord Cairns in *Shaw v Foster*.[159] The vendor-trustee, he explained, 'was not a mere dormant trustee, he was a trustee having a personal and substantial interest in the property, a right to protect that interest, and an active right to assert that interest if anything should be done in derogation of it. The relation, therefore, of trustee and cestui que trust subsisted, but subsisted subject to the paramount right of the vendor and trustee to protect his own interest as vendor of the property.' For a full discussion of the special position of a vendor-trustee, reference should be made to works on vendor and purchaser;[160] for present purposes it is sufficient to observe by way of illustration that, on the one hand, like any other trustee, he is under a duty to use reasonable care to maintain the property in a reasonable state of preservation,[161] though, by way of qualification, he will be under no liability to the purchaser for neglect or even misfeasance if the contract ultimately goes off.[162] Further, a vendor who, after entering into a contract for the sale of property, sold that property to another person for valuable consideration, has been held accountable as a trustee to the original purchaser for the proceeds of sale.[163] And if the vendor has made a planning application he may be under an obligation not to withdraw it without the consent of the purchaser.[164] On the other hand, by way of contrast with an ordinary trustee the vendor-trustee is entitled to retain for his own benefit the rents and profits until the date fixed for completion, and is entitled to retain possession of the property until the contract is completed by payment of the purchase price.

It may be added that a property adjustment order in ancillary proceedings pursuant to the Matrimonial Causes Act 1973, s 24(1)(a) ordering a husband to transfer his interest in the matrimonial home to his wife likewise confers an equitable interest in the property on her conditional only upon the making of the decree absolute.[165]

---

[159] (1872) LR 5 HL 321 at 339. See also *Bunny Industries Ltd v FSW Enterprises Pty Ltd* [1982] Qd R 712 where this discussion is referred to; *Jerome v Kelly* [2004] UK HL 25, [2004] 2 All ER 935, Per Lord Walker at [30]–[32].

[160] Eg Emmet on *Title*, 19th edn, Chapter 6; (1959) 23 Conv 173 (V G Wellings). See also Law Com No 191, which recommends that this trust should remain unaltered. See also *Englewood Properties Ltd v Patel* [2005] EWHC 188 (Ch), [2005] 3 All ER 307; *Bevin v Smith* [1994] 3 NZLR 648.

[161] See eg *Cumberland Consolidation Holdings Ltd v Ireland*, supra, CA; *Phillips v Lamdin* [1949] 2 KB 33, [1949] 1 All ER 770. See also [1995] Cambrian LR 33 (A Dowling).

[162] *Plews v Samuel* [1904] 1 Ch 464.

[163] *Lake v Bayliss* [1974] 2 All ER 1114, noted (1974) 38 Conv 357 (F R Crane).

[164] *Sinclair-Hill v Sothcott* (1973) 26 P & CR 490, doubted *Englewood Properties Ltd v Patel*, supra.

[165] *Mountney v Treharne* [2002] EWCA Civ 1174, [2002] 3 WLR 1760.

5 UNDERTAKING BY PURCHASER

In *Binions v Evans*[166] the Tredegar Estate entered into an agreement with the defend-ant, the widow of a former employee, that she should be permitted to reside in a specified cottage rent free for the remainder of her life or until she determined the arrangement by four weeks notice. The Estate subsequently sold the cottage to the plaintiffs expressly subject to the agreement and because of that provision at a reduced price. Some months later the plaintiffs brought proceedings for possession against the defendant. The majority of the Court of Appeal held that the effect of the agreement was to make the defendant a tenant for life under the Settled Land Act and the plaintiff accordingly bound by her interest. Lord Denning MR did not agree. He thought—wrongly, as it has now been held[167]—that she had from the outset a licence conferring an equitable interest in the land but, on the hypothesis that this was not so, said that on the sale at a reduced price 'subject to' the defendant's rights the court would 'impose on the purchaser a constructive trust for her benefit, for the simple reason that it would be utterly inequitable for the purchaser to turn the widow out contrary to the stipulation subject to which he took the premises'.

It is now clear that Lord Denning went too far when he said that a constructive trust would be imposed whenever the owner of land sells it to a purchaser and at the same time stipulates that he shall take it 'subject to' a contractual licence. While taking this view in *Ashburn Anstalt v Arnold*,[168] the Court of Appeal was equally clear that the facts of *Binions v Evans*[169] did give rise to a constructive trust. In the circumstances it was a proper inference that on the sale to the plaintiffs, the intention of the Estate and the plaintiffs was that the plaintiffs should give effect to the tenancy agreement. If they had failed to do so, the Estate would have been liable to damages to the defendant.

In *Lyus v Prowsa Developments Ltd*[170] the plaintiff contracted with developers to buy a plot with a house to be built according to agreed specifications. Before the house was built or the contract completed the developers went into liquidation and the bank mortgagees, who were not bound by the plaintiff's contract and were accordingly in a position to sell free from it, sold to the first defendants. It was, however, a term of the

---

[166] [1972] Ch 359, [1972] 2 All ER 70, CA applied *DHN Food Distributors Ltd v London Borough of Tower Hamlets* [1976] 3 All ER 462, CA; *Lyus v Prowsa Developments Ltd* [1982] 2 All ER 953; [1983] 46 MLR 96 (P H Kenny); [1983] Conv 64 (Paul Jackson); *Ungurian v Lesnoff* [1990] Ch 206, [1989] 3 WLR 840, discussed [1990] Conv 223 (P Sparkes), (1991) 107 LQR 596 (J Hill), (1991) 5 Tru LI 12 (Bernadette Griffin); *Dent v Dent* [1996] 1 All ER 659, [1996] 1 WLR 683. *Binions v Evans* is discussed in (1972) 88 LQR 336 (P V Baker); (1973) 117 Sol Jo 23 (B W Harvey); (1972) 36 Conv 266 (Jill Martin); (1972) 36 Conv 277 (D J Hayton); (1975) 35 MLR 551 (A J Oakley); (1973) 32 CLJ 123 (R J Smith); (1977) 93 LQR 561 (J A Hornby). See also [1978] Conv 250; (2004) 120 LQR 667 (B McFarlane).

[167] See *Ashburn Anstalt v Arnold* [1989] Ch 1, [1988] 2 All ER 147, CA.

[168] [1989] Ch 1, [1988] 2 All ER 147, CA.   [169] [1972] Ch 359, [1972] 2 All ER 70, CA.

[170] [1982] 2 All ER 953 noted (1984) 47 MLR 476 (P Bennett). See [1985] CLJ 280 (M P Thompson); (1983) 80 LSG (Constance Whippman); [2000] Conv 398 (Susan Bright) and *Bahr v Nicolay (No 2)* (1988) 62 ALJR 268. The position may be affected by the Contracts (Rights of Third Parties) Act 1999.

contract that the property was sold subject to, but with the benefit of, the plaintiff's agreement. The first defendants resold to the second defendants, subject to the plaintiff's contract so far, if at all, as it may have been enforceable against the first defendants. The plaintiff successfully contended that the 'subject to' clause imposed a constructive trust on the first defendants and it was admitted that if this was so the second defendants were similarly bound.[171] In approving this decision in *Ashburn Anstalt v Arnold*[172] the Court of Appeal observed that there was no point in making the conveyance subject to the contract unless the parties intended the purchaser to give effect to it. Further, on the sale by the bank, a letter had been written to the bank's agents by the first defendant's solicitors, giving an assurance that their client would take reasonable steps to make sure the interests of contractual purchasers were dealt with quickly and to their satisfaction. But there is no rule that the sale of land 'subject to' a contractual licence automatically gives rise to a constructive trust, rather the reverse. To establish a constructive trust very special circumstances must be proved showing that the transferee of the property undertook a new liability to give effect to provisions for the benefit of third parties. It is the conscience of the transferee which has to be affected and it has to be affected in a way which gives rise to an obligation to meet the legitimate expectations of the third party.[173] It has been suggested[174] that if a 'subject to' clause does create a trust the true analysis is that it arises because that is what the parties intended. It is therefore not a constructive trust at all, but rather an express trust.

6 EXECUTOR DE SON TORT

An executor de son tort is one who, without due authority, takes possession of or intermeddles with the property of a deceased person. Such a person may be, but is not necessarily, a constructive trustee.[175] There would appear to be no justification for imposing a constructive trust where the executor de son tort is a complete stranger, save in the most exceptional circumstances. But where, for instance, a widow enters into possession as executrix de son tort and seeks to establish title by adverse posses-

---

[171] Quaere whether this admission was rightly made. The way in which Dillon J distinguished *Miles v Bull (No 2)* [1969] 3 All ER 1585 is unconvincing vis-a-vis the second defendant. See (1983) 80 LSG 1783 (Constance Whippman) asking what was the fraud or unconscionable conduct on the part of the second defendant, and drawing attention to the failure to refer to the Land Registration Act 1925, ss 59(6) and 74 (both now repealed). The apparent force of s 74 is reduced by the decision in *Williams & Glyn's Bank Ltd v Boland* [1981] AC 487, [1980] 2 All ER 408, HL.

[172] [1989] Ch 1, [1988] 2 All ER 147, CA. See (1990) 20 VUWLR 23 (B Davies).

[173] *IDC Group Ltd v Clark* [1992] 1 EGLR 187; *Lloyd v Dugdale* [2001] EWCA Civ 1754, [2002] WTLR 863 noted [2002] Conv 584 (M Dixon).

[174] (1983) 133 NLJ 798 (C T Emery & B Smythe).

[175] See the full discussion in [1974] Conv 176 (F Hinks).

sion against her adult children, it would be quite a different matter. In *James v Williams*,[176] where it has been pointed out[177] that the contrary Court of Appeal decision in *Pollard v Jackson*[178] was not cited, the intestate died leaving three adult children. No letters of administration were taken out, but William, one of the children, took it upon himself to take possession of the property as if he owned it. Nearly 24 years after the intestate's death William himself was dead and the defendant claimed title to the property through him. One of the other children commenced proceedings against the defendant contending that she was entitled to a one-third share in the property. The defence was based on the Limitation Act 1980 which provides for a 12-year limitation period in an action to recover any land. The defence failed on the ground that on the facts William had been a constructive trustee of the property, and the plaintiff's claim was accordingly not barred by the Act.[179]

[176] [2000] Ch 1, [1999] 3 All ER 309, CA.
[177] By N Asprey in (2000) 20 T & ELJ 19; (2000) 150 NLJ 942 (G Miller).
[178] (1993) 67 P & CR 327, CA.
[179] By s 21(1) of the 1980 Act no limitation period applies to an action by a beneficiary under a trust to recover trust property in possession of the trustee or previously received by the trustee and converted to his use. See p 538 et seq, infra.

9

RESULTING TRUSTS

1 FAILURE TO DISPOSE OF THE EQUITABLE INTEREST

(a) THE PRINCIPLE INVOLVED

'Equity', it has been said,[1] 'abhors a beneficial vacuum.' Accordingly, where a settlor conveys or transfers property to trustees, but fails to declare the trusts upon which it is to be held; or where the expressed trusts fail altogether on the ground,[2] for instance, of uncertainty, or non-compliance with statutory requirements as to writing;[3] or where they fail partially on similar grounds, or because the trusts expressed only dispose of a part of the equitable interest; in any such case the entire equitable interest, or such part thereof as has not been effectively disposed of, remains vested in the settlor or, in technical language, is said to result to him, and the property is accordingly said to be held by the trustees upon a resulting trust for him.[4] Ex hypothesi in these cases the transfer is on trust, and accordingly the resulting trust does not establish the trust but merely carries back to the transferor the beneficial interest that has not been disposed of. The same principle applies to a devise or bequest by a testator to trustees upon trusts which fail similarly either altogether or in part, when the trustees will hold on a resulting trust, wholly or pro tanto, for the persons entitled to residue, or, if the gift which fails is a gift of residue, or if there is no residuary gift, then for the persons entitled on intestacy.[5] We have, indeed, already come across an application of the principle in connection with alleged half-secret trusts which have not been

---

[1] *Vandervell v IRC* [1966] Ch 261 at 291, [1965] 2 All ER 37 at 46, CA, per Diplock LJ. Contrast dicta in *Wood Preservation Ltd v Prior* [1969] 1 All ER 364, CA, esp, per Lord Donovan, at 367 and in *Conservative and Unionist Central Office v Burrell* [1980] 3 All ER 42 at 61 et seq, per Vinelott J; affd [1982] 2 All ER 1, CA. See, generally, (1999) 25 Mon LR 110 (J Glover).

[2] The special considerations which apply where the trusts fail on the ground of illegality, or because they offend against public policy, are discussed in chapter 11, p 217, infra.

[3] *Hodgson v Marks* [1971] Ch 892, [1971] 2 All ER 684, CA.   [4] Or, if he is dead, for his estate.

[5] See eg *Morice v Bishop of Durham* (1805) 10 Ves 522; *Chichester Diocesan Fund v Simpson* [1944] AC 341, [1944] 2 All ER 60, HL.

established.[6] Another illustration is where there has been a marriage settlement in contemplation of a particular marriage and the contract to marry has been 'definitely and absolutely put an end to';[7] the trustees of the settlement will in such a case hold the property on a resulting trust for the person who put the property into the settlement. And the same result has been reached where a decree of nullity has been pronounced.[8]

Of a very different character is the so-called '*Quistclose* trust'.[9] In that case Rolls Razor Ltd had not got the funds to pay the dividend which it had declared. Quistclose agreed to lend the necessary money, nearly £210,000, on condition 'that it is used to pay the forthcoming dividend due on July 24 next'. A cheque for the exact amount was handed over and paid into a separate account at Barclays Bank with whom it was agreed the account would only be used to meet the dividend due on July 24. Before that date Rolls Razor went into liquidation and the dividend could no longer lawfully be paid. Barclays sought to set the sum in the separate account against Rolls Razor's overdraft. It was decided that that money was held on trust for Quistclose. The fact that the contract between Quistclose and Rolls Razor was one of loan did not prevent a trust from arising.[10] Moreover Barclays had notice that the money was trust money and not part of the assets of Rolls Razor, and was accordingly bound by the trust.

Dicta of Lord Wilberforce in the *Quistclose* case[11] suggested that there were two successive trusts, a primary trust for payment to identifiable beneficiaries, such as

---

[6] See eg *Johnson v Ball* (1851) 5 De G & Sm 85; *Re Keen* [1937] Ch 236, [1937] 1 All ER 452, CA. The result is the same in a fully-secret trust if the apparent beneficiary admits that he is or is proved to be a mere trustee— *Re Boyes* (1884) 26 Ch D 531.

[7] Per Pearson J in *Essery v Cowlard* (1884) 26 Ch D 191 at 193. In this case the parties had in fact lived together without marriage and had had three children; *Bond v Walford* (1886) 32 Ch D 238. For a case where no trusts were sufficiently declared see *Re Wilcock* (1890) 62 LT 317. Cf *Burgess v Rawnsley* [1975] Ch 429, [1975] 3 All ER 142, CA.

[8] *Re Ames' Settlement* [1946] Ch 217, [1946] 1 All ER 689, considered by Lord Browne-Wilkinson in *Westdeutsche Landesbank Girozentrale v Islington London Borough Council* [1996] 2 All ER 961, HL, at 997–998. See also *Re d'Altroy's Will Trusts* [1968] 1 All ER 181, discussed in (1969) 32 MLR 210 (J Tiley); *Re Rodwell* [1970] Ch 726, [1969] 3 All ER 1363. But note the power of the Divorce Court under the Matrimonial Causes Act 1973, s 24. Section 16 of the Act now provides that a decree of nullity in respect of a voidable marriage shall end the marriage from the date of the decree absolute and not retrospectively.

[9] From *Barclays Bank Ltd v Quistclose Investments Ltd* [1970] AC 567, [1968], 3 All ER 651, HL, which was applied in *Re EVTR Ltd* [1987] BCLC 646, CA, discussed (1987) 131 Sol Jo 1439 (D W Fox); (1988) 85 LSG 36/14 (I M Hardcastle); *Lord v Australian Elizabethan Theatre Trust* (1991) 102 ALR 681, discussed (1992) 18 Mon LR 147 (Fiona Burns); *R v Common Professional Examination Board, ex p Mealing-McCleod* (2000) Times, 2 May, CA. But no trust in *Daly v Sydney Stock Exchange Ltd* (1986) 65 ALR 193, discussed (1987) 61 ALJ 241 (J G Starke), where no condition was imposed on the loan. Nor in *Re Miles* (1988) 85 ALR 216 where the *Quistclose* principle was said to be limited to cases involving the actual payment of money, by the party claiming to be the beneficiary of a resulting trust, for the purpose of discharge of debts by the payee, that purpose having failed. Also distinguished in *Peter Cox Investment Pty Ltd (in liquidation) v International Air Transport Association* (1999) 161 ALR 105. See also (1993) 23 QLSJ 145 (Tina Cockburn); [1992] Ox JLS 333 (M Bridge); [1994] Denning LJ 93 (G McCormack); *The Quistclose Trust: Critical Essays*, ed W Swadling.

[10] *Neste Oy v Lloyds Bank plc* [1983] 2 Lloyd's Rep 658; *Re E Dibbens & Sons Ltd (in liquidation)* [1990] BCLC 577. Normally payment by way of loan is inconsistent with the creation of a resulting trust. In *Hussey v Palmer* [1972] 3 All ER 744, CA, it is submitted that the view of Cairns LJ at 749 on this point is to be preferred to that of Phillimore LJ at 748. See (1973) 37 Conv 65 (D J Hayton).

[11] Supra, HL, at 580, 654–6.

creditors or shareholders, and a secondary trust in favour of the lender arising on the
failure of the primary trust. The matter was considered in some detail by Lord Millett
in *Twinsectra v Yardley*,[12] who pointed out several objections to this approach, in
particular that it could not apply to a trust for an abstract purpose. There was, he said,
no reason to make an arbitrary distinction between money paid for an abstract
purpose and money paid for a purpose which could be said to benefit an ascertained
class of beneficiaries. Other analyses were discussed and dismissed, and the conclusion
reached, it is submitted rightly, that in cases such as these the beneficial interest
remains throughout in the lender subject only to the borrower's power or duty to
apply the money in accordance with the lender's instructions. If the purpose fails, the
money is returnable to the lender, not under some new trust in his favour which only
comes into being on the failure of the purpose, but because the resulting trust in his
favour is no longer subject to any power on the part of the borrower to make use of
the money. In the latter case money was loaned to a firm of solicitors on an undertaking that the money would be retained by them until such time as it was applied in the
acquisition of property on behalf of Y and that it would be utilized solely for that
purpose. Money in a client account is held on trust, and the only question is as to the
terms of the trust. Here the solicitors held the money on a resulting trust for the
lender, but subject to a power to apply it towards the acquisition of property by Y in
accordance with the undertaking.

Where the expressed trusts are in part valid but do not exhaust the beneficial
interest there will be a resulting trust whether the expressed trusts are of a non-
charitable, or of a charitable nature, unless the terms of the trust expressly or by
implication exclude a resulting trust,[13] or, in the case of a charitable trust the cy-près
doctrine applies. A case involving a non-charitable trust was *Re the Trusts of the Abbott
Fund*,[14] in which a fund had been raised by subscription for the maintenance and
support of two distressed ladies. On the death of the survivor, a portion of the fund
remained unapplied in the hands of the trustees. It was held that there was a resulting
trust of the balance of the fund for the subscribers thereto. Again in *Re Gillingham Bus
Disaster Fund*,[15] following an accident in which a number of cadets were killed and
injured, a fund was raised by subscription for the benefit of the victims and then to
other worthy causes in memory of the boys who were killed. The trust for worthy
causes was void for uncertainty. Consequently it was held that the balance of the fund
not applied for the benefit of the victims was held on a resulting trust for the subscribers. It was further held in that case that the position was unaffected by the fact
that a large number of the subscribers, such as contributors to street collections, were,

---

[12] [2002] 2 All ER 377, HL, noted (2003) 119 LQR 8 (T M Yeo and H Tjio); (2002) 16 Tru LI 165
(N Richardson); (2002) 16 Tru LI 223 (J Glister). Though Lord Millett delivered a dissenting speech, there does
not seem to have been any disagreement on this point. His observations on *Quistclose* were, however, obiter.

[13] *Davis v Richards and Wallington Industries Ltd* [1991] 2 All ER 563, [1990] 1 WLR 1511.

[14] [1900] 2 Ch 326.

[15] [1958] Ch 300, [1958] 1 All ER 37; affd [1959] Ch 62, [1958] 2 All ER 749, CA, though the present point
did not arise on appeal.

as it was assumed, unascertainable, but the better view seems to be that where money is raised by means of entertainments, raffles and sweepstakes, or street collections, the donor parts with his money out and out, and there is no resulting trust.[16]

Another type of case in which there may be a resulting trust is where the provisions of a settlement fail to cover the events which in fact happen. In *Re Cochrane's Settlement Trusts*[17] there was a post-nuptial settlement in an unusual form. Husband and wife each brought property into the settlement, the beneficial limitations of which were that income was payable to the wife for life 'so long as she shall continue to reside with the husband' and after her death 'or the prior determination of the trust in her favour' to the husband for life with a gift over of capital, 'from and after the decease of the survivor of them'. The wife ceased to reside with the husband, who later died, leaving the wife surviving him. It was held that during the remainder of the life of the wife there were resulting trusts in favour of the estate of the husband and in favour of the wife of the income of their respective parts of the trust fund.

Where charitable trusts are declared which fail in whole or in part, there may likewise be a resulting trust though here, as already mentioned, it will often be ousted by the cy-près doctrine, which will be discussed later in connection with charitable trusts. In the absence of the requirements for the application of the cy-près doctrine, there has been held to be a resulting trust both in cases where the trust has failed altogether, and in cases where the court has had to deal with a surplus after the particular charitable purpose has come to an end. In *Re Ulverston and District New Hospital Building Trusts*[18] a fund was opened for the building of a new hospital, but the scheme became impracticable so that there was a total failure ab initio of the purpose of the fund. It was held that so far as money had been received from identifiable[19] sources there was a resulting trust for the subscribers. There will likewise be a resulting trust for the subscribers where there is a surplus after the particular charitable trust has been fulfilled,[20] and for the settlor or his representatives

---

[16] *Re West Sussex Constabulary's Widows, Children and Benevolent (1930) Fund Trusts* [1971] Ch 1, [1970] 1 All ER 544, criticized on another ground (1971) 87 LQR 466 (Michael Albery); and see (1958) 74 LQR 190, 489 (P S Atiyah); (1973) 37 Conv 126 (Penelope Pearce and A Samuels).

[17] [1955] Ch 309, [1955] 1 All ER 222. The resulting trust may, however be ousted by the doctrine of acceleration—*Re Flower's Settlement Trusts*, [1957] 1 All ER 462, CA; *Re Dawson's Settlement* [1966] 3 All ER 68—or the court may even, in a clear case, supply words to fill in a gap in the limitations with the result that there will be no place for a resulting trust—*Re Akeroyd's Settlement* [1893] 3 Ch 363, CA; *Re Cory* [1955] 2 All ER 630, [1955] 1 WLR 725.

[18] [1956] Ch 622, [1956] 3 All ER 164, CA. See also *Re University of London Medical Sciences Institute Fund* [1909] 2 Ch 1, CA.

[19] As to anonymous subscribers see the Charities Act 1993, s 14 and p 330, infra.

[20] *Re British Red Cross Balkan Fund* [1914] 2 Ch 419—the subscribers are entitled to the surplus rateably in proportion to their subscriptions. The actual decision is suspect as the objects would seem to have been charitable in which case the surplus should have been applied cy-près to some other charitable purpose: *Barlow Clowes International Ltd (in liquidation) v Vaughan* [1992] 4 All ER 22, CA. As to the cy-près doctrine see p 325 et seq, infra.

where a charitable trust for a limited period or a limited purpose has come to an end.[21]

(b) THE PRELIMINARY QUESTION OF CONSTRUCTION

In various circumstances where at first sight one might think that there was a resulting trust it has been held that on the true construction of the relevant documents a resulting trust does not arise.

(i) Donor/settlor parts with his money out and out without any intention of retaining any interest therein

If the settlor or donor has expressly, or by necessary implication, abandoned any beneficial interest in the property, there is no resulting trust, and the undisposed-of equitable interest[22] necessarily falls to the Crown as bona vacantia. This, according to the better view,[23] is the position in relation to money raised by means of street collections. The result is even clearer in the case of money raised by means of enter-tainments, raffles and sweepstakes. Here, as Goff J pointed out in *Re West Sussex Constabulary's Fund Trusts*[24] it is quite impossible to apply the doctrine of resulting trusts for two reasons. First the relationship is one of contract and not of trust. The purchaser pays his money as the price of what is offered and what he receives. His motive need not be to aid the cause at all. Secondly, there is in such cases no direct contribution to the fund at all. It is only the profit, if any, which is ultimately received, and there may even be none.

(ii) Defunct voluntary associations[25]

If a number of persons associate together for whatever purpose involving the acquisi-tion of cash or property of any magnitude, then for practical purposes some one or more persons have to act as treasurers or holders of the property; in any sophisticated association they will be trustees. Usually the association's affairs will be run by a committee, though in a small association the committee might comprise all the mem-bers. A trust deed may provide that the property is to be dealt with as directed by the committee, or in accordance with the rules. In all such cases, unless under the rules the property is to be devoted wholly to charity, or unless and to the extent that other trusts were declared, the only persons interested in the property are the members. In such a case if the association is dissolved the remaining assets are held on trust for the

---

[21] *Gibson v South American Stores (Gath & Chaves) Ltd* [1950] Ch 177, [1949] 2 All ER 985, CA; *Re Cooper's Conveyance Trusts* [1956] 3 All ER 28; *Bankes v Salisbury Diocesan Council* [1960] Ch 631, [1960] 2 All ER 372. See (1957) 21 Conv 213; and note the effect of the Perpetuities and Accumulations Act 1964, s 12.

[22] *Westdeutsche Landesbank Girozentrale v Islington London Borough Council* [1996] 2 All ER 961, HL, per Lord Browne-Wilkinson at 991.

[23] *Re West Sussex Constabulary's Widows, Children and Benevolent (1930) Fund Trusts* [1971] Ch 1, [1970] 1 All ER 544. See also, in a very different context, *Universe Tankships Inc of Monrovia v International Transport Workers' Federation* [1981] ICR 129, CA; revsd [1983] 1 AC 366, [1982] 2 All ER 67, HL.

[24] Supra.   [25] See generally (1981) 7 Mon LR 141 (A S Sievers).

members of the association at the date of dissolution equally, to the exclusion of any claim on behalf of the Crown as bona vacantia. Nor does it raise a case of resulting trust.[26]

The Crown will, however, be able to claim as bona vacantia any surplus after contractual claims have been met where a society becomes defunct or moribund by its members all dying or becoming so reduced in numbers that it is impossible either to continue the society or to dissolve it by instrument. And exceptionally as in *Cunnack v Edwards*[27] the combined effect of the rules of the society and statute may make a claim by the members impossible so that again the Crown will take the surplus as bona vacantia.

(iii) Gift subject to carrying out a particular trust

In some cases the court has to decide whether on the true construction of a will[28] there is a gift to a donee on trust, when any property not required to carry out the expressed trust will be held on a resulting trust for the testator's estate,[29] or whether there is a beneficial gift to a donee subject to carrying out some specified trust or obligation, in which case the donee will take beneficially any surplus remaining after the trust or obligation has been carried out.[30] Extrinsic evidence will not be admitted to show that someone who on the construction of the will is a mere trustee was intended by the testator to take beneficially.[31]

(iv) Trust for assistance of certain persons by stated means

In *Re Andrew's Trust*[32] a fund was subscribed for the education of the children of a deceased clergyman. When the children were all of age and their education had been

---

[26] *Re St Andrew's Allotment Association's Trusts* [1969] 1 All ER 147; *Re Sick and Funeral Society of St John's Sunday School Golcar* [1973] Ch 51, [1972] 2 All ER 439; *Re Bucks Constabulary Widows and Orphans Fund Friendly Society (No 2)* [1979] 1 All ER 623; *Re GKN Bolts & Nuts Ltd Sports & Social Club* [1982] 2 All ER 855. Contra, *Re West Sussex Constabulary's Widows, Children and Benevolent (1930) Fund Trusts*, supra. None of these cases appears to have been cited in either *Re Grant's Will Trusts* [1979] 3 All ER 359 or *Conservative and Unionist Central Office v Burrell* [1980] 3 All ER 42 where Vinelott J seems to say that on the basis of an implied contractual term subscribers (not, semble, current members) are entitled to the return of their subscriptions so far as not used for the purposes for which they were subscribed. This point was not discussed on appeal [1982] 2 All ER 1, CA, where the relationship between contributors and the treasurer was said to be one of mandate and agency. See also [1982] NZLJ 335 (C E F Rickett); [1983] Conv 150 (P Creighton); (1983) 133 NLJ 87 (C T Emery); [1983] Conv 315 (R Griffith); (1983) 127 Sol Jo 792 (G Holgate); [1987] Conv 415 (P St J Smart).

[27] [1896] 2 Ch 679, CA.

[28] The cases all seem to have arisen on wills, but there seems no reason why the same problem should not arise on an inter vivos disposition.

[29] This was the decision in *Re West* [1900] 1 Ch 84 and *Re Rees' Will Trusts* [1950] Ch 204, [1949] 2 All ER 1003, CA.

[30] This was the decision in *King v Denison* (1813) 1 Ves & B 260 and *Croome v Croome* (1888) 59 LT 582, CAS, affd (1889) 61 LT 814, HL.

[31] *Re Rees' Will Trusts*, supra, CA. Cf *Re Tyler's Fund Trusts* [1967] 3 All ER 389, [1967] 1 WLR 1262.

[32] [1905] 2 Ch 48; *Re Osoba* [1978] 2 All ER 1099; varied [1979] 2 All ER 393, CA. See [1978] 37 CLJ 219 (C E F Rickett).

completed, there remained a surplus. It was held that it should be divided equally among the children and not on a resulting trust for the subscribers. It is interesting to compare this case with the somewhat similar facts of *Re the Trusts of the Abbott Fund*[33] where it will be recalled it was held that there was a resulting trust for the subscribers. If a trust is constituted for the assistance of certain persons by certain stated means there is a sharp distinction between cases where the beneficiaries have died and cases where they are still living. If they are dead, as in *Re the Trusts of the Abbot Fund*,[34] the court is ready to hold that there is a resulting trust, for the major purpose of the trust can no longer in any sense be carried out. But if the beneficiaries are still living, the major purpose of providing help and benefit for the beneficiaries can still be carried out even after the stated means have all been accomplished, and so the court will be ready to treat the stated means as being merely indicative and not restrictive. Accordingly in *Re Andrew's Trust*[35] the fund was treated as having been subscribed for the benefit of the children generally, with particular reference to their education. Accordingly there was nothing to form the subject matter of a resulting trust.

(v) The rule in Lassence v Tierney[36]

Finally, mention should be made of the rule 'that if you find an absolute gift to a legatee in the first instance, and trusts are engrafted or imposed on that absolute interest which fail, either from lapse or invalidity or any other reason then the absolute gift takes effect so far as the trusts have failed to the exclusion of the residuary legatee or next of kin[37] as the case may be'.[38]

(c) PENSION FUND SURPLUSES

Pension fund schemes vary widely and the position with regard to any surplus depends on the terms of the scheme. In the most usual type of scheme the employee contributes a specified proportion of his salary and the employer's contribution is on a 'balance of cost' basis, that is, he has to contribute the sum required to bring the total contribution up to what is necessary to meet the funding level. In such a scheme if, on dissolution, there is a surplus it is not clear who is entitled to it. In *Re Courage Group's Pension Schemes*[39] Millett J was of the opinion that any surplus arises from past overfunding not by the employer and employees pro rata to their respective contributions, but by their employer alone to the full extent of its past contributions and only subject thereto by the employees. Writing extrajudicially[40] Vinelott J said

---

[33] [1900] 2 Ch 326. See p 170, supra.   [34] [1900] 2 Ch 326. See p 170, supra.   [35] Supra.

[36] (1849) 1 Mac & G 551, also known as the rule in *Hancock v Watson* [1902] AC 14, HL; *Watson v Holland* [1985] 1 All ER 290.

[37] Who could, of course, only claim on a resulting trust.

[38] Per Lord Davey in *Hancock v Watson* [1902] AC 14 at 22, HL.

[39] [1987] 1 All ER 528; *Wrightson Ltd v Fletcher Challenge Nominees Ltd* [2002] 2 NZLR 1, PC. See (2001) Tru LI 130 (N Davis).

[40] (1994) 8 Tru LI 35.

that Millett J in that case gave 'compelling reasons for the conclusion that in the case of a balance of cost scheme the surplus belongs to the employer'.[41]

In *Davis v Richards and Wallington Industries Ltd*[42] Scott J distinguished between the proportion of the fund derived from employees' contributions and the proportion attributable to the employer's contributions. It was held that, in so far as the surplus was derived from the employers' overpayments, there was a resulting trust for them. However a resulting trust was excluded in relation to the employees' contributions because it would lead to an unworkable result and it would conflict with the statutory provisions giving tax advantages to an approved scheme: in so far as the surplus was so derived, it devolved in the Crown as bona vacantia.[43]

2 TRANSFER INTO AND PURCHASE IN THE NAME OF ANOTHER AND RELATED CASES

(a) PURCHASE IN THE NAME OF ANOTHER OR IN THE JOINT NAMES OF THE PURCHASER AND ANOTHER

Whenever someone buys either real or personal property and has it conveyed or registered or otherwise put into the name of another, or of himself and another jointly, it is presumed that the other holds the property on trust for the person who has paid the purchase money. The classic statement of the law is to be found in the judgment of Eyre CB in *Dyer v Dyer*.[44]

The clear result of all the cases, without a single exception, is that the trust of a legal estate, whether freehold, copyhold, or leasehold; whether taken in the names of the purchasers and others jointly, or in the names of others without that of the purchaser; whether in one name or several; whether jointly or successive—results to the man who advances the purchase-money.[45]

Although *Dyer v Dyer*[46] refers only to interests in land, the principle has always

---

[41] But see s 37 of the Pensions Act 1995 providing safeguards to scheme members in relation to the payment of a surplus to the employer. See also *National Grid Co plc v Mayes* [2001] ICR 544, HL, noted [2001] 30 Ind LJ 318 (R Nobles).

[42] [1991] 2 All ER 563 noted [1990] Ind LJ 204 (R Nobles); [1991] Conv 366 (Jill Martin); [1992] Conv 41 (S Gardner); *Re UEB Industries Ltd Pension Plan* [1992] 1 NZLR 294; (1990) 4 TL & P 163 (Meryl Thomas); (1991) 5 TL & P 60 (R Ellison). See also *Re William Makin & Son Ltd* [1993] BCC 453, discussed (1996) 10 Tru LI 15 (Marina Milner); (2000) 14 Tru LI 66 (Lord Millett).

[43] A proportion of the fund derived from transfers from other schemes: this also devolved as bona vacantia.

[44] (1788) 2 Cox Eq Cas 92 at 93: cited with approval by Lord Upjohn in *Pettitt v Pettitt* [1970] AC 777, [1969] 2 All ER 385, HL.

[45] It has been held in Australia—*Little v Little* (1988) 15 NSWLR 43—that regard is to be had to contributions to the purchase money only, and not to incidental costs, fees, disbursements or the aggregate costs of the acquisition.

[46] *Supra.*

been treated as equally applicable to pure personalty.[47] The same principle governs analogous cases, as in *Re Howes*,[48] where a testatrix put £500 on deposit at a bank in the name of her niece.[49] She never informed the niece of what she had done, retained the deposit note and purported to dispose of the money by a codicil to her will. It was held that even though this was not strictly a purchase, the equitable principle gave rise to a resulting trust to the testatrix. It also applies in a similar way where there is a joint advance by two or more persons, but the conveyance or transfer is taken in the name of one only. For instance, if X advances £60,000 and Y advances £30,000 towards the purchase of property which is conveyed into the name of X alone, X will hold the property as to one-third on a resulting trust for Y.[50]

There is no need for the conveyance or other instrument of transfer to contain any reference to the fact that the purchase price has been paid by someone other than the transferee. Parol evidence is always admissible to establish who in fact advanced the money,[51] and this is so, even though the consideration is expressed to be paid by the nominal purchaser. The fact of the advance must, of course, be satisfactorily proved by evidence, which may, however, be circumstantial evidence, such as that the nominal purchaser had not the means to provide the purchase money.[52] Evidence must also show that the money was intended to be advanced by the person alleging the resulting trust in the character of purchaser: if the evidence merely established a loan of some or all the money used for the purchase, there would be no resulting trust and the person lending the money would be a mere creditor.[53] If the fact of the advance is established, absence of writing is immaterial, even in the case of land, since the statutory provisions as to writing expressly exclude the creation and operation of resulting, implied and constructive trusts.[54]

The resulting trust of a property purchased in the name of another, in the absence of contrary intention, arises once and for all at the date on which the property is acquired. Because of the liability assumed by the mortgagor in a case where moneys are borrowed by the mortgagor to be used in the purchase, the mortgagor is treated as having provided the proportion of the purchase price attributable to the moneys so borrowed. Subsequent payments of the mortgage instalments are not part of the purchase price already paid to the vendor, but are sums paid for dis-

---

[47] *The Venture* [1908] P 218, CA; *Re Policy No 6402 of the Scottish Equitable Life Assurance Society* [1902] 1 Ch 282; *Shephard v Cartwright* [1955] AC 431, [1954] 3 All ER 649, HL; *Bateman Television Ltd v Bateman and Thomas* [1971] NZLR 453, CA.

[48] (1905) 21 TLR 501; *Abrahams v Trustee of the Property of Abrahams* [1999] BPIR 637 (wife paid husband's share of informal lottery syndicate: presumption of resulting trust in respect of husband's share of winnings).

[49] She was not in loco parentis to the niece, so the presumption of advancement did not apply—see p 180 et seq, infra.

[50] *Diwell v Farnes* [1959] 2 All ER 379, CA; *Bull v Bull* [1955] 1 QB 234, [1955] 1 All ER 253, CA. The presumption is that if the contributions are equal they take jointly, but if their contributions are unequal they take as tenants in common in shares proportionate to their contributions.

[51] *Heard v Pilley* (1869) 4 Ch App 548.

[52] *Willis v Willis* (1740) 2 Atk 71; *Groves v Groves* (1829) 3 Y & J 163.

[53] *Aveling v Knipe* (1815) 19 Ves 441; *Carlton v Goodman* [2002] EWCA Civ 545, [2002] 2 FLR 259.

[54] Law of Property Act 1925, s 53(2) replacing the Statute of Frauds (1677), s 8.

charging the mortgagor's obligations under the mortgage.[55] Payment for subsequent improvements to the property will not increase the payer's interest under a resulting trust.[56]

An attempt was made in *Savage v Dunningham*[57] to extend the principle of *Dyer v Dyer*[58] to an informal flat-sharing arrangement where the tenancy agreement was in the name of the defendant, but the rent and other expenses were shared equally between the plaintiffs and the defendant. It was held that 'purchase money' does not include rent, and accordingly the sharing of the rent[59] did not establish a resulting trust in favour of the plaintiffs. Rent, unlike purchase money, is not paid for the acquisition of a capital asset, but for the use of property during the term.

The presumption of a resulting trust may also apply where the parties were at the relevant time husband and wife. Further discussion of this aspect of resulting trusts will be found at p 182 et seq below.

As to a claim that there is a resulting trust, which involves setting up a transaction which is fraudulent, illegal, or contrary to public policy, see chapter 11, sections 3 and 7, infra.

It must be remembered that if there is a specific declaration in the conveyance as to the parties' interests, this will prevail and, as was again stressed by Ward LJ in *Carlton v Goodman*,[60] it should be the invariable standard practice of conveyancers to ensure that such a declaration is inserted. Thus if a conveyance of property to X and Y were to contain an express declaration that the property is to be held by them as joint tenants, the fact that X may have paid all the mortgage instalments in respect of the property would not be relevant in determining how the property was held.[61]

---

[55] *Curley v Parkes* [2004] EWCA Civ 1515, unrep, noted [2005] Conv 79 (M J Dixon) expressing surprise that no claim was made on the basis of constructive trust.

[56] Unless there is a specific agreement to the contrary or, exceptionally, such an agreement can be inferred. See *Harwood v Harwood* [1991] 2 FLR 274, CA. As to improvements to matrimonial property, see p 200, infra. See (1994) 8 Tru LI 43 (P Matthews) arguing that all subsequent payments and contributions are irrelevant in considering the initial share in the property under a resulting trust.

[57] [1974] Ch 181, [1973] 3 All ER 429.   [58] Supra.

[59] A fortiori the sharing of the other expenses.

[60] [2002] EWCA Civ 545, [2002] 2 FLR 259. There, though the woman had had a relationship with the man (now deceased), they had never lived together. The deceased had provided the deposit and discharged all the payments on the property bought in their joint names. The woman's involvement in the purchase was limited to joining in the mortgage as the deceased did not have sufficient income to finance a mortgage by himself: the involvement was so circumscribed and temporary that it could not fairly be described as a contribution to the purchase price. She therefore held the legal estate on a resulting trust for the deceased's estate. If necessary so to find, there was a common intention that she should hold the house on trust solely for the benefit of the deceased. The same point had been made by Dillon LJ in *Walker v Hall* [1984] FLR 126, CA. See (1983) 127 Sol Jo 554 (D G Barnsley).

[61] *Grindal v Hooper* (1999) 144 Sol Jo LB 33.

(b) VOLUNTARY CONVEYANCE OR TRANSFER INTO THE NAME OF
    ANOTHER OR INTO THE JOINT NAMES OF THE GRANTOR AND
    ANOTHER

It is necessary to draw a distinction between land and pure personalty.

(i) As to land, the position is still curiously unsettled, not withstanding s 60(3) of the
Law of Property Act 1925, which provides:

In a voluntary conveyance a resulting trust for the grantor shall not be implied merely by
reason that the property is not expressed to be conveyed for the use or benefit of the grantee.

At first instance in *Lohia v Lohia*,[62] it was held that the effect of that section is that a
voluntary conveyance does not give rise to a presumption of a resulting trust. On
appeal, however, it was held to be unnecessary to decide the matter and the members
of the court preferred not to express a concluded view, so the 'knotty question'
remains unresolved.

(ii) As to pure personalty, it seems to be settled that on a transfer into the joint names
of the transferor and another, there is a presumption of a resulting trust for the
transferor. A clear example is *Re Vinogradoff*,[63] where a testatrix, during her lifetime,
had transferred an £800 War Loan into the joint names of herself and her infant
granddaughter aged four years. After the death of the testatrix, it was held that her
granddaughter held the War Loan on a resulting trust for the testatrix's estate. According to Lord Browne-Wilkinson[64] the resulting trust only comes into effect when the
transferee becomes aware of the circumstances giving rise to it, but a different view
has been expressed, extrajudicially, by Lord Millett.[65]

It also seems that there is a presumption of a resulting trust where there is a transfer
into the name of another alone.[66]

---

[62] [2001] WTLR 101 on appeal (2002) 16 Tru LI 231.

[63] [1935] WN 68. See also *Batstone v Salter* (1875) 10 Ch App 431; *Standing v Bowring* (1885) 31 Ch D 282,
CA; *Young v Sealey* [1949] Ch 278, [1949] 1 All ER 92.

[64] *Westdeutsche Landesbank Girozentrale v Islington London Borough Council* [1996] AC 669, [1996] 2 All
ER 961, HL.

[65] In Cornish et al (eds) *Restitution: Past, Present and Future*, 201. Also by W Swadling in (1998) 12 Tru
LI 228.

[66] *Crane v Davis* (1981) *Times*, 13 May; *Fowkes v Pascoe* (1875) 10 Ch App 343 at 348; *Vandervell v IRC*
[1967] 2 AC 291, [1967] 1 All ER 1, HL. See also *Seldon v Davidson* [1968] 2 All ER 755, CA, (not followed in
Australia: *Joaquin v Hall* [1976] VR 788), where it was held that a payment of money was prima facie a loan,
not a gift, in the absence of circumstances raising the presumption of advancement—as to which see infra,
p 180 et seq.

(c) REBUTTING THE PRESUMPTION OF A RESULTING TRUST

'Trusts', it has been said,[67] 'are neither created nor implied by law to defeat the intentions of donors or settlors; they are created or implied or are held to result in favour of donors or settlors in order to carry out and give effect to their true intentions, expressed or implied . . .' Accordingly, the presumed intention of a person who purchases property in the name of another whether alone or jointly, that that other shall be a bare trustee for him, will not prevail if evidence establishes that the true intention is otherwise. The same is true where there is a voluntary conveyance or transfer which gives rise to a presumption of a resulting trust. Even parol evidence[68] may suffice to establish that at the relevant time the true intention of the person who provided the purchase money or transferred the property was that the person into whose name the property was conveyed or transferred solely or jointly with his own should take some beneficial interest. The relevant time is, of course, the date of the purchase or transfer and if the evidence[69] establishes an intention at that time to make an absolute gift, the donor cannot subsequently change his mind and recall the property which he has had put in the then intended donee's name.[70]

It has been suggested[71] that, in the absence of any presumption of advancement, where a transfer or payment is made by mistake, or where there is a failure of consideration, the transferee holds the property on a resulting trust for the transferor, there being no positive evidence of donative intent. The better view,[72] however, seems to be that evidence of the mistake or failure of consideration is inconsistent with a presumed intention that the transferee is to be a trustee for the transferor, and accordingly no resulting trust arises. There may, of course, be a personal restitutionary claim at common law.

Evidence to rebut a resulting trust may establish that there is no resulting trust at all, and that the person in whose name the property is purchased was intended to take absolutely and beneficially,[73] but it may merely rebut the presumption of a resulting trust in part, leaving it to prevail as to the remainder.[74] In particular, the courts, it seems, will be very ready to accept evidence, where there has been a purchase in or transfer into the joint names of the person providing the purchase money or transferring the property, and another, that the intention was that the former should receive

---

[67] Per Lindley LJ in *Standing v Bowring* (1885) 31 Ch D 282 at 289, CA, and see generally *Vandervell v IRC*, supra, HL. The presumption was rebutted in *Aroso v Coutts & Co* [2002] 1 All ER(Comm) 241, noted (2001) 31 T & ELJ 9 (R Walford), and in *Vajpeyi v Yusaf* [2003] EWHC (Ch) [2004] WTLR 989 noted (2003) 147 Sol Jo 1301 (M Pawlowski).

[68] *Fowkes v Pascoe* (1875) 10 Ch App 343.

[69] As to what evidence is admissible see *Shephard v Cartwright* [1955] AC 431, [1954] 3 All ER 649, HL.

[70] *Re Gooch* (1890) 62 LT 384; *Shephard v Cartwright*, supra, HL.

[71] *Equity and Contemporary Legal Developments* (ed Goldstein) 335 (P Birks); Chambers *Resulting Trusts*.

[72] (1996) 16 LS 110 (W Swadling); *Westdeutsche Landesbank Girozentrale v Islington London Borough Council* [1996] 2 All ER 961, HL, per Lord Browne-Wilkinson at 985, 986. See [1997] JBL 48 (G McCormack); [1997] 10 Tru LI 84 (C Mitchell); (1977–78) 8 KCLJ 147 (P Oliver).

[73] *Currant v Jago* (1844) 1 Coll 261.

[74] *Napier v Public Trustee (Western Australia)* (1980) 32 ALR 153.

the income during his life, that is, to this extent the resulting trust prevails, but that the property should belong to the other after his death, that is, the resulting trust is rebutted as to the remainder.[75] Indeed, in cases where stock has been transferred or money paid into a bank account in joint names, the person providing the stock or money has been held entitled on the evidence not only to the income during his life, but also to sell and transfer the stock or withdraw the money. Nevertheless on that person's death an intention that the other should take beneficially what is left in the joint names had been established and held to be valid.[76]

It may be added that the presumption of a resulting trust naturally weakens with the passage of time, at any rate if there has been acquiescence as where the person in whose name the property has been purchased is allowed to remain in possession.[77]

(d) THE PRESUMPTION OF ADVANCEMENT

In addition to rebutting the presumption of a resulting trust by evidence as to the true intention, the existence of certain special relationships between the person who provides the purchase money or who transfers the property and the person into whose name the property is conveyed or transferred, either alone or jointly, gives rise to a presumption of advancement, which displaces the presumption of a resulting test.[78] Although the law is commonly expressed in such a way, it is perhaps more accurate to say that the special relationship will be treated as prima facie evidence that the person who paid the purchase money or transferred the property intended to make a gift to the person into whose name the property was conveyed or transferred.[79] In any case evidence is admissible to rebut the presumption of advancement in whole or in part and to reinstate wholly or partially the presumption of a resulting trust by showing that the intention of the person who paid the purchase money or transferred the property was that he should retain the whole or some part of the equitable interest.

(i) Father and child

Perhaps the primary relationship which has consistently been held to give rise to a presumption of advancement is that of father and child. There have been many cases

---

[75] *Fowkes v Pascoe* (1875) 10 Ch App 343, CA; *Batstone v Salter* (1875) 10 Ch App 431; *Standing v Bowring* (1885) 31 Ch D 282, CA; *Young v Sealey* [1949] Ch 278, [1949] 1 All ER 92. It is submitted that there is no difference in principle between realty and personalty—see (1966) 30 Conv 223 (E L G Tyler). See also (1992) 6 Tru LI 57 (J G Miller).

[76] *Beecher v Major* (1865) 2 Drew & Sm 431; *Young v Sealey*, supra. (Gift not defeated by the Wills Act 1837, although it appeared in fact to be testamentary in nature. The earlier decisions on similar facts were followed notwithstanding that the point on the Wills Act had apparently not been raised.) See also *Re Figgis* [1969] 1 Ch 123, [1968] 1 All ER 999; *Aroso v Coutts & Co* [2002] 1 All ER (Comm) 241; *Griffiths v Floyd* [2004] WTLR 667 (Isle of Man HC), and see 62 TELTJ 9 (S Phelps and Tamara Glassman).

[77] *Groves v Groves* (1829) 3 Y & J 163; *Clegg v Edmondson* (1857) 8 De GM & G 787.

[78] See (2001) 26 T & ELJ 16 (H Landau).

[79] This sentence in the text applied in *Re Dagle* (1990) 70 DLR (4th) 201.

where on the purchase or transfer of property by a father into the name of his child[80] the question has been whether the evidence was sufficient to rebut the presumption of advancement arising by virtue of the relationship. Thus in the Canadian decision *B v B*[81] a father bought an Irish Hospitals Sweepstake in the name of his 12-year old daughter. It proved to be the winning ticket and won £50,000. It was held that the father had failed to discharge the onus upon him to rebut the presumption of advancement. The winnings accordingly belonged to the daughter. The fact that property is conveyed or transferred into the joint names of a child and a stranger does not prevent the presumption of advancement from applying.[82]

The Privy Council, in *Comr of Stamp Duties v Byrnes*,[83] said that the fact that a son permits his father to receive the profits during his lifetime is not evidence which rebuts the presumption, as it is merely an act of reverence and good manners, but a later case shows that the retention of the title deeds to the property by the father may have a different result.[84] The presumption of advancement was rebutted in *Re Gooch*,[85] where a father bought shares in a company in the name of his son in order to qualify the son to be a director. The son always handed the dividends received on the shares to his father, and later handed over the actual share certificates. And it seems that the fact that the son in his father's solicitor is by itself a fact which will rebut the presumption.[86] Most recently the view which has been applied in husband and wife cases[87] that the presumption of advancement is a judicial instrument of last resort has been held equally applicable in father and child cases. Evidence that a house had been put in the son's name to enable a mortgage to be obtained, and the existence of proposals that the beneficial interest should be shared, was held sufficient to rebut the presumption.[88]

The presumption of advancement also arises where a man is in loco parentis[89] to the person into whose name the property is conveyed or transferred, that is to say, where he has taken upon himself what is regarded in equity as the father's natural office and duty of making provision for the child.[90]

The mere relationship of mother[91] and child has been held not to give rise to any

[80] There is no presumption of advancement on a purchase or transfer of property by a child into the name of its father.

[81] (1976) 65 DLR (3d) 460; *Casimir v Alexander* [2001] WTLR 939.

[82] *Crabb v Crabb* (1834) 1 My & K 511.   [83] [1911] AC 386, PC.

[84] *Warren v Gurney* [1944] 2 All ER 472, CA.

[85] (1890) 62 LT 384. See also *Stock v McAvoy* (1872) LR 15 Eq 55.

[86] *Garrett v Wilkinson* (1848) 2 De G & Sm 244.   [87] See p 182, infra.

[88] *McGrath v Walls* [1995] 2 FLR 114. See (1995) 139 Sol Jo 826 (Ann Kenny); *Lavelle v Lavelle* [2004] EWCA Civ 223, [2004] 2 FCR 418; *Kyriakides v Pippas* [2004] EWHC 646, [2004] 2 FCR 434.

[89] The meaning of the term in loco parentis seems to be the same here as in connection with satisfaction, discussed fully in chapter 32, section 3(c), infra.

[90] *Currant v Jago* (1844) 1 Coll 261; *Soar v Foster* (1858) 4 K & J 152; *Shephard v Cartwright* [1955] AC 431, [1954] 3 All ER 649, HL; *Re Paradise Motor Co Ltd* [1968] 2 All ER 625, CA. But see *Tucker v Burrow* (1865) 2 Hem & M 515 at 526, 527.

[91] A fortiori, stepmother and stepchild—*Todd v Moorhouse* (1874) LR 19 Eq 69 at 71.

presumption of advancement,[92] the reason given being that equity does not recognize any obligation on the part of the mother to provide for her child. In practice, however, as Jessel MR observed[93] 'in the case of a mother . . . it is easier to prove a gift than in the case of a stranger: in the case of a mother very little evidence beyond the relationship is wanted, there being very little additional motive required to induce a mother to make a gift to her child.' Moreover it has recently been held,[94] so far as concerns the rule against double portions,[95] that both parents should nowadays be taken to be in loco parentis unless the contrary is proved, and it is thought that this view would now also be taken in relation to the presumption of advancement generally.

(ii) Husband and wife[96]

Questions often arise between husband and wife as to the ownership of property, more often than not after the break-up of a marriage. In some circumstances a wife may place reliance on the presumption of advancement. Certain important principles should, however, be referred to before investigating the different situations that may arise. First, property rights have to be ascertained as at the time of purchase or transfer, and the rights so ascertained cannot be altered by subsequent events unless there has been an agreement to vary them. In particular, as Lord Morris said in *Pettitt v Pettitt*,[97] 'the fact of a break-down of the marriage is irrelevant in the determination of a question as to where ownership lay before the break-down: the break-down will then merely have caused the need for a decision but will not of itself have altered whatever was the pre-existing position as to ownership.'[98]

Secondly, as Lord Upjohn explained in the same case,[99] 'the beneficial ownership of

---

[92] *Bennet v Bennet* (1879) 10 Ch D 474; *Gross v French* (1974) 232 Estates Gazette 1319; affd (1975) 238 Estates Gazette 39, CA; *Sekhon v Alissa* [1989] 2 FLR 94, noted [1990] Conv 213 (G Kodilinye); *Lattimer v Lattimer* (1978) 82 DLR (3d) 587. Contra, particularly in the case of a widowed mother, *Sayre v Hughes* (1868) LR 5 Eq 376; *Garrett v Wilkinson* (1848) 2 De G & Sm 244. In Australia the presumption has been held to apply equally to a gift by a mother to a child: *Brown v Brown* (1993) 31 NSWLR 582; *Nelson v Nelson* (1995) 184 CLR 538. The paragraph in the text was cited in the Canadian case of *Cohen v Cohen* (1985) 60 Alberta Rep 234 where Montgomery J said that whatever the law may have been in the past, today there should be a presumption of gift when a mother transfers property to her child, though on the evidence he held that in the case before him the presumption was rebutted and the child held on trust for the mother and this view was followed in *Dreger v Dreger* [1994] 10 WWR 293 (presumption rebutted by evidence) and *Nelson v Little Estate* (2004) 250 Sask R 237.

[93] In *Bennet v Bennet*, supra, at 479–480.

[94] *Re Cameron (decd)* [1999] Ch 386, [1999] 2 All ER 924.   [95] See p 745 et seq, infra.

[96] Note the wide powers of the court under s 24 of the Matrimonial Causes Act 1973. This section does not apply to formerly engaged couples notwithstanding s 2 of the Law Reform (Miscellaneous Provisions) Act 1970 which provides that the rules applied to determine property disputes between husband and wife apply also to property disputes between formerly engaged couples—*Mossop v Mossop* [1988] Fam 77, [1988] 2 All ER 202, CA, noted [1988] Conv 284 (JEM). See, Law Com No 115; (1993) 23 Fam Law 231 (J Dewar). See *R v Harrow London Borough Council, ex p Coker* (1989) *Times*, 14 March, CA, an unusual case where a third party sought, unsuccessfully, to rely on the presumption.

[97] [1970] AC 777 at 803, [1969] 2 All ER 385 at 397, HL.

[98] He added that it might be relevant on s 17 application—see p 200, infra.

[99] *Pettitt v Pettitt*, supra, at 813, 405; *Pink v Lawrence* (1977) 36 P & CR 98, CA; *Brykiert v Jones* (1981) 2 FLR 373, CA (conveyance to husband or wife in 1948 contained express declaration of trust in favour of

the property in question must depend on the agreement of the parties determined at the time of its acquisition.[100] If the property in question is land there must be some lease or conveyance which shows how it was acquired. If that document declares not merely in whom the legal title is to vest but in whom the beneficial title is to vest that necessarily concludes the question of title as between the spouses for all time,[101] and in the absence of fraud or mistake at the time of the transaction the parties cannot go behind it at any time thereafter even on death or the break-up of the marriage. . . . But the document may be silent as to the beneficial title. . . . If there is no . . . available evidence then what are called the presumptions come into play.' Accordingly if 'the relevant conveyance contains an express declaration of trust which comprehensively declares the beneficial interests in the property or its proceeds of sale, there is no room for the application of the doctrine of resulting, implied or constructive trusts unless or until the conveyance is set aside or rectified; until that event the declaration contained in the document speaks for itself.'[102]

The presumptions to which Lord Upjohn referred are the presumption of a resulting trust on a purchase in the name of, or voluntary conveyance to, another—and the presumption of advancement. As to the latter, it can be taken as settled, in the light of clear statements by three of the Law Lords in *Pettitt v Pettitt*[103] that the strength of this presumption has been much diminished with changing conditions of society.

---

purchasers as joint tenants: marriage came to grief and wife left matrimonial home in 1951: wife entitled to assert her claim to a half share on sale in 1981); *Bernard v Josephs* [1982] Ch 391, [1982] 3 All ER 162, CA; *Re Gorman (a bankrupt)* [1990] 1 All ER 717, [1990] 1 WLR 616, Ch D.

100 The agreement may be in writing or oral: *Lloyds Bank plc v Rosset* [1991] 1 AC 107, HL, at 132, [1990] 1 All ER 1111, HL, at 1118; *Mortgage Corpn v Shaire* [2001] 4 All ER 364, [2001] 3 WLR 639.

101 Presumably this means concludes for all time the question of title as at the date of acquisition. It may be varied by subsequent agreement. The author shares the opinion of H K Bevan and F W Taylor in (1966) 30 Conv 354, 438 and E H Scamell in (1967) CLP 120, that the view stated in the text is the better one. It was held in *Robinson v Robinson* (1976) 241 Estates Gazette 153, a decision which Vinelott J in *Re Gorman (a bankrupt)* supra, found difficult to understand, in a case of man and mistress, that this principle did not apply in the case of a registered transfer where neither party had executed the transfer and 'therefore neither effectively declared or settled respective beneficial interests in the property'. Cf *Pariser v Wilson* (1973) 229 Estates Gazette 786.

102 Per Slade LJ in *Goodman v Gallant* [1986] Fam 106, [1986] 1 All ER 311, CA, noted (1986) 45 CLJ 205 (S Juss). This principle was applied in *Turton v Turton* [1988] Ch 542, [1987] 2 All ER 641, to the erstwhile home of an unmarried couple many years after they had parted. The woman was held to be entitled to her half share under the trust though she had made no contribution directly or indirectly to the purchase price and had only lived with the man for about five years. See also *Wright v Johnson* [2001] EWCA Civ 1667, [2002] P & CR 210. But in *City of London Building Society v Flegg* [1988] AC 54, [1987] 3 All ER 435, HL, notwithstanding express trusts for named beneficiaries, the property was deemed to be held on resulting trusts for the named beneficiaries and the respondents (who had provided over half of the purchase price) as tenants in common.

103 [1970] AC 777 [1969] 2 All ER 385, HL, per Lord Reid at 793, 389, Lord Hodson at 811, 404, and Lord Diplock at 824, 414. Lord Upjohn, however, thought the presumptions as useful as ever, though he said that they only come into play in the absence of evidence. It was said that it 'must be applied with caution in modern social conditions' in *Harwood and Harwood* [1991] 2 FLR 274, CA, though on the facts of that case there was nothing to displace it. It was held still to exist in Canada, and applied, in *Mehta Estate v Mehta Estate* (1993) 104 DLR (4th) 24 (happily married couple killed together in air crash), noted (1993) 22 Man LJ 185 (C H C Edwards).

Lastly, in *Gissing v Gissing*,[104] Viscount Dilhorne referred to *Pettitt v Pettitt*[105] as establishing that there is not one law of property applicable where a dispute as to property is between spouses, and another law of property where the dispute is between other persons. In some cases before *Pettitt v Pettitt*[106]—and indeed in some after it—the phrase 'family assets' is used. This may be a useful loose expression to refer to possessions of a family, but it has no legal meaning, and family assets are not a special class of property known to the law. English law knows no doctrine of community of goods or joint family property, and such a doctrine could only be established by legislation. Property law principles apply equally to married and unmarried couples, though the presumption of advancement can only apply between husband and wife.

(a) *Purchase or transfer by a husband into the name of his wife, or into the joint names of his wife and himself.* The classic statement of the presumption of advancement in this situation is that of Malins VC in *Re Eykyn's Trusts*,[107] cited with approval by Lord Upjohn in *Pettitt v Pettitt*:[108]

The law of the court is perfectly settled that when a husband transfers money or other property into the name of his wife only, then the presumption is, that it is intended as a gift or advancement to the wife absolutely at once . . . And if a husband invests money, stock or otherwise, in the names of himself and his wife, then also it is an advancement for the benefit of the wife absolutely if she survives her husband, but if he survives her, then it reverts to him as joint tenant with his wife.

Though, as mentioned above, the House of Lords has stated that the strength of presumption is now greatly diminished the Court of Appeal relied on it in *Tinker v Tinker*.[109] The court did not attempt to explain why it applied the presumption without hesitation in this case, which contrasts with all the other husband and wife cases since *Pettitt v Pettitt*[110] where the presumption has been treated as of little or no importance. All the other relevant cases have in fact involved contributions to the purchase by both husband and wife—a situation which is discussed in (c) below—and *Tinker v Tinker*[111] may be distinguished on that ground, for there the husband had provided the whole of the purchase price of the house which he had put into his wife's name. It may be that the strength of the presumption of advancement is less impaired in the situation under consideration, that is, where there has been a purchase or transfer by a husband into the name of his wife, and no contribution is made by the wife.

It has always, of course, been possible to rebut the presumption by evidence that no gift was intended. The older cases, particularly those in which the presumption of

---

[104] [1971] AC 886, [1970] 2 All ER 780, HL.   [105] Supra, HL.   [106] Supra, HL.
[107] (1877) 6 Ch D 115 at 118, where it was held that the presumption of advancement was unaffected by the fact that the property was placed in the name also of another person. It makes no difference whether one is dealing with realty or personalty—see (1966) 30 Conv 223 (E C G Tyler).
[108] Supra.
[109] [1970] P 136, [1970] 1 All ER 540, CA, where the evidence in fact supported the presumption.
[110] Supra.   [111] Supra.

advancement was upheld, must, however, be read with care in the light of the change in the weight to be attached to the presumption. The presumption of advancement was rebutted in *Re Salisbury-Jones*,[112] where the wife entered into a mortgage of her property under which the husband was a surety. When the husband was called upon to pay the money due under the mortgage it was held that in so doing he was discharging a legal obligation and there was no question of his making a gift to his wife. He was therefore entitled as against her to all the remedies of a surety.

The presumption has been applied not only to a once and for all purchase or transfer, but also to analogous transactions, such as a purchase of land with the aid of an instalment mortgage which is paid off by the husband over a period of years, when the payment of each instalment is, as it were, a supplementary gift.[113] Since *Pettitt v Pettitt*,[114] however, the court will, it seems, be slow to apply the presumption in such case, at any rate where the wife has made a contribution.[115] It may be noted that by the Married Women's Property Act 1964 money derived from any allowance made by a husband for the expenses of the matrimonial home or for similar purposes,[116] or any property acquired out of that money, is to be treated as belonging to the husband and wife in equal shares, in the absence of any agreement between them to the contrary.

Special mention should be made of joint bank accounts[117] between husband and wife where both parties have power to draw cheques on the account. Prima facie in such a case during their joint lives each spouse has power to draw cheques not only for the joint benefit of both, but also for his or her own separate benefit, and accordingly if either spouse draws on the account to purchase a chattel or an investment in his or her name alone, that spouse will be the sole owner of the chattel or investment both at law and in equity. If the purchase were in joint names[118] they would prima facie be joint tenants. And on the death of one spouse the survivor will be entitled to the balance of the account.[119] These prima facie rules may be displaced by the evidence. On the one hand, this may rebut the presumption of advancement and show that a

---

[112] [1938] 3 All ER 459, applied to a guarantee of an overdraft; *Anson v Anson* [1953] 1 QB 636, [1953] 1 All ER 867.

[113] *Moate v Moate* [1948] 2 All ER 486; *Silver v Silver*, supra.

[114] [1970] AC 777, [1969] 2 All ER 385, HL.   [115] *Falconer v Falconer* [1970] 3 All ER 449, CA.

[116] This phrase was held not to include mortgage repayments towards the purchase of the matrimonial home in *Tymoszczuk v Tymoszczuk* (1964) 108 Sol Jo 676 where it was held that the Act was retrospective. This decision was doubted on both points by Goff J in *Re John's Assignment Trusts* [1970] 2 All ER 210n. See Law Com No 175; (1985) 135 NLJ 797 (S P de Cruz).

[117] See (1969) 85 LQR 530 (M C Cullity).

[118] Vaisey J's dictum in *Jones v Maynard* [1951] Ch 572 at 575, [1951] 1 All ER 802 at 804, to the effect (semble) that if the husband draws on the account to purchase investments in his wife's name, the presumption of advancement will apply and the wife will be entitled, seems to be right on principle. It is less certain whether the general rule of a resulting trust for the wife (see p 187, infra) would apply to a similar purchase by the wife in the husband's name.

[119] The authorities for the above propositions are *Re Young* (1885) 28 Ch D 705; *Re Bishop* [1965] Ch 450, [1965] 1 All ER 249. The same principle was applied where a father transferred funds into a joint account with one of his children: *MacInnis Estates v MacDonald* (1995) 394 APR 321. See Law Com No 175. Cf *Public Trustee v Gray-Masters* [1977] VR 154, where the parties were unmarried and it was held that the presumption of resulting trust was rebutted.

banking account placed in joint names is to be held beneficially for the husband[120] alone. Thus in *Marshall v Crutwell*[121] a husband in failing health transferred his banking account from his own name into the names of himself and his wife and directed his bankers to honour cheques drawn either by himself or his wife. He afterwards paid considerable sums into the account. All cheques were thereafter drawn by the wife at the direction of her husband, and proceeds were applied in payment of household and other expenses. After his death the wife claimed to be entitled to the balance, but it was held that the transfer of the account was not intended to be a provision for the plaintiff, but merely a mode of conveniently managing her husband's affairs. It has recently been observed,[122] however, that it is likely that today a court would take a different view of the facts.

The presumption was not rebutted in *Re Figgis*,[123] where the joint account had been in existence for nearly 50 years, but had only been operated by the wife during the First World War, and, without the husband's knowledge, during his last illness. This case involved both a current and a deposit account, and as to the latter the judge observed that in the nature of things it was far less appropriate than a current account as a provision made for convenience. He added that even if the current account had been opened merely for convenience, in his view this could change and later become an advancement for the wife. On the other hand, where one spouse has drawn on the account to purchase an investment in his or her name alone, the evidence may show, as in *Jones v Maynard*,[124] that the parties intended 'a common purse and a pool of their resources'.[125] In that case the investment purchased out of the joint[126] account by the husband in his sole name was accordingly directed to be held by him as to one half on trust for his wife.

If at the relevant time, that is, the time of the purchase or transfer, the relationship of husband and wife was in existence, the presumption of advancement will be applied notwithstanding that the parties were subsequently divorced,[127] or, in the case of a voidable marriage, that a decree of nullity has been pronounced.[128] The presumption may be even stronger where the parties were engaged to be married, provided that the marriage was subsequently duly solemnized.[129] There is, however, no presumption of

---

[120] *Hoddinott v Hoddinott* [1949] 2 KB 406, CA.

[121] (1875) LR 20 Eq 328; *Simpson v Simpson* [1992] 1 FLR 601. A fortiori where the account is fed by the wife alone, she alone is beneficially entitled—*Heseltine v Heseltine* [1971] 1 All ER 952, CA.

[122] *Aroso v Coutts & Co* [2002] 1 All ER (Comm) 241, per Lawrence Collins J at 249.

[123] [1969] 1 Ch 123, [1968] 1 All ER 999.   [124] Supra.   [125] *Jones v Maynard*, supra, at 803.

[126] Technically, it seems, it was not a joint account, as it remained in the name of the husband alone, but it was said to be a joint account 'to all intents and purposes', because both spouses had power to draw on it.

[127] *Thornley v Thornley* [1893] 2 Ch 229.   [128] *Dunbar v Dunbar* [1909] 2 Ch 639.

[129] *Moate v Moate* [1948] 2 All ER 486. Cf *Zamet v Hyman* [1961] 3 All ER 933, CA and see (1975) 119 Sol Jo 108 (E Ellis); (1976) 120 Sol Jo 141 (N V Lowe); *Cavalier v Cavalier* (1971) 19 FLR 199. There is a statutory presumption of gift in relation to an engagement ring, even though the marriage does not take place—Law Reform (Miscellaneous Provisions) Act 1970, s 3(2), though the gift may be expressly made on the condition that it is to be returned if the agreement is terminated: ibid, s 3(1), and see *Shaw v Fitzgerald* [1992] 1 FLR 357.

advancement if the purported marriage is void.[130] Nor has the presumption ever been applied where a man and woman are living together without having gone through any ceremony of marriage at all.[131]

(b) *Purchase or transfer by a wife into the name of her husband or into the joint names of her husband and herself.* Here there is no presumption of advancement, and accordingly the husband will hold on a resulting trust for the wife.[132] Thus in *Mercier v Mercier*[133] husband and wife had a joint banking account almost entirely composed of the wife's income. Land was purchased and paid for out of the joint account, but conveyed into the name of the husband alone. In holding that the husband held the property on a resulting trust for his wife, it was pointed out that there was no distinction in principle between payment out of capital or income. And in *Pearson v Pearson*,[134] where the matrimonial home was conveyed into joint names, but the wife not only provided the initial payment but paid all the mortgage instalments, it was held that the wife alone was entitled. In *Pettitt v Pettitt*,[135] however, Lord Upjohn observed:

If a wife puts property into her husband's name it may be that in the absence of all other evidence he is a trustee for her, but in practice there will in almost every case be some explanation (however slight) of this (today) rather unusual course. If a wife puts property into their joint names I would myself think that a joint beneficial tenancy was intended, for I can see no other reason for it.

In *Heseltine v Heseltine*[136] a wealthy wife transferred two sums of £20,000 to her relatively poor husband for the purpose of equalizing their property for estate duty purposes, and a further sum of £20,000 to enable the husband, as a candidate for membership of Lloyd's, to sign a certificate that he was worth £90,000. One might expect the court to have held that there was a presumption of a resulting trust, rebutted by the evidence. In fact after the break-up of the marriage it was held that all these sums were held by the husband on trust for the wife. Lord Denning MR called it 'a resulting trust which resulted from all the circumstances of the case', but in fact the

---

[130] *Soar v Foster* (1858) 4 K & J 152—'marriage' with deceased wife's sister, at that time illegal. So held notwithstanding the judicial observation that 'any moralist would say that a man was bound to make provision for the woman with whom he had so cohabitated'. Whether or not a decree of nullity has been pronounced would seem to be irrelevant.

[131] *Crisp v Mullings* (1974) 233 Estates Gazette 511 reversed without discussing this point (1975) 239 Estates Gazette 119, CA; *Napier v Public Trustee (Western Australia)* (1980) 32 ALR 153; *Calverley v Green* (1984) 59 ALJR 111, and see (1986) ALJ 31 (F Bates), (1985) 8 UNSWLJ 1 (Rebecca Bailey-Harris); (1986) 12 NZULR 79 (Julie K Maxton).

[132] *Re Curtis* (1885) 52 LT 244; *Rich v Cockell* (1804) 9 Ves 369. Law Com No 175 (1988) proposed that the presumption of advancement should apply equally to both spouses.

[133] [1903] 2 Ch 98, CA.   [134] (1965) *Times*, 30 November.

[135] Supra, at 815, 407; *Knightly v Knightly* (1981) unreported but noted 131 NLJ 479, CA.

[136] [1971] 1 All ER 952, CA. Possibly the wife could have had the transfers set aside on the grounds of undue influence. This case also raises difficulties as to what has been called the 'floating trust' concept, and the idea of a 'trust for the family'—See (1971) 115 Sol Jo 614 (S Cretney).

court seems to have imposed a constructive trust, though it is doubtful whether it was justified in doing so on the facts.

An established, though limited, exception to the presumption of a resulting trust arises where a husband and wife are living together and the wife consents to or acquiesces in the husband receiving income from her property, when to that extent only there will be a presumption of gift.[137] But if without the wife's knowledge the husband sold the property and misappropriated the proceeds of sale, he would not only be liable to replace the capital, but also to account for the income that would have been produced after the date of the sale, for whatever the position may have been as to income arising before that date, the wife not having known of the sale could not have assented or acquiesced thereafter.[138] The same principles underlie what is known as the equity of exoneration,[139] which has been said not to have 'any less part to play now than it had in the days when the equitable doctrine was being formulated'.[140] This applies where a married woman charges her property with money for the purpose of paying her husband's debts and the money raised by her is so applied. In such case she is prima facie regarded in equity and as between herself and him, as lending him and not giving him the money raised on her property and as entitled to have the property exonerated by him from the charge she has created. The presumption of the equity of exoneration, however, may be rebutted by evidence showing that the proper inference is that the money was intended to be given, not merely lent, as might be the case, for instance, where the debts have been incurred with the assent of the wife in order to maintain the husband and wife in a standard of living above their income.[141]

It has recently been pointed out[142] that in view of completely changed social conditions the guide that the older cases can provide is often not very valuable. In considering how the equity of exoneration should work as between a husband and a wife, the courts should take into account the relationship which husbands and wives bear, or ought to bear, to one another in their family affairs in current times. On the facts in Re Pittortou[143] where the husband and wife were each beneficially entitled to a half share subject to the building society mortgage, the wife was prima facie entitled, by the equity of exoneration, to require the second charge to secure the husband's debts to be met primarily out of the husband's share in the net proceeds of sale. But to the extent that the husband's indebtedness represented payments made for the benefit of the household, it should be discharged out of the proceeds of sale before division.

---

[137] *Caton v Rideout* (1849) 1 Mac & G 599; *Edward v Cheyne (No 2)* (1888) 13 App Cas 385, HL. The presumption is, of course, rebuttable: *Re Young* (1913) 29 TLR 391.

[138] *Dixon v Dixon* (1878) 9 Ch D 587.

[139] *Clinton v Hooper* (1791) I Ves 173; *Hudson v Carmichael* (1854) Kay 613.

[140] *Re Pittortou* [1985] 1 All ER 285, per Scott J at 289.

[141] *Paget v Paget* [1898] 1 Ch 470, CA explained in *Hall v Hall* [1911] 1 Ch 487; *Re Berry (a bankrupt)* [1978] 2 NZLR 373.

[142] *Re Pittortou* [1985] 1 All ER 285, citing the unreported decision of Walton J in *Re Woodstock (a bankrupt)* (19 November 1979).

[143] Supra. See *Official Trustee in Bankruptcy v Citibank Savings Ltd* (1995) 38 NSWLR 116.

(c) *Contributions*[144] by both spouses to purchase price of property.[145] In this situation the role of the presumption of advancement is now negligible. Even if the property is conveyed into the name of the wife alone the strength of the presumption has diminished virtually to vanishing point.[146]

(d) Even in the absence of an express declaration of trust, the prima facie entitlement arising under the presumptions of resulting trust and advancement may be defeated by establishing a common intention constructive trust, which is discussed in the immediately following chapter.

[144] Including contributions before marriage with a view to setting up the matrimonial home—*Ulrich v Ulrich* [1968] 1 All ER 67, CA. Where the purchase is with the aid of a mortgage, credit may be given for mortgage liability. Thus if H contributes £40,000, W £20,000 and £40,000 is raised by a mortgage to which they are both parties, H will prima facie be entitled to 3/5 and W to 2/5. See *Marsh v Von Sternberg* [1986] 1 FLR 526; *Savill v Goodall* [1993] 1 FLR 755, CA. As to mortgage instalments paid by a spouse continuing to live in the matrimonial home after the other spouse has left, see *Shinh v Shinh* [1977] 1 All ER 97; *Suttill v Graham* [1977] 3 All ER 1117, CA; *Bernard v Josephs* [1982] Ch 391, [1982] 3 All ER 162, CA; *Re Paulou (a bankrupt)* [1993] 3 All ER 955, [1993] 1 WLR 1046. See also [1992] Fam Law 45 (S Johnson).

[145] See generally (1978) 94 LQR 26 (A A S Zuckerman); (1978–80) 6 U Tas LR 97 (J Wade); (1987) 3 QITLJ 61 (Lindy Willmott).

[146] Even Lord Upjohn in *Pettitt v Pettitt* [1970] AC 777, [1969] 2 All ER 385, HL, thought that a wife would not be able to rely on the presumption of advancement unless the husband's contribution was very small. See *Falconer v Falconer* [1970] 3 All ER 449, CA.

10

COMMON INTENTION CONSTRUCTIVE TRUSTS; PROPRIETARY ESTOPPEL; LICENCES

It might well be asked why three apparently disparate subjects should be included in the same chapter. The justification is that in recent years in a number of cases, mainly arising out of informal arrangements in a family setting, the court has taken the view that justice demanded that the claimant should have a remedy in circumstances where it was at least doubtful whether he was entitled to one under existing rules as previously understood. The matters to be discussed concern the ways in which the courts have sought to achieve what they considered to be a just result. The different ways overlap and interact.

1 COMMON INTENTION CONSTRUCTIVE TRUST

(a) THE CORRECT APPROACH TO DETERMINATION OF BENEFICIAL INTERESTS

The common intention constructive trust has been developed mainly in connection with disputes relating to claims to beneficial interests in the matrimonial home or quasi-matrimonial home.[1] In the typical case property has been purchased as a home by a couple who, whether or not married, intend to live in it as man and wife, but has been conveyed into the name of one of them only, let us assume the man as is more often the case. How can the woman claim a share of the beneficial interest? If there is a

---

[1] See the Law Commission's Discussion Paper on 'Sharing Homes', Law Com No 278, July 2002. Recent literature includes (1995) 15 LS 356 (M Howard and J Hill); (1995) 145 NLJ 423, 456 (P Milne); [1995] Fam Law 560 (T Lawrence-Cruttenden and A Odutola); (1996) 16 LS 324 (Nicola Glover and P Todd); [1998] Conv 202 (Ursula Riniker); (1998) 18 LS 369 (Simone Wong); (1999) 19 LS 468 (Anne Barlow and Craig Lind); (2001) 10(2) Nott LJ 20 (M Pawlowski); [2002] Fam Law 743 (S Bridge); [2002] Fam Law 834 (R Probert); (2003) 23 LS 624 (Joanna Miles); (2004) 24 LS 414 (J Mee); [2004] Conv 208 (C Rotherham).

written declaration or agreement as to their respective beneficial interests, this will govern the situation. Again if the woman has made a direct contribution to the cost of acquisition she will have a claim under a resulting trust. Failing either of these possibilities in order to succeed she must establish a common intention between her and the defendant, acted on by her, that she should have a beneficial interest. If she can do that, equity will not allow the defendant to deny that interest and will construct a trust to give effect to it. And where she has a share under a resulting trust she may yet be able to establish a larger share under a constructive trust.

In the case of married couples questions usually only arise on divorce, when it is seldom necessary to decide their exact property rights. Where there are matrimonial proceedings the matter can and should be dealt with under the provisions of the Matrimonial Causes Act 1973, which enable the court to do what is just in all the circumstances.[2] Questions of ownership yield to the higher demands of relating the means of both to the needs of each, the first consideration being given to the welfare of children.[3] However, there are cases where it is necessary to determine their rights under property law. For example, in *Re Cummins*[4] the husband was dead, and the question was whether his widow could claim a beneficial interest in assets standing in the husband's name immediately prior to his death. Again in *Lloyds Bank plc v Rosset*[5] the wife sought to claim a beneficial interest in the house which she argued would not be subject to the claims of her husband's creditor, the bank. The matrimonial legislation does not apply to unmarried couples but the Civil Partnership Act 2004,[6] not yet in force, contains provisions corresponding to those in Part 2 of the Matrimonial Causes Act 1973 in connection with civil partnerships.

The leading cases are the House of Lords decisions in *Pettitt v Pettitt*,[7] *Gissing v Gissing*[8] and *Lloyds Bank plc v Rosset*[9] as explained in a series of subsequent cases of

---

[2] See *Fielding v Fielding* [1978] 1 All ER 267, [1977] 1 WLR 1146n, CA.
[3] See *Hammond v Mitchell* [1992] 2 All ER 109, [1991] 1 WLR 1127.
[4] [1972] Ch 62, [1971] 3 All ER 782, CA. It is too late to make application under the Act after remarriage: s 28(3).
[5] [1991] 1 AC 107, [1990] 1 All ER 1111, HL.   [6] Section 72 and Sch 5.
[7] Supra, HL. See the discussion in *Thwaites v Ryan* [1984] VR 65.
[8] [1971] AC 886, [1970] 2 All ER 780, HL; see (1984) 14 Fam Law 40 (Diana Parkes).
[9] [1991] 1 AC 107, [1990] 1 All ER 1111, HL; *Ivin v Blake* [1995] 1 FLR 70, CA, noted [1995] Fam Law 72 (S Cretney); [1996] Conv 462 (Anna Lawson); *Mortgage Corpn v Shaire* [2001] 4 All ER 364. In *Re Schuppan (a bankrupt) (No 2)* [1997] 1 BCLC 256 it was held that the principle in *Lloyds Bank plc v Rosset*, namely that an agreement made prior to the acquisition of property that it should be shared beneficially gave rise to a constructive trust where the person asserting a claim to a beneficial interest against the party entitled to the legal estate had altered his position to his detriment in reliance on that agreement, was applicable where the property was acquired through or held by a company owned by the legal owner instead of being owned by the legal owner directly. See also *McHardy & Sons (a firm) v Warren* [1994] 2 FLR 338, CA, noted [1994] Fam Law 567 (J Dewar), in which case it was held that where a parent paid a deposit on the first matrimonial home it is an 'irresistible conclusion' that the bride and groom are to have equal interests in the home; and *Halifax Building Society v Brown* [1996] 1 FLR 103, CA, where it was held that a loan to a married couple from one of their parents to finance a deposit on a house was capable of founding an inference of a common intention to share the property beneficially even if the house was conveyed into the husband's name alone.

which the most recent is *Oxley v Hiscock*.[10] One complication is the relationship with proprietary estoppel.[11] In *Grant v Edwards*[12] Browne-Wilkinson V-C said there was much to be said for the view, in this sort of case, that there is no difference between constructive trust and proprietary estoppel, and in *Stokes v Anderson*[13] Nourse LJ seems to have thought the same. More recently in *Yaxley v Gotts*[14] Robert Walker LJ observed that the common intention constructive trust is 'closely akin to, if not indistinguishable from, proprietary estoppel'. This development reached its conclusion in *Oxley v Hiscock*[15] where Chadwick LJ said:

. . . the time has come to accept that there is no difference in outcome, in cases of this nature, whether the true analysis lies in constructive trust or in proprietary estoppel.

Subject to what has been said about matrimonial legislation (and prospectively civil partnerships), and, in the rare cases where it is applicable, the presumption of advancement, what is settled is that, in determining their property rights the same principles apply between married and unmarried couples, though cohabitation in marriage (and prospectively civil partnerships), in contrast to a less permanently intended relationship, may have a bearing on the ascertainment of their common intention and on the determination of an appropriate apportionment of their respective rights to the property in which they live.[16] What follows is, of course, subject to any express declaration of trust in the conveyance.[17]

A recent decision not involving the matrimonial or quasi-matrimonial home is *Re West Norwood Cemetery*.[18] In that case P was the registered owner of exclusive rights of burial in plot 177. According to the report, after the burial of his mother's remains in the plot, P, one of seven children, made it clear to his siblings that he did not want the remains of his father (D) to be buried there. Nevertheless five of P's siblings arranged for D's ashes to be buried in the plot, in all likelihood by forging P's signature on the burial form. When the burial authority discovered the facts it petitioned the Consistory Court for a faculty for the exhumation of D's ashes. The court held that the grant to P of exclusive rights of burial was not definitive of those rights. About a quarter of the cemetery bill had been paid by other members of the family, including D, who had acted to his detriment by contributing without insisting that his name appear on the grant. The judge said that 'since there was a common intention among family members that D should have a right of interment in plot 177, a constructive trust was established and P had no right to refuse his consent to D's interment thereby defeating the common purpose of the trust'. The report fails to

---

[10] [2004] EWCA Civ 546, [2004] 3 All ER 703, discussed p 198, infra. See the unusual case of *Buggs v Buggs* [2003] EWHC 1538 (Ch), [2004] WTLR 799, discussed [2003] Conv 411 (M P Thompson).

[11] See pp 209, 210, infra.   [12] [1986] Ch 638, [1986] 2 All ER 426, CA.

[13] [1991] FCR 539, CA.   [14] [2000] Ch 162, [2000] 1 All ER 711.

[15] Supra, CA, at [66]. For the position in Australia, see *Austin v Keele* (1987) 61 ALJR 605 (the last appeal to the Privy Council from Australia) and (2004) 23 UQLJ 54 (D Jensen).

[16] *Bernard v Josephs* [1982] Ch 391, [1982] 3 All ER 162, CA, noted [1982] Conv 444 (Jean Warburton); (1983) CLJ 30 (K Gray). See (1980) 96 LQR 248 (A A S Zuckerman); (1980) WILJ 3 (A J Bland).

[17] See p 183 supra.   [18] (2005) *Times*, 20 April (Consistory Court).

show what evidence there was that P, who had the legal title, shared this 'common intention', which was vital to the result. The judge continued by holding that the same result was achieved by the law of proprietary estoppel: by contributing to the project D and P's siblings had acted to their detriment in reliance on the belief that D would have a right to be buried there. The report does not show what evidence there was that P encouraged or even acquiesced in that belief. The necessary evidence to establish a constructive trust and/or proprietary estoppel may well have been before the court, but it does not appear in the brief report.

(b) FAMILY HOME TAKEN IN JOINT NAMES

Unless the facts are very unusual,[19] both the man and the woman are entitled to a share in the beneficial interest on the basis of a resulting trust. Where the house is bought outright, their shares will depend on a more or less precise arithmetical calculation of the extent of their contributions to the purchase price. Where it is bought with the aid of a mortgage, then the court has to assess each of the parties' respective contributions in a broad sense; nevertheless the court is only entitled to look at the financial contributions, or their real or substantial equivalent, to the acquisition of the house.[20] Prima facie, if the purchase is financed in whole or in part on mortgage, the person who assumed liability for the mortgage payments, as between the joint owners, is to be treated as having contributed the mortgage moneys.[21]

Since, as we have seen, a resulting trust is based on presumed intention, it is open to a claimant to show that the intention of the parties was that their beneficial interests should be other than those which would arise purely on the basis of contributions. This may be done by establishing a common intention constructive trust or proprietary estoppel which may be applicable where the property is in joint names in the same way as discussed in the following subsection where it is in the name of one party only.

(c) HOME TAKEN IN THE NAME OF ONE ONLY OF THE TWO PARTIES

In practice this usually proves to be the name of the man, but this is not legally significant. The claimant in this situation, in order to secure a beneficial interest, has to establish a constructive trust by showing that it would be inequitable for the legal owner to claim sole beneficial ownership. The first and fundamental question, Lord Bridge stated in *Lloyds Bank plc v Rosset*,[22] which must always be resolved is whether,

---

[19] As they were in *Young v Young* (1984) 134 NLJ 944, CA, where the house was in joint names, but the man had made no substantial contribution and was held to have no beneficial interest.

[20] *Burns v Burns* [1984] Ch 317, [1984] 1 All ER 244, CA, per May LJ at 344, 264.

[21] *Re Gorman (a bankrupt)* [1990] 1 All ER 717, [1990] 1 WLR 616, Ch DC; *Huntingford v Hobbs* [1993] 1 FLR 736, CA, noted [1992] Conv 347 (Helen Norman); [1993] Fam Law 176 (P Wylie); *Byford v Butler* [2003] EWHC 1267 (Ch), [2004] 1 FLR 56, noted [2003] Conv 533 (Heather Cowan).

[22] [1991] 1 AC 107, [1990] 1 All ER 1111, HL, noted [1990] Conv 314 (M P Thompson); (1991) 54 MLR 126 (S Gardner); (1991) 5 Tru LI 9 (Jean Warburton).

independently of any inference to be drawn from the conduct of the parties in the course of sharing the house as their home and managing their joint affairs, there has at any time prior to acquisition, or exceptionally at some later date, been any agreement, arrangement or understanding reached between them that the property is to be shared beneficially, though it is not necessary that the agreement extends to defining the extent of the respective shares. This 'common intention', which has been said to mean 'a shared intention communicated between them',[23] can only be based on evidence of express discussions between the parties, however imperfectly remembered and however imprecise their terms may have been. Once a finding to this effect is made it will only be necessary for the party asserting a claim to a beneficial interest against the party entitled to the legal estate to show that he or she has acted to his or her detriment or significantly altered his or her position in reliance on the agreement in order to give rise to a constructive trust or proprietary estoppel. Thus in *Grant v Edwards*[24] the defendant told the plaintiff with whom he was cohabiting that her name was not to go on to the title because, if the property were acquired jointly, it would operate to her prejudice in the matrimonial proceedings between her and her husband. This showed that she was intended to have a beneficial interest otherwise no such excuse would have been needed.[25]

The judge in *Hammond v Mitchell*[26] did not say whether in his view the reasons given by the plaintiff for the bungalow being put in his name were valid: he held, however, that there was express discussion in relation to the bungalow which, although not directed with any precision as to proprietary interests, was sufficient to amount to an understanding at least that the bungalow was to be shared beneficially. The common intention that has to be established must relate to the beneficial ownership of the property. Lord Bridge observed in *Lloyds Bank plc v Rosset*[27] that neither a common intention by spouses that a house is to be renovated as a 'joint venture' nor a

---

[23] *Springette v Defoe* [1992] 2 FLR 388 at 393, CA, per Dillon LJ. A common intention by laymen to own their home jointly will be taken to mean an intention to own it equally: *Savill v Goodall* [1993] 1 FLR 755, CA. In the unusual case of *Mollo v Mollo* [2000] WTLR 227, discussed (2000) 17 T & ELJ 7 (M Cohn and M Watson) a divorced couple bought a house in the woman's name, principally to serve as a home for their adult sons. It was decided that she held it for herself and her ex-husband in proportion to their contributions on the basis of constructive trust or proprietary estoppel.

[24] [1986] Ch 638, [1986] 2 All ER 426, CA, noted [1986] Conv 291 (Jean Warburton); (1986) 45 CLJ 394 (D Hayton). See (1987) 50 MLR 94 (Brenda Sufrin). *Eves v Eves* [1975] 3 All ER 768, [1975] 1 WLR 1338, CA was said in *Grant v Edwards* and *Lloyds Bank plc v Rosset*, supra, HL, to be explicable in the same way. In that case the parties had lived together, intending to marry when they were free to do so, and had two children. A house was purchased, in the man's name. He told the plaintiff that it was to be their house, but that it would have to be in his name alone as she was under 21. This was simply an excuse to avoid a conveyance into joint names. She made no financial contribution, but did a great deal of work to the house and garden 'much more than many wives would do'. After they had parted the plaintiff successfully claimed a share of the beneficial interest.

[25] Strictly there was, as Mustill LJ pointed out, no common intention, but the defendant could not be heard to say so in view of the untruthful excuse he has given to the plaintiff.

[26] [1992] 2 All ER 109, [1991] 1 WLR 1127, noted [1992] Conv 218 (Anna Lawson); (1993) 56 MLR 224 (P O'Hagan); (1992) 22 Fam Law 523 (Linda Clarke & Rod Edmonds).

[27] Supra, HL, at 130, 1117.

common intention that the house is to be shared by parents and children as the family home throws any light on their intentions with respect to its beneficial ownership.

Unlike the above cases in the first category, there is a second category of case above there is no evidence to support a finding of an agreement or arrangement to share the beneficial interest, however reasonable it might have been for the parties to have made such an agreement if they had applied their minds to the question. Here the court, relying entirely on the conduct of the parties, may first infer from it a common intention to share the property beneficially. If the inference can properly be drawn the same conduct may be relied on to show that the party has acted to his or her detriment or has significantly altered his position in reliance on the inferred agreement. Lord Bridge[28] said that while direct contributions to the purchase price by a party who is not the legal owner, whether initially or by payment of mortgage instalments, would readily justify the court in drawing the inference of a common intention,[29] it was very doubtful whether anything less would do.[30] If the conduct does not justify the court in drawing the necessary inference, the court cannot impute to the parties a common intention they did not have by forming its own opinion as to what reasonable persons in the position of parties would have intended.

Burns v Burns,[31] which like most of the cases involved an unmarried couple, illustrates the difficulty of inferring a common intention in the absence of direct contributions. There a house had been purchased and conveyed into the name of the man alone in 1963. There was no express trust, and no express agreement to create an interest for the benefit of the woman plaintiff, who had made no real or substantial contribution towards the purchase price either directly or indirectly. The court declined to infer a common intention that she was to have a beneficial interest merely from the facts that she had lived with the defendant, by whom she had two children, for 19 years, had looked after the family's well-being by performing the domestic duties of the household and had brought up their children, or from the fact that she had bought chattels for the household out of her earnings and had redecorated the house. She was not, May LJ said 'entitled to any share in the beneficial interest in [the family] home even though over a very substantial number of years she may have worked just as hard as the man in maintaining the family, in the sense of keeping

---

[28] In *Lloyds Bank plc v Rosset*, supra, HL.

[29] If the court refused to draw such an inference, there would be a resulting trust in proportion to the contribution made.

[30] But in *Burns v Burns* [1984] Ch 317, [1984] 1 All ER 244, CA and *Grant v Edwards*, supra, CA, it seems to have been thought that indirect contributions would suffice provided that they are referable to the acquisition of the property. The need for referability was repeated in *Windeler v Whitehall* [1990] 2 FLR 505. See also *Layton v Martin* [1986] 2 FLR 227; *R v Robson* (1990) 92 Cr App Rep 1, CA.

[31] Supra, CA, noted (1984) 43 CLJ 227 (R Ingleby); [1984] Conv 381 (S Coneys); *Thomas v Fuller-Brown* [1988] 1 FLR 237, CA; *Howard v Jones* [1989] Fam Law 231, CA (claim also failed in last two cases on ground of no common intention). See also *Winkworth v Edward Baron Development Co Ltd* [1987] 1 All ER 114, [1986] 1 WLR 1512, HL, noted [1987] Conv 217 (Jean Warburton), where the wife was held to have no equitable interest, there being no connection between her contribution and the acquisition of the matrimonial home and [2003] Fam Law 834 (D Burles)

house, giving birth to and looking after and helping to bring up the children of the union'. In *Le Foe v Le Foe*,[32] however, the judge held, after citing *Burns v Burns*,[33] that by virtue of the wife's indirect contributions to the mortgage he was entitled to infer that the parties commonly intended that the wife should have a beneficial interest in the former matrimonial home.

In the unusual case of *Re Share (Lorraine)*,[34] where the property was in the sole name of the wife, it was her trustee in bankruptcy who sought to claim that she had a beneficial interest. It was held, however, that the husband was the sole beneficial owner. He had paid the deposit, all of the mortgage instalments and the insurance payments, and the evidence was that at the time of the purchase (when the husband was married to a different woman) it was agreed that the property should belong to the husband alone.

(d) DETRIMENTAL RELIANCE

Even if a common intention is established, a claimant (let us assume the woman) will not succeed unless she establishes that she has acted to her detriment on the basis of that common intention. Thus in *Midland Bank Ltd v Dobson*[35] it had been the common intention of husband and wife when the family home had been purchased 30 years earlier that they should share the beneficial interest. However the wife's claim failed: on the ground of resulting trust because she had made no contribution directly or indirectly to the purchase price, and on the ground of constructive trust because she had not demonstrated that she was induced to act to her detriment on the basis of a common intention of ownership of the house or that there was otherwise any nexus between the acquisition of the property and something provided or foregone by her. There is little authority on what is necessary for a claimant to prove that she so acted, but there must be some link between the common intention and the acts relied on as a detriment. In *Grant v Edwards*[36] Nourse LJ said that in his view the conduct required 'must be conduct on which the woman could not reasonably have been expected to embark unless she was to have an interest in the home'. In the same case Browne-Wilkinson VC said:[37] 'Setting up house together, having a baby and making payments to general housekeeping expenses (not strictly necessary to enable the mortgage to be paid) may all be referable to the mutual love and affection of the parties and not specifically referable to the claimant's belief that she has an interest in the house.' However, he went on, 'once it has been shown that there was a common intention that the claimant should have an interest in the house, any act done by her to her detriment relating to the joint lives of the parties is . . . sufficient detriment to qualify. The

---

32 [2001] 2 FLR 970, noted [2002] Conv 273 (M P Thompson).   33 Supra, CA.
34 [2002] 2 FLR 88.   35 [1986] 1 FLR 171, CA. See (1996) 16 LS 218 (Anna Lawson).
36 Supra, CA, at 433, and see p 194 n 1 supra. See also *Ungarian v Lesnoff* [1990] Ch 206, [1989] 3 WLR 840, noted [1990] CLJ 25 (Mika Oldham); *Cooke v Cooke* [1987] VR 625.
37 Supra CA, at 439, applied *Lloyds Bank plc v Rosset* [1989] Ch 350, [1988] 3 All ER 915, CA. See (1991) 54 MLR 126 (S Gardner).

acts do not have to be inherently referable to the house.' In *Churchill v Roach*[38] all the acts relied upon as constituting detriment occurred before the alleged common intention arose and could not therefore constitute the detrimental reliance required to establish a constructive trust. It may be added that a party who fails to establish a claim under a common intention constructive trust may yet, if she has made a contribution to the purchase price, be able to claim a share under a resulting trust.[39]

(e) QUANTUM OF THE CLAIMANT'S BENEFICIAL INTEREST

This question was considered in detail by Chadwick LJ, with whose judgment the other members of the court agreed, in *Oxley v Hiscock*.[40] Where the evidence establishes the shares which the parties have agreed each should have, this will prevail. Where this is not the case Chadwick LJ, in his careful review of the cases both before and after the important case of *Midland Bank plc v Cooke*,[41] explained how the approach of the courts had changed.[42] The earlier cases, such as *Walker v Hall*[43] adopted a property-based approach so that in the absence of specific evidence of the parties' intention each would have an interest proportionate to his or her contribution to the cost of acquisition under a resulting trust. Thus in *Springette v Defoe*[44] Dillon LJ said that 'the court does not as yet sit, as under a palm tree, to exercise a general discretion to do what the man in the street, on a general overview of the case, might regard as just'.

A turning point in this area of the law, said Chadwick LJ, was *Grant v Edwards*,[45] where the extent of the interest was said to depend on the common intention of the parties, either expressed or, more usually to be inferred from all the circumstances. Identifiable contributions to the purchase of the house would often be important factors, but contributions by way of labour or other unquantifiable actions of the

---

[38] [2004] 2 FLR 989.

[39] See *Re Densham (a bankrupt)* [1975] 3 All ER 726 (claim to a half share under a common intention constructive trust void as against the trustee in bankruptcy by reason of the Bankruptcy Act 1914 (repealed), but entitled to a one ninth share under a resulting trust as a consequence of contributions to the purchase price).

[40] [2004] EWCA Civ 546, [2004] 3 All ER 703, noted (2004) 120 LQR 541 (S Gardner); [2005] Conv 79 (M J Dixon); [2004] Conv 496 (M P Thompson); (2004) 154 NLJ 952 (E Atkinson); [2004] Fam Law (S Edwards); (2004) 62 T & ELTJ 6 (Constance Mahoney); (2004) 135 PLJ (M Pawlowski). In this case Chadwick LJ expressed himself as dealing with cases where each party has made some financial contribution to the purchase; *Cox v Jones* [2004] EWHC 1486 (Ch), [2004] 2 FLR 1010 was not such a case, but Mann J did not think that that made any difference.

[41] [1995] 4 All ER 562, CA.

[42] He cited *Drake v Whipp* [1996] 2 FCR 296 per Peter Gibson LJ at 298 who said '. . . as is notorious, it is not easy to reconcile every judicial utterance in this well-travelled area of the law'.

[43] [1984] FLR 126, CA; *Turton v Turton*, [1988] Ch 542, [1987] 2 All ER 641, CA. See also *Springett v Defoe* [1992] 2 FCR 561, CA, as explained by Chadwick LJ in *Oxley v Hiscock*, supra, CA.

[44] Supra, CA, at 567. See the observations on this case in *Oxley v Hiscock*, supra, CA.

[45] [1986] Ch 638, [1986] 2 All ER 426, CA, referred to by Lord Bridge with evident approval in *Lloyds Bank plc v Rosset*, supra, HL. For facts see p 194, supra.

claimant might also be relevant.[46] The claimant in that case was awarded a half
interest in the house, which was not proportionate to the 'qualifying contribution' in
terms of the indirect contribution to the acquisition or enhancement of the house. In
his judgment Browne-Wilkinson V-C suggested that the law of proprietary estoppel
might provide useful guidance, though the case was not decided on that basis.

Having considered the earlier cases Chadwick LJ came to *Midland Bank plc v
Cooke*[47] where the Court of Appeal increased the wife's share of 6.74% awarded by the
judge at first instance, being the proportion represented by her half share of the
wedding gift from the husband's parents to the total purchase price of the property, to
50%. In that case Waite LJ said that in cases where the party without legal title has
successfully asserted an equitable interest through direct contribution, the duty of the
judge in determining (in the absence of direct evidence of intention) what proportions the parties must be assumed to have intended for their beneficial ownership, is
to undertake a survey of the whole course of dealing between the parties relevant to
their ownership and occupation of the property and their sharing of its burdens and
advantages. His scrutiny should not confine itself to the limited range of acts of direct
contribution of the sort that are needed to found a beneficial interest in the first
place, but should take into consideration all conduct which throws light on the question what shares were intended. It was further held that the court may infer an
agreement as to the proportions of their beneficial interests notwithstanding positive
evidence that the parties neither discussed nor intended any such agreement.[48] A
similar approach was taken in *Drake v Whipp*[49] where Peter Gibson LJ said, 'in constructive trust cases, the court can adopt a broad brush approach to determining the
parties' respective shares', and look at the parties' entire course of conduct together.

In *Oxley v Hiscock*[50] Chadwick LJ said that the question of quantum arises only after
a common intention has been established that each party shall have a beneficial interest. In many cases, he said, the answer to the question will be provided by evidence of
what they said and did at the time of the acquisition, but where there is no evidence of
any such discussion—or even where there is positive evidence that there was no
discussion on the point—the question must be answered. It must, he continued:

now be accepted that (at least in this court and below) the answer is that each is entitled to
that share which the court considers fair having regard to the whole course of dealing
between them in relation to the property. And, in that context, 'the whole course of dealing
between them in relation to the property' includes the arrangements which they make from

---

[46] *Risch v McFee* [1991] FCR 168, CA (interest free loan); *Springett v Defoe*, supra, CA (discount under the
right to buy—Housing Act 1985, Part V).

[47] Supra, CA, at 574.

[48] This last proposition was criticized in [1997] Conv 66 (M Dixon) but seems to have been accepted by
Chadwick LJ in *Oxley v Hiscock*, supra, CA.

[49] *Drake v Whipp*, supra, CA, noted [1997] Conv 467 (Alison Dunn); [1996] Fam Law 298 (Diane Wragg);
[1996] Fam Law 484 (Mark Pawlowski). See also *Carlton v Goodman* [2002] EWCA Civ 545, [2002] 2 FLR
259; *Chan Pui Chun v Leung Kam Ho* [2002] EWCA Civ 1075, [2003] 1 FLR 23.

[50] Supra, CA.

time to time in order to meet the outgoings (for example, mortgage contributions, council tax and utilities, repairs, insurance and housekeeping) which have to be met if they are to live in the property as their home.

In supplying or imputing a common intention in this way an outcome is arrived at which is no different from that which is reached by an analysis in the terms of proprietary estoppel.

Chadwick LJ went on to observe that the courts had not found it easy to reconcile the present position with the traditional property-based approach. He identified three strands of reasoning: (1) that the parties are taken to have agreed at the time of acquisition of the property that their respective shares are not to be quantified then, but are left to be determined by the court when their relationship comes to an end or the property is sold on the basis of what is then fair having regard to the whole course of dealing between them;[51] (2) that the court undertakes a survey of the whole course of dealing between the parties and treats what has taken place while the parties have been living together in the property as evidence of what they intended at the time of the acquisition.[52] Both of these approaches, particularly the second, Chadwick LJ thought artificial. He preferred (3) the view that the court makes such order as the circumstances require in order to give effect to the beneficial interest in the property of the one party, the existence of which the other party (having the legal title) is estopped from denying.[53]

(f) DATE OF VALUATION OF SHARES

Prima facie, if persons are entitled to property in aliquot shares as tenants in common under a trust, the value of their respective shares must be determined at the date when the property is sold, but that may have to give way to circumstances. For example, one of the parties may buy out the other, in which case the value of that party's share may have to be determined at a different date.[54]

Valuation is not to be made as at the date of separation, save in the unlikely circumstance that it was agreed that the parties' respective beneficial shares should be valued at that point of time if and when it should occur. The parties' separation will doubtless indicate that the purpose of the trust has failed and the effect may well be to trigger off a demand for a sale. But it does not give rise to any discretion in the court

---

[51] See per Lord Diplock in *Gissing v Gissing* [1971] AC 886, [1970] 2 All ER 780, HL, at 909, 793, adopted by Nourse LJ in *Stokes v Anderson*, supra, CA, at 543.

[52] As suggested by Waite LJ in *Midland Bank plc v Cooke*, supra, CA, at 574.

[53] This was suggested by Browne-Wilkinson V-C in *Grant v Edwards* [1986] Ch 638, [1986] 2 All ER 426, CA, at 657, 439, approved by Robert Walker LJ in *Yaxley v Gotts* [2000] Ch 162, [2000] 1 All ER 711, CA, at 177, 722. It underlies the decision of this court in *Drake v Whipp*, supra, CA, at 302.

[54] *Gordon v Douce* [1983] 2 All ER 228, CA per Fox LJ at p 230. *Bernard v Josephs*, supra, CA; *Turton v Turton* supra, CA. See [1987] Conv 378 (Jean Warburton); [1988] Fam Law 72 (J Montgomery); (1989) 86 LSG 31/31 (I M Hardcastle).

to impose on the parties a valuation of their interests at a date which is earlier than the date of the realization.

Events after the date of separation may be very relevant in relation to the equitable accounting that must take place before the money is distributed: if, for example, one party stays in possession paying mortgage instalments, rates and other outgoings prima facie he must on the one hand be given credit for paying the other's share of these payments, while on the other hand he must be debited with an occupation rent for using the other's share of the house.[55]

(g) IMPROVEMENTS

So far as improvements to matrimonial property are concerned s 37 of the Matrimonial Proceedings and Property Act 1970 provides[56] that where a husband or a wife makes a substantial[57] contribution to the improvement of real or personal property in which either or both of them has or have a beneficial interest, the party so contributing shall unless otherwise agreed be treated as having acquired by virtue of his or her contribution a share or an enlarged share, as the case may be, in that beneficial interest of such an extent as may have been then agreed or, in default of such agreement, as the court may in all the circumstances consider just.

The Civil Partnership Act 2004,[58] not yet in force, contains similar provisions in relation to civil partners.

(h) SECTION 17 OF THE MARRIED WOMEN'S PROPERTY ACT 1882[59]

This section provides as follows: 'In any question between husband and wife[60] as to the title or to possession of property, either party . . . may apply [to a court which] may make such order with respect to the property in dispute . . . as it thinks fit.' So far as title to property is concerned, it was finally settled by the House of Lords in *Pettitt v Pettitt*,[61] after a long series of cases demonstrating acute differences of opinion in the Court of Appeal, that s 17 is a purely procedural section which confers no jurisdiction to transfer any proprietary interest from one spouse to the other or to create new

---

[55] See *Dennis v McDonald* [1982] Fam 63, [1982] 1 All ER 590, CA, and the cases cited in n 144, p 189, supra. See also (1992) 22 Fam Law 545 (S Johnson); [1995] Conv 391 (Elizabeth Codie) and cf *Jones (AE) v Jones (FW)* [1977] 2 All ER 231, CA.

[56] The section was said by Lord Denning MR in *Davis v Vale* [1971] 2 All ER 1021, CA, at 1025 to be declaratory of the pre-existing law. It is made applicable to engaged couples by the Law Reform (Miscellaneous Provisions) Act 1970, s 2. See (1970) 120 NLJ 1008 (R T Oerton) and the correspondence at 1082.

[57] As to what is meant by 'substantial' see *Samuels (WA)'s Trustee v Samuels* (1973) 233 Estates Gazette 149.

[58] Section 65.

[59] As amended. It applies also to previously engaged couples: Law Reform (Miscellaneous Provisions) Act 1970, s 2(2), and see *Shaw v Fitzgerald* [1992] 1 FLR 357.

[60] Including the parties to a polygamous or potentially polygamous union married according to the law of their domicile—*Chaudhry v Chaudhry* [1975] 3 All ER 687 point not decided on appeal [1976] Fam 148, [1976] 1 All ER 805n, CA.

[61] [1970] AC 777, [1969] 2 All ER 385, HL.

proprietary rights in either spouse.[62] By an extension contained in s 39 of the Matrimonial Proceedings and Property Act 1970 an application may be made for three years after the marriage has been dissolved or annulled. Usually, however, there is no point in going on with an application under s 17 once there has been a divorce. The proper course is to take out proceedings under the Matrimonial Causes Act 1973, which gives wide powers to the court to do what is just having regard to all the circumstances.[63]

It should be added that it is equally clear from *Pettitt v Pettitt*[64] that where the question is not one of title to property, but whether an established property right can be enforced, it is agreed that the court has a discretion to restrain or postpone the enforcement of a spouse's legal rights, in relation, for instance, to sale of the property or to possession, having regard to the mutual matrimonial duties of the spouses.

The Civil Partnership Act 2004,[65] not yet in force, contains similar provisions in relation to civil partners.

2 PROPRIETARY ESTOPPEL

(a) THE PRINCIPLES INVOLVED

In *Dillwyn v Llewellyn*[66] a father placed one of his sons in possession of land belonging to the father, and at the same time signed a memorandum that he had presented the land to the son for the purpose of furnishing him with a dwelling-house, but no formal conveyance was ever executed. The son, with the assent and approbation of the father, built at his own expense a house upon the land and resided there. After the father's death the question arose what estate, if any, the son had in the land. The judgment of Lord Westbury LC does not makes it clear whether he considered the

---

[62] The court has power to order a sale of the property. Having declared the respective shares of husband and wife in the property, it may order the sale by one party to the other of his or her share at the price defined by the declared value of the vendor's interest, and in an appropriate case may order payment of the sum so assessed—*Bothe v Amos* [1976] Fam 46, [1975] 2 All ER 321, CA.

[63] See *Fielding v Fielding* [1978] 1 All ER 267, CA.

[64] Supra. Note that the Family Law Act 1996, ss 30 et seq confers rights of occupation on a husband or wife in relation to a dwelling house that has been a matrimonial home so long as the marriage subsists. The phrase 'husband or wife' is prospectively amended to 'spouse or civil partner' by the Civil Partnership Act 2004. See also Insolvency Act 1986, ss 335A and 336, as amended.

[65] Sections 66–68.

[66] (1862) 4 De G F & J 517. Cf *Ramsden v Dyson* (1866) LR 1 HL 129; *Plimmer v Wellington Corpn* (1884) 9 App Cas 699, PC; *Chalmers v Pardoe* [1963] 3 All ER 552, PC. See, generally, (1983) 42 CLJ 257 (M P Thompson); (1984) 13 AALR 45 (E K Teh); [1988] Conv 346 (P T Evans); (1988) 23 Ir Jur NS 38 (L Bentley and P Coughlan); (1989) 12 Sydney LR 17 (S Stoljar); (1990) 10 Ox JLS 42 (M Garner); (1991) 13 Adel LR 225 (Linda Kirk); (1994) 14 LS 151 (Margaret Halliwell); [1996] Conv 193 (Christine Davis). See also (1993) 13 Ox JLS 99 (Christine Davis); (1996) 20 MULR 805; (1997) 19 Syd LR 32 (A Robertson) and (2002) 146 Sol Jo (M Pawlowski).

case to be one of gift or of contract, but he did say, after repeating the rule that equity will not complete an imperfect gift, that the subsequent acts of the donor might give the donee a right or ground of claim which he did not have under the original gift. The ratio of his actual decision in this case seems to be that putting the son into possession and the subsequent expenditure incurred with the approbation of the father were grounds for equity intervening to complete the imperfect gift by compelling a conveyance of the fee simple to the son,[67] though it has been thought that the case is to be explained on a contractual basis.[68]

Scarman LJ in *Crabb v Arun District Council*[69] adopted a passage from the judgment of Fry J in *Willmott v Barber*[70] in which he had in effect said that in order for P (who may in fact be either plaintiff or defendant) to succeed in a plea of proprietary estoppel he must establish five points, namely:

(i)   P must have made a mistake as to his legal rights.

(ii)   P must have expended some money or must have done some act (not necessarily upon D's land) on the faith of his mistaken belief.

(iii) D, the possessor of the legal right which P claims it would be inequitable for D to enforce, must have known of the existence of his own right which is inconsistent with the right claimed by P.

(iv)   D must have known of P's mistaken belief of his, P's, right.

(v)   D must have encouraged P in his expenditure of money or in the other acts which he has done, either directly or by abstaining from asserting his legal right.

However it has been said now to be clear that it is not essential to establish the five 'probanda', as they are called,[71] though they continue to be referred to from time to time.[72] There are many cases of proprietary estoppel which do not involve a mistaken

---

[67] See (1963) 79 LQR 238 (D E Allan).

[68] Eg Wynn-Parry J at first instance in *Re Diplock* [1947] Ch 716 at 781–784, [1947] 1 All ER 522 at 549. See *J T Developments Ltd v Quinn* (1990) 62 P & CR 33, CA, where to found an estoppel it had to be shown that the plaintiffs had created or encouraged an expectation that the defendants would have a new lease and that the defendants had expended money on the property in reliance on the expectation and with the knowledge of the plaintiffs.

[69] [1976] Ch 179, [1975] 3 All ER 865, CA, noted (1976) 40 Conv 156 (F R Crane), and applied *Griffiths v Williams* [1977] LS Gaz R 1130, CA. See also *Western Fish Products Ltd v Penwith District Council* [1981] 2 All ER 204, CA; *Waltons Stores (Interstate) Ltd v Maher* (1988) 76 ALR 513; (1979) 8 Sydney LR 578 (J D Davies); [2001] 22 Adel LR 157.

[70] (1880) 15 Ch D 96.

[71] *Lloyds Bank plc v Carrick* [1996] 4 All ER 630, CA, per Morritt LJ, noted (1996) 112 LQR 549 (Patricia Ferguson); [1996] Conv 295 (M P Thompson).

[72] See *Coombes v Smith* [1986] 1 WLR 808, where the judge went through Fry LJ's five points and held that the plaintiff failed to establish any of them; *Matharu v Matharu* [1994] 2 FLR 597, CA, noted [1994] Fam Law 624 (J Dewar); (1995) 58 MLR 413 (P Milne); [1995] Conv 61 (Mary Welstead), where the majority of the court held that the five points were established and the defendant was accordingly entitled to a remedy. The estoppel claim failed in *A-G of Hong Kong v Humphreys Estate (Queen's Gardens) Ltd* [1987] AC 114, [1987] 2 All ER 387, PC, which shows that where there is an agreement subject to contract it is very difficult to establish an estoppel preventing a party from withdrawing.

belief on either side, and where to insist on the five probanda is inappropriate.[73] Accordingly in *Taylor Fashions Ltd v Liverpool Victoria Trustees Co Ltd*[74] Oliver J said that what is required is:

a very much broader approach which is directed to ascertaining whether, in particular individual circumstances, it would be unconscionable for a party to be permitted to deny that which, knowingly or unknowingly, he has allowed or encouraged another to assume to his detriment rather than to inquiring whether the circumstances can be fitted within the confines of some preconceived formula serving as a universal yardstick for every form of unconscionable behaviour.

'The fundamental principle that equity is concerned to prevent unconscionable conduct permeates all the elements of the doctrine.'[75] The principle in its broadest form is that where one person (A) has acted to his detriment on the faith of a belief which was known to and encouraged[76] by another person (B) that he either has or is going to be given a right in or over B's property, B cannot insist on his legal rights if to do so would be inconsistent with A's belief.[77] There must be a sufficient link between the promises relied upon and the conduct which constitutes the detriment,[78] but the promises relied on do not have to be the sole inducement for the conduct: it is sufficient that they are *an* inducement.[79] Once it has been established that promises were made, and that there has been conduct by the complainant of such a nature that inducement may be inferred, then the burden of proof shifts to the defendant to establish that he did not rely on the promises.[80] The effect is that promises unsupported by consideration which are initially revocable may become

---

[73] See eg *Inwards v Baker* [1965] 2 QB 29, [1965] 1 All ER 446, CA, discussed infra p 208; *ER Ives Investments Ltd v High* [1967] 2 QB 379, [1967] 1 All ER 504, CA, discussed infra p 208.

[74] Supra, at 915, 916, CA. Oliver LJ cited this after his elevation to the Court of Appeal in *Habib Bank Ltd v Habib Bank AG Zurich* [1981] 2 All ER 650, CA, and it received the approbation of the other members of the court. See also *Hammersmith and Fulham London Borough Council v Top Shop Centres Ltd* [1990] Ch 237, [1989] 2 All ER 655; *Lim Teng Huan v Ang Swee Chuan* [1992] 1 WLR 113, PC, noted [1992] Conv 173 (Say Hak Goo); *Austotel Pty Ltd v Franklin's Selfservice Pty Ltd* (1989) 16 NSWLR 582, (NSWCA); *Pridean Ltd v Forest Taverns Ltd* (1998) 75 P & CR 447, CA; *Jones v Stones* [1999] 1 WLR 1739, CA.

[75] *Gillett v Holt* [2000] 2 All ER 289, CA, per Robert Walker LJ at 301, noted (2000) 59 CLJ 453 (M Dixon), (2000) 15 T & ELJ 6 (J McDonnell); [2001] Conv 78 (M P Thompson). Where the pleadings fail to make the allegations normally necessary to support a claim on the basis of proprietary estoppel, the court may nevertheless grant relief on that basis if the evidence relied on would have supported such a plea: *Strover v Strover* (2005) Times 30 May.

[76] Or, it seems, merely allowed—*Inwards v Baker* [1965] 2 QB 29, [1965] 1 All ER 446, CA, at 37, 448; *Ward v Kirkland* [1967] Ch 194, [1966] 1 All ER 609.

[77] See *Re Basham (decd)* [1987] 1 All ER 405, [1986] 1 WLR 1498, per Mr Nugee QC at 410, 1503, cited by Balcombe LJ in *Wayling v Jones* (1993) 69 P & CR 170, CA, at 172, and by Robert Walker LJ in *Gillett v Holt* supra, CA, at 302, and noted [1987] Conv 211 (Jill Martin); (1988) 46 CLJ 216 (D J Hayton).

[78] See *Wayling v Jones*, supra, CA, at 173, cited *Gillett v Holt*, supra, CA; *Keelwalk Properties Ltd v Walker* [2002] EWCA Civ 1076, [2002] 3 EGLR 79.

[79] See *Wayling v Jones* supra, CA, at 173, cited *Gillett v Holt*, supra, CA; *Amalgamated Investment and Property Co Ltd (in liq) v Texas Commerce International Bank Ltd* [1982] QB 84, [1981] 1 All ER 923, affd on other grounds [1982] QB 84, [1981] 3 All ER 577, CA.

[80] See *Wayling v Jones* supra, CA, at 173, cited *Gillett v Holt*, supra, CA; *Greasley v Cooke* [1980] 3 All ER 710, [1980] 1 WLR 1306, CA; *Grant v Edwards* [1986] Ch 638, [1986] 2 All ER 426, CA.

binding and irrevocable as a consequence of the promisee's detrimental reliance. Thus, for example, if B gives repeated assurances to A that he will leave certain property to A by his will, and A acts to his detriment on the faith of those assurances, A may have a remedy in equity against B if B subsequently changes his mind.[81] However if there is a relevant unforeseen change of circumstances, the probable reaction of the just bystander (and it has been said that it is by reference to his conscience that these matters should be judged) might be that the assurance given could be rescinded by the B and replaced by a different arrangement, and this would be the proper conclusion as long as it satisfied the equity that arose before the change of circumstances.[82]

It was said in *Jennings v Rice*[83] that the expectation need not be focused on any specific property, but in the most recent case, *Lissimore v Downing*,[84] it was said that that dictum must be read in context. In the opinion of the judge the basic rule is that the representation made or assurance provided or expectation raised must relate to some specific property (which may include the whole of the B's property or his residuary estate) or be expressed in terms which enable an objective assessment to be made of what is being promised.

Somewhat surprisingly, under the doctrine of proprietary estoppel a promise to confer an interest in property which is so equivocal in its terms that it would be incapable of giving rise to a binding contract may be capable of conferring on the promisee a right in equity to a transfer of the whole property. This is said to be an instance of equity supplementing the law.[85]

Finally it may be added, on general principles, that when a person seeks the aid of the court to override someone's strict legal rights on equitable grounds, aid will not be given to one who has violated the principle of equity that 'he who comes to equity must come with clean hands'.[86]

(b) DETRIMENTAL RELIANCE

It is settled law that detriment is required, but in this context detriment is not a narrow or technical concept. The detriment need not consist of the expenditure of money or other quantifiable financial detriment, so long as it is something substantial.

---

[81] *Gillett v Holt* supra, CA. Generally, of course, a will may be revoked and a representation by a living person as to his testamentary intentions is not binding. It is the detrimental reliance which may prevent that person from changing his mind. See *Taylor v Dickens* [1998] 3 FCR 455 and the criticism of that decision in *Gillet v Holt*, supra, CA.

[82] *Uglow v Uglow* [2004] EWCA Civ 987, [2004] WTLR 1183.

[83] [2002] EWCA Civ 159, [2003] 1 P & CR 100, citing *Re Basham* [1987] 1 All ER 405, and see per Robert Walker LJ in *Gillett v Holt*, supra, CA, at 302.

[84] [2003] 2 FLR 308.

[85] *Jones v Watkins* [1987] CA Transcript 1200 per Slade LJ, cited by Robert Walker LJ in *Gillett v Holt* supra, CA.

[86] *J Willis & Son v Willis* [1986] 1 EGLR 62, CA (aid refused to one who had put forward a wholly fraudulent document. It seems to be a case of proprietary estoppel, though referred to as 'promissory estoppel', 'equitable estoppel' or 'quasi estoppel').

The requirement must be approached as part of a broad inquiry as to whether repudiation of an assurance is or is not unconscionable in all the circumstances.[87] The issue of detriment must be judged at the moment when the person who has given the assurance seeks to go back on it. Whether the detriment is sufficiently substantial is to be tested by whether it would be unjust or inequitable to allow the assurance to be disregarded—that is, again, the essential test of unconscionability. The detriment alleged must, of course, be pleaded and proved.[88] Further it must be a personal detriment. Accordingly in *Lloyd v Dugdale*[89] the majority shareholder in a company was not permitted to rely on a form of derivative estoppel, derived from the company.

In order to show that the person to whom the assurance was made was induced to act to his detriment it is not necessary to show that he would have left the maker of the assurance if the promise had not been made, but only that he would have left him if the promise had been withdrawn. Once the claimant shows that the promise was made, and that his conduct was such that inducement could be inferred, the burden of proof shifts to the maker of the promise to show that the claimant did not, on fact, rely on the promise.[90]

In *Gillett v Holt*,[91] at the defendant's suggestion, the claimant left school at 15, against his headmaster's advice and despite his parents' misgivings, to work on the defendant's farm, which he continued to do for nearly 40 years. With his wife and children the claimant provided the defendant, a bachelor, with a surrogate family, and he was given repeated assurances that he would inherit the farm business. However in 1995 he was summarily dismissed, and the last of a series of wills left him nothing: an earlier will had left everything to him. The Court of Appeal, reversing the judge below, had no hesitation in finding the necessary detriment. 'Mr Gillett and his wife devoted

---

[87] *Gillett v Holt* [2000] 2 All ER 289, CA, discussed [2001] Conv 13 (Rosalyn Wells) who argues that the decision does not make it easy to ascertain to what extent the court can take into account matters of a personal nature as opposed to matters which have a financial or property element. In *Greasley v Cooke* [1980] 3 All ER 710 (see [1981] Conv 154 (Ruth Annand)) the plaintiffs had given assurances to the defendant that she could remain in the house which had been her home for many years for as long as she wished, and it was held that it was to be presumed that the defendant had acted on the faith of those assurances. The burden of proof was on the plaintiffs to rebut this presumption, and since they had failed to do so an equity was raised in favour of the defendant, which should be satisfied by allowing her to stay on in the house for as long as she wished. In (1981) 125 Sol Jo 539, M P Thompson observed that the facts are difficult to distinguish from those in *Maddison v Alderson* (1983) 8 App Cas 467, not cited in *Greasley v Cooke*, where the contrary conclusion was reached. A passage of the judgment of Lord Denning MR in *Greasley v Cooke*, at 713, which suggests that any action in reliance on an assurance is sufficient, whether or not the action is detrimental has been explained by Dunn LJ in *Watts v Storey* (1983) 134 NLJ 631, CA.

[88] *Gillett v Holt*, supra, CA; *Jiggins v Brisley* [2003] EWHC 841 (Ch), [2003] WTLR 1141. Contrast *Christian v Christian* (1981) 131 NLJ 43, CA, where the claim failed because the plaintiff had not shown a detriment; *Bostock v Bryant* (1990) 61 P & CR 23, CA where there was no detriment sufficient to make it unconscionable for the licence to be determined. See (1981) 44 MLR 461 (G Woodman); [1982] CLJ 290 (Susan J Burridge). The detriment was insufficient to establish a claim in *Churchill v Roach* [2004] 2 FLR 989, but a claim under the Inheritance (Provision for Family and Dependants) Act 1975 was established.

[89] [2001] EWCA Civ 1754, [2002] WTLR 863, noted [2002] Conv 584 (M Dixon).

[90] *Wayling v Jones* (1995) 69 P & CR 170, CA, noted (1995) 111 LQR 389 (Elizabeth Cooke); *Grundy v Ottey* [2003] EWCA Civ 1176, [2003] WTLR 1253, noted [2004] Conv 137 (M P Thompson).

[91] Supra, CA. See (2004) 130 PLJ 22 (Barbara Rich).

the best years of their lives to working for Mr Holt and his company, showing loyalty and devotion to his business interests, his social life and his personal wishes, on the strength of clear and repeated assurances of testamentary benefit.'[92]

(c) HOW THE EQUITY MAY BE SATISFIED [93]

If the equity is established, it is then for the court to say, in the light of the circumstances at the date of the hearing, taking into account the conduct of the parties up to that date, what is the appropriate way in which it can be satisfied.[94] However, the court approaches its task in a cautious way, in order to achieve 'the minimum equity to do justice to the plaintiff'.[95] Thus in *Dillwyn v Llewelyn*,[96] *Pascoe v Turner*[97] and *Voyce v Voyce*[98] there was an order for the conveyance of the fee simple estate, in *Taylor Fashions Ltd v Liverpool Victoria Trustees Co Ltd*[99] a decree of specific performance of the renewal option in the lease, while in *Unity Joint Stock Mutual Banking Association v King*[100] a lien was imposed for the amount expended where a father had allowed his sons to occupy and expend money on his land.

The law was recently reviewed by the Court of Appeal in *Jennings v Rice*[101] where a widow died at the age of 93 without children and wholly intestate leaving an estate of £1.285 million including a house and furniture valued at £435,000. The claimant (the appellant in the Court of Appeal) was a self-employed bricklayer who started to work for the deceased as a part-time gardener in 1970 at the rate of 30p per hour. As time went on his job was extended to running errands, taking the deceased shopping and doing minor maintenance work in the house. In the late 1980s she stopped paying him, but did give him £2,000 towards the purchase of his home. As the deceased became more physically incapacitated the claimant came to perform other services, including personal services, for her and after she suffered a burglary the claimant

---

[92] Ibid, per Robert Walker LJ at 310. Further examples are to be found in the cases referred to in the following section.

[93] Useful articles include (1997) 17 LS 258 (Elizabeth Cooke); (1998) 18 LS 360 (A Robertson); (1999) 115 LQR 438 (S Gardner); [2003] Conv 225 (M P Thompson).

[94] *Burrows and Burrows v Sharpe* [1991] Fam Law 67, CA, discussed (1992) 142 NLJ 320 (S Jones); [1992] Conv 54 (Jill Martin). See *Roebuck v Mungovin* [1994] 2 AC 224 where Lord Browne-Wilkinson observed that the effect of an estoppel is to give the court the power to do what is equitable in all the circumstances.

[95] The phrase used by Scarman LJ in *Crabb v Arun District Council* [1976] Ch 179, [1975] 3 All ER 865, CA, at 198, 880, and cited by Robert Walker LJ in *Gillett v Holt* [2000] 2 All ER 289, CA, at 311. See also *Grundy v Ottey* [2002] EWCA Civ 1176, [2003] WTLR 1253; *Wormall v Wormall* (2004) *Times* 1 Dec, CA (declaration satisfied minimum equity); (2004) 54 T & ELJ 8 (Barbara Rich).

[96] (1862) 4 De G F & J 517. See also *Jackson v Crosby (No 2)* (1979) 21 SASR 280.

[97] [1979] 2 All ER 945, CA. See p 207, n 104.

[98] (1991) 62 P & CR 290, CA, noted [1992] Conv 54 (Jill Martin).   [99] Supra.

[100] (1858) 25 Beav 72. See *Savva v Costa* (1981) 131 NLJ 1114, CA. In *Giumelli v Giumelli* [1999] ALJR 547, noted [1999] CLJ 476 (D Wright), the order was for the payment of a sum of money. See also (2001) 22 Adel LR 123 (Fiona Bruce).

[101] [2002] EWCA Civ 159, [2003] 1 P & CR 100, noted (2002) 118 LQR 519 (M Pawlowski); [2003] Conv 225 (M P Thompson); *Grundy v Ottey* [2003] EWCA Civ 1176, [2003] WTLR 1253; *Uglow v Uglow* [2004] EWCA Civ 987. [2004] WTLR 1183.

began to stay overnight to provide security. On several occasions the deceased led the claimant to believe he would receive all or part of her property on her death. The claimant had clearly acted to his detriment in giving up spare time in the evenings and at weekends to look after the deceased and eventually staying overnight, all unpaid. The judge at first instance, taking account of what the cost of full-time nursing care would have been, awarded the claimant £200,000. The respondent accepted the decision but, in the appeal, the claimant asserted that he was entitled to the whole estate or at least the house and furniture. In dismissing the appeal and affirming the judge's decision Aldous LJ said:

> ... once the elements of proprietary estoppel are established an equity arises. The value of that equity will depend upon all the circumstances including the expectation and the detriment. The task of the court is to do justice. The most essential requirement is that there must be proportionality between the expectation and the detriment.

Robert Walker LJ agreed with Aldous LJ's decision observing that the court must take a principled approach and cannot exercise a completely unfettered discretion according to the individual judge's notion of what is fair in any particular case. The equity arises not from the claimant's expectation alone, though this may be the starting point: it is the combination of this with detrimental reliance and the unconscionability of allowing the benefactor (or his estate) to go back on his assurances. Factors that may be taken into account include misconduct on the part of the claimant,[102] particularly oppressive conduct on the part of the defendaant,[103] the need for a clean break,[104] a change in the amount of the benefactor's assets and his circumstances, the effects and potential effects of taxation,[105] and other claims there may be on the benefactor's bounty. On the facts of the instant case it would have been disproportionate to award the claimant the whole estate or even the house and furniture valued at £435,000.[106]

---

[102] See *J Willis & Son v Willis* [1986] 1 EGLR 62, CA, referred to in n 86, p 204, supra.

[103] *Crabb v Arun DC* [1976] Ch 179, [1975] 3 All ER 865, CA (defendants estopped from denying that the claimant had a right of way over their land. On the faith of their words and conduct the claimant had sold off a portion of his land leaving him, if the defendants had been allowed to succeed, with a useless piece of land to which there was no access). M P Thompson, loc cit, has pointed out that there was some misunderstanding of this decision in *Jennings v Rice*, supra, CA. It was applied to an unusual set of facts in *Salvation Army Trustee Co Ltd v West Yorkshire Metropolitan CC* (1908) 41 P & CR 179.

[104] *Pascoe v Turner* [1979] 2 All ER 945, CA, noted [1979] MLR 574 (Brenda Sufrin); (1979) 129 NLJ 1193 (R D Oughten), where the deserted mistress was perhaps lucky, having spent only about £250 on repairs and improvements, for the court to order conveyance of the fee simple to her. The court took the view that the equity could in all the circumstances only be satisfied by compelling the defendant to give effect to his promise and her expectations. Contrast *Sledmore v Dalby* (1996) 72 P & CR 196, CA, noted (1997) 113 LQR 232 (M Pawlowski); [1997] CLJ 34 (P Milne); [1997] Conv 458 (J R Adams), where the claimant had to be content with something less than his expectation, the need for proportionality being at the heart of the judgment.

[105] *Gillett v Holt*, supra, CA (for facts see p 205, supra).

[106] Similarly in *Campbell v Griffin* [2001] EWCA Civ 990, [2001] WTLR 981, noted (2001) 31 T & ELJ 17 (T Sisley); [2003] Conv 157 (M P Thompson), it would have been disproportionate to award the claimant a life interest in the whole property: he was entitled to the sum of £35,000 charged on the property worth £160,000.

Illustrative cases include *Inwards v Baker*,[107] where the defendant was, in 1931, considering building a bungalow on land which he would have to purchase. His father, who owned some land, suggested that the defendant should build the bungalow on his land and make it a little bigger. The defendant accepted that suggestion and built the bungalow himself, with some financial assistance from his father, part of which he repaid. He had lived in the bungalow ever since. In 1951 the father died and in 1963 the trustees of his will claimed possession from the defendant. The court held that the defendant was entitled to remain in possession of the bungalow as a licensee so long as he desired to use it as his home. In *E R Ives Investments Ltd v High*,[108] the facts were very different and the application of the principle was varied accordingly. The defendant and the predecessors in title of the plaintiff had, in 1949, entered into an agreement whereby the defendant agreed that the foundations of the plaintiff's building should remain on the defendant's land, and it was further agreed that the defendant should have a right of access across the plaintiff's land. The agreement was never put into a formal document. Subsequently the defendant, with the encouragement of the plaintiff's predecessors in title built a garage, the only access to which was across the plaintiff's land. The plaintiff, who took with full knowledge of the facts, nevertheless brought an action for damages for trespass and an injunction to restrain the defendant from further trespass. On the basis of the above principle the Court of Appeal affirmed the dismissal of the action by the county court judge.[109]

In *Baker v Baker*[110] a father gave up his secure tenancy and moved in with his son and daughter-in-law to a property partially bought with his money on the basis that he would live there rent-free for the rest of his life. The father left following a family dispute and it was held that what he was entitled to was compensation for the loss of rent-free accommodation for the rest of his life.

In relation to unregistered land it seems to be accepted that a right arising from proprietary estoppel is capable of binding third parties. It is not registrable as a

---

107 Supra, CA. See also *Jones (A E) v (F W) Jones* [1977] 2 All ER 231, CA (a tenant in common entitled to one quarter of proceeds of sale of a house held on trust for sale held entitled to stay in possession of the house for the rest of his life without paying any rent to his stepmother, his deceased father's administratrix, who was entitled to the other three quarters. He had given up work elsewhere and moved into the house, and also paid money, in the reasonable expectation, induced by his father, that it would be his home for the rest of his life); *Re Sharpe* [1980] 1 All ER 198; *Matharu v Matharu* [1994] 2 FLR 597, CA.

108 [1967] 2 QB 379, [1967] 1 All ER 504, CA, foll. *Thatcher v Douglas* [1996] NLJR 282, CA. See (1967) 31 Conv 332 (F R Crane); (1967) 30 MLR 580 (H W Wilkinson); (1968) 32 Conv 96 (R E Poole); (1995) 59 MLR 637 (G Battersby).

109 The court also relied on the principle of *Halsall v Brizell* [1957] Ch 169, [1957] 1 All ER 371; viz that he who takes the benefit (on the facts here, of keeping his foundations in the defendant's land) must accept the burden (of allowing the defendant the agreed access). It is probably necessary that the benefit and burden both arise under the same deed: *IDC Group Ltd v Clark* [1992] 1 EGLR 187. See *Tito v Waddell (No 2)* [1977] Ch 106 at 289 et seq, [1977] 3 All ER 129 et seq; *Rhone v Stephens* [1994] 2 AC 310, HL: *Thamesmead Town Ltd v Allotey* (1998) 30 HLR 1052, CA; and [1998] CLJ 522 (Christine Davis).

110 (1993) 25 HLR 408, CA; *Cheese v Thomas* [1994] 1 All ER 35, CA—both cases discussed (1994) NLJ 264 (Jill Martin); [1994] CLJ 232 (M Dixon). See also *Dodsworth v Dodsworth* (1973) 228 EG 1115, CA; *Griffiths v Williams* [1977] LS Gaz R 1130, CA.

land charge and will not bind a purchaser for value without notice.[111] In relation to registered land the Land Registration Act 2002[112] provides, for the avoidance of doubt, that an equity by estoppel has effect from the time the equity arises as an interest capable of binding successors in title, and, where the claimant is in actual occupation, it may constitute an overriding interest both in respect of first registration *and in* respect of registered dispositions.[113] It has been strongly argued[114] that the person whose conduct gives rise to a proprietary estoppel claim is personally liable to the claimant and may remain so even after the transfer of the relevant property to a third party. The authors of this view accept, however, that there is no authority which unequivocally supports it.

(d) FLEXIBILITY

The flexibility of equity is shown not only in the range of orders that have been made, tailored to the circumstances of the case, but in the way it may be varied according to changing circumstances. Thus in *Williams v Staite*[115] Goff LJ said: 'In the normal type of case ... whether there is an equity and its extent will depend ... simply on the initial conduct said to give rise to the equity, although the court may have to decide how, having regard to supervening circumstances, the equity can best be satisfied', or, as Cumming-Bruce LJ put it in the same case 'the rights in equity [do not] necessarily crystallize forever at the time when the equitable rights come into existence'. Thus in *Crabb v Arun District Council*[116] where the court directed that the person setting up the equity should have an easement, the court felt that had the matter been dealt with earlier it would have ordered the party setting up the equity to make compensation; and in *Dodsworth v Dodsworth*[117] the court took into account the fact that the lady who had offered to share her house had died.

(e) RELATIONSHIP WITH CONSTRUCTIVE TRUST

As we have seen[118] according to Chadwick LJ in *Oxley v Hiscock*[119] it is now accepted that in cases concerning the property interests of unmarried couples in the quasi-matrimonial home there is no difference in outcome whether the true analysis lies in constructive trust or proprietary estoppel, and in *Yaxley v Gotts*[120] all the members of

---

[111] *Inwards v Baker* [1965] 2 QB 29, [1965] 1 All ER 446, CA; *E R Ives Instruments Ltd v High* [1967] 2 QB 379, [1967] 1 All ER 504, CA; *Williams v Staite* [1979] Ch 291, [1978] 2 All ER 928, CA; *Lloyds Bank plc v Carrick* [1996] 4 All ER 630, CA. But see *Ashburn Anstalt v Arnold* supra, CA, and *United Bank of Kuwait plc v Sahib* [1997] Ch 107, [1996] 3 All ER 215, CA; (1984) 100 LQR 376 (S Moriarty); [1991] Conv 36 (G Battersby); (1994) 14 LS 147 (S Baughen).

[112] Section 116. See [2003] CLJ 661 (B McFarlane).   [113] Schedule 1, para 2; Sch 3, para 2.

[114] [2005] Conv 14 (Susan Bright and B McFarlane).   [115] [1979] Ch 291, [1978] 2 All ER 928, CA.

[116] Supra.   [117] (1973) 228 EG 1115, CA.   [118] See Section 1(e), supra, p 197.

[119] [2004] EWCA Civ 546, [2004] 3 All ER 703.

[120] [2000] 1 All ER 711, CA, discussed (1999) 11 T & ELJ 4 (A Allston); [2000] NLJ Easter Supp 21 (P Milne); (2000) 59 CLJ 23 (Louise Tee); [2000] Conv 245 (M P Thompson); (2000) 116 LQR 11 (R J Smith);

the court agreed that although there are large areas where the two concepts do not overlap, in the area of a joint enterprise for the acquisition of land (which may be, but is not necessarily, the matrimonial home) the two concepts coincide. In *Hyett v Stanley*,[121] again in a judgment agreed by all the members of the court, it was said in terms that the two doctrines have not been assimilated. It has been contended[122] that there are fundamental distinctions between the two doctrines. In both cases the claimant must show that he has acted to his detriment: however in the case of constructive trust a common intention must be established, while in proprietary estoppel the unilateral act of the defendant must raise an expectation in the claimant which it would be unconscionable for the defendant to deny. Further the evidentiary requirements for a constructive trust are more stringent than those for proprietary estoppel.

It should be noted that proprietary estoppel may enable a claimant to enforce an oral contract for the grant of an interest in land, notwithstanding s 2 of the Law of Property (Miscellaneous Provisions) Act 1989, provided that this does not run contrary to the public policy underlying the Act.[123]

3 THE *PALLANT V MORGAN* EQUITY

The *Pallant v Morgan*[124] equity, as it has been called,[125] is closely related to proprietary estoppel and constructive trust. In that case there was an agreement between the claimant's and the defendant's respective agents that they would not compete against each other for lot 16 at auction, but that the defendant's agent alone should bid. The proper inference from the facts was that the defendant's agent, when he bid for lot 16, was bidding at auction for both parties on an agreement that there should be an arrangement between the parties on the division of the lot if he were successful, as he was. There was too much uncertainty as to the terms of the arrangement for a decree of specific performance to be ordered, but the claimant was none the less entitled to a remedy. If the parties could not agree on a division the property would have to be re-sold and the proceeds divided equally between them. Unlike proprietary estoppel the claimant had not suffered any detriment as a consequence of his agent's agreement not to bid, for he would have been outbid by the defendant's agent. However the

---

(2000) 63 MLR 912 (Imogen Moore); [2000] All ER Rev 244–245 (P J Clarke); *Birmingham Midshires Mortgage Services Ltd v Sabberwal* (1999) 80 P & CR 256, noted (2000) 116 LQR 341 (C Harpum); (2000) 22 T & ELJ 16 (N Jones and P J Kirby), per Robert Walker LJ at 263.

121 [2003] EWCA Civ 942, [2003] 3 FCR 253, not cited in *Oxley v Hiscock*, supra, CA.

122 By Patricia Ferguson in (1993) 109 LQR 114, but see (1993) 109 LQR 485 (D Hayton).

123 *Yaxley v Gotts*, supra, CA; *James v Evans* [2000] 3 EGLR 1, CA; *Kinane v Mackie-Conteh* [2005] EWCA Civ 45, [2005] WTLR 345. See (2001) 30 Tru LI 21 (R Stone) and p 655, infra.

124 [1953] Ch 43, [1952] 2 All ER 951. See [2001] Conv 35 (N Hopkins); (2003) 23 LS 311 (Sarah Nield).

125 *Banner Homes Group plc v Luff Developments Ltd* [2000] 2 All ER 117, CA, per Chadwick LJ at 137, noted [2001] Conv 265 (M P Thompson).

defendant had obtained an advantage by keeping the claimant out of the bidding, as he obtained lot 16 for less than he would have had to pay if the claimant had been bidding against him.

In *Banner Homes Group plc v Luff Developments Ltd*[126] Chadwick LJ, observing that this was the first case in which the *Pallant v Morgan* equity had been before the Court of Appeal, laid down a series of relevant propositions. These are:

(i)   A *Pallant v Morgan* equity may arise where the arrangement or understanding on which it is based precedes the acquisition of the relevant property by one of the parties to the arrangement. It is the pre-acquisition arrangement which colours the subsequent acquisition by the defendant and leads to his being treated as a trustee if he seeks to act inconsistently with it.

(ii) It is unnecessary that the arrangement or understanding should be contractually enforceable. Indeed, if it is, there is unlikely to be any need to invoke the *Pallant v Morgan* equity; equity can act through the remedy of specific performance and will recognize the existence of a corresponding trust.

(iii) It is necessary that the pre-acquisition arrangement or understanding should contemplate that one party (the acquiring party) will take steps to acquire the relevant property, and that, if he does so, the other party (the non-acquiring party) will obtain some interest in that property. Further it is necessary that (whatever private reservations the acquiring party may have) he has not informed the non-acquiring party before the acquisition (or, more accurately, before it is too late for the parties to be restored to a position of no advantage/ no detriment) that he no longer intends to honour the arrangement or understanding.

(iv) It is necessary that, in reliance on the arrangement or understanding, the non-acquiring party should do (or omit to do) something which confers an advantage on the acquiring party in relation to the acquisition of the property; or is detrimental to the ability of the non-acquiring party to acquire the property on equal terms. It is the existence of the advantage to the one, or detriment to the other, gained or suffered as a consequence of the arrangement or understanding, which leads to the conclusion that it would be inequitable or unconscionable to allow the acquiring party to retain the property for himself, in a manner inconsistent with the arrangement or understanding which enabled him to acquire it.

(v)   Although in many cases the advantage/disadvantage will be found in the agreement of the non-acquiring party to keep out of the market, that is not a necessary feature. Further, although there will usually be advantage to the one and co-relative disadvantage to the other, the existence of both advantage and

---

[126] Supra, CA. See *Hooper v Gorvin* [2001] WTLR 575, criticized [2001] Conv 293 (P Kenny); *Cox v Jones* [2004] EWHC 1486 (Ch), [2004] 2 FLR 1010, noted [2004] Fam Law 7 (Rebecca Bailey-Harris); [2005] Conv 168 (Rebecca Probert); [2000] All ER Rev 244 (P J Clarke).

detriment is not essential—either will do. What is essential is that the circumstances make it inequitable for the acquiring party to retain the property for
himself in a manner inconsistent with the arrangement or understanding on
which the non-acquiring party has acted.

4 LICENCES

(a) AT COMMON LAW

In the context of property law a licence is a purely personal permission which allows
the licensee to do some act which would otherwise be a trespass and the traditional
common law view is that it is not a proprietary interest.[127] The basic distinction at
common law was between a bare licence, for example, permission to the child next
door to enter to recover his ball, and a licence coupled with a proprietary interest in
land or chattels, for example, a licence to the purchaser of felled timber on the
vendor's land to enter the vendor's land to carry it away. The former was revocable at
any time on reasonable notice,[128] even if under seal or made for valuable consideration; the latter was irrevocable until the purpose for which the licence was given had
been fulfilled.

The common law approach is illustrated by *Wood v Leadbitter*[129] where the plaintiff
bought a ticket for admission to the grandstand at Doncaster races. Having been
forcibly removed after refusing to depart peacefully, he sued for assault. The defence
was that as his licence had been revoked he was a trespasser and the defendant was
entitled to remove him using no more force than was reasonably necessary. The
defence succeeded. It made no difference that he had given a valuable consideration
for the privilege of going on to the stand.

(b) EQUITABLE INTERVENTION

(i) Hurst v Picture Theatres Ltd [130]

Here X, having bought a 6d tally, surrendered it to an usherette at a Kensington
cinema and was shown to an unreserved seat. Under the mistaken belief that he had

---

[127] As to what is meant by this phrase in this context see *Hounslow London Borough Council v Twickenham Garden Developments Ltd* [1971] Ch 233, [1970] 3 All ER 326.

[128] *Ministry of Health v Bellotti* [1944] KB 298, CA: *Greater London Council v Jenkins* [1975] 1 All ER 354, CA. See [1996] CLJ 229 (Tamara Kerbel); [2001] CLJ 89(J Hill).

[129] (1845) 13 M & W 838. The decision turned very much on the pleadings. The only issue to be decided was whether the plaintiff continued to have the leave and licence of the defendant when he was removed. It was held he had not because it had been withdrawn. On the pleadings the question did not arise whether or not the effect of the contract was to prevent the plaintiff from being treated as a trespasser until the races were over.

[130] [1915] 1 KB 1, CA.

not paid he was asked to see the manager and on his refusal was eventually removed by the porter under protest, offering no resistance. In an action for assault and false imprisonment there was pleaded a right to revoke the licence and thereafter eject X as a trespasser. The ratio least stressed[131] by the court was that there was a contract by implication not to revoke the licence before its purpose had been fulfilled and that as an injunction would lie to restrain the breach of such a contract there was no justification for treating X as a trespasser. This ground was approved by both the Court of Appeal and the House of Lords in *Wintergarden Theatre (London) Ltd v Millennium Productions Ltd*[132] and adopted by Megarry J in *Hounslow London Borough Council v Twickenham Garden Developments*.[133] These cases assume the possibility of an irrevocable licence entirely divorced from the grant of any interest of a proprietary nature.[134] As Megarry J explained in the last case mentioned a licence is a contractual licence if it is conferred by a contract; it is immaterial whether the right to enter the land is the primary purpose of the contract or is merely secondary. It is not an entity distinct from the contract which brings it into being, but merely one of the provisions of that contract. A contractual licensee cannot be treated as a trespasser so long as his contract entitles him to be on the land, whether or not his contract was specifically enforceable. Not only may an injunction be granted to restrain a breach but in an appropriate case a decree of specific performance may be granted.[135] And in *Tanner v Tanner*[136] where it was held on appeal, reversing the judge below, that the defendant had a contractual licence to occupy the house so long as the children were of school age and the accommodation was reasonably required by the defendant, damages were awarded to compensate the plaintiff for having been wrongly turned out following the judgment at first instance.

It may be added that nowadays, particularly where informal family-type arrangements are involved, the courts may find a contractual licence on very slight evidence.[137]

(ii) Proprietary estoppel

If an equity is made out, in appropriate circumstances, it may be satisfied by conferring a licence. This as we have seen,[138] was the decision of the court in *Inwards v Baker*,[139] *Re Sharpe*[140] and *Greasley v Cooke*.[141] The terms of the licence vary according

---

[131] The other rationes are untenable: that X had an 'interest' in seeing the picture, and that the absence of a deed of grant would be relieved in equity since the Judicature Acts.

[132] [1948] AC 173, [1947] 2 All ER 331.   [133] [1971] Ch 233, [1970] 3 All ER 326.

[134] Of course the licence may be revocable according to its terms—*Abbeyfield (Harpenden) Society Ltd v Woods* [1968] 1 All ER 352n.

[135] *Verrall v Great Yarmouth Borough Council* [1981] QB 202, [1980] 1 All ER 837, CA.

[136] [1975] 3 All ER 776, CA. Lord Denning MR was prepared, if need be, to impose the equivalent of a contract on the defendant. See [1976] 92 LQR 168 (J L Boston). *Tanner v Tanner* was distinguished on the facts in *Coombes v Smith* [1986] 1 WLR 808.

[137] See eg *Horrocks v Forray* [1976] 1 All ER 737, CA; *Hardwick v Johnson* [1978] 2 All ER 935, CA; *Chandler v Kerley* [1978] 2 All ER 942, CA.

[138] See p 208, supra.   [139] [1965] 1 All ER 446, CA.   [140] [1980] 1 All ER 198.

[141] [1980] 3 All ER 710, CA.

to the circumstances—in the first and last of these cases as long as the plaintiff wished, in *Re Sharpe*[142] until the loan was repaid.

(iii) Constructive trust

In *Re Sharpe*,[143] Browne-Wilkinson J felt bound by the authority of *Binions v Evans*[144] and *DHN Food Distributions Ltd v London Borough of Tower Hamlets*[145] to hold that, without more, an irrevocable licence to occupy gave rise to a property interest. The Court of Appeal has now held, in *Ashburn Anstalt v Arnold*[146] that a contractual licence does not create a property interest, though the facts of a particular case may give rise to a constructive trust.

(iv) Reason and justice

In *Hardwick v Johnson*[147] the majority of the court based their decision on contractual licence. Lord Denning MR, however, said the court would look at all the circumstances and spell out the most fitting relationship; and would find the terms of that relationship according to what reason and justice require. He cited in support Lord Diplock's speech in *Pettitt v Pettitt*[148] where he said the court imputes to the parties a common intention which they never in fact had by forming its own opinion as to what intention reasonable men would have formed in those circumstances. Yet in *Gissing v Gissing*[149] Lord Diplock himself recognized that the majority of their Lordships had rejected his view, and his speech in the latter case was in different terms. Lord Denning referred to constructive trust and personal licence as alternative relationships and held that this was a personal, not a contractual, licence—'an equitable licence of which the court has to spell out the terms'. With respect, the introduction of yet another category of licence, the equitable licence imputed in equity, simply adds more confusion to an already confused area. The approach of the majority is to be preferred, though it is arguable that a more natural inference from the evidence was that the contractual licence was conditional on the continuance of the marriage.[150]

(c) THE LICENSEE'S RIGHTS AGAINST THIRD PARTIES

(i) Contractual licences

The traditional view is that a licence is a purely personal transaction, creating no property rights, and does not affect a subsequent purchaser, even though he takes with

---

[142] Supra.   [143] Supra.   [144] Supra.   [145] Supra.

[146] [1989] Ch 1, [1988] 2 All ER 147, CA, and see [1980] Conv 207 (Jill Martin).

[147] [1978] 2 All ER 935, [1978] 1 WLR 683, CA.   [148] [1970] AC 777, [1969] 2 All ER 385, HL.

[149] [1971] AC 886, [1970] 2 All ER 780, HL.

[150] See (1980) 12 MULR 356 (I J Hardingham); *Chandler v Kerley* [1978] 2 All ER 942 at 945, per Lord Scarman.

notice.[151] The only exception is a licence coupled with an interest in land where the proprietary interest is binding on the third party and probably similarly with an interest in chattels.

As we have seen it is now clear that a contractual licence can be specifically enforced and its breach prevented by injunction. But as Lord Wilberforce pointed out in *National Provincial Bank Ltd v Ainsworth*[152] 'this does not mean that the right is any less of a personal character or that a purchaser with notice is bound by it; what is relevant is the nature of the right, not the remedy which exists for its enforcement.'

Lord Denning, however, took a different view in *Errington v Errington and Woods*[153] maintaining that 'this infusion of equity means that contractual licences now have a force and validity of their own and cannot be revoked in breach of the contract. Neither the licensor nor anyone who claims through him can disregard the contract except a purchaser for value without notice.' After a long period of uncertainty the Court of Appeal positively affirmed the traditional view in *Ashburn Anstalt v Arnold*[154] and it seems the law can now be regarded as settled.

(ii)   Estoppel licences

The position is considered in relation to proprietary estoppel at p 209, supra.

(iii)   Contractual licence giving rise to constructive trust

If a contractual licence gives rise to a constructive trust, then it logically follows that a third party may be bound on ordinary trust principles. Lord Denning's view[155] that a constructive trust will be imposed whenever a purchaser takes property subject to a contractual licence can no longer be supported. The Court of Appeal, in *Ashburn Anstalt v Arnold*,[156] accepted, however, that on the facts, a case involving a contractual licence could give rise to a constructive trust. Thus, as we have seen, it was said to have been right for a constructive trust to have been imposed in *Binions v Evans*[157] and *Lyus v Prowsa Developments Ltd*.[158] But the court will not impose a constructive trust unless it is satisfied that the conscience of the estate owner is affected. The mere fact

---

[151]   *King v David Allen & Sons, Billposting Ltd* [1916] 2 AC 54, HL; *Clore v Theatrical Properties Ltd* [1936] 3 All ER 483, CA. Cf *Pennine Raceway Ltd v Kirklees Metropolitan Council* [1982] 3 All ER 628, CA (licensee 'interested in the land' for the purposes of the Town and Country Planning Act 1971, s 164, now repealed and replaced by the Town and Country Planning Act 1990, s 107).

[152]   [1965] AC 1175, [1965] 2 All ER 472, HL. See (1972) 36 Conv 266 (Jill Martin); [1982] Conv 118 at 177 (Ann Everton), who suggests the category of quasi-proprietary right for a licence.

[153]   [1952] 1 KB 290 at 299, [1952] 1 All ER 149 at 155—as pointed out in *Ashburn Anstalt v Arnold* [1989] Ch 1, [1988] 2 All ER 147, CA, the actual decision can be supported on other grounds; *Binions v Evans* [1972] Ch 359, [1972] 2 All ER 70, CA; *DHN Food Distributors Ltd v London Borough of Tower Hamlets* [1976] 3 All ER 462, CA.

[154]   [1989] Ch 1, [1988] 2 All ER 147, CA, noted [1988] Conv 201 (M P Thompson); (1988) 51 MLR 226 (J Hill).

[155]   See *Binions v Evans* [1972] Ch 359, [1972] 2 All ER 70, CA; *DHN Food Distributors Ltd v London Borough of Tower Hamlets* [1976] 3 All ER 462, CA.

[156]   [1989] Ch 1, [1988] 2 All ER 147, CA.   [157]   [1972] 2 All ER 70, CA, discussed supra, p 165.

[158]   [1982] 2 All ER 953.

that land is expressed to be conveyed 'subject to' a contractual licence gives notice to the purchaser, but does not necessarily imply that he is to be under an obligation, not otherwise existing, to give effect to the licence. Moreover a constructive trust of land should not be imposed in reliance on inferences from slender materials, and the case was not made out in *Ashburn Anstalt v Arnold*[159] itself.

(iv) Rights of licensees against a trespasser

Where the defendant is not claiming through the licensor but is a mere trespasser, a licensee, whether or not he is in actual occupation, can obtain an order for possession, if that is a necessary remedy to vindicate and give effect to such rights of occupation as by contract with his licensor he enjoys. The remedy is not limited to a party with title to or an estate in the land, and is available to a licensee even though he has no right to exclude the licensor himself.[160]

---

[159] Supra, CA; *Canadian Imperial Bank of Commerce v Bello* (1991) 64 P & CR 48, CA.

[160] *Manchester Airport plc v Dutton* [2000] 1 QB 133, sub-nom *Dutton v Manchester Airport plc* [1999] 2 All ER 675, CA, noted [1999] Conv 535 (E Paton and Gwen Seabourne). It is cogently argued that this case is wrongly decided (2000) 116 LQR 354 (W Swadling). A contractual licensee in possession has contractual rights against the licensor, but it is only the fact of possession that enables him to bring conversion or trespass against a third party who interferes with his possession. Contrast *Hunter v Canary Wharf Ltd* [1997] AC 655, [1997] 2 All ER 426, HL, not cited in *Dutton*, where it was held that only someone with a right to the land, such as a freeholder, a tenant in possession or a licensee with exclusive possession, can sue in nuisance, and see *Countryside Residential (North Thames) Ltd v (1) a Child; (2) persons unknown* (2001) 81 P & CR 10, CA.

11

UNLAWFUL TRUSTS

It is against the policy of the law to enforce certain trusts, and the following are the more important categories of trust which are liable to be declared void. No attempt is made here to give an exhaustive list, and in any case there is no reason why a novel kind of trust should not be declared void on the ground of public policy. As Danckwerts LJ said in *Nagle v Feilden*:[1] 'The law relating to public policy cannot remain immutable. It must change with the passage of time. The wind of change blows on it.' Some cases are really isolated instances, such as *Brown v Burdett*.[2]

One instance of change relates to trusts for illegitimate children. The fact that a person is illegitimate has never prevented him from being a beneficiary under a trust, but in dispositions made before 1 January 1970 an illegitimate child might face two difficulties. First, if he claimed under a gift to a class of children, he would have had to displace the presumption that 'children' means 'legitimate children'. Secondly, he would have had to establish that on the facts the rule that a disposition in favour of illegitimate children not in being when the disposition takes effect is void as being contrary to public policy did not apply. These difficulties do not arise in respect of a disposition made after 31 December 1969. By s 15(1) of the Family Law Reform Act 1969, now repealed and replaced by the Family Law Reform Act 1987 the presumption referred to was reversed, and by s 15(7) the public policy rule was abolished.

1 TRUSTS WHICH OFFEND AGAINST THE RULE AGAINST PERPETUITIES

Since the Perpetuities and Accumulations Act 1964 it will only be rarely that the rule against perpetuities will make void a limitation contained in an instrument taking effect after the commencement of the Act.[3] Until amended by the Act, however, the

---

[1] [1966] 2 QB 633, [1966] 1 All ER 689, CA, admittedly in a different context. In *Re Canada Trust Co and Ontario Human Rights Commission* (1990) 69 DLR (4th) 321, it was held that a trust premised on notions of racism and religious superiority was against public policy. However a valid charitable trust when founded in 1923 and saved by the cy-près doctrine—see p 325 et seq, infra.

[2] (1882) 21 Ch D 667 (trust to block up a house for 20 years), applied *Re Boning* [1997] 2 Qd R 12. As to the validity of a testamentary direction for the destruction of a pet, see (1987) 9 U Tas LR 51 (P Jamieson).

[3] 16 July 1964. With one limited exception (in s 8(2)) the Act has no retrospective effect—s 15(5).

rule was one of the commonest causes of the failure of a trust. In its unamended form it laid down that a future interest[4] in any kind of property, real or personal, would be void ab initio if it might possibly vest outside the perpetuity period, namely, the compass of a life or any number of lives in being[5] at the time when the instrument creating it came into effect, and 21 years thereafter, with the possible addition of the period of gestation in the case of some person entitled being en ventre sa mère at the end of the period. The main alteration made by the 1964 Act was to change the rule from one concerned with possibilities to one concerned with actual events—the wait and see principle. The Act[6] also enables the trust instrument to specify a perpetuity period of a fixed number of years not exceeding 80. The rule is discussed at length in books on the law of real property.[7]

The government accepted Law Commission proposals[8] for reform in 2001, but no steps have yet been taken towards implementation.

2 TRUSTS WHICH OFFEND AGAINST THE RULE AGAINST PERPETUAL TRUSTS

Closely related to and sometimes confused with the rule against perpetuities is the rule that a gift which requires capital to be retained beyond the perpetuity period is void. This rule is sometimes known as the rule against inalienability, and it should perhaps be made clear that it cannot be evaded merely by giving a power to change investments sufficiently wide to enable the property given to be disposed of, if the proceeds of sale are required to be re-invested and the capital fund has to be retained in perpetuity. This rule, which does not apply to charities, is, like the rule against perpetuities, discussed in books on the law of real property.[9]

3 THE EFFECT OF DECLARING A TRUST VOID AS OFFENDING AGAINST THE POLICY OF THE LAW

In the types of case discussed in the two preceding sections, the usual result of an expressed trust being declared void will be that the property must be held on a

---

[4] Since 1925 a future interest, other than a revisionary lease, must be an equitable interest under a trust. For a possible qualification see (1908) 24 LQR 431 (D T Oliver).

[5] Including the life of a person en ventre sa mère at the relevant time. 'Lives' means 'human lives'. Insofar as *Re Dean* (1889) 41 Ch D 552 suggests the contrary it is generally thought to be wrong—see Morris and Leach, *The Rule against Perpetuities*, 2nd edn, p 63 and *Re Kelly* [1932] IR 250.

[6] In s 1.

[7] See eg Cheshire and Burn, *Modern Real Property*, 16th edn, p 308 et seq; Megarry and Wade, *The Law of Real Property*, 6th edn, p 298 et seq; Morris and Leach, *The Rule against Perpetuities*, 2nd edn, and Supp.

[8] Law Com No 251 (1998).

[9] See eg Megarry and Wade, op cit, p 357 et seq; Morris and Leach, op cit, p 321 et seq.

resulting trust for the settlor, or, where the trust arises under a will, the property will fall into the residuary estate[10] of the testator. The particular provisions of the instrument creating the trust must, however, be taken into account. Suppose, for instance, the limitations under a trust were to X for life, with remainder for life to X's first son to become a barrister, remainder in fee simple to Y. Suppose further that when the limitation came into effect X had no children though he subsequently had sons who survived him by more than 21 years. Before the Perpetuities and Accumulations Act 1964, the second limitation would have been void ab initio as infringing the rule against perpetuities, and even now will become void for the same reason if no son has become a barrister within 21 years of the death of X. Neither before nor after the Act, however, would there have been a resulting trust, but the vested remainder of Y would have been or would be accelerated.[11]

In the types of case discussed in the following three sections, the question is not strictly one as to the validity of the trust itself but as to the validity of a condition to which the trust is made subject. It is a question of construction whether a condition is a condition precedent, that is, where the gift is not intended to take effect unless and until the condition is fulfilled, or a condition subsequent, that is, where the gift vests immediately, but is liable to be divested if and when the condition is fulfilled, the court in general, it seems, preferring the latter construction where the intention is not made clear.[12] If a condition subsequent is void,[13] the gift, whether of realty or personalty, remains good and is not liable to be determined by breach of the condition, the presence of a gift over being irrelevant. In the case of conditions precedent it seems that a distinction has to be drawn between gifts of realty and gifts of personalty. If a gift of real property is made dependent upon a condition precedent which is void, the gift fails. In the case of a gift of personal property where a condition precedent is illegal and void, a further distinction is drawn according to whether the illegality involves malum in se, or malum prohibitum. In the former case, the gift fails, as in the case of real property, but in the latter case the gift is good, and will pass to the donee unfettered by the condition. Unfortunately 'the difference between malum prohibitum and malum in se has never been very precisely defined or considered';[14] malum in se seems to mean some act which is intrinsically and morally wrong, such as

---

[10] If the subject of the gift is residue, or if there is no residuary gift, it will become property undisposed of by will and devolve accordingly.

[11] Cf *Re Flower's Settlement Trusts* [1957] 1 All ER 462, CA; *Re Allan's Will Trusts* [1958] 1 All ER 401; *Re Boning* [1997] 2 Qd R 12, and see Perpetuities and Accumulations Act 1964, s 6; (1973) 32 CLJ 246 (A M Pritchard).

[12] See eg *Re Johnston* [1980] NI 229.

[13] The requirement of certainty is stricter for a condition subsequent than a condition precedent; *Blathwayt v Baron Cawley* [1976] AC 397, [1975] 3 All ER 625, HL; *Re Barlow's Will Trusts* [1979] 1 All ER 296; *Re Waring's Will Trusts* [1985] NI 105. See (1977) 8 Sydney LR 400 (P Butt); [1980] Conv 263 (Lindsay McKay); (1982) 126 Sol Jo 518 (N D M Parry). On testamentary conditions generally see (1998) 20 UQLJ 38 (K Mackie).

[14] Per Romer J in *Re Piper* [1946] 2 All ER 503 at 505. See Sheppard's *Touchstone*, p 132; *Re Moore* (1888) 39 Ch D 116, CA; *Re Elliott* [1952] Ch 217, [1952] 1 All ER 145; (1955) 19 Conv 176 (V T H Delaney).

murder, malum prohibitum some act which offends against a rule of law but is not wrong in itself, such as smuggling. It has been held in Canada that a condition precedent in a will intended to promote the divorce of the testator's son from his wife is malum prohibitum.[15]

Finally, it was held in *Re Hepplewhite's Will Trusts*[16] that where a testator leaves a gift of personalty subject to several conditions precedent, some of which are valid and some of which are invalid as contrary to public policy, the valid conditions are separable from the others and the gift is good subject thereto but disregarding the invalid conditions.[17]

4 TRUSTS TENDING TO PREVENT THE CARRYING OUT OF PARENTAL DUTIES

The cases have usually arisen on the validity of a condition subsequent, and in deciding the matter the courts have referred to the principle set out in Sheppard's *Touchstone*,[18] that 'if the matter of the condition tend to provoke or further the doing of some unlawful act, or to restrain or forbid a man the doing of his duty; the condition for the most part is void.' Thus in *Re Sandbrook*[19] a testatrix, having given the bulk of her residuary estate to trustees on trust for two grandchildren, declared that if one or both of them should 'live with or be or continue under the custody, guardianship or control of their father, . . . or be in any way directly under his control', they should forfeit their interest. It was held that the case fell directly within the principle laid down in Sheppard's *Touchstone*. The condition, Parker J said,[20] 'is inserted in the will with the direct object of deterring the father of these two children from performing his parental duties with regard to them, because it makes their worldly welfare dependent on his abstaining from doing what it is certainly his duty to do, namely, to bring his influence to bear and not give up his right to the custody, the control and education of his children.' It was accordingly declared to be void, with the result that the gift remained valid and not liable to be determined by breach of the condition. Similarly in *Re Piper*,[21] where a condition precedent in a will against residence with the father was held void as being calculated to bring about the separation of parent and child. The fact that the father had been divorced before the date of the will was held not to affect the matter. The condition was further held to be malum prohibitum, and, accordingly, the gift to the children, being a gift of personalty, took effect free from it.

---

[15] *Re McBride* (1980) 107 DLR (3d) 233.   [16] (1977) *Times*, 21 January.

[17] Presumably only where it involves malum prohibitum.   [18] Page 132.

[19] [1912] 2 Ch 471. See also *Re Morgan* (1910) 26 TLR 398 (bequest to grandchildren on condition of living with mother if she and father live separately); *Re Boulter* [1922] 1 Ch 75, [1921] All ER Rep 167 (condition against children residing abroad); *Re Johnston* [1980] NI 229.

[20] *Re Sandbrook* [1912] 2 Ch 471 at 476.

[21] [1946] 2 All ER 503. See (1947) 11 Conv 218 (J H C Morris).

Dicta in *Blathwayt v Lord Cawley*[22] have however cast doubt on whether the principle was correctly applied in *Re Borwick*.[23] In that case a condition subsequent under which children becoming Roman Catholics would forfeit their interests was held void on the ground that it operated to restrain or hamper their parents from doing their parental duty in regard to the religious instruction of their children. Their Lordships have now made it reasonably clear that not every condition which might affect or influence the way in which a child is brought up, or in which parental duties are exercised, is void on the principle set out above. In particular a condition as to religious upbringing is not necessarily void because it may compel parents to make a choice between material prosperity and spiritual welfare for their children. A condition such as that in *Re Sandbrook*[24] with the direct object of deterring a father from performing his parental duty and from exercising any control at all over his children is quite different from one tending to influence him to exercise his authority in a particular way. The mere fact that the existence of a condition may affect a parent's action does not necessarily mean it is void as offending against public policy.

5 TRUSTS DESIGNED OR TENDING TO INDUCE A FUTURE SEPARATION OF HUSBAND AND WIFE, OR TO ENCOURAGE AN INVASION OF THE SANCTITY OF THE MARRIAGE BOND

Where a husband and wife have decided upon an immediate separation, trusts contained in a deed of separation entered into at that time are valid and will be enforced;[25] the point is that the separation in such case is not in any way induced by the trusts contained in the deed. By contrast, trusts which are made in contemplation of the future separation of a husband and wife then living together are void, for their existence might tend to bring about a separation which would not otherwise take place.[26]

A condition contained in a bequest to a married woman that she should live apart from her husband has been held[27] contra bonos mores and void on this ground. Again in the case of the will of a testatrix giving her residue to her son absolutely with a proviso modifying the gift so long as the son's wife should be alive and married to him, but declaring that the absolute gift should take effect if the wife should die or the marriage be otherwise terminated, it was held that the provision was designed, or tended, to encourage an invasion of the sanctity of the marriage bond, and was,

---

[22] Supra, HL. [23] [1933] Ch 657, [1933] All ER Rep 737. [24] [1912] 2 Ch 471.

[25] *Wilson v Wilson* (1848) 1 HL Cas 538; *Vansittart v Vansittart* (1858) 2 De G & J 249.

[26] *Westmeath v Westmeath* (1831) 1 Dow & Cl 519; *Re Moore* (1888) 39 Ch D 116, CA.

[27] *Wren v Bradley* (1848) 2 De G & Sm 49; *Re Freedman* (21 December 1942, unreported) referred to in *Re Caborne* [1943] Ch 224, [1943] 2 All ER 7.

therefore, void as being against public policy.[28] The facts were somewhat similar and the decision the same in *Re Johnson's Will Trusts*,[29] where a testator gave his residue of over £11,000 on protective trusts for his daughter for life, with a proviso cutting down her interest to £50 pa so long as she was married and living with her husband, but giving her the whole income in the event of her husband's death, or her divorce or separation from him. The result will be the same where the provision in question operates indirectly.[30]

The effect of each particular provision has to be carefully considered in every case. Thus in *Re Lovell*,[31] a man, by his will, gave an annuity to his mistress, a married woman living apart from her husband 'provided and so long as she shall not return to live with her present husband . . . or remarry'. It was held that the provision was valid, as its object was not to induce her to continue to live apart from her husband and not to remarry, but to make provision for her until she returned to her husband or remarried. A similar decision was reached in *Re Thompson*,[32] where a testator gave his daughter an annuity of £300, if still married to her present husband, but the income of the whole estate if she should become a widow, or remarried to another person, or divorced and not remarried to her present husband. It was held that the provision was not contrary to public policy as the purpose was not to induce a divorce, but to prevent the income coming into the hands of the husband, regarded by the testator as a spendthrift. It has been suggested,[33] however, that this decision disregards the rule that the law looks to the general tendency of the disposition, and not to the possibility of public mischief occurring in the particular instance.

6 TRUSTS IN RESTRAINT OF MARRIAGE

The law is difficult,[34] being complicated both by the differences in the rules relating to general and partial restraints and also by the distinctions that have to be drawn between dispositions of realty, where the rules are based on the common law, and dispositions of personalty, where the rules adopted by the Court of Chancery came to it, with considerable modifications, from Roman Law by way of the Ecclesiastical Courts.[35]

So far as realty is concerned there is no clear decision, but the weight of opinion is

---

[28] *Re Caborne* [1943] Ch 224, [1943] 2 All ER 7; *Re Hope Johnstone* [1904] 1 Ch 470.

[29] [1967] Ch 387, [1967] 1 All ER 553.

[30] See *Wilkinson v Wilkinson* (1871) LR 12 Eq 604 (condition against residence by wife in place where her husband lived and had his business).

[31] [1920] 1 Ch 122.   [32] [1939] 1 All ER 681.

[33] By Simonds J in *Re Caborne*, supra. Cf *Re Fentem* [1950] 2 All ER 1073; *Re Johnson's Will Trusts*, supra.

[34] 'Proverbially difficult', at least as to personalty, per Younger J in *Re Hewett* [1918] 1 Ch 458 at 463.

[35] See *Re Whiting's Settlement* [1905] 1 Ch 96 at 115–116, CA, per Vaughan Williams LJ; *Bellairs v Bellairs* (1874) LR 18 Eq 510 at 513 per Jessel MR.

in favour of the view that a general restraint is prima facie void.[36] It seems, however, that whatever the form of the disposition it will readily be treated as a limitation until marriage, which is valid, if the intention appears to be, not to promote celibacy, but to make provision until marriage takes place.[37]

As far as personalty[38] is concerned, it is settled that a general restraint is prima facie void,[39] whether the restraint is general in so many words, or whether, although in terms partial, it is from its nature probable that in practice it would amount to a prohibition of marriage.[40] However, where the intention was not to promote celibacy, but, for instance, to make provision for the child of the person restrained,[41] or to ensure that after the death of the person restrained the property given would be dealt with in a particular manner,[42] the restraint has been held good. On principle one might have thought that the court would not be entitled to look behind the general tendency of the provision, and examine its motive and intention in the light of the particular circumstances and the ground of the public policy involved. However, in the cases above referred to, the court has regarded itself as entitled to make the necessary inquiry.[43] It is clear, however, that a gift until marriage is perfectly good,[44] the intention in such a case being assumed to be to provide for the beneficiary while unmarried, and not to prevent a marriage from taking place.

Partial restraints, whether with regard to realty or to personalty, are prima facie valid,[45] and accordingly the following conditions have been held good: against marriage with any person born in Scotland or of Scottish parents,[46] against marriage with a person who did not profess the Jewish religion and was not born a Jew,[47] against marriage with a domestic servant, or a person who had been a domestic servant,[48] against marriage with either of two named persons,[49] or against marriage without the consent of named persons.[50] For this purpose a condition in restraint of a second or

---

[36] White and Tudor, *Leading Cases in Equity*, 9th edn, vol 1, p 487; *Jarman on Wills*, 8th edn, vol II, p 1528; (1896) 12 LQR 36 (Cyprian Williams). Contra, *Theobald on Wills*, 16th edn, p 665.

[37] *Jones v Jones* (1876) 1 QBD 279, DC.

[38] Or a mixed fund representing the proceeds of sale of real estate and personalty—*Bellairs v Bellairs*, supra.

[39] *Bellairs v Bellairs*, supra; *Re Bellamy* (1883) 48 LT 212; *Re Hewett* [1918] 1 Ch 458.

[40] *Re Lanyon* [1927] 2 Ch 264—marriage with a blood relation, however remote.

[41] *Re Hewett*, supra, where the woman restrained was the testator's mistress and the child the fruit of their irregular union. See *Williams on Wills*, 7th edn, vol 1, p 346.

[42] *Re Fentem* [1950] 2 All ER 1073—a gift by a testatrix to her brother for life, with remainder to his personal representatives. The condition was attached only to the gift over after the brother's death.

[43] See also *Jones v Jones*, supra. Cf *Re Caborne* [1943] Ch 224, [1943] 2 All ER 7.

[44] *Morley v Rennoldson* (1843) 2 Hare 570; *Webb v Grace* (1848) 2 Ph 701.

[45] Unless void on some other ground, such as uncertainty. See eg *Clayton v Ramsden* [1943] AC 320, [1943] 1 All ER 16, HL; *Re Moss's Trusts* [1945] 1 All ER 207; *Blathwayt v Baron Cawley* [1976] AC 397, [1975] 3 All ER 625, HL; *Re Tepper's Will Trusts* [1987] Ch 358, [1987] 1 All ER 970.

[46] *Perrin v Lyon* (1807) 9 East 170.

[47] *Hodgson v Halford* (1879) 11 Ch D 959. Cf *Re Selby's Will Trusts* [1965] 3 All ER 386 (condition precedent). See (1999) 19 LS 339 (Davina Cooper and Didi Herman).

[48] *Jenner v Turner* (1880) 16 ChD 188.   [49] *Re Bathe* [1925] Ch 377; *Re Hanlon* [1933] Ch 254.

[50] *Dashwood v Lord of Bulkeley* (1804) 10 Ves 230; *Lloyd v Branton* (1817) 3 Mer 108.

subsequent marriage, whether of a man or a woman, and whether the gift was by one spouse to the survivor, or by a stranger, is regarded as a partial restraint, and it is accordingly prima facie valid.[51]

There is, however, an important difference in the effect of a partial restraint imposed on realty and personality respectively. Lord Radcliffe[52] has stated the position in these words:

For, whereas a condition subsequent in partial restraint of marriage was effective to determine the estate in the case of a devise of realty even without any new limitation to take effect on the forfeiture, so that a residuary devisee or heir came in of his own right,[53] it was early determined and consistently maintained that a condition subsequent in partial restraint of marriage, when annexed to a bequest of personality,[54] was ineffective to destroy the gift unless the will in question contained an explicit gift over of the legacy to another legatee. And for this purpose a mere residuary bequest was not treated as a gift over.

In the latter case, where there is no gift over, the condition is said to be merely in terrorem, that is, intended merely in a monitory sense. Lord Radcliffe,[55] after emphasizing that it is impossible to give an account of the origin of the rule that is wholly logical, suggested that rather than base the rule on an artificial presumed intention, it is better to say simply that it is the presence in the will of the express gift over that determines the matter in favour of forfeiture.

7 TRUSTS WHICH ARE NOT MERELY UNLAWFUL BUT ALSO FRAUDULENT

As we have seen,[56] where the object of a trust is unlawful, in general there will be a resulting trust for the settlor, or where the trust is declared by will, the property given will fall into the residuary estate of the testator. This is so not only when the trust offends against a technical rule such as the rule against perpetuities, but also where the trust is calculated to encourage an offence prohibited by statute.[57] Where, however, the object is not merely against the policy of the law, but is also fraudulent, further considerations have to be taken into account.

If the matter is still in the stage of contract or covenant, the fraud or illegality will, of course, make it unenforceable. This is not a matter of trust, but a matter of

---

51   *Leong v Lim Beng Chye* [1955] AC 648, [1955] 2 All ER 903, PC; *Allen v Jackson* (1875) 1 Ch D 399, CA.
52   Giving the judgment of the Judicial Committee of the Privy Council in *Leong v Chye* supra, at 660, 906.
53   *Haughton v Haughton* (1824) 1 Mol 611; *Jenner v Turner*, supra.
54   And possibly, where realty and personality are given together: *Duddy v Gresham* (1878) 2 LR Ir 442.
55   *Leong v Lim Beng Chye* [1955] AC 648 at 662, [1955] 2 All ER 903 at 908, PC.
56   See p 218, supra.   57   *Thrupp v Collett* (1858) 26 Beav 125.

contract. As Lord Jauncey put it in *Tinsley v Milligan*,[58] 'it is trite law that the court will not give its assistance to the enforcement of executory provisions of an unlawful contract whether the illegality is apparent ex facie the document or whether the illegality of purpose of what would otherwise be a lawful contract emerges during the course of the trial.'

We are concerned, however, to consider at this point cases where a man, having conveyed or transferred property to another for some fraudulent and illegal purpose, subsequently claims that that other holds the property upon a resulting trust for him. The law on this matter was reviewed by the House of Lords in *Tinsley v Milligan*.[59] The facts were that a house, to the purchase of which the parties contributed equally, was conveyed into the sole name of the appellant to enable the respondent to make false claims to the Department of Social Security for benefits. The appellant claimed possession, and relied on the clean hands doctrine to prevent the respondent from asserting a trust. The planned illegality of defrauding the DSS was in fact carried out, but without needing to make use of the conveyance, and the respondent, as it was said, 'made her peace with the DSS' soon after the action began, so there was no continuing illegality.

More recently, in *Tribe v Tribe*,[60] the plaintiff had transferred his shareholding in his family company to his son for a pretended consideration which was not paid and was not intended to be paid. The transaction was carried out for the illegal purpose of deceiving his creditors by creating the appearance that he no longer owned any shares in the company. The illegal purpose, however, was never carried into effect: negotiations with the creditors were brought to a satisfactory conclusion without resorting to deception. When the plaintiff sought a retransfer of the shares the son unsuccessfully contended that evidence of the illegal purpose could not be admitted in order to rebut the presumption of advancement in his favour.

In both these last two cases property had been put into the name of X with the mutual intention of concealing Y's interest in the property for a fraudulent or illegal purpose. Before *Tinsley v Milligan*[61] the general rule was that in such a case Y could not recover the property irrespective of whether the presumption of advancement

---

[58] [1994] 1 AC 340, [1993] 3 All ER 65, HL, discussed [1993] JBL 513 (A G J Berg); (1993) 143 NLJ 1577 (Bron Council); [1994] LMCLQ 163 (Nili Cohen); (1994) 57 MLR 441 (H Stowe); (1994) 45 NILQ 378 (S H Goo); (1994) 110 LQR 3 (R A Buckley); (1994) 14 Ox JLS 295 and (1995) 111 LQR 135 (N Enonchong); *Birkett v Acorn Business Machines Ltd* [1999] 2 All ER (Comm) 429, CA. See also *Nelson v Nelson* (1995) 132 ALR 133, and for a comparative study with French law (1995) 44 AALR 196 (M Enonchong).

[59] [1994] 1 AC 340, [1993] 3 All ER 65, HL, applied *Lowson v Coombes* [1999] Ch 373, CA, noted (1999) 8 T & ELJ 3 (D Reade); [1999] Conv 242 (M P Thompson), where a married man bought a house jointly with his mistress, but it was conveyed into her sole name with the illegal purpose of frustrating any potential claim by his wife under s 37(2)(*b*) of the Matrimonial Causes Act 1973; *Webb v Chief Constable of Merseyside Police* [2000] 1 All ER 209, CA; *Mortgage Express v Robson* [2001] EWCA Civ 887, [2001] 2 All ER (Comm) 881. See [2004] Conv 439 (M Halliwell).

[60] [1996] Ch 107, [1995] 4 All ER 236, CA noted [1996] CLJ 23 (G Virgo). See also (1996) 112 LQR 545 (F D Rose).

[61] [1994] 1 AC 340, [1993] 3 All ER 65, HL.

arose between the parties or not, but it now appears that a distinction must be made.[62] In any case, however, as Millet LJ has observed[63] Y's action will fail if it would be illegal for him to retain any interest in the property. Thus the claims rightly failed in *Curtis v Perry*,[64] where a ship was registered in the name of one partner only to enable profits to be made by government contracts into which the other partner, who alleged a trust, could not enter, being a member of Parliament; and in *Ex Yallop*,[65] where to admit the alleged resulting trust would have defeated the purpose of the statute requiring registration.

(a) WHERE THERE IS NO PRESUMPTION OF ADVANCEMENT

In *Tinsley v Milligan*[66] all the Law Lords agreed that at law property in chattels and land can pass under a contract which is illegal, and the transferee can enforce property rights so acquired provided that he does not need to rely on the illegal contract for any purpose other than providing the basis of his claim to a property right. It is irrelevant that the illegality of the underlying agreement was either pleaded or emerged in evidence: if the transferee has acquired legal title under the illegal contract that is enough. Moreover the same principles apply at law and in equity. Neither at law nor in equity may a party rely on his own fraud or illegality in order to found a claim or rebut a presumption, but the common law and equity alike will assist him to protect and enforce his property rights if he can do so without relying on the fraud or illegality.

This was the situation in *Tinsley v Milligan*[67] where it was not disputed that apart from the question of illegality the respondent would have been entitled in equity to a half share in the property. In principle this should be simply on the basis of a resulting trust by reason of her equal contribution to the purchase price, but Lord Browne-Wilkinson said that she had established a resulting trust by showing that she had contributed to the purchase price and that there was a common understanding between her and the appellant that they should own the house equally. The clear theoretical distinction between a resulting and a constructive trust is again being blurred.

Whatever the basis of the equitable interest there was no need for the respondent to allege or prove why she had allowed the house to be conveyed into the sole name of the appellant. 'The test is whether of necessity reliance is placed by the claimant on the illegality in proving his claim.'[68] Both Nourse and Millett LJJ in *Tribe v Tribe*[69] agreed that where he can rely on a resulting trust the transferor will normally be able to recover his property if the illegal purpose has not been carried out. However where

---

[62] In Australia the distinction was rejected by all the members of the court in *Nelson v Nelson*, supra.

[63] In *Tribe v Tribe*, supra, CA, at 252, 259.   [64] (1802) 6 Ves 739.   [65] (1808) 15 Ves 60.

[66] Supra, HL. See [1999] LMCLQ 465 (Imogen Cotterill).   [67] Supra, HL.

[68] Per Peter Gibson LJ in *Silverwood v Silverwood* (1997) 74 P & CR 453, 457, CA, where *Tinsley v Milligan*, supra, HL, was applied.

[69] Supra, CA.

the illegal purpose has been carried out Nourse and Millett LJJ expressed different views. Nourse LJ said it was inherent in the decision in *Tinsley v Milligan*[70] that it makes no difference whether or not the illegal purpose has been carried into effect, as it clearly had been in that case. Millett LJ said that there is no invariable rule: a claim may fail where the illegal purpose has been carried out and the transferee can rely on the transferor's conduct as inconsistent with his retention of a beneficial interest.[71] It is not clear, however, what is the essential difference between the facts of *Tinsley v Milligan*[72] and the case put by Millett LJ, namely that a transferor would not in his view be able to recover property transferred to a nephew in order to conceal it from creditors with whom he had subsequently settled on the footing he had no interest in the property transferred.

In the most recent case, *Collier v Collier*,[73] although the dispute was between father and daughter, the case turned on whether the father could rely on an express agreement that his daughter would hold the leases he had granted to her on trust for him, when the admittedly effective grants were intended to further an illegal purpose. It was held that he could not, unless he could resort to the doctrine of locus poenitentiae, which was not available on the facts. Mance LJ observed that if the presumption of advancement were to be applicable, the father would likewise fail as he could only rebut it by disclosing his illegal purpose.

(b) WHERE THERE IS A PRESUMPTION OF ADVANCEMENT

In cases where the presumption of advancement applies, such as *Tribe v Tribe*,[74] the plaintiff can only recover if he brings evidence which rebuts the presumption and shows that no gift was intended. It was held in that case that he can do this by leading evidence of an illegal purpose behind the transfer, provided that he has withdrawn from the transaction before the illegal purpose has been wholly or partly carried into effect. In the opinion of Millett LJ voluntary withdrawal from an illegal transaction when it has ceased to be needed is sufficient. Unless and until the illegal purpose begins to be carried into effect it is often said that he has a locus poenitentiae, but Nourse LJ said that this was a name which tended to mislead. Both Nourse and Millett LJJ refused to become embroiled in the application of that doctrine to executory contracts.

In *Tribe v Tribe* itself the illegal purpose was not carried out, as we have seen, and the plaintiff was able to rebut the presumption of advancement. In *Gascoigne v Gascoigne*,[75] however, where the husband intended to defeat his creditors by putting property in his wife's name while retaining the beneficial interest, and had acted upon

---

[70] Supra, HL.

[71] Millett LJ did not think that cases such as *Re Great Berlin Steamboat Co* (1884) 26 Ch D 616, CA (money placed to credit of a company to enable it to have a fictitious credit in case of inquiries at their bankers) had been impliedly overruled in *Tinsley v Milligan*, supra, HL.

[72] Supra, HL.   [73] [2002] EWCA Civ 1095, [2002] BPIR 1057.   [74] Supra, CA.

[75] [1918] 1 KB 223, DC; *Re Emery's Investments' Trusts* [1959] Ch 410, [1959] 1 All ER 577.

that dishonest intention, it was held that the wife was entitled to retain the property conveyed to her for her own use, notwithstanding that she was a party to the fraud; and in *Tinker v Tinker*[76] the husband, on the purchase of the matrimonial home, had it conveyed into his wife's name, to avoid its being taken by his creditors in case his business failed. It was found as a fact that he had acted honestly, not fraudulently. This evidence of his intention was held to strengthen the presumption of advancement, and accordingly the husband had no claim to the house when the marriage broke up, although the wife had made no contribution to its purchase.[77]

(c) REIMBURSEMENT OF BENEFITS

In the Australian case of *Nelson v Nelson*,[78] Mrs Nelson had purchased property in the name of her children to enable her to obtain a subsidized loan from the Commonwealth by making a declaration that she did not own or have a financial interest in a house other than the one for which a subsidy was sought. The loan was obtained, but all the members of the court were prepared to admit evidence to rebut the presumption of advancement,[79] tainted though it was by illegality and notwithstanding that the illegal purpose had been carried out. They held that there was a resulting trust in favour of Mrs Nelson. The majority, applying the maxim that he who seeks equity must do equity, went on to hold that Mrs Nelson must do equity by reimbursing the Commonwealth to the extent of the benefit she had received. The minority allowed the appeal unconditionally, saying, however, that the Commonwealth should be informed and would presumably require repayment. The majority view has its attractions, but if a plaintiff, notwithstanding the illegality, is held to have an equitable property interest under a resulting trust, the English courts might well prefer the minority view. The maxim has normally been applied in relation to dealings between the parties, for example, where a person seeks to enforce a claim to an equitable interest in property, the court has required as a condition of giving effect to that equitable interest that an allowance be made for costs incurred and for skill and labour expended in connection with the administration of the property.[80] In England, by reason of the decision in *Tribe v Tribe*,[81] the problem could only arise where there is no presumption of advancement.

---

[76] [1970] P 136, [1970] 1 All ER 540, CA, somewhat unconvincingly distinguished in *Heseltine v Heseltine* [1971] 1 All ER 952, CA. See (1971) 115 Sol Jo 614 (S Cretney); (1980) 9 AALR 28 (G Kodilinye).

[77] Note, however, that such a conveyance into the wife's name may constitute a postnuptial settlement which the court has jurisdiction to vary under s 24(1)(c) of the Matrimonial Causes Act 1973.

[78] (1995) 132 ALR 133. See (1996) 10 Tru LI 51 (P H Pettit); (1996) 19 UQLJ 150 (P Butler); (1997) 60 MLR 102 (P Creighton); [1997] ALJ 195 (D Maclean); (1997) 19 Sydney LR 240.

[79] As to that presumption, see p 180, supra.

[80] *Re Berkeley Applegate (Investment Consultants) Ltd* [1989] Ch 32, [1988] 3 All ER 71.

[81] Supra, CA.

8 LAW COMMISSION CONSULTATION PAPER 154[82]

The Law Commission consider that the law relating to the effect of illegality on trusts is in need of reform, by reason of the complexity and uncertainty of the law and its potential to give rise to unjust decisions. While accepting the need to retain an illegality doctrine, they propose the abandonment of the reliance principle laid down in *Tinsley v Milligan*[83] and *Tribe v Tribe*,[84] and the giving of a statutory discretion to the courts to declare an illegal trust to be invalid or valid. The court would be required to take into account:

(1) the seriousness of the illegality

(2) the knowledge and intention of the illegal trust beneficiary

(3) whether invalidity would tend to deter the illegality

(4) whether invalidity would further the purpose of the rule which renders the trust 'illegal'

(5) whether invalidity would be a proportionate response to the claimant's participation in the illegality

They further propose that there should be no role for the clean hands doctrine.

---

[82] The Law Commission intend to publish a report in 2005.   [83] Supra, HL.   [84] Supra, CA.

12

VOIDABLE TRUSTS

1 TRANSACTIONS AT AN UNDERVALUE

(a) GENERAL

Where a settlor has become bankrupt the relevant provisions of the Insolvency Act 1986 are designed to enable the trustee of the bankrupt's estate to recover the trust property for the benefit of the creditors. Section 339(1) provides that the trustee of the bankrupt's estate may apply to the court for an order under that section where an individual has been adjudged bankrupt and has at a relevant time entered into a transaction[1] with any person[2] at an undervalue. On such an application the court may make such order as it thinks fit for restoring the position to what it would have been if that individual had not entered into that transaction.[3]

(b) MEANING OF UNDERVALUE

An individual enters into a transaction at an undervalue if:

(a) he makes a gift to that person or he otherwise enters into a transaction with that person on terms that provide for him to receive no consideration,
(b) he enters into a transaction with that person in consideration of marriage,[4] or
(c) he enters into a transaction with that person for a consideration the value of which, in

---

[1] See p 233 n 16 for a case on the same words in s 423.

[2] The expression 'any person' in the corresponding provision dealing with companies (s 238) has been held to have its literal meaning, unrestricted as to persons or territory. The safeguards are that the court's power to make an order is discretionary and, in the case of persons who are abroad, the leave of the court must be obtained for service abroad: *Re Paramount Airways Ltd* [1993] Ch 223, [1992] 3 All ER 1, CA.

[3] Section 339(2). The value is to be assessed as at the date of the transaction: *Re Thoars (decd)* [2002] EWCHC 2416 (Ch), [2003] BPIR 489. Contrast s 423(2) discussed p 233, infra. See, generally, (1987) 17 Fam Law 316 (N Furey); [2001] CWLR 206 (A Keay).

[4] When the Civil Partnership Act 2004 is brought into force there will be added 'or the formation of a civil partnership'.

money or money's worth, is significantly less than the value, in money or money's worth, of the consideration provided by the individual.[5]

(c) THE RELEVANT TIME

A transaction at an undervalue can only be upset by the court if it was entered into at a relevant time. This is defined in s 341(1) as a time in the period of five years ending with the day of the presentation of the bankruptcy petition on which the individual is adjudged bankrupt.

Within the five year period, a distinction is drawn between a time which is less than two years, and one which is two years or more, before the end of the five year period. There are no qualifications if the transaction was entered into within two years of the bankruptcy, but within the period of two to five years before the bankruptcy a time is not a relevant time unless the individual was insolvent at that time, or becomes insolvent in consequence of the transaction. However this qualification is presumed to be satisfied, unless the contrary is shown, in relation to any transaction at an undervalue which is entered into by an individual with a person who is an associate of his.[6] For the purposes of these provisions a person is insolvent if he is unable to pay his debts as they fall due, or the value of his assets is less than the amount of his liabilities taking into account his contingent and prospective liabilities.[7]

Special provisions are made in the case of criminal bankruptcy.[8] In this case a transaction is treated as having been entered into at a relevant time if it was entered into at any time on or after the date specified in the criminal bankruptcy order on which the petition was based.[9]

---

[5] Section 339(3). Though not essential it is preferable for the court to arrive at precise figures for the incoming and outgoing values where it is possible to do so: *Ramlort Ltd v Reid* [2004] EWCA Civ 800, [2004] BPIR 985. It was held in *Re Kumar (a Bankrupt)* [1993] 2 All ER 700 that the compromise of a claim to financial provision in matrimonial proceedings was capable of being consideration in money or money's worth for the purpose of determining whether a transaction had been entered into at an undervalue, though it was not on the facts; and that where a husband transferred his interest in the matrimonial home to his wife, having regard to the difference in value between the equity of redemption and the amount of the mortgage, the wife's assumption of sole liability for the mortgage was significantly less than the consideration provided by the husband and was not sufficient to prevent the transaction being at an undervalue. See also *Clarkson v Clarkson* [1994] BCC 921, CA; *National Bank of Kuwait v Menzies* [1994] 2 BCLC 306, CA; *Re Brabon* [2000] BCC 1171.

[6] Section 341(2). 'Associate' is defined in s 435. A person is an associate (i) of an individual if that person is the individual's husband or wife, or is a relative, or the husband or wife of a relative, of the individual or of the individual's husband or wife, (ii) of any person with whom he is in partnership and the husband or wife or a relative of any individual with whom he is in partnership, and (iii) of any person by whom he is employed. Further, a person in his capacity of trustee of a trust is, with certain exceptions, an associate of another person if the beneficiaries of the trust include, or the terms of the trust confer a power that may be exercised for the benefit of, that other person or an associate of that other person. 'Relative' is defined in s 435(8). The Civil Partnership Act 2004, not yet in force, will extend references to a husband or wife to a civil partner.

[7] Section 341(3).

[8] Under s 264(1)(d), repealed from a date to be appointed: Criminal Justice Act 1988, s 170, Sch 16. Note the power of the court to make confiscation orders under ibid ss 71, et seq as amended.

[9] Section 341(4). By sub-s (5) no order is to be made under s 339 where an appeal is pending. Both these sub-sections repealed from a date to be appointed by the Criminal Justice Act 1988, s 170, Sch 16.

(d) THE ORDER OF THE COURT

Without prejudice to the generality of the power of the court to make such order as it thinks fit,[10] s 342 spells out particular orders that the court may make. Under ss 1(a) and (b) these clearly include orders to direct trustees to vest appropriate property, whether in its original form or in any form which represents it, in the trustee of the bankrupt's estate. The power of the court to make an order is not limited to the person with whom the bankrupt entered into the transaction, but a third party will be protected in his interest if he can show that he acquired it in good faith and for value.[11] However it is presumed that the interest was acquired otherwise than in good faith if at the time of its acquisition the third party had notice of the relevant surrounding circumstances[12] and of the relevant proceedings,[13] or was in some way connected with either party to the original transaction.[14]

It may be added that the fact that a settlement or transfer of property had to be made in order to comply with a property adjustment order under the Matrimonial Causes Act 1973 does not prevent it being a transaction in respect of which an order may be made under s 339.[15]

2 TRANSACTIONS DEFRAUDING CREDITORS

(a) GENERAL

The substance of ss 423–425 of the Insolvency Act 1986 is to empower the court to make an appropriate order to protect the interests of persons who are the victims of certain specific transactions. Section 423, like s 339, relates to transactions entered

---

[10] The court does not start with a presumption in favour of monetary compensation as opposed to setting aside the transaction: *Ramlort Ltd v Reid* [2004] EWCA Civ 800, [2004] BPIR 985.

[11] Section 342(2) as amended by the Insolvency (No 2) Act 1994, s 2(1).

[12] Ie, the fact that the individual in question entered into the transaction at an undervalue: Insolvency Act 1986, s 342(4) as substituted by the Insolvency (No 2) Act 1994, s 2(3).

[13] A person has notice of the relevant proceedings if he has notice (a) of the fact that the petition on which the individual in question is adjudged bankrupt has been presented, or (b) of the fact that the individual in question has been adjudged bankrupt: Insolvency Act 1986, s 342(5) added by the Insolvency (No 2) Act 1994, s 2(3).

[14] Insolvency Act 1986, s 342(2A), added by the Insolvency (No 2) Act 1994, s 2(2). See (1994) 138 Sol Jo 710 (R Potterton and Sue Cullen).

[15] See s 39 of the Matrimonial Causes Act 1973 as amended by s 235(1) and Sch 8 para 23 of the Insolvency Act 1985 and s 439(2) and Sch 14 to the Insolvency Act 1986.

into[16] at an undervalue[17] but, unlike s 339, is not restricted to transactions taking place within a certain period. Again s 423 applies whether or not insolvency proceedings have been taken while, as we have seen, s 339 only applies where an individual has been adjudged bankrupt. In these respects s 423 is wider than s 339. In one respect, however, it is narrower. Section 339 does not call for any intent on the part of the bankrupt: all that has to be established is the transaction at an undervalue at a relevant time. Under s 423, the court only has jurisdiction if it is satisfied that the transaction was entered into for the purpose:[18]

    (a) of putting assets beyond the reach of a person[19] who is making, or may at some time make, a claim against him, or

    (b) of otherwise prejudicing the interests of such a person in relation to the claim which he is making or may make.[20]

The power of the court under s 423 is somewhat wider than under s 339. There is the same power in s 423(2) for the court to make such order as it thinks fit for '(a) restoring the position to what it would have been if the transaction had not been entered into', but while s 339(2) stops at that point s 423(2) continues 'and (b) protecting the interests of persons who are victims of the transaction'. A victim of a transaction is a person who is, or is capable of being, prejudiced by it.[21]

(b) WHO MAY APPLY FOR AN ORDER

An application for an order under s 423 cannot be made except:

    (a) in a case where the debtor has been adjudged bankrupt, . . . by the official receiver, by the trustee of the bankrupt's estate . . . or, (with the leave of the court), by a victim of the transaction;

    (b) in a case where a victim of the transaction is bound by a voluntary arrangement

---

[16] *Department for Environment, Food and Rural Affairs v Feakins* (2004) *Times* 20 Dec (a person can enter into a transaction at an undervalue by simply participating in an arrangement which resulted in the under-valued transaction); *Beckenham MC Ltd v Centralex Ltd* [2004] EWHC 1287 (Ch), [2004] BPIR 1112 (s 423 prima facie applies to a transfer by a trustee, but transaction will normally, but not always, be protected by s 423(2)).

[17] Defined in s 423(1) in similar terms to s 339(3) set out p 231, supra, and likewise prospectively amended. Section 423 is concerned with actual value, not book value: *Pena v Coyne* [2004] EWHC 2684 (Ch), [2004] 2 BCLC 703. See *Agricultural Mortgage Corpn Ltd v Woodward* [1995] 1 BCLC 1; *Barclays Bank plc v Bean* [2004] 3 EGLR 71, and generally, [1998] Conv 362 (G Miller).

[18] Note that the wording of s 423 is subjective: *Pagemanor Ltd v Ryan* [2002] BPIR 593. What must be shown is that the bankrupt was substantially motivated by one or other of the aims set out in s 423(3)(a) and (b) in entering into the transaction in question: *IRC v Hashim* [2002] EWCA 981, [2002] 2 BCLC 489, applied *Kubiangha v Ekpenyong* [2002] EWHC 1567 (Ch), [2003] BPIR 623. See (2002) 36 T & ELJ 21 (Suzanne Popovic-Monyag) discussing *Stone v Stone* (2001) 55 OR(3d) 491; [2003] Conv 272 (A Keay).

[19] The section does not require the applicant to establish that the purpose of the transaction was to put assets beyond the applicant's reach: *Jyske Bank (Gibraltar) Ltd v Spjeldnaes* [1999] 2 BCLC 101.

[20] Section 423(3). See *Midland Bank plc v Wyatt* [1997] 1 BCLC 242.

[21] Section 423(5). See *Chohan v Saggar* [1994] 1 BCLC 706, CA.

approved under . . . Part VIII of the Act,[22] the supervisor of the voluntary arrangement or any person who (whether or not so bound) is such a victim, or;

(c) in any other case, a victim of the transaction.

It is expressly provided[23] that whoever makes the application, it is to be treated as made on behalf of every victim of the transaction.

(c) THE ORDER OF THE COURT

Section 425 contains provisions corresponding to those in s 342[24] modified only to allow for the fact that s 423, unlike s 339, is not restricted to cases where the individual who entered into the transaction at an undervalue has been adjudged bankrupt.

(d) ASSET PROTECTION TRUSTS

The so-called asset protection trust, the term is imprecise, has primarily been developed in the United States, and is designed to hold assets beyond the reach of creditors, including the revenue authorities. It has made little headway in England, partly, no doubt, because of the above provisions. Further s 357 provides for criminal penalties, and a professional adviser involved in arranging such a trust to defraud creditors could become liable in a criminal conspiracy or in aiding and abetting a s 357 crime.[25] A trust, however, may be, and commonly is, drafted quite properly with the purpose and effect of avoiding tax, and the protective trust, as we have seen,[26] may operate to defeat the claims of the creditors of a spendthrift life tenant.

3 VOLUNTARY SETTLEMENT OF LAND FOLLOWED BY CONVEYANCE FOR VALUABLE CONSIDERATION

Under section 173 of the Law of Property Act 1925 a voluntary settlement of land made with intent to defraud a subsequent purchaser is voidable at the instance of such a purchaser, being a bona fide purchaser for value. The onus of establishing an actual

---

[22] Ie a proposal made by the debtor to his creditors for a composition in satisfaction of his debts or a scheme of arrangement of his affairs. The procedure under Part VIII is additional to the provisions in the Deeds of Arrangement Act 1914.

[23] Section 424(2).

[24] Discussed supra, p 232. In unusual circumstances monetary compensation was ordered in place of setting aside the transaction in *Pena v Coyne (No 2)* [2004] EWHC 2685 (Ch), [2004] 2 BCLC 730. See *Moon v Franklin* [1996] BPIR 196.

[25] *Midland Bank plc v Wyatt* [1997] 1 BCLC 242, and see [1994] PCB 96 (R Citron and M Steiner); 239 (J McLeuchlan and M Steiner); [1997] PCB 77 (P Willoughby).

[26] See p 79 et seq, supra.

intent to defraud rests on the party alleging it.[27] This provision does not affect a bona fide purchaser for value who purchased the interest of a beneficiary under the settlement prior to the disposition for value.[28]

4 PROVISIONS FOR PROTECTION OF SPOUSE AND FAMILY

(a) SECTION 37 OF THE MATRIMONIAL CAUSES ACT 1973

By virtue of this section a wife[29] who has brought proceedings for financial relief under the Act against her husband may apply to the court for an order setting aside any 'reviewable' disposition[30] which the court is satisfied[31] was made with the intention, that is, the husband's subjective intention (which need not be his sole or even his dominant intention), of defeating the claim for financial relief. It is open to the court to conclude that in making the disposition he knew and intended the inevitable result of his action.[32] If the application is made before financial relief has been granted, the wife must show that if the disposition were set aside the court would grant her financial relief or different financial relief. A disposition is a 'reviewable disposition' unless it was 'made for valuable consideration (other than marriage) to a person who, at the time of the disposition, acted in relation to it in good faith and without notice of any intention on the part of the other party to defeat the applicant's claim for financial relief.'[33] 'Notice' includes constructive as well as actual notice.[34] This provision operates to protect intermediate bona fide dealing for value between the date of the disposition and the date of its being set aside.

Where the disposition was made three years or more before the application the wife

---

[27] *Moore v Kelly* [1918] 1 IR 169.

[28] *Prodger v Langham* (1663) 1 Keb 486.

[29] Including a former wife. Though less often needed in practice the section applies equally to an application by a husband, or former husband. When the Civil Partnership Act 2004 has been brought into force corresponding provisions will apply to a civil partner and a former civil partner: s 72 (1), Sch 5, Part 14.

[30] 'Disposition' is defined by s 37(6) in terms wide enough to include a trust. The court may also restrain a threatened disposition of property, even though it be land situated abroad, *Hamlin v Hamlin* [1986] Fam 11, [1985] 2 All ER 1037, CA. See also *Shipman v Shipman* [1991] 1 FLR 250. The section only applies to transactions effected by the other spouse, and does not apply to transactions effected by a third party for the benefit of that spouse: *McGladdery v McGladdery* [2000] 1 FCR 315, CA.

[31] As to the standard of proof see *K v K* (1982) *Times*, 16 February, CA; *Kemmis v Kemmis* [1988] 1 WLR 1307, CA noted [1989] Conv 204 (Jane Fortin); *Trowbridge v Trowbridge* [2002] EWHC 3114 (Ch), [2004] 2 FCR 79.

[32] *Kemmis v Kemmis*, supra, CA.

[33] Section 37(4). See *Whittingham v Whittingham* [1979] Fam 9, [1978] 3 All ER 805 per Balcombe J, affd CA on other grounds at 813; *Green v Green* [1981] 1 All ER 97.

[34] *Kemmis v Kemmis*, supra, CA; *Sherry v Sherry* [1991] 1 FLR 307, CA, noted [1991] Conv 370 (Jane Fortin).

must prove affirmatively the husband's intention to defeat her claim. Where, however, the disposition was made less than three years before the application, this intention is presumed, if the effect of the disposition would be to defeat the claim, or, where an order for relief is already in force, if it has had this effect: the presumption can be rebutted by evidence to the contrary, but the onus of proof in this case rests on the husband.[35]

(b) THE INHERITANCE (PROVISION FOR FAMILY AND DEPENDANTS) ACT 1975

This Act[36] enables the court to review dispositions (including dispositions by way of trust) effected by the deceased otherwise than for full valuable consideration and made with the intention,[37] though not necessarily the sole, or even the dominant, intention,[38] of defeating applications for financial provision in whole or in part. The Act applies to dispositions made less than six years before the date of the death of the deceased.

5 SHAM TRUSTS

What appears on the face of it to be a trust may be set aside as a sham if the truth of the matter is that the settlor retains full beneficial entitlement and there is no intention that the apparent beneficiaries shall obtain any benefit. The definition in *Snook v London and West Riding Investments Ltd*[39] is constantly cited, namely that '. . . if it has any meaning in law, [sham] means acts done or documents executed by the parties to the "sham" which are intended by them to give to third parties or to the court the appearance of creating between the parties legal rights and obligations different from the actual rights and obligations (if any) which the parties intend to create'.

Arden LJ in *Hitch v Stone*[40] said that the authorities established the following points:

---

[35] Section 37(5). The onus was discharged in *Shipman v Shipman* [1991] 1 FLR 250.

[36] Sections 10–14. When the Civil Partnership Act 2004 is brought into force the 1975 Act will apply in relation to a civil partnership as it applies to marriage: s 71, Sch 4, Part 2.

[37] On a balance of probabilities.

[38] *Re Dawkins, Dawkins v Judd* [1986] 2 FLR 360; *Kemmis v Kemmis*, supra, CA.

[39] [1967] 2 QB 786, [1967] 1 All ER 518, CA, at 802, 528. Cf *Bhopal & Kaur v Wilia* (1999) 32 HLR 302, CA (oral agreement for a tenancy at a rent of £300 per month. Written agreement for tenancy at £450 per month to mislead vendor's bank held to be a sham giving rise to no legal rights or obligations). See [2004] PCB 95 (D Harris); [1999] NZLJ 462 (R Holmes).

[40] [2001] EWCA Civ 63, [2001] STC 214, applied *Re Esteem Settlement* [2003] JLR 188(Jersey Royal Court), discussed (2003) 52 T & ELJ 14 (Kerry Lawrence and Victoria Connolly). See *Midland Bank plc v Wyatt* [1995] 3 FCR 11; *Abdel Rahman v Chase Bank (CI) Trust Co Ltd* [1991] JLR 105(Jersey Royal Court), noted [1993] PCB 94 (R C Lawrence III). See also [1996] PCB 228 (P Willoughby); (1999) 6 T & ELJ 11 (Catriona Syed); [1999] NZLJ 462 (R Holmes); [2000] PCB 28, 105 (J Mowbray); [2005] PCB 69 (D Hochberg).

(i)   the court in addition to examining the document itself may examine external evidence;

(ii) the test of intention is subjective. The parties must have intended to create rights and obligations other than those appearing on the face of document, and further must have intended to give third parties a false impression of what the rights and obligations created were;

(iii) the mere fact that the act or document is uncommercial, or artificial, does not mean that it is a sham. For it to be a sham the parties must have intended to be bound by some other arrangement;

(iv) the fact that parties subsequently depart from the terms set out in an agreement does not necessarily mean that they never intended that it should be effective and binding;

(v)   a trust deed is not a sham unless both the settlor and the trustee intended that the true arrangement should be different from that appearing in the trust deed.

Another apparent trust which may, perhaps, be set aside as a sham is what is sometimes referred to as a 'Red Cross trust'. This is a trust in a wide discretionary form set up with a single named beneficiary, such as the Red Cross, but with the trustees having wide powers to add the settlor and his family, and where there is evidence that the Red Cross is not intended to benefit.[41]

There is an irreducible core of obligations owed by the trustees to the beneficiaries and enforceable by them which is fundamental to the concept of a trust. If the beneficiaries have no trusts enforceable against the trustees there are no trusts and an apparent trust document will have no effect as such. In so holding in *Armitage v Nurse*,[42] Millett LJ refused to accept that these core obligations included the duties of skill and care, prudence and diligence. The duty of the trustees to perform the trusts honestly and in good faith for the benefit of the beneficiaries was, he said, the minimum necessary to give substance to the trusts and, in his opinion, was sufficient.

6 ILLUSORY TRUSTS

Illusory trusts are really examples of sham trusts, but merit separate treatment as they are subject to a long line of authority.

---

[41] This is sometimes called a 'black hole' trust. See [2002] PCB 42, 110 (P Matthews). See also *TR Technology Investment Trusts plc* [1988] BCLC 256, and the Isle of Man litigation in *Steele v Paz Ltd (in liquidation)* (10 October 1995, unreported), extracts from which appear in Butterworths *Offshore Cases and Materials* (1996) vol 1 at p 338.

[42] [1998] Ch 241, [1997] 2 All ER 705, CA.

(a) TRUSTS FOR THE BENEFIT OF CREDITORS[43]

If a valid trust is created it cannot be revoked, unless the settlement itself contains a power of revocation. There appears to be an exception to this rule where a debtor conveys or transfers property to trustees for the benefit of his creditors. Such a disposition is prima facie revocable by the debtor, but the true view in such a case is that the apparent beneficiaries have never acquired any equitable interest in the property at all. The trustees, in the eye of equity, hold the property conveyed or transferred to them on trust for the debtor himself absolutely. The debtor 'proposes only a benefit to himself by the payment of his debts—his object is not to benefit his creditors'.[44] The trustees are in effect mere mandatories or agents[45] of the debtor, who, it has been said,[46] 'is merely directing the mode in which his own property shall be applied for his own benefit, and . . . the general creditors, or the creditors named on the schedule, are merely persons named there for the purpose of showing how the trust property under the voluntary deed shall be applied for the benefit of the volunteers'. The deed, in substance, operates merely as a power to the trustees which is revocable by the debtor.

(b) WHERE THE TRUST BECOMES IRREVOCABLE

In various circumstances, the court will draw the inference that the prima facie rule does not represent the intention of the debtor, and that the deed accordingly creates a true trust for the benefit of the creditors, or at any rate some of them. This will clearly be the case as regards those creditors who have executed the deed,[47] or who have acted on the deed, for instance by forbearing to sue,[48] or have expressly assented, not necessarily formally, to the trust,[49] or where they have been expressly or impliedly told by the debtor that they may look to the trust property for the payment of their debts.[50] Mere communication of the trust to a creditor which is not dissented from by him may well be sufficient by itself to make the trust irrevocable, but the law on this point is confused.[51]

A deed has been held to be irrevocable where the obvious intention of the transaction would be frustrated if the debtor retained a power of revocation. Thus in *New, Prance and Garrard's Trustee v Hunting*[52] the debtor conveyed the property to trustees

---

[43] See generally (1957) 21 Conv 280 (L A Sheridan).

[44] *Bill v Cureton*, supra, at 511, per Pepys MR.

[45] See *Acton v Woodgate* (1833) 2 My & K 492, per Leach MR.

[46] *Garrard v Lord Lauderdale* (1830) 3 Sim 1 at 12, per Shadwell VC; affd (1931) 2 Russ & My 451.

[47] *Montefiore v Browne* (1858) 7 HL Cas 241; *Mackinnon v Stewart* (1850) 1 Sim NS 76; *Johns v James* (1878) 8 Ch D 744, CA.

[48] *Nicholson v Tutin* (1855) 2 K & J 18; *Re Baber's Trusts* (1870) LR 10 Eq 554.

[49] *Harland v Binks* (1850) 15 QB 713.   [50] *Synnot v Simpson* (1854) 5 HL Cas 121.

[51] In favour of a trust *Adnitt v Hands* (1887) 57 LT 370, DC; *Re Sanders' Trusts* (1878) 47 LJ Ch 667; contra, *Cornthwaite v Frith* (1851) 4 De G & Sm 552; *Re Michael* (1891) 8 Morr 305, DC. See also *Mackinnon v Stewart*, supra; *Montefiore v Browne*, supra.

[52] [1897] 2 QB 19, CA; affd on another ground [1899] AC 419, HL. See also *Radcliffe v Abbey Road & St John's Wood Permanent Building Society* (1918) 87 LJ Ch 557.

on trust to raise £4,200 to make good breaches of trust committed by the debtor. The obvious purpose, it was said, was thereby to mitigate the penal consequences of the breaches of trust, which purpose required the creation of an irrevocable binding trust.

The effect of the death of the debtor is not clear. If the trust is to commence only after the debtor is dead, it seems that it makes it irrevocable.[53] Where the trust is to pay either during the debtor's lifetime or after his death the authorities are contradictory as to whether the death of the debtor makes the trust irrevocable.[54]

Lastly, it has been held that the mandatory theory does not apply to an assignment made to a creditor as trustee for himself and other creditors; the debtor cannot revoke such a deed after it has been communicated to the assignee.[55]

(c) DEEDS OF ARRANGEMENT ACT 1914

This Act considerably reduces the practical importance of the law as stated above. It provides that a deed of arrangement[56] made by a debtor for the benefit of his creditors generally, or, if he was insolvent at the date of the execution thereof, for the benefit of any three or more of them, shall be void if not registered with the registrar appointed by the Board of Trade within seven days of its execution.[57] Further, if a deed of arrangement is expressed to be or is in fact for the benefit of a debtor's creditors generally, it will be void unless it has received the written assent of a majority in number and value of the creditors within 21 days after registration.[58]

It should also be noted that a deed of arrangement affecting unregistered land may be registered under the Land Charges Act 1972,[59] and if not so registered will be void as against a purchaser for valuable consideration.[60] In the case of registered land the procedure to protect the priority of a deed of arrangement is to enter a notice in the register.[61]

---

[53] *Re Fitzgerald's Settlement* (1887) 37 Ch D 18, CA; *Priestley v Ellis* [1897] 1 Ch 489.

[54] In favour of a continued power of revocation—*Garrard v Lord Lauderdale*, supra (assumed without discussion); *Re Sanders' Trusts* (1878) 47 LJ Ch 667; contra, *Montefiore v Browne*, supra; *Priestley v Ellis*, supra.

[55] *Siggers v Evans* (1855) 5 E & B 367.   [56] Defined in s 1.

[57] Section 2, subject to the Administration of Estates Act 1925, s 22(1).

[58] Deeds of Arrangement Act 1914, s 3, as amended by the Insolvency Act 1985, s 235 and Sch 8, para 22, and the Insolvency Act 1986, s 439(2) and Sch 14.

[59] Land Charges Act 1972, s 7(1).   [60] Ibid, ss 7(2) and 17(2).

[61] Land Registration Act 2002, ss 32, 29(2)(a)(ii).

13

CHARITABLE TRUSTS

1 DIFFERENCE BETWEEN CHARITABLE AND NON-CHARITABLE TRUSTS

Although in most ways the rules relating to charitable and non-charitable trusts are the same, there are certain very important differences, which may go to the very validity of the trust, for instance, in relation to certainty and perpetuity, or may have important economic results, for instance, in relation to income tax. It seems convenient to begin by discussing the most important of these differences, in order to appreciate the reasons why it may be necessary to contend that a trust is or is not charitable. Other differences will appear incidentally from time to time.

(a) CERTAINTY

(i) Basic position

The ordinary rule, as we have seen,[1] is that a private trust will fail if there is no certainty of objects, and thus, for instance, gifts for public or for benevolent purposes, or for worthy causes,[2] are void for uncertainty since the words used have no technical legal meaning. Where, however, there is a clear intention to give property for charitable purposes the gift will not fail on that ground. 'Charity' and 'charitable' are words with a technical legal meaning, and accordingly if trustees are given discretion to distribute property amongst charitable objects, the court can determine whether any object chosen is charitable or not, and, as we shall see,[3] a procedure is available for selecting the objects of a gift to charity where the settlor or testator either makes no provisions for the purpose or the provisions are for the any reason ineffective. The certainty required is certainty of intention to devote the property exclusively to charitable purposes. Thus a gift 'for the relief and benefit of the deserving poor and needy *in the district in which I farmed*' (italics added) was held to be a valid charitable gift by

---

[1] Chapter 3, section 2(c), p 50, supra.

[2] *Re Gillingham Bus Disaster Fund* [1958] Ch 300, [1958] 1 All ER 37; affd [1959] Ch 62, [1958] 2 All ER 749, CA; *Re Atkinson's Will Trusts* [1978] 1 All ER 1275, [1978] 1 WLR 586; *A-G of the Cayman Islands v Wahr-Hansen* [2001] WTLR 345, PC.

[3] Chapter 14, section 5, p 321 et seq, infra.

a Canadian court in *Re Daley's Estate*.[4] The purposes being exclusively charitable, the vagueness of the italicized phrase did not matter.

Although a gift for charity may be good notwithstanding that the particular objects are left undefined by the trust instrument, the gift will none the less fail if the trust is drafted in such a way that it is possible, without a breach of trust, for the whole of the gift to be devoted to non-charitable purposes. It was for this reason that gifts have wholly failed in numerous cases, such as *Blair v Duncan*,[5] where there was a bequest 'for such charitable or public purposes, as my trustee thinks proper'; *Houston v Burns*,[6] where residue was given 'for such public, benevolent or charitable purposes . . . as [my trustees] in their discretion shall think proper'; and *A-G of the Bahamas v Royal Trust Co*,[7] where residue was given 'for any purposes for and/or connected with the education and welfare of Bahamian children and young people'. In each of these cases the words were construed disjunctively so that the trustees, according to the terms of the trust, could quite properly have applied the whole fund for, in the first case public, in the second case public or benevolent and in the third case, welfare purposes, none of which is exclusively charitable. A trust is charitable only in so far as the trust funds are exclusively devoted to charitable purposes.[8] But it is not necessarily fatal that it is impossible for a benefit to be withdrawn after a beneficiary ceases to qualify.[9]

However, as Lord Millett has pointed out,[10] a charitable trust is not precluded from co-existing with a private trust either (so to speak) vertically or horizontally. Thus a testator may validly leave his estate to be held (by the same trustees) as to part on charitable trusts and as to part on private trusts.[11] Alternatively a trust instrument may provide for trustees to pay or apply income for charitable purposes for 21 years and then to hold it on non-charitable trusts for individual beneficiaries.[12]

(ii) Charitable Trusts (Validation) Act 1954

The principle that to be charitable trust funds must be exclusively devoted to charitable purposes still remains in full force in respect of trust instruments coming into

---

[4] (1988) 64 Sask LR 175.

[5] [1902] AC 37, HL. See also *Barralet v A-G* [1980] 3 All ER 918, sub nom *Re South Place Ethical Society* [1980] 1 WLR 1565, where the promotion of human welfare in harmony with advancing knowledge was said to be plainly a non-charitable object.

[6] [1918] AC 337, [1918–19] All ER Rep 817, HL; *Chichester Diocesan Fund and Board of Finance Inc v Simpson* [1944] AC 341, [1944] 2 All ER 60, HL.

[7] [1986] 3 All ER 423, PC, discussed [1987] NLJ Annual Charities Review 20 (S P de Cruz); (1987) 131 Sol Jo 1537 (N D M Parry).

[8] The existence of a power to revoke existing charitable trusts and declare new non-charitable trusts does not affect the charitable nature of the original trusts unless and until they are revoked—*Gibson v South American Stores (Gath and Chaves) Ltd* [1950] Ch 177, [1949] 2 All ER 985, CA.

[9] *Joseph Rowntree Memorial Trust Housing Association Ltd v A-G* [1983] 1 All ER 288.

[10] In *Latimer v Commissioners of Inland Revenue* [2004] UKPC 13, [2004] 1 WLR 1466, sub nom *Re Crown Forestry Rental Trust* [2004] 4 All ER 558 at [31], noted (2004) 18 Tru LI 155 (Debra Morris).

[11] *Public Trustee v Commissioners of Inland Revenue* [1971] NZLR 77.

[12] *Re Sir Robert Peel's School at Tamworth, ex p the Charity Commissioners* (1868) LR 3 Ch App 543.

operation on or after 16 December 1952,[13] but is qualified by the above Act in respect of what the Act calls 'imperfect trust provisions' contained in instruments coming into operation before that date.

An 'imperfect trust provision' is defined[14] as one declaring the objects for which property is to be held or applied, and so describing those objects that, consistently with the terms of the provision, the property can be used exclusively for charitable purposes, but can nevertheless be used for purposes which are not charitable. Where the Act applies, an imperfect trust provision has effect as respects the period before commencement of the Act,[15] as if the whole of the declared objects were charitable; and as respects the period after the commencement as if the provision required the property to be held or applied for the declared objects in so far only as it authorized use for charitable purposes.

The Act may apply not only to a gift which is expressed to be for charitable purposes as well as for other non-charitable purposes, but also to a gift such as, for example, a gift for worthy causes, in which charity is not expressly mentioned but where the terms of the gift in fact include both charitable and non-charitable purposes, and the gift can accordingly in fact be used exclusively for charitable purposes. One test might be to ask whether anyone, such as the founder or a person interested in a non-charitable application, would have a legitimate complaint if the whole were applied to charity.[16] It did not apply to a trust for institutions as opposed to one for objects or purposes.[17]

(iii) Primary trust for non-charitable purposes, residue to charity

Where there is a trust under which a fund or the income thereof is to be applied primarily to purposes which are not charitable and accordingly void, and as to the balance or residue to purposes which are charitable, if, on the one hand, as a matter of construction, the gift to charity is a gift of the entire fund or income subject to the payments thereout required to give effect to the non-charitable purpose, the amount set free by the failure of the non-charitable gift will be caught by and pass under the charitable gift.[18] On the other hand, if the gift of the residue is to be read as a gift of the mere balance of the fund after deducting the amount of the sum previously given out of it, the gift will wholly fail, on the ground that no ascertainable part of the fund or the income is devoted to charity, unless the amount applicable to the non-charitable purpose can be quantified. If this can be done the gift will fail, quoad that amount only, and will take effect in favour of the charitable purpose as regards the

---

[13] The Act is more fully discussed in the 3rd edn, p 158 et seq. A strong argument for a new Act to similar effect to apply to future such dispositions is put by Sheridan in (1993/94) 2 CLPR 1. See the Report for 1977, paras 71–80.

[14] By s 1(1).   [15] 30 July 1954.

[16] *Ulrich v Treasury Solicitor* [2005] EWHC 57 (Ch), [2005] 1 All ER 1059.

[17] *Re Harpur's Will Trusts* [1962] Ch 78, [1961] 3 All ER 588, CA.

[18] *Re Parnell* [1944] Ch 107; *Re Coxen* [1948] Ch 747, [1948] 2 All ER 492.

remainder.[19] Exceptionally and anomalously if the primary non-charitable trust is the maintenance in perpetuity of a tomb not in a church, it is simply ignored, even though it may be capable of being quantified, and the whole fund or income is treated as being devoted to charitable purposes.[20]

(iv) Non-charitable trusts ancillary to charitable trusts

Purposes merely ancillary to a main charitable purpose, which if taken by themselves would not be charitable, will not vitiate the claim of an institution to be established for purposes that are exclusively charitable.[21] Thus in *Re Coxen*[22] a fund of some £200,000 was given to the Court of Aldermen for the City of London upon trust:

(i)   to apply annually a sum not exceeding £100 to a dinner for the Court of Aldermen upon their meeting upon the business of the trust,

(ii) to pay one guinea to each alderman who attended during the whole of a committee meeting in connection with the trust, and

(iii) to apply the balance for a specified charitable purpose.

It was held that all the trusts were charitable as the provisions in favour of the aldermen were given for the better administration of the principal charitable trust and not for the personal benefit of the recipients. And a trust for the erection of a synagogue for religious educational and social purposes was likewise held to be exclusively charitable on the ground that the social activities were merely ancillary to the strictly religious activities.[23]

As explained by Slade J in *McGovern v A-G*[24] a distinction of critical importance has to be drawn between:

(a)   the designated purposes of the trust,

(b)   the designated means of carrying out those purposes, and

(c)   the consequences of carrying them out.

Trust purposes of an otherwise charitable nature do not lose their charitable status merely because, as an incidental consequence of the trustees' activities, there may enure to private individuals benefits of a non-charitable nature. Thus the Incorporated Council of Law Reporting was held to be charitable notwithstanding that publication of the law reports supplies members of the legal profession with the tools of their trade.[25] On the same principle a student's union, if it exists to further and

---

[19] *Re Vaughan* (1886) 33 Ch D 187; *Re Taylor* (1888) 58 LT 538; *Re Porter* [1925] Ch 746.

[20] *Re Birkett* (1878) 9 Ch D 576; *Re Vaughan*, supra; *Re Rogerson* [1901] 1 Ch 715.

[21] *Incorporated Council of Law Reporting for England and Wales v A-G* [1972] Ch 73, [1971] 3 All ER 1029, CA, per Russell LJ at pp 84, 1033; *Stratton v Simpson* (1970) 125 CLR 138.

[22] Supra, *Royal College of Surgeons of England v National Provincial Bank Ltd* [1952] AC 631, [1952] 1 All ER 984, HL. Contrast *Re Barnett* (1908) 24 TLR 788.

[23] *Neville Estates Ltd v Madden* [1962] Ch 832, [1961] 3 All ER 769.

[24] [1982] Ch 321, [1981] 3 All ER 493. See *Public Trustee v A-G of New South Wales* (1997) 42 NSWLR 600.

[25] *Incorporated Council of Law Reporting for England and Wales v A-G*, supra, CA.

does further the educational purposes of a college or university, may be charitable notwithstanding the personal benefits conferred on union members.[26] But the charitable purposes must be predominant, and any benefits to individual members of a non-charitable character which result from its activities must be of a subsidiary or incidental character.[27] Again many charities are membership organizations whose members may be entitled to special benefits such as reduction or waiver of admission charges, for example, the National Trust. If the benefits are only given to encourage members and to carry out the main charitable purpose, they will not deprive the organization of charitable status.

Similarly, trust purposes of an otherwise charitable nature do not lose it merely because the trustees, by way of furtherance of such purposes, have incidental powers to carry on activities which are not themselves charitable. The distinction is between (i) those non-charitable activities authorized by the trust instrument which are merely subsidiary or incidental to a charitable purpose, and (ii) those non-charitable activities so authorized which in themselves form part of the trust purpose. In the latter but not the former case, the reference to non-charitable activities will deprive the trust of its charitable status. In drawing this distinction Slade J recognized[28] that it might be easier to state than to apply in practice. And Scott J in *A-G v Ross*[29] said that the activities of an organization after its formation may serve to indicate that the power to carry on non-charitable activities was in truth not incidental or supplementary at all but was the main purpose for which the organization was formed. Such activities will, however, only be relevant if they are intra vires and of a nature and took place at a time which gives them probative value on the question whether the main purpose for which the organization was formed was charitable or non-charitable.

The problem has arisen with increasing frequency in relation to trading by or on behalf of charities. The Charity Commissioners[30] point out that there are three main aspects:

(i)   whether trading by a charity is permissible,

(ii)   whether charities may properly establish subsidiary or associated non-charitable trading companies for the purpose of raising funds, and

(iii)   whether trading by an institution on a non-profit making basis for the benefit of a local community can be charitable.

As to (i) a charity may properly engage in trading in the course of carrying out its primary purposes, for example, a charity for the relief of the disabled may run shops

---

[26] *London Hospital Medical College v IRC* [1976] 2 All ER 113; *A-G v Ross* [1985] 3 All ER 334; Contrast *IRC v City of Glasgow Police Athletic Association* [1953] AC 380, [1953] 1 All ER 747; and see [1978] Conv 92 (N P Gravells); [1986] T L & P 47 (Jean Warburton). The Attorney-General's Guidance on Expenditure by Student Unions is set out in App A to the Report for 1983.

[27] See *A-G v Ross* [1985] 3 All ER 334, and RR 8.   [28] In *McGovern v A-G*, supra.

[29] [1985] 3 All ER 334.

[30] Report for 1980, paras 5–12. See also Report for 1984, App C and see CC 35; (2001) 7 CPLR 109 (R Venables and J Kessler).

for the sale of goods made by disabled people employed in that charity's workshops, and a charity for the advancement of the Christian religion may sell bibles. A power to trade otherwise than in carrying out the primary purpose does not necessarily prevent an institution from being a charity. It is a question of degree, and it may not be easy to draw the line between a charity which is merely raising funds and furthering its activities by trading and what is in substance a trading institution wearing a charitable mantle.

As to (ii) this is permissible if it is within the investment powers of the charity and as an investment is not too speculative for a charity.

As to (iii) although, if the village shop goes, it may in one sense be of benefit to the community to set up a community shop, this is not regarded as being within a category recognized by law as charitable.

(v) Apportionment[31]

It must be remembered that where there is a power of selection or appointment between two or more persons or objects, the whole may be appointed to one to the total exclusion of the other or others, unless there is some express provision that each object is to have a minimum amount.[32] In the first place, if each object taken by itself is a valid object, whether charitable or non-charitable, the trust will be good even though the share that each object is to take is not declared by the trust instrument, and even though the trustees, having been given a power of selection, apportionment, division or appointment, fail to exercise it. In such case the court will divide the property between the objects equally, unless there is some contrary intention in the trust instrument.[33] Secondly, this principle was applied in *Re Clarke*[34] to a case where residue was given to:

(i)   indefinite charitable objects,

(ii)   a definite charitable object,

(iii) another definite charitable object,

(iv)   such indefinite charitable and non-charitable objects as the executors should think fit,

and the residue was directed to be divided among the four objects or sets of objects in such shares and proportions as the executors should determine. It was held that the power of distribution or appointment given to the executors was void, as they could

---

[31] It does not seem that it should make any difference whether trustees are directed to apportion a fund between different objects as opposed to being given a power of selection, division or appointment.

[32] Section 158 of the Law of Property Act 1925 replacing earlier legislation.

[33] *Salusbury v Denton* (1857) 3 K & J 529; *Re Douglas* (1887) 35 Ch D 472, CA; *Hunter v A-G* [1899] AC 309 at 324; HL, per Lord Davey. It seems doubtful whether the principle was properly applied in *Hoare v Osborne* (1866) LR 1 Eq 585.

[34] [1923] 2 Ch 407; *Re King* [1931] WN 232. The gift failed in *Re Wright's Will Trusts* (1981) (1999) 13 Tru LI 48, CA, where apportionment was not possible. The whole of the gift, if valid, could have been devoted to non-charitable purposes.

appoint the whole fund to object (iv), which was void for uncertainty, and this was clearly correct. It was further held, however, that the principle of *Lambert v Thwaites*[35] applied. In this case, it will be recalled, it was held that on its true construction the will set up a trust for all the children giving them vested interests, liable to be divested if the power of appointment was exercised. Similarly here the residue was held to have vested in the four objects equally: prima facie their interests were liable to be divested by exercise by the executors of their power of distribution or appointment, but this power being void, their interests were indefeasible. The gifts to objects (i), (ii) and (iii) were accordingly good, but the gift of the remaining one-fourth share to object (iv) failed on the ground of uncertainty, and went to the persons entitled on intestacy.

The principle of the trust power cases such as *Walsh v Wallinger*[36] does not, however, enable one, in, for instance, a gift to 'such charitable or benevolent objects as my trustees shall select', to imply a gift over in default of appointment to charitable and benevolent objects in equal shares so as to save the gift as to one-half for charity. The courts are unwilling to make any apportionment in this sort of case,[37] and, as we have seen,[38] numerous decisions, including many in the House of Lords, have held such gifts altogether void. In this sort of case there is no gift to objects, but only a power given to the trustees to distribute among an uncertain group of objects, and the court will not imply any gift in default of appointment when, as has been said[39] 'charitable purposes are mixed up with other purposes of such a shadowy and indefinite nature that the court cannot execute them'.

(vi) Liverpool City Council v A-G[40]

Here there was a gift of land to a local authority which covenanted to use and maintain it 'as a public park or recreation ground and for no other purpose'.[41] It was held, in the absence of any of the formalities applicable to a transfer of land to be held on charitable trusts, that no charitable trust requiring the authority to maintain the land for recreational purposes in perpetuity had been created. It was not established that there was an intention that the corporation's legal ownership was to be held beneficially for charitable purposes.

(b) PERPETUITIES

In general the rule against perpetuities, which is shortly stated in Section 1 of chapter 11, applies to gifts to charity. As Lord Selborne LC said,[42] 'if the gift in trust for charity

---

[35] (1866) LR 2 Eq 151, discussed in chapter 2, section 2(d), p 34, supra.

[36] (1830) 2 Russ & M 78; see chapter 2, section 2(d), p 34, supra.

[37] See per Lord Wright in *Chichester Diocesan Fund v Simpson and Board of Finance Inc* [1944] AC 341 at 356, [1944] 2 All ER 60 at 66, HL.

[38] See p 241, supra.   [39] *Hunter v A-G* [1899] AC 309 at 323, HL, per Lord Davey.

[40] (1992) *Times*, 1 May, noted (1992/93) 1 CLPR 153 (Debra Morris).

[41] It was conceded that the provision of a recreation ground is a charitable purpose: see p 274, infra.

[42] *Chamberlayne v Brockett* (1872) 8 Ch App 206 at 211; *Re Lord Stratheden and Campbell* [1894] 3 Ch 265; *Re Mander* [1950] Ch 547, [1950] 2 All ER 191.

is itself conditional upon a future and uncertain event, it is subject . . . to the same rules and principles as any other estate depending for its coming into existence upon a condition precedent. If the condition is never fulfilled, the estate never arises; if it is so remote and indefinite as to transgress the limits of time prescribed by the rules of law against perpetuities, the gift fails ab initio.'[43] Thus gifts to charity to take effect on the appointment of the next lieutenant-colonel of a volunteer corps,[44] or when a candidate for the priesthood comes forward from a particular church,[45] have been held void on the ground that the event might not occur until after the expiration of the perpetuity period.[46] The general rule applies equally when the limitation to charity is by way of a gift over following a gift in favour of private individuals.[47]

Exceptionally, however, the rule against perpetuities has no application to a gift to one charity with a gift over to another charity upon some contingency, notwithstanding that the contingency may occur outside the perpetuity period.[48] The exception, however, does not cover the case of a gift over from a charity to an individual. The gift over in such case is subject to the rule.[49]

(c) THE RULE AGAINST PERPETUAL TRUSTS

As has been seen,[50] gifts for non-charitable purposes are generally void, and, in the exceptional cases where they are valid, must, if they are to be effective at all, be limited so as not to continue beyond the perpetuity period. Trusts for charitable purposes are, however, completely unaffected by the rule against perpetual trusts, and it is no objection to a charitable trust that it may continue for ever and that it may never be possible to expend the capital as opposed to the income of the property subject to the trust.

It is convenient to mention at this point some of the cases that have arisen in connection with the upkeep of tombs. Though the upkeep of a tomb, other than a tomb in a church, is not a charitable purpose, it may nevertheless be possible to some extent to effect the desired purpose. If the provision is limited to the perpetuity period it is apparently valid, though unenforceable, and various devices may be adopted which may, in practice, provide for its upkeep for an even longer period. First, if the gift is for the upkeep of the whole of a churchyard, including the particular tomb in question, the gift is charitable even though the motive for it may be the non-charitable one of maintaining one particular tomb. Secondly, advantage may be taken of the principle

---

[43] But see now the Perpetuities and Accumulations Act 1964, s 3.

[44] *Re Lord Stratheden and Campbell*, supra.   [45] *Re Mander*, supra.

[46] But see the Perpetuities and Accumulations Act 1964, s 3.

[47] *Re Bowen* [1893] 2 Ch 491, [1891–94] All ER Rep 238; *Re Wightwick's Will Trusts* [1950] Ch 260, [1950] 1 All ER 689.

[48] *Christ's Hospital v Grainger* (1849) 1 Mac & G 460; *Re Tyler* [1891] 3 Ch 252, CA; *Royal College of Surgeons of England v National Provincial Bank Ltd* [1952] AC 631, [1952] 1 All ER 984, HL. Cf *Re Martin* [1952] WN 339.

[49] *Re Bowen*, supra; *Gibson v South-American Stores (Gath & Chaves) Ltd* [1950] Ch 177, [1949] 2 All ER 985, CA; *Re Cooper's Conveyance Trusts* [1956] 3 All ER 28.

[50] Chapter 3, p 55 et seq, infra.

of *Christ's Hospital v Grainger*[51] by granting property to one charity with a gift over to another charity if the tomb is not kept in repair. Care must be taken, however, not to impose any trust for the non-charitable purpose of maintaining the tomb on the subject-matter of the gift—failure to observe this point led to a failure of the scheme in *Re Dalziel*.[52] From a practical point of view the validity of this device depends on the trust income exceeding the sums needed for the upkeep of the tomb and on the availability of other income to carry out the necessary maintenance. This device would appear to be equally available in relation to any non-charitable purpose trust which is not void for some reason, such as uncertainty or administrative unworkability. Thirdly it may be noted that a burial authority may undertake the maintenance of a private grave for a period not exceeding 100 years from the date of the agreement.[53]

(d) EXEMPTIONS FROM RATES AND TAXES[54]

The income of bodies of persons or trusts established in the United Kingdom[55] for charitable purposes only, so far as it is applied accordingly,[56] is generally wholly exempt from income tax,[57] corporation tax,[58] and there is a similar exemption in relation to capital gains tax.[59]

---

[51] (1849) 1 Mac & G 460. See section 1B of this chapter, supra.

[52] [1943] Ch 277, [1943] 2 All ER 656.

[53] Local Authorities' Cemeteries Order 1977, SI 1977/204, art 10(7) and a monument or memorial for a period not exceeding 99 years: Parish Councils and Burial Authorities (Miscellaneous Provisions) Act 1970, s 1(1).

[54] See [1972] BTR 345; (1999) 62 MLR 333 (M Chesterman). The cost in terms of lost revenues to central and local government is estimated to be £2.2–2.5 billion.

[55] *Camille and Henry Dreyfus Foundation Inc v IRC* [1956] AC 39, [1955] 3 All ER 97, HL (foundation established in State of New York which carried out all its activities in the USA not entitled to exemption in respect of royalties received from a company resident in the UK).

[56] The Revenue may disallow a claim if it is not satisfied that the income has been used for charitable purposes. See *IRC v Educational Grants Association Ltd* [1967] Ch 993, [1967] 2 All ER 893, CA; *IRC v Helen Slater Charitable Trust Ltd* [1982] Ch 49, [1981] 3 All ER 98, CA (held to have been so applied where a charitable corporation, acting intra vires, made an outright transfer of money applicable to charitable purposes to another charity so as to pass to that other charity full title to the money. The opinion was expressed by the court that it would also cover the case where income was retained by the charity or otherwise capitalized—but see (1982) 98 LQR 1; *Sheppard v IRC (No 2)* [1993] STC 240. See also [2000] BTR 144 (Jean Warburton).

[57] Income and Corporation Taxes Act 1988, ss 505–506 as amended. If a charity carries on a trade its profits will only be exempt if they are applied solely to the purposes of the charity, and either (i) the trade is exercised in the course of the actual carrying out of a primary purpose of the charity, or (ii) the work in connection with the trade is mainly carried out by beneficiaries of the charity: s 505(1)(e). Note that under Extra Statutory Concession C4 if certain conditions are fulfilled the profits from bazaars, jumble sales and the like may not be charged to tax. A way round the liability of trading income to tax is to allow the trade to be carried on by a company whose shares are held by the charity and which covenants to make payments to the charity equal to its profits. See Report for 1988, paras 41–44, and NLJ Christmas Appeals Supp 12 (P R Framjee).

[58] Ibid, s 9(4).

[59] Taxation of Chargeable Gains Act 1992, s 256(1). The donor may obtain relief from capital gains tax on gifts to charities—ibid, s 257, as amended.

In relation to non-domestic rates relief is available where at the relevant time the rate-payer is a charity or trustees for a charity, and the hereditament is wholly or mainly used for charitable purposes.[60] A charity is entitled to 80% relief in respect of a hereditament of which it is in occupation in whole or in part,[61] and the charging authority may increase the relief to 100%.[62]

Charities are generally liable to Value Added Tax.[63] However in relation to charities various items are zero rated, including the sale by a charity of goods which have been donated to it, whether new or used, and the sale of donated goods by a taxable person who has covenanted to give all the profits of the sale to a charity.[64] There is also an exemption in respect of fund-raising events by charities.[65]

Transfers, conveyances and leases to charities are exempt from stamp duty.[66]

There is no charge to inheritance tax in respect of gifts to charities.[67]

Under gift aid arrangements a charity can reclaim income tax at the basic rate and capital gains tax where the gift was made by a UK taxpayer, and payments made are deductible by the donor in computing his income for higher rates of tax. The donor must make an appropriate declaration stating, inter alia, that the gift is to be treated as a qualifying donation for the purposes of s 25 of the Finance Act 1990.[68] Relief is also given for donations under a payroll deduction scheme.[69] Further donations to charity by companies are, subject to certain conditions, deductible in computing their profits.[70]

---

[60] By the Local Government Finance Act 1988, s 64(10), it is provided that for this purpose a hereditament is to be treated as 'wholly or mainly used for charitable purposes, if (a) it is used wholly or mainly for the sale of goods donated to a charity; and (b) the proceeds for sale (after deduction of expenses) are applied for the purposes of a charity. It does not appear to provide relief to trading shops run by charities, that is shops wholly or mainly used to sell goods bought under normal trading conditions, or to 'fifty-fifty' shops in which goods are deposited for sale and the net proceeds of sale are divided between the donor and the charity. See *Royal Society for the Protection of Birds v Brighton Borough Council* [1982] RA 33. As to a charity setting up a trading company see (1988) 3 TL & P 98 (Judith Hill and J de Souza).

[61] Local Government Finance Act 1988, s 43(5), (6). Likewise in the case of unoccupied hereditaments where it appears that when next in use the hereditament will be wholly or mainly used for charitable purposes: ibid, s 45(5), (6). Note *Kent County Council v Ashford Borough Council* [1998] RA 217.

[62] Ibid, ss 47, 48. Certain hereditaments, including places of religious worship and property used for the disabled, are wholly exempt from non-domestic rating: ibid, s 51, Sch 5 paras 11 (as amended by the Local Government Finance Act 1992, s 104 and Sch 10, para 3), 16.

[63] See (1995/96) 3 CLPR 37, 133 (1996/97) 4 CLPR 105; and (1997/98) 5 CLPR 77 (Jean Warburton).

[64] Value Added Tax Act 1994, s 30 and Sch 8 Group 15 as amended by the Finance Act 1997, ss 33, 34.

[65] Ibid, Sch 9 Group 12.   [66] Finance Act 1982, s 129, as amended.

[67] Inheritance Tax Act 1984, s 23. See *Re Benham's Will Trusts* [1995] STC 210, discussed (1995/96) 3 CLPR 11 (R Grierson) and (1998) 142 Sol Jo 1060 (J Sunnocks), not followed *Re Ratcliffe (decd)* [1999] STC 262.

[68] Finance Act 1990, s 25 as amended by the Finance Act 2000, s 39, and see SI 2000/2074. As to gift aid schemes and companies see Finance Act 2000, s 40. As to income tax and corporation tax relief for gifts of qualifying investments to a charity by an individual or a company see Income and Corporation Taxes Act 1988, s 587B as amended and (2000) 7 CLPR 23 (R Venables and J Kessler).

[69] Income and Corporation Taxes Act 1988, s 202 and Finance Act 2000, s 38.

[70] Income and Corporation Taxes Act 1988, s 338, as substituted by the Finance Act 2000, s 338A inserted by the Finance Act 2000, s 339 as amended.

2 DEFINITION OF CHARITY

(a) GENERAL

There is no statutory definition of charity or charitable purpose, a situation which has met with much criticism on the ground that the lack of a definition results in apparently arbitrary decisions as to whether an organization is charitable, and makes it difficult to give clear advice.[71] In 2001 the Prime Minister commissioned a review of the law and regulation of charities and other not-for-profit organizations. This was carried out by the Prime Minister's Strategy Unit and published as 'Private Action, Public Benefit'. Following an open public consultation the Government published 'Charities and the Not-For-Profits: a Modern Legal Framework', which led to the Charities Bill introduced in the House of Lords on 29 December 2004 following pre-legislative scrutiny of a draft Bill by a joint committee. This provided for the first time a statutory definition of 'charity' and 'charitable purpose'. Unfortunately the Bill was lost on the prorogation of Parliament in spring 2005 prior to the general election, but it was reintroduced in the Queen's speech in May 2005 and will, hopefully, become law in the 2005–06 session. The proposed statutory definition builds on the existing law, and, even if enacted, it will continue to be necessary to be familiar with most of the current law.

As the law stands, in order for a trust to be legally charitable, its purposes must fall within the spirit and intendment of the preamble to the Statute 43 Eliz 1 c 4, sometimes referred to as the Charitable Uses Act 1601.[72] This proposition, which appears to go back to *Morice v Bishop of Durham*,[73] has recently been reaffirmed by the House of Lords[74] notwithstanding the repeal of the preamble. The purposes set out in the preamble are, in modernized English, as follows:

The relief of aged, impotent and poor people; the maintenance of sick and maimed soldiers and mariners, schools of learning, free schools and scholars in universities; the repair of bridges, ports, havens, causeways, churches, seabanks and highways; the education and preferment of orphans; the relief, stock or maintenance for houses of correction; the marriages of poor maids, the supportation, aid and help of young tradesmen, handicraftmen

---

[71] But as recently as 1989 the White Paper (Cm 694): 'A Framework For The Future' concluded that there would be few advantages in attempting a wholesale redefinition of charitable status, and many real dangers in doing so.

[72] Repealed by the Mortmain and Charitable Uses Act 1888, the preamble, however, being to some extent preserved by s 13(2). The 1888 Act was itself repealed by the Charities Act 1960, but s 38(4) provides that, 'any reference in any enactment or document to a charity within the meaning, purview and interpretation of the Charitable Uses Act 1601, or of the preamble to it, shall be construed as a reference to a charity within the meaning which the word bears as a legal term according to the law of England and Wales'.

[73] (1804) 9 Ves 399; affd (1805) 10 Ves 522. See Gareth Jones, op cit, p 120 et seq, who also discusses the paradoxical effect of the Mortmain Act 1736 in persuading the courts to preserve a liberal definition of charity.

[74] *Scottish Burial Reform and Cremation Society Ltd v Glasgow City Corpn* [1968] AC 138 [1967] 3 All ER 215, HL; see also *Re Banfield* [1968] 2 All ER 276; *Ashfield Municipal Council v Joyce* [1978] AC 122, PC.

and persons decayed; the relief or redemption of prisoners or captives; and the aid or ease of any poor inhabitants concerning payment of fifteens, setting out of soldiers and other taxes.

While, as Lord Upjohn said in *Scottish Burial Reform and Cremation Society Ltd v Glasgow City Corpn*[75] 'it may seem almost incredible to anyone not familiar with this branch of the English law that this should still be taken as the test, it is undoubtedly the accepted test, though only in a very wide and broad sense'. In the same case, however, Lord Wilberforce pointed out[76] that the requirement that the purpose in order to be charitable must be within the spirit and intendment of the preamble does not mean quite what it says; 'for it is now accepted that what must be regarded is not the wording of the preamble itself, but the effect of decisions given by the courts as to its scope, decisions which have endeavoured to keep the law as to charities moving according as new social needs arise or old ones become obsolete or satisfied.' The process was described by Lord Reid:[77] 'The courts appear to have proceeded first by seeking some analogy between an object mentioned in the preamble and the object with regard to which they had to reach a decision. Then they appear to have gone further, and to have been satisfied if they could find an analogy between an object already held to be charitable and the new object claimed to be charitable.' The result, in Lord Upjohn's words,[78] is that 'the spirit and intendment' of the preamble to the Statute of Elizabeth have been stretched almost to breaking point. In recent tax cases,[79] the view that a benignant construction should be given if possible, so as to save the gift, has been reaffirmed.

Be this as it may, the accepted classification of the multitude of single instances is set out in the speech of Lord Macnaghten in *Income Tax Special Purposes Comrs v Pemsel*:[80] 'Charity', he said, 'in its legal sense comprises four principal divisions: trusts for the relief of poverty; trusts for the advancement of education; trusts for the advancement of religion; and trusts for other purposes beneficial to the community, not falling under any of the preceding heads.' Lord Macnaghten went on to observe that 'the trusts last referred to are not the less charitable in the eye of the law, because incidentally they benefit the rich as well as the poor, as indeed, every charity that deserves the name must do either directly or indirectly'. But it is very doubtful whether a trust would be declared to be charitable which excluded the poor.[81] Lord Macnaghten's

---

[75] [1968] AC 138 at 151, [1967] 3 All ER 215 at 221, HL.

[76] In *Scottish Burial Reform and Cremation Society Ltd v Glasgow City Corpn*, supra, HL, at 154, 223.

[77] In *Scottish Burial Reform and Cremation Society Ltd v Glasgow City Corpn*, supra, HL at 147, 218.

[78] *Scottish Burial Reform and Cremation Society Ltd v Glasgow City Corpn*, supra, HL, at 153, 222. Cf *Dingle v Turner* [1972] AC 601, [1972] 1 All ER 878, HL.

[79] *Guild v IRC* [1992] 2 AC 310, [1992] 2 All ER 10, HL; *IRC v McMullen* [1981] AC 1 at 11, [1980] 1 All ER 884 at 890, HL. See also *Re Le Cren Clarke (decd)* [1996] 1 All ER 715, sub nom *Funnell v Stewart* [1996] 1 WLR 288.

[80] [1891] AC 531 at 583, HL, based on the classification put forward by Sir Samuel Romilly as counsel in *Morice v Bishop of Durham* (1805) 10 Ves 522.

[81] *Re Macduff* [1896] 2 Ch 451 at 666, CA, per Lindley LJ; *Re Resch's Will Trusts, Le Cras v Perpetual Trustee Co Ltd* [1969] 1 AC 514, [1967] 3 All ER 915, PC. But see *Joseph Rowntree Memorial Trust Housing Association Ltd v A-G* [1983] Ch 159, [1983] 1 All ER 288, noted (1983) 46 MLR 782 (R Nobles).

classification has constantly been referred to in later cases. Lord Wilberforce, in *Scottish Burial Reform and Cremation Society Ltd v Glasgow City Corpn*[82] reaffirmed its value and its usefulness in solving many problems, but made three observations. These were 'first, that, since it is a classification of convenience, there may well be purposes which do not fit neatly into one or other of the headings: secondly, that the words used must not be given the force of a statute to be construed; and, thirdly, that the law of charity is a moving subject which may well have evolved even since 1891.'[83]

Whether or not a trust is charitable is a question of law[84] to be decided by the judge in the light of the circumstances in which the institution or trust came into existence and the sphere in which it operates.[85] In reaching his decision the judge[86] is completely unaffected by the settlor's or testator's opinion as to whether the purpose he has indicated is charitable or not.[87] Otherwise, as Russell J observed,[88] 'trusts might be established in perpetuity for the promotion of all kinds of fantastic (though not unlawful) objects, of which the training of poodles to dance might be a mild example'. Equally the motive of the settlor or testator will not prevent a gift from being charitable if the purpose is one which is charitable in the eye of the law. Thus a bequest to provide for the erection of a stained glass window in a church was held to be charitable notwithstanding that the motive of the testatrix was to perpetuate her memory and not to beautify the church or to benefit the parishioners.[89] As Farwell J said in *Re Delany*,[90] 'the care of the aged, poor and the like is a charity . . . whether the persons who devote their lives to it are actuated by the love of God, a desire for their own salvation, or mere pique, or disgust with the world'.

Generally the trust instrument comes into existence before, or at the same time as, the trust fund. Sometimes, however, the order may be reversed, as may be the case, for instance, where a fund is set up as a result of a public appeal which does not clearly define the trusts. The first question is to establish whether it is a private or a charitable trust.[91] If it is charitable, the position was thus explained by Cozens-Hardy LJ in *A-G v Mathieson*:[92]

---

[82] [1968] AC 138 at 154, [1967] 3 All ER 215 at 223, HL.

[83] Ie when *Comrs for Special Purposes of Income Tax v Pemsel*, supra, was decided.

[84] *Royal Choral Society v IRC* [1943] 2 All ER 101, CA.

[85] *Incorporated Council of Law Reporting for England and Wales v A-G* [1972] Ch 73 at 91, [1971] 3 All ER 1029 at 1038; CA, per Sachs LJ.

[86] Commonly in practice the Charity Commissioners on an application for registration—see p 314, infra.

[87] *Re Hummeltenberg* [1923] 1 Ch 237; *National Anti-Vivisection Society v IRC* [1948] AC 31, [1947] 2 All ER 217, HL; Cf *Re Cox* [1955] AC 627, [1955] 2 All ER 550, PC. Similarly where the trust instrument purports to leave the matter to the opinion of the trustees—*Re Wootton's Will Trust* [1968] 2 All ER 618.

[88] In *Re Hummeltenberg*, supra at 242, approved by the House of Lords in *National Anti-Vivisection Society v IRC*, supra.

[89] *Re King* [1923] 1 Ch 243; *Re Delius* [1957] Ch 299, [1957] 1 All ER 854.

[90] [1902] 2 Ch 642 at 647, 648; *Northern Ireland Valuation Comr v Redemptorist Order Trustees* [1971] NI 114, CA.

[91] See Report for 1981, paras 408, App A, and (1982) 132 NLJ 223 (H Picarda) discussing the Penlee Lifeboat Disaster Fund. This was held not to be charitable, and the £3 million raised was divided among eight families.

[92] [1907] 2 Ch 383 at 394, CA, applied *Re Trust Deed relating to the Darwin Cyclone Tracy Relief Fund Trust* (1979) 39 Fed LR 260.

When money is given by charitable persons for somewhat indefinite purposes, a time comes when it is desirable, and indeed necessary, to prescribe accurately the terms of the charitable trust, and to prepare a scheme for that purpose. In the absence of evidence to the contrary, the individual or the committee entrusted with the money must be deemed to have implied authority for and on behalf of the donors to declare the trusts to which the sums contributed are to be subject. If the individual or the committee depart from the general objects of the original donors, any deed of trust thus transgressing reasonable limits might be set aside by proper proceedings instituted by the Attorney-General, or possibly by one of the donors. But unless and until set aside or rectified, such a deed must be treated as in all respects decisive of the trusts which, by the authority of the donor, are to regulate the charity.

It should be added that it is quite clear that the mere making of a charge for the services rendered does not prevent an organization, otherwise charitable, from being charitable.[93] There are numerous cases where beneficiaries only receive benefits from a charity by way of bargain, for example, a private hospital,[94] fee paying schools,[95] and special housing for the elderly.[96] Nor is it necessarily fatal that incidentally it could happen that the bargain might produce a profit for the beneficiary.[97]

We must now turn to consider Lord Macnaghten's four heads of charity, which will be discussed in turn. One should add the warning, however, that it is often arguable that the facts of a case bring it under more than one head of charity, or that it does not decisively fit into one rather than another category,[98] and the court may well declare a trust to be charitable without making it clear exactly on what ground it does so.

It must also be remembered that even if the purposes of a charity fall within these four heads, a trust will not be charitable unless in addition:

(i) its purposes are wholly and exclusively charitable,[99]

(ii) the required element of public benefit is present.[100]

(b) TRUSTS FOR THE RELIEF OF POVERTY[101]

'Poverty, of course, does not mean destitution. It is a word of wide and somewhat indefinite import, and, perhaps, it is not unfairly paraphrased for present purposes as meaning persons who have to "go short" in the ordinary acceptation of that term, due

---

[93] It is irrelevant that a commercial undertaking comes into the field and supplies similar services on a commercial basis. See *Scottish Burial Reform and Cremation Society Ltd v Glasgow City Corpn* [1968] AC 138, [1967] 3 All ER 215, HL.

[94] *Re Resch's Will Trusts, Le Cras v Perpetual Trustee Co Ltd* [1969] 1 AC 514, [1967] 3 All ER 915, PC. See (1993) 1 Dec Ch Com 18.

[95] *The Abbey, Malvern Wells Ltd v Ministry of Town and Country Planning* [1951] Ch 728, [1951] 2 All ER 154.

[96] *Joseph Rowntree Memorial Trust Housing Association Ltd v A-G* [1983] Ch 159, [1983] 1 All ER 288.

[97] *Joseph Rowntree Memorial Trust Housing Association Ltd v A-G*, supra.

[98] *Re Hopkins' Will Trusts* [1965] Ch 669 at 678, 679, [1964] 3 All ER 46 at 51; *Scottish Burial Reform and Cremation Society Ltd v Glasgow City Corpn*, supra.

[99] This is discussed at p 240, et seq, supra.   [100] This is discussed at p 276 et seq, infra.

[101] See Report for 1978, paras 61–63 and App A. See, also, (2000) 20 LS 222 (Alison Dunn).

regard being had to their status in life and so forth.'[102] 'There may be a good charity for the relief of persons who are not in grinding need or utter destitution ... [but] relief connotes need of some sort, either need for a home, or for the means to provide for some necessity or quasi-necessity, and not merely an amusement, however healthy.'[103] The Charity Commissioners take the view that, generally speaking, anyone who cannot afford the normal things in life which most people take for granted would probably qualify for help,[104] and have suggested ways in which poor people may be assisted.[105] The fact that no one in receipt of an income less than a certain amount is eligible to benefit does not necessarily prevent a trust from being charitable.[106]

In accordance with these dicta, gifts for ladies in reduced circumstances,[107] for the aid of distressed gentlefolk,[108] and to provide a nursing home for persons of moderate means,[109] have all been held charitable. Neighbourhood law centres formed for the purpose of giving legal aid and advice to poor persons have also been registered as charities,[110] as have the grant of low interest or interest free loans to enable poor people to purchase freehold or leasehold housing accommodation.[111]

The intention that the gift shall be for the relief of poverty may be inferred from the nature of the gift, as in *Re Lucas*,[112] where the income of a fund was given 'to the oldest respectable inhabitants in Gunville to the amount of 5s per week each'. It was held that the smallness of the amounts payable showed that the purpose of the gift was to assist the aged poor. It is, of course, sufficient if the gift is to an institution the object of which is the relief of poverty.[113]

By way of contrast a gift to provide a contribution towards the holiday expenses of workpeople was held not to be charitable on the ground that, although employed at a very small wage, the workpeople could not be described as poor people within the meaning of the Statute of Elizabeth.[114] And it has been held that the working classes do not constitute a section of the poor for the purpose of the law of charity,[115] though

---

[102] *Re Coulthurst* [1951] Ch 661; [1951] 1 All ER 774, CA, per Evershed MR at 666, 776.

[103] *IRC v Baddeley* [1955] AC 572; [1955] 1 All ER 525, HL, per Lord Simonds at 585, 529.

[104] Charity Commission Leaflet CC4, para 3.

[105] See Charity Commission Leaflet CC4, paras 10–11; (1995) 4 Dec Ch Com 1.

[106] *Re De Carteret* [1933] Ch 103; *Re Lacy* [1899] 2 Ch 149.

[107] *Shaw v Halifax Corpn* [1915] 2 KB 170, CA.   [108] *Re Young* [1951] Ch 344, [1950] 2 All ER 1245.

[109] *Re Clarke* [1923] 2 Ch 407.

[110] See 1974 Report, paras 67–72. It does not matter that the work could equally well be done by a solicitor in private practice, or that there may be a contractual relationship between the centre and a beneficiary. There might however be a difficulty if the centre undertook a large amount of work under the Legal Aid Scheme, giving rise to payments which might be used to increase the salaries of the centre's employees.

[111] See Report for 1990, App A (e); (1995) 3 Dec Ch Com 7 (Garfield Poverty Trust); (1995) 4 Dec Ch Com 13 (Habitat for Humanity Great Britain).

[112] [1922] 2 Ch 52; *Re Dudgeon* (1896) 74 LT 613; *Re Wall* (1889) 42 Ch D 510.

[113] *Biscoe v Jackson* (1887) 35 Ch D 460, CA (soup-kitchens).

[114] *Re Drummond* [1914] 2 Ch 90, [1914–15] All ER Rep 223.

[115] *Re Sanders' Will Trusts* [1954] Ch 265, [1954] 1 All ER 667, compromised on appeal (1954) *Times*, 22 July, CA, where it was said at first instance that the term 'working class' is now an anachronism. Cf *Westminster City Council v Duke of Westminster* [1991] 4 All ER 136; *Dano Ltd v Earl Cadogan* (2003) *Times*, 14 Mar.

a gift for the purpose of the construction of a working men's hostel has been held to fall on the other side of the line.[116] Charity funds should not be used to replace state benefits; they should be used in a way which will actually benefit the recipient in addition to any assistance that he can receive from the state.[117]

It is convenient to mention here, since the statute of Elizabeth refers in one phrase to 'the relief of aged, impotent and poor people', that a series of decisions has held that these words are to be read disjunctively so that a gift may be charitable if the beneficiaries conform to any one of these descriptions. The cases were reviewed by Peter Gibson J in *Joseph Rowntree Memorial Trust Housing Association Ltd v A-G*[118] who stressed, however, that there must be a need which is to be relieved by the charitable gift, such need being attributable to the aged or impotent condition of the person to be benefited. The schemes in that case were charitable: the charity had identified a particular need for special housing to be provided for the elderly in specified ways.

(c) TRUSTS FOR THE ADVANCEMENT OF EDUCATION

Schools of learning, free schools and scholars in universities are specifically mentioned in the Statute of Elizabeth, and many other educational purposes have been held to come within its spirit and intendment. Schools are not, however, necessarily charities. While many independent non-profit-making schools, including well-known public schools, are charities, privately owned schools run for profit are not, nor are county schools funded by the state which do not usually have assets held on charitable trusts or dedicated to charitable purposes.[119]

Education is not restricted to the narrow sense of a master teaching a class,[120] and includes the education of artistic taste,[121] 'the promotion or encouragement of those arts and graces of life which are, perhaps, the finest and best part of the human character',[122] and the improvement of a useful branch of human knowledge and its

---

[116] *Re Niyazi's Will Trusts* [1978] 3 All ER 785.   [117] See CC4 paras 21–25.

[118] [1983] Ch 159, [1983] 1 All ER 288; In *Re Dunlop* [1984] NI 408. As to aged persons see *Re Robinson* [1951] Ch 198, [1950] 2 All ER 1148; *Re Cottam's Will Trusts* [1955] 3 All ER 704 (a gift to a local authority to provide flats for aged persons to be let at economic rents). As to impotent persons see *Re Lewis* [1955] Ch 104, [1954] 3 All ER 257, ('to ten blind girls, Tottenham residents if possible, the sum of £100 each'); (1951) 67 LQR 164; (1955) 71 LQR 16 (R E Megarry); (1958) 21 MLR at pp 140, 141 (P S Atiyah); [1970] ASCL 199 (J D Davies).

[119] See 1995 NLJ Annual Charities Review 18 (Debra Morris) where the differences between types of school are explained. As to the possible removal of charitable status from independent schools, see [1996] Conv 24 (J Jaconelli).

[120] *Re Koeppler Will Trusts* [1984] Ch 243, [1984] 2 All ER 111 (intensive discussion process); revsd [1986] Ch 423, [1985] 2 All ER 869, CA, but approved on this point.

[121] *Royal Choral Society v IRC* [1943] 2 All ER 101, CA.

[122] Per Vaisey J in *Re Shaw's Will Trusts* [1952] Ch 163 at 172, [1952] 1 All ER 49 at 55 (the wife of G Bernard Shaw). Cf Farwell J in *Re Lopes* [1931] 2 Ch 130 at 136, 'a ride on an elephant may be educational. At any rate it brings the reality of the elephant and its uses to the child's mind, in lieu of leaving him to mere book learning. It widens his mind, and in that broad sense is educational.'

public dissemination.[123] So far as research is concerned Slade J has summarized the law as follows:[124]

(1) A trust for research will ordinarily qualify as a charitable trust if, but only if (a) the subject-matter of the proposed research is a useful subject of study; and (b) it is contemplated that knowledge acquired as a result of the research will be disseminated to others; and (c) the trust is for the benefit of the public, or a sufficiently important section of the public. (2) In the absence of a contrary context, however, the court will be readily inclined to construe a trust for research as importing subsequent dissemination of the results thereof. (3) Furthermore, if a trust for research is to constitute a valid trust for the advancement of education, it is not necessary either (a) that a teacher/pupil relationship should be in contemplation or (b) that the persons to benefit from the knowledge to be acquired should be persons who are already in the course of receiving 'education' in the conventional sense. (4) In any case where the court has to determine whether a bequest for the purposes of research is or is not of a charitable nature, it must pay due regard to any admissible extrinsic evidence which is available to explain the wording of the will in question or the circumstances in which it was made.

It may be added that it is not enough that the object should be educational in the sort of loose sense in which all experience may be said to be educative.[125]

In accordance with these principles, gifts to endow and build a Cambridge college,[126] to found lectureships and professorships,[127] and to augment fellows' stipends[128] have all been held to be charitable. Of special interest is *Incorporated Council of Law Reporting for England and Wales v A-G*.[129] The main object of the Council is the preparation and publication of law reports, not for profit, for the purposes of providing essential material for the study of law—in the sense of acquiring knowledge of what the law is, how it is developing, and how it applies to the enormous range of human activities which it affects. This was held to be for the advancement of education, as would be the institution and maintenance of a library for the study of any other learned subject or science. As regards the subjects of education, a wide variety have been held to be educational, including the promotion and advancement of the

---

[123] *Incorporated Council of Law Reporting for England and Wales v A-G* [1972] Ch 73 at 102, [1971] 3 All ER 1029 at 1046, CA, per Buckley LJ.

[124] In *McGovern v A-G* [1982] Ch 321, [1981] 3 All ER 493; *Re Hopkins' Will Trusts* [1965] Ch 669 at 680, [1964] 3 All ER 46 at 52, per Wilberforce J. See (1965) 29 Conv 368 (M Newark and A Samuels); (1975) 39 Conv 183 (G Susan Plowright).

[125] *IRC v Baddeley* [1955] AC 572 at 585, [1955] 1 All ER 525 at 529, HL, per Lord Simonds.

[126] *A-G v Lady Downing* (1766) Amb 550; (1769) Amb 571.

[127] *A-G v Margaret and Regius Professors in Cambridge* (1682) 1 Vern 55.

[128] *The Case of Christ's College, Cambridge* (1757) 1 Wm Bl 90.

[129] [1972] Ch 73, [1971] 3 All ER 1029, CA. Russell LJ reached the same result, but on the ground that the case fell under Lord Macnaghten's fourth head. The fact that the reports are used by members of the legal profession for earning fees is incidental and does not detract from the exclusively charitable character of the Council's objects. See (1972) 88 LQR 171.

art and science of surgery,[130] of choral singing in London,[131] of organists and organ music,[132] of the music of a particular composer,[133] of Egyptology,[134] of a search for the Bacon-Shakespeare manuscripts,[135] of economic and sanitary science,[136] of industry and commerce,[137] of legal education,[138] of zoology,[139] of English classical drama and the art of acting,[140] and of ethical principles;[141] in New Zealand, the education of the public in the facts of human reproduction;[142] and, in Australia, the endowment of an annual prize for portrait painting.[143] Even a trust[144] for 'the teaching, promotion and encouragement in Ireland of self-control, elocution, oratory, deportment, the arts of personal contact, of social intercourse, and the other arts of public, private, professional and business life', described by the judge[145] as 'a sort of finishing school for the Irish people' has been held to be charitable, as have trusts for the Boy Scouts,[146] for an annual chess tournament for boys and young men in the city of Portsmouth,[147] and to provide an annual treat or field day for schoolchildren, on the ground that this would

---

[130] *Royal College of Surgeons of England v National Provincial Bank Ltd* [1952] AC 631, [1952] 1 All ER 984, HL.

[131] *Royal Choral Society v IRC* [1943] 2 All ER 101, CA (It is irrelevant and, according to Lord Greene, curious, that incidentally people may find pleasure either in providing education or in being educated), applied *Re Perpetual Trustees Queensland Ltd* [2000] QdR 647. See also *Canterbury Orchestra Trust v Smitham* [1978] 1 NZLR 787 distinguishing between a trust for the advancement of musical education—charitable, and a society formed to promote music merely for the amusement of its members—not charitable.

[132] *Re Levien* [1955] 3 All ER 35.

[133] *Re Delius' Will Trusts* [1957] Ch 299, [1957] 1 All ER 854—a gift by the widow of the composer Delius for the advancement of his musical works. All the counsel in the case agreed that the works were of a high standard. In *Re Pinion* [1965] Ch 85, [1964] 1 All ER 890, CA, the testator sought to found a small museum with his own paintings and his collection of paintings and antiques. On expert evidence that as a means of education the collection was worthless, it was held the gift was not charitable.

[134] *Re British School of Egyptian Archaeology* [1954] 1 All ER 887.

[135] *Re Hopkins' Will Trusts* [1965] Ch 669, [1964] 3 All ER 46.

[136] *Re Berridge* (1890) 63 LT 470, CA.

[137] *Re Town and Country Planning Act 1947 Crystal Palace Trustees v Minister of Town & Country Planning* [1951] Ch 132, [1950] 2 All ER 857n. See Report for 1987 (Business in the Community charitable); *Re Tennant* [1996] 2 NZLR 633.

[138] *Smith v Kerr* [1902] 1 Ch 774, CA—a gift to Clifford's Inn—one of the Inns of Chancery established to provide legal education.

[139] *Re Lopes* [1931] 2 Ch 130; *North of England Zoological Society v Chester RDC* [1959] 3 All ER 116, CA. Contrast the narrower meaning of 'education' in the Value Added Tax Act 1994: *North of England Zoological Society v Customs and Excise Comrs* [1999] STC 1027.

[140] *Re Shakespeare Memorial Trust* [1923] 2 Ch 398.

[141] *Barralet v A-G* [1980] 3 All ER 918 sub nom *Re South Place Ethical Society* [1980] 1 WLR 1565 (both 'the study and dissemination of ethical principles' and 'the cultivation of a rational religious sentiment' held to be for the advancement of education, alternatively charitable within the fourth class).

[142] *Auckland Medical Aid Trust v IRC* [1979] 1 NZLR 382.

[143] *Perpetual Trustee Co Ltd v Groth* (1985) 2 NSWLR 278.

[144] *Re Shaw's Will Trusts* [1952] Ch 163, [1952] 1 All ER 49.   [145] Vaisey, J, supra, at 167, 52.

[146] *Re Webber* [1954] 3 All ER 712 at 713.

[147] *Re Dupree's Deed Trusts* [1945] Ch 16, [1944] 2 All ER 443. See (1977) 41 Conv 8.

encourage nature study[148] though not trusts for artistic purposes,[149] or to present artistic dramatic works.[150] The Charity Commissioners have, however, now stated their opinion that the promotion of the arts is charitable in and of itself and that there is no need to refer to education.[151]

Although a trust for mere sport is not charitable,[152] it has long been settled that a gift for sport in a school is charitable as being for the advancement of education, which involves development of the body as well as the mind.[153] Without casting any doubt on *Re Nottage*,[154] the House of Lords extended *Re Mariette*[155] by holding, in *IRC v McMullen*,[156] that a trust to promote the physical education and development of pupils at schools and universities as an addition to such part of their education as relates to their mental education by providing facilities and assistance to Association Football and other games and sports is charitable. And an Australian court has held that a trust for the establishment of a rose garden in the grounds of a university is a charitable gift for the advancement of education, since such a garden 'must of its very nature be conducive to the inspiration in all but the most blasé of students of a state of mind better attuned to the academic tasks ahead'.[157]

Though charitable education purposes include the discussion of political issues, political propaganda masquerading as education is not charitable.[158] Education for some purposes may lack the necessary element of public benefit and therefore not be charitable as in the illustrations of schools or colleges for prostitutes, or pickpockets, given by Harman LJ,[159] and the college for training spiritualistic mediums in *Re Hummeltenberg*.[160] Thus it was held in *Southwood v A-G*[161] that a trust for the advancement of the education of the public in the subject of militarism and disarmament and

---

[148] *Re Mellody* [1918] 1 Ch 228. Cf *Re Pleasants* (1923) 39 TLR 675.

[149] *Re Ogden* (1909) 25 TLR 382, CA (too wide: might include 'merely providing for one or two individuals paints and paint-brushes', per Lord Greene MR in *Royal Choral Society v IRC*, supra, CA, at 107, who had no doubt that the education of artistic taste was charitable).

[150] *Associated Artists Ltd v IRC* [1956] 2 All ER 583 ('too wide and too vague').

[151] See Report for 1991, App D (b).

[152] *Re Nottage* [1895] 2 Ch 649, CA (yacht racing); *IRC v City of Glasgow Police Athletic Association* [1953] AC 380, [1953] 1 All ER 747, HL. See the Recreational Charities Act 1958, discussed at p 274 et seq, infra, *Re Laidlaw Foundation* (1985) 13 DLR (4th) 491, and (1986) 1 TL & P 22 (Della Evans).

[153] *Re Mariette* [1915] 2 Ch 284, [1914–15] All ER Rep 794; *London Hospital Medical College v IRC* [1976] 2 All ER 113.

[154] Supra, CA.   [155] Supra.

[156] [1981] AC 1, [1980] 1 All ER 884, HL, who left open the question whether the trust might also fall within Lord Macnaghten's fourth head.

[157] *McGrath v Cohen* [1978] 1 NSWLR 621. Cf *Re the Worth Library* [1995] 2 IR 301, and see (1994) 45 NILQ 364 (Hilary Delany).

[158] *Bonar Law Memorial Trust v IRC* (1933) 17 TC 508; *Re Hopkinson* [1949] 1 All ER 346; *Re Bushnell* [1975] 1 All ER 721, nor is campaigning in the sense of seeking to influence public opinion on political matters: *Webb v O'Doherty* (1991) Times, 11 February. See p 268, post. See also Report for 1991, App D (a) in connection with a proposed Margaret Thatcher Foundation.

[159] In *Re Pinion* [1965] Ch 85 at 105, [1964] 1 All ER 890 at 893, CA; *Re Shaw* [1957] 1 All ER 745 at 752, compromised CA, [1958] 1 All ER 245n.

[160] [1923] 1 Ch 237, [1923] All ER Rep 49.

[161] [2000] NLJR 1017, CA, noted (2000) 14 Tru LI 233 (J Garton).

related fields was not charitable because the court could not determine whether or not the trust's object of securing peace by demilitarization promoted the public benefit.

It may be added that the mere fact that membership of an institution may confer some benefit on the members does not necessarily prevent the institution from being a charitable body. The test is whether the main object of the institution is the promotion and advancement of a science (using this word in a wide sense) or the protection and advantage of those practising a particular profession.[162]

(d) TRUSTS FOR THE ADVANCEMENT OF RELIGION[163]

This is a separate head of charity under Lord Macnaghten's classification, although the only matter relating to the purposes of religion referred to in the Statute of Elizabeth is the repair of churches. Many religious purposes, however, have been held to fall within its spirit and intendment. It is generally accepted that 'the Court of Chancery makes no distinction between one religion and another . . . [or] one sect and another . . . [unless] the tenets of a particular sect inculcate doctrines adverse to the very foundations of all religion and . . . subversive of all morality . . . If the tendency were not immoral and although this Court might consider the opinions sought to be propagated foolish or even devoid of foundation' the trust would nevertheless be charitable.[164] 'As between different religions the law stands neutral, but it assumes that any religion is at least likely to be better than none.'[165] The courts are understandably reluctant to judge the relative worth of different religions or the truth of competing religious doctrines, all of which may have a place in a tolerant and culturally diverse society.

These propositions are undoubtedly true so far as the various Christian denominations are concerned; there is no doubt as to the charitable character of religious trusts not only for the established church, but also for nonconformist bodies,[166] Unitarians,[167] Roman Catholics,[168] and the Exclusive Brethren.[169] More controversially two

---

[162] *Royal College of Surgeons of England v National Provincial Bank Ltd* [1952] AC 631, [1952] 1 All ER 984, HL; *Royal College of Nursing v St Marylebone Corpn* [1959] 3 All ER 663, CA: *London Hospital Medical College v IRC*, supra; *A-G v Ross* [1985] 3 All ER 334. See also Report for 1976, paras 30–36 and 50–53.

[163] See (1996) 8 Auck ULR 25 (S T Woodfield); [1999] Jur R 303 (Christine Barker) (2001) 21 LS 36 (PW Edge and Joan M Loughren).

[164] Per Romilly MR in *Thornton v Howe* (1862) 31 Beav 14 at 19; *Gilmour v Coats* [1949] AC 426, [1949] 1 All ER 848, HL; *Re Watson, Hobbs v Smith* [1973] 3 All ER 678.

[165] Per Cross J in *Neville Estates Ltd v Madden* [1962] Ch 832 at 853, [1961] 3 All ER 769 at 781. See (1992/93) 1 CLPR 87 (A Longley); (1996) 8 Auck ULR 25 (S T Woodfield). P Edge argues, in (1995/96) 3 CLPR 29, that this head of charity should be abolished, to which M King responded in (1995/6) 3 CLPR 179.

[166] Since the Toleration Act 1688. See eg *Re Strickland's Will Trusts* [1936] 3 All ER 1027, appeal dismissed by consent, [1937] 3 All ER 676, CA (Baptist); *Re Manser* [1905] 1 Ch 68 (Quakers).

[167] Since the Doctrine of Trinity Act 1813. Eg *Re Nesbitt's Will Trusts* [1953] 1 All ER 936.

[168] Since the Roman Catholic Charities Act 1832. Eg *Dunne v Byrne* [1912] AC 407, [1911–13] All ER Rep 1105, PC; *Re Flinn* [1948] Ch 241, [1948] 1 All ER 541. As to whether there has been, or now is, an anti-Roman Catholic bias see (1981) 2 JLH 207 (M Blakeney); [1990] Conv 34 (C E F Rickett).

[169] *Holmes v A-G* (1981) *Times*, 12 February; *Broxtowe Borough Council v Birch* [1981] RA 215. See also *Radmanovich v Nedeljkovic* (2001) 52 HSWCR 641.

trusts associated with the Unification Church[170] have been registered as charitable, as has a trust for the publication of the works of Joanna Southcote.[171] Similarly with regard to organizations which exist for the advancement of religion, such as the Church Army,[172] the Salvation Army,[173] the Church Missionary Society,[174] the Society for the Propagation of the Gospel in Foreign parts,[175] the Sunday School Association,[176] the Protestant Alliance and kindred institutions,[177] and even, it has been held, a society of clergymen, in connection with a trust to provide dinners, on the ground that the free meals would increase the usefulness of the society by attracting a greater number of clergymen to the meetings.[178] Also a faith healing movement of a religious nature.[179] But not, it has been decided, the Oxford Group Movement.[180]

Beyond the Christian religion, trusts for the advancement of the Jewish religion are undoubtedly charitable.[181] So far as wholly distinct religions such as Islam or Buddhism are concerned, there are clear dicta[182] in favour of charitable status, and this is assumed in regulations[183] made under the Charities Act 1993. Moreover the Charity Commissions have registered trusts for the advancement of the Hindu,[184]

---

[170] Popularly known as the Moonies. The Attorney-General appealed against the refusal of the Charity Commissioners to accede to his request to remove the trusts from the register, but the appeal was eventually discontinued—see the statement of the Attorney-General in Hansard, 3 Feb 1988, 977 et seq, and the debate in the Lords, 10 Feb, 247 et seq.

[171] *Thornton v Howe*, supra, Joanna Southcote claimed that she was with child by the Holy Ghost, and would give birth to a second Messiah. As the law then was, the effect of holding the gift charitable was that, being given out of land, it failed by reason of the Mortmain Act 1736 and went to the heir-at-law.

[172] *Re Smith* (1938) 54 TLR 851.   [173] *Re Fowler* (1914) 31 TLR 102, CA; *Re Smith*, supra.

[174] *Re Clergy Society* (1856) 2 K & J 615.   [175] *Re Maguire* (1870) LR 9 Eq 632.

[176] *R v Income Tax Special Comrs, ex p Essex Hall* [1911] 2 KB 434, CA.

[177] *Re Delmar Charitable Trust* [1897] 2 Ch 163 (societies having as their object 'to maintain and defend the doctrines of the Reformation, and the principles of civil and religious liberty against the advance of Popery').

[178] *Re Charlesworth* (1910) 26 TLR 214.

[179] *Re Le Cren Clarke (decd)* [1996] 1 All ER 715, sub nom *Funnell v Stewart* [1996] 1 WLR 288 noted [1996] Lpool LR 63 (Debra Morris); (1996) 112 LQR 557 (Rachael Fletcher).

[180] *Re Thackrah* [1939] 2 All ER 4; *Oxford Group v IRC* [1949] 2 All ER 537, CA (the movement is probably a social movement founded on Christian ethics rather than a movement for the advancement of religion).

[181] Since the Religious Disabilities Act 1846, according, inter alia, to *Neville Estates Ltd v Madden* [1962] Ch 832, [1961] 3 All ER 769. But a Jewish religious trust was held charitable in *Strauss v Goldsmid* (1837) 8 Sim 614. See (1993/94) 2 CLPR 155 (H Picarda).

[182] *Barralet v A-G* [1980] 3 All ER 918 sub nom *Re South Place Ethical Society* [1980] 1 WLR 1565 where two of the essential attributes of religion were said to be faith and worship—faith in a god and worship of that god. This was said to be too narrow a test by the High Court of Australia in *Church of the New Faith v Comrs for Pay Roll Tax* (1983) 57 ALJR 785, noted (1984) 100 LQR 340; (1984) 14 MULR 539 (M Darian Smith); [1984] Conv 449 (St John Robilliard), where Scientology was held to be a religion in Victoria. It has not been granted charitable status in England. It is accepted that Buddhism is a religion, though it does not have the attributes stated in *Barralet v A-G*, supra. The wider Australian view has been applied in New Zealand—*Centrepoint Community Growth Trust v IRC* [1985] 1 NZLR 673. See (1981) 131 NLJ 436 (H Picarda); (1989) 63 ALJ 834 (W Sadurski); (1999) 5 CLPR 153 (Francesca Quint and T Spring).

[183] SI 1962/1421; SI 1963/2074. See the Interpretation Act 1978, s 17(2)(*b*).

[184] *Varsani v Jesani* [1999] Ch 219, [1998] 3 All ER 273, CA.

Sikh, Islamic and Buddhist religions. Neither the objects of the Theosophical Society[185] nor those of the South Place Ethical Society[186] or the Church of Scientology[187] are for the advancement of religion, and it has not been thought arguable that gifts for the maintenance of a masonic temple[188] or a college for training spiritualistic mediums[189] are charitable on this ground, and the same must surely be true of an atheistic society.[190]

The advancement of religion means the promotion of spiritual teaching in a wide sense, and the maintenance of the doctrine on which it rests, and the observances that serve to promote and manifest it,[191] such as saying masses in public.[192] Gifts for religious purposes or to religious societies have been held to be prima facie good as being restricted to such purposes as are charitable,[193] though, as we shall see,[194] religious purposes are not necessarily charitable for they may, for instance, lack the vital element of public benefit and similarly a religious body may engage in a number of subsidiary activities which are not purely religious. A trust in favour of such a body simpliciter may nevertheless be a good charitable trust, but the income can only be applied to the activities of the body which are purely religious.[195] A trust, however, which is so worded as to permit the income to be used by a religious body in activities which are not purely religious is not a good charitable trust.[196]

A gift for missionary purposes is ambiguous and may comprise objects which are not charitable,[197] but the court will readily find in the context of surrounding circumstances evidence to show that the gift is restricted to the popular sense of Christian missionary work which is charitable.[198] Gifts in popular language such as to 'the

---

[185] *Re Macaulay's Estate* [1943] Ch 435n, HL ('to form a nucleus of Universal Brotherhood of Humanity without distinction of race, creed, caste or colour'). Cf *Re Price* [1943] Ch 422 [1943] 2 All ER 505 (Anthropological Society).

[186] *Barralet v A-G*, supra ('the study and dissemination of ethical principles' and 'the cultivation of a rational religious sentiment'—society concerned with man's relations with man, not man's relations with God: nor did it have attributes referred to in n 182, supra). See (1981) 131 NLJ 761 (A Hoffer).

[187] *R v Registrar General, ex p Segerdal* [1970] 2 QB 697, [1970] 3 All ER 886, CA, but see supra, n 182.

[188] *Re Porter* [1925] Ch 746.   [189] *Re Hummeltenberg* [1923] 1 Ch 237, [1923] All ER Rep 49.

[190] The point did not arise in *Bowman v Secular Society Ltd* [1917] AC 406, [1916–17] All ER Rep 1, HL, where it was held that there is nothing contrary to law in an attack on or a denial of the truth of Christianity unaccompanied by vilification, ridicule or irreverence. Christianity is not part of the law of England.

[191] *Keren Kayemeth Le Jisroel Ltd v IRC* [1931] 2 KB 465 at 477, CA, per Hanworth MR affd [1932] AC 650, [1932] All ER Rep 971, HL; *Oxford Group v IRC* [1949] 2 All ER 537, CA; *Berry v St Marylebone Corpn* [1958] Ch 406, [1957] 3 All ER 677, CA.

[192] *Re Hetherington* [1990] Ch 1, [1989] 2 All ER 129; (noted [1989] CLJ 373 (J Hopkins); [1989] Conv 453 (N D M Parry). See p 59, supra.

[193] *Re White* [1893] 2 Ch 41, CA. Sed quaere. See the doubts suggested in *Dunne v Bryne* [1912] AC 407 at 411, [1911–13] All ER Rep 1105 at 1108, PC; *Re Smith's Will Trusts* [1962] 2 All ER 563, CA. However this principle was confirmed and applied by Browne-Wilkinson-VC in *Re Hetherington*, supra, at 135.

[194] See p 276 et seq, infra.

[195] *Oxford Group v IRC* [1949] 2 All ER 537 at 539, CA, per Tucker LJ; *Re Banfield* [1968] 2 All ER 276.

[196] *Oxford Group v IRC*, supra.

[197] *Scott v Brownrigg* (1881) 9 LR Ir 246; *McCracken v A-G for Victoria* [1995] 1 VR 67 (for Christian purposes).

[198] *Re Kenny* (1907) 97 LT 130; *Re Moon's Will Trusts* [1948] 1 All ER 300.

service of God'[199] or 'for God's work'[200] have also been held to be applicable only to charitable purposes for the advancement of religion, but not a gift for 'good works'.[201]

More clearly analogous to the repair of churches referred to in the Statute of Elizabeth, the erection, maintenance or repair of any church, chapel or meeting house or any part of the fabric thereof is charitable, and there have been held charitable gifts in connection with, inter alia, stained glass windows,[202] the spire,[203] chancel,[204] gallery,[205] seating,[206] organ,[207] and a monument in a church.[208] By a slight extension gifts for the upkeep of a churchyard or burial ground,[209] are charitable, even though restricted to some particular denomination,[210] but not a gift for the erection or repair of a particular tomb in a churchyard,[211] though it was held otherwise in the case of a gift to erect and maintain headstones to the graves of the pensioners of certain alms houses.[212]

Trusts for the support of the clergy are clearly charitable, even though subject to a condition such as promoting some specific doctrine,[213] wearing a black gown in the pulpit,[214] or even preaching an annual sermon in commemoration of the testator.[215] Also charitable was a gift to a society for the relief of infirm, sick and aged Roman Catholic secular priests in the Clifton diocese, on the ground that this would tend to make the ministry more efficient, by making it easy for the sick and old to retire and give place to the young and healthy,[216] and somewhat similarly in the case of a gift for retired missionaries.[217]

Somewhat less obviously charitable perhaps is a gift for the benefit of a church choir,[218] and a case which seems to be at least on the extreme limits is *Re Pardoe*,[219] where a trust to endow the ringing of a peal of bells on 29 May in each year to commemorate the restoration of the monarchy to England was held to be for the advancement of religion as calculated to bring back 'happy thoughts' which would necessarily connote 'a feeling of gratitude to the Giver of all good gifts'.[220] This

---

[199] *Re Darling* [1896] 1 Ch 50.   [200] *Re Barker's Will Trusts* (1948) 64 TLR 273.

[201] *Re How* [1930] 1 Ch 66, [1929] All ER Rep 354.

[202] *Re King* [1923] 1 Ch 243; *Re Raine* [1956] Ch 417, [1956] 1 All ER 355.

[203] *Re Palatine Estate Charity* (1888) 39 Ch D 54.   [204] *Hoare v Osborne* (1866) LR 1 Eq 585.

[205] *A-G v Day* [1900] 1 Ch 31.   [206] *Re Raine*, supra.

[207] *A-G v Oakaver* (1736) cited in 1 Ves Sen 536.   [208] *Hoare v Osborne*, supra.

[209] *Re Douglas* [1905] 1 Ch 279; *Re Vaughan* (1886) 33 Ch D 187 (per North J at 192, 'I do not see any difference between a gift to keep in repair what is called "God's House" and a gift to keep in repair the churchyard round it, which is often called "God's Acre". ').

[210] *Re Manser* [1905] 1 Ch 68 (Quakers). Cf *Re Eighmie* [1935] Ch 524 and see *Scottish Burial Reform and Cremation Society Ltd v Glasgow City Corpn* [1968] AC 138, [1967] 3 All ER 215, HL.

[211] *Hoare v Osborne* (1866) LR 1 Eq 585; *Re Vaughan*, supra; *Re Hooper* [1932] 1 Ch 38.

[212] *Re Pardoe* [1906] 2 Ch 184.   [213] *A-G v Molland* (1832) 1 You 562.

[214] *Re Robinson* [1897] 1 Ch 85, CA. Condition was subsequently removed—*Re Robinson* [1923] 2 Ch 332.

[215] *Re Parker's Charity* (1863) 32 Beav 654; cf *Re Hussey's Charities* (1861) 7 Jur NS 325.

[216] *Re Forster* [1939] Ch 22, [1938] 3 All ER 767.

[217] *Re Mylne* [1941] Ch 204, [1941] 1 All ER 405. Contrast *Hester v CIR* [2005] 2 NZLR 172.

[218] *Re Royce* [1940] Ch 514, [1940] 2 All ER 291.   [219] [1906] 2 Ch 184.

[220] Per Kekewich J at 186.

principle was not applied, however, where the bells were directed to be rung half-muffled on the anniversary of the testator's death.[221]

It is convenient to consider at this point the effect of a gift to a person not as an individual but as the holder of a particular office. The relevant principles are not in fact restricted to gifts for the advancement of religion, and would apply equally, for instance, to a gift to the head of a school or college,[222] but they have been worked out mainly in connection with gifts to bishops and vicars.[223] The principles are, in fact, relatively easy to state, but their application has led to very fine distinctions. The basic principle is that in determining whether or not trusts are charitable, the character of the trustee is prima facie irrelevant. What matters is the purpose of the trust not the character of the trustee. Where, however, there is a gift to a person who holds an office the duties of which are in their nature wholly charitable, and the gift is made to him in his official name and by virtue of his office, then, if the purposes are not expressed in the gift itself, the gift is assumed to be for the charitable purposes inherent in the office. But where the purposes of the gift are expressed in terms not confining them to purposes which are in the legal sense charitable, they cannot be confined to charitable purposes merely by reference to the character of the trustee.

Thus a gift to the bishop of a diocese, or the vicar or vicar and church-wardens of a particular parish, simpliciter, is a valid charitable gift, for the bishop or vicar must use the gift exclusively for the charitable purposes inherent in his office. The gift is equally charitable where the gift is followed by words which merely indicate that the bishop or vicar is to have a full discretion in settling the particular mode of application within the charitable purposes of the gift. Thus gifts were held charitable in *Re Garrard*,[224] where there was a legacy 'to the vicar and churchwardens—to be applied by them in such a manner as they shall in their sole discretion think fit', in *Re Flinn*,[225] where residue was given to 'His Eminence the Archbishop of Westminster Cathedral London for the time being . . . to be used by him for such purposes as he shall in his absolute discretion think fit', and in *Re Rumball*,[226] where residue was given to 'the Bishop for the time being of the Diocese of the Windward Islands to be used by him as he thinks fit in his diocese'.

Where, however, the added words set out the purposes for which the gift is to be held, it must be seen whether or not those declared purposes are charitable. Thus in *Dunne v Bryne*,[227] residue was left to 'the Roman Catholic Archbishop of Brisbane and his successors to be used and expended wholly or in part as such archbishop may judge most conducive to the good of religion in his diocese'. It was held this was not charitable since a thing could be most conducive to the good of religion without being charitable in the legal sense, or even in itself religious. This principle was applied in *Re*

---

[221] *Re Arber* (1919) *Times*, 13 December.

[222] Cf *Re Spensley's Will Trusts* [1954] Ch 233, [1954] 1 All ER 178, CA.

[223] See (1960) 24 Conv 306 (V T H Delaney).

[224] [1907] 1 Ch 382, [1904–7] All ER Rep 237; *Re Norman* [1947] Ch 349, [1947] 1 All ER 400.

[225] [1948] Ch 241, [1948] 1 All ER 541.   [226] [1956] Ch 105, [1955] 3 All ER 71, CA.

[227] [1912] AC 407, [1911–13] All ER Rep 1105, PC.

Stratton,[228] where there was a gift to the vicar of a parish 'to be by him distributed at his absolute discretion among such parochial institutions or for such parochial purposes as he shall select' and in *Farley v Westminster Bank Ltd*,[229] where the gift was to the vicars and churchwardens of two named churches 'for parochial work'. A gift for parochial purposes or for parish work means that the gift is not a gift for ecclesiastical or religious purposes in the strict sense, but that it is a gift for the assistance and furtherance of those various activities connected with the parish church which are to be found in every parish but which include many objects which are not charitable in the legal sense of the word. On the other hand, a gift to the vicar of a church 'to be used for his work in the parish' has been held to be charitable,[230] for the added words merely had the effect of imposing a limitation on the scope of the trust which would have been created simply by a gift to the vicar. Again gifts to the vicar of St Alban's Church 'for such objects connected with the Church as he shall think fit',[231] and to the vicar and churchwardens of St George's Church 'for any purpose in connection with the said church which they may select'[232] have been held to be charitable. In both cases the objects or purposes were construed as relating to the church—its fabric and services—in contrast to the parish. The court in both cases refused to import into the objects or purposes parochial activities, holding that the funds were to be held in each case on the more limited, and, accordingly, charitable trusts.

(e) TRUSTS FOR OTHER PURPOSES BENEFICIAL TO THE COMMUNITY

In putting forward the classification[233] of charitable trusts adopted by Lord Macnaghten in *Income Tax Special Purposes Comrs v Pemsel*[234] Sir Samuel Romilly called this fourth head the most difficult, and it is indeed impossible to devise any simple test to decide whether or not any particular purpose is within it. It is not sufficient under this head that a gift is for the public benefit: it must be beneficial in a way which the law regards as charitable, which brings one back to the question whether the particular purpose is within the spirit and intendment of the Statute of Elizabeth as revealed in the cases. The position was explained by Viscount Cave LC in *A-G v National Provincial and Union Bank of England*[235] as follows:

Lord Macnaghten[236] did not mean that all trusts for purposes beneficial to the community are charitable, but that there were certain charitable trusts which fell within that category:

---

[228] [1931] 1 Ch 197, [1930] All ER Rep 255, CA.

[229] [1939] AC 430, [1939] 3 All ER 491, HL; *Ellis v IRC* (1949) 31 TC 178.

[230] *Re Simson* [1946] Ch 299, [1946] 2 All ER 220.

[231] *Re Bain* [1930] 1 Ch 224, [1929] All ER Rep 387, CA.

[232] *Re Eastes* [1948] Ch 257, [1948] 1 All ER 536.

[233] In *Morice v Bishop of Durham* (1805) 10 Ves 522.   [234] [1891] AC 531 at 583, HL.

[235] [1924] AC 262 at 265, HL. See also *Williams' Trustees v IRC* [1947] AC 447, [1947] 1 All ER 513, HL; *Scottish Burial Reform and Cremation Society Ltd v Glasgow City Corpn* [1968] AC 138, [1967] 3 All ER 215, HL.

[236] In *Pemsel's Case*, supra.

and accordingly to argue that because a trust is for a purpose beneficial to the community it is therefore a charitable trust is to turn round his sentence and to give it a different meaning. So here it is not enough to say that the trust in question is for public purposes beneficial to the community or for the public welfare; you must also show it to be a charitable trust.

More recently, however, the Court of Appeal put forward a more pragmatic approach. In *Incorporated Council of Law Reporting for England and Wales v A-G*[237] Russell LJ stated that the courts in substance accept that if a purpose is shown to be beneficial to the community or, as it is sometimes put, of general public utility it is prima facie charitable in law, but have left open a line of retreat based on the spirit and intendment of the statute in case they are faced with a purpose (for example, a political purpose) which could not have been within the contemplation of the statute even if the then legislators had been endowed with the gift of foresight into the circumstances of later centuries. If prima facie charitable, the onus is on those who say it is not to show some sufficient reason to support their contention. Dillon J has, however, doubted whether this more generous approach is permissible in the light of earlier House of Lords decisions.[238] He thought the approach of analogy was the correct one. It should be added, as regards benefit to the community, that in some cases the purpose may be so manifestly beneficial to the public that it would be absurd to call evidence on the point, though in others it may be much more debatable. If the court regards the element of public benefit as incapable of proof one way or the other it will have to refuse to recognize the trust as charitable.[239]

In the light of the above principles, let us now look at some of the most important kinds of purpose that have commonly come before the courts.

As might be expected in English courts, gifts in favour of animals generally, or a class of animals, as opposed to gifts for specific animals,[240] may be charitable; not, however, on the ground that they benefit the animals, but on the ground that they produce a benefit to mankind. Thus in *Re Wedgwood*[241] a trust for the protection and benefit of animals was held to be charitable on this ground, Swinfen Eady LJ observing[242] 'a gift for the benefit and protection of animals tends to promote and encourage kindness towards them, to discourage cruelty, and to ameliorate the condition of the brute creation, and thus to stimulate humane and generous sentiments in

---

[237] [1972] Ch 73, [1971] 3 All ER 1029, CA, esp per Russell LJ at 88, 1036; *IRC v McMullen* [1979] 1 All ER 588, CA; revsd [1981] AC 1, [1980] 1 All ER 884, HL without discussing this point. See *Brisbane City Council v A-G for Queensland* [1979] AC 411, [1978] 3 All ER 30, PC, per Lord Wilberforce, at 422, 33.

[238] *Barralet v A-G* [1980] 3 All ER 918 sub nom *Re South Place Ethical Society* [1980] 1 WLR 1565 referring especially to *Williams Trustees v IRC* supra, HL.

[239] *McGovern v A-G* [1981] 3 All ER 493 at 504. But see [1982] Conv 387 (T G Watkin).

[240] *Re Dean* (1889) 41 Ch D 552. Perhaps this was the point in the judge's mind in *Re Green's Will Trust* [1985] 3 All ER 455, when he dismissed an objection that 'cruelly treated animals are too small a section of the animal community'.

[241] [1915] 1 Ch 113, [1914–15] All ER Rep 322, CA; *Re Grove-Grady* [1929] 1 Ch 557, [1929] All ER Rep 158, CA, compromised on appeal sub nom *A-G v Plowden* [1931] WN 89, HL; *National Anti-Vivisection Society v IRC* [1948] AC 31, [1947] 2 All ER 217, HL. See, generally, on animal welfare trusts (1987) 13 Mon LR 1 (P Jamieson).

[242] At 122 and 327.

man towards the lower animals; and by these means promote feelings of humanity and morality generally, repress brutality, and thus elevate the human race.' Accordingly a bequest 'for the establishment of a hospital in which animals, which are useful to mankind, should be properly treated and cured and the nature of their diseases investigated, with a view to public advantage' was held to be charitable in *University of London v Yarrow*[243] and in *Re Douglas*[244] the Home for Lost Dogs was said to be a charitable institution. Again in *Re Moss*[245] a gift to a lady 'for her to use at her discretion for her work for the welfare of cats and kittens needing care and protection' was held to be charitable on evidence that for many years she had carried on the work of receiving, sheltering and caring for unwanted or stray cats, the judge observing[246] that 'the care of and consideration for animals which through old age or sickness or otherwise are unable to care for themselves are manifestations of the finer side of human nature, and gifts in furtherance of these objects are calculated to develop that side and are therefore, calculated to benefit mankind'.

In *Re Grove-Grady*,[247] however, where the purpose was to provide 'a refuge or refuges for the preservation of all animals, birds or other creatures not human ... so that [they] shall there be safe from molestation or destruction by man' the gift was held not to be charitable. The purpose was held not to afford any advantage to animals that are useful to mankind in particular, or any protection from cruelty to animals generally, and not to denote any elevating lesson to mankind.

In that case Russell LJ observed,[248] 'the authorities have, in my opinion, reached the furthest admissible point of benevolence in construing, as charitable, gifts in favour of animals, and, for myself, I am not prepared to go any further'. This probably represents the weight of judicial opinion, and Lord Sterndale pin-pointed an anomaly when he said,[249] 'I confess I find considerable difficulty in understanding the exact reason why a gift for the benefit of animals, and for the prevention of cruelty to animals generally, should be a good charitable gift, while a gift for philanthropic purposes which, I take it, is for the benefit of mankind generally, should be bad as a charitable gift.' Though it is hard to believe that in any true sense gifts in favour of animals come within the spirit and intendment of the Statute of Elizabeth, their charitable character is, within limits, firmly settled. To be charitable, however, the gift must be regarded as producing a benefit to mankind, and in this sense be for the public benefit. In this context there seems much to be said for the approach of the Australian court in *A-G for New South Wales v Sawtell*[250] which accepted that since 1929, when *Re Grove-Grady*[251] was decided, there has been a radical change in the recognition throughout the world of the value to mankind in the preservation of wild

---

[243] (1857) 1 De G & J 72 at 79.

[244] (1887) 35 Ch D 472, CA. Also the RSPCA—see *Re Wedgwood*, supra.

[245] [1949] 1 All ER 495.   [246] At 497, 498.   [247] Supra, CA; *Re Howey* [1991] 2 NZLR 16.

[248] At 588, 171.

[249] *Re Tetley* [1923] 1 Ch 258 at 266, CA; affd sub nom *A-G v National Provincial and Union Bank of England* [1924] AC 262, HL.

[250] [1978] 2 NSWLR 200.   [251] Supra, CA.

life in general. The court accordingly, on the basis of arguments and evidence not considered in *Re Grove-Grady* held that a trust for the preservation of native wild life (both flora and fauna) was a valid charitable gift. Before leaving animals it may be noted that one ground on which the National Anti-Vivisection Society was held by the House of Lords not to be a charitable institution was that it lacked the element of public benefit.[252] It may be added that the validity of cases[253] which decided that vegetarian societies whose object was to stop the killing of animals for food were charitable, seems very doubtful in the light of the *National Anti-Vivisection Society's Case*,[254] though Lord Simonds expressly refused[255] to express an opinion as to whether they were rightly decided.

'Equity has always refused to recognize [political] objects as charitable.'[256] Political objects include:

(i) furthering the interests of a political party

(ii) procuring, or opposing,[257] changes in the law of this, or a foreign, country

(iii) procuring a reversal of government policy or a particular decision of government authority in this, or a foreign, country.[258]

The alternative ground upon which the *National Anti-Vivisection Society's Case*[259] was decided was that a, if not the, main object of the society was to obtain an alteration of the law, and that this was a political object. The law, it is said,[260] cannot stultify itself by holding that it is for the public benefit that the law itself should be changed; the court must decide on the principle that the law is right as it stands. To do otherwise, even if the court could, on the evidence, form a prima facie opinion that the proposed change in the law would be for the public benefit, would be to usurp the functions of the legislature, and might prejudice the reputation of the judiciary for political impartiality. Again, campaigning, in the sense of seeking to influence public

---

[252] *National Anti-Vivisection Society v IRC* [1948] AC 31, [1947] 2 All ER 217, HL. See (1994) 2 Dec Ch Com 1 (Animal Abuse, Injustice & Defence Society held not charitable).

[253] *Re Cranston* [1898] 1 IR 431, CA; *Re Slatter* (1905) 21 TLR 295.   [254] Supra.

[255] *National Anti-Vivisection Society v IRC*, supra, HL at 73, 238.

[256] Per Lord Parker in *Bowman v Secular Society Ltd* [1917] AC 406 at 442, [1916–17] All ER Rep 1 at 18, HL. See [1995] NLJ Annual Charities Review 24 (P Luxton); (1996) NLJ Christmas App Supp 30 (G Griffiths); (1999) 50 NILQ 298 (Alison Dunn); [1999] CLP 254 (GFK Santow); (2002) 8 Cant LR 345 (Nicola Silke). The possible effect of the Human Rights Act 1998 is discussed in (2002) KCLJ (G Moffat). See also *Public Trustee v A-G of New South Wales* (1997) 42 NSWLR 600.

[257] *Re Koeppler Will Trusts* [1984] Ch 243, [1984] 2 All ER 111; revsd [1986] Ch 423, [1985] 2 All ER 869, CA, without affecting relevant dictum; *Molloy v CIR* [1981] 1 NZLR 689.

[258] *McGovern v A-G* [1982] Ch 321, [1981] 3 All ER 493 (Amnesty International Trust not charitable), noted (1982) 45 MLR 704 (R Nobles) and see (1982) 10 NZULR 169 (C E F Rickett); (1983) 46 MLR 385 (F Weiss); [1984] Conv 263 (Caroline J Farder). Cf *R v Radio Authority, ex p Bull* [1997] 2 All ER 561, CA.

[259] [1948] AC 31, [1947] 2 All ER 217, HL.

[260] See *National Anti-Vivisection Society v IRC*, supra, especially per Lord Wright at 50, 224–225 and per Lord Simonds at 62, 232. Lord Parker, dissenting, thought that political objects here should be restricted to those whose only means of attainment is a change of law. Elsewhere in their speeches both Lord Wright and Lord Simonds frankly recognized that in changing conditions the same purpose may at one time be beneficial, and at another injurious, to the public. See p 282, infra.

opinion on political matters, is not a charitable activity. As is commonly the case in charity matters, the cases run to find distinctions; thus a gift to a temperance society whose object was the promotion of temperance mainly by political means was held not to be charitable,[261] while in a subsequent case the Court of Appeal held that a gift for the promotion of temperance generally was.[262]

The Charity Commissioners have issued guidelines,[263] based on court decisions, on political activities and campaigning by charities. A body whose stated purposes include the attainment of a political purpose cannot be charitable, but a body whose purposes are exclusively charitable can engage in political or campaigning activity if the trustees are satisfied on reasonable grounds:

(a) that the activities will be an effective means of furthering the purposes of the charity, and

(b) that they will do so to an extent justified by the resources applied.

The trustees must have regard to the following points:

(i) the activities must be permitted under the governing document,

(ii) they must weigh the possible benefits for their charity and beneficiaries against any possible reputational or other risks, and

(iii) the charity must comply with the general law and with any other regulatory requirements.

It may be added that there is nothing to prevent an organization which has some purposes that, taken by themselves, are exclusively charitable, and other related purposes that are political and non-charitable, in effect dividing itself into two by founding an entirely separate organization restricted to carrying out such of the purposes as are charitable, while the original organization concentrates on the political purposes.[264] And a charity will not lose its charitable status merely because its trustees or officers are also the trustees or officers of a political and non-charitable body operating in the same field, or, as individuals, engage in politics.[265] Further if a charitable organization improperly uses some of its funds for purposes which are not charitable, it does not thereby lose its charitable status. Such an act would constitute a breach of trust making the trustees personally liable for the improper expenditure in question.

---

[261] *IRC v Temperance Council of Christian Churches of England and Wales* (1926) 136 LT 27.

[262] *Re Hood* [1931] 1 Ch 240, CA.

[263] See CC9 which contains examples of activities in which charities may, or must not, engage. See the Report of an Inquiry into the campaigning activities of Oxfam, and (1999) 5 CLPR 219 (Debra Morris).

[264] Eg the National Council of Civil Liberties—non charitable—and the Cobden Trust, an educational charity formed to undertake 'the promotion of research into civil liberties and an understanding of the civil rights, liberties and duties of citizens and public servants in Britain'.

[265] Report for 1976, para 101.

A gift for the relief of the sick is charitable,[266] falling by close analogy within the phrase 'the relief of the impotent' in the Statute of Elizabeth,[267] and it has always been assumed that gifts for the ordinary hospitals which, before the National Health Service Act 1946, were supported by voluntary contributions and were generally referred to as voluntary hospitals, were charitable, as opposed to private nursing homes run for profit.[268] There have also been held charitable gifts to a hospital to provide accommodation for the use of relatives of patients who were critically ill,[269] and to provide a home of rest for nurses, for this would be calculated to increase the efficiency of the hospital by providing the means of restoring the efficiency of the nurses.[270] The hospital cases have been extended so as to render charitable Homes of Rest, as they were called, for lady teachers,[271] for the sisters of a charitable community and such persons as the Mother Superior should appoint,[272] and generally so as to 'afford the means of physical and/or mental recuperation to persons in need of rest by reason of the stress and strain caused or partly caused by the conditions in which they ordinarily live and/or work'.[273]

To increase the efficiency of the armed forces or the police forces is a charitable purpose and gifts calculated to have this effect are accordingly charitable, for instance, gifts for the benefit of a volunteer corps,[274] and to promote the defence of the United Kingdom from the attack of hostile aircraft.[275] This principle was said to be unassailable in *IRC v City of Glasgow Police Athletic Association*,[276] but doubt was cast on whether it had been correctly applied in earlier cases where there had been held charitable gifts to maintain a library and purchase plate for an officers' mess, and for the promotion of sport in a regiment as calculated to improve the physical efficiency of the army.[277] The Charity Commissioners have held that the principle does not extend to the purpose of eliminating waste in the public service so as to increase its efficiency.[278] Nor is a gift for the welfare benefit or assistance of members of the Royal Navy whether past, present, or future, charitable as it could be used purely for the benefit of ex-members of the navy not being necessarily poor or aged or in any other way objects of charity.[279]

The relief of human suffering or distress, which has been termed a 'charity of

---

[266] See CC6 and Report for 1978, paras 61–63 and App B. Including faith healing: *Re Le Cren Clarke (decd)* [1996] 1 All ER 715, sub nom *Funnell v Stewart* [1996] 1 WLR 288, noted [1996] NLJ Annual Charities Review 14 (P Luxton).

[267] *Re Resch's Will Trusts, Le Cras v Perpetual Trustee Co Ltd* [1969] 1 AC 514, [1967] 3 All ER 915, PC.

[268] See *Re Smith's Will Trusts* [1962] 2 All ER 563, CA.

[269] *Re Dean's Will Trusts* [1950] 1 All ER 882.   [270] *Re White's Will Trusts* [1951] 1 All ER 528.

[271] *Re Estlin* (1903) 72 LJ Ch 687.   [272] *Re James* [1932] 2 Ch 25.

[273] *Re Chaplin* [1933] Ch 115; *Re Banfield* [1968] 2 All ER 276.

[274] *Re Lord Stratheden and Campbell* [1894] 3 Ch 265.

[275] *Re Driffill* [1950] Ch 92, [1949] 2 All ER 933.

[276] [1953] AC 380, [1953] 1 All ER 747, HL. See also *Downing v Taxation Comr of Commonwealth of Australia* (1971) 125 CLR 185.

[277] *Re Good* [1905] 2 Ch 60.

[278] *Re Gray* [1925] Ch 362. There would seem to be less doubt about this case than about *Re Good*, supra.

[279] Report for 1983, paras 35, 36.

compassion',[280] is clearly within the spirit and intendment of the Statute of Elizabeth, and there have accordingly been held charitable the Royal National Life-boat Institution,[281] and a trust for the provision of a fire brigade.[282] One has to look with care, however, at the sort of case where there is a trust, commonly as the result of a public appeal, in relation to a specified disaster which has already happened. Such a trust was held to be charitable in the case of disastrous floods in the Lyn Valley, in relation to a trust to relieve hardship and suffering by the local people and others who were in the area at the time of the disaster and suffered by it.[283] But if the victims are a specific and identifiable group the trust may be non-charitable on the ground that it lacks the necessary element of public benefit.[284] Thus it was conceded in *Re Gillingham Bus Disaster Fund*,[285] where a bus ran into a column of cadets killing 24 and injuring others, that the funeral expenses and care of the boys were not, for this reason, charitable objects. To get over this difficulty the Charity Commissioners advise that the trust deed in this sort of case should utilize the poverty exception[286] and restrict the benefits to those in need.[287] There has also been held charitable a trust for the founding of a children's home,[288] but the Court of Appeal has decided by a majority that a gift for the general benefit and general welfare of the children for the time being in a home provided and maintained by a local authority was not charitable as it might be possible to use the fund for non-charitable purposes, such as, it was suggested, the provision of television sets for juvenile delinquents and refractory children, or even the inmates of a Borstal institution.[289]

The National Trust is a charitable body,[290] and likewise a trust to preserve two ancient cottages.[291] Of a very different character were the purposes of the appellant company in *Scottish Burial Reform and Cremation Society Ltd v Glasgow City Corpn*[292] namely, primarily, to promote and afford facilities for cremation. These were held to

---

[280] *Re Meyers* [1951] Ch 534, [1951] 1 All ER 538. Nor a gift of a house for the use of ex-officers at a small rent during their lives—*Re Good*, supra.

[281] *Thomas v Howell* (1874) LR 18 Eq 198.

[282] *Re Wokingham Fire Brigade Trusts* [1951] Ch 373, [1951] 1 All ER 454.

[283] *Re North Devon and West Somerset Relief Fund Trusts* [1953] 2 All ER 1032.

[284] See p 276 et seq. The size of the group may be relevant. This may explain the different results in the last cited and next cited cases.

[285] [1958] Ch 300, [1958] 1 All ER 37; affd [1959] Ch 62, [1958] 2 All ER 749 and see *Re Hobourn Aero Components Ltd's Air Raid Distress Fund* [1946] Ch 194, [1946] 1 All ER 501, CA.

[286] Discussed p 283 et seq, infra.

[287] See Report for 1965 paras 54–58 and Report for 1966, paras 9–12. Guidelines proposed by the Attorney-General are set out in CC40.

[288] *Re Sahal's Will Trusts* [1958] 3 All ER 428.

[289] *Re Cole* [1958] Ch 877, [1958] 3 All ER 102, CA. There seems much to be said for the dissenting judgment of Lord Evershed MR.

[290] *Re Verrall* [1916] 1 Ch 100. Note that a trust to erect and maintain the statue of a person internationally respected and of historical importance (Earl Mountbatten of Burma) was held to be charitable by the Commissioners—Report for 1981, paras 68–70. See (1983) 133 NLJ 1107 (H Picarda).

[291] *Re Cranstoun* [1932] 1 Ch 537; *Re Corelli* [1943] Ch 332, [1943] 2 All ER 519. See Report for 1990, App A (b), (1995) 3 Dec Ch Com 1 (Settle and Carlisle Railway Trust).

[292] [1968] AC 138, [1967] 3 All ER 215, HL.

be charitable under the fourth head, through an extension of the burial ground cases which, though apparently at first held charitable as being for the advancement of religion, are probably best regarded as falling on the borderline between that head and the fourth head of trusts otherwise beneficial to the community.[293] Different again, and also charitable, are the purposes of the Incorporated Council of Law Reporting for England and Wales, which publishes law reports, not for profit, in order to further the sound development and administration of the law in this country.[294] By analogy the Charity Commissioners have taken the view that family conciliation services can be charitable as advancing the administration of the law, divorce being a judicial process.[295] The promotion or advancement of industry (including a particular industry such as agriculture)[296] or of commerce has been said, obiter, to be a charitable object, provided that the purpose is the advancement of the benefit of the public at large and not merely the promotion of the interests of those engaged in the manufacture and sale of their products,[297] but this has been doubted by the Charity Commissioners, except perhaps in relation to agriculture.[298] More recently[299] they have indicated that they would register as a charity a company with objects directed to the advancement of industry and commerce by promoting, or assisting in promoting, opportunities for employment, particularly in areas where involuntary unemployment is causing suffering by reason of poverty and ill-health. However, in *IRC v Oldham Training Enterprise Council*[300] the second main object, namely promoting trade, commerce or enterprise, and the ancillary object of providing support services and advice to and for new businesses, disqualified the institution from having charitable status, for they conferred freedom to provide private benefits to individuals engaged in trade, commerce or enterprise.

Trusts which have been held not to be charitable include a trust to provide knickers for boys living in a certain area,[301] a trust to encourage emigration,[302] the trust under George Bernard Shaw's will to provide for research into and propaganda on the advantages of a reform of the alphabet,[303] a trust to strengthen the bonds between

---

[293] See the cases cited supra p 262 in nn 209 and 210.

[294] *Incorporated Council of Law Reporting for England and Wales v A-G* [1972] Ch 73, [1971] 3 All ER 1029, CA. (Also for the advancement of education in the opinion of the majority of the court—see p 256, supra.)

[295] Report for 1983, paras 28–34.

[296] *Brisbane City Council v A-G for Queensland* [1979] AC 411, [1978] 3 All ER 30, PC.

[297] *IRC v White* [1980] TR 155.   [298] Report for 1980, para 99.

[299] Report for 1987. See also (1994) 2 Dec Ch Com 5 (Public Concern at Work—objects the promotion of ethical standards of conduct and compliance with the law—charitable). As to the relief of unemployment as a charitable purpose see (1999) 6 CLPR 23 (P Somerfield).

[300] [1996] STC 1218, noted [1997] BTR 59 (A Roycroft).

[301] *Re Gwyon* [1930] 1 Ch 255 (not for the relief of poverty and not saved by restriction to a particular area).

[302] *Re Sidney* [1908] 1 Ch 488, CA. Contrast *Re Tree* [1945] Ch 325 (a trust to help poor emigrants, charitable as being for the relief of poverty).

[303] *Re Shaw* [1957] 1 All ER 745; compromised on appeal, [1958] 1 All ER 245n, CA. The money given up by the residuary legatees under the compromise was spent on the creation of a 48 letter alphabet and the publication of a bi-alphabetical edition of *Androcles and the Lion*, more than 50,000 copies of which were distributed before the compromise money was exhausted.

South Africa and the United Kingdom,[304] a trust to promote and aid the improvement of international relations,[305] and a trust the twin purposes of which were the formation of an informed international public opinion and the promotion of greater co-operation in Europe and the West in general.[306] The Charity Commissioners have taken the view that the provision of a service for charities is not necessarily a charitable purpose of itself, and accordingly refused to register as a charity a company formed to provide catering staff at cost exclusively for charities such as voluntary hospitals and old people's homes,[307] though a different view was taken in regard to the provision to charitable organizations of advice and assistance in the field of information technology so as to improve their efficiency.[308] Again it has been held that it is not open to one charity to subscribe to the funds of another charity unless the recipient charity is expressly or by implication a purpose or object of the donor charity.[309]

In *Re Smith*[310] a gift of residue 'unto my country England to and for . . . own use and benefit absolutely' was held to be charitable, and this may be justified on the ground that, where no purpose is defined, a charitable purpose may be implicit in the context.[311] There is considerable difficulty as regards gifts limited to a particular locality. One line of cases[312] establishes the principle that if the purposes are not charitable per se, the localization of them will not make them charitable. The difficulty is really caused by *Goodman v Saltash Corpn*,[313] unfortunately a decision of the House of Lords. Always cited in this context are words of Lord Selborne LC.[314] 'A gift subject to a condition or trust for the benefit of the inhabitants of a parish or town or of any particular class of such inhabitants is (as I understand the law) a charitable trust.' Accordingly it would seem that under such a charitable trust the trust funds may properly be used for public or benevolent purposes in a parish, though a gift for public or benevolent purposes in a parish would not be charitable.

---

[304] *Re Strakosch* [1949] Ch 529, [1949] 2 All ER 6, CA.

[305] *Buxton v Public Trustee* (1962) 41 TC 235.

[306] *Re Koeppler Will Trusts* [1984] Ch 243, [1984] 2 All ER 111 (void for uncertainty), noted [1985] Conv 56 and 412 (T G Watkin). On appeal [1986] Ch 423, [1985] 2 All ER 869, CA, it was held that on its true construction the gift was for the furtherance of the work of the Wilton Park project. This was for the advancement of education and charitable, notwithstanding that the ultimate aims and aspirations of the testator were for the non-charitable purposes set out in the text above.

[307] Report of the Charity Commissioners for 1969, para 20.

[308] See Report for 1990, App A (f).

[309] *Baldry v Feintuck* [1972] 2 All ER 81. Nor can a charity give a gratuitous guarantee in respect of the liability of a third party with whom it has no legal tie—*Rosemary Simmons Memorial Housing Association Ltd v United Dominions Trust Ltd* [1987] 1 All ER 281. See [1988] Conv 275 (Jean Warburton).

[310] [1932] 1 Ch 153, CA. See (1940) 56 LQR 49 (M Albery).

[311] *Williams' Trustees v IRC* [1947] AC 447 at 459, [1947] 1 All ER 513 at 521, HL; *Re Strakosch* [1949] Ch 529, [1949] 2 All ER 6, CA.

[312] *Houston v Burns* [1918] AC 337, [1918–19] All ER Rep 817, HL; *Re Gwyon* [1930] 1 Ch 255; *Williams' Trusts v IRC*, supra; *Re Sanders' Will Trusts* [1954] Ch 265, [1954] 1 All ER 667, compromised on appeal (1954) Times, 22 July, CA.

[313] (1882) 7 App Cas 633, HL, applied *Peggs v Lamb* [1994] Ch 172, [1994] 2 All ER 15.

[314] At 642.

This anomalous[315] situation will not be extended. Being a House of Lords decision, it must be followed by lower courts in an appropriate case, as was done in *Re Norton's Will Trusts,*[316] where the gift was 'for the benefit of the church and parish', but the Court of Appeal felt able to distinguish it in *Re Endacott,*[317] where the testator gave his residuary estate 'to North Tawton Devon Parish Council for the purpose of providing some useful memorial to myself', and Jenkins LJ has even observed[318] that the line of cases based on *Goodman v Saltash Corpn*[319] 'should not now be regarded as authoritative save in so far as they can be explained on the ground that the particular purpose was regarded as falling within the spirit and intendment of the preamble to the Statute of Elizabeth I'. More recently, in *A-G of the Cayman Islands v Wahr-Hansen*[320] Lord Browne-Wilkinson said that 'For reasons that are obscure, [the locality] cases have been benevolently construed. They are now so long established that ... they remain good law.' They are exceptions to the well established principle that general words are not to be artificially construed so as to be impliedly limited to charitable purposes only. *Re Endacott*[321] was itself distinguished by a Canadian court in *Re Levy Estate,*[322] where a gift of residue was held not to lose its charitable status by reason of a direction that it was 'to be in the form of a dedication honouring and recognizing the deceased'. This was said to be a corollary to and not to defeat the main charitable intention.

(f) RECREATIONAL CHARITIES

On general principles, a purely recreational trust will not be charitable because it is not within the spirit and intendment of the preamble to the Statute of Elizabeth, and accordingly it was held in *Re Nottage*[323] that a gift to promote mere sport, whether a particular sport or sport in general,[324] is not charitable: the fact that it is beneficial to the public is not enough.

A Canadian court gave a generous interpretation of this proposition in favour of charity in *Re Laidlaw Foundation.*[325] In that case the sedentary nature of modern society was contrasted with society in 1895 when the people who needed to exercise on a regular basis in order to maintain health were the wealthy who could afford yachts. Most people by the very nature of their way of life exercised on a regular basis

---

[315] See the discussion by Lord Simonds in *Williams' Trusts v IRC,* supra, at 459, 521; *IRC v Baddeley* [1955] AC 572, [1955] 1 All ER 525, HL.

[316] [1948] 2 All ER 842. Cf *Verge v Somerville* [1924] AC 496, [1924] All ER Rep 121, PC.

[317] [1960] Ch 232, [1959] 3 All ER 562, CA. Cf *Murray v Thomas* [1937] 4 All ER 545.

[318] In the Court of Appeal in *Baddeley v IRC* [1953] Ch 504 at 527, [1953] 2 All ER 233 at 246.

[319] (1882) 7 App Cas 633, HL.   [320] [2001] 1 AC 75, [2000] 3 All ER 642, PC.   [321] Supra, CA.

[322] [1987] 62 OR (2d) 212.

[323] [1895] 2 Ch 649, [1895–99] All ER Rep 1203, CA (annual cup in perpetuity for the most successful yacht of the season). As to sport in a school, see *Re Mariette,* referred to at p 258, supra, and, as to sport in the army, *Re Gray,* referred to at p 269, supra.

[324] *IRC v City of Glasgow Police Athletic Association* [1953] AC 380, [1953] 1 All ER 747, HL. See (2001) 32 T & ELJ 13 (S Lloyd and M Kelly).

[325] (1985) 13 DLR (4th) 491. See [2000] NZLJ 69 (J Willis and B Gully).

daily either in their work or by walking. In modern conditions, it was held, the promotion of amateur athletic sports under controlled conditions promotes health, and is akin to cases which have decided that the promotion of health is a charitable purpose. Furthering participation in organized, competitive amateur sports is in itself educational, both in the sense of training in discipline and maintenance of a healthy body and further in respect to education resulting from the inter-change of people from different cultures in cases where the competitions involve more than local participants. In this country, however, the Charity Commissioners refused to follow the Canadian approach considering that it paid insufficient regard to the decision in *Re Nottage*.[326] They refused to accept the claim of Birchfield Harriers[327] and the North Tawton Rugby Union Football Club, a small village club,[328] to charitable status. Now, however, while still accepting that the promotion of a particular sport for its own sake is not charitable, they have held that promotion of community participation in healthy recreation by providing facilities for playing particular sports can be a charitable purpose. They were particularly concerned with community amateur sports clubs, which may be charitable provided that the sport is capable of improving physical health or fitness (not, for example, angling or snooker) and that the club has an open membership.[329] It may be added that it has long been accepted that the provision of land for use as a recreation ground by the community at large or by the inhabitants of a particular area is charitable.[330]

The decision of the House of Lords in *IRC v Baddeley*[331] that a trust 'for the promotion of the moral social and physical well-being of persons resident [in a certain area] by the provision of facilities for moral social and physical training and recreation and by promoting and encouraging all forms of such activities as are calculated to contribute to the health and well-being of such persons' was not charitable raised doubts as to the charitable status of many institutions, and in particular many village halls, and for the removal of these doubts there was passed the Recreational Charities Act 1958.[332] The Act itself is, however, by no means free from difficulties of interpretation, and it is doubtful whether *IRC v Baddeley*[333] would be decided differently today by reason of its provisions.

The main provisions are contained in s 1(1) of the Act, which provides that:

... it shall be and be deemed always to have been charitable to provide, or assist in the

---

[326] Supra, CA.   [327] See Report for 1989, paras 48–55.

[328] (1997) 5 Dec Ch Com 7. See (1997/98) 5 CLPR 77 (P Smith) supporting the view that a gift for sporting purposes should be charitable.

[329] See RR11.

[330] *Re Hadden* [1932] 1 Ch 133, [1931] All ER Rep 539; *IRC v Baddeley*, supra, HL; *Re Morgan* [1955] 2 All ER 632; *Bath and North East Somerset Council v A-G* [2002] EWHC 1623 (Ch), [2002] WTLR 1257; *Strathalbyn Show Jumping Club v Mayes* (2001) 79 SASR 54. Cf (1976) 54 CBR 784 (Donovan Waters).

[331] Supra.

[332] See generally (1959) 23 Conv 15 (Spencer G Maurice) and the Charity Commission publication RR 4 (Aug 2000).

[333] Supra.

provision of, facilities for recreation or other leisure-time occupation,[334] if the facilities are provided in the interests of social welfare.

In construing this provision the Charity Commissioners have taken the view that there is no requirement for an educative element in the provision of recreational facilities.[335]

The meaning of the requirement of social welfare[336] is to some extent explained in sub-s (2), which provides that the requirements shall not be treated as satisfied unless:

(a) the facilities are provided with the object of improving the conditions of life for the persons for whom the facilities are primarily intended;[337] and

(b) either—

    (i) those persons have need of such facilities as aforesaid by reason of their youth, age, infirmity or disablement, poverty or social and economic circumstances; or—

    (ii) the facilities are to be available to the members or female members of the public at large.

In *Guild v IRC*[338] the House of Lords unanimously approved the dissenting judgment of Bridge LJ in *IRC v McMullen*[339] and rejected the argument that facilities are not provided in the interests of social welfare unless they are provided with the object of improving the conditions of life for persons who suffer from some form of social disadvantage. It suffices if they are provided with the object of improving the conditions of life for members of the community generally.

Subject to the requirement of social welfare, sub-s (3) provides that the Act:

. . . applies in particular to the provision of facilities at village halls, community centres and women's institutes, and to the provision and maintenance of grounds and buildings to be used for purposes of recreation or leisure-time occupation, and extends to the provision of facilities for those purposes by the organising of any activity.

All this means, it has been said,[340] is 'that the facilities with which the section as a whole is dealing may be provided at these places: that is to say, on the particular premises belonging to or associated with the examples given.'

It is specifically provided that nothing in s 1 is to derogate from the principle that a

---

[334] See *Re Samford Hall Trust* [1995] 1 Qd R 60.

[335] *Re Fairfield (Croydon) Ltd* (1997) 5 Dec Ch Com 14. The provision of a cyber cafe in an area of social and economic deprivation may constitute a charitable recreational facility within the Act.

[336] The view of the Charity Commissioners in RR 4 is that the phrase 'the interests of social welfare' implies elements of both altruism and social obligation.

[337] The same provision has been held in Australia not to include the conduct of registered horse racing: *Re Hoey* [1994] 2 Qd R 510.

[338] [1992] 2 AC 310, [1992] 2 All ER 10, HL, noted [1992] Conv 361 (Helen Norman); (1992) 51 CLJ 429 (J Hopkins); (1992/93) 1 CLPR 45 (Debra Morris); *Russell's Executor v IRC* 1992 SC (HL) 71, HL.

[339] [1979] 1 All ER 588, [1979] 1 WLR 130, CA; revsd [1981] AC 1, [1980] 1 All ER 884, HL on another ground—see p 258.

[340] *IRC v McMullen*, supra, per Walton J at first instance at 242.

trust or institution to be charitable must be for the public benefit.[341] The Charity Commissioners are of the opinion that community associations and other recreational organizations which otherwise meet the requirements of the Recreational Charities Act 1958, and which are established for identifiable racial minority groups (including those defined by religion), can properly be regarded as being charitable where the group in question is in special need of the recreational facilities provided by the organization because of the group's social and economic circumstances.[342] Another point is that it seems that under s 1(2)(b)(ii), a trust cannot be charitable by virtue of the Act if it is available only to male members of the public at large, or, apparently, if it is available only to members or female members of the public in a particular geographical area. It has, however, been held that s 1(2)(b)(ii) does not require that the facilities should be available to members of the public at large primarily or without being subject to the primary intention of benefit to others.[343]

The provisions of the 1958 Act do not appear directly to affect the principle that a gift for mere sport is not charitable, though in practice the result would now seem to be otherwise where sporting facilities are provided in the interests of social welfare, for instance, organized games in a youth club. However it is by no means clear that the Act would affect a case such as *IRC v City of Glasgow Police Athletic Association*[344] where it was held that although the association had official importance and a public aspect, its provision of recreation for members was an essential non-charitable purpose which was not subsidiary or incidental to the furtherance of a public purpose, and, therefore, the association was not a body established for charitable purposes only. Members of the police would hardly seem to fall within s 1(2)(b)(i).

(g) THE REQUIREMENT OF PUBLIC BENEFIT[345]

Even if it has been established that the purposes of a trust fall within one of the four heads of charity under Lord Macnaghten's classification, the trust will still not be legally charitable unless it can also be shown that it is for the benefit of the community (or public) or an appreciably important section of the community (or public). This requirement, that there are enough potential beneficiaries, applies equally to charities under Lord Macnaghten's fourth head, where the different public benefit requirement refers to the kind of benefit being conferred.[346] As will be seen trusts for the relief of poverty constitute an exception to the general rule, but in relation to

---

[341] See *Wynn v Skegness UDC* [1966] 3 All ER 336, [1967] 1 WLR 52.

[342] (1995) 4 Dec Ch Com 18.

[343] *Wynn v Skegness UDC*, supra. As to the meaning of need in s 1(2)(b)(i) see *Belfast City YMCA Trustees v Valuation Comr for Northern Ireland* [1969] NI 3, CA, esp Curran LJ at 23.

[344] [1953] AC 380, [1953] 1 All ER 747, HL.

[345] See generally (1956) 72 LQR 187 (G Cross); (1958) 21 MLR 138 (P S Aityah); (1993/94) 2 CLPR 203 (J Callman). For a discussion of the difficulties of making a donation to a charity coupled with an undertaking by the charity to benefit a specified individual see (1999) 6 CLPR 31 (R Venables and Judith Morris).

[346] See p 264 et seq, supra and [1982] Conv 387 (T G Watkin).

the other heads of charity the requirement of public benefit has frequently proved a trap for the unwary. Thus in *Gilmour v Coats*[347] a trust for an association of strictly cloistered and purely contemplative nuns, though undoubtedly for the advancement of religion, was held not to be charitable as lacking the element of public benefit. So far as the intercessory prayers of the nuns were alleged to be productive of public benefit, the court could not consider it; the court could only act on evidence before it and no temporal court could determine the truth of any religious belief. And the benefit alleged to be derived by others from the example of pious lives was held to be too vague and intangible to satisfy the test of public benefit.[348] Elsewhere Farwell J has observed[349] that 'there is, in truth, no charity in attempting to improve one's own mind or save one's own soul. Charity is necessarily altruistic and involves the idea of aid or benefit to others.'

Whether or not the required element of public benefit is present is a question of law for the judge to decide on the evidence before him. However, as Lord Simonds has pointed out[350] 'when a purpose appears broadly to fall within one of the familiar categories of charity, the court will assume it to be for the benefit of the community, and, therefore, charitable unless the contrary is shown, and further the court will not be astute in such a case to defeat upon doubtful evidence the avowed benevolent intention of the donor.'

The most baffling problem[351] in this context is to determine whether or not the common characteristic which is shared by a number of persons is or is not such as to make them a section of the public. The test which has been most consistently applied during the last 50 or so years, often referred to as the '*Compton* test',[352] was approved by the majority of the House of Lords in *Oppenheim v Tobacco Securities Trust Co Ltd*.[353] According to this test in order to constitute a section of the public the possible beneficiaries must not be numerically negligible, and the quality which distinguishes

---

[347] [1949] AC 426, [1949] 1 All ER 848, HL; *Cocks v Manners* (1871) LR 12 Eq 574, per Wickens VC at 585, 'A voluntary association of women for the purpose of working out their own salvation by religious exercises and self-denial seems to me to have none of the requisites of a charitable institution.' These cases were rightly distinguished in *Re Banfield* [1968] 2 All ER 276. Contrast the decision of the Charity Commissioners in Report for 1989, paras 56–62, (1995) 3 Dec Ch Com 11 (the Society of the Precious Blood), and see (2001) 21 LS 26 (P W Edge and Joan M Loughren); (2001) 7 CLPR 151 (T Haddock).

[348] As Greene MR said in the Court of Appeal, sub nom *Re Coats' Trusts* [1948] Ch 340 at 353, [1949] 1 All ER 521 at 528, 'they are to be paid, not to do good, but to be good'.

[349] In *Re Delany* [1902] 2 Ch 642 at 648, 649.

[350] In *National Anti-Vivisection Society v IRC* [1948] AC 31 at 65, [1947] 2 All ER 217 at 233, HL: *Re Watson* [1973] 3 All ER 678. See Report for 1991 App D(b) where the public benefit element is regarded as self-evident in relation to charities for the promotion of education, or of the arts generally. Evidence would be needed, however, if the education provided, or the arts promoted, were of a particular nature or type.

[351] See eg *Re Mead's Will Trust Deed* [1961] 2 All ER 836 at 840 (members of a trade union not a section of the public for a trust under Lord Macnaghten's fourth head) where Cross J, as he then was, said despairingly not only that this is a very difficult question, but that 'there appears to be no principle by reference to which it can be answered'.

[352] *Re Compton* [1945] Ch 123, [1945] 1 All ER 198, CA; *Re Hobourn Aero Components Ltd's Air Raid Distress Fund* [1946] Ch 194, [1946] 1 All ER 501, CA.

[353] [1951] AC 297, [1951] 1 All ER 31, HL.

them from other members of the public, so that they form by themselves a section of it, must be a quality which does not depend on their relationship to a particular individual. It must be essentially impersonal and not personal. A section of the public in this sense has been contrasted with a fluctuating body of private individuals. Applying this test the inhabitants of a named place normally constitute a section of the public. The principle, as expressed a little differently by Peter Gibson J in *Re Koeppler Will Trusts*,[354] is that 'the beneficiaries must not be a private class qualifying by reason of some relationship unconnected with the charitable purpose'.

In *Re Compton* itself a trust for the education of the lawful descendants of three named persons was held not to be for a section of the public and thus not charitable, and the same result was reached in the *Oppenheim* case, where the trust was again for the advancement of education and the potential beneficiaries were the children of employees and former employees of one or other of a group of companies. They were held not to constitute a section of the public, notwithstanding that the number of employees was over 110,000. In the *Oppenheim* case, counsel had pointed out some of the anomalies that may flow from an application of the *Compton* test. In his speech in the House of Lords, Lord Simonds first set out counsel's argument:

Admittedly, those who follow a profession or calling—clergymen, lawyers, colliers, tobacco-workers and so on—are a section of the public, and how strange then it would be if, as in the case of railwaymen, those who follow a particular calling are all employed by one employer. Would a trust for the education of men employed on the railways by the Transport Board not be charitable? And what of service of the Crown, whether in the civil service or the armed forces? Is there a difference between soldiers and soldiers of the King?

His comment was short but clear, 'My Lords, I am not impressed by this sort of argument . . .'[355] The Charity Commission take the view that a class whose distinguishing feature is an impersonal quality may be a sufficient section of the community even though its constituent members also happen to share some personal characteristic (for example, being tenants or related to tenants of a single landlord).[356]

The *Compton* test was, however, regarded as inadequate by Lord MacDermott, giving the only dissenting speech in the *Oppenheim*[357] case, and his views have since received strong support from obiter dicta of Lord Cross in *Dingle v Turner*,[358] dicta in which all the other Law Lords concurred. In the opinion of Lord Cross the distinction between personal and impersonal relationships is unsatisfactory—as Lord MacDermott had

---

[354] [1984] 2 All ER 111 at 125; revsd [1986] Ch 423, [1986] Ch 423, [1985] 2 All ER 869, CA, without affecting this dictum.

[355] Per Lord Simonds in *Oppenheim v Tobacco Securities Trust Co Ltd*, supra, at 34, 35, 307.

[356] RR8, para B10.

[357] Supra, HL. The same judge, in *Baptist Union of Ireland (Northern) Corpn Ltd v IRC* [1945] NI 99 (NI CA) said that the test is whether the purpose is substantially altruistic in character and this test was adopted in *Educational Fees Protection Society Inc v IRC* [1992] 2 NZLR 115. Contrast *IRC v Baddeley* [1955] AC 572 at 606, [1955] 1 All ER 525 at 543, HL, per Lord Reid.

[358] [1972] AC 601, [1972] 1 All ER 878, HL noted (1972) 36 Conv 209; (1974) 33 CLJ 63 (Gareth Jones). See also [1987] Conv 14 (Norma Dawson).

pointed out in the *Oppenheim*[359] case it is accepted that the poor and the blind are sections of the public, but what is more personal than poverty or blindness? Further the attempt to elucidate the phrase 'a section of the public' by contrasting it with 'a fluctuating body of private individuals' is unhelpful, since a particular group of persons might equally well answer both descriptions. At the end of the day, Lord Cross said, one is left where one started with the bare contrast between 'public' and 'private' and in his view the question whether or not the potential beneficiaries of a trust can fairly be said to constitute a section of the public is (as it was generally thought to be before *Re Compton*[360]) a question of degree. In the light of these dicta the precise standing of the *Compton* test is uncertain. It may still be considered binding at first instance, but the House of Lords might well take a different view, particularly if the trust in question should be other than for the advancement of education.

In *Dingle v Turner*[361] Lord Cross went on to say that in his view much must depend on the purpose of the trust. 'It may well be', he said, 'that, on the one hand, a trust to promote some purpose, prima facie charitable, will constitute a charity even though the class of potential beneficiaries might fairly be called a private class and that, on the other hand, a trust to promote another purpose, also prima facie charitable, will not constitute a charity even though the class of potential beneficiaries might seem to some people fairly describable as a section of the public.' This, it is submitted, is eminently reasonable and entirely consistent with the view that whether or not a class constitutes a section of the public is a question of degree, taking into account all the facts of the case. It is difficult however to see that an application of the *Compton* test can permit any variation in the meaning of the phrase 'a section of the public' according to the kind of charitable purpose involved. Yet there are clear statements and decisions recognizing that such variation exists, though unfortunately they do not advert to the difficulties of reconciling this with the *Compton* test. For instance, Lord Somervell, in *IRC v Baddeley*[362] declared himself unable to accept the principle 'that a section of the public sufficient to support a valid trust in one category must, as a matter of law, be sufficient to support a trust in any other category . . . There might well be a valid trust for the promotion of religion benefiting a very small class. It would not follow at all that a recreation ground for the exclusive use of the same class would be a valid charity, though it is clear . . . that a recreation ground for the public is a charitable purpose.' In that case the majority of the Law Lords took the view that the social purposes were too wide to fall within Lord Macnaghten's fourth class and the trusts were for that reason not charitable. Lord Simonds[363] however went on to express the view that had the purpose fallen within the fourth head, the trusts would still not have been charitable as the prospective beneficiaries—members and potential

---

[359] [1951] AC 297, [1951] 1 All ER 31, HL.   [360] Supra, CA.

[361] Supra, HL at 624, 889. See (1976) 27 NILQ 198 (J C Brady).

[362] Supra, HL, at 615, 549. See also per Lord Simonds in *National Anti-Vivisection Society v IRC* [1948] AC 31 at 65, [1947] 2 All ER 217 at 233, HL.

[363] Lord Reid took a contrary view and Lords Porter and Tucker expressly refused to express an opinion on the point.

members of the Methodist church in West Ham and Leyton—were 'a class within a class' and did not constitute a section of the public.[364]

By contrast in the case of religious trusts a similar group has been held to constitute a section of the public, as in *Neville Estates Ltd v Madden*[365] where the group— members for the time being of the Catford Synagogue—was even narrower than persons of the Jewish faith living in Catford. In this case the judge accepted that the members of the Catford Synagogue were no more a section of the public than the members of the Carmelite priory in *Gilmour v Coats*,[366] and justified the contrasting result on the ground that the nuns of the priory lived secluded from the world, while the members of the synagogue spent their lives in the world. The court, he said,[367] is 'entitled to assume that some benefit accrues to the public from the attendance at places of worship of persons who live in this world and mix with their fellow citizens'. Likewise in *Re Hetherington*[368] it was held that the celebration of a religious rite in public—in that case saying masses—confers a sufficient public benefit because of the edifying and improving effect of such celebration on the members of the public who attend. The same assumption can be made in relation to attendance at an educational course.[369] It should be added that it would appear that in order for a class to form a section of the public the qualifications for membership must be relevant to the purposes of the trust.[370]

Several further separate points should be noted. First, the charitable nature of a trust is not affected by the fact that, by its very nature, only a limited number of persons are likely to avail themselves or are, perhaps, even capable of availing themselves, of its benefits, for example, a trust for the relief of anyone in the community suffering from a particular and very rare disease. If potential beneficiaries are further limited to only some of those who are suffering (for example, those living in a specified area) the trust will only be charitable where the potential beneficiaries

---

[364] See also *Williams' Trustees v IRC* [1947] AC 447 at 457, [1947] 1 All ER 513 at 520, HL, per Lord Simonds, who, in relation to similar trusts, expressed the opinion that Welsh people, defined as persons of Welsh nationality by birth or descent or born or educated or at any time domiciled in the Principality of Wales or the county of Monmouth, did not constitute an identifiable community for this purpose. The trust has since been registered as a charity on the grounds that the imprecision of the beneficiary class does not prevent it from being a section of the public, and that insofar as the purposes were too wide it was saved by the Charitable Trusts (Validation) Act 1954. See Report for 1977, paras, 71–80. See also (1977) 41 Conv 8.

[365] [1962] Ch 832, [1961] 3 All ER 769. See *Re Dunlop* [1984] NI 408 where it was said that the advancement of religion stands upon a different footing than the relief of poverty or the advancement of education. It is not designed to confer benefits upon those who receive it as an end in itself, but to advance the ultimate purpose of spreading the word of God and accomplishing the divine purpose.

[366] [1949] AC 426, [1949] 1 All ER 848, HL. See p 277, supra.

[367] *Neville Estates Ltd v Madden*, supra, at 853, 751. It is difficult to reconcile this with *Re Warre's Will Trusts* [1953] 2 All ER 99; criticized in Tudor, *Charities*, 9th edn, 2–068.

[368] [1990] Ch 1, [1989] 2 All ER 129. It was said in that case that it would be otherwise where the celebration was in private. See (1989) 139 NLJ 1767 (J M Q Hepworth); (1990) 32 Mal LR 114 (C H Sherrin).

[369] *Re Koeppler Will Trusts* [1984] 2 All ER 111 at 126; revsd [1986] Ch 423, [1985] 2 All ER 869, CA, without affecting this dictum.

[370] *Davies v Perpetual Trustee Co Ltd* [1959] AC 439, PC.

constitute a sufficiently important section of the community.[371] In our multicultural society there are some groups which, though numerically small, nevertheless suffer some common disadvantage, and accordingly many organizations have been registered as charities which are designed to cater for the education, social and personal safety needs of Asian women and girls in a particular area. If the benefits of such an organization are available to anyone who, being suitably qualified, chooses to take advantage of them, it has a public character.

Secondly, anything in the nature of a mutual benefit society[372] does not have the necessary quality of public benefit, as in *Re Hobourn Aero Components Ltd's Air Raid Distress Fund*[373] where voluntary collections from employees of the munition factories belonging to a certain company were to be used to relieve, without a means test, the distress suffered by the employees from air raids. This was held not to be charitable, Greene MR observing,[374] 'the point to my mind, which really puts this case beyond reasonable doubt is the fact that a number of employees of this company, actuated by motives of self-help, agreed to a deduction from their wages to constitute a fund to be applied for their own benefit without any question of poverty coming into it. Such an arrangement seems to me to stamp the whole transaction as one having a personal character, money put up by a number of people, not for the general benefit, but for their own individual benefit.' This principle does not, however, apply with full force in the case of trusts for religious purposes, which may be valid even though in favour of the members of a religious organization.[375]

Thirdly, in deciding the question of law whether or not an element of public benefit is present, it is unsettled whether regard should be had to the fiscal privileges accorded to charities. In *Dingle v Turner*[376] Lord Cross, with whose speech Lord Simon concurred, thought that it should, but the other three Law Lords expressed their doubts, and there is no case in which fiscal privileges have been expressly taken into account. Lord Cross however said that in his opinion the *Compton*[377] and *Oppenheim*[378] cases had been influenced by fiscal considerations—a trust for the education of children of employees of a company represents a fringe benefit for the employees and does not deserve fiscal privileges. There is not the same risk of abuse in the case of trusts for the relief of poverty, whose privileged position Lord Cross thought might be thus justified on practical grounds. Lord Cross even suggested that for the same sort of reason a trust to promote religion among the employees of a company might be charitable, provided the benefits were purely spiritual, though purposes under Lord Macnaghten's fourth head would normally be on a par with educational trusts.

---

[371] See per Lord Simonds in *IRC v Baddeley* [1955] AC 572 at 592, [1955] 1 All ER 525 at 533, HL.

[372] Unless it comes within the 'poverty' exception discussed in the following subsection by reason of a means test for benefits.

[373] [1946] Ch 194, [1946] 1 All ER 501, CA; *IRC v City of Glasgow Police Athletic Association* [1953] AC 380, [1953] 1 All ER 747, HL. Cf *London Hospital Medical College v IRC* [1976] 2 All ER 113.

[374] Supra, at 200, 506.   [375] *Neville Estates Ltd v Madden* [1962] Ch 832, [1961] 3 All ER 769.

[376] [1972] AC 601, [1972] 1 All ER 878, HL. See (1977) 40 MLR 397 (N P Gravells); [1978] Conv 277 (T G Watkin).

[377] [1945] Ch 123, [1945] 1 All ER 198, CA.   [378] [1951] AC 297, [1951] 1 All ER 31, HL.

Fourthly, it must be borne in mind that the courts' understanding of public benefit and, indeed, of what purposes are charitable, may vary with the passing of time. Thus in *National Anti-Vivisection Society v IRC*[379] Lord Wright observed[380] 'where a society has a religious object it may fail to satisfy the test (of public benefit) if it is unlawful, and the test may vary from generation to generation as the law successively grows more tolerant ... It cannot be for the public benefit to favour trusts for objects contrary to the law. Again eleemosynary trusts may, as economic ideas and conditions and ideas of social service change, cease to be regarded as being for the benefit of the community, and trusts for the advancement of learning or education may fail to secure a place as charities, if it is seen that the learning or education is not of public value.'

Lastly, it may be added that it appears that a trust may be charitable, and the test of public benefit passed, where the persons to benefit are all outside the jurisdiction.[381] The Charity Commissioners have recently reaffirmed their view[382] that if the objects of an institution are for the relief of poverty, the promotion of religion or the advancement of education, the public benefit element is presumed whether the charity is operating within the United Kingdom or wholly outside it. The element of public benefit can always be challenged and the criterion to be applied is the same for all charities, namely the one adopted by the English courts. Accordingly the Commissioners doubt whether the courts would regard it as charitable to support in a foreign country a religion permitted in that country but deemed, if carried on in the United Kingdom, contrary to the public benefit. In relation to charities falling under the fourth head, the Commissioners now consider that in determining the charitable status of institutions operating abroad one should first consider whether the organization would be regarded as a charity if its operation was confined to the United Kingdom. If it would, then the organization will be presumed also to be charitable even though operating abroad, unless it would be contrary to the public policy of this country to recognize it.[383] It is, however, necessary to distinguish between the objects of a charity and the means by which that object is to be carried out. If the object itself is contrary to the law of the foreign state in which it is to operate then the trust will not be charitable. On the other hand, if only the means of carrying out the object is

---

379 [1948] AC 31, [1947] 2 All ER 217, HL.

380 Supra, at 42, 220. Also per Lord Simonds at pp 69, 236.

381 *Income Tax Special Purposes Comrs v Pemsel* [1891] AC 531, HL ('for the general purposes of maintaining, supporting and advancing the missionary establishments among heathen nations of the Protestant Episcopal Church'); *Re Robinson* [1931] 2 Ch 122 ('to the German Government for the time being for the benefit of its soldiers disabled in the late war'); *Re Niyazi's Will Trusts* [1978] 3 All ER 785, [1978] 1 WLR 910 (working men's hostel in Cyprus); and cases on foreign missions such as *Re Kenny* (1907) 97 LT 130; *Re Redish* (1909) 26 TLR 42. Sed quaere. See (1965) 29 Conv 123 (D M Emrys Evans).

382 (1993) 1 Dec Ch Com 16, modifying their previous view in relation to charities falling under the fourth head. See *Re Jacobs* (1970) 114 Sol Jo 515. In *Re Levy's Estate* (1989) 58 DLR (4th) 375 (followed in *Re Gray* (1990) 73 DLR (4th) 161) a Canadian court held that a gift for charitable purposes in Canada is equally valid for the same charitable purposes abroad. See also (1990) 4 TL & P 74 (G Kodilinye).

383 This view was said to be clearly right in *Re Carapiet's Trusts* [2002] EWHC 1304, [2002] WTLR 989.

contrary to such laws then there will be a failure in the trusts and a case for cy-près application.

(h) EXCEPTIONS TO THE REQUIREMENT OF PUBLIC BENEFIT

The major anomalous head of charity for which the requirement of public benefit is not essential or is at least greatly modified is trusts for the relief of poverty. The law of charity in relation to poverty has followed its own line, and a series of cases, beginning with *Isaac v Defriez*,[384] has established the validity of trusts for 'poor relations' and other groups of persons who are not normally regarded as forming for this purpose a section of the community. Thus a trust for the relief of poverty was held to be charitable in *Gibson v South American Stores (Gath and Chaves Ltd)*[385] where the beneficiaries were selected by the tie of common employment, and in *Re Young's Will Trusts*,[386] where there was a gift to the trustees of the Savage Club 'upon trust to be used by them as they shall in their absolute discretion think fit for the assistance of my fellow members by way of pensions or grants who may fall on evil days'. The existing cases on this matter were considered by the Court of Appeal in *Re Scarisbrick*,[387] where, following life interests to her children, a testatrix gave half her residue to such relations, that is, relations in any degree, of her children as should be in needy circumstances. It was held that the exceptional rule in relation to trusts for the relief of poverty applied just as much to a trust for immediate distribution as to a perpetual trust. The distinction is between (a) a gift for the relief of poverty among poor people of a particular description, which is charitable even though the class of potential beneficiaries would not normally be regarded as forming a section of the public, and even though it includes specified individuals,[388] and (b) a gift to particular poor persons, which is not charitable even though the relief of poverty may be the motive of the gift. Most of the earlier cases were reviewed by the House of Lords in *Dingle v Turner*,[389] where the validity of the poverty exception was confirmed. Their Lordships agreed that it was a natural development of the 'poor relations' decisions to hold as charitable trusts for 'poor employees' of an individual or company (the case before the House), or poor members of a club or society, and they held that it would be illogical to draw a distinction between different kinds of poverty trusts.

There seems to be a second minor and equally anomalous exception to the

---

[384] (1754) Amb 595; *A-G v Price* (1810) 17 Ves 371.

[385] [1950] Ch 177, [1949] 2 All ER 985, CA; *Re Coulthurst* [1951] Ch 661, [1951] 1 All ER 774, CA.

[386] [1955] 3 All ER 689; *Re Hilditch* (1985) 39 SASR 469 ('poor and distressed Freemasons who shall be members or past members' of the specified lodge).

[387] [1951] Ch 622, [1951] 1 All ER 822, CA; *Re Cohen* [1973] 1 All ER 889.

[388] *Re Segelman (decd)* [1996] Ch 171, [1995] 3 All ER 676, noted [1996] NLJ Annual Charities Review 12 (P Luxton); [1996] Conv 379 (Elise Histed).

[389] [1972] AC 601, [1972] 1 All ER 878, HL. See [1978] Conv 277 (T G Watkin). The Goodman Committee Report recommended that the poverty exception should be abolished.

requirement of public benefit in what the Privy Council has called[390] 'the ancient English institution of educational provision for "Founder's Kin" in certain schools and colleges'. Such foundations giving preference to descendants of the donor are valid, 'though there seems to be virtually no direct authority as to the principle on which they rested and they should probably be regarded as belonging more to history than to doctrine'.[391] Most founder's fellowships at Oxford and Cambridge were abolished by the Oxford University Act 1854 and the Cambridge University Act 1856, respectively, but some still exist, and there have been at least two new foundations during the twentieth century.

Though hardly an exception to the rules as to public benefit, it is convenient to refer at this point to a way in which it may be possible, from a practical point of view, to evade it. It was held in *Re Koettgen*[392] that the charitable character of the primary trust for the advancement of education being of a sufficiently public nature, its validity was unaffected by the expression of the testator's imperative wish that in selecting beneficiaries the trustees should give preference to the employees of a particular company and members of their families. It was held that it was at the stage when the primary class of eligible persons was ascertained that the question of the public nature of the trust arose to be decided. Doubts have been raised,[393] however, as to whether this decision is consistent with the principle of *Oppenheim v Tobacco Securities Trust Ltd*.[394]

Finally it should be remembered that it does not follow from the general rule that in order to be charitable a trust must be for the public benefit, that a trust for the public benefit is necessarily charitable.[395]

(i) 'CHARITY' FOR THE PURPOSES OF THE CHARITIES ACT 1993

(i) Statutory definition

In this Act, which provides a code for the administration of charities, 'charity' is defined[396] as meaning 'any institution, corporate or not, which is established[397] for

---

[390] In *Caffoor v Income Tax Comr, Columbia* [1961] AC 584 at 602, [1961] 2 All ER 436 at 444, PC. See, generally, Squibb, *Founder's Kin*.

[391] *Caffoor v Income Tax Comrs, Columbia*, supra; *Spencer v All Souls College* (1762) Wilm 163; *Re Compton* [1945] Ch 123, [1945] 1 All ER 198, CA.

[392] [1954] 1 All ER 581. Contrast *Vernon v IRC* [1956] 3 All ER 14; *Trustees of George Drexler Ofrex Foundation v IRC* [1966] Ch 675, [1965] 3 All ER 529; *Re Martin* (1977) 121 Sol Jo 828. See the Report for 1976, paras 45–49, and Report for 1978, paras 86–89. See also *Public Trustee v Young* (1980) 24 SASR 407 where the preference clause was held to be simply an administrative direction to the trustee not affecting the charitable nature of the trust. Zelling J doubted the need today for a requirement of public benefit.

[393] *Caffoor v Income Tax Comrs, Columbia*, supra; *IRC v Educational Grants Association Ltd* [1967] Ch 993, [1967] 2 All ER 893, CA.

[394] Supra.   [395] See supra, p 264.

[396] In s 96(1). As to Oxbridge colleges and chartered universities see (1999) 6 CLPR 151 (D Palfreyman); [2001] 2 ELJ 134 (G R Evans).

[397] The relevant date is the foundation date. *Incorporated Council for Law Reporting for England and Wales v A-G* [1972] Ch 73 at 91, [1971] 3 All ER 1029 at 1038, CA, per Sachs LJ.

charitable purposes[398] and is subject to the control[399] of the High Court in the exercise of the court's jurisdiction with respect to charities'. 'Institution' is itself defined[400] as including any trust or undertaking, and trust is defined in relation to a charity as meaning 'the provisions establishing it as a charity and regulating its purposes and administration, whether those provisions take effect by way of trust or not'. 'Charity' therefore clearly includes both the ordinary case of trustees holding property upon charitable trusts and a company incorporated for charitable purposes. The Act does not, however, apply to an institution established for charitable purposes outside England and Wales, that is, an institution constituted in accordance with the law of a foreign country, though if constituted here its objects may be located abroad.[401]

(ii) Trustee holding separate funds on special trusts

If a trustee[402]—which may be a corporate charity with its own corporate property— holds separate funds on special trusts, each fund will, prima facie, constitute a separate institution and accordingly a separate charity for the purposes of the Act. However the Charity Commissioners may direct that for all or any of the purposes of the Act an institution established for any special purposes of or in connection with a charity (being charitable purposes) shall be treated as forming part of that charity or as forming a distinct charity;[403] and may also direct that two or more charities having the same charity trustees shall be treated as a single charity.[404] Thus, for instance, if a donor gives a fund to a school (being a charity) for the purpose of endowing a scholarship, the commissioners may direct that the fund should not be treated as a distinct charity and need not be separately registered under s 3.[405] A special trust does not, by itself, constitute a charity for the purposes of the statutory provisions relating to charity accounts.[406]

(iii) Exclusions from statutory definition

The Act specifically excludes from the definition[407] of charity any ecclesiastical corporation (that is, any corporation in the Church of England, whether sole or aggregate, which is established for spiritual purposes) in respect of the corporate property of the corporation, except a corporation aggregate having some purposes which are

---

[398] Ie exclusively charitable according to the law of England and Wales—s 97(1). The definition thus excludes a discretionary trust for 'charities' and non-charities.

[399] It seems from *Construction Industry Training Board v A-G* [1973] Ch 173, [1972] 2 All ER 1339, CA, that it is sufficient that the institution should be subject to the control of the court in some significant respect, even though in other respects the jurisdiction of the courts is ousted. See (1993/94) 2 CLPR 149 (O Hyams). It is very doubtful whether it is necessary for there to be a trustee within the jurisdiction: *Re Carapiet's Trusts* [2002] EWHC 1304, [2002] WTLR 989.

[400] Charities Act 1993, s 97(1).

[401] *Gaudiya Mission v Brahmachary* [1998] Ch 341, [1997] 4 All ER 957, CA.

[402] Eg *Re Royal Society's Charitable Trusts* [1956] Ch 87, [1955] 3 All ER 14.

[403] Charities Act 1993, s 95(5).   [404] Ibid, s 96(6) added by the Charities (Amendment) Act 1995.

[405] Discussed infra, p 314 et seq.   [406] Ie ss 41–49, Charities Act 1993: ibid, s 97(1).

[407] Ibid, s 96(2).

not ecclesiastical in respect of its corporate property held for those purposes,[408] or any trust of property for purposes for which the property has been consecrated.

(iv) Exempt charities

Certain charities listed in the Second Schedule to the Act[409] and known as 'exempt charities' are not subject to the mandatory provisions of the Act. These exempt charities, which are subject to their own special provisions as to supervision, include universities and colleges, specified national institutions such as the British Museum and the National Gallery, and other institutions administered by them or on behalf of any of them, the Church Commissioners and any institution administered by them, and Industrial and Provident Societies and Friendly Societies. Though free from the supervisory provisions of the Act, exempt charities may take advantage of its enabling provisions.

(v) Excepted charities

Quite distinct from exempt charities are excepted charities, who may be excepted from some of the obligations of the Act though in general subject to it.[410]

(j) THE OPINION OF THE CHARITY COMMISSION

The Charity Commission, which acts on the same basis as the courts, has summarized the essential characteristics of a charity in the following terms.[411]

A charity:

(a) has aims all of which are, and continue to be, recognized by law as exclusively charitable ie that are:
  (i) directed to the provision of something of clear benefit to others in society;
  (ii) not concerned with benefiting individuals in a way which outweighs any benefit to the public;
  (iii) directed to things that overall are not harmful to humankind;
  (iv) certain and lawful;
  (v) not for the pursuit of party or other political aims;
(b) is independent;
(c) is able to show that any personal, professional or commercial advantage, is or will continue to be incidental to carrying out its charitable aims;

---

[408] Also any Diocesan Board of Finance within the meaning of the Endowments and Glebe Measure 1976 for any diocese in respect of the diocesan glebe land of that diocese within the meaning of that Measure— s 96(2)(b).

[409] See (1992/93) 1 CLPR 209 (Judith Hill and Elizabeth Hakett). Also certain institutions added by Order in Council under para (c) of the Schedule eg the Royal College of Art by SI 2000/1826. See CC23.

[410] The obligations from which they may be excepted include the duty to register under s 3 and in connection with annual accounts, s 46.

[411] See RR1—the first of a series of publications relating to the review of the register.

(d) does not impose conditions on access or membership that in practice restricts the availability of facilities in a way that results in the organization as a whole not benefiting the public.

The Charity Commission also offer guidance on the charitable status of various bodies.[412]

(k) HUMAN RIGHTS ACT 1998

Where a local authority, in pursuance of its duty to provide accommodation, had arranged for accommodation to be provided by a charitable foundation, it was held that the foundation was not a public authority within the meaning of the Human Rights Act 1998.[413]

---

[412] See eg RR2 on bodies promoting urban and rural regeneration; RR3 on bodies for the relief of employment; RR5 on the promotion of Community Capacity Building.

[413] MR *(on the application of Heather) v Leonard Cheshire Foundation* [2002] 2 All ER 936, CA.

14

THE ADMINISTRATION
OF CHARITIES

The law relating to the administration of charities was revised by the Charities Act 1960 following the comprehensive Nathan Committee report.[1] Since then the charity world has changed dramatically. There has been an enormous increase in the number and variety of charities, and a substantial increase in the funds flowing through them. The Charity Commissioners in their 2003–04 Annual Report state that the total annual income to 31 March 2004 of 'main' registered charities exceeded £34 billion. Most registered charities had an income of £10,000 or less; just over 7% received 90%, and the largest 499 received 46%, of that income. The assets of registered charities exceed £75 billion.

A growing number of charities now rely on fund raising rather than endowments, and they are increasingly dependent on the commercial operations of associated business interests. Many more charities are set up as companies, and new fund raising methods are constantly being invented.[2] Further, there has been a significant growth of the so-called 'contract culture', under which charities enter into agreements to provide services in exchange for payment from public bodies such as local authorities and health authorities.[3] In the light of these developments it became clear that the supervision under which charities operate needed some updating. The Charities Act 1992 was accordingly passed to modernize the law. Its objectives were to achieve a balance between on the one hand proper control by the Charity Commission and proper accountability by charities, and on the other hand the freedom and corresponding responsibilities of individual organizations to develop and do business. It was intended to produce a stronger and more modern framework of supervision which would equip the Charity Commission for a more active role, narrow the scope for abuse, encourage trustees to shoulder their responsibilities, and ensure continuing public confidence in the sector. Most of the Charities Act 1992 (other than Parts II and III), together with most of the Charities Acts 1960 and 1985, have now been consolidated in the Charities Act 1993.

---

[1] Cmd 8710 published in December 1952.

[2] On broadcast advertising by charities, see [1990] Conv 106 (Debra Morris).

[3] See Charity Commission leaflet CC37; (2000) 20 LS 409 (Debra Morris); (2000) 14 T & ELJ 93 (J Garton); (2001) 23 JSW & FL 65 (A Cartwright and Debra Morris).

It was soon recognized that these changes were inadequate and the Charities Bill,[4] which was lost as a consequence of the May 2005 general election, would have made many amendments relating to the regulation of charities and their administration. Though the proposed amendments were substantial, the basic framework of the 1993 Act would have remained. This chapter sets out the law as it stands.

Charities are independent of the state, and even if set up by a governmental body cannot be directed by that body how to act.[5]

1 LEGAL FRAMEWORK OF CHARITY[6]

(a) CHARITABLE TRUST

A charity is, perhaps, most commonly constituted by means of a charitable trust. This is basically the same institution as a private trust: it is created, either inter vivos or by will, in the same way as a private trust but is set up exclusively to carry out charitable purposes as described in the preceding chapter.

(b) CORPORATE CHARITIES

There is no reason why a company formed in the ordinary way under the Companies Acts should not have objects which are exclusively charitable.

A charity may also be incorporated by Royal Charter,[7] by statute[8] or under the provisions of the Industrial and Provident Societies Act 1965.[9]

A company formed exclusively for charitable purposes does not, by reason only of that attribute, hold its property on trust: prima facie it owns its property beneficially as absolute owner, though it can, of course, only properly apply it to its charitable purposes. The Trustee Act 2000 does not apply to such corporate property. However where a charitable company is a trustee of a separate charity the Act applies to its actions as such trustee.

Like any other corporate body a corporate charity is liable to be sued. Its charitable

---

[4] See p 250, supra.   [5] See RR7.

[6] See (1993/94) 2 CLPR 113 (Judith Hill); [1997] Conv 106, [1999] Conv 20 (Jean Warburton). Model forms are provided by the Charity Commissioners—GD1 for corporate charities, GD2 for charities set up under a trust and GD3 for charities set up as unincorporated associations. The Charities Bill, lost on the prorogation of Parliament in spring 2005, would have created a new legal form, the charitable incorporated organization, specifically to meet the needs of charities.

[7] See eg *Re Royal Society's Charitable Trusts* [1956] Ch 87, [1955] 3 All ER 14.

[8] See eg *Re Shipwrecked Fishermen and Mariners' Royal Benevolent Society Charity* [1959] Ch 220, [1958] 3 All ER 465.

[9] Charities incorporated under this Act are exempt charities: Charities Act 1993, Sch 2 para (y). See p 286, supra.

status gives it no immunity.[10] The directors (assuming they have acted properly) will, if the funds of the charity are insufficient to satisfy the liability, not be personally liable. The third party's claim will remain unsatisfied. Contrast the case of a charitable trust where any claim will have to be made against the trustees and though they will (assuming they have acted properly) be entitled to reimbursement out of the trust funds, they will be personally liable in so far as this is insufficient.[11]

(c) UNINCORPORATED ASSOCIATIONS

It is possible for a group of persons to join together for some exclusively charitable purpose without setting up a trust and without being incorporated. The rules of the association will normally provide for it to be run by an elected committee,[12] and for any property held for this purpose to be vested in a small number of the members of the committee as trustees. However such trustees will not be the charity trustees for the purposes of the Charities Act 1993: the committee, as the persons having the general control and management of the administration of the charity, will be the charity trustees for those purposes.[13] Moreover by reason of the fact that an unincorporated association is not a separate entity in law,[14] all the members of the association may be personally liable in respect of the acts of committee members who, in purporting to act on behalf of the association, may be regarded as acting as agents of the members thereof, unless those acts fall outside their actual or ostensible authority having regard to the rules of the association. In an employment law case on unlawful discrimination an industrial tribunal held that the employer was the membership of the charity as a whole, but on appeal the Employment Appeal Tribunal held that, since employees of unincorporated associations, including charities, must have continuity of employment despite changes in the composition of the management committee, their contracts of employment were made with the management committee and its members for the time being.[15]

---

[10] *Mersey Docks Trustees v Gibbs* (1866) LR 1 HL 93. It has been held in Canada that all property of a charity 'whether owned beneficially or on trust for one or more charitable purposes' is available to pay the claims of trust victims against the charity: *Re Christian Brothers of Ireland in Canada* (2000) 184 DLR (4th) 445, noted (2003) 119 LQR 44 (D R Wingfield).

[11] See p 410, infra, and as to reimbursement p 483 et seq. As to charity trustees and exemption clauses see Law Com CP 171, paras 2.69–2.88.

[12] In a very small association the committee might comprise all the members.

[13] See Charities Act 1993, s 97(1) and p 291, infra.   [14] See p 60 et seq, supra.

[15] *Affleck v Newcastle Mind* [1999] ICR 852, EAT.

2 CHARITY TRUSTEES AND PERSONS AND BODIES HAVING POWERS AND DUTIES IN CONNECTION WITH CHARITIES

(a) TRUSTEES OF A CHARITABLE TRUST; CHARITY TRUSTEES; TRUSTEES FOR A CHARITY

(i) Kinds of trustees

Trustees in relation to charities are of three kinds which to some extent overlap. They are:

(a) trustees of a charitable trust. Where a charity exists as a charitable trust its trustees are fundamentally in the same position as trustees of a private trust, and in general have the same powers, duties and liabilities.[16] Unlike the trustees of a private trust, however, they need not act unanimously but the decision and act of a majority will be treated as the decision and act of the whole body of trustees and thus bind a dissenting minority;[17] moreover s 34 of the Trustee Act 1925, which restricts the number of trustees of land to four, does not apply to land vested in trustees for charitable purposes.[18] There is no requirement of a minimum number of trustees, but in some circumstances, the Charity Commissioners may appoint additional trustees.[19] Trustees of a charitable trust are clearly trustees for the purposes of the Charities Act 1993.

(b) charity trustees. Except in so far as the context otherwise requires, 'charity trustees' for the purposes of the Charities Act 1993[20] 'means the persons having the general control and management of the administration of a charity',[21] and therefore includes not only trustees in the sense with which we are familiar, but also, for instance, the directors in the case of a charity incorporated under the Companies Acts or, in the case of an unincorporate association the executive or management committee.

(c) trustees for a charity. The funds of a charity may be vested in trustees other than the charity trustees who have the general control and management of the administration. Such trustees may be custodian trustees,[22] but this is not necessarily the case.[23] They are not charity trustees for the purposes of the Charities Act 1993.

---

[16] As to investment see (1995/96) 3 CLPR 65 (H P Dale and M Gwinnell).

[17] *Wilkinson v Malin* (1832) 2 Cr & J 636; *Perry v Shipway* (1859) 1 Giff 1; *Re Whiteley* [1910] 1 Ch 600.

[18] Trustee Act 1925, s 34(3)(a). A power to execute instruments may be delegated to two or more trustees—Charities Act 1993, s 82. As to the appointment of new trustees see Charities Act 1993, s 83.

[19] See Charities Act 1993, ss 16, 18 discussed pp 297–301, post.

[20] But not for trust law generally—see (1995/96) 3 CLPR 65 (H P Dale and M Gwinnell).

[21] Section 97(1). There are an estimated 1.1 million charity trustees.   [22] See p 386 et seq, infra.

[23] See p 290, supra.

(ii) Qualifications for trusteeship

Until 1 January 1993 anyone who could be a trustee could be a charity trustee, unless the governing document contained a relevant disqualification provision. Now by virtue of s 72 of the Charities Act 1993[24] a person is disqualified[25] for being a charity trustee or trustee for a charity if:

(a) he has been convicted of any offence involving dishonesty or deception;[26]

(b) he has been adjudged bankrupt or sequestration of his estate has been awarded, and he has not been discharged;[27]

(c) he has made a composition or arrangement with, or granted a trust deed for, his creditors and has not been discharged in respect of it;

(d) he has been removed from the office of charity trustee or trustee for a charity by an order made by the Commissioners[28] or by the High Court on the grounds of any misconduct or mismanagement in the administration of the charity for which he was responsible or to which he was privy, or which he by his conduct contributed to or facilitated;[29]

(e) he has been removed, under the Law Reform (Miscellaneous Provisions) (Scotland) Act 1990[30] from being concerned in the management or control of any body;

(f) he is subject to a disqualification order or disqualification undertaking under the Company Directors Disqualification Act 1986 to a disqualification order under Part II of the Companies (Northern Ireland) Order 1989, or to an order under s 429(2)(b) of the Insolvency Act 1986 (as amended by the Enterprise Act 2000) (failure to pay under county court administration order).[31]

There is no automatic vacation of office of a disqualified trustee,[32] and acts done by him are not invalid by reason only of that disqualification.[33] However a person who acts as a charity trustee or trustee for a charity while disqualified is guilty of an offence.[34] Moreover the Commissioners may call upon him to repay to the charity the whole or part of any sums[35] he received from the charity while so acting.[36]

---

[24] As amended by the Insolvency Act 2000.

[25] With some exceptions the Commissioners may waive this disqualification: s 72(4). See (1993) 1 Dec Ch Com 26 and (1994) 2 Dec Ch Com 12 for factors taken into account.

[26] Unless it is a spent conviction under the Rehabilitation of Offenders Act 1974, s 72(2).

[27] A person is not disqualified for being a charity trustee or trustee for a charity which is a company if he has leave under s 11 of the Company Directors Disqualification Act 1986 to act as director of the charity: s 72(3).

[28] Under s 18(2)(i) of the Charities Act 1993 or its predecessors.

[29] The Commissioners are required to keep a register available for public inspection of all persons who have been removed from office under this head: s 72(6), (7).

[30] Section 7—powers of Court of Session to deal with management of charities.

[31] In relation to a charity which is a company the disqualification order may grant him leave to act, and in the case of an order under s 429(2)(b) the court which made the order may grant leave.

[32] See (1994) 2 Dec Ch Com 11.   [33] Section 73(3).

[34] Punishable on summary conviction to imprisonment for up to six months or a fine up to the statutory maximum, or both; and on conviction on indictment to imprisonment up to two years or a fine, or both: Charities Act, s 73(1). See subsection (i), p 314, infra.

[35] Or the monetary value of any benefit in kind.

[36] Section 73(4), (5). This does not apply in the case of an exempt charity.

(iii) Application of statutory powers relating to trustees generally

The unrepealed provisions of the Trustee Act 1925[37] apply to charity trustees. In general the Trustee Act 2000 applies to charitable trustees, but there are modifications and limitations in relation to the appointment of agents, nominees and custodians and in relation to remuneration.[38]

The Trusts of Land and Appointment of Trustees Act 1996, which provides, in s 6(1), that for the purpose of exercising their functions as trustees, the trustees of land have in relation to the land all the powers of an absolute owner, applies to trustees of a charity, though it is expressly provided that the powers are not to be exercised in contravention of an order of any court or of the Commissioners.[39]

(iv) Payment of charity trustees

Like other trustees, charity trustees are not permitted to receive any benefit (which includes money, services, facilities or other benefits including a token honorarium) from their trust unless they have express legal authority to do so from a clause in the charity's governing document, or by the authority of the Charity Commissioners or the court. Where the charity has such a power, the trustees must always consider when exercising it whether to do so is in the best interests of the charity at that time.[40]

(v) Insurance against personal liability of trustees

To overcome possible reluctance on the part of potential trustees to accept office because of the risks involved, a charity may be able to take out insurance to cover a trustee for personal liability for acts either properly undertaken in the administration of a charity or undertaken in breach of trust but under an honest mistake. The policy should exclude claims in respect of a trustee committing wrongful acts knowingly, or in reckless disregard whether the acts constitute a breach of trust or not. Unless the constitution of the charity expressly permits such payments, the authorization of the Charity Commissioners is required.[41]

(vi) Advice of the charity commissioners

Any charity trustee may make a written application to the Commissioners for their opinion or advice[42] on any matter affecting the performance of his duties as such. A charity trustee or trustee for a charity who acts in accordance with such opinion or advice is deemed to have acted in accordance with his trust unless he knows or has

---

[37] With the exception of s 15.

[38] See p 443 et seq, infra, p 454 et seq, infra. As to insurance see CC49.

[39] Trusts of Land and Appointment of Trustees Act 1996, s 6(6)(7). See also s 6(8).

[40] See CC11 listing factors to be taken into account. See also Trustee Act 2000, ss 28, 30 discussed p 443 et seq, infra.

[41] 1995, paras 20–24 (1994) 2 Dec Ch Com 24–27, 30. See [1996] Conv 12 (C Baxter); [1999] T & ELJ (S Harwood); (2003) 52 T & ELJ 8, (2004) 53 T & ELJ 12 (M King). As to insurance against the costs of a successful defence to a criminal prosecution see (1995) 4 Dec Ch Com 28.

[42] Which, semble, need not be in writing.

reasonable cause to suspect that the opinion or advice was given in ignorance of material facts, or that the decision of the court has been obtained on the matter or proceedings are pending to obtain one.[43] This provision may be useful to the trustees as a body, and may also be of particular value to an individual trustee who is concerned that the majority of his co-trustees insist on pursuing a course of action which he believes to be a breach of trust. The accuracy of the commissioners' opinion or advice may be challenged under the procedure set up by s 33, discussed below,[44] but a common law action in negligence cannot be brought on the ground that the opinion or advice is not only wrong but was given negligently.[45] The main reason for holding that there is no liability in negligence is the existence of the statutory scheme which provides an effective right of appeal against the substance of the matter. There is no question either of the commissioners being in any sense above the law or of aggrieved persons with sufficient *locus standi* not having a remedy. Further reasons are that to allow the concurrent exercise of rights in negligence actions at common law and rights of appeal in charity proceedings could only multiply costs, and that it would be contrary to the general good of charities for the commissioners' decision to be subject to attack by so wide a class of persons as potential objects of charity.

(vii) Incorporation of charity trustees

By s 50 of the 1993 Act the Charity Commissioners are empowered, where they consider that the incorporation of the trustees would be in the interests of the charity, to grant to the charity trustees of a charity[46] a certificate of incorporation of the trustees as a body corporate. Except as regards property vested in the official custodian for charities,[47] the certificate of incorporation vests in the body corporate all the property belonging to or held in trust for the charity, but the liability of the trustees is unaffected.[48] After incorporation the trustees may sue and be sued in their corporate name[49] and the requirements for the execution of documents are simplified.[50] However the charity itself is not incorporated but continues to be an unincorporated trust.

---

[43] Charities Act 1993, s 29. A trustee of an exempt charity may take advantage of this section. See generally Report for 1982, paras 24–27.

[44] Pages 304–307.

[45] *Mills v Winchester Diocesan Board of Finance* [1989] Ch 428, [1989] 2 All ER 317.

[46] Other than one which should be, but is not, registered under s 3 of the Charities Act 1993 as to which see p 314 et seq, post.

[47] See subsection (d), p 302, infra.

[48] Sections 51, 54. 50 certificates of incorporation were granted in 1996. It thus becomes unnecessary to change the names on documents such as share certificates and land certificates on a change of trustees. This difficulty can, however, be avoided without incorporation by the use of a custodian trustee.

[49] Charities Act 1993, s 50(4)(a).

[50] Charities Act 1993, s 60. Note, however, s 82 which achieves a somewhat similar result without incorporation—see p 291, n 18, ante.

(b) CHARITABLE COMPANIES

A charitable company is normally limited by guarantee, and a model memorandum and articles of association are provided by the Charity Commissioners.[51]

(i) Alteration of objects clause

There is no provision in the Charities Acts to prevent a corporate charity from altering its objects so that it ceases to be exclusively charitable. However a company which is a charity cannot alter (a) the objects clause in its memorandum of association, or (b) any other provision in its memorandum of association or its articles of association, which is a provision directing or restricting the manner in which property of the company may be used or applied, without the prior written consent of the Commissioners.[52]

Where an alteration is made which has the effect that the body ceases to be a charity, it does not affect the application of property held by the company at the time of the alteration.[53]

(ii) Ultra vires transactions

The provisions of the Companies Act 1985[54] that in favour of a person dealing with a company in good faith, any transaction decided on by the directors is deemed to be one which is within the capacity of the company to enter into, and that the power of the directors to bind the company is deemed to be free of any limitation under the memorandum or articles, do not apply to the acts of a company which is a charity except in favour of a person who:

(a) gives full consideration in money or money's worth in relation to the act in question, and

(b) does not know that the act is not permitted by the company's memorandum or, as the case may be, is beyond the powers of the directors, or who does not know at the time the act is done that the company is a charity.[55]

(iii) Certain acts by a charitable company

Approval of payment to a director in respect of loss of office or retirement is,[56] for example, ineffective without the prior written consent of the Commissioners.[57]

---

[51] The June 2003 revision is available on the internet. See also (2004) 54 T & ELJ 11 (Sarah Chiappini). Exceptionally the Charity Bank, limited by shares, was recently registered as a charity.

[52] Charities Act 1993, s 64(2). A copy of the consent must be delivered to the registrar of companies: s 64(3).

[53] Ibid, s 64(1).

[54] Sections 35 and 35A. See (1987) 2 TL & P 46 (Jean Warburton). See *Bayoumi v Women's Total Abstinence Educational Union Ltd* [2003] EWCA Civ 1548, [2004] 3 All ER 110.

[55] Ibid, s 65 (1). Subsection (2) protects a subsequent purchaser for value without notice.

[56] See Companies Act 1985, s 312. See also Companies Act 1985, ss 313(1), 319(3), 320(1), 337(2) and 322(2)(c).

[57] Charities Act 1993, s 66.

(iv) Name and status of a charitable company

Where a company is a charity and its name does not include the word 'charity' or 'charitable', the fact that the company is a charity must be stated in English in legible characters in (inter alia) all its business letters, notices and other official publications, cheques, conveyances, invoices and receipts.[58]

(v) Winding up

A petition for the winding up of a charitable company under the Insolvency Act 1986 may be presented by the Attorney-General, as well as by any person authorized by that Act.[59] It may also be presented by the Commissioners with the agreement of the Attorney-General, if, at any time after they have instituted an inquiry under s 8,[60] they are satisfied as mentioned in s 18(1)(a) or (b).[61]

The Commissioners, again only with the agreement of the Attorney-General, may apply for a declaration that the dissolution of a company is void, or that a company whose name has been struck off the register of companies should have it restored.[62]

(vi) Offences committed by a body corporate

Where any offence under the Charities Act 1993, or the Charities Act 1992 or any regulations made under it, is committed by a body corporate and is proved to have been committed with the consent or connivance of, or to be attributable to any neglect on the part of, any director,[63] manager, secretary or other similar officer of the body corporate, or any person who was purporting to act in any such capacity, he as well as the body corporate is guilty of that offence.[64]

(c) THE CHARITY COMMISSIONERS

(i) General function and object of the commissioners

There are a Chief Charity Commissioner and four other commissioners appointed by the Secretary of State; at least two of them must be persons who have a seven year general qualification within the meaning of the Courts and Legal Services Act 1990. The general function[65] of the Commissioners is stated to be to promote 'the effective use of charitable resources by encouraging the development of better methods of administration, by giving the charity trustees information or advice on any matter affecting the charity, and by investigating and checking abuses', and their general object,[66] 'so to act in the case of any charity (unless it is a matter of altering its

---

[58] Ibid, s 68. See also Companies Act 1985, ss 30(7), 349(1) and Charities Act 1993, s 67.

[59] Ibid, s 63(1).   [60] See p 298, infra.   [61] Charities Act 1993, s 63(2). See p 299.

[62] Ibid, s 63(3)–(5).

[63] In relation to a body corporate whose affairs are managed by its members, 'director' means a member of the body corporate: Charities Act 1992, s 75; Charities Act 1993, s 95.

[64] Charities Act 1992, s 75; Charities Act 1993, s 95.

[65] Charities Act 1993, s 1(3).   [66] Section 1(4).

purposes) as best to promote and make effective the work of the charity in meeting the needs designated by its trusts'. In their report for 2000/2001 the Commission state their objectives to be:

(1) to ensure that charities are able to operate for their proper purposes within an effective legal, accounting and governance framework;

(2) to improve the governance, accountability, efficiency and effectiveness of charities;

(3) to identify and deal with abuses and poor procedures.

The Commission issue numerous publications to assist and give guidance to actual and potential charity trustees, and from time to time issue consultation documents in relation to possible changes in the law. They are all available on the internet.[67]

To reassure charity trustees that in seeking the assistance of the Commission they will not run any danger of losing their independence in the administration of their charity, it is expressly provided that the Commissioners should themselves have no power to act in the administration of a charity.[68] They are required to make an annual report to the Secretary of State, a copy of which he must lay before each House of Parliament.[69] To assist them in carrying out their duties the Commissioners may by order require any person to furnish them with information in his possession which relates to any charity, and to furnish them with a copy or extract of any relevant documents in his custody or under his control, or to transmit the document itself for inspection.[70]

The Charity Commissioners have jurisdiction over funds raised via a charitable appeal, even if the appeal was made by an organization which is not charitable.[71]

The Charity Commissioners' services have traditionally been provided free to charities. Provision was made in the Charities Act 1992 for fees to be charged, and this is continued in the 1993 Act.[72]

(ii) Concurrent jurisdiction with the High Court

The Commissioners have the same powers[73] as are exercisable by the High Court in charity proceedings for (a) establishing schemes,[74] (b) for appointing, discharging or removing a charity trustee or trustee for a charity, or removing an officer or employee,

---

[67] http://www.charity-commission.gov.uk/publications.   [68] Section 1(4).   [69] Section 1(5).

[70] Charities Act 1993, s 9(1). The right is extended to require that the information be in a legible form where it is otherwise recorded: s 9(5). This section does not apply to documents relating only to an exempt charity: s 9(4).

[71] See Report for 1998, pp 23, 24.

[72] Section 85. The Charity Commissioners' Fees (Copies and Extracts) Regulations 1992, SI 1992/2986 prescribe the fees payable where they furnish a copy of, or extract from, any document kept by them under s 57 (records of applications for, and certificates of, incorporation of charity trustees), or s 84 (supply of copies of documents open to public inspection).

[73] It will be recalled that the supervisory powers of the Act as opposed to the enabling powers do not extend to exempt charities.

[74] Discussed in section 5, p 321 et seq infra.

and (c) for vesting or transferring property. The power can, however, be exercised only on the application of the charity, or on an order of the court for a scheme to be settled by the Commissioners,[75] or, in the case of a charity other than an exempt charity, on the application of the Attorney-General.[76] The Commissioners may also discharge a charity trustee or trustee for a charity on his application.[77] The Commissioners have no jurisdiction under these provisions to try or determine the title to any property as between a charity or trustee for a charity and any person claiming adversely thereto, or any question as to the existence or extent of any charge or trust.[78] Moreover the Commissioners are not to exercise their jurisdiction in any case which, by reason of its contentious character, or of any special question of law or of fact which it may involve, or for other reasons, the Commissioners may consider more fit to be adjudicated on by the court.[79] There are provisions for appeal to the High Court with a certificate from the Commissioners or leave of a Chancery Judge.[80]

(iii) General power to institute inquiries

The Commissioners may from time to time institute inquiries with regard to charities or a particular charity or class of charities, either generally or for particular purposes.[81] The inquiry may be conducted by the Commissioners themselves, or they may appoint someone else to conduct it and report to them, and in either case there is power to compel the attendance of witnesses and take evidence on oath.[82] They may direct any person to furnish accounts and statements in writing with respect to any matter in question at the inquiry on which he has or can reasonably obtain information, to furnish copies of relevant documents in his custody or under his control, and to attend and give evidence or produce any such documents.[83] The report of the inquiry, or some other statement of the results of the inquiry, may be printed and published, or published in some other way so as to bring it to the attention of persons who may wish to make representations about the action to be taken.[84]

---

[75] Under s 16(2).

[76] Charities Act 1993, s 16(1), (4) and by s 16(5), in the case of non-exempt charities whose income from all sources does not in the aggregate exceed £500 a year, on the application of a charity trustee or any other person interested in the charity, or, in the case of any local charity, any two or more inhabitants of the area. The figure of £500 may be altered by statutory instrument—Charities Act 1993, s 16(15).

[77] Section 16(8). In many cases a trustee will be able to retire under s 39 of the Trustee Act 1925, or, as a last resort, pay into court under s 63 of the Trustee Act 1925—see chapter 15, section 3(c), p 376, infra.

[78] Section 16(3).   [79] Ibid, s 16(10).

[80] Section 16(12), (13), (14); *Childs v A-G* [1973] 2 All ER 108, [1973] 1 WLR 1497. By sub-s 11 the A-G has an unqualified right of appeal. As to the joinder of the Charity Commissioners in an appeal see *Weth v A-G* [1999] 1 WLR 686, CA.

[81] Ibid, s 8(1).

[82] Charities Act 1993, s 8. The section does not apply to exempt charities. See Report for 1976, paras 128–132. See also the Report of an Inquiry into War on Want submitted to the commission on 15 February 1991.

[83] Section 8(3). It is an offence knowingly or recklessly to provide false or misleading information, or wilfully to alter, suppress, conceal or destroy any relevant document: s 11. See subsection (i), p 314, infra.

[84] Charities Act 1993, s 8(6).

(iv) Power to act for protection of charities

Section 18, which does not apply to an exempt charity, gives the Commissioners wide powers to act for the protection of charities.[85] If at any time after they have instituted an inquiry the Commissioners are satisfied that:

(a) there is or has been any misconduct or mismanagement[86] in the administration of the charity, or

(b) that it is necessary or desirable to act for the purpose of protecting the property of the charity or securing a proper application for the purposes of the charity of that property or of property coming to the charity.

They may take various steps. Those steps are:

(i) The suspension for a period not exceeding 12 months of any trustee, charity trustee or other person connected with the charity from the exercise of his office or employment pending consideration being given to his removal;

(ii) the appointment of additional charity trustees;

(iii) the vesting in or transfer to the official custodian for charities of any property held by or in trust for the charity;

(iv) orders not, without the approval of the Commissioners, to part with charity property, to make payments to the charity in discharge of a debtor's liability, or to enter into transactions or make payments in the administration of the charity;[87]

(v) to appoint a receiver and manager in respect of the property and affairs of the charity.[88]

If the Commissioners are satisfied as to *both* (a) and (b) they may:

(i) order the removal of any trustee, charity trustee or other person connected with the charity who has been responsible for or privy to the misconduct or mismanagement or has by his conduct contributed to it or facilitated it; and/or

(ii) by order establish a scheme for the administration of the charity.[89]

As an indication of the scale of the Commissioners' activities, in the year to 31 March 2004 the Commissioners made 1021 uses of their regulatory powers.

The Commissioners may remove a charity trustee by order made of their own motion:[90]

(a) where, within the last five years, the trustee—

---

[85] Unless they are acting under sub-s (1), they must give notice of their intention to each of the charity trustees, except any that cannot be found or has no known address in the UK: s 18(12).

[86] This includes the payment of excessive sums by way of remuneration or reward to persons acting in the affairs of the charity: ibid; s 18(3).

[87] Contravention of an order referred to in (iv) is an offence: s 18(14) and see subsection (i), p 314 infra.

[88] Charities Act 1993, s 18(1), (11). Detailed provisions relating to the appointment of a receiver and manager are contained in s 19 and SI 1992/2355. See Report for 1995, paras 28, 29.

[89] Charities Act 1993, s 18(2).

[90] Section 18(4). Section 18(4)(c) is unaffected by the Mental Capacity Act 2005.

(i) having previously been adjudged bankrupt or had his estate sequestrated, has
     been discharged, or
(ii) having previously made a composition or arrangement with, or granted a trust
     deed for, his creditors, has been discharged in respect of it;

(b) where the trustee is a corporation in liquidation;
(c) where the trustee is incapable of acting by reason of mental disorder within the
     meaning of the Mental Health Act 1983;
(d) where the trustee has not acted, and will not declare his willingness or unwillingness
     to act;
(e) where the trustee is outside England and Wales or cannot be found or does not act,
     and his absence or failure to act impedes the proper administration of the charity.

Similarly, they may appoint a person to be a charity trustee, and make orders with
regard to the vesting and transfer of property:[91]

(a) in place of a charity trustee removed by them under this section or otherwise;
(b) where there are no charity trustees, or where by reason of vacancies in their number
     or the absence of incapacity of any of their number the charity cannot apply for the
     appointment;
(c) where there is a single charity trustee, not being a corporation aggregate, and the
     Commissioners are of the opinion that it is necessary to increase the number for
     the proper administration of the charity;
(d) where the Commissioners are of opinion that it is necessary for the proper adminis-
     tration of the charity to have an additional charity trustee, because one of the existing
     charity trustees who ought nevertheless to remain a charity trustee either cannot be
     found or does not act or is outside England and Wales.

The provisions for appeal against an order of the Commissioners under s 16[92] are
applied to orders under s 18,[93] save that there is no need for a certificate of leave in the
case of an order appointing a receiver and manager, or removing a person from his
office or employment.[94] The Commissioners can only be joined as defendants to such
an appeal if they are 'proper' defendants,[95] and in general it is neither necessary nor
desirable for them to be joined.[96]

(v) Publicity for proceedings under ss 16 and 18

Before making any order under the Act to establish a scheme for the administration of
a charity, the Commissioners must give at least a month's public notice of the proposal, inviting representations to be made to them;[97] likewise in respect of an order to
appoint, discharge or remove a charity trustee or trustee for a charity.[98] A like notice
must be given to the person concerned if it is proposed to remove without his consent

---

[91] Section 18(5), (6).   [92] See p 298, supra.   [93] Section 18(8), (10).   [94] Section 18(9).
[95] Within CPR Sch 1, RSC Ord 108, r 5(2).
[96] *Weth v A-G* [1999] 1 WLR 686, CA. The Attorney-General will normally be defendant. This case and the
unreported case of *Scargill v Charity Comrs* are discussed in (1999) 8 T & ELJ 10 (Ann Phillips).
[97] Section 20(1).   [98] Section 20(2).

a charity trustee or trustee for a charity, or an officer, agent or employee of a charity.[99] Any representations received must be taken into account before proceeding with the proposals with or without modifications.[100]

(vi) Power to authorize dealings with charity property

Section 26(1)[101] of the Charities Act 1993 gives the Commissioners wide powers to authorize dealings with charity property if they consider that any action proposed or contemplated in the administration of a charity is expedient in the interests of the charity whether or not it would otherwise be within the powers exercisable by the charity trustees. The order may be made so as to authorize a particular transaction, compromise or the like, or a particular application of property, or so as to give a more general authority.[102] In practice the procedure of establishing a scheme[103] is preferred for this last purpose. In particular the order may authorize a charity to use common premises, or employ a common staff, or otherwise combine for any purpose of administration, with any other charity,[104] and it may give directions as to the manner in which any expenditure is to be borne and as to other connected matters.[105] It may be added that the Commissioners may provide books in which any deed, will or other document relating to a charity may be enrolled and may accept for safe keeping any document of or relating to a charity.[106]

(vii) Power to give directions about dormant bank accounts

Where the Commissioners are informed by a relevant institution[107] that it holds an account[108] in the name of or on behalf of a particular charity which is dormant,[109] and that it is unable, after making reasonable inquiries, to locate that charity or any of its trustees, they may direct that it be transferred to such other charity as they consider appropriate, subject to the willingness of that other charity to accept the transfer.[110] It will then be held for the purposes of the transferee charity, but subject to any restrictions on expenditure to which it was previously subject.[111]

---

[99] Section 20(3).   [100] Section 20(4).

[101] This section was used in August 1962 to authorize the sale of the Leonardo cartoon by the Royal Academy of Arts at a price lower than that obtainable on the open market, on condition that upon sale it should be held on trust for exhibition to the public, and in 1979 to authorize investment in the Pooh Properties—Report for 1979, para 116.

[102] Ibid, s 26(2).   [103] See section 5, p 321 et seq, infra.   [104] Ibid, s 26(2).

[105] Ibid, s 26(3), (4). See CC38.

[106] Section 30. Exempt charities may take advantage of this provision.

[107] Primarily banks and building societies—see Charities Act 1993, s 28(8)(b).

[108] Other than one held in the name of or on behalf of an exempt charity: s 28(10).

[109] Defined in s 28(8)(a) as one in which no transaction other than a payment in (or internal transaction by the institution) has been effected for the last five years.

[110] Section 28(1), (2), (3).   [111] Section 28(4).

(d) THE OFFICIAL CUSTODIAN FOR CHARITIES

The Official Custodian for Charities, a corporation sole having perpetual succession and using an official seal, was created by s 3 of the 1960 Act and continues in existence under s 2 of the 1993 Act.[112] His role was significantly reduced by the Charities Act 1992 in pursuit of the policy that the responsibility for managing charities' affairs should be placed squarely on the shoulders of the trustees. Under that Act provisions were made[113] for divesting the official custodian of all property held by him with the exception of land, and property (other than land) vested in him by order of the Commissioners under their power to act for the protection of charities.[114] This property is to be transferred to the charity trustees or any trustee for the charity, or to a person nominated by the charity trustees. The process is effectively complete.

Charity land may become vested in the Official Custodian by an order of the court,[115] either directly vesting the land in the Official Custodian, or authorizing or requiring the persons in whom the land is vested to transfer it to him or appointing any person to transfer it to him.[116] It simplifies the ownership of charity land and may make dealing with the land easier and cheaper. Property other than land can only be vested in the official custodian by an order of the commissioners under s 18.

Where property is vested in the Official Custodian in trust for a charity, he must not exercise any powers of management, but has the same powers, duties and liabilities, and is entitled to the same rights and immunities, and is subject in the same way to the control and orders of the court as a corporation appointed custodian trustee under s 4 of the Public Trustee Act 1906,[117] except that he has no power to charge fees.[118] Accordingly charity trustees may bring proceedings in their own name without the need to obtain the permission of or to join in the proceedings the Official Custodian for Charities.[119]

(e) THE ATTORNEY-GENERAL

The Attorney-General acts in charity cases on behalf of the Crown as parens patriae. As a general rule he is a necessary party to charity proceedings, in which he represents all the objects of the charity.[120] It has always been recognized that it is his duty to intervene for the purpose of protecting charities and affording advice and assistance to the court in the administration of charitable trusts.[121] Until the Charities Act 1992

---

[112] See CC13.

[113] Charities Act 1992, ss 29–30, as amended by Charities Act 1993, Sch 6, para 29. As to land subject to the Reverter of Sites Act 1987, see Charities Act 1993, s 23, as amended by the Trusts of Land and Appointment of Trustees Act 1996.

[114] Ie Charities Act 1960, s 20, now Charities Act 1993, s 18.

[115] Or, under s 16, of the Commissioners.   [116] Section 21.

[117] See chapter 16, section 4, p 386, infra.   [118] Charities Act 1993, s 22(1).

[119] *Muman v Nagasena* [1999] 4 All ER 178, [2000] 1 WLR 299, CA.

[120] See *Brooks v Richardson* [1986] 1 All ER 952, [1986] 1 WLR 385.

[121] *Wallis v Solicitor-General for New Zealand* [1903] AC 173, PC; *Re Royal Society's Charitable Trusts* [1956] Ch 87, [1955] 3 All ER 14; *Re Belling* [1967] Ch 425, [1967] 1 All ER 105. Cf Charities Act 1993, s 33(7).

no-one other than the Attorney-General was entitled to maintain an action against supposed trustees to establish the existence of a charitable trust and only the Attorney-General or the trustees of a charity could bring proceedings to recover charity property from a third person.[122] 'So far as the enforcement of the trust is a matter of public interest,' it was said,[123] 'the guardian of that interest was the Attorney-General.' The Charities Act 1993 now provides that with his agreement the Commissioners may of their own motion exercise the same powers as the Attorney-General with respect to the taking of legal proceedings with reference to charities or the property or affairs of charities, or the compromise of claims with a view to avoiding or ending such proceedings.[124] The Commissioners are under a duty to inform the Attorney-General if it appears to them that it is desirable that he should bring proceedings with reference to a charity.[125]

One particular power possessed by the Attorney-General and the court is to authorize charity trustees to make ex gratia payments out of funds held on charitable trusts. This power is not to be exercised lightly on slender grounds, but only in cases where it can fairly be said that, if the charity were an individual, it would be morally wrong of him to refuse to make the payment.[126] By the 1993 Act[127] the same power is conferred on the Commissioners, under the supervision, however, and subject to the directions of the Attorney-General. A refusal to exercise the power by the Commissioners does not prevent an application to the Attorney-General.[128]

The Law Officers Act 1997 allows the Solicitor General to exercise both the statutory and non-statutory functions of the Attorney-General and for his acts to have effect as if done by the Attorney-General.

(f) LOCAL AUTHORITIES

Provisions designed to encourage co-operation and partnership between charity trustees and local authorities are contained in ss 76–79 of the 1993 Act.

Section 76 authorizes the council of a county or of a district or London borough

---

[122] *Hauxwell v Barton-upon-Humber UDC* [1974] Ch 432, [1973] 2 All ER 1022. Contrast the position with regard to 'charity proceedings' discussed pp 304, 305, infra.

[123] *Bradshaw v University College of Wales* [1987] 3 All ER 200, per Hoffman J at 203.

[124] Charities Act 1993, ss 63(1), 32(1), (5). The power does not extend to the presentation of a petition for the winding up of a charity under ss 63(1), 32(2).

[125] Ibid, s 33(7).

[126] *Re Snowden* [1970] Ch 700, [1969] 3 All ER 208; *Hobday v A-G of New South Wales* [1982] 1 NSWLR 160; and see [1968] 32 Conv 384 (P H Pettit); Report for 1969, paras 26–31 and Report for 1976, paras 113–116; [1994] PCB 416 (J Burchfield). Accordingly the Attorney-General could not authorize the return of Nazi-looted Old Master drawings to the heirs of the previous owner in contravention of the express provisions in s 3(4) of the British Museum Act 1963, notwithstanding that the trustees felt under a moral obligation to do so. Legislation has been proposed to enable such property looted between 1936 and 1945 to be returned.

[127] Section 27. See CC7 and (2001) 32 T & ELJ 17 (P Hamlin).   [128] Section 27(4).

and the Common Council of the City of London to maintain an index[129] of local charities[130] or of any class of local charities in the council's area, and to publish information therein contained. The index is to be open to public inspection at all reasonable times.

Charity trustees in applying their funds should seek to avoid overlapping with the statutory welfare services or otherwise directly relieving public funds.[131] Guidance Notes issued by the Charity Commissioners[132] state that trustees are in breach of trust if by making a grant they bring about a reduction in a statutory benefit to which a person otherwise has a right; but they are acting within their trusts in relieving need, hardship and distress so long as they do not replace funds from the state.

Section 78(1) empowers any local council[133] to make, with any charity established for purposes similar or complementary to services provided by the council, arrangements for co-ordinating the activities of the council and those of the charity in the interests of persons who may benefit from those services or from the charity. This is carried a stage further by s 142 of the Local Government Act 1972[134] which empowers a local authority to make or assist in the making of, arrangements under which the public may obtain information concerning the services provided by the authority, government departments, charities and voluntary bodies within the area of the local authority concerned.

It is convenient to mention here that s 79 of the Charities Act 1993 contains special provisions relating to parochial charities.[135] These provisions relate in the main to the transfer of property by the trustees to the parish council or their appointees, and to the appointment of charity trustees by the parish council or parish meeting.

(g) THE COURT

The court has an inherent general jurisdiction[136] over charitable trusts and may accordingly enforce them, take steps to redress a breach of trust, direct a scheme[137] in

---

[129] The Commissioners must provide, on request, copies of relevant entries in the register of charities (discussed, infra, p 314, et seq). The index may also contain informal references to local branches of national charities which are ineligible to be placed on the register. These have no legal consequences but may be of considerable practical value.

[130] Defined by s 96(1) in relation to any area as 'a charity established for purposes which are by their nature or by the trusts of the charity directed wholly or mainly to the benefit of that area or of part of it'. As to reviews of local charities by local authority see s 77.

[131] See Report for 1978, paras 61 and 62.

[132] See CC3, para 63, CC4, paras 21–22, CC37, paras 21–32.

[133] This includes councils not included in ss 76 and 77 and is defined for this purpose in s 78(1).

[134] As amended by the Local Government Act 1986, s 3.

[135] Defined by s 96(1). Voluntary and grant maintained schools within the meaning of the Education Act 1996 are excluded: s 79(9) as amended by the Education Act 1996, Sch 37, para 119. See CC29.

[136] *A-G v Sherborne Grammar School Governors* (1854) 18 Beav 256. Including, as incidental to the administration of a charity estate, jurisdiction to alien charity property where the alienation is clearly for the charity's benefit and advantage: *Oldham Borough Council v A-G* [1993] Ch 210, [1993] 2 All ER 432, CA.

[137] Either by directing a reference to chambers to settle the scheme, or by reference to the Commissioners under s 16(2) discussed infra, p 322. In a simple case, or where the fund is very small, the court may act directly without any reference.

order to enforce the more complete attainment of the charitable objects and alter and amend the trusts under the cy-près doctrine. In addition to proceedings by the Attorney-General and the Commissioners the Charities Act 1993 provides that charity proceedings, that is, proceedings 'brought under the court's jurisdiction with respect to charities, or brought under the court's jurisdiction with respect to trusts in relation to the administration of a trust for charitable purposes[138] may be taken either by the charity, or by any of the charity trustees, or by 'any person interested in the charity', or by any two or more inhabitants of the area of the charity, if it is a local charity.[139] In *Re Hampton Fuel Allotment Charity*[140] the Court of Appeal said that there were insuperable difficulties in attempting comprehensive definition of the phrase 'any person interested in the charity'. The interest which ordinary members of the public, whether or not subscribing to a charity, and whether or not potential beneficiaries, have in seeing that a charity is properly administered is the responsibility of the Attorney-General. To qualify as a plaintiff in his own right a person needs to have an interest materially greater than or different from that possessed by ordinary members of the public. The Court of Appeal referred with apparent approval to Megarry V-C's reference in *Haslemere Estates Ltd v Baker*[141] to those 'who have some good reason for seeking to enforce the trusts of a charity or secure its due administration', which Megarry V-C contrasted with 'those who merely have some claim adverse to the charity, and seek to improve their position at the expense of the charity'. A person who founds and finances a charity may well qualify as a person interested in that charity, though his executors would not.[142]

Except in the case of an exempt charity, however, or where the proceedings are brought by the Attorney-General or by the Commissioners under s 32[143] no charity

---

[138] Section 33(8). *See Brookes v Richardson* [1986] 1 All ER 952, discussed [1986] All ER Rev 203 (P J Clarke). 'Charity proceedings' probably includes an application for judicial review of the decision of a charitable public body exercising its discretionary power in the management of trust property: *Scott v National Trust for Places of Historic Interest or Natural Beauty* [1998] 2 All ER 705, sub nom *Ex p Scott* [1998] 1 WLR 226 (National Trust decision to end deer hunting with hounds on trust land: judicial review refused as alternative remedy available under the Charities Act 1993). It does not cover proceedings by way of construction of a testamentary document to determine whether a provision was effective to create a charitable trust, where only the Attorney-General, or the trustees, can start an action: *Re Belling* [1967] Ch 425, [1967] 1 All ER 105; *Mills v Winchester Diocesan Board of Finance* [1989] Ch 428, [1989] 2 All ER 317. In appropriate circumstances a case may be heard and judgment given in private notwithstanding the Human Rights Act 1998: *In re Trusts of X Charity* [2003] EWHC 257 (Ch), [2003] 1 WLR 2751.

[139] Section 33(1). See (1988) 2 TL & P 128 (J Thurston).

[140] [1989] Ch 484, sub nom *Richmond upon Thames London Borough Council v Rogers* [1988] 2 All ER 761, CA.

[141] [1982] 3 All ER 525. *Gunning v Buckfast Abbey Trustees* (1994) Times, 9 June (fee-paying parents of children at a preparatory school run by a charitable trust entitled to bring proceedings though neither subscribers to nor beneficiaries of the charity), noted (1993/94) 2 CLPR 250 (Debra Morris); (1995) 9 Tru LI 130 (R Nolan); *Royal Society for the Protection of Cruelty to Animals v A-G* [2001] 3 All ER 530 (disappointed applicant for membership has not a sufficient interest).

[142] *Re Hampton Fuel Allotment Charity*, supra, CA; *Bradshaw v University College of Wales, Aberystwyth* [1987] 3 All ER 200.

[143] Charities Act 1993, s 33(6).

proceedings relating to a charity[144] can be proceeded with in any court unless the taking of the proceedings is authorized by the Commissioners, who should not, however, without special reasons, give such authorization where in their opinion the case can be dealt with by them under the powers of the Act.[145] The object of this 'protective filter', as it has been called,[146] is to prevent money of the charity being spent unnecessarily on legal proceedings. If the Commissioners refuse their authorization, an application for leave may nevertheless be sought from a Chancery judge.[147]

The jurisdiction is based primarily on the existence of a trust. The point has several times been raised where a testator has given property to a non-existent institution and where there is clearly a general charitable intention. In such case if the gift is by way of trust, the court has jurisdiction and will direct a scheme; but if it is by way of direct gift the court has no jurisdiction and the matter falls within the royal prerogative and will be disposed of by the Crown by sign-manual, acting as it is said as parens patriae.[148]

The inherent jurisdiction was limited in relation to charities established by royal charter or by statute,[149] though it always had jurisdiction to see that the provisions of the charter or the statute were observed. There is, moreover, a difficulty as to jurisdiction over corporate charities. Where a corporate body holds property on charitable trusts there is clearly jurisdiction, but in many cases a corporation with exclusively charitable purposes simply holds property as part of its corporate funds. If jurisdiction depends on the existence of a trust a problem arises. It may be possible in the case of a charity incorporated by charter to evade the difficulty by holding that the corporate charity holds its property on trust for its charitable purposes,[150] but this argument is not available in the case of a company incorporated under the Companies Acts with exclusively charitable objects, for a company does not hold its property on trust either for its members or the objects set out in its memorandum of association. However it has been held[151] that the court has jurisdiction not only where there is a trust in the strict sense, but also, in the case of a corporate body, where under the terms of its constitution it is legally obliged to apply the assets in question for exclusively charit-

---

[144] This does not include a charitable institution established in a foreign jurisdiction but operating here: *Gaudiya Mission v Kamalaksha DAS Brahmachary* [1998] Ch 341, [1997] 4 All ER 957. See p 285, supra.

[145] Charities Act 1993, s 33(2), (3). Section 33(4) excludes an order for the taking of proceedings in a pending cause or matter or for the bringing of an appeal.

[146] By Nicholls J in *Re Hampton Fuel Allotment Charity*, supra, at 410. See also *Muman v Nagasena* [1999] 4 All ER 178, [2000] 1 WLR 299, CA.

[147] Ibid, s 33(5).

[148] See *Re Bennett* [1960] Ch 18, [1959] 3 All ER 295, (1974) 52 CBR 372 (Lyn L Stevens). See also Report for 1964, paras 64–66. The power was delegated to the Attorney-General in 1986: the average number of directions made by the Attorney-General over the 5 years to 1996 is 50, but only 37 in 1996.

[149] See now p 321, infra.

[150] Even, it seems, although the charity came into existence before the creation of trusts—*A-G v St Cross Hospital* (1853) 17 Beav 435 (hospital founded in twelfth century).

[151] *Liverpool and District Hospital for Diseases of the Heart v A-G* [1981] Ch 193, [1981] 1 All ER 994. The particular terms of the trust or constitution in question may, however, operate substantially or partially to oust the jurisdiction of the court.

able purposes. In any event such a company incorporated under the Companies Act is clearly a charity for the purposes of the Charities Act 1993, provision being made for its being wound up on a petition presented by the Attorney-General or by a person authorized by the Insolvency Act 1986.[152] Further, the statutory definition of charity[153] includes a corporate 'institution' established for charitable purposes; 'institution' is defined[154] to include a trust, and trust is defined in relation to a charity as meaning the provisions establishing it as a charity and regulating its purposes and administration, whether those provisions take effect by way of trust or not.

(h) VISITORS

(i) Position apart from statute[155]

Ecclesiastical and eleemosynary corporations[156] are subject to the jurisdiction of visitors in relation to their internal management.[157] Ecclesiastical corporations are those which exist for the furtherance of religion and perpetuating the rights of the Church. For present purposes eleemosynary corporations[158] are such as are constituted for the perpetual distribution of the free alms or bounty of the founder of them to such persons as he has directed, originally mainly hospitals[159] and colleges. The universities of Oxford and Cambridge are civil and not eleemosynary corporations and so have no visitor. However the colleges of those universities are eleemosynary corporations, though it must be remembered that in most cases only the master, fellows and scholars, and not exhibitioners or commoners, are members of the foundation.[160] Most of the more modern universities, other than those which have become

---

[152] Charities Act 1993, s 63(1). The affairs of the first company to be wound up under the predecessor of this section came before the court in *Liverpool and District Hospital for Diseases of the Heart v A-G*, supra. See [1984] Conv 112 (Jean Warburton).

[153] Ibid, s 96(1).   [154] Ibid, s 97.

[155] See, generally, (1992/93) 1 CLPR 63 (H Picarda); (1994) 18 UQLJ 106 (S Robinson); (2002) 1 ELJ 135 (T Birtwistle).

[156] *Blackstone's Commentaries* 470. As to civil corporations see pp 481, 482, where he pointed out that the Court of King's Bench (now presumably the Queen's Bench Division) has a supervisory jurisdiction, but it is doubtful whether the court acts in the capacity of visitor. In relation to universities in Nigeria see (1991) ICLQ 699 (M A Ikhariale) and in Western Australia (1995) 25 UWALR 146 (P Whalley and D Price).

[157] The judges have a visitatorial jurisdiction over the Inns of Court, notwithstanding that an Inn of Court is not a corporation, does not have statutes, nor does it have a founder who nominated a visitor to hear and determine internal disputes: *R v Visitors to the Inns of Court, ex p Calder* [1994] QB 1, [1993] 2 All ER 876, CA; *Joseph v Council of Legal Education* [1994] ELR 407, CA; *R v Council of Legal Education, ex p Halstead* (1994) *Times*, 11 August and 7 October, DC.

[158] This phrase is not a term of art with a judicially established definition. The narrowest possible meaning has been said to be charities for the relief of poverty. In *Re Armitage's Will Trusts* [1972] Ch 438, [1972] 1 All ER 708, it was said to cover all charities directed to the relief of individual distress whether due to poverty, age, sickness or other similar individual afflictions.

[159] In the old sense of institutions for the maintenance of the needy, infirm or aged.

[160] The position of Oxford colleges is discussed by D Palfreyman in (1997/98) 5 CLPR 85. Cf *Herring v Templeman* [1973] 3 All ER 569, CA where it was held that a student at a teacher-training college was outside the visitatorial jurisdiction for although he was a student there he was in no position of membership. As to the visitor in New Zealand universities see (1985) 11 NZULR 382 (F M Brookfield).

universities under the Further and Higher Education Act 1992[161] have been founded by royal charter and are eleemosynary corporations: moreover such charters normally, perhaps always, provide that all the undergraduates are members of the university.[162]

Ecclesiastical corporations are generally visitable by the Ordinary.[163] So far as elee-mosynary corporations are concerned the founder is said to be a legislator,[164] and may accordingly appoint visitors, and if no visitor is appointed by him, he and his heirs[165] are visitors by operation of law.[166] This principle applies where the founder is the Crown. Thus if a university is founded by royal charter, and the charter reserves to the Crown the right to appoint a visitor and no appointment has been made, the Crown is the visitor.[167] Visitatorial jurisdiction never fails through lack of a visitor.[168] If the founder's heirs die out, or cannot be found,[169] or cannot act by reason of insanity[170] the visitatorial power becomes vested in the Crown. In any case where visitatorial powers are exercisable by the Crown, they are in practice exercised by the Lord Chancellor on behalf of the Crown, acting in a capacity distinct from his judicial capacity,[171] or such other person as the Crown may nominate.[172] And, as it would be contrary to natural justice that a man should be judge in his own cause, the Court of Queen's Bench[173] has assumed jurisdiction where otherwise the same person would be both visitor and visited.[174] No technical words are required for the appointment of

---

[161] Section 77. The only other non-charter university is the University of Newcastle upon Tyne, created by the Universities of Durham and Newcastle upon Tyne Act 1963, which expressly provided that the Lord Chancellor should be its visitor. Polytechnics which became universities following the 1992 Act had previously under the Education Reform Act 1988 become, and remain, corporate bodies having no visitor. As public institutions discharging public functions their decisions are subject to judicial review on conventional grounds: *R v Manchester Metropolitan University, ex p Nolan* [1994] ELR 380, QBD. In the case of these 'new universities' the role of the court will frequently amount to performing the reviewing role which would otherwise be performed by the visitor: *Clark v University of Lincolnshire and Humberside* [2000] 3 All ER 752, [2000] 1 WLR 1988, CA.

[162] *Patel v University of Bradford Senate* [1978] 3 All ER 841; affd [1979] 2 All ER 582, CA; (1970) 86 LQR 531 (J W Bridge); (1978) 4 Dal LJ 647 (W Ricquier); (1979) 12 MULR 291 (Peter Willis); (1981) 97 LQR 610 (P M Smith); (1985) Dal LJ 313 (C B Lewis).

[163] As to cathedral churches see Cathedrals Measure 1963, s 6; Church of England (Miscellaneous Provisions) Measure 1976, s 4.

[164] *Spencer v All Souls' College* (1762) Wilm 163; *Phillips v Bury*, supra; *Thomas v University of Bradford* [1987] AC 795, [1987] 1 All ER 834, HL.

[165] The effect of the abolition of inheritance by the Administration of Estates Act 1925, s 45 is not clear.

[166] *Phillips v Bury*, supra; *Eden v Foster* (1726) 2 P Wms 325.

[167] *Thomas v University of Bradford*, supra, HL.

[168] *Re Wislang's Application* [1984] NI 63 at 93, per Kelly LJ.

[169] *Ex p Wrangham* (1795) 2 Ves 609; *A-G v Earl of Clarendon* (1810) 17 Ves 491.

[170] *A-G v Dixie* (1805) 13 Ves 519.

[171] *Casson v University of Aston in Birmingham* [1983] 1 All ER 88.

[172] In *R v HM the Queen in Council, ex p Vijayatunga* [1990] 2 QB 444, sub nom *R v University of London Visitor, ex p Vijayatunga* [1989] 2 All ER 843, CA, the Crown nominated a Committee of the Lords of the Privy Council, in *R v Lord President of the Privy Council, ex p Page* [1993] AC 682, sub nom *Page v Hull University Visitor* [1993] 1 All ER 97, the Lord President of the Privy Council, and in *Thomas v University of Bradford (No 2)* [1992] 1 All ER 964, Visitor, a Lord of Appeal in Ordinary.

[173] And presumably the High Court would now act in the same way.

[174] *R v Bishop of Chester* (1728) 2 Stra 797; *R v Bishop of Ely* (1788) 2 Term Rep 290.

a visitor by the founder,[175] who may either appoint a general visitor, or divide up the visitatorial power among two or more persons,[176] or appoint special visitors for a particular purpose. If a visitatorial power is prima facie general, it requires particular words to abridge it in any respect. The mere fact that in certain respects the visitor's powers are limited in the way they can be exercised does not cut him down from being a general visitor to a special visitor.[177]

The nature of the visitatorial power has been said to be forum domesticum, the private jurisdiction of the founder,[178] and in any dispute arising under the domestic law of the institution the power of the visitor is absolute[179] and exclusive.[180] This is because the founder of such a body is entitled to reserve to himself or to a visitor whom he appoints the exclusive right to adjudicate upon the domestic laws which the founder has established for the regulation of his bounty. Even where the contractual rights of an individual (such as those contained in a contract of employment between a university teacher and his university) are in issue, if those contractual rights are themselves dependent upon rights arising under the regulating documents of the charity, the visitor has an exclusive jurisdiction over disputes relating to such employment.[181]

What is meant by the 'domesticity' of the visitatorial jurisdiction was explained by Lord Griffiths giving the leading speech in *Thomas v University of Bradford*,[182] who adopted a passage from an article by Dr P M Smith.[183] Dr Smith had pointed out that the basis of the visitatorial jurisdiction is the supervision of the statutes, ordinances, regulations etc of the foundation, which leads to a distinction between any matter concerning the application or the interpretation of those internal laws which is within his jurisdiction, and questions concerning rights and duties derived otherwise than from such internal laws which are outside it:

---

[175] *A-G v Middleton* (1751) 2 Ves Sen 327; *St John's College, Cambridge v Todington* (1757) 1 Burr 158.

[176] *A-G v Middleton*, supra. [177] *Oakes v Sidney Sussex College, Cambridge* [1988] 1 All ER 1004.

[178] Per Hardwicke LC in *Green v Rutherford* (1750) 1 Ves Sen 462 at 472. See (1980) 7 Mon LR 59 (R T Sadler); (1981) U Tas LR 2 (R T Sadler).

[179] *R v Bishop of Chester* (1748) 1 Wm Bl 22 Wright J said 'Visitors have an absolute power; the only absolute one I know of in England', and in *Page v Hull University Visitor*, supra, HL, Lord Browne-Wilkinson said 'the position of the visitor is anomalous, indeed unique'. Where any question as to the validity of an act by the trustees of a charity was under the scheme governing it to be determined by the Charity Commissioners, the Commissioners were in the position of a visitor: *R v Charity Comrs, ex p Baldwin* [2001] WTLR 137.

[180] *Thorne v University of London* [1966] 2 QB 237, [1966] 2 All ER 338, CA (the court has no jurisdiction to hear a complaint that failure in degree examinations in, inter alia, the law of trusts, was a result of negligence of the examiners); *Herring v Templeman* [1973] 2 All ER 581; affd on different grounds [1973] 3 All ER 569, CA; *Patel v University of Bradford Senate*, supra, CA; *Re University of Melborne, ex p De Dimone* [1981] VR 378; *R v University of Nottingham, ex p K* [1998] ELR 184, CA. See (1974) 37 MLR 324 (D Christie); (1974) 33 CLJ 23 (S A de Smith). It may be noted that even if there is no visitor the court will not hear a complaint as to the application of university regulations relating to degrees and satisfaction of examiners where the university regulations provide a proper complaints procedure: *M v London Guildhall University* [1998] ELR 149, CA.

[181] *Page v Hull University Visitor* [1993] 1 All ER 97 at 102, HL, per Lord Browne-Wilkinson.

[182] [1987] AC 795, [1987] 1 All ER 834, HL. See (1986) 136 NLJ 484, 519, 567, 571 and 665 (P M Smith); [1987] Pub L (Bridgid Hadfield); [1987] 46 CLJ 384 (C Lewis); (1987) 16 AALR 376 (G L Peiris); (1989) 8 CJQ 152 (G G Howells); (1998) Denning LJ 1 (M J Beloff).

[183] Loc cit at p 568.

Thus a matter or dispute is 'domestic' so as to be within the visitatorial jurisdiction if it involves questions relating to the internal laws of the foundation of which he is visitor or rights and duties derived from such internal laws. Conversely, an issue which turns on the enforcement of or adjudication on terms entered into between an individual and his employer, notwithstanding that they may also be in the relationship of member and corporation, and which involves no enforcement of or adjudication concerning the domestic laws of the foundation, is *ultra vires* the visitor's authority and is cognizable in a court of law or equity.

Subject to any special provisions in the statutes of the foundation, the ordinary duties and powers of the visitor concern the election and removal of members[184] of the corporation and its officers, the internal management of the corporation, construction of the statutes of the foundation, and judging claims and complaints by members. He is 'a judge, not for the single purpose of interpreting laws, but also for the application of laws, that are perfectly clear: requiring no interpretation; and, farther, for the interpretations of questions of fact; involving no interpretation of laws.'[185] It is his function to ensure due compliance with the terms of the charter and statutes. If there is a threat to do an act in breach of the charter or statutes it is the visitor's function to prohibit such breach.[186] His jurisdiction extends beyond members to other persons who claim rights under the domestic law.[187]

The jurisdiction covers all questions of disputed membership, including claims by persons to become members of the foundation, such as rejected candidates for fellowships,[188] and disputes where the issue is whether or not the person concerned is entitled to be reinstated or admitted to a university,[189] but does not otherwise extend to questions between the foundation and people outside it not arising under the domestic law.[190] It also covers academic matters such as the award of degrees and admission to courses, though when dealing in educational matters with actions properly taken within the structures and discretions approved under statutory process, visitors should respect the exercise of such discretions, rather than replacing them with their own views on matters of academic judgment.[191] Contrary to the view

---

184 This includes not only corporations, but all persons who can be described as members of the institution or as being on the foundation—*Hines v Birkbeck College* [1986] Ch 524, [1985] 3 All ER 156; *Thomas v University of Bradford*, supra, HL.

185 Per Sir Samuel Romilly in his argument in *Ex p Kirkby Ravensworth Hospital* (1808) 15 Ves 305 at 311, cited by Lord Griffiths in *Thomas v University of Bradford*, supra, HL, at 815, 842 and said to have long been accepted as authoritative.

186 *Pearce v University of Aston in Birmingham (No 2)* [1991] 2 All ER 469, Visitor.

187 *Oakes v Sidney Sussex College, Cambridge*, supra.

188 *R v Hertford College* (1878) 3 QBD 693, CA.

189 *Patel v University of Bradford Senate* [1978] 3 All ER 841; affd [1979] 2 All ER 582, CA—doubted as to first admission [1979] Pub L 209 (W T M Ricquier). See also *Casson v University of Aston in Birmingham* [1983] 1 All ER 88; *Thomas v University of Bradford*, supra, HL.

190 *Oakes v Sidney Sussex College, Cambridge*, supra; *Thomas v University of Bradford*, supra, HL.

191 *R v Council of Legal Education, ex p Eddis* (1995) 7 Admin LR 357; *O' v Inns of Court Law School* [1999] ELR 364, Visitor; *Jhamat v Inns of Court School of Law* [1999] ELR 450, Visitor; *R v University of Cambridge, ex p Persaud* [2001] ELR 64.

expressed by Lord Hailsham LC,[192] the House of Lords has now[193] said that there is no reason why the visitor should not award damages in an appropriate case.

If the matter falls within his jurisdiction, a visitor can be compelled to exercise it.[194] The exercise of the visitatorial power is a judicial act so that the dictates of natural justice, which require, for example, that both sides should be heard, must be observed.[195] Provided, however, that he acts judicially, the mode of the exercise of his power is left to the discretion of the visitor, who enjoys untrammelled jurisdiction to investigate and correct wrongs done in the administration of the internal law of the foundation to which he is appointed. He has a general power to right wrongs and to redress grievances. According to the circumstances he may act as a review court or an appellate tribunal, and he may, indeed should, investigate the basic facts to whatever depth is appropriate.[196]

Judicial review is not available to quash the decision of the visitor on the ground of an alleged error of law. The visitor is not applying the general law of the land but a peculiar, domestic law of which he is the sole arbiter and of which the courts have no cognisance. If the visitor has power under the regulating documents to enter into the adjudication of the dispute (that is, is acting within his jurisdiction in the narrow sense) he cannot err in law in reaching his decision since the general law is not the applicable law. Therefore he cannot be acting ultra vires and unlawfully by applying his view of the domestic law in reaching his decision. The court has no jurisdiction either to say that he erred in his application of the general law (since the general law is not applicable to the decision) or to reach a contrary view as to the effect of the domestic law (since the visitor is the sole judge of such domestic law).[197] Judicial review lies only where the visitor has acted outside his jurisdiction (in the narrow sense), or abused his powers, or acted in breach of the rules of natural justice.[198] The delegation of the powers of a university visitor to another could amount to a failure

---

[192] In *Casson v University of Aston in Birmingham*, supra, at 91.

[193] *Thomas v University of Bradford*, supra, HL. In line g6 on p 848 of the All ER report insert 'visitor' after 'university'. See *Re Macquarie University, ex p Ong* (1989) 17 NSWLR 113; *Bayley-Jones v University of Newcastle* (1990) 22 NSWLR 425.

[194] *Whiston v Dean and Chapter of Rochester* (1849) 7 Hare 532.

[195] *R v Bishop of Ely* (1788) 2 Term Rep 290.

[196] *R v University of London Visitor, ex p Vijayatunga*, supra, CA; *R v Cranfield University Senate, ex p Bashir* [1999] ELR 317, CA. See also *Thomas v University of Bradford (No 2)* [1992] 1 All ER 964, Visitor, noted (1992/93) 1 CLPR 73 (Suzy Hughes). But note *R v Visitors to the Inns of Court, ex p Calder* [1994] QB 1, [1993] 2 All ER 876, CA, where the decision was quashed on the ground that the visitors had misapprehended their role and had acted as a reviewing, rather than an appellate, tribunal, and see [1992] Pub L 41 (J H Baker).

[197] *R v Lord President of the Privy Council, ex p Page* [1993] AC 682, sub nom *Page v Hull University Visitor* [1993] 1 All ER 97, noted (1993) 109 LQR 155 (H W R Wade); *R v Visitor of the University of Leicester* [2003] EWCA Civ 1082, [2003] ELR 562; *Denman v Lord Chancellor's Department* [2004] EWHC 930 (Admin), [2004] ELR 484. See also (1995) 7 E & L 63 (J W Parlour and L R V Burwood).

[198] *Page v Hull University Visitor*, supra, HL, and see *R v Visitors to the Inns of Court, ex p Calder*, supra, CA; *Joseph v Council of Legal Education* [1994] ELR 407, CA (jurisdiction of visitor exclusive); *Ex p Toms, Latimer and Nightingale* (1994) Times, 5 May; (1993/94) 2 CLPR 103 (P M Smith).

on the visitor's part to exercise his jurisdiction fully and such a failure would be amenable to judicial review.[199]

Thus if by the statutes of the foundation he is to conduct a general visitation not more than once in five years, he has no power to visit more often. General visitation has been said to be at least obsolescent,[200] but a general visitor has a standing constant authority at all times to hear complaints and redress grievances of particular members of the foundation.[201] Apart from judicial review the courts have no power to interfere with the visitor acting within his jurisdiction, but statute may impinge on the situation. Thus if in proceedings under the Employment Rights Act 1996 a question arises concerning the interpretation or application of the internal laws of the university the proceedings will not be adjourned and the question will have to be resolved for the purpose of the case by the tribunal hearing the application.[202]

It should be added that if a corporation holds property as a trustee on a special trust, the court has jurisdiction in the ordinary way and the matter is outside the jurisdiction of the visitor.[203]

(ii) Higher Education Act 2004

The jurisdiction of the visitor in relation to disputes arising in a 'qualifying institution'[204] is considerably reduced by the provisions of the above Act.

(i) Student complaints. Part 2 of the Act provides for the setting up of a student complaints scheme for the review of a 'qualifying complaint'. This is widely defined in s 12 as—

a complaint about an act or omission of a qualifying institution which is made by a person—

(a) as a student or former student at that institution, or
(b) as a student or former student at another institution . . . undertaking a course of study, or programme of research, leading to the grant of one of the qualifying institution's awards.

This is subject to the important restriction that a complaint is not a qualifying complaint to the extent that it relates to matters of academic judgment.[205]

Complementarily to the scheme, s 20 provides that the visitor of a qualifying institution has no jurisdiction in respect of an application for admission to the qualifying institution as a student, or in respect of a complaint by a person referred to in (a) or (b) set out above.

---

[199] *R (Varma) v Visitor to Cranfield University* (2004) *Times*, 23 July.

[200] *Patel v University of Bradford Senate*, supra; per Megarry V-C at first instance at 846.

[201] *Philips v Bury* (1694) Carth 180, Holt KB 715.

[202] *Thomas v University of Bradford* [1987] AC 795, [1987] 1 All ER 834, HL.

[203] *Green v Rutherford* (1750) 1 Ves Sen 462 at 472; *Whiston v Dean and Chapter of Rochester*, supra; *Thomas v University of Bradford*, supra, HL.

[204] Defined in the Higher Education Act 2004, s 11 as including a university whose entitlement to grant awards is conferred or confirmed by an Act of Parliament, a Royal Charter, or an order made by the Privy Council under the Further and Higher Education Act 1992 s 76.

[205] Cf the cases cited at p 310, n 191, and text thereto.

(ii) Staff disputes. Section 46, which repeals and replaces s 206 of the Education Reform Act 1988, provides that the visitor of a qualifying institution has no jurisdiction in respect of—

(a) any dispute relating to a member of staff which concerns his appointment or employment or the termination of his appointment or employment,

(b) any other dispute between a member of staff and the qualifying institution in respect of which proceedings could be brought before any court or tribunal,[206] or

(c) any dispute as to the application of the statutes or other internal laws of the institution in relation to a matter falling within paragraph (a) or (b).

(iii) The Human Rights Act 1998

There is as yet no authority as to the effect on the visitational jurisdiction of the incorporation of Art 6(1) of the European Convention for the Protection of Human Rights and Fundamental Freedoms into English law, but it has been contended[207] that it is likely to have a highly significant impact on the role of the visitor in universities. The contentions are: first, that although a student will continue to be contractually obliged to take any complaint through the relevant university complaints procedures, any delay at a chartered university in organizing a hearing before the visitor will amount to a breach of Art 6(1) such as to enable an aggrieved student to take his case directly to court.

Secondly that, even if taken reasonably promptly, the visitor's decision will no longer be final. Recourse to the courts will lie not only for breaches of natural justice or acts in excess of jurisdiction, but also for any breach of ordinary public law principles.

Thirdly that, whether the student wishes to challenge the visitor's decision or goes directly to court the judge hearing the case will normally be obliged to hear evidence as to the substantive merits and factual basis of the case.

It may be added that a private law action may, perhaps, replace an application for judicial review, for s 8(2) of the Human Rights Act 1998 gives the court power to award damages against a university which issues an improper grade or delays for an unreasonable length of time in dealing with a student's complaint, if it can be shown that the student has suffered some loss as a result, provided that the claim is made in private law and not by way of an application for judicial review.[208] Further, by s 8(1) the court may grant such relief or remedy, or make such order, within its powers as it considers just and appropriate.

---

[206] In determining whether a dispute falls within (b) it is to be assumed that the visitor does not have jurisdiction to determine the dispute.

[207] See (1999) 11 E & L 165 (T Kaye); (2001) 13 E & L 279 (M Arthur).

[208] See *Moran v University College, Salford (No 2)* [1994] ELR 187.

(i) THE DIRECTOR OF PUBLIC PROSECUTIONS

Proceedings for certain specified offences may only be instigated by or with the consent of the Director of Public Prosecutions.[209] The offences specified relate to the omission of a registered charity's status on official publications,[210] supplying false or misleading information,[211] failure to comply with orders made by the Charity Commissioners,[212] failure to comply with requirements as to annual reports and annual returns,[213] and acting as a trustee while disqualified.[214]

3 REGISTRATION OF CHARITIES

(a) THE REGISTER OF CHARITIES

Section 3 of the Charities Act 1993, replacing provisions contained in the Charities Act 1960, provides that the Commissioners shall continue to keep a register of charities containing the name and such other particulars of, and information relating to the charity, as they think fit. The purposes of the register are to provide evidence of charitable status; to provide a way for charities to be accountable, for example, by making basic information publicly available; and to enable large charities to be actively monitored—the Charity Commission currently do this in relation to charities with an income or expenditure in excess of £10,000 pa.

If the Commissioners are satisfied[215] that a body seeking registration is established for purposes which are charitable in law, they are under a duty to register it as a charity. Registration is accordingly no evidence that the institution is efficiently and properly managed or that the trustees and servants of the charity are of good character.[216] The computerized register is to be open to public inspection in legible form at all reasonable times. It is now available on the internet.

It is the duty of the charity trustees of any charity which is neither registered nor excepted from registration to apply for it to be registered, and to supply all the documents and information required for this purpose.[217] Though no time limit is specified before which the duty must be carried out, any person who makes default may be required by order of the commissioners to make it good, and failure to obey their order is punishable as a contempt of court.[218] The same sanction applies to the further duty of the charity trustees of any institution which is for the time being registered to notify the Commissioners if it ceases to exist, or if there is any change in

---

209 Charities Act 1993, s 94.   210 See ibid, s 5(4), (5) and p 317, infra.
211 See ibid, s 11 and p 298, supra.   212 See ibid, s 18(14) and p 299, supra.
213 See ibid, s 49 and pp 320, 321, infra.   214 See ibid, s 73(1) and p 292, supra.
215 Section 10 authorizes exchange of information between the Commissioners and government departments, local authorities, constables and any other body or person discharging functions of a public nature.
216 See the Press Notice relating to the Unification Church reprinted in the Report for 1982, Appendix C.
217 Charities Act 1993, s 3(7)(a).   218 Ibid, ss 87 and 88.

its trusts, or in the particulars of it entered in the register.[219] The commissioners are themselves under a duty[220] to remove from the register any institution which no longer appears to them to be a charity,[221] and also any charity which ceases to exist or does not operate.[222]

(b) EXCEPTIONS FROM REQUIREMENT OF REGISTRATION

The excepted charities fall into four categories:[223]

(a) Exempt charities.[224]

(b) Any charity which is excepted by order or regulations. Regulations have been made excepting all universities which are not exempt charities;[225] all voluntary schools, within the meaning of the Education Acts 1944–1973, being charities and having no permanent endowment other than the premises of, or connected with, the school;[226] charities for the promotion of the efficiency of the armed forces,[227] certain religious charities,[228] and charities comprising funds, not being permanent endowments, belonging to units of the Boy Scouts Association or the Girl Guides Association, which are being accumulated for the purposes of the unit and which produce an income of more than £15 a year.[229]

(c) Any charity having neither any permanent endowment, nor the use and occupation of any land, and whose income from all sources does not in aggregate amount to more than £1,000 a year.[230] The conditions are cumulative and must all be fulfilled if the charity is to be excepted. The phrase 'permanent endowment' is somewhat misleading for, as defined by ss 97 and 96(3) it does not necessarily mean that the endowment must be retained as capital in perpetuity. A charity is deemed to have a permanent endowment for the purposes of the Act unless all the property held for the purposes of the charity may be expended for those purposes without distinction between capital and income. If capital is subject to restrictions not attached to income, the charity has a permanent endowment even though the capital may be entirely expended in appropriate circumstances.

---

[219] Ibid, s 3(7)(b). This provision does not apply to schemes for the administration of a charity made otherwise than by the court: and if a relevant document is already in the possession of the Commissioners it suffices to refer to it: s 3(11).

[220] Ibid, s 3(4).   [221] See the Report for 1967. Appendix D, Part II.

[222] It is not clear when a charity can be said not to operate. Presumably it does not cover the case where the trustees fail to act, where the proper course is merely to compel them to do so, or have new trustees appointed who will.

[223] Charities Act 1993, s 3(5). See [1988] Sol Jo Charities Supp 14 (J M Fryer).

[224] See chapter 13, subsection 2(i)(iv), p 286, supra.   [225] SI 1966/965.

[226] SI 1960/2366.   [227] SI 1965/1056. The regulation has certain exceptions.

[228] SI 1996/180 (expiry date deferred to 1 October 2007: SI 2002/1598).   [229] SI 1961/1044.

[230] The amount may be altered by statutory instrument: s 3(12).

(d) No charity is required to be registered in respect of any registered place of worship.[231] This means in effect the meeting-places, recorded by the Registrar-General of Births, Deaths and Marriages, for the religious worship of Protestant Dissenters or other Protestants, Roman Catholics, Jews and any other body or denomination of persons other than the Church of England,[232] so long as it continues to be used bona fide as a place of religious worship. The exception extends to ancillary premises held on the same trusts as the meeting-place so recorded such as a forecourt, yard, garden, burial-ground, vestry or caretaker's house and, on a certificate of the Commissioners, a Sunday-school house or building.

An excepted charity, other than an exempt charity, may be entered on the register if the Commission are satisfied that there is a public interest in their registration, at the request of the charity, for instance to publicize its work or to establish its charitable status, but may at any time, and must at the request of the charity, be removed from the register.

The Charity Commission and the Home Office have issued a joint consultation document[233] on the question whether the current arrangements for voluntary registration should be changed.

(c) EFFECT OF REGISTRATION

Registration of an institution has the effect that for all purposes other than rectification of the register it is conclusively presumed to be or have been a charity at any time when it is or was on the register of charities.[234] To some extent the presumption operates retrospectively. Thus in *Re Murawski's Will Trusts*[235] the question was whether at the date of the testatrix's death in 1964 the Bleakholt Animal Sanctuary was a charity. The Sanctuary was not registered as a charity until 1968. On evidence that at all material times before and after registration its objects were identical, the court felt bound to hold that the Sanctuary was a charity at the date of death. Provision is of course made for claims and objections to registration, on referral of registration, being adjudicated upon. This is done by the Commissioners with an appeal to the High Court.[236] And any question affecting the registration or removal from the register of an institution may be reconsidered by the Commissioners on a change of circumstances.[237]

---

[231] For a definition, by reference to the Places of Worship Registration Act 1855 and the Charitable Trusts Act 1853, see Charities Act 1993, s 3(14).

[232] It will be remembered that a corporation in the Church of England is not a charity for the purpose of the Act—s 96(2) discussed in chapter 13, section 2(i)(iii) supra.

[233] Available on the internet. The consultation period ended on 16 October 2000.

[234] Charities Act 1993, s 4(1).   [235] [1971] 2 All ER 328.

[236] See s 4(2)–(4). (1993) 1 Dec Ch Com 1.

[237] Ibid, s 4(5). See (1983) 80 LSG 2142, (1984) 81 LSG 3475 and [1985] Sol Jo 880 (J M Fryer). On 31 March 2004 there were 188,739 registered charities, 165,131 being main charities, the remainder being

Conversely it should be observed that refusal of registration by the Commissioners on the ground that the purposes of an organization are not charitable does not conclusively establish that the organization is not charitable. Thus the refusal by the Commissioners to register the Over Seventies Housing Association did not prevent that body from arguing that it was a charity and therefore entitled to rating relief, though the argument in fact failed.[238]

(d) CHANGE OF NAME

The Commissioners have power to direct a registered charity, other than an exempt charity,[239] within 12 months of registration, to change its name on the ground that it is the same as, or too like, that of another charity;[240] that it may mislead the public as to the true nature of the purposes of the charity or of the activities it carries on; that it includes any specified word or expression whose inclusion is likely to mislead the public as to the status of the charity;[241] that it is likely to give the impression that the charity is connected in some way with the government, a local authority, or with any other body of persons or any individual, when that is not the case; or that the name is in the opinion of the Commissioners offensive.[242]

(e) STATUS TO APPEAR ON OFFICIAL PUBLICATION ETC

Where the gross income of a registered charity in its last financial year exceeded £10,000, the fact that it is a registered charity must be stated on all official publications including appeal documents, cheques, orders for goods, bills, receipts and invoices.[243] There seems to be no reason why these requirements should not apply to charitable companies which, however, are covered by more stringent requirements. The overlap is presumably inadvertent.[244]

---

subsidiaries, branches or constituents of group charities. During the year there were 6,234 new registrations and 5,210 charities were removed from the register. Nearly 25% of registered charities are for the relief of poverty. The other heads over 10% are education; social welfare and culture; health and sickness; and children, young people and students. Appeals to the High Court are rare.

[238] *Over Seventies Housing Association v Westminster City Council* (1974) 230 EG 1593.

[239] Charities Act 1993, s 6(9).   [240] For specified words and expressions see SI 1992/1901.

[241] See (1995) 4 Dec Ch Com 23; (1996/7) 4 CLPR 1 (Debra Morris).

[242] Charities Act 1993, s 6. Consequential provisions in the case where the charity is a company are contained in s 7. Where a charity operates under more than one name, all will be registered: see (1995) 4 Dec Ch Com 22.

[243] Ibid, s 5(1)–(3); SI 1995/2696 increasing original limit. Breach of these provisions is an offence: s 5(4), (5).

[244] See ibid, s 68 discussed in section 2(b)(iv), supra, p 296. Unlike s 68, s 5 does not cover business letters (other than those which solicit money or other property), or conveyances.

(f) REVIEW OF THE REGISTER[245]

The Charity Commission are carrying out a rolling review of the register. They have the same power as the court when determining whether an organization has charitable status and the same powers to take into account changing social and economic circumstances—whether to recognize a purpose as charitable for the first time or to recognize that a purpose has ceased to be charitable. The Commission interprets and applies the law in accordance with the principles laid down by the courts, to which an appeal may be made against the Commission's decision.[246]

Thus, on the one hand, in *Re Stephens*[247] it had been held that teaching shooting was a charitable purpose as promoting the security of the nation and the defence of the realm. On this basis a number of civilian rifle and pistol clubs were registered as charities. Following the Falklands and Gulf conflicts it was seen that the skills required of modern uniformed personnel were quite different from those required when *Re Stephens* was decided in 1892 in the immediate aftermath of the First Boer War, and clubs (whose principal concern was the benefit of members through recreational and sporting shooting) were in no sense a reserve for the armed forces. Most were accordingly removed from the register.

On the other hand in *Re Strakosch*[248] it had been held both that the appeasement of racial feelings between different ethnic groups in a community was a political purpose and also that such a purpose was too vague and might include very wide objects some plainly not charitable. In their Report for 1983 the Commission took the view that the authority of that case had been undermined by the race relations legislation, and accepted that promoting good race relations, endeavouring to eliminate discrimination on grounds of race and encouraging equality of opportunity between persons of different racial groups are prima facie charitable purposes.

4 CHARITY ACCOUNTS, AUDIT, ANNUAL REPORTS AND ANNUAL RETURNS

(a) GENERAL PROVISIONS[249]

(i) Duties in relation to accounts

Charity trustees must ensure that accounting records are kept in respect of the charity which are sufficient to show and explain all the charity's transactions and to disclose

---

[245] See RR1 and RR6. See also (2001) 32 T & ELJ 6 (Sarah Chiappini); ibid 10 (Catriona Syed).

[246] See RR1a 'Recognising New Charitable Purposes'; RR2 'Promotion of Urban and Rural Regeneration'; RR12 'Promotion of Human Rights'. See (2001) 21 LS 36 (P W Edge and Joan M Loughrey).

[247] (1892) 8 TLR 792.   [248] [1949] Ch 529, [1949] 2 All ER 6, CA.

[249] See CC8 and 61, and the *Statement of Recommended Practice* (SORP 2005) issued by the Charity Commissioners.

at any time, with reasonable accuracy, the financial position of the charity at that time.[250] They must prepare in respect of each financial year a statement of account complying with prescribed requirements,[251] though there are less stringent requirements where the charity's gross income in any financial year does not exceed £100,000.[252] Accounting records and statement of accounts must be preserved for six years from the end of the financial year of the charity.[253]

(ii) Annual audit or examination of accounts[254]

A distinction is made according to the size of the charity. If the charity's gross income or total expenditure in the relevant year[255] exceeds £250,000[256] the accounts must be audited by a person who is eligible for appointment as a company auditor,[257] or is a member of a specified body[258] and is under the rules of that body eligible for appointment as auditor of the charity.[259] In the case of smaller charities the trustees may elect for such an audit, but it suffices if the accounts are examined by an independent person who is reasonably believed by the trustees to have the requisite ability and practical experience to carry out a competent examination of the accounts.[260] Very small charities, that is, where the gross income or total expenditure in the relevant year does not exceed £10,000, are exempted from the requirement of having their annual accounts audited or examined.[261] If the requirement of an audit (or examination) has not been complied with within 10 months from the end of the relevant year, the Commissioners may order an audit (even in the case of a smaller charity),[262] at the expense of the charity trustees personally.[263]

(iii) Annual reports

Where in any financial year of a charity its gross income or total expenditure exceeds £10,000, the charity trustees must within 10 months[264] from the end of the charity's financial year transmit to the Commissioners an annual report on the activities of the charity, with a statement of accounts and the report of the auditor or independent examiner, as the case may be, attached. Regulations may prescribe what the reports

---

[250] Charities Act 1993, s 41(1), (2).   [251] Ibid, s 42(1), (2).

[252] Ibid, s 42(3). See SI 1995/2696 increasing original limit. As to the meaning of 'income', see (1993/94) 2 CLPR 111 (C McCall). The prescribed requirements are set out in SI 2005/572, which also defines 'financial year'.

[253] Ibid, ss 41(3), 42(4). By ss 41(4), 42(5) the obligation continues on the last charity trustees of a charity which has ceased to exist within six years unless the Commissioners consent in writing to the records being destroyed or otherwise disposed of.

[254] The duties of an auditor or independent examiner are set out in SI 1995/2724 as amended.

[255] Or in either of the two financial years of the charity immediately preceding the relevant year: ibid, s 43(1).

[256] Limit increased from £100,000 by SI 1995/2696.   [257] See the Companies Act 1989, s 25.

[258] Ie under regulations made by the Secretary of State under the Charities Act 1993, s 44.

[259] Ibid, s 43(2).

[260] Ibid, s 43(3). As to Commissioners' directions and guidance see s 43(7) and CC63.

[261] Deregulation and Contracting Out Act 1994, s 28.

[262] Ibid, s 43(4), (5).   [263] Ibid, s 43(6). In default, from the funds of the charity.

[264] Unless the Commissioners allow a longer period.

should contain.[265] Smaller charities may be required to transmit a report on the request of the Commissioners.

The annual reports and documents attached thereto are kept by the Commissioners for such period as they think fit, during which time they are open to public inspection at all reasonable times.[266]

(b) SPECIAL PROVISIONS RELATING TO PARTICULAR KINDS OF CHARITIES

(i) Exempt charities

Charity trustees of these charities are required to keep proper books of account and to prepare consecutive statements of account consisting on each occasion of an income and expenditure account relating to a period of not more than 15 months and a balance sheet relating to the end of that period. The documents must be preserved for at least six years, unless the charity ceases to exist and the Commissioners consent in writing to their being destroyed or otherwise disposed of.[267]

None of the duties discussed in (a) above applies to exempt charities which are subject to adequate alternative supervision.[268]

(ii) Unregistered charities within s 3(5)(c)

These are subject to the duty to keep accounting records, and to prepare annual statements of account. They are not however subject to the provisions relating to an annual audit or the submission of annual reports.[269] Other charities which are not required to be registered and are not registered (other than exempt charities) may be requested by the Commissioners to provide annual reports.[270]

(iii) A charity which is a company

Here the company law provisions relating to accounts apply, and not the provisions in relation to accounts and audit discussed in (a) above.[271] Further the Commissioners may require that the condition and accounts of the charity be investigated by a qualified auditor, who is entitled to access to all relevant documents and to require statements from the charity trustees and its officers and employees. The auditor reports to the Commissioners, with a copy to the charity trustees.[272]

The duty to transmit annual reports applies to a charity which is a company.[273]

---

[265] Ibid, s 45, as amended by the Deregulation and Contracting Out Act 1994, s 29; SI 1995/2724. Persistent default in transmitting a report is an offence: s 49 and see Section 2(i), p 314, supra.

[266] Ibid, ss 45(6); 47(1).   [267] Charities Act 1993, s 46(1), (2).   [268] Ibid, s 46(1).

[269] Ibid, s 46(3).   [270] Ibid, s 46(4)–(8).

[271] Ibid, ss 41(5), 42(7), 43(1). See the Companies Act 1985, Part VII as amended (1994) 138 Sol Jo Spring Charity Supp 32 (Pesh Framjee).

[272] Charities Act 1993, s 69. The expenses of the audit are paid by the Commissioners.

[273] Modified in that instead of the report of the auditor or independent examiner there must be attached a copy of the charity's annual accounts prepared under Part VII of the Companies Act 1985, and the auditor's report thereon: Charities Act 1993, s 45(5).

(c) PUBLIC RIGHT TO A COPY OF CHARITY'S ACCOUNTS

The charity trustees of every charity must, on written request, provide a copy of the charity's most recent accounts to any person requesting them, subject to payment of a reasonable fee.[274]

(d) ANNUAL RETURNS

Unless the Commissioners dispense with the requirement, every registered charity must, within 10 months from the end of the charity's financial year, submit an annual return in the form and containing the information prescribed by regulations made by the Commissioners.[275] This requirement does not apply in relation to any financial year of a charity in which neither the gross income nor the total expenditure exceeds £10,000.[276]

5 SCHEMES

(a) GENERAL

As we have seen,[277] a charitable trust does not fail for uncertainty, and an order for the direction of a scheme is the device available to the court under its inherent jurisdiction to remedy uncertainty either in the substance of the trust[278] or the mode of administration, to get over some administrative difficulty or to amend the rules of the charity.[279] A scheme is not necessarily, or even generally, a scheme for the application of property cy-près,[280] under which, as will be seen later,[281] the purpose of a trust may be varied. It may be directed where the exact ambit of the charitable purpose is not clear,[282] where the trustees are dead,[283] or disclaim or refuse to act,[284] or have misapplied the trust property,[285] where the income of the charity has substantially increased,[286]

---

[274] Ibid, s 47(2), (3). Persistent default in relation to this provision is an offence: s 49, and see subsection 2(i), p 314, supra.

[275] Ibid, s 48. The Commissioners may allow a longer period. Persistent default in transmitting the return is an offence: s 49.

[276] Deregulation and Contracting Out Act 1994, s 30.   [277] Chapter 13, subsection 1(a), p 240, supra.

[278] There must be a trust—*Re Bennett* [1960] Ch 18, [1959] 3 All ER 295, and supra, p 306.

[279] *Re Gott* [1944] Ch 193, [1944] 1 All ER 293. The details of the scheme will be settled by the Master in Chambers.

[280] *Re Robinson* [1931] 2 Ch 122. As to cy-près see section 6, p 325, infra.   [281] Infra, p 325, et seq.

[282] *Re White* [1893] 2 Ch 41, CA; *Re Gott*, supra.

[283] *Moggridge v Thackwell* (1803) 7 Ves 36 (affd (1807) 13 Ves 416, HL); *Re Willis* [1921] 1 Ch 44, CA. Cf *Marsh v A-G* (1860) 2 John & H 61.

[284] *Reeve v A-G* (1843) 3 Hare 191; *Re Lawton* [1936] 3 All ER 378; *Re Lysaught* [1966] Ch 191, [1965] 2 All ER 888.

[285] *A-G v Coopers' Co* (1812) 19 Ves 187.   [286] *Re Campden Charities* (1881) 18 Ch D 310, CA.

and in other cases where it is an appropriate remedy.[287] But sometimes even a charitable trust cannot be saved by a scheme. Thus 'if it is of the essence of a trust that the trustees selected by the settlor and no-one else shall act as the trustees of it and those trustees cannot or will not undertake the office, the trust must fail.'[288] The terms of particular schemes vary considerably. Some are very simple and do no more, for example, than change the name of a charity or set up a new body of trustees to administer it, while others are long and complicated and contain detailed provisions for the future regulation of the charity. The court has, of course, a discretion whether to order a scheme or not, even where the effect would be to defeat a gift over; however it refused to do so in *Re Hanbey's Will Trusts*[289] where the proposed scheme, in defeating the gift over, would defeat the intention of the testator rather than give effect to it.

As we have seen, the Commissioners have the same power as the court for establishing a scheme, though generally only on the application of the charity.[290] Where a court directs a scheme for the administration of a charity to be established, the court may refer the matter to the Commissioners for them to prepare or settle a scheme and the court order may direct such scheme to come into effect without further reference to the court.[291] Further, where in the case of a charity, other than an exempt charity, the Commissioners are satisfied that the charity trustees ought to apply for a scheme, but have unreasonably refused or neglected to do so, and the Commissioners have given the charity trustees an opportunity to make representations to them, the Commissioners may proceed as if an application for a scheme had been made by the charity.[292] Their power under this last provision does not, however, enable them to alter the purposes of a charity, unless 40 years have elapsed from the date of its foundation.

(b) STATUTORY EXTENSIONS OF THE JURISDICTION

(i) The inherent jurisdiction of the court over charities founded by royal charter was limited, though the limits were not altogether clear.[293] Now it is provided[294] that a

---

287 Eg *Re Robinson* [1923] 2 Ch 332 (removing 'abiding' condition that a black gown should be worn in the pulpit); *Re Dominion Students' Hall Trust* [1947] Ch 183 (removing colour bar from trust for Dominion students); *Re Lysaght*, supra (removing provision for religious discrimination); *Re J W Laing Trust* [1984] 1 All ER 50 (obligation to distribute whole of capital and income within 10 years of settlor's death removed where trust fund set up in 1922 with £15,000 and now worth £24m). See also [1987] NLJ Christmas Appeals Supp viii (P Luxton) who argues that the courts have sometimes, and in particular in relation to public schools, in effect varied the purpose of a trust by treating it as a matter of an administrative nature.

288 Per Buckley J in *Re Lysaght* [1966] Ch 191 at 207, [1965] 2 All ER 888 at 896.

289 [1956] Ch 264, [1955] 3 All ER 874.

290 See p 297, supra. 650 schemes were made in the year to March 2001. A scheme may, within limits, confer a power on trustees enabling amendments to the governing document of a charity to be made by the trustees themselves: (1995) 3 Dec Ch Com 29.

291 Section 16(2).   292 Section 16(6).

293 *Re Whitworth Art Gallery Trusts* [1958] Ch 461, [1958] 1 All ER 176; cf *Re Royal Society's Charitable Trusts* [1956] Ch 87, [1955] 3 All ER 14.

294 Section 15(1).

scheme relating to such a charity or the administration of its property may be made by the court[295] notwithstanding that it cannot take effect without the alteration of the charter. In such case the scheme must be so framed as not to come into effect unless or until Her Majesty thinks fit to make an appropriate amendment to the charter.[296]

(ii) The inherent jurisdiction of the court over a charity regulated by statute is also limited in a somewhat similar way to that over charities founded by royal charter.[297] The court[298] has now been given statutory jurisdiction with respect to certain charities relating to allotments, seamen's and regimental funds, and some educational and local charities.[299]

(iii) In the case of other charities regulated by statute, the Commissioners, but not the court, are now empowered,[300] if they consider that a scheme should be established, to settle a scheme to which effect may be given by order of the Secretary of State made by statutory instrument.[301] The Commissioners can only proceed under these provisions on the like application as would be required if they were proceeding (without an order of the court) under s 16.[302]

(iv) Temporary cy-près scheme. Under s 17(8) where the Commissioners are satisfied:

i   that the whole of the income of a charity cannot in existing circumstances be effectively applied for the purpose of the charity; and

ii   that, if those circumstances continue, a scheme might be made for applying the surplus cy-près; and

iii that it is for any reason not yet desirable to make such a scheme;

they may authorize the charity trustees to apply a limited[303] amount of income for any purposes for which it might be made applicable by a cy-près scheme.

(v) A special scheme-making power is conferred on the Commissioners by the Reverter of Sites Act 1987 in relation to sites conveyed to trustees for specific purposes under Acts such as the School Sites Act 1841, where the site has ceased to be used for

---

[295] Or, in a proper case, by the Commissioners acting under s 16(1).

[296] By Order in Council—s 15(2). See eg SI 1999/656 and 667.

[297] *London Parochial Charities' Trustees v A-G* [1955] 1 All ER 1; *Re Shipwrecked Fishermen and Mariners' Royal Benevolent Society Charity* [1959] Ch 220, [1958] 3 All ER 465.

[298] And, in a proper case, the Commissioners—s 16(1).

[299] Section 15(3) and Sch 4, as amended by the Education Act 1996, Sch 37, para 121.

[300] By s 17. The procedure set out in this section also applies where the Commissioners wish to insert some provision in a scheme which otherwise would be beyond their powers, or where in any case it is proper for the scheme to be subject to Parliamentary review. See eg Reports for 1977, paras 132–145 and 1983, paras 61–72. The provisions for publicity in s 20 apply to proceedings under s 17—see p 300, supra.

[301] The most recent are SIs 1995/1047 and SI 1997/2240.   [302] See pp 298, 322, supra.

[303] Up to £300 income accrued before the date of the order and up to £100 out of income accruing in each of the next three years: s 17(9).

the particular purpose and the person to whom the site should revert cannot be ascertained.[304]

(c) COMMON INVESTMENT SCHEMES AND COMMON DEPOSIT SCHEMES

It is a frequent occurrence for a single body of trustees, particularly of a large charity, to hold and administer a number of separate funds associated with the main charity, each fund being held on separate (though possibly similar or even identical) trusts, and legally constituting a separate charity. Before the Charities Act 1960 the funds of such separate trusts had in general to be kept separate, even though held by the same trustees and held on similar trusts. Exceptionally particular statutes[305] authorized particular bodies to amalgamate various trust funds held by them and to administer the amalgam as a single fund, and the court and the Commissioners sometimes made schemes, known as pooling schemes, to the like effect, but this was only possible where the separate trusts were administered by a single body of trustees.[306] Common investment schemes were introduced by the 1960 Act and the relevant provisions are now contained in s 24 of the 1993 Act which authorizes the court or the Commissioners where two or more bodies of trustees wish to unite in pooling the endowments of the charities which they administer, to make and bring into effect schemes for the establishment of common investment funds under trusts which provide:

(i)   for property transferred to the fund by or on behalf of a charity participating in the scheme to be invested under the control of trustees appointed to manage the fund; and

(ii)   for the participating charities to be entitled . . . to the capital and income of the fund in shares determined by reference to the amount or value of the property transferred to it by or on behalf of each of them and to the value of the fund at the time of the transfer.[307]

Such a scheme may involve the appointment of an entirely distinct body of trustees to manage the pooled endowments. A common investment scheme may be made on the application of any two or more charities[308]—it will be remembered that for the purposes of the Act each separate trust fund is prima facie a separate charity,[309] even where the trustees are the same persons[310]—and the scheme may make provision for,

---

[304] See Report for 1987, App C; Report for 1988, paras 78–82. See also *Re Picklenash School, Newport* (1993) unreported, but noted [1994] NLJ Charities App Supp 23 (H Picarda).

[305] Eg Liverpool University Act 1931; Birmingham University Act 1948. Cf Administration of Justice Acts 1965 and 1982 and SI 1965/1467 as amended by 1972/528.

[306] *Re Royal Society's Charitable Trusts* [1956] Ch 87, [1955] 3 All ER 14.

[307] See (1996/7) 4 CLPR 21 (R Marlow).

[308] All charities have power to participate in common investment schemes, unless expressly excluded by the trust instrument—s 24(7).

[309] See chapter 13, subsection 2(i)(ii), p 285, supra.

[310] *Re University of London Charitable Trusts* [1964] Ch 282, [1963] 3 All ER 859.

and for all matters connected with, the establishment, investment, management and winding up of the common investment fund.[311] It may provide for a charity to deposit sums on such terms as to repayment and interest as may be set out in the scheme.[312] The common investment fund is itself deemed for all purposes to be a charity, and if the scheme admits only exempt charities, the fund is an exempt charity for the purposes of the Act.[313] The Commissioners have indicated that they will not be willing to make such schemes involving two or more bodies of trustees, unless there is some nexus, either geographical or functional, between the participating charities.[314]

Common deposit schemes were introduced by the 1992 Act and the provisions are now contained in s 25 of the 1993 Act. It provides:

(a) for sums to be deposited by or on behalf of a charity participating in the scheme and invested under the control of trustees appointed to manage the fund, and

(b) for any such charity to be entitled to repayment of any sums so deposited and to interest thereon at a rate determined under the scheme.[315]

With minor modifications[316] the provisions of s 24 are incorporated in s 25.

The provisions of the Trustee Act 2000 relating to investments; the acquisition of land; and agents, nominees and custodians do not apply to trustees managing a fund under a common investment scheme or a common deposit scheme.[317]

6 THE CY-PRÈS DOCTRINE

(a) GENERAL POSITION[318]

In the case of a private trust, if the trust fails the beneficial interest results to the settlor or testator. This may be the position also in the case of a charitable trust, though in practice the trust property is commonly saved for charity by the cy-près doctrine. Where this doctrine applies, even though the particular charitable trust fails, the trust property is applied for other charitable purposes cy-près, that is as near as possible,[319]

---

[311] Section 24(4).   [312] Section 24(5).   [313] Section 24(8).

[314] Reports of the Charity Commissioners for 1962 and 1963, paras 48 and 46 respectively.

[315] Section 35(1).

[316] Different paragraphs are substituted for sub-s 4(*b*), (*c*) and sub-s (5) does not apply: s 25(2), (3).

[317] Trustee Act 2000, s 38: there is an exception in s 38(*a*) in relation to a common investment fund.

[318] For a review of cases in other common law jurisdictions see (1972) 1 AALR 101 (L A Sheridan), and for comparison with the law in the USA see [1987] NLJ Annual Charities Review 34 (P Luxton). Text below cited *Re Fitzpatrick* (1984) 6 DLR (4th) 644. See also (1993/94) 2 CLPR 182 (L A Sheridan); (1995/6) 3 CLPR 9 (Jean Warburton).

[319] *Re Prison Charities* (1873) LR 16 Eq 129; but the cy-près application may still be made even though there is no possible object closely resembling the one that has failed—*A-G v Ironmongers Co* (1841) Cr & Ph 208; affd (1844) 10 Cl & Fin 908, HL. Chesterman, *Charities, Trusts and Social Welfare*, pp 225–227, argues that s 13 has, by implication, altered the meaning of cy-près to purposes that are suitable and effective having regard inter alia to the spirit of the gift.

to the original purposes which cannot be carried out. The doctrine applies equally to an incorporated charity.[320] The procedure is for the establishment of a scheme by the court or the Commissioners.[321] There are one, and often two, conditions that have to be satisfied in order for the doctrine to apply, and these, as affected by the relevant provisions of the Charities Act 1993, are considered below. The Act now imposes a statutory duty on the trustees of a charitable trust to take steps, in an appropriate case, for trust property to be applied cy-près.[322]

Before considering the cy-près doctrine in detail, one particular situation should be mentioned. Where before the Perpetuities and Accumulations Act 1964, there was a gift to charity for a limited period only, at the end of the period the undisposed interest resulted to the grantor, notwithstanding the grantor had in fact purported to make some disposition over, if this was void for perpetuity. There was no case for cy-près application.[323] There is still no case for cy-près application, and there will still be a resulting trust, unless the case falls within s 12 of the Perpetuities and Accumulations Act 1964, which provides that if and when it appears that the event which might cause the interest to determine must occur, if at all, outside the perpetuity period ascertained in accordance with the Act, the resulting trust becomes void and the determinable interest becomes absolute,[324] whether or not it is followed by a gift over.

(b) IMPOSSIBILITY OR IMPRACTICABILITY

Before the Charities Act 1960 the rule was that cy-près application was only possible where it was impossible or impracticable to carry out the declared trust. The rule covered both the case where the declared trust was initially impossible,[325] and the case of supervening impossibility,[326] and also cases where there was a surplus of funds after

---

[320] *Liverpool and District Hospital for Diseases of the Heart v A-G* [1981] Ch 193, [1981] 1 All ER 994 and see p 293, supra.

[321] Generally the Commissioners—s 33(3) discussed at p 306, supra.

[322] Section 13(5). The duty was previously proclaimed by Lord Simonds in *National Anti-Vivisection Society v IRC* [1948] AC 31 at 74, [1947] 2 All ER 217 at 238, HL.

[323] *Re Rendell* (1888) 38 Ch D 213; *Re Blunt's Trusts* [1904] 2 Ch 767; *Re Cooper's Conveyance Trusts* [1956] 3 All ER 28. Contrast *Re Bowen* [1893] 2 Ch 491; *Re Peel's Release* [1921] 2 Ch 218, and see (1961) 25 Conv 56 (J D Davies).

[324] See (1964) 80 LQR 486 at 527 (Morris and Wade). The resulting trust or possibility of reverter will still be valid if the determining event in fact happens within the perpetuity period and the same would be true of an express gift over.

[325] Eg *Biscoe v Jackson* (1887) 35 Ch D 460, CA—trust to establish a soup kitchen and cottage hospital in Shoreditch, but no land available for the purpose. An unusual case of initial impracticability was *Re Lysaght* [1966] Ch 191, [1965] 2 All ER 888, where insistence on the provision for religious discrimination would have resulted in the trustee disclaiming the trusteeship. This would have occasioned complete failure of the trust as it was the exceptional case where the trust was conditional on acceptance of the office by the named trustee. See also *Harris v Skevington* [1978] 1 NSWLR 176, where the legacy was held to be impractical and void because the donee by its constitution had no power to effectuate the particular charitable intention.

[326] Eg *A-G v Ironmongers Co* (1841) Cr & Ph 208; affd, sub nom *Ironmongers Co v A-G* (1844) 10 Cl & Fin 908, HL—trust for redemption of Barbary slaves.

the particular charitable purpose had been fulfilled.[327] Although impossibility and impracticability were generously construed,[328] the court had no jurisdiction to apply cy-près so long as any lawful object of the testator's bounty was available, however inexpedient such object might appear to the court as compared with other objects, and Romilly MR pointed out[329] that in several cases the court had considered itself bound to carry into effect 'charities of the most useless description'.

The old rule was considerably modified by s 13(1) of the Charities Act 1960, now replaced without amendment by s 13(1) of the 1993 Act which provides that, subject to any other necessary conditions being fulfilled, cy-près application may be directed in any of five sets of circumstances, namely:

(a) where the original purposes,[330] in whole or in part—
   (i) have been as far as may be fulfilled; or
   (ii) cannot be carried out, or not according to the directions given[331] and to the spirit of the gift; or
(b) where the original purposes provide a use for part only of the property available by virtue or the gift; or
(c) where the property available by virtue of the gift and other property applicable for similar purposes can be more effectively used in conjunction, and to that end can suitably, regard being had to the spirit of the gift, be made applicable to common purposes; or
(d) where the original purposes were laid down by reference to an area which then was but has since ceased to be a unit for some other purpose, or by reference to a class of persons or to an area which has for any reason since ceased to be suitable, regard being had to the spirit of the gift, or to be practical in administering the gift;[332] or
(e) where the original purposes, in whole or in part, have, since they were laid down—
   (i) been adequately provided for by other means;[333] or
   (ii) ceased, as being useless or harmful to the community or for other reasons, to be in law charitable; or
   (iii) ceased in any other way to provide a suitable and effective method of using the

---

[327] *Re Monk* [1927] 2 Ch 197, CA; *Re North Devon and West Somerset Relief Fund Trusts* [1953] 2 All ER 1032; *Re Raine* [1956] Ch 417, [1956] 1 All ER 355.

[328] Eg *Re Dominion Students' Hall Trust* [1947] Ch 183 (removing colour bar from trust for Dominion students); *Re Canada Trust Co and Ontario Human Rights Commission* (1990) 69 DLR (4th) 321 (Ont CA); *Toronto Aged Men's and Women's Homes v The Loyal True Blue and Orange Home* (2004) 68 OR (3d) 777—an unusual application of the doctrine.

[329] In *Philpott v St George's Hospital* (1859) 27 Beav 107 at 111; *Re Weir Hospital* [1910] 2 Ch 124, CA.

[330] Where the application of the trust property has been altered or regulated by a scheme or otherwise, 'original purposes' means the purposes for which the property is for the time being applicable—s 13(3).

[331] See *Re J W Laing Trust* [1984] Ch 143, [1984] 1 All ER 50, discussed [1985] Conv 313 (P Luxton).

[332] This paragraph applied *Peggs v Lamb* [1994] Ch 172, [1994] 2 All ER 15.

[333] Eg where the object of the charity has become the statutory responsibility of the central or local government authorities.

property[334] available by virtue of the gift, regard being had to the spirit of the gift.[335]

The court is also given a limited power to enlarge the area of a charity's operations, without any need to show that any of the above conditions are fulfilled.[336] There has been little authority on this section, but it was held in *Re Lepton's* Charity[337] that, in relation to a trust for payment of a fixed annual sum out of the income of a fund to charity A and payment of the residue of that income to charity B, the 'original purposes' referred to in the section should be construed as referring to the trust as a whole. It has been held that mere sale of charitable property and reinvestment of the proceeds in the acquisition of other property to be held on precisely the same charitable trusts, or for precisely the same charitable purposes, does not require a scheme, but the court may act under its general jurisdiction.[338] In Victoria, Australia, there is a statutory provision in similar terms to s 13. A Victorian court has held[339] that the words 'spirit of the gift' in the section corresponding to sub-ss 13(1)(*a*)(ii) and 13(1)(*e*)(iii) effect a shift in emphasis in the application of the cy-près doctrine; that is away from the previous position of requiring the impossibility or impracticability of the testator's original objective being achieved to those circumstances which frustrate the purposes as revealed by the terms of the will, or by evidence, being attained. On the facts the fundamental purpose and objective of the testator to benefit all Victorian charities for ever was being frustrated by a term in the will restricting eligibility to charities in existence at the testator's death, and the restriction was accordingly removed.

As we shall see, it might have been important under the old law to know whether the case was one of initial or supervening impossibility. Suppose a testator gave a fund to trustees on trust for an individual for life, and then to found a defined institution of a charitable nature, and that at the date of the testator's death the fund would have been adequate to carry out the charitable purpose, but was inadequate when the life tenant died, say, 30 years later. Would this be a case of initial impossibility? The question of initial impossibility or impracticability must be determined as at the time when the gift was made, not when it falls into possession so far as charity is concerned, that is, in the case of a gift by will, on the death of the testator. The proper inquiry, in the case of a gift by will is, therefore, whether at the date of the death of the testator it was practicable to carry the intentions of the testator into effect or whether at that

---

[334] A requirement that capital and income should be wholly distributed within ten years of the settlor's death is not a 'purpose' within s 13, nor a method of 'using the property'. Cy-près application under s 13 was therefore not appropriate—*Re J W Laing Trust*, supra—but see p 322, supra.

[335] *Varsani v Jesani* [1998] 3 All ER 273, CA (case held to fall within this head where the original purpose was to promote the faith of Swaminarayan and the adherents were now divided into two groups each believing that they alone were continuing to profess the true faith—cy-près scheme directed).

[336] Section 13(4) and Sch 3.   [337] [1972] Ch 276, [1971] 1 All ER 799.

[338] *Oldham Borough Council v A-G* [1993] Ch 210, [1993] 2 All ER 432, CA, noted (1992/93) 1 CLPR 157 (Debra Morris).

[339] *Forrest v A-G* [1986] VR 187.

date there was any reasonable prospect that it would be practicable to do so at some future time. If there is a negative answer to both parts of this inquiry, it is a case of initial impossibility or impracticability.[340]

If there is a vested gift to charity which is not only to take effect at some future time but is also liable to be defeated on the happening of some event such as the birth of issue to the person holding a life interest, an inquiry as to its practicability should be approached on the footing that the gift will not be defeated, but will take effect at some future time in possession.[341]

(c) GENERAL CHARITABLE INTENTION

We must now turn to the distinction which has been drawn between initial and supervening impossibility, and consider whether a general charitable intention is required for the other cy-près occasions introduced by s 13(1).

(i) Initial impossibility or impracticability

Here the general rule was and is that cy-près application is only permitted if a paramount intention of charity on the part of the donor is established. The classic statement of the law is contained in the judgment of Parker J in *Re Wilson*,[342] where he said the authorities were to be divided into two classes:

First of all, we have a class of cases where, in form, the gift is given for a particular charitable purpose, but it is possible, taking the will as a whole, to say that, notwithstanding the form of the gift, the paramount intention, according to the true construction of the will, is to give the property in the first instance for a general charitable purpose rather than a particular charitable purpose, and to graft on to the general gift a direction as to the desires or intentions of the testator as to the manner in which the general gift is to be carried into effect.

If this is the proper construction and the particular purpose is initially impossible, the gift will be applied cy-près.[343] He continued:

Then there is the second class of cases, where, on the true construction of the will, no such paramount general intention can be inferred, and where the gift, being in form a particular gift—a gift for a particular purpose—and it being impossible to carry out that particular purpose, the whole gift is held to fail.[344]

---

[340] *Re Moon's Will Trusts* [1948] 1 All ER 300; *Re Wright* [1954] Ch 347, [1954] 2 All ER 98, CA; *Re Woodhams* [1981] 1 All ER 202. The principle has been applied where the donee had no power under its constitution to effectuate the particular charitable intention, but might be given such power by an amendment to its constitution—*Harris v Skevington* [1978] 1 NSWLR 176. Cf *Harris v Sharp* (1989) [2003] WTLR 1541, CA.

[341] *Re Tacon* [1958] Ch 447 at 454, [1958] 1 All ER 163 at 166, CA—but different considerations may be applicable to the case of a strictly contingent gift, per Evershed MR.

[342] [1913] 1 Ch 314 at 320, 321; *Re Pettit* [1988] 2 NZLR 513. See [1957] CLJ 87 (J C Hall) who observes that the meaning of the phrase 'general charitable intention' is obscure and its application extremely difficult.

[343] *Biscoe v Jackson* (1887) 35 Ch D 460, CA; *Re Hillier* [1954] 2 All ER 59, CA; *Re Lysaght* [1966] Ch 191, [1965] 2 All ER 888.

[344] *Re Good's Will Trusts* [1950] 2 All ER 653; *Re Ulverston and District New Hospital Building Fund* [1956] Ch 622, [1956] 3 All ER 164, CA.

Another way of putting it is to say that the distinction is between, on the one hand, the case where the scheme prescribed by a testator can be regarded as the mode by which a general charitable purpose is to be carried into effect and where the mode is not of the substance of the gift; and, on the other hand, the case where no part of the scheme prescribed by the testator can be disregarded as inessential without frustrating the testator's evident intention. One way of approaching the question whether a prescribed scheme or project which has proved impracticable is the only way of furthering a desirable purpose that the testator or settlor contemplated or intended is to ask whether a modification of that scheme or project, which would enable it to be carried into effect at the relevant time, is one which would frustrate the intention of the testator or settlor as disclosed by the will or trust instrument interpreted in the light of any admissible evidence of surrounding circumstances.[345] It is a question of construction, and the court will not necessarily infer a general charitable intention merely because the gift is of residue and failure to draw the inference will result in intestacy.[346]

(ii) Anonymous donors eg contributors to a collecting box on a flag day

This is now dealt with by s 14(1) of the 1993 Act which provides, with retrospective effect, that:

Property given for specific charitable purposes which fail[347] shall be applicable cy-près as if given for charitable purposes generally, where it belongs—
    (a) to a donor who, after
        (i)   the prescribed[348] advertisements and inquiries have been published and made, and
        (ii)   the prescribed[348] period beginning with the publication of those advertisements has expired,
    cannot be identified or cannot be found; or
    (b) to a donor who has executed a disclaimer in the prescribed[348] form of his right to have the property returned.

Further sub-s (3) provides that:

For the purposes of this section property shall be conclusively presumed (without any advertisement or inquiry) to belong to donors who cannot be identified, in so far as it consists—

---

[345] *Re Woodhams* [1981] 1 All ER 202; *Re Currie* [1985] NI 299; *National Trust Co v Canadian Diabetes Association* (1993) 109 DLR (4th) 232. See (1984) 128 Sol Jo 760 (Jean Warburton).

[346] See *Re Crowe* unreported, but noted in Report for 1979 paras 40–45. It does not appear whether the judge was referred to cases which suggest that in such a case the court will be very ready to draw the inference— *Re Raine* [1956] Ch 417, [1956] 1 All ER 355; *Re Griffiths* (23 July 1958, unreported), but cited in *Re Roberts* [1963] 1 All ER 674 at 680n. See (1956) 72 LQR 170 (R E Megarry).

[347] They are deemed to 'fail' by sub-s (7): 'where any difficulty in applying property to those purposes makes that property or the part not applicable cy-près available to be returned to the donors'. See also sub-s (10) as to definition of 'donor' and 'property'.

[348] Ie prescribed by regulations made by the Commissioners: ibid s 14(8). The Charities (Cy-près Advertisements, Inquiries and Disclaimers) Regulations 1993 set out the forms and prescribe a period of three months.

(a) of the proceeds of cash collections made by means of collecting boxes or by other
means not adapted for distinguishing one gift from another; or

(b) of the proceeds of any lottery, competition, entertainment, sale or similar money-
raising activity, after allowing for property given to provide prizes or articles for sale
or otherwise to enable the activity to be undertaken.

Trustees who follow this procedure will not be liable to any person who fails to make a
claim within the prescribed[349] period.[350] And under sub-s (4):

The court may by order direct that property not falling within sub-s (3) above shall for the
purposes of this section be treated (without any advertisement or inquiry) as belonging to
donors who cannot be identified, where it appears to the court either—
(a) that it would be unreasonable, having regard to the amounts likely to be returned to
the donors, to incur expense with a view to returning the property; or
(b) that it would be unreasonable, having regard to the nature, circumstances and
amounts of the gifts, and to the lapse of time since the gifts were made, for the donors
to expect the property to be returned.

Provision is made for a donor who cannot be identified or found to recover his
contribution to property applied cy-près under these provisions less any expenses
properly incurred by the charity trustees, except in respect of property to which sub-s
(3) or (4) applies. The scheme may direct that a sum be set aside for an appropriate
period to meet any such claims. Any claim must be made within six months of the
scheme being made.[351]

The first case in which the Commissioners used their powers under s 14 concerned
the Mile End Memorial Hall Fund.[352] It is a useful illustration of how these provisions
work in practice. The facts were that a fund had been opened in 1945 to provide a
memorial hall at Mile End but it was clear in 1964 that the trusts had failed for the
fund then amounted to only £372. Of this £346 had been raised by whist drives,
dances and concerts and the balance of £26 represented the subscription of 63 subscribers. A public meeting was held to discuss the fund, at which it was agreed to apply
it to the extension of a war memorial and a church hall, objects which the Commissioners considered satisfactory under the cy-près doctrine. By virtue of s 14(3)(b)
there was no difficulty with regard to the £346, but 62 of the 63 subscribers could be
traced and so could not come under s 14(1)(a). These persons were invited to execute
a written disclaimer[353] so as to bring their subscriptions within s 14(1)(b). Only one of
these persons desired the return of his subscription (which was, of course, returned)
and the remainder could also be applied cy-près. The final result was a cy-près scheme
allowing the trustees to use the money as proposed, subject to a provision for the

---

[349] See n 348, supra.   [350] Section 14(2).

[351] Ibid, s 14(5). Under s 14(6) there will normally be pro rata distribution if the amount set aside proves
to be inadequate.

[352] Reported in the Report of the Charity Commissioners for 1965, paras 19, 20, 21.

[353] Under the 1960 Act a written disclaimer was called for under s 14(1)(b), not a disclaimer in a prescribed form.

retention of a small sum for twelve months to cover a possible claim by the one subscriber who could not be identified or found.

(iii) Supervening impossibility

Here it is not necessary to show a paramount intention of charity. Once money is effectually dedicated to charity in perpetuity, whether in pursuance of a general or a particular charitable intention, the testator's next of kin or residuary legatees are for ever excluded and no question of subsequent failure can affect the matter so far as they are concerned. It is a case for cyprès application.[354]

The distinction between initial and supervening impossibility has commonly not been taken account of in cases where there is a surplus over what is needed to carry out a designated purpose. It is submitted that these should properly be regarded as cases of supervening impossibility not requiring a general charitable intention for cyprès application, but the weight of authority seems to assume that a general charitable intention is required.[355]

(iv) Cy-près application on occasions introduced by s 13(1)

Though there are dicta suggesting the contrary in *Re J W Laing Trust*,[356] it is generally thought that there is no need to show a general charitable intention on occasions introduced by s 13(1).[357]

(d) GIFT TO A SPECIFIED CHARITABLE INSTITUTION WHICH ONCE EXISTED, BUT CEASED TO EXIST BEFORE THE DEATH OF THE TESTATOR[358]

Prima facie the gift lapses in the same way as if it had been a gift to an individual. Thus in *Re Rymer*[359] there was a legacy 'to the rector for the time being of St Thomas's Seminary for the education of priests in the diocese of Westminster for the purposes of such seminary'. Shortly before the testator's death the Seminary had been closed, the building sold, and the students transferred to another seminary near Birmingham. It was held that the legacy lapsed and fell into residue. However, as Wilberforce J observed in *Re Roberts*,[360] 'the position is that the courts have gone very far in the

---

[354] *Re Slevin* [1891] 2 Ch 236, CA; *Re Wright* [1954] Ch 347, [1954] 2 All ER 98, CA; *Re Tacon* [1958] Ch 447, [1958] 1 All ER 163, CA; *Re Fitzpatrick* (1984) 6 DLR (4th) 644. But see [1983] Conv 107 (P Luxton).

[355] *Re Stanford* [1924] 1 Ch 73; *Re Monk* [1927] 2 Ch 197, CA; *Re North Devon and West Somerset Relief Fund Trusts* [1953] 2 All ER 1032. Contrast *Re King* [1923] 1 Ch 243; and see *Re Raine* [1956] Ch 417.

[356] [1984] Ch 143, [1984] 1 All ER 50 per Peter Gibson J at 149, 53. See [1984] Conv 319 (Jean Warburton).

[357] See Picarda, *The Law and Practice of Charities*, 3rd edn, p 297; Luxton, *The Law of Charities*, para 15.51.

[358] See generally (1969) 32 MLR 283 (J B E Hutton); (1972) 36 Conv 198 (R B M Cotterrell); (1974) 38 Conv 187 (Jill Martin); (1980) 39 CLJ 88 (C E F Rickett).

[359] [1895] 1 Ch 19, CA (a decision which has not received much favour in the courts per Wilberforce J in *Re Roberts* [1963] 1 All ER 674 at 681); *Re Tacon*, supra, CA; *Re Slatter's Will Trusts* [1964] 2 All ER 469. The gift was held to lapse in *Re Prescott* [1990] 2 IR 342, (donee body had ceased to exist before the date of the will).

[360] Supra, at 678; *Re Broadbent's Will* [2001] WTLR 967, noted [2002] PCB 243 (G Duncan).

decided cases to resist the conclusion that a legacy to a charitable institution lapses, and a number of very refined arguments have been found acceptable with a view to avoiding that conclusion'. In practice much depends on difficult and debatable questions of construction, and the courts may not infrequently be thought to have adopted a somewhat strained construction of the testator's words in order to reach the desired result. There are the following possibilities.

(i) No lapse on the ground that although the specified institution may apparently have disappeared the charity has not ceased to exist

Re Faraker[361] is the leading case in a series of decisions[362] which have established that so long as there are funds held in trust for the purposes of a charity the charity continues in existence and is not destroyed by any alteration in its constitution, name or objects made in accordance with law, or even amalgamation with another charity. The vital point seems to be that there is a fund in existence for ever dedicated to charity. The *Re Faraker*[363] principle is readily applied where the gift is construed as a gift to augment the funds of the named charity and there is no difficulty where, as is common, the charity was founded as a perpetual charity which no-one has power to terminate. Where, however, a charitable organization was founded, not as a perpetual charity, but as one liable to termination, and its constitution provided for the disposal of its funds in that event, then if the organization has determined and its funds have been disposed of, the charity has ceased to exist and there is nothing to prevent the operation of the doctrine of lapse.[364] There is, however, some doubt as to whether the principle was properly applied in *Re Vernon's Will Trusts*[365] a case of an incorporated charity which had been dissolved, where its work was being carried on by another body in unbroken continuance of the work originally conducted by the dissolved charity. The funds of the incorporated charity had, however, vested in the Ministry of Health under the National Health Service Act 1946 free from any trusts, and accordingly the funds had ceased to be dedicated to charity.

(ii) Gift construed as a gift for the purposes of the specified institution

It is well established that a gift for a particular purpose will lapse if the particular purpose has ceased to exist before the death of the testator[366] on a similar principle to that applied in *Re Rymer*.[367] Thus in *Re Spence*[368] there was a gift for the benefit of the

---

[361] [1912] 2 Ch 488, CA.

[362] Including *Re Lucas* [1948] Ch 424, [1948] 2 All ER 22, CA (more fully reported in All ER—see *Re Spence* [1979] Ch 483, [1978] 3 All ER 92); *Re Bagshaw* [1954] 1 All ER 227; *Re Roberts*, supra; *Re Slatter's Will Trusts*, supra; *Re Broadbent's Will*, supra, CA.

[363] Supra, CA.

[364] *Re Stemson's Will Trusts* [1970] Ch 16, [1969] 2 All ER 517; *Re Finger's Will Trusts* [1972] Ch 286, [1971] 3 All ER 1050.

[365] Decided in 1962 but not reported until [1972] Ch 300n, [1971] 3 All ER 1061n; see *Re Finger's Will Trusts*, supra at 295, 1057.

[366] *Re Wilson* [1913] 1 Ch 314; *Re Tacon*, supra; *Re Slatter's Will Trusts* [1964] Ch 512, [1964] 2 All ER 469 noted (1964) 28 Conv 313 (J T Farrand).

[367] Supra, CA.

[368] [1979] Ch 483, [1978] 3 All ER 92. See also *Re Lucas*, supra, CA; *Re Currie* [1985] NI 299.

patients at the Old Folks Home at Hillworth Lodge, Keighley. At the date of the will there were patients at that home. When the testatrix died, there was no longer any home there, but offices instead; and so there were no longer any patients there, or any possibility of them. The gift was a gift for a charitable purpose which at the date of the will was capable of accomplishment and at the date of death was not. Accordingly it was held to fail.

In practice, charitable purposes are not easily destroyed and may continue, thus giving no occasion for lapse, notwithstanding the fact that the original organization or machinery for carrying out those purposes no longer exists.[369] This approach was used in several cases[370] in relation to gifts to hospitals taken over by the Minister of Health under the National Health Service Act 1946 between the date of the will and the date of death. The courts commonly held that the gift was to be construed as being for the work previously carried on by the hospital, and where the work was now being carried on by the appropriate Hospital Management Committee, directed payment to the Committee on trust to apply the money for the purposes of the particular hospital which was the object of the testator's bounty.

(iii) The approaches in (i) and (ii) above in the light of the general statement made by Buckley J in re Vernon's Trusts[371]

In this case Buckley J stated the principles to be applied to gifts to unincorporated charities on the one hand and corporate charities on the other. He expressed the logical view that every gift to an unincorporated charity must take effect as a gift for the purpose which the charity exists to serve. Such a gift will not fail for want of a trustee, and effect will be given to it by way of the scheme notwithstanding the disappearance of the charity in the lifetime of the testator,[372] unless there is something positive to show that the continued existence of the donee was essential to the gift. In the case of a gift to a corporate charity, however, Buckley J said that there is simply a gift to the corporate body beneficially, which will lapse if that body ceases to exist before the death of the testator, unless there is positive evidence that that body took on trust for charitable purposes.[373] It has not ceased to exist if it is in insolvent liquidation but not yet formally dissolved, and accordingly a gift to it will take effect

---

[369] *Re Watt* [1932] 2 Ch 243n; *Re Morrison* (1967) 111 Sol Jo 758.

[370] Eg *Re Morgan's Will Trusts* [1950] Ch 637, [1950] 1 All ER 1097; *Re Meyers* [1951] Ch 534, [1951] 1 All ER 538. The courts seem to have construed the purposes of the hospitals to these cases as that of carrying on their work on the particular premises, and this construction accordingly could not have saved a gift where the premises had ceased to be used for hospital work—*Re Hutchinson's Will Trusts* [1953] Ch 387, [1953] 1 All ER 996.

[371] [1972] Ch 300n, [1971] 3 All ER 1061n; *Re Edis's Trusts* [1972] 2 All ER 769. In Australia it has been held that the presumption is that there is a trust for the purposes of the charity whether it is corporate or unincorporate—*Sir Moses Montefiore Jewish Home v Howell & Co (No 7) Pty Ltd* [1984] 2 NSWLR 406.

[372] In restating this proposition in *Re Finger's Will Trusts* [1972] Ch 286, [1971] 3 All ER 1050. Goff J added the proviso that the work was still being carried on. In principle it would seem sufficient for the purpose to be capable of being carried out.

[373] Which situation applied was the main dispute in *Rabin v Gerson Berger Association Ltd* [1986] 1 All ER 374, CA. As to legacies to charitable corporations, see generally (1997) NLJ Easter App Supp 17 (P Luxton).

and be available to the creditors of the company and not for the charitable objects of the corporation.[374]

Re Vernon's Will Trusts[375] was adopted by Goff J in *Re Finger's Will Trusts*.[376] In that case questions arose over two shares of residue, one given to the National Radium Commission, an unincorporated charity, and the other to the National Council for Maternity and Child Welfare, a corporate charity. Both charities had been dissolved between the date of the will and the date of death. Applying the above principles it was held that the gift to the unincorporated charity, the National Radium Commission did not fail. It was a purpose trust for the work of the commission, which was not dependent on the continued existence of the named charitable organization. The charitable purposes of the commission could still be carried out and the appropriate share of residue was accordingly applicable under a scheme. The gift of the share to the corporate charity however failed, for the will did not show an intention that the gift should be held on trust for the purposes of the charity. It was an absolute gift to a corporate body which had ceased to exist before the death of the testatrix. This gift could not be claimed by the National Association for Maternity and Child Welfare, to which the Council had transferred its funds on its dissolution and which to all intents and purposes carried on the work of the Council. As will be seen later, the failure of the gift to the Council gave rise to the further question whether the share should pass on intestacy or was applicable cy-près.

The law as stated in *Re Vernon's Will Trusts*[377] and *Re Finger's Will Trusts*[378] is not without its difficulties—Goff J in the latter case himself pointed out that the distinction between corporate and unincorporate charities produced anomalies. One such anomaly had appeared in *Re Meyers*,[379] and an absurd result had only been avoided by reliance on the special context in the will. In that case there were legacies to both unincorporate and corporate hospitals, all of which had been taken over by the Ministry of Health under the 1946 Act. There was no difficulty in construing the legacies to the unincorporated hospitals as gifts for the purposes of the work they carried on, and on that construction, as we have seen under (ii) above they were valid. Prima facie, however, the gifts to the corporate hospitals were gifts to them beneficially (and not for the purposes of the work they carried on). and should accordingly lapse. Such a result, the judge observed, would be contrary to common sense and would produce an unacceptable difference between the gifts to corporate and unincorporated hospitals. On the true construction of that particular will he felt able to decide that the legacies were given to the corporate hospitals for the purposes of the work they carried on, and should go to the appropriate hospital management committees on trust to apply them for those purposes.

The main difficulty, however, it is submitted, lies in the proposition, as stated by

---

[374] *Re ARMS (Multiple Sclerosis Research) Ltd* [1997] 1 WLR 877, noted [1997] Co Law 213 (Alison Dunn).
[375] [1972] Ch 300n, [1971] 3 All ER 1061n.
[376] Supra. The facts as stated below have been slightly simplified.   [377] Supra.
[378] Supra.   [379] [1951] Ch 534, [1951] 1 All ER 538.

Buckley J,[380] that 'if the gift [to an unincorporated charity] is to be permitted to take effect at all, it must be a bequest for a purpose, ie that charitable purpose which the named charity exists to serve'. A gift to an unincorporated charity, it would seem to follow, must always be a gift for its purposes as under (ii) above. Both the *Re Rymer*[381] and *Re Faraker*[382] lines of cases, however, appear to assume the possibility of a gift to a charity (including an unincorporated charity) as distinct from a gift to a charitable purpose. A case which appears to raise the difficulty squarely, but which was not apparently referred to in either *Re Vernon's Will Trusts*[383] or *Re Finger's Will Trusts*[384] is *Re Bagshaw*.[385] Here there was a legacy to the Bakewell and District War Memorial Cottage Hospital, the correct name of an unincorporated charity. Between the date of the will and the date of death the hospital run by the charity had been taken over under the National Health Service Act 1946 and was now carried on by the defendant Hospital Management Committee. The charity had changed its name to the Bakewell and District 1914–18 War Memorial Charity, and also changed its purposes. On the basis of the principles laid down in *Re Vernon's Will Trusts* and *Re Finger's Will Trusts* one should, it seems, construe the legacy as a gift for the purposes of the work being carried on in the hospital buildings at the date of the will. The work was in fact being continued on the same premises by the appropriate hospital management committee. On the posited basis one would expect the legacy to be payable to the hospital management committee as explained in (ii) above. Such an argument was put forward but failed. It was held that this was a gift to the charity correctly described by the testatrix as the Bakewell and District War Memorial Cottage Hospital. It was further held that the principle of *Re Faraker*[386] applied and that the legacy was accordingly payable to the Bakewell and District 1914–18 War Memorial Charity for its general purposes.

(iv) Cy-près application

If the gift would otherwise fail, it may be possible to apply the cy-près doctrine. The non-existence of the specified charity at the date of death is treated as a case of initial impossibility, and the gift will be applied cy-près, provided a general charitable intention can be established. In *Re Harwood*[387] it was said to be very difficult to find such an intention where a testator had selected a particular charity and taken some care to identify it. Though difficult, it depends on the circumstances and is not impossible, as is shown by *Re Finger's Will Trusts*.[388] In that case, as we have seen, the bequest of a

---

[380] In *Re Vernon's Will Trusts*, supra at 303, 1064.   [381] [1895] 1 Ch 19, CA.

[382] [1912] 2 Ch 488, CA.   [383] [1972] Ch 300n, [1971] 3 All ER 1061n.

[384] [1972] Ch 286, [1971] 3 All ER 1050.   [385] [1954] 1 All ER 227.   [386] Supra, CA.

[387] [1936] Ch 285, [1935] All ER Rep 918 (gift to the Wisbech Peace Society, Cambridge). The assumption that the purposes of a peace society are charitable is probably wrong: they would seem to be political—see *Re Koeppler Will Trusts* [1984] Ch 243, [1984] 2 All ER 111; (1999) 6 CLPR 1 (H Picarda). See also *Re Collier (decd)* [1998] 1 NZLR 81, criticized, it is submitted rightly, in [1998] NZLJ 55 (C Rickett).

[388] Supra. The Australian courts have, indeed, held that there is no rule or principle that it is more difficult to conclude that a testator had a general charitable intention where there is a gift to a named charity which existed at the date of the will but ceased to exist before death than in the case where the named charity never existed at all—*A-G for New South Wales v Public Trustee* (1987) 8 NSWLR 550.

share of residue to the National Council for Maternity and Child Welfare failed. Taking account of the facts that virtually the whole estate was dedicated to charitable purposes, that the Council had been mainly, if not exclusively, a co-ordinating body, and that the testatrix regarded herself as having no relatives, the judge found a general charitable intention and directed cy-près application.

The principle of *Re Harwood*[389] applies as much to a gift for a particular purpose as to a gift to a particular institution.[390]

(e) SPECIFIED INSTITUTION CEASING TO EXIST BEFORE THE GIFT BECOMES PAYABLE OR IS IN FACT PAID OVER

In the case where the specified institution was in existence at the death of the testator there is no lapse and the testator's next of kin or residuary legatees are for ever excluded.[391] The property will be applied to charity, though it is not clear whether the correct view is that it falls to be administered by the Crown, who in practice applies it to analogous charitable purposes,[392] or that it is a case of cy-près application by the court.[393]

(f) GIFT TO WHAT APPEARS TO BE A SPECIFIED CHARITABLE INSTITUTION, BUT WHICH IT TURNS OUT HAS NEVER EXISTED

This is, in effect, a case of initial impossibility and a class of case, moreover, in which the court will lean in favour of a general charitable purpose, and will accept even a small indication of the testator's intention as sufficient to show that a gift for a general charitable purpose and not a particular charitable body was intended.[394] Harman LJ once declared[395] that the court has leaned so far over in this sort of case that it has become almost prone, and, expressing his preference for an upright posture, he held that there was no general charitable intention in a case of this kind, where residue was also given to charity, for this would be to favour one charity against another. There may be other circumstances in the will which may negative the existence of a general charitable intention and thus prevent a cy-près application.[396]

It is respectfully submitted that Harman LJ's preference for an upright posture showed some weakening in *Re Satterthwaite's Will Trusts*[397] where, simplifying the facts slightly, residue was to be divided equally between an anti-vivisection society (not in law charitable), seven animal charities and the 'London Animal Hospital'.

---

[389] Supra.   [390] *Re Spence* [1978] 3 All ER 92.

[391] *Re Slevin* [1891] 2 Ch 236, CA; *Re Soley* (1900) 17 TLR 118; *Re Tacon*, supra; *Re Fitzpatrick* (1984) 6 DLR (4th) 644.

[392] *Re Slevin*, supra.   [393] *Re Soley*, supra; *Re Tacon*, supra.

[394] *Re Davis* [1902] 1 Ch 876; *Re Harwood* [1936] Ch 285, [1935] All ER Rep 918; *Re Pettit* [1988] 2 NZLR 513. Similarly if there are two or more possible claimants, but the one intended by the testator cannot be identified—*Re Songest* [1956] 2 All ER 765, CA; *Re Conroy* (1973) 35 DLR (3d) 752.

[395] *Re Goldschmidt* [1957] 1 All ER 513 at 514; (1957) 73 LQR 166.

[396] *Re Tharp* [1942] 2 All ER 358.   [397] [1966] 1 All ER 919, CA.

None of the claimants was able to establish a claim to this last share, which it was held must be applied cy-près, the Court finding a general charitable intention in the dispositions of residue notwithstanding that 'one-ninth of residue was given to an anti-vivisection society which in law—unknown to the average testator—is not charitable'.[398]

In *Re Jenkins' Will Trusts*,[399] heard after *Re Satterthwaite's Will Trusts*[400] had been decided but before it had been reported, a one-seventh share of residue was given to an anti-vivisection society expressly to be used for non-charitable purposes, and the other six one-seventh shares to animal charities. The gift of the one-seventh share to the anti-vivisection society was held to fail as being impressed with a non-charitable purpose, and Buckley J held that he could not find a general charitable intention in the residuary gift so as to enable him to apply this one-seventh share cy-près. It is not easy to distinguish this decision convincingly from *Re Satterthwaite's Will Trusts*[401] on this point. However even if *Re Satterthwaite's Will Trusts* had been followed and a general charitable intention had been established it is submitted that the cy-près doctrine would not have been applicable. The doctrine operates where there is failure of a gift for a particular charitable purpose, and not where there is failure of a gift for a non-charitable purpose.

It may be added that where the trust is in favour of a non-existent institution in a particular locality in a foreign country, cy-près application may, it appears, nevertheless be made and the trustees directed to make payment to an appropriate organization in that foreign country.[402]

7 SMALL CHARITIES: POWER TO TRANSFER PROPERTY OR MODIFY OBJECTS

The following provisions apply to a charity whose gross income in its last financial year did not exceed £5,000 and which does not hold any land on trusts which stipulate that the land is to be used for the purposes, or any particular purposes, of the charity. They do not, however, apply to an exempt charity or a charitable company.[403]

Where the provisions do apply the charity trustees may resolve[404] that all the property should be transferred to another specified charity,[405] being either a registered

---

[398] *Re Satterthwaite's Will Trusts*, supra, at 925, per Russell LJ.

[399] [1966] Ch 249, [1966] 1 All ER 926.

[400] Supra. It is strange that this case was apparently not referred to in *Re Jenkins' Will Trusts* as the same person was counsel for the Attorney-General in both cases.

[401] Supra.   [402] See the Canadian decision of *Re Barnes* (1976) 72 DLR (3d) 651.

[403] Charities Act 1993, s 74(1). The Secretary of State may by order alter the specified sum of £5,000: s 74(11). See CC44.

[404] By a majority of not less than two thirds of the trustees voting on the resolution: s 74(3).

[405] Or divided between two or more specified charities: s 74(2)(*b*). And see s 74(12).

charity or a charity which is not required to be registered.[406] The charity trustees have no power to pass such a resolution unless they are satisfied:

(i)   that the existing purposes of the transferor charity have ceased to be conducive to a suitable and effective application of the charity's resources, and

(ii) that the purposes of the charity or charities specified in the resolution are as similar in character to the purposes of the transferor charity as is reasonably practicable.

They must also have obtained written confirmation from the charity trustees of the transferee charity or charities that they are willing to accept the transfer.[407]

Alternatively the charity trustees may resolve that the trusts of the charity should be modified by replacing all or any of the purposes of the charity with other charitable purposes.[408] The conditions that have to be fulfilled for the trustees to have power to pass such a resolution are:

(a)   that the existing purposes of the charity (or, as the case may be, such of them as it is proposed to replace) have ceased to be conducive to a suitable and effective application of the charity's resources; and

(b)   that the purposes specified in the resolution are as similar in character to those existing purposes as is practical in the circumstances.[409]

Finally, without the need to satisfy any special conditions, the charity trustees may resolve to modify any of their powers exercisable in the administration of the charity or the procedure to be followed in connection therewith.[410]

Whichever resolution is passed the charity trustees must give such public notice thereof as they think reasonable, and send a copy to the Commissioners, together with a statement of their reasons for passing it.[411] The Commissioners may call for additional information and explanation from the charity trustees, and must take into account any representations made to them by persons appearing to be interested in the charity.[412] Within three months of receipt of the resolution the Commissioners must notify the trustees in writing either that they concur with the resolution or that they do not.[413] If they notify their concurrence with a resolution to transfer, the charity trustees must arrange for the transfer to take place,[414] if the resolution was for modification, the trusts of the charity are deemed to have been modified in accordance with the terms of the resolution as from the date specified in the notification.[415]

---

[406] Section 74(2)(a).   [407] Section 74(4).   [408] Section 74(2)(c).
[409] Section 74(5).   [410] Section 74(2)(d).   [411] Section 74(6).
[412] Section 74(7). Representations must be received within six weeks of receipt of the resolution by the Commissioners.
[413] Section 74(8). Virtually all are approved—1250 in 1996.
[414] Section 74(9)(a). At the request of the charity trustees the Commissioners have power to make appropriate vesting orders; s 74(10).
[415] Section 74(9)(b).

8 VERY SMALL CHARITIES: POWER TO
SPEND CAPITAL

The following provisions apply to a charity if it has a permanent endowment[416] which does not consist of or comprise any land, and its gross income in its last financial year did not exceed £1,000. They do not, however, apply to an exempt charity or to a charitable company.[417]

Where the provisions apply and the charity trustees are of the opinion that the property of the charity is too small, in relation to its purposes, for any useful purpose to be achieved by the expenditure of income alone, they may resolve[418] that the charity ought to be freed from the restrictions with respect to expenditure of capital to which its permanent endowment is subject.[419] Before passing such a resolution, however, they must consider whether any reasonable possibility exists of effecting a transfer under s 74.[420]

If a resolution is passed, the procedure is the same as under s 74.[421] If the Commissioners notify their concurrence with the resolution the charity trustees, from the date of the notification, can expend any property of the charity without regard to any restrictions relating to the permanent endowment.[422] When all the funds have been spent the charity ceases to exist.

9 DISCRIMINATION

(a) RACE RELATIONS ACT 1976

Apart from statute, it does not seem that a provision in a trust instrument discriminating against potential beneficiaries on the ground, for instance, of colour or religion is regarded as being against public policy or otherwise unlawful even in the case of a charitable trust. This was impliedly assumed in *Re Dominion Students' Hall Trusts,*[423] a case concerning a colour bar, and expressly stated in *Re Lysaght,*[424] a case concerning a provision excluding students of the Jewish or Roman Catholic faith from benefit, though the judge stigmatized this provision as 'unamiable' and 'undesirable'.

The Race Relations Act 1976, now declares that discrimination, as defined in the

---

[416] As to the meaning of 'permanent endowment' see p 315, supra.
[417] Section 75(1). The Secretary of State may by order alter the specified sum of £1,000: s 75(9). See CC44.
[418] By a majority of not less than two thirds of the trustees voting on the resolution: s 75(3).
[419] Section 75(2).   [420] Section 75(4). For s 74 see pp 338–339, supra.
[421] See 75(5) to (7), and pp 338–339, supra. Virtually all are approved—705 in 1996.
[422] Section 75(8).   [423] [1947] Ch 183, and see supra, p 327.
[424] [1966] Ch 191, [1965] 2 All ER 888.

Act, on racial grounds, that is, on the grounds of colour, race, nationality, or ethnic[425] or national[426] origins, is unlawful. For the purposes of the Act, a person discriminates against another if on any of these grounds he treats that other in certain specified situations less favourably than he treats or would treat other persons. The specified situations would prima facie seem to include the administration of a charitable, though not a private, trust.

Section 34, however, contains two special provisions relating to charities. By sub-s (1) a provision in a charitable instrument (whenever it took or takes effect) which provides for conferring benefits on persons of a class defined by reference to colour is to have effect for all purposes as if it provided for conferring the like benefits on persons of the class which results if the restriction by reference to colour is disregarded.[427] Thus, for example, a trust 'to educate black children in the East End of London' would become a trust 'to educate children in the East End of London'.[428] Otherwise by sub-ss (2) and (3) the Act does not affect a provision in a charitable instrument which provides for conferring benefits on persons of a class defined otherwise than by reference to colour, nor does it render unlawful any act which is done in order to give effect to such a provision.

It should be observed, however, that in the administration of a charitable trust a cy-près scheme may be made for the removal[429] of a discriminatory provision saved by s 34(2) and (3), or one altogether outside the scope of the Act, such as a provision for religious discrimination.

(b) SEX DISCRIMINATION ACT 1975

Though in general the Sex Discrimination Act 1975 applies to charities—for example, in advertising for and selecting paid staff—there is an important exception in s 43.[430] This provides that where a charitable instrument contains a provision for conferring benefits on persons of one sex only (disregarding any benefits to persons of the

---

[425] For a group to constitute itself an ethnic group it must regard itself, and be regarded by others, as a distinct community by virtue of certain characteristics. Of these, two are essential ie (i) a long shared history and (ii) a cultural tradition of its own. Other common but not essential characteristics include (iii) a common geographical origin, (iv) a common language, (v) a common literature, (vi) a common religion and (vii) being a minority: *Mandla v Dowell Lee* [1983] 2 AC 548, [1983] 1 All ER 1062, HL, discussed [1983] Pub L 348 (St J A Robilliard); (1984) 128 Sol Jo 274 (A N Khan); (1984) 43 CLJ 218 (G T Pagone). The decision is analysed in detail in (1984) 100 LQR 120 (Helen Beynon and Nigel Love). Gypsies have been held to be a racial group: *Commission for Racial Equality v Dutton* [1989] QB 783, [1989] 1 All ER 306, CA, but Rastafarians have been held not to be a separate ethnic group: *Crown Supplies (Property Services Agency) v Dawkins* [1993] ICR 517, CA, discussed (1993) 143 NLJ 610 (Neil Parpworth).

[426] The Scots and the English are separate racial groups defined by reference to 'national origins', in the sense that England and Scotland are nations, but not by reference to ethnic origins: *Northern Joint Police Board v Power* [1997] IRLR 610, EAT.

[427] Or, where the original class is defined by reference to colour only, on persons generally.

[428] Section 34(1) is severely criticized in [1981] Conv 131 (T G Watkin); (1983) 47 MLR 759 (I B McKenna).

[429] As was done both in *Re Dominion Students' Hall Trust*, supra and *Re Lysaght*, supra.

[430] As amended by the Sex Discrimination Act 1975 (Amendment of Section 43) Order 1977, SI 1977/528.

opposite sex which are exceptional or are relatively insignificant) nothing done by the charity trustees to comply with that provision is made unlawful by the Act. This exception applies equally to national single-sex organizations such as the Boy Scouts and Girl Guides, and to small parochial charities for elderly spinsters, retired school-masters and so on. It was held, in *Hugh-Jones v St John's College, Cambridge*[431] to cover the award of a research fellowship available only to men.

There are special provisions for educational charities in s 78. In the case of these charities the trustees may apply to the Secretary of State for an order removing or modifying the restrictions so that the benefits can be made available to both sexes, and the Secretary of State may make the order if satisfied that to do so would conduce to the advancement of education without sex discrimination. However if the trust was created by gift or bequest, no order can be made until 25 years after the date it took effect, unless the donor or his personal representatives, or the personal representatives of the testator, have consented in writing.

10 DISPOSITIONS OF CHARITY LAND

The primary rule is that no land (except an advowson) held by or in trust for a charity (with the exception of an exempt charity)[432] can be sold, leased or otherwise disposed of without an order of the court or of the Commissioners.[433] This rule, however, will in many cases be inoperative, because it is qualified by a provision that it is not to apply to certain dispositions of such land made to a person who is not a 'connected person',[434] or a trustee for, or nominee of, a connected person.[435] There are two categories of disposition:

---

[431] [1979] ICR 848, EAT—college also excluded from liability under s 51, relating to things done under pre-Act statute. Sections not overriden by directive of the Council of the European Communities.

[432] Charities Act 1993, s 36(1)(*a*).

[433] Ibid, s 36(1). See CC28. See also *Bayoumi v Women's Total Abstinence Educational Union Ltd* [2003] EWCA Civ 1548, [2004] 3 All ER 110 (the subsection has no application to an agreement for the sale, etc of charity land) and [2004] PCB 118 (T Dumont and Fiona Wilson). In the view of the Commissioners the section does not apply in relation to sales of land left in wills to charities, either as specific devisees or residuary legatees—(1995) 4 Dec Ch Com 26. By sub-s (9) the restrictions do not apply to a disposition expressly authorized by statute or a legally established scheme; to certain dispositions to another charity; and to certain leases to carry out the charity's purposes on the demised premises, eg in the case of a charity whose purposes include the provision of subsidized accommodation for the poor, a letting of premises at less than a market rent. Nor by s 40 do they apply in many cases of the release of a rentcharge.

[434] This term is defined in the Charities Act 1993, Sch 5: in summary it means (a) charity trustee or trustee for the charity; (b) a donor of any land to the charity; (c) specified relatives of anyone in (a) or (b); (d) an officer, agent or employee of the charity; (e) the spouse (or civil partner after the Civil Partnership Act 2004 has been brought into force) of anyone in (a)–(d); (f) an institution controlled by any person or persons in (a)–(e); (g) a body corporate in which any person or persons in (a)–(f) have a substantial interest.

[435] Ibid, s 36(2).

(a) A LEASE FOR SEVEN YEARS OR LESS (OTHER THAN ONE GRANTED WHOLLY OR PARTLY IN CONSIDERATION OF A FINE)

The primary rule does not apply provided that before entering into an agreement for the lease the charity trustees:

(a) obtain and consider the advice on the proposed lease by a person who they reasonably believe to have the requisite ability and practical experience to provide them with competent advice thereon; and

(b) decide that they are satisfied, having considered that advice, that the terms on which the lease is proposed to be made are the best that can reasonably be obtained for the charity.[436]

(b) ANY OTHER DISPOSITION OF LAND

The primary rule does not apply provided that before entering into an agreement for the sale, lease (other than one under (i) above) or other disposition of the land the charity trustees—

(a) obtain and consider a written report on the proposed disposition from a qualified surveyor[437] instructed by the trustees and acting exclusively for the charity;

(b) advertise the proposed disposition as advised by the surveyor (unless he advises against advertisement); and

(c) decide that they are satisfied, having considered the surveyor's report, that the terms on which the disposition is proposed to be made are the best that can reasonably be obtained for the charity.[438]

There are further restrictions where any land is held by or in trust for a charity and the trusts on which it is so held stipulate that it is to be used for the purposes or any particular purposes of the charity, that is, what is sometimes called 'functional land'. In that case the charity trustees must give public notice of the proposed disposition, inviting representations which they are under a duty to take into consideration.[439] This restriction does not, however, apply where other property is to be acquired by way of replacement of the property disposed of, or where the disposition comprises a lease for two years or less (other than one granted wholly or partly in consideration of a fine).[440]

---

[436] Ibid, s 36(2), (5).

[437] Defined in s 36(4) as someone holding a specified professional qualification, who is reasonably believed by the charity trustees to have ability in, and experience of, the valuation of land of the particular kind, and in the particular area, in question. As to the contents of report, see SI 1992/2980.

[438] Ibid, s 36(3). See *Bayoumi v Women's Total Abstinence Educational Union Ltd* [2003] EWCA Civ 1548, [2004] 3 All ER 110.

[439] Ibid, s 26(6). The requirements of this sub-section may be waived by the Commissioners: s 36(8).

[440] Ibid, s 36(7).

None of the provisions in s 36 applies to a mortgage of land.[441] However a separate section[442] provides that no mortgage of land held by or in trust for a charity, (except an exempt charity)[443] can be granted without an order of the court or the Commissioners, but it is likewise subject to an important qualification. It does not apply to a mortgage by way of security for the repayment of a loan where the charity trustees have, before executing the mortgage, obtained and considered proper advice,[444] in writing, on the following matters:

(a) whether the proposed loan is necessary in order for the charity trustees to be able to pursue the particular course of action in connection with which the loan is sought by them;

(b) whether the terms of the proposed loan are reasonable having regard to the status of the charity as a prospective borrower; and

(c) the ability of the charity to repay on those terms the sum proposed to be borrowed.[445]

11 CONTROL OF FUND RAISING FOR
CHARITABLE INSTITUTIONS

Part II of the Charities Act 1992 contains new provisions for the control of fund raising.[446]

The statutory control imposed by Part II of the Charities Act 1992 extends beyond charities by reason of the fact that in the relevant Part[447] of that Act 'charitable institution' is defined so as to include an institution (other than a charity) which is established for charitable, benevolent or philanthropic purposes.

The Act[448] makes it unlawful for a professional fund raiser[449] to solicit money or other property in any manner whatever, including by means of a statement published in any newspaper, film or radio or television programme, for the benefit of a charitable institution unless he does so in accordance with an agreement with the institution

---

[441] Charities Act 1993, s 36(10)(*b*). Nor do they apply to any disposition of an advowson: s 36(10)(*c*).

[442] Ibid, s 38(1).   [443] Ibid, s 38(7).

[444] Ie the advice of a person (a) who is reasonably believed by the charity trustees to be qualified by his ability in and practical experience of financial matters; and (b) who has no financial interest in the making of the loan in question. Such advice may be given in the course of his employment by the charity or the charity trustees: ibid, s 38(4).

[445] Ibid, s 38(2), (3).

[446] See, generally, CC20. Note that when a member of the public puts money in a collecting tin the property in the money passes at once to the charity: *R v Dyke and Munro* [2002] 1 Cr App R 30, CA.

[447] Charities Act 1992, Part II.   [448] Ibid, s 59(1).

[449] As defined ibid, s 58(1), (2), (3); Deregulation and Contracting Out Act 1994, s 25(3).

satisfying the prescribed requirements.[450] Compliance with this requirement may be enforced by means of an injunction, but in no other way.[451]

In his solicitation a professional fund raiser[452] must indicate the institution or institutions[453] which are to benefit, and in general terms the method by which his remuneration in connection with the appeal is to be determined.[454] If the solicitation is made in the course of a radio or television programme inviting payment by credit card or debit card a professional fund raiser must also give full details of the donor's right to have any payment of £50 or more refunded by serving written notice on the fund raiser within seven days of the solicitation.[455] Where a payment of £50 or more is made in response to a telephone solicitation, the fund-raiser must within seven days give the donor a written statement indicating the institutions benefiting and the arrangements for remuneration as mentioned above, and giving full details of the right to have the payment refunded and any agreement to make a payment of £50 or more cancelled.[456]

Charitable institutions are given the right to prevent unauthorized fund raising by seeking an injunction. They may do so where the person in question is using methods of fund raising to which the institution objects; where the court is satisfied that that person is not a fit and proper person to raise funds for the institution; or where he has represented that charitable contributions are to be given to or applied for the benefit of the institution, which, however, does not wish to be associated with the particular promotional or other fund raising venture in which that person is engaged.[457]

It is an offence for a person to solicit money or other property for the benefit of an institution representing it to be a registered charity[458] when that is not the case, but it is a defence for the accused to prove that he believed on reasonable grounds that the institution was a registered charity.[459]

[450] Ie prescribed by regulations made under s 64(2)(a): see SI 1994/3024. An agreement which does not satisfy the prescribed requirements is not enforceable against the institution, nor does it give any entitlement to remuneration or expenses, save by order of the court: s 59(4), (5). It is likewise made unlawful for a commercial participator (defined in s 58(1), as amended) to represent that charitable contributions are to be given to or applied for the benefit of a charitable institution without such an agreement: s 59(2). As to a commercial participator see (1995/96) 3 CLPR 17 (Judith Hill).

[451] Ibid, s 59(3).

[452] There are corresponding provisions relating to a commercial participator: s 60(3).

[453] On, where the solicitation is for purposes rather than institutions, how the proceeds are to be distributed between different charitable institutions: s 60(2).

[454] Section 60(1).   [455] Sections 60(4), 61(1), (4).

[456] Sections 60(5), (6), 61(2), (3), (4).   [457] Section 62.

[458] Ie registered under the Charities Act 1993, s 3.

[459] Charities Act 1992, s 63, as amended by the Deregulation and Contracting Out Act 1994, s 26. A person guilty of an offence is liable on summary conviction to a fine not exceeding level 5 on the standard scale.

12 PUBLIC CHARITABLE COLLECTIONS

Part III of the Charities Act 1992 contains new provisions for the control of public charitable collections.[460] It is understood that this Part of the Act is still under consideration but there is no timetable for implementation.

The Charities Act 1992 Part III imposes controls on public charitable collections, that is, charitable appeals made in any public place or by means of visits from house to house. Again the provision extends beyond charity in the legal sense for 'charitable appeal' is defined as an appeal to members of the public to give money or other property (whether for consideration or otherwise) which is made in association with a representation that the whole or any part of its proceeds is to be applied for charitable, benevolent or philanthropic purposes.[461] The Act provides that no public charitable collection is to be conducted in the area of a local authority except in accordance with a permit issued by the authority or an order made by the Charity Commissioners.[462]

There are detailed provisions relating to applications for permits, the determination of applications, the withdrawal of permits and appeals against the refusal or withdrawal of a permit.[463] The grounds on which a permit may be refused are set out in the Act.[464]

The Charity Commissioners can only make an order authorzing a public charitable collection in relation to a charity in the strict sense. On the application of a charity they may make such an order where they are satisfied that the charity proposes to promote public charitable collections throughout England and Wales, or a substantial part thereof, in connection with its charitable purposes, or to authorize other persons to promote such charitable collections.[465]

---

[460] They replace the Police, Factories etc (Miscellaneous Provisions) Act 1916 and the House-to-House Collections Act 1939. See, generally (1992/93) 1 CLPR 35 (P Luxton); (2000) 63 MLR 791 (Christine Barker).

[461] Charities Act 1992, s 65.

[462] Ibid, s 66. The promoter of a collection in breach of this provision is guilty of an offence and liable on summary conviction to a fine not exceeding level 4 on the standard scale.

[463] Ibid, ss 67 (as amended by the Deregulation and Contracting Out Act 1994, s 27), 68, 70, 71. It is an offence (as under s 66) knowingly or recklessly to furnish false information on an application, and there are offences relating to the improper use of prescribed badges or certificates (or ones nearly resembling them): s 74.

[464] Ibid, s 69.   [465] Ibid, s 69.

15

TRUSTEES. APPOINTMENT AND DETERMINATION OF APPOINTMENT

1 APPOINTMENT OF TRUSTEES

(a) APPOINTMENT BY THE SETTLOR

The first trustees are normally appointed by the settlor or testator who creates the trust.

In the case of a trust created by will the fact that the trustees appointed all predecease the testator,[1] or otherwise cease to exist,[2] or even that no trustees were originally appointed by the testator at all,[3] or that they all disclaim the trust, or that the trustee appointed is legally incapable of taking,[4] will not cause the trust to fail, even though the will may contain no provisions for the appointment of trustees. In such a case the court will be able to appoint trustees under the powers hereafter discussed. In the meantime the personal representatives will be deemed to be constructive trustees, and accordingly it could not be successfully contended that the trust was not completely constituted.

In the case of a voluntary trust purported to be created inter vivos, it seems clear that there can be no valid trust if the document relied upon as constituting the trust is a purported conveyance or transfer to trustees who are not named or otherwise identified, or who are already dead, or have otherwise ceased to exist or are not capable grantees. Such a document would be a nullity and completely ineffective to constitute a trust. If, however, a trust is once completely constituted, it is another matter. Accordingly where there is a conveyance or transfer to named persons, as trustees, a trust is validly created notwithstanding an effective disclaimer[5] by the trustees, and even though the settlor has died without having communicated the trust to the trustees. The reasoning in such case is that the conveyance or transfer is valid

---

[1] *Re Smirthwaite's Trusts* (1871) LR 11 Eq 251.   [2] *A-G v Stephens* (1834) 3 My & K 347, semble.

[3] *Dodkin v Brunt* (1868) LR 6 Eq 580; *Pollock v Ennis* [1921] 1 IR 181.

[4] *Sonley v Clock Makers' Co* (1780) 1 Bro CC 81.

[5] As to disclaimer generally see section 3(a) of this chapter, p 373, infra.

until disclaimer,[6] and accordingly the property passes to the trustees and the trust is completely constituted. On disclaimer the trust property is by operation of law revested in the settlor, or his personal representatives, if he is dead, subject to the trusts, notwithstanding the fact that a disclaimer is often said to make the conveyance void ab initio.[7] Again in such a case the court has power to appoint new trustees.[8] To the above propositions, which are sometimes compendiously comprehended in the maxim that a trust will not fail for want of a trustee, there is one qualification which we have already met in connection with charities.[9] 'If it is of the essence of a trust that the trustees selected by the settlor and no-one else shall act as the trustees of it and those trustees cannot or will not undertake the office, the trust must fail.'[10]

Apart from his power to appoint the first trustees when creating the trust, the settlor has, as such, no power to appoint new or additional trustees, unless such a power is expressly reserved to him by the trust instrument. It should be mentioned that in the case of an inter vivos trust there is no reason why the settlor should not himself be one of the original trustees, and he will inevitably be the sole original trustee if the trust is created by the settlor simply declaring himself a trustee of property already vested in him alone.

(b) APPOINTMENT UNDER AN EXPRESS POWER

It is not usual to insert an express power of appointing new trustees, as the statutory power hereafter discussed is usually regarded as adequate. The operation and effect of an express power is, of course, a question of construction of the particular words used, and it seems that such a power will be strictly construed.[11] It is doubtful whether under an express power the donee of the power can appoint himself to be a new trustee, either alone or jointly with other persons, even assuming that such an

---

[6] Disclaimer does not need to be in any particular form—*Re Moss* (1977) 77 DLR (3d) 314. A transfer of property to a person without his knowledge, if made in proper form, vests the property in him at once, subject to his right to repudiate it when he learns of it: in other words assent is presumed until dissent is signified: *Siggers v Evans* (1855) 5 E & B 367; *Standing v Bowring* (1885) 31 Ch D 282, CA. In *Dewar v Dewar* [1975] 2 All ER 728 it was held that a statement by the donee that he would only accept it as a loan did not prevent it from being an effective gift unless the donor agreed that it should be a loan, not citing the conflicting decision of *Hill v Wilson* (1873) 8 Ch App 888 as pointed out in (1976) 35 CLJ 47 (J W A Thornely) and (1975) 38 MLR 700 (S Roberts). See also (2001) 117 LQR 127 (J Hill); (1999) 28 UWALR 65 (N Crago). Cf *Re Smith (decd)* [2001] 3 All ER 552.

[7] Such a statement signifies that as regards the person to whom the grant is made, he is in respect of his liabilities, his burdens and his rights, in exactly the same position as though no conveyance has been made to him. *Mallott v Wilson* [1903] 2 Ch 494; but see *Re Stratton's Deed of Disclaimer* [1958] Ch 42, [1975] 2 All ER 594, CA; *J W Broomhead (Vic) Pty Ltd v J W Broomhead Pty Ltd* [1985] VR 891. It is contended in [1981] Conv 141 (P Matthews) that disclaimer should in fact make the conveyance void ab initio with consequent failure of the trust, unless established on some other ground.

[8] *Jones v Jones* (1874) 31 LT 535; *Mallott v Wilson* [1903] 2 Ch 494.

[9] Chapter 14, section 5(a), supra, p 322.

[10] Per Buckley J in *Re Lysaght* [1966] Ch 191 at 207, [1965] 2 All ER 888 at 896.

[11] See eg *Stones v Rowton* (1853) 17 Beav 308; *Re Norris* (1884) 27 Ch D 333. See also *Re Papadimitriou* [2004] WTLR 1141 (Isle of Man HC) (power given to protector).

appointment is prima facie, as a matter of construction, within the power.[12] Kay J has stated the equitable objection:

A man should not be judge in his own case; ... he should not decide that he is the best possible person, and say that he ought to be the trustee. Naturally no human being can be imagined who would not have some bias one way or the other as to his own personal fitness, and to appoint himself among other people, or excluding them to appoint himself, would certainly be an improper exercise of any power of selection of a fiduciary character such as this is.[13]

In order to avoid duplication, cases on the construction in express powers of common form phrases which appear in the statutory power in identical or similar terms are discussed in relation to the latter, with an identifying note. They are not, of course, direct decisions on the statute, but are likely to be applied by analogy, and, conversely, decisions on statutory phrases would almost certainly be followed in a case on an express power in similar terms.

(c) APPOINTMENT UNDER THE PROVISIONS OF S 36 OF THE TRUSTEE ACT 1925

The statutory power contained in this section applies to all trusts, unless a contrary intention appears.[14] Such a contrary intention is not, it seems, to be inferred from the mere fact that there is an express power in certain circumstances, and accordingly this would not prevent the appointment of new trustees under the statutory power in other circumstances to which the express power did not apply.[15]

Subsection (1) of s 36 provides as follows:

Where a trustee, either original or substituted, and whether appointed by a court or other-wise, is dead, or remains out of the United Kingdom for more than twelve months, or desires to be discharged from all or any of the trusts or powers reposed in or conferred on him, or refuses or is unfit to act therein, or is incapable of acting therein, or is an infant, then, subject to the restrictions imposed by this Act on the number of trustees—

(a) the person or persons nominated for the purpose of appointing new trustees by the instrument, if any, creating the trust; or

(b) if there is no such person, or no such person able and willing to act, then the surviving or continuing trustees or trustee for the time being, or the personal representatives of the last surviving or continuing trustee;

may, by writing, appoint one or more other persons (whether or not being the persons exercising the power) to be a trustee or trustees in the place of the trustee so deceased,

---

[12] *Re Skeats' Settlement* (1889) 42 Ch D 522; *Re Newen* [1894] 2 Ch 297; see, however, the explanation of these cases in *Montefiore v Guedalla* [1903] 2 Ch 723; doubted in *Re Sampson* [1906] 1 Ch 435.

[13] *Re Skeats' Settlement*, supra, per Kay J at 527.

[14] Trustee Act, 1925, s 69(2). Eg when there is a foreign trustee the power may be varied to prevent his removal by reason of remaining outside the UK for more than 12 months.

[15] *Re Wheeler and De Rochow* [1896] 1 Ch 315; *Re Sichel's Settlements* [1916] 1 Ch 358.

remaining out of the United Kingdom, desiring to be discharged, refusing, or being unfit or being incapable, or being an infant, as aforesaid.

It has been held[16] that as an appointment has to be 'in place of' a retiring trustee, the section cannot be construed so that the appointment of one new trustee would be effective to discharge two retiring trustees.

The unanimous view of textbook writers, the assumption of practitioners, and the only inference to be drawn from the cases, is that a trustee in this section does not include a personal representative, notwithstanding that the definition section[17] specifically provides that 'trustee, where the context admits, includes a personal representative'. In the face of such unanimity of opinion, it is not surprising that no litigant has yet been brave, or perhaps one should say rash, enough even to argue the contrary. It is, however, not easy to find in s 36 a context which clearly supplies the necessary contrary intention and it is noteworthy that in s 41 of the Trustee Act 1925,[18] which gives power to the court to appoint new trustees in certain circumstances, it was thought necessary to provide expressly that nothing therein contained gives power to appoint a personal representative. Of course if a personal representative has become a trustee, the statutory, or any other, power to appoint a new trustee will apply: the circumstances in which this transformation takes place were discussed in chapter 2, section 2(e), p 37, supra.

We must now consider the provisions of the subsection set out above in more detail.

(i) The circumstances in which the statutory power may be exercised

These can be put under eight heads:

(i) 'where a trustee . . . is dead.' It is specifically provided by sub-s(8) that this includes the case of a person nominated trustee in a will but dying before the testator, thus resolving the doubts previously caused by the differing views of the judges.[19] The statutory provision does not cover the case, which is seldom likely to occur in practice, where under an inter vivos trust a trustee appointed is already dead. In the absence of direct authority the cases cited in the previous note provide a close analogy, but, as stated, leave the point doubtful. Perhaps the better view is that of Parker VC in *Re Hadley,*[20] from which it would follow that in the case of such prior death the power of appointment would be exercisable. It will be remembered, however, that if all the trustees appointed under an inter vivos trust are already dead at the date of the deed there will be no valid trust at all.[21]

(ii) 'where a trustee . . . remains out of the United Kingdom[22] for more than twelve

---

[16] *Adam & Co International Trustees Ltd v Theodore Goddard (a firm)* (2000) 144 Sol Jo LB 150. The principle would apply to an appointment in place of any other specified category of trustee.

[17] Trustee Act 1925, s 68(17).   [18] Discussed at p 359, infra.

[19] *Walsh v Gladstone* (1844) 14 Sim 2; *Winter v Rudge* (1847) 15 Sim 596; *Re Hadley* (1851) 5 De G & Sm 67 (all cases on express powers, where doubts still remain).

[20] Supra.   [21] See p 347 supra.

[22] This means Great Britain and Northern Ireland—Trustee Act 1925, s 68(1), (20).

months.'[23] This means an uninterrupted period of 12 months, and it was accordingly held in *Re Walker*[24] that the event upon which the power arose had not happened when the period had been broken by a week's visit to London. If, however, the event has happened and the power has become exercisable, the trustee who has remained out of the United Kingdom can be removed against his will.[25] This head should be excluded where the trust includes a power to appoint non-resident trustees.

(iii) 'where a trustee . . . desires to be discharged from all or any of the trusts or powers reposed in or conferred on him.' It will be observed that this provision specifically authorizes a trustee to retire from a part only of the trusts or powers reposed in or conferred on him, thus getting over the difficulty caused by cases which held that this could only be done with the aid of the court.[26]

(iv) 'where a trustee . . . refuses . . . to act therein.'[27] This seems to cover the case of a trustee who disclaims the trust.[28]

(v) 'where a trustee . . . is unfit to act therein.'[29] It seems that a trustee who is bankrupt is, prima facie, unfit to act,[30] though in *Re Wheeler and De Rochow*[31] the court did not rely on this saying that, whether or not a trustee who became bankrupt was for that reason alone unfit to act, one who became bankrupt and absconded certainly was.

(vi) 'where a trustee . . . is incapable of acting therein.'[32] The better view[33] seems to be that the incapacity to act must be personal incapacity, such as old age, with con-

---

[23] For the protection of purchasers, s 38 of the Trustee Act 1925 provides '(1) A statement contained in any instrument coming into operation after the commencement of this Act by which a new trustee is appointed for any purpose connected with land, to the effect that a trustee has remained out of the United Kingdom for more than twelve months or refuses or is unfit to act, or is incapable of acting . . . shall, in favour of a purchaser of a legal estate, be conclusive evidence of the matter stated. (2) In favour of such purchaser any appointment of a new trustee depending on that statement, and any vesting declaration, express or implied, consequent on the appointment, shall be valid.'

[24] [1901] 1 Ch 259. Cf *Re Moravian Society* (1858) 26 Beav 101; *Re Arbib and Class's Contract* [1891] 1 Ch 601, CA (both decisions on express provisions).

[25] *Re Stoneham's Settlement Trusts* [1953] Ch 59, [1952] 2 All ER 694.

[26] *Savile v Couper* (1887) 36 Ch D 520; *Re Moss' Trusts* (1888) 37 Ch D 513. Cf s 39 Trustee Act 1925, discussed at p 377, infra (retirement without appointment of new trustees).

[27] Trustee Act 1925, s 38, applies—see note 23, supra.

[28] *Viscountess D'Adhemar v Bertrand* (1865) 35 Beav 19.

[29] Trustee Act 1925, s 38, applies—see note 23, supra.

[30] See *Re Roche* (1842) 2 Dr & War 287; *Re Hopkins* (1881) 19 Ch D 61 at 63 CA, per Jessel MR; *Re Matheson* (1994) 121 ALR 605 and (1979) 53 ALJ 648 (R P Meagher).

[31] [1896] 1 Ch 315. Cf *Re Barker's Trusts* (1875) 1 Ch D 43 and *Re Adams' Trust* (1879) 12 Ch D 634 where the question concerned the power of the court to appoint in place of a bankrupt trustee.

[32] Trustee Act 1925, s 38, applies—see note 23, supra.

[33] See eg *Re Bignold's Settlement Trusts* (1872) 7 Ch App 223; *Turner v Maule* (1850) 15 Jur 761; *Re Watts' Settlement* (1851) 9 Hare 106, all decisions on express powers.

sequent bodily and mental infirmity,[34] or mental disorder,[35] but not bankruptcy.[36] Where a trustee who is incapable by reason of mental disorder is also entitled in possession to some beneficial interest in the trust property, it is specially provided[37] that no appointment of a new trustee in his place shall be made,[38] unless leave to make the appointment has been given by the authority having jurisdiction under Part VII of the Mental Health Act 1983.

The Law of Property Act 1925[39] requires that if land subject to a trust of land is vested, solely or jointly, in a trustee who is incapable by reason of mental disorder of exercising[40] his functions as a trustee, he must be discharged before the legal estate is dealt with. This has been modified by the insertion of a new subsection[41] which removes the need for a discharge if there is an attorney under an enduring power of attorney,[42] whenever created,[43] entitled to act for the incapable trustee.[44]

It was held during the First World War that an alien enemy was incapable of acting, on the ground that he could not bring an action to protect the trust property.[45] This decision does not appear to have been cited to the court during the Second World War in a case where the court refused to lay down a rule, but said that on the facts before it there was no evidence that the trustee, resident in enemy occupied territory, was really incapable of acting.[46] The court in fact rather avoided the issue by itself appointing a new trustee under s 41 of the Trustee Act 1925.[47]

---

[34] *Re Lemann's Trusts* (1883) 22 Ch D 633; *Re Weston's Trusts* [1898] WN 151 (cases on appointment by the court).

[35] *Re East* (1873) 8 Ch App 735 (express power); *Re Blake* [1887] WN 173, CA. Cf *Kirby v Leather* [1965] 2 QB 367 at 387, [1965] 2 All ER 441 at 446, CA, per Winn LJ; compromised sub nom *Leather v Kirby* [1965] 3 All ER 927n, HL.

[36] *Turner v Maule*, supra; *Re Watts' Settlement*, supra (both cases on express powers).

[37] Trustee Act 1925, s 36(9) as substituted by the Mental Health Act 1959, s 149(1) and Sch 7 and the Mental Health Act 1983, s 148 and Sch 4, para 4. When the Mental Capacity Act 2005, Sch 6, para 2 has been brought into force—

  (i)   the words in line 2 of the text from: 'is incapable' to 'disorder' should be replaced by: 'lacks capacity to exercise his functions as trustee and'
  (ii) the words in lines 5–6 of the text from: 'the authority' to 'Act 1983' should be replaced by: 'the Court of Protection'.

[38] Except by the person or persons nominated to appoint new trustees by the trust instrument.

[39] Section 22(2) as amended by the Trusts of Land and Appointment of Trustees Act 1996, s 25(1), Sch 3, para 4(6).

[40] When the Mental Capacity Act 2005, Sch 6, para 4 has been brought into force the words in the text from: 'is incapable' in the previous line to 'exercising' should be replaced by: 'lacks capacity (within the meaning of the Mental Capacity Act 2005) to exercise'.

[41] Subsection (3) inserted by the Trustee Delegation Act 1999, s 9(1).

[42] See the Enduring Powers of Attorney Act 1985 and pp 461, 462, infra where the prospective effect of the Mental Capacity Act 2005, not yet in force, is discussed.

[43] Trustee Delegation Act 1999, s 9(2).

[44] When the Mental Capacity Act 2005, Sch 6, para 4 has been brought into force the last two lines in the text from: 'if there' to end should be replaced by: 'at a time when the donee of an enduring power of attorney or lasting power of attorney (within the meaning of the Mental Capacity Act 2005) is entitled to act for the trustee who lacks capacity in relation to the dealing'.

[45] *Re Sichel's Settlement* [1916] 1 Ch 358.   [46] *Re May's Will Trusts* [1941] Ch 109.

[47] Discussed in subsection (f), p 359, et seq.

The question whether a trustee becomes incapable of acting by going abroad is now less likely to arise in the case of the statutory power by reason of the provision already discussed that a new trustee may be appointed in place of a trustee who remains out of the United Kingdom for more than 12 months. In cases on express powers, it was held in two early cases that a trustee did not become incapable of acting by going abroad, even in such places as Australia[48] and China,[49] at that time very remote. In *Mesnard v Welford,*[50] however, it was held that a trustee who had been absent for 20 years and established a business in New York, was incapable of acting as a trustee of leasehold property in London, and in *Re Lemann's Trusts*[51] residence abroad was given as an obvious illustration of incapacity.

One case is specially provided for by the section itself.[52] Where a trustee is a corporation, and the corporation is or has been dissolved, it is deemed to be and to have been from the date of the dissolution incapable of acting in the trusts or powers reposed in or conferred on the corporation.

(vii) 'where a trustee . . . is an infant.' Although the appointment of an infant to be a trustee in relation to any settlement or trust is void,[53] an infant may be a trustee under a resulting, implied or constructive trust.[54]

(viii) 'where a trustee has been removed under a power contained in the instrument creating the trust.'[55] In such a case the statutory power arises and operates in the case of a trustee who is removed, as if he were dead, and in the case of a corporation, as if the corporation desired to be discharged from the trust. It should be observed that this provision applies only in the case where a trustee has been removed under a power contained in the trust instrument. It does not confer any power to remove a trustee.

(ii) The persons who can exercise the statutory power

The section, it will be observed, has a primary and a secondary category.

(i) 'The person or persons nominated for the purpose of appointing new trustees.' There is no need for the nomination to refer to the statutory power[56] and it is usual for the trust deed simply to provide that X shall have power to appoint new trustees. If someone is nominated to appoint new trustees in certain cases only, it should be noted that he is not regarded as nominated to exercise the statutory power in other cases not specifically mentioned.[57] As there is no need for the person nominated to

---

[48] *Re Harrison's Trusts* (1852) 22 LJ Ch 69.   [49] *Withington v Withington* (1848) 16 Sim 104.

[50] (1853) 1 Sm & G 426 (express power). See *Re Bignold's Settlement Trusts* (1872) 7 Ch App 223 (appointment by court).

[51] (1883) 22 Ch D 633 (appointment by court).   [52] Trustee Act 1925, s 36(3).

[53] Law of Property Act 1925, s 20. Note Law of Property Act, s 15 which provides that the parties to a conveyance are presumed to be of full age until the contrary is proved.

[54] See eg *Re Vinogradoff* [1935] WN 68.   [55] Trustee Act 1925, s 36(2).

[56] See *Re Walker and Hughes' Contract* (1883) 24 Ch D 698.

[57] *Re Wheeler and De Rochow* [1896] 1 Ch 315; *Re Sichel's Settlements* [1916] 1 Ch 358.

appoint new trustees to have any beneficial interest under the trust, it is not surprising that it has been held that if a beneficiary is nominated to appoint new trustees, he may continue to exercise the power of appointment after alienating his interest, and without obtaining the consent of the alienees.[58] A curious point arises where two or more persons are jointly nominated to appoint new trustees. Here, unless a contrary intention can be found as a matter of construction, the old rule still applies that a bare power, given to two or more persons by name and not annexed to an estate or office, does not survive, but determines on the death of the first of the named persons to die.[59]

(ii) 'The surviving or continuing trustees or trustee for the time being, or the personal representatives of the last surviving or continuing trustee.' Power to appoint new trustees is given to persons in this second category where there is no one nominated to appoint, or where there is 'no such person able and willing to act'. It was held that there was no person able and willing to act where the persons jointly nominated were a husband and wife, who were at the relevant time living apart and unable to agree on the selection of new trustees,[60] and likewise where the donee of the power of appointment could not be found.[61]

A continuing trustee normally means a trustee who is to continue to act after the appointment of the new trustee has taken effect.[62] It is, however, specifically provided that the provisions of s 36 'relative to a continuing trustee include a refusing or retiring trustee, if willing to act in the execution of the provisions' of that section.[63] It is accordingly possible for all the surviving trustees together, or a sole trustee, to retire and at the same time to appoint new trustees or a new trustee to act in their or his place, which could not be done if this power was given to the continuing trustees or trustee in the prima facie sense. In thus obviating one difficulty, another has arisen; namely, whether the continuing trustees or trustee stricto sensu can validly make an appointment without the concurrence of a refusing or retiring trustee. The answer seems to be that such an appointment is valid, unless it is shown that the refusing or retiring trustee was competent and willing to act, the onus being upon those who allege that this is so to establish it.[64] In practice it is desirable that a refusing or retiring trustee should join in the deed of appointment of new trustees, if this is possible.

[58] *Hardaker v Moorhouse* (1884) 26 Ch D 417 (express power). But see *Re Bedingfield and Herring's Contract* [1893] 2 Ch 332 at 337.

[59] *Re Harding* [1923] 1 Ch 182, [1922] All ER Rep 557. The rule was held not to be abrogated by the Trustee Act 1893, s 22, now replaced by the Trustee Act 1925, s 18. Cf *Bersel Manufacturing Co Ltd v Berry* [1968] 2 All ER 552, HL.

[60] *Re Sheppard's Settlement Trusts* [1888] WN 234.   [61] *Cradock v Witham* [1895] WN 75.

[62] *Travis v Illingworth* (1865) 2 Drew & Sm 344; *Re Norris* (1884) 27 Ch D 333 (both cases on express powers); *Re Coates to Parsons* (1886) 34 Ch D 370. The last two cases disapprove contrary dicta in *Re Glenny and Hartley* (1884) 25 Ch D 611. These cases would still apply to the construction of the word 'continuing' in the case of an express power.

[63] Trustee Act 1925, s 36(8). A trustee who is compulsorily removed because he has remained out of the United Kingdom for more than 12 months is not a refusing or retiring trustee within the subsection and accordingly his concurrence is not required to an appointment of new trustees—*Re Stoneham's Settlement Trusts* [1953] Ch 59, [1952] 2 All ER 694.

[64] *Re Coates to Parsons* (1886) 34 Ch D 370.

The phrase 'the last surviving or continuing trustee' has been held to include a sole trustee,[65] but where all the trustees of a will predecease the testator, the last of them to die does not come within the meaning of the phrase and consequently his personal representatives are not entitled to appoint.[66] Where the section does apply, it seems that the personal representatives of a last surviving or continuing trustee are not bound to exercise the statutory power of appointment.[67]

Subsection (4) provides that:

the power of appointment given . . . to the personal representatives of a last surviving or continuing trustee shall be . . . exercisable by the executors for the time being (whether original or by representation) of such surviving or continuing trustee who have proved the will of their testator or by the administrators for the time being of such trustee without the concurrence of any executor who has renounced or has not proved.

But, by sub-s (5):

a sole or last surviving executor intending to renounce, or all the executors where they all intend to renounce, shall have . . . power, at any time before renouncing probate, to exercise the power of appointment given by this section, . . . if willing to act for that purpose and without thereby accepting the office of executor.

Although a non-proving executor can exercise the power of appointment, his title to do so can only be proved by a proper grant of representation.[68]

(iii) Mode of appointment

An appointment under s 36 is merely required to be in writing, though it is normally made by deed in order to get the benefit of the vesting provisions contained in s 40.[69] It need not be contained in an instrument expressly executed for that purpose, if it can properly be construed as having that effect.[70] If the trust deed in terms requires an appointment to be made with some unusual form of execution or attestation or solemnity, such provisions are ineffective by reason of s 159 of the Law of Property Act 1925, though the section expressly provides that it does not operate to defeat any direction making the consent of some person necessary to a valid appointment.[71] The appointment cannot, however, be made by will, that is to say a last surviving trustee cannot appoint a new trustee to take office at his own death in place of himself.[72]

(iv) Appointment of additional trustees

Even under subsection (1) the number of trustees may be increased, for this section authorizes the appointment of 'one or more other persons . . . to be a trustee or

---

[65] *Re Shafto's Trusts* (1885) 29 Ch D 247.   [66] *Nicholson v Field* [1893] 2 Ch 511.
[67] *Re Knight's Will* (1884) 26 Ch D 82 at 89, per Pearson J (not discussed on appeal).
[68] *Re Crowhurst Park, Sims-Hilditch v Simmons* [1974] 1 All ER 991.
[69] Discussed in section 2 of this chapter, p 370, infra.
[70] *Re Farnell's Settled Estates* (1886) 33 Ch D 399 (express power).
[71] Cf *Lancashire v Lancashire* (1848) 2 Ph 657 (express power).
[72] *Re Parker's Trusts* [1894] 1 Ch 707.

trustees in the place of the trustee' who has already ceased or upon the appointment ceases to hold office. Subsection (6), however, authorizes the appointment of an additional trustee or trustees in some circumstances, even where there is no vacancy in the trusteeship. Subsection (6), as amended by the Trusts of Land and Appointment of Trustees Act 1996, provides as follows:

Where, in the case of any trust, there are not more than three trustees—
    (a) the person or persons nominated for the purpose of appointing new trustees by the instrument, if any, creating the trust; or
    (b) if there is no such person, or no such person able and willing to act, then the trustee or trustees for the time being;

may, by writing, appoint another person or other persons[73] to be an additional trustee or additional trustees, but it shall not be obligatory to appoint any additional trustee, unless the instrument, if any, creating the trust, or any statutory enactment provides to the contrary, nor shall the number of trustees be increased beyond four by virtue of any such appointment.

(v) Effect of appointment

The Trustee Act 1925, s 36(7), which applies equally to a trustee appointed under s 19 or 20 of the Trusts of Land and Appointment of Trustees Act 1996,[74] provides:

Every new trustee appointed under this section as well before as after all the trust property becomes by law, or by assurance, or otherwise, vested in him, shall have the same powers, authorities, and discretions, and may in all respects act as if he had been originally appointed a trustee by the instrument, if any, creating the trust.

(d) APPOINTMENT BY BENEFICIARIES UNDER THE TRUSTS OF LAND AND APPOINTMENT OF TRUSTEES ACT 1996

Where—

    (a) there is no person nominated[75] for the purpose of appointing new trustees by the instrument, if any, creating the trust, and

    (b) the beneficiaries under the trust are of full age and capacity and (taken together[76]) are absolutely entitled to the property subject to the trust

---

[73] Under this provision he cannot appoint himself: *Re Power's Settlement Trusts* [1951] Ch 1074, [1951] 2 All ER 513, CA. Contrast s 36(1), p 349, supra. The Law Reform Committee in their 23rd Report, Cmnd 8733, para 2(6), recommended the amendment of sub-s (6) to bring into line with sub-s (1).

[74] See s 21(3). Section 20 of the 1996 Act is prospectively amended by the Mental Capacity Act 2005—see n 82, infra.

[75] Presumably this means no such person at the relevant time, so that if X alone is nominated and he is dead, the section will apply.

[76] This is thought to encompass the situation where beneficiaries are entitled in succession, or are objects of a discretionary trust, as well as being co-owners. Contrast the wording in s 6(2) which appears to be restricted to joint tenants and tenants in common.

they may give a written direction to the trustees or trustee for the time being[77] to appoint by writing[78] to be a trustee or trustees the person or persons specified in the direction.[79] The direction may be by way of substitution for a trustee or trustees directed to retire,[80] or as an additional trustee or trustees up to the statutory maximum.[81] The section does not expressly require or empower the trustees to comply with the direction but this is thought to be implicit.

It is further provided[82] that where—

(a) a trustee is incapable by reason of mental disorder of exercising his functions as trustee,

(b) there is no person who is both entitled and willing and able to appoint a trustee in place of him under s 36(1) of the Trustee Act 1925, and

(c) the beneficiaries under the trust are of full age and capacity and (taken together) are absolutely entitled to the property subject to the trust

the beneficiaries may give[83] to—

(a) a receiver of the trustee,

(b) an attorney acting for him under the authority of a power of attorney created by an instrument registered under the Enduring Powers of Attorney Act 1985 s 6, or

(c) a person authorized for the purpose by the authority having jurisdiction under Part VII of the Mental Health Act 1983

a written direction to appoint by writing the person or persons specified in the direction to be a trustee or trustees in place of the incapable trustee.

For the purposes of the above provisions the direction may be a single direction given by all, or individual directions given by each, of course in the latter case specifying the same persons.[84] These provisions can be excluded (in whole or in part) in any

---

[77] Or, if there are none, the personal representatives of the last person who was a trustee. 'Trustee for the time being' includes any trustee being directed to retire—see Section 3(c)(vi), infra, p 379.

[78] In practice, it should be by deed to take advantage of s 40 of the Trustee Act 1925—see Section 2, infra, p 370.

[79] Trusts of Land and Appointment of Trustees Act 1996, s 19(1), (2)(b). As to restrictions on who may be specified see ibid s 21(4).

[80] See, Section 3(c)(vi), infra, p 379.   [81] See, Section 1(h), infra, p 365.

[82] Ibid, s 20(1). When the Mental Capacity Act 2005, Sch 6, para 41 has been brought into force the words in (a): 'is incapable by reason of mental disorder of exercising' will be substituted by: 'lacks capacity (within the meaning of the Mental Capacity Act 2005) to exercise'.

[83] Ibid, s 20(2). When the Mental Capacity Act 2005, Sch 6, para 41 has been brought into force there will be substituted—

(i) for (a) 'a deputy appointed for the trustee by the Court of Protection'

(ii) in (b) for the words from 'a power of attorney' to the end, 'an enduring power of attorney or lasting power of attorney registered under the Mental Capacity Act 2005'

(iii) in (c) for the words from 'the authority' to the end, 'the Court of Protection'

[84] Ibid, s 21(1), (2).

disposition on or after 1 January 1997 creating the trust.[85] They may also be excluded in a pre-1997 trust by an irrevocable deed to that effect executed by the settlor (or if more than one settlor such as are alive and of full capacity).[86]

(e) APPOINTMENT BY DONEE OF AN ENDURING POWER OF ATTORNEY

The donee of an enduring power of attorney[87] created after the commencement of the Trustee Delegation Act 1999[88] has been given a new but limited power to appoint new trustees. These provisions are designed to prevent the 'two-trustee rules'[89] from frustrating the new power for an attorney under an enduring power of attorney to exercise the trustee functions of the donor as provided by s1 of the 1999 Act. For example A holds land for himself and B. A appoints X as his attorney under an enduring power. A loses mental capacity and the power is registered. X wants to sell the land but cannot satisfy the 'two-trustee rules' unless a new trustee is appointed.

An attorney who intends to exercise a trustee function in relation to land, the capital proceeds of a conveyance of land or income from land under s 1 of the 1999 Act, s 25 of the Trustee Act 1925, or the instrument creating the trust may appoint a new, additional trustee if the attorney is either both a trustee and an attorney under a registered power of attorney for the other trustee or trustees (to a maximum of two), or an attorney under a registered power for all the trustees (to a maximum of three).[90] A registered power means an enduring power of attorney registered under s 6 of the Enduring Powers of Attorney Act 1985.[91] The power may be excluded or limited by the instrument creating the power of attorney or in the instrument creating the trust.[92]

The Mental Capacity Act 2005, when brought into force will repeal the Enduring Powers of Attorney Act 1985.[93] It will introduce a lasting power of attorney,[94] in effect to replace an enduring power of attorney. Then existing enduring powers of attorney will, however, continue to exist but will become governed by the provisions in Sch 4 to the 2005 Act, and will be capable of registration under that Act. The definition of a registered power will be amended so as to include both an enduring power of attorney and a lasting power of attorney registered under the 2005 Act,[95] and the above provisions[96] will accordingly apply to both.

---

[85] Ibid, s 21(5).   [86] Ibid, s 21(6)–(8).   [87] See p 461 et seq, infra.
[88] Ie 1 March 2000; Trustee Delegation Act 1999, s 8(2).   [89] See p 367, infra.
[90] Trustee Act 1925, s 36(6A), (6B) inserted by the Trustee Delegation Act 1999, s 8(1).
[91] Trustee Act 1925, s 36(6C), inserted by the Trustee Delegation Act 1999, s 8(1).
[92] Trustee Act 1925, s 36(6D), likewise inserted.
[93] Mental Capacity Act 2005 s 67(2). Sch 7. There are transitional provisions and savings in Sch 5, Part 2.
[94] Ibid, ss 9–14 and Sch 1. See p 462, infra.
[95] The amendments are made by s 67(1), Sch 6, para 3.
[96] Ie those contained in the Trustee Act 1925, s 36(6A), (6B).

(f) APPOINTMENT BY THE COURT

(i) Under the statutory power contained in the Trustee Act 1925

Section 41(1)[97] of the Act provides as follows:

The court[98] may,[99] whenever it is expedient to appoint a new trustee or new trustees, and it is found inexpedient difficult or impracticable so to do without the assistance of the court, make an order appointing a new trustee or new trustee either in substitution for or in addition to any existing trustee or trustees, or although there is no existing trustee.

In particular and without prejudice to the generality of the foregoing provision, the court may make an order appointing a new trustee in substitution for a trustee who is incapable, by reason of mental disorder within the meaning of the Mental Health Act 1983, of exercising his functions as trustee, or is a bankrupt, or is a corporation which is in liquidation or has been dissolved.[100]

Cases in which the court has made an appointment under the statutory power, apart from those specifically referred to in the section, include the following: where all the named trustees predeceased the testator;[101] where no trustees were named;[102] where a trustee had gone abroad with the intention of residing there permanently;[103] where a trustee was incapable of acting by reason of old age and consequent bodily and mental infirmity;[104] where a trustee was, so far as was known, in enemy occupied territory;[105] where there was a doubt as to whether the statutory, or an express, power of appointment was exercisable;[106] where the persons who should have exercised a power of appointment,[107] or one of them in the case of a joint power,[108] were resident abroad; where an infant had been nominated to appoint new trustees, for though an appointment by an infant may not be void, it is at least liable to be set aside and accordingly it would not be safe to act upon it;[109] and where there was friction

---

[97] As amended by the Mental Health Act 1959, s 149(1) and Sch 7, Pt I, and the Criminal Law Act 1967, s 10 and Sch 3, Pt III and the Mental Health Act 1983, s 148 and Sch 4, para 4. When the Mental Capacity Act 2005, Sch 6, para 3 has been brought into force the words in para 2 of the subsection from 'is incapable' to 'exercising' should be replaced by 'lacks capacity to exercise'.

[98] Defined in s 67(1). It normally means the High Court, or, where the estate or fund subject to the trust does not exceed £30,000, the County Court—see p 4, n 14, infra.

[99] The court delayed making an appointment in *Re Pauling's Settlement (No 2)* [1963] Ch 576, [1963] 1 All ER 857 in order to protect the old trustees against possible liability for costs and estate duty.

[100] It has been held on similar provisions in Australia that although a trustee who becomes bankrupt will be removed almost as of course, in its discretion the court will not replace a corporate trustee in liquidation as a matter of course, but will approach the question with an open mind and assess where the balance of interest lies: *Wells v Wily* [2004] NSWSC 607, (2004) 83 FLR 284.

[101] *Re Smirthwaite's Trusts* (1871) LR 11 Eq 251.   [102] *Re Gillett's Trusts* (1876) 25 WR 23.

[103] *Re Bignold's Settlement Trusts* (1872) 7 Ch App 223.

[104] *Re Lemann's Trusts* (1883) 22 Ch D 633; *Re Phelps' Settlement Trusts* (1885) 31 Ch D 351, CA; *Re Weston's Trusts* [1898] WN 151.

[105] *Re May's Will Trusts* [1941] Ch 109.

[106] *Re Woodgate's Settlement* (1956) 5 WR 448; *Re Bignold's Settlement Trusts*, supra.

[107] *Re Humphry's Estate* (1855) 1 Jur NS 921.   [108] *Re Somerset* [1887] WN 122.

[109] *Re Parsons* [1940] Ch 973, [1940] 4 All ER 65; and see (1941) 57 LQR 25 (R E Megarry).

between trustees, there being no dispute as to the facts, even though this involved removing a trustee against her will.[110]

There are authorities suggesting that the court will not under s 41 interfere with an appointment of new trustees by a person having the statutory or an express power to do so,[111] even on an application by all the beneficiaries,[112] and even though the person with the power of appointment may have intended to exercise it corruptly.[113] An Australian court has held,[114] however, it is thought rightly, that a court is not deprived of its statutory power to appoint a new trustee where there are circumstances which render it expedient to do so simply because there is an appointor who is capable of appointing and is willing to act. The exercise of the power will depend on a number of other circumstances as to whether it is expedient to make an appointment.

Even a decree for administration of the trusts by the court does not take away a power of appointing new trustees, though after decree the exercise of the power is subject to the supervision of the court.[115] In such case, if the person with the power of appointment nominates a fit and proper person, he must be appointed and the court will not appoint another person whom it might think more suitable. If, however, the court does not approve of the person nominated it will call for a fresh nomination. Persistent nomination of unsuitable persons would, however, amount to a refusal to appoint and the court would then make its own choice.[116]

The exercise by the court of its power to appoint trustees under s 41 frequently involves the removal of an existing trustee, possibly against his will. This section, however, as a matter of construction does not empower the court simply to discharge a trustee, unless at the same time it reappoints the continuing trustees in place of themselves and the retiring trustee. This, however, the court will not do in practice, either from want of jurisdiction or from a refusal to exercise it.[117]

It should be observed that s 41(4) provides in express terms that 'nothing in this section gives power to appoint an executor or administrator',[118] though the section will, of course, apply if the personal representative has become a trustee.[119] The court

---

[110] *Re Henderson* [1940] Ch 764, [1940] 3 All ER 295. Cf *Letterstedt v Broers* (1884) 9 App Cas 371, PC.

[111] *Re Higginbottom* [1892] 3 Ch 132; *Re Brockbank* [1948] Ch 206, [1948] 1 All ER 287; *Re Merry* [2003] WTLR 424 (Canada). Aliter, where the donee of the power is an infant—*Re Parsons*, supra.

[112] But see now s 19 of the Trusts of Land and Appointment of Trustees Act discussed supra p 356.

[113] *Re Hodson's Settlement* (1851) 9 Hare 118. The abuse could, however, be dealt with by the court under its inherent jurisdiction in an action to restrain the corrupt exercise of the power and for the execution of the trusts by the court.

[114] *Pope v DRP Nominees Pty Ltd* (1999) 74 SASR 78.

[115] The last proposition only applies when there has been a general administration order; it does not apply to an order for partial administration, unless an enquiry is ordered as to the appointment of new trustees, or proceedings are taken for this purpose—*Re Cotter* [1915] 1 Ch 307.

[116] *Re Gadd* (1883) 23 Ch D 134, CA; *Tempest v Lord Camoys* (1882) 21 Ch D 571, CA; *Re Norris* (1884) 27 Ch D 333. See *Yusuof bin Ahmad bin Talib v Hong Kong Bank Trustees (Singapore) Ltd* (1989) 3 MLJ 84.

[117] *Re Chetwynd's Settlement* [1902] 1 Ch 692. See also *Re Dewhirst's Trusts* (1886) 33 Ch D 416, CA; *Re Gardiner's Trusts* (1886) 33 Ch D 590.

[118] The court has such power in some circumstances under the Supreme Court Act 1981, s 114(4), and the Administration of Estates Act 1925, s 23(2).

[119] See p 38, ante.

has now, however, been given a wide jurisdiction to appoint substituted personal representatives under s 50 of the Administration of Justice Act 1985.[120]

(ii) Under its inherent jurisdiction

Prior to the Trustee Act 1850 the court had no statutory power to appoint new trustees, but appointments were commonly made by the Court of Chancery under its inherent jurisdiction to supervise trusts and trustees.[121] There was nothing in the Act of 1850 or in the subsequent legislation replacing it to take away this jurisdiction. The statutory power should, however, be invoked if it is available, and in view of the wide wording of s 41, it is seldom necessary to rely on the inherent jurisdiction,[122] unless it is desired to remove a trustee against his will and there is a dispute as to the facts.[123]

(iii) Under the Trustee Act 1925, s 54

This section[124] gives the authority having jurisdiction under Part VII of the 1983 Act[125] concurrent jurisdiction with the High Court where a mental patient is a trustee and a receiver is acting for him,[126] except where the trust is being administered by the High Court, in relation to matters consequent on the making of provision by the said authority for the exercise of a power of appointing trustees or retiring from a trust. The object of this provision is to prevent the necessity of cases being transferred from one department to another.

Significant amendments will be made to s 54 when the Mental Capacity Act 2005 is brought into force.[127] The effect of these amendments will be that where a person lacks capacity to exercise his functions as a trustee and a deputy is appointed for him by the Court of Protection or an application for the appointment of a deputy has been made but not determined, then, except as regards a trust which is being administered by the High Court, the Court of Protection will have concurrent jurisdiction with the High Court in relation to, inter alia, matters consequent on the making of provision by the Court of Protection for the exercise of a power of appointing trustees or retiring from a trust. Subject to this, the Court of Protection will not be permitted to make an order, or give a direction or authority, in relation to a person who lacks capacity to exercise his functions as trustee, if the High Court may make an order to that effect under the 2005 Act.

---

[120] See p 37, ante.

[121] See eg *Buchanan v Hamilton* (1801) 5 Ves 722; *Ockleston v Heap* (1847) 1 De G & Sm 640.

[122] *Dodkin v Brunt* (1868) LR 6 Eq 580. Here the court relied on the inherent jurisdiction.

[123] See p 378, infra.

[124] As substituted by the Mental Health Act 1959 s 149(1) and Sch 7, Part I and amended by the Mental Health Act 1983, s 148, and Sch 4, para 4.

[125] Ie the Lord Chancellor, any judge of the Supreme Court nominated by the Lord Chancellor, the Master of the Court of Protection, the Public Trustee (subject to the directions of the Master) and any officer of that court nominated by the Lord Chancellor—Mental Health Act 1983, ss 111(2), 112 and 93(1) and (4), as amended by the Public Trustee and Administration of Funds Act 1986, s 2(3).

[126] Also where an application for the appointment of a receiver has been made but not yet determined.

[127] See Sch 6, para 3(4).

(iv) Under the Judicial Trustees Act 1896 and the Public Trustee Act 1906

These statutes are considered in chapter 16.

(v) Effect of appointment by the court

The Trustee Act 1925, s 43, provides:

Every trustee appointed by a court of competent jurisdiction shall, as well before as after the trust property becomes by law, or by assurance, or otherwise, vested in him, have the same powers, authorities, and discretions, and may in all respects act as if he had been originally appointed a trustee by the instrument, if any, creating the trust.

(g) THE PERSONS WHO MAY BE APPOINTED TRUSTEE

(i) General

So far as legal capacity is concerned, in general[128] any person who has capacity to hold property has capacity to be a trustee. There are however, statutory disqualifications in relation to charity trustees,[129] and trustees of an occupational pension scheme established under a trust.[130] The Crown, it seems, can be a trustee,[131] at any rate if it deliberately chooses to act as such,[132] but in practice should never be appointed a trustee if only by reason of the doubts and difficulties in enforcing the trust.[133] A local authority cannot be a trustee of an ecclesiastical charity or a charity for the relief of poverty.[134] A minor cannot be validly appointed a trustee either of real or personal property,[135] though it seems that he can hold property, other than a legal estate in land,[136] upon a resulting, implied or constructive trust.[137]

Where an appointment of a new trustee is made by the court, it will be guided by certain rules in deciding who should be appointed. The Court of Appeal in *Re Tempest*[138] set out three principles. First, that in selecting a person for the office of trustee the court will have regard to the wishes of the author of the trust, expressed in,

---

[128] As to aliens see the Status of Aliens Act 1914, s 17, as amended by the British Nationality Act 1948. There are limitations on capacity as to ships and aircraft. As to ships, see the Merchant Shipping Act 1995 and SI 1993/3138 as amended by SI 1994/541, and as to aircraft, SI 2000/1562, art 4(3).

[129] See p 292, supra.

[130] Pensions Act 1995, ss 29, 30. See also ss 3–6 as to prohibition from being, or suspending, such a trustee by the Occupational Pensions Regulatory Authority.

[131] *Penn v Lord Baltimore* (1750) 1 Ves Sen 444 at 453, per Hardwicke LC; *Lonrho Exports Ltd v Export Credits Guarantee Department* [1996] 2 Lloyd's Rep 645, 659. As to an officer of state, see *Town Investments Ltd v Department of the Environment* [1978] AC 359, [1977] 1 All ER 813, HL.

[132] *Civilian War Claimants Association Ltd v R* [1932] AC 14 at 27, HL, per Lord Atkin. Note, however, that circumstances which may at first sight appear to constitute the Crown as a trustee may well be explicable by reference to the governmental powers and obligations of the Crown and may not set up a true trust at all— *Tito v Waddell (No 2)* [1977] Ch 106, [1977] 3 All ER 129, and see p 74, supra.

[133] See *Dyson v A-G* [1911] 1 KB 410, CA; *Esquimalt and Nanaimo Rly Co v Wilson* [1920] AC 358, PC; Hanbury, *Essays in Equity*, pp 87–89; Holdsworth, *History of English Law*, vol IX, pp 30–32.

[134] Local Government Act 1972, s 139(3).   [135] Law of Property Act 1925, s 20.

[136] Cf Law of Property Act 1925, s 1(6).   [137] *Re Vinogradoff* [1935] WN 68.

[138] (1866) 1 Ch App 485.

or plainly deduced from, the instrument containing it. Secondly, that the court will not appoint a person with a view to the interest of some of the beneficiaries, in opposition to the interest of others. Thirdly, that the court will have regard to the question whether the appointment will promote or impede the execution of the trust. It appears from the same case, however, that the mere fact that a continuing trustee refuses to act with a proposed new trustee would not be sufficient to induce the court to refrain from appointing him. A more recent case[139] suggests a fourth principle, namely, that the court should not appoint a person who would be in a position where there would be a conflict between his duty and his interest.

In applying these principles the courts have held that certain categories of persons will not normally be appointed trustees, though in every case 'the rule is not imperative, and when there are special circumstances, the court will exercise its discretion in judging whether the case is one in which the rule may be departed from'.[140] Thus neither the tenant for life, nor any other beneficiary, will normally be appointed.[141] If, perhaps because it is impossible to obtain the services of an independent trustee,[142] beneficiaries are appointed, an undertaking may be required in some such form as in *Re Lightbody's Trusts*,[143] where two beneficiaries were appointed trustees, and they were required to undertake that if either of them became a sole trustee he would use every endeavour to obtain the appointment of a co-trustee. Further, the court will not normally appoint the husband of a tenant for life;[144] indeed, it has been said that no near relative of parties interested should be appointed except in cases of absolute necessity.[145] This dictum was applied by an Australian court in *Re John Albert Roberts*[146] where the Public Trustee was trustee of the deceased's estate for the widow and their children. The court refused, on the widow's application, to appoint her as trustee in substitution for the Public Trustee. The same rule applies to the solicitor of the tenant for life, or, presumably for any other of the beneficiaries,[147] to a solicitor of an existing trustee,[148] and to the partner of an existing solicitor-trustee. It may be noticed that there is no principle that would prevent a bank from being appointed a trustee merely because one or all of the beneficiaries happen to be customers of the bank, but the special facts may justify the court in refusing to appoint a particular bank, where, for example, the trustee has a discretionary power to advance to the life

---

[139] *Re Parsons* [1940] Ch 973, [1940] 4 All ER 65.

[140] *Ex p Conybeare's Settlement* (1853) 1 WR 458, per Turner LJ.

[141] *Ex p Conybeare's Settlement*, supra; *Re Clissold's Settlement* (1864) 10 LT 642; *Forster v Abraham* (1874) LR 17 Eq 351.

[142] Since the Public Trustee Act 1906, it may be possible to appoint the Public Trustee (but see pp 384, 447, infra), or a trust corporation or other professional trustee may be appointed: see p 388, infra and pp 443–445 as to their remuneration.

[143] (1884) 52 LT 40. Similarly in *Re Parrott* (1881) 30 WR 97 (husband of tenant for life).

[144] *Re Parrott* (1881) 30 WR 97; *Re Coode* (1913) 108 LT 94.

[145] *Wilding v Bolder* (1855) 21 Beav 222 and see *Re Parsons*, supra.   [146] (1983) 70 Fed LR 158.

[147] *Re Spencer's Settled Estates* [1903] 1 Ch 75; *Re Cotter* [1915] 1 Ch 307.

[148] *Re Norris* (1884) 27 Ch D 333, where a solicitor trustee appointed his son and partner as co-trustee. The trusts were being administered by the court, and the court refused to sanction the appointment.

tenant out of capital, and the life tenant has a large overdraft with the bank proposed as trustee.[149]

It is generally said that the donee of a power of appointment should in making his appointment be guided by the same principles as would guide the court. In practice, however, persons whom the court would not normally appoint are frequently appointed, and such appointment will not normally be upset by the court.[150] Again it has been said that it is the duty of a trustee to consult beneficiaries before appointing a new trustee,[151] but although it is a desirable and usual practice to do so, the duty seems to be unenforceable for, as has been seen,[152] the court will not normally interfere with an appointment made by a person having power to do so, even at the instance of all the beneficiaries.

In conclusion, it may be observed that the settlor himself is, of course, legally quite uninhibited in the choice of the original trustees, and the same appears to be the case where beneficiaries direct the appointment of trustees under the Trusts of Land and Appointment of Trustees Act 1996.[153] In practice, however, this is a vital matter and the choice of the trustees will affect the smooth running of the trusts and the safety of the interests of the beneficiaries. Qualities to be looked for include integrity, a willingness to spend time and trouble on the trust affairs, the ability to get on with cotrustees and beneficiaries; knowledge of financial matters, business acumen and common sense: and Megarry VC has observed that there are some who are temperamentally unsuited to being trustees.[154]

(ii) Exporting a trust

The power of the court to supervise a trust and give a remedy for breach of trust depends upon the trustees being within the jurisdiction of the court: the court acts in personam. If, therefore, trustees within the jurisdiction are replaced as trustees by persons who are outside the jurisdiction the court ceases to be able to deal with the trust. This is referred to as exporting, or sometimes emigrating, a trust. Because of the effect it has persons outside the jurisdiction should not, therefore, normally be appointed. However, it is well established that there is no absolute bar to the appointment of persons resident abroad as trustees of an English trust. In *Re Whitehead's Will Trusts*[155] Pennycuick J held that the court would only make such an appointment in exceptional circumstances, and said that it would not be right for donees of a power to

---

[149] *Re Northcliffe's Settlements* [1937] 3 All ER 804, CA. Cf *Re Pauling's Settlement Trusts* [1964] Ch 303, [1963] 3 All ER 1, CA.

[150] *Re Earl of Stamford* [1896] 1 Ch 288 (solicitor of tenant for life); *Re Coode* (1913) 108 LT 94 (husband of tenant for life); *Re Norris*, supra (as to the appointment of a father and son, solicitors in partnership). As to the case where the donee of the power of appointment is an infant see *Re Parsons* [1940] Ch 973, [1940] 4 All ER 65; (1941) 57 LQR 25 (R E Megarry).

[151] *O'Reilly v Alderson* (1849) 8 Hare 101.   [152] See p 360, ante.

[153] Section 19. See section 1(d), supra.

[154] *Cowan v Scargill* [1985] Ch 270, [1984] 2 All ER 750. See (1988) 2 TL & P 86 (C Bell).

[155] *Re Whitehead's Will Trust* [1971] 2 All ER 1334. See Matthews, *Trusts: Migration and Change of Proper Law.*

do so out of court save in like exceptional circumstances. If they were to do so presumably the court would be likely to interfere at the instance of beneficiaries. The most obvious exceptional circumstances are where the beneficiaries have settled permanently in some country outside the United Kingdom and what is proposed to be done is to appoint new trustees in that country.[156] The court, however, refused to appoint trustees resident in Jersey in *Re Weston's Settlements*[157] where the appointment was sought as part of a tax avoidance scheme which would have involved removing the trusts from England to Jersey.

In *Richard v Mackay*[158] Millett J considered that the language of Pennycuick J in *Re Whitehead's Will Trust*[159] was too restrictive for the circumstances of the present day. Though when the court is invited to exercise an original discretion of its own, the applicants must make out a positive case for the court to exercise discretion as they request, it is a different matter where the transaction is proposed to be carried out by the trustees in the exercise of their discretion, entirely out of court, and the trustees merely seek the authorization of the court for their own protection. In that case the court is concerned to ensure that the proposed exercise of the trustees' power is lawful and within the power and that it does not infringe the trustees' duty to act as ordinary, reasonable and prudent trustees might act, but it requires only to be satisfied that the trustees can properly form the view that the proposed transaction is for the benefit of beneficiaries or the trust estate. On the facts, the proposed export of about a quarter of the trust funds to a proposed similar trust in Bermuda was lawful. This approach was approved by Vinelott J in *Re Beatty's Will Trusts (No 2)*,[160] and the proposed export of the trust regarded as acceptable, although one of the three principal beneficiaries was to continue to be domiciled and resident in the United Kingdom.

(iii) Trustees of a trust for religious purposes

In the case of a charitable trust for religious purposes in general only members of the church, denomination or sect in question will be appointed. It has been held in New Zealand,[161] and the law is probably the same in England, that there is no absolute rule and the court has an unfettered discretion when it is called upon to act.[162]

(h) THE NUMBER OF TRUSTEES

Apart from statute, on the one hand a sole trustee can act effectively, while on the other hand there is no limit to the number of trustees who may be appointed.

---

[156] *Re Whitehead's Will Trust* [1971] 2 All ER 1334.   [157] [1969] 1 Ch 223, [1968] 3 All ER 338, CA.
[158] (1987) unreported until (1997) 11 Tru LI 23.
[159] Supra. See *Royal Society for the Protection of Animals v A-G* [2001] 3 All ER 530.
[160] (1987) unreported until (1997) 11 Tru LI 77.
[161] *Mendelssohn v Centrepoint Community Growth Trust* [1999] 2 NZLR 88. The relevant statutory provisions are similar.
[162] Ie under the Trustee Act 1925, s 41 discussed p 359, supra.

Statutory provisions, however, impose limitations in many cases on both the maximum and minimum number of trustees.

(i) Maximum number of trustees

Section 34(2) of the Trustee Act 1925 as amended by the Trusts of Land and Appointment of Trustees Act 1996 provides as follows:

In the case of settlements[163] and dispositions creating trusts of land[164] . . .—

    (a) the number of trustees thereof shall not in any case exceed four, and where more than four persons are named as such trustees, the four first named (who are able and willing to act) shall alone be the trustees, and the other persons named shall not be trustees unless appointed on the occurrence of a vacancy;

    (b) the number of the trustees shall not be increased beyond four.

It should be noted that this subsection is in terms restricted to settlements and dispositions creating trusts of land,[165] and accordingly does not apply to trusts of pure personalty; further, sub-s (3) provides that the restrictions on the number of trustees do not apply:

    (*a*) in the case of land vested in trustees for charitable, ecclesiastical, or public[166] purposes;[167] or

    (*b*) where the net proceeds of the sale of the land are held for like purposes; or

    (*c*) to the trustees of a term of years absolute limited by a settlement on trusts for raising money, or of a like term created under the statutory remedies[168] relating to annual sums charged on land.

On the appointment of a trustee the number of trustees may, subject to the above restrictions, be increased.[169] However, where an additional trustee or additional trustees is or are appointed under the provisions of s 36(6) of the Trustee Act 1925,[170] the number of trustees cannot be increased beyond four, whether or not the trust involves land.

---

[163] Defined in Trustee Act 1925, s 68(15), and Settled Land Act 1925, s 1.

[164] Defined in ibid, s 68(6), as amended by the Trusts of Land & Appointment of Trustees Act 1996.

[165] See also s 34(3), where, however, the words 'creating trusts' would appear to have been omitted after the word 'disposition'. The section applies to appointments under s 19 of the Trusts of Land and Appointment of Trustees Act 1996: ibid s 19(3).

[166] Trusts of land belonging to an unincorporated society coming within the provisions of the Literary and Scientific Institutions Act 1854 are public trusts—*Re Cleveland Literary and Philosophical Society's Land* [1931] 2 Ch 247.

[167] No land held on such trusts is or is deemed to be settled land: Trusts of Land and Appointment of Trustees Act 1996, s 2(5). This Act repealed and reversed the previous position in the Settled Land Act 1925, s 29(1).

[168] See Law of Property Act 1925, s 121.

[169] Trustee Act 1925, s 37(1)(*a*), which appears to apply to appointments under both an express and the statutory power. As to the latter, s 36(1) by itself would seem to have the same result.

[170] See p 355 supra.

(ii) Minimum number of trustees

Obviously as a result of deaths of trustees the number may be reduced to one, or, indeed, to none at all,[171] and legislation cannot prevent this happening. There are, however, two sets of relevant provisions.

First, in some cases it is provided that for some purposes a sole trustee (not being a trust corporation)[172] cannot act effectively. The two-trustee rules, as they are sometimes called, require that, save where a sole trustee is a trust corporation:

(i) capital moneys arising from land must be paid to, or at the direction of, at least two trustees;[173]

(ii) a valid recept for such capital moneys must be given otherwise than by a sole trustee;[174] and

(iii) a conveyance or deed must be made by at least two trustees to overreach any powers or interests affecting a legal estate in land.[175]

These provisions apply notwithstanding anything to the contrary contained in the relevant instruments.

Secondly, the better view, it is submitted, is that, provided no contrary intention was expressed in the power of appointment, equity did not insist upon the original number of trustees being maintained. Accordingly, on the appointment of new trustees the number of trustees might be increased[176] or reduced.[177] It followed that there was in general no obligation to keep up the number of trustees, and where, as was commonly the case, the power of appointment was vested in the continuing trustees, failure to replace the trustees who ceased for any reason to hold office was not normally a breach of trust. This was carried to the limit by the Court of Appeal, which held in *Peacock v Colling*[178] that, at any rate where the will contemplated a sole trustee acting, a sole continuing trustee was justified in refusing to appoint a second trustee, and consequently his failure to do so was not a breach of trust.

There are now statutory provisions[179] to the effect that on the appointment of a trustee[180] it shall not be obligatory:

---

[171] But note Trustee Act 1925, s 18(2), discussed at p 375, infra.

[172] See chapter 16, section 5, p 388, infra.

[173] Settled Land Act 1925, ss 18(1)(*c*), 94(1); Law of Property Act 1925, s 27(2), as substituted by the Law of Property (Amendment) Act 1926 and amended by the Trusts of Land and Appointment of Trustees Act 1996.

[174] Trustee Act 1925, s 14(2) as amended by the Law of Property (Amendment) Act 1926 and the Trusts of Land and Appointment of Trustees Act 1996.

[175] Law of Property Act 1925, s 2(1), (2) as amended by the Trusts of Land and Appointment of Trustees Act 1996.

[176] *Meinertzhagen v Davis* (1844) 1 Coll 335. See now Trustee Act 1925, s 37(1)(*a*).

[177] *Emmet v Clark* (1861) 3 Giff 32; *Re Cunningham and Bradley's Contract for Sale to Wilson* [1877] WN 258 (the statement in this case that there is a different rule in relation to charity trustees seems to be ill-founded—see *Re Worcester Charities* (1847) 2 Ph 284; *Re Shrewsbury Charities* (1849) 1 Mac & G 84).

[178] (1885) 53 LT 620, CA. Cf *Re Rendell's Trusts* (1915) 139 LT Jo 249.

[179] Trustee Act 1925, s 37(1)(*c*), as amended by the Trusts of Land and Appointment of Trustees Act 1996, Sch 3, para 12.

[180] Presumably under either an express or the statutory power.

(i) subject to the provisions discussed above[181] to appoint more than one trustee where only one trustee was originally appointed, or

(ii) to fill up the original number of trustees where more than two trustees were originally appointed.

The same section[182] further provides, however, that:

except where only one trustee was originally appointed, and a sole trustee when appointed will be able to give valid receipts for all capital money,[183] a trustee shall not be discharged from his trust unless there will be either a trust corporation or at least two persons[184] to act as trustees to perform the trust.

A sole surviving trustee even of pure personalty accordingly cannot retire from the trust and appoint a sole trustee (not being a trust corporation) to act in his stead where more than one trustee was originally appointed, and in many cases a sole trustee, even though he be the first and only trustee originally appointed, is in the same position.[185] It has been held,[186] however, that s 37(1)(c) can be overridden by a provision in the trust instrument since it is ancillary to s 36, which can certainly be overridden under s 69(2),[187] and as consolidating legislation could not change the underlying law.

(iii) Appointment by the court

The court has always had power and now has statutory jurisdiction under s 41 of the Trustee Act 1925 to increase the number of trustees on an appointment of new trustees,[188] or by appointing an additional trustee or trustees where there is no vacancy.[189] An appointment by the court is commonly made at the request of one or more of the beneficiaries, but although it has been held in some cases that a beneficiary was entitled to have a second,[190] or even a third,[191] trustee appointed, it is doubtful whether in strictness even all the beneficiaries acting together have an absolute right to require the appointment of even a second trustee.[192] Again, the court has always had power to reduce the number of trustees, and on the appointment of new

---

[181] See also Trustee Act 1925, s 37(2), which provides 'Nothing in this Act shall authorise the appointment of a sole trustee, not being a trust corporation, where the trustee, when appointed, would not be able to give valid receipts for all capital money arising under the trust'.

[182] Ibid, s 37(1)(c).   [183] Ie where there is a trust of pure personalty.

[184] Prior to the 1996 Act the subsection referred to 'individuals' not 'persons' and there was doubt as to whether corporate trustees were included. The amendment removes the doubt.

[185] Ie where a sole trustee when appointed will be unable to give valid receipts for all capital money.

[186] London Regional Transport Pension Fund Trustee Co Ltd v Hatt [1993] PLR 227 on this point, but relevant part of judgment cited and discussed by M Jacobs in (1993) 7 Tru LI 72.

[187] See p 349, supra.

[188] See eg Birch v Cropper (1848) 2 De G & Sm 255; Plenty v West (1853) 16 Beav 356.

[189] See eg Grant v Grant (1865) 34 LJ Ch 641; Re Gregson's Trusts (1886) 34 Ch D 209.

[190] Grant v Grant, supra.   [191] Viscountess D'Adhemar v Bertrand (1865) 35 Beav 19.

[192] Re Badger's Settlement (1915) 113 LT 150. But the position may be different since 1925 where there is a sole trustee who cannot give a valid receipt for capital moneys, and see now s 19 of the Trusts of Land and Appointment of Trustees Act 1996 discussed, supra, p 356.

trustees may do so under the statutory jurisdiction,[193] even in disregard of directions contained in the trust deed,[194] though it is not likely to take this course without special circumstances being established.[195] As we have seen,[196] the court either cannot, or will not, under the statutory jurisdiction, reduce the number of trustees save on the appointment of new trustees, though it has inherent jurisdiction to do so in an action to administer the trust.

In deciding how many trustees should be appointed the court will, of course, comply with the restriction limiting the number of trustees to four, in those cases where s 34 of the Trustee Act 1925 applies, and in practice will never appoint a sole trustee where such trustee would not be able to give a valid receipt for capital moneys. Quite apart from statutory provisions, there are obvious dangers in the trust property being under the control of a sole trustee, and consequently it has been said[197] that 'the court never commits a trust to the care of a single trustee, even in cases where no more than one was originally appointed' and one judge even affirmed[198] 'I do not think it right to leave it to two'. It seems, however, that although the court is reluctant to appoint a single trustee,[199] it will do so if special circumstances would make it more beneficial to the parties interested,[200] for instance where the trust fund is small and shortly to be distributed and the appointment of a second trustee would incur disproportionate expense.

(i) SEPARATE SETS OF TRUSTEES FOR DISTINCT TRUSTS

On an appointment[201] out of court of a trustee for the whole or any part of trust property, s 37(1)(b) of the Trustee Act 1925 provides:

a separate set of trustees, not exceeding four, may be appointed for any part of the trust property held on trusts distinct from those relating to any other part or parts of the trust property, notwithstanding that no new trustees or trustee are or is to be appointed for other parts of the trust property, and any existing trustee may be appointed or remain one of such separate set of trustees, or, if only one trustee was originally appointed, then, save as hereinafter provided,[202] one separate trustee may be so appointed.

The section apparently applies in a case where different parts of the trust property are for the time being held on distinct trusts, even though upon a certain event the trusts, may ultimately coalesce.[203]

[193] *Re Fowler's Trusts* (1886) 55 LT 546; *Re Leslie's Hassop Estates* [1911] 1 Ch 611.
[194] *Re Leslie's Hassop Estates*, supra.   [195] *Re Fowler's Trusts* (1886) 55 LT 546.
[196] See p 360, supra.
[197] Per Romilly MR in *Viscountess D'Adhemar v Bertrand* (1865) 35 Beav 19, 20.
[198] *Bulkeley v Earl of Eglinton*, supra, at 994, per Page Wood VC. This statement goes too far.
[199] Ie an individual as opposed to a trust corporation.
[200] *Sitwell v Heron* (1850) 14 Jur 848; *Re Reynault* (1852) 16 Jur 233.
[201] Presumably under either an express or the statutory power.
[202] By sub-s (2) set out supra, p 368, in n 181.   [203] *Re Hetherington's Trusts* (1886) 34 Ch D 211.

On an appointment of new trustees by the court,[204] it has always been possible for separate sets of trustees to be appointed for different parts of the trust property held on distinct trusts,[205] though applications to the court are now much less common by reason of the existence of the statutory power just mentioned.

(j) LIABILITY[206] OF THE ORIGINAL TRUSTEES AND THE PURPORTED NEW TRUSTEES UNDER AN INVALID APPOINTMENT

If a purported appointment of new trustees in place of existing trustees is invalid, the existing trustees remain trustees and will be liable as such in case there is any loss to the trust estate, even though they act upon the assumption that the appointment was valid and take no further part in the administration of the trust. A purported new trustee under the invalid appointment may also be liable as a trustee de son tort if he on the like assumption has acted in the trust. These propositions are neatly illustrated by *Pearce v Pearce*,[207] where A and B were trustees. A deed was prepared appointing C a new trustee in the place of B. It was executed by C, but not by the other parties, so that the appointment was invalid. At the same time the trust fund was transferred by A and B to A and C. Afterwards A and C authorized the husband of the tenant for life to receive the fund, and it was lost. It was held that both B and C were liable for the loss, in addition, of course, to A.

2 VESTING OF THE TRUST PROPERTY

(a) NEW TRUSTEES

When new trustees are appointed it is clearly vital that the trust property shall be vested in them jointly with the continuing trustees, if any. Dealing first with an appointment out of court, the vesting of the trust property in the new trustees (including any continuing trustees) can be done by means of an ordinary conveyance or transfer by the old trustee or trustees in whom the property is vested, in the form appropriate to the particular kind of trust property. There will not always, however, be a need for this to be done, as by statute the trust property is in many cases automatically vested in the new and any continuing trustees, provided that the new trustees are appointed by deed.

---

[204] It is not clear whether the Trustee Act 1925, s 37, applies to an appointment by the court, though it seems to have been assumed that the original provision in s 5 of the Conveyancing Act 1881 did so apply in *Re Paine's Trusts* (1885) 28 Ch D 725; *Re Hetherington's Trusts*, supra. But see *Re Moss' Trusts* (1888) 37 Ch D 513.

[205] See eg the cases cited in n 204 above.

[206] See, generally, chapter 24, infra, and in particular s 61 of the Trustee Act 1925, discussed section 3(f), p 546, infra.

[207] (1856) 22 Beav 248.

The relevant provisions are contained in s 40 of the Trustee Act 1925, sub-s (1) of which is in the following terms:

Where by a deed[208] a new trustee is appointed to perform any trust, then:

(*a*) if the deed contains a declaration[209] by the appointor to the effect that any estate or interest in any land subject to the trust, or in any chattel so subject, or the right to recover or receive any debt or other thing in action so subject, shall vest in the persons who by virtue of the deed become or are the trustees for performing the trust, the deed shall operate,[210] without any conveyance or assignment, to vest in those persons as joint tenants and for the purposes of the trust the estate interest or right to which the declaration relates; and

(*b*) if the deed ... does not contain such a declaration, the deed shall, subject to any express provision to the contrary therein contained, operate as if it had contained such a declaration by the appointor extending to all the estates interests and rights with respect to which a declaration could have been made.

There are similar provisions in s 40(2) vesting the trust property in the continuing trustees on the discharge of a trustee under s 39,[211] or under s 19 of the Trusts of Land and Appointment of Trustees Act 1996.[212]

Certain cases are, however, expressly excluded from the operation of the section by sub-s (4), and unfortunately they include some of the most usual kinds of trust property.[213] They comprise the following:

(*a*) land conveyed by way of mortgage for securing money subject to the trust except land conveyed on trust for securing debentures or debenture stock;

(*b*) land held under a lease[214] which contains any covenant, condition or agreement against assignment or disposing of the land without licence or consent, unless, prior to the execution of the deed containing expressly or impliedly the vesting declaration, the requisite licence or consent has been obtained, or unless, by virtue of any statute or rule of law, the vesting declaration, express or implied, would not operate as a breach of covenant or give rise to a forfeiture;

(*c*) any share, stock, annuity or property which is only transferable in books kept by a company or other body, or in manner directed by or under an Act of Parliament.

---

[208] An instrument in writing suffices in the case of trustees for a listed trade union: Trade Union and Labour Relations (Consolidation) Act 1992, s 13(1)–(3).

[209] See also sub-s (3), which deals with the possibility that there may be defects in the form of an express vesting declaration.

[210] Even where the estate, interest or right is not vested in the person making the appointment. Cf s 9, Law of Property Act 1925. This provision conveniently covers the case where, for instance, the person who appoints the new trustees is not himself a trustee. The section presumably does not enable a legal estate outstanding in some third party holding adversely to the trust to be vested in the new trustees, or even, it seems, according to *Re King's Will Trusts* [1964] Ch 542, [1964] 1 All ER 833, where the trustee holds the legal estate in some other capacity, such as personal representative.

[211] Discussed p 377, infra.

[212] Discussed p 356, supra. Section 19 added to s 40(2) by Sch 3, para 3(14) of the 1996 Act.

[213] Paragraph (a) and (c) do not apply in the case of trustees for a listed trade union: Trade Union and Labour Relations (Consolidation) Act 1992, s 13(4).

[214] Defined by the subsection to include an underlease and an agreement for a lease or underlease.

There are special reasons why it is necessary to exclude the implied vesting provisions in each of these cases. In the first case, concerning mortgages, the object is to keep the trusts off the face of the mortgagor's title; trustees who lend money on a mortgage of land do not disclose the fact in the mortgage deed, nor is it disclosed in the transfer of mortgage which must be executed on the appointment of new trustees.[215] The second case, concerning leases, is to avoid the possibility of an inadvertent breach of covenant which would render the lease liable to be forfeited. The last case is necessary because the legal title to such property as stocks and shares depends upon the appropriate entry having been made in a register consequent upon the completion of a proper instrument of transfer and the whole system would break down if the legal title could pass in any other manner. A company deals with the registered shareholder as the legal owner of the shares, and does not recognize the existence of any trust which may affect them.

(b) VESTING ORDERS

Wide powers to make vesting orders are given to the court under ss 45–56[216] of the Trustee Act 1925. In particular, it is provided that where the court appoints or has appointed a trustee, or where a trustee has been appointed out of court under any statutory or express power, the court may make a vesting order vesting land or any interest therein in the persons who on the appointment are the trustees in any such manner and for any such estate or interest as the court may direct,[217] and may likewise make an order vesting in such persons the right to transfer or call for a transfer of stock, or to receive the dividends or income thereof, or to sue for or recover a thing in action.[218]

It should be mentioned that by rule 6 of the Judicial Trustee Rules 1972, on the appointment of a judicial trustee the court is required to make such vesting or other orders as may be required for vesting the trust property in the judicial trustee either as sole trustee or jointly with other trustees as the case requires.

---

215 The Law of Property Act 1925, s 112, as amended by the Decimal Currency Act 1969, s 10(1), provides that a purchaser shall not be deemed to have notice of any trust by reason of the fact that the transfer bears only a 50p stamp and not any higher ad valorem duty. See also the Law of Property Act 1925, s 113.

216 A vesting order can only be made in relation to property within the territorial jurisdiction of the court: *Webb v Webb* [1992] 1 All ER 17, further proceedings [1994] QB 696, [1994] 3 All ER 911, ECJ. A new section was substituted for s 54 by the Mental Health Act 1959, s 149(1) and Sch 7, Pt 1, which also amended s 55. These sections were slightly amended by the Mental Health Act 1983, s 148 and Sch 4, para 4(c) and (d). Cf *Re Harrison's Settlement Trusts* [1965] 3 All ER 795. Sections 54 and 55 are prospectively amended by the Mental Capacity Act 2005, Sch 6, para 3(4), (5).

217 Trustee Act 1925, s 44. Alternatively by s 50, if it is more convenient the court may appoint a person to convey the land or any interest therein.

218 Trustee Act 1925, s 51.

3 TERMINATION OF TRUSTEESHIP

(a) DISCLAIMER[219]

A person who is appointed a trustee cannot be compelled to accept the office. He may disclaim[220] the office, which will also amount to a disclaimer of the estate,[221] at any time before acceptance, but once he has accepted it, it cannot thereafter be disclaimed.[222] Acceptance may be either express, or implied from the acts or conduct of the alleged trustee. Execution by the trustee of the trust deed will normally be regarded as an express acceptance of the trust,[223] and where a person is appointed by will to be executor and trustee, it seems that if he takes out probate of the will, he will be treated as having thereby also accepted the trust.[224] It is sometimes said that in the absence of evidence to the contrary, acceptance will be presumed,[225] but the position is far from certain.

Whether by his conduct a person is deemed to have accepted the trust depends upon the view which the court takes of the facts of the case.[226] In general, any interference with the subject matter of the trust by a person appointed trustee will be regarded as an acceptance of the trust, unless it can clearly be explained on some other ground. Thus where a man has permitted an action to be brought in the name of himself and the other trustees,[227] or given directions as to the sale of the trust property and made enquiries as to the accounts,[228] he has been held to have accepted the trust. In another case[229] there was a bequest of £1,100 and certain leasehold property to trustees. The only relevant act of the trustees was an assignment of the leasehold property to a beneficiary who had become absolutely entitled. It was held that the execution of the assignment amounted to an acceptance of the trusts not only of the leasehold property but also of the sum of £1,100, for there cannot be part acceptance and part disclaimer. Acceptance of part is regarded as acceptance of the whole, and accordingly prevents a disclaimer of any other parts.[230] Conversely partial disclaimer is impossible: to be effective disclaimer must be 'of the totality of the office and estate and ab initio'.[231]

On the other hand, a person appointed a trustee has been held not to have accepted the trust merely by holding the deed for about six months for safe custody,[232] and

---

[219] The effect of a valid disclaimer is discussed in section 1(a) of this chapter, p 347, supra.

[220] At the cost of the trust estate—*Re Tryon* (1844) 7 Beav 496.

[221] *Re Birchall* (1889) 40 Ch D 436, CA.

[222] *Re Sharman's Will Trusts* [1942] Ch 311, [1942] 2 All ER 74, and see *Re Lister* [1926] Ch 149, CA.

[223] *Jones v Higgins* (1866) LR 2 Eq 538.

[224] *Mucklow v Fuller* (1821) Jac 198; *Re Sharman's Will Trust*, supra.

[225] See eg Underhill and Hayton *Law of Trusts and Trustees*, 16th edn, p 451—the corresponding statement in an earlier edition was cited with approval in *Re Sharman's Will Trusts* [1942] Ch 311, [1942] 2 All ER 74.

[226] See *White v Barton* (1854) 18 Beav 192.   [227] *Montfort v Cadogan* (1810) 17 Ves 485.

[228] *James v Frearson* (1842) 1 Y & C Ch Cas 370.   [229] *Urch v Walker* (1838) 3 My & Cr 702.

[230] *Re Lord and Fullerton's Contract* [1896] 1 Ch 228, CA.

[231] Per Sargant LJ in *Re Lister* [1926] Ch 149 at 166, CA.   [232] *Evans v John* (1841) 4 Beav 35.

similarly in another, perhaps rather doubtful case, where the alleged trustee had actually signed a legacy duty receipt which he need not have done if he were not a trustee.[233] Again, the court has sometimes allowed that the dealing with the subject matter of the trust which is alleged to constitute acceptance of the trust was merely carried out in the capacity of agent to a trustee who had accepted,[234] though the court would doubtless be suspicious of such an explanation of his conduct by an alleged trustee.[235]

If the trust has not been accepted it may be disclaimed, the proper form being by a deed poll.[236] As has been said,[237] 'It is most prudent that a deed of disclaimer[238] should be executed by a person named trustee, who refused to accept the trust, because such deed is clear evidence of the disclaimer, and admits of no ambiguity; but there may be conduct which amounts to a clear disclaimer, and such appears to be the case here.' The conduct referred to was that of the alleged trustee who purchased real property and took a conveyance from one who could only have a title thereto on the basis of a disclaimer having been effected.[239] An effective disclaimer may be made by an alleged trustee in the pleadings in an action brought against him for enforcement of the trust,[240] or even by his counsel at the bar.[241]

Although it has been said[242] that 'a disclaimer, to be worth anything, must be an act where by one entitled to an estate immediately and before dealing with it renounces it', the better view is that although a disclaimer ought to be made without delay, there is no rule that it must be executed within any particular time,[243] and in several reported cases a disclaimer after 20 years or so has been held to be valid.[244] It is submitted that mere inaction by the alleged trustee over a long period may by itself be sufficient evidence of disclaimer, and the longer the period of inaction, the stronger the presumption of disclaimer.[245]

It has been said that one of several trustees cannot disclaim[246] but it is submitted, with respect, that this obiter dictum cannot stand in the light of numerous cases

---

233 *Jago v Jago* (1893) 68 LT 654.

234 *Dove v Everard* (1830) 1 Russ & M 231; *Lowry v Fulton* (1838) 9 Sim 104.

235 *Conyngham v Conyngham* (1750) 1 Ves Sen 522.

236 *Re Schar* [1951] Ch 280, [1950] 2 All ER 1069.

237 Per Leach MR in *Stacey v Elph* (1833) 1 My & K 195 at 199.

238 It has been held that what is in form a deed of release which logically involves a prior acceptance, may operate as a disclaimer if this was the intention (*Nicolson v Wordsworth* (1818) 2 Swan 365).

239 See also *Re Gordon* (1877) 6 Ch D 531; *Re Birchall* (1889) 40 Ch D 436, CA.

240 *Norway v Norway* (1834) 2 My & K 278; *Bray v West* (1838) 9 Sim 429.

241 *Foster v Dawber* (1860) 1 Drew & Sm 172.

242 Per Kelly CB in *Bence v Gilpin* (1868) LR 3 Exch 76 at 81.   243 *Jago v Jago* (1893) 68 LT 654.

244 *Doe d Chidgey v Harris* (1847) 16 M & W 517 (16 years); *Peppercorn v Wayman* (1852) 5 De G & Sm 230 (20 or 21 years).

245 *Re Clout and Frewer's Contract* [1924] 2 Ch 230; *Rajabali Jumabhoy v Ameerali R Jumabhoy* [1997] 3 SLR 802 (Singapore).

246 Per Vaisey J in *Re Schar* [1951] Ch 280 at 285, [1950] 2 All ER 1069 at 1072.

where such a disclaimer has been held to be effective,[247] thus making the title of those trustees who do accept valid ab initio. Finally it should perhaps be mentioned that just as acceptance of a trust makes a subsequent disclaimer impossible, so a valid disclaimer precludes the possibility of a subsequent acceptance.

(b) DEATH

Trustees are invariably joint tenants and accordingly on the death of one of two or more trustees the trust estate, by reason of the ius accrescendi, devolves on the surviving trustees or trustee. It is now provided by statute, affirming the equitable rule,[248] that the office likewise devolves on the surviving trustees or trustee. The terms of s 18(1) of the Trustee Act 1925 are as follows:

Where a power or trust is given to or imposed on two or more trustees jointly, the same may be exercised or performed by the survivors or survivor of them for the time being.

It should be remembered that this provision does not abrogate the old rule that a bare power, given to two or more persons by name and not annexed to an estate or office, does not survive.[249] However it has been said[250] that:

Every power given to trustees which enables them to deal with or affect the trust property is prima facie given them ex officio as an incident of their office, and passes with the office to the holders or holder thereof for the time being: whether a power is so given ex officio or not depends in each case on the construction of the document giving it, but the mere fact that the power is one requiring the exercise of a very wide personal discretion is not enough to exclude the prima facie presumption . . .; the testator's reliance on the individuals to the exclusion of the holders of the office for the time being must be expressed in clear and apt language.

Upon the death of a sole or last surviving trustee, the trust estate, since 1925, devolves on his personal representatives,[251] and it is provided by s 18(2) of the Trustee Act 1925, that such personal representatives (excluding an executor who has renounced or has not proved),[252] 'shall be capable of exercising or performing any power or trust which was given to, or capable of being exercised by, the sole or last surviving or continuing trustee, or other trustees or trustee for the time being of the trust'. It will be observed that this provision does not impose any obligation on the personal representatives to act, and it would seem therefore that the old law still applies, that 'such a personal representative of a deceased trustee has an absolute right to decline

---

[247] See eg *Peppercorn v Wayman* (1852) 5 De G & Sm 230; *Re Birchall* (1899) 40 Ch D 436, CA. McGarvie J agreed with the view in the text in *J W Broomhead (Vic) Pty Ltd v J W Broomhead Pty Ltd* [1985] VR 891, saying that Vaisey J's opinion is inconsistent with authority.

[248] See eg *Warburton v Sandys* (1845) 14 Sim 622.

[249] *Re Harding* [1923] 1 Ch 182, [1922] All ER Rep 557, see p 354, supra.

[250] Per Farwell J in *Re Smith* [1904] 1 Ch 139 at 144; *Re De Sommery* [1912] 2 Ch 622.

[251] Administration of Estates Act 1925, ss 1–3, as amended. See (1977) 41 Conv 423 (P W Smith).

[252] Trustee Act 1925, s 18(4).

to accept the position and duties of trustee if he chooses so to do'.[253] Presumably, however, if such a personal representative chose to accept[254] the trust, he would thereafter be liable as a trustee in the ordinary way. Even if personal representatives do accept the trust, they can only act until the appointment of new trustees. In practice, they are themselves likely to be the appropriate persons to appoint new trustees, but if some other person has such a power which is validly exercised, it will operate forthwith to oust the personal representatives for all purposes from the trust.[255]

Finally it should be mentioned that all the above provisions are subject to the restrictions imposed in regard to receipt by a sole trustee, not being a trust corporation.[256]

(c) RETIREMENT AND REMOVAL

(i) Under an express power in the trust instrument

An express power of retirement or removal is not usually inserted under most kinds of trust. A power of removal is, however, commonly found in an equitable mortgage to a bank by a deposit of title deeds, when the mortgagor often declares himself a trustee of the legal estate for the bank, which is given an express power to remove the mortgagor as trustee and appoint itself or some other person in his place.[257]

(ii) Under the provisions of s 36 of the Trustee Act 1925

As we have seen,[258] a trustee who desires to be discharged from all or any of the trusts may retire on the appointment of a new trustee in his place, and on the appointment of a new trustee an existing trustee may be removed against his will if he remains out of the United Kingdom for more than 12 months, or refuses or is unfit to act therein, or is incapable of acting.

It should be noted that it has been held[259] that the appointment of a single trustee under s 36(1) would be effective to discharge only one of two or more trustees: the other trustee or trustees would only be effectively discharged by retirement under s 39. The decision has, however, met with convincing criticism.[260]

---

[253] Per Vaughan Williams LJ in *Re Benett* [1906] 1 Ch 216 at 255, CA; *Re Ridley* [1904] 2 Ch 774.

[254] Taking out probate is not, of course, any evidence of an intention to accept a trust of which the deceased was trustee.

[255] *Re Routledge's Trusts* [1909] 1 Ch 280.   [256] Trustee Act 1925, s 18(3).

[257] *London and County Banking Co v Goddard* [1897] 1 Ch 642; and see Key and Elphinstone's *Precedents in Conveyancing*, 15th edn, vol 2, p 237.

[258] See section 1(c), p 349, supra. Similarly under an appropriate express power of appointment.

[259] *Adam & Co International Trustees Ltd v Theodore Goddard (a firm)* [2000] 144 SJ LB 149.

[260] [2003] Conv 15 (F Barlow).

(iii) Under the provisions of s 39 of the Trustee Act 1925[261]

Under these provisions a trustee may be able to retire without a new appointment. Section 39 provides as follows:

Where a trustee is desirous of being discharged from the trust, and after his discharge there will be either a trust corporation or at least two persons to act as trustees to perform the trust, then, if such trustee as aforesaid by deed declares that he is desirous of being discharged from the trust, and if his cotrustees and such other person, if any, as is empowered to appoint trustees, by deed consent[262] to the discharge of the trustee, and to the vesting in the cotrustees alone of the trust property, the trustee desirous of being discharged shall be deemed to have retired from the trust, and shall, by the deed, be discharged therefrom under this Act, without any new trustee being appointed in his place.

It appears that under this provision, as contrasted with the provisions of s 36, a trustee cannot retire from part of the trusts, as there is no phrase equivalent to 'all or any of the trusts or powers'. However, if separate sets of trustees have been appointed under s 37, it is submitted that a trustee will be able to retire therefrom under s 39, on the ground that the distinct trust is to be regarded as a trust and not merely part of a trust.

(iv) Under the provisions of s 41 of the Trustee Act 1925

As we have seen the court may, under this section, on the appointment of a new trustee, remove an existing trustee. It will not, however, simply discharge a trustee without appointing a new trustee,[263] nor will it exercise its statutory jurisdiction to remove a trustee where there is a dispute as to the facts.[264]

It was said in one case[265] that 'no person can be compelled to remain a trustee and act in the execution of the trust' but retirement without good cause was discouraged by the rule that if a trustee retired from mere caprice, he would have to pay the costs,[266] though he might be justified in wishing to retire and accordingly be allowed his costs when circumstances arising in the administration of the trust had altered the nature of his duties and involved him in difficulties and responsibilities which he had never contemplated.[267] However, since the Trustee Act 1925 recognizes that a trustee has a right to retire if he desires to do so,[268] it would seem that a trustee should now

---

[261] As amended by the Trusts of Land and Appointment of Trustees Act 1996, Sch 3, para 3(13). Note that in relation to trustees for a listed trade union references to a deed are to be construed as references to an instrument in writing: Trade Union and Labour Relations (Consolidation) Act 1992, s 13(1)–(3).

[262] By the Public Trustee Act 1906, s 5(2) where the Public Trustee has been appointed a trustee, a cotrustee may retire under these provisions notwithstanding that there are not more than two trustees, and without any consents being obtained.

[263] See pp 359–360, supra. Also *Re Harrison's Settlement Trusts* [1965] 3 All ER 795.

[264] *Re Combs* (1884) 51 LT 45, CA, applied *Popoff v Actus Management Ltd* [1985] 5 WWR 660. Cf *Re Dove's Will Trust* [1939] WN 230.

[265] *Forshaw v Higginson* (1855) 20 Beav 485 at 487, per Romilly MR.

[266] *Forshaw v Higginson*, supra; *Howard v Rhodes* (1837) 1 Keen 581.

[267] *Forshaw v Higginson*, supra; *Gardiner v Downes* (1856) 22 Beav 395.

[268] See *Re Duke of Norfolk's Settlement Trusts* [1981] 3 All ER 220 at 231, CA, per Brightman LJ.

normally be allowed the costs of an application to the court, if for any reason he is unable to take advantage of the statutory provisions.

Where a sole trustee wishes to retire, and it is impossible to find anyone who is willing to become the new trustee,[269] the court will not discharge him, so as to leave the trust without a trustee. An order may, however, be made in such a case for the administration of the trust by the court, and although the trustee retains his office, the court will take care in working out the order that the trustee does not suffer.[270] Similar considerations will presumably apply,[271] where one of two trustees wishes to retire, and the sole continuing trustee would not be able to give valid receipts for capital moneys.[272]

(v) By the court under its inherent jurisdiction

The court has an inherent jurisdiction to remove a trustee in an action[273] for the administration or execution of a trust, without necessarily appointing a new trustee, and notwithstanding that the facts may be in dispute.[274] The Privy Council observed in *Letterstedt v Broers*[275] that there was little authority to guide them in deciding in what circumstances the jurisdiction should be exercised and they were not prepared to lay down any general rule beyond the very broad principle that their main guide must be the welfare of the beneficiaries. It seems that although friction and hostility between a trustee and the beneficiaries is not necessarily or even normally a sufficient ground for the removal of a trustee,[276] the court may think it proper to take this into account and accordingly in some circumstances to remove a trustee, even though he has not been guilty of any breach of trust.[277]

Clarke v Heathfield (No 2)[278] was an unusual case in which the court removed the trustees of the funds of the National Union of Mineworkers and appointed a receiver to act until new trustees were appointed, or, on a change of heart, the removed trustees were restored. Factors leading to the removal included the attempt by the trustees to place the trust property abroad and out of reach of sequestrators appointed by the court, placing the trust funds in jeopardy, and by their actions making the trust funds unavailable for the purposes for which they were contributed by the general membership.

Provided that the individual trustees are subject to the jurisdiction of the English courts, there is power to remove them and appoint new trustees, and to make such in

---

269 Since the Public Trustee Act 1906, it will usually be possible to appoint the Public Trustee (but see p 384, infra) or a trust corporation may be appointed.

270 *Courtenay v Courtenay* (1846) 3 Jo & Lat 519; *Re Chetwynd's Settlement* [1902] 1 Ch 692.

271 Cf *Re Chetwynd's Settlement*, supra.   272 See section 1(h), p 365, supra.

273 If there is a substantial dispute of fact the claim should be made under CPR Part 7, not CPR Part 8.

274 *Re Chetwynd's Settlement* [1902] 1 Ch 692; *Re Wrightson* [1908] 1 Ch 789; *Re Henderson* [1940] Ch 764, [1940] 1 All ER 295; *Scott v Scott* [1991] 5 WWR 185; *Porteous v Rinehart* (1998) 19 WAR 495.

275 (1884) 9 App Cas 371 at 385, PC, applied *Re Whitehouse* [1982] Qd R 196; *Titterton v Oates* [2001] WTLR 319 (Supreme Ct of Aust Capital Territory).

276 *Forster v Davies* (1861) 4 De GF & J 133; *Re Wrightson*, supra.

277 *Letterstedt v Broers*, supra; *Re Consiglio Trusts* (1973) 36 DLR (3d) 658.   278 [1985] ICR 606.

personam orders as may be necessary to achieve vesting of the trust assets in the new trustees. This is so whether or not the trust assets are situated in England, and whether or not the proper law of the trusts in question is English law.[279]

(vi) At instance of beneficiaries under the Trusts of Land and Appointment of Trustees Act 1996

The provisions of s 19 of the 1996 Act, discussed above,[280] which in certain circumstances enable beneficiaries to direct the appointment of trustees, apply equally to enable them to direct the retirement of trustees from the trust.[281] Where a trustee has been given such a direction and—

(a) reasonable arrangements have been made for the protection of any rights of his in connection with the trust,

(b) after he has retired there will be either a trust corporation or at least two persons to act as trustees to perform the trust, and

(c) either another person is to be appointed to be a new trustee on his retirement or the continuing trustees by deed consent to his retirement

he must make a deed declaring his retirement and is deemed to have retired and to have been discharged from the trust.[282]

Further, as we have seen,[283] in certain circumstances a trustee who is incapable by reason of mental disorder of exercising his functions as trustee can in effect be removed by a substitute appointment following a direction by the beneficiaries under s 20 of the Trusts of Land and Appointment of Trustees Act 1996.

The above provisions do not apply in relation to a trust created by a disposition in so far as the disposition so provides.[284]

(vii) By consent of the beneficiaries

If all the cestuis que trust, being sui iuris, consent to the retirement of a trustee, none of them will thereafter be able to call that trustee to account for anything that happens after the date of such retirement. In truth this is merely a special application of the rule[285] that a beneficiary who has concurred in or consented to a breach of trust cannot have any right of action in respect thereof.

---

[279] *Chellaram v Chellaram* [1985] Ch 409, [1985] 1 All ER 1043; (1985) 135 NLJ 18 (D Hayton).

[280] Section 1(d), p 356, supra.   [281] Ibid, s 19(2)(a).

[282] Trusts of Land and Appointment of Trustees Act 1996, s 19(3). By sub-s (4) the retiring trustee and the continuing trustees (together with any new trustee) must do anything necessary to vest the trust property in the continuing trustees (together with any new trustee).

[283] See p 357, supra and note prospective amendments to s 20 referred to in nn 82 and 83.

[284] Section 21(5). As to pre-1997 trusts see sub-ss (6), (7), (8) and p 358 supra.

[285] Discussed in chapter 24, section 3(b), p 534, infra.

(viii) By payment into court

Under the Trustee Act 1925, s 63,[286] trustees may pay into court money or securities belonging to a trust. It has been said[287] that 'payment of a trust fund into court is a retiring from the trust', and it is settled that having done so the trustees cannot prevent a cestui que trust from having the fund paid out to him,[288] nor can the trustees any longer exercise any of their discretionary powers.[289] It seems, however, that he does not in fact altogether cease to be a trustee, neither is the court nor the Accountant-General constituted a co-trustee.[290] He remains a trustee for the purpose of receiving notices,[291] and would be a necessary party to an action in relation to the fund.[292]

---

[286] Discussed in chapter 22, section 11(d), p 494, infra.

[287] Per Page Wood VC in *Re Williams' Settlement* (1858) 4 K & J 87 at 88.

[288] *Re Wright's Trusts* (1857) 3 K & J 419.

[289] *Re Tegg's Trust* (1866) 15 LT 236; *Re Nettleford's Trusts* (1888) 59 LT 315.

[290] *Thompson v Tomkins* (1862) 6 LT 305; *Barker v Peile* (1865) 2 Drew & Sm 340.

[291] *Thompson v Tomkins,* supra.   [292] *Barker v Peile,* supra.

16

SPECIAL KINDS OF TRUSTEES

1 JUDICIAL TRUSTEES

By the Judicial Trustees Act 1896[1] the High Court[2] is empowered, on application made by or on behalf of the person creating or intending to create a trust, or of a trustee or beneficiary, to appoint a person, known as a judicial trustee, to be a trustee of that trust. The object of the Act has been said[3] to have been 'to provide a middle course in cases where the administration of the estate by the ordinary trustees had broken down and it was not desired to put the estate to the expense of a full administration. In those circumstances, a solution was found in the appointment of a judicial trustee, who acts in close concert with the court and under conditions enabling the court to supervise his transactions.' The provisions of the Act do not seem, however, to have found much favour with practitioners: it is often possible, and thought more convenient, to deal with cases where a judicial trustee could be applied for, by appointing a corporate trustee.

A judicial trustee may be appointed either jointly with any other person, or as sole trustee, and if sufficient cause is shown, in place of all or any existing trustees.[4] It is expressly provided that the appointment is to be made at the discretion of the court, and it follows that no one can claim to be entitled as of right to have an appointment made.[5] Thus the court in one case refused to make an appointment on the application of the mortgagees of one fifth of the reversion where one of two trustees wished to be discharged, and the tenant for life was prepared to appoint in his place a person to whom no objection was made.[6]

The Act does not contain any definition of 'trust', and it was held in *Re Marshall's Will Trusts*[7] that that word must be given its ordinary meaning, the judge for the purpose of the case before him adopting the definition given by Underhill,[8] and

---

[1] Section 1(1). See, generally (2003) 51 T & ELJ 11 (J Ellis and P Hewitt).
[2] Proceedings under the Act are assigned to the Chancery Division.
[3] Per Jenkins J in *Re Ridsdel* [1947] Ch 597 at 605, [1947] 2 All ER 312 at 316–317.
[4] Judicial Trustees Act 1896, s 1(1). In *Re Martin* [1900] WN 129, Kekewich J expressed the opinion that the union of a judicial trustee and a private trustee was undesirable.
[5] Ibid, s 1(1). *Re Ratcliff* [1898] 2 Ch 352.   [6] *Re Chisholm* (1898) 43 Sol Jo 43.
[7] [1945] Ch 217, [1945] 1 All ER 550.
[8] *Law of Trusts and Trustees*, 8th edn, p 3. The definition is modified in the current (16)th edition.

holding that Settled Land Act trustees were trustees within that definition. In one respect, however, the meaning of trust is considerably extended for the purpose of the Judicial Trustees Act, which by s 1(2) expressly provides that 'the administration of the property of a deceased person, whether a testator or intestate, shall be a trust, and the executor or administrator a trustee, within the meaning of this Act'. Accordingly the court, by appointing a judicial trustee, can in effect appoint a new personal representative,[9] which, as we have seen,[10] it has no power to do either under the provisions of the Trustee Act 1925,[11] or the inherent jurisdiction.[12] Unless, however, the will appointed separate executors for different parts of the estate, the court has no powers to appoint a judicial trustee of the trusts affecting a part only of the estate. Unless this were done, the executorship would be indivisible, and there would not be created separate trusts within the meaning of the Act of 1896 with regard to particular assets.[13] It may be added that the court now has a wide statutory jurisdiction to appoint substituted personal representatives under s 50 of the Administration of Justice Act 1985, and the court may treat an application to the court under that section as including an application for the appointment of a judicial trustee.

By s 1(3) of the Act 'any fit and proper person nominated for the purpose in the application may be appointed a judicial trustee, and, in the absence of such nomination, or if the court is not satisfied of the fitness of a person so nominated, an official of the court[14] may be appointed.' An official of the court cannot, however, be appointed or act as judicial trustee for any persons in their capacity as members or debenture holders of, or being in any other relation to, any corporation or unincorporate body, or any club, or of a trust which involves the carrying on of any trade or business unless the court, with or without special conditions to ensure the proper supervision of the trade or business, specifically directs.[15] The Public Trustee Act 1906[16] provides that the Public Trustee may, if he thinks fit, be appointed to be a judicial trustee.

Except where the judicial trustee is an official of the court, the court may require a judicial trustee to give security approved by the court duly to account for what he receives as judicial trustee and to deal with it as the court directs. Security is normally by guarantee. It will not, however, normally require security to be given when the application is made by a person creating or intending to create a trust.[17]

---

9 *Re Ratcliff* [1898] 2 Ch 352.   10 See p 359, supra.

11 Section 41(1), prospectively amended by the Mental Capacity Act 2005, Sch 6, para 3.

12 Note, however, the Supreme Court Act 1981, s 114(4) and the Administration of Estates Act 1925, s 23(2).

13 *Re Wells* [1967] 3 All ER 908.

14 'Official of the Court' means the holder of any paid office in or connected with the Supreme Court, and includes the Official Solicitor to the Supreme Court—Judicial Trustees Act 1896, s 5, and Judicial Trustee Rules 1983, SI 1983/370, r 2.

15 Ibid, r 15.

16 Section 2(1)(*d*). See also *Re Johnston* (1911) 105 LT 701 which seems to be authority for the proposition that where there is an existing judicial trustee, and it is desired to appoint the Public Trustee as an ordinary trustee, there must first be an order that there shall cease to be a judicial trustee of the trust.

17 Judicial Trustee Rules 1983, r 6.

Once appointed a judicial trustee is, in general,[18] 'in the position of any other trustee and exercises all the powers of any other trustee'. The court may give such directions as it thinks fit in relation to the custody of trust funds, property and documents. A judicial trustee, or any person interested in the trust, may request the court to give directions as to the trust or its administration, including a direction that there shall cease to be a judicial trustee. The Judicial Trustee rules also contain provisions relating to remuneration and accounts, and provide that in any case of default by a judicial trustee the court may give such directions as it thinks proper, including, if necessary, directions for the discharge of the judicial trustee and the appointment of another and the payment of costs.[19]

2 THE OFFICIAL SOLICITOR

The office can be traced back to mediaeval times, but only became statutory when the Supreme Court Act 1981[20] provided that the Official Solicitor should be an Officer of the Supreme Court to be appointed by the Lord Chancellor. The office has been merged to a large extent with the office of Public Trustee, discussed in the following section, though they continue to have separate corporate functions. They are housed in the same building and the same person has been appointed as Official Solicitor and Public Trustee. In general both will continue to accept work on a 'last resort' basis— broadly where failure to do so would result in an injustice, and there is no other suitable person willing and able to undertake the work.

The main situations where the Official Solicitor accepts a trust[21] are so as to be an impartial trustee where disputes between the trustees and/or beneficiaries as to the administration of a trust are such that decisions cannot be made; to be trustee to facilitate the sale and purchase of real property where a trustee of the land is under a disability; and to be trustee of property held for a person under a disability pursuant to an order of the court following court proceedings. In particular the Official Solicitor will consider accepting new matters which the Public Trustee cannot undertake because of the statutory restrictions imposed on him. Appointment of the Official Solicitor as a trustee requires the authority of the court.

---

[18] Per Jenkins J in *Re Ridsdel* [1947] Ch 597 at 601, [1947] 2 All ER 312 at 314.

[19] Judicial Trustee Rules 1983, rr 7–14; Practice Note [2003] 3 All ER 974, [2003] 1 WLR 1653.

[20] Section 90.

[21] The total number of cases currently in hand of trusts, grants of administration and guardianships of minors' estates is about 1,300.

3 THE PUBLIC TRUSTEE

(a) GENERAL POWERS AND DUTIES

The Public Trustee, a corporation sole with perpetual succession and an official seal, is an office created by the Public Trustee Act 1906. Its main purpose was to provide a public body which could be considered by testators as a safe appointment as executor of a will, or as trustee of a trust. The need for such a body has been eroded by the availability of alternative suitably qualified professional help in the private sector.[22]

The Public Trustee may act, either alone or jointly with any person or body of persons,[23] as an ordinary trustee,[24] a judicial trustee, or as custodian trustee,[25] but he may decline to accept any trust, though he cannot do so on the ground only of the small value of the trust property.[26] He is not permitted to accept any trust exclusively for religious or charitable purposes,[27] nor any trust under a deed of arrangement for the benefit of creditors,[28] nor the trust of any instrument made solely by way of security for money,[29] He must not, as a general rule, accept any trust which involves the management or carrying on of any business.[30]

(b) MODE OF APPOINTMENT

The Public Trustee may be appointed as ordinary trustee of any will or settlement or other instrument creating a trust, either as an original or a new trustee, or as an additional trustee, in the same cases and in the same manner and by the same persons or by the court, as if he were a private trustee.[31] He can always be appointed, and act,[32] as sole trustee, even though two or more trustees were originally appointed,[33] and notwithstanding a direction in the trust instrument that the number of trustees shall

---

[22] See section 5, infra, p 388.

[23] Public Trustee Act 1906, s 2(2). See, generally, (1989) 10 JLH 228 (P Polden); (2002) 33 T & ELJ 18 (Catherine Sanders).

[24] He can accept trusteeship only of an English trust—*Re Hewitt's Settlement* [1915] 1 Ch 228.

[25] Public Trustee Act 1906, s 2(1) as amended. This section read together with s 15 and Public Trustee Rules 1912, r 6, enables the Public Trustee to act as executor and administrator, and in effect by s 6(2) to be appointed as a new executor or administrator, either solely or jointly with the continuing executors or administrators; he is, by s 3, also authorized to administer an estate, in lieu of administration by the court, where the gross capital is less than £1,000.

[26] Public Trustee Act 1906, s 2(3).

[27] Ibid, s 2(5). Eg a trust where the sole object involved the selection of charitable objects for the testator's bounty—*Re Hampton* (1918) 88 LJ Ch 103.

[28] Public Trustee Act 1906, s 2(4).   [29] Public Trustee Rules 1912, r 6.

[30] For exceptions see the Public Trustee Act 1906, s 2(4) and Public Trustee Rules 1912, r 7.

[31] Public Trustee Act 1906, s 5(1).

[32] *Re Duxbury's Settlement Trusts* [1995] 3 All ER 145, [1995] 1 WLR 425, CA, noted [1996] Conv 50 (J Snape).

[33] Ibid, s 5(1).

not be less than some specified number.[34] Indeed, the court may order that the Public Trustee be appointed as a new or additional trustee, notwithstanding an express direction to the contrary in the trust instrument.[35] Provision is, however, made for giving notice to the beneficiaries of any proposed appointment of the Public Trustee either as a new or additional trustee, and within 21 days of such notice any beneficiary can apply to the court for an order prohibiting the appointment being made.[36] In deciding whether it is expedient to make such an order, the court will not in ordinary circumstances take into account the fact of the expense that will be incurred by the appointment.[37]

The Public Trustee may be appointed to be custodian trustee of any trust:

(a) by order of the court made on the application of any person on whose application the court may order the appointment of a new trustee; or

(b) by the testator, settlor, or other creator of any trust; or

(c) by the person having power to appoint new trustees.[38]

There is no provision in the case of appointment as custodian trustee for giving notice to the beneficiaries.

An appointment of the Public Trustee as a judicial trustee is made by the court under the provisions of the Judicial Trustees Act 1896.

No appointment of the Public Trustee as an ordinary trustee or as custodian trustee should be made (except by a testator)[39] unless and until the Public Trustee has given his formal consent to act.[40] This is usually incorporated in the deed of appointment. It seems, however, that if formal consent is given at some time after the appointment, the appointment thereupon becomes effective and incapable of being withdrawn.[41] In any case, even under a will, the appointment will only become effective if and when the formal consent is given.[42]

(c) POSITION OF PUBLIC TRUSTEE AFTER APPOINTMENT

The general position is set out in s 2(2) of the Act, which provides that the Public Trustee:

---

[34] *Re Leslie's Hassop Estates* [1911] 1 Ch 611 (appointment by the court); *Re Moxon* [1916] 2 Ch 595 (appointment by persons having statutory power of appointment).

[35] Public Trustee Act 1906, s 5(3); *Re Leslie's Hassop Estates*, supra.

[36] Public Trustee Act 1906, s 5(4). It was said in *Re Hope Johnstone's Settlement Trusts* (1909) 25 TLR 369 that the Public Trustee should only be appointed if there was no other way out of the difficulty, but in *Re Drake's Settlement* (1926) 42 TLR 467, Romer J stated that these observations were only intended to refer to settlements of the kind with which the judge was dealing (spendthrift settling his own property, after payment of debts, mainly for his own benefit) and were not of general application.

[37] *Re Firth* [1912] 1 Ch 806.   [38] Public Trustee Act 1906, s 4(1).

[39] Public Trustee Rules 1912, r 8(1). Rule 8(3) provides that a person appointed by will to be co-trustee with the Public Trustee should give the Public Trustee notice of his appointment.

[40] Ibid, r 8(1) and (2).   [41] *Re Shaw* [1914] WN 141.

[42] Public Trustee Rules 1912, r 8(2); *Re Shaw*, supra.

shall have all the same powers, duties, and liabilities, and be entitled to the same rights and immunities and be subject to the control and orders of the court, as a private trustee acting in the same capacity.

He has no more power than a private trustee, where he is in the position of having conflicting interests, to make a bargain with himself, and he must accordingly in such circumstances come to the court for sanction to such a bargain.[43] The more important regulations and provisions affecting the Public Trustee are referred to in their respective contexts.

(d) VESTING OF THE ESTATE OF AN INTESTATE IN THE PUBLIC TRUSTEE

Section 9 of the Administration of Estates Act 1925, as substituted by the Law of Property (Miscellaneous Provisions) Act 1994, s 14, provides that where a person dies intestate his real and personal estate vests in the Public Trustee until the grant of administration, and likewise where he dies testate but there is no executor or, before the grant of probate, there ceases to be any executor, able to obtain probate. The vesting of the estate in the Public Trustee is to prevent it being ownerless, but it does not, of course, confer any beneficial interest on him, nor does it impose on him any duty, obligation or liability in respect thereof. However if, for instance, the estate included a tenancy the Public Trustee would be the proper person on whom a notice to quit should be served.[44]

(e) PUBLIC TRUSTEE AND ADMINISTRATION OF FUNDS ACT 1986

The effect of the 1986 Act was to merge the office of the Public Trustee with the Courts Funds Office and the property division of the Court of Protection. Section 1 of the Act provides that the office of Public Trustee and the office of Accountant-General of the Supreme Court may be held by one person, which means that funds in court and trust work may be brought together under the same person.

4 CUSTODIAN TRUSTEES

The office of custodian trustee was created by the Public Trustee Act 1906. The idea is quite simply that the trust property shall for greater security be vested in a custodian trustee, while the management of the trust remains in the hands of the other trustees who are known as the managing trustees. It is accordingly provided, on the one hand,[45] that the trust property shall be transferred to the custodian trustee as if he

---

[43] *Re New Haw Estates Trust* (1912) 107 LT 191.
[44] See *Practice Direction* [1995] 3 All ER 192, [1995] 1 WLR 1120.   [45] Ibid s 4(2)(*a*).

were a sole trustee, and for that purpose vesting orders may, where necessary, be made under the Trustee Act 1925, and, on the other hand,[46] that the management of the trust property and the exercise of any power or discretion exercisable by the trustees under the trust shall remain vested in the trustees other than the custodian trustee. The custodian trustee is not to be reckoned as a trustee in determining the number of trustees for the purposes of the Trustee Act 1925.[47] An incidental advantage of having a custodian trustee is that when new managing trustees are appointed there is no need to go to the trouble and expense of vesting the trust property in the new trustees. The trust property remains vested in the custodian trustee throughout, and he, of course, is a corporate trustee who will never normally need to be replaced.

The Public Trustee Act 1906[48] which, as we have seen, provided that the Public Trustee could act as a custodian trustee, also declared that the provisions relating to a custodian trustee should apply in like manner (including a power to charge) to any banking or insurance company or other body corporate entitled by the rules[49] made thereunder to act as custodian trustee.

The more important provisions regulating the relationship between the custodian trustee and the managing trustees are set out in s 4(2) of the Act.

It provides that as between the custodian trustee and the managing trustees, the custodian trustee is to have the custody of all securities and documents of title relating to the trust property, but the managing trustees are to have free access and are entitled to take copies. The custodian trustee must concur in and perform all acts necessary to enable the managing trustees to exercise their powers of management, without being liable for any act or default on the part of the managing trustees, unless he concurs in a breach of trust. All sums payable to or out of the income or capital of the trust property must be paid to or by the custodian trustee, who may, however, allow income to be paid to the managing trustees or as they direct. The power of appointing new trustees, when exercisable by the trustees, is exercisable by the managing trustees alone, but the custodian trustee has the same power of applying to the court for the appointment of a new trustee as any other trustee.

The Public Trustee cannot be appointed to act in the dual capacity of custodian trustee and managing trustee;[50] and accordingly where, the Public Trustee being custodian trustee, the managing trustee died, and it was desired that the Public Trustee

---

[46] Ibid, s 4(2)(b). The differences between a custodian trustee and managing trustees are discussed in *Forster v Williams Deacon's Bank Ltd* [1935] Ch 359, [1935] All ER Rep 374, CA.

[47] Public Trustee Act 1906, s 4(2)(g). The relevant provision is discussed at p 366, supra.

[48] Public Trustee Act 1906, s 4(3).

[49] The Public Trustee Rules 1912, r 30 as amended. These amended rules, inter alia, implement Council Directive No 73/81/EEC/OJ No L194, 16.7.73, p 1 by authorizing corporations constituted in other EEC Member States to act as custodian trustees if they comply with the conditions prescribed for UK corporations, including the requirement of a place of business in the UK through or at which the trust business is carried on. See *Re Bigger* [1977] Fam 203, [1977] 2 All ER 644.

[50] A corporation capable of being appointed custodian trustee under the Rules is in the same position. *Forster v Williams Deacon's Bank Ltd* [1935] Ch 359, [1935] All ER Rep 374, CA; *Arning v James* [1936] Ch 158.

should manage the trust, it was admitted that his custodian trusteeship had to be terminated before he could be appointed an ordinary trustee.[51]

The custodian trusteeship can be brought to an end by an order of the court, on an application for this purpose brought by the custodian trustee, or any of the managing trustees, or any beneficiary. Before making the order, the court requires to be satisfied that it is the general wish of the beneficiaries, or that on other grounds it is expedient, to terminate the custodian trusteeship.[52]

5 TRUST CORPORATIONS

In various circumstances it may be advantageous to have a corporate trustee, and when this is the case it will commonly be desirable that the corporate trustee shall be a trust corporation. While almost any corporate trustee could provide continuity of administration, a trust corporation[53] can in addition be expected to provide financial stability and professional expertise in managing the trust, and can act alone in cases where at least two individual trustees would otherwise be required by statute.[54] The most familiar trust corporations are large banks and insurance companies having trustee departments, often separately incorporated, which offer their services as professional trustees. Clearly they will not be prepared to act unless they are remunerated, and they will now normally be entitled to remuneration whether or not there is an express charging clause.[55] These are special provisions where they are appointed by the court.[56]

Technically, 'trust corporation', for the purposes of the relevant 1925 Property Acts[57] is defined therein as meaning the Public Trustee or a corporation either appointed by the court in any particular case[58] to be a trustee or entitled by rules made under the Public Trustee Act 1906, s 4(3), to act as custodian trustee;[59] it also, as a result of the Law of Property (Amendment) Act 1926, s 3, includes the Treasury Solicitor, the Official Solicitor, and other officials prescribed by the Lord Chancellor, a trustee in bankruptcy and a trustee under a deed of arrangement, and in relation to charitable, ecclesiastical and public trusts, local or public authorities and other corporations prescribed by the Lord Chancellor.[60]

---

[51] *Re Squire's Settlement* (1946) 115 LJ Ch 90.   [52] Public Trustee Act 1906, s 4(2)(*i*).

[53] But not only a trust corporation; where, for instance, a reputable firm of accountants has formed its own trust company, with unlimited liability, such a company may be able to offer sufficient de facto protection to the beneficiaries, as well as professional skills.

[54] See p 367 supra.   [55] See the Trustee Act 2000, ss 28, 29 and pp 444–445, infra.

[56] See chapter 20, section 1(a)(iv) and 1(a)(v), pp 446, 447, infra.

[57] Law of Property Act 1925, Settled Land Act 1925, Trustee Act 1925, Administration of Estates Act 1925, and the Supreme Court Act 1981 replacing the Supreme Court of Judicature (Consolidation) Act 1925.

[58] Including a corporation appointed by the Charity Commissioners under the Charities Act 1993; ibid, s 35.

[59] See p 386 supra.

[60] In addition some other bodies are created as a trust corporation for special limited purposes, eg the Church of England Pensions Board by the Clergy Pensions Measure 1961, s 31.

17

DUTIES OF TRUSTEES

Jessell MR has pointed out[1] that 'it is a fallacy to suppose that every trustee[2] has the same duties and liabilities'. As has been mentioned,[3] for instance, the vendor under a contract for the sale of land is in a special position. And it seems that the only power of a bare trustee to deal with the trust assets is to retain them: for all other purposes he can only deal with the assets as directed by the beneficiaries.[4] More generally it is uncertain to what extent the following rules relating to a trustee's powers and duties apply to a constructive trustee. The question is little discussed in the cases, and it 'is a mistake to suppose that in every situation in which a constructive trust arises the legal owner is necessarily subject to all the fiduciary obligations and disabilities of an express trustee'.[5] Prima facie however an express trustee is under an obligation to carry out the duties, and has the powers, about to be considered.

Before considering these duties in detail a general picture should perhaps be drawn. On accepting a trust, new trustees 'are bound to inquire of what the property consists that is proposed to be handed over to them and what are the trusts',[6] and they should examine all the relevant documents in order to ascertain that everything is in order. Thereafter 'the duty of a trustee is properly to preserve the trust fund, to pay the income and the corpus to those who are entitled to them respectively, and to give all his cestuis que trust, on demand, information with respect to the mode in which the trust fund has been dealt with, and where it is.'[7] 'A trustee cannot assert a title of his own to trust property',[8] neither can he divest himself of the trust property, nor of a

---

[1] *Earl of Egmont v Smith* (1877) 6 Ch D 469 at 475; *Knox v Gye* (1872) LR 5 HL 656 per Lord Westbury. Cf *Henderson v Merrett Syndicates Ltd* [1995] 2 AC 145 per Lord Browne-Wilkinson at 206: 'The phrase "fiduciary duties" is a dangerous one, giving rise to a mistaken assumption that all fiduciaries owe the same duties in all circumstances. That is not the case.'

[2] As to a trustee in bankruptcy, see *Re Debtor, ex p Debtor v Dobwell (Trustee)* [1949] Ch 236, [1949] 1 All ER 510; *Ayerst v C & K (Construction) Ltd* [1976] AC 167, [1975] 2 All ER 537, HL. As to the director of a company, see *Selangor United Rubber Estates, Ltd v Cradock (No 3)* [1968] 2 All ER 1073, [1968] 1 WLR 1555.

[3] Chapter 8, section 4, p 163 supra.

[4] *Koorootang Nominees Pty Ltd v Australia and New Zealand Banking Group Ltd* [1998] 3 VR 16.

[5] *Lonrho plc v Fayed (No 2)* [1991] 4 All ER 961, 971, 972 [1992] 1 WLR 1, 12 per Millett J.

[6] *Hallows v Lloyd* (1888) 39 Ch D 686 at 691 per Kekewich J.

[7] *Low v Bouverie* [1891] 3 Ch 82 at 99, CA, per Lindley LJ.

[8] Per Page-Wood V-C in *Frith v Cartland* (1865) 2 Hem & M 417 at 420, [1861–73] All ER Rep 608 at 610. Nor can he set up, as against his cestuis que trust, the adverse title of a third party—*Newsome v Flowers* (1861) 30 Beav 461.

power given to him as incident to the execution of his trust.[9] If he 'ventures to deviate from the letter of his trust, he does so under the obligation and at the peril of afterwards satisfying the court that the deviation was necessary or beneficial'.[10] Prima facie, a trustee must act personally, and an undertaking which fetters a trustee in the exercise of his discretionary powers is invalid.[11] 'As a general rule a trustee sufficiently discharges his duty if he takes in managing trust affairs all those precautions which an ordinary prudent man of business would take in managing similar affairs of his own.'[12] It is the paramount duty of trustees 'to exercise their powers in the best interests of the present and future beneficiaries of the trust',[13] and accordingly the pursuit of the interests of his beneficiaries may require him to disregard the dictates of commercial morality.[14] It has been said[15] that a 'paid trustee is expected to exercise a higher standard of diligence and knowledge than an unpaid trustee, and . . . a bank which advertises itself largely in the public press as taking charge of administrations is under a special duty'. Brightman J expressed a similar opinion in *Bartlett v Barclays Bank Trust Co Ltd*[16] saying that 'a professional corporate trustee is liable for breach of trust if loss is caused to the trust fund because it neglects to exercise the special care and skill which it professes to have'. On this basis not all paid trustees will necessarily be subject to the same higher duty of care. It may depend not merely on the fact of payment, but also on the status of the trustee and the special skills he offers.[17] As between beneficiaries with conflicting interests, a trustee must act impartially and it is 'an inflexible rule of a Court of Equity that a person in a fiduciary position . . . is not, unless otherwise expressly provided, entitled to make a profit; he is not allowed to put himself in a position where his interest and duty conflict.' So far as his powers are concerned the well-established principle is that 'a trustee shall not be permitted to use the powers which the trust may confer upon him at law, except for the legitimate purposes of his trust'.[18]

In the exercise of a discretionary power the duty of trustees is to exercise 'the power for the purpose for which it is given, giving proper consideration to the matters which

---

[9] *Re Mills* [1930] 1 Ch 654, [1930] All ER Rep 355, CA; cf *Re Wills's Trust Deeds* [1964] Ch 219, [1963] 1 All ER 390; *Muir v IRC* [1966] 3 All ER 38, [1966] 1 WLR 1269, CA.

[10] *Harrison v Randall* (1851) 9 Hare 397 at 407, per Turner VC.

[11] See *Re Gibson's Settlement Trusts* [1981] Ch 179, [1981] 1 All ER 233. But see Chapter 21, infra.

[12] *Speight v Gaunt* (1883) 9 App Cas 1 at 19, HL, per Lord Blackburn; *Learoyd v Whiteley* (1887) 12 App Cas 727; *Eaton v Buchanan* [1911] AC 253, HL. See (1973) 37 Conv 48 (D R Paling).

[13] *Cowan v Scargill* [1985] Ch 270, per Megarry V-C at 286, 287.

[14] See *Taylors Fashions Ltd v Liverpool Victoria Trustees Co Ltd* [1981] 1 All ER 897 at 900, 901, per Oliver J and p 467, infra.

[15] Per Harman J in *Re Waterman's Will Trusts* [1952] 2 All ER 1054 at 1055; *Steel v Wellcome Custodian Trustees Ltd* [1988] 1 WLR 167. Contra, *Jobson v Palmer* [1893] 1 Ch 71 per Romer J; *Australian Securities Commission v A S Nominees Ltd* (1995) 133 ALR 1

[16] [1980] Ch 515, [1980] 1 All ER 139, discussed [1980] Conv 155 (G A Shindler). See Law Reform Committee 23rd Report (Cmnd 8733), paras 2.12–2.16; (1996) 146 NLJ 348 (Ann Kenny).

[17] *Bray v Ford* [1896] AC 44 at 51, HL, per Lord Herschell. A similar distinction is made in relation to the statutory duty of care imposed by the Trustee Act 2000, s 1: see p 394, infra.

[18] Per Wigram VC in *Balls v Strutt* (1841) 1 Hare 146 at 149.

are relevant and excluding from consideration matters which are irrelevant'.[19] Relevant matters may not be limited to simple matters of fact but will on occasion include taking advice from appropriate experts, whether the experts are lawyers, accountants, actuaries, scientists or whomsoever. It is, however, for advisers to advise and for trustees to decide: trustees may not (except in so far as they are authorized to do so[20]) delegate the exercise of their discretions, even to experts.[21] In reaching decisions as to the exercise of their fiduciary powers, trustees have to try to weigh up competing factors, which may be incommensurable in character. In that sense they have to be fair. But they are not a court and are not under any general duty to give a hearing to both sides—indeed in many situations 'both sides' is a meaningless expression. Further it seems that the legitimate expectation of potential beneficiaries should be taken into account.[22]

1 DUTIES ON THE ACCEPTANCE OF THE TRUST

As we have seen,[23] a trustee cannot be compelled to accept the office of trustee, 'but having once accepted it . . . he must discharge its duties, so long as his character of trustee subsists'.[24] The law does not recognize any distinction between active and passive trustees, and a trustee will be fully liable to the beneficiaries for any loss that occurs, where he has left the management of the trust to a co-trustee, even though the co-trustee may be the solicitor to the trust.[25] A trustee who has accepted the trust has been ordered by the court to concur with the other trustees in all proper and necessary acts of administration,[26] though in practice it would normally in such a case be possible and more convenient to appoint a new trustee in his place. Before he accepts a trusteeship to which any discretionary power is annexed, a trustee must disclose any circumstances in his situation which might tend to induce him to exercise any such

---

[19] *Edge v Pensions Ombudsman* [1999] 4 All ER 546, CA, per Chadwick LJ at 567. In relation to pensions trusts it has been said that in exercising their distributive powers, trustees and managers of pensions funds should regard themselves more as giving effect to a contract than exercising discretionary trust powers: (2002) 16 Tru LI 214 (Lord Scott of Foscote). See *Wong v Burt* [2004] NZCA 174, [2005] WTLR 291, discussed (2005) 63 T & ELTJ 8 (R Myint).

[20] See chapter 21, infra.

[21] *Scott v National Trust for Places of Historic Interest or Natural Beauty* [1998] 2 All ER 705; *Dundee General Hospitals Board of Management v Walker* [1952] 1 All ER 896, HL; *Re Hastings-Bass (decd)* [1975] Ch 25, [1974] 2 All ER 193; *Mettoy Pension Trustees Ltd v Evans* [1991] 2 All ER 513, [1990] 1 WLR 1587.

[22] *Scott v National Trust for Places of Historic Interest or Natural Beauty*, supra.

[23] See chapter 15, section 3(a), p 373 supra.

[24] *Moyle v Moyle* (1831) 2 Russ & M 710 at 715, per Brougham LC. He will not be liable for failing to act in a trust of which he has no notice—*Youde v Cloud* (1874) LR 18 Eq 634.

[25] *Bahin v Hughes* (1886) 31 Ch D 390, CA; *Robinson v Harkin* [1896] 2 Ch 415; *Re Turner* [1897] 1 Ch 536.

[26] *Ouchterlony v Lord Lynedoch* (1830) 7 Bli NS 448, HL.

power unfairly. If he fails to do so and nevertheless accepts the trust, he cannot afterwards exercise the discretionary power for his own benefit.[27]

On their appointment it is the right and duty of trustees to see that their appointment has been properly made,[28] and to ascertain of what the trust property consists and the trusts upon which they are to hold it.[29] 'They ought also to look into the trust documents and papers to ascertain what notices appear among them of incumbrances and other matters affecting the trust.'[30] To enable this to be done effectively, a trustee, being an individual, can be required to produce to his successors in office entries relating to the administration of the trust recorded by him in a diary or other document, and where there are two or more trustees they can be required to produce the minutes of their meetings. A retiring trustee is expected to answer his successor's requests for information about the trust and its affairs and is expected to exercise due care in doing so. If through negligence he misled his successor and loss resulted to the trust estate he would have no defence to a common law action in negligence.[31] Similarly in the case of a corporate trustee, new trustees may even be able to demand production of the internal correspondence and memoranda of such a trustee: each individual document has to be considered on its merits.[32] But a trustee is not affected by knowledge merely because a former trustee or a co-trustee has knowledge.[33]

The trustees should ensure that the legal title to the trust property is duly transferred to them, and if this is not possible, that their equitable rights are appropriately protected by notice to the legal owners, or otherwise.[34] If any part of the trust property is outstanding it is their duty to press for the payment or transfer of such trust property to them.[35] They must not be deterred by considerations of delicacy, or regard for the feelings of relatives or friends.[36] If the payment or transfer is not completed within a reasonable time the best course generally is to ask for the directions of the court as to whether they should bring appropriate legal proceedings for the purpose,[37] for while it has always been true that if they do not ask for the directions of the court, they will not be liable where their failure to sue was based on a well-founded belief that an action would be fruitless, the burden of proving that such belief was well-founded would rest on the trustees who asserted it.[38] However it now seems that

---

[27] *Peyton v Robinson* (1823) 1 LJOS Ch 191.   [28] *Harvey v Olliver* (1887) 57 LT 239.

[29] *Harvey v Olliver*, supra; *Hallows v Lloyd* (1888) 39 Ch D 686; *Nestle v National Westminster Bank plc* [1994] 1 All ER 118, [1993] 1 WLR 1260.

[30] *Hallows v Lloyd*, supra at 691, per Kekewich.

[31] See *Mond v Hyde* [1999] QB 1097, [1998] 3 All ER 833, CA.

[32] *Tiger v Barclays Bank Ltd* [1952] 1 All ER 85, CA.

[33] *Re Miller's Deed Trusts* [1978] LS Gaz R 454.

[34] But see Trustee Act 1925, s 22(1) and (2) as amended by the Trustee Act 2000, Sch 2, para 22.

[35] See eg *M'Gachen v Dew* (1851) 15 Beav 84; *Westmoreland v Holland* (1871) 23 LT 797.

[36] *Re Brogden* (1888) 38 Ch D 546, CA.

[37] *Re Beddoe* [1893] 1 Ch 547 at 557, CA; *Bennett v Burgis* (1846) 5 Hare 295. See *Young v Murphy* (1994) 13 ACSR 722.

[38] *Re Brogden*, supra, CA; *Re Hurst* (1890) 63 LT 665; affd (1892) 67 LT 96, CA.

under s 15 of the Trustee Act 1925[39] trustees who have discharged the duty of care set out in s 1(1) of the Trustee Act 2000[40] will not be liable in any case where failure to sue is the result of the positive exercise of their discretion and not the result of a mere passive attitude of leaving matters alone.[41] Again, where a settlement contains a covenant to settle after-acquired property, a new trustee is entitled, unless there are circumstances which should put him on enquiry, to assume that everything has been duly attended to up to the time of his becoming trustee.[42]

New trustees are bound to see that the trust funds are properly invested,[43] and the investment should be in the names of all the trustees.[44] Title deeds and non-negotiable securities may, however, be kept in the custody of one of the trustees, and in such case a co-trustee cannot, in the absence of special circumstances, require that they be removed from such custody and placed at a bank in a box accessible only to the trustees jointly.[45] Trustees have statutory power, and in respect of some securities, a duty to appoint custodians of trust assets and documents. This is discussed later.[46]

In the case of a trust of chattels, the trustees should ensure that there is a proper inventory,[47] which should be signed by a tenant for life who is let into possession.[48] If the trust property includes a lease containing a covenant that the tenant will at all times personally inhabit the demised premises, it seems that the covenant will bind the trustees.[49] In conclusion it should be observed that no trustee can be bound by a release of a power made by a previous holder of the office, even where the power is capable of release, which is commonly not the case.[50]

2 STATUTORY 'DUTY OF CARE'

The Trustee Act 2000[51] establishes a new precisely defined duty of care applicable to trustees when carrying out their functions under the Act. As in the law generally, the phrase 'duty of care' signifies a duty to take care to avoid causing injury or loss. The new duty is intended to bring certainty and consistency to the standard of competence and behaviour expected of trustees. It is additional to existing fundamental duties such as the duty to act in the best interests of the beneficiaries and to comply with the terms of the trust.

---

[39] As amended by the Trustee Act 2000, Sch 2, para 20. Discussed generally in chapter 22, section 5, p 470, infra.

[40] See section 2, this page.   [41] *Re Greenwood* (1911) 105 LT 509.

[42] *Re Strahan* (1856) 8 De GM & G 291, CA.

[43] *Re Strahan*, supra, and see chapter 18, p 412, infra.   [44] *Lewis v Nobbs* (1878) 8 Ch D 591.

[45] *Re Sisson's Settlement* [1903] 1 Ch 262; *Cottam v Eastern Counties Rly Co* (1860) 1 John & H 243.

[46] See p 457 et seq, infra.   [47] *England v Downs* (1842) 6 Beav 269.

[48] *Temple v Thring* (1887) 56 LT 283.   [49] *Lloyds Bank Ltd v Jones* [1955] 2 QB 298, CA.

[50] *Re Will's Trust Deeds* [1964] Ch 219, [1963] 1 All ER 390; *Muir v IRC* [1966] 3 All ER 38, CA and see (1968) 84 LQR 64 (A J Hawkins).

[51] Section 1. As to its application to pension schemes, see s 36(2).

The new duty does not, however, alter the principles relating to the exercise of discretionary powers by trustees. The decision whether to exercise a discretion remains a matter for the trustees to determine. That decision is not subject to the new duty of care, though it is subject to the control of the court as discussed later.[52] However once trustees have decided to exercise a discretionary function which is subject to the new duty, the manner in which they exercise it will be measured against the appropriate standard of care.

Whenever the duty applies a trustee must exercise such care and skill as is reasonable in the circumstances, having regard in particular—

(a) to any special knowledge or experience that he has or holds himself out as having, and

(b) if he acts as trustee in the course of a business or profession, to any special knowledge or experience that it is reasonable to expect of a person acting in the course of that kind of business or profession.

Thus in relation to the purchase of stocks and shares, a higher standard may be expected of a trustee who is an investment banker, specializing in equities, than of a motor mechanic, particularly if the investment banker is acting as a trustee in the course of his investment banking business.

The statutory functions under the Act are set out in Sch 1. The duty of care accordingly applies to a trustee—

(i) When exercising the general power of investment, or when exercising statutory duties relating to the exercise of a power of investment or to the review of investments.[53]

(ii) When exercising the statutory power to acquire land or any power in relation to land so acquired.[54]

(iii) When entering into arrangements under which a person is, under the Act, authorized to exercise functions as an agent, or is appointed to act as a nominee or custodian; or when carrying out his duties in relation to the review of an agent, nominee or custodian.[55]

(iv) When exercising the power under s 15 of the Trustee Act 1925 to do any of the things referred to in that section.[56]

---

[52] See pp 498–501, infra.   [53] See ss 3–7, Sch 1 para 1, and p 418, infra.

[54] See ss 8–10, Sch 1 para 2, and p 422, infra.

[55] See ss 11–27, Sch 1 Para 3(1), and p 454 et seq, infra. Entering into arrangements includes (a) selecting the person who is to act, (b) determining any terms on which he is to act, and (c) if the person is being authorized to exercise asset management functions, the preparation of a policy statement under s 15: Sch 1, para 3(2).

[56] Schedule 1, para 4, Section 15 of the 1925 Act gives trustees wide powers to compound liabilities. See p 470 et seq, infra.

(v) When exercising the statutory power to insure property.[57]

(vi) When exercising the power under s 22(1) or (3) of the Trustee Act 1925 to do any of the things referred to there.[58]

The same duty of care applies to trustees when carrying out equivalent functions to those referred to above conferred by the trust instrument.[59] However the duty of care does not apply if or in so far as it appears from the trust instrument that the duty is not meant to apply.[60]

3 DUTY OF TRUSTEES TO ACT UNANIMOUSLY

'There is no law that I am acquainted with which enables the majority of trustees to bind the minority. The only power to bind is the act of [them all].'[61] Subject to any contrary provision in the trust instrument, only the joint exercise by trustees of their powers and discretions will be valid,[62] and only a receipt by all the trustees will give a good discharge to a purchaser.[63] Accordingly if one of two or more trustees enters into a contract to sell trust property, whether purporting to act as absolute owner, or on behalf of himself and his co-trustees (who have not authorized the sale beforehand and have refused to ratify it afterwards), the sale cannot be enforced against the trust estate.[64] The trust fund should be under the joint control of all the trustees,[65] and if one trustee obtains control of some or all of the fund, and misapplies it, his co-trustees will be fully liable,[66] though they may escape liability if they can show that the trustee properly obtained control of the fund and that the co-trustees acted promptly to get the money invested in their joint names.[67] Nor, it seems, will trustees be liable

---

[57] See s 19 of the Trustee Act 1925 as substituted by s 34 of the Trustee Act 2000, Sch 1, para 5 of the 2000 Act, and p 468 infra.

[58] Schedule 1, para 6. Section 22 of the 1925 Act confers wide powers on trustees in relation to reversionary interests, valuations and audit: see p 462, infra. Section 22 has been amended by the Trustee Act 2000, Sch 2, para 22 by substituting for the phrase 'in good faith' a reference to the duty of care in s 1(1) of the 2000 Act.

[59] Schedule 1, paras 1–6.   [60] Schedule 1, para 7.

[61] *Luke v South Kensington Hotel Co* (1879) 11 Ch D 121 at 125, CA, per Jessel MR; *Re Mayo* [1943] Ch 302, [1943] 2 All ER 440; *Phipps v Boardman* [1965] Ch 992, [1965] 1 All ER 849, CA; affd sub nom *Boardman v Phipps* [1967] 2 AC 46, [1966] 3 All ER 721, HL. The reason behind the rule is, perhaps, to make trustees more cautious—see (1986) 36 UTLJ 186 (A I Ogus). The desirability of the rule is challenged in [1991] Conv 30 (J Jaconelli).

[62] But a trustee will not be liable and the joint act of the trustees will be valid if a dissenting trustee, acting bona fide, modifies his original view in deference to the views of his cotrustees and agrees to the proposed act—*Re Schneider* (1906) 22 TLR 223.

[63] *Lee v Sankey* (1872) LR 15 Eq 204; *Re Flower and Metropolitan Board of Works* (1884) 27 Ch D 592. And see Trustee Act 1925, s 14(2), (3), discussed chapter 22, section 3, infra.

[64] *Naylor v Goodall* (1877) 47 LJ Ch 53.   [65] *Consterdine v Consterdine* (1862) 31 Beav 330.

[66] *Rodbard v Cooke* (1877) 36 LT 504; *Lewis v Nobbs* (1878) 8 Ch D 591.

[67] *Thompson v Finch* (1856) 8 De GM & G 560.

for moneys belonging to the trust which their co-trustee gets into his possession without their knowledge or consent and by a fraud upon them.[68]

Exceptionally, one of several trustees may be authorized, on the grounds of practical convenience, to receive income,[69] though no trustee should be authorized to do this whose co-trustees have any reason to believe that he is liable to misapply the income,[70] and on general principles his co-trustees must see to the money being brought under their joint control with all due despatch. Where the trust property includes an investment in a limited company, the Articles of Association in practice invariably provide that trusts shall not be recognized,[71] and that in the case of joint holders, dividends will be payable to the first named, who can give an effectual receipt therefor.[72]

The different rules in relation to charity trustees[73] and personal representatives[74] have already been discussed, and decisions of trustees of an occupational pension scheme established under a trust may, unless the scheme provides otherwise, be taken by agreement of a majority of the trustees.[75]

4 DUTIES IN RELATION TO INFORMATION, ACCOUNTS AND AUDIT

(a) DUTY TO ACCOUNT AND GIVE INFORMATION[76]

(i) Rights of beneficiaries vis-à-vis the trustees

The extent to which a beneficiary can claim disclosure of trust documents was recently reviewed by the Privy Council in *Schmidt v Rosewood Trust Ltd.*[77] The judgment of the Board is, of course, technically not binding in England, but it is thought that it is likely to be followed. The claim has sometimes been based on proprietary right. The clearest statement to this effect is that of Lord Wrenbury in *O'Rourke v*

---

[68] *Bernard v Bagshaw* (1862) 3 De GJ & Sm 355—crossed cheque entrusted to co-trustee for delivery to beneficiary. Cf *Re Bennison* (1889) 60 LT 859, where trustee was held liable on similar facts with the essential difference that the beneficiary should not have been paid by cheque, the strict duty of the trustees being to purchase stock to satisfy a specific legacy.

[69] *Townley v Sherborne* (1633) J Bridg 35.   [70] *Gough v Smith* [1872] WN 18.

[71] See Companies Act 1985, s 360 and Companies (Tables A–F) Regulations 1985, reg 5—SI 1985/805; Gower & Davies, *Principles of Modern Company Law*, 7th edn, p 342.

[72] Ibid, art 121.   [73] In chapter 14, section 2(a), p 291 supra.   [74] In chapter 2, p 39, supra.

[75] Pensions Act 1995, s 32.   [76] As to charities see p 318 et seq, supra.

[77] [2003] UKPC 26, [2003] 3 All ER 76 (technically not binding in England but likely to be followed). It has been adopted in New Zealand: *Foreman v Kingstone* [2004] 1 NZLR 841, and noted in (2003) 17 Tru LI 90 (D Pollard); (2003) 46 T & ELJ 5 (R Colquitt); (2003) 147 Sol Jo 737 (Dawn Goodman and Henrietta Lobes); [2003] PCB 358 (C McCall); (2003) 153 NLJ 1300 (K Noel-Smith); (2003) 23 ET & PJ 1 (L Smith); (2003) 52 T & ELJ 21 (G Brown); [2004] 120 LQR 1 (J D Davies). See [2004] PCB 23 (Lightman J). See also *Broere v Mourant & Co* [2004] JCA 009, [2004] WTLR 1417; *Re the Internine and the Intertraders Trusts* [2004] JLR 325.

Darbishire[78] who said: 'The beneficiary is entitled to see all trust documents because they are trust documents and because he is a beneficiary. They are in this sense his own.' However Lord Walker, delivering the judgment of the Board, said that this could not be regarded as a reasoned or binding decision that a beneficiary's right or claim to disclosure of trust documents or information must always have the proprietary basis of a transmissible interest in trust property. That was not an issue in *O'Rourke v Darbishire*.

The alleged proprietary right came into conflict in *Re Londonderry's Settlement*[79] with the principle that trustees exercising a discretionary power are not bound to disclose to their beneficiaries the reasons actuating them in coming to a decision. Though, as pointed out in *Schmidt v Rosewood Trust*,[80] the judgments in that case are not easy to reconcile, the conclusion was that the need to protect the confidentiality in communications between trustees as to the exercise of their dispositive discretions, and in communications made to the trustees by other beneficiaries, could override the prima facie proprietary right of the beneficiaries to disclosure of information.

Their Lordships in *Schmidt v Rosewood Trust Ltd*[81] considered that, although the right to seek disclosure of trust documents might sometimes not inappropriately be described as a proprietary right, the more principled and correct approach is to regard this right as one aspect of the court's inherent jurisdiction to supervise, and if necessary to intervene in, the administration of trusts. The right to seek the court's intervention does not depend on entitlement to a fixed and transmissible beneficial interest. The object of a discretionary trust, and also the object of a mere power of a fiduciary character, may also be entitled to protection from a court of equity, although the circumstances in which he may seek protection, and the nature of the protection he may expect to obtain, will depend on the court's discretion. In *Hartigan Nominees Pty Ltd v Rydge*[82] Kirby P said that for an applicant to have a proprietary right might be sufficient, but was not necessary. While expressing general agreement with the approach of Kirby P and Sheller JA in that case, the Board disagreed on this point, saying that a proprietary right was neither sufficient nor necessary: there may be

---

[78] [1920] AC 581, HL, at 626–627. [79] [1963] Ch 918, [1964] 3 All ER 855, CA.

[80] Supra, PC.

[81] Supra, PC. As to pension schemes see *Wilson v Law Debenture Trust Corpn* [1995] 2 All ER 337, discussed 145 NLJ 1414 (P O'Hagan) and see (1997) 11 Tru LI 11, 43 (D Pollard); (2003) 17 Tru LI 170 (D Pollard and Judith Clixby). Meryl Thomas in (1997) JBL 514 argues for increasing the obligation of disclosure in occupational pension schemes. For statutory duties, see Pensions Act 1995, s 41, as amended. As to the position where trustees are directors of a company see *Butt v Kelson* [1952] Ch 197, sub nom *Re Butt* [1952] 1 All ER 167 and (1980) 30 UTLJ 151 (D Hughes). Cf *Hughes v Transport and General Workers' Union* [1985] IRLR 382, noted (1986) 15 Ind LJ 46 (R W Rideout). See [1996] PCB 302 (P Willoughby); (2000) 13 T & ELJ 9 (C Sly).

[82] (1992) 29 NSWLR 403, noted (1993) 67 ALJ 703 (D Maclean). Here it was held that a memorandum of wishes provided by the instigator of a discretionary trust was not a document which the trustees were obliged to disclose to a beneficiary if the memorandum was provided on a confidential basis, though the trustees could take it into account in the exercise of their discretion. See (1995) 7 Bond LR 5 (D Davies); (2001) 26 T & ELJ 21, and 27 T & ELJ 6 (D Benest); [2001] PCB 145 (P Stibbard); [2004] PCB 23 (Lightman J). See also *R v Rabiotti Settlements* [2001] Fam Law 808 (Jersey Royal Court); *Morris v Morris* (1993) 9 WAR 140.

circumstances in which even a vested and transmissible interest is not a sufficient basis for requiring disclosure of trust documents. Especially when there are issues as to personal or commercial confidentiality, the court may have to balance the competing interests of different beneficiaries, the trustees themselves and third parties. Disclosure may have to be limited and safeguards may have to be put into place.

It remains to be seen whether the principles laid down by the Board in *Schmidt v Rosewood Trust*[83] will be held to be applicable to modify the law as previously understood in relation to trust accounts as distinct from other information relating to the trust. As long ago as *Pearse v Green*[84] it was said to be '. . . the first duty of an accounting party [including a trustee] . . . to be constantly ready with his accounts', and this was recently reaffirmed by Millett LJ in *Armitage v Nurse*[85] who stated, 'Every beneficiary is entitled to see the trust accounts, whether his interest is in possession or not', and if a trustee fails to produce accounts he may become liable to pay the costs of proceedings by a beneficiary to obtain them.[86] There is no suggestion in *Schmidt v Rosewood Trust* that trust accounts should be treated differently from other trust documents.

It was held in *Low v Bouverie*,[87] inter alia, that it is 'no part of the duty of a trustee to tell his cestui que trust what incumbrances the latter has created, nor which of his incumbrancers have given notice of their respective charges' on the ground that 'it is no part of the duty of a trustee to assist his cestui que trust in selling or mortgaging his beneficial interest and in squandering or anticipating his fortune'. Now, however, it is provided by s 137(8) of the Law of Property Act 1925 that any person interested in the equitable interest may require, subject to the payment of costs, production of all notices in writing of dealings with the equitable interest which have been served on the trustees. But trustees are not under any duty to proffer information to their beneficiary, or to see that he has proper advice, merely because they are trustees for him and know that he is entering into a transaction with his beneficial interest with some person or body connected in some way with the trustees, such as a company in which the trustees own some shares beneficially.[88]

Trustees under an express trust where there is a minor beneficiary, are under a positive duty to inform him of his interest on his coming of age.[89] It seems, however,

---

[83] Supra, PC.

[84] *Pearse v Green* (1819) 1 Jac & W 135 per Plumer MR at 140; *Kemp v Burn* (1863) 4 Giff 348; *Foreman v Kingstone* [2004] 1 NZLR 841 (noted [2005] Conv 93 (G Griffiths)). See, generally, (1974) 124 NLJ 452 (D Paling). As to judicial trustees see Judicial Trustees Act 1896 as amended by the Administration of Justice Act 1982, s 57 and the Judicial Trustee Rules 1983, SI 1983/370, rr 9–13.

[85] [1997] 2 All ER 705 at 720. See [2004] PCB 23 (Lightman J).

[86] *James v Newington* [2004] JRC 059, [2004] WTLR 863.

[87] [1891] 3 Ch 82 at 99, CA, per Lindley LJ.

[88] *Tito v Waddell (No 2)* [1977] Ch 106 at 243, [1977] 3 All ER 129 at 242, 243. It has, however been suggested that in some cases there might be a duty to see that the beneficiaries were at least warned to take proper professional advice—(1977) 41 Conv 438 (F R Cane).

[89] *Hawksley v May* [1956] 1 QB 304, [1955] 3 All ER 353. As to whether this involves an obligation to inform the beneficiary of the rule in *Saunders v Vautier* (1841) Cr & Ph 240, discussed infra in section 5 see (1970) 34 Conv 29 (Alec Samuels). See [2004] PCB 23 (Lightman J).

that executors are under no such duty,[90] the distinction being said to be due to the fact that a will is open to public inspection.

It may be mentioned that trustees may well be held personally liable for the costs of any proceedings made necessary by their failure to carry out the above duties.[91]

(ii) Right of beneficiaries to seek information from a third party

It is convenient to mention here that, exceptionally, the court, under its equitable jurisdiction,[92] can order a defendant, who is not otherwise an appropriate party to proceedings, to identify the name and address of a third party. Thus in *Re Murphy's Settlements*[93] the court, in proceedings brought by a discretionary beneficiary, ordered the settlor (who had reserved the power of appointment of trustees) to give the plaintiff information as to the names and addresses of the trustees of the settlement.[94]

(b) AUDIT[95]

There are three statutory provisions. First, s 22(4) of the Trustee Act 1925 provides:

Trustees may, in their absolute discretion, from time to time, but not more than once in every three years unless the nature of the trust or any special dealings with the trust property make a more frequent exercise of the right reasonable, cause the accounts of the trust property to be examined or audited by an independent accountant, and shall, for that purpose, produce such vouchers and give such information to him as he may require.[96]

Secondly, s 13 of the Public Trustee Act 1906, 'an exceedingly drastic enactment',[97] enables any trustee or beneficiary to apply to the Public Trustee for an audit of the whole accounts of a trust at any time whatever, subject to the proviso that the application cannot be made within one year after there has been a prior audit. There is no limit backwards beyond which the audit is not to be extended, and the audit can only be prevented by an application to the court to stay the exercise of the prima facie right conferred by the Act. The sanction against insisting improperly on an investigation of

---

[90] *Re Lewis* [1904] 2 Ch 656, CA; *Re Mackay* [1906] 1 Ch 25; *Hawksley v May*, supra. See (1995) 145 NLJ 1408 (J Sunnocks).

[91] See eg *Re Skinner* [1904] 1 Ch 289; *Re Holton's Settlement Trusts* (1918) 119 LT 304. Illiteracy and consequent inability to keep accounts is no defence—an agent could be employed (*Wroe v Seed* (1863) 4 Giff 425).

[92] Cf what Neuberger J referred to in *Re Murphy's Settlements* [1998] 3 All ER 1, sub nom *Murphy v Murphy* [1999] 1 WLR 282, noted (1999) 115 LQR 206 (C Mitchell), as 'the discovery jurisdiction'—see *Norwich Pharmacal Co v Customs and Excise Comrs* [1974] AC 133, [1973] 2 All ER 942, HL; *Ashworth Security Hospital v MGN Ltd* [2002] UKHL 29, [2002] 4 All ER 193.

[93] Supra.

[94] Subject to an opportunity being given to him to put in evidence as to the inconvenience or cost or other problem the order would cause. The order was extended to similar information in relation to a settlement made by the settlor's wife (now deceased) where the settlor did not have a power of appointment of trustees.

[95] As to charities, see p 318 et seq, supra.

[96] The sub-s provides for the costs to be apportioned between capital and income by the trustees: in default capital and income bear the costs respectively attributable to them.

[97] Per Parker J in *Re Oddey* [1911] 1 Ch 532 at 537, [1911–13] All ER Rep 744 at 745.

the trust accounts is the liability of the applicant to be ordered to pay the costs of the audit.[98] The section has been invoked only occasionally and its operation has not been found to be particularly effective because there are no powers to enforce the Public Trustee's findings. The Law Reform Committee accordingly recommends[99] its repeal.

Lastly there is provision for annual audit by the court in the case of a judicial trustee.[100]

5 DUTY OF TRUSTEES TO HAND OVER THE TRUST FUNDS TO THE RIGHT PERSONS

(a) THE EXTENT OF THE DUTY

Trustees are under a duty to distribute income and capital to beneficiaries without demand,[101] but must take care to distribute the trust property only to the beneficiaries who are properly entitled thereto. Accordingly trustees have been held liable to the person rightly entitled where they have paid the wrong persons through acting on the faith of a marriage certificate which turned out to be a forgery,[102] or through acting on the wrong construction of the trust instrument.[103] Strictly, it remains a breach of trust notwithstanding the fact that the payment is made upon legal advice,[104] though, as is explained elsewhere,[105] this may be a factor which would induce the court to relieve the trustees under s 61 of the Trustee Act 1925. Since the Family Law Reform Act 1987, there is no special protection given in relation to any illegitimate relationship, and the practical course is for trustees to take advantage of s 27 of the Trustee Act 1925, discussed below. Exceptionally under s 45 of the Adoption Act 1976, a trustee or personal representative is not under a duty to enquire before conveying or distributing any property whether any adoption has been effected or revoked if that could affect entitlement to the property, and will not be liable for any conveyance or distribution made without notice of a claim. This does not, however, prejudice the right of a person to follow the property into the hands of any person, other than a purchaser, who has received it.

If a trustee has received notice of a claim against the trust funds which is, prima facie, a reasonably arguable claim, he will be liable to the claimant if he deals with the trust funds in disregard of that notice should the claim subsequently prove to be well

---

98 *Re Oddy*, supra; *Re Utley* (1912) 106 LT 858.   99 23rd Report, Cmnd 8733, para 4.48.

100 Judicial Trustee Rules, SI 1972/1096, rr 13–15.

101 *Hawkesley v May* [1956] 1 QB 304, [1995] 3 All ER 353.

102 *Eaves v Hickson* (1861) 30 Beav 136; *Sporle v Barnaby* (1864) 11 LT 412.

103 *Re Hulkes* (1886) 33 Ch D 552; *Ministry of Health v Simpson* [1951] AC 251, [1950] 2 All ER 1137, HL.

104 *National Trustees Co of Australasia Ltd v General Finance Co of Australasia Ltd* [1905] AC 373, PC.

105 See chapter 24, section 3(f), p 546, infra.

founded.[106] It should be noted, however, that under the rule in *Cherry v Boultbee*[107] where a person entitled to participate in a fund is also bound to make a contribution in aid of that fund, he cannot be allowed to participate unless and until he has fulfilled his duty to contribute.[108] Trustees will not be liable if they have accounted to an apparent beneficiary on the face of the trust documents, without notice of any facts or documents which might indicate that some other person is in fact entitled. Thus if a power of appointment has been exercised, apparently properly, in favour of X and the trustees having made all reasonable inquiries pay the trust funds to him, they will not be liable to pay again if it turns out that there was a prior appointment to Y of which the trustees had no notice.[109] Again, a payment to the apparent beneficiary will be a good discharge to the trustees, if they have no notice of the fact that the beneficiary has assigned or charged his interest,[110] and it seems they can safely pay to a person entitled in default of appointment on apparently satisfactory evidence that no appointment has ever been made.[111]

Conversely, trustees will be liable to pay again if they ignore a derivative title of which they have notice, whether actual or constructive.[112] Trustees have a right to call upon anyone who claims to be a beneficiary to prove his title,[113] but they cannot raise questions where the validity or invalidity of the doubt is not essential to their safety,[114] nor, on distribution of the fund, can they require delivery of the assignment or other documents whereby the beneficiary established his derivative title.[115]

Where the trustees have a reasonable doubt as to title of a claimant, as for instance, where he claims under an appointment which may be a fraud on a power,[116] they should apply to the court and act under its directions.[117] Again in appropriate

[106] *Guardian Trust and Executors Company of New Zealand v Public Trustee of New Zealand* [1942] AC 115, PC; *Sinel Trust Ltd v Rothfield Investments Ltd* [2003] WTLR 593 (Jersey CA).

[107] (1829) 2 Keen 319.

[108] *The Russell-Cooke Trust Company v Richard Prentis & Co Ltd (in liquidation)* [2003] EWHC 1206 (Ch), [2003] WTLR 1529.

[109] *Cothay v Sydenham* (1788) 2 Bro CC 391.

[110] *Leslie v Baillie* (1843) 2 Y & C Ch Cas 91; *Re Lord Southampton's Estate* (1880) 16 Ch D 178.

[111] *Re Cull's Trusts* (1875) LR 20 Eq 561; *Williams v Williams* (1881) 17 Ch D 437.

[112] *Hallows v Lloyd* (1888) 39 Ch D 686; *Re Neil* (1890) 62 LT 649; *Davis v Hutchings* [1907] 1 Ch 356. As to priorities relating to equitable interests in both pure personalty and land consider the rule in *Dearle v Hall* (1828) 3 Russ 1 as affected by ss 136–138 of the Law of Property Act 1925 (as amended by the Trusts of Land and Appointment of Trustees Act 1996), discussed [1999] Conv 311 and (1999) 28 AALR 87, 197 (J De Lacy). Registered land is governed by the same rules as unregistered land since the Land Registration Act 1986.

[113] *Hurst v Hurst* (1874) 9 Ch App 762.

[114] *Devey v Thornton* (1851) 9 Hare 222—where beneficiary is dead cannot raise doubts as to the title of apparently properly constituted executors or administrators.

[115] *Re Palmer* [1907] 1 Ch 486.

[116] It is submitted that cases such as *Campbell v Home* (1842) 1 Y & C Ch Cas 664; *Firmin v Pulham* (1848) 2 De G & Sm 99, charging trustees with costs where the appointment was held to be valid would not be followed. The courts are now more ready to allow costs, partly by reason of the simpler and less expensive procedure available.

[117] *Talbot v Earl of Radnor* (1834) 3 My & K 252; *Merlin v Blagrave* (1858) 25 Beav 125.

circumstances the court may make a *Re Benjamin*[118] order enabling trustees to distribute on the footing that a theoretical beneficiary had predeceased a testator or as the case may be. An alternative practical solution to the problem of a missing beneficiary, particularly in the case of a small trust, may be to take out missing beneficiary insurance.[119]

It may be added that as between the trustees and a person who is wrongly paid, the trustees, under the law of restitution based on the principle of unjust enrichment, have a right to recover the payment if it was paid under a mistake, whether of fact or law, subject to the defences available in the law of restitution such as the defence of change of position,[120] or estoppel by representation. Estoppel is a rule of evidence which prima facie defeats a claim completely, but it does not operate in full where it would be clearly inequitable or unconscionable for the defendant to retain the whole mistaken payment.[121]

(b) SECTION 27 OF THE TRUSTEE ACT 1925

This section,[122] which applies notwithstanding a provision to the contrary in the trust instrument,[123] gives considerable protection to trustees on the distribution of the trust property. Subsection 1 provides that trustees of a settlement, trustees of land, trustees for sale of personal property or personal representatives may give notice[124] of their intention to distribute by advertisement in the *London Gazette* and, where land is involved, in a newspaper circulating in the district in which the land is situated,[125] and 'such other like notices, including notices elsewhere than in England and Wales, as would, in any special case, have been directed by a court of competent jurisdiction in

---

[118] [1902] 1 Ch 723; *Re Green's Will Trusts* [1985] 3 All ER 455. If the beneficiary turns out to be alive, the court order will not prevent him from pursuing the remedies dealt with in chapter 25, but the trustees will be protected by the court order.

[119] See *Re Evans (decd)* [1999] 2 All ER 777.

[120] *Kleinwort Benson Ltd v Lincoln City Council* [1999] 2 AC 349, [1998] 4 All ER 513, HL, critically noted [1999] CLJ 21 (S Hedley); [1999] Conv 40 (M P Thompson), reversing the rule that money is not recoverable in restitution on the ground that it was paid under a mistake of law; *Nurdin & Peacock plc v D B Ramsden & Co Ltd* [1999] 1 All ER 941, noted (1999) 58 CLJ 478 (G Virgo); *Deutsche Morgan Grenfell Group plc v IRC* [2003] EWHC 1779 (Ch), [2003] 4 All ER 645. See also [1998] SJLS 468 (A Abdullah); [2000] CLP 205 (P Birks); [2002] RLR 9 (R Sutton); [2003] RLR 26 (D Sheehan). As to overpayments to pension scheme beneficiaries, see (2000) 14 Tru LI 201 (A Simmonds).

[121] *Scottish Equitable plc v Derby* [2001] 3 All ER 818, CA; *National Westminster Bank plc v Somer International (UK) Ltd* [2002] 1 All ER 198, CA, both noted (2001) 60 CLJ 465 (P Key).

[122] As amended by the Law of Property Amendment Act 1926, s 7 and Schedule, and the Trusts of Land and Appointment of Trustees Act 1996. It has been pointed out that on a strict construction the section does not apply to trustees of personalty where there is no trust for sale, including pension scheme trustees: (1995) 9 Tru LI 127 (P Docking).

[123] Trustee Act 1925, s 27(3).

[124] At any rate in the case of a trust arising under a will, as soon as possible— *Re Kay* [1897] 2 Ch 518.

[125] On similar language in other statutes it has been held that *The Sporting Life* circulates in Westminster (*R v Westminster Betting Licensing Committee, ex p Peabody Donation Fund* [1963] 2 QB 750, [1963] 2 All ER 544, DC), and that *The Times* is a local paper circulating in Rickmansworth (*Re Southern Builders and Contractors (London) Ltd* (1961) *Times*, 10 October).

an action for administration'.[126] The notice must require any person interested to send particulars of his claim to the trustees within the time, not being less than two months, fixed in the notice.[127] The notices should follow the wording of s 27 so as to indicate that it is not merely the claims of creditors which are required to be sent in, but also those of beneficiaries.[128]

At the expiration of the time fixed by the notice, the trustees, provided they make all appropriate searches, can safely distribute having regard only to those claims, whether formal or not, of which they have notice, whether as a result of the advertisement or otherwise.[129] The trustees will be as fully protected as if they had administered under an order of the court.[130] So far as claimants are concerned, however, it is expressly provided that nothing in the section prejudices the right of any person to follow the property, or any property representing the same, into the hands of any person, other than a purchaser, who may have received it.[131]

(c) PROTECTION AGAINST LIABILITY IN RESPECT OF RENTS AND COVENANTS

At one time where a trust estate included a lease the trustees were at risk if they distributed the rest of the estate without retaining sufficient funds to meet any liability which might arise under the lease in the future. This might delay for a long time the distribution of a large part of the estate. It is now provided[132] that where a trustee, liable as such:

(a) satisfies all liabilities under the lease which have accrued and been claimed, and,

(b) sets apart a sufficient sum to answer any future claim in respect of any fixed and ascertained sum which the lessee agreed to lay out on the property, and,

(c) conveys the property to a purchaser, legatee, devisee or other person entitled to call for a conveyance thereof

he may distribute the remainder of the trust estate to those entitled thereto without any personal liability in respect of any subsequent claim under the lease. The section operates without prejudice to the right of the lessor to follow the trust assets into the

---

[126] See *Re Bracken* (1889) 43 Ch D 1, CA; *Re Holden* [1935] WN 52.

[127] Or the last of the notices, if more than one is given.

[128] *Re Aldhous* [1955] 2 All ER 80, [1955] 1 WLR 459.

[129] Trustee Act 1925, s 27(2). The Law Reform Committee, 23rd Report, Cmnd 8733, para 5.1, recommends similar protection where trustees have received the advice of counsel to distribute notwithstanding a possible adverse claim, provided they first write to the potential creditor and no claim is made within three months.

[130] *Re Frewen* (1889) 60 LT 953.   [131] Trustee Act 1925, s 27(2)(*a*).

[132] Trustee Act 1925, s 26(1) as amended by the Law of Property (Amendment) Act 1926. It has been extended to cover an authorized guarantee agreement under the Landlord and Tenant (Covenants) Act 1995, s 16 which Act, by Sch 1, para 1, has added s 26(1A) to the 1925 Act.

hands of those who have received them, and applies notwithstanding anything to the contrary in the trust instrument.[133]

(d) RIGHT TO A DISCHARGE ON TERMINATION OF TRUSTS

In general, a trustee cannot demand a release by deed from the beneficiaries on handing over the trust property in accordance with the terms of the trust.[134] As Kindersley VC explained in *King v Mullins*,[135] 'in the case of a declared trust; where the trust is apparent on the face of a deed; the fund clear; the trust clearly defined; and the trustee is paying either the income or the capital of the fund; if he is paying it in strict accordance with the trusts, he has no right to require a release under seal.' He has, however, a right to a receipt for the funds paid over, and an acknowledgement that the accounts are settled.[136] But if he is a trustee of two separate trusts, he cannot refuse to pay over funds to which a beneficiary is clearly entitled under one trust by reason of some dispute in connection with the other.[137]

In some cases, however, a release may be demanded. In *King v Mullins*[138] Kindersley VC continued, on the facts of the case before him, that where 'there was no writing to indicate either what the trusts were or the amount of the trust fund; and . . . what the trustee has been asked to do is not in accordance with the tenor of the trusts' . . . it is 'not illegal in the trustee to demand a release by deed'. Again, where the beneficial interest has been resettled, although the trustees of the original settlement are not entitled to a release from the trustees of the resettlement, but only an acknowledge-ment of the receipt of the money paid,[139] it has been said[140] that in such case they are entitled to a release from the cestui que trust to whom the money was due.

---

[133] Ibid, s 26(2).   [134] *Chadwick v Heatley* (1845) 2 Coll 137; *Re Roberts' Trusts* (1869) 38 LJ Ch 708.

[135] (1852) 1 Drew 308 at 311, where the different position of an executor is contrasted.

[136] *Chadwick v Heatley*, supra; *Re Heming's Trust* (1856) 3 K & J 40. See (1981) 78 LSG 477 (A Mithani and M P Green).

[137] *Price v Loaden* (1856) 21 Beav 508.

[138] Supra; *Plimsoll v Drake* (1995) 4 Tas R 334 (release under seal can be required where at request of the beneficiaries, being sui iuris and together absolutely entitled, the trustee acts otherwise than in accordance with terms of trust).

[139] *Re Cater's Trusts (No 2)* (1858) 25 Beav 366; *Tiger v Barclays Bank Ltd* [1951] 2 KB 556, [1951] 2 All ER 262; affd, but not on this point, [1952] 1 All ER 85, CA. Cf *Re Hoskins' Trusts* (1877) 5 Ch D 229; on appeal 6 Ch D 281, CA.

[140] *Re Cater's Trusts (No 2)*, supra.

6 DUTIES WHERE BENEFICIARY IS SOLELY AND BENEFICIALLY ENTITLED

(a) ENTIRE EQUITABLE INTEREST PRESENTLY VESTED IN A BENEFICIARY OF FULL AGE AND CAPACITY

Such a beneficiary can require the trustee to convey the trust property to him and thus bring the trusts to an end, notwithstanding that the trust instrument may contain contrary provisions. It would, of course, be quite a different matter if the beneficiary merely had a contingent interest, contingent, for instance, upon his attaining a specified age.[141] Trustees may be validly empowered by the trust instrument to pay a beneficiary at an earlier age than 18, but even so a minor beneficiary cannot compel payment before coming of age.[142] A leading case is *Saunders v Vautier*,[143] which is commonly cited to support the general principle, though the ratio has been more narrowly stated by Lord Davey[144] to be 'that where there is an absolute vested gift made payable at a future event, with direction to accumulate the income in the meantime, and pay it with the principal, the court will not enforce the trust for accumulation in which no person has any interest but the legatee or (in other words) the court holds that a legatee[145] may put an end to an accumulation which is exclusively for his benefit'. A Canadian court applied the principle more widely in *Re Lysiak*[146] where a testator left all his estate to his wife and son who resided in the Soviet Union and gave his executors the 'sole discretion to dispose of . . . all my estate in such manner and at such time as they see fit, and until they are absolutely satisfied that the beneficiaries are free and unhindered to receive the said benefits without interference from the regime under which they are presently residing'. It was held that on the construction of the will the interests of the beneficiaries were absolutely vested, and the attempt to give the executors a right to postpone the distribution of the estate was

---

[141] See per Page Wood VC in (1859) John 265 at 272; *Re Johnston* [1894] 3 Ch 204. The rule has been abolished in some jurisdictions and the premature termination of the trust made subject to the approval of the court. See (1984) 62 CBR 618 (Jane M Glenn).

[142] *Re Somech* [1957] Ch 165, [1956] 3 All ER 523, and see s 21 of the Law of Property Act 1925, whereby a married minor can give a valid receipt for income.

[143] (1841) Cr & Ph 240; *IRC v Executors of Hamilton-Russell* [1943] 1 All ER 474, CA; *Stephenson v Barclays Bank Trust Co Ltd* [1975] 1 All ER 625. The principle has been applied to a gift to X for life, with power to appoint by deed or will, or by will alone, and a gift in default to X's personal representatives—*Re Canada Permanent Trust Co and Bell* (1982) 131 DLR (3d) 501, but not to a gift of life interests to children with power to appoint by will and gift over in default to children's or testator's issue where children had agreed to appoint to each other by irrevocable wills—*Re Saracini and National Trust Co* (1987) 39 DLR (4th) 436 (appeal dismissed (1989) 69 OR (2d) 640) nor in *Re Lee's Estate* (1986) 84 Fed LR 268). See also *Don King Productions Inc v Warren* [1998] 2 All ER 608; affd [2000] Ch 291, [1999] 2 All ER 218, CA, noted [1999] LMCLQ 353 (A Tettenborn).

[144] In *Wharton v Masterman* [1895] AC 186 at 198, HL.

[145] Assuming, of course, he is of full age and capacity—*Re Jump* [1903] 1 Ch 129.

[146] (1975) 55 DLR (3d) 161.

ineffective. Conversely, if the beneficiary absolutely entitled refused to accept a transfer of the trust funds in such a case the trustees would be entitled, if they wished, to pay them into court.[147] Again, where there is a gift of an annuity, the annuitant is entitled to demand in lieu thereof payment of the cash which would be needed to purchase it.[148] The general principle applies in the same way where the beneficiary is a charity, whether corporate or incorporate,[149] but not where the alleged beneficiary is 'charity' in the abstract, there being provisions for the future ascertainment of particular charitable institutions.[150] It may also be observed that although an indefinite gift of income to an individual carries the right to corpus,[151] this is not so in the case of a similar gift to charity, for such a gift could be enjoyed by the charity to its fullest extent in perpetuity.[152]

(b) ENTIRE EQUITABLE INTEREST VESTED IN TWO OR MORE BENEFICIARIES, EACH OF FULL AGE AND CAPACITY

Provided they are both or all agreed, they can bring the trust to an end by requiring the trust funds to be paid over to them or as they may direct. This principle has been held applicable not only to joint tenants and tenants in common, but also to the certificate holders under a unit trust[153] and cases where the beneficiaries are entitled in succession.[154] It also applies to the objects of a discretionary trust where there are individuals who are, in effect, combining on a compromise basis.[155] However it has been held in Australia that in such a case it is not open to the trustees of two separate charitable trusts to take action which would have the effect of varying the trusts upon which they hold or are entitled to receive property.[156] It is important to remember, moreover, as Lord Maugham has pointed out,[157] that 'the rule has no operation unless all the persons who have any present or contingent interest in the property, are sui iuris and consent'. Accordingly it seems that the principle will not apply where the only beneficiaries who do not consent are the unborn issue of a woman in fact past the age of child-bearing, for there remains the theoretical possibility of further beneficiaries coming into existence.[158] It is irrelevant for this purpose that the trustees, in

---

147 *IRC v Executors of Hamilton-Russell*, supra.

148 *Re Robbins* [1907] 2 Ch 8, CA, and cf *Parkes v Royal Botanic Society of London* (1908) 24 TLR 508. As to the valuation of the annuity see *Re Castle* [1916] WN 195; *Westminster Bank v IRC* [1954] 1 All ER 240, [1954] 1 WLR 242.

149 *Wharton v Masterman* [1895] AC 186, HL.   150 *Re Jefferies* [1936] 2 All ER 626.

151 *Re Levy* [1960] Ch 346, [1960] 1 All ER 42, CA.

152 *Re Levy*, supra; *Re Beesty's Will Trusts* [1966] Ch 223, [1964] 3 All ER 82.

153 *Re AEG Unit Trust (Managers) Ltd's Deed* [1957] Ch 415, [1957] 2 All ER 506.

154 *Anson v Potter* (1879) 13 Ch D 141; *Re White* [1901] 1 Ch 570.

155 *Re Nelson* [1928] Ch 920n, CA; *Re Smith* [1928] Ch 915; *Re Beckett's Settlement* [1940] Ch 279.

156 *Sir Moses Montefiore Jewish Home v Howell & Co (No 7) Pty Ltd* [1984] 2 NSWLR 406.

157 *Berry v Geen* [1938] AC 575 at 582, sub nom *Re Blake, Berry v Geen* [1938] 2 All ER 362 at 366, HL; *Biggs v Peacock* (1882) 22 Ch D 284, CA.

158 *Re Whichelow* [1953] 2 All ER 1558.

an appropriate case, may properly distribute the trust funds on the basis that a particular woman is past the age of child-bearing.[159]

In the case of any land subject to a trust of land, where each of the beneficiaries interested in the land is a person of full age and capacity who is absolutely entitled to the land, the trustees have power to convey the land to the beneficiaries even though they have not required the trustees to do so, and the beneficiaries must do whatever is necessary to secure that it vests in them.[160] Further the trustees may, where beneficiaries are absolutely entitled in undivided shares to land subject to the trust, partition the land and provide for the payment of equality money.[161] Subject to obtaining the consent of the beneficiaries, the trustees must give effect to any such partition by conveying the partitioned land in severalty in accordance with their rights.[162] Both the above powers may be restricted or excluded by a provision in the disposition creating a trust of land,[163] and if a consent is required to be obtained a power cannot be exercised without it.[164]

(c) WHERE ONE OF SEVERAL BENEFICIARIES, BEING SUI IURIS, IS ABSOLUTELY ENTITLED IN POSSESSION TO A SHARE IN THE TRUST PROPERTY

In general, according to Cozens-Hardy MR in *Re Marshall*,[165] 'the right of a person, who is entitled indefeasibly in possession to an aliquot share of property, to have that share transferred to him is one which is plainly established by law'. So far as personalty is concerned, the rule will normally be applied, even though this may result in the undistributed shares losing value. However in very special circumstances, where it would unduly prejudice the other beneficiaries, such a beneficiary may be unable to insist on a transfer.[166] Thus the principle discussed later,[167] that trustees are bound to hold an even hand among their beneficiaries, was successfully relied on in *Lloyds Bank*

---

[159] See eg *Re Westminster Bank Ltd's Declaration of Trust* [1963] 2 All ER 400n; *Re Pettifor's Will Trusts* [1966] Ch 257, [1966] 1 All ER 913; *Re Levy Estate Trusts* [2000] CLY 5263 and contrast *Re Cazenove* (1919) 122 LT 181. See also p 518, infra.

[160] Trusts of Land and Appointment of Trustees Act 1996, s 6(2). If the beneficiaries fail to do what is necessary, the court may order them to do so. In relation to the conveyance by trustees of unregistered land to a beneficiary, see ibid, s 16(4), (15). For some of the difficulties in construing this subsection see the *Encyclopaedia of Forms and Precedents*, vol 40(2) (5th edn, 2002 Reissue), paras 399, 400.

[161] Ibid, s 7(1). By sub-s 5 the trustees may act on behalf of a minor and retain his share on trust for him.

[162] Ibid, s 7(2)(3).

[163] Ibid, s 8(1), except in the case of charitable, ecclesiastic or public trusts; s 8(3).

[164] Ibid, s 8(2), and see s 10 and chapter 22, section 12(c), p 501, infra.

[165] [1914] 1 Ch 192 at 199, CA; *Stephenson v Barclays Bank Trust Co Ltd* [1975] 1 All ER 625; *Crowe v Appleby* [1975] 3 All ER 529, [1975] 1 WLR 1539; affd without reference to this point [1976] 2 All ER 914, [1976] 1 WLR 885, CA.

[166] *Re Sandeman's Will Trusts* [1937] 1 All ER 368; *Re Weiner's Will Trusts* [1956] 2 All ER 482. See Law Reform Committee, 23rd Report, Cmnd 8733, para 3.64–3.65.

[167] See chapter 19, infra.

plc v Duker[168] to prevent a beneficiary from calling for his share in specie. In this case the deceased's estate included 999 shares in a private company. The beneficiary, Duker, was entitled to 46/80 of the estate and asked for a transfer to him of 574 shares (the nearest whole number to 46/80 of 999). The other beneficiaries argued successfully against this on the ground that since the majority holding was worth more per share than the other shares, Duker would get more than his 46/80ths of the total value received by the beneficiaries as a body if the shares were transferred to him. The shares were directed to be sold on the general market and Duker, of course would be entitled to 46/80ths of the proceeds of sale. In Australia the rule has been extended to enable beneficiaries entitled in succession to combine to require payment or transfer of part of their interests in the fund, subject to the court retaining a discretion to refuse to order an inappropriate payment or transfer.[169] The question does not appear to have arisen in England.

In relation to land the courts have taken a different view because, as Cozens-Hardy MR went on to explain[170] 'it is a matter of notoriety, of which the court will take judicial notice, that an undivided share of real estate never fetches quite its proper proportion of the proceeds of sale of the entire estate; therefore, to allow an undivided share to be elected to be taken as real estate by one of the beneficiaries would be detrimental to the other beneficiaries.'[171] However an application may be made to the court under s 14 of the Trusts of Land and Appointment of Trustees Act 1996,[172] and once all the shares are vested in possession in persons of full age and capacity, then, as we have seen, either the beneficiaries or the trustees may take steps to bring the trust to an end.

7 RIGHT OF BENEFICIARIES TO OCCUPY TRUST LAND[173]

A beneficiary who is beneficially entitled to an interest in possession in land subject to a trust of land is entitled by reason of his interest to occupy the land at any time if at that time

(a) the purposes of the trust include making the land available for his occupation, or

(b) the land is held by the trustees so as to be so available.[174]

---

168 [1987] 3 All ER 193, [1987] 1 WLR 1324.   169 *Quinton v Proctor* [1998] 4 VR 469.

170 In *Re Marshall*, supra, CA, at 199.

171 *Re Horsnaill* [1909] 1 Ch 631; *Re Kipping* [1914] 1 Ch 62, CA. As to whether in a suitable case an appropriation could be required, quaere—per Harman J in *Re Weiner's Will Trusts*, supra.

172 Discussed p 494, infra.

173 See, generally, [1998] CLJ 123 (D G Barnsley).

174 Trusts of Land and Appointment of Trustees Act 1996, s 12(1). By sub-s (2) the beneficiary has no such right if the land is either unavailable or unsuitable for occupation by him. 'Beneficiary' is defined in s 22. See [1997] Conv 254 (J G Ross Martyn).

Where two or more beneficiaries are so entitled to occupy land, the trustees of land may exclude or restrict the entitlement of any one or more (but not all) of them, provided that the exclusion or the extent of the restriction is not unreasonable,[175] and may from time to time impose reasonable conditions on any beneficiary in relation to his occupation.[176] Thus in *Rodway v Landy*[177] trustees were held entitled, in relation to a single building which lent itself to physical partition, to exclude or restrict one beneficiary's entitlement to occupy one part, and at the same time exclude or restrict the other beneficiary's entitlement to occupy the other part. It was further held that a condition requiring a beneficiary to contribute to the cost of adapting the property to make it suitable for his occupation was a condition within s 23(3).

In exercising their powers the trustees of land must have regard to—

(a) the intentions of the creator(s) of the trust,

(b) the purposes for which the land is held, and

(c) the circumstances and wishes of each of the beneficiaries entitled to occupy the land.[178]

Moreover they must not exercise these powers so as to prevent any person who is in occupation of land from continuing in occupation, or in a manner likely to result in any such person ceasing to occupy the land, unless he consents or the court has given approval.[179]

There is a difficulty as to the construction of the phrase 'beneficially entitled to an interest in possession in land', which also appears in s 9 (delegation by trustees)[180] and s 11 (consultation with beneficiaries),[181] in relation to an express trust for sale. One view[182] is that in such a case, notwithstanding s 3 which abolished the doctrine of conversion in relation to trusts for sale, the life tenant beneficiary does not have an interest in possession in the land but only in the income, and accordingly no right of occupation can arise under s 12. The alternative view,[183] which it is submitted is to be preferred, is that the effect of s 3 is to give the beneficiary under a trust for sale an interest in land: s 12 may therefore apply. This view is supported by the fact that it was thought necessary to provide in s 22(3) that an annuitant is not to be regarded as entitled to an interest in possession in land. Further, in relation to ss 9 and 11 it would be surprising if these sections, which respectively replace ss 29 and 26(3) of the Law of Property Act 1925, were to exclude the life tenant under a trust for sale as a person to

---

[175] Ibid, s 13(1), (2).

[176] Ibid, s 13(3). In particular conditions requiring payment of outgoings or expenses or the assumption of other obligations in relation to the land: ibid, s 13(5); and compensating a beneficiary whose entitlement has been excluded or restricted: ibid, s 13(6).

[177] [2001] 2 WLR 1775, CA, noted (2001) 30 T & ELJ 5 (R Pearce).   [178] Ibid, s 13(4).

[179] Ibid, s 13(7). In determining whether to give approval the court must have regard to the matters set out in s 13(4): s 13(8).

[180] This is discussed at p 462, infra.   [181] This is discussed at p 497, infra.

[182] See the annotation to ibid, s 12, in Current Law Statutes 1996 (P Kenny).

[183] See Whitehouse and Hassall, *Trusts of Land, Trustee Delegation and the Trustee Act 2000*, 2nd edn, para 2.21.

whom functions could be delegated, or who must be consulted, when they were clearly persons coming within the earlier provisions. Admittedly the language in ss 29 and 26(3) is different, but it is submitted that a purposive construction should be applied in relation to s 3. Another approach is to take account of the fact that, before 1997, despite the equitable doctrine of conversion, the interests of beneficiaries under a trust for sale of land were treated as interests in land for the purposes of various statutory provisions.[184] It is submitted that interest in land in ss 9, 11 and 12 of the Trusts of Land and Appointment of Trustees Act 1996[185] equally is apt to include the interest of a beneficiary under a trust for sale. It should be added that the term 'interest in possession' is primarily used by way of contrast to 'interest in remainder', and accordingly a life tenant under a trust for sale falls within ss 9, 11 and 12. Further support for the view being advanced is to be found in amendments to other legislation made by the 1996 Act. Thus the references in ss 18 and 38 of the Limitation Act 1980 to interests in the proceeds of sale of land have been deleted, but it is surely inconceivable that the effect of these deletions was intended to exclude the operation of the Act where land is held on trust for sale: it must have been assumed that they have 'equitable interests in land' within the Act.

The right to occupy trust land does not extend to a beneficiary under a discretionary trust, but there is no reason why the trust instrument should not provide that the trustees may permit a discretionary beneficiary to occupy the trust land upon such terms and conditions as they think fit.

If a settlor does not wish any beneficiary to enjoy a right of occupation it is important that it should be clearly indicated in the trust instrument. The Act does not appear to contemplate the exclusion of s 12, but a statement of the intention of the settlor in the trust instrument is likely to be effective in practice.[186]

8 RIGHTS AND LIABILITIES IN RELATION TO STRANGERS TO THE TRUST

A trustee is personally liable on the contracts into which he enters on behalf of the trust. Thus in *Marston Thompson Evershed plc v Bend*[187] the plaintiff lent money to finance a new club house at a rugby club. The loan was secured by a mortgage of the

---

[184] See per Pennycuick V-C in *Elias v Mitchell* [1972] Ch 652 at 664, [1972] 2 All ER 153 at 159; *Ahmed v Kendrick* (1987) 56 P & CR 120, CA; and *Williams and Glyn's Bank Ltd v Boland* [1981] AC 487, [1980] 2 All ER 408, HL.

[185] Section 9 is prospectively amended by the Mental Capacity Act 2005, Sch 6, para 41.

[186] This may be backed up by a provision restricting the investment powers of trustees under s 6(1), (3) (as amended by the Trustee Act 2000, Sch 2, para 45) so as to exclude buying land for beneficial occupation—see s 8(1). See also Trustee Act 2000, ss 8, 9(b).

[187] Unreported, but noted (1997) 39 LSG 38; *Perring v Draper* [1997] EGCS 109. See (1996) 10 Tru LI 45 (R Ham); (1999) 4 T & ELJ 4 (Jennifer Chambers); (1999) 6 T & ELJ 4 (D Hayton).

club's property which was held in the name of the four defendant trustees. The defendants had signed the loan agreement, which expressly described them as trustees, and had covenanted to repay the capital and interest on demand. The club failed to repay the debt and the defendants were held personally liable to the full extent of the debt. An express statement that liability is limited is needed to avoid exposure to personal risk. But a proviso which is so wide as to exclude all liability may not be upheld.[188]

Trustees may likewise be personally liable in tort in respect of their acts or omissions in connection with the administration of the trust, and this includes vicarious liability for their employees or their agents. Thus in *Benett v Wyndham*[189] woodcutters properly employed by a trustee to fell a tree on a settled estate negligently allowed a bough to fall on and injure a passerby, who was held entitled to recover damages from the trustee.

A trustee may generally sue and be sued on behalf of or as representing the property of which he is trustee, and a beneficiary has no direct cause of action against a third party save in special circumstances such as a failure, excusable or inexcusable, by the trustees in the performance of the duty owed by the trustees to the beneficiary to protect the trust estate or to protect the interests of the beneficiary in the trust estate.[190] Where he can do so he sues in right of the trustees and in the room of the trustees, who should be joined as defendants. He is not enforcing a right reciprocal to some duty owed directly to him by the third party.[191] Thus in *Field v Finnenich & Co*[192] a plaintiff was allowed to sue on a cause of action vested in personal representatives where the personal representatives refused to sue and there was no one interested in the estate except the plaintiff and the widow of the deceased and the widow had a personal interest in the defeat of the action. Conversely creditors do not have a direct action against either the trust estate or the beneficiaries.

---

[188] See *Watling v Lewis* [1911] 1 Ch 414.

[189] (1862) 4 De G F & J 259; *Re Raybould* [1900] 1 Ch 199 (nuisance). As to a trustee's right to an indemnity from the trust estate see p 483 et seq, infra.

[190] *Hayim v Citibank NA* [1987] AC 730, PC; *Morla Professional Services Pty Ltd v Richard Walter Pty Ltd (in liq)* (1999) 169 ALR 419. *Bradstock Trustee Services Ltd v Nabarro Nathanson (a firm)* [1995] 4 All ER 888; *Fried v National Australia Bank Ltd* [2001] FCR 322 (Aust). See (1997) 11 Tru LI 60 (G McCormack) where it is suggested that in general beneficiaries cannot sue external fund managers.

[191] *Parker-Tweedale v Dunbar Bank plc* [1991] Ch 12, [1990] 2 All ER 577, CA.

[192] [1971] 1 All ER 1104.

18

THE INVESTMENT OF TRUST FUNDS

1 INTRODUCTION[1]

(a) HISTORICAL BACKGROUND

The law of trusts developed largely in the context of the family settlement where there was a life tenant entitled to income, and on his death the capital of the settlement would pass to the remaindermen. Of course the limitations of the settlement might be very complex and there might be a number of persons concurrently and/or successively entitled to income before the capital finally became vested in possession in one or more remaindermen. It is a basic duty of trustees to act fairly between the different classes of beneficiary, and accordingly in choosing investments they are under a duty to hold a balance between them and must take care not unduly to favour the tenant for life against the remaindermen or vice versa.[2] It is submitted that it is the portfolio of investments that should be balanced, not each individual investment within it. The idea is that they should invest the trust funds in such a way as to provide a reasonable income for the life tenant and at the same time maintain the value of the capital for the remaindermen. In the view of Hoffman J (as he then was) at first instance in *Nestle v National Westminster Bank plc*[3] this means the value in monetary terms rather than the real value. 'Preservation of real values', he said, 'can be no more than an aspiration which some trustees may have the good fortune to achieve.' Another matter which is little discussed in the cases is whether the personal circumstances of individual beneficiaries and the relationship between them should be taken into account. In *Nestle v*

---

[1] See, generally, [1987] PCB 22, 87 (A Duckworth); (1998) 12 Tru LI 158 (G McCormack). As to modern portfolio theory see Longstretch, *Modern Investment Management and the Prudent Man Rule*; (2000) 14 Tru LI 75 (I N Legair).

[2] *Raby v Ridehalgh* (1855) 7 De G M & G 104; *Re Dick* [1891] 1 Ch 423 at 431, CA; affd sub nom *Hume v Lopes* [1892] AC 112, HL. The meaning is thought to be the same whether one speaks of the obligation of a trustee to administer the trust fund impartially, or fairly, having regard to the different interests of beneficiaries, or to preserving an equitable balance between them: see *Nestle v National Westminster Bank plc* [1994] 1 All ER 118, [1993] 1 WLR 1260, CA. See *Re Smith* (1971) 16 DLR (3d) 130; affd (1971) 18 DLR (3d) 405, where the trustee was removed from office for breach of this duty; *Re Mulligan (decd)* [1998] 1 NZLR 481; *Edge v Pensions Ombudsman* [2000] Ch 602, [1999] 4 All ER 546 CA.

[3] See (1984) 62 CBR 577 (R E Scane); (1995) 16 NZULR 349 (A S Butler); (1997) 10 Tru LI 102 (Emma Ford).

National Westminster Bank plc[4] Staughton LJ thought that they should, observing: 'If the life tenant is living in penury and the remainderman already has ample wealth, common sense suggests that a trustee should be able to take that into account.' A trustee who has a lien on the trust funds[5] is entitled to take into account his own interest, but must act impartially as between himself and the beneficiaries.[6]

(b) NON-FINANCIAL CONSIDERATIONS

Until recently there was little direct authority on the questions whether trustees could properly take non-financial considerations into account in making decisions. In *Cowan v Scargill*,[7] however, Megarry VC stated the law in clear and unambiguous terms, holding that the defendants were in breach of their fiduciary duties in refusing approval of an investment plan for the pension scheme unless it was amended so as to prohibit any increase in overseas investment, to provide for the withdrawal of existing overseas investments at the most opportune time, and to prohibit investment in energies which are in direct competition with coal.

The duty of trustees to exercise their powers in the best interests of the present and future beneficiaries, known in the United States as 'the duty of undivided loyalty to the beneficiaries',[8] is paramount. When the purpose of the trust is to provide financial benefits for the beneficiaries, as is usually the case, the best interests of the beneficiaries are normally their financial interests. It follows that a power of investment must be exercised so as to yield the best return for the beneficiaries, judged in relation to the risks of the investments in question; and the prospects of the yield of income and capital appreciation have both to be considered in judging the return from the investment:

In considering what investments to make trustees must put on one side their own personal interests and views. Trustees may have strongly held social or political views. They may be firmly opposed to any investment in South Africa or other countries, or they may object to any form of investment in companies concerned with alcohol, tobacco, armaments or many other things. In the conduct of their own affairs, of course, they are free to abstain from making any such investments. Yet if under a trust investments of this type would be more

---

[4] (29 June 1988, unreported), affd [1994] 1 All ER 118, [1993] 1 WLR 1260, CA.   [5] See p 485, infra.
[6] *X v A* [2000] 1 All ER 490, discussed (1999) 12 T & ELJ 4 (E Rajah); [2000] Conv 560 (Ann Kenny).
[7] [1985] Ch 270, [1984] 2 All ER 750, criticized (1984) 13 Ind LJ 167 (R Nobles) and (1986) 102 LQR 32 (J H Farrar and J K Maxton). See [1985] Conv 52 (Penelope Pearce and Alec Samuels); [1990] LSG 87/23/17 (Nancy Convey); (1990) 4 TL & P 25 (P Dodding & I Pittaway); (1991) 5 Tru LI 157 (R Ellison); [1992] 55 MLR 587 (P Luxton); (1995) 9 Tru LI 71 (Lord Nicholls); (1998) 19 Co Law 39 (G McCormack) and for a general discussion of some of the special considerations in the case of a pension fund (1985) 14 Ind LJ 1 and (1987) 16 Ind LJ 164 (R Nobles). See also (1980) 68 Calif LR 518 (R B Ravikoff and M P Curzon); (1980) 79 Mich LR 72 (J H Langheim and R A Posner); (1987) 2 TL & P 9 (Tony Thurnham) and (1987) 61 ALJ 329 (F J Finn and P A Zeigler).
[8] See *Blankenship v Boyle* 329 F Supp 1089 at 1095 (1971).

beneficial to the beneficiaries than other investments, the trustees must not refrain from making the investments by reason of the views that they hold.[9]

This was applied by Lord Murray in the Scottish case of *Martin v City of Edinburgh District Council*[10] where he held that a breach of trust by the council had been proved where it had acted 'in pursuing a policy of disinvesting in South Africa without considering expressly whether it was in the best interests of the beneficiaries and without obtaining professional advice on this matter'.

One interpretation might be that trustees should not take their personal views into account even if there is a choice between two equally beneficial investments, though if they do so in such a case it would in practice be difficult to sustain an attack upon their action. This interpretation is, perhaps, too extreme. In *Martin v City of Edinburgh District Council*,[11] Lord Murray considered the general proposition that trustees have a duty not to fetter their investment discretion for reasons extraneous to the trust purposes, including reasons of a political or moral nature, and presumably matters of conscience. He thought this acceptable if it means that a trustee has a duty to apply his mind genuinely and independently to a trust issue which is before him, and not simply to adhere to a decision which he has made previously in a different context, or to a policy or other principle to which he is committed. Lord Murray, however, did not consider the proposition either reasonable or practicable if it means that each individual trustee in genuinely applying his mind and judgment to a trust decision, must divest himself of all personal preferences, of all political beliefs, and of all moral, religious and other conscientiously held beliefs. What he must do is to recognize that he has those preferences, commitments or principles, but nonetheless do his best to exercise fair and impartial judgment on the merits of the issue before him. If he realizes that he cannot do that, then he should abstain from participating in deciding the issue, or, in the extreme case, resign as a trustee. Further, as discussed later,[12] trustees may even have to act dishonourably (though not illegally) if the interests of their beneficiaries require it.

Megarry VC's statement of the law, that the best interests of the beneficiaries are normally their financial interests, leaves scope for the exceptional case. As he went on to observe:

. . . if the only actual or potential beneficiaries of a trust are all adults with very strict views on moral and social matters, condemning all forms of alcohol, tobacco and popular entertainments, as well as armaments, I can well understand that it might not be for the 'benefit'[13] of such beneficiaries to know that they are obtaining rather larger financial returns under the trust by reason of investments in those activities than they would have received if the trustees had invested the trust funds in other investments. The beneficiaries might well

---

[9] *Cowan v Scargill*, supra, at 761, per Megarry VC, discussed (1984) 81 LSG 229 (S C Butler); [1985] JBL 45 (Constance Whippman).

[10] 1988 SLT 329.   [11] Supra.

[12] See *Buttle v Saunders* [1950] 2 All ER 193, discussed p 467, infra.

[13] See p 514, et seq, discussing the meaning of 'benefit' under the Variation of Trusts Act 1958.

consider that it was far better to receive less than to receive more from what they consider to be evil and tainted sources . . . But I would emphasize that such cases are likely to be very rare, and in any case I think that under a trust for the provision of financial benefits the burden would rest, and rest heavy, on him who asserts that it is for the benefit of the beneficiaries as a whole to receive less by reason of the exclusion of some of the possibly more profitable forms of investment.

The same general approach applies to charities.[14] Charity trustees may hold property for functional purposes, for example the National Trust owns historic houses, and many charities need office accommodation in which to carry out essential administrative work. Charity trustees may also hold property for the purpose of generating money, whether from income or capital growth, with which to further the work of the charity. Where property is so held by trustees as an investment the trustees should normally seek to obtain therefrom the maximum return, whether by way of income or capital growth, which is consistent with commercial prudence. In most cases the best interests of the charity require that the trustees' choice of investments should be made solely on the basis of well-established investment criteria, including the need for diversification. Exceptionally if trustees are satisfied that investing in a company engaged in a particular type of business would conflict with the very objects their charity is seeking to achieve, they should not so invest.[15] Another exceptional case might be where trustees' holdings of particular investments might hamper a charity's work either by making potential recipients of aid unwilling to be helped because of the source of the charity's money, or by alienating some of those who support the charity financially. In this case the trustees would need to balance the difficulties they would encounter, or likely financial loss they would sustain, if they were to hold the investments, against the risk of financial detriment if those investments were excluded from their portfolio.[16]

For the avoidance of doubt it may be added that if an investment clause prohibits or restricts certain kinds of investment, it is the duty of the trustees to comply with the prohibition or restriction. And the clause might empower or require trustees to take non-financial considerations into account.[17]

---

[14] See CC14.

[15] Eg cancer research charities and tobacco shares. It is very unlikely that this would disable the trustees from choosing a properly diversified portfolio.

[16] *Harries v Church Comrs for England* [1993] 2 All ER 300, [1992] 1 WLR 1241 (trustees could properly adopt an ethical investment policy which left open an adequate width of alternative investments) noted [1992] Conv 115 (R Nobles). See (1982) 45 MLR 268 (Helen Beynon); Report of the Charity Commissioners for 1987, paras 41–45; [1988] NLJ Christmas Appeals Supp ii (A Phillips); (2001) 7 CPLR 137 (R Meakin); (2002) 36 T & ELJ 18 (C Cutbill).

[17] *Harries v Church Comrs for England*, supra.

2 EXPRESS POWER OF INVESTMENT

The effect of any particular express provision is, of course, a question of construction of the particular words used.[18] Some general observations may, however, be made. First, express investment clauses are now construed more generously than was once the case. The older view[19] was that they 'should be construed strictly for the protection of trustees and remaindermen'. The modern view is that the words of such a clause will be given a natural and not a restrictive interpretation. Accordingly it was held in *Re Harari's Settlement Trusts*,[20] where the earlier authorities are discussed, that there was no justification for implying any restriction on the meaning of an investment clause authorizing trustees to invest 'in or upon such investments as to them may seem fit'.

Secondly, questions have arisen as to the meaning of the word 'invest' as used in an investment clause. The judicial definition most commonly referred to is that of P O Lawrence J in *Re Wragg*,[21] that 'to invest' includes 'as one of its meanings "to apply money in the purchase of some property from which interest or profit is expected and which property is purchased in order to be held for the sake of the income which it will yield".' There the investment clause was held to authorize the purchase of real property for the sake of the income it would produce, but this case was distinguished in *Re Power*[22] where it was held that a power to invest in the purchase of freehold property did not authorize the purchase of a freehold house with vacant possession for the occupation of the beneficiaries.

Thirdly, mention may be made of the construction placed on particular provisions contained in express investment clauses in various cases. A power to invest in 'stocks' has been held to authorize an investment in fully-paid shares,[23] and, conversely, a power to invest in shares an investment in stock,[24] while a power to invest in 'securities' has been held to include any stocks or shares or bonds by way of investment.[25] Only a very clear provision will be treated as authorizing an investment on personal security, in the sense that there is no security beyond the liability of the borrower to repay, as opposed to a loan on the security of personal property. In *Khoo Tek Keong v Ching Joo Tuan Neoh*[26] there was a very wide investment clause empowering the

---

[18] It is a part of the duty of trustees to acquaint themselves with the scope of their powers and in any case of doubt to obtain legal advice and if necessary, the opinion of the court: *Nestle v National Westminster Bank plc* [1994] 1 All ER 118, [1993] 1 WLR 1260, CA,

[19] See eg *Re Maryon-Wilson's Estate* [1912] 1 Ch 55 at 66–67, CA, per Farwell LJ; *Bethell v Abraham* (1873) LR 17 Eq 24; *Re Braithwaite* (1882) 21 Ch D 121.

[20] [1949] 1 All ER 430; *Re Peczenik's Settlement* [1964] 2 All ER 339.

[21] [1919] 2 Ch 58 at 64, 65, [1918–19] All ER Rep 233 at 237; *Re Peczenik's Settlement*, supra.

[22] [1947] Ch 572, [1947] 2 All ER 282. But see now Section 4, p 422, infra.

[23] *Re McEacharn's Settlement Trusts* [1939] Ch 858. Cf *Re Willis* [1911] 2 Ch 563.

[24] *Re Boys' Will Trusts* [1950] 1 All ER 624.

[25] *Re Douglas' Will Trusts* [1959] 2 All ER 620; affd [1959] 3 All ER 785, CA, but no appeal on this point. As to the meaning of 'ordinary preferred stock or shares' see *Re Powell-Cotton's Re-Settlement* [1957] Ch 159, [1957] 1 All ER 404.

[26] [1934] AC 529, PC. See also *Pickard v Anderson* (1872) LR 13 Eq 608.

trustees 'to invest all moneys liable to be invested in such investments as they in their absolute discretion think fit', but it was held that this did not authorise them to invest in personal security in the above sense, though it did authorize a loan on the security of personal property. One may contrast with this case *Re Laing's Settlement*[27] where the trustees were expressly authorized to invest 'upon such personal credit without security as the trustees or trustee shall in their or his absolute and uncontrolled discretion think fit'. On these clear words the trustees were held to be authorized to advance by way of loan, even to the tenant for life, on his personal security which, it was pointed out, was not really an advance on security at all.

Fourthly, it should be observed that if the trust instrument directs and requires trustees to make some specified investment they are under a duty to do so, even if it is one of which they disapprove, and accordingly they will not be under any liability in doing so even though this may result in a loss to the trust estate.[28]

Fifthly, an investment clause usually confers an express power to vary investments. In the absence of such a provision it has been held in a series of cases[29] that a power to vary is implied in a power of investment, the court observing in one case[30] that it would be most unfortunate if it were not so.

Sixthly, there is a conflict of authority as to whether a power of investment 'with the consent of X' gives X a beneficial power which he can use for his own benefit, or effectively release, or whether it gives X a fiduciary power which he should use in the interests of all the beneficiaries, and which he is unable to release. In the absence of a controlling context, the former view is perhaps to be preferred.[31]

Lastly, a settlor or testator can, it seems, validly confer on a trustee or someone else a power to enlarge the original investment clause.[32]

3 THE STATUTORY POWER UNDER THE TRUSTEE ACT 2000

(a) BACKGROUND

Under the Trustee Act 1925, investment by trustees was restricted in the main to fixed interest investments which would ultimately be repayable at par, in particular

[27] [1899] 1 Ch 593; *Re Godwin's Settlement* (1918) 119 LT 643.

[28] *Beauclerk v Ashburnham* (1845) 8 Beav 322; *Cadogan v Earl of Essex* (1854) 2 Drew 227; *Re Hurst* (1890) 63 LT 665; affd (1892) 67 LT 96, CA. See (1972) 36 Conv 260 (Penelope Pearce).

[29] Including *Hume v Lopes* [1892] AC 112, HL; *Re Pope's Contract* [1911] 2 Ch 442; *Re Pratt's Will Trusts* [1943] Ch 326, [1943] 2 All ER 375.

[30] *Re Pope's Contract*, supra, per Neville J.

[31] *Re Wise* unreported discussed in (1954) 218 LT 116 following *Dicconson v Talbot* (1870) 6 Ch App 32 rather than *Re Massingberd's Settlement* (1890) 63 LT 296, CA.

[32] *Re Jewish Orphanage Endowments Trusts* [1960] 1 All ER 764. Cf *Soldiers', Sailors' and Airmen's Families Association v A-G* [1968] 1 All ER 448n.

excluding investment in 'equities'. This was designed to maintain the capital value of
the trust fund in money terms, and thus protect the beneficiaries from loss and the
trustees from the risk of a claim for breach of trust by imprudent investment. The
legislators did not, however, foresee the subsequent far-reaching changes in the econ-
omy and the investment situation, in particular, inflation. There is no real safety in the
capital of a trust retaining a paper value of £10,000 if in the meantime the real value of
the pound has, as a result of inflation, been reduced to fifty pence. And to a somewhat
lesser extent the same is true in relation to income beneficiaries.

The individual investor was often able to provide a hedge against inflation by
investing in investments which themselves appreciated in value in money terms so as
to keep pace with the progress of inflation. In particular he could invest in equity
stock and shares which represent the right, not to a fixed money income and a fixed
capital sum, but to a share in the companies' profits and assets and are thus ultimately
associated with real values and not with money values. The real value may thus be
maintained, or may even increase, but there is the risk of a reduction in value if the
share price falls. The Trustee Investments Act 1961 was passed, somewhat belatedly, to
enable trustees to invest more widely. Subject to certain safeguards it empowered
trustees to invest up to half the trust funds, later increased to three quarters, in the
equity stock and shares of financial, industrial and commercial companies quoted on
a recognized investment exchange.

Long before the turn of the century the 1961 Act was in turn generally agreed to be
outdated. The Trustee Act 2000 was passed to remedy the situation. This Act embraces
modern portfolio theory in which the main concern of the investor is to balance
overall growth and overall risk. It repealed Part I of the Trustee Act 1925, which
contained the provisions relating to investments, and, subject to savings, the Trustee
Investments Act 1961 and went on to give to trustees the wide powers of investment
commonly included in any contemporary professionally drawn trust.

(b) THE GENERAL POWER OF INVESTMENT

Part II of the Trustee Act 2000 is revolutionary in that it replaces the previous system,
under which a trustee was only permitted to make specified 'authorized' investments,
by one under which a trustee may make any kind of investment that he could make if
he were absolutely entitled to the assets of the trust. This is called 'the general power
of investment'.[33] The general power of investment does not, however, permit a trustee
to make investments in land other than in loans secured on land, but there are special
provisions in relation to the acquisition of land in s 8, discussed below.[34]

---

[33] Trustee Act 2000, s 3(1), (2).

[34] Ibid, s 3(3), and see p 422, infra. A person invests in a loan secured on land if he has rights under any
contract under which (a) one person provides another with credit, and (b) the obligation of the borrower to
repay is secured on land. 'Credit' includes any cash loan or other financial accommodation and 'cash' includes
money in any form: ibid, s 3(4)–(6).

The general power of investment, which applies to trusts whenever created,[35] is additional to any powers of investment conferred on trustees otherwise than by the Act, but is subject to any restriction or exclusion imposed by the trust instrument (provided it was made after 2 August 1961),[36] or by any enactment or any provision of subordinate legislation.[37]

Part II does not apply to trustees of pension schemes, authorized unit trusts, or funds established under schemes made under ss 24 or 25 of the Charities Act 1993.[38]

(c) GENERAL PRINCIPLES TO BE APPLIED

(i) The rules developed by equity

The mere fact that a certain type of investment is authorized by the trust instrument or by statute does not mean that it is necessarily proper to invest in it in any particular case: if it is too risky it will constitute a breach of trust. However wide the provisions of an express investment clause may be, it is submitted that they do not absolve trustees from their duty to consider whether a proposed investment is such as in its nature it is prudent and right for them as trustees to make. Even if they are given power to invest at their absolute discretion and as if they were absolute owners they cannot invest in an investment which is one that a prudent man of business would have eschewed.[39] The general principles were restated in the leading case of *Learoyd v Whiteley*.[40] In the Court of Appeal Lindley LJ said:[41]

care must be taken not to lose sight of the fact that the business of the trustee, and the business which the ordinary prudent man is supposed to be conducting for himself, is the business of investing money for the benefit of persons who are to enjoy it at some future time, and not for the sole benefit of the person entitled to the present income. The duty of a trustee is not to take such care only as a prudent man would take if he had only himself to consider; the duty rather is to take such care as an ordinary prudent man would take if he were minded to make an investment for the benefit of other people for whom he felt morally bound to provide.

In *Learoyd v Whiteley*[42] itself, although the power of investment was wide enough to

---

[35] Ibid, s 7(1). A provision in a trust instrument made before the commencement of Part II which operates under the 1961 Act as a power to invest under that Act, or confers power to invest under that Act, is to be treated as conferring the general power of investment: s 7(3).

[36] Ibid, s 7(2). This is to ensure that old restrictions overcome by the 1961 Act do not revive to restrict the benefits of the new general power of investment.

[37] Ibid, s 6(1)–(3).

[38] Ibid, ss 36–38. As to ss 24 and 25 of the Charities Act 1993 see pp 324, 325 supra.

[39] *Khoo Tek Keong v Ching Joo Tuan Neogh* [1934] AC 529, PC; *Chapman v Browne* [1902] 1 Ch 785, CA; *Bartlett v Barclays Bank Trust Co Ltd* [1980] Ch 515, [1980] 1 All ER 139.

[40] (1887) 12 App Cas 727, HL. See *Jones v AMP Perpetual Trustee Co of NZ Ltd* [1994] 1 NZLR 690.

[41] *Re Whiteley* (1886) 33 Ch D 347 at 355, CA; *Nestle v National Westminster Bank plc* [1994] 1 All ER 118, [1993] 1 WLR 1260, CA.

[42] Supra, HL.

cover a mortgage on a freehold brickfield, it was held to be a breach of trust since the property was of a hazardous and wasting character:

> This does not mean that a trustee is bound to avoid all risk and in effect act as an insurer of the trust fund . . . The distinction is between a prudent degree of risk on the one hand, and hazard on the other. [The court will not] be astute to fix liability on a trustee who has committed no more than an error of judgment, from which no business man, however prudent, can expect to be immune.[43]

Particular decisions need to be looked at with care for what a prudent man should do depends on the economic and financial conditions of the time, not on what judges may have said should be done in different conditions in the past.[44] Referring to the 'classic statement' of Lindley LJ cited above, Hoffman J[45] said that it set an extremely flexible standard capable of adaptation to current economic conditions and contemporary understanding of markets and investments. 'For example', he continued, 'investments which were imprudent in the days of the gold standard may be sound and sensible in times of high inflation. Modern trustees acting within their investment powers are entitled to be judged by the standards of current portfolio theory, which emphasizes the risk level of the entire portfolio rather than the risk attaching to each investment taken in isolation.'

Another aspect was demonstrated in *Re David Feldman Charitable Foundation*.[46] Mr Feldman set up an incorporated charity with a gift of $180,000, of which he, his solicitor and his accountant were directors. Shortly afterwards the charity lent $175,000 to Mr Feldman's company, on the security of a promissory note. This was within the charity's powers of investment. Though there was no loss to the trust estate it was held that by reasons of the conflict of interest the loan to Mr Feldman's company was an improper investment and a breach of trust.

These equitable rules have been in effect superseded first by the Trustee Investments Act 1961, and subsequently by the Trustee Act 2000, which embodies and enlarges the equitable principles.

(ii) the statutory provisions

The Trustee Act 2000 provides that in exercising any power of investment, whether arising under the Act or otherwise, and whenever created, a trustee must have regard to the standard investment criteria. The standard investment criteria, in relation to a trust, are—

> '(a) the suitability to the trust of investment of the same kind as any particular investment proposed to be made or retained and of that particular investment as an investment of that kind, and

---

[43] *Bartlett v Barclays Bank Trust Co Ltd* [1980] Ch 515, [1980] 1 All ER 139.

[44] *Nestle v National Westminster Bank plc*, supra, CA.

[45] In *Nestle v National Westminster Bank plc* at first instance, unrep, affd on appeal, supra, CA. See (1987) 62 NYULR 52 (J N Gordon); (2003) 12 Tru LI 74 (P U Ali).

[46] (1987) 58 OR (2d) 626.

(b) the need for diversification of investments of the trust, in so far as is appropriate to the circumstances of the trust.'[47]

'Suitability' includes considerations as to the size and risk of the investment and the need to produce an appropriate balance between income and capital growth to meet the needs of the trust. It will also include any relevant ethical considerations as to the kind of investments which it is appropriate for the trust to make.

The Act also requires trustees to review the investments of the trust from time to time and to consider whether, having regard to the standard investment criteria, they should be varied.[48]

(d) OBTAINING ADVICE

Section 5(1) of the Trustee Act 2000 provides that before exercising any power of investment[49] a trustee must obtain and consider proper advice about the way in which, having regard to the standard investment criteria, the power should be exercised. Likewise, by s 5(2), when reviewing the investments of the trust he must obtain and consider proper advice about whether, having regard to the standard investment criteria, the investments should be varied. 'Proper advice' is the advice of a person who is reasonably believed by the trustee to be qualified to give it by his ability in and practical experience of financial and other matters relating to the proposed investment.[50] The trustee is not, on the one hand, required to act on such advice, but he is not entitled to reject it merely because he sincerely disagrees with it, unless in addition to being sincere he is acting as an ordinary prudent man would act.[51] Nor, on the other hand, is he necessarily protected if he follows it: but, clearly, it would be difficult to establish a breach of trust if a trustee had bona fide relied on such advice, and such reliance would also normally enable him to obtain relief under s 61 of the Trustee Act 1925.[52]

By way of exception to the above requirements, s 5(3) provides that a trustee need not obtain such advice if he reasonably concludes that in all the circumstances it is unnecessary or inappropriate to do so. This would be the case, for example, if the proposed investment is small, so that the cost of obtaining advice would be disproportionate to the benefit to be gained from doing so, or where the trustees themselves possess skills and knowledge making separate advice unnecessary.

In the present investment situation the position of trustees is not easy.[53] The sort of investment which will produce a high rate of interest which will suit the life tenant, is

---

[47] Trustee Act 2000, ss 4(1), (3), 7(1).   [48] Ibid, s 4(2).

[49] Whether arising under the statutory power or otherwise; and whenever created: ibid, s 7(1).

[50] Trustee Act 2000, s 5(4).

[51] *Cowan v Scargill* [1985] Ch 270, [1984] 2 All ER 750, per Megarry V-C.

[52] Discussed in chapter 24, section 3(f), p 546, supra.

[53] See (1975) 39 Conv 318 (D Paling). For a discussion of the problem in the USA see (1978) 126 U Penn LR 1171.

likely to be fixed interest investment whose real value may well be eroded by inflation by the time the remaindermen come into possession, while equities which it is hoped will show a capital appreciation and thus safeguard the position of remaindermen, may not produce a high enough rate of interest to satisfy the tenant for life.

4 ACQUISITION OF LAND

Part III of the Trustee Act 2000 provides that a trustee may acquire freehold or leasehold land in the United Kingdom—

(a) as an investment,

(b) for occupation by a beneficiary, or

(c) for any other reason.[54]

As with Part II, the powers conferred by Part III are additional to any powers conferred on trustees otherwise than by the Act, but are subject to any restriction or exclusion imposed by the trust instrument or by any enactment or any provision of subordinate legislation.[55]

For the purposes of exercising his functions as a trustee, a trustee who acquires land under these provisions has all the powers of an absolute owner in relation to the land.[56] Thus, for example, a trustee has power to hold land jointly with other persons, powers of sale and leasing, and power to grant mortgages in respect of land.

The above provisions, which apply to trusts whenever created,[57] are broadly modelled on s 6(3), (4) of the Trusts of Land and Appointment of Trustees Act 1996, but are in wider terms than that section as originally enacted. Section 6, which is still in force in relation to trustees of land, has, however, been amended by the 2000 Act so as to give trustees of land the powers conferred by s 8 of the latter Act as set out above. Unlike the 1996 Act the 2000 Act is not restricted to trustees of land, but applies to trustees generally. An express duty was imposed on trustees of land by s 6(5) of the 1996 Act to have regard to the interests of the beneficiaries in exercising their powers under that section. This provision is not replicated in the 2000 Act, but since it is thought merely to have made statutory the pre-existing equitable duty of trustees, the omission of an equivalent provision does not diminish the obligations of trustees.

---

[54] Ibid, s 8(1). 'Freehold or leasehold land' is defined in s 8(2): in relation to England and Wales it means a legal estate in land: s 8(2)(*a*).

[55] Ibid, s 9.   [56] Ibid, s 8(3).

[57] Ibid, s 10(2). But not to settled land under the Settled Land Act 1925, or to a trust to which the Universities and College Estates Act 1925 applies: ibid, s 10(1).

Part III does not apply to trustees of pension schemes, trustees of authorized unit trusts, or trustees managing funds established under schemes made under ss 24 or 25 of the Charities Act 1993.[58]

5 TRUSTEES HOLDING A CONTROLLING INTEREST IN A COMPANY

As already mentioned,[59] the duty of a trustee is to conduct the business of the trust in such a way as an ordinary prudent man would conduct a business of his own. In *Re Lucking's Will Trusts*[60] Cross J had to consider how this general principle should be applied to trustees holding a controlling interest in a private company. First he asked himself, 'What steps, if any, does a reasonably prudent man who finds himself a majority shareholder in a private company take with regard to the management of the company's affairs?' To this question he gave answer: 'He does not, I think, content himself with such information as to the management of the company's affairs as he is entitled to as a shareholder, but ensures that he is represented on the board. He may be prepared to run the business himself as managing director or, at least, to become a non-executive director while having the business managed by someone else. Alternatively, he may find someone who will act as his nominee on the board and report to him from time to time as to the company's affairs.' Trustees holding a controlling interest, he concluded, ought in the same way to ensure so far as they can that they have such information as to the progress of the company's affairs as directors would have, and act on that information appropriately. It has since been explained[61] this is not to be read as imposing on such trustees a necessary requirement that one of them or a nominee must be on the board of directors. These are merely examples of what may in some circumstances be convenient methods for trustees to adopt, but other methods may be equally satisfactory and convenient in other circumstances. Every case will depend on its own facts.

In *Re Lucking's Will Trusts*[62] itself trustees held a majority shareholding. One of the trustees was indeed on the board of the company, but he had failed to supervise adequately the drawings of the managing director in effect appointed by him, as a consequence of which the company lost some £15,000 on the managing director's bankruptcy. The failure of supervision was clearly a failure of the trustee-director's duty to the company qua director; the judge held that, being partly a representative of the trust, it was also a failure of his duty qua trustee, for which he was liable to the beneficiaries.

---

[58] Ibid, ss 36–38. As to ss 24 and 25 of the Charities Act 1993 see pp 324, 325 supra.
[59] Supra, pp 390, 419.   [60] [1967] 3 All ER 726. See (1980) 30 UTLJ 151 (D Hughes).
[61] For instance by Brightman J in *Bartlett v Barclays Bank Trust Co Ltd* [1980] Ch 515, [1980] 1 All ER 139; *Re Poyiadjis* [2004] WTLR 1169 (Isle of Man HC).
[62] Supra.

6 SETTLED LAND AND LAND HELD UPON A TRUST OF LAND

Capital money arising under a settlement within the Settled Land Act 1925 may be invested or otherwise applied in investment in securities either under the general power of investment in s 3 of the Trustee Act 2000 or under a power to invest conferred on the trustees of the settlement by the settlement; or in various other modes set out in s 73(1)[63] of the Settled Land Act 1925. Most of the modes are closely connected with the management of the settled land, but there is included[64] the purchase of land in fee simple, or of leasehold land held for 60 years or more unexpired at the time of purchase. The investment or other application of capital money by the trustees must normally be made according to the discretion of the trustees, but subject to any consent required or direction given by the settlement with respect to the investment or other application by the trustees of trust money of the settlement.[65] Any investment must be in the names or under the control of the trustees.[66] The trustees, in exercising their power to invest or apply capital money must, so far as practicable, consult the tenant for life, and, so far as consistent with the general interest of the settlement, give effect to his wishes.[67]

The general power of investment[68] applies to trustees of land as to other trustees, as does the power to acquire freehold and leasehold land.[69] As we have seen[70] the power under the Trusts of Land and Appointment of Trustees Act 1996 for trustees of land to acquire land has been brought into line with the provisions of the Trustee Act 2000.

7 PERSONAL REPRESENTATIVES

The provisions of the Trustee Act 2000 apply in relation to a personal representative administering an estate according to the law as it applies to a trustee carrying out a trust for beneficiaries, with appropriate modifications.[71]

It may be noted that s 41[72] of the Administration of Estates Act 1925, gives a power of appropriation to personal representatives, though it is important to remember that it does not apply to trustees. Subsection 2 of this section provides that any property duly appropriated under the statutory power shall thereafter be treated as an authorized

---

[63] As amended by the Trustee Act 2000, Sch 2, para 10(1).   [64] Settled Land Act 1925, s 73(1)(xi).
[65] Settled Land Act 1925, s 75(2)(*a*) as substituted by the Trustee Act 2000, Sch 2, para 10(1).
[66] Settled Land Act 1925, s 75(2)(*b*) as likewise substituted.
[67] Ibid, s 75(4) as likewise substituted. See also s 75(4A), (4B), (4C) and s 75A.
[68] See Trustee Act 2000, s 3 and p 418, supra.   [69] See ibid, s 8 and p 418, supra.
[70] See p 418, supra.   [71] Trustee Act 2000, s 35.
[72] As amended. The section will be further amended when the Mental Capacity Act 2005, Sch 6, para 5 is brought into force.

investment, and may be retained or dealt with accordingly. The Law Reform Committee recommends[73] that trustees should be given a similar power of appropriation in all cases in which the property to be appropriated would, once appropriated, be held on trusts separate from those applying to any other trust property.

8 ALTERATION OF POWER OF INVESTMENT

Since the Trustee Act 2000 trustees will generally have wide powers of investment either under that Act or under an express investment clause. There are accordingly far fewer cases where trustees will have any need to apply to the court for an enlargement of their investment powers. A case could arise, however, where there is an express investment clause giving only limited powers of investment, or where the trust instrument imposes some restriction on the statutory power.

In respect of charities, a power of investment may be altered by way of scheme,[74] or under the provisions of s 57 of the Trustee Act 1925.[75]

In the case of a private trust s 57 of the 1925 Act is equally available,[76] and there is also jurisdiction under the Variation of Trusts Act 1958.[77] It has been said[78] where the beneficial interests under a will or settlement were unaffected, an application for extension of investment powers should be brought under s 57 of the Trustee Act 1925 rather than under the Variation of Trusts Act 1958. The reasons for this were said to be that the trustees were the natural persons to make the application, the consent of every adult beneficiary was not essential and the court was not required to give its consent on behalf of every category of beneficiary separately but—more realistically— would consider their interests collectively in income and capital.

---

[73] 23rd Report, Cmnd 8733, para 4.42.

[74] *Re Royal Society's Charitable Trusts* [1956] Ch 87, [1955] 3 All ER 14; *Re University of London Charitable Trusts* [1964] Ch 282, [1963] 3 All ER 859; *Steel v Wellcome Custodian Trustees Ltd* [1988] 1 WLR 167 (in exceptional case, power given to invest as if trustees were absolutely and beneficially entitled), discussed (1988) 85 LSG 45/26 (N J Reville); [1988] Conv 380 (Brenda Dale), and see chapter 14, section 5, supra.

[75] *Re Shipwrecked Fishermen & Mariners' Royal Benevolent Society Charity* [1959] Ch 220, [1958] 3 All ER 465; *Re Kolb's Will Trusts* [1962] Ch 531, [1961] 3 All ER 811, not following the view expressed by Vaisey J in *Re Royal Society's Charitable Trusts*, supra. See chapter 23, section 2(b), p 506, post.

[76] *Mason v Farbrother* [1983] 2 All ER 1078 and see the cases cited in note 75, supra.

[77] Considered generally, p 511, et seq, infra.

[78] In *Anker-Petersen v Anker-Petersen* [1991] 16 LS Gaz R 32.

9 CLAIMS BY BENEFICIARIES IN RELATION TO THE INVESTMENT OF TRUST FUNDS

It may be difficult for beneficiaries to succeed in a claim based on mismanagement by the trustees of the trust investments. In *Nestle v National Westminister Bank plc*[79] it was held or assumed by all the members of the court that the trustees had at all relevant times been under a misunderstanding as to the scope of the investment clause in the will, in relation to which it was said to be inexcusable not to have taken legal advice. Further they had failed to carry out regular reviews of the trust investments. These were symptoms of incompetence or idleness (though on the part of the predecessors of the National Westminister Bank), but not without more breaches of trust. In order to succeed the beneficiary had to show that through one or other or both of these causes, the trustees made decisions which they should not have made or failed to make decisions which they should have made, and further that loss to the trust estate had resulted therefrom. Staughton LJ admitted that this put on the beneficiary a burden which it might be difficult to discharge, and she failed to do so in *Nestle v National Westminister Bank plc*[80] itself. It has subsequently been held that, irrespective of breaches of trust during the decision-making process, the beneficiaries of a trust do not have a claim against trustees in respect of an investment decision they have made unless they could establish that the decision was one that no reasonable trustee could have made.

It may be added that if a decision by trustees is objectively right, they will not be liable even if it was in fact made on wholly wrong grounds.[81]

10 OCCUPATIONAL PENSION SCHEMES ESTABLISHED UNDER A TRUST

Parts II (investment) and III (acquisition of land) do not apply to the trustees of any pension scheme.[82] However the Pensions Act 1995 provides that the trustees of such a scheme have, subject to any restriction imposed by the scheme, the same power to make an investment of any kind as if they were absolutely entitled to the assets of the

---

[79] [1994] 1 All ER 118, [1993] 1 WLR 1260, CA, noted [1993] Conv 63 (Ann Kenny); [1997] PCB 232 (S Lofthouse). Contrast *Re Mulligan (decd)* [1998] 1 NZLR 481 where the trustees were held liable having taken no steps over a period of 40 years to protect the capital from inflation. See [1998] Conv 352 (G Watt and M Stauch), where it is argued that courts should be prepared to acknowledge as a breach of trust any inprudent investment conduct, and to judge, in retrospect and with common sense, the probable extent of the loss caused to the fund by the breach. See also *Wight v Olswang* [2001] WTLR 291, CA.

[80] Supra, CA.

[81] *Cowan v Scargill* [1985] Ch 270, [1984] 2 All ER 750; *Nestle v National Westminster Bank plc*, supra, CA.

[82] Trustee Act 2000, s 36(3).

scheme.[83] Their duties in relation to investment cannot be excluded by an exemption clause.[84]

Similar provisions as to choosing investments to those laid down in s 4(3) of the Trustee Act 2000 are enacted by s 36 of the Pensions Act 1995, and the trustees are required to provide and maintain a written statement of the principles governing their decisions about investments.[85]

---

[83] Pensions Act 1995, s 34.   [84] Ibid, s 33.

[85] Ibid, ss 35, 36. See s 40 as to restrictions on employer-related investments.

19

EVENHANDEDNESS
AS BETWEEN
THE BENEFICIARIES

One aspect of this duty that we have already come across[1] is the obligation to maintain an even hand as between the life tenant and remaindermen in considering the choice of investments. The most elaborate development, however, in connection with the conflicting interests of tenant for life and remainderman,[2] concerns the duties to convert, and to apportion income.

1 THE DUTY TO CONVERT

Where the will or settlement contains a direction, express or implied,[3] to convert, then the precise duty of the trustees will depend upon the terms of the direction, as affected by statutory provisions.[4] In the absence of any such direction, there is no duty to convert in the case of an inter vivos settlement, which must necessarily deal with specific property,[5] nor does any such duty arise in the case of a devise of real estate, whether specific or residuary,[6] or in the case of a specific legacy of personal estate.[7] A

---

[1] See p 412, supra. For another aspect of the duty see *Re Leigh's Settlement Trusts* [1981] CLY 2453.

[2] The different position of personal representatives in the course of administration of the deceased's estate is discussed in *Re Hayes's Will Trusts* [1971] 2 All ER 341. For the special case where trustees are authorized to continue a farming business, and the stock of sheep and cattle increases, see *Re Richards* [1974] 2 NZLR 60. See also *Re McClintock* (1976) 70 DLR (3d) 175; *Josephs v Canada Trust Co* (1992) 90 DLR (4th) 242; revsd (1994) 106 DLR (4th) 384. As to pension schemes see (2000) 14 Tru LI 130 (SEK Hulme).

[3] See eg *Flux v Best* (1874) 31 LT 645 and cf *Re Holloway* (1888) 60 LT 46.

[4] Section 4 of the Trusts of Land and Appointment of Trustees Act 1996 provides, with retrospective effect: 'In the case of every trust for sale of land created by a disposition there is to be implied, despite any provision to the contrary made by the disposition, a power for the trustees to postpone sale of the land; and the trustees are not liable in any way for postponing sale of the land, in the exercise of their discretion, for an indefinite period.'

[5] *Re Van Straubenzee* [1901] 2 Ch 779. But see (1972) 50 CBR 116 (M C Cullity).

[6] *Re Woodhouse* [1941] Ch 332, [1941] 2 All ER 265. See (1981) 59 CBR 687 (J Smith).

[7] See eg *Bethune v Kennedy* (1835) 1 My & Cr 114; *Re Van Straubenzee*, supra, and the cases cited infra in connection with enjoyment in specie.

duty to convert may, however, be implied in the case of a residuary bequest contained in a will under what is known as the rule in *Howe v Earl Dartmouth*.[8] Under this rule, wasting property, such as royalties in respect of copyright[9] and hazardous investments[10] should be converted in order to do justice to the remainderman, who might otherwise get nothing at all, or property much depreciated in value: reversionary interests and other property not producing income should be converted in order to do justice to the tenant for life, who might otherwise obtain nothing from these parts of the trust property. The traditional reasoning behind the rule is no longer appropriate to contemporary conditions in which the remainderman may well prefer the hazard of an investment which stands a chance of maintaining its real value, as against one which, while maintaining its value on paper, is certain to depreciate in real terms in an inflationary situation. Conversely the tenant for life may well prefer a 'safe' investment such as consols bringing in, at the date of writing, nearly 5 per cent interest. The Law Reform Committee recommends[11] that the duty to convert under *Howe v Earl Dartmouth*, together with the rules as to apportionment under both that case and *Re Earl of Chesterfield's Trust*[12] should be subsumed in a new statutory duty to hold a fair balance between the beneficiaries, in particular those entitled to capital and those entitled to income. Coupled with such a general duty should be an express power for such purposes to convert income into capital and vice versa.

The rule in *Howe v Earl Dartmouth*, it has been observed,[13] 'has been since affirmed, as often as it has been referred to, and is unquestionably the law. But the testator may take the case of any particular bequest out of this rule . . .' There are a large number of reported cases where the question has been whether on the true construction of the will an intention is to be found that the rule in *Howe v Earl Dartmouth* shall not apply.

Dicta are to be found in *Hinves v Hinves*[14] and other cases[15] to the effect that small indications of intention will prevent the application of the rule, but the true view, it is submitted, is that expressed by Cozens-Hardy MR in *Re Wareham*,[16] 'that the rule in *Howe v Earl Dartmouth* must be applied, unless it appears on the construction of the particular will that the testator has shown an intention that the rule shall not apply. The burden of providing this rests on the tenant for life who claims to enjoy the property in specie.' The willingness of the courts to hold that the duty to convert

---

[8] (1802) 7 Ves 137—a decision of Lord Eldon; *Hinwes v Hinves* (1844) 3 Hare 609. See, generally: (1943) 7 Conv 128 (S J Bailey); (1952) 16 Conv 349 (L A Sheridan). The suggestion in (1996) 146 NLJ 960 (R Wallington), that the incidental effect of the Trusts of Land and Appointment of Trustees Act 1996 is to exclude the rule (and the rule in *Re Earl of Chesterfield's Trusts* (1883) 24 Ch D 643) is not, it is submitted, valid.

[9] *Re Sullivan* [1930] 1 Ch 84.

[10] Unauthorized investments, ie those not authorized by the trust instrument or the Trustee Act 2000, are always deemed to be more or less hazardous—*Macdonald v Irvine* (1878) 8 Ch D 101, CA.

[11] 23rd Report (1982), Cmnd 8733, paras 3.27–3.28. See (1984) 62 CBR 577 (R E Scane).

[12] See p 434 et seq, infra.   [13] Per Romilly MR in *Morgan v Morgan* (1851) 14 Beav 72 at 82.

[14] (1844) 3 Hare 609 at 611.   [15] Eg *Morgan v Morgan*, supra; *Simpson v Lester*, supra.

[16] [1912] 2 Ch 312 at 315, CA; *Macdonald v Irvine* (1878) 8 Ch D 101, CA; see also *Re Eaton* (1894) 70 LT 761.

has been excluded has been criticized[17] as being inappropriate in a modern context. A testator nowadays, it is suggested,[18] 'is planning for the transmission of wealth, not for the custody of sacred icons'.

Whether the rule in *Howe v Earl Dartmouth* is held to be excluded is thus in each case a question of the true construction of the particular will. The intention that the rule shall not apply may be express, or may be implied from directions in the will which are inconsistent with the application of the rule. Typically the rule will be excluded if the court finds an intention that the tenant for life should enjoy the property in specie,[19] or that the remainderman should take the identical property comprised in the residuary gift,[20] or, which indeed follows from either of the preceding intentions, that all the beneficiaries in turn shall enjoy the estate as existing at the time of the death.[21] The intention to exclude the rule may alternatively be found not in directions as to the beneficial enjoyment, but in directions in relation to conversion. Thus the rule will be excluded by implication if the court finds an intention that the property should be converted at some time fixed by the will by reference to a given number of years after the testator's death, or to the falling in of a life;[22] or that the residuary estate should be divided on the death of the tenant for life.[23] The same result follows from finding an intention that whether the property should be sold, and, if so, when it should be sold, should be left to the discretion of the trustees or of some other person, for instance by giving trustees power to retain existing investments, or to sell and convert the same as they should in their absolute discretion think fit,[24] or by giving them a mere power to sell if and when they should consider it expedient.[25] But a power to vary securities supports the application of the rule by showing the testator intended a conversion.[26] Contrary to what was at one time thought to be the law, in considering whether the rule in *Howe v Earl Dartmouth* is excluded, there is no distinction between hazardous and wasting investments,[27] and reversionary interests are in the same position.[28]

---

[17] (1984) 62 CBR 577 (R E Scane).   [18] Op cit at p 601.

[19] See eg *Marshall v Bremner* (1854) 2 Sm & G 237; *Boys v Boys* (1860) 28 Beav 436.

[20] *Harris v Poyner* (1852) 1 Drew 174; *Holgate v Jennings* (1857) 24 Beav 623.

[21] *Re Gough* [1957] Ch 323, [1957] 2 All ER 193.

[22] *Alcock v Sloper* (1833) 2 My & K 699; *Rowe v Rowe* (1861) 29 Beav 276.

[23] *Re Barratt* [1925] Ch 550. Cf *Re Evans' Will Trusts* [1921] 2 Ch 309.

[24] *Re Bates* [1907] 1 Ch 22; *Re Wilson* [1907] 1 Ch 394. In *Re Bates*, supra, Kekewich J put it another way, namely, that the power to retain the shares added them to the list of authorized investments. See (1978) 56 CBR 128 (Donovan Waters).

[25] *Re Pitcairn* [1896] 2 Ch 199; and see *Re Rogers* [1915] 2 Ch 437.

[26] *Morgan v Morgan* (1851) 14 Beav 72; *Re Llewellyn's Trust* (1861) 29 Beav 171.

[27] *Re Nicholson* [1909] 2 Ch 111.   [28] *Re Pitcairn* [1896] 2 Ch 199.

2 THE DUTY TO APPORTION

If there is no duty to convert, express[29] or implied, whether as a matter of construction or as a rule of law under the rule in *Howe v Earl Dartmouth*, the tenant for life is of course entitled to the income in specie, if any,[30] and the remainderman will in turn become entitled to the capital in specie. Suppose, however, there is a duty to convert, no matter how it arises, and suppose, moreover, there is some lapse of time before the conversion actually takes place. In such circumstances if the tenant for life during such period were to take the income in specie, this would be liable to result in unfairness—in the case of a wasting asset, for instance, it might be unfair to the remainderman, for the tenant for life might get a large income for a number of years and the remainderman get nothing at all, while in the case of a reversionary interest producing no income, it might, conversely, be unfair to the tenant for life. Equity will not allow failure to carry out a duty to affect the rights of the beneficiaries, and, basing itself on the maxim that equity looks upon that as done which ought to be done, has laid down somewhat elaborate rules as to the apportionment that is to take place in such circumstances. There is, of course, no reason why the testator should not make what provision he likes with regard to the intermediate income, and if expressly or by implication he gives the income in specie pending sale to the tenant for life, his wish will prevail.[31] Similarly he may make what provisions he chooses where the property in question is a reversionary interest producing no income.[32] In practice it is very common for a professionally drawn will to contain appropriate express provisions.

It may be noted that the rule in *Howe v Lord Dartmouth* is often taken to refer not only to the duty to convert, for which the case is an authority, but also to the duty to apportion when conversion is delayed, which at most is a corollary of the main rule.[33] Indeed, it is commonly taken[34] to refer to the corresponding duty to apportion in the case of an express trust for conversion, which would be more properly called the rule in *Gibson v Bott*.[35] Subject to any such expression of a contrary intention, the rules as to apportionment are the same however the duty to convert arises.

Assuming that there is a duty to convert, the income to which the tenant for life is entitled depends to a large extent upon the type of property, in accordance with the following rules.

---

[29] There is no duty to convert where trustees are merely given a discretionary power to convert if and when they think fit—*Re Leonard* (1880) 43 LT 664.

[30] *Re Pitcairn* [1896] 2 Ch 199; *Rowlls v Bebb* [1900] 2 Ch 107, CA.

[31] *Re Crowther* [1895] 2 Ch 56; *Re Elford* [1910] 1 Ch 814.

[32] *Re Pitcairn*, supra; *Rowlls v Bebb*, supra.

[33] See (1952) 16 Conv 349 (L A Sheridan); (1943) 7 Conv 128 and 191 (S J Bailey).

[34] *Re Brooker* [1926] WN 93; *Re Trollope's Will Trusts* [1927] 1 Ch 596; *Re Berton* [1939] Ch 200, [1938] 4 All ER 286.

[35] (1802) 7 Ves 89. The distinction was taken by Romer J in *Re Parry* [1947] Ch 23, [1946] 2 All ER 412.

(i) Authorized investments

The tenant for life is of course entitled to the whole income of authorized investments as from the date of death.[36] Where there is a trust for sale of land, there is a trust of land under the Trusts of Land and Appointment of Trustees Act 1996, under which the land is an authorized investment,[37] and the tenant for life is accordingly entitled to the actual income.

It will be convenient to mention at this point the position where there is an authorized investment upon some security such as a mortgage, the interest upon which falls into arrears, if when the security is realized it is not sufficient to pay the capital debt and arrears of interest in full. The loss in such case has to be shared between the tenant for life and the remainderman, the sum actually realized being apportioned upon the principles laid down in Re Atkinson,[38] namely, in the proportion which the amount due for arrears of interest bears to the amount due in respect of the capital debt. The tenant for life, in making this calculation, is only allowed simple interest.[39]

(ii) Unauthorized pure personalty

The following rules as to how this apportionment is to be carried out where there is no express power to postpone conversion are mainly taken from the decision of Farwell J in Re Fawcett.[40] The tenant for life is not in this case entitled to the actual income, but there has to be an apportionment. In most cases the tenant for life is likely, as a result of such apportionment, to receive less than the actual income, though in some cases it may operate in his favour. There is no longer any distinction made between unauthorized investments which could only be realized at a serious loss to the estate, and those which could easily be realized without such loss.

(i)   Where unauthorized investments are retained unsold at the end of one year from the death of the testator, the tenant for life is entitled to receive, not the actual income, but interest at the rate of 4 per cent per annum from the date of death until realization, on the value taken one year after the date of death, that is, at the end of the executors' year, by which time the conversion ought to have taken place.

(ii) Where unauthorized investments are sold during the year following the death of the testator, the tenant for life is entitled to receive from the date of death until realization the like interest on the net proceeds of sale.[41]

---

[36]   Meyer v Simonsen (1852) 5 De G & Sm 723; Brown v Gellatly (1867) 2 Ch App 751.

[37]   See ss 1, 6(3) as amended by the Trustee Act 2000, Sch 2, para 45 and Re Gough [1957] Ch 323, [1957] 2 All ER 193.

[38]   [1904] 2 Ch 160, CA; Re Walker's Settlement Trusts [1936] Ch 280. Principles applied Trust Company of Australia Ltd v Braid [1998] 4 VR 97.

[39]   Re Moore (1885) 54 LJ Ch 432.

[40]   [1940] Ch 402. See also Dimes v Scott (1828) 4 Russ 195; Meyer v Simonsen (1852) 5 De G & Sm 723; Brown v Gellatly (1867) 2 Ch App 751.

[41]   Re Berry [1962] Ch 97, [1961] 1 All ER 529.

(iii) Subject to head (vi) below, upon realization, whether during or after the end of the executors' year, the net proceeds of sale must be reinvested in authorized investments and thereafter rule (i) above will apply.

(iv) The unauthorized investments for the time being unsold must be treated en bloc as one aggregate.[42]

(v) Any excess of income from unauthorized investments beyond the interest payable to the life tenant under heads (i) and (ii) above, must be invested in authorized investments, to the income of which thereafter rule (i) above will apply.

(vi) Interest in respect of unauthorized investments is payable out of the interest arising from them or, in so far as that is insufficient, out of the proceeds of their realization; any interest for the time being in arrears is payable (but calculated as simple interest only) out of subsequent income from unauthorized investments, which are for the time being retained, and out of the proceeds of their sale when realized.

(vii) Neither excess income from unauthorized investments which at the end of any accounting period is available under head (v) above for investment in authorized investments, nor proceeds of realization of unauthorized investments not required at the date of realization to pay interest under head (vi) above which are accordingly available to be invested in authorized investments, are applicable towards payment of subsequently accruing interest in respect of unauthorized investments still retained.

(iii) Unauthorized pure personalty—the effect of a power to postpone conversion

The preliminary point is whether the inclusion of such a power shows an intention that the tenant for life should enjoy the income in specie until a conversion takes place. This depends upon whether the power is inserted for the benefit of the tenant for life, or merely for the more convenient realization of the estate.[43] In order to entitle the tenant for life in specie there must be something more than a bare power to postpone. Where the necessary indications of the testator's intention are found, and even though there is an express provision excluding the rules as to apportionment, the tenant for life will prima facie only be entitled to the income in specie so long as the trustees postpone the sale in proper exercise of their discretion.[44]

In the absence of any indication that the tenant for life is to take the income in specie, there must be an apportionment notwithstanding the power to postpone

---

[42] *Re Owen* [1912] 1 Ch 519.   [43] *Re Inman* [1915] 1 Ch 187.

[44] This seems right on principle, and may be inferred from *Rowlls v Bebb* [1900] 2 Ch 107, CA (dealing however with a reversionary interest); *Re Godfree* [1914] 2 Ch 110. See also *Re Slater* (1915) 113 LT 691 at 693; *Re Chance* [1962] Ch 593, [1962] 1 All ER 942.

conversion.[45] The difference made by the insertion of a power to postpone was fully discussed by Romer J in *Re Parry*.[46] It means, he pointed out, that there is no duty upon the executor to sell at once, or within a year, or at any other time, and accordingly there is no reason for assuming a notional conversion at once, or within a year, or at any other time:

The essential equity, however—the balance between the successive interests—remains equally compelling even where there is no immediate obligation to convert and property is retained for the benefit of the estate as a whole. It is accordingly rational, and indeed obvious, to substitute a valuation of the testator's assets in the place of a hypothetical sale; and, if so, it is difficult to think of a better date for the valuation than the day when the testator died and the assets passed to his executors.[47]

Accordingly the tenant for life is entitled to receive interest at the rate of 4 per cent per annum from the date of the death until realization, on the value taken at the date of death. Subject to the consequential variations due to the different date of valuation, the directions set out in rule (iii) above, heads (iii)–(vii) will, however, presumably apply.

(iv) Reversionary interests—the rule in *Re Earl of Chesterfield's Trusts*[48]

Here the property is producing no income, and accordingly until it falls in there is nothing to apportion. When it eventually does fall in, or is realized, an apportionment has to be made in order to be fair to the tenant for life. The apportionment is made by ascertaining the sum which, put out at interest at 4 per cent per annum on the day of the testator's death, and accumulating at compound interest calculated at that rate with yearly rests and deducting income tax, would, with the accumulations of interest, have produced, at the day of receipt, the amount actually received. The sum so ascertained must be treated as capital, and the residue as income payable to the tenant for life. The rule applies not only to a reversionary interest in its strict sense,[49] but to other sums which have to be treated as postponed capital payments even though they may have some appearance of income. Thus the rule has been applied to a policy of assurance on the life of another which fell in some years after the death of the testator,[50] to sums payable to the estate after the testator's death in consideration of past service,[51] to the instalments of the purchase price of a business sold by the testator and payable after his death,[52] to a determinable annuity, and payments analogous

---

[45] *Re Chaytor* [1905] 1 Ch 233; *Re Parry* [1947] Ch 23, [1946] 2 All ER 412; *Re Berry* [1962] Ch 97, [1961] 1 All ER 529. In *Re Parry* counsel reserved the right to contend before a higher tribunal that the power to postpone excluded the duty to apportion.

[46] Supra, where the relevant cases are carefully considered.

[47] Per Romer J in *Re Parry* [1947] Ch 23 at 45, [1946] 2 All ER 412 at 422.

[48] (1883) 24 Ch D 643 following with some variation *Wilkinson v Duncan* (1857) 23 Beav 469; *Beavan v Beavan* (1869) 24 Ch D 649n. See p 429 n 8.

[49] *Re Hobson* (1885) 53 LT 627; *Re Flower* (1890) 62 LT 216 revsd on other grounds (1890) 63 LT 201, CA; *Rowlls v Bebb* [1900] 2 Ch 107, CA. Cf *Re Holliday* [1947] Ch 402, [1947] 1 All ER 695.

[50] *Re Morley* [1895] 2 Ch 738.

[51] *Re Payne* [1943] 2 All ER 675. Cf *Re Fisher* [1943] Ch 377, [1943] 2 All ER 615.

[52] *Re Hollebone* [1919] 2 Ch 93, [1918–19] All ER Rep 323.

thereto,[53] and to payment of a sum due from an insolvent estate which was grossly insufficient to satisfy a bond debt.[54] It was also applied to sums paid in respect of claims under Part I of the Town and Country Planning Act 1954[55] in *Re Chance*,[56] which also decides that it makes no difference that when the asset ultimately comes in, it brings with it or contains within it interest. It is the fact that the asset is not producing anything in the meantime that gives rise to the claim by the tenant for life for recoupment. But the court has refused to apply the rule where the interest of the testator at the date of death was not a reversionary interest, but an absolute interest, the income of which was temporarily charged in favour of a third person.[57]

(v) Reversionary interests—the effect of a power to postpone conversion

On similar principles to those discussed under rule (iii) above, a mere power to postpone does not affect the duty to apportion when the reversion eventually falls in or a sale eventually takes place. The apportionment must be carried out according to the principles set out in rule (iv) above. If, however, there is a power to postpone which is properly[58] exercised then there may be other indications in the will that it is the testator's intention that no apportionment is to take place, and if so this will be effective. In practice, it is usual to exclude the operation of the rule in *Re Earl of Chesterfield's Trusts*.

(vi) Rate of interest

It will have been observed that in making an apportionment, both in the case of wasting or hazardous investments, and in the case of reversionary interests, the rate of interest is stated to be 4 per cent. There was, however, a period in the early part of this century when the rate was reduced to 3 per cent. The rate was restored to 4 per cent in *Re Baker*[59] and *Re Beech*[60] and has ever since continued to be applied.[61] Perhaps the time has come for a reappraisal, as has happened in other contexts. For example

---

[53] *Re Hey's Settlement Trusts* [1945] Ch 294; *Re Guinness's Settlement* [1966] 2 All ER 497. Contrast, however, *Crawley v Crawley* (1835) 7 Sim 427, followed in *Re Whitehead* [1894] 1 Ch 678 where the court simply ordered each payment to be treated as capital and invested accordingly, the tenant for life thereafter to receive the income on the investments. It is to be noted that *Crawley v Crawley*, supra, was decided before the rule in *Re Earl of Chesterfield's Trusts* was settled, and it is submitted that on such facts an apportionment under the rule should be made.

[54] *Cox v Cox* (1869) LR 8 Eq 343; and see *Re Duke of Cleveland's Estate* [1895] 2 Ch 542. For unusual applications of the rule see *Re Godden* [1893] 1 Ch 292; *Re Hengler* [1893] 1 Ch 586—this doubtful case is difficult to reconcile with *Re Owen* [1912] 1 Ch 519 and seems to depend on a wrong admission by counsel that the rule in *Re Earl of Chesterfield's Trusts* applied.

[55] *Re Chance* [1962] Ch 593, [1962] 1 All ER 942. [56] Supra.

[57] *Re Holliday* [1947] Ch 402, [1947] 1 All ER 695.

[58] *Rowlls v Bebb* [1900] 2 Ch 107, CA; *Re Hey's Settlement Trusts* [1945] Ch 294; *Re Guinness's Settlement* [1966] 2 All ER 497. See (1984) 62 CBR 577 (R E Scane).

[59] [1924] 2 Ch 271.

[60] [1920] 1 Ch 40 followed in *Re Fawcett* [1940] Ch 402; *Re Parry* [1947] Ch 23, [1946] 2 All ER 412; *Re Berry* [1962] Ch 97, [1961] 1 All ER 529.

[61] In *Re Ellis* [1935] Ch 193, [1934] All ER Rep 58. Farwell J refused to take judicial notice of the fact that a trustee could not then get 4 per cent on trustee securities, saying this was a matter for evidence.

the rate of interest on judgment debts, which was originally fixed at 4 per cent by the Judgments Act 1838, is now 8 per cent.[62] In Canada it has been held[63] that the life tenant is entitled to an annual income that would be a fair equivalent for what he would have received had the assets been converted and the proceeds of such conversion invested in accordance with the provisions of the will.

(vii) Unauthorized investment by trustees

For the avoidance of doubt, it may be observed that the above rules as to apportionment only apply to property found in a particular state of investment at the date of the death. They have no application where trustees commit a breach of trust by making an unauthorized investment. Trustees in such a case 'have discharged their liability in favour of the cestuis que trust who are entitled to the capital in remainder, when they have made good the capital and any increase which that capital has received.'[64] Increase here 'does not mean increase by way of interest, but increase by way of profit—some accumulations, something by way of accretion to the capital.'[65] Accordingly if the tenant for life has received more than 4 per cent, he cannot be called upon to account for the balance over that amount to the remainderman, even though it be the trustee himself who is the tenant for life.[66] If the unauthorized investment proves to be insufficient, the loss[67] has to be thrown rateably on the tenant for life and remainderman. The sum available has to be divided in the proportion which the dividends which the tenant for life would have received had the wrongful investment not been made bear to the value of the sum wrongly invested. The tenant for life must, of course, give credit for moneys actually received, though he is not liable to refund any over payment.[68]

3 WHERE STOCK OR SHARES ARE SOLD OR PURCHASED BY TRUSTEES CUM DIVIDEND

In such cases the general rule is that there is no apportionment between capital and income.[69] This is purely a rule of convenience as a result of which the beneficiaries have to take the rough with the smooth in order to ease the burden falling on trustees. The court, however, may depart from the general rule where its application would cause a glaring injustice, though it seems that this jurisdiction will only be exercised in

---

[62] SI 1993/564. See CPR 40.8 and *Cremer v General Carriers SA* [1974] 1 All ER 1, [1974] 1 WLR 341.

[63] *Re Lauer and Stekl* (1974) 47 DLR (3d) 286; affd (1975) 54 DLR (3d) 159n.

[64] *Stroud v Gwyer* (1860) 28 Beav 130 at 141, per Romilly MR; *Slade v Chaine* [1908] 1 Ch 522, CA.

[65] *Slade v Chaine*, supra, at 526, per Kekewich J.   [66] *Re Hoyles* [1912] 1 Ch 67.

[67] For present purposes it is assumed that any personal remedy against the trustee who has committed the breach of trust is worthless.

[68] *Re Bird* [1901] 1 Ch 916.

[69] *Bulkeley v Stephens* [1896] 2 Ch 241. Cf *Re Henderson* [1940] Ch 368, [1940] 1 All ER 623.

extreme circumstances.[70] If at the date of the purchase of stock or shares, however, dividends have been earned and declared, though not paid, they must go to capital when they are ultimately paid and not to the tenant for life.[71]

4 THE 'WINDFALL' PRINCIPLE

Questions sometimes arise as to whether the tenant for life or remainderman is entitled to extraordinary payments made by a company, which may be given some name such as 'cash bonus' or 'capital profits dividend'. It is a basic principle that a limited company not in liquidation can make no payment by way of return of capital to its shareholders except as a step in an authorized reduction of capital. Any other payment made by it by means of which it parts with moneys or other property to its shareholders must and can only be made by way of dividing profits. Accordingly, whatever the payment may be called, if it is paid to a trustee shareholder it will prima facie belong to the person beneficially entitled to the income of the trust estate, that is, the tenant for life as opposed to the remainderman.[72] As Vaisey J put it,[73] 'These accretions to the normal income of the trust fund are sometimes metaphorically described as "windfalls", and when they have left the parent tree, I can see no principle for notionally replacing them on the boughs from which they have fallen.'

Thus in *Re Bates*[74] a company sold some of its assets at a price well above the value as appearing in the company's balance sheet. The profit on the sale was distributed as a cash bonus, and it was held that the tenant for life was entitled to the whole payment. Similarly in *Re Tedlie*[75] a company sold a considerable part of its assets to another company, receiving in payment shares and a sum of cash. Following this transaction the company had a large surplus of assets over debts, capital and what was required for carrying on the business retained. Shares[76] and cash were paid to the shareholders, and it was held that a trustee shareholder must pay the whole to the tenant for life. Again in *Re Whitehead's Will Trusts*[77] the question arose where trustees,

---

[70] *Bulkeley v Stephens*, supra; *Re Firth* [1938] Ch 517, [1938] 2 All ER 217; *Re Maclaren's Settlement Trusts* [1951] 2 All ER 414. *Re Winterstoke's Will Trusts* [1938] Ch 158, [1937] 4 All ER 63, seems out of line with the other cases, and in *Re Ellerman's Settlement Trusts* [1984] LSG R 430 (more fully reported and noted in [1986] TL & P 62, sub nom *Hitch v Ruegg*) Nourse J said it was wrong and ought not to be followed.

[71] *Re Sir Robert Peel's Settled Estates* [1910] 1 Ch 389.

[72] *Hill v Permanent Trustee Co of New South Wales Ltd* [1930] AC 720, PC; *Re Doughty* [1947] Ch 263, [1947] 1 All ER 207, CA; *Re Harrison's Will Trusts* [1949] Ch 678; see generally (1951) 67 LQR 195 (S J Bailey); *Manukan City Council v Lawson* [2001] 1 NZLR 599.

[73] *Re Kleinwort's Settlement Trusts* [1951] Ch 860 at 863, [1951] 2 All ER 328 at 330.

[74] [1928] Ch 682.

[75] (1922) 126 LT 644. See also the Thomas Tilling cases—*Re Sechiari* [1950] 1 All ER 417; *Re Kleinwort's Settlement Trusts* [1951] Ch 860, [1951] 2 All ER 328; *Re Rudd's Will Trusts* [1952] 1 All ER 254—discussed (1953) 17 Conv 22 (A J Bland).

[76] Ie the shares in the other company.

[77] [1959] Ch 579, [1959] 2 All ER 497; *Thomson's Trustees v Thomson* [1955] SC 476.

as holders under a unit trust, received what were called capital distributions. The court held that in case of doubt the trustees must enquire into the course of any such distribution and treat it as income or capital just as if they were the direct shareholders of the shares included in the portfolio.

These rules, however, cease to be applicable where a company has taken the necessary steps to capitalize its profits. All limited companies having a share capital now have power,[78] if authorized by their articles,[79] to increase their capital. If, instead of paying out its profits as dividend, a company uses the profits to pay for a new issue of shares which are issued as bonus shares to the shareholders, trustee-shareholders must hold the bonus shares as part of the capital of the trust and must not hand them over to the tenant for life as income. The point is that if the company does this it is not in fact parting with its money at all, and the money ceases for all time to be divisible as profits and can only be paid to the shareholders on a reduction of capital or in a winding-up. The same principle has been applied even though no new paid-up capital in the strict sense of the word has been created, as where the profits are used to pay for an issue of unsecured loan stock.[80] 'The real application of the principle is to assets, from which any further character of divisible profits has been taken away, whatever may be the substituted character thereafter impressed upon them.'[81]

Thus in the leading case of *Bouch v Sproule*[82] the directors of a company proposed to distribute certain accumulated profits as a bonus dividend, to allot new shares to each shareholder, and to apply the bonus dividend in payment of the new shares. This proposal was carried out and it was held that the real nature of the transaction was that the undivided profits should be appropriated as an increase of the capital stock, and the tenant for life accordingly had no claim either to the bonus dividend or to the new shares. Lord Herschell in this case approved the statement of Fry LJ in the court below[83] that the company alone decides whether to capitalize its profits or not, and provided its decision is properly carried out, its decision will bind beneficiaries claiming under a shareholder. Whether there has been capitalization of profits or not is therefore a question of fact in each case. In considering this question from one point of view Atkin LJ observed,[84] 'the intention of the company is dominant for all purposes. Did the company intend to distribute as profits or as capital?' From another point of view, however, Lord Sumner has said,[85] 'the only intention, that the company has, is such as is expressed in or necessarily follows from its proceedings. It is hardly a paradox to say that the form of a company's resolutions and instruments is their substance.'[86] Accordingly although the question is as to the intention of the company

---

[78] Companies Act 1985, s 121(1).

[79] If not so authorized, the articles can be altered for the purpose.

[80] *Re Outen's Will Trusts* [1963] Ch 291, [1962] 3 All ER 478.

[81] Per Lord Summer in *IRC v Fisher's Executors* [1926] AC 395 at 410, HL. Cf *IRC v Parker* [1966] AC 141, [1966] 1 All ER 399, HL.

[82] (1887) 12 App Cas 385, HL.   [83] (1885) 29 Ch D 635 at 653, CA.

[84] *IRC v Burrell* [1924] 2 KB 52 at 68, CA.   [85] *IRC v Fisher's Executors* [1926] AC 395 at 411, HL.

[86] See also *IRC v Blott* [1921] 2 AC 171, HL; *Re Taylor* [1926] Ch 923; *IRC v Wright* [1927] 1 KB 333, CA.

the court will not be bound by a company's statement as to what it intended to do or as to the effect of what it has done, if it has failed to take the necessary steps for effective capitalization.[87] If the intention of the company to capitalize is clear, however, the fact that an option is given to the shareholders to take cash instead of new shares makes no difference and since, in practice, the cash offer is always less favourable than the offer of bonus shares, the trustees will be under a duty to accept the offer in its most favourable, that is to say its capitalized, form.[88] If, however, there is such an option given but no intention to capitalize, then if the cash option is properly exercised, the cash will go to the tenant for life,[89] but if the trustees, as they normally should, accept the offer of new shares as being more advantageous, the tenant for life will only be entitled to so much of the value of the new shares as represented the dividend applied by the trustees in taking them up, the balance of such value forming part of the capital of the trust.[90] The point is that the issue of new shares in such circumstances necessarily depreciates the value of the old ones.

Even though the above rules may appear to operate harshly in a particular case, there is authority to support the view that the courts have power to make an apportionment only where the trustees have been guilty of some breach of trust.[91]

The question arose in an acute form in *Sinclair v Lee*.[92] Here ICI was about to reorganize its structure by demerging its original undertaking into two parts each of which would be carried on as a separate undertaking by a separate company, namely ICI and a new company (ZG). The shareholders of ICI would be issued with paid-up shares in ZG in addition to their existing holdings in ICI. These ZG shares would compensate ICI shareholders for the depreciation in the value of ICI shares caused by the transfer of assets from ICI to ZG. Nicholls V-C recognized that as between tenant for life and remainderman an application of established principles in their full width would produce the absurd result that the ZG shares should go to the tenant for life. In seeking to avoid this result he observed that the principle of company law prohibiting payments by way of return of capital to its shareholders is concerned with the protection of the company's creditors and others dealing with the company. This is far removed from the trustee's duty to hold a fair balance between income and capital beneficiaries. The rules laid down in the cases should be treated as guidelines not to be applied slavishly where to do so would produce a result manifestly inconsistent with the presumed intention of the testator or settlor. Approaching the matter in this way

---

[87] *Re Piercy* [1907] 1 Ch 289; *Re Bates* [1928] Ch 682; *Re Thomas* [1916] 2 Ch 331 at 343, CA, per Cozens Hardy MR.

[88] *Re Evans* [1913] 1 Ch 23; *Re Malam* [1894] 3 Ch 578.

[89] *Re Despard* (1901) 17 TLR 478. The question whether it was proper for the trustees to exercise the cash option does not seem to have been raised, though it would seem that the effect of the whole transaction must have been to reduce the value of the trust shares.

[90] *Re Northage* (1891) 64 LT 625; *Re Malam* [1894] 3 Ch 578. See (1975) 39 Conv 355 (W H Goodhart).

[91] *Re Kleinwort's Settlement Trusts*, supra; *Re Maclaren's Settlement Trusts* [1951] 2 All ER 414; *Re Rudd's Will Trusts*, supra; *Re Morris's Will Trusts* [1960] 3 All ER 548.

[92] [1993] Ch 497, sub nom *Re Lee (decd)* [1993] 3 All ER 926, noted [1993] PCB 294 (D Brownbill); [1993] PCB 301 (S Taube).

Nicholls V-C decided that the ZG shares were to be held by the trustees as capital of the fund.

Finally, it should be noted that, where the company is being wound up, the situation is entirely different, and distributions made to shareholders are capital.[93] And as a result of statute,[94] the same rule applies to a distribution out of moneys in a company's share premium account.[95]

5 ALLOCATION OF EXPENDITURE

As we shall see,[96] trustees are entitled to be indemnified out of the capital and income of their trust fund against all obligations incurred by the trustees in the due performance of their duties and the due exercise of their powers. The trustees must then debit each item of expenditure either against income or against capital. The general rule is that income must bear all ordinary outgoings[97] of a recurrent nature, such as rates and taxes and interest on charges and incumbrances, while capital must bear all costs, charges and expenses incurred for the benefit of the whole estate. Obviously in so far as it is thrown on to capital, the income beneficiaries will lose the income of the sums expended.

In the leading case of *Re Bennett*[98] capital was ordered to pay the expenses of the yearly audit and inventory of a business where money employed in the business was a capital asset of the trust. Likewise it was held in *Carver v Duncan*[99] that premiums paid by trustees in respect of inheritance tax protection and on endowment policies, and fees paid to investment advisers, were capital expenses and not income expenses.

There is, of course, nothing to prevent a settlor from authorizing or directing his trustees to pay income expenses out of capital or to pay capital expenses out of income. Though such a provision is perfectly valid and effective, it does not alter the nature of the expenses.[100]

---

[93] *Re Armitage* [1893] 3 Ch 337, CA; *Re Palmer* (1912) 28 TLR 301; *IRC v Burrell* [1924] 2 KB 52, CA.

[94] Companies Act 1985, ss 130–132.

[95] *Re Duff's Settlement* [1951] Ch 923, [1951] 2 All ER 435, CA.   [96] See p 483 et seq, infra.

[97] 'Outgoing' has been said to mean 'some payment which must be made in order to secure the income of the property'—per Lindley LJ in *Re Bennett* [1896] 1 Ch 778 at 784, CA.

[98] Supra, CA.

[99] [1985] AC 1082, [1985] 2 All ER 645, HL. As to insurance premiums, see Trustee Act 1925, s 19, discussed p 468, infra.

[100] *Carver v Duncan*, supra, HL.

6 LAW COMMISSION CONSULTATION PAPER 175[101]

The Law Commission in 2004 proposed a new scheme for the classification and apportionment of trust receipts and expenses. Subject to any provisions to the contrary in the trust instrument, they propose, inter alia, (i) instead of the 'windfall' principle, cash distributions to trustee-shareholders by corporate entities (or distributions which could have been taken in cash) should be classified as income. All other distributions by corporate entities should be classified as capital; (ii) trustees should have power to allocate investment returns and trust expenses as income or capital insofar as necessary to maintain a balance between income and capital; (iii) all existing equitable rules of apportionment should be abolished; (iv) the duty under the rule in *Howe v Earl Dartmouth* to convert unauthorized, hazardous or wasting assets should be abolished. Express and statutory trusts for sale would be unaffected.

---

[101] Discussed (2004) 62 T & ELTJ 12 (Carolyn O'Sullivan) and, in relation to charities, (2005) 63 T & ELTJ 12 (R Venables).

20

THE FIDUCIARY NATURE
OF TRUSTEESHIP

DUTY NOT TO PROFIT FROM HIS TRUST

In *Bray v Ford*,[1] Lord Herschell said:[2] 'It is an inflexible rule of a Court of Equity that a person in a fiduciary position . . . is not, unless otherwise expressly provided, entitled to make a profit; he is not allowed to put himself in a position where his interest and duty conflict.' The rule does not apply, however, where the trustee or other fiduciary has been put in that position by the testator or settlor under whose dispositions his trust or other fiduciary obligation arose.[3] Thus, for example, a trustee can be given an express power to distribute a fund among a class including himself, and can exercise the power in his own favour.[4] Moreover in exceptional circumstances the court has jurisdiction to relax the rule.[5]

Where the rule does apply it suffices for liability that the 'reasonable man looking at the relevant facts and circumstances of the particular case would think that there was a real sensible possibility of conflict; not that you could imagine some situation arising which might, in some conceivable possibility in events not contemplated as real sensible possibilities by any reasonable person, result in a conflict.'[6] The liability arises from the mere fact of a profit having been made by the fiduciary. 'The profiteer,

---

[1] [1896] AC 44, HL; *Regal (Hastings) Ltd v Gulliver* [1967] 2 AC 134n, [1942] 1 All ER 378, HL; *Guinness plc v Saunders* [1990] 2 AC 663, [1990] 1 All ER 652, HL, but according to Oliver LJ in *Swain v Law Society* [1981] 3 All ER 797, [1982] 1 WLR 17, CA, at 813, 36, 'the rule is not so much that it is improper for him to put himself in that position but that, if he does so, he is obliged by his trust to prefer the interest of his beneficiary'.

[2] At 51; *Brown v IRC* [1965] AC 244, [1964] 3 All ER 119, HL, per Lord Upjohn at 127; *Marley v Mutual Security Merchant Bank and Trust Co Ltd* [2001] WTLR 483, PC. See (1996) 10 Tru LI 49 (J Mowbray).

[3] *Sargeant v National Westminster Bank plc* (1990) 61 P & CR 518, CA, applied to a pensions scheme in *Edge v Pensions Ombudsman* [1998] Ch 512, [1998] 2 All ER 547; affd [2000] Ch 602, [1999] 4 All ER 546, CA.

[4] See [1998] PCB 239 (J Mowbray).

[5] *Re Drexel Burnham Lambert UK Pension Plan* [1995] 1 WLR 32, discussed (1994) 8 Tru LI 112 (D Griffiths), where the matter arose in connection with a pension scheme under which a trustee was himself an employee and a member of the scheme. There is now a statutory exception to the rule: Pensions Act 1995, s 39.

[6] *Boardman v Phipps* [1967] 2 AC 46 at 124, [1966] 3 All ER 721 at 756, HL, per Lord Upjohn; *Queensland Mines Ltd v Hudson* (1978) 52 ALJR 399, PC. See p 146, supra.

however honest and well intentioned, cannot escape that risk of being called upon to account.'[7] We have already seen that he becomes a constructive trustee of profits received by virtue of his position as trustee.[8] Other aspects of this general principle must be considered.

(a) DUTY TO ACT WITHOUT REMUNERATION[9]

As early as 1734,[10] it was said to be 'an established rule that a trustee . . . shall have no allowance for his care and trouble: the reason of which seems to be, for that on these pretences, if allowed, the trust estate might be loaded, and rendered of little value'. In general the rule applies to a trustee who spends much time and trouble in managing a business to the great advantage of the beneficiaries. Prima facie a solicitor-trustee is in no different position,[11] but he will now usually be entitled to remuneration under the provisions of the Trustee Act 2000 discussed below. Nor is he now likely to need to rely on the rule in *Clack v Carlon*[12] under which, where a solicitor-trustee could properly employ an outside solicitor, he 'may employ his partner to act as solicitor for himself and his co-trustees with reference to the trust affairs, and may pay him the usual charges, provided that it has been expressly agreed between himself and his partner that he himself shall not participate in the profits or derive any benefit from the charges.'[13] Nor will he need to rely on the rule in *Cradock v Piper*,[14] which permits a solicitor-trustee or his firm to receive the usual profit costs for work done in a legal proceedings, not on behalf of the solicitor-trustee alone, but on behalf of himself and a co-trustee, provided that the costs of appearing for and acting for the two have not added to the expense which would have been incurred if he or his firm had appeared only for his co-trustee.

The rule has never meant and does not mean that there is necessarily anything illegal or improper in a trustee receiving remuneration, but the onus is on the trustee to point to some provision in the trust instrument or some rule of law which establishes his right thereto.[15] A trustee may establish his right to remuneration upon any of the following grounds.

---

[7] Per Lord Russell of Killowen in *Regal (Hastings) Ltd v Gulliver*, supra, at 386. See (1983) 46 MLR 289 (W Bishop and D D Prentice) bringing in economic considerations.

[8] Supra, p 141 et seq.

[9] See, generally, [1984] Conv 275 (N D M Parry); (1995) 9 Tru LI 50 (P Matthews). He can, of course, claim out-of-pocket expenses.

[10] *Robinson v Pett* (1734) 3 P Wms 249 at 251.

[11] *Moore v Frowd* (1837) 3 My & Cr 45; *Todd v Wilson* (1846) 9 Beav 486.   [12] (1861) 30 LJ Ch 639.

[13] *Re Doody* [1893] 1 Ch 129, per Stirling J at 134.

[14] (1850) 1 Mac & G 664; *Re Corsellis* (1887) 34 Ch D 675, CA. See (1983) 46 MLR 289 (W Bishop and D D Prentice); (1998) 19 JLH 189 (Chantal Stebbings).

[15] See *Dale v IRC* [1954] AC 11 at 27, [1953] 2 All ER 671 at 674, HL, per Lord Normand.

(i) Charging clause in the trust instrument

There has never been any doubt but that the trust instrument may authorize the payment of remuneration to a trustee,[16] though a provision to this effect always receives a strict interpretation from the courts.[17] Thus if a solicitor-trustee is given the right to charge for his professional services, he can only charge for services strictly professional, and not for business 'not strictly professional which might have been performed, or would necessarily have been performed in person by a trustee not being a solicitor'.[18] Further where a will appoints a trustee, and there is a charging clause, the right of the trustee is for some purposes treated as a legacy.[19] Accordingly if the assets are insufficient it will abate proportionately with the other legacies, and will be avoided by s 15 of the Wills Act 1837 if the trustee was an attesting witness.

Section 28 of the Trustee Act 2000 introduces new rules for the construction of express charging clauses, but only where the trustee is a trust corporation or is acting in a professional capacity.[20] These new rules apply where there is a provision in the trust instrument entitling a trustee to payment out of trust funds[21] in respect of services[22] provided by him to or on behalf of the trust, whenever created.[23] The section does not apply, however, to the extent that the trust instrument makes inconsistent provision.[24]

Reversing the old rules such a trustee is now to be treated as entitled under the trust instrument to receive payment out of the trust funds in respect of services even if they are services which are capable of being provided by a lay trustee.[25] Further, in relation to deaths occurring on or after 1 February 2001[26] any payments to which a trustee is entitled in respect of services are to be treated as remuneration for services and not as a gift (a) for the purposes of s 15 of the Wills Act 1837. This change enables trustees to be paid for work done in connection with testamentary trusts even where they witness the will under which the trust arises. And (b) for the purposes of determining

---

[16] *Webb v Earl of Shaftesbury* (1802) 7 Ves 480; *Willis v Kibble* (1839) 1 Beav 559. Cf *Space Investments Ltd v Canadian Imperial Bank of Commerce Trust Co (Bahamas) Ltd* [1986] 3 All ER 75, [1986] 1 WLR 1072, PC (bank trustee authorized to deposit trust money with itself as banker: on insolvency of bank no priority for trust beneficiaries).

[17] *Re Gee* [1948] Ch 284, [1948] 1 All ER 498.

[18] Per Warrington J in *Re Chalinder and Herington* [1907] 1 Ch 58 at 61; and see *Re Chapple* (1884) 27 Ch D 584; *Clarkson v Robinson* [1900] 2 Ch 722.

[19] *Re Pooley* (1888) 40 Ch D 1, CA; *Re White* [1898] 2 Ch 217, CA; *Re Brown* [1918] WN 118. However it is earned income for the purposes of tax: *Dale v IRC* [1954] AC 11, [1953] 2 All ER 671, HL.

[20] Ie in the course of a profession or business which consists of or includes the provision of services in connection with the management or administration of trusts generally or a particular kind of trust, or any particular aspect thereof: Trustee Act 2000, s 28(5).

[21] 'Trust funds' means income or capital funds of the trust: ibid, s 39(1).

[22] Ibid, s 33(1). On the wording of this subsection it seems that, in contrast to expenses, the services may have been provided before the commencement of the Act.

[23] Ibid, s 33(1).   [24] Ibid, s 28(1).

[25] Ibid, s 28(2). This subsection applies to a trustee of a charitable trust who is not a trust corporation only if he is not a sole trustee and a majority of the other trustees agree: ibid, s 28(3). A person acts as a lay trustee if he is not a trust corporation and does not act in a professional capacity: ibid, s 28(6).

[26] See ibid, s 33(2).

their priority as against other payments due from the deceased's estate (Administration of Estates Act 1925, s 34(3)). Thus in relation to the administration of the estate, the trustee's charges are an expense of administration.

(ii) No express provision in trust instrument relating to remuneration

There are new statutory provisions in the Trustee Act 2000 which apply where there is no provision (either for or against) about the entitlement of a trustee to remuneration in the trust instrument, or in any enactment or any provision of subordinate legislation.[27] It is now provided that a trustee who is a trust corporation, but who is not a trustee of a charitable trust, is entitled to receive reasonable remuneration out of the trust funds[28] for any services[29] it provides to or on behalf of the trust.[30] A trustee who acts in a professional capacity,[31] but who is not a trust corporation, a trustee of a charitable trust or a sole trustee is likewise entitled, but in his case only if each other trustee has agreed in writing that he may be remunerated for the services.[32] 'Reasonable remuneration' means, in relation to the provision of services by a trustee, such remuneration as is reasonable in the circumstances for the provision of those services to or on behalf of that trust by that trustee.[33] In determining the level of remuneration that is reasonable in the circumstances, regard must be had not only to the nature of the services provided, but also to the nature of the trust and the attributes of the trustee. The above provisions apply to trusts whenever created.[34]

The above provisions apply even if the services in question could be provided by a lay trustee; and they apply equally to a trustee who has been duly authorized to exercise functions as an agent of the trustees, or to act as a nominee or custodian.[35]

The above provisions do not apply to trustees of charitable trusts. However the Secretary of State has power to make regulations for the provision of remuneration of trustees of charitable trusts.[36]

(iii) Contract with the cestuis que trust

Such a contract by a trustee for remuneration may be valid, though it would be viewed with great jealousy by the courts.[37] If, however, the trustee, having accepted the trust, merely contracted to carry out his existing duties as trustee, it could be

---

[27] Trustee Act 2000, s 29(5).

[28] 'Trust funds' means income or capital funds of the trust: ibid, s 39(1).

[29] Ibid, s 33(1) and see p 444, n 22, supra.

[30] Ibid, s 29(1). 'Trust funds' means income or capital funds of the trust: ibid, s 39(1).

[31] See ibid, s 28(5) and p 444, n 20, supra.   [32] Ibid, s 29(2).

[33] Ibid, s 29(3), which also provides that a trust corporation which is a recognized provider of banking services may make any reasonable charges for the provision of such services in the course of, or incidental to, the performance of its function as a trustee.

[34] Ibid, s 33(1).   [35] Ibid, s 29(4), (6).

[36] Ibid, s 30. No regulations had been made at the date of writing.

[37] Ayliffe v Murray (1740) 2 Atk 58.

argued that the obligation to pay the remuneration was invalid, on the ground of insufficiency of consideration, unless the contract were by deed.[38]

(iv) Order of the court

The court, under the inherent jurisdiction, can authorize the payment of remuneration to a trustee, whether appointed by the court or not.[39] The payment of remuneration may be authorized either prospectively or retrospectively, and the jurisdiction extends to increasing the remuneration authorized by the trust instrument.[40] Though the existence of the jurisdiction is undoubted, it has been said[41] that it should be exercised only sparingly and in 'exceptional cases'.

Many of the earlier cases were discussed by the Court of Appeal in *Re Duke of Norfolk's Settlement Trusts*[42] where it was pointed out that in exercising this jurisdiction the court has to balance two influences which are to some extent in conflict. The first is that the office of trustee is, as such, gratuitous; the court will accordingly be careful to protect the interests of the beneficiaries against claims by the trustees. The second is that it is of great importance to the beneficiaries that the trust should be well administered. If the court concludes, having regard to the nature of the trust, to the experience and skill of a particular trustee and to the amounts which he seeks to charge when compared with what other trustees might require to be paid for their services and to all the other circumstances of the case, that it would be in the interests of the beneficiaries to authorize the remuneration, or increased remuneration, then the court may properly do so.

---

[38] Cf Cheshire, Fifoot and Furmston, *The Law of Contract*, 14th edn, p 100 et seq; (1956) 71 LQR 490 (A L Goodhart). But see *Williams v Roffey Bros & Nicholls (Contractors) Ltd* [1991] 1 QB 1, [1990] 1 All ER 512, CA, noted (1990) 53 MLR 536 (J Adams and R Brownsword), where it was said that today the rigid approach to the concept of consideration to be found in *Stilk v Myrick* (1809) 2 Camp 317, was neither necessary nor desirable. The courts should now be more ready to find the presence of consideration so as to reflect the intention of the parties to the contract where the bargaining powers are not unequal and where the finding of consideration reflects the true intention of the parties. See also [1991] JBL 19 (R Hooley).

[39] *Re Masters* [1953] 1 All ER 19, [1953] 1 WLR 81; *Re Jarvis* [1958] 2 All ER 336, [1958] 1 WLR 815 (constructive trustee). The jurisdiction extends to other fiduciaries—see *Boardman v Phipps* [1967] 2 AC 46, [1966] 3 All ER 721, HL; *O'Sullivan v Management Agency and Music Ltd* [1985] QB 428, [1985] 3 All ER 351, CA (remuneration allowed even though guilty of undue influence): *Badfinger Music v Evans* [2001] WTLR 1. The courts are, perhaps, even more reluctant to sanction the remuneration of trustees in the case of a charity: see Report of the Charity Commissioners for 1990, App D(c). See also their Reports for 1981, para 64, and for 1988, para 38.

[40] *Boardman v Phipps*, supra, HL; *Re Keeler's Settlement Trusts* [1981] Ch 156, [1981] 1 All ER 888; *Re Duke of Norfolk's Settlement Trusts* [1982] Ch 61, [1981] 3 All ER 220, CA, and see (1981) 40 CLJ 243 (C M G Ockleton); [1982] Conv 231 (K Hodkinson); (1982) 98 LQR 181; (1982) 45 MLR 211 (B Green); (1982) 126 Sol Jo 195 (D W Fox).

[41] Per Upjohn J in *Re Worthington* [1954] 1 All ER 677 at 678, [1954] 1 WLR 526 at 528. In *Re Barbour's Settlement* [1974] 1 All ER 1188 at 1192, [1974] 1 WLR 1198 at 1203, Megarry J doubted whether the phrase was intended to exclude the disastrous consequences following from inflation merely because inflation is not an exception but the rule.

[42] Supra, CA, criticized (1982) 79 LSG 217 (Ann M Kenny), doubting whether the court should authorize an increase of remuneration to professional trustees who have made a bad bargain. See also *Re Berkeley Applegate (Investment Consultants) Ltd* [1989] Ch 32, [1988] 3 All ER 71; *Foster v Spencer* [1996] 2 All ER 672.

An application asking the court to exercise its jurisdiction to authorize the payment of remuneration should be made very promptly on assumption of office or after there has been a radical change in circumstances,[43] though this principle need not be rigorously applied where the individual concerned has been ignorant of his liability to account.[44]

(v) Statutory provisions

By s 42 of the Trustee Act 1925 it is provided that:

where the court appoints a corporation, other than the Public Trustee, to be a trustee[45] either solely or jointly with another person, the court may authorise the corporation to charge such remuneration for its services as trustee as the court may think fit.

The Judicial Trustees Act 1896 provides[46] that the court may assign remuneration to a person whom it appoints as a judicial trustee.

The Public Trustee is authorized[47] to charge fees fixed by the Lord Chancellor, irrespective of any provision in the trust instrument, and fees not exceeding those chargeable by the Public Trustee may likewise be charged by any body properly appointed to be a custodian trustee.[48] It is not, however, possible to take advantage of this latter provision by appointing a bank, for instance, separately as custodian trustee and managing trustee.[49]

(vi) Custom

The existence of any valid custom is very doubtful. In *Brown v IRC*[50] a Scottish solicitor had received money from a number of his clients, too small in individual amounts or held for too short a time to make individual investment worthwhile in the interest of the client, but which, in the aggregate, amounted to a large floating sum. This money was put on deposit so as to earn interest for the solicitor which he claimed to be entitled to retain. There was no question of professional malpractice, for the practice had been recognized as proper by the Council of the Law Society of Scotland, whose opinion, however, was held to be ill-founded. The solicitor had based his claim on the grounds of implied agreement and custom. Both grounds proved to be inadequately supported by evidence, and dicta of their Lordships[51] leave it very doubtful whether such a custom would be recognized by the law of either Scotland or England.

---

[43] See *Re Duke of Norfolk's Settlement Trusts*, at first instance, [1979] Ch 37 at 58, [1978] 3 All ER 907.

[44] *Re Keeler's Settlement Trusts* [1981] 1 All ER 888 at 893.

[45] By s 68(17) 'trustee' is defined so as to include a personal representative—*Re Youngs Estate* (1934) 151 LT 221; *Re Masters* [1953] 1 All ER 19.

[46] Section 1(5).   [47] Public Trustee Act 1906, s 9, as amended.   [48] Ibid, s 4(3).

[49] *Forster v Williams Deacon's Bank Ltd* [1935] Ch 359, CA; *Arning v James* [1936] Ch 158.

[50] [1965] AC 244, [1964] 3 All ER 119, HL.

[51] *Brown v IRC*, supra, per Lord Evershed at 125, Lord Guest at 126 and Lord Upjohn at 128. As to solicitors, the law in England is now governed by the Solicitors Act 1974, s 73.

(vii) Foreign remuneration

It appears from *Re Northcote's Will Trusts*[52] that if in the course of administering assets abroad, trustees receive remuneration without their volition, they will not be called to account. In that case executors took out an English grant, and on doing so were required by the Inland Revenue to undertake to obtain a grant in New York State in respect of American assets. They duly obtained such a grant, and got in the American assets, for doing which the law of that State allowed them agency commission. It was held that in those circumstances there was no equity against the trustees requiring them to disgorge money which had come to them without their volition.

(b) DISABILITIES OF TRUSTEE RELATING TO PURCHASE OF TRUST PROPERTY OR EQUITABLE INTEREST

Before *Tito v Waddell (No 2)*,[53] it was common practice for the rules dealt with in this subsection to be treated as part of the duty of a trustee not to profit from his trust. In that case, however, Megarry V-C said that in cases falling within these rules what equity in fact does is to subject trustees to particular disabilities. Whether a rule is classified as a duty or a disability may be important in connection with the applicability of the Limitation Act 1980.[54]

(i) Purchase by a trustee of the trust property[55]—'the self-dealing rule'[56]

'Any trustee purchasing[57] the trust property is liable to have the purchase set aside, if in any reasonable time the cestui que trust chooses to say, he is not satisfied with it.'[58] The transaction is voidable at the instance of the beneficiaries,[59] even though the

---

[52] [1949] 1 All ER 442.   [53] [1977] Ch 106 at 247, 248, [1977] 3 All ER 129 at 246, 247.

[54] See p 538 et seq, infra.

[55] See (1936) 49 HLR 521 (A W Scott); (1955) 8 CLP (O R Marshall). The rule does not apply to the purchase of the equity of redemption by a mortgagee—*Alec Lobb (Garages) Ltd v Total Oil GB Ltd* [1983] 1 All ER 944 at 965. This point not discussed on appeal [1985] 1 All ER 303, CA, where decision was affirmed in part. As to solicitors, see *Longstaff v Birtles* (2001) *Times*, 18 Sept, CA.

[56] Per Megarry V-C in *Tito v Waddell (No 2)*, supra, at 241, 228; 240, 241, 255. See (1990) 10 Co Law 191 (D Hayton) as to the position of an investment manager appointed under an express provision in the trust instrument, and (1993) 137 Sol Jo 500 (L Price) as to the use of brokers/market makers. Cf *Kane v Radley-Kane* [1999] Ch 274, [1998] 3 All ER 753, noted [1998] T & ELJ 7 (O Clutton), where it was held to be a breach of the self-dealing rule for a sole personal representative of an intestate estate to appropriate to herself unquoted shares in satisfaction of her statutory legacy, unless she had been authorized to do so by the other beneficiaries, or the court had sanctioned the appropriation.

[57] The rule applies equally to the grant of a lease—*Re Dumbell, ex p Hughes* (1802) 6 Ves 617; *A-G v Earl of Clarendon* (1810) 17 Ves 491. Also to a trustee who concurs in a transaction in which he has an interest and which cannot be carried into effect without his concurrence—*Re Thompson's Settlement* [1986] Ch 99, [1985] 2 All ER 720 discussed (1985) 135 NJL 1201 (L Cane); [1986] TL & P 66 (C H Sherrin).

[58] *Campbell v Walker* (1800) 5 Ves 678 at 680, per Arden MR.

[59] Note that one of several beneficiaries cannot insist on the property being reconveyed to the trust without the consent of the other beneficiaries. His remedy is to demand a resale as discussed p 450, infra—*Holder v Holder* [1966] 2 All ER 116 at 128 (this point did not arise on appeal [1968] Ch 353, [1968] 1 All ER 665, CA).

particular dealing may in fact be perfectly fair,[60] and even beneficial to the trust estate.[61] The rule cannot be evaded by carrying out the transaction by means of a nominee,[62] and it applies to a sale to someone such as a partner, where the trustee may directly or indirectly benefit from the transaction:[63] it seems strictly not to apply to a sale by a trustee to his wife, but such a transaction would be viewed by the courts with great suspicion:[64] it does not apply to a sale to a company of which the trustee is a member, though the circumstances may throw upon the company the onus of showing that the sale was fair and honest,[65] and the rule will apply if the company is a mere nominee for the trustee.[66] There is no objection to a trustee completing a purchase where the contract came into existence before the fiduciary relationship.[67]

If a trustee sells to a stranger to the trust, and subsequently repurchases the trust property for himself, the sale cannot always be set aside. If the sale to the stranger has not been completed the vendor trustee is never allowed to purchase the benefit of the contract for himself.[68] After the sale to a stranger has been completed, however, a subsequent re-purchase by the trustee may be good provided that the court is satisfied that there was no agreement or understanding for re-purchase at the time of the sale to the stranger, that the original sale price was adequate and the sale bona fide; in order to set aside a re-purchase by a trustee it is not enough merely to show that the trustee had a hope that he would be able to purchase at some time in the future, or that, having in fact re-purchased, he ultimately made a profit on a re-sale many years later.[69]

The right to avoid the purchase is valid not only as against the trustee, but also against any subsequent purchaser with notice.[70] Alternatively if the trustee has re-sold at a profit, the beneficiaries can adopt the sale and require the trustee to account for

---

[60] See eg *Campbell v Walker*, supra—sale by public auction, trustee taking no unfair advantage; *Dyson v Lum* (1866) 14 LT 588.

[61] It was early settled that the right of the beneficiary does not depend on the trustee making a profit—*Ex p Lacey* (1802) 6 Ves 625; *Ex p Bennett* (1805) 10 Ves 381.

[62] *Silkstone and Haigh Moore Coal Co v Edey* [1900] 1 Ch 167; *Re Walters* [1954] Ch 653, sub nom *Re Sherman* [1954] 1 All ER 893.

[63] *Ex p Moore* (1881) 45 LT 558; *Re Sparks, ex p Forder* [1881] WN 117, CA. And see *Hickley v Hickley* (1876) 2 Ch D 190, perhaps a doubtful decision.

[64] *Burrell v Burrell's Trustees* 1915 SC 333; *Ferraby v Hobson* (1847) 2 Ph 255; (1949) 13 Conv 248 (J G Fleming). It will depend on the circumstances. 'Manifestly there are wives and wives' per Megarry V-C in *Tito v Waddell (No 2)*, supra.

[65] *Farrar v Farrar's Ltd* (1888) 40 Ch D 395, CA. Aliter where the trustee is a substantial shareholder and director—*Re Thompson's Settlement*, supra, said to be the high-water mark of the application of the rule in *Hillsdown Holdings plc v Pensions Ombudsman* [1997] 1 All ER 862.

[66] *Silkstone and Haigh Moore Coal Co v Edey*, supra.

[67] *Vyse v Foster* (1874) LR 7 HL 318; *Re Mulholland's Will Trusts* [1949] 1 All ER 460.

[68] *Parker v McKenna* (1874) 10 Ch App 96 at 125, per Mellish LJ; *Williams v Scott* [1900] AC 499, PC; *Delves v Gray* [1902] 2 Ch 606.

[69] *Baker v Peck* (1861) 4 LT 3; *Re Postlethwaite* (1888) 60 LT 514, CA.

[70] *Cookson v Lee* (1853) 23 LJ Ch 473; *Aberdeen Town Council v Aberdeen University* (1877) 2 App Cas 544, HL. It follows that, at any rate in the case of land, the trustee will find it almost impossible to find a purchaser. On setting aside a sale to a trustee, he is liable to account for the rents and profits, but without interest—*Silkstone and Haigh Moore Coal Co v Edey* [1900] 1 Ch 167.

the profit.[71] If the trustee has not re-sold, the court may require him to offer the property for re-sale: if a greater price is offered than that paid by the trustee, the sale to the trustee will be set aside; otherwise he will be held to his bargain.[72] On general principles the beneficiaries, having full knowledge of the facts,[73] may waive their rights and affirm the purchase by the trustee, and after a long period of acquiescence will be deemed to have done so under the equitable doctrine of laches:[74] mere lapse of time will not be enough, though it may be some evidence of laches.

The rule applies in all its stringency to a trustee who has recently retired, whether or not with a view to the sale,[75] but ceases to apply after a long period of retirement, such as 12 years,[76] unless there are circumstances of doubt or suspicion. It does not apply to a trustee who disclaims the trust,[77] nor, it seems, to trustees who have no active duties to perform.[78] Normally, of course, the rule applies equally to an executor, but it was held, on appeal, not to do so on the special facts of *Holder v Holder*.[79] The defendant in that case was, as it was assumed, technically an executor by reason of the fact that he had intermeddled with the estate. His interference had, however, been of a minimal character, and ceased before he executed a deed of renunciation, which at all relevant times had been wrongly assumed to have been effective. He had taken no part in the arrangements for the sale, which had been by public auction, and the beneficiaries had not looked to him to protect their interests.

There are some exceptions to the general rule. In the first place, the court can give the trustee leave to purchase the trust property, but it will not do so, if the beneficiaries object, until all other ways of selling the property at an adequate price have failed.[80] Dicta in *Holder v Holder*,[81] however, suggest that the court might now be prepared to exercise its discretion more readily than indicated by some of the earlier cases. Secondly, a provision in the trust instrument authorizing a purchase by a trustee will be effective according to its terms.[82] Thirdly, under s 68 of the Settled Land Act 1952 the tenant for life, who holds the legal estate on trust for all the beneficiaries, is permitted to purchase the settled land.

---

[71] *Baker v Carter* (1835) 1 Y & C Ex 250.

[72] *Re Dumbell, ex p Hughes* (1802) 6 Ves 617; *Ex p Lacey* (1802) 6 Ves 625; *Dyson v Lum* (1866) 14 LT 588; *Holder v Holder* [1966] 2 All ER 116, at first instance.

[73] *Randall v Errington* (1805) 10 Ves 423; *Holder v Holder*, supra, CA and see p 536, infra.

[74] Right not lost in *Aberdeen Town Council v Aberdeen University*, supra, HL (80 years); *Re Walters* [1954] Ch 653, sub nom *Re Sherman* [1954] 1 All ER 893 (19 years).

[75] *Wright v Morgan* [1926] AC 788, [1926] All ER Rep 201, PC.

[76] *Re Boles and British Land Co's Contract* [1902] 1 Ch 244.

[77] *Stacey v Elph* (1833) 1 My & K 195; *Clark v Clark* (1884) 9 App Cas 733, PC.

[78] *Parkes v White* (1805) 11 Ves 209—trustees to preserve contingent remainders.

[79] [1968] Ch 353, [1968] 1 All ER 665, CA.

[80] *Farmer v Dean* (1863) 32 Beav 327; *Tennant v Trenchard* (1869) 4 Ch App 537.

[81] Supra, CA, at 402, 403, 398; 680, 677.

[82] Where the two trustees were also agricultural tenants of the trust property it was held that they were entitled to sell the freehold subject to the agricultural tenancies and were under no duty to co-operate in its sale in any other way: *Sargeant v National Westminster Bank plc* (1990) 61 P & CR 518, CA. See *Edge v Pensions Ombudsman* [1998] Ch 512, [1998] 2 All ER 547; affd [2000] Ch 602, [1999] 4 All ER 546, CA.

Finally it may be noted that the rule sometimes causes difficulty in the case of family trusts, as it may make transfers between trusts with common trustees impossible without the sanction of the court. The Law Reform Committee[83] has recommended that, so long as the common trustees are not beneficiaries under either of the trusts concerned, the trustees should be able to do business with one another with the common trustees playing such part as is thought fit, provided that the market value of any property dealt with has been certified by a truly independent valuer as being the proper market price for that property.

(ii) Purchase by the trustee from the beneficiary of his equitable interest—'the fair-dealing rule'[84]

There is no rigid rule that a trustee cannot purchase the equitable interest of a beneficiary, but if challenged in proper time the trustee, if he is to uphold the bargain, must establish that he dealt with the beneficiary at arm's length, that the bargain was beneficial to the beneficiary, that he made full disclosure to the beneficiary and that the transaction was fair and honest.[85]

A trustee would be assisted in upholding a purchase by showing that the purchase was arranged by the beneficiary,[86] or that he pressed the trustee to purchase,[87] or that no other purchaser could be found.[88] These principles, and not those discussed in sub-s (i) above, also apply where a trustee purchases the trust property with the consent of the beneficiaries, for this is in effect a purchase from the beneficiaries.[89] For a purchase to be set aside it must be possible to restore the parties to their original positions, but the court will be slow to hold that *restitutio in integrum* is impossible.[90]

The same principles apply to other persons in a fiduciary position.[91] Indeed, as Vinelott pointed out in *Movitex Ltd v Bulfield*,[92] a trustee who is in breach of the fair-dealing rule is not strictly guilty of a breach of trust, but of the duty he owes to the beneficiary to make full disclosure and to deal fairly with him arising from his fiduciary position. Thus, for instance, on a purchase by a solicitor from his client 'the solicitor must establish that the sale was as advantageous to the client as it could have been if the solicitor had used his utmost endeavours to sell the property to a stranger, and that the burthen of proving this lies on the solicitor, or any persons claiming

---

[83] 23rd Report, Cmnd 8733, paras 3.56–3.59.

[84] Per Megarry V-C in *Tito v Waddell (No 2)* [1977] Ch 106 at 225, 240, 241, [1977] 3 All ER 129 at 228, 241.

[85] *Ex parte Lacey* (1802) 6 Ves 625 at 626. *Coles v Trecothick* (1804) 9 Ves 234 at 247; *Tito v Waddell*, supra. See also *Thomson v Eastwood* (1877) 2 App Cas 215 at 236, HL, per Lord Cairns, approved in *Dougan v Macpherson* [1902] AC 197, HL, where the trustee failed to disclose a valuation to the beneficiary.

[86] *Coles v Trecothick*, supra.   [87] *Morse v Royal* (1806) 12 Ves 355; *Luff v Lord* (1864) 34 Beav 220.

[88] *Clark v Swaile* (1762) 2 Eden 134 (actually a case of solicitor and client).

[89] See *Williams v Scott* [1900] AC 499, PC; *Coles v Trecothick*, supra.

[90] *Tate v Williamson* (1866) 2 Ch App 55.   [91] *Hill v Langley* (1988) *Times*, 28 January.

[92] [1988] BCLC 104.

through him.'[93] In practice, a solicitor who wishes to buy from his client should see to it that the client is independently advised.[94]

[93] *Spencer v Topham* (1856) 22 Beav 573 at 577 per Romilly MR. Here the sale was upheld, although the solicitor re-sold two years later at a considerable profit; *Luddy's Trustee v Peard* (1886) 33 Ch D 500 and cf *Johnson v Fesemeyer* (1858) 3 De G & J 13.

[94] *Cockburn v Edwards* (1881) 18 Ch D 449, CA; *Barron v Willis* [1900] 2 Ch 121, CA; affd sub nom *Willis v Barron* [1902] AC 271, HL.

21

APPOINTMENT OF AGENTS, NOMINEES AND CUSTODIANS: DELEGATION OF TRUSTS

1 THE EQUITABLE RULES AS TO DELEGATION

The original principle was that 'trustees who take on themselves the management of property for the benefit of others have no right to shift their duty on other persons'.[1] It was early recognized, however, that administration of a trust would often be impracticable unless exceptions were permitted, and thus it can now be said that 'the law is not that trustees cannot delegate: it is that trustees cannot delegate unless they have authority to do so'.[2] Lord Hardwicke[3] said that trustees could 'act by other hands' on the ground of legal necessity,[4] or what he called moral necessity, from the usage of mankind. The ground of moral necessity, which was much the more important of these exceptions, was fully discussed, particularly by the Court of Appeal, in *Speight v Gaunt*[5] which, as Kay J pointed out in *Fry v Tapson*,[6] 'did not lay down any new rule, but only illustrated a very old one, viz, that trustees acting according to the ordinary course of business, and employing agents as a prudent man of business would do on his own behalf, are not liable for the default of an agent so employed'. In deciding whether the employment of an agent by a trustee was proper, the standard adopted was the conduct of the ordinary prudent man of business in managing his own affairs.

In appointing an agent the trustees must exercise their personal discretion in

---

[1] Per Landgale MR in *Turner v Corney* (1841) 5 Beav 515 at 517.

[2] *Pilkington v IRC* [1964] AC 612 at 639, [1962] 3 All ER 622 at 630, HL, per Lord Radcliffe.

[3] In *Ex p Belchier* (1754) Amb 218.

[4] An illustration would be where a broker is employed to purchase investments, it being impossible to purchase them in any other way.

[5] (1883) 22 Ch D 727, CA; affd (1883) 9 App Cas 1, HL; *Learoyd v Whiteley* (1887) 12 App Cas 727, HL.

[6] (1884) 28 Ch D 268 at 280.

making their choice of agent;[7] an important, if obvious, limitation is that they must only employ an agent to do work within the scope of the usual business of the agent.[8]

2 PART IV OF THE TRUSTEE ACT 2000

Part IV of the Trustee Act 2000 contains new provisions for the appointment of agents, nominees and custodians, which apply whenever the trust was created.[9] The powers conferred by Part IV are additional to any other powers the trustees may have, but are subject to any restriction or exclusion imposed by the trust instrument or by any enactment or any provision of subordinate legislation.[10] The previous more limited provisions in the Trustee Act 1925 have been repealed.

(a) THE APPOINTMENT OF AGENTS

Sections 11–15 confer powers of collective delegation on trustees. Section 11(1) provides that trustees may authorize any person to exercise any or all of their delegable functions as their agent. A distinction is made between charitable and non-charitable trusts. In the case of the latter, the trustees' delegable functions consist of any function other than—

(a) any function relating to whether or in what way any assets of the trust should be distributed,

(b) any power to decide whether any fees or other payment due to be made out of the trust funds should be made out of income or capital,

(c) any power to appoint a person to be a trustee of the trust, or

(d) any power conferred by any other enactment or the trust instrument which permits the trustees to delegate any of their functions or to appoint a person to act as a nominee or custodian.[11]

In the case of a charitable trust, the trustees' delegable functions are—

(a) any function consisting of carrying out a decision that the trustees have taken;

(b) any function relating to the investment of assets subject to the trust;[12]

---

[7] *Re Weall* (1889) 42 Ch D 674. *Robinson v Harkin* [1896] 2 Ch 415. A direction in a will that a particular person is to be solicitor to the trust imposes no trust or duty on the trustees to employ him—*Foster v Elsley* (1881) 19 Ch D 518.

[8] *Fry v Tapson* (1884) 28 Ch D 268. *Wilkinson v Wilkinson* (1825) 2 Sim & St 237. *Rowland v Witherden* (1851) 3 Mac & G 568, and see Per Kay J in *Re Dewar, Dewar v Brooke* (1885) 52 LT 489 at 492, 493.

[9] Trustee Act 2000, s 27. Part IV applies in relation to a trust having a sole trustee: ibid, s 25(1).

[10] Ibid, s 26.   [11] Ibid, s 11(2).

[12] Including, in the case of land acquired as an investment, managing the land and creating or disposing of an interest in land: ibid, s 11(3)(b).

(c) any function relating to the raising of funds for the trust otherwise than by means of profits of a trade which is an integral part of carrying out the trust's charitable purpose;[13]

(d) any other function prescribed by an order[14] made by the Secretary of State.[15]

The only restrictions on whom the trustees can appoint as their agents are that they cannot authorize a beneficiary to exercise any function as their agent,[16] and they cannot authorize two or more persons to exercise the same function unless they are to exercise it jointly.[17] The persons whom the trustees authorize to exercise functions as their agent may, however, include one or more of their number,[18] and a person so authorized may also be appointed to act as their nominee or custodian.[19]

The statutory duty of care[20] is limited to trustees. It does not apply to an agent in the performance of his agency, though such a person will owe a separate duty of care to the trust under the general law of agency. In particular an agent is subject to any specific duties or restrictions attached to the functions. This is provided for in s 13(1), which gives as an example the case where trustees exercise their new power to delegate their investment function. This was not possible prior to the Trustee Act 2000, except under a specific provision in the trust instrument. In such a case the agent must have regard to the standard investment criteria in accordance with s 4, though the requirement to obtain advice[21] does not apply if the agent is the kind of person from whom it would have been proper for the trustees, in compliance with the requirement, to obtain advice.[22] Another case would be where charity trustees delegate functions in relation to land, when the agent would be required to comply with the restrictions on dispositions and mortgages of charity land under ss 36–39 of the Charities Act 1993.[23]

Trustees of land are, under s 11(1) of the Trusts of Land and Appointment of Trustees Act 1996 under duties to consult beneficiaries and give effect to their wishes.[24] Section 13(3)–(5) of the Trustee Act 2000 provides that trustees must ensure that, in delegating any of their functions under the 2000 Act, they do so on terms that that does not prevent them from complying with their duties under the 1996 Act.

The statutory power of trustees to employ agents does not apply to trustees of authorized unit trusts, or to trustees managing a fund under a common investment scheme or common deposit scheme under ss 24 or 25 of the Charities Act 1993.[25] It does apply to trustees of a pension scheme, but subject to restrictions.[26]

---

[13] Ibid, sub-s 3(c) must be read together with in the definition of a trade in sub-s (4). A distinction is made between general fund-raising activities, and fund-raising activities which are an integral part of carrying out the trust's charitable purpose: for example the charging of fees by a school operating as a charitable trust.

[14] Made by statutory instrument as prescribed by sub-s (5).   [15] Ibid, 11(3).

[16] Ibid, 12(3). This prevents the use of s 11 of the 2000 Act to avoid the restrictions on delegation by trustees of land to a beneficiary under s 9 of the Trusts of Land and Appointment of Trustees Act 1996 (prospectively amended by the Mental Capacity Act 2005, Sch 6, para 41). See p 462, infra.

[17] Trustee Act 2000, s 12(2).   [18] Ibid, s 12(1).   [19] Ibid, s 12(4).

[20] Ibid, s 1: see p 393, supra.   [21] Under ibid, s 5.   [22] Ibid, s 13(2).

[23] As amended by the Land Registration Act 2002, Sch 11, para 29. See p 342, supra. [24] See p 497, infra.

[25] Trustee Act 2000, ss 37, 38.   [26] Ibid, s 36(4)–(7).

(b) TERMS OF AGENCY

In general trustees are free to determine the terms as to remuneration and other matters of the appointment of an agent. The exercise of the power to delegate is subject to the statutory duty of care.[27]

Certain terms, however, may only be authorized by the trustees where it is reasonably necessary for them to do so. These terms are—

(a) a term permitting the agent to appoint a substitute;

(b) a term restricting the liability of the agent or his substitute to the trustees or any beneficiary;

(c) a term permitting the agent to act in circumstances capable of giving rise to a conflict of interest.[28]

These provisions are a response to the realities of modern fund management and are designed to ensure that adequate protection is given to beneficiaries by imposing a test of reasonable necessity on the trustees. The appointment of a fund manager will often be necessary to the efficient and effective management of assets of the trust, and would in practice be impossible if the trustees could not accept the terms in (b) and (c) above.

Special restrictions apply where trustees delegate any of their asset management functions. In this case the delegation must be contained in an agreement made in writing or evidenced in writing. Further the trustees must prepare a 'policy statement', giving guidance as to how the functions should be exercised, with a view to ensuring that the functions are exercised in the best interests of the trust. The agreement with the agent must include a term to the effect that the agent will secure compliance with the policy statement and any revision or replacement thereof. For example, if trustees delegate their powers of investment to an agent, they must enter into an agreement with the agent at the outset setting out the investment objectives of the trust. Such an agreement may include considerations as to the liquidity of assets to meet the needs of the trust, the desired balance between capital growth and income yield, and any 'ethical' considerations relevant to the investment policy of the trust. The policy statement may expand upon the manner in which the duties imposed by s 4 should be discharged in respect of the trust. In relation to the delegation of functions relating to the acquisition and management of land on behalf of the trust, the policy statement may include considerations as to the value and type of property which may be acquired, and the quality of title required. Where relevant it may also consider the terms upon which land may be let, sold or charged. The requirement for a policy statement only applies where the trustees delegate their discretion in relation to the matters concerned. It does not apply in cases where

---

[27] Ie under the Trustee Act 2000, s 1 and Sch 1, para 3(1)(*a*) and (*d*).   [28] Ibid, s 14(1)–(3).

the trustees obtain investment advice but take decisions on investment matters themselves.[29]

(c) APPOINTMENT OF NOMINEES AND CUSTODIANS

A nominee is a person appointed by trustees to hold trust property in his name. Thus, a person may be registered as the owner of certain shares in a company but may in fact hold them as nominee for a trust. The fact of the trust will not appear in the share register. A person is defined as a custodian in relation to assets if he undertakes the safe custody of the assets or of any documents or records concerning the assets.[30]

The trustees of a trust may appoint a person to act as a nominee or as a custodian in relation to such of the assets of the trust as they may determine.[31] Further, if they retain or invest in securities payable to bearer, they have a duty to appoint a person to act as a custodian of the securities.[32]

The appointment in each case must be in or evidenced in writing.[33]

To be eligible for appointment as a nominee or custodian, a person must either—

(a) carry on a business which consists of or includes acting as a nominee or custodian, or

(b) be a body corporate controlled by the trustees,[34] or

(c) be a solicitor's nominee company recognized under s 9 of the Administration of Justice Act 1985.[35]

It is intended that the use of such bodies corporate will enable trustees to use special purpose vehicles for nominee or custodianship purposes.

The trustees may appoint one of themselves, if that one is a trust corporation, or two (or more) of their number, if they are to act as joint nominees or joint custodians.[36] The person appointed as nominee or custodian may also be appointed as custodian or nominee, as the case may be, or as agent.[37]

The terms of appointment of nominees and custodians are similar to those applicable to agents.[38]

---

[29] Ibid, s 15(1)–(4). The asset management functions of trustees are their functions relating to (a) the investment of assets subject to the trust, (b) the acquisition of property which is to be subject to the trust, and (c) managing property which is subject to the trust and disposing of, or creating or disposing of an interest in, such property: s 15(5).

[30] Trustee Act 2000, s 17(2).

[31] Ibid, ss 16(1), 17(1). A nominee cannot, however, be appointed in relation to settled land.

[32] Ibid, s 18(1), unless exempted by a provision in the trust instrument or any enactment or provision of subsequent legislation: ibid, s 18(2). The section does not impose a duty on a sole trustee if that trustee is a trust corporation: s 25(2).

[33] Ibid, ss 16(2), 17(3), 18(3). For the restrictions applicable to most charity trustees see s 19(4).

[34] This is determined in accordance with s 840 of the Income and Corporation Taxes Act 1988: Trustee Act 2000, s 19(3).

[35] Ibid, s 19(1), (2). As to when a body is controlled by trustees see s 19(3).   [36] Ibid, s 19(5).

[37] Ibid, s 19(6), (7).   [38] Ibid, s 20(1)–(3). See s 14 and p 456, supra.

The above provisions do not apply to any trust which has a custodian trustee or in relation to any assets vested in the official custodian for charities.[39]

(d) REVIEW OF AND LIABILITY FOR AGENTS, NOMINEES AND CUSTODIANS

Statutory provisions for the review of, and liability for, agents, nominees and custodians apply whether they were authorized or appointed under the provisions discussed above, or under express powers in the trust instrument, unless they would be inconsistent with the terms of the trust instrument.[40]

Once an agent, nominee or custodian has been authorized or appointed, the trustees have a duty to keep under review the arrangements under which that person acts for the trust, and how those arrangements are being implemented. This obligation means that the trustees must keep under review the question of whether the agent, nominee or custodian is a suitable person to act for the trust, and whether the terms of his appointment are appropriate. In addition, the trustees must keep under review the manner in which the agent, nominee or custodian is performing his functions. The duty to keep under review does not oblige trustees to review the arrangements at specific intervals or in a particular way.[41]

Trustees have a further duty which comes into effect if circumstances make it appropriate, when they must consider whether there is a need to exercise any power of intervention[42] that they have.[43] It might become appropriate where the agent, nominee or custodian is not carrying out his functions effectively, or where the trustees have cause to doubt the suitability of the person in question to continue to act for the trust.

Trustees are under a positive duty, if they consider that there is a need to do so, to exercise their power of intervention.[44]

If the agent has been authorized to exercise asset management functions, the above duties extend to keeping under review and, where necessary, revising or replacing, any policy statement prepared in connection with the delegation of asset management functions.[45]

(e) REMUNERATION OF AN AGENT, NOMINEE OR CUSTODIAN

Trustees may provide for the remuneration of a person, other than a trustee, who has been authorized to exercise functions as an agent of the trustees, or who has been appointed to act as a nominee or custodian.[46] He may be remunerated out of the trust

---

[39] Ibid, ss 16(3), 17(4) and 18(4).   [40] Trustee Act 2000, s 21(1)–(3).   [41] Ibid, s 22(1)(*a*).
[42] This includes a power to give directions and a power to revoke the authorization or appointment of the agent, nominee or custodian: ibid, s 22(4).
[43] Ibid, s 22(1)(*b*).   [44] Ibid, s 22(1)(*c*).   [45] Ibid, s 22(2), (3).
[46] Ie an agent, nominee or custodian authorized or appointed under Part IV of the Trustee Act 2000 or any other enactment or any provision of subordinate legislation, or by the trust instrument: ibid, s 32(1). Note that Part IV does not apply to trustees of authorized unit trusts, or to trustees managing a common

funds[47] for services if (a) he was engaged on terms entitling him to be remunerated for those services, and (b) the amount does not exceed such remuneration as is reasonable in the circumstances for the provision of those services by him to or on behalf of the trust.[48]

The trustees may likewise reimburse the agent, nominee or custodian out of the trust funds for any expenses properly incurred by him in exercising functions as an agent, nominee or custodian.[49]

(f) LIABILITY OF TRUSTEE FOR AGENTS, NOMINEES AND CUSTODIANS

A trustee is not liable for any act or default of an agent, nominee or custodian unless he has failed to comply with the statutory duty of care applicable to him when entering onto the arrangements under which the person acts as agent, nominee or custodian; or when carrying out his duties under s 22 (duty to keep under review).[50]

If a trustee has agreed a term under which the agent, nominee or custodian is permitted to appoint a substitute, the trustee is not liable for any act or default of the substitute unless he has failed to comply with the duty of care applicable to him when agreeing the term, or when carrying out his duties under s 22 in so far as they relate to the use of the substitute.[51]

(g) PROTECTION OF THIRD PARTIES

A failure by the trustees to act within the limits of their statutory powers in authorizing a person to exercise a function of theirs as an agent, or in appointing a person to act as a nominee or custodian does not invalidate the authorization or appointment.[52] Third parties, therefore, do not need to satisfy themselves that the trustees have complied with the requirements of the Act, for example that a person authorized to act as an agent is not a beneficiary. The trustee will, of course, be liable for any loss to the trust estate flowing from a failure to comply with the requirements of the Act.

investment scheme or a common deposit scheme under ss 24 or 25 of the Charities Act 1993 (as to which see p 310, supra): Trustee Act 2000, ss 37, 38. Part IV applies to trustees of a pension scheme subject to restrictions: see ibid, s 36(4)–(8).

[47] 'Trust funds' means income or capital funds of the trust: ibid, s 39(1).   [48] Ibid, s 32(2).

[49] Ibid, s 32(3). In contrast to services it seems the expenses must be incurred on or after the coming into force of the section: ibid, s 33(1).

[50] Ibid, s 23(1). As to the duty of care, see s 1, Sch 1, para 3 and p 393, supra.

[51] Ibid, s 23(2). See s 1, Sch 1, para 3.   [52] Ibid, s 24.

3 DELEGATION BY POWER OF ATTORNEY UNDER S 25 OF THE TRUSTEE ACT 1925 AS SUBSTITUTED BY S 5(1) OF THE TRUSTEE DELEGATION ACT 1999

Under this section a power of delegation is conferred on trustees individually not collectively,[53] and delegation under it leaves the trustee liable for the acts or defaults of the donee of the power of attorney in the same manner as if they were the acts or defaults of the donor.[54] Section 25(1), as substituted, provides as follows:

Notwithstanding any rule of law or equity to the contrary, a trustee may, by power of attorney, delegate[55] the execution or exercise of all or any of the trusts, powers and discretions vested in him as trustee, either alone or jointly with any other person or persons.

It will be observed that this provision authorizes the delegation of powers[56] and discretions, including investment decisions,[57] as well as merely ministerial acts. The persons who may be donees of a power of attorney under this section include a trust corporation.[58] A delegation under this section runs from the date of execution (or other date if specified) and continues for a period of 12 months or any shorter period provided by the instrument creating the power.[59] Written notice containing details of the power must be given by the trustee within seven days to each of the other trustees and any person who has power to appoint a new trustee, whether alone or jointly. The notice must contain the reason why the power is given, though this need not appear in the power itself. Failure to give notice does not, however, prejudice a person dealing with the donee of the power.[60] The Powers of Attorney Act 1971 gives protection to the donee of a power of attorney and third persons where the power of attorney has been revoked without their knowledge. The donee will not incur any liability, and in favour of the third party the transaction will be valid.[61]

The section[62] provides a form of power of attorney, to be executed as a deed,[63] which may be used by a single trustee wishing to delegate all his trustee functions in relation

---

[53] Contrast the power to appoint agents under s 11 of the Trustee Act 2000 discussed supra, p 454. However it seems that each of two or more trustees may effect separate powers of attorney in favour of the same third party: see [1978] Conv 854 (J T Farrand).

[54] Trustee Act 1925, s 25(7) as substituted.

[55] A further power may be being granted when the first expires, but doubts have been expressed as to whether it is an appropriate exercise of the power to renew the delegation annually: (1993) 137 SJ 535 (L Price).

[56] But not including the power under s 25 itself—s 25(8) as substituted.

[57] See Law Reform Committee, 23rd Report, Cmnd 8733, paras 4.16–4.18, 4.20; (1990) 106 LQR 87 (D Hayton).

[58] Trustee Act 1925, s 25(3) as substituted.

[59] Trustee Act 1925, s 25(2) as substituted. It applies only to powers of attorney granted on or after 1 March 2000.

[60] Ibid, s 25(4) as substituted.   [61] Powers of Attorney Act 1971, s 5.

[62] Section 25(5), (6) of the Trustee Act 1925 as substituted by the Trustee Delegation Act 1999, s 5(1). These subsections are new.

[63] See the Law of Property (Miscellaneous Provisions) Act 1989, s 1(3).

to a single trust to a single attorney. A power of attorney differing in immaterial respects only will have the same effect as a power in the prescribed form.

4 ENDURING POWERS OF ATTORNEY ACT 1985

The purpose of this Act is to alter the general rule so as to enable powers of attorney to be created which will survive any subsequent mental incapacity of the donor. In order to be an enduring power of attorney, as it is called, the power must be in the pre-scribed[64] form, have been executed in the prescribed manner by the donor and the attorney and incorporate the prescribed explanatory information. However, to be effective during the mental incapacity of the donor it must be duly registered[65] follow-ing notice to at least three specified relatives, but there is no requirement to give notice to co-trustees or anyone with a power to appoint new trustees.[66] The court is under a duty to register unless one of the grounds of objection specified in s 6(5) of the Act, including that the power purported to have been created is not valid as an enduring power of attorney, or that the application is premature because the donor is not yet mentally incapable, is established to the satisfaction of the court. The burden of proof remains throughout on the objectors.[67] It has been held that an enduring power of attorney is not rendered invalid by reason of the fact that at the time of execution of the power the donor was incapable by reason of mental disorder from managing his property and affairs. It suffices that he understood the nature and effect of the power.[68] An instrument which appoints more than one person to be an attorney cannot create an enduring power unless the attorneys are appointed to act jointly or jointly and severally.[69]

As originally enacted s 2(8) of the Enduring Powers of Attorney Act 1985 provided that a power of attorney granted under s 25 of the Trustee Act 1925 could not be an enduring power. This subsection was repealed by the Trustee Delegation Act 1999, s 6, in relation to powers created after the commencement of that Act. The repeal allows an enduring power of attorney to be used to delegate functions under s 25 of the 1925 Act.

The 1985 Act will be repealed by the Mental Capacity Act 2005 when it is brought

---

[64] Ie under s 2(2). See SI 1990/1376.   [65] See (1991) 141 NLJ 933 (R Kerridge).

[66] Cf Trustee Act 1925, s 25(4) as substituted.

[67] *Re W* [2001] 4 All ER 88, CA; *Re F* [2004] EWHC 725 (Ch), [2004] 3 All ER 277 and see (2000) 22 T & ELJ 9 (Caroline Bielanska).

[68] *Re K* [1988] Ch 310, [1988] 1 All ER 358. But see (1989) 13 NZULR 253 (R Munday) who argues that the intention of the Act may be partially frustrated by reason of a misunderstanding of the basic law of agency, which, he says, can only empower an agent to do acts which the principal has capacity to do himself. He criticizes *Re K* and contends that an enduring power can only be executed effectively before senility has begun to manifest itself in the donor.

[69] Enduring Powers of Attorney Act 1985 s 11(1), and see *Re E* [2000] Ch 364, [2000] 3 All ER 1004, where revocation of a power is also considered.

into force. The 2005 Act[70] provides for the replacement of an 'enduring power of attorney'[71] by a 'lasting power of attorney'. A lasting power of attorney is designed to survive any subsequent mental incapacity of the donor. It must be in the prescribed form, have been executed in the prescribed manner and contain the prescribed information about its purpose and effect. It does not become effective unless and until it has been registered with the Public Guardian,[72] and specified notification requirements have been complied with. A power of attorney under s 25 of the Trustee Act 1925 may be a lasting power of attorney.

5 DELEGATION UNDER THE TRUSTS OF LAND AND APPOINTMENT OF TRUSTEES ACT 1996

Trustees of land may, by power of attorney, delegate to any beneficiary or beneficiaries of full age and beneficially entitled to an interest in possession in land[73] subject to the trust any of their functions as trustees which relate to the land.[74] The delegation may be for any period or indefinite.[75] It must be given by all the trustees jointly and may be revoked by any one or more of them.[76] Where a beneficiary to whom alone functions have been delegated ceases to be a person beneficially entitled to an interest in possession in land subject to the trust, the power is revoked.[77]

Beneficiaries to whom functions have been delegated are, in relation to their exercise, in the same position as trustees, but they are not trustees for any other purpose.[78] Protection is given to a person who in good faith deals with a person to whom the trustees have purported to delegate functions.[79]

In deciding whether, under the above provisions, to delegate any of their functions, and, where the delegation is not irrevocable, in carrying out their obligations in relation to keeping the delegation under review, the duty of care under s 1 of the Trustee Act 2000 applies.[80] Unless the trustee fails to comply with this duty he is not liable for any act or default of the beneficiary or beneficiaries.[81]

A power of attorney under these provisions cannot be an enduring power under the Enduring Powers of Attorney Act 1985.[82]

---

[70] Sections 9–14 and Sch 1.

[71] There are provisions in Sch 4 relating to enduring powers of attorney created before the commencement of the 2005 Act, and transitional provisions consequent on the repeal in Sch 5, Part 2.

[72] This is a new office created by ibid, s 57.   [73] As to the meaning of this phrase, see p 409, supra.

[74] Trusts of Land and Appointment of Trustees Act 1996, s 9(1).   [75] Ibid, s 9(5).

[76] Ibid, s 9(3), unless expressed to be irrevocable and to be given by way of security.

[77] Ibid, s 9(4), which also provides for cases of delegation to two or more beneficiaries.

[78] Ibid, s 9(7). In particular not for the purpose of any enactment permitting the delegation of functions by trustees or imposing requirements relating to payment of capital money.

[79] Ibid, s 9(2).   [80] Ibid, s 9A(1)–(5) inserted by the Trustees Act 2000, Sch 2, para 47.

[81] Ibid, s 9A(6) likewise inserted.

[82] Ibid, s 9(6), prospectively amended by the Mental Capacity Act 2005, Sch 6, para 41.

6 DELEGATION UNDER S 1 OF THE TRUSTEE DELEGATION ACT 1999

This section created a new statutory exception to the general rule that a trustee must exercise in person the functions vested in him as a trustee. It provides that, where the donee of a power of attorney created on or after 1 March 2000,[83] who is not otherwise authorized[84] to exercise trustee functions,[85] would only be prevented from doing an act because doing it would involve the exercise of a function of the donor as a trustee, the donee may nevertheless do that act if:

(a) it related to land,[86] the capital proceeds of a conveyance[87] of land, or income from land, and

(b) at the time when the act is done the donor has a beneficial interest in the land, proceeds or income.[88]

The person creating the trust or the donor may, however, exclude or restrict this provision in the document creating the trust, or the power of attorney, as the case may be.[89]

Subject to the provisions in the trust instrument, although a trustee is not liable for permitting the donee to exercise a function by virtue of sub-s (1), he remains liable for the acts and defaults of the donee in exercising such function in the same manner as if they were the acts or defaults of the donor.[90]

The above provisions are of particular benefit to co-owners of land who are essentially trustees for themselves. First it enables them to delegate without having to comply with the restrictions which apply where trustees hold land only for third parties.[91] Secondly it enables a co-owner of land to make effective provision for the disposal of the co-owned land if he becomes mentally incapable.[92] Finally it ensures

---

[83] The date when the section came into force. For the exceptional case where it applies to a pre-Act power see s 4(6).

[84] Trustee Delegation Act 1999, s 1(8), ie under a statutory provision or a provision in a trust instrument, under which the donor of the power is expressly authorized to delegate the exercise of all or any of his trustee functions by power of attorney.

[85] Ie those which he has as trustee either alone or jointly with another person or persons: s 1(2)(b).

[86] Defined in s 11(1) by reference to the Trustee Act 1925. Further by s 10(1)–(3) a reference to land in a power of attorney created after the commencement of the Act includes, subject to any contrary intention expressed in the instrument creating the power, a reference to any estate or interest of the donor of the power of attorney in the land at the time that the donee acts. In the few remaining cases where the doctrine of conversion continues to operate a person who has a beneficial interest in the proceeds of sale of land is treated for the purposes of ss 1 and 2 as having a beneficial interest in the land: s 1(7).

[87] Defined in s 1(2)(a) by reference to the Law of Property Act 1925.   [88] Section 1(1), (2)(b), (9).

[89] Section 1(3), (5).   [90] Section 1(4), (5).

[91] See s 25 of the Trustee Act 1925 as substituted by s 5(1) of the Trustee Delegation Act 1999, and see p 460, supra.

[92] So assumed in the Explanatory Notes to the Bill, but a doubt has been raised as s 1 does not actually refer in terms to an enduring power of attorney.

that the donee is able to deal with the proceeds of sale and income from the land as well as the land itself.

It follows from the terms of s 1(1) that a person dealing with a donee under that section needs to know whether the donor has a beneficial interest in the relevant property. To avoid the difficulties that might otherwise arise in investigating the title of the beneficial interest, it is provided that in favour of a purchaser[93] a signed statement by the donee made when doing the act in question or within three months thereafter that the donor has such a beneficial interest is conclusive evidence thereof.[94]

7 ATTORNEY ACTING FOR A TRUSTEE AND THE 'TWO-TRUSTEE RULE'

The Trustee Delegation Act 1999 contains provisions intended to strengthen and clarify the operation of the 'two-trustee rules'[95] by making it clear that so long as there are at least two trustees, the rules could be satisfied either by two people acting in different capacities or by two people acting jointly in the same capacity, but not by one person acting in two capacities. It achieves this by providing that the rules are not satisfied by money being paid to or dealt with as directed by, or a receipt for money being given by, a 'relevant attorney' or by a conveyance or deed being executed by such an attorney.[96] 'Relevant attorney' is defined as meaning a person (other than a trust corporation within the meaning of the Trustee Act 1925)[97] who is acting either—

(a) both as a trustee and as attorney for one or more other trustees, or

(b) as attorney for two or more trustees,

and who is not acting together with any other person or persons.[98] These provisions apply whenever the power under which a relevant attorney is acting was created.[99]

Applying the above provisions, where A and B are the only trustees, if A and B each appoint X as attorney, X (acting alone) would not satisfy the two-trustee rules. However, if A appointed X as his attorney and B appointed Y as his, X and Y could act together and satisfy the requirement. Similarly, if A appointed X and Y as his joint attorneys and B appointed X and Y as his joint attorneys, X and Y can satisfy the requirement.

---

[93] 'Purchaser' has the same meaning as in Part I of the Law of Property Act 1925: s 2(1) of the 1999 Act.

[94] Section 2(1)–(3). As to liability for a false statement see s 2(4).   [95] See p 367, supra.

[96] Trustee Delegation Act 1999, s 7(1).   [97] See p 388, supra.

[98] Trustee Delegation Act 1999, s 7(2).

[99] Ibid, s 7(3), subject to transitional provisions in s 4. Section 4 and part of s 7(3) are prospectively repealed by the Mental Capacity Act 2005, Sch 7.

22

POWERS OF TRUSTEES

1 INTRODUCTION

Trustees commonly have many and varied powers which may be conferred on them by the trust instrument or by statute. Many of them will be administrative, but they may be dispositive, giving them power to decide which of potential beneficiaries shall take an interest and what the extent of that interest shall be. Trustees may even be given power to amend the terms of the trust, but any such power must be exercised for the purpose for which it was granted.[1] Such a power must not be exercised beyond the reasonable contemplation of the parties.[2]

Some trustees' powers have already been discussed:[3] other important powers are discussed below.

2 POWER OF SALE[4]

(a) EXISTENCE OF A POWER OF SALE

(i) Land

Trustees of land, for the purpose of exercising their functions as trustees, have in relation to the land all the powers of an absolute owner, which must include a power of sale.[5]

Apart from statute, trustees who purchase land in breach of trust can sell it and

---

[1] *Hole v Garnsey* [1930] AC 472.   [2] *Society of Lloyd's v Robinson* [1999] 1 WLR 756, HL.

[3] Eg the power of investment (Chapter 18, supra), and the power to appoint agents (Chapter 21, supra).

[4] See [1999] Conv 84 (R Mitchell).

[5] Trusts of Land and Appointment of Trustees Act 1996, s 6(1), and see the Trustee Act 2000, s 8(4). If the land is settled land as defined by the Settled Land Act 1925, the power of sale given by that Act is conferred on the tenant for life, not the trustees of the settlement: Settled Land Act 1925, ss 1 (as amended by the Trusts of Land and Appointment of Trustees Act 1996), 38.

make a good title even to a purchaser with notice, provided only that all the beneficiaries are not at once competent and desirous to take the land in specie.[6]

(ii) Property other than land

Here there may be an express trust for or power of sale, or one may be implied, for instance under the rule in *Howe v Lord Dartmouth*.[7] In other cases a power may exist under statutory provisions such as s 4(2) of the Trustee Act 2000,[8] or s 16 of the Trustee Act 1925.[9]

Where the trustees were assumed to have no power of sale, it was held in *Re Hope's Will Trust*[10] that the court could order a sale under s 57 of the Trustee Act 1925.[11]

(b) STATUTORY PROVISIONS RELATING TO SALES

The Trustee Act 1925 contains various provisions, which are chiefly of interest to the conveyancer, and for present purposes need not be considered in detail. By s 12(1), as amended by the Trusts of Land and Appointment of Trustees Act 1996, where a trustee has a duty or power to sell property he

may sell or concur with any other person in selling[12] all or any part of the property, either subject to prior charges or not, and either together or in lots,[13] by public auction or by private contract, subject to any such conditions respecting title or evidence of title or other matter as the trustee thinks fit, with power to vary any contract for sale, and to buy in at any auction, or to rescind any contract for sale and to re-sell, without being answerable for any loss.

A duty or power to sell or dispose of land, moreover, 'includes a duty or power to sell or dispose of part thereof, whether the division is horizontal, vertical, or made in any other way'.[14] Further, no beneficiary can impeach a sale made by a trustee on 'the

---

[6] *Re Patten and Edmonton Union Poor Guardians* (1883) 48 LT 870; *Re Jenkins and HE Randall & Co's Contract* [1903] 2 Ch 362.

[7] Discussed in chapter 19, p 428 seq, supra.

[8] See p 421, supra. The duty to review investments and vary them where appropriate implies a power to sell existing investments.

[9] This section, which applies equally to land, provides that in any case where trustees are authorized to pay or apply capital money subject to the trust for any purpose or on any manner, they have power to raise the money required by sale of all or any part of the trust property for the time being in possession. This section applies notwithstanding any contrary provision in the trust instrument, but does not apply to charity trustees, nor to the trustees of a settlement, not being also the statutory owners. It empowers trustees to raise money by mortgage as well as by sale. It does not however enable them to raise money on the security of the trust property for the purpose of acquiring further land by way of investment—*Re Suenson-Taylor's Settlement Trusts* [1974] 3 All ER 397.

[10] [1929] 2 Ch 136, [1929] All ER Rep 561.   [11] Discussed in chapter 23, Section 2(b), infra.

[12] Apart from statute trustees could, and indeed should, concur with other persons, if they can thereby get a higher price: *Re Cooper and Allen's Contract for Sale to Harlech* (1876) 4 Ch D 802. There must be a proper apportionment and the apportioned part due to the trustees paid to them, unless there is some special provision in the trust instrument—*Re Parker and Beech's Contract* (1887) 56 LT 96, CA.

[13] See *Re Judd and Poland and Skelcher's Contract* [1906] 1 Ch 684, CA.

[14] Trustee Act 1925, s 12(2) as amended.

ground that any of the conditions subject to which the sale was made may have been unnecessarily depreciatory, unless it also appears that the consideration for the sale was thereby rendered inadequate',[15] and it cannot after the execution of the conveyance be impeached as against the purchaser on such ground 'unless it appears that the purchaser was acting in collusion with the trustee at the time when the contract for sale was made'.[16]

In general it must be remembered that the trustees 'have an overriding duty to obtain the best price which they can for their beneficiaries',[17] even though accepting a higher offer may mean resiling from an existing offer at a late stage in the negotiations contrary to the dictates of commercial morality. Trustees must, however, act with proper prudence, and may accept an existing lower offer if to probe a higher one would involve a serious risk that both offers would fall through.

3 POWER TO GIVE RECEIPTS

Notwithstanding anything to the contrary in the instrument, if any, creating the trust,[18] s 14(1) of the Trustee Act 1925 as amended by the Trustee Act 2000 provides:

The receipt in writing of a trustee for any money, securities, investments, or other personal property or effects payable, transferable, or deliverable to him under any trust or power shall be a sufficient discharge to the person paying, transferring, or delivering the same and shall effectually exonerate him from seeing to the application or being answerable for any loss or misapplication thereof.

By sub-s (2),[19] however, this section does not affect the statutory provisions[20] which require the proceeds of sale or other capital money arising under a trust of land not to be paid to fewer than two persons as trustees, except where the trustee is a trust corporation. Nor, it seems clear, does the section alter the rule[21] that where there are two or more trustees, a valid receipt can only be given by all of them acting jointly.

---

[15] Ibid, s 13(1). Cf *Dance v Goldingham* (1873) 8 Ch App 902; *Dunn v Flood* (1885) 28 Ch D 586, CA. Both decided prior to any statutory conditions.

[16] Trustee Act 1925, s 13(2). This does not prevent an action against the trustees for breach of trust. See also ibid, s 17.

[17] *Buttle v Saunders* [1950] 2 All ER 193 at 195 per Wynn Parry J; *Re Cooper and Allen's Contract for Sale to Harlech*, supra; (1950) 14 Conv 228 (E H Bodkin); (1975) 39 Conv 177 (A Samuels).

[18] Trustee Act 1925, s 14(3).

[19] As amended by the Law of Property (Amendment) Act 1926 and the Trusts of Land and Appointment of Trustees Act 1996.

[20] Law of Property Act 1925, s 27(2), as substituted by the Law of Property (Amendment) Act 1926 and amended by the Trusts of Land and Appointment of Trustees Act 1996. There are corresponding provisions in respect of strict settlements: Settled Land Act 1925, s 94(1).

[21] Discussed in chapter 17, section 3, p 395, supra.

4 POWER TO INSURE

The traditional view was that unless there was some express provision in the trust instrument, trustees were under no duty to insure the trust property, and accordingly would not be liable for failure to insure if the trust property should be destroyed or damaged.[22] Nor, originally, did they have any power to insure, unless conferred by a trust instrument expressly or by implication.[23] There are now statutory provisions.

Section 19 of the Trustee Act 1925 as substituted by the Trustee Act 2000[24] confers power on all trustees, whenever the trust was created,[25] to insure any trust property against such risks as they think fit, and to pay the premiums out of the income or capital funds of the trust.[26] Where property is held on a bare trust, however, this is subject to any direction given by the beneficiary (or each of them) that any specified property is not to be insured, or only insured on specified conditions.[27] The rationale behind this qualification is said to be that where the beneficiaries are together absolutely entitled to the trust property, they have power under the general law of trusts to bring the trust to an end.[28] Property is held on a bare trust if the beneficiary (each beneficiary if more than one) is of full age and (taken together if more than one) is absolutely entitled to the trust property.[29] To the extent that such directions are given the trustees may not delegate their power to insure.[30]

These provisions do not impose a duty to insure. The imposition of such a duty might cause difficulties if the trustees had no funds out of which to pay premiums, and a trust fund comprising trustee investments such as government bonds would be secure without insurance. In *Re McEacharn*[31] Eve J held that insurance was not to be maintained at the expense of the tenant for life, but expressly decided nothing as to whether the trustees ought to insure the premises at the expense of the estate generally because he had not been asked that question. The Australian courts[32] have adopted the American approach[33] that a trustee would normally be under a duty to insure. It is submitted that a failure by trustees to exercise a power to insure (whether statutory or

---

[22] *Re McEacharn* (1911) 103 LT 900.

[23] *Re Bennett* [1896] 1 Ch 778, CA. Where there is a power to insure there has never been any doubt that a trustee may insure the whole beneficial interest in property in which he holds only the legal estate, and that he may recover from the insurers the entire diminution of its value notwithstanding that the beneficial owners were not co-assureds. He is, of course, accountable to the beneficiaries for such insurance proceeds as he may receive: see *Lonsdale & Thompson Ltd v Black Arrow Group plc* [1993] Ch 361, [1993] 3 All ER 648.

[24] Section 34. In relation to land see also s 6(1) of the Trusts of Land and Appointment of Trustees Act 1996.

[25] Ibid, s 34(3).

[26] Section 19(1), (5) of the Trustee Act 1925 as substituted.

[27] Ibid, s 19(2) as substituted.   [28] See *Saunders v Vautier* (1841) 4 Beav 115 and p 405 supra.

[29] Ibid, s 19(3) as substituted.

[30] Ibid, s 19(4) as substituted. This is so that the beneficiaries can ensure compliance with their directions.

[31] Supra.   [32] *Pateman v Heyen* (1993) 33 NSWLR 188.

[33] See *Scott on Trusts* 4th edn, Vol IIA, 484.

express), in circumstances where a reasonable person would have done so, would constitute a breach of the trustees' paramount duty to act in the best interests of the beneficiaries.[34] Moreover the statutory duty of care applies to a trustee when exercising the statutory power to insure property, or any corresponding power, however conferred.[35] It will cover, for example, the selection of an insurer and the terms on which the insurance cover is taken out.

The following section[36] deals with the application of insurance moneys, the general effect of which is that money receivable by trustees or any beneficiary[37] under a policy of insurance against the loss or damage of any property subject to a trust or to a settlement within the meaning of the Settled Land Act 1925, is capital money for the purposes of the trust or settlement as the case may be. Detailed provisions for the carrying through of the application in different circumstances are set out in sub-s (3). In particular, sub-s 3(c), as amended by the Trusts of Land and Appointment of Trustees Act 1996, provides that money receivable in respect of land subject to a trust of land or personal property held on trust for sale is to be held upon the trusts and subject to the powers and provisions applicable to money arising by a sale under such trust. By sub-s 4, subject to obtaining the specified consents, the trustees are empowered to apply the money in rebuilding, reinstating, repairing or replacing the property lost or damaged. Subsection (5), moreover, expressly saves the other rights, whether statutory or otherwise, of any person to require the insurance money to be applied in rebuilding, reinstating, or repairing the property lost or damaged—for instance, under the Fires Prevention (Metropolis) Act 1774, s 83, which despite its title, is of general application.[38]

---

[34] The old case of *Bailey v Gould* (1840) 4 Y & C Ex 221 which suggests that trustees are not under a duty to insure trust property unless there is an obligation to insure imposed by the trust instrument is of doubtful authority in contemporary conditions.

[35] Trustee Act 2000, s 1 and Sch 1, para 5.

[36] Ibid, s 20 as amended by the Trustee Act 2000, s 34(3).

[37] By s 20(2) of the Trustee Act 1925, if receivable by a beneficiary it must be paid by him to the trustees, or into court.

[38] *Sinnott v Bowden* [1912] 2 Ch 414, [1911–13] All ER Rep 752. This Act provides that on the request of any person interested the insurers must cause the insurance money to be laid out and expended towards rebuilding, reinstating or repairing the house or building burnt down, demolished or damaged by fire, unless all the persons interested agree as to its disposition, to the satisfaction of the insurers.

5 POWER TO COMPOUND LIABILITIES

Section 15 of the Trustee Act 1925[39] provides as follows:

A personal representative, or two or more trustees[40] acting together,[41] or, subject to the restrictions imposed in regard to receipts by a sole trustee not being a trust corporation, a sole acting trustee where by the instrument, if any, creating the trust, or by statute, a sole trustee is authorised to execute the trusts and powers reposed in him, may, if and as he or they think fit—

(a) accept any property, real or personal, before the time at which it is made transferable or payable; or

(b) sever and apportion any blended trust funds or property; or

(c) pay or allow any debt or claim on any evidence that he or they think sufficient; or

(d) accept any composition or any security, real or personal, for any debt[42] or for any property, real or personal, claimed; or

(e) allow any time of payment of any debt; or

(f) compromise,[43] compound, abandon, submit to arbitration, or otherwise settle any debt, account, claim, or thing whatever relating to the testator's or intestate's estate or to the trust;

and for any of those purposes may enter into, give, execute, and do such agreements, instruments of composition or arrangement, releases, and other things as to him or them seem expedient, without being responsible for any loss occasioned by any act or thing so done by him or them if he has or they have discharged the duty of care set out in s 1(1) of the Trustee Act 2000.

The section, particularly (f), is drafted in very wide terms, and will not be restrictively construed. It is thought advantageous that trustees should enjoy wide and flexible powers of compromising and settling disputes, bearing in mind that such powers, however wide, must be exercised with due regard for the interests of those whose interests it is the duty of the trustees to protect. If the person who has a claim adverse to the trust happens also to be a beneficiary under it, in an appropriate case the consideration may include the surrender of his interest. The trustees must listen to the beneficiaries and pay attention to their wishes but have power to agree a proposed

---

[39] As amended by the Trustee Act 2000, Sch 2, para 20. Apart from statute see *Blue v Marshall* (1735) 3 P Wms 381.

[40] Including a judicial trustee. *Re Ridsdel* [1947] Ch 597, [1947] 2 All ER 312, see also *Re Shenton* [1935] Ch 651, [1935] All ER 920, DC.

[41] It is submitted that under this section trustees have no power to compromise a claim by one of themselves, unless, perhaps, there is a provision in the trust deed allowing trustees to act although personally interested. According to *Re Houghton* [1904] 1 Ch 622, however, one executor can, on other grounds, compromise a claim by a co-executor.

[42] Including a statutory debt: *Bradstock Group Pensions Scheme Trustees Ltd v Bradstock Group plc* [2002] WTLR 1281, discussed (2002) 152 NLJ 1284 (Sarah Boon).

[43] 'Compromise' in other contexts has been held to require either some dispute as to the claimant's rights, or some difficulty in enforcing them—*Mercantile Investment and General Trust Co v River Plate Trust, Loans and Agency Co* [1894] 1 Ch 578; *Chapman v Chapman* [1954] AC 429, [1954] 1 All ER 798, HL.

compromise even though all the beneficiaries oppose it. The section has been held to be concerned with external disputes, that is, cases in which there is some issue between the trustees on behalf of the trust as a whole and the outside world, as opposed to internal disputes where one beneficiary under the trust is at issue with another beneficiary under the trust.[44] It has, however, been held to extend to the claim of one who alleges that he is a beneficiary.[45]

Re Ridsdel[46] decides the fairly obvious point that although a payment under s 15(f) must be made in compromise of a claim, it does not follow that, to justify a compromise payment, it must be established that the claim, if there had not been a compromise, would have succeeded. As the judge observed, if this were so the power of compromise would be reduced in effect to a nullity. Further, it seems that the section only protects a trustee where he has done some act or at least exercised some active discretion and will not avail him where he has adopted a mere passive attitude of leaving matters alone.[47] In exercising the power, the only criterion is whether the compromise is desirable and fair as regards all the beneficiaries.[48]

6 POWERS IN RELATION TO REVERSIONARY INTERESTS

Provisions in s 22 of the Trustee Act 1925 as amended by the Trustee Act 2000 give considerable protection to trustees where trust property includes any share or interest in property not vested in the trustees, or the proceeds of the sale of any such property, or any other thing in action. Subsection (1) provides that on the same falling into possession, or becoming payable or transferable the trustees may:

(a) agree or ascertain the amount or value thereof or any part thereof in such manner as they may think fit;

(b) accept in or towards satisfaction thereof, at the market or current value, or upon any valuation or estimate of value which they may think fit, any authorised investments;

(c) allow any deductions for duties, costs, charges and expenses which they may think proper or reasonable;

(d) execute any release in respect of the premises so as effectually to discharge all accountable parties from all liability in respect of any matters coming within the scope of such release;

without being responsible in any such case for any loss occasioned by any act or thing so done by them if they have discharged the duty of care set out in s 1(1) of the Trustee Act 2000.

---

[44] *Re Earl of Strafford* [1978] 3 All ER 18; affd [1980] Ch 28, [1979] 1 All ER 513, CA, not followed in Australia: *Re Irismay Holdings Pty Ltd* [1996] 1 Qd R 172.

[45] *Re Warren* (1884) 51 LT 561; *Eaton v Buchanan* [1911] AC 253, HL.

[46] Supra.   [47] *Re Greenwood* (1911) 105 LT 509.   [48] *Re Earl of Strafford*, supra, CA.

Subsection (2) restricts the obligations of trustees during the period before such property falls into possession, but it is expressly provided that nothing therein contained 'shall relieve the trustees of the obligation to get in and obtain payment or transfer of such share or interest or other thing in action on the same falling into possession'.

7 POWER OF MAINTENANCE OF MINORS

(a) EXPRESS POWERS

In view of the wide statutory power hereafter discussed, it is no longer so usual or vital to insert express powers of maintenance, and it is not proposed to deal with them in great detail, particularly as much turns in each case on the construction of the particular words used. A primary question may be whether the alleged power is not in fact an imperative trust to apply the income, or so much of it as may be required, for or towards the maintenance of the minor. Thus there was held to be an imperative trust in *Re Peel*,[49] and a line of cases[50] which the Court of Appeal has accepted as binding, though agreeing that criticism is well founded, has decided that 'a trust to apply the whole or part as the trustees may think fit of the income for the maintenance of the children is an obligatory trust and compels the trustees to maintain the children where that trust occurs in the marriage settlement to which the father is a party'.[51] Accordingly the father in such case, notwithstanding his own ability to maintain his children, can compel the trustees to apply an adequate portion of the income for this purpose. It was made clear, however, that this line of cases is not to be extended.

Where the trustees have, on the construction of the instrument, a true discretionary power of maintenance, they must, in exercising it, have regard exclusively to the best interests of the minors and ignore those of the settlor or any other person. They are not, however, necessarily precluded from exercising the power by, for instance, paying children's school fees, where to do so would confer an incidental (and unintended) benefit on their father, who is bound by a consent order in divorce proceedings to pay such fees; but they can only properly do so if they honestly consider that, despite these consequences, it would be in the best interests of the minors.[52] Nor, it is thought, should they be forgetful of the principles which the court would apply in granting

---

[49] [1936] Ch 161, [1935] All ER Rep 179.
[50] Including *Meacher v Young* (1834) 2 My & K 490; *Thompson v Griffin* (1841) Cr & Ph 317.
[51] Per Jessel MR in *Wilson v Turner* (1883) 22 Ch D 521 at 515, CA.
[52] *Fuller v Evans* [2000] 1 All ER 636; *Re Lofthouse* (1885) 29 Ch D 921, CA. Applied to a statutory trust— *Re Sayers and Philip* (1974) 38 DLR (3d) 602.

maintenance.[53] In general the court will not interfere with or overrule the bona fide exercise by trustees of their discretion.[54] Where, however, trustees fail to exercise their discretion one way or the other, the court may make an appropriate order. Thus, on the one hand, past maintenance has been allowed where the trustees were apparently unaware of their discretionary power,[55] and, on the other hand, a father has been compelled to repay the whole of the income paid to him by the trustees without their exercising any discretion at all;[56] and where trustees had failed to exercise any discretion as to which of two funds the allowance for maintenance should be paid out of, the court exercised it by directing that it should be paid primarily out of that fund from which it was most for the minor's benefit that it should be taken.[57]

It may be added that it has been held that a provision in an express maintenance clause that no income is to be applied while the minor is in the custody or control of the father, or while the father has anything to do with the education or bringing up of the child, is valid.[58]

(b) STATUTORY POWER

(i) The present law

The current provision is contained in s 31 of the Trustee Act 1925 as amended in relation to instruments made on or after 1 January 1970, by the Family Law Reform Act 1969, which reduced the age of majority to 18.[59] Terms in the section such as 'infant', 'infancy' and 'minority' are to be construed accordingly. As thus amended, s 31(1), the language of which, it has been said, 'is by no means easy to follow',[60] provides as follows:

Where any property is held by trustees in trust[61] for any person for any interest whatsoever, whether vested or contingent, then, subject to any prior interests or charges affecting that property—

(i) during the infancy of any such person,[62] if his interest so long continues, the trustees may, at their sole discretion, pay to his parent or guardian, if any, or otherwise apply for or towards his maintenance, education, or benefit,[63] the whole or such part, if

---

[53] See p 478, infra.   [54] See p 498, infra.   [55] *Stopford v Lord Canterbury* (1840) 11 Sim 82.

[56] *Wilson v Turner*, supra.   [57] *Re Wells* (1889) 43 Ch D 281.

[58] *Re Borwick's Settlement* [1916] 2 Ch 304.

[59] The 1969 Act does not apply to interests under a pre-1970 settlement, but does apply to an appointment thereunder incorporating s 31 made after 1969: *Begg-MacBrearty v Stilwell* [1996] 4 All ER 205, [1996] 1 WLR 951.

[60] Per Evershed MR in *Re Vestey's Settlement* [1951] Ch 209 at 216, [1950] 2 All ER 891 at 897, CA. See, generally (1953) 17 Conv 273 (B S Ker).

[61] This does not include a sum of income allocated to a minor as being the object of a discretionary trust—*Re Vestey's Settlement*, supra.

[62] In a class gift to persons contingently on attaining the age of 21, it does not matter that one or more members of the class have attained that age—*Re Holford* [1894] 3 Ch 30, CA.

[63] The same words in s 53 of the Trustee Act 1925 were said to be of the widest import in *Re Heyworth's Contingent Reversionary Interest* [1956] Ch 364 at 370, [1956] 2 All ER 21 at 23.

any, of the income of that property as may, in all the circumstances, be reasonable, whether or not there is—

(a) any other fund applicable to the same purpose; or

(b) any person bound by law to provide for his maintenance or education, and

(ii)   if such person on attaining the age of eighteen years has not a vested[64] interest in such income, the trustees shall thenceforth pay the income of that property and of any accretion thereto under subsection (2) of this section to him, until he either attains a vested interest therein or dies, or until failure of his interest . . .

The principal function of s 31, it has been said,[65] 'appears to be to supply a code of rules governing the disposal of income, especially during a minority, in cases where a settlor or testator has made dispositions of capital and either (a) being an unskilled draftsman, has not thought about income, or, (b) being a skilled draftsman, has been content to let the statutory code apply'.

A settlor may adopt the section with variations,[66] or exclude it by a contrary intention,[67] express or implied, which may be shown even by a direction for accumulation,[68] notwithstanding that the direction itself is void.[69] The provisions of s 31 are inapplicable if on a fair reading of the relevant instrument one can say that their application would be inconsistent with the purport of the instrument.[70] Obviously, as the subsection makes clear, the power of maintenance cannot affect prior interests and charges, and by sub-s 3 it only applies in the case of a contingent interest if the limitation or trust carries the intermediate income of the property, expressly including a future or contingent legacy by the parent of, or a person standing in loco parentis to, the legatee, if and for such period as, under the general law, the legacy carries interest[71] for the maintenance of the legatee.[72]

In many cases, quite irrespective of the relationship between the testator and the devisee or legatee, a testamentary disposition will carry the intermediate income (unless otherwise disposed of)[73] under s 175 of the Law of Property Act 1925, which provides that this shall be so[74] in the case of a contingent or future specific devise or

---

64 This provision does not apply if such person has a vested interest, even if it is liable to be divested—*Re McGeorge* [1963] Ch 544, [1963] 1 All ER 519.

65 *Re Delamere's Settlement Trusts* [1984] 1 All ER 584 at 587, CA, per Slade LJ.

66 Eg by substituting 'they may in their absolute discretion think fit' for 'may, in all the circumstances, be reasonable' and deleting the proviso at the end of sub-s (1).

67 Trustee Act 1925, s 69(2) as explained in *IRC v Bernstein* [1961] Ch 399, [1961] 1 All ER 320, CA; *Re Evans' Settlement* [1967] 3 All ER 343 (both actually decisions on s 32 Trustee Act 1925); *Re McGeorge*, supra.

68 *Re Ransome's Will Trusts* [1957] Ch 348, [1957] 1 All ER 690; *IRC v Bernstein*, supra.

69 *Re Ransome's Will Trusts*, supra. See [1979] 43 Conv 423 (J G Riddall).

70 *IRC v Bernstein*, supra, at 412, 325, CA, per Lord Evershed MR; *Re Delamere's Settlement Trusts*, supra, CA.

71 At 5 per cent, provided the income available is sufficient—Trustee Act 1925, s 31(3).

72 It is thought that s 31(3) embraces also cases (ii) and (iii) on p 475, infra, and that the specific mention of case (i) is only for the purpose of establishing a suitable rate of interest: see Ker in (1953) 17 Conv 273 at 279.

73 See *Re Reade-Revell* [1930] 1 Ch 52; *Re Stapleton* [1946] 1 All ER 323.

74 Subject to the provisions relating to accumulations in ss 164–166 of the Law of Property Act 1925 and s 13 of the Perpetuities and Accumulations Act 1964.

bequest of property, whether real or personal; a contingent residuary devise of free-hold land, and a specific or residuary devise of freehold land to trustees upon trust for persons whose interests are contingent or executory. Further, apart from the section, a contingent gift of residuary personalty carries the intermediate income,[75] but prob-ably not a residuary bequest, whether vested or contingent, expressly deferred to a future date which must come sooner or later.[76]

A future or contingent pecuniary legacy is not within s 175, and prima facie does not carry the intermediate income. Exceptionally, however, the court presumes an intention that it does carry the intermediate income in three cases,[77] namely,

(i) where the legacy is given by a testator to his minor child, or to a minor to whom he stands in loco parentis,[78] no other fund being provided for his maintenance.[79] This exception applies to a contingent legacy,[80] but only where the contingency is the attainment of full age by the minor legatee or previous marriage,[81]

(ii) where the will indicates, expressly or by implication, an intention that the income should be used for the maintenance of a minor legatee, not necessarily standing in any special relationship to the testator. It does not matter in this case that the legacy is contingent on some event other than the attainment of majority, or previous marriage.[82] The exception has been held to apply where trustees have been given a discretionary power to apply the whole or any part of the share to which the legatee might be entitled in or towards his advance-ment in life or otherwise for his benefit,[83] or, in another case, for the purpose of his education,[84]

(iii) where a legacy is, expressly or by implication, directed to be set aside so as to be available for the legatee so soon as the contingency happens.[85]

The trustees, in deciding whether to exercise their statutory power, and, if so, to what extent, are directed[86] to have regard to the age of the minor and his requirements and generally to the circumstances of the case, and in particular to what other income, if any, is applicable for the same purposes; and where they have notice that the income of more than one fund is applicable, then, so far as practicable, unless the entire income of the funds is used or the court otherwise directs, a proportionate part only

---

[75] *Countess of Bective v Hodgson* (1864) 10 HL Cas 656; *Re Taylor* [1901] 2 Ch 134.

[76] *Re Geering* [1964] Ch 136, [1962] 3 All ER 1043; *Re McGeorge* [1963] Ch 544, [1963] 1 All ER 519; *Re Nash* [1965] 1 All ER 51; and see (1963) 79 LQR 184 (PVB).

[77] *Re Raine* [1929] 1 Ch 716.

[78] Only the father comes within the exception qua parent; if the mother is to come within it, it must be shown she was in loco parentis—*Re Eyre* [1917] 1 Ch 351.

[79] *Re Moody* [1895] 1 Ch 101; *Re George* (1877) 5 Ch D 837, CA.

[80] *Re Bowlby* [1904] 2 Ch 685, CA.   [81] *Re Abrahams* [1911] 1 Ch 108.

[82] *Re Jones* [1932] 1 Ch 642.   [83] *Re Churchill* [1909] 2 Ch 431. Cf *Re Stokes* [1928] Ch 716.

[84] *Re Selby-Walker* [1949] 2 All ER 178.

[85] *Re Medlock* (1886) 54 LT 828; *Re Clements* [1894] 1 Ch 665; *Re Woodin* [1895] 2 Ch 309, CA.

[86] Trustee Act 1925, s 31(1) proviso.

of the income of each fund should be applied. The principle stated in *Fuller v Evans*,[87] discussed in relation to express powers, applies equally to the statutory powers.

It has been held[88] that s 31 does not exclude the operation of the Apportionment Act 1870. This may produce a somewhat anomalous result where income is received after a beneficiary has attained the age of eighteen. In so far as such income is apportioned in respect of the period before he was eighteen, the income cannot be applied for maintenance, because the trustees cannot exercise their discretion in advance so as to affect the income when it is received, and they cannot apply it in arrear, because the infancy will have ceased.

(ii) Destination of any balance of the income not applied under sub-s (1)

Subsection (2), as amended by the Trustee Act 2000, provides that any such balance shall be accumulated during the minority (or until his interest previously determines), though during this period the accumulations, or any part thereof, may be applied as if they were income arising in the current year. Subsection (2) further provides for the destination of the accumulations as follows:

    (i)   If any such person—
        (a) attains the age of eighteen years, or marries under that age, and his interest in such income during his infancy or until his marriage is a vested interest; or
        (b) on attaining the age of eighteen years or on marriage under that age becomes entitled to the property from which such income arose in fee simple, absolute or determinable, or absolutely, or for an entailed interest;
        the trustees shall hold the accumulations in trust for such person absolutely, but without prejudice to any provision with respect thereto contained in any settlement by him made under any statutory powers during his infancy, and so that the receipt of such person after marriage, and though still an infant, shall be a good discharge; and
    (ii)   In any other case the trustees shall, notwithstanding that such person had a vested interest in such income, hold the accumulations as an accretion to the capital of the property from which such accumulations arose, and as one fund with such capital for all purposes, and so that, if such property is settled land, such accumulations shall be held upon the same trusts as if the same were capital money arising therefrom.

When the Civil Partnership Act 2004 is brought into force, sub-s (2) will be amended so that references to marriage will include the formation of a civil partnership. In *Re Sharp's Settlement Trusts*[89] it was accepted that in (i)(b) the words 'in fee simple, absolute or determinable' apply exclusively to realty; that the word 'absolutely' applies exclusively to personalty; and that the words 'for an entailed interest' apply alike to

---

[87] [2000] 1 All ER 636. See p 472, supra.

[88] *Re Joel's Will Trusts* [1967] Ch 14, [1966] 2 All ER 482. The Law Reform Committee, 23rd Report, Cmnd 8733, para 3.41 recommends a change in the law.

[89] [1973] Ch 331, [1972] 3 All ER 151.

realty and personality. It was further held that a person cannot be said to be entitled 'absolutely' if his interest is liable to be divested, for instance by the exercise of a power of appointment. As Pennycuick VC pointed out in that case the words of the subsection produce the anomalous result that a person having a determinable interest in realty qualifies to take accumulations at 18 while a person having the like interest in personalty would not because his interest is not absolute.

The effect of para (ii), where it applies, is to engraft upon the vested interest originally conferred on the minor a qualifying trust of a special nature which confers on the minor a title to the accumulations if, and only if, he attains the age of majority or marries (or, prospectively, forms a civil partnership). If he dies before attaining 18 or marrying (or, prospectively, entering into a civil partnership) his interest, even though vested, is defeated and the accumulations rejoin the general capital of the trust property from which they arose. The 'capital of the property from which such accumulations arose' is the share which the infant ultimately obtains. Accordingly, in a gift to a class of or including minors the accumulations of income allocated to a minor but not used for his maintenance under sub-s (1) continue to be held on trust for him, even though his share in the capital may subsequently be reduced by an increase in the size of the class. If the minor dies before attaining a vested interest, his share accrues to the other shares and carries the accumulations with it, becoming a part of the common fund of capital.[90]

It should be added that although the section applies to a vested annuity as if the annuity were the income of property held by trustees in trust to pay the income thereof to the annuitant for the same period for which the annuity is payable, sub-s (4), in contrast to sub-s 2(ii), provides that accumulations made during the minority of the annuitant must be held in trust for the annuitant or his personal representative absolutely.

(iii) Interests arising under instruments made before 1 January 1970

Such interests are unaffected by the Family Law Reform Act 1969, which has to be read in its original form, that is, 21 instead of 18 in sub-s 1(ii) and 2(i)(*a*) and (*b*), and references to 'infant', 'infancy' and 'minority' being construed in relation to an age of majority of 21.[91]

(c) POWER OF THE COURT

Although it will now seldom be necessary to invoke it, the court has an inherent jurisdiction to allow maintenance out of a minor's property. As Lord Redesdale explained in *Wellesley v Wellesley*[92] the court has an unquestionable jurisdiction 'with

---

[90] *Re Joel's Will Trusts*, supra; *Re Sharp's Settlement Trusts*, supra. The Law Reform Committee, 23rd Report, Cmnd 8733, para 3.41, recommends a change in the law.

[91] Note the qualification in s 1(4) and Sch 3, para 5. Note also s 1(4), (7) and Sch 3, para 1.

[92] (1828) 2 Bli NS 124 at 133, 134, HL.

respect to the income of the property, to take care of it for the benefit of the children, to apply it for the benefit of the children, as far as it may be beneficial for them that it should be so applied, and to accumulate any surplus, if any surplus there should be'. Although income will primarily be used, in exceptional circumstances the court will even resort to capital for maintenance.[93]

The court has normally applied the rule 'that however large a child's fortune may be, whilst the father is of ability to maintain the child, he must perform his duty, and no part of the child's fortune is to be applied for that purpose'.[94] The rule, however, is not strictly applied, and the surrounding circumstances, such as the means of the father, the size of the minor's fortune, and even the effect on other members of the family, have been taken into account.[95]

As has been mentioned, where trustees have been given a power of maintenance, the court will not normally interfere with its exercise, and even where they have not been given any such power, if they in fact use income[96]—or even capital[97]—for maintenance, the court will, in a proper case, allow the payment in the accounts.

8 POWER OF ADVANCEMENT[98]

(a) EXPRESS POWERS

Before 1926 an express power of advancement was frequently conferred on trustees under settlements of personalty, though since 1925 reliance is commonly placed on the statutory power hereafter discussed. In *Pilkington v IRC*,[99] Viscount Radcliffe explained that the general purpose and effect of such a power was to enable trustees:

in a proper case to anticipate the vesting in possession of an intended beneficiary's contingent or reversionary interest by raising money on account of his interest and paying or applying it immediately for his benefit. By so doing they released it from the trusts of the settlement and accelerated the enjoyment of his interest (though normally only with the consent of a prior tenant for life); and where the contingency upon which the vesting of the beneficiary's title depended failed to mature or there was a later defeasance or, in some

---

[93] *Ex p Green* (1820) 1 Jac & W 253; *Ex p Chambers* (1829) 1 Russ & M 577; *Robison v Killey* (1862) 30 Beav 520 at 521.

[94] Per Langdale MR in *Douglas v Andrews* (1849) 12 Beav 310 at 311.

[95] See *Hoste v Pratt* (1798) 3 Ves 730; *Jervoise v Silk* (1813) Coop G 52. As to means of the mother see *Haley v Bannister* (1820) 4 Madd 275; *Douglas v Andrews*, supra, and pp 181, 182, supra.

[96] *Brown v Smith* (1878) 10 Ch D 377, CA. As to charging past maintenance on corpus see *Re Hambrough's Estate* [1909] 2 Ch 620; *Re Badger* [1913] 1 Ch 385, CA.

[97] *Prince v Hine* (1859) 25 Beav 634; *Worthington v M'Craer* (1856) 23 Beav 81.

[98] See, generally, (1958) 22 Conv 413 (D W M Waters). Powers of advancement are not affected by s 96(3) of the Mental Health Act 1983—*Re C W H T* [1978] Ch 67, [1978] 1 All ER 210.

[99] [1964] AC 612 at 633, [1962] 3 All ER 622 at 627, HL.

cases, a great shrinkage in the value of the remaining trust funds, the trusts as declared by the settlement were materially varied through the operation of the power of advancement.

The exact scope of a power of advancement, of course, depends upon the words of the particular clause under consideration. 'Advancement' is itself a word appropriate to an early period of life'[100] and means the establishment in life of the beneficiary who was the object of the power or at any rate some step that would contribute to the furtherance of his establishment. To avoid uncertainties, other words were commonly inserted, such as a phrase as 'or otherwise for his benefit' being of the widest import.[101] Viscount Radcliffe has explained[102] the combined phrases 'advancement and benefit' as meaning 'any use of the money which will improve the material situation of the beneficiary', and it has been held to authorize, for instance, a payment for the purpose of discharging the beneficiary's debts,[103] a payment made to the beneficiary's husband, on his personal security, for the purpose of setting him up in trade,[104] payments for the maintenance and education of a beneficiary,[105] and, of particular importance in modern conditions, an advancement made in order to avoid tax, although the beneficiary may not require it at the time it is made for any special purpose.[106]

However wide the power, the trustees must, of course, be satisfied that the proposed exercise will benefit the beneficiary.[107] The courts, however, do not take too narrow a view of what represents a benefit. At any rate in the case of a wealthy beneficiary who regards himself as being under a moral obligation to make charitable donations, it may be for his benefit for the trustees to raise capital and pay it over to a charity in order to relieve him of his moral obligation. The trustees cannot, however, do this against the beneficiary's will, for it is of the essence of the matter that the beneficiary himself should recognize the moral obligation.[108] It has also been held to be proper, under a power to apply the capital of a fund for the benefit of a beneficiary, to re-settle it on the beneficiary's children, including unborn children, with a view to avoiding tax, in a case where the beneficiary himself was already well provided for.[109]

Four final points may be added. First, if the power is given only during minority, and the beneficiary has attained 18,[110] or for a limited purpose which can no longer be effected,[111] the power ceases to be exercisable, and the trustees will, of course, be

---

[100] *Re Kershaw's Trusts* (1868) LR 6 Eq 322.

[101] *Re Halstead's Will Trusts* [1937] 2 All ER 570; *Pilkington v IRC*, supra, HL, at 633, 627, but see *Re Pinto's Settlement* [2004] WTLR 879 (Jersey Royal Court).

[102] In *Pilkington v IRC*, supra, HL at 628, 635, HL.   [103] *Lowther v Bentinck*, (1874) LR 19 Eq 166.

[104] *Re Kershaw's Trusts* (1868) LR 6 Eq 322.

[105] *Re Breed's Will* (1875) 1 Ch D 226; *Re Garrett* [1934] Ch 477, [1934] All ER Rep 129.

[106] *Pilkington v IRC*, supra, HL (on the statutory power).

[107] *Re Moxon's Will Trusts* [1958] 1 All ER 386 (on the statutory power); *Re Pauling's Settlement Trusts* [1964] Ch 303, [1963] 3 All ER 1, CA. Cf *Molyneux v Fletcher* [1898] 1 QB 648.

[108] *Re Clore's Settlement Trusts* [1966] 2 All ER 272.

[109] *Re Earl of Buckinghamshire's Settlement Trusts* (1977) *Times*, 29 March.

[110] *Clarke v Hogg* (1871) 19 WR 617; Family Law Reform Act 1969, s 1.

[111] *Re Ward's Trusts* (1872) 7 Ch App 727.

personally liable to refund if they exercise the power improperly.[112] Secondly, where a beneficiary has an interest which will determine if he does any act whereby if the income were payable to him he would be deprived of the right to receive the same it will not normally be forfeited if that beneficiary consents to the exercise of a power of advancement—whether express or statutory.[113] This is expressly provided for in the statutory protective trusts under s 33 of the Trustee Act 1925. Thirdly, on basic equitable principles the exercise of the power must be bona fide, and, accordingly, it was held to be a breach of trust in *Molyneux v Fletcher*[114] where trustees advanced money to a beneficiary on the understanding that the money advanced would be used to repay a debt owed to one of the trustees by the beneficiary's husband. Fourthly, where a power of advancement is exercised for a particular purpose specified by the trustees, the advancee is under a duty to carry out that purpose and the trustees are under a duty to see that he does so, and are under a duty not to leave the advancee free to spend the advance in any way he chooses.[115]

(b) THE STATUTORY POWER CONTAINED IN S 32 OF THE TRUSTEE ACT 1925

Subsection (1) provides as follows:

Trustees may at any time or times pay or apply any capital money subject to a trust, for the advancement or benefit, in such manner as they may, in their absolute discretion, think fit, of any person entitled to the capital of the trust property or of any share thereof, whether absolutely or contingently on his attaining any specified age or on the occurrence of any other event, or subject to a gift over on his death under any specified age or on the occurrence of any other event, and whether in possession or in remainder or reversion, and such payment or application may be made notwithstanding that the interest of such person is liable to be defeated by the exercise of a power of appointment or revocation, or to be diminished by the increase of the class to which he belongs.

It adopts without qualification the accustomed wording 'for the advancement or benefit, in such manner as they may, in their absolute discretion, think fit' which, as we have seen in connection with express powers, is of the widest import. It applies to contingent interests even where there is a double contingency such as surviving the life interest and attaining a specified age.[116] Like s 31, a settlor may incorporate this section with variations,[117] or exclude it altogether by a contrary intention, express or

---

[112] *Simpson v Brown* (1864) 11 LT 593.   [113] *Re Rees' Will Trusts* [1954] Ch 202, [1954] 1 All ER 7.

[114] [1898] 1 QB 648.   [115] *Re Pauling's Settlement Trusts*, supra, CA, at 334.

[116] *Re Garrett* [1934] Ch 477, [1934] All ER Rep 129.

[117] Eg by altering or omitting proviso (a), infra. See *Henley v Wardell* (1988) *Times*, 29 January, where the extension of the power was held, as a question of construction, not to exclude s 32(1)(c), discussed infra, p 482. In accumulation and maintenance settlements the section is often restricted to ensure that the exercise or possibility of its exercise cannot infringe the conditions in s 71 of the Inheritance Tax Act 1984—see *Inglewood v IRC* [1983] 1 WLR 366, CA.

implied.[118] In exceptional circumstances the Jersey Court of Appeal has held that a trustee may exercise a power of advancement in favour of a beneficiary against his express wishes. The principle underlying the rule that no one can be forced to accept a gift was said not to preclude an indirect benefit being conferred against the objection of a donee of the power of advancement.[119]

One question is whether trustees can exercise the statutory power by transferring the sum advanced to new trustees to be held upon new trusts containing powers and discretions not contemplated in the original trust instrument. Trustees have often wished to do this in cases where the beneficiary being advanced had no immediate need of the money, and the creation of the new trusts was designed primarily to avoid tax.[120] In *Pilkington v IRC*[121] the House of Lords, reversing the decision of the Court of Appeal, held that it is within the scope of s 32 to exercise the power of advancement by way of re-settlement, and, further, that it can make no difference whether the trustees require re-settlement as a condition of advancement, or themselves appoint new trusts. It is irrelevant whether they actually raise money or merely appropriate certain investments to the new trusts, and it is also irrelevant whether or not the trustees of the new trusts are the same persons as the trustees of the original trust. It is not clear whether, in any absence of specific powers in the original settlement, the re-settlement can validly include discretionary trusts for this would involve the delegation of dispositive, not merely administrative or ministerial, discretions, in contravention of the principle 'delegatus non potest delegare'.[122]

When a re-settlement is made under a power which came into existence before the coming into force of the Perpetuities and Accumulations Act 1964 on 16 July 1964, one must bear in mind the operation of the rule against perpetuities, particularly where the trustees have to appoint new trusts themselves because the beneficiary being advanced is a minor and therefore incapable of making a settlement. In such case as regards the rule against perpetuities there is an effective analogy between powers of advancement and special powers of appointment, and failure to realize this meant, in *Re Abraham's Will Trusts*,[123] that many of the declared trusts were void for perpetuity, so that the character of the settlement was wholly altered. It followed that the trustees had never addressed their minds to the question whether the settlement, as modified by the rule against perpetuities, was 'for the advancement or benefit' of

---

[118] Trustee Act 1925, s 69(2); *Re Rees' Will Trusts* [1954] Ch 202, [1954] 1 All ER 7; *IRC v Bernstein* [1961] Ch 399, [1961] 1 All ER 320, CA; *Re Evans' Settlement* [1967] 3 All ER 343, [1967] 1 WLR 1294.

[119] *Re Esteem Settlement* [2002] WTLR 337 (on the facts a distribution to a beneficiary's creditor in reduction of his debt would not be a payment for the benefit of the beneficiary), discussed (2002) 34 T & ELJ 34 (Gillian Robinson).

[120] See *Swires v Renton* [1991] STC 490.

[121] [1964] AC 612, [1962] 3 All ER 622, HL. See (1981) 9 NZULR 247 (J Prebble).

[122] *Re Morris' Settlement Trusts* [1951] 2 All ER 528; *Re Hunter's Will Trusts* [1963] Ch 372, [1962] 3 All ER 1050; *Re Hay's Settlement Trusts* [1981] 3 All ER 786, and see (1963) 27 Conv 65 (F R Crane); [1994] PCB 317, 402 (R Oerton).

[123] [1969] 1 Ch 463, [1967] 2 All ER 1175. See also *Pilkington v IRC* per Upjohn LJ in CA [1961] Ch at 488, 489, [1961] 2 All ER at 340, 341; and per Lord Radcliffe in HL at [1964] AC 641, 642, [1962] 3 All ER at 631, 632.

the beneficiary, as required by s 32. There had accordingly never been a valid exercise by the trustees of the power of advancement and the purported settlement by the trustees was ineffective.

Even in *Re Abrahams' Will Trusts*[124] it was recognized that this drastic result would not necessarily follow where the rule against perpetuities operated to invalidate only a comparatively small part of the settlement and the Court of Appeal in *Re Hastings-Bass*[125] declared the principle of *Re Abrahams' Will Trusts*[126] to be limited to cases where the effect of the perpetuity rule had been to alter the intended consequences of an advancement so drastically that the trustees could not reasonably be supposed to have addressed their minds to the question relevant to the true effect of the transaction. On this basis the advancement in *Re Hastings-Bass* was good, notwithstanding the failure for perpetuity of the ulterior trusts in the sub-settlement. The primary duty-saving aspect of the scheme, giving a clear benefit to the beneficiary being advanced, was not prejudiced thereby, and the indirect or contingent benefits that the beneficiary might have obtained under the ulterior trusts were mere make-weights.

Where the power of advancement came into existence after 15 July 1964, the effect of the Perpetuities and Accumulations Act 1964 is that it is most unlikely that the exercise of the power of advancement will be invalid, for the interests under the re-settlement will be valid unless and until it becomes established that the interests thereunder must vest, if at all, after the end of the perpetuity period.

By the proviso to sub-s (1) the statutory power is subject to certain important restrictions, namely:

(*a*) the money so paid or applied for the advancement or benefit of any person shall not exceed altogether in amount one-half of the presumptive or vested share or interest of that person in the trust property;[127] and

(*b*) if that person is or becomes absolutely and indefeasibly entitled to a share in the trust property the money so paid or applied shall be brought into account as part of such share;[128] and

(*c*) no such payment or application shall be made so as to prejudice any person entitled to any prior life or other interest, whether vested or contingent, in the money paid or applied unless such person is in existence and of full age and consents in writing to such payment or application.

Under proviso (*c*) it has been held that the objects of a discretionary trust are not persons whose consent to the exercise of the power is required, even where these

---

[124] Supra.   [125] [1975] Ch 25, [1974] 2 All ER 193 and see p 498, infra.   [126] Supra.

[127] The court may remove the limit on an application under the Variation of Trusts Act 1958: *D (a child) v O* [2004] EWHC 1036 (Ch), [2004] 3 All ER 280.

[128] The rule that advancements are brought into account on a cash basis may result in injustice in times of inflation: *Re Marquis of Abergavenny's Estate Act Trusts* [1981] 2 All ER 643, [1981] 1 WLR 843. The Law Reform Committee, 23rd Report, Cmnd 8733, paras 4.43–4.47 recomends that they should be brought into account on an index-linked or fractional basis.

discretionary trusts have come into operation.[129] But if there is a person whose consent is required, the court has not got power to dispense with it.[130]

Section 32 does not apply to capital money arising under the Settled Land Act 1925.[131]

(c) POWER OF THE COURT

The court may, in exceptional circumstances, apply capital for the maintenance or advancement of an infant,[132] or allow such payment made by the trustee without any express power to do so,[133] and may also exercise its statutory jurisdiction for this purpose under s 53 of the Trustee Act 1925,[134] or under the Variation of Trusts Act 1958.[135]

9 RIGHT TO REIMBURSEMENT FOR COSTS AND EXPENSES

(a) REIMBURSEMENT OUT OF THE TRUST ESTATE[136]

Trustees are personally liable on any contracts they enter into in relation to the trust: creditors have no direct action against either the trust estate or the beneficiaries. However, s 31(1) of the Trustee Act 2000,[137] provides—

A trustee—
(a) is entitled to be reimbursed from the trust funds,[138] or
(b) may pay out of the trust funds,
expenses properly incurred by him when acting on behalf of the trust.

The section applies equally to a trustee who has been duly authorized to exercise functions as an agent of the trustees, or to act as a nominee or custodian.[139]

---

[129] *Re Harris' Settlement* (1940) 162 LT 358; *Re Beckett's Settlement* [1940] Ch 279.

[130] *Re Forster's Settlement* [1942] 1 All ER 180, Quaere, if an application were made under Trustee Act 1925, s 57.

[131] Section 32(2) as substituted by the Trusts of Land and Appointment of Trustees Act 1996, Sch 3, para 8.

[132] Eg to pay the expenses of emigration—*Re Mary England's Estate* (1830) 1 Russ & M 499; *Clay v Pennington* (1837) 8 Sim 359.

[133] *Worthington v M'Craer* (1856) 23 Beav 81.

[134] Discussed in chapter 23, section 2(a), p 505, infra.

[135] Discussed in chapter 23, section 3, infra.

[136] In relation to charity trustees see (1979) 95 LQR 99 (A J Hawkins).

[137] Replacing legislation going back to the Law of Property Amendment Act 1859, s 31 (Lord St Leonard's Act). See (1996) 10 Tru LI 45 (R Ham).

[138] 'Trust funds' means income or capital funds of the trust: Trustee Act 2000, s 39(1).

[139] Ibid, s 31(2).

The right of reimbursement has been held to include, inter alia, calls on shares which the trustee has been obliged to pay,[140] and damages and costs awarded to a third party in an action against the trustee as legal owner of the trust property.[141]

Where trustees duly authorized by will carry on a business[142] they are personally liable on the contracts into which they enter.[143] They are, however, entitled to an indemnity[144] which, though good as against the beneficiaries, will not prevail against the testator's creditors at the date of death, unless they have assented to the business being carried on, and such assent will not be inferred from their merely standing by with knowledge that the business was being carried on and abstaining from interfering.[145] Agents, such as solicitors, employed by the trustees, even though described as solicitors to the trust, are in law retained by the trustees and therefore have no direct claim against the trust estate. The trustees will, of course, be entitled to an indemnity in respect of the agent's proper fees.

Trustees may, if they wish, pay claims which are statute-barred, and will be entitled to the usual indemnity in respect thereof, notwithstanding that the beneficiaries do not wish the claim to be paid.[146]

As between the beneficiaries, the trustees' costs and expenses are normally payable out of capital,[147] but so far as the trustees are concerned their right to 'indemnity against all costs and expenses properly incurred by them in the execution of the trust is a first charge on all the trust property, both income and corpus'.[148] This indemnity, which thus gives the trustees a lien on the trust property, takes priority to the claims both of beneficiaries and third parties,[149] and is unaffected by the fact that a beneficiary has assigned his equitable interest to a stranger.[150] The lien extends to all

---

[140] *Re National Financial Co* (1868) 3 Ch App 791; *James v May* (1873) LR 6 HL 328.

[141] *Benett v Wyndham* (1862) 4 De GF & J 259; *Re Raybould* [1900] 1 Ch 199.

[142] Under a will, the personal representatives are impliedly authorized to carry on the business for the purpose of winding it up so soon as reasonably possible. In general, the rules apply equally whether the trust is created inter vivos or by will, though most of the cases are on wills—*Re Johnson* (1880) 15 Ch D 548.

[143] *Farhall v Farhall* (1871) 7 Ch App 123; *Re Morgan* (1881) 18 Ch D 93, CA, esp per Fry J at first instance at 99. As to the possibility of contracting in terms which avoid personal liability see *Re Robinson's Settlement* [1912] 1 Ch 717, CA; *Hunt Bros v Colwell* [1939] 4 All ER 406, CA. See (1987) 2 TL & P 51 (D Goddard). In Australia it has been held that a trustee's right to indemnity out of the trust assets for personal liabilities incurred in the performance of the trust constitutes a beneficial interest in the trust assets: *Chief Comr of Stamp Duties v Buckle* (1995) 38 NSWLR 574.

[144] *Re Evans* (1887) 34 Ch D 597, CA; *Dowse v Gorton* [1891] Ac 190, HL; *Re Oxley* [1914] 1 Ch 604, CA. If they are only authorized to use certain assets in the business, their indemnity will be against these assets only. *Re Johnson*, supra. Cf *Strickland v Symons* (1884) 26 Ch D 245, CA.

[145] *Dowse v Gorton*, supra; *Re Oxley*, supra.

[146] *Budgett v Budgett* [1895] 1 Ch 202; contrast the position of executors—*Re Wenham* [1892] 3 Ch 59.

[147] *Carter v Sebright* (1859) 26 Beav 374 (costs of appointment of new trustees).

[148] Per Selborne LC in *Stott v Milne* (1884) 25 Ch D 710 at 715, CA; *Re Exhall Coal Co* (1866) 35 Beav 449. Except where trustees pay off an interest-bearing debt of the estate, the court has no jurisdiction to award interest on expenses: *Foster v Spencer* [1996] 2 All ER 672.

[149] *Re Knapman* (1881) 18 Ch D 300, CA; *Dodds v Tuke* (1884) 25 Ch D 617; *Re Turner* [1907] 2 Ch 126, CA.

[150] *Re Knapman*, supra.

liabilities of the trustee as such, and in *X v A*[151] was held to include liabilities under Part IIA of the Environmental Protection Act 1990 even though they were contingent upon a number of matters, including the commencement of Part IIA. Trustees who have such a lien may at any time apply to the court to enforce it; they are not bound to wait until the trust property happens to be turned into money.[152] Exceptionally, however, the court may refuse to enforce the lien, where to do so would destroy the trusts altogether, though in such a case the court has held the trustees entitled to the possession of the title deeds, and prohibited any disposition of the trust property without discharging the trustees' lien.[153] In any case where the trustees have committed a breach of trust, they can only claim their indemnity after they have first made good to the trust estate the loss caused by the breach of trust.[154] As we shall see,[155] where the trustee mixes his own moneys and trust moneys, the trust has a first and paramount charge over the mixed fund, and, similarly, where a trustee expends his own money in the purchase or improvement of trust property, the claim of the trustee for indemnity is subject to the prior claim of the beneficiaries under the trust.[156]

In some cases the above principles have been extended so as to give the trustee an indemnity and a lien on the trust property where the trustee has expended his own money in the preservation of the trust property, as by paying the premiums on an insurance policy.[157] The court in one case even allowed a partial indemnity where the trustee, under the impression that he would be repaid out of the estate, had bona fide used his own moneys together with trust moneys in rebuilding the mansion house, although this was a breach of trust which the court considered it would have had no jurisdiction to authorize had it been asked to do so.[158] The indemnity was, however, limited to the amount which happened to be in court,[159] this being about half the sum advanced and clearly less than the amount by which the estate had benefited. Again, in *Rowley v Ginnever*,[160] a constructive trustee of property, who expended money in improving what he bona fide believed to be his own property, was held to be entitled to be recouped his expenditure to the extent of the improved value.

Creditors, or victims of tort, have no direct action against either the trust estate or the beneficiaries. However they may be entitled to be subrogated to the rights of the trustees against the estate,[161] though they cannot be in a better position than the trustees, and if, for instance, the trustees have committed a breach of trust, this must first be made good. Each trustee has a separate right of indemnity, which will not

---

[151] [2000] 1 All ER 490. [152] *Re Pumfrey* (1882) 22 Ch D 255.

[153] *Darke v Williamson* (1858) 25 Beav 622.

[154] *McEwan v Crombie* (1883) 25 Ch D 175; cf *Re Knott* (1887) 56 LJ Ch 318.

[155] See chapter 25, section 2(b), p 557. [156] *Re Pumfrey* (1882) 22 Ch D 255.

[157] *Re Leslie* (1883) 23 Ch D 552; *Re Smith's Estate* [1937] Ch 636. See *Foskett v McKeown* [1998] Ch 265, [1997] 3 All ER 392, CA, revsd [2001] 1 AC 102, [2000] 3 All ER 97, HL.

[158] *Jesse v Lloyd* (1883) 48 LT 656. [159] A somewhat haphazard solution on no clear principle.

[160] [1897] 2 Ch 503.

[161] *Benett v Wyndham* (1862) 4 De GF & J 259; *Re Blundell* (1888) 40 Ch D 370; *Re Raybould* [1900] 1 Ch 199. See (1997) NLJ Easter App Supp 28 (Emma Ford); *Belar Pty Ltd (in liq) v Mahaffey* [2000] 1 Qd R 477.

necessarily be affected by the fact that another trustee has committed a breach of trust. Since a creditor may sue the trustee with a subsisting indemnity, it follows that he does not lose his right of subrogation by reason of the fact that one of two or more trustees is a defaulter.[162] Nevertheless the position is that the right of a third party against the trust fund is indirect and uncertain, and this may make him reluctant to enter into contractual relations with trustees. This may cause difficulty, particularly to large commercial trusts, such as pension funds. It may well be that an appropriate and effective power could be expressly given. However, because of doubts as to whether this is permissible the Law Reform Committee[163] proposes legislation to make it clear that a power to create a charge upon the trust fund as a continuing entity can be conferred upon trustees by the trust deed, enabling them to give the maximum possible security to third parties.

(b) PERSONAL LIABILITY OF CESTUI QUE TRUST TO INDEMNIFY TRUSTEES

The general principle, it has been said,[164] is that a trustee is entitled to an indemnity for liabilities properly incurred in carrying out the trust and that that right extends beyond the trust property and is enforceable in equity against a beneficiary who is sui juris. The basis of the principle is that the beneficiary who gets the benefit of the trust should bear its burdens unless he can show some good reason why his trustee should bear the burdens himself.

Hardoon v Belilios[165] has been thought to restrict the principle to the case where there is a sole beneficiary, but it has been applied by Australian courts[166] to cases where there were several beneficiaries. *Hardoon v Belilios*[167] was explained as being a case where there was only one beneficiary and the Privy Council chose not to state the principle more widely than necessary for the case before it.

Where the settlor is also a beneficiary, Jessel MR stated in *Jervis v Wolferstan*,[168] 'I take it to be a general rule that where persons accept a trust at the request of another, and that other is a cestui que trust, he is personally liable to indemnify the trustees for any loss accruing in the due execution of the trust.' In any case where a cestui que trust is personally liable to indemnify his trustee, his liability is not terminated by an assignment of his beneficial interest.[169]

---

[162] *Re Frith* [1902] 1 Ch 342.

[163] 23rd Report, Cmnd 8733, paras 2.17–2.24. As to whether a trustee's indemnity can be excluded to the prejudice of third parties, see *RWG Management Ltd v Corporate Affairs Comr* [1985] VR 385.

[164] *J W Broomhead (Vic) Pty Ltd v J W Broomhead Pty Ltd* [1985] VR 891 per McGarvie J at 936, 937; *Hurst v Bryk* [1999] Ch 1, [1997] 2 All ER 283, CA.

[165] [1901] AC 118, PC.

[166] McGarvie J in *J W Broomhead (Vic) Pty Ltd v J W Broomhead Pty Ltd*, supra; *Balkin v Peck* (1998) 43 NSWLR 706; *Ron Kingham Real Estate Pty Ltd v Edgar* [1999] 2 Qd R 439. See (1990) 64 ALJ 567 (R A Hughes).

[167] Supra, PC.   [168] (1874) LR 18 Eq 18 at 24; *Hobbs v Wayet* (1887) 36 Ch D 256.

[169] *Matthews v Ruggles-Brice* [1911] 1 Ch 194.

It may be added that, unless the rules provide to the contrary, members of a club are assumed not to be under any liability beyond their subscriptions, and are under no obligation to indemnify trustees of club property.[170]

(c) COSTS OF LEGAL PROCEEDINGS

The Civil Procedure Rules[171] provide that where a trustee is a party to any proceedings in that capacity he is entitled to the costs of those proceedings, in so far as they are not recovered from or paid by any other person, out of the trust funds, and the costs are assessed on the indemnity basis. It does not matter that in the proceedings he is incidentally defending himself against charges made against him personally in relation to his administration of the trust provided it is for the benefit of the trust.[172] As Ungoed-Thomas J explained in *Re Spurling's Will Trusts*,[173] 'if costs of successfully defending claims to make good to a trust fund for alleged breach of trust were excluded, it would drive a coach and four through the very raison d'etre which Sir George MR invoked[174] for the principle which he lays down; namely, the safety of trustees, and the need to encourage persons to act as such by protecting them "if they have done their duty or even if they have committed an innocent breach of trust".' To this last proposition *Re Dargie*,[175] which unfortunately does not appear to have been cited to the court in *Re Spurling's Will Trusts*,[176] suggests one qualification, namely that trustees are not necessarily entitled to costs on an indemnity basis in hostile litigation designed to define and secure the personal rights of the trustees as individuals.

In practice, the prudent course is for the trustees to apply to the court for directions before taking part in any legal proceedings:[177] if they are given leave to sue or defend, the order will normally entitle them to an indemnity for all their costs out of the trust property, though it is essentially for the discretion of the court.[178] On such an application the court is acting in an essentially administrative capacity: the proposed

---

[170] *Wise v Perpetual Trustee Co Ltd* [1903] AC 139, PC.

[171] CPR 48.4. See Practice Note [2001] 3 All ER 574 as to a prospective costs order.

[172] *Walters v Woodbridge* (1878) 7 Ch D 504, CA; *Re Dunn* [1904] 1 Ch 648. See (1987) 2 TL & P 55 (J Thurston).

[173] [1966] 1 All ER 745 at 758. See *National Trustees Executors and Agency Co of Australasia Ltd v Barnes* (1941) 64 CLR 268.

[174] *In Turner v Hancock* (1882) 20 Ch D 303 at 305.   [175] [1954] Ch 16, [1953] 2 All ER 577.

[176] Supra.

[177] *Re Beddoe* [1893] 1 Ch 547, CA; *Re Biddencare* [1994] 2 BCLC 160; *McDonald v Horn* [1995] 1 All ER 961, CA. The application should be made in separate proceedings: *Alsop Wilkinson (a firm) v Neary* [1995] 1 All ER 431, [1996] 1 WLR 1220.

[178] *Evans v Evans* [1985] 3 All ER 289, sub nom *Re Evans* [1986] 1 WLR 101, CA (merits of the claimant's case an important consideration); *National Anti-Vivisection Society Ltd v Duddington* (1989) *Times*, 23 November (other factors where a pre-emptive order for costs is sought include the likelihood that at the trial the court would order costs to be paid out of the fund, and the justice of the case). See *Holding and Management Ltd v Property Holdings and Investment Trust plc* [1990] 1 All ER 938, [1989] 1 WLR 1313, CA (trustee not entitled to indemnity where not a party to proceedings truly in capacity of trustee); *STG Valmet Trustees Ltd v Brennan* [2002] WTLR 273 (CA for Gibraltar).

defendants are not entitled to be heard on the application or to be furnished with the evidence on which the court is asked to act.[179]

If trustees go ahead without the leave of the court, they do so at their own risk as to costs: if they fail, they will not receive their costs unless they establish that they were properly incurred.[180] Even if they have been advised by counsel that they have a good case, they will not receive their costs unless the court is satisfied that it would have authorized the claim or defence, as the case may be, had an appropriate application been made to them.[181] Of course, even if it is proper to bring or defend the proceedings, excessive or unnecessary costs therein will be disallowed.[182] And where the costs are due to breach of trust or misconduct by the trustees, the court has a discretion which it will usually exercise against the trustees.[183] It was said in *Carroll v Graham*[184] that trustees holding a merely neutral position, and not intending to argue, ought not to appear by separate counsel on appeal, but the contrary view seems to have prevailed, that trustees ought to appear in the Court of Appeal, because it is necessary for them to see that the order which relates to the administration of the estate is properly carried out.[185]

In a case where the dispute is between rival claimants to a beneficial interest in the subject matter of the trust, the duty of the trustees is to remain neutral and offer to submit to the court's directions, leaving it to the rivals to fight their battles.[186] If, however, they actively defend the trust and succeed, for example, in challenging a claim by the settlor to set aside for undue influence, they may be entitled to costs out of the trust, for they have preserved the interests of the beneficiaries under the trust.[187] But if they fail, then in particular in the case of hostile litigation, although in an exceptional case the court may consider that the trustee should have his costs,[188] ordinarily the trustees will not be entitled to any indemnity, for they have incurred expenditure and liabilities in an unsuccessful attempt to prefer one class of beneficiaries (for example, the express beneficiaries specified in the trust instrument) over another (for example, the trustee in bankruptcy or creditors) and so have acted unreasonably and otherwise than for the benefit of the trust estate.[189]

Where it appears that the cost of an application is out of proportion to the amount

---

[179] *Re Moritz* [1960] Ch 251; *Craig v Humberclyde Industrial Finance Group Ltd* [1999] 1 WLR 129, [1998] 2 BCLC 526, CA.

[180] *Re Beddoe,* supra; *Re Yorke* [1911] 1 Ch 370; *Dagnall v J L Freedman & Co (a firm)* [1993] 2 All ER 161, [1993] 1 WLR 388, HL.

[181] *Singh v Bhasin* [2000] 2 WTLR 275; *Re Beddoe,* supra; *Breadner v Granville-Grossman* [2001] WTLR 377. See (1999) 5 T & ELJ 10 (A Penny).

[182] *Re England's Settlement Trusts* [1918] 1 Ch 24; *Re Robertson* [1949] 1 All ER 1042; *Re Whitley* [1962] 3 All ER 45, [1962] 1 WLR 922.

[183] *Easton v Landor* (1892) 62 LJ Ch 164, CA; *Re Knox's Trusts* [1895] 2 Ch 483, CA; *Re Chapman* (1895) 72 LT 66, CA.

[184] [1905] 1 Ch 478, CA.   [185] *Re Stuart* [1940] 4 All ER 80, CA; *Chettiar v Chettiar,* supra, PC.

[186] *Alsop Wilkinson (a firm) v Neary* [1995] 1 All ER 431, adopted in New Zealand, *Re Schroder's Will* [2004] 1 NZLR 695.

[187] See *Re Holden* (1887) 20 QBD 43, DC.

[188] See *Bullock v Lloyds Bank Ltd* [1955] Ch 317, [1954] 3 All ER 726.

[189] *Alsop Wilkinson (a firm) v Neary* [1995] 1 All ER 431.

at stake, the Law Reform Committee recommends[190] that trustees should be empowered to take the advice of counsel (in the case of trusts having adult beneficiaries only) or Queen's Counsel practising in the Chancery Division or Conveyancing Counsel of the Court (where there are minor beneficiaries) and to distribute on the basis of that advice if no adult beneficiary starts proceedings within three months of being sent a copy of the relevant opinion.

(d) COSTS OF BENEFICIARIES

CPR 48.4 does not apply to the costs of beneficiaries, but the courts have sometimes been willing to extend to other parties to trust litigation an entitlement to costs in any event by analogy with that accorded to trustees. In *Re Buckton*[191] Kekewich J said trust litigation can be divided into three categories. First, there are proceedings brought by trustees to have the guidance of the court as to the construction of the trust instrument or some question arising in the course of administration. In such cases the costs of all parties are usually treated as necessarily incurred for the benefit of the estate and ordered to be paid out of the fund. Secondly, there are cases in which the application is made by someone other than the trustees, but raises the same kind of point as in the first category and would have justified an application by the trustees. This second category is treated in the same way as the first. Thirdly, there are cases in which a beneficiary is making a hostile claim against the trustees. This is treated in the same way as ordinary common law litigation and costs usually follow the event. It is not always easy to determine into which category a particular case falls.[192]

In a case which clearly falls within the first or second category, parties other than the trustees can in general assume, that an order will be made at the trial for their costs to be paid out of the fund. However the claimant was held not to be entitled to costs out of the trust fund in *D'Abo v Paget (No 2)*[193] where she had successfully brought an action against the trustees and her sister (the first defendant). The trustees had been willing and able to bring the proceedings. The sole reason that the claimant brought the proceedings was to make a claim for costs in the event that the first defendant lost. In exceptional cases trustees can ask for a prospective order that they are to have their costs in any event. The court will be reluctant to make such an order unless it is clear that the judge would be bound to do so at the trial.[194]

---

[190] 23rd Report, Cmnd 8733, paras 5.2–5.3.

[191] [1907] 2 Ch 406. See *The Trustee Corporation Ltd v Nadir* [2000] BPIR 541.

[192] *McDonald v Horn* [1995] 1 All ER 961, CA; *Breadner v Granville-Grossman* [2001] WTLR 377. Cf *R v Lord Chancellor, ex p Child Poverty Action Group* [1998] 2 All ER 755.

[193] (2000) *Times*, 10 August, noted (2000) 22 T & ELJ 13 (J Godwin-Austen) where it was said that a more robust attitude to costs was appropriate under the new Civil Procedure Rules, but, subject to that qualification, the guidelines in *Re Buckton*, supra, had not been superseded.

[194] Such pre-emptive costs orders have been made at the request of, or with the support of, the trustee bringing the proceedings. See *Re Exchange Securities and Commodities Ltd (No 2)* [1985] BCLC 392; *Re Charge Card Services Ltd* [1986] BCLC 316; *Re Westdock Realisations Ltd* [1988] BCLC 354; *Alsop Wilkinson (a firm) v Neary* [1995] 1 All ER 431; *Chessels v British Telecommunications plc* [2002] WTLR 719.

The principles behind CPR 48.4 were applied in *Wallersteiner v Moir (No 2)*[195] to enable a minority shareholder bringing a derivative action on behalf of a company to obtain the authority of the court to sue as if he were a trustee suing on behalf of a fund, with the same entitlement to be indemnified out of the assets against his costs and any costs he may be ordered to pay to the other party. This was extended in *McDonald v Horn*[196] to an action primarily for breach of trust by the beneficiaries of a pension fund. Pension funds are a special form of trust[197] and there is a compelling analogy between a minority shareholder's action for damages on behalf of a company and an action by a member of a pension fund to compel trustees or others to account to the fund.

10 TRUSTEES OF LAND

Trustees of land[198] have, by virtue of the Trusts of Land and Appointment of Trustees Act 1996,[199] in relation to the land subject to the trust all the powers of an absolute owner. They have this power, however, only for the purpose of exercising their functions as trustees. Thus they have management powers, such as letting and mortgaging, but if the land is sold the question becomes one of investing the sale proceeds which in general falls outside the scope of the Act, though, as we have seen,[200] the Act gives trustees of land power to acquire land not only as an investment but also for occupation by a beneficiary or for any other reason.

The powers under the 1996 Act are subject to general equitable principles. Thus it is expressly provided that in exercising their powers trustees of land shall have regard to the rights of the beneficiaries,[201] and that the powers shall not be exercised in contravention of, or of any order made in pursuance of, any other enactment or any rule of law or equity.[202] As we have already seen,[203] in the exercise of their functions relating to land trustees of land have a duty to consult with beneficiaries, and, in favour of a purchaser, there are limits on the number of consents that can be required.

The powers under s 6 can be restricted or excluded by a provision in the disposition

---

[195] [1975] QB 373, [1975] 1 All ER 849, CA.

[196] Supra, CA; *Mackin v National Power plc* [2001] WTLR 741 and see [2001] CJQ 208.

[197] See p 18 supra.

[198] Including trustees holding under a bare trust—see p 72 supra.

[199] Section 6(1) and see Trustee Act 2000 s 8(4).

[200] See s 6(3) as amended by the Trustee Act 2000, Sch 2, para 45(1) and p 422, supra.

[201] Section 6(5). 'Beneficiary' is defined in s 22.

[202] Section 6(6). This includes an order of the court or of the Charity Commissioners: s 6(7). See also s 6(8).

[203] See p 497, supra.

creating the trust, except in the case of charitable, ecclesiastical or public trusts,[204] and if a consent is required to be obtained a power cannot be exercised without it.[205]

11 APPLICATIONS TO THE COURT

(a) PROCEEDINGS FOR ADMINISTRATION, OR DETERMINATION OF QUESTION

In addition to its statutory jurisdiction,[206] the court has an inherent jurisdiction to administer trusts. Trustees, and any person claiming to be interested in the relief sought as beneficiary, may apply to the court by means of the alternative Part 8 procedure for directions and for the determination, without an administration of the trust, of any question arising in the administration of the trust.[207] When a trustee surrenders his discretion to the court, the court should be put in possession of all the material necessary to enable that discretion to be exercised. If that exercise calls for the obtaining of expert advice or valuation, it is the trustee's duty to obtain that advice and place it fully and fairly before the court. It should always be borne in mind that in exercising its jurisdiction to give directions on a trustee's application the court is essentially engaged solely in determining what ought to be done in the best interests of the trust estate and not in determining the rights of adversarial parties.[208]

It is also possible to apply by a Part 8 claim for the administration of the trust.[209] The court, however, is not bound to make an administration order if the questions

---

[204] Ibid, s 8(1), (3), and see s 8(4). See [1997] Conv 263 (G Watt) for possible ways of escaping s 8(1) provisions.

[205] Ibid, s 8(2), and see s 8(4). Purchases are protected under ibid, s 16(3).

[206] Trustee Act 1925, ss 41 and 44. *See Chellaram v Chellaram* [1985] 1 All ER 1043.

[207] CPR Sch 1, RSC Ord 85, r 2. See generally, (1994) 138 Sol Jo 789, 850, 878 (Dawn Goodman); (2000) 15 T & ELJ 20 (C Cutbill) and correspondence at (2000) 19 T & ELJ 5. A Part 8 claim may be brought, eg for the construction of the trust instrument; as to whether the trustees should bring or defend an action (*Re Moritz* [1960] Ch 251, [1959] 3 All ER 767; *Re Eaton* [1964] 3 All ER 229n); as to whether a fund may be distributed on the basis that a person is dead (*Re Newson-Smith's Settlement* [1962] 3 All ER 963n) or a woman past childbearing (*Re Westminster Bank Ltd's Declaration of Trust* [1963] 2 All ER 400n). New Zealand authority suggests that such an application is inappropriate where there are substantial factual disputes and/or the possibility of a breach of trust: *Neagle v Rimmington* [2002] 3 NZLR 826. As to the participation of beneficiaries in the hearing see *Smith v Croft* [1986] 2 All ER 551, [1986] 1 WLR 580, and *Re Permanent Trustee Australia Ltd* (1994) 33 NSWLR 547. See (1978) 56 CBR 128 (Donovan Waters).

[208] *Marley v Mutual Security Merchant Bank and Trust Co Ltd* [1991] 3 All ER 198, PC. Contrast the case where trustees merely seek the approval by the court of a proposed exercise by them of their discretion: see p. 365, infra. As to costs see Practice Note [2001] 3 All ER 574 and p 487, supra.

[209] As to the effect of an order on a trustee's powers, see (1968) 84 LQR 64 (A J Hawkins).

between the parties can be properly determined without it,[210] and in fact will only undertake the administration of a trust as a last resort. It has been said[211] that:

a general administration order will be made only in three categories of cases:
  (1) where the trustees cannot pull together, or,
  (2) the circumstances of the estate give rise to ever-recurring difficulties requiring the frequent direction of the court, or,
  (3) where a prima facie doubt is thrown on the bona fides or the discretion of one or more of the trustees.

The beneficiary's real right is to approach the court for the appropriate order for performance of the trust, a specific order if that will meet the case, or a general decree, if that is called for, subject to the beneficiary paying the costs of any unnecessary application and subject also to the restrictions which the court has over the years put on that right to approach it.

A trustee may have to pay the costs of an application personally if he does not make out his case for administration by the court, and the court holds the view that some other process would have dealt with the difficulty more satisfactorily.[212]

The Administration of Justice Act 1985[213] may enable costs to be saved where the proceedings raise a question of construction of the terms of a will or a trust. Where an opinion in writing of a person who has a ten year High Court qualification[214] has been obtained on the question by the personal representatives or trustees, the High Court may, on the application of the personal representatives or trustees and without hearing argument, make an order authorizing them to take such steps in reliance on the opinion as are specified in the order. The court must not make such an order, however, if a dispute exists which would make such action inappropriate.

It should be observed that a settlor[215] or testator cannot deprive a beneficiary of his right to go to the court, at any rate on questions of law. The reasons for this rule were explained by Danckwerts J in *Re Wynn's Will Trusts*[216] where he said:[217]

a provision which refers the determination of all questions and matters of doubt arising in the execution of the trusts of a will to the trustees, and which attempts to make such determination conclusive and binding upon all persons interested under the will, is void and of no effect; because it is both repugnant to the benefits which are conferred by the will upon the beneficiaries; and also because it is contrary to public policy as being an attempt to oust the jurisdiction of the court to construe the will and control the construction and administration of a testator's will and estate.

It is submitted that the rule applies to invalidate not only wide general clauses such

---

[210] CPR Sch 1, RSC Ord 85, r 5.

[211] Per Young J in *McLean v Burns Philip Trustee Co Pty Ltd* (1985) 2 NSWLR 623.

[212] See *Re Wilson* (1885) 28 Ch D 457; *Re Blake* (1885) 29 Ch D 913, CA.

[213] Section 48, as amended by the Courts and Legal Services Act 1990, s 71(2), Sch 10, para 63.

[214] Ie, has a right of audience in relation to all proceedings in the High Court: Courts and Legal Services Act 1990, s 7(3)(b).

[215] The cases concern wills but the same principles would seem applicable in inter vivos trusts. See (1983) 133 NLJ 915 (P Matthews).

[216] [1952] Ch 271, [1952] 1 All ER 341.   [217] Supra, at 278–279, 346.

as that mentioned by the judge, but any clause which purports to give trustees power to decide on a question of law, as opposed to one which gives trustees power to decide on a question of fact, provided in this last case that the state of affairs on which the trustees have to form their opinion is sufficiently defined. Thus, on the one hand, in *Re Raven*[218] a provision that in case of doubt the trustees should decide the identity of the institution intended to benefit was held to be void, while, on the other hand, in *Re Coxen*[219] a gift over 'if, in the opinion of my trustees, she shall have ceased permanently to reside therein' was held to be validly made dependent on the decision of the trustees, who were described as 'judges of fact for this purpose'. A similar distinction is drawn where contracting parties seek to oust the jurisdiction of the court.[220] The converse of this is that a private person cannot impose on a judge a jurisdiction or duty to adjudicate by providing for instance, for a power of revocation 'with the consent of a judge of the Chancery Division'.[221]

(b) SURRENDER OF DISCRETION

When trustees have a discretionary power and are in doubt how they ought to exercise it, they can go to the court and obtain directions as to what is the proper thing for them to do.[222] The court will not, however, accept from trustees the surrender for the future of a discretion which involves considering from time to time changing circumstances. The trustees must apply their minds to future problems as and when they arise, though if they cannot arrive at a satisfactory answer they may seek the court's directions from time to time.[223]

(c) APPEAL BY THE TRUSTEES

Contrasting views were expressed in *Re Londonderry's Settlement*[224] as to whether trustees should initiate an appeal from a decision of the court. Harman LJ said[225] 'Trustees seeking the protection of the court are protected by the court's order and it is not for them to appeal' but Salmon LJ stated[226] 'In my view the trustees were fully justified in bringing this appeal. Indeed it was their duty to bring it since they believed rightly that an appeal was essential for the protection of the general body of beneficiaries.' It is submitted that trustees should not normally appeal, but that they have a

---

[218] [1915] 1 Ch 673, [1914–15] All ER Rep 353; *Re Wynn's Will Trusts*, supra.

[219] [1948] Ch 747, [1948] 2 All ER 492; *Re Tuck's Settlement Trusts* [1978] Ch 49, [1978] 1 All ER 1047, CA.

[220] See *Re Davstone Estates Ltd's Leases* [1969] 2 All ER 849, and cases there cited.

[221] *Re Hooker's Settlement* [1955] Ch 55, [1954] 3 All ER 321. Cf *Allen v Distillers Co (Biochemicals) Ltd* [1974] QB 384, [1974] 2 All ER 365; *Anthony v Donges* [1998] 2 FLR 775.

[222] *Talbot v Talbot* [1968] Ch 1, [1967] 2 All ER 920, CA. See *Thrells Ltd v Lomas* [1993] 2 All ER 546, [1993] 1 WLR 456 (conflict of interest).

[223] *Re Allen-Meyrick's Will Trusts* [1966] 1 All ER 740, [1966] 1 WLR 499; *Gailey v Gordon* [2003] 2 NZLR 192.

[224] [1965] Ch 918, [1964] 3 All ER 855, CA.   [225] At 930, 858.   [226] At 936, 862.

discretionary power to do so which they may exercise in exceptional circumstances. It
will only be very rarely, however, that they will be justified in bringing an appeal.

(d) PAYMENT INTO COURT

The statutory power[227] for trustees, or the majority of them, to pay trust funds into
court is one which it is now seldom advisable for them to adopt, as they are likely to be
made liable for at least the costs of payment out if they neglect some less expensive or
more convenient procedure, such as advertising for claimants under s 27,[228] or raising
a question for the decision of the court under the Civil Procedure Rules Part 8.[229]
Moreover, 'a trustee cannot pay into court merely to get rid of a trust he has undertaken to perform', and the fact that he has been so advised by counsel will not assist
him.[230] Payment into court does not affect the trusts on which the trust funds are
held.[231]

Subject to what had been said, trustees may be justified in paying into court where
there is a bona fide doubt as to whom they should pay,[232] or where they cannot get a
valid discharge from the cestuis que trust, by reason of their incapacity, or otherwise.[233] But trustees have been held liable to pay costs where payment in was made
when the trustees knew that the person claiming the fund was on his way from
Australia to establish his claim,[234] and would be held liable if they paid in instead of
paying a beneficiary entitled in default of appointment, satisfactory evidence having
been produced that no appointment had been made.[235]

(e) APPLICATIONS UNDER THE TRUSTS OF LAND AND APPOINTMENT OF TRUSTEES ACT 1996

Any person who is a trustee of land or has an interest in property subject to a trust of
land may apply to the court for an order under s 14 of the above Act.[236] On the

---

[227] Trustee Act 1925, s 63 (as amended by the Administration of Justice Act 1965, s 36 and Sch 3). See,
generally, (1968) 84 LQR 64 (A J Hawkins).

[228] Discussed in chapter 17, section 5(b), p 402, supra.   [229] *Re Giles* (1886) 55 LJ Ch 695.

[230] Per Romilly MR in *Re Knight's Trusts* (1859) 27 Beav 45 at 49.

[231] See *Harman v Federal Comr of Taxation* (1991) 104 ALR 117.

[232] *Re Maclean's Trusts* (1874) LR 19 Eq 274; *Hockey v Western* [1898] 1 Ch 350, CA; *Re Davies' Trusts*
(1914) 59 Sol Jo 234.

[233] *Re Parker's Will* (1888) 39 Ch D 303 (more fully reported in 58 LJ Ch 23), CA; *Re Salomons* [1920] 1 Ch
290. Cf Administration of Estates Act 1925, s 42.

[234] *Re Elliot's Trusts* (1873) LR 15 Eq 194.

[235] *Re Cull's Trusts* (1875) LR 20 Eq 561 (though trustees were here allowed costs as it was the first case of
its kind and the trustees had been advised by counsel); see also *Re Foligno's Mortage* (1863) 32 Beav 131; *Re
Leake's Trusts* (1863) 32 Beav 135.

[236] Section 14(1). In *Oke v Rideout* [1998] CLY 4876 discussed (1999) 4 T & ELJ 18 (M Warner) it was held
that a trustee with no beneficial interest was entitled to apply despite a conflict of interest, but on the facts and
applying the criteria in s 15 the application was refused.

application the court may make any such order relating to the exercise by the trustees of any of their functions,[237] or declaring the nature or extent of a person's interest in property subject to the trust, as the court thinks fit.[238] In determining an application the matters to which the court must have regard include—

(a) the intentions of the person or persons (if any) who created the trust,

(b) the purposes for which the property subject to the trust is held,

(c) the welfare of any minor who occupies or might reasonably be expected to occupy any land subject to the trust as his home, and

(d) the interests of any secured creditor of any beneficiary.[239]

The use of the word 'include' has been held in the county court to indicate that the matters specifically referred to are not exclusive, and that all other relevant matters should be taken into account. The principles that were applied in relation to the predecessor to s 14, namely, s 30 of the Law of Property Act 1925, were applicable. These are, first, that the purpose of the provision is to enable the court as a matter of discretion to do what is equitable. Secondly, where there is a conflict between a chargee's interest in a matrimonial home and the interest of an innocent spouse, the interest of the charge will prevail except where there are exceptional circumstances. And, thirdly, where there is a collateral purpose of the trust still subsisting the court should not defeat that purpose by ordering a sale.[240] However, more recently, in the High Court, it has been held that under the 1996 Act the court has a wider discretion than previously when deciding whether to order the sale of a home at the suit of a chargee. The increased flexibility is to the benefit of families and to the detriment of banks and other chargees. Old authorities should not be overthrown but should be regarded with caution, and in many cases are unlikely to be of great, let alone decisive, assistance.[241]

---

[237] Including an order relieving them of any obligation to obtain the consent of, or to consult, any person in connection with the exercise of any of their functions.

[238] Ibid, s 14(2). The court may not, however, make an order under this section as to the appointment or removal of trustees: s 14(3). Following *Smith v Smith* (1975) 120 Sol Jo 100 on the corresponding provision of the Law of Property Act 1925, the discretion of the court would not be limited in any way by s 11 (consultation with beneficiaries).

[239] Ibid, s 15(1). In relation to s 13, discussed p 409 supra, the court must also have regard to the circumstances and wishes of each of the beneficiaries entitled to occupy the land: s 15(2); and in all other applications (except the power to convey to beneficiaries under s 6(2), discussed p 407, supra) the circumstances and wishes of any beneficiaries of full age and entitled to an interest in possession in property subject to the trust (or the majority according to the value of their combined interests); s 15(3).

[240] *TSB Bank plc v Marshall* [1998] 2 FLR 769, Cty Ct, noted (1998) 142 Sol Jo 1076 (M Draper).

[241] *Mortage Corpn v Shaire* [2001] 4 All ER 364 discussed [2000] Conv 315 (S Pascoe); [2000] Conv 329 (M P Thompson); [2001] CLJ 44 (Mika Oldham); [2001] Fam Law 275 (M Pawlowski and Sarah Greer). It remains a powerful consideration whether the creditor is receiving proper recompense for being kept out of his money: *Bank of Ireland Home Mortgages Ltd v Bell* [2001] 2 All ER Comm 920, CA, noted [2002] Conv 61 (Rebecca Probert); *Re MCA* [2002] EWHC 611 (Admin/Fam), [2002] 2 FLR 274. Note that if the court refuses to order a sale, a mortagee can sue on the personal covenant which will almost certainly force the mortagor into bankruptcy: *Alliance and Leicester plc v Slayford* [2001] 1 All ER (Comm) 1, CA, noted [2002] Conv 53 (M P Thompson).

There are special provisions on an application for the sale of land by a trustee of a bankrupt's estate. On such an application the court must make such order as it thinks just and reasonable having regard to—

(a) the interests of the bankrupt's creditors;

(b) where the application is made in respect of land which includes a dwelling house which is or has been the home of the bankrupt or the bankrupt's spouse or former spouse—

    (i) the conduct of the spouse or former spouse, so far as contributing to the bankruptcy,

    (ii) the needs and financial resources of the spouse or former spouse, and

    (iii) the needs of any children; and

(c) all the circumstances of the case other than the needs of the bankrupt.[242]

Moreover where an application is made after the end of the period of one year beginning with the first vesting of the bankrupt's estate in a trustee, the court must assume, unless the circumstances of the case are exceptional, that the interests of the bankrupt's creditors outweigh all other considerations.[243]

When the Civil Partnership Act 2004 is brought into force the section will be extended to include a civil partner or former civil partner.

12 CONTROL OF TRUSTEE'S POWERS

So far as a trustee's duties are concerned, he is under an obligation to carry them out, and if he fails to do so will be liable for breach of trust. In relation to the exercise of a discretionary power, however, his obligation is limited to a duty to consider from time to time whether he should exercise it, and in particular he must consider a request by a person within the ambit of a power for it to be exercised in his favour.[244] A trustee who considers whether or not to exercise a power and acts bona fide is not likely to have his decision upset.

(a) CONTROL BY BENEFICIARIES

As we have seen,[245] all the beneficiaries, being sui iuris, can together terminate the trusts. They cannot, however, bind the trustees by their actions, unless power has been

---

[242] Insolvency Act 1986, s 335A(1), (2) inserted by the Trusts of Land and Appointment of Trustees Act 1996. Where s 335A applies s 15 of the 1996 Act is excluded: s 15(4). See *Judd v Brown* (1999) 79 P & CR 491, CA.

[243] Insolvency Act 1986, s 335A(3).

[244] *Re Manisty's Settlement* [1974] Ch 17 at 26, [1973] 2 All ER 1203 at 1210.

[245] Chapter 17, section 6, supra, p 405.

delegated to them by the trust document or under some statutory provision such as s 9 of the Trusts of Land and Appointment of Trustees Act 1996.[246] Thus in *Napier v Light*[247] there was a trust for sale of land under which the plaintiff was the remainderman and his mother the life beneficiary. The plaintiff originally purported to grant a tenancy to the defendant, but from 1952 onwards the tenancy was treated as being between the defendant and the plaintiff's mother. It was held that the trustees were not bound in the absence of any evidence of delegation by them, or of acquiescence with knowledge of the tenancy which might have given rise to an estoppel. Moreover the plaintiff, who had become solely entitled in equity and acquired the legal title from the trustees, was not estopped from denying the tenancy by reason of the fact that he had been the original purported landlord.

The same case also makes it clear that the beneficiaries even though they represent the entire beneficial interest and are all sui iuris cannot, so long as the trust continues, direct or control the trustees in the bona fide exercise of their powers and discretions under the trust. The point has arisen in connection with the appointment of new trustees, and in one such case, *Re Brockbank*,[248] Vaisey J observed, 'If the court, as a matter of practice and principle, refuses to interfere with the legal power to appoint new trustees,[249] it is, in my judgment, *a fortiori* true that the beneficiaries cannot do so.'

The principle remains generally valid, although substantially reversed in relation to the appointment of new trustees.[250] However in relation to trusts of land s 11 of the Trusts of Land and Appointment of Trustees Act 1996[251] requires that, subject to any contrary provision in the disposition,[252] trustees of land shall, in the exercise of any function relating to land subject to the trust,[253] 'so far as practicable, consult the beneficiaries of full age and beneficially entitled to an interest in possession in the land',[254] and, 'so far as consistent with the general interest of the trust, give effect to the wishes of those beneficiaries, or (in case of dispute) of the majority (according to the value of their combined interests)'. A purchaser of unregistered land is not concerned to see that this requirement has been complied with.[255] The requirement is

---

[246] Section 9 is prospectively amended by the Mental Capacity Act 2005, Sch 6, para 41.

[247] (1974) 236 EG 273, CA.

[248] [1948] Ch 206 at 210, [1948] 1 All ER 287 at 289; *Stephenson v Barclays Bank Trust Co Ltd* [1975] 1 All ER 625.

[249] As is clearly the case—*Tempest v Lord Camoys*, supra, CA; *Re Higginbottom* [1892] 3 Ch 132.

[250] Trusts of Land and Appointment of Trustees Act 1996, ss 19–21. See the prospective amendments to s 20 referred to in a 82, p 357, supra.

[251] The section does not apply to a trust arising under a will made before 1997, nor to one created by a pre-1997 disposition unless the person who created it, being of full capacity, executes an appropriate deed: ibid, s 11(2)–(4).

[252] Ibid, s 11(2)(a). The corresponding provision in s 26(3) of the Law of Property Act 1925 (repealed) applied only to statutory trusts for sale unless a contrary intention appeared.

[253] See *Crawley Borough Council v Ure* [1996] QB 13, [1996] 1 All ER 724, CA; *Notting Hill Housing Trust v Brackley* [2001] WTLR 1327.

[254] As to the meaning of this phrase, see p 409, supra.   [255] Ibid, s 16(1), (7).

often excluded, for many draftsmen consider it to be unduly burdensome, and its meaning to be in some respects uncertain. However in many circumstances where consultation is not mandatory it is nevertheless good practice to consult.

Apart from this section Romer LJ in a case[256] where the trust fund comprised shares in a private company, stated:

the beneficiaries are entitled to be treated as though they were the registered shareholders in respect of trust shares with the advantages and disadvantages (eg restrictions imposed by the articles) which would be involved in that position and that they could compel the trustee directors, if necessary, to use their votes as the beneficiaries—or as the court, if the beneficiaries themselves are not in agreement—should think proper, even to the extent of altering the articles of association if the trust shares carry votes sufficient for that purpose.

As Upjohn J has pointed out in *Re Whichelow*,[257] however, it is difficult to reconcile this statement with the principle upon which *Re Brockbank*[258] and the cases cited in note 249, p 497, supra, were decided. None of these cases was cited in *Hayim v Citibank NA*[259] where, on unusual facts, it seems to have been assumed that the beneficiary (itself an executor) could give binding directions to the trustee.

(b) CONTROL BY THE COURT

The jurisdiction of the court to interfere with discretionary powers of trustees against their will is limited.[260] It has been held that where the trustees are expressly given an uncontrollable discretion by the trust instrument, the court will not interfere in the absence of mala fides, even though the court may be clearly of opinion that the trustees are not acting judiciously.[261] Where there is a simple or unenlarged discretion, some judges have asserted the jurisdiction of the court to control the exercise by trustees of discretionary powers given to them, and have interfered where the trustees have 'not exercised a sound discretion', as it was put by Fry J in *Re Roper's Trusts*.[262] However the better view, which seems to be supported by dicta in the more recent

---

[256] *Butt v Kelson* [1952] Ch 197 at 207, sub nom *Re Butt* [1952] 1 All ER 167 at 172, CA—the other members of the Court of Appeal concurred in the judgment; *Kirby v Wilkins* [1929] 2 Ch 444 at 454. See (1980) 30 UTLJ 151 (D Hughes).

[257] [1953] 2 All ER 1558, [1954] 1 WLR 5.   [258] Supra.

[259] [1987] AC 730, PC, noted [1988] Conv 60 (P McLoughlin).

[260] See, generally, (1957) 21 Conv 55 (L A Sheridan); (1967) 31 Conv 117 (A J Hawkins); (1975) 25 UTLJ 99 (M Cullity); [1992] JBL 261 (R L Nobles). N D M Parry in [1989] Conv 244 agrees that, whether or not the discretion is qualified, the court should have jurisdiction to intervene on the ground of mala fides in the sense of dishonesty, or impropriety in the sense of failing to take into account of all (or only) legally relevant factors. Cf *Asea Brown Boveri Superannuation Fund No 1 Pty Ltd v Asea Brown Boveri Pty Ltd* [1999] 1 VR 144. For a discussion of the position in New Zealand see [1999] NZLJ 209 (R Peterson).

[261] *Gisborne v Gisborne* (1877) 2 App Cas 300, HL; *Tabor v Brooks* (1878) 10 Ch D 273.

[262] (1879) 11 Ch D 272; *Re Hodges* (1878) 7 Ch D 754 (decided immediately after, and without reference to, *Gisborne v Gisborne*, supra, HL).

cases,[263] is that the court will not interfere if the power is exercised bona fide, and the terms of the power are duly observed, except on the ground of fraud, mala fides or improper exercise of the power[264] or where the trustees had failed or refused to consider whether or not to[265] exercise a discretionary power.[266] In particular the court will not normally intervene positively to exercise a power, but it did so in the pensions trust cases of *Mettoy Pension Trustees Ltd v Evans*[267] and *Thrells Ltd v Lomas*[268] where the person with the power could not exercise it because of a conflict of interest. Again in the family trust case of *Klug v Klug*[269] one trustee wished to exercise a discretionary power of advancement while the other trustee refused to exercise her discretion for extraneous reasons. The court directed that the advancement should be made.

In many cases it will be appropriate to apply what is commonly referred to as the Rule in *Hastings-Bass*[270] where it was held that the court should not interfere with the bona fide exercise by a trustee of a discretionary power vested in him, notwithstanding that it does not have the full effect which he intended,[271] unless (1) what he has achieved is unauthorized by the power conferred on him, or (2) it is clear that he would not have acted as he did (a) had he not taken into account considerations which he should not have taken into account, or (b) had he not failed to take into

---

[263] *Re Whichelow* [1953] 2 All ER 1558; *Re Gulbenkian's Settlement Trusts* [1970] AC 508 at 518, [1968] 3 All ER 785 at 787, HL, per Lord Reid; *Re 90 Thornhill Road, Tolworth, Surrey* [1970] Ch 261, sub nom *Barker v Addiscott* [1969] 3 All ER 685.

[264] It would be an improper exercise of a power for trustees to act capriciously, which was explained in *Re Manisty's Settlement* [1974] Ch 17, [1973] 2 All ER 1203 as meaning where they act 'for reasons which . . . could be said to be irrational, perverse, or irrelevant to any sensible expectation of the settlor; for example, if they chose a beneficiary by height or complexion . . .'.

[265] In *Turner v Turner* [1984] Ch 100, [1983] 2 All ER 745, the trustees had executed deeds of appointment on their face effective, but executed in breach of their duties in that they signed, in all good faith, without having given any attention to the contents of the deeds. It was held that the purported appointments must be set aside.

[266] *Tempest v Lord Camoys* (1882) 21 Ch D 571, [1881–5] All ER Rep 836, CA; *Re Hays Settlement Trusts* [1981] 3 All ER 786, [1982] 1 WLR 202; *Wendt v Orr* [2004] WASC 28, [2005] WTLR 223; *Edge v Pensions Ombudsman* [2000] Ch 602, [1999] 4 All ER 546, CA noted [2000] ALJ 47 (D Maclean). At first-instance [1998] Ch 512, [1998] 2 All ER 547, Scott V-C observed that the duty of impartiality which applies in the exercise of an investment power—see p 412 infra – is inapposite where what is in point is a discretionary power to choose between different beneficiaries. See [1998] PCB 239 (J Mowbray).

[267] [1991] 2 All ER 513, [1990] 1 WLR 1587.   [268] [1993] 2 All ER 546, [1993] 1 WLR 456.

[269] [1918] 2 Ch 67 (the refusing trustee, the beneficiary's mother, refused because her daughter had married without her consent).

[270] *Re Hastings-Bass (decd)* [1975] Ch 25, [1974] 2 All ER 193, CA, applied *Green v Cobham* [2000] STC 820; *Abacus Trust Company (Isle of Man) Ltd v NSPCC* [2001] WTLR 953; *Re Green GLG Trust* [2003] WTLR 377 (Jersey Royal Court). The Rule was restated in a positive form by Warner J in *Mettoy Pension Trustees Ltd v Evans* [1991] 2 All ER 513 at 552–553; [1990] 1 WLR 1587 at 1621. See (2001) 31 T & ELJ 20 (I Burman); [2002] Conv 67 (I Dawson); (2002) 42 E & ELJ 11 (R Wilson); (2002) 16 Tru LI 202 (J Hilliard); [2004] Conv 208 (J Hilliard).

[271] The Rule appears to apply not only to cases where trustees fail to appreciate the legal consequences of their action, but also to cases where they fail to appreciate the fiscal or other consequences: see [2002] PCB 102 (Dawn Goodman and C Graves). However the question has been raised whether the actual or potential adverse tax considerations of the exercise of the power are relevant facts for the purposes of the Rule: [2002] PCB 226 (Sir Robert Walker).

account considerations which he ought to have taken into account. Some cases[272] suggest that the word 'would' should read 'might': it was said in *Abacus Trust Company (Isle of Man) Ltd v Barr*[273] that the choice between the two criteria remains open. A successful challenge to a decision under the Rule in *Hastings-Bass* results in the decision being held voidable and not void.[274]

In *Burrell v Burrell*[275] Mann J noted that *Barr's Case* might be said to introduce an additional requirement of a breach of duty or default on the part of the trustee or on the part of its advisers or agents if the principle in *Hastings-Bass* is to be invoked. Whether this is so was left open, as both in the case before him and in *Barr's Case* if there was such a requirement, it was met.

The problem was approached somewhat differently in *Harris v Shuttleworth*[276] where the trust deed governing a pension fund gave the trustees conclusive power to determine all questions. Nevertheless it was said to be clear that the court had control over the trustees, though it was not a court of appeal from their decisions. The court adopted the principles that have been laid down in respect of domestic tribunals, namely, (a) the trustees must ask themselves the correct questions; (b) they must direct themselves correctly in law, in particular they must adopt a correct construction of the trust deed; and (c) they must not arrive at a perverse decision, that is one at which no reasonable body of trustees could arrive, and they must take into account all relevant and no irrelevant factors.

It should be added that trustees exercising a discretionary power are not bound to disclose to their beneficiaries the reasons actuating them in coming to a decision,[277] though if they do give reasons, their soundness can be considered by the court.[278] However if a decision taken by trustees is directly attacked in legal proceedings, the trustees may be compelled either legally (through discovery or subpoena) or practically

---

272 *Stannard v Fisons Pensions Trust* [1992] IRLR 27, CA; *Kerr v British Leyland (Staff) Trustees Ltd* [2001] WTLR 1071, CA; *AMP(UK) plc v Barker* [2001] WTLR 1237.

273 [2003] EWHC 114 (Ch), [2003] Ch 409, sub nom *Re Barr's Settlement Trusts* [2003] 1 All ER 763, discussed (2003) 17 Tru LI 114 (B Green); [2003] PCB 173 (E Nugee); [2004] CLJ 283 (M Conaglen).

274 *Re Barr's Settlement Trusts*, supra. Under the rule in *Re Hastings-Bass* [1975] Ch 25, [1974] 2 All ER 193 the court may be able to declare something which the trustees have done to be void, but it is very doubtful whether a court can hold that a trust takes effect as if the trustees had done something which they never did at all: *Breadner v Granville-Grossman* [2000] 4 All ER 705, discussed [2000] All ER Rev, p 248 (P J Clarke).

275 [2005] EWHC 145 (Ch), [2005] WTLR 313.

276 [1994] ICR 991, CA; *Wild v Pensions Ombudsman* [1996] 2 FLR 680. See also *Boe v Alexander* (1987) 15 BCLR (2d) 106, approved and applied *Pelensky v Alberta Stock Exchange* [1993] 1 WWR 561; *Re Schipper and Guaranty Trust Co of Canada* (1989) 69 OR (2d) 386.

277 See p 397, ante.

278 *Re Beloved Wilkes' Charity* (1851) 3 Mac & G 440; *Re Londonderry's Settlement* [1965] Ch 918, [1964] 3 All ER 855, CA; *Wilson v Law Debenture Trust Corp* [1995] 2 All ER 337. See (1965) 81 LQR 192 (R E Megarry).

(in order to avoid adverse inferences being drawn) to disclose the substance of the reasons for their decision.[279]

A related question faced a Canadian court in *Re Billes*[280] where a testator had given his trustees an absolute power to convert existing assets as well as an equal and absolute power to retain. The trustees were deadlocked and the court held that it had jurisdiction to intervene and 'cast a deciding vote'. The court's jurisdiction arose because the trustees were under a duty to exercise one power or the other, and until they did so they were failing to discharge their duty with the result that the testator's intention was frustrated and the beneficiaries might suffer.

(c) PROVISIONS OF THE TRUST INSTRUMENT: PROTECTORS

The settlor may reserve some control over the trustees, for instance by requiring them to obtain his consent to the exercise of specified powers, or he may require them to obtain the consent of a named person or persons.[281] In the case of overseas settlements with foreign trustees it is a common practice to appoint 'protectors' for this purpose. Tax considerations may explain why the settlor appoints a protector rather than reserve powers to himself. The exact status and powers of the protector depend on the terms of his appointment: prima facie his powers are fiduciary.[282]

Though it does not affect the liability of trustees towards their beneficiaries, if a disposition creating a trust of land (not being a charitable, ecclesiastical or public trust) requires the consent of more than two persons to the exercise of any function relating to the land, in favour of a purchaser the consent of any two of them will suffice.[283] Further in favour of a purchaser if a person whose consent is required is not of full age, his consent is not required but the trustees must obtain the consent of his parent or guardian.[284]

A drawback to the appointment of a protector is that it complicates the administration of the trust and makes it more expensive.

---

[279] *Scott v National Trust for Places of Historic Interest or Natural Beauty*, supra; *Maciejewski v Telstra Super Pty Ltd* (1998) 44 NSWLR 601, discussed (1999) 11 Bond LR 14 (Lisa Butler) who argues that a trustee's discretion should be somewhat circumscribed: in particular in the limited field of superannuation trustees should be required to disclose to beneficiaries reasons for their decisions.

[280] (1993) 148 DLR (3d) 512 and see *Kordyban v K* (2003) 13 BCLR (4th) 50.

[281] See Trusts of Land and Appointment of Trustees Act, s 8(2).

[282] See [1996] PCB 169, 245, 328 (A Duckworth); [1995] PCB 36 (H Rosen); [1995] PCB 109 (Deborah Hartnett and W Norris); [1995] PCB 288 (J Conder); [1996] PCB 24, 122 (Colloquium Report); (2004) 62 TELTJ 24 (R Ticehurst); *IRC v Schroder* [1983] STC 480. It seems that the court has the same inherent jurisdiction as in respect of trustees to appoint a person to exercise the protector's powers, or, as a last resort, to exercise those powers itself: see *Steele v Paz Ltd (in liquidation)* (10 October, unreported), extracts from which appear in Butterworths *Offshore Cases and Materials* (1996) vol 1 at p 338. It has an inherent power to remove a protector only in exceptional circumstances, eg, to protect the assets of the trust: *Re Papadimitriou* [2004] WTLR 1141 (Isle of Man HC).

[283] Trusts of Land and Appointment of Trustees Act 1996, s 10(1), (2).

[284] Ibid, s 10(3).

A protector, who may be called by some other name, such as adviser, appointor, or management committee may be given a wide variety of powers, for instance, to remove and appoint trustees and settle their remuneration, to add to a class of discretionary beneficiaries, to make or approve distribution decisions, to change the governing law of the trust, or to terminate the trust by triggering a final vesting provision. There are limits, however, to the powers which he may be given. He cannot be given power to determine questions of law arising in the construction or administration of the trust,[285] and it is doubtful whether he could be empowered to deprive the beneficiaries of their right to inspect the trust documents,[286] or to release the trustees from liability for breach of trust.

---

[285] See *Re Wynn's Will Trusts* [1952] Ch 271, [1952] 1 All ER 341 and p 492, ante.
[286] See *Re Londonderry's Settlement* [1965] Ch 918, [1964] 3 All ER 855, CA, and pp 396–399, ante.

23

VARIATION OF TRUSTS

1 DUTY NOT TO DEVIATE FROM THE TERMS OF THE TRUST[1]

The fundamental principle is that a trustee must faithfully observe the directions contained in the trust instrument and, 'as a rule, the court has no jurisdiction to give, and will not give, its sanction to the performance by trustees of acts with reference to the trust estate which are not, on the face of the instrument creating the trust, authorized by its terms'.[2] The House of Lords has made it clear in *Chapman v Chapman*[3] that under the inherent jurisdiction the exceptions to this rule are very limited. These exceptions will now be discussed, and in the next sections we shall consider inroads made upon the rule by statute. Two other exceptions are more conveniently considered elsewhere, namely the rule that if all the beneficiaries being of full age and capacity act together they can consent to what would otherwise be a breach of trust so as to free the trustees from any liability,[4] and, indeed, even bring the trust to an end,[5] and the cy-près doctrine in relation to charities.[6]

Adopting the classification used by Lord Morton in *Chapman v Chapman*[7] the cases under the inherent jurisdiction can be grouped under four heads.

(i) '*Cases in which the court has effected changes in the nature of an infant's property, eg by directing investment of his personalty in the purchase of freeholds.*' As a consequence of the substantial assimilation of the law relating to realty and the law relating to personalty, this head is no longer of practical importance.

(ii) '*Cases in which the court has allowed the trustees of settled property to enter into some*

---

[1] See generally (1965) 43 CBR 181 (A J McClean). Cf *Re Baker* (1984) 47 OR (2d) 415.

[2] *Re New* [1901] 2 Ch 534 at 544, CA, per Romer LJ.

[3] [1954] AC 429, [1954] 1 All ER 798, HL; affmg the judgment of the majority in CA, [1953] Ch 218, [1953] 1 All ER 103.

[4] See chapter 24, section 3(b), p 534 et seq, infra. If the proposed act can affect only some of the beneficiaries, only those who may be affected need consent in order to protect the trustees—but those beneficiaries must all be of full age and capacity.

[5] See chapter 17, section 6, p 405 supra.   [6] See chapter 14, section 6, p 325, supra.

[7] [1954] AC 429 at 451, [1954] 1 All ER 798 at 807, 808, HL.

business transaction which was not authorized by the settlement.' These are emergency situations not foreseen or anticipated by the settlor and where the consent of the beneficiaries cannot be obtained because some of them are under disability or not yet in existence.[8]

This exception includes, and can perhaps be regarded as,[9] an extension of the principle of the salvage cases, where, in the case of absolute necessity, such as repairs vital to prevent further damage to settled land, the court has sanctioned a transaction such as the mortgage or sale of part of a minor's beneficial interest.[10] The Court of Appeal in *Re Montagu*,[11] following earlier cases,[12] made it quite clear that the fact that the proposed scheme would benefit the minor, or indeed all the beneficiaries, was not enough. The application failed in *Re Montagu*[13] itself, Lopes LJ observing,[14] 'If the buildings were falling down it would be a case of actual salvage and would stand differently.'

The proposal put forward in *Re New*,[15] was that the trustees, as holders of certain shares, should be empowered to concur in a proposed reconstruction of a mercantile company, as a result of which they would receive shares and debentures in the proposed new or reconstructed company. In sanctioning the scheme the court put the trustees on an undertaking to apply for leave to retain such shares and debentures if they desired to retain them for more than a year. This decision, it was said two years later in *Re Tollemache*,[16] 'constitutes the high-water mark of the exercise by the court of its extraordinary jurisdiction in relation to trusts'. In the later case what was sought, and refused, was authority for the trustees to acquire a mortgage of the tenant for life's interest, a transaction which it was claimed could not prejudice the remaindermen and would enable the tenant for life to enjoy a large addition to her income by reason of that fact that a higher rate of interest was payable under the mortgage than was being received on the authorized trust investments.

(iii) *'Cases in which the court has allowed maintenance out of income which the settlor or testator directed to be accumulated.'* Unlike the previous two exceptions, this exception involves modification or re-moulding of the beneficial trusts. The classic explanation of this exception was given by Pearson J in *Re Collins*,[17] namely:

that where a testator has made a provision for a family, using that word in the ordinary sense in which we take the word, that is the children of a particular stirps in succession or otherwise, but has postponed the enjoyment, either for a particular purpose or generally for the increase of the estate, it is assumed that he did not intend that these children should be left unprovided for or in a state of such moderate means that they should not be educated

---

[8] See *Re New* [1901] 2 Ch 534, CA per Romer LJ at 544. Cf *Re Lotzkar* (1984) 57 BCLR 364.

[9] See (1954) 17 MLR 420 (O R Marshall).

[10] *Re Jackson* (1882) 21 Ch D 786; *Conway v Fenton* (1888) 40 Ch D 512; *Re De Teissier's Settled Estates* [1893] 1 Ch 153.

[11] [1897] 2 Ch 8, CA.   [12] Eg *Calvert v Godfrey* (1843) 6 Beav 97; *Re Jackson*, supra.

[13] Supra.   [14] At 11.   [15] Supra.   [16] [1903] 1 Ch 955 at 956, CA, per Cozens-Hardy LJ.

[17] (1886) 32 Ch D 229 at 232; *Havelock v Havelock* (1881) 17 Ch D 807.

properly for the position and fortune which he designs them to have, and the court has accordingly found from the earliest time that where an heir-at-law is unprovided for, maintenance ought to be provided for him. Lord Hardwicke has extended that to the case of a tenant for life . . .[18]

The jurisdiction here does not depend on the minority of the life tenant,[19] nor is it confined to cases of emergency or necessity.[20]

(iv) '*Cases in which the court has approved a compromise on behalf of infants and possible after-born beneficiaries.*' There is no doubt that the court has jurisdiction where rights are in dispute: but if the court approves a compromise in such case it is not really altering the trusts, which are, ex hypothesi, still in doubt and unascertained. The House of Lords, however, in *Chapman v Chapman*[21] decided that there was no jurisdiction to sanction an alteration or re-arrangement of beneficial interests where there was no compromise of disputed rights, and the Court of Appeal has since decided that there cannot be said to be any disputed rights where there is merely an ambiguity in, for instance, an investment clause and it would be to the common advantage of all the beneficiaries to have a new clause substituted therefor.[22]

2 STATUTORY EXCEPTIONS TO DUTY NOT TO DEVIATE FROM THE TERMS OF THE TRUST

(a) SECTION 53 OF THE TRUSTEE ACT 1925[23]

The section provides as follows:

Where an infant is beneficially entitled to any property the court may, with a view to the application of the capital or income thereof for the maintenance, education, or benefit[24] of the infant, make an order—

   (a) appointing a person to convey such property; or
   (b) in the case of stock, or a thing in action, vesting in any person the right to transfer or

---

[18] Instead of presumed intent, Farwell J in *Re Walker* [1901] 1 Ch 879 based the jurisdiction on the construction of the will, and Denning LJ, dissenting in *Re Downshire Settled Estates* [1953] Ch 218 at 273, [1953] 1 All ER 103 at 134, CA, simply on the benefit to the children.

[19] *Revel v Watkinson* (1748) 1 Ves Sen 93.

[20] *Haley v Bannister* (1820) 4 Madd 275, where maintenance was allowed to a father although the mother had ample means of her own to bring up the children.

[21] [1954] AC 429, [1954] 1 All ER 798, HL. See (1954) 17 MLR at 427–431 (O R Marshall); *Re Barbour's Settlement, National Westminster Bank Ltd v Barbour* [1974] 1 All ER 1188.

[22] *Re Powell-Cotton's Re-Settlement* [1956] 1 All ER 60, CA. Contrast *Mason v Farbrother* [1983] 2 All ER 1078.

[23] See (1957) 21 Conv 448 (O R Marshall).

[24] These are words of the widest import—*Re Heyworth's Settlement* [1956] Ch 364 at 370, [1956] 2 All ER 21 at 23.

call for a transfer of such stock, or to receive the dividends or income thereof, or to sue for and recover such thing in action, upon such terms as the court may think fit.

Under this section it was held in *Re Gower's Settlement*[25] that where there was an infant tenant in tail in remainder of Blackacre with divers remainders over, the court could effectually authorize a mortgage of Blackacre (subject to the interests having priority over the infant's tenancy in tail) framed so as to vest in the mortgagee a security which would be as effective a bar against the infant's issue taking under the entail and the subsequent remaindermen as if the infant were of full age and had executed the conveyance in accordance with the Fines and Recoveries Act 1833.

It was expressly assumed in *Re Gower's Settlement*[26] that the requirement of the section that the mortgage should be made 'with a view to the application of the capital or income thereof for the maintenance, education or benefit of the infant' was satisfied. It was held that there was no such 'application' in *Re Heyworth's Settlements*[27] where it was proposed to put an end to the trusts created by the settlement by selling the infant's contingent reversionary interest to the life tenant for an outright cash payment. This decision was distinguished in *Re Meux's Will Trusts*[28] where the proceeds of sale were to be settled. It was held that the sale and settlement of the proceeds of the sale were to be regarded as a single transaction, which did constitute an 'application' for the purpose of the section.[29] And in *Re Bristol's Settled Estates*[30] a person was appointed to execute a disentailing assurance to bar the infant's entail with a view to a settlement being made with the assistance of the court under the Variation of Trusts Act 1958.

(b) SECTION 57(1) OF THE TRUSTEE ACT 1925

This section, which does not apply to trustees of a settlement for the purposes of the Settled Land Act 1925,[31] provides as follows:

Where in the management or administration of any property vested in trustees any sale, lease, mortgage, surrender, release, or other disposition, or any purchase, investment, acquisition, expenditure, or other transaction, is in the opinion of the court expedient, but the same cannot be effected by reason of the absence of any power for that purpose vested in the trustees by the trust instrument, if any, or by law, the court may by order confer upon the trustees, either generally or in any particular instance, the necessary power for the purpose, on such terms, and subject to such provisions and conditions, if any, as the court may think fit and may direct in what manner any money authorised to be expended, and the costs of any transaction, are to be paid or borne as between capital and income.[32]

---

[25] [1934] Ch 365, [1934] All ER Rep 796; *Re Lansdowne's Will Trusts* [1967] Ch 603, [1967] 1 All ER 888.
[26] Supra.   [27] [1956] Ch 364, [1956] 2 All ER 21.
[28] [1958] Ch 154, [1957] 2 All ER 630; *Re Lansdowne's Will Trusts*, supra.
[29] Cf *Re Ropner's Settlement Trust* [1956] 3 All ER 332n, [1956] 1 WLR 902—a decision on similar words in s 32 of the Trustee Act 1925.
[30] [1964] 3 All ER 939, [1965] 1 WLR 469.   [31] Trustee Act 1925, s 57(4).
[32] An application may be made by the trustees, or any of them, or any beneficiary: see *Rennie v Proma Ltd* [1990] 1 EGLR 119, CA.

Although it was conceded by counsel before the House of Lords in *Chapman v Chapman*[33] that this section could not apply, Lord Morton stated his agreement with the comments on the section contained in the majority judgment in the Court of Appeal,[34] which is authority for the following propositions. It was presumably the intention of Parliament, in enacting this section, to confer new powers on the court rather than to codify or define the existing powers under the inherent jurisdiction, though it may well be that the new extended jurisdiction does in some degree overlap the old. The section envisages

(i)   an act unauthorized by a trust instrument,[35]

(ii)   to be effected by the trustees thereof,

(iii) in the management or administration of the trust property,

(iv)   which the court will empower them to perform,

(v)   if in its opinion the act is expedient, that is expedient for the trust as a whole.[36]

Of primary importance is the interpretation of the words 'management' and 'administration', which are largely, though very possibly not entirely, synonymous. The subject-matter of both words in s 57 is trust property which is vested in trustees, and 'trust property' cannot by any legitimate stretch of the language include the equitable interests which a settlor has created in that property. The application of both words is confined to the managerial supervision and control of trust property on behalf of beneficiaries, and the section accordingly does not permit the remoulding of the beneficial interests. The object of s 57, it was said,[37] is:

to secure that trust property should be managed as advantageously as possible in the interests of the beneficiaries, and, with that object in view, to authorize specific dealings with the property which the court might have felt itself unable to sanction under the inherent jurisdiction, either because no actual 'emergency' had arisen or because of inability to show that the position which called for intervention was one which the creator of the trust could not reasonably have foreseen, but it was no part of the legislative aim to disturb the rule that the court will not re-write a trust or to add to such exceptions to that rule as had already found their way into the inherent jurisdiction.

Later in the judgment the majority adopted the statement of Farwell J in *Re Mair*,[38] that 'if and when the court sanctions an arrangement or transaction under s 57, it must be taken to have done it as though the power which is being put into operation had been inserted in the trust instrument as an overriding power'. Perhaps Farwell J put it even more clearly later in his judgment where he said[39] 'the effect of the court

---

[33] [1954] AC 429, [1954] 1 All ER 798, HL.   [34] [1953] Ch 218, [1953] 1 All ER 103, CA.

[35] *Re Pratt* [1943] Ch 326, [1943] 2 All ER 375.

[36] *Re Craven's Estate* [1937] Ch 423, [1937] 3 All ER 33.

[37] Per Evershed MR and Romer LJ in *Re Downshire Settled Estates* [1953] Ch 218, 248, 264 and 265; [1953] 1 All ER 103, 119, 129 and 132. And see *Municipal and General Securities Co Ltd v Lloyds Bank Ltd* [1950] Ch 212, [1949] 2 All ER 937.

[38] [1935] Ch 562 at 565.   [39] Supra at 738, 566.

permitting the exercise by trustees of some power which is not in the trust document itself, and, therefore, something which the trustees could not do except by the direction of the court, is the same as though that power had been inserted as an overriding power in the trust document.'

Applications under s 57 are almost invariably heard and disposed of in private and accordingly not reported. There are, however, a few reported cases which show that in the exercise of its jurisdiction under this section the court has authorized the sale of settled chattels,[40] a partition of land,[41] and a sale of land where the necessary consent could not be obtained.[42] It has authorized two residuary estates left on identical charitable trusts to be blended into one fund.[43] It has, apparently commonly, authorized capital money to be expended on paying off the tenant for life's debts, on having its replacement secured by a policy of insurance so that the beneficial interests remain unaltered,[44] but although it has in exceptional circumstances sanctioned a similar expenditure of capital to purchase the life tenant's interest, it is doubtful whether it would do so in an ordinary case, as it would come 'at least very near to altering the beneficial interests of the tenant for life'.[45] The court has also authorized the sale of a reversionary interest which under the trust instrument was not to be sold until it should fall into possession.[46] Finally, as has already been seen,[47] the section may be used to extend trustees' powers of investment.

(c) SECTION 64 OF THE SETTLED LAND ACT 1925

This section gives the court jurisdiction to authorize the tenant for life of settled land within the Act to effect any transaction. The section has five requirements:

(i) a transaction, as defined in sub-s (2),[48]

(ii) affecting or concerning the settled land or any part thereof,

(iii) not being a transaction otherwise authorized by the 1925 Act or the settlement,

---

[40] *Re Hope's Will Trust* [1929] 2 Ch 136. [41] *Re Thomas* [1930] 1 Ch 194, [1929] All ER Rep 129.

[42] *Re Beale's Settlement Trusts* [1932] 2 Ch 15, [1931] All ER Rep 637.

[43] *Re Harvey* [1941] 3 All ER 284. The contrary decision in *Re Royal Society's Charitable Trusts* [1956] Ch 87, [1955] 3 All ER 14, where *Re Harvey* does not appear to have been cited, would seem to be wrong in the light of *Re Shipwrecked Fishermen and Mariners' Royal Benevolent Society Charity* [1959] Ch 220, [1958] 3 All ER 465.

[44] *Re Salting* [1932] 2 Ch 57; *Re Mair*, supra. These cases must be read in the light of the observations of the majority of the Court of Appeal in *Re Downshire Settled Estates* [1953] Ch 218 at 249–251, [1953] 1 All ER 103 at 119–121; and see *Re Forster's Settlement* [1954] 3 All ER 714.

[45] *Re Forster's Settlement*, supra, at 720, per Harman J.

[46] *Re Cockerell's Settlement Trusts* [1956] Ch 372, [1956] 2 All ER 172. [47] See p 425, supra.

[48] As amended by the Settled Land and Trustee Acts (Court's General Powers) Act 1943 and the Statute Law (Repeals) Act 1969, to include 'any sale, exchange, assurance, grant, lease, surrender, reconveyance, release, reservation, or other disposition, and any purchase or other acquisition, and any covenant, contract, or option, and any application of capital money, and any compromise or other dealing, or arrangement'.

(iv) which in the opinion of the court would be for the benefit of (a) the settled land or any part of it or (b) the persons interested under the settlement, and

(v) being one which could have been effected by an absolute owner.

According to the majority judgment of the Court of Appeal in *Re Downshire Settled Estates*[49] the jurisdiction under this section is more ample in regard to the subject-matter to which it relates than is s 57 of the Trustee Act 1925. The jurisdiction here is not limited to managerial and administrative acts, but also enables the court to authorize alterations in the beneficial interests, including the variation of the beneficial interests of beneficiaries who are of full age and capacity and who do not consent.[50] It extends to the conveyance by the tenant for life of the settled land to trustees of a new settlement to be held by them on trust for sale.[51] It is, however, essential that the court should be satisfied that the transaction proposed is for the benefit of either the settled land or some part thereof, or of the persons interested under the settlement—but not necessarily of both; also that the transaction affects or concerns the settled land or any other land.[52] The last qualification is satisfied by transactions indirectly, as well as directly, operating upon the settled land (or other land), provided that in the former case the effect is real and substantial by ordinary commonsense standards, as distinct from that which is oblique or remote and merely incidental. If, however, there is no relevant property[53] which is, or is deemed to be, subject to the settlement, the settlement permanently ceases to be a settlement for the purposes of that Act.[54]

The section was used in *Re Scarisbrick Resettlement Estates*[55] to raise money by the sale of investments representing capital to enable the tenant for life to continue to live in Scarisbrick Hall, his continued residence being essential for the preservation of the hall. In other cases[56] the court has authorized alterations in beneficial interests with the object of avoiding estate duty. Lastly, in *Raikes v Lygon*[57] it was held that s 64 is wide enough to allow trustees of settled property to transfer part of the property to another settlement in order to maintain other settled property of which the trustees remained the owners, even though under the second settlement bodies not beneficiaries under the first settlement would become potential beneficiaries. The transaction was said simply to involve an application of part of the capital of the settled property in a fiscally efficient way to maintain other parts of the settled property, the price of

---

[49] [1953] Ch 218, [1953] 1 All ER 103, CA.

[50] *Hambro v Duke of Marlborough* [1994] Ch 158, [1994] 3 All ER 332, noted [1994] Conv 492 (Elizabeth Cooke).

[51] *Hambro v Duke of Marlborough*, supra.

[52] Whether settled or not and whether within or without England.

[53] Defined in s 2(4) of the Trusts of Land and Appointment of Trustees Act 1996.   [54] Ibid, s 2(4).

[55] [1944] Ch 229, [1944] 1 All ER 404. See also *Re Mount Edgcumbe Settled Estates* [1950] Ch 615, [1950] 2 All ER 242.

[56] *Re Downshire Settled Estates*, supra, CA, where the real object of the scheme was to preserve the land for future holders of the plaintiff's title; *Re Simmons' Trusts* [1956] Ch 125, [1955] 3 All ER 818.

[57] [1988] 1 All ER 884, [1988] 1 WLR 281.

the fiscal saving being the introduction, as long stops, of certain bodies which were non-beneficiaries under the first settlement.

(d) SETTLED LAND AND TRUSTEE ACTS (COURT'S GENERAL POWERS) ACT 1943

This Act[58] permanently extends[59] the jurisdiction of the court under s 57 of the Trustee Act 1925 and s 64 of the Settled Land Act 1925, giving it power, in certain circumstances, taking all relevant matters into account,[60] to authorize any expense of action taken or proposed in or for the management of settled land, or of land subject to a trust of land, to be treated as a capital outgoing, notwithstanding that in other circumstances that expense could not properly have been so treated.

The circumstances referred to are that the court is satisfied that the action taken or proposed was or would be for the benefit of the persons entitled under the settlement, or under the trust of land; and either

(i)   that the available income from all sources of a person who, as being bene-ficially entitled to possession or receipt of rents and profits of the land or to reside in a house comprised therein, might otherwise have been expected to bear the expense has been so reduced as to render him unable to bear that expense, or unable to bear it without undue hardship, or

(ii) where there is no such person, that the income available for meeting that expense has become insufficient.

(e) MATRIMONIAL CAUSES ACT 1973

The court has wide powers in matrimonial proceedings to make, inter alia, an order varying for the benefit of the parties to the marriage and of the children of the family or either or any of them any ante-nuptial or post-nuptial settlement made on the parties to the marriage.

(f) MENTAL HEALTH ACT 1983

The court has wide powers under ss 95 and 96 in relation to the settlement of any property of the patient and the variation of any settlement so made. These provisions will be repealed when the Mental Capacity Act 2005 is brought into force, and replaced by similar provisions contained in ss 16 and 18 of, and Sch 2 to, that Act.

---

[58] Section 9, as amended by the Emergency Laws (Miscellaneous Provisions) Act 1953, and the Trusts of Land and Appointment of Trustees Act 1996.

[59] *Re Scarisbrick Resettlement Estates* [1944] Ch 229, [1944] 1 All ER 404.

[60] Section 1(3) of the Settled Land and Trustee Acts (Court's General Powers) Act 1943.

(g) OCCUPATIONAL PENSION SCHEMES

Special provisions for the modification of occupational pension schemes are contained in the Pensions Act 1995, ss 67–72.

3 THE VARIATION OF TRUSTS ACT 1958[61]

This Act gives the court a discretionary power to approve on behalf of any of four classes of persons, any arrangement varying or revoking all[62] or any of the trusts upon which property is held, or enlarging the powers of the trustees of managing or administering any of the property subject to the trusts. The jurisdiction given to the court by the Act is not confined to settlements governed by English law.[63]

The word 'arrangement' used in the Act has been said[64] to be 'deliberately used in the widest possible sense so as to cover any proposal which any person may put forward for varying or revoking the trusts', and there is some authority as to the extent of the jurisdiction of the court in these matters. In looking at the cases it seems that the maxim 'equity looks to the intent rather than the form' has, in effect, been applied. On the one hand, Wilberforce J has pointed out[65] that if the arrangement, though presented as a 'variation', is in truth a complete new re-settlement, the court has no jurisdiction to approve it. If an arrangement changes the whole substratum of the trust, then it may well be that it cannot be regarded as a variation. On the other hand, Megarry J has said[66] that 'if an arrangement, while leaving the substratum, effectuates the purpose of the original trust by other means, it may still be possible to regard that arrangement as merely varying the original trusts, even though the means employed are wholly different, and even though the form is completely changed.'

The nature of the court's jurisdiction under the Act was explained in *Re Holmden's Settlement Trusts*[67] where Lord Reid said:

Under the Variation of Trusts Act 1958, the court does not itself amend or vary the trusts of the original settlement. The beneficiaries are not bound by variations because the court has made the variation. Each beneficiary is bound because he has consented to the variation. If he was not of full age[68] when the arrangement was made, he is bound because the court was authorized by the Act of 1958 to approve of it on his behalf and did so by making an order. If

---

[61] Discussed (1963) 27 Conv 6 (D M Evans); (1969) 33 Conv 113 and 183 (J W Harris).

[62] *Re Seale's Marriage Settlement* [1961] Ch 574, [1961] 3 All ER 136.

[63] *Re Ker's Settlement Trusts* [1963] Ch 553, [1963] 1 All ER 801; *Re Paget's Settlement* [1965] 1 All ER 58, [1965] 1 WLR 1046.

[64] *Re Steed's Will Trusts* [1960] Ch 407 at 419, [1960] 1 All ER 487 at 492, CA, per Evershed MR.

[65] In *Re T's Settlement Trusts* [1964] Ch 158 at 162, sub nom *Re Towler's Settlement Trusts* [1963] 3 All ER 759 at 762.

[66] In *Re Ball's Settlement* [1968] 2 All ER 438 at 442, [1968] 1 WLR 899 at 905.

[67] [1968] AC 685, [1968] 1 All ER 148, HL.

[68] The principle here stated to apply to a minor must apply equally to any other class of person under s 1(1).

he was of full age and did not in fact consent he is not affected by the order of the court and he is not bound. So the arrangement must be regarded as an arrangement made by the beneficiaries themselves. The court merely acted on behalf of or as representing those beneficiaries who were not in a position to give their consent and approval.

As Mummery LJ observed in *Goulding v James*[69] the 1958 Act is viewed as a statutory extension of the consent principle embodied in the rule in *Sanders v Vautier*,[70] which recognizes the rights of beneficiaries, being sui juris and together absolutely entitled to the trust property, to exercise their proprietary rights to overbear and defeat the intention of a testator or settlor to subject property to the continuing trusts, powers and limitations of a will or trust instrument.

Unfortunately in *Re Holmden's Settlement Trusts*[71] no mention seems to have been made of the difficulty raised by s 53(1)(*c*) of the Law of Property Act 1925[72] which would seem to require that the beneficiaries, other than those on whose behalf the court was giving its approval, should sign some document in writing. The difficulty was, however, carefully considered by Megarry J in *Re Holt's Settlement*,[73] who accepted with some hesitation two grounds which were put forward by counsel to defeat the argument based on s 53(1)(*c*). First, that by conferring an express power on the court to do something by order, Parliament in the Act of 1958 had provided by necessary implication an exception to s 53(1)(*c*). Secondly, that where, as on the facts before him, the arrangement consisted of a specifically enforceable agreement made for valuable consideration, the beneficial interest would have passed to the respective purchasers on the making of the agreement. This would be a case of constructive trust excluded from the operation of s 53(1)(*c*) by sub-s (2).[74] The result appears to have been accepted as correct, and no point on s 53(1)(*c*) has been raised in subsequent reported cases.

(a) PERSONS ON WHOSE BEHALF THE COURT MAY ACT

The four classes of persons referred to in the Act are therein defined[75] as follows:

(a) any person having, directly or indirectly, an interest, whether vested or contingent, under the trusts who by reason of infancy or other incapacity is incapable of assenting, or

(b) any person (whether ascertained or not) who may become entitled, directly or indirectly, to an interest under the trusts as being at a future date or on the happening of a future event a person of any specified description or a member of any specified

---

[69] [1997] 2 All ER 239, CA.   [70] [1841] 4 Beav 115. See p 405, supra.

[71] [1968] AC 685, [1968] 1 All ER 148, HL.   [72] Discussed p 89 et seq, supra.

[73] [1969] 1 Ch 100, [1968] 1 All ER 470.

[74] See pp 89, 163 supra. This last ground carries more weight since *Neville v Wilson* [1997] Ch 144, [1996] 3 All ER 171, CA.

[75] Variation of Trusts Act 1958, s 1(1).

class of persons, so however that this paragraph shall not include any person[76] who would be of that description, or a member of that class, as the case may be, if the said date had fallen or the said event had happened at the date of the application to the court,[77] or

(c) any person unborn, or

(d) any person[78] in respect of any discretionary interest of his under protective trusts where the interest of the principal beneficiary[79] has not failed or determined.

The first part of paragraph (b) gives jurisdiction in relation to any person, whether ascertained or not, who may become entitled to an interest under the trusts as being at some future date a person answering a specified description. This looks to someone who may become entitled in the future, and excludes one who already has an interest, albeit remote. Thus the court in *Knocker v Youle*[80] had no power to give its consent on behalf of persons who had a merely contingent interest (in some cases a double contingency), which, moreover, was liable to be defeated by the exercise of general testamentary power of appointment. It has been argued,[81] however, that 'interest' in s 1(1)(b) means 'vested interest' and that the court's jurisdiction is not excluded in the case of persons having a contingent interest.

Prospective next of kin, of course, do not have even a contingent interest. They have only a *spes successionis*, a hope of succeeding, and are the typical category of persons who fall within the first part of paragraph (b). They may, however, be excluded from the jurisdiction of the court if they fall within the second part of that paragraph. There has been discussion of the construction of the second half of paragraph (b), which excludes the jurisdiction of the court in relation to persons falling within it. It apparently excludes only ascertained persons who would fit the description in the first half of the paragraph upon the occurrence of a single contingency. Thus in *Re Suffert's Settlement*[82] the court had no jurisdiction to give its consent on behalf of cousins who would have been entitled as next of kin if the life tenant applicant had died on the date

---

[76] It seems to be assumed that this is to be construed as 'any ascertained person', see Underhill and Hayton, *Law of Trusts and Trustees*, 16th edn, p 507.

[77] Ie, per Buckley, J, obiter, in *Re Suffert's Settlement* [1961] Ch 1, [1960] 3 All ER 561, and per Warner J in *Knocker v Youle* [1986] 2 All ER 914, the date on which the originating summons (now claim form) was issued. Underhill and Hayton, loc cit, suggests it may be the date on which the application is heard by the court.

[78] Including an unascertained or unborn person—*Re Turner's Will Trusts* [1960] Ch 122, [1959] 2 All ER 689. It appears that under this paragraph approval may be given on behalf of, and even against the wishes of, an adult ascertained beneficiary.

[79] Defined by s 1(2) by reference to s 33 of the Trustee Act 1925. See *Re Wallace's Settlement* [1968] 2 All ER 209, [1968] 1 WLR 711.

[80] [1986] 2 All ER 914, discussed [1986] 136 NLJ 1057 (P Luxton).

[81] See *Buschau v Rogers Communications Inc* (2004) 236 DLR (4th) 18 (further proceedings (2004) 239 DLR (4th) 610) where it was observed that J G Riddall appears to have resiled from his criticism of the case in [1987] Conv 144.

[82] Supra. See Harris, *Variation of Trusts*, pp 33–41 and n 77, supra.

of the application to the court, and in *Re Moncrieff's Settlement Trusts*[83] the court had no jurisdiction in relation to an adopted son who would have been entitled had the life tenant applicant died on the date of the application to the court. In the latter case the court did, however, have jurisdiction in relation to persons who would have been entitled as next of kin in that event had the adopted son predeceased the life tenant.

By the proviso, except as regards the last class under paragraph (d), the court must not approve an arrangement on behalf of any person unless the carrying out thereof would be for the benefit of 'that person'.[84] In *Re Cohen's Settlement Trusts*[85] there was a class of persons unborn. It was held that the court was not concerned with the interests of the class as a whole, but with the individual members of it. Accordingly the court could not approve a variation where, among persons yet unborn who might become entitled to beneficial interests under the settlement in its original form, there might be a person or persons who by the effect of the proposed variation would be deprived of the beneficial interest he or they might otherwise have taken without obtaining any counter-balancing advantage.

Finally it should be noted that the court may make an order even though there may be persons with potential interests in the estate who are not parties and who will not be bound by the order. In such a case the trustees will not be free, except at their own risk, to treat the trusts as effectively varied until they have obtained the consent of such persons.[86]

(b) MEANING OF BENEFIT IN THE PROVISO

It is clear that a proposed arrangement may well involve some sort of risk to the beneficiary upon whose behalf the court is asked to give its approval, but this will not prevent the court giving its sanction if it is a risk that an adult would be prepared to take.[87] Thus, for example, it is no bar to the court giving approval on behalf of an unborn person that in some circumstances such a person would obtain no benefit,

---

[83] [1962] 3 All ER 838n, [1962] 1 WLR 1344.

[84] Proviso to s 1(1) of the Variation of Trusts Act 1958; *Re Clitheroe's Settlement Trusts* [1959] 3 All ER 789; *Re Hessian* (1996) 153 NSR (2d) 122, 450 APR 122. It was held that the peculiar discretionary trust in *Re Bristol's Settled Estates* [1964] 3 All ER 939, [1965] 1 WLR 469, did not fall within para (d). In *Re T Settlement* [2002] JLR 204 the Royal Court of Jersey held that it was to the benefit of minor and unborn beneficiaries to vary the trust to enable tax due from the settlor, a non-beneficiary, to be paid by the settlement, in discharge of a moral obligation. By s 1(3) in the case of a patient under the Mental Health Act 1983 the question is to be determined by the authority of the person having jurisdiction within Part VII of that Act. As prospectively amended by the Mental Capacity Act 2005, Sch 6, para 9, s 1(3) will provide that in the case of a person who lacks capacity (within the meaning of that Act) to give his assent the question is to be determined by the Court of Protection.

[85] [1965] 3 All ER 139, [1965] 1 WLR 1229.

[86] *Re Suffert's Settlement*, supra; *Re Hall's Will Trusts* [1985] NI 118.

[87] *Re Cohen's Will Trusts* [1959] 3 All ER 523, [1959] 1 WLR 865. The court may require the risk to be covered by insurance. See *Re Brook's Settlement* [1968] 3 All Er 416, [1968] 1 WLR 1661 for a discussion of the risk that may be involved in the possibility of the judge taking what turns out later to have been a wrong view of the law.

where probably in fact the arrangement would be to his advantage. This is simply the risk that the court is entitled to take, if it thinks fit, on behalf of the unborn person.[88] The court, however, starts from the principle that the beneficiary should not be materially worse off as a result of the variation, whatever happens.[89] It may be added that the fact that as between the adult beneficiaries the arrangement does not represent a fair bargain does not prevent the court from approving the arrangement in a proper case.[90]

According to obiter dicta of Megarry J in *Re Holt's Settlement*,[91] the benefit referred to is 'plainly not confined to financial benefit, but may extend to moral or social benefit'. It was, he said, 'speaking in general terms, ... most important that young children "should be reasonably advanced in a career and settled in life before they are in receipt of an income sufficient to make them independent of the need to work" '. Thus it might, under the Act, be a 'benefit' to an infant to suffer the financial detriment of a postponement in the date of the absolute vesting of his interest, though on the facts of that case the financial advantages of the proposed arrangement were overwhelming, and there was no need for any 'balance sheet' of advantages and disadvantages. The principle that an element of financial benefit is unnecessary actually formed part of the ratio decidendi in *Re CL*[92] where the court approved an arrangement on behalf of an elderly, wealthy widow who was a patient under the Mental Health Act 1959. Under the arrangement she gave up life interests in trust funds for no consideration at all, for the benefit of adopted daughters. The object was to save estate duty and the actual cost to the patient would be trifling, taking account of income tax and sur-tax, the patient's spending income being substantially in excess of her requirements. It may be added that it has been held, on similar legislation in Canada, that non-financial considerations carry greater weight where the contingent beneficiaries on whose behalf the court is asked to give consent stand no real chance of becoming entitled, and where the persons who are likely to be affected have given their consent to the proposed variation.[93]

Neither of these cases appears to have been cited in *Re Weston's Settlements*[94] where Lord Denning MR expressed a similar view:[95] 'The court should not consider merely the financial benefit to the infants or unborn children, but also their educational and

---

[88] *Re Holt's Settlement* [1969] 1 Ch 100, [1968] 1 All ER 470.
[89] *Re Robinson's Settlement Trusts* [1976] 3 All ER 61, [1976] 1 WLR 806, where the court considered some of the implications of the change from estate duty to inheritance tax.
[90] *Re Berry's Settlement* [1966] 3 All ER 431n, [1966] 1 WLR 1515.
[91] [1969] 1 Ch 100, [1968] 1 All ER 470. See *Re an Estate Trust* [2001] WTLR 571 (Jersey Royal Court).
[92] [1969] 1 Ch 587, [1968] 1 All ER 1104 (Ct of Protection).
[93] *Re Tweedie* (1975) 64 DLR (3d) 569.
[94] [1969] 1 Ch 223, [1968] 3 All ER 338, CA. See also *Re Remnant's Settlement Trusts* [1970] Ch 560, [1970] 2 All ER 554 (forfeiture clause on practising Roman Catholicism a deterrent in the selection of a husband and a source of possible family dissension: deletion accordingly a benefit) criticized by McPherson J in *Re Christmas' Settlement Trusts* [1986] 1 Qd R 372, who thought this extended the notion of benefit much further than could fairly be justified. The criticism seems valid. Cf *Re Tinker's Settlement* [1960] 3 All ER 85n, [1960] 1 WLR 1011, not cited in *Re Remnant's Settlement Trusts*.
[95] At 245, 342.

social benefit. There are many things in life more worthwhile than money.' In this case the proposed scheme involved the appointment by the court[96] of new trustees resident outside the jurisdiction and variation of the trusts to enable the trust property to be discharged from the trusts of the existing English settlement and made subject to similar trusts under a Jersey settlement. The object was admittedly tax avoidance. Applying the principle mentioned above Lord Denning said:

One of these things [more worthwhile than money] is to be brought up in this our England, which is still 'the envy of less happier lands'. I do not believe it is for the benefit of children to be uprooted from England and transported to another country simply to avoid tax ... The Court of Chancery should not encourage or support [the avoidance of tax]—it should not give its approval to it—if by so doing it would imperil the true welfare of the children, already born or yet to be born.

Accordingly he dismissed the appeal from the judge's refusal to approve the scheme. The decision was criticized in *The Times*[97] on the grounds that these were matters of judgment for parents, and that the court was trespassing on the preserves of family life. Professor Crane[98] however, is not wholly convinced by this criticism and thinks that the mathematics should carry less weight when the application involves removing the trust from the jurisdiction of the court.

(c) PRINCIPLES TO BE APPLIED

The law has recently been reviewed by the Court of Appeal in *Goulding v James*.[99] Here F left her residuary estate to her daughter (D) for life, with remainder to her grandson (G) contingently on his attaining the age of 40. If G died before F or before attaining the age of 40, the residuary estate was left to F's great grandchildren living at the death of G. The arrangement proposed by D and G was that 10 per cent of the residuary estate should be put into a trust fund for the great-grandchildren (this being considerably more than the current value of their interest in residue) and the balance of the fund divided between D and G. The first instance judge refused to approve the arrangement, on the ground that it was the complete opposite of what was provided for under the will and the settled intention of F. In reversing this decision Mummery LJ, who gave the leading judgment in the Court of Appeal, said that the discretion of the court whether or not to approve a proposed arrangement is fettered only by the proviso to s 1(1), which prohibits the court from approving an arrangement which is not for the benefit of the classes referred to in s 1(1)(a), (b) or (c). Actuarial benefit of the person or persons on whose behalf approval is sought does not, however, oblige the court to give its approval. The court is concerned whether the arrangement as a whole, in all the circumstances, is such that it is proper to approve it. The court's concern involves, inter alia, a practical and business-like consideration of the

---

96 Under s 41 of the Trustee Act 1925, discussed p 359 et seq, supra.   97 1 August 1968.
98 (1968) 32 Conv 431. See also (1969) 85 LQR 15 (P V Baker).
99 [1997] 2 All ER 239, CA, noted (1997) 60 MLR 719 (P Luxton).

arrangement, including the total amounts of the advantages which the various parties obtain, and their bargaining strength. In many cases, the intentions and wishes of the testator or settlor carry little, if any, weight on the issue of approval on behalf of those who have not the capacity to give consent themselves, and on the facts of the case approval should be given. *Re Steed's Will Trusts*,[100] where the Court of Appeal had refused to approve an arrangement which 'cut at the root of the testator's wishes and intentions', was held not to have laid down any rule, principle or guideline of general application on the importance of the intentions and wishes of a settlor or testator. It was clearly distinguishable: there the testator had manifested a particular purpose in creating a protective trust, namely to protect the life tenant from improvident dealings with property in favour of certain members of her family. The result of the proposed arrangement, coupled with an appointment which the life tenant had made by irrevocable deed to herself of the reversion, would have been that the applicant life tenant would have become absolutely entitled to the property. The Court of Appeal was satisfied that the testator's purpose was still justified. In the opinion of Mummery LJ in those circumstances there was overwhelming reason for refusal of the order.

It does not matter that the object of the proposed variation is to improve the position of the beneficiaries from the point of view of taxation or death duties, and this is in fact the most frequent motive behind applications under the Act.[101] The court will not, however, sanction an arrangement involving approval of an appointment which was a fraud on a power.[102] Where evidence of fraud is not clear Megarry J has explained[103] what the attitude of the court should be: 'If to a fair, cautious and enquiring mind the circumstances of the appointment, so far as known, raise a real and not a merely tenuous suspicion of a fraud on the power, the approval of the court ought to be withheld until that suspicion is dispelled.' He added that although the court should act as an alert and persistent watchdog, it ought not to be required to discharge the functions of a bloodhound or a ferret.

On an application under the Act the court may remove the limit on the statutory power of advancement.[104] The Act, however, almost certainly does not empower the court to direct a settlement of an infant's property, though in special circumstances it may defer an infant's right to capital.[105] Nor does it enable the court to get round the

---

[100] [1960] Ch 407, [1960] 1 All ER 487, CA. The approval of the court was sought on behalf of a para (d) person, the 'spectral husband' of the applicant, who was unmarried and past the age of childbearing.

[101] See *Re Holmden's Settlement Trusts* [1966] Ch 511 at 517, [1966] 2 All ER 661 at 665, CA per Denning MR; affd [1968] AC 685, [1968] 1 All ER 148, HL; *Re Sainsbury's Settlement* [1967] 1 All ER 878; (1968) 32 Conv 194 (G R Bretten). Note, however, that in *Re Weston's Settlements* [1968] 1 All ER 720 (affd on different grounds by CA [1969] 1 Ch 223, [1968] 3 All ER 338) Stamp J refused to sanction what he called 'a cheap exercise in tax avoidance' as distinct from 'a legitimate avoidance of liability to taxation'. A distinction without a difference?

[102] *Re Robertson's Will Trusts* [1960] 3 All ER 146n, [1960] 1 WLR 1050.

[103] *Re Wallace's Settlement* [1968] 2 All ER 209, [1968] 1 WLR 711. See also *Re Brook's Settlement* [1968] 3 All ER 416; (1969) 32 MLR 317 (S Cretney).

[104] See *D (a child) v O* [2004] EWHC 1036 (Ch), [2004] 3 All ER 780 and p 482, supra.

[105] *Re T's Settlement Trusts* [1964] Ch 158, sub nom *Re Towler's Settlement Trusts* [1963] 3 All ER 759.

absence of any inherent jurisdiction to order the payment out to trustees of moneys in court, being a sum recovered by way of damages by an infant, on terms that would defer the infant's entitlement beyond the age of majority. The payment out to trustees of sums in court does not give rise to the kind of trust contemplated by the Act, and, in any event, since the money recovered as damages is the infant's money absolutely, to impose such terms would not constitute a variation at all, but would be a new trust made on behalf of an absolute owner.[106] An application under the Act has been held[107] not to be appropriate to cover the contingency of the birth of a child to a woman believed in fact to be past the age of child-bearing. In administration the court may direct that funds be dealt with on the footing that at a certain age, normally in the middle or late fifties, a woman has become incapable of child-bearing. In a clear case no application to the court is necessary, but if an application is made to the court it will be to the ordinary administrative jurisdiction.[108] As a result of medical advances (including fertility treatment), the assumptions made by the court in 1966 as to the age at which a woman becomes incapable of child-bearing are now of doubtful validity. An application to the administrative jurisdiction may be combined with an application for an order under the Act in relation to other persons.[109]

As has been seen, in *Re Weston's Settlement*[110] Lord Denning decided the case on the ground that the required benefit to the persons on whose behalf the court was asked to give consent had not been established. Harman LJ preferred to dismiss the appeal on the ground that the linchpin[111] of the scheme was the exercise by the court of its power to appoint new trustees, and that the judge was entitled in the exercise of his discretion to refuse to exercise it so as to remove the trusts to Jersey. The settlements, he said, were English settlements and should remain so unless some good reason connected with the trusts themselves could be put forward.[112]

Re Weston's Settlement[113] must not, however, be taken to decide that it is never possible to export a trust. The court did not overrule, though it did distinguish *Re Seale's Marriage Settlement*.[114] There the whole family had emigrated to Canada and become Canadian citizens. The children were being educated there. Irrespective of

106 *Allen v Distillers Co (Biochemicals) Ltd* [1974] QB 384, [1974] 2 All ER 365. See (1984) 81 LSG 977 (G W Thomas).

107 *Re Pettifor's Will Trusts* [1966] Ch 257, [1966] 1 All ER 913. See (2001) 27 T & ELJ 10 (H Legge). In *Figg v Clarke* [1997] 1 WLR 603 it was said one should apply to the court for a declaration of the trustees' right of distribution rather than for the exercise by the court of its administrative jurisdiction.

108 As to the test to be applied, see *Re Levy Estate Trust* [2000] 5 CL 635, discussed (2000) 21 T & ELJ 6 (R Oughton).

109 *Re Westminster Bank Ltd's Declaration of Trust* [1963] 2 All ER 400n, [1963] 1 WLR 820.

110 [1969] 1 Ch 223, [1968] 3 All ER 338, CA, discussed pp 515–516, supra.

111 Though commonly new trustees outside the jurisdiction could be appointed otherwise than by the court under an express, or the statutory, power.

112 Danckwerts, LJ, agreed with both Lord Denning MR and Harman LJ.

113 Supra, CA. The trust instrument may give power to export a trust by appointing non-resident trustees, and to transfer the trust property out of the jurisdiction.

114 [1961] Ch 574, [1961] 3 All ER 136.

tax advantages there were manifest administrative advantages in having the trust administered locally. This decision has been followed since *Re Weston's Settlement*[115] in *Re Windeatt's Will Trusts*,[116] and was extended in *Re Chamberlain*[117] where, to obtain freedom from capital gains tax, the court gave its approval to an English settlement being transferred to Guernsey, a country with which the beneficiaries under the settlement—who had long since ceased to be domiciled and resident in the United Kingdom—had no connection.

(d) RELATIONSHIP TO OTHER STATUTORY PROVISIONS

It is expressly provided[118] that the jurisdiction given by the Act is additional to that given by s 57 of the Trustee Act 1925 and s 64 of the Settled Land Act 1925. Although in most ways the jurisdiction under the 1958 Act is wider, there are differences between these provisions which mean that it may sometimes be necessary to bring proceedings under one of the other Acts. Thus under s 57 of the Trustee Act 1925 the court must be satisfied that the proposed transaction is expedient, but there is no requirement that all or any of the beneficiaries must give their consent for an order to be effective. Under the 1958 Act, as we have seen, approval of an arrangement will only be fully effective if all the beneficiaries who are sui juris give their consent: moreover in giving its approval on behalf of beneficiaries who are unable to give their consent, the court can in general only do so if the proposed arrangement is for their benefit. Where jurisdictions overlap, practitioners seem to prefer to proceed under the 1958 Act.

---

[115] [1969] 1 Ch 223, [1968] 3 All ER 338, CA.

[116] [1969] 2 All ER 324, [1969] 1 WLR 692. See (1976) 40 Conv 295 (T G Watkin).

[117] (9 May 1976, unreported). See (1976) 126 NLJ 1034 (J B Morcom).

[118] Variation of Trusts Act 1958, s 1(6). As prospectively amended by the Mental Capacity Act 2005, Sch 6, para 9, s 1(6) provides only that nothing in the section is to be taken to limit the powers of the Court of Protection. It is thought unlikely that the omission of references to s 57 of the Trustee Act 1925 and s 64 of the Settled Land Act 1925 affects the result.

24

BREACH OF TRUST

1 PERSONAL LIABILITY OF TRUSTEES TO BENEFICIARIES

(a) GENERAL POSITION

At common law there are two principles fundamental to the award of damages: first, that the defendant's wrongful act must cause the damage complained of; second, that the plaintiff is to be put in the same position as he would have been in if he had not sustained the wrong for which he is now getting his compensation or reparation. Although equity approaches liability for making good a breach of trust from a different starting point, and though the detailed rules of equity as to causation and the quantification of loss differ from those applicable at common law, the principles underlying both systems are the same. Under both systems liability is fault based.[1]

The basic right of a beneficiary is to have the trust duly administered in accordance with the provisions of the trust instrument, if any, and the general law. Failure in such due administration, whether by a positive act, for instance, investing the trust funds in unauthorized investments, or by a failure to act,[2] for instance, neglecting to get the trust funds transferred into his name, constitutes a breach of trust,[3] for which the trustee will be liable. The liability extends to all loss thereby caused directly or indirectly[4] to the trust estate and, even where no loss can be shown, to any profit which has accrued to the trustee.[5] It is equally a breach of trust whether committed

---

[1] The law in this area was reviewed by Lord Browne-Wilkinson in *Target Holdings Ltd v Redferns (a firm)* [1996] AC 421, [1995] 3 All ER 785, HL. See *Friends' Provident Life Office v Hillier Parker May and Rowden (a firm)* [1997] QB 85 [1995] 4 All ER 260, CA; [1997] Conv 14 (D Capper); (2001) 60 CLJ 337 (D Capper); [2003] NZLJ 225 (C Rickett).

[2] *Grayburn v Clarkson* (1868) 3 Ch App 605. See [1983] Conv 127 (P Pearce and A Samuels). See also *Nichols v Wevill Estate* [1996] 2 WWR 408 (failure to act with care in exercising discretion).

[3] See *Tito v Waddell (No 2)* [1977] 3 All ER 129 at 246, 247; where Megarry V-C referred to two American definitions: 'every omission or violation by a trustee of a duty which equity lays on him . . . is a breach of trust' (*Corpus Juris Secundum*, vol 90, pp 225, 228 para 247); 'a trustee commits a breach of trust if he violates any duty which he owes as a trustee to the beneficiaries' (*Scott on Trusts*, 3rd edn, vol 3, p 1605, para 201).

[4] *Bateman v Davis* (1818) 3 Madd 98; *Lander v Weston* (1855) 3 Drew 389.

[5] Where the breach of trust results in a profit for which the trustees have to account this is the limit of their liability—*Vyse v Foster* (1872) 8 Ch App 309; affd (1874) LR 7 HL 318.

fraudulently by a trustee for his own purposes, or innocently, for the benefit of the trust estate and ignorant of the fact it was a breach of trust.

There can, however, be cases where, although there is an undoubted breach of trust, the trustee is under no liability at all to a beneficiary. Thus if trustees have committed a judicious breach of trust[6] by investing in an unauthorized investment which proves to be very profitable to the trust, although a beneficiary could nevertheless insist that the unauthorized investment be sold and the proceeds invested in authorized investments, the trustees would be under no liability to pay compensation either to the trust fund or the beneficiary because the breach has caused no loss to the trust fund.[7] In considering the liability of trustees it is immaterial how the trust was created, and whether it was for valuable consideration, or by the voluntary gift of the very trustees who are now being sued.[8]

It is settled law that a shareholder cannot recover damages that are merely reflective of the company's loss, in respect of which the company has a cause of action (the reflective loss principle).[9] Where a claimant brings an action not as a shareholder but as a beneficiary under a trust against a trustee shareholder for a profit, the reflective loss principle would preclude the claim only if it could be shown by the defendant that the whole of the claimed profit reflected what the company had lost and which it had a cause of action to recover.[10]

Finally it should be observed that not every legal claim arising out of a relationship of trustee and beneficiary will give rise to a claim for a breach of trust. In *Bristol and West Building Society v Mothew*[11] the defendant solicitor held money in trust for the plaintiff society but with the society's instructions to apply it in the completion of a transaction of purchase and mortgage. The solicitor by an oversight gave incorrect information to the plaintiff society, which might have revoked its instructions had the correct information been given. The defendant acting on the unrevoked instructions paid the money over to the vendor. He was held liable in negligence at common law, but was held not to be guilty of a breach of trust. Though he knew that he was a trustee for the society, he did not realize that he had misled the society and could not know that his authority had determined (if indeed it had). He could not be bound to repay the money to the society so long as he was ignorant of the facts which had brought his authority to an end, for it would be those facts which would affect his conscience and subject him to an obligation to return the money to the society.

---

[6] It has been judicially observed that the great use of a trustee is to commit judicious breaches of trust— *National Trustees Co of Australasia v General Co of Australasia* [1905] AC 373 at 375, 376, PC, per Lindley LJ. It has been suggested that there is no such thing as a judicious breach of trust where the breach of trust involves a deliberate breach of the terms of the trust deed, whether or not the breach is in the best economic interests of the beneficiaries: (1998) 12 Tru LI 44 (Vicki Vann).

[7] *Target Holdings Ltd v Redferns (a firm)* [1996] AC 421, [1995] 3 All ER 785, HL.

[8] *Smith v French* (1741) 2 Atk 243; *Drosier v Brereton* (1851) 15 Beav 221.

[9] *Prudential Assurance Co Ltd v Newman Industries Ltd (No 2)* [1982] Ch 204, [1982] 1 All ER 354, CA.

[10] *Shaker v Al-Bedrawi* [2002] EWCA Civ 1452, [2002] 4 All ER 835

[11] [1998] Ch 1, [1996] 4 All ER 698, CA, discussed (1999) 13 Tru LI 74 (S Elliott).

(b) MEASURE OF DAMAGE

(i) Equitable compensation for breach of trust[12]

This is designed to make good a loss in fact suffered by the beneficiaries and which, using hindsight and common sense, can be seen to have been caused by the breach:[13] compensation is to be assessed as at the date of judgment and not at an earlier date.

The equitable rules have largely been developed in traditional family trusts where the fund is held on trust for a number of beneficiaries having different, usually successive, interests. Here, if trust assets are wrongfully paid away, the only way in which all the beneficiaries' rights can be protected is by restoring to the trust fund what ought to be there. In such a case the basic rule is that a trustee in breach of trust must restore or pay to the trust estate either the assets which have been lost to the estate by reason of the breach or compensation for such loss. Courts of Equity did not award damages but, acting in personam, ordered the defaulting trustee to restore the trust estate. If specific restitution of the trust property is not possible, then the liability of the trustee is to pay sufficient compensation to the trust estate to put it back to what it would have been had the breach not been committed. Even if the immediate cause of the loss is the dishonesty or failure of a third party, the trustee is liable to make good that loss to the trust estate if, but for the breach, such loss would not have occurred. Thus the common law rules of remoteness of damage and causation do not apply. However, there does have to be some causal connection between the breach of trust and the loss to the trust estate for which compensation is recoverable, viz the fact that the loss would not have occurred but for the breach.[14] And a beneficiary who subsequent to the breach receives a benefit from the trustees' actions must give credit for it, and cannot recover compensation if on balance he has suffered no loss.[15]

(ii) Bare trusts

The position is modified where the trusts have come to an end and the trustees hold the trust fund on a bare trust for a beneficiary absolutely entitled. In relation to a breach of trust in such a case there is no reason for compensating the breach of trust by way of an order for restitution and compensation *to the trust fund* as opposed to the beneficiary himself. In *Target Holdings Ltd v Redferns (a firm)*[16] Lord

---

[12] See (2004) 18 Tru LI 116 (J Edelman and S Elliott).

[13] *Target Holdings Ltd v Redferns (a firm)*, supra, HL. The principles laid down in this case were held to be applicable to claims for fraudulent breach of trust in *Collins v Brebner* [2000] Lloyd's Rep PN 587, CA. See also *Greater Pacific Investments Ltd (in liq) v Australian National Industries Ltd* (1996) 39 NSWLR 143 and (2003) 26 UNSWLJ 349 (R P Meagher and A Maroya).

[14] *Target Holdings Ltd v Redferns (a firm)* [1996] AC 421, [1995] 3 All ER 785, HL, discussed (1995) 9 Tru LI 86 (Janet Ulph); (1996) 112 LQR 27 (C E F Rickett); [1996] LMCLQ 161 (R Nolan); 8 KCLJ 86 (R Davern). See *Bristol and West Building Society v May May & Merrimans (a firm)* [1996] 2 All ER 801; *Bristol and West Building Society v Mothew*, supra, CA, both noted [1997] CLJ 39 (R Nolan); [1997] LMCLQ 26 (A Alcock). See also *Bank of New Zealand v New Zealand Guardian Trust Co Ltd* [1999] 1 NZLR 213.

[15] *Hulbert v Avens* [2003] EWHC 76 (Ch), [2003] WTLR 387.

[16] Supra, HL. See (1998) 114 LQR 214 (P J Millett); (2003) 25 Sydney LR 31 (C E F Rickett).

Browne-Wilkinson did not wholly rule out the possibility that even in those circumstances an order to reconstitute the fund may be appropriate.[17] However in the ordinary case where a beneficiary becomes absolutely entitled to the trust fund the court orders, not restitution to the trust estate, but payment of compensation directly to the beneficiary.

Lord Browne-Wilkinson further stated that although the same fundamental principles apply, it is wrong to lift wholesale the detailed rules developed in the context of traditional trusts and then seek to apply them to trusts of quite a different kind. *Target* itself was a commercial case where the defendant solicitors held moneys as bare trustee for the plaintiff lender as part of a series of conveyancing transactions under which they had implied authority to pay the money to or to the order of a third party, C, when the property had been transferred and C had executed charges in the plaintiff's favour. In breach of trust the defendants paid moneys to X, but within a short time the legal estate became vested in C and a legal charge executed in favour of the plaintiff. This position was the one the plaintiff had all along intended. What the plaintiff did not intend was that its security should be grossly inadequate. It had lent £1.7m on the basis of a valuation of the property at £2m made by the second defendant against whom judgment in default had been obtained but which was in insolvent liquidation. The property was eventually sold by the plaintiff as mortgagee for £500,000. The plaintiff alleged that it was the victim of a fraud by third parties who had induced it to advance the £1.7m, and that it had in consequence suffered a loss of £1.2m (the loan less the proceeds of the realization).

The way in which the case came before their Lordships was that Warner J at first instance had refused to give the plaintiff summary judgment and had given the defendants leave to defend the breach of trust claim, conditional on the payment into court of £1m. The Court of Appeal allowed the plaintiff's appeal against refusal to give summary judgment and gave judgment for £1,490,000 less the net sum to be realized on the subsequent sale of the property. The House of Lords had to act on the assumption (which it thought would very likely not be established at the trial) that if the defendants had not, in breach of trust, provided moneys to X, the moneys would have been available from some other source and the series of transactions would have gone through. On this assumption the plaintiff obtained exactly what it would have obtained had no breach occurred, and accordingly would have suffered no compensatable loss. The defendants were therefore entitled to leave to defend to give them an opportunity to justify the assumption. However if at the trial it was shown that the defendants' breach of trust in making the trust moneys available was essential to the success of the scheme which would not have proceeded without it, the plaintiff would indeed be entitled to recover the total sum advanced to C less the proceeds of the security.

---

[17] Perhaps he had in mind a case where the beneficiary is a minor or under disability.

(iii) Improper retention on sale

Where the trustees were under a duty to sell unauthorized investments, and neglected or delayed doing so, they will be liable for the difference between the price for which they could have been sold at the proper time, and the price eventually obtained on the actual sale.[18] Conversely where trustees improperly realized a proper investment they will be liable either to replace the investment sold, or to pay the difference in the price between the amount actually obtained and the value of such an investment at the date of the commencement of the proceedings or the date of judgment.[19]

(iv) Unauthorized investments

Where trustees have made an unauthorized investment, they are liable for all loss which is incurred when it is realized.[20] If an unauthorized investment has brought in a greater income than an authorized investment would have done which income has been paid to the tenant for life, the trustees cannot call upon him to pay the excess income to capital, nor can it be set off against future income[21] even if the tenant for life and the trustee are the same person.[22] This rule may be contrasted with the position where trustees fail to convert under the rule in *Howe v Earl of Dartmouth*,[23] or an express trust for sale.[24] Of course, as we have seen, if the unauthorized investment causes a loss to capital, the trustees must make it good.

In the case of an unauthorized investment, the beneficiaries, if they are sui iuris and together comprehend the entire equitable interest, can, if they so agree, adopt the unauthorized investment as part of the trust property.[25] It may well be that if they do this, they can nevertheless call on the trustee to make good any loss to the trust estate; the law is not clear.[26] 'But if there is not unanimity, then it is not trust property, but the trustee who has made it must keep the investment himself. He is debtor to the trust for the money which has been applied in its purchase.'[27] More accurately, per-haps, the duty of the trustee to sell the unauthorized investment if the cestuis que trust do not choose to adopt it is subject to the right of the trustee to take it over on

---

[18] *Grayburn v Clarkson* (1868) 3 Ch App 605; *Dunning v Earl of Gainsborough* (1885) 54 LJ Ch 991. See (1977) 55 CBR 342 (Donovan Waters). As to the position where there is a power to postpone sale and the trustees postpone for too long causing loss and where there have been fluctuations in value, see *Fales v Canada Permanent Trust Co* (1976) 70 DLR (3d) 257.

[19] *Re Massingberd's Settlement* (1890) 63 LT 296, CA, referred to the earlier date but Vinelott J in *Re Bell's Indenture* [1980] 3 All ER 425, [1980] 1 WLR 1217, said, without citing any authority, that this was wrong in principle and that the later date should be used. *Scott on Trusts*, 4th edn, Vol III, s 208.3, p 1687 could be used to support this view. See (1978) 77 Mich LR 95 (R V Wellman).

[20] *Knott v Cottee* (1852) 16 Beav 77.

[21] *Slade v Chaine* [1908] 1 Ch 522, CA; *Learoyd v Whiteley* (1887) 12 App Cas 727, HL.

[22] *Re Hoyles (No 2)* [1912] 1 Ch 67.   [23] (1802) 7 Ves 137.

[24] *Dimes v Scott* (1828) 4 Russ 195, and see chapter 19, p 428, supra.

[25] *Re Patten and Edmonton Union Poor Guardians* (1883) 52 LJ Ch 787; *Re Jenkins and HE Randall & Co's Contract* [1903] 2 Ch 362; *Wright v Morgan* [1926] AC 788, [1926] All ER Rep 201, PC.

[26] *Re Lake* [1903] 1 KB 439; contra, semble, *Thornton v Stokill* (1855) 1 Jur NS 751.

[27] *Wright v Morgan*, supra, at 206, 799, PC; *Sharp v Jackson* [1899] AC 419, HL.

replacing the trust funds.[28] Until this is done the cestuis que trust retain a lien on the unauthorized investment.

(v) Failure to invest

Where, however, trustees were not directed to invest in one specified investment, but were given a choice, and yet made no investment at all, it has been held that they are only liable to replace the trust fund, on the ground that it would be impossible to say which investment they would have chosen and for what other sum they could be held liable.[29] It is doubtful whether such a case would be decided in this way today. It is thought that the courts might well prefer to apply obiter dicta of Dillon and Staughton LJJ in *Nestle v National Westminster Bank plc*[30] to the effect that trustees who fail to follow a proper investment policy may be required to make good to the trust fair compensation. If trustees were directed to make a specific investment, and either made no investment at all or invested in something else, they will be required to provide the amount of that specified investment which could have been purchased with the trust funds at the time when the investment should have been made.[31]

(vi) Profits

If the breach of trust has resulted in some profit accruing to the trust estate, this must be held by the trustees as a part of the trust property.[32] Profits may be assessed on the basis of the highest intermediate value of the property between the date of breach and the date of judgment, provided that there was an opportunity to realize the property during the period of the continuing breach. No distinction is made between shares and other types of property where investment is only a secondary consideration.[33]

If trustees have committed more than one breach of trust, a gain in one cannot be set off against a loss in another: the gain on the one transaction becomes subject to the trusts, and the trustees are liable to replace the loss on the other.[34] The rule was slightly relaxed in *Bartlett v Barclays Bank Trust Co Ltd*[35] where the trustee was controlling shareholder in a company which made speculative investments in property development. The trustee was held liable for the loss that occurred on one of these

---

[28] *Re Salmon* (1889) 42 Ch D 351, CA; *Re Lake,* supra; *Head v Gould* [1898] 2 Ch 250.

[29] *Shepherd v Mouls* (1845) 4 Hare 500; *Robinson v Robinson* (1851) 1 De GM & G 247.

[30] [1994] 1 All ER 118, [1993] 1 WLR 1260, CA. See (1992) 142 NLJ 1279 (Jill Martin).

[31] *Byrchall v Bradford* (1822) 6 Madd 235; *Pride v Fooks* (1840) 2 Beav 430. See *Elder's Trustee and Executor Co Ltd v Higgins* (1963) 113 CLR 426 (failure to exercise option to purchase). Account will be taken of any payments, such as calls on shares, that they would necessarily have made if they had properly carried out the directions as to investment: *Briggs v Massey* (1882) 51 LJ Ch 447, CA.

[32] See p 141 et seq, supra.

[33] *Jaffray v Marshall* [1994] 1 All ER 143, [1993] 1 WLR 1285 (no doubt was cast on this proposition in *Target Holdings Ltd v Redferns (a firm),* supra, HL, though it was said to have been wrongly applied to a claim for compensation for breach of trust); *Nant-y-glo and Blaina Ironworks Co v Grave* (1879) 12 Ch D 738.

[34] *Dimes v Scott* (1828) 4 Russ 195; *Wiles v Gresham* (1854) 2 Drew 258; affd 5 De GM & G 770; *Re Barker* (1898) 77 LT 712. The general rule is even clearer where there are in fact two separate funds, even though the trustees and the trusts may be the same—*Wiles v Gresham,* supra.

[35] [1980] Ch 515, [1980] 1 All ER 139. *Cf Fletcher v Green* (1864) 33 Beav 426.

investments, but was allowed to set off a profit arising from another investment which had stemmed from exactly the same investment policy.

(vii) Exemplary or punitive damages

There do not appear to be any cases in which exemplary or punitive damages have been awarded for breach of trust.[36] The Law Commission recommended[37] that punitive damages should be available for equitable wrongdoing, but the government has stated that it does not intend to take forward the draft legislation proposed, having regard to the balance of opinion disclosed at consultation.

(viii) Equitable compensation for breach of the duty of skill and care

This resembles common law damages in that it is awarded by way of compensation to the plaintiff for his loss. There is no reason in principle why the common law rules of causation, remoteness of damage and measure of damages should not be applied by analogy in such a case.[38]

(ix) Breach of fiduciary duty

It has been said[39] that the considerations which apply to a breach of trust 'apply to a claim for breach of a fiduciary duty: fiduciary duties are equitable extensions of trustee duties'. The claimant for breach of a fiduciary duty must show that the loss he has suffered has been caused by the defendant's breach of duty. Furthermore it seems that unless the breach could properly be regarded as the equivalent of fraud, the claimant is not entitled to be placed financially in the same position as he was in before the breach occurred but only in the same position as he would have been in if the breach of duty had not occurred. As Evans LJ explained in *Swindle v Harrison*[40] the positions are not necessarily the same: the claimant's position might have deteriorated, or for that matter improved, during the intervening period by reason of independent, extraneous events. In *Nationwide Building Society v Various Solicitors (No 3)*[41] it was said that the correct approach to equitable compensation for breach of fiduciary duty, except where the fiduciary had acted dishonestly or in bad faith, is to

---

[36] See *Vyse v Foster* (1872) 8 Ch App 309 per James LJ at 333. Contra *Aquaculture Corpn v New Zealand Green Mussel Ltd* [1990] 3 NZLR 299 noted (1991) 107 LQR 209 (J Beatson); (1991) 21 VUWLR 391 (P Michalik); *Harris v Digital Pulse Property Ltd* (2003) 197 ALR 626. See (1995) 69 ALJ 773 (P M McDermott); (1996) 19 UQLJ 125 (D Jensen); (2004) 18 Tru LI 116 (J Edelman and S Elliott); (2004) 67 MLR 16 (S Elliott and C Mitchell).

[37] Law Com No 247 (1997). It seems to assume the equitable wrongdoing includes breach of trust.

[38] *Bristol and West Building Society v Mothew* [1998] Ch 1, [1996] 4 All ER 698, CA; *Swindle v Harrison* [1997] 4 All ER 705, CA; *ICS Ltd v West Bromwich B S* [1999] Lloyd's PN 496. See also [2002] MLR 588 (S B Elliott) and note the comments of the High Court of Australia in *Youyang Property Ltd v Minter Ellison* (2003) 196 ALR 482 at 491, noted (2003) 119 LQR 545 (S Elliott and J Edelman), and see p 522, supra.

[39] Per Mummery LJ in *Swindle v Harrison* [1997] 4 All ER 705, CA, noted (1997) 11 Tru LI 72 (Lusina Ho); (1998) 114 LQR 181 (Hans Tjio and T M Yeo). See (2003) 119 LQR 246 (M Conaglen). See also *Maguire v Makaronis* (1997) 188 CLR 449, noted (1998) 114 LQR 9 (S Moriarty).

[40] Supra, CA at 714.

[41] [1999] PNLR 608. See *JJ Harrison (Properties) Ltd v Harrison* [2001] EWCA Civ 1467, [2002] 1 BCLC 162.

assess what actual loss had resulted from the breach, having regard to the scope of the duty broken.

(c) TAX

In assessing compensation for breach of trust, tax payable by the beneficiaries is not taken into account. The obligation of a trustee who is held liable for breach of trust is fundamentally different from the obligation of a contractual or tortious wrongdoer. The trustee's obligation is to restore to the trust estate the assets of which he has deprived it. The tax liability of individual beneficiaries, who have claims qua bene-ficiaries to the capital and income of the trust estate, does not enter into the picture because it arises not at the point of restitution to the trust estate but at the point of distribution of capital or income out of the trust estate. Accordingly a trustee is not entitled to have an order for compensation qualified so as to restrict the compensation payable to the net loss respectively suffered by the beneficiaries by reason of non-payments of distributions which ought properly to have been made, even though the breach of trust has not enriched the defaulting trustee. The principle of *British Trans-port Commission v Gourley*,[42] that damages for loss of earnings should take into account the tax that would have been payable, does not apply.[43]

(d) INTEREST

Where a trustee is required to replace a loss caused to the trust estate, he is normally liable, in addition, to pay interest. Traditionally the rate was 4 per cent, but this has been said to be unrealistic in modern conditions. Some relatively recent cases[44] have held that the proper rate of interest is 1 per cent above bank rate, while in others it has been said to be that allowed from time to time on the courts' special account.[45]

---

[42] [1956] AC 185, [1955] 3 All ER 796, HL. See (1987) 103 LQR 211 (W Bishop and J Kay).

[43] *Bartlett v Barclays Bank Trust Co Ltd (No 2)* [1980] Ch 515, [1980] 2 All ER 92, noted [1980] Conv 449 (G A Shindler); *a fortiori Re Bell's Indenture* [1980] 3 All ER 425, [1980] 1 WLR 1217, where trust funds had been dissipated in breach of trust, and the estate duty office had waived the duty which would have been payable on the deaths of the life tenants if the funds had not been dissipated. It was held that a trustee who had taken trust moneys for his own benefit or for the benefit of others and who was therefore liable to restore them, could not benefit from his breach of trust by retaining sums which would have been paid in tax if the breach of trust had not been committed.

[44] *Belmont Finance Corpn Ltd v Williams Furniture Ltd (No 2)* [1980] 1 All ER 393, CA; *O'Sullivan v Management Agency Music Ltd* [1985] QB 428 [1985] 3 All ER 351, CA. In *Guardian Ocean Cargoes Ltd v Banco do Brasil SA (No 3)* [1992] 2 Lloyd's Rep 193, Hirst J awarded compound interest at 1% over the New York prime rate applicable from time to time.

[45] See CPR 7.0.17 and *Bartlett v Barclays Bank Trust Co Ltd (No 2)* [1980] Ch 515, [1980] 2 All ER 92, where the judge pointed out that since to some extent high interest rates reflect and compensate for the continual erosion in the value of money, it was arguable that a proportion of the interest should go to capital. Most recently, in *Re Evans (decd)* [1999] 2 All ER 777, a case 'involving the non-professional administrator of a small estate in times of more gentle inflation', 8% was awarded. See also *Wallersteiner v Moir (No 2)* [1975]

It is still the law that in special circumstances a trustee may be liable for a higher rate.[46] The earlier cases established that if he had actually received more he was liable for what he had actually received. If he ought to have received more, he was liable for what he ought to have received, as, for instance, where he called in a mortgage carrying a high rate of interest.[47] If he was fairly presumed to have received more, as where he had used the trust money for his own purposes, he used normally to be charged an extra 1 per cent over the normal rate: in particular where he had employed the trust money in trade, the beneficiaries had the option of claiming that higher rate, or alternatively the actual profits,[48] or, if the trustee had mixed his own moneys and the trust moneys, a proportionate share of the profits.[49] They could not however, claim profits for part of the time and interest for the remainder.[50]

Prima facie the liability is for simple interest only, but compound interest may be awarded in cases where it has been withheld or misapplied by a trustee or anyone else in a fiduciary position, by way of recouping from such a defendant an improper profit made by him. The cases commonly refer to situations where the defendant has used trust moneys in his own trade, but it is thought that the better view is that it extends to all cases where a fiduciary has improperly profited from his trust.[51] It may well be that there is jurisdiction in equity to award compound interest in cases where the defendant owes no fiduciary duty but where money has been obtained and retained by fraud, but the law is not settled.[52]

(e) JOINT AND SEVERAL LIABILITY TO BENEFICIARIES

It is settled that where two or more trustees are liable for a breach of trust, their liability is joint and several: this means that the beneficiaries can claim the whole loss from any one trustee,[53] or two or more jointly, or all of them, and even where a

---

QB 373, [1975] 1 All ER 849, CA (1975) 39 Conv 309 (J T Farrand), (1985) 101 LQR 30 (F A Mann) and (1993) 67 ALJ 471; [2001] Conv 313 (S Elliott).

[46] See CPR 7.0.9; *Jones v Foxall* (1852) 15 Beav 388; *A-G v Alford*, supra, explained in *Berwick-on-Tweed Corpn v Murray* (1857) 7 De GM & G 497.

[47] See *Jones v Foxall* (1852) 15 Beav 388.

[48] *Vyse v Foster* (1872) 8 Ch App 309; affd (1874) LR 7 HL 318; *Gordon v Gonda* [1955] 2 All ER 762, CA. An inquiry may be ordered as to what use the defendant made of the trust money and what return on it he received: *Mathew v T M Sutton Ltd* [1994] 4 All ER 793.

[49] *Docker v Somes* (1834) 2 My & K 655; *Edinburgh Corpn v Lord Advocate* (1879) 4 App Cas 823, HL.

[50] *Heathcote v Hulme* (1819) 1 Jac & W 122; *Vyse v Foster* (1872) 8 Ch App 309 at 334.

[51] *Westdeutsche Landesbank Girozentrale v Islington London Borough Council* [1996] AC 669, [1996] 2 All ER 961, HL, noted (1996) 112 LQR 521 (M Cope); *Equiticorp Industries Group Ltd v The Crown (No 3) (Judgment No 51)* [1996] 3 NZLR 690.

[52] *Clef Aquitaine SARL v Laporte Materials (Barrow) Ltd (sued as Sovereign Chemicals Industries Ltd)* [2001] QB 488, [2000] 3 All ER 493, CA, citing *President of India v La Pintada Cia Navegacion SA* [1985] AC 104, [1984] 2 All ER 773, HL; *Westdeutsche Landesbank Girozentrale v Islington London Borough Council*, supra, HL.

[53] *Walker v Symonds* (1818) 3 Swan 1 at 75; *Re Harrison* [1891] 2 Ch 349; *McCheane v Gyles (No 2)* [1902] 1 Ch 911. But if all the trustees are dead, an action cannot normally be brought against the personal representatives of one trustee, not being the survivor of the trustees, without joining the personal

judgment is obtained against all of them, may execute the whole judgment against any one.[54] The beneficiaries are not concerned with the liability of the trustees inter se. So far as the beneficiaries are concerned 'all parties to a breach of trust are equally liable; there is between them no primary liability'.[55] The above rules apply equally where the trustees comprise or include constructive trustees.[56] The liability continues against the estate of a deceased or bankrupt trustee,[57] but the estate of a deceased trustee is not liable for what he left in a proper state of investment at his death.[58] Since the liability is joint and several, beneficiaries who have recovered in part from one trustee, may prove in the bankruptcy of another trustee for the whole amount of the loss, and not merely for the balance though they cannot, of course, in the aggregate recover more than their loss.[59]

Retired trustees remain liable for their own breaches of trust but are not normally liable for breaches of trust committed by their successors. If, however, a trustee is asked to commit a breach of trust, and refuses, he should take care before appointing, or resigning in order to enable the appointment of, a new trustee who he has reason to believe may be more accommodating. The position, according to Kekewich J in *Head v Gould*,[60] is:

that in order to make a retiring trustee liable for a breach of trust committed by his successor you must shew, and shew clearly, that the very breach of trust which was in fact committed was not merely the outcome of the retirement and new appointment, but was contemplated by the former trustee when such retirement and appointment took place. ... It will not suffice to prove that the former trustees rendered easy or even intended, a breach of trust, if it was not in fact committed. They must be proved to have been guilty as accessories before the fact of the impropriety actually perpetrated.

Again, a new trustee is not liable for breaches of trust committed by his predecessors, and 'is entitled to assume that everything has been duly attended to up to the time of his becoming trustee'.[61] However, if he discovers a breach of trust, he should take appropriate steps to remedy it, if necessary by proceedings against the old trustees, as part of his duty to get in the trust property and to see that it is in a proper state of investment.[62]

---

representatives of the survivor, or having new trustees appointed and joining them as defendants—*Re Jordan* [1904] 1 Ch 260.

[54] *A-G v Wilson* (1840) Cr & Ph 1, 28; *Fletcher v Green* (1864) 33 Beav 426.

[55] Per Leach MR in *Wilson v Moore* (1833) 1 My & K 126 at 146; (affd (1834) 1 My & K 337); *Edwards v Hood-Barnes* [1905] 1 Ch 20.

[56] See chapter 8, p 139, supra. *Blyth v Fladgate* [1891] 1 Ch 337; *Cowper v Stoneham* (1893) 68 LT 18.

[57] See eg *Dixon v Dixon* (1878) 9 Ch D 587; *Edwards v Hood-Barnes* [1905] 1 Ch 20.

[58] *Re Palk* (1892) 41 WR 28.   [59] *Edwards v Hood-Barnes*, supra.

[60] [1898] 2 Ch 250 at 273–274.   [61] *Re Strahan* (1856) 8 De GM & G 291 at 309, per Turner LJ.

[62] See chapter 17, section 1, supra.

(f) LIABILITY FOR CO-TRUSTEE

It has been recognized since *Townley v Sherborne*[63] in 1634 that a trustee is not liable for the acts and defaults of his co-trustee. An innocent trustee is, however, liable for his own acts or defaults. Accordingly he has been said to be liable for his own breach of trust in relation to a co-trustee in three cases:

(i)   where he hands over money to a co-trustee without securing its due application,

(ii) where he permits a co-trustee to receive money without making due inquiry as to his dealing with it,[64] and

(iii) where he becomes aware of a breach of trust by a co-trustee, either committed or meditated, and fails to take the needful steps to obtain restitution or redress.[65] As Jonathan Parker J observed:[66] 'A trustee is himself in default if, by his own neglect, he allows his fellow trustees to enter into a transaction in breach of trust.'

(g) TRUSTEE-BENEFICIARY

It is settled that if a trustee, who is also a beneficiary, is in default and liable to the trust estate, he will not be allowed to claim, as against his beneficiaries, any beneficial interest in the trust estate, until he has made good his default.[67] It makes no difference that he acquired his beneficial interest derivatively, for instance, under the will or on the intestacy of an original beneficiary.[68] And if the trustee has assigned his beneficial interest, his assignee is in no better position, even though the default takes place after the assignment.[69] But if the same persons happen to be the trustees of two separate trusts, even though created by the same will, then their beneficial interest under one cannot be impounded to make good their default in connection with the other.[70]

(h) INJUNCTION

An injunction may be obtained in appropriate circumstances to restrain an apprehended breach of trust. This is discussed in chapter 28, section 8, infra.

---

[63] (1633) J Bridge 35. For a recent illustration see *Re Lucking's Will Trusts* [1967] 3 All ER 726, [1968] 1 WLR 866.

[64] See eg *Wyman v Paterson* [1900] AC 271, HL.

[65] *Styles v Guy* (1849) 1 Mac & G 422, which referred to a duty to keep watch on co-trustees.

[66] *Segbedzi (Minors) v Segbedzi* (1999) [2001] WTLR 83, CA.

[67] *Re Rhodesia Goldfields Ltd* [1910] 1 Ch 239. See *Selangor United Rubber Estates Ltd v Cradock (No 4)* [1969] 3 All ER 965, [1969] 1 WLR 1773.

[68] *Jacubs v Rylance* (1874) LR 17 Eq 341; *Re Dacre* [1916] 1 Ch 344, CA.

[69] *Doering v Doering*, supra; *Re Towndrow* [1911] 1 Ch 662.   [70] *Re Towndrow* [1911] 1 Ch 662.

2 LIABILITY OF TRUSTEES INTER SE

The equitable rule was that as between themselves trustees were equally liable, and one who was compelled to pay more than his fair share could enforce contribution from the others.[71] The right extended to the personal representatives of a deceased trustee, where the breach of trust took place before, even though the loss only occurred after, his death.[72] The rule applied as between so-called active and passive trustees for, as pointed out in *Bahin v Hughes*,[73] a passive trustee by doing nothing may neglect his duty more than a trustee who acts honestly, though erroneously.

The equitable rule has now been superseded by the Civil Liability (Contribution) Act 1978 which provides that any person liable in respect of any damage suffered by another person—defined to include damage based on breach of trust—may recover contribution from any other person liable in respect of the same damage. The amount of the contribution recoverable is such as may be found by the court to be just and equitable having regard to the extent of that person's responsibility for the damage in question, and may be nil or a hundred per cent. This gives the court a discretion to depart from the equitable rule of equal contribution, but would not otherwise appear to alter the position.

The Act does not, however, apply to an indemnity, and there are three cases where a trustee is liable to indemnify his co-trustees:

(i)   where a trustee has got the money into his hands and made use of it,[74]

(ii) where the active trustee was a solicitor, who was relied on by the other trustees.[75] A solicitor-trustee is not, however, necessarily bound to indemnify a co-trustee merely because he is a solicitor: he will be under no such obligation if it appears that the co-trustee was an active participator in the breach of trust, and is not proved to have participated merely in consequence of the advice and control of the solicitor,[76]

(iii) where a trustee is also, or subsequently becomes, a beneficiary, he is bound, at any rate where he has received some benefit by the breach of trust,[77] to indemnify his co-trustee to the extent of his interest in the trust fund, and not merely to the extent of any benefit he may have received by the breach of trust.[78] A

---

[71] *Chillingworth v Chambers* [1896] 1 Ch 685, CA; *Robinson v Harkin* [1896] 2 Ch 415.

[72] *Jackson v Dickinson* [1903] 1 Ch 947.

[73] (1886) 31 Ch D 390, CA; *Bacon v Camphausen* (1888) 58 LT 851; *Goodwin v Duggan* (1996–97) 41 NSWLR 158. See (1977) 55 CBR 342 (Donovan Waters).

[74] *Bahin v Hughes* at 395, supra, CA; *Goodwin v Duggan*, supra.

[75] *Chillingworth v Chambers*, supra, CA; *Re Linsley* [1904] 2 Ch 785. The principle is not confined to solicitors: *Bahin v Hughes* (1886) 31 Ch D 390, 395–397 per Cotton LJ; *Re Partington* (1887) 57 LT 654, 662, and see *Blair v Canada Trust Co* (1986) 32 DLR (4th) 515.

[76] *Head v Gould* [1898] 2 Ch 250.

[77] *Chillingworth v Chambers*, supra at 707, per Kay LJ: contrast Lindley LJ at 700.

[78] *Chillingworth v Chambers*, supra, CA.

new trustee who is also a beneficiary, however, although he may be liable to the other beneficiaries for failure to have an existing breach of trust put right on his appointment, is not liable to indemnify the original trustees under this head, but is himself entitled to be indemnified by the original trustees who were responsible for the breach the primary cause of the loss.[79]

Finally, it may be noted that where one only of two or more trustees is excused under s 61,[80] it is strongly arguable that the effect must be to leave the other trustee or trustees fully liable without the possibility of obtaining contribution from the excused trustee.[81]

3 DEFENCES OF A TRUSTEE TO PROCEEDINGS FOR BREACH OF TRUST

(a) EXEMPTION CLAUSES

(i) The present law

The efficacy of a trustee exemption clause was affirmed by the Court of Appeal in *Armitage v Nurse*[82] where a clause in the settlement provided that no trustee should be liable for any loss or damage to the fund or its income 'unless such loss or damage shall be caused by his own actual fraud'. It was held that the clause was effective no matter how indolent, imprudent, lacking in diligence, negligent or wilful he might have been, so long as he had not acted dishonestly. The test of dishonesty was considered by Sir Christopher Slade, with whose judgment the other members were content to agree, in *Walker v Stones*.[83] At first instance Rattee J, purporting to apply dicta in *Armitage v Nurse*,[84] derived two propositions, first that the deliberate

---

[79] *Re Fountaine*, not reported on this point in [1909] 2 Ch 382, CA, but referred to in Underhill and Hayton, *Law of Trusts and Trustees*, 16th edn, p 947.

[80] Discussed p 546 et seq, infra.

[81] See *Fales v Canada Permanent Trustee Co* (1976) 70 DLR (3d) 257 and (1977) 55 CBR 342 (Donovan Waters). The argument is even stronger under the 1978 Act for the excused trustee is not liable for the damage.

[82] [1997] 2 All ER 705, CA, noted [1998] CLJ 33 (N McBride). The Law Commission in Law Com CP 171, para 2.54 have expressed the opinion that the authority of *Armitage v Nurse* is not entirely free from doubt. In [1998] Conv 100 G McCormack argues that trustee exemption clauses should be subject to a strict construction. As to an occupational pension scheme see Pensions Act 1995, s 33; (1999) 13 Tru LI 2 (N Moore). See also (1999) 8 T & ELJ 6 (Lord Millett); (2000) 20 T & ELJ 22 (R Vas); [1999] PCB 227 (S M Smith); [2000] All ER Rev 251 (P J Clarke).

[83] [2000] 4 All ER 412, [2000] 2 WLR 623, CA, noted (2000) 15 Tru LI 18 (M Doherty and R Fletcher); [2001] PCB 215 (P Stibbard). The test of dishonesty is the same as that in *Royal Brunei Airlines Sdn Bhd v Newman Industries Ltd* [1995] 2 AC 378, [1995] 3 All ER 97, PC.

[84] Supra, CA.

commission of a breach of trust is not necessarily dishonest.[85] Second, it is only dishonest if the trustee committing it does so 'either knowing that it is contrary to the interests of the beneficiaries or being recklessly indifferent whether it is contrary to their interests or not'. These two propositions appeared to be accepted by the Court of Appeal, but there was a third proposition, namely: 'It seems to me impossible to call a trustee's conduct "dishonest" in any ordinary sense of that word, even if he knew he was acting in breach of the terms of the trust, if he so acted in a genuine (even if misguided) belief that what he was doing was for the benefit of the beneficiaries.' This last proposition required qualification. At least in the case of a solicitor-trustee, a qualification is necessary to take account of the case where the trustee's so-called 'honest belief', though actually held, is so unreasonable that, by any objective standard, no reasonable solicitor-trustee could have thought that what he did or agreed to do was for the benefit of the beneficiaries. A person may act dishonestly, even though he genuinely believes that his action is morally justified. It was added that the test of honesty may vary from case to case, depending on, among other things, the role and calling of the trustee.

It is not contrary to public policy to exclude liability for gross negligence by an appropriate clause clearly worded to that effect. Further a trustee does not lose the protection of an exemption clause by ceasing to be a trustee.[86] However, where there is a doubt on the construction of a trust whether a trustee would be exempted from liability for breach of trust by a trustee exemption clause, such doubt should be resolved against the trustee and the clause construed so as not to protect him.[87] It may be added that it has been suggested[88] that in the case of a professional trustee an exemption clause might be invalidated by the Unfair Contract Terms Act 1977, but this seems unlikely in the light of *Bogg v Raper*[89] where it was held that the solicitor draftsman of a will was entitled to rely on the provisions of an exemption clause contained therein. Indeed the author of the suggestion now doubts whether it is right.[90]

There are special provisions in relation to trustees of debentures,[91] pension trust schemes[92] and authorized unit trust schemes.[93]

---

[85] Cf per Lindley MR in *Perrins v Bellamy* [1899] 1 Ch 797 at 798; 'My old master, the late Lord Justice Selwyn, used to say, "The main duty of a trustee is to commit *judicious* breaches of trust" . . .' (Lindley MR's emphasis).

[86] *Seifert v Pensions Ombudsman* [1997] 1 All ER 214.

[87] *Wright v Olswang* (1998) *Times*, 17 September, revsd (1999) *Times*, 18 May, CA, on a question of construction without affecting this point. It was further held, and affirmed on the appeal, that where a settlement had two trustee exemption clauses, one protecting all trustees from liability for breach of trust and one which expressly did not apply to paid trustees, then paid trustees could not rely on the general exemption.

[88] [1980] Conv 333 and (1986) 1 TL & P 43 (W Goodhart). See also (1995) 9 Tru LI 21 (R Ham); (1996) 146 NLJ 348 (Ann Kenny).

[89] (1998) *Times*, 22 April, CA, where, however, the point does not appear to have been argued.

[90] (1996) 10 Tru LI at 42.   [91] Companies Act 1985, s 192.

[92] Pensions Act 1995, ss 33, 34(6). See (2004) 18 Tru LI 132 (I Greenstreet).

[93] Financial Services and Markets Act 2000, s 253.

(ii) The Law Commission proposals[94]

The Law Commission have published a Consultation Paper containing proposals, inter alia, that a professional trustee should not be able to rely on any provision in a trust instrument excluding liability for breach of trust arising from negligence and that clauses purporting to do so should not be given effect. They also considered duty exclusion clauses and extended powers clauses, which may have the effect of protecting trustees from liability for breach of trust. They did not propose that such clauses should be prohibited, but did propose that in determining whether professional trustees have been negligent, the court should have the power to disapply duty exclusion clauses or extended powers clauses where reliance on such clauses would be inconsistent with the overall purposes of the trust and it would be unreasonable in the circumstances for the trustee to be exempted from liability.

(b) CONSENT OR CONCURRENCE OF THE CESTUI QUE TRUST

A beneficiary who consents to or concurs in a breach of trust,[95] or subsequently confirms it or grants a release to the trustees,[96] or even merely acquiesces in it,[97] will not, in general, be able to succeed in a claim against the trustees[98] whether or not he has derived any benefit thereby.[99] In order to have this result, as will be elaborated later, the beneficiary must, at the relevant time, have been fully cognizant of the circumstances affecting his rights. Although a beneficiary whose interest is reversionary is not bound to assert his title until his interest falls into possession, he may in the meantime assent to a breach of trust so as to bar his claims in respect thereof, though the mere fact that he knows of the breach of trust and does nothing about it will not by itself be enough.[100] Further, the concurrence, release or acquiescence of a person not sui iuris is generally ineffective;[101] but although, accordingly, as Wigram VC said,[102] 'the release of infants is worth nothing in law', the court will not permit an infant who, by fraudulently misrepresenting his age, persuades trustees to pay him money in breach of trust, to claim the money over again on attaining his majority.[103]

---

94 Law Com CP 171. See [2003] PCB 404 (C Groves and Judith Ingham); [2003] Conv 185 (Ann Kenny).

95 *Brice v Stokes* (1805) 11 Ves 319; *Nail v Punter* (1832) 5 Sim 555; *Evans v Benyon* (1887) 37 Ch D 329, CA. See *Spellson v George* (1992) 26 NSWLR 666.

96 *Farrant v Blanchford* (1863) 1 De GJ & Sm 107.

97 *Walker v Symonds* (1818) 3 Swan 1; *Stafford v Stafford* (1857) 1 De G & J 193.

98 *A fortiori*, a beneficiary who is also a trustee cannot claim from a co-trustee in respect of a breach of trust in which they have both joined—*Butler v Carter* (1868) LR 5 Eq 276.

99 *Fletcher v Collis* [1905] 2 Ch 24, CA.

100 *Life Association of Scotland v Siddal* (1861) 3 De GF & J 58.

101 *Lord Montfort v Lord Cadogen* (1810) 19 Ves 635.

102 *Overton v Banister* (1844) 3 Hare 503 at 506.

103 *Overton v Banister*, supra; *Wright v Snowe* (1848) 2 De G & Sm 321. Cf s 3 of the Minors' Contracts Act 1987 which provides that where a contract is unenforceable against a defendant (or he repudiates it) because he was a minor when the contract was made, the court may, if it is just and equitable to do so, require the defendant to transfer to the plaintiff any property acquired by the defendant under the contract, or any property representing it.

Again, on general principles, a consent or release obtained by undue influence will not avail a trustee.[104] 'A consent which is not a free one is no consent at all.'[105]

Whether a beneficiary has consented to or concurred in a breach of trust is a question of fact. No particular formalities are required.[106] Similarly, a release does not need to be a formal release under seal in order to be effective; any expression of an intention to waive the breach of trust, if supported by some consideration, however slight, will be regarded as equivalent to a release.[107] A release may even be inferred from conduct,[108] but a beneficiary does not waive his rights in respect of a breach of trust merely by accepting a part of what is due to him with the knowledge that the trustee has committed a breach of trust.[109] Where a trustee relies on acquiescence by the beneficiary he must, it seems, show more than the mere passing of time and failure to act. If a long time has passed, however, very slight acts may suffice to establish acquiescence, and Campbell LC has even said[110] that 'although the rule be that the onus lies on the party relying on acquiescence to prove the facts from which the consent of the cestui que trust is to be inferred, it is easy to conceive cases in which, from great lapse of time, such facts might and ought to be presumed'.[111]

There are many cases which stress that, whether relying on concurrence,[112] release, or acquiescence, a trustee must establish full knowledge on the part of the beneficiary.

Accordingly releases[113] have been set aside where executed under a mistake of fact,[114] where a solicitor-trustee was allowed costs to which he was not entitled, the beneficiary not being professionally advised,[115] and where the release was executed shortly after the beneficiary attained his majority and purported to involve the examination of complicated accounts.[116] In a different context the House of Lords has recently observed[117] that, like any other contractual provision, a release will be construed so as to give effect to what the contracting parties intended, having regard to

---

[104] *Farrant v Blanchford* (1863) 1 De GJ & Sm 107; *Lloyd v Attwood* (1859) 3 De G & J 614.

[105] Per Stuart VC in *Stevens v Robertson* (1868) 18 LT 427 at 428.

[106] See *Rehden v Wesley* (1861) 29 Beav 213 at 215, per Romilly MR.

[107] *Stackhouse v Barnston* (1805) 10 Ves 453.

[108] *Egg v Devey* (1847) 10 Beav 444. Note the observations of Nicholls J in *John v James* [1991] FSR 397 at 439.

[109] *Re Cross* (1882) 20 Ch D 109, CA.

[110] *Life Association of Scotland v Siddal*, supra at 77. Cf *Knight v Bowyer* (1858) 2 De G & J 421 at 443, per Turner LJ.

[111] In the following cases, acquiescence was established—*Jones v Higgins* (1866) LR 2 Eq 538; *Sleeman v Wilson* (1871) LR 13 Eq 36, in the following cases it was not—*Griffiths v Porter* (1858) 25 Beav 236; *Re Jackson* (1881) 44 LT 467.

[112] *Buckeridge v Glasse* (1841) Cr & Ph 126.

[113] See *Farrant v Blanchford* (1863) 1 De GJ & Sm 107 at 119; *Thomson v Eastwood* (1877) 2 App Cas 215, HL.

[114] *Hore v Becher* (1842) 12 Sim 465.

[115] *Todd v Wilson* (1846) 9 Beav 486 distinguishing *Stanes v Parker* (1846) 9 Beav 385 where the beneficiary was professionally advised. See also *Aspland v Watte* (1855) 20 Beav 474.

[116] *Wedderburn v Wedderburn* (1838) 4 My & Cr 41; *Parker v Bloxam* (1855) 20 Beav 295.

[117] See *Bank of Credit and Commerce International SA (in liquidation) v Ali* [2001] UKHL 8 [2001] 1 All ER 961, HL, noted [2001] JBL 107 (D Sheehan); [2002] MLR 425 (Kay Wheat); *Ramsden v Hylton* (1751) 2 Ves Sen 304; *Lindo v Lindo* (1839) 1 Beav 496.

the parties' relationship and all the relevant facts surrounding the transaction so far as known to the parties. Although a party could, at any rate in a compromise agreement supported by valuable consideration, agree to release claims or rights of which he was not, and could not, be aware, the court would be slow to infer that he had done so in the absence of clear language to that effect.

Where a trustee relies on acquiescence he must establish knowledge of the relevant facts by the person alleged to have acquiesced, but 'one cannot lay down a hard and fast rule to this effect that knowledge of the legal consequences of known facts is or is not essential to the success of the plea'.[118] Further, a nice distinction has to be drawn between knowledge by the beneficiary of what he is doing and its legal effect, and knowledge of the fact that what he is concurring in is a breach of trust. At any rate where a trustee relies on the concurrence of a beneficiary—and on principle there seems no reason why the rule in relation to release or acquiescence should be any different—Wilberforce J in *Re Pauling's Settlement*[119] accepted the view of the Court of Appeal in *Evans v Benyon*[120] as correctly representing the law. There it was said that a person who, knowing that a trustee was distributing a settled fund, consented to and was active in the distribution, could not afterwards claim against the trustee even though he did not know at the time that he was beneficially interested and although he did not know that the division was a breach of trust.[121] All the members of the Court of Appeal in *Holder v Holder*[122] expressly approved the general statement of the law made by Wilberforce J in *Re Pauling's Settlement*,[123] where he said,[124] after reviewing the authorities:

The result of these authorities appears to me to be that the court has to consider all the circumstances in which the concurrence of the cestui que trust was given with a view to seeing whether it is fair and equitable that, having given his concurrence, he should afterwards turn round and sue the trustees: that, subject to this, it is not necessary that he should know that what he is concurring in is a breach of trust, provided that he fully understands what he is concurring in, and that it is not necessary that he should himself have directly benefited by the breach of trust.

---

[118] Per Cross J at first instance in *Holder v Holder* [1966] 2 All ER 116 at 128. Note the observations of Nicholls J in *John v James* [1991] FSR 397 at 459.

[119] [1961] 3 All ER 713. The Court of Appeal expressed no opinion on this point in the same case on appeal in [1964] Ch 303, [1963] 3 All ER 1.

[120] (1887) 37 Ch D 329, CA; *Re Hulkes* (1886) 33 Ch D 552.

[121] Note, however, that the court was in fact of opinion that he knew both of his beneficial interest and of the breach of trust.

[122] [1968] Ch 353, [1968] 1 All ER 665, CA; *Re Freeston's Charity* [1979] 1 All ER 51, CA; *Spellson v George* (1992) 26 NSWLR 666.

[123] Supra. See *Gold v Rosenberg* (1995) 129 DLR (4th) 152, appeal dismissed (1998) 35 OR (3d) 736.

[124] At p 730. The proposition that it is not necessary that a consenting beneficiary should know that what he is concurring in is a breach of trust may be of a quite narrow as opposed to a general application—note the facts of *Evans v Benyon*, supra, CA. In other circumstances such lack of knowledge may be a fact relevant to the issue of fairness and equity: see *Spellson v George* (1992) 26 NSWLR 666 at 676, per Hope A-JA.

(c) IMPOUNDING THE BENEFICIAL INTEREST OF THE BENEFICIARY

Quite apart from statute, a beneficiary who instigated or requested a trustee to commit a breach of trust could be called upon to indemnify the trustee, in respect of his liability to make good the loss to the trust estate, out of his beneficial interest;[125] where the beneficiary had merely consented to the breach of trust, the trustee had no right to impound his beneficial interest by way of indemnity,[126] unless the beneficiary had obtained a personal benefit from the breach of trust, when the trustee was apparently entitled to an indemnity out of the beneficial interest, though only to the extent of the benefit.[127] The right does not depend on possession of the trust fund, and so will continue in favour of a former trustee where a new trustee is appointed.[128]

The equitable right has been extended by statute, now represented by s 62 of the Trustee Act 1925. Section 62(1)[129] provides as follows:

Where a trustee commits a breach of trust at the instigation or request or with the consent in writing[130] of a beneficiary, the court may, if it thinks fit, make such order as to the court seems just, for impounding all or any part of the interest of the beneficiary in the trust estate by way of indemnity to the trustee or persons claiming through him.

The statement with regard to the corresponding provision of the 1888 Act applies here,[131] namely, that it 'was intended to enlarge the power of the court as to indemnifying trustees, and to give greater relief to trustees, and was not intended and did not operate to curtail the previously existing rights and remedies of trustees, or to alter the law except by giving greater power to the court'.[132] Although the section gives the court a discretion, it is a judicial discretion, and in any case where it would have impounded the interest of a beneficiary before the statutory provisions, it will be bound to make a similar order under the Act.[133] Accordingly, the power to impound is not lost on the one hand by an assignment, even for value, of the beneficial interest,[134] nor, on the other hand, by the appointment of new trustees.[135]

In order to rely successfully on s 62, the trustee must establish that the beneficiary at least knew the facts which rendered what he was instigating, or requesting, or consenting to, a breach of trust. It is not enough, therefore, to show that the beneficiary pressed for a particular investment if it also appears that he left it to the

---

[125] *Sawyer v Sawyer* (1885) 28 Ch D 595, CA; *Chillingworth v Chambers* [1896] 1 Ch 685, CA.
[126] *Sawyer v Sawyer*, supra; *Fletcher v Collis* [1905] 2 Ch 24, CA.
[127] *Booth v Booth* (1838) 1 Beav 125; *Chillingworth v Chambers*, supra.
[128] *Re Pauling's Settlement (No 2)* [1963] Ch 576, [1963] 1 All ER 857.
[129] As amended by the Married Women (Restraint upon Anticipation) Act 1949, s 1(4) and Sch 2.
[130] The words 'in writing' apply only to consent and not to instigation or request—*Griffith v Hughes* [1892] 3 Ch 105; *Re Somerset* [1894] 1 Ch 231, CA.
[131] *Re Pauling's Settlement (No 2)*, supra.
[132] *Bolton v Curre* [1895] 1 Ch 544 at 549, per Romer J; *Fletcher v Collis* [1905] 2 Ch 24, CA.
[133] *Re Somerset* [1894] 1 Ch 231, CA; *Bolton v Curre*, supra. [134] *Bolton v Curre*, supra.
[135] *Re Pauling's Settlement (No 2)*, supra.

trustees to determine whether it was a proper one for the moneys proposed to be advanced.[136]

It should also be observed that, again apart from statute, it has always been the practice of the court when administering the estate of a deceased person or a trust, 'in cases where trustees have under an honest mistake overpaid one beneficiary, in the adjustment of the accounts between the trustees and the cestui que trust, to make allowance for the mistake in order that the trustee may so far as possible be recouped the money which he has inadvisedly paid'.[137] The overpaid beneficiary will not however be compelled to refund the overpayment, but further payments will be withheld until the accounts have been put straight.[138] Exceptionally it has been held that a trustee-beneficiary who has overpaid the other beneficiaries and underpaid himself is not allowed to correct his mistake,[139] though it is obviously different where he has overpaid himself.[140] Further, this principle only applies to trusts and estates, and not, for instance, to overpayments made under a covenant.[141]

(d) LIMITATION

The rules as to the limitation of actions against trustees are set out in s 21 of the Limitation Act 1980. There may be applied to the relevant provisions of the Act the remarks of Kekewich J in *Re Timmis*[142] on the corresponding provisions in the earlier legislation:

The intention of the statute was to give a trustee the benefit of the lapse of time when, although he had done something legally or technically wrong, he had done nothing morally wrong or dishonest, but it was not intended to protect him where, if he pleaded the statute, he would come off with something he ought not to have, that is, money of the trust received by him and converted to his own use.

(i) Situations where there is no period of limitation

Somewhat curiously s 21 begins by laying down the circumstances in which a trustee cannot rely upon the Act, that is, where he remains liable indefinitely. Subsection (1) provides as follows:

No period of limitation prescribed by this Act shall apply to an action by a beneficiary under a trust, being an action—

---

[136] *Re Somerset* [1894] 1 Ch 231, CA; *Mara v Browne* [1895] 2 Ch 69, revsd, but not on this point [1896] 1 Ch 199, CA.

[137] Per Neville J in *Re Musgrave* [1916] 2 Ch 417 at 423; *Re Robinson* [1911] 1 Ch 502; *Re Ainsworth* [1915] 2 Ch 96.

[138] *Downes v Bullock* (1858) 25 Beav 54; affd sub nom *Bullock v Downes* (1860) 9 HL Cas 1; *Bate v Hooper* (1855) 5 De GM & G 338; *Burns & Geroff v Leda Holdings Pty Ltd* [1988] 1 Qd R 214, but contrast *Hood v Clapham* (1854) 19 Beav 90.

[139] *Re Horne* [1905] 1 Ch 76, but see *Re Reading* [1916] WN 262.   [140] *Re Reading, supra.*

[141] *Re Hatch* [1919] 1 Ch 351, [1918–19] All ER Rep 357.   [142] [1902] 1 Ch 176 at 186.

(a) in respect of any fraud or fraudulent breach of trust to which the trustee was a party or privy; or

(b) to recover from the trustee trust property or the proceeds of trust property in the possession of the trustee, or previously received by the trustee and converted to his use.

(ii) Construction of sub-s (1)(a)

Subsection (1)(*a*) has been held to be limited to cases of fraud or fraudulent breach of trust properly so called, that is to say to cases involving dishonesty.[143] Further Lord Davey observed,[144] on similar words in the 1888 Act, that 'if fraud, or a non-discovery of fraud, is to be relied on to take a case out of the Statute of Limitations, it must be the fraud of or in some way imputable to the person who invokes the aid of the Statute of Limitations'.

(iii) Construction of sub-s (1)(b)

As regards possession, or receipt and conversion to the trustee's use, under sub-s 1(*b*) the slight change in the wording from the 1888 Act probably does not alter the substance.[145] Accordingly, on the one hand, the subsection applied, and the trustees were unable to rely on the defence of limitation where they paid themselves annuities, by mistake without deduction of tax.[146] Likewise where a trustee remained in occupation of trust property for his own purposes,[147] and where a company director through an abuse of the trust and confidence reposed in him as a director had taken a transfer of the company's property to himself.[148] In *James v Williams*[149] an executor de son tort who, knowing he was not solely entitled, took possession of property and acted as if it belonged to him was held to be a constructive trustee and thus within s 21(1) and unprotected. This decision has been much criticized[150] as taking no account of

---

[143] *Armitage v Nurse* [1998] Ch 241, [1997] 2 All ER 705, CA: *Gwembe Valley Development Co Ltd (in receivership) v Koshy (No 3)* [2003] EWCA Civ 1048, [2004] 1 BCLC 131, where it was held that the subsection applies to a company director who dishonestly makes an unauthorized profit in breach of his fiduciary duty. Cf *Woodland-Ferrari v UCL Group Retirement Benefits Scheme* [2002] 3 All ER 670, [2002] 3 WLR 1154.

[144] *Thorne v Heard* [1895] AC 495, HL; and see *G L Baker Ltd v Medway Building and Supplies Ltd* [1958] 2 All ER 532, order discharged on another ground [1958] 3 All ER 540, CA.

[145] *Re Howlett* [1949] Ch 767, [1949] 2 All ER 490. On a corresponding provision in Tasmania it was held in *Stilbo Property Ltd v MCC Property Ltd (in liquidation)* (2002) 11 Tas R 63 that it covers claims for income or profit derived from trust property whenever received.

[146] *Re Sharp* [1906] 1 Ch 793. See *Nelson v Rye* [1996] 2 All ER 186, [1996] 1 WLR 1378, noted [1997] Conv 225 (J Stevens). Millett LJ pointed out in *Paragon Finance plc v D B Thakerer & Co (a firm)* [1999] 1 All ER 400, CA, that though the manager was a fiduciary, there was no trust as there was no obligation on him to keep the alleged trust property separate from his own.

[147] *Re Howlett*, supra (held chargeable with an occupation rent).

[148] *J J Harrison (Properties) Ltd v Harrison* [2001] EWCA Civ 1467, [2002] 1 BCLC 162 (liable for profits on a resale). See also *Re Pantone 485 Ltd* [2002] 1 BCLC 266.

[149] [2001] Ch 1, [1999] 3 All ER 309, CA. Cf *Gwembe Valley Development Co Ltd (in receivership) v Kosby (No 3)* [2003] EWCA Civ 1048, [2004] 1 BCLC 131.

[150] Underhill, *Law of Trusts and Trustees*, 16th edn, pp 924 n 20, 952 n 1; Lewin, *Law of Trusts*, 17th edn, 44-38; *Nolan v Nolan* [2004] VSCA 109, [2004] WTLR 1261 (Australia).

Paragon Finance plc v D B Thakerer & Co (a firm).[151] On the other hand, the subsection was held not to apply, and the trustees thus able to rely on the Act, where, for instance, the trustee had used the trust funds in the maintenance of an infant beneficiary,[152] where the trust funds had been lost,[153] and where the trust funds had been lent on mortgage, and the mortgagor used the moneys to pay off a debt to a bank in which one of the trustees was a partner.[154]

(iv) Limited protection to trustees

It is clear that sub-s 1(*b*) prevents a trustee, however honest, from putting forward a defence on the ground of limitation in respect of a claim to recover trust property (or its proceeds) in his hands, though he may sometimes, as we shall see, be able to rely on the equitable doctrines of laches and acquiescence.[155] Exceptionally some protection is now[156] given to a trustee who acts honestly and reasonably[157] in distributing the trust property among all those whom he believes to constitute the class of beneficiaries entitled to it, including himself. A late-comer who has a claim to a share in the distributed estate but whose claim is barred by the Limitation Act as regards the other beneficiaries, used to be able to claim the whole of his share from a trustee-beneficiary up to the amount the trustee had paid himself. Now such a trustee will be liable only in respect of the share which he would have had to pay to the late-comer had all the beneficiaries, including himself, been sued in time. Thus if the trustee had distributed one-third of the trust property to himself and one-third to each of two other beneficiaries in ignorance of the existence of a fourth, he is liable to pay the newcomer only the difference between the one-third share he has taken and the one-quarter share which is truly his.

(v) The basic limitation provision

Subject to s 21(1) discussed above, s 21(3) provides that no action by a beneficiary to recover trust property or in respect of any breach of trust[158] shall be brought after the expiration of six years from the date on which the right of action accrued. It has no application, however, to claims by the Attorney-General to enforce public charitable trusts.[159]

---

[151] Supra, CA.   [152] *Re Page* [1893] 1 Ch 304; *Re Timmis* [1902] 1 Ch 176.

[153] *Re Tufnell* (1902) 18 TLR 705; *Re Fountaine* [1909] 2 Ch 382, CA.

[154] *Re Gurney* [1893] 1 Ch 590.   [155] See p 545, infra.   [156] Limitation Act 1980, s 21(2).

[157] Cf Trustee Act 1925, s 61, discussed p 546, infra.

[158] See *Tito v Waddell (No 2)* [1977] Ch 106, [1977] 3 All ER 129, and pp 448, 520, supra.

[159] *A-G v Cocke* [1988] Ch 414, [1988] 2 All ER 391, noted [1988] Conv 292 (Jean Warburton).

(vi) Extension of limitation period

The general provisions as to the extension of the period of limitation by reason of disability,[160] fraud, deliberate concealment and mistake[161] apply to actions against trustees. 'Fraud' is here used in the equitable sense to denote conduct by the defendant or his agent such that it would be against conscience for him to avail himself of the lapse of time.[162] Further the periods of limitation may be extended, in appropriate cases, under the provisions of the Limitation (Enemies and War Prisoners) Act 1945.

(vii) Running of time

Where s 21(3) applies time runs from the date of the breach of trust, not from the time the loss accrued,[163] for instance, where trustees pay annuities to other persons, by mistake not deducting tax,[164] where they fail to convert in accordance with the directions of the trust instrument,[165] or where they invest on insufficient security.[166] By a proviso to this subsection, however, the right of action is not to be deemed to have accrued to any beneficiary entitled to future interest in the trust property until the interest falls into possession. It has accordingly been held that where a person has two separate interests in property, one in possession and one reversionary, he will not be barred as to the latter merely because he is barred as to the former.[167]

(viii) Parasitic claim

Section 21(4) provides that no beneficiary whose own claim has been barred can derive any benefit from a judgment or order obtained by any other beneficiary. Thus if a trust fund is lost, and the claim of the tenant for life is barred, the trustees, if compelled to replace the trust fund by the remainderman, will be personally entitled to the income so long as the life interest subsists.[168]

(ix) To whom the Act applies

The Act applies to trustees as defined in the Trustee Act 1925 and accordingly includes trustees holding on implied and constructive trusts and personal representatives.[169]

Before the 1888 Act came into force in 1890 a claim against an express trustee was never barred by lapse of time. So far as constructive trusts were concerned it will be

---

[160] Section 28.

[161] Section 32. As to deliberate concealment see *Cave v Robinson Jarvis & Rolf (a firm)* [2002] UKHL 18, [2002] 2 All ER 641; *Williams v Fanshaw Porter & Hazelhurst (a firm)* [2004] EWCA Civ 157, [2004] 2 All ER 616.

[162] *Bartlett v Barclays Bank Trust Co Ltd* [1980] Ch 515, [1980] 1 All ER 139.

[163] *Re Somerset* [1894] 1 Ch 231, CA; *Want v Campain* (1893) 9 TLR 254.

[164] *Re Sharp* [1906] 1 Ch 793.   [165] *Re Swain* [1891] 3 Ch 233.

[166] *Re Bowden* (1890) 45 Ch D 444; *Re Somerset,* supra, and see *How v Earl of Winterton* [1896] 2 Ch 626, CA (failure to accumulate); *Re Tufnell* (1902) 18 TLR 705 and *Re Fountaine* [1909] 2 Ch 382, CA (allowing co-trustee, a solicitor, to receive trust moneys).

[167] *Mara v Browne* [1895] 2 Ch 69, revsd, but not on this point [1896] 1 Ch 199, CA. As to a discretionary beneficiary see *Armitage v Nurse* [1998] Ch 24, CA; *Johns v Johns & anr* [2004] NZCA 42, [2005] WTLR 529.

[168] *Re Somerset,* supra.

[169] Limitation Act 1980, s 38(1); Trustee Act 1925, s 68(17).

remembered that there are two distinct categories of constructive trust.[170] The first category is where the constructive trustee, although not expressly appointed as a trustee, has assumed the duties of a trustee before the events which are alleged to constitute the breach of trust. Before 1890 this category of constructive trust was treated in the same way as an express trust and often confusingly described as such. The other category of constructive trust is the so-called remedial constructive trust which is not in reality a trust at all, but merely a remedial mechanism by which equity gives relief against fraud. Before 1890 the Court of Chancery gave effect to the reality of the situation by applying the statutes of limitation by analogy to the fraud which gave rise to the defendant's liability. The definitions of trust and trustee in the 1980 Act are not materially different from those in the 1888 Act. Read literally and without regard to the evident purpose of the Act it might be thought that the definitions abolish the difference between the two categories of constructive trust. The matter was carefully considered by Millett LJ in *Paragon Finance plc v D B Thakerar & Co (a firm)*,[171] in a judgment with which the other members of the court agreed, and it is thought that it can now be regarded as settled that this is not so and that the Limitation Act 1980 applies in the case of a constructive trust in the second category.

(x) Action for breach of fiduciary duty

An action for breach of fiduciary duty simpliciter has been said to be outside the provisions of the Act and therefore not subject to a period of limitation.[172] However the same distinction has to be drawn as that in relation to trustees between those whose fiduciary obligations preceded the acts complained of and those whose liability in equity was occasioned by the acts of which complaint was made.[173] It is clear that it is not possible, either in a case where a breach of fiduciary duty gives rise to a constructive trust, or in an action for breach of an express trust, to avoid any limitation period imposed by the Act by treating the case as one of breach of fiduciary duty.[174] Further the court will apply the statute by analogy where there is a 'correspondence' between the remedies available at law and in equity. Thus no distinction in point of limitation is to be made between an action for damages for fraud at common law and its counterpart in equity based on the same facts.[175]

---

[170] See p 66 et seq, supra.

[171] [1999] 1 All ER 400, CA. See also *Coulthard v Disco Mix Club Ltd* [1999] 2 All ER 457; *Clarke (exor of Will of Francis Bacon, decd) v Marlborough Fine Art (London) Ltd* (2001) *Times*, 5 July; *Gwembe Valley Development Co Ltd (in receivership) v Koshy (No 3)* [2003] EWCA Civ 1048, [2004] 1 BCLC 131 (dishonest fiduciary liable to account for all profits whether received directly or indirectly), noted (2004) 60 T & ELJ 7 (A Thompson).

[172] *A-G v Cocke*, supra; *Nelson v Rye* [1996] 2 All ER 186, [1996] 1 WLR 1378.

[173] *Paragon Finance plc v D B Thakerar & Co (a firm)*, supra, CA.   [174] *Nelson v Rye*, supra.

[175] *Knox v Gye* (1872) LR 5 HL 656, HL; *Paragon Finance plc v D B Thakerar & Co (a firm)*, supra, CA; *Coulthard v Disco Mix Club Ltd* [1999] 2 All ER 457; *Johns v Johns & anr*, supra. See also *Companhia de Seguros Imperio v Heath (REBX) Ltd* [2001] 1 WLR 112; (2001) 20 CJQ 171 (A McGee and G Scanlon).

(xi) Action for an account

A claim to an account in equity, absent any trust, has no equitable element; it is based on legal not equitable rights and the Act will apply.[176] Accordingly an action for an account brought by a principal against his agent is barred by the statutes of limitation unless the agent is more than a mere agent and is a trustee of the money which he received.[177] It may be added that where an account is sought as ancillary to another claim, the period of limitation, if any, appropriate to the main claim would also be applied to the ancillary one.[178]

(xii) Relationship between ss 21 and 22

Section 22 provides for a 12-year period of limitation in an action in respect of any claim to the personal estate of a deceased person. Time in this case runs from the date when the right to receive the share or interest accrued, which may be an earlier date than the date on which he can first bring an action to recover it.[179] In the case of an immediate legacy, this means the end of the executor's year[180] but a later date may be specified expressly or by implication in the will,[181] and there can be no right to receive the interest until there are sufficient assets to cover the claim in the hands of the personal representatives.[182]

The relationship between ss 21(3) and 22 is not altogether clear. Under the law in operation before the Act of 1939 it was vital to ascertain whether a personal representative had become a trustee. If the personal representative had not become a trustee the action was one to recover a legacy under s 8 of the Real Property Limitation Act 1874 and the period was 12 years, whereas if the personal representative had become an express trustee s 8 of the Trustee Act 1888 applied and the period of the limitation was only six years. An illustration of the first situation was *Re Richardson*[183] where the widow of a testator who died in 1909 was entitled to the whole residue absolutely. After the widow's death in 1917, the beneficiaries under her will claimed an account of the testator's estate. It was held that as the only duty of the personal representative was to administer the estate as such, the appropriate period of limitation was 12 years, and accordingly the claim must succeed. The second type of situation is illustrated by

---

[176] *How v Earl Winterton* [1896] 2 Ch 626 at 639 per Lindley LJ; *Paragon Finance plc v D B Thakerar & Co (a firm)* [1999] 1 All ER 400, CA.

[177] *Burdick v Garrick* (1870) LR 5 Ch App 233; *Paragon Finance plc v D B Thakerar & Co (a firm)*, supra, CA, disapproving *Nelson v Rye*, supra.

[178] *Tito v Waddell (No 2)* [1977] Ch 106 at 250–252, [1977] 3 All ER 129 at 248–250.

[179] *Hornsey Local Board v Monarch Investment Building Society* (1889) 24 QBD 1, CA; contra, Kekewich J in *Re Pardoe* [1906] 1 Ch 265 (overruled on another point [1906] 2 Ch 340; CA), but previous decision of Court of Appeal not cited.

[180] *Re Loftus (dec'd)* [2005] EWHC 406(Ch), [2005] 2 All ER 700. Strictly this case only decides that this is the earliest date from which time can begin to run.

[181] *Prior v Horniblow* (1836) 2 Y & C Ex 200; *Rudd v Rudd* [1895] 1 IR 15, CA.

[182] *Re Johnson*, supra; *Re Ludlam* (1890) 63 LT 330; cf *Re Owen* [1894] 3 Ch 220.

[183] [1920] 1 Ch 423, CA. Cf *Re Barker* [1892] 2 Ch 491; *Re Lacy* [1899] 2 Ch 149.

Re Oliver,[184] where a testatrix who died in 1890 gave the residue of her real and personal estate to her executors on trust for sale and conversion, and directed them to set aside £2,000 out of the proceeds to be held by them upon trust for L during her widowhood, and on her death or remarriage to fall into residue. Subject to this life interest the residue was given to her six children in equal shares. L died in 1916 and in an action brought in 1925 it was held that there was a trust for the residuary legatees and their claim was accordingly statute barred. After 1925, the Trustee Act 1888 would prima facie have applied wherever a man died intestate, by reason of the express trusts set up by the Administration of Estates Act 1925.[185]

Some writers[186] take the view that the same distinction has to be drawn under the Act of 1980, but it is submitted that the better view is that this distinction is no longer relevant.[187] Section 22 of the 1980 Act, re-enacting s 20 of the Act of 1939 is more widely worded than the corresponding provision of the Real Property Limitation Act 1874 and it is submitted that an 'action in respect of [a] claim to the personal estate of a deceased person'[188] remains such notwithstanding that the personal representative may for some purposes have become a trustee. This view is supported by *Re Diplock*[189] in two ways. In a general way it is supported by the indication of the proper approach to s 20 of the 1939 Act given by Lord Simonds in the House of Lords, in a speech concurred in by all the other Law Lords present, when he said[190] 'there is nothing in the ancestry of the section which justifies, much less requires, a narrower meaning being given to its words than they ordinarily bear'. More specifically, it is supported by the observations of the Court of Appeal[191] as to the position of an administrator on intestacy. The court affirmed the proposition that after 1925 and before the 1939 Act such an administrator would be a trustee for the next-of-kin and that the relevant period of limitation would apparently be six years under the Trustee Act 1888. However, under the 1939 Act, such a case would, it was said, be governed by s 20 and the limitation period would accordingly be 12 years, thus increasing the statutory period applicable.

(xiii) Law Commission Report No 270[192]

The Draft Bill appended to this Report provides for a core regime, which would extend to claims for breach of trust and related claims, including claims in respect of

---

[184] [1927] 2 Ch 323; *Re Swain* [1891] 3 Ch 233; *Re Timmis* [1902] 1 Ch 176.

[185] Sections 33 (as amended by the Trusts of Land and Appointment of Trustees Act 1996 and the Trustee Act 2000) and 46 (as amended).

[186] Preston and Newsom, *Limitation of Actions*, 4th edn, p 51; Halsbury's *Laws of England*, (4th edn, Reissue) vol 28, para 1047; Williams, *Law of Wills*, 8th edn, pp 295, 296.

[187] Franks, *Limitations of Actions*, pp 49, 50.   [188] Limitation Act 1939, s 20.

[189] [1948] Ch 465, [1948] 2 All ER 318, CA; affd sub nom *Ministry of Health v Simpson* [1951] AC 251, [1950] 2 All ER 1137, HL.

[190] At 276, 277, 1148, respectively.

[191] *Supra*, at 511–513, 342, 343, semble; approved by the House of Lords supra, at 276, 1147.

[192] The report was accepted in principle by the government in July 2002, but no steps have yet been taken towards its implementation. It is discussed in [2003] CJQ 41 (R James).

the personal estate of a deceased person. It lays down a primary limitation period of three years from the time when the claimant knew, or ought reasonably to have known, that he had a cause of action, a period which the court would have no discretion to disapply. There would be a long-stop limitation period of 10 years, starting from the date of the accrual of the cause of action. The present law in relation to future interests and to parasitic claims would be substantially continued,[193] and a cause of action to recover property held on a bare trust would not accrue unless and until the trustee acted in breach of trust.

The primary limitation would not run during the claimant's minority; the long-stop period, however, would, but not so as to bar an action before the claimant reached the age of 21. Adult disability (including supervening disability) would suspend the primary limitation period, but not the long-stop period. However the long-stop period would not run where the defendant had dishonestly concealed relevant facts.

Neither limitation period would apply to a claim for breach of trust or to recover trust property brought by the Attorney-General or the Charity Commissioners in relation to a charity.

(e) LACHES

Where the Limitation Act 1980 does not apply[194] the question arises whether it can be barred by the plaintiff's delay in bringing the action, that is, by laches in the narrow sense.[195] In practice, lapse of time is commonly pleaded together with acquiescence, which indeed, on one view,[196] is included in the scope of the word laches in the wide sense. Mere delay by itself will never,[197] or almost never,[198] bar the plaintiff, but the court has to look at all the circumstances, in particular the period of delay, the extent to which the defendant's position has been prejudiced by the delay, and the extent to which that prejudice was caused by the actions of the plaintiff, and then decide whether the balance of justice or injustice is in favour of granting the remedy or withholding it. It is not necessary to show a causal link between the delay and the prejudice, but the plaintiff's knowledge that the delay will cause prejudice is a factor to be taken into account.[199]

---

[193] See (vii) and (viii), p 541, supra.

[194] *Re Pauling's Settlement Trust* [1961] 3 All ER 713 at 735; affd on this point [1964] Ch 303, [1963] 3 All ER 1, CA.

[195] See Brunyate, *Limitation of Actions*, pp 188–189; *Orr v Ford* (1989) 167 CLR 316 at 335–346, per Deane J. See also (1992) 22 VUWLR 51 (Lucy Trevelyan).

[196] Another view is that it is simply evidence of acquiescence. *Morse v Royal* (1806) 12 Ves 355; *Life Association of Scotland v Siddal* (1861) 3 De GF & J 58.

[197] *Rochefoucauld v Boustead* [1897] 1 Ch 196, CA; *Re Lacey* [1907] 1 Ch 330, CA. Contrast *Re Sharpe* [1892] 1 Ch 154, CA, per Lindley LJ at 168.

[198] *Nelson v Rye* [1996] 2 All ER 186, 201 [1996] 1 WLR 1378, 1392 per Laddie J.

[199] *Nelson v Rye*, supra; *Lindsay Petroleum Co v Hurd* (1874) LR 5 PC 221 (where there is an important statement of the doctrine); *Erlanger v New Sombrero Phosphate Co* (1878) 3 App Cas 1218, HL; *John v James* [1991] FSR 397. See also *Baburin v Baburin (No 2)* [1991] 2 Qd R 240.

It has recently been made clear that the modern approach to laches or acquiescence does not require an exhaustive inquiry into whether the circumstances could fit within the principles established in previous cases. A broader approach should be adopted, namely whether it is unconscionable for the party concerned to be permitted to assert his beneficial rights.[200]

The Law Commission recommend that nothing in the proposed new Limitation Act should be taken to prejudice any equitable jurisdiction of the court to refuse an application for equitable relief (whether final or interlocutory) on the grounds of delay (or because of any other equitable defence such as acquiescence) even though the limitation period applicable to the claim in question has not expired.

(f) SECTION 61 OF THE TRUSTEE ACT 1925[201]

This section provides:

If it appears to the court that a trustee ... is or may be personally liable for any breach of trust ... but has acted honestly and reasonably, and ought fairly to be excused for the breach of trust and for omitting to obtain the directions of the court in the matter in which he committed such breach, then the court may relieve him either wholly or partly from personal liability for the same.

'The provisions of the section', it has been said,[202] 'were intended to enable the court to excuse breaches of trust where the circumstances of the particular case showed reasonable conduct, but it was never meant to be used as a sort of general indemnity clause for honest men who neglect their duty.' The onus of showing that he acted not only honestly but also reasonably rests on the trustee,[203] and unless both these matters are established 'the court cannot help the trustees; but if both are made out, there is then a case for the court to consider whether the trustee ought fairly to be excused for the breach, looking at all the circumstances'.[204] By 'fairly' is meant in fairness to the trustee and to other people who may be affected.[205] Although the court has refused to fetter its discretion and insists that each case must be dealt with

---

[200] *Frawley v Neill* (1999) 143 Sol Jo LB 98, CA, noted (2000) 13 T & ELJ 19 (C Taylor); As to the application of the doctrine of laches in a commercial setting see *Patel v Shah* [2005] EWCA Civ 157, [2005] WTLR 359, noted [2005] Conv 174 (G Watt) and (2005) 63 T & ELTJ 18 (J Davey).

[201] Re-enacting, with slight alterations, Judicial Trustees Act 1896, s 3, decisions on which are usually applicable to s 61. The section need not be specially pleaded—*Singlehurst v Tapscott Steamship Co* [1899] WN 133, CA, though it is better that it should be. In relation to a charitable corporation; see *Re Freeston's Charity* [1978] 1 All ER 481; affd [1979] 1 All ER 51, [1978] 1 WLR 741, CA. Cf Companies Act 1985, s 727(1) and *Coleman Taymar Ltd v Oakes* [2001] 2 BCLC 749. See generally (1955) 19 Conv 420 (L A Sheridan).

[202] *Williams v Byron* (1901) 18 TLR 172 at 176, per Byrne J.   [203] *Re Stuart* [1897] 2 Ch 583.

[204] Per Sir Ford North, giving the advice of PC in *National Trustees Co of Australasia v General Finance Co of Australasia* [1905] AC 373 at 381 on the corresponding provision of the Victorian Trusts Act 1901; *Re Turner* [1897] 1 Ch 536.

[205] *Marsden v Regan* [1954] 1 All ER 475, CA. The above passage was cited and applied by Coleman J in *Canadian Imperial Bank of Commerce v Valley Credit Union Ltd* (1989) 56 Man R (2d) 50 at 65.

according to its own circumstances,[206] it is helpful to look at some of the decisions, particularly on the question of reasonableness. Before doing so it may be observed that the courts have said that the section should not be narrowly construed.[207] It can even be applied to cases where a trustee has paid the wrong person,[208] and the maxim ignorantia iuris non excusat does not in the least prevent the court from granting relief.[209] There must, however, have been a breach of trust—the section cannot be used to excuse trustees from a breach of trust they wish to commit in the future.[210] On another point it seems clear that the court will be much less ready to grant relief to a professional trustee who is being paid for his services in performing his duties.[211]

Turning to the cases, in *Re Stuart*[212] the court said it was fair to consider whether the trustee would have acted in the same way if he had been dealing with his own property. If he would, it is a point in his favour, though not enough by itself to show that he acted reasonably.[213] The taking and acceptance of advice by someone reasonably believed to be qualified to give it has a similar effect.[214] In *Chapman v Browne*[215] the trustees were held not to have acted reasonably, where they never really considered whether the security was one which it was right and proper for a trustee to take, and in *Wynne v Tempest*[216] the court refused relief where a trustee had left the trust money in the hands of his co-trustee, a solicitor, without sufficient reason. Indeed Kekewich J regarded it not merely as a failure to act reasonably, but as dishonest in this context, where a trustee 'does nothing, swallows wholesale what is said by his co-trustee, never asks for explanation, and accepts flimsy explanations'.[217]

A further illustration of refusal of relief by the court is *Ward-Smith v Jebb*[218] where the court would assist neither a solicitor trustee nor his lay co-trustee, who had made payments out of a trust fund on the erroneous assumption that a certain person was entitled by reason of the Adoption of Children Act 1949, having failed to observe the provisions of the Act, which made it quite clear that it did not apply on the facts of the case. Accepting the general rule that a trustee must exercise that degree of care which a prudent man would exercise in respect of his own affairs, Buckley J applied it to the facts before him by saying:[219] 'A prudent man, whose affairs were affected by a statute would either satisfy himself that he fully understood its effect or would seek legal

---

[206] *Re Turner*, supra; *Re Kay* [1897] 2 Ch 518.   [207] *Re Allsop* [1914] 1 Ch 1, CA.

[208] *Re Allsop*, supra; *Re Wightwick's Will Trusts* [1950] Ch 260, [1950] 1 All ER 689. But see *Ward-Smith v Jebb* (1964) 108 Sol Jo 919, discussed infra.

[209] *Holland v Administrator of German Property* [1937] 2 All ER 807, CA.

[210] *Re Rosenthal* [1972] 3 All ER 552, [1972] 1 WLR 1273.

[211] *National Trustees Co of Australasia v General Finance Co of Australasia* [1905] AC 373, PC; *Re Windsor Steam Coal Co (1901) Ltd* [1929] 1 Ch 151, CA; *Re Pauling's Settlement Trusts* [1964] Ch 303, [1963] 3 All ER 1, CA.

[212] [1897] 2 Ch 583; *Re Barker* (1898) 77 LT 712.

[213] Per Farwell J in *Re Lord De Clifford's Estate* [1900] 2 Ch 707 at 716, 'The fact that he has acted with equal foolishness in both cases will not justify relief under this statute.'

[214] *Marsden v Regan* [1954] 1 All ER 475, CA.   [215] [1902] 1 Ch 785, CA.

[216] (1897) 13 TLR 360; *Re Second East Dulwich etc Building Society* (1899) 68 LJ Ch 196.

[217] *Re Second East Dulwich etc Building Society*, supra, at 198.   [218] (1964) 108 Sol Jo 919.

[219] Ibid.

advice. A solicitor trustee could not be heard to say that it was reasonable to apply a lower standard to him.' The lay trustee was in no better position, in the absence of any evidence that he had relied on the advice of the solicitor or any other legal adviser. The question of any indemnity between the two trustees was not before the court. Finally, as is expressly provided by the section, the court may relieve the trustee either wholly, or to a limited extent as it did in *Re Evans (decd)*.[220]

On the other hand, in *Re Lord De Clifford's Estate*[221] executors were relieved where, during five years' administration of the estate, and knowing that large sums were required for administration purposes, they paid various sums to their solicitors in reliance on their statements that they were required for those purposes. Over 90 per cent of the sums were in fact so applied, but the balance was lost on the solicitors' bankruptcy. Similarly where executors failed to call in a small debt, where the terms of the will might fairly bring a business man to the conclusion there was no duty to do so.[222] According to the circumstances it may[223] or may not be reasonable to act without seeking the directions of the court.

(g) DISCHARGE IN BANKRUPTCY

A claim in respect of a breach of trust is provable in bankruptcy,[224] and in general, an order of discharge releases a bankrupt from all the bankruptcy debts.[225] This provision applies to all claims in respect of a breach of trust, except where the debt was incurred in respect of any fraud or fraudulent breach of trust to which the bankrupt trustee was a party.[226] Although, as stated, in the case of a non-fraudulent breach of trust the discharge bars the right to the original debt due from the trustee, his duties, character and functions as debtor are perfectly distinct from those which belong to him as trustee, and those of the trustee are not affected by the bankruptcy. Accordingly it is the duty of defaulting trustee to prove in his own bankruptcy just as much as if he were a perfect stranger to it, and it is a clear breach of trust for him to fail to do so. This further breach of trust subsequently attaching to the trustee in that character is unaffected by the discharge, and the trustee accordingly remains liable for it, to the amount of the dividends he would have received under the bankruptcy.[227]

---

[220] [1999] 2 All ER 777 (claimant and defendant entitled equally to intestate's estate. Defendant, sole administratrix, wrongfully distributed estate in belief that the claimant had long predeceased the intestate. Defendant relieved against the claim of the underpaid claimant to the extent that it could not be satisfied out of a property derived from the intestate's estate which was still at her disposal).

[221] [1900] 2 Ch 707; *Perrins v Bellamy* [1899] 1 Ch 797, CA.

[222] *Re Grindey* [1898] 2 Ch 593, CA; *Re Mackay* [1911] 1 Ch 300.

[223] *Re Gee* [1948] Ch 284, [1948] 1 All ER 498.

[224] Insolvency Act 1986, s 382(1), (3) and (4), amended from a date to be appointed by the Criminal Justice Act 1988, s 170, Sch 16, by the repeal of sub-s 1(*c*).

[225] Ibid, s 281(1).   [226] Ibid, s 281(3). See *Mander v Evans* [2001] 3 All ER 811.

[227] *Orrett v Corser* (1855) 21 Beav 52.

4 CRIMINAL LIABILITY OF TRUSTEES[228]

Under the Theft Act 1968 a trustee is liable for theft 'if he dishonestly appropriates property belonging to another with the intention of permanently depriving the other of it'.[229] For the purposes of the Act, in the case of trust property, the persons to whom it belongs are to be regarded as including 'any person having a right to enforce the trust',[230] that is, the beneficiaries (including, it is thought, potential beneficiaries under a discretionary trust) or, in the case of a charitable trust, the Attorney-General. In the case of unenforceable trusts, it would presumably include the person entitled to the residue, from which it would follow that it would not be theft if the trustee was himself solely entitled to the residue.[231] Though in general a person cannot steal land, a trustee can and will do so if 'he appropriates the land or anything forming part of it by dealing with it in breach of the confidence reposed in him'.[232]

Mention may be made of the difficult decision in *A-G's Reference (No 1 of 1985)*[233] where the court seemed anxious lest the imposition of a constructive trust might bring within the Theft Act 1968 'a host of activities which no layman would think were stealing'. The facts were that the salaried manager of a tied public house was under contract to sell on his employer's premises only goods supplied by his employer and to pay all the takings into his employer's account. He bought beer elsewhere and sold it to customers in the public house making a secret profit, of which he was held not to be a constructive trustee.[234] It was held that there was no difference in principle between the facts of this case and a bribe and at that time it was generally assumed that a fiduciary was not a constructive trustee of a bribe he received. In the light of *A-G for Hong Kong v Reid*[235] it seems unlikely that this assumption is valid, and this casts doubt on this ground of the decision in *A-G's Reference (No 1 of 1985)*.[236] A further ground for the decision seems very doubtful. It was said that there could be no trust until the profit is identifiable as a separate piece of property. Equity, however, has never found any difficulty in relation to mixed funds.[237] The actual decision may perhaps be supported on the basis of absence of mens rea: the manager clearly knew that he was breaking the terms of his contract, but the idea that he might be stealing from his employers the profit element in the transactions may well never have occurred to him.

Finally, it may be mentioned that under the Debtors Act 1869, s 4, a trustee who has been ordered by the court to pay any sum in his possession or under his control is, on default, liable to imprisonment for a period of up to a year.

---

[228] See (1975) 39 Conv 29 (R Brazier).

[229] Theft Act 1968, s 1(1). As to 'borrowing' trust funds see (1985) 5 LS 183 (Glanville Williams). See also *Re Wain* (1993) unreported but noted (1994) 2 Dec Ch Com 34.

[230] Theft Act 1968, s 5(2).

[231] Nor, of course, would the trustee in such case be liable for breach of trust.

[232] Theft Act 1968, s 4(2)(a).   [233] [1986] QB 491, [1986] 2 All ER 219, CA.

[234] Disregarding the use by the manager of his employer's property.

[235] [1994] 1 AC 324, [1994] 1 All ER 1, PC. See pp 149–150, supra.   [236] Supra, CA.

[237] See pp 557 et seq, infra.

25

FOLLOWING AND TRACING

It may be helpful to begin by giving an illustration of the sorts of circumstances which may call for following or tracing. Suppose a trustee (T), now bankrupt so that any remedy against him would be inadequate, in breach of trust had transferred an asset of the trust to X, who has transferred it to Y. The beneficiaries (B) can *follow* the asset through X into the hands of Y, assert their equitable title, and call on Y to restore the asset to the trust. B will normally succeed in their claim unless Y can show that either he or X was a bona fide purchaser for value of the asset without notice of the trust. Suppose further that X and Y are volunteers, and that Y has sold the asset to Z, a bona fide purchaser for value without notice, and used the proceeds of sale to purchase another asset. B can no longer *follow* the original asset, but they can *trace* it into the substituted asset held by Y. Alternatively suppose X was a purchaser for value without notice of the trust and had given T a cheque for its full value which he paid into a new account in his own name. Suppose further that the account has been exhausted in the purchase by T of shares in his own name which he continues to hold. B can *trace* the original asset into the account and out of the account into the shares.

This illustration adopts the new approach which appears to have been established by Lord Millett in *Foskett v McKeown*.[1] He said, in relation to beneficiaries under a trust, that following and tracing:

. . . are both exercises in locating assets which are or may be taken to represent an asset belonging to the [claimants] and to which they assert ownership. The processes of following and tracing are, however distinct. Following is the process of following the same asset as it moves from hand to hand. Tracing is the process of identifying a new asset as the substitute for the old.

It enables the claimant to substitute the traceable proceeds for the original asset as the subject matter of his claim. Though there are undoubtedly two different processes the distinction has by no means always been made in this way, and the past language of judges and academics must be looked at with care. Unfortunately Lord Millett

---

[1] [2001] 1 AC 102, [2000] 3 All ER 97, HL noted [2001] Conv 94 (J Stevens); [2000] 63 MLR 905 (R Grantham and C Rickett); (2000) 14 Tru LI 194 (P Jaffey); [2001] LMCLQ 1 (D Fox); [2001] NZLJ 276 (C Cato and M Connell); [2003] RLR 56 (C Rotherham); (2001) 117 LQR 366 (A Berg). Lord Millet's opinion set out above was not expressly referred to by any of the other Law Lords. Lord Browne-Wilkinson and Lord Hoffman can, perhaps, be taken to have implicitly agreed, and neither Lord Steyn nor Lord Hope expressed dissent. See also (2001) 117 LQR 412 (A Burrows); [2001] CLP 231 (P Birks); [2002] CLP 262 (P Jaffey).

did not explain the change of approach from that he had previously expressed, extrajudicially,[2] that it is '. . . necessary to distinguish between two kinds of tracing: (i) following the same asset from one person to another; and (ii) following an asset into a changed form in the same hands.' The change is one of classification and terminology rather than of susbtance. The matter is complicated by the fact that one set of facts may well involve both following and tracing.

Lord Millett explained the law of tracing as follows:

The transmission of a claimant's property rights from one asset to its traceable proceeds is part of our law of property, not of the law of unjust enrichment. There is no 'unjust factor' to justify restitution (unless 'want of title' be one, which makes the point). The claimant succeeds if at all by virtue of his own title, not to reverse unjust enrichment. Property rights are determined by fixed rules and settled principles. They are not discretionary. They do not depend upon ideas of what is 'fair, just and reasonable'. Such concepts, which in reality mask decisions of legal policy, have no place in the law of property.[3]

A beneficiary of a trust is entitled to a continuing beneficial interest not merely in the trust property but in its traceable proceeds also, and his interest binds everyone who takes the property or its traceable proceeds except a bona fide purchaser for value without notice.

Lord Millett further stated that tracing is neither a claim nor a remedy.[4] After the process is complete the beneficiaries may be able to make a claim.[5] Where a beneficiary can follow a trust asset into the hands of a third party, without the intervention of a bona fide purchaser for value without notice, he can assert his equitable proprietary interest and require the asset to be restored to the trust. Where one asset is exchanged for another, a claimant can elect whether to follow the original asset into the hands of the new owner or to trace its value into the new asset in the hands of the original owner, though he cannot, of course, recover twice. In practice his choice is often dictated by circumstances. If, for instance, the asset had been transferred to a bona fide purchaser for value without notice of the trust, it would be pointless to try to follow it even if it could physically be located. In this case, or if the trust property had ceased to exist in traceable form, the beneficiary will seek to claim against the trustee. He has a choice of remedy where the trustee has wrongfully misappropriated

---

[2] (1991) 107 LQR 71.

[3] Dicta of Millett LJ, as he then was, in *Boscawen v Bajwa* [1995] 4 All ER 769, CA, at 776, which, surprisingly, was not cited by any of their Lordships in *Foskett v McKeown*, supra, HL, are difficult to reconcile with this statement. There he seemed to say that the claim following successful completion of a tracing exercise is based on unjust enrichment, to which there could, applying *Lipkin Gorman (a firm) v Karpnale* [1991] 2 AC 548, [1992] 4 All ER 512, HL, be raised the defence of innocent change of position.

[4] *Foskett v McKeown*, supra, HL at 128, 120. Unfortunately he did not refer to *Agip (Africa) Ltd v Jackson* [1990] 1 Ch 265, [1992] 4 All ER 385; affd [1991] Ch 547, [1992] 4 All ER 451, CA, where he said, at 285, 398: 'Tracing at common law, unlike its counterpart in equity, is neither a cause of action nor a remedy but serves as evidential purpose.'

[5] The successful completion of a tracing exercise may be preliminary to a personal claim (as in *El Ajou v Dollar Land Holdings plc* [1993] 3 All ER 717; revsd [1994] 2 All ER 685, CA, on a company law point) or a proprietary one, to the enforcement of a legal right (as in *F C Jones & Sons (a firm) v Jones* [1997] Ch 159, [1996] 4 All ER 721, CA) or an equitable one.

trust property and used it exclusively to acquire other property for his own benefit. He may either assert his beneficial ownership of the proceeds or bring a personal claim against the trustee for breach of trust and enforce an equitable lien or charge on the proceeds to secure restoration of the trust fund. If the traceable proceeds are worth more than the original asset it will be to his advantage to assert his beneficial owner-ship and obtain the profit for himself. If they are worth less he will take the whole of the proceeds either by asserting his beneficial ownership or by enforcing his lien, and have a personal claim for the deficiency.

In so far as he does not rely on his personal claim, his remedies are proprietary and can be maintained not only against the wrongdoing trustee but also against anyone who derives title from him other than a bona fide purchaser without notice of the breach of trust. It matters not how many successive transactions there may have been, so long as tracing is possible and no bona fide purchaser for value without notice has intervened.

The proprietary remedy may have various advantages. Suppose, for instance, a trustee, who has since become bankrupt, used the trust funds in clear breach of trust to buy a diamond brooch which he gave to Marilyn. The beneficiary can, of course, bring a personal action against the trustee for breach of trust, but the effect of the bankruptcy will be to make the remedy worthless, or at best lead to a claim to a dividend in the bankruptcy. If, however, Marilyn still has the brooch, the beneficiary can trace the trust funds into her hands in their altered form, assert his proprietary right, and require that the brooch be transferred to the trust. One advantage of a proprietary remedy is that if a trustee becomes bankrupt, the trust property does not pass to the trustee in bankruptcy and does not become available to the trustee's creditors.[6] Further, as we shall see, a proprietary remedy may enable the beneficiary to take advantage of any increase there may be in the value of the property, and entitle him to any income which the property has produced in the defendant's hands.

So far we have been considering the position in equity. Following and tracing, however, are available at law as well as in equity, but the rules are generally thought to be more restricted. Lord Millett[7] has said that there is nothing inherently legal or equitable about the tracing exercise and that there is no sense in maintaining different rules for tracing at law and in equity. These observations were obiter, and elsewhere[8] he has accepted that presently differences exist. It has been pointed out[9] that a more restricted right to trace at law may be justified because a legal right, unlike an equitable one, is not defeated by a bona fide purchase without notice. Since we are concerned with the position of beneficiaries under a trust we will concentrate on the rules in equity, but it will be helpful first to refer briefly to the rules at law.

---

[6] See Insolvency Act 1986, s 283(3).

[7] In *F C Jones & Sons (a firm) v Jones*, supra, CA, at 169, 729; and *Foskett v McKeown*, supra, HL, at 128, 121.

[8] *Agip (Africa) Ltd v Jackson*, supra, at first instance *El Ajou v Dollar Land Holdings plc*, supra, at first instance.

[9] [2001] Conv 94 (J Stevens).

1 FOLLOWING AND TRACING AT COMMON LAW

These are preliminary steps towards obtaining an appropriate remedy necessary in some circumstances. Completion of the process enables the defendant to be identified as the recipient of the plaintiff's money or chattels.[10] In the case of chattels he may then be liable in conversion. Conversion does not, however, lie for money taken and received as currency, but there may be a remedy by the old action for money had and received, nowadays called a personal claim in restitution at common law.[11]

At common law the legal owner of an asset who is deprived of its possession has a right to follow or trace it no matter into whose hands it might come, notwithstanding that it may change its form, so long as the means of identifying the asset in its original or converted form continue to exist. The right is not restricted to tangible assets, such as the sovereigns in a bag or a strong box referred to in the older cases, but applies equally to a chose in action, such as a banker's debt to his customer.[12] In *Lipkin Gorman (a firm) v Karpnale Ltd*[13] Cass, one of the partners in a firm of solicitors, had withdrawn some £223,000 from the firm's client account and lost it in gambling at the Playboy Club, owned and operated by the defendant. Cass himself had been convicted of theft, and was presumably not worth suing. It was held that the claimant solicitors could trace their original property, a chose in action that is a debt owed to them by the bank, into its product, cash drawn from their client account at the bank, and thence follow it into the hands of the defendant. The defendant, the recipient, albeit innocent, of the stolen money traced into his hands, was further held, under the law of restitution, obliged to pay an equivalent sum to the true owner where he had not given full consideration for it and had thus been unjustly enriched at the expense of the true owner.

One difficulty which may arise is as to the continued identification of the asset, particularly if at some stage of the chain of events it has been converted into money. Lord Goff, in *Lipkin Gorman (a firm) v Karpnale Ltd*[14] has recently restated the rule that 'at common law, property in money, like other fungibles, is lost as such when it is

---

[10] See *Agip (Africa) Ltd v Jackson*, supra, CA; *Bank Tejarat v Hong Kong & Shanghai Banking Corp (CI) Ltd* [1995] 1 Lloyd's Rep 239, discussed (1995) 9 Tru LI 91 (P Birks).

[11] See *Lipkin Gorman (a firm) v Karpnale Ltd*, supra, HL, and *Westdeutsche Landesbank Girozentrale v Islington London Borough Council* [1996] 2 All ER 961, HL, per Lord Goff at 967.

[12] *Agip (Africa) Ltd v Jackson*, supra, CA; (1991) 107 LQR 71 (P Millett) (1992) 55 MLR 377 (E McKendrick); [1992] Conv 124 (Margaret Halliwell); [1995] CLJ 377 (A J Oakley); [1995] LMCLQ 240 (L D Smith); (1995) 9 Tru LI 113 (Sarah Worthington). But see (1979) 95 LQR 78 (S Khurshid and P Matthews).

[13] Supra, HL, noted (1991) 107 LQR 521 (P Watts); [1991] CLJ 407 (W R Cornish); (1992) 55 MLR 377 (E McKendrick); [1992] Conv 124 (Margaret Halliwell). See also (2002) 31 CLWR 165 (S Baughen); *F C Jones & Sons v Jones*, supra, CA, noted [1997] 113 LQR 21 (N H Andrews and J Beatson); (1997) 8 KCLJ 123 (C Mitchell); (1997) 6 Nott LJ 90 (G McMeel); (1997) 11 Tru LI 12 (P Birks).

[14] Supra, HL, at 527. See (1992) 45(2) CLP 69 (P Birks); All ER Rev 1992, pp 263, 264 (W J Swadling).

mixed with other money', and it was mixing which caused the common law claims to fail in *Agip (Africa) Ltd v Jackson*[15] and *El Ajou v Dollar Land Holdings.*[16] Professor Goode, however, has argued forcefully[17] that the inability of the common law to allow money to be followed into a mixed fund is a myth. In any case it is clear that mixing can only refer to mixing by a prior recipient. Mixing by the defendant himself is irrelevant for the cause of action for money had and received is complete when the plaintiff's money is received by the defendant. But mixing by a prior recipient will defeat a claim because it will prevent proof that the money received by the defendant was the money paid by the plaintiff.[18]

With regard to physical mixtures, in *Indian Oil Corpn Ltd v Greenstone Shipping SA*[19] it was held that justice required that in a case of wrongful mixing of similar goods the mixture should be held in common and that each party should be entitled to receive out of the bulk a quantity equal to that of his goods which went into the mixture, any doubt as to that quantity being resolved in favour of the innocent party. This was carried one stage further in *Glencore International AG v Metro Trading Inc,*[20] another case concerning oil, where it was held that when one person wrongfully blends his own oil with oil of a different grade belonging to another person with the result that a new product is produced, that new product is owned by them in common, the proportions in which the contributors own the new blend reflecting both the quantity and the value of the oil which each has contributed. Any doubts about the quantity or value of the oil contributed by the innocent party are to be resolved against the wrongdoer. But if the 'mixing' destroys the claimant's contribution there is nothing he can trace.[21] The essence of tracing through a mixed fund is the ability to re-divide the mixed fund into its constituent parts pro rata according to the value of the contributions made to it. There was, however, an inevitable limitation at common law as the common law did not recognize equitable interests in property. A beneficiary under a trust could not at law follow the property in the hands of the trustee, though he could take steps in equity to compel the trustee to follow the trust property into the hands of a stranger to the trust.

It should be added that the right at law is not restricted to cases where there is fiduciary relationship.[22]

---

[15] Supra, CA. See *Solomon v Williams* [2001] BPIR 1123.   [16] Supra, CA.

[17] (1976) 92 LQR 360.

[18] *Agip (Africa) Ltd v Jackson* [1992] 4 All ER 385 at 399, per Millett J affd [1991] Ch 547, [1992] 4 All ER 451, CA.

[19] [1988] QB 345, [1988] 3 All ER 893, noted (1987) 46 CLJ 369 (P Stein).

[20] [2001] 1 All ER (Comm) 103. See (2003) 66 MLR 368 (R W J Hickey).

[21] See eg *Borden (UK) Ltd v Scottish Timber Products Ltd* [1981] Ch 25, [1979] 3 All ER 961, CA.

[22] *Sinclair v Brougham* [1914] AC 398 at 420, HL, per Haldane LC.

2 TRACING IN EQUITY

(a) GENERAL POSITION

In *Re Diplock's Estate*[23] Caleb Diplock, who died in 1936, by his will directed his executors to apply his residuary estate of over a quarter of a million pounds 'for such charitable institution or institutions or other charitable or benevolent object or objects in England as my acting executors or executor may in their or his absolute discretion select'. The executors had distributed over £200,000 among 139 charitable institutions before the validity of this disposition was successfully challenged by the next-of-kin.[24] Having exhausted their primary remedy against the personal representatives for their misapplication of the residuary estate,[25] the next-of-kin sought to recover the balance from the wrongly paid charities, claiming alternatively in personam and in rem. The claim in personam was allowed by the House of Lords, affirming the Court of Appeal. The claim in rem, that is, the right of the next-of-kin to trace their claims into the hands of the charities, did not come before the House of Lords but was considered at length by the Court of Appeal. It is, of course, the claim in rem with which we are now concerned.[26]

The general principle laid down in *Re Diplock's Estate* is that whenever there is an initial fiduciary relationship,[27] the beneficial owner of an equitable proprietary[28] interest in property can follow or trace it into the hands of anyone holding the property, except a bona-fide purchaser for value without notice whose title, is, as

---

[23] [1948] Ch 465, [1948] 2 All ER 318, CA, affd sub-nom *Ministry of Health v Simpson* [1951] AC 251, [1950] 2 All ER 1137, HL. See generally (1976) 92 LQR 528 (R M Goode); *Equity and Contemporary Legal Developments* (ed S Goldstein) 407 (P J Millett); *Re Goldcorp Exchange Ltd (in receivership)* [1994] 2 All ER 806, PC, noted [1994] CLJ 443 (L S Sealy); (1994) 110 LQR 509 (E McKendrick); [1995] CLJ 377 (A J Oakley); (1995) 9 Tru LI 43 (P Birks); (1995) 9 Tru LI 78 (P Oliver); (1996) 70 ALJ 54 (April Mountfort); (1996) 17 Co Law 3 and [1996] JBL 225 (G McCormack). See generally (1995) 6 Cant LR 123 and (1996) 8 Otago LR 467 (S R Scott); (1996) 34 Osg Hall LJ 321 (C Rotherham); [1997] LMCLQ 65 (Christa Bond); (1999) 115 LQR 438 (S Evans); (2003) 26 UNSWLJ 377 (Margaret Stone and A McKeogh).

[24] *Chichester Diocesan Fund v Simpson* [1944] AC 341, [1944] 2 All ER 60, HL, and see chapter 3, section 2(c), supra.

[25] Not surprisingly, the executors could not satisfy the claims of the next-of-kin and terms of compromise were approved by the court. It is believed that at least one of the executors committed suicide as a consequence of taking on the executorship.

[26] Supra, CA.

[27] *Re Diplock's Estate*, supra, CA; *Agip (Africa) Ltd v Jackson*, supra, CA; *Boscawen v Bajwa* [1995] 4 All ER 769, [1996] 1 WLR 328, CA; *Westdeutsche Landesbank Girozentrale v Islington London Borough Council* [1996] AC 669, [1996] 2 All ER 961, HL. But see (1976) 40 Conv 277 (R A Pearce). Heydon, Gummow & Austin, *Cases & Materials on Equity & Trusts* 4th edn, para 3702 ask, in the light of *Stamp Duties Comr (Queensland) v Livingston* [1965] AC 694, [1964] 3 All ER 692, PC, discussed, supra p 38, why the next-of-kin were allowed to trace in *Re Diplock's Estate* itself.

[28] See (1959) 75 LQR 234 (R H Maudsley) at 243 et seq; [1975] CLP 64 (A J Oakley). But note that in the administration of a deceased's estate a mere unsatisfied creditor has a similar equitable right to follow assets of the estate into the hands of devisees and legatees and those claiming through them for the purpose of obtaining payment—see *Salih v Atchi* [1961] AC 778, PC.

usual, inviolable.[29] The requirement of a fiduciary relationship has been much criticized,[30] and Peter Leaver QC[31] appears to have treated *Foskett v McKeown*[32] as deciding that there is no longer any necessity for there to be a pre-existing fiduciary relationship in order for tracing to be permitted. However the dictum of Lord Millett[33] which he cites does not form part of the ratio decidendi and it is thought that Rimer J in *Shalson v Russo*[34] was right to take the view that the requirement remains. It may well be, however, that the requirement would not survive an appeal to the House of Lords in some future case. Trustees, of course, occupy a fiduciary position, and there is probably a rebuttable presumption that bailees and agents do so. It may also be established by evidence in other situations.[35]

The wide meaning given to fiduciary relationship may have important repercussions in commercial transactions for if an appropriate reservation of title clause is incorporated into a contract of sale not only may the property sold remain the property of the vendor until he has been fully paid, but on a sub-sale the head vendor may be able to trace the proceeds of sale and recover them in priority to other creditors.[36] Stolen moneys have been said to be traceable in equity on the ground that when property is obtained by fraud equity imposes a constructive trust on the fraudulent recipient,[37] but this has been doubted by Rimer J in *Shalson v Russo*,[38] pointing out that a thief has no title to property he steals and it is accordingly difficult to see how he can become a trustee of it: the true owner retains the legal and beneficial title.

---

[29] *Sinclair v Brougham* [1914] AC 398, [1914–15] All ER Rep 622, HL; *Re Diplock's Estate* [1948] Ch 465 at 539, [1948] 2 All ER 318 at 356, CA; *McTaggart v Boffo* (1975) 64 DLR (3d) 441, where Lieff J cited and applied the statement in the text; *Millican v Robinson* [1993] 6 WWR 539. *Polly Peck International plc v Nadir (No 2)* [1992] 4 All ER 769 at 781, 782, per Scott LJ, CA. *Clarke v Cutland* [2003] EWCA Civ 810, [2003] 4 All ER 733.

[30] (1959) 75 LQR 234 (R H Maudsley); Goff and Jones, *The Law of Restitution*, 6th edn, paras 2-031–033.

[31] Sitting as a deputy judge of the High Court in *Bracken Partners Ltd v Gutteridge* [2003] EWHC 1064 (Ch), [2003] 2 BCLC 84, appeal dismissed [2003] EWCA Civ 1875, [2004] 1 BCLC 377.

[32] [2000] 3 All ER 97, HL.

[33] In *Foskett v McKeown*, supra, HL at 121. See *Governor and Company of the Bank of Scotland v A Ltd* [2001] EWCA Civ 52, [2001] 3 All ER 58 per Lord Woolf at [30].

[34] [2003] EWHC 1637 (Ch), [2003] WTLR 1165 at 1199.

[35] *Hendy Lennox (Industrial Engines) Ltd v Grahame Puttick Ltd* [1984] 2 All ER 152, [1984] 1 WLR 485. See [1975] CLP 39 (J D Stephens).

[36] See eg *Aluminium Industrie Vaasen BV v Romalpa Aluminium Ltd* [1976] 2 All ER 552, CA; *Armour v Thyssen Edelstahlwerke AG* [1991] 2 AC 339, [1990] 3 All ER 481, HL, noted (1991) 54 MLR 726 (R Bradgate). *Re Highway Foods International Ltd* [1995] 1 BCLC 209; *Chaigley Farms Ltd v Crawford, Kaye & Grayshire Ltd* [1996] BCC 957, noted [1997] CLJ 28 (L S Sealy); [1998] Conv 52 (J de Lacy). See, generally, [1996] Denning LJ 23 (M D J Conaglen); (1997) 9 SAcLJ Pt II 250 (V Yeo).

[37] *Westdeutsche Landesbank Girozentrale v Islington London Borough Council* [1996] AC 669, [1996] 2 All ER 961, HL, noted [1996] CLJ 432 (G Jones), per Lord Browne-Wilkinson at 716, 998; *Lipkin Gorman v Karpnale Ltd* [1991] 2 AC 548, [1992] 4 All ER 512, HL, per Lord Templeman at 565–566, 522. See also *El Ajou v Dollar Land Holdings plc* [1993] 3 All ER 717, noted (1994) 15 Co Law 148 (R Nolan), revsd [1994] 2 All ER 685, CA, on a company law point.

[38] [2003] EWHC 1637 (Ch), [2003] WTLR 1165, noted (2003) 49 T & ELJ 7. The principle in relation to property obtained by fraud was reaffirmed in *Commerzbank Aktiengesellschaft v IMB Morgan plc* [2004] EWHC 2771 (Ch), [2005] 1 Lloyd's Rep 298 (not involving stolen property).

Further a recipient of money under a contract subsequently found to be void for mistake or as being ultra vires does not hold the money on a resulting trust. In these cases the transferor intended that the whole legal and beneficial ownership should pass to the transferee.[39] It is a different matter where a transfer of property to an agent of the transferor was obtained by fraudulent misrepresentation and the transferor never intended that the whole legal and beneficial interest should pass to the transferee.[40]

(b) MIXING OF TRUST PROPERTY WITH THE TRUSTEE'S[41] OWN PROPERTY

In *Foskett v McKeown*[42] Lord Millett cited with approval Page Wood V-C in *Frith v Cartland*:[43] '. . . if a man mixes trust funds with his own, the whole will be treated as trust property, except so far as he may be able to distinguish what is his own', and went on to say that this does not exclude a pro rata division where this is appropriate, as in the case of money and other fungibles like grain, oil and wine.

Equity, by contrast with the position at common law, recognized and protected equitable interests, and the metaphysical approach of equity, coupled with and encouraged by the far reaching remedy of a declaration of charge, enabled equity to identify money in a mixed fund. 'Equity, so to speak, is able to draw up a balance sheet, on the right hand side of which appears the composite fund, and on its left hand side the two or more funds of which it is deemed to be made up.'[44]

In relation to physical mixtures the rule is the same in equity as at law. Pro rata division is the best that the wrongdoer and his donees can hope for. If this is not possible the beneficiary takes the whole; there is no question of confining him to a lien. *Jones v De Marchant*[45] illustrates the rules, namely that an innocent recipient who

[39] *Westdeutsche Landesbank Girozentrale v Islington London Borough Council*, supra, HL. In this case Lords Browne-Wilkinson and Lloyd thought that the 'bewildering authority' of *Sinclair v Brougham* [1914] AC 398, HL, should be overruled, and Lord Slynn agreed it should be departed from. Lord Woolf, however, was unwilling to go so far, and Lord Goff was not prepared to depart from it. Further, in the light of the *Westdeutsche* case the reasoning in *Chase Manhattan Bank NA v Israel-British Bank (London) Ltd* [1981] Ch 105, [1979] 3 All ER 1025, that a person who pays money to another under a mistake of fact retains an equitable property in it and that the conscience of that other is subjected to a fiduciary duty to respect his proprietary right, 'is at best doubtful' (*Hillsdown Holdings plc v Pensions Ombudsman* [1997] 1 All ER 862 per Knox J), though the actual result may be supported on the ground that the retention of the moneys after the recipient bank learned of the mistake may well have given rise to a constructive trust—see per Lord Browne-Wilkinson at 997. Notwithstanding criticism of this dictum in Goff and Jones, *Restitution*, 6th edn, paras 4.35 and 4.36, the judge in *Papamichael v National Westminster Bank plc* [2003] EWHC 164 (Comm), [2003] 1 Lloyd's Rep 341 agreed with it. It has not, however, been followed in Singapore: *Re Pinkroccade Educational Services Pte Ltd* [2002] 4 SLR 867. See [1997] JBL 48 (GCG McCormack); (1997) 10 Tru LI 84 (C Mitchell); (2000) 12 Bond LR 30 (DSK Ong).

[40] *Collings v Lee* [2001] 2 All ER 332, CA, noted (2001) 60 CLJ 477 (R Nolan).

[41] Trustee in this section is used, where the context admits, to include other fiduciary agents.

[42] [2001] 1 AC 102, [2000] 3 All ER 97, HL, at 133, 125; *Re Global Finance Group Pty Ltd (in liq), ex parte Read & Herbert* (2002) 26 WAR 385.

[43] (1865) 2 Hem & M 417, 420.

[44] *Re Diplock's Estate* [1948] Ch 465 at 520, [1948] 2 All ER 318 at 346, CA.

[45] (1916) 28 DLR 561.

receives misappropriated property by way of gift obtains no better title than his donor, and that if a proportionate sharing is inappropriate the wrongdoer and those who derive title under him take nothing. In that case the claimant's husband used 18 beaver skins belonging to his wife, together with four of his own, and had them made up into a coat which he gave to his mistress, the defendant, who knew nothing of the true ownership of the skins. The coat was clearly not divisible and the claimant on the above principles was held entitled to recover the coat. The determinative factor was that the mixing was the act of the wrongdoer through whom the mistress acquired the coat otherwise than for value.

Most cases in practice will be where a trustee in breach of trust has mixed money in his own bank account with trust moneys. In this case the moneys in the account belong to the trustee personally and to the beneficiaries under the trust rateably according to the amounts respectively provided. On a proper analysis there are 'no moneys in the account' in the sense of physical cash. Immediately before the improper mixture, the trustee had a chose in action being his right against the bank to demand payment of the credit balance in the account. Immediately after the mixture, the trustee had the same chose in action but its value reflected in part the amount of the beneficiaries' money wrongly paid in. The credit balance on the account belongs to the trustee and the beneficiaries rateably according to their respective contributions.[46]

Commonly the mixing takes place in an active banking account when, under the rule in *Re Hallett's Estate*,[47] the trustee is presumed to draw out his own moneys first, and is deemed not to draw on the trust moneys until his own moneys have been exhausted, no matter in what order the moneys were paid in. This is said to be based on a presumption against a breach of trust—or rather a further breach of trust, for any mixing of trust moneys and other moneys is of course improper. Thus if a trustee has £1,000 of his own money in his account, pays in first £2,000 of trust moneys and then a further £1,000 of his own money, and subsequently withdraws £2,000 for his own purposes, the beneficiaries are entitled to say that the £2,000 remaining in the account is trust property. The presumption is not, however, extended to enable a beneficiary to claim, once the trust funds have been drawn upon, that any subsequent payment in of private moneys is to be treated as being made in replacement of such withdrawals in breach of trust. Thus if in the illustration given above the £2,000 had been withdrawn before the £1,000 private moneys had been paid in, the beneficiary would only have been able to claim £1,000 of the balance in the account as trust property. Tracing is only possible to such an amount of the balance ultimately standing to the credit of the trustee as does not exceed the lowest intermediate balance standing to the credit of the account after the date of the mixing and before the date when the claim is made.[48] It is, of course, impossible to trace through an overdrawn

---

[46] See *Foskett v McKeown*, supra, HL, per Lord Browne-Wilkinson at 110, 103.

[47] (1880) 13 Ch D 696, CA.

[48] *James Roscoe (Bolton) Ltd v Winder* [1915] 1 Ch 62; *Dewar v Nustock Pastoral Co Pty Ltd* (1994) 10 State Rep (W A) 1.

bank account because in that case there is no fund into which the trust moneys can be traced. This is so whether the account was already overdrawn at the time the relevant money was paid in, or was then in credit but subsequently became overdrawn.[49]

The rule in *Re Hallett's Estate*[50] does not, however, operate so as to derogate from the basic principle that the beneficiary is entitled to a first charge on the mixed fund or any property which is purchased thereout. In *Re Oatway*[51] the trustee had mixed his own and trust moneys in a banking account. He drew on this account to purchase shares, leaving a balance exceeding the amount of the trust moneys paid in. He subsequently made further drawings which exhausted the account, so that it was useless to proceed against the account: these later drawings were dissipated and did not result in traceable assets. On these facts it was held that the beneficiary had a charge on the shares for the trust money paid into the account. The original charge on the mixed fund would, it was said, continue on each and every part thereof, notwithstanding changes of form, unless and until the trust money paid into the mixed account was restored and the trust money reinstated by the due investment of the money in the joint names of the proper trustees. Equity's power to charge a mixed fund with the repayment of trust moneys enables the claimant to follow the money, not because it is his, but because it is derived from a fund which is treated as if it were subject to a charge in his favour.[52]

Since equity treats money in a mixed account as charged with the repayment of the claimant's money, if it is paid out into a number of different accounts the claimant can claim a similar charge over each of the recipient accounts. He is not bound to choose between them.[53]

Re Oatway[54] did not raise the question whether a beneficiary is entitled to any profit made out of the purchase of property by a trustee out of a fund consisting of his personal moneys which he mixed with the trust moneys. In such a case of a mixed substitution, that is where a trustee buys property partly with his own money and partly with trust money, *Foskett v McKeown*[55] now lays down that where a trustee wrongfully uses trust money to provide part of the cost of acquiring an asset, the beneficiary is entitled at his option either to claim a proportionate share of the asset or to enforce a lien upon it to secure his personal claim against the trustee for the

---

[49] *Bishopsgate Investment Management Ltd v Homan* [1995] Ch 211, [1995] 1 All ER 347, CA, noted [1996] Conv 129 (Alison Jones); *Shalson v Russo* [2003] EWHC 1637 (Ch), [2003] WTLR 1165. If the payment in put the account into credit and it continued in credit, to that extent tracing would be possible subject to the lowest intermediate balance rule. The possibility of 'backward tracing' apparently accepted by Dillon LJ was approved by Millett LJ, writing extrajudicially, in KCLJ 6 (1995–96) 1, 12. However the contrary view expressed by Leggatt LJ is preferred by Oakley in [1995] CLJ 377. See also (1994) 8 Tru LI 102 (L Smith); [1995] LMCLQ 446 (Louise Gallifer).

[50] Supra.   [51] [1903] 2 Ch 356.   [52] *Boscawen v Bajwa* [1995] 4 All ER 769, CA, at 778.

[53] *El Ajou v Dollar Land Holdings plc* [1993] 3 All ER 717, 735, revsd [1994] 2 All ER 685, CA, on a company law point.

[54] Supra.

[55] [2001] 1 AC 102, [2000] 3 All ER 97, HL, overruling a dictum of Jessel MR to the contrary in *Re Hallett's Estate*, supra, CA. In (2001) 117 LQR 366, Berg argues that the beneficiaries should have been held entitled to the whole of the profit. See also (2001) 117 LQR 412 (A Burrows).

amount of the misapplied money. It does not matter whether the trustee mixed the trust money with his own in a single fund before using it to acquire the asset, or made separate payments (whether simultaneously or sequentially) out of differently owned funds to acquire a single asset.

In *Re Tilley's Will Trusts*[56] a sole trustee, who was also a life tenant of the trust, had mixed the trust moneys with her own moneys in her bank account, which became overdrawn on the purchase of an asset, though subsequent payments in of her own moneys left the account in credit to an amount exceeding the amount of the trust fund. The trustee carried out many property dealings, had ample overdraft facilities and had no need, nor, as the judge found, any intention of relying on the trust moneys for the purchase. Ungoed-Thomas J's view[57] was 'that if, having regard to all the circumstances of the case objectively considered, it appears that the trustee has in fact, whatever his intention, laid out trust moneys in or towards a purchase, then the beneficiaries are entitled to the property purchased and any profits which it produces to the extent to which it has been paid for out of the trust moneys'. Applying this test he nevertheless held that the trust moneys were not so laid out: they were not invested in properties at all but merely went in reduction of the trustee's overdraft which was in reality the source of the purchase moneys. The application of the test was perhaps unduly favourable to the trustee.

(c) MIXING OF TWO TRUST FUNDS, OR OF TRUST MONEYS WITH MONEYS OF AN INNOCENT VOLUNTEER

Where the contest is between two claimants to a mixed fund made up of moneys held on behalf of the two of them respectively and mixed together by the trustee, they share pari passu, and if property is acquired by means of the mixed fund, each is entitled to a charge pari passu and neither is entitled to priority over the other.[58] Further, as against the trustee, they can agree to take the property itself, so as to become tenants in common in shares proportional to the amounts for which either could claim a charge.[59] The same rules apply where moneys of a beneficiary and an innocent volunteer are mixed, whether the mixing is done by the innocent volunteer or the trustee,[60] though it has been argued[61] that this puts the innocent volunteer in too favourable a position. The suggestion is that it is unreasonable that, as is the law, an innocent volunteer who purchases, say, £2,000 stock, half with his own and half with trust moneys, and then withdraws half and spends it on living expenses is regarded as

---

[56] [1967] Ch 1179, [1967] 2 All ER 303.   [57] Supra, at 1193, 313.

[58] *Foskett v McKeown* [2001] 1 AC 102, [2000] 3 All ER 97, HL; *Re Diplock's Estate* [1948] Ch 465 at 533, 534, 539, [1948] 2 All ER 318 at 353, 354, 356, CA; *Sinclair v Brougham* [1914] AC 398, HL. See Maudsley (1959) 75 LQR 234, pp 246 et seq.

[59] *Sinclair v Brougham*, supra, at 643, 442, per Lord Parker; *Re Tilley's Will Trusts*, supra.

[60] *Re Diplock's Estate*, supra at 524, 536, 539, and at 349, 354, 357, CA; *Sinclair v Brougham*, supra.

[61] Maudsley, op cit. But see [1983] Conv 135 (K Hodkinson) pointing out that if an innocent volunteer dissipates an unmixed fund, there is no action in rem against him.

withdrawing it rateably from the trust funds and his own funds and is accordingly entitled to share the remaining half equally with the beneficiary. The position, as will be seen, might be even more extreme if the funds were in an active banking account to which the rule in Clayton's *Case*[62] applied, when the innocent volunteer might be entitled to the whole remaining funds.

The above rules as to mixing are modified where the mixing takes place in an active banking account. Where a trustee mixes the funds of two separate trusts,[63] or a volunteer mixes trust moneys with his own moneys,[64] the rule in *Clayton's Case*[65] applies. This rule of convenience, based on so-called presumed intention, is to the effect that withdrawals out of the account are presumed to be made in the same order as payments in, that is to say, first in, first out. It was reaffirmed, in *Barlow Clowes International Ltd (in liquidation) v Vaughan*[66] as the prima facie rule, though it was also said that, being a rule of convenience, it will not be applied if to do so would be impracticable or result in injustice. More recently, in *Russell-Cooke Trust Co v Prentis*[67] Lindsay J said that it was plain from *Barlow Clowes* that the rule could be 'displaced by even a slight counterweight. Indeed in terms of its actual application between beneficiaries who have in any sense met a shared misfortune, it might be more accurate to refer to the exception that is, rather than the rule in, *Clayton's* case.' In *Barlow Clowes* itself the rule in *Clayton's* case was not applied and the available assets were ordered to be distributed pari passu among all unpaid investors rateably in proportion to the amounts due to them, and a similar result was reached in *Commerzbank Aktiengesellschaft v IMB Morgan plc*.[68]

The North American solution has not found favour in England. It was held to be impractical on the facts in *Barlow Clowes*, and Lindsay J said[69] it was complicated and could be difficult to apply. This solution involves treating credits to a bank account made at different times and from different sources as a blend with the result that when

---

[62] *Devaynes v Noble, Clayton's Case* (1816) 1 Mer 529 at 572.

[63] *Re Hallett's Estate* (1880) 13 Ch D 696; *Re Stenning* [1895] 2 Ch 433.

[64] *Re Diplock's Estate*, supra, at 364, 554, CA.

[65] Supra. For application in another context see: *Re Yeovil Glove Co Ltd* [1965] Ch 148, [1964] 2 All ER 849, CA. Held inapplicable in *Re Eastern Capital Futures Ltd (in liquidation)* [1989] BCLC 371. See *Re Global Finance Group Pty Ltd (in liq) ex parte Read and Herbert* (2002) 26 WAR 385, discussed (2003) 52 T & ELJ 11, (2004) 53 T & ELJ 18 (J Hockley). For an unorthodox view, see (1963) 79 LQR 388 (D A McConville).

[66] [1992] 4 All ER 22, CA, noted (1993) 137 Sol Jo 770 (R S J Marshall); [1993] Conv 370 (Jill Martin). See *Re Registered Securities Ltd* [1991] 1 NZLR 545 where it was said that the presumed intent must give way to an express contrary intention or to circumstances which point to a contrary conclusion. See also [1995] CLJ 377 (A J Oakley).

[67] [2002] EWHC 2227 (Ch), [2003] 2 All ER 478, noted [2003] Conv 339 (M Pawlowski); [2005] CLJ 45 (M Conaglen). After a full consideration of the cases both in England and Australia, it was held in *Re French Caledonia Travel Service Pty Ltd (in liq)* (2004) 204 ALR 353 that *Clayton's Case* does not apply in Australia to allocate losses suffered by beneficiaries where funds are mixed, regardless of whether or not there is sufficient information to enable an allocation of withdrawals to deposits to be made in any particular case.

[68] [2004] EWHC 2771 (Ch), [2005] 1 Lloyd's Rep 298.

[69] In *Russell-Cooke Trust Co v Prentis*, supra.

a withdrawal is made from the account it is treated as a withdrawal in the same proportions as the different interests in the account bear to each other at the moment before the withdrawal is made.[70]

The rule, where it applies, will not be extended beyond banking accounts and only applies where there is one unbroken account. Moreover, the rule will not apply if the fund is 'unmixed', and a specific withdrawal is earmarked as trust money. Accordingly in *Re Diplock's Estate*[71] a charity which paid £1,500 trust moneys into its current account, and later drew out the same sum which it placed in a Post Office Savings Bank account and treated as 'Diplock' money was held bound by its own appropriation. The whole sum could accordingly be traced by the next of kin, the rule in *Clayton's Case*[72] not being applicable.

(d) IDENTIFICATION

Tracing is only possible so long as the fund can be followed in a true sense, that is so long as, whether mixed or unmixed, it can be located and identified. It presupposes the continued existence of the money either as a separate fund or as part of a mixed fund or as latent in property acquired by means of such a fund. If, on the facts of any individual case, such continued existence is not established, equity is as helpless as the common law itself.[73] Thus tracing is impossible where an innocent volunteer spends the trust money on a dinner,[74] or on education or general living expenses. Where trust money is used in the alteration and improvement of property which the defendant already owns, it was said in *Re Diplock's Estate*[75] that this would not necessarily increase its value, in which case the money would have disappeared leaving no monetary trace behind. However it has been said more recently[76] that where the value of the defendant's land has been enhanced by the use of the plaintiff's money the court may treat the land as charged with the payment to the plaintiff of a sum representing that increase in value: the most that a claimant can hope for is a proprietary lien to recover the money expended.[77]

---

[70] *Re Ontario Securities Commission and Greymac Credit Corpn* (1986) 30 DLR (4th) 1, appeal dismissed (1988) 52 DLR (4th) 767n; *Re Elliott* (2002) 333 AR 39. See [1997] Denning LJ 431 (Sarah Lowrie and P Todd).

[71] [1948] Ch 465 at 551, 552, [1948] 2 All ER 318 at 363, 364, CA (revsd on the facts at 559, 429–432); *Boscawen v Bajwa* [1995] 4 All ER 769, CA, at 778.

[72] (1816) 1 Mer 529.

[73] It has been pointed out, eg by Goulding in [1992] Conv 367, that this seems to have been overlooked or disregarded in *Agip (Africa) Ltd v Jackson* [1991] Ch 547, [1992] 4 All ER 451, CA, where there was said to be no difficulty about the mechanics of tracing in equity although at one stage Lloyds Bank had taken a delivery risk and paid out of its own money. *See McTaggart v Boffo* (1975) 64 DLR (3d) 441.

[74] *Re Diplock's Estate*, supra, at 521, 347, CA.

[75] Supra, at 547, 361, CA. Another difficulty in such case might be as to whether the charge should be on the whole of the land or only on that part which was altered or reconstructed.

[76] *Boscawen v Bajwa*, supra CA, per Millett LJ at 777.

[77] *Foskett v McKeown* [2001] 1 AC 102, [2000] 3 All ER 97, HL, per Lord Browne-Wilkinson at 133, 102. In *Re Esteem Settlement* [2002] JLR 53 the Royal Court of Jersey held that the claimant could trace his money spent on improvements into the increased value of the property. On the one hand there can be no tracing if

In *Foskett v McKeown*[78] M effected a life assurance policy on his own life which he later declared to be held on trust for his children. He paid the first two premiums out of his own funds but at least the fourth and fifth premiums were paid out of funds in a bank account under M's name to which the claimants were entitled under an express trust. The claimants' money had been moved in and out of various bank accounts where in breach of trust it had been inextricably mixed by M with his own money. M committed suicide and the death benefit of £1m was paid out to the trustees. Under the terms of the policy the same benefit would have been paid even if only the first two premiums had been paid. The claimants claimed to be entitled to a share proportionate to the premiums paid.

The essence of the competing arguments was whether the correct analogy was with an improvement of property, as discussed above, or with a mixed bank account, as discussed earlier.[79] It was held by the majority that the correct analogy was with a bank account. The claimants could trace the premiums paid out of their funds into the policy, that is, the bundle of rights to which the policyholder was entitled in return for the premiums and which collectively constituted a chose in action. That chose in action represented the traceable proceeds of the premium, and it followed that the claimants were entitled to a proportionate share of the policy in so far as they could show that the premiums were paid with their money. Such an interest arose immediately upon the payment of the premiums, and thus the claimants were entitled to the insurance money paid on M's death in the same shares and proportions as they were entitled in the policy immediately before his death.

Re Diplock's Estate[80] also appears to hold that the right to trace comes to an end if an innocent volunteer uses the trust money to pay off a debt, even though secured, and even though the money was given to him for this purpose. The effect of such payment was said to be that the debt is extinguished and any security ceases to exist, and the cestui que trust cannot claim to be subrogated to the rights of the creditor.[81] In *Boscawen v Bajwa*,[82] however, Millett LJ could see no reason why in the case of a secured debt subrogation should not be available, and explained *Re Diplock's Estate*[83] as a case where in the particular circumstances it was considered unjust to grant the remedy of subrogation. Those circumstances would today, he said, be regarded as relevant to a change of position defence rather than as going to liability.

It may be added that a volunteer who has received trust property cannot be made subject to a personal liability to account for it as a constructive trustee if he has parted

---

there is no increase in value attributable to the claimant's money. On the other hand, if tracing is possible, the claimant will be entitled not merely to a lien to recover the money expended but to a proportionate share of any subsequent increase in total value.

[78] Supra, HL.   [79] See p 558, supra.

[80] Supra, at 549, 362, CA. See [1995] CLJ 290 (L D Smith).

[81] *Re Diplock's Estate*, supra, at 521, 347, CA.

[82] Supra, CA. And see *Banque Financiere de la Cite v Parc (Battersea) Ltd* [1998] 1 All ER 737, HL, discussed [1998] JBL 323 (M Bridge); (1998) 114 LQR 341 (P Watts).

[83] Supra, CA.

with it without having previously acquired some knowledge of the existence of the trust.[84]

(e) CLAIM INEQUITABLE

The general principle that a remedy will not be granted in a case where it would lead to an inequitable result, was said, in *Re Diplock's Estate*,[85] to be an additional reason why trust moneys used by an innocent volunteer in alterations to his house could not be traced. The equitable remedy is a declaration of charge, enforceable by sale. This would be equitable where the land was purchased with moneys of the innocent volunteer mixed with trust moneys, but it would be different where the innocent volunteer has contributed not money but the land itself. It is not clear how this relates to the defence of change of position recognized in *Lipkin Gorman (a firm) v Karpnale Ltd*.[86]

(f) INTEREST

Where a tracing claim succeeds, it appears that the claimant is entitled to interest, that is, the interest in fact earned by the trust moneys or the property into which they have been traced.[87]

3 THE CLAIMS IN PERSONAM

It is convenient to mention here the alternative claim by the next of kin in *Re Diplock's Estate*[88] against the innocent recipients by means of a direct action in personam in equity. The House of Lords expressly affirmed the Court of Appeal judgment on this point, which had asserted the right of an unpaid or underpaid creditor, legatee or next of kin to bring a direct action in equity against the persons to whom the estate had been wrongfully distributed. Contrary to what had previously been commonly thought, it makes no difference whether the wrongful distribution was due to a mistake of law or fact; it does not matter that the wrongful recipient has no title at all and was a stranger to the estate, and there is no requirement that the estate must be administered by the court. The Court of Appeal observed:[89] 'as regards the conscience of the defendant on which in this, as in other jurisdictions, equity is said to act, it is prima facie, at least, a sufficient circumstance that the defendant, as events have proved, has received some share of the estate to which he was not entitled.' Nevertheless it

---

[84] *Re Montagu's Settlement Trusts* [1987] Ch 264, [1992] 4 All ER 308; *Agip (Africa) Ltd v Jackson* [1992] 4 All ER 385 at 403, per Millett J, affd [1991] Ch 457, [1992] 4 All ER 451, CA; *Westdeutsche Landesbank Girozentrale v Islington London Borough Council* [1996] AC 669, [1996] 2 All ER 961, HL.

[85] Supra, at 547–548, 361, CA.   [86] [1991] 2 AC 548, [1992] 4 All ER 512, HL.

[87] *Re Diplock's Estate* [1948] Ch 465, at 517, 557, [1948] 2 All ER 318 at 345, 346, CA.   [88] Supra.

[89] In *Re Diplock's Estate*, supra, at 503, 337, CA.

seems somewhat inequitable that an innocent volunteer can be called upon to refund—admittedly without interest—until the claim is barred by the Limitation Act, for he may well alter his position on the assumption that the payment was valid.[90] However in the light of *Lipkin Gorman v Karpnale Ltd*[91] it may be that a defence of change of position would now have a chance of success.

The claim, in any case, is subject to the qualification that the primary remedy is against the wrongdoing executor or administrator, and the direct claim in equity against those overpaid or wrongly paid is limited to the amount which the beneficiary cannot recover in the primary action.[92] And it seems that no claim will lie if when the payment was made to the defendant the assets were sufficient to pay all claims in full but a deficiency has subsequently arisen.[93]

It must be made clear that it is uncertain whether a direct action in equity lies in similar circumstances in the execution of a trust as opposed to the administration of the estate of a deceased person. In the House of Lords, Lord Simonds, whose speech was concurred in by all the other Law Lords, said:[94]

it is important in the discussion of this question to remember that the particular branch of the jurisdiction of the Court of Chancery with which we are concerned relates to the administration of assets of a deceased person. While in the development of this jurisdiction certain principles were established which were common to it and to the comparable jurisdiction in the execution of trusts, I do not find in history or in logic any justification for an argument which denies the possibility of an equitable right in the administration of assets because, as it is alleged, no comparable right existed in the execution of trusts.

However, though the claims failed on other grounds, Templeman J in *Butler v Broadhead*[95] was inclined to think that there was a sufficient analogy between the position of an executor and the liquidator of a company in a winding up to enable equity to intervene in favour of unpaid creditors against overpaid contributories; and Oliver J took a similar view in *Re J Leslie Engineers Co Ltd*[96] where a liquidator sought to recover the company's money wrongfully procured by its controlling director and paid to the respondent after the commencement of the winding up.

---

[90] (1957) 73 LQR 48 (G H Jones), cf (1961) 24 MLR 85 (R Goff).

[91] [1991] 2 AC 548, [1992] 4 All ER 512, HL. In this case it was held that change of position is a good defence to a claim for restitution based on unjust enrichment. But an illegal change of position cannot be relied on: *Barros Mattos Jnr v MacDaniels Ltd* [2004] EWHC 1188 (Ch), [2004] 3 All ER 299, criticized [2005] LMCLQ 6 (A Tettenborn).

[92] *Re J Leslie Engineers Co Ltd* [1976] 2 All ER 85, [1976] 1 WLR 292. The same qualification appears to apply to the claim in rem: *Re Diplock's Estate*, supra, at 556, 365. The qualification has been statutorily modified in some jurisdictions; eg the Western Australian Trustees Act, s 65(7), provides that the volunteer must be sued first. See also Queensland Trusts Act 1973, s 109; New Zealand Administration Act 1969, s 50.

[93] *Fenwick v Clarke* (1862) 4 De GF & J 240; *Peterson v Peterson* (1866) LR 3 Eq 111.

[94] *Ministry of Health v Simpson* [1951] AC 251 at 265–266, [1950] 2 All ER 1137 at 1140, HL. But see *G L Baker Ltd v Medway Building and Supplies Ltd* [1958] 3 All ER 540, CA; *Eddis v Chichester Constable* [1969] 1 All ER 546; affd without reference to this point [1969] 2 Ch 345, [1969] 2 All ER 912, CA. Professor Goode considers the restriction to be justified: (1976) 92 LQR 528, 541, but Professor Martin argues for coherence in equity's treatment of the rights of beneficiaries of trusts and beneficiaries of estates: [1998] Conv 13.

[95] [1975] Ch 97, [1974] 2 All ER 401.   [96] Supra.

It would now appear that a claim could be made by an application of the law of restitution based on the principle of unjust enrichment, under which, it is submitted, as between trustees and a person who is wrongly paid, the trustees have a right to recover the payment if it was paid under a mistake, whether of fact or law, subject to the defences available in the law of restitution such as the defence of change of position.[97] This defence requires some causal link between the innocent receipt of the mistaken payment and the defendant's change of position, which makes it inequitable for the recipient to be required to make restitution.[98] The change of position must have occurred after the receipt of the mistaken payment.[99] Since the emphasis is upon whether it would be unjust or inequitable to allow restitution, the defence may be defeated if it can be shown that the recipient acted in bad faith, even though he was not (subjectively) dishonest.[100]

[97] *Lipkin Gorman (a firm) v Karpnale Ltd* [1991] 2 AC 548, [1992] 4 All ER 512, HL; *Kleinwort Benson Ltd v Lincoln City Council* [1999] 2 AC 349, [1998] 4 All ER 513, HL; See [2002] RLR 69 (D Sheehan).

[98] *Scottish Equitable plc v Derby* [2001] EWCA Civ 369, [2001] 3 All ER 818; *Maersk Air Ltd v Expeditors International (UK) Ltd* [2003] 1 Lloyd's Rep 491. See also [2000] CLP 205 (P Birks); (2004) 15 KCLJ 301 (H Liu).

[99] *South Tyneside Metropolitan BC v Svenska International plc* [1994] 4 All ER 972, doubted Goff and Jones, *The Law of Restitution* (6th edn) at 4-004.

[100] *Niru Battery Manufacturing Co v Milestone Trading Ltd* [2003] EWCA Civ 1446, [2004] 1 All ER (Comm) 193, noted [2005] CLJ 35 (G Virgo) and *Commerzbank AG v Gareth Price-Jones* [2003] EWCA Civ 1663, unrep, both noted [2004] CLJ 276 (A Burrows); (2004) 120 LQR 373 (P Birks).

26

INJUNCTIONS I—NATURE, DAMAGES IN LIEU, ENFORCEMENT

1 MEANING AND NATURE OF AN INJUNCTION

(a) MEANING AND JURISDICTION

An injunction is an order[1] of the court directing a person or persons to refrain from doing some particular act or thing or, less often, to do some particular act or thing. It is an equitable remedy which originally could only be obtained in the Court of Chancery or the Court of Exchequer in equity.[2] A limited power to grant injunctions was first given to the common law courts by the Patent Law Amendment Act 1852 and then, by the Common Law Procedure Act 1854,[3] the common law courts were given so wide a jurisdiction to grant injunctions in all cases of breach of contract or other injury that, as Baggalay LJ observed,[4] they had a more extensive jurisdiction as regards the granting of injunctions than the Court of Chancery itself.

These statutes have been repealed and the Judicature Acts[5] have transferred to the High Court all the jurisdiction, including the jurisdiction to grant injunctions, previously exercised both by the Court of Chancery and the common law courts. The jurisdiction may, of course, be exercised by every division of the High Court, though in practice most applications for an injunction are made to the Chancery Division.[6]

---

[1] The Supreme Court Act 1981, s 31(2) provides that an injunction may be granted on an application for judicial review. In *Re M* [1994] 1 AC 377, sub nom *M v Home Office* [1993] 3 All ER 537, HL, noted [1994] CLJ 1 (T R S Allan) it was held that the language of the section being unqualified in its terms, there was no warrant for restricting its application so that in respect of ministers and other officers of the Crown alone the remedy of an injunction, including an interim injunction, was not available, but the jurisdiction should be exercised only in the most limited circumstances. So far as final relief was concerned, a declaration would continue to be an appropriate remedy. See (1996) 146 NLJ (J Algazy).

[2] The equity jurisdiction of the Court of Exchequer was abolished by the Court of Chancery Act 1841.

[3] Common Law Procedure Act 1854, ss 79 and 82.

[4] In *Quartz Hill Consolidated Gold Mining Co v Beall* (1882) 20 Ch D 501 at 509, CA.

[5] Judicature Act 1873, s 16, now the Supreme Court Act 1981, s 19(2).

[6] Under s 38 of the County Courts Act 1984 (as substituted by s 3 of the Courts and Legal Services Act 1990), in proceedings in which a county court had jurisdiction, the county court has the same remedies available to it as the High Court, save that it cannot grant a search order or a freezing injunction, except in family cases. The jurisdiction extends to a district judge sitting as a small claims arbitrator: *Joyce v Liverpool*

Section 37(1) of the Supreme Court Act 1981 replacing earlier provisions, now provides that 'the High Court may by order grant . . . an injunction (whether interlocutory or final) in all cases in which it appears to the court to be just and convenient to do so. Any such order may be made either unconditionally or on such terms and conditions as the court thinks just.'

The effect of this provision, which applies equally to the grant of an injunction and the appointment of a receiver, has given rise to more difficulty than one might expect.

(i) Jurisdiction—the narrow issue

An attractive view is 'that, where there is a legal right which was, independently of the [Judicature Act], capable of being enforced either at law or in equity, then whatever may have been the previous practice, the High Court may interfere by injunction in protection of that right'.[7] In other words where, before the Judicature Acts, some court would have had power to grant some remedy, there is now jurisdiction:

to superadd to what would have been previously the remedy, a remedy by way of injunction, altering therefore not in any way the rights of the parties so as to give a right to those who had no legal right before, but enabling the court to modify the principle on which it had previously proceeded in granting injunctions, so that where there is a legal right the court may, without being hampered by its old rules, grant an injunction where it is just or convenient to do so for the purpose of protecting or asserting the legal rights of the parties.[8]

In contrast a series of cases[9] appears to decide that the Act gave no power to the court to grant an injunction in a case in which no court could have granted one before the Act. Donaldson MR, however, has commented[10] that 'it is in the highest degree inconvenient if judges exercising jurisdiction in 1979 have to try and find out what was the extent of the jurisdiction of their predecessors over a century ago', and has indicated[11] that he does not accept that 'the pre-Judicature practices of the Court of

City Council [1996] QB 252, [1995] 3 All ER 110, CA. As to sequestration of a company's assets see *Rose v Laskington* [1990] 1 QB 562, [1989] 3 All ER 306, DC.

7 Per Cotton LJ in *North London Rly Co v Great Northern Rly Co* (1883) 11 QBD 30 at 40, CA; *Den of Airlie Steamship Co Ltd v Mitsui & Co Ltd* (1912) 106 LT 451, CA; *Duchess of Argyll v Duke of Argyll* [1967] Ch 302 at 344, [1965] 1 All ER 611 at 634. Cf *Montgomery v Montgomery* [1965] P 46, [1964] 2 All ER 22.

8 Per Cotton LJ ubi supra, at 39. Dicta to some extent supporting this view may be found in *Anglo-Italian Bank v Davies* (1878) 9 Ch D 275, CA (Jessel MR and Cotton LJ); *Smith v Cowell* (1880) 6 QBD 75, CA (Lord Esher); *Thomas v Williams* (1880) 14 Ch D 864 (Fry J); *Quartz Hill Consolidated Gold Mining Co v Beall* (1882) 20 Ch D 501, CA (Jessel MR); *Manchester and Liverpool District Banking Co v Parkinson* (1888) 22 QBD 173, CA: *Monson v Tussauds Ltd* [1894] 1 QB 671, CA (Lopes LJ). See *Aslatt v Southampton Corpn* (1880) 16 Ch D 143; *Hedley v Bates* (1880) 13 Ch D 498; *Richardson v Methley School Board* [1893] 3 Ch 510.

9 *North London Rly Co v Great Northern Rly Co* (1883) 11 QBD 30, CA; *Holmes v Millage* [1893] 1 QB 551, CA; *Kitts v Moore* [1895] 1 QB 253, CA; *Morgan v Hart* [1914] 2 KB 183, CA. See also *Gouriet v Union of Post Office Workers* [1978] AC 435 at 576, [1977] 3 All ER 70 at 112, HL, per Lord Edmund-Davies, saying that the section 'dealt only with procedure and had nothing to do with jurisdiction'; *Mercedes-Benz AG v Leiduck* [1995] 3 All ER 929, PC, per Lord Mustill at 939, 940.

10 In *Bremer Vulkan Schiffbau und Maschinenfabrik v South India Shipping Corpn* [1979] 3 All ER 194 at 202; affd on other grounds [1980] 1 All ER 420, CA; but revsd [1981] 1 All ER 289, HL.

11 In *Parker v Camden London Borough Council* [1986] Ch 162, [1985] 2 All ER 141, CA.

Chancery . . . should rule us from their graves'. Colman J faced the problem head on in *Soinco SACI v Novokuznetsk Aluminium Plant*,[12] a case concerning the appointment of a receiver by way of equitable execution.[13] He accepted that application of the rule laid down in cases such as *Morgan v Hart*[14] would require him to reject the application, but refused to accept that he must treat 'the rules of the Court of Chancery before the Judicature Acts as carved in stone and as expressing immutable principles incapable of development beyond 1873 unless changed by Parliament'. He appointed a receiver.

(ii) Jurisdiction—the wider issue

In *South Carolina Insurance Co v Assurantie Maatschappij de Zeven Provincien NV*[15] Lord Brandon said that although the terms of s 37(1) of the 1981 Act and its predecessors are very wide, the power conferred by them has been circumscribed by judicial authority dating back many years.[16] In his view[17] the authorities establish that the power of the court to grant injunctions is, subject to two exceptions, limited to two situations. Situation (1) is when one party to an action can show that the other party either has invaded, or threatens to invade, a legal or equitable right of the former for the enforcement of which the latter is amenable to the jurisdiction of the court. Situation (2) is where one party to an action has behaved, or threatens to behave, in a matter which is unconscionable. Cases illustrating this proposition include *Day v Brownrigg*[18] where the plaintiff lived in a house that for some sixty years had been called 'Ashford Lodge'. The defendant's adjoining house had been known for some forty years as 'Ashford Villa'. The plaintiff was held to have no claim to an injunction when the defendant altered the name of his house to 'Ashford Lodge', notwithstanding the resulting inconvenience. The plaintiff had suffered no legal injury because

---

[12] [1998] QB 406, [1997] 3 All ER 523.   [13] See p 700, infra.   [14] Supra, CA.

[15] [1987] AC 24, [1986] 3 All ER 487, HL, noted (1987) 104 LQR 157; (1988) 47 CLJ 177 (C F Forsyth). See *Australian Broadcasting Corporation v Lenah Game Meats Pty Ltd* (2001–02) 208 CLR (Aust) 199, where it was held that when an interim injunction is sought it is necessary to identify the legal (which may be statutory) or equitable rights which are to be determined at the trial and in respect of which final relief is sought (which need not be injunctive in nature). The equivalent of the Supreme Court Act 1981, s 37(1) does not expand the jurisdiction of the court to permit the grant of an interim injunction where no legal or equitable rights are to be determined. As to New Zealand see [2004] NZLJ 173 (C Chapman).

[16] The view of Lord Denning in *Chief Constable of Kent v V* [1983] QB 34, [1982] 3 All ER 36, CA, that s 37(1) of the Supreme Court Act 1981 has conferred on the High Court a new and wider jurisdiction was decisively rejected by Lord Bridge, with whom all the other Law Lords agreed, in *Pickering v Liverpool Daily Post and Echo Newspapers plc* [1991] 2 AC 370, [1991] 1 All ER 622, HL. For the position where a declaration is sought see *Kingdom of Spain v Christie Manson and Woods Ltd* [1986] 3 All ER 28.

[17] Lord Bridge and Lord Brightman agreed with Lord Brandon, but Lord Goff, with whom Lord Mackay agreed, was reluctant to accept the proposition that the power of the court to grant injunctions is restricted to certain exclusive categories. Lord Goff's view was supported by Lords Browne-Wilkinson and Keith in *Channel Tunnel Group Ltd v Balfour Beatty Construction Ltd* [1993] AC 334, [1993] 1 All ER 664, HL. See also *Department of Social Security v Butler* [1995] 4 All ER 193, [1995] 1 WLR 1528, CA.

[18] (1878) 10 Ch D 294, CA; *Sports and General Press Agency Ltd v Our Dogs Publishing Co Ltd* [1917] 2 KB 125, CA; *The Siskina* [1979] AC 210, [1977] 3 All ER 803, HL; *Richards v Richards* [1984] AC 174, [1983] 2 All ER 807, HL.

there is no right of property in the name of a house, or, it may be added, of a political party.[19] Again a husband has no legal right enforceable at law or in equity to stop his wife having, or a registered medical practitioner performing, a legal abortion and accordingly he cannot obtain an injunction for this purpose.[20] And in *Medina Housing Association Ltd v Case*[21] the claimant had obtained a possession order on the grounds of the tenant's anti-social behaviour in breach of the terms of the tenancy agreement from the county court judge. At the same time he granted an injunction in effect prohibiting the defendant from continuing her anti-social behaviour for some five years after the tenancy came to an end. The Court of Appeal held that the judge had no jurisdiction to grant an injunction extending beyond the time when the possession order would become effective, thereby bringing to an end the claimant's contractual rights.

The two exceptions referred to by Lord Brandon are, first, in relation to an injunction granted to one party to an action to restrain the other party from beginning, or continuing, proceedings against the former in a foreign court.[22] This may be granted where the foreign court is not the forum conveniens for the trial of the dispute, though the party who has brought proceedings in the foreign court may not, by doing so, have invaded any legal or equitable right of the other party, nor acted in an unconscionable manner. The second exception relates to the freezing or Mareva injunction[23] which is now, however, expressly recognized by s 37(3) of the 1981 Act. More recently judicial approval[24] has been given to a passage in Spry, *Equitable Remedies*:[25]

The powers of courts with equitable jurisdiction to grant injunctions are, subject to any relevant statutory restrictions, unlimited. Injunctions are granted only when to do so accords with equitable principles, but this restriction involves, not a defect of powers, but an adoption of doctrines and practices that change in their application from time to time . . . The preferable analysis involves a recognition of the great width of equitable powers, an historical appraisal of the categories of injunctions that have been established and an acceptance that pursuant to general equitable principles injunctions may issue in new categories when this course appears appropriate.

Three further points should be added. First in *Re Oriental Credit Ltd*[26] Harman J shared Lord Goff's reluctance[27] to accept fetters on the statutory power under s 37, and granted an injunction in the aid of, and ancillary to, an order made by the registrar under s 561 of the Companies Act 1985,[28] on the ground that the defendant

---

[19] *Kean v McGivan* [1982] FSR 119, CA (Social Democratic Party).

[20] *Paton v Trustees of British Pregnancy Advisory Service* [1979] QB 276, [1978] 2 All ER 987, noted (1979) 42 MLR 325 (I M Kennedy). The position is different in Canada: *Tremblay v Daigle* (1989) 59 DLR (4th) 609. See also *Patel v Patel* [1988] 2 FLR 179, CA; *Burris v Azadani* [1995] 4 All ER 802, [1995] 1 WLR 1372, CA.

[21] [2002] EWCA Civ 2001, [2003] 1 All ER 1084.   [22] See cases cited at p 627, infra, n 74.

[23] See p 640 et seq, infra.

[24] *Broadmoor Hospital Authority v R* [2000] 2 All ER 727, CA, per Lord Woolf at 732; *Venables v News Group Newspapers Ltd* [2001] 1 All ER 908, per Butler-Sloss P at 918.

[25] 5th edn, p 323. See [2002] CJQ 29 (Linda Clarke).   [26] [1988] Ch 204, [1988] 1 All ER 892.

[27] See p 569, n 17, supra. See also *Re I (a minor)* [1987] NLJ Rep 613.

[28] This provides for a summons for a private examination and gives the court a power of arrest.

had a public duty to obey that order though the section created no cause of action and no legal or equitable right in the liquidation. Secondly, in some family proceedings it seems that the infringement of a legal or equitable right may not be a pre-condition to an injunction. Non-molestation orders are commonly made between both spouses[29] and former spouses,[30] apparently without the infringement of a legal or equitable right being considered essential, and likewise a wide ranging variety of orders have been made in wardship proceedings.[31] Thirdly, an interim injunction does not have to be ancillary to a claim for substantive relief to be granted in *this* country by an order of the *English* court. Thus the court had power to grant an interim injunction in support of a cause of action which the parties had agreed should be the subject of a foreign arbitration and notwithstanding that proceedings in England had been stayed, since the cause of action remained potentially justiciable before the English court.[32]

The words 'just and convenient'[33] do not confer an arbitrary or unregulated discretion on the court;[34] 'what is right or just must be decided, not by the caprice of the judge, but according to sufficient legal reasons or on settled legal principle'.[35] When it is said that equitable remedies are discretionary, what is meant is that the court is entitled to take into account certain collateral matters, such as the conduct of the parties, in addition to considering their bare legal rights, in deciding whether to grant an equitable remedy. It may be added that it follows that an appeal court will be slow to interfere with an order made by the trial judge in his discretion, unless it appears that he has acted on wrong principles.

Further it should be noted that where statute provides that a statutory duty is enforceable by injunction the court has little, if any, discretion to exercise.[36]

(b) REMEDY IN PERSONAM

In granting an injunction 'the court acts in personam, and will not suffer anyone within its reach to do what is contrary to its notions of equity, merely because the act to be done may be, in point of locality, beyond its jurisdiction'.[37] A person who is residing abroad, and physically outside the jurisdiction, is nevertheless within the reach of the court if service out of the jurisdiction can properly be made upon him

---

[29] Eg *Horner v Horner* [1982] Fam 90, [1982] 2 All ER 495, CA, where the meaning of molestation is discussed.

[30] Eg *Vaughan v Vaughan* [1973] 3 All ER 449, [1973] 1 WLR 1159, CA.

[31] See eg *Re C (a minor) (No 2)* [1990] Fam 39, [1989] 2 All ER 791, CA.

[32] *Channel Tunnel Group Ltd v Balfour Beatty Construction Ltd* [1993] AC 334, [1993] 1 All ER 664, HL, noted [1993] LMCLQ 465 (J Hill).

[33] See p 568, supra.   [34] Per Davey LJ in *Harris v Beauchamp Bros* [1894] 1 QB 801 at 809, CA.

[35] Per Jessel MR in *Beddow v Beddow*, supra, at 93. See (1959) 17 MULR 133 (Patricia Loughlon).

[36] *Taylor v Newham London Borough Council* [1993] 2 All ER 649, [1993] 1 WLR 444, CA. In this case Bingham MR found it almost impossible to imagine circumstances in which a discretion would arise or be properly exercisable.

[37] Per Cranworth LC in *Carron Iron Co v Maclaran* (1855) 5 HL Cas 416 at 436, 437; *Hope v Carnegie* (1868) LR 7 Eq 254. See, however, *'Morocco Bound' Syndicate Ltd v Harris* [1895] 1 Ch 534. Cf *Chellaram v Chellaram* [1985] Ch 409, [1985] 1 All ER 1043.

under rules of court,[38] and the same is true of a company incorporated abroad.[39] The court, however, will consider carefully before it grants an injunction in these cases, and, as a general rule, will not adjudicate on questions relating to the title or the right to the possession of immovable property out of the jurisdiction,[40] nor will it give effect to a contractual or equitable right in personam which the lex situs would treat as incapable of creation.[41]

Until recently it has been generally thought that the court has no jurisdiction to grant an injunction against the world at large, relying on the dictum of Lord Eldon in *Iveson v Harris*[42] that '. . . you cannot have an injunction except against a party to the suit'. It was said in *Venables v News Group Newspapers Ltd*,[43] however, that we are now entering into a new era following the implementation of the Human Rights Act 1998, and the requirements that the courts act in a way that is compatible with the convention,[44] and have regard to European jurisprudence: this adds a new dimension enabling the court to grant an injunction openly contra mundum, or against the world.

An injunction may be granted against a defendant by description, provided that the description is sufficiently certain so as to identify both those who are included and those who are not. Thus in *Bloomsbury Publishing Group Ltd v News Group Newspapers Ltd*[45] injunctive relief was granted against a defendant referred to as '. . . the person or persons who have offered the publishers of the Sun, the Daily Mail and the Daily Mirror newspapers a copy of the book *Harry Potter and the Order of the Phoenix* by JK Rowling . . .', referred to at an earlier hearing[46] as effectively a 'John Doe' order. In a subsequent unreported case[47] the claimant had been the victim of a hoaxer who had written forged letters in her name, published in the national press, expressing views which she did not hold and which led to her receiving vicious hate mail. Evans J granted an injunction restraining 'John Doe' from continuing to send such letters. Although the hoaxer might not learn of the existence of the injunction, if served on the media it would effectively prevent publication.[48] Finally in *South Cambridgeshire DC v Persons Unknown*[49] an interim injunction was granted, under the statutory power

---

[38] Now CPR 6.17–6.31. See *Re Liddell's Settlement Trusts* [1936] Ch 365, [1936] 1 All ER 239, CA, applied *Re D (a minor)* [1992] 1 All ER 892 [1992] 1 WLR 315, CA.

[39] *Hospital for Sick Children v Walt Disney Productions Inc* [1968] Ch 52, [1967] 1 All ER 1005, CA.

[40] *Deschamps v Miller* [1908] 1 Ch 856.   [41] *Bank of Africa Ltd v Cohen* [1909] 2 Ch 129, CA.

[42] (1802) 7 Ves 251, 257.

[43] [2001] 1 All ER 908; *X (a woman formerly known as Mary Bell) v O'Brien* [2003] EWHC 1101 (QB), [2003] FCR 686, both discussed at p 633, infra. See *Re Z (a minor)* [1997] Fam 1, [1995] 4 All ER 961 where the Court of Appeal affirmed the grant of an injunction in rem.

[44] Ie the Convention for the Protection of Human Rights and Fundamental Freedoms 1950.

[45] [2003] EWHC 1205 (Civ), [2003] 3 All ER 736, [2003] 1 WLR 1633. Any other person who knowing of the order assisted in its breach would be liable for contempt of court: see p 591, infra.

[46] [2003] EWHC 1087 (Ch) unrep.

[47] Referred to by S Smith and A Sithamparanathan in a feature in the *Times* on 23 December 2003.

[48] See n 45, supra, and p 591, infra.

[49] As inserted by the Planning and Compensation Act 1991: [2004] EWCA Civ 1280, (2004) *Times*, 11 November, discussed [2005] JPEL 595 (R Langham). The court also ordered that service of the claim form and the injunction be effected by placing copies in clear plastic envelopes and nailing them to gateposts, etc on the site.

contained in the Town and Country Planning Act 1990 s 187B, against persons unknown restraining them from perpetrating identified breaches of planning control.

(c) WHERE A PARTICULAR REMEDY IS PROVIDED BY STATUTE

If a right of property which is created or confirmed by statute is infringed, it is settled that the fact that a particular remedy is provided for an infringement of that right by statute does not oust the jurisdiction of the court to grant an injunction. Even though the statutory remedy may be the only remedy available for the past infringement, the court may grant an injunction to prevent further infringements in the future,[50] unless the statute expressly or by implication provides to the contrary.[51] If no right of property is created the question whether legislation which makes the doing or omitting to do a particular act a criminal offence renders the person guilty of such offence liable also in a civil action for damages or an injunction at the suit of any person who thereby suffers loss or damage is a question of construction of the legislation.[52] The presumption is that there is no civil action at the suit of a private individual. The exceptions are discussed later.[53]

(d) INJUNCTIONS AGAINST PERSONS UNDER DISABILITY

The fact of disability is not in itself a bar to the granting of an injunction against the person under disability or to the enforcement of an order which has been made. In the case of mental incapacity the question is whether the person under that disability understands the proceedings and the nature and requirements of the order sought. In the case of a person incapable of understanding what he is doing or that it is wrong, an injunction should not be granted against him since he would not be capable of complying with it. An injunction could not have the desired deterrent effect, nor could any breach be the subject of effective enforcement proceedings since he would have a clear defence to an application for committal to prison for contempt.[54]

In the case of a person under the age of 17, he may well understand the order and its consequences. However the court has no power to commit him to prison for breach of an injunction. The court should investigate other alternatives, in particular the possibility of a fine. If this would be an appropriate means of enforcement, the penal notice attached to the injunction should substitute the threat of a fine for the threat of imprisonment. But in the vast majority of cases where the minor is still of school age, or unemployed, it would be inappropriate to grant an injunction.[55]

---

[50] *Stevens v Chown* [1901] 1 Ch 894; *Devonport Corpn v Tozer* [1903] 1 Ch 759, CA; *Carlton Illustrators v Coleman & Co* [1911] 1 KB 771.

[51] *Evans v Manchester, Sheffield and Lincolnshire Rly Co* (1887) 36 Ch D 626; *Stevens v Chown*, supra.

[52] *Cutler v Wandsworth Stadium Ltd* [1949] AC 398, [1949] 1 All ER 544, HL.

[53] See chapter 28, section 7, infra.

[54] *Wookey v Wookey, Re S (a minor)* [1991] Fam 121, [1991] 3 All ER 365, CA.   [55] Ibid.

2 CLASSIFICATION OF INJUNCTIONS

(a) PROHIBITORY AND MANDATORY

The prohibitory or restrictive injunction, by which a person is directed to refrain from doing some particular act or thing, is the original basic form, the mandatory injunction, by which a person is directed to perform some positive act, being a later development. This is demonstrated by the fact that until the turn of the previous century an order, even though mandatory in substance, had to be drafted in a prohibitory form. Thus the court would not, for instance, make an order directing a building to be pulled down, but would order the defendant not to allow it to remain on the land. Since the decision in *Jackson v Normandy Brick Co*[56] however, it has been the rule that if an injunction is mandatory in substance, it should be made in direct mandatory form.

At one time it was thought that particular caution had to be exercised by the court in granting a mandatory injunction[57] but it is now settled that there is no distinction in principle between granting a prohibitory and a mandatory injunction: every injunction requires to be granted with care and caution, but it is not more needed in one case than the other.[58] The court will not hesitate to grant a mandatory injunction in an appropriate case,[59] but whenever it does so, it must be careful to see that the defendant knows exactly what he has to do, and this means not as a matter of law but as a matter of fact.[60]

There is obviously an analogy between a mandatory injunction and a decree of specific performance. As we shall see there are certain contracts of which specific performance cannot be obtained,[61] and one cannot get round this by making a claim for a mandatory injunction. Thus, for example, the court will not grant an injunction ordering the defendant to do something which is impossible,[62] or which cannot be enforced, or which is unlawful.[63] Again the court will not normally make an order

---

[56] [1899] 1 Ch 438, CA. Occasionally orders were made in the positive form even before this date—*Bidwell v Holden* (1890) 63 LT 104. See [1981] Conv 55 (C D Bell); [1983] Conv 29 (R Griffith).

[57] *Great North of England, Clarence and Hartlepool Junction Rly Co v Clarence Rly Co* (1845) 1 Coll 507; *Isenberg v East India House Estate Co Ltd* (1863) 3 De GJ & Sm 263.

[58] *Smith v Smith* (1875) LR 20 Eq 500; *Lawrence v Hornton* (1890) 59 LJ Ch 440.

[59] *Hermann Loog v Bean* (1884) 26 Ch D 306, CA; *Kelsen v Imperial Tobacco Co (of Great Britain and Ireland) Ltd* [1957] 2 QB 335; *Evans v BBC and IBA* (1974) *Times*, 27 Feb (mandatory injunction to ensure political programme during election campaign transmitted as originally arranged). See *Charrington v Simons & Co Ltd* [1971] 2 All ER 588, CA; *John Trenberth Ltd v National Westminster Bank Ltd* (1979) 39 P & CR 104, and see p 620, infra.

[60] *Redland Bricks Ltd v Morris* [1970] AC 652, [1969] 2 All ER 576, HL; *Stephen & Co Ltd v Post Office* [1978] 1 All ER 939, [1977] 1 WLR 1172, CA.

[61] See chapter 29, section 2, infra. See also *Sanderson Motors (Sales) Pty Ltd v Yorkstar Motors Pty Ltd* [1983] 1 NSWLR 513.

[62] *A-G v Colney Hatch Lunatic Asylum* (1868) 4 Ch App 146.

[63] *Pride of Derby and Derbyshire Angling Association Ltd v British Celanese Ltd* [1953] Ch 149 at 198, [1953] 1 All ER 179 at 181, CA, per Evershed MR.

requiring a defendant to perform personal services,[64] nor one to enforce an obligation entered into by a person that he will not apply to Parliament, or that he will not oppose an application to Parliament by another person,[65] or to compel the sale and delivery of chattels not specific or ascertained.[66]

(b) PERPETUAL AND INTERIM

A perpetual injunction is one which has been granted after the right thereto has been established in an action in which both sides have been fully heard: it is intended to settle finally the relations between the parties in connection with the matter in dispute, so as to relieve the plaintiff from the need to bring a series of actions as his rights are from time to time infringed by the defendant. The word 'perpetual' does not necessarily signify that the order is to remain permanently effective: for instance, where a man has entered into a valid contract not to enter into competition with his former employer in a defined area for, say, three years after leaving the employment any injunction granted will be limited to that specific period.

An interim injunction, previously[67] called an interlocutory injunction, on the other hand, is only a temporary measure framed normally so as to continue in force until the trial of the action, or until further order.[68] In an appropriate case, however, one may be granted even though from a practical point of view it disposes of the matter. This has been done, for instance, where it has been applied for in order to remove a trespasser, who had plainly no defence to the action and merely sought to delay his eviction as long as possible;[69] and again, to prevent a member of a private association from being deprived of his right to vote at the annual general meeting.[70] Generally, where an injunction though in form interim will be irreversible in effect, the court will not grant it unless it feels a high degree of assurance that the claimant would be successful at the trial in obtaining the remedy which he seeks at the interlocutory stage.[71]

Exceptionally an interim injunction may be granted after judgment. In a case

[64] *Lumley v Wagner* (1852) 1 De GM & G 604. Cf *Hill v CA Parsons & Co Ltd* [1972] Ch 305, [1971] 3 All ER 1345, CA; and see pp 673–676, infra.

[65] *Bilston Corpn v Wolverhampton Corpn* [1942] Ch 391, [1942] 2 All ER 447.

[66] *Sky Petroleum Ltd v VIP Petroleum Ltd* [1974] 1 All ER 954, [1974] 1 WLR 576—an exceptional case where order made: decision said to be 'almost certainly wrong' by Professor Goode (1976) 92 LQR at 383, n 98, and 540. See p 668, infra.

[67] Ie before the Civil Procedure Rules 1998.

[68] If an application for an interim injunction is dismissed, the judge has jurisdiction to grant the unsuccessful applicant a limited interim injunction in the same terms pending appeal against the dismissal— *Erinford Properties Ltd v Cheshire County Council* [1974] Ch 261, [1974] 2 All ER 448. See *Ketchum International plc v Group Public Relations Holdings Ltd* [1996] 4 All ER 374, CA.

[69] *Manchester Corpn v Connolly* [1970] Ch 420, [1970] 1 All ER 961, CA.

[70] *Woodford v Smith* [1970] 1 All ER 1091n. Contrast with this case and that cited in the previous footnote *Cayne v Global Natural Resources plc* [1984] 1 All ER 225, CA.

[71] *Ford Sellar Morris Developments Ltd v Grant Seward Ltd* [1989] 2 EGLR 40.

involving a freezing injunction,[72] Bingham J observed[73] that 'an injunction is to be regarded as interlocutory, whether given before judgment or after, if it is not finally determinative of the rights of the parties but is merely in aid of the court's procedure and safeguarding the rights of the parties in the proceedings.'

Generally an interim injunction will only be granted on notice so as to give the defendant a full opportunity to resist the claim. In a case of urgency, however, it may be granted without notice to the other party.[74] Though the claimant is under a duty to make the fullest possible disclosure of all material facts within his knowledge,[75] it is an anomaly that the court should have power to act against a defendant without having heard his side of the story. Though it is essential that the court should have such a power it must be used only in circumstances in which it is really necessary to act immediately.[76]

The temporary character of an interim injunction means that it is generally of a prohibitory nature, though in exceptional circumstances it may be mandatory.[77] This is not because different principles apply to the grant of mandatory and prohibitory interim injunctions—in every case the fundamental principle is that the court should take whichever course appears to carry the lower risk of injustice if it should turn out that the successful party at this stage should ultimately fail. In practice this means that the features which justify describing an injunction as 'mandatory' will usually also have the consequence of creating a greater risk of injustice if it is granted rather than withheld at the interim stage. The merits threshold is a flexible one, and in some circumstances the court requires a high degree of assurance that the claimant will be able to establish his right at a trial.[78] Cases in which mandatory interim injunctions were granted include *Von Joel v Hornsey*,[79] where the defendant, knowing that the plaintiff wished to serve a writ upon him deliberately evaded service of the writ for some days and in the meantime hurried on with the building of which the plaintiff, as he well knew, was complaining. Another case is *Esso Petroleum Co Ltd v Kingswood Motors (Addlestone) Ltd*[80] where there was a five-year solus tie agreement between

---

[72] See pp 640–653, infra.   [73] In *Hill Samuel & Co Ltd v Littaur* [1985] NLJ Rep 57, 58.

[74] Likewise an injunction will normally only be varied or discharged on notice, *London City Agency (J C D) Ltd v Lee* [1970] Ch 597, [1969] 3 All ER 1376. As to the procedures see *Pickwick International Inc (GB) Ltd v Multiple Sound Distributors Ltd* [1972] 3 All ER 384.

[75] *Bank Mellat v Nikpour* [1985] FSR 87, CA; *Memory Corpn plc v Sidhu (No 2)* [2000] 1 WLR 1443, CA.

[76] *Ansah v Ansah* [1977] Fam 138, [1977] 2 All ER 638, CA; *G v G* [1990] 1 FLR 395, CA; *Re First Express Ltd* [1992] BCLC 824.

[77] *Daniel v Ferguson* [1891] 2 Ch 27, CA; *Astro Exito Navegacion SA v Southland Enterprise Co Ltd (No 2)* [1983] 2 AC 787, [1982] 3 All ER 335, CA (an interlocutory mandatory order compelling the execution of a contractual obligation), noted (1983) 99 LQR 5; *Locabail International Finance Ltd v Agroexport and Atlanta (UK) Ltd* [1986] 1 All ER 901, CA.

[78] *Films Rover International Ltd v Cannon Film Sales Ltd* [1986] 3 All ER 772, discussed (1988) 47 CLJ 34 (N H Andrews); *Leisure Data v Bell* [1988] FSR 367, CA; *Channel Tunnel Group Ltd v Balfour Beatty Construction Ltd* [1992] 2 All ER 609 at 626, CA, per Staughton LJ affd [1993] AC 334, [1993] 1 All ER 664, HL, without discussing this point; *Edwin Shirley Productions Ltd v Workspace Management Ltd* [2001] 2 EGLR 10.

[79] [1895] 2 Ch 774, CA. But refused in *Shepherd Homes Ltd v Sandham* [1971] Ch 340, [1970] 3 All ER 402 (breach of negative covenant).

[80] [1974] QB 142, [1973] 3 All ER 1057.

Esso and Kingswood. As part of a scheme to defeat the tie, Kingswood's garage was conveyed to a third party, Impact. The facts were somewhat complex, but the judge had no doubt that Impact had unlawfully procured a direct breach of Kingswood's contract with Esso. Accordingly a mandatory injunction was granted ordering a reconveyance of the garage to Kingswood. Finally a mandatory order was made in *Parker v Camden London Borough Council*[81] where the defendant landlord was admittedly in breach of its obligation to keep in repair the services for space heating and heating water. The breach, during a spell of cold weather, was causing severe hardship to the plaintiff tenants, particularly the elderly and the young, giving rise to an immediate fear as to the health of the tenants, going even to the risk of death.

In an appropriate case at the trial of the action where the defendant intends to appeal the judge may refuse to grant a successful claimant a perpetual injunction forthwith, but pending appeal by the defendant may instead continue an interim injunction. This may be done where, if the defendant were to succeed on appeal, he would otherwise have no claim for compensation for the loss he might suffer by being subject to the injunction between the trial and appeal. If only an interim injunction is granted, it may be made subject to the usual undertaking in damages.[82] The claimant would be given the right to come back to court to ask for a perpetual injunction if the defendant failed to enter an appeal in due time or if an appeal were not prosecuted with due diligence.[83]

(c) QUIA TIMET INJUNCTION

Although an injunction is directed to the future, it is, in general, based on some infringement or, in the case of an interim injunction, alleged infringement of the claimant's rights. It is, however, possible to obtain injunctions, both interim and perpetual, based on an injury by the defendant[84] which is merely threatened or apprehended, although no infringement of the claimant's rights has yet occurred.[85] The House of Lords, in *Redland Bricks Ltd v Morris*,[86] said that there are two types of cases. First, where the defendant has as yet done no hurt to the plaintiff but is threatening and intending (so the plaintiff alleges) to do works which will render irreparable harm to him or his property if carried to completion: such cases are normally concerned with negative injunctions. Secondly, the type of case where the plaintiff has been fully recompensed both at law and in equity for the damage he has suffered but where he

---

[81] [1986] Ch 162, [1985] 2 All ER 141, CA. The actual order was for an inspection of the boiler installations with a view to an appropriately drafted injunction being granted if necessary. Also in *London and Manchester Assurance Co Ltd v O and H Construction Ltd* [1989] 2 EGLR 185.

[82] See p 595 et seq, infra.   [83] *American Cyanamid Co v Ethicon Ltd* [1979] RPC 215 at 275 et seq.

[84] *Trawnik v Gordon Lennox* [1985] 2 All ER 368, [1985] 1 WLR 532, CA.

[85] As to the power of a county court see p 567, n 6, supra. As to quia timet injunctions in libel and slander actions see *British Data Management plc v Boxer Commercial Removals plc* [1996] 3 All ER 707, CA; and as to an injunction restraining someone from using the plaintiff's name or trademark as a domain name on the Internet, see *British Telecommunications plc v One in a Million* [1998] FSR 265.

[86] [1970] AC 652, [1969] 2 All ER 576, HL.

alleges that the earlier actions of the defendant may lead to future causes of action. The typical case is where the defendant has withdrawn support from the plaintiff's land. Such withdrawal of support only constitutes a cause of action when damage is suffered, and any further damage arising from the original withdrawal will constitute a fresh cause of action. In such cases a mandatory injunction may well be the appropriate remedy. Professor Jolowicz contends, however, that the term quia timet injunction should be restricted to the first type of case.[87]

The jurisdiction to grant a quia timet injunction has been said to be 'as old as the hills',[88] but 'no one can obtain a quia timet order by merely saying "Timeo" '.[89] Chitty J said[90] 'that the plaintiff must show a strong case of probability that the apprehended mischief will, in fact, arise'; in other words the plaintiff must prove that the threatened or intended act would be an inevitable violation of his right. Inevitable has been explained as meaning, in this context, a 'very great probability',[91] or that 'the result is one which all reasonable men skilled in the matter would expect would happen'.[92] More recently Russell LJ has suggested[93] that the degree of probability of future injury is not an absolute standard. 'What is to be aimed at', he said, 'is justice between the parties having regard to all the relevant circumstances.'

Not surprisingly, in the light of what has been said above, the dividing line between the cases is not altogether clear. It may be helpful to look at a few cases on either side. On the one hand the court thought that there was a sufficient degree of probability in *Dicker v Popham, Radford & Co*,[94] where the defendant was erecting a building which, if completed, would infringe the plaintiff's alleged right to light; in *Goodhart v Hyett*,[95] where the plaintiff had a right to have pipes to convey water through the defendant's land, and the defendant was building a house over part of the line of pipes, which would render their repair more difficult and expensive: and in *Torquay Hotel Co Ltd & Cousins*[96] where defendant members of a trade union had begun to picket the plaintiff's hotel in order to prevent the delivery of fuel oil. The evidence was that the defendants threatened or intended to interfere with the delivery of fuel oil, if necessary for months, by placing pickets. This showed a manifest intention to interfere directly and deliberately with the execution of contracts for the supply of fuel oil to the plaintiff's hotel, which warranted the granting of a quia timet injunction. On the other hand, the court will not grant an injunction where there is nothing more than a mere possibility of future injury, or mere speculation of possible mischief which may

---

[87] (1975) 34 CLJ 224.   [88] *A-G v Long Eaton UDC* [1915] 1 Ch 124, CA per Cozens-Hardy at 127.

[89] Per Lord Dunedin in *A-G for Dominion of Canada v Ritchie Contracting and Supply Co Ltd* [1919] AC 999 at 1005, PC.

[90] *A-G v Manchester Corpn* [1893] 2 Ch 87 at 92; *Redland Bricks Ltd v Morris* [1970] AC 652, [1969] 2 All ER 576, HL.

[91] Per Jessel MR in *Pattisson v Gilford* (1874) LR 18 Eq 259 at 264.

[92] Per Chitty J in *Phillips v Thomas* (1890) 62 LT 793 at 795.

[93] In *Hooper v Rogers* [1974] 3 WLR 329 at 334, CA. This approach was followed in Australia in *Kestrel Coal Property Ltd v Construction, Forestry, Mining & Energy Union* [2001] 2 Qd R 634.

[94] (1890) 63 LT 379; *Hepburn v Lordan* (1865) 2 Hem & M 345.   [95] (1883) 25 Ch D 182.

[96] [1969] 2 Ch 106, [1969] 1 All ER 522, CA.

never happen at all.[97] Thus the plaintiff failed to make out a case of sufficient probability, and an injunction was refused, in *Fletcher v Bealey*,[98] to restrain a defendant from polluting a river by depositing chemicals, from which in time a noxious liquid would flow, on certain land close to the river, on the ground that the liquid could be prevented from reaching the river, and that by the time the flow began some method of rendering it innocuous might have been discovered; in *A-G v Manchester Corpn*,[99] to restrain the erection of a smallpox hospital, on the ground that the danger to the health of the neighbourhood was not sufficiently established; and in *Draper v British Optical Association*,[100] to restrain the holding of a meeting to consider the removal of the plaintiff from the defendant association, for it was to be assumed that they would not remove him unless entitled to do so.

In particular, a quia timet injunction will readily be granted where the plaintiff establishes his right, and the defendant has claimed and insisted on his right to do an act which would be an infringement of the plaintiff's right,[101] or has threatened or given notice of his intention to do such act.[102] In any case it is not as a rule a sufficient defence to a claim for an injunction for the defendant to say that he has no present intention of doing the act in question.[103] Conversely in *Lord Cowley v Byas*,[104] an injunction was refused where the defendant not only stated that he had no present intention of using the land as a cemetery, but said also that if he should at any time thereafter wish to do so, he would give the plaintiff two months' prior notice of his intention in order to give him an opportunity to bring proceedings to try and prevent his doing so. The general principle seems to be that 'it would be wrong for [the] court in quia timet proceedings to grant relief by way of injunction to compel the defendants to do something which they appear to be willing to do without the imposition of an order of the court'.[105]

Where a mandatory injunction is sought in quia timet proceedings the question of the cost to the defendant of doing works to prevent or lessen the likelihood of a future apprehended wrong must be an element to be taken into account. On the one hand, where the defendant has acted wantonly and quite unreasonably in relation to his neighbour he may be ordered to repair his wanton and unreasonable acts by doing positive work to restore the status quo even if the expense to him is out of all proportion to the advantage thereby accruing to the claimant. On the other hand, where the defendant has acted reasonably, although in the event wrongly, the cost of remedying by positive action his earlier activities is more important for two reasons.

---

[97] *Worsley v Swann* (1882) 51 LJ Ch 576, CA.

[98] (1885) 28 Ch D 688 (the plaintiff's right to bring another action later in case of actual injury or imminent danger, was expressly reserved).

[99] [1893] 2 Ch 87; *A-G v Nottingham Corpn* [1904] 1 Ch 673.   [100] [1938] 1 All ER 115.

[101] *Shafto v Bolckow, Vaughan & Co* (1887) 34 Ch D 725; *Philips v Thomas* (1890) 62 LT 793.

[102] *McEacharn v Colton* [1902] AC 104, PC; *Thornhill v Weeks* [1913] 1 Ch 438.

[103] *Hext v Gill* (1872) 7 Ch App 699; *Leckhampton Quarries Co Ltd v Ballinger* (1904) 20 TLR 559.

[104] (1877) 5 Ch D 944, CA; *Jenkins v Hope* [1896] 1 Ch 278.

[105] *Bridlington Relay Ltd v Yorkshire Electricity Board* [1965] Ch 436 at 445, [1965] 1 All ER 264 at 269, per Buckley J.

First, because ex hypothesi no legal wrong has occurred (for which the claimant has not been recompensed) and may never occur or only on a small scale. Secondly, because if ultimately heavy damage does occur the claimant is in no way prejudiced for he has his action at law and all his consequential remedies in equity. The cost to the defendant of carrying out a mandatory order must be balanced against the anticipated possible damage to the plaintiff, and if, on such balance, it seems unreasonable to inflict such expenditure on one who for this purpose is no more than a potential wrongdoer then the court must exercise its jurisdiction accordingly.[106]

3 DAMAGES IN LIEU OF AN INJUNCTION

(a) JURISDICTION

Whether before Lord Cairns' Act[107] the Court of Chancery had power to award damages is not altogether clear.[108] If it had such power it would only exercise it in exceptional circumstances, and there seems to be no reported case of its exercise since Lord Cairns' Act which by s 2 empowered the court to award damages in addition to or in substitution for an injunction 'in all cases in which the Court of Chancery has jurisdiction to entertain an application for an injunction'.[109] This statutory power enabled the court to give damages in some cases where damages could not have been obtained in a court of common law, where, for instance, the injury was merely threatened or apprehended,[110] where the writ was issued prematurely for a common law action[111] or where the right was purely equitable,[112] and it applied even though the damage was only nominal.[113] Again at common law damages are recoverable only in respect of causes of action which are complete at the date of the writ; damages for future or repeated wrongs, for instance a continuing trespass, must be made the subject of fresh proceedings. Damages in substitution for an injunction, however, relate to the future, not the past, and inevitably extend beyond the damages to which

---

[106]   *Redland Bricks Ltd v Morris* [1970] AC 652, [1969] 2 All ER 576, HL.

[107]   Chancery Amendment Act 1858. For a valuable discussion of this Act see (1975) 34 CLJ 224 (J A Jolowicz); [1981] Conv 286 (T Ingman and J Wakefield). As to its application to the county court, see p 567, n 6, supra. See also (1985) 34 ICLQ 317 (A Burgess); (1989) 12 Dal LJ 131 (P M McDermott).

[108]   See *Grant v Dawkins* [1973] 3 All ER 897 at 899, 900; Spry, *Equitable Remedies*, 5th edn, pp 623–625, and p 7 supra. It is clear that an account might be ordered in certain cases where the defendant had made a profit. As to equitable damages in Singapore see (1988) 30 Mal LR 79 (Soh Kee Bun).

[109]   Or specific performance. Since the same principles apply the cases referred to below include cases on specific performance.

[110]   *Leeds Industrial Co-operative Society Ltd v Slack* [1924] AC 851, HL.

[111]   *Oakacre Ltd v Claire Cleaners (Holdings) Ltd* [1982] Ch 197, [1981] 3 All ER 667, discussed p 664, infra.

[112]   Eg a restrictive covenant, in respect of a subsequent purchaser to whom the burden did not pass at common law—*Eastwood v Lever* (1863) 4 De GJ & Sm 114; *Baxter v Four Oaks Properties Ltd* [1965] Ch 816, [1965] 1 All ER 906.

[113]   *Sayers v Collyer* (1884) 28 Ch D 103, CA.

the claimant may be entitled at law. They compensate the claimant for those future wrongs which an injunction would have prevented, and make it impossible for him to bring an action in respect thereof in the future.[114] Although Lord Cairns' Act has been repealed,[115] the jurisdiction has been preserved, as explained by the House of Lords in *Leeds Industrial Co-operative Society Ltd v Slack*.[116] The relevant provision of Lord Cairns' Act is now substantially re-enacted in s 50 of the Supreme Court Act 1981 and the present position is that all divisions of the High Court now have both this jurisdiction and also, under the Judicature Acts,[117] the jurisdiction which the common law courts had to award damages before 1875. It may be added that in a proper case the court may grant damages as to the past and an injunction as to the future.[118] It may also in an appropriate case award a restricted injunction and damages as compensation for the restriction.[119]

The object of Lord Cairns' Act was said, in *Ferguson v Wilson*,[120] to be to prevent a litigant being bandied about from one court to another and to enable the Court of Chancery to do complete justice by awarding damages where, before the Act, it would have refused an injunction and left the plaintiff to bring his action for damages at law. Since Lord Cairns was himself a member of the court in which this explanation was given it is presumably accurate, but it seems at first sight to be contradicted by cases[121] which appear to hold that the court could only exercise the jurisdiction to award damages where it would have granted an injunction before the Act, or in cases where the injunction was refused by reason of a change in circumstances between the filing of the bill and the trial, but would have been granted on the facts at the time of the filing of the bill. As Professor Jolowicz observes[122] this 'comes close to the reductio ad absurdum that the jurisdiction to award damages under the Act exists only when, by definition, it should not be exercised'.

The difficulty, as pointed out by Professor Jolowicz,[123] lies in defining the scope of the jurisdiction conferred by the Act which grants a discretionary power to substitute damages in lieu of a remedy which is itself discretionary. The correct view appears to be that damages may be granted in substitution for an injunction in any case where as at the date of the writ the court *could* (not *would*) have granted an injunction apart

---

[114] *Jaggard v Sawyer* [1995] 2 All ER 189, [1995] 1 WLR 269, CA.

[115] By the Statute Law Revision Act 1883, s 3.   [116] Supra.

[117] See now Supreme Court Act 1981, s 49.

[118] *Martin v Price* [1894] 1 Ch 276, CA; *Gilling v Gray* (1910) 27 TLR 39.

[119] *Chiron Corpn v Organon Teknika Ltd (No 10)* [1995] FSR 325.

[120] (1866) 2 Ch App 77 per Turner LJ (a case on specific performance). But Jessel MR thought in *Aynsley v Glover* (1874) LR 18 Eq 544 at 555, that the Act was designed to prevent a man obtaining an extortionate sum as the price of giving up his legal right to an injunction, for instance, against some comparatively trifling infringement of a right to light by a property developer. Cf Buckley J in *Cowper v Laidler* [1903] 2 Ch 337 who did not think it extortionate to ask a price which a property for exceptional reasons in fact commands.

[121] Eg *Aynsley v Glover*, supra; *Holland v Worley* (1884) 26 Ch D 578 (where Pearson J observed that the authorities added to rather than removed the difficulties); *Proctor v Bayley* (1889) 42 Ch D 390, CA.

[122] (1975) 34 CLJ 224 at 240.   [123] Op cit, pp 240–242.

from Lord Cairns' Act.[124] If the plaintiff does not make out even a prima facie claim to equitable relief, there can, of course, be no question of damages under Lord Cairns' Act. Thus in *Ferguson v Wilson*[125] itself specific performance of the alleged contract for the allotment of shares to the plaintiff was impossible because the shares had already been allotted to third parties. Accordingly it was held that damages could not be awarded under Lord Cairns' Act. But if he makes out a case which requires the court to exercise its general equitable discretion as to whether in all the circumstances an injunction should be awarded it is a different matter. If, in the exercise of that discretion, the judge decides against an injunction, he should then consider whether to award damages under Lord Cairns' Act, by reference to the circumstances as they exist at the date of the hearing.

In this context *Price v Strange*[126] suggests that the courts will be slow to hold that a matter alleged as a defence to a claim for equitable relief goes to jurisdiction rather than discretion. That case concerned want of mutuality[127] in a claim for specific performance, which was unhesitatingly held to go to discretion. Likewise the fact that it concerned a contract to do repairs was held not to go to jurisdiction, for although the court does not often order specific performance of a contract to build or do repairs it can do so in exceptional circumstances.[128] It has further been held that the jurisdiction to grant damages in lieu of specific performance exists in any case where, when the proceedings were begun, the court had jurisdiction to grant specific performance, and continues notwithstanding that thereafter, but before judgment, specific performance has become impossible,[129] and also, it is thought, where a right to decree equitable relief has accrued after the commencement of the action.[130]

It is not necessary for the plaintiff to include a claim for damages in his claim. Nor, conversely, need he ask for an injunction if he recognises that he is unlikely to obtain one, though he should make it clear whether he is claiming damages for past injury at common law, or damages under the Act in substitution for an injunction.[131]

(b) PRINCIPLES TO BE APPLIED

The result of the Act was, where it applied, to give the court a discretion whether to grant an injunction or to award damages in substitution therefor. The court has assumed a similar discretion where, as a result of the Judicature Acts, it has both the

---

124 *Jaggard v Sawyer* [1995] 2 All ER 189, [1995] 1 WLR 269, CA; *Hooper v Rodgers* [1975] Ch 43, [1974] 3 All ER 417.

125 Supra. See *Surrey County Council v Bredero Homes Ltd* [1993] 3 All ER 705, [1993] 1 WLR 1361, CA, as explained in *Jaggard v Sawyer*, supra, CA.

126 [1978] Ch 337, [1977] 3 All ER 371, CA.   127 See p 676 infra.

128 See p 671, infra. Goff LJ in *Price v Strange*, supra, at 385, 386, CA thought the same was true of a contract for personal services, but Buckley LJ at 394 seems to have thought this went to the jurisdiction.

129 *Johnson v Agnew* [1978] Ch 176, [1978] 3 All ER 314, CA; appeal dismissed on other grounds [1980] AC 367, [1979] 1 All ER 883, HL.

130 See McDermott, *Equitable Damages*, p 82 et seq.

131 *Jaggard v Sawyer*, supra, CA. Cf *Surrey County Council v Bredero Homes Ltd*, supra, CA.

equitable jurisdiction to grant an injunction and the common law jurisdiction to award damages. The courts do not seem to distinguish between these two discretions in considering whether to award an injunction or damages.

In exercising their discretion, the courts have made it clear that if, according to ordinary principles, a plaintiff has made out his case for an injunction, the court will not award damages in substitution therefore, except under very exceptional circumstances. The mere fact that an injunction would almost certainly do no good to the plaintiff does not seem to be sufficient.[132] In particular, as Lindley LJ said in *Shelfer v City of London Electric Lighting Co*,[133] 'ever since Lord Cairns' Act was passed the Court of Chancery has repudiated the notion that the legislature intended to turn that court into a tribunal for legalizing wrongful acts; or in other words, the court has always protested against the notion that it ought to allow a wrong to continue simply because the wrongdoer is able and willing to pay for the injury he may inflict', even if the wrongdoer is in some sense a public benefactor.[134] Lord Sumner expressed the same idea in colourful language in *Leeds Industrial Co-operative Society Ltd v Slack*,[135] which involved the infringement of a right to light. 'For my part', he said, 'I doubt, as Sir George Jessel doubted,[136] whether it is complete justice to allow the big man, with his big building and his enhanced rateable value and his improvement of the neighbourhood, to have his way, and to solace the little man for his darkened and stuffy little house by giving him a cheque that he does not ask for.' But the objection that the court should not legalize wrongful acts carries much less weight if put forward by the defendant, the plaintiff being content with the award of damages.[137]

In *Shelfer v City of London Electric Lighting Co*[138] A L Smith LJ gave it as his opinion that 'as a good working rule' damages in substitution for an injunction may[139] be given if:

(i)   the injury to the plaintiff's legal right is small, and
(ii) is one which is capable of being estimated in money, and
(iii) is one which can be adequately compensated by a small money payment, and
(iv) the case is one in which it would be oppressive to the defendant to grant an injunction.

---

[132] Per Stamp J at first instance in *Sefton v Tophams Ltd* [1964] 3 All ER 876 at 894. Lord Cairns' Act was not discussed at either stage of the appeal.

[133] [1895] 1 Ch 287 at 315, 316, CA, referred to with approval in *Elliott v London Borough of Islington* [1991] 1 EGLR 167, CA.

[134] *Shelfer v City of London Electric Lighting Co*, supra, CA, per Lindley LJ; *Biogen Inc v Medeva plc* [1993] RPC 475 discussing the point in relation to life saving drugs.

[135] [1924] AC 851 at 872, HL.

[136] In *Krehl v Burrell* (1878) 7 Ch D 551 at 554; affd (1879) 11 Ch D 146, CA.

[137] *Sampson v Hodson-Pressinger* [1981] 3 All ER 710, 125 Sol Jo 623, CA.

[138] [1895] 1 Ch 287 at 322, 323, CA. Cf *Aynsley v Glover* (1874) LR 18 Eq 544.

[139] The word 'may' was emphasized by Lord Donaldson, with whom the other LJJ agreed, in *Elliott v London Borough of Islington* [1991] 1 EGLR 167, CA.

It was pointed out in *Slack v Leeds Industrial Co-operative Society Ltd*,[140] where the rule was accepted as valid, that it must be read in its context, including in particular the judge's preceding observation that if the plaintiff's legal right has been invaded, he is prima facie entitled to an injunction. It came in for more severe criticism in *Fishenden v Higgs and Hill Ltd*[141] where it was said[142] 'to be the high water mark of what might be called definite rules'. It was further said[143] that the rule was not intended to be exhaustive or to be rigidly applied, and that the tests were, as A L Smith LJ himself recognized, of imperfect application—what, for instance, is meant by a 'small' injury, or 'adequate' compensation. Another member of the court,[144] after observing that the rule was contained in an obiter dictum, observed that, though it might have been valid in the sort of case then before the court, that is nuisance by noise and vibration, it was 'not a universal or even sound rule in all cases of injury to light'. However, in the more recent cases the Court of Appeal has accepted the rule without qualification or criticism, pointing out that it has been applied time and again over the years. Thus in *Jaggard v Sawyer*[145] the award of damages at first instance was confirmed by the Court of Appeal, Millett LJ observing that the outcome of any particular case usually depends on the application of the fourth of A L Smith's rules. By way of contrast in *Kennaway v Thompson*[146] the judge at first instance had awarded £15,000 damages, but the Court of Appeal granted an injunction restricting the activities of a club which organized motor boat races causing a nuisance by noise to the plaintiff. None of the first three conditions in A L Smith LJ's 'good working rule' was satisfied.

The exercise of the court's discretion has been discussed in several cases. On the

---

[140] [1924] 2 Ch 475, CA. Dicta in *Woollerton and Wilson Ltd v Richard Costain Ltd* [1970] 1 All ER 483 doubting whether the rule applied to trespass where only nominal damages are recoverable were disapproved in *Jaggard v Sawyer* [1995] 2 All ER 189, CA.

[141] (1935) 153 LT 128, CA.   [142] Per Hanworth MR at 138.

[143] Some assistance is obtained from *Slack v Leeds Industrial Co-operative Society Ltd*, supra, which says that this is meant comparatively and not absolutely, and *Fishenden v Higgs and Hill Ltd*, supra, which decided that it does not matter if 'comparatively small damages' constitute absolutely a 'not inconsiderable sum'.

[144] Maugham LJ at 144.

[145] [1995] 2 All ER 189, [1995] 1 WLR 269, CA; *Daniells v Mendonca* (1999) 78 P & CR 401, CA (rule applied: mandatory injunction granted).

[146] [1981] QB 88, [1980] 3 All ER 329, CA, discussed (1981) 131 NLJ 108 (B S Markesinis and A M Tettenborn); (1982) 41 CLJ 87 (Stephen Tromans) who argues that the time is ripe for a review of the rule in *Shelfer's Case* and that the courts should exercise their discretion more readily in favour of damages; *Wakeham v Wood* (1981) 43 P & CR 40, CA (conditions not satisfied—mandatory injunction awarded); *Morris v Redland Bricks Ltd* [1967] 3 All ER 1, CA, where however the LJJ disagreed as to the application of the rule of the facts. Note, however, that this decision was reversed on appeal in the House of Lords, sub nom *Redland Bricks Ltd v Morris* [1970] AC 652, [1969] 2 All ER 576, where this point was not discussed. All their Lordships agreed with Lord Upjohn that the Court of Appeal should not have considered Lord Cairns' Act at all. The question at issue was said to be simply whether or not a mandatory quia timet injunction should be granted. Lord Cairns' Act was said not to be applicable because neither party had sought to rely on it, but the better view is that the Act applies whether or not the parties themselves invoke it—see (1975) 34 CLJ 224 (J A Jolowicz). See *Hooper v Rogers* [1975] Ch 43, [1974] 3 All ER 417, where on similar facts Lord Cairns' Act was applied. See also (1977) 36 CLJ 369; (1978) 37 CLJ 51 (P H Pettit).

one hand Lord Macnaghten has stated[147] that while the amount of damages that it is supposed could be recovered does not furnish a satisfactory test, an injunction and not damages should be awarded if the injury cannot fairly be compensated by money; or if the defendant has acted in a high-handed manner, or if he has endeavoured to steal a march upon the plaintiff or to evade the jurisdiction of the court. Jessel MR has suggested[148] that as a general rule an injunction should be awarded if the defendant knew he was doing wrong and took his chance about being disturbed in doing it. And it has been held[149] that in general damages will not be granted in lieu of an injunction against the pollution of a stream, or nuisance by noise or smell,[150] as it is impossible to measure what the future damage would be; or in the case of a continuing trespass where refusal of an injunction would in effect compel the landowner to grant a right to the trespasser.[151] On the other hand Lord Macnaghten, in the same case,[152] observed that where there is a real question as to whether the plaintiff's rights have been infringed, and the defendant has acted fairly and not in an unneighbourly spirit, the court should incline to damages rather than an injunction, and Lindley LJ has suggested,[153] as examples of circumstances where the court would exercise its discretion by awarding damages, trivial and occasional nuisances; cases in which a plaintiff has shown that he only wants money; vexatious and oppressive cases; cases where the plaintiff has so conducted himself as to render it unjust to give him more than pecuniary relief, and cases where damages is really an adequate remedy. And in several cases[154] it has been held that a fairly weak case of acquiescence by the plaintiff may be a ground for awarding damages in lieu of an injunction.

Most of the cases in which an injunction has been refused and damages awarded are cases where the plaintiff has sought a mandatory injunction to pull down a building which infringes his right to light or which has been built in breach of a restrictive covenant. In such cases the court is faced with a fait accompli and to grant an injunction would subject the defendant to a loss out of all proportion to that which would be suffered by the plaintiff if it were refused. A similar situation arises where a prohibitory injunction is sought to restrain access to the defendant's house which, if

---

[147] In *Colls v Home and Colonial Stores Ltd* [1904] AC 179 at 193, HL; *Shelfer's Case*, CA, supra; *Wakeham v Wood*, CA, supra.

[148] *Smith v Smith* (1875) LR 20 Eq 500; *Pugh v Howells* (1984) 48 P & CR 298, CA discussed (1985) 135 NLJ 1005 (H W Wilkinson). But see *Ketley v Gooden* (1996) 73 P & CR 305, where delay in seeking relief was an important factor against the award of an injunction.

[149] *Pennington v Brinsop Hall Coal Co* (1877) 5 Ch D 769.

[150] *Wood v Conway Corpn* [1914] 2 Ch 47, CA.

[151] Damages in lieu were however awarded in *Tollemache and Cobbold Breweries Ltd v Reynolds* (1983) 268 Estates Gazette 52, CA, having regard to the minor nature of the trespass and the appellant's behaviour.

[152] *Colls v Home and Colonial Stores Ltd*, supra, HL; *Kine v Jolly* [1905] 1 Ch 480, CA.

[153] In *Shelfer v City of London Electric Lighting Co* [1895] 1 Ch 287 at 317, CA.

[154] *Sayers v Collyer* (1884) 28 Ch D 103, CA, esp per Fry LJ at 110; *H P Bulmer Ltd and Showerings Ltd v J Bollinger SA* [1977] 2 CMLR 625 at 681, per Goff LJ. In *Ludlow Music Inc v Robbie Williams* [2001] FSR 271 an injunction was refused, although the appropriate compensation might be substantial, where there was clearly an element of acquiescence, and the evidence suggested strongly that the claimants were only interested in money.

granted, would render the house land-locked and incapable of beneficial enjoyment.[155] One may note also *Sharp v Harrison*[156] where Astbury J stated the general proposition that damages and not an injunction should be granted where the plaintiff had not really suffered any damage and an injunction would inflict damage upon the defendant out of all proportion to the relief which the plaintiff ought to obtain.

Finally Lord Denning MR has indicated, obiter, that damages should be awarded where the effect of an injunction would be 'to stop a great enterprise and render it useless'.[157]

(c) MEASURE OF DAMAGE

Where damages are recoverable in respect of the same cause of action either at common law or under Lord Cairns' Act the same compensatory principle applies to both situations.[158] As previously mentioned Lord Cairns' Act applies equally to claims for specific performance and claims for an injunction and in *Wroth v Tyler*[159] the point arose in a specific performance action. Specific performance of a contract for the sale of land was refused and the question was whether the damages should be £1,500, the difference between the contract price and the market price of the property as at the date of the breach that is the date fixed for completion, or £5,500 being the same difference as at the date of the trial. Though damages are normally assessed as at the date of the breach, Megarry J took the view that damages under Lord Cairns' Act are not necessarily the same as at common law, and awarded damages of £5,500. In *Johnson v Agnew*[160] the House of Lords disagreed with this case in so far as it might be taken to hold that the measure of damage differs in common law from equity. Though damages are normally assessed as at the date of the breach, this is not an absolute rule either at common law or under Lord Cairns' Act. As Lord Wilberforce observed:[161]

In cases where a breach of a contract of sale has occurred, and the innocent party reasonably

---

[155] *Jaggard v Sawyer* [1995] 2 All ER 189, [1995] 1 WLR 269, CA. Contrast cases such as *Goodson v Richardson* (1874) 9 Ch App 221.

[156] [1922] 1 Ch 502.

[157] *Allen v Gulf Oil Refining Ltd* [1980] QB 156, [1979] 3 All ER 1008, CA, at 1016.

[158] *Johnson v Agnew* [1980] AC 367, [1979] 1 All ER 883, HL; *Jaggard v Sawyer*, supra, CA. See (1980) CLJ 58 (A J Oakley); (1981) 97 LQR 445 (S M Waddams); (1999–2000) 4 Deak LR 61 (T H Ong); Jones and Goodhart, *Specific Performance*, 2nd edn, pp 280 et seq. Exceptionally, an account of profits may be the most appropriate remedy for breach of contract: *A-G v Blake* [2001] 1 AC 268, [2000] 4 All ER 385, HL; *Experience Hendrix LCC v PPX Enterprises Inc* [2003] EWCA Civ 323, [2003] 1 All ER (Comm) 830, noted (2003) RLR 101 (J Edelman); [2003] LMCLQ 301 (Pey-Woan Lee); (2004) 120 LQR 26 (M Graham). See (2002) 118 LQR 377 (J Beatson); [2003] CLJ 605 (D Campbell and P Wylie).

[159] [1974] Ch 30, [1973] 1 All ER 897; *Tito v Waddell (No 2)* [1977] Ch 106 at 334, 335, [1977] 3 All ER 129 at 318, 319; *Suleman v Shahsavari* [1989] 2 All ER 460, [1988] 1 WLR 1181; *Souster v Epsom Plumbing Contractors Ltd* [1974] 2 NZLR 515; *Semelhago v Paramadevan* [1996] 2 SCR 415. See [1974] 48 ALJ 273 (R P Austin); (1975) 91 LQR 337 (Michael Albery); (1997) 76 CBR 551 (N Siebrasse) where *Wroth v Tyler* is said to be wrong in principle.

[160] Supra, HL.

[161] Supra, HL, at 896. All the other Law Lords agreed with the speech of Lord Wilberforce.

continues to try to have the contract completed, it would to me appear more logical and just rather than tie him to the date of the original breach, to assess damages as at the date when (otherwise than by his default) the contract is lost.

In a few cases damages may be awarded in substitution for an injunction under Lord Cairns' Act where damages could not be recovered at common law: for example, in lieu of a quia timet injunction, or for breach of a restrictive covenant to which the defendant was not a party.[162] An instance of this is *Wrotham Park Estate Co v Parkside Homes Ltd*,[163] where the houses were built in breach of a restrictive covenant, and a mandatory injunction to demolish them was refused. The value of the covenantee's retained land was not diminished by the breach, but he was nevertheless awarded substantial damages in lieu of the injunction, assessed by reference to the sum he might reasonably have demanded as a quid pro quo for relaxing the covenant. This method of assessment was approved and applied by the Court of Appeal in *Jaggard v Sawyer*,[164] and approved by the House of Lords in *A-G v Blake*.[165]

[162] See p 580, supra.

[163] [1974] 2 All ER 321, [1974] 1 WLR 799; *Bracewell v Appleby* [1975] Ch 408, [1975] 1 All ER 993; *Carr-Saunders v Dick McNeil Associates Ltd* [1986] 2 All ER 888, [1986] 1 WLR 922. See (1979) 95 LQR 581 (Harris, Ogus and Phillips); (1953) 99 LQR 443 (Gareth Jones).

[164] Supra, CA, noted [1995] 14 CJQ 16 (F M) considering *Surrey County Council v Bredero Homes Ltd* [1993] 3 All ER 705, [1993] 1 WLR 1361, CA, noted (1993) 109 LQR 518 (P Birks); [1993] LMCLQ 453 (A Burrows), where the court refused to extend this method of assessment to a claim for damages at common law for breach of contract. In *A-G v Blake*, supra, HL, Lord Nicholls said that in so far as the *Bredero Homes* Ltd decision is inconsistent with the approach adopted in the *Wrotham* Park case the latter approach is to be preferred. See *Stoke-on-Trent City Council v W & J Wass Ltd* [1988] 3 All ER 394, [1988] 1 WLR 1405, CA; *Gafford v Graham* (1999) 77 P & CR 73, CA, noted (1998) 114 LQR 555 (P Milne). See also [1995] Conv 141 (T Ingman).

[165] Supra, HL. Subsequently applied *Amec Development Ltd v Jury's Hotel Management (UK) Ltd* (2001) 82 P & CR 286, noted (2001) 66 PLJ 16 (B Leighton). See [2001] Conv 453 (D Halpern); [2001] LMCLQ 9 (J Edelman); (2002) 22 LS 208 (D Campbell and D Harris).

4 ENFORCEMENT OF AN INJUNCTION[166]

(a) POWERS OF THE COURT

(i) Enforcement against defendant

A person who is restrained by injunction from doing a particular act is liable for contempt of court,[167] if he in fact does the act, and it is no answer to say that the act was not contumacious in the sense that, in doing it, there was no direct intention to disobey the order: an act, however, which is merely casual or accidental and unintentional would not give rise to liability.[168] It is not sufficient by way of answer to an allegation that a court order has not been complied with, for the person concerned to say that he 'did his best'. Nor is bona fide reliance on legal advice which turns out to be wrong, though this may be relevant as mitigation.[169] The party enjoined is, of course liable for its agents, and has some responsibility for the acts of its licensees. There is implied in the standard form of an injunction a requirement on the party enjoined to take such steps as are within its power to prevent its independent con-tractors from performing acts which, if performed by the party enjoined, would be in breach; failure unreasonably to exercise such power would be a contempt of court.[170]

---

[166] An undertaking given to the court has all the force of an injunction: *Roberts v Roberts* [1990] 2 FLR 111, CA; *Kensington Housing Trust v Oliver* (1997) 30 HLR 608, CA, but the procedural requirements for enforce-ment are not so strict as in the case of an order—*Hussain v Hussain* [1986] Fam 134, [1986] 1 All ER 961, CA. But it is not a contempt of court to refuse to comply with a declaratory order—*Webster v Southwark London Borough Council* [1983] QB 698, [1983] 2 WLR 217; *D v D* (1990) *Times*, 16 November, CA. Where a breach by the defendant of an undertaking to the court necessarily involves a breach of a contract between the plaintiff and the defendant the court may, on the hearing of an application to commit the defendant for breach of the undertaking, award damages without need for the plaintiff to bring a separate action: *Midland Marts Ltd v Hobday* [1989] 3 All ER 246. In this case Vinelott J said, at 250, that the court cannot impose a fine and direct that the fine be paid to someone other than the Crown, but a different view has been taken in New Zealand: *Taylor Bros Ltd v Taylors Group Ltd* [1991] 1 NZLR 91 (NZ CA). Contempt proceedings in industrial disputes are discussed by John Bowers in (1985) 135 NLJ 1143; and in relation to the disobeying spouse by M Chesterman and P Waters (1985) 8 UNSWLJ 106.

[167] This is technically 'civil contempt', ie contempt by a party to proceedings in matters of procedure. A finding of contempt may be made against a government department or a minister of the Crown in his official capacity: *Re M* [1994] 1 AC 377, sub nom *M v Home Office* [1993] 3 All ER 537, HL, noted [1994] Pub L 568 (M Gould) where Lord Templeman said that to hold otherwise would be to 'establish the proposition that the executive obeyed the law as a matter of grace, not of necessity, a proposition that would reverse the result of the Civil War'. A finding of contempt can, of course, be made against a minister personally provided the contempt related to his own default. See also *R v IRC, ex p Kingston Smith (a firm)* [1996] STC 1210.

[168] *Fairclough v Manchester Ship Canal* (1897) 41 Sol Jo 225, CA; *Heatons Transport (St Helens) Ltd v Transport and General Workers Union* [1973] AC 15, [1972] 3 All ER 101, HL; *Director General of Fair Trading v Pioneer Concrete UK Ltd* [1995] 1 AC 456, HL; *Bird v Hadkinson* [1999] BPIR 653. In *Pereira v Beanlands* [1996] 3 All ER 528 it was said that the word 'defiant' was possibly one which combined some of the flavour of both 'contumelious' and 'contumacious' in more everyday language.

[169] *Z Bank v DI* [1994] 1 Lloyd's Rep 656. *Parker (t/a NBC Services) v Rasalingham (t/a Micro Tec)* (2000) *Times*, 25 July.

[170] *World Wide Fund for Nature v THQ/Jakks Pacific LLC* [2004] FSR 161 CA.

In the case of a company disobedience to an injunction by its employees, acting in the course of their employment, amounts to contempt of court by the employing company notwithstanding that the act of disobedience contravenes a specific instruction given by senior management, unless the conduct of the employees could be described as merely casual or accidental and unintentional.[171]

The quality of non-compliance, which varies over an enormous range, from a flat defiance of the court's authority to a genuine wholehearted use of the best endeavours to comply with the order which, nevertheless, has been unsuccessful, is of the utmost importance to the court in deciding what penalty should be imposed. The penalty in fact reflects faithfully the court's view of the conduct of the person to whom the order was addressed.[172] However the history which led to the imposition of an injunction is not relevant when sentencing for breach of the injunction which has to be examined for what it is and sentenced accordingly.[173] An injunction, or an undertaking given, operates until it is revoked on appeal or by the court itself, and must be obeyed whether or not it should have been granted or accepted in the first place.[174]

The traditional sanction for contempt of court is imprisonment in the case of an individual, or sequestration in the case of a corporation, though in the case both of an individual and a corporation it seems the court could always impose the lesser penalty of a fine,[175] or merely order the offending party to pay costs and, if it thought fit, damages.[176] These powers remain and rules of court[177] now provide that one or more of the following means are available for enforcing an injunction against both an individual and a body corporate, viz:

(i)   with the permission of the court, a writ of sequestration against the property of that person;

(ii)   where that person is a body corporate, with the permission of the court, a writ of sequestration against the property of any director or other officer of the body;[178]

---

[171] *Director General of Fair Trading v Pioneer Concrete (UK) Ltd,* supra, HL.

[172] *Howitt Transport Ltd v Transport and General Workers Union* [1973] ICR 1 per Donaldson J esp at 10 and 11. See *A-G v Newspapers Publishing plc* (1990) *Times,* 28 February, CA, discussed (1991) 141 NLJ 173 (A Halpin).

[173] *Cambridgeshire County Council v D* [1999] 2 FLR 42, CA (sentence of 12 months' imprisonment reduced to three months for writing love letters to his pregnant girlfriend in breach of an injunction taken out by the local authority to prevent violence on the girlfriend in its care).

[174] *Johnson v Walton* [1990] 1 FLR 350, CA.

[175] *Ronson Products Ltd v Ronson Furniture Ltd* [1966] Ch 603, [1966] 2 All ER 381; *The Jarlinn* [1965] 3 All ER 36, [1965] 2 Lloyd's Rep 191; *The Calyx* [1966] 1 Lloyd's Rep 701 (Mayor's and City of London Court). The fine may be large, eg £525,000—see *Messenger Newspapers Group Ltd v National Graphical Association* [1984] IRLR 397. But is limited to £2,500 in the case of an inferior court—Contempt of Court Act 1981, s 14(2); Criminal Justice Act 1991 s 17(3)(a), Sch 4 Pt I.

[176] *Fairclough v Manchester Ship Canal,* supra; *Re Agreement of Mileage Conference Group of the Tyre Manufacturers' Conference Ltd* [1966] 2 All ER 849 (RPC).

[177] CPR Sch 1, RSC Ord 45, r 5. See *AMIEU v Mudginberri Station Pty Ltd* (1986) 66 ALR 577; *A-G for Tuvalu v Philatelic Distribution Corpn Ltd* [1990] 2 All ER 216, [1990] 1 WLR 926, CA.

[178] An officer of a company is not liable in contempt merely by virtue of his office and his knowledge that the order sought to be enforced was made. He will only be liable if he can otherwise be shown to be in contempt under the general law of contempt—*Director General of Fair Trading v Buckland* [1990] 1 All ER 545, [1990] 1 WLR 920.

(iii)   subject to the provisions of the Debtors Act 1869 and 1878, an order of committal against that person or, where that person is a body corporate, against any such officer.

The High Court has jurisdiction to commit for contempt whenever contempt involves a degree of fault or misconduct, including negligence.[179] However the power is discretionary and is not automatically available at the demand of the plaintiff whose rights are being infringed. Indeed where an application for committal is a wholly disproportionate response to a trivial or blameless breach of a court order, the court will dismiss the application with costs in favour of the respondent.[180]

The fundamental purpose of proceedings for contempt of court consisting of disobedience of an injunction is to uphold the supremacy of the rule of law and the court's authority to administer it. It is punitive in character. That it provides the beneficiary of such an order with an enforcement remedy is incidental.[181] Nevertheless the court seldom takes the initiative in punishing a person who disobeys an injunction. The initiative is normally taken by the beneficiary of the order who is entitled to consult his own interests in deciding whether or not to enforce it, and if he chooses not to the court will not, generally speaking, intervene. Where a public element is involved the Attorney-General may intervene if he thinks fit. If neither the litigant nor the Attorney-General seeks to enforce the order, the court may act to punish the contempt of its own volition, but will only do so in exceptional cases of clear contempts which cannot wait to be dealt with.[182] However once proceedings for contempt have been launched they cannot be abandoned without the leave of the court, for the court itself has a major interest in the proceedings.[183]

Five final points may be added. First, under CPR Sch 1, RSC Ord 45, r 8 the court without prejudice to its powers in relation to contempt may direct that an act to be done be carried out by some person appointed by the court at the cost of the disobedient party. Secondly, the court has jurisdiction to commit for contempt for breach of an injunction even though the injunction has ceased to have effect,[184] or has

---

[179] *Guildford Borough Council v Valler* (1993) *Times*, 15 October, CA; *Heaton's Transport (St Helens) Ltd v Transport and General Workers Union* [1973] AC 15 at 109, [1972] 3 All ER 101 at 117, HL, per Lord Wilberforce.

[180] *Adam Phones Ltd v Goldschmidt* [1999] 4 All ER 486.

[181] *Re Supply of Ready Mixed Concrete* [1992] QB 213, sub nom *Director-General of Fair Trading v Smiths Concrete Ltd* [1991] 4 All ER 150, CA overruled *Re supply of Ready Mixed Concrete (No 2); Director-General of Fair Trading v Pioneer Concrete (UK) Ltd* [1995] 1 AC 456, [1995] 1 All ER 135, HL, without affecting this point.

[182] *Clarke v Chadburn* [1985] 1 All ER 211, [1985] 1 WLR 78, where Megarry V-C debated whether the law was satisfactory.

[183] *Re Supply of Ready Mixed Concrete*, supra, CA.

[184] *Jennison v Baker* [1972] 2 QB 52, [1972] 1 All ER 997, CA, where it was held on this point that the county court has the same power as the High Court.

been discharged as having been irregularly obtained.[185] Thirdly, an act done in disobedience to an order of the court is an illegal and invalid act which cannot effect any change in the rights and liabilities of others.[186] Fourthly, the contempt jurisdiction of the court is quite separate from the criminal jurisdiction of any other court notwithstanding that it may arise out of the same set of factual circumstances. The judge at first instance was accordingly held to have acted rightly in *Szczepanski v Szczepanski*[187] in refusing to adjourn contempt proceedings pending completion of criminal proceedings. Fifthly, when imposing a sentence of imprisonment for contempt of court, the court has no jurisdiction to direct that the contemnor should not be released from prison until a certain date. This would override the early release provisions in the Criminal Justice Act 1991.[188] Finally, there is no general rule that a court will not hear an application for his own benefit by a person in contempt unless and until he has purged his contempt, though it may do so in the circumstances of a particular case.[189]

(ii) Enforcement against third parties

A third party who assists, that is, by aiding and abetting, a breach of an injunction is an accessory to breach of the injunction and equally liable with the defendant for what is a civil contempt.[190]

Further in the case of an interim, but not a final injunction,[191] a third party may be liable for criminal contempt even though he is acting independently of the party against whom the order was made. This is where his act constitutes a wilful interference with the administration of justice in the proceedings in which the order was made. One species of such interference is the deliberate publication information which the court has ordered someone else to keep confidential. Such publication interferes with the administration of justice because it destroys the subject matter of proceedings. Once the information has been published the court can no longer do justice between the parties by enforcing the obligation of confidentiality.[192]

(b) SERVICE OF THE INJUNCTION

Unless the court dispenses with the requirement, a mandatory injunction cannot be enforced unless a copy of the order has been served personally on the person required

---

[185] *Wardle Fabrics Ltd v G Myristis Ltd* [1984] FSR 263.   [186] *Clarke v Chadburn*, supra.

[187] [1985] FLR 468, CA, where the appellant had been committed to prison for 12 months; *Keeber v Keeber* [1995] 2 FLR 748, CA.

[188] *Thompson v Mitchell* (2004) *Times*, 13 Sept.

[189] *Raja v van Hoogstraten* [2004] EWCA Civ 968, [2004] 4 All ER 793.

[190] *Acrow (Automation) Ltd v Rex Chainbelt Inc* [1971] 3 All ER 1175, CA; *A-G v Punch Ltd* [2002] UKHL 50, [2003] 1 All ER 289.

[191] *Jockey Club v Buffham* [2002] EWHC 1866 (QB), [2003] QB 462, noted [2003] CLJ 241 (A T H Smith). See also (2002) 33 VUWLR 51 and (2003) 81 CBR 207 (J Berryman).

[192] *A-G v Times Newspapers Ltd* [1992] UKHL 50, [2003] 1 All ER 289, noted (2003) 119 LQR 384 (P Devonshire); (2003) 24 Co Law 310 (Rinita Sarker).

to do the act in question.[193] In the case of a prohibitory injunction, however, it suffices if the defendant was present when the order was made, or has been notified informally by telephone or telegram or in some other way.[194] A defendant who has merely had informal notice will not, however, be committed for contempt if he can establish a bona fide and reasonable belief that no injunction has in fact been granted.[195] In the case of an undertaking, the defendant is presumed to have known that he has given it, though if he can satisfy the court that he was unaware of the terms of an undertaking given on his behalf, but not by him personally, this may be a mitigating circumstance.[196]

The court has a general power to dispense with service of a copy of an order if it thinks it just to do so.[197] In the case of a mandatory order the power is exercisable not only prospectively, that is before the expiration of the time limited for compliance with it, but also retrospectively, that is, after the occurrence of the events alleged to constitute its breach.[198]

(c) COMMITTAL TO PRISON

Guidance as to the proper approach was given by Lord Woolf MR in *Nicholls v Nicholls*.[199] Since committal orders involve the liberty of the subject it is particularly important that the relevant rules are duly complied with. However, where defects have occurred in a committal order, or in an application to commit, but the contemnor has had a fair trial and the order for committal has been made on valid grounds, the court will not, in the absence of prejudice to the contemnor, set aside the order, since it has power to rectify the order and it would be contrary to the interests of justice to set aside the order purely on the grounds of a technicality.

By s 14(1) of the Contempt of Court Act 1981, imprisonment must be for a fixed term not exceeding two years in the case of committal by a superior court,[200] including for this purpose a county court,[201] or one month in the case of committal by an inferior court. Both the High Court and the county court have power on making an order of committal to prison to suspend the order conditional on compliance with stated conditions, and have power to impose consecutive sentences of imprisonment in appropriate cases.[202] The reasons for a committal to custody for contempt are

---

[193] CPR Sch 1, RSC Ord 45, r 7(2) and (7). In the case of a body corporate, if enforcement is sought against an officer, personal service on that officer is normally required—Ord 45, r 7(3).

[194] CPR Sch 1, RSC Ord 45, r 7(6). See *Blome v Blome* (1976) 120 Sol Jo 315 and (1977) 40 MLR 220 (P H Pettit).

[195] *Re Bishop, ex p Langley* (1879) 13 Ch D 110, CA.

[196] *Hussain v Hussain* [1986] Fam 134, [1986] 1 All ER 961, CA. See *Watkinson v AJ Wright (Electrical) Ltd* [1996] 3 All ER 31.

[197] CPR Sch 1, RSC Ord 45, r 7(7).

[198] *Davy International Ltd v Tazzyman* [1997] 3 All ER 183, CA.

[199] [1997] 2 All ER 97, CA, applying *M v P* [1992] 4 All ER 833, CA.

[200] As defined in s 19. See *Villiers v Villiers* [1994] 2 All ER 149, [1994] 1 WLR 493, CA.

[201] County Courts (Penalties for Contempt) Act 1983.

[202] *Lee v Walker* [1985] QB 1191, [1985] 1 All ER 781, CA. See *Re R (a minor)* [1994] 2 FCR 629, CA.

twofold: first, to punish the contemnor for disobedience of an order of the court and, second, to attempt to coerce him to comply with the order. Once the contemnor has been sufficiently punished for disobeying a court order he should not be punished further for continuing to do the same thing. If it becomes clear that continuance of imprisonment will have no coercive effect, and he has been punished enough, there is no justification for continuing to keep him in prison.[203] And a person cannot be committed more than once for a single breach.[204] Though as a general rule the court should not commit where there is a reasonable alternative available[205] a prison sentence may be appropriate where there has been flagrant defiance of an order.[206]

It may be added that on an application to the court to purge contempt, the judge can only say 'yes', 'no' or 'not yet'. He cannot release him on terms that the remaining part of sentence be suspended.[207]

(d) FAMILY LAW ACT 1996

Section 47 provides that if the court makes an occupation order (as defined by s 39) or a non-molestation order (as defined by s 42(1)), and it appears to the court that the respondent has used or threatened violence against the applicant or a relevant child (as defined in s 62(2)) it must attach a power of arrest to one or more provisions of the order unless satisfied that in all the circumstances of the case the applicant or child will be adequately protected without such power of arrest.[208]

The effect of this is to empower a constable to arrest without warrant a person whom he has reasonable cause of suspecting of being in breach of any such provision. The person arrested must be brought before a judge within 24 hours.[209]

---

[203] *Enfield London Borough Council v Mahoney* [1983] 2 All ER 901, [1983] 1 WLR 749, CA (refusal to deliver up the Glastonbury Cross).

[204] *Kumari v Jalal* [1996] 4 All ER 65, [1997] 1 WLR 97, CA (failure to comply with delivery order by a fixed date: committal and continued non-compliance after release).

[205] *Danchevsky v Danchevsky* [1975] Fam 17, [1974] 3 All ER 934, CA.

[206] *Burton v Winters* [1993] 3 All ER 847, CA, where the maximum sentence of two years was held to be justified; *Aubrey v Damollie* [1994] 1 FCR 131, CA.

[207] *Harris v Harris* [2002] 1 All ER 185, CA.

[208] There are restrictions to attaching a power of arrest in the case of without notice orders: s 47(3), (4), (5).

[209] Excluding Christmas Day, Good Friday, or any Sunday—Family Law Act 1996, s 47(7).

27

INJUNCTIONS II —
PRINCIPLES GOVERNING
GRANT OF INJUNCTIONS

1 INTERIM INJUNCTIONS

(a) INTRODUCTORY CONSIDERATIONS

In *American Cyanamid Co v Ethicon Ltd*[1] Lord Diplock explained the rationale of interim injunctions as follows:

When an application for an interlocutory injunction to restrain a defendant from doing acts alleged to be in violation of the plaintiff's legal right[2] is made on contested facts, the decision whether or not to grant an interlocutory injunction has to be taken at a time when ex hypothesi the existence of the right or the violation of it, or both, is uncertain and will remain uncertain until final judgment is given in the action. It was to mitigate the risk of injustice to the plaintiff during the period before that uncertainty could be resolved that the practice arose of granting him relief by way of interlocutory injunction . . . The object of the interlocutory injunction is to protect the plaintiff against injury by violation of his right for which he could not be adequately compensated in damages recoverable in the action if the uncertainty were resolved in his favour at the trial.

An interim injunction is never granted as a matter of course:[3] it is always a matter of discretion. However it is a judicial discretion and in appropriate circumstances it is a 'matter of right that upon proper terms the property shall be maintained *in statu quo* pending the trial'. As one would expect, the plaintiff has a harder task on a without

---

[1] [1975] AC 396, [1975] 1 All ER 505, HL, most recently reaffirmed in *Bath and North East Somerset DC v Mowlem plc* [2004] EWCA Civ 722, [2004] BLR 153. See (1981) 40 CLJ 307 (Christine Gray), and for a general discussion of the position in Canada (1982) 60 CBR 1 (B M Rogers and G W Hately). As to American law see (1978) 91 HLR 525 (J Leubsdorf). See also *Smith v Peters* (1875) LR 20 Eq 511, 513 cited with approval in *Astro Exito Navegacion SA v Southland Enterprise Co Ltd (No 2)* [1982] QB 1248, [1982] 3 All ER 335, CA; *Bayer AG v Winter* [1986] 1 All ER 733, CA.

[2] An injunction to restrain a defendant from presenting a winding-up petition is in a different category to which special rules apply — *Bryanston Finance Ltd v de Vries (No 2)* [1976] Ch 63, [1976] 1 All ER 25, CA.

[3] *Potter v Chapman* (1750) Amb 98. *Saunders v Smith* (1838) 3 My & Cr 711 at 728 per Cottenham LC (where an injunction was refused to restrain the sale of the first edition of Smith's Leading Cases, as being an infringement of copyright in various law reports).

notice application.[4] Claimants who seek relief without notice are under a duty to make full and frank disclosure of all the material facts. Those who fail in that duty, and those who misrepresent matters to the court, expose themselves to the very real risk of being denied interim relief whether or not they have a good arguable case or even a strong prima facie case.[5] On the other hand the rule must not be allowed itself to become an instrument of injustice, nor be carried to extreme lengths.[6] In every case the court retains a discretion to continue or to grant interim relief even if there has been non-disclosure or worse. In deciding how that discretion should be exercised the court will have regard to all the circumstances of the case, including the degree and extent of the culpability with regard to the non-disclosure or misrepresentation.[7]

The discretion is vested in the judge of first instance and accordingly on an appeal from the judge's grant or refusal of an interim injunction the function of an appellate court is not to exercise an independent discretion of its own. It must not interfere merely on the ground that the members of the appellate court would have exercised the discretion differently. It may however interfere on the ground that the judge's exercise of his discretion was based on a misunderstanding of the law or of the evidence before him, or on an inference that particular facts existed or did not exist which new evidence shows to be wrong, or that there has been a change of circumstances that would have justified the trial judge in acceding to an application to vary his order.[8]

At the hearing of an interim injunction the court does not decide finally on the rights of the parties but confines itself to the immediate object of the proceedings and so far as possible will not prejudge the case.[9] It will impose only such a restraint as may be required to stop the mischief complained of and to keep things as they are until the hearing.[10] The court has jurisdiction to make at this stage an order which would not be appropriate at the final trial.[11]

(b) UNDERTAKINGS

The Civil Procedure Rules[12] provide that on the grant of an interim injunction the claimant must enter into the 'usual undertaking' unless the court otherwise orders.[13]

---

[4] *Eothen Films Ltd v Industrial and Commercial Education—Macmillan Ltd* [1966] FSR 356, CA.

[5] *Behbehani v Salem* [1989] 2 All ER 143, [1989] 1 WLR 723n, CA; *W v H (Family Division: without notice orders)* [2001] 1 All ER 300.

[6] *Brink's—MAT Ltd v Elcombe* [1988] 3 All ER 188, [1988] 1 WLR 1350, CA.

[7] See the cases referred to in the previous two notes.

[8] *Hadmor Productions Ltd v Hamilton* [1983] 1 AC 191, [1982] 1 All ER 1042, HL, discussed (1984) 128 Sol Jo 325 (A N Khan); *The Abidin Daver* [1984] AC 398, [1984] 1 All ER 470, HL. *Bouygues Offshore SA v Caspian Shipping Co* [1998] 2 Lloyd's Rep 461, CA.

[9] *Skinners' Co v Irish Society* (1835) 1 My & Cr 162; *Preston v Luck* (1884) 27 Ch D 497, CA.

[10] *Blakemore v Glamorganshire Canal Navigation*, supra.

[11] *Fresh Fruit Wales Ltd v Halbert* (1991) *Times*, 29 January, CA.

[12] CPR PD 25.5(1). See, generally, [1994] CLJ 546 (A A S Zuckerman).

[13] If omitted in the court order by mistake it may be inserted under the 'slip rule'—CPR 40.12. However, it is the practice not to require the usual undertaking if (a) the applicant is legally aided, or, (b) the applicant is a

This applies in the Chancery and Queen's Bench Divisions, but not in the Family Division where it will be assumed that there is no undertaking as to damages unless it has been expressly given.[14] The usual undertaking requires that the claimant will abide by any order as to damages which the court may make if it should eventually turn out that he was not entitled to the interlocutory injunction and the defendant has suffered damage thereby.[15] Though the undertaking is extracted for the defendant's benefit it is in fact given to the court[16] and non-performance is accordingly a contempt of court. The court therefore retains a discretion not to enforce the undertaking if the conduct of the defendant makes it inequitable to do so;[17] but if the undertaking is enforced the measure of damages payable under it is not discretionary.

Damages, it has been said,[18] are to be assessed on the same basis as damages for breach of contract would be assessed if the undertaking had been a contract between the claimant and the defendant, that the claimant would *not* prevent the defendant from doing that which he was restrained from doing by the terms of the injunction. It has been suggested[19] that this basis may be too narrow in some cases, and that in an appropriate case the courts will have to examine the principles more closely.

Contrary to the view expressed by Jessel MR,[20] an undertaking is perfectly valid and enforceable even though the injunction was obtained by the claimant bona fide,

public authority enforcing the general law. As to lack of means of the applicant see *Bunn v British Broadcasting Corpn* [1998] 3 All ER 552. The undertaking does not extend to the costs of third parties: *Miller Brewing Co v Mersey Docks and Harbour* Co [2003] EWHC 1606 (Ch), [2004] I P & T 542, but see p 647, infra.

[14] *W v H (Family Division: without notice orders)* [2001] 1 All ER 300, where Munby J summarizes the history of the rule.

[15] Possibly exemplary damages if the injunction was obtained fraudulently or maliciously—*Smith v Day* (1882) 21 Ch D 421, per Brett LJ at 428; *Digital Equipment Corpn v Darkcrest Ltd* [1984] Ch 512, [1984] 3 All ER 381. Note that the court will not make an order as to damages until either the plaintiff has failed on the merits of the trial, or it is established before the trial that the injunction ought not to have been granted in the first instance—*Ushers Brewery Ltd v P S King & Co (Finance) Ltd* [1972] Ch 148, [1971] 2 All ER 468; *Colledge v Crossley*, supra, CA. The cross-undertaking in damages extends to all defendants in an action not just to those against whom the injunction was granted: *Dubai Bank Ltd v Galadari (No 2)* (1989) *Times*, 11 October. See also *Barratt Manchester Ltd v Bolton Metropolitan Borough Council* [1998] 1 All ER 1, CA; *A Bank v A Ltd* (2000) *Times*, 18 July. The possibility of a claim where a freezing order is made for an excessive sum is discussed in [2004] 36 Sol Jo 1081 (Z Mavrogardato).

[16] *Digital Equipment Corpn v Darkcrest Ltd*, supra; *Cheltenham and Gloucester Building Society v Ricketts* [1993] 4 All ER 276, [1993] 1 WLR 1545, CA; *Balkanbank v Taher* [1994] 4 All ER 239, 256 (where, in dismissing an appeal [1995] 2 All ER 904, [1995] 1 WLR 1056, CA, it was held that on the proper construction of a consent order providing for an inquiry as to damages, the court still retained a discretion whether to award damages at all).

[17] As to the possible courses of action where an interlocutory injunction is discharged before trial, see *Cheltenham and Gloucester Building Society v Ricketts*, supra, CA.

[18] *F Hoffman-La Roche & Co AG v Secretary of State for Trade and Industry* [1975] AC 295 at 361, [1974] 2 All ER 1128 at 1150, HL, per Lord Diplock. The undertaking remains effective even though the action is dismissed—*Ross v Buxton* [1888] WN 55, or the plaintiff discontinues his action. *Newcomen v Coulson* (1878) 7 Ch D 764. See *Tharros Shipping Co Ltd v Bias Shipping Ltd* [1994] 1 Lloyd's Rep 577.

[19] *R v Medicines Control Agency, ex p Smith & Nephew Pharmaceuticals Ltd* [1999] RPC 705, per Jacob J at 714, 715.

[20] In *Smith v Day* (1882) 21 Ch D 421, CA, where the history of undertakings is discussed.

without any misrepresentation, suppression of the facts, or other default on his part.[21] It makes no difference whether in granting the injunction the judge made an error of law or of fact.[22] The court has technically no power to compel the claimant to enter into an undertaking, but it has power in practice since it can indicate that an injunction will be refused unless the undertaking is given.[23]

It is not unusual, on an application for an injunction, for no injunction to be granted but for the defendant to offer and the claimant to accept an undertaking by the defendant in terms similar to those claimed in the injunction.[24] In such cases a cross-undertaking in damages, similar to the usual undertaking above mentioned, will automatically be inserted in the order, unless the contrary is expressly agreed at the time.[25]

Where an injunction is granted on the usual undertaking, the court may, if it doubts the claimant's ability to pay any damages that may be ordered under the undertaking, make the injunction conditional on the claimant's depositing a specified sum of money with the parties' solicitors,[26] or giving security to the satisfaction of the court.[27]

Likewise the court may require the defendant to enter into an undertaking as a condition of refusing an injunction: thus the defendant, in appropriate circumstances, may be required to undertake to keep an account to assist the court, should the claimant succeed at the trial, in ascertaining what damage he has suffered in the meantime.[28]

Finally, special mention should be made of the position where an injunction is sought by the Attorney-General on behalf of the Crown. In general when the Crown applies for an interim injunction in an action brought against a subject to enforce or protect its proprietary or contractual rights, it should be put on the same terms as a subject as respects the usual undertakings as to damages.[29] There is, however, a kind of action by the Crown which has no counterpart in ordinary litigation between subject and subject. This has been called a 'law enforcement action', in which civil proceedings are brought by the Crown to restrain a subject from breaking a law where the breach is harmful to the public or some section of it, but does not necessarily effect any proprietary or contractual rights of the Crown. The action is brought by the

---

[21] *Griffith v Blake* (1884) 27 Ch D 474, CA. [22] *Hunt v Hunt* (1884) 54 LJ Ch 289.

[23] See eg *F Hoffman-La Roche & Co A-G v Secretary of State for Trade and Industry* [1975] AC 295 at 361, [1974] 2 All ER 1128 at 1150, HL, per Lord Diplock. The undertaking is nonetheless regarded as voluntary, and a party is not normally entitled to appeal against it: *Secretary of State for Trade and Industry v Bell Davis Trading Ltd* [2004] EWCA Civ 1066, [2005] 1 BCLC 516 (an exceptional case where an appeal was allowed).

[24] But if the defendant wishes to appeal, an injunction, not an undertaking, is appropriate—*McConnell v McConnell* (1981) 131 NLJ 116. It was pointed out in *London and Manchester Assurance Co Ltd v O and H Construction Ltd* [1989] 2 EGLR 185 that an undertaking is just as binding and even more effective than an order, because it does not need service and a penal notice endorsed on it in order to bite. See *Gantenbrink v BBC* [1995] FSR 162.

[25] *Practice Note* [1904] WN 203; *Oberrheinische Metallwerke GmbH v Cocks* [1906] WN 127; *W v H (Family Division: without notice orders)* [2001] 1 All ER 300.

[26] *Baxter v Claydon* [1952] WN 376.

[27] *Harman Pictures N V v Osbourne* [1967] 2 All ER 324, [1967] 1 WLR 723.

[28] *Mitchell v Henry* (1880) 15 Ch D 181, CA; *Holophane Ltd v Berend & Co Ltd* (1897) 15 RPC 18. See also *Wall v London and Northern Assets Corpn* [1898] 2 Ch 469, CA; *Wright v Hennessey* (1894) 11 TLR 14, DC.

[29] See *F Hoffman-La Roche and Co A-G v Secretary of State for Trade and Industry* [1975] AC 295, [1974] 2 All ER 1128, HL.

Attorney-General, as guardian of the public interest, who may sue ex officio or under the relator procedure. Under this latter procedure a member of the public, known as the relator, may seek the Attorney-General's consent to the institution of proceedings in which the Attorney-General is the nominal claimant. If the Attorney-General gives his consent, the relator becomes responsible for the conduct of the proceedings and is liable for the costs, and, if an interim injunction is sought, the relator will be called upon to give the usual undertaking.

Where, however, the Attorney-General sues ex officio, the court will consider the propriety of requiring such an undertaking in the light of the particular circumstances of the case. It seems that an undertaking is unlikely to be thought proper where the Attorney-General is proceeding directly under a statute which provides expressly that compliance with some provision of the Act shall be enforceable by civil proceedings by the Crown for an injunction. This was the position in *F Hoffman-La Roche & Co A-G v Secretary of State for Trade and Industry*,[30] where the interim injunction was granted without any undertaking being given. A similar view has been taken in relation to a law enforcement action by a local authority under s 222 of the Local Government Act 1972,[31] an application by the Director-General of Fair Trading for an interim injunction to restrain the publication of misleading advertisements,[32] and an application by the Securities and Investments Board for interim injunctions under the Financial Services Act 1986, including a worldwide freezing injunction.[33]

Analogous to a law-enforcement action is an action by the Attorney-General in the exercise of the Crown's power to act as protector of charity. In such an action the Crown is not asserting any proprietary or contractual claim of its own and it is not therefore a case in which the cross-undertaking will be demanded as of course. However, in *A-G v Wright*[34] the Crown was asserting proprietary rights on behalf of the charity and was seeking to recover property alleged to belong to or to be owed to the charity. It was thought right to protect the interests of the defendant by a cross-undertaking limited to the funds of the charity.

(c) THE APPROACH OF THE COURTS

Until *American Cyanamid Co v Ethicon Ltd*[35] it was the accepted rule that in order to get an interim injunction, the claimant must first make out a prima facie case. In that

---

[30] Supra, HL. Contrast *Customs and Excise Comrs v Anchor Foods Ltd* [1999] 3 All ER 268 where, on the unusual facts of the case, a cross-undertaking was required.

[31] *Kirklees Metropolitan Borough Council v Wickes Building Supplies Ltd* [1993] AC 227, [1992] 3 All ER 717, HL, discussed (1992) 136 Sol Jo 1084 (Ruth Galinsky); *Chisholm v Kirklees Metropolitan Borough Council* [1993] ICR 826.

[32] *Director General of Fair Trading v Tobyward Ltd* [1989] 2 All ER 266, [1989] 1 WLR 517; *Re Agreement between Members of the Institute of Insurance Brokers* [1991] ICR 822.

[33] *Securities and Investment Board v Lloyd-Wright* [1993] 4 All ER 210. As to a worldwide freezing injunction see p 650 et seq, infra.

[34] [1987] 3 All ER 579.

[35] [1975] AC 396, [1975] 1 All ER 504, HL. See (1975) 91 LQR 168 (Peter Prescott); (1975) 38 MLR 672 (A Gore); (1976) 35 CLJ 82 (P Wallington); (1980) 30 UTLJ 240 (R Grant Hammond).

case Lord Diplock, in a speech with which all the other Law Lords agreed, appeared to have laid down that there is no such rule. The court must be satisfied that the claim is not 'frivolous or vexatious'; in other words, that there is 'a serious question to be tried', or 'a real prospect of succeeding in his claim to a permanent injunction at the trial'.[36] But unless the material available to the court at the hearing of the application fails to disclose that the claimant has any real prospect of succeeding in his claim for a permanent injunction at the trial, the court should at once proceed to consider whether the balance of convenience lies in favour of granting or refusing the interim relief that is sought.[37]

Shortly afterwards, in two cases in the Court of Appeal, *Fellowes & Son v Fisher*[38] and *Hubbard v Pit*[39] it was noted that the previous House of Lords decision of *J T Stratford & Son v Lindley*[40] had not been cited to the House in the *American Cyanamid* case. There all the members of the House of Lords had expressed the view that a claimant was not entitled to an interim injunction unless he established a prima facie case. Notwithstanding this the Court of Appeal in the two cases cited agreed that the *American Cyanamid* case had laid down an entirely different approach to be followed in connection with interim relief from that which had hitherto been habitually applied, and accepted that the principles stated by Lord Diplock in the *American Cyanamid Case* must be followed even on the assumption that the two House of Lords decisions were in conflict. It was the more recent decision, and the point was not argued in the earlier case.

In *Series 5 Software v Clarke*[41] Laddie J has sought to reinterpret the decision. He stresses the discretionary nature of the jurisdiction to grant an interim injunction and the absence of fixed rules. The view of the court as to the relative strength of the parties' cases is in his opinion a major factor to take into account. Laddie J found it difficult to accept that Lord Diplock had performed a volte face within four months, because in *F Hoffman-La Roche & Co A-G v Secretary of State for Trade and Industry*[42] he had said that the claimant must first satisfy the court that there was a strong prima facie case. On the other hand, though he referred to *NWL Ltd v Woods*,[43] decided after the change of approach had been highlighted by the two Court of Appeal cases cited above, he did not quote Lord Diplock's statement in that case that the *American Cyanamid* case 'enjoins the judge on an application for an interim injunction to direct his attention to the balance of convenience as soon as he has satisfied himself that there is a serious question to be tried', which seems consistent with the interpretation of the *American Cyanamid* case in the Court of Appeal decisions mentioned, to which

---

[36] In *Mothercare Ltd v Robson Books Ltd* [1979] FSR 466 Megarry V-C pointed out that this phrase could give rise to misunderstanding. All that has to be seen is whether the claimant has prospects of success which, in substance and reality, exist.

[37] The court was not satisfied in *John Hayter Motor Underwriting Agencies Ltd v R B H S Agencies Ltd* [1977] 2 Lloyd's Rep 105, CA; but was in *Losinka v Civil and Public Services Association* [1976] ICR 473, CA.

[38] [1976] QB 122, [1975] 2 All ER 829, CA.   [39] [1976] QB 142, [1975] 3 All ER 1, CA.

[40] [1965] AC 269, [1964] 3 All ER 102, HL.   [41] [1996] 1 All ER 853.

[42] [1975] AC 295, [1974] 2 All ER 1128, HL.   [43] [1979] 3 All ER 614, [1979] 1 WLR 1294, HL.

Laddie J did not refer. Laddie J has adhered to his view in subsequent cases,[44] and his approach has received the support of Robert Walker LJ.[45] In *Rilett v Greet and Greet*[46] Park J referred to the judgment of Laddie J as 'thought-provoking', but applied the *American Cyanamid* principles: on appeal[47] it was argued that the judge below should have complied with *Series 5* guidelines to which Chadwick LJ responded that the judge was not at liberty to disregard the well-settled approach founded on *American Cyanamid*. It is far from clear that the reinterpretation will prevail and it seems appropriate, therefore, to consider the traditional approach.

It has been observed[48] that the principles laid down in the *American Cyanamid* case[49] apply even though the life of the injunction may be brief and the decision on the application for an interim injunction may influence future proceedings. The principles are not, however, applicable where it is clear that if an injunction were granted to the claimants they would not pursue their claim to trial. They apply in cases, such as the *American Cyanamid* case itself, where the application for the interim injunction is merely a holding operation pending a contemplated trial. If the grant of an injunction would have the effect of putting an end to the action the court should approach the case on the broad principle: what can the court do in its best endeavour to avoid injustice?[50] On this basis an interim injunction was granted in *Dyno-Rod v Reeve*[51] in respect of a restrictive covenant in a franchising agreement although the action could not be tried before all or a substantial proportion of the period of restraint had expired.

(d) THE PRINCIPLES LAID DOWN IN THE *AMERICAN CYANAMID* CASE

Lord Goff has pointed out[52] that in many cases the court will be able to decide the application on the basis of the first two principles (the first stage). It is only where there is doubt as to the adequacy of either or both of the respective remedies in damages that the court proceeds to the second stage, the balance of convenience. In any event it has been made clear that the House in the *American Cyanamid* case[53] did not intend to lay down rigid rules, and indeed the principles themselves contain flexible words such as 'normally'. As was reaffirmed by Lord Goff in *Factortame Ltd v Secretary of State for Transport (No 2)*,[54] they are guidelines rather than rules.

---

[44] See eg *Barclays Bank plc v RBS Advanta* [1996] RPC 307 and *Antec International Ltd v South Western Chicks (Warren) Ltd* [1997] FSR 278.

[45] See eg *Barnsley Brewery Co Ltd v RBNB* [1997] FSR 462; *SIG Architectural Products Ltd v Castle House Windows Ltd* (1996) unrep but referred to in [1997] JBL 486

[46] [1999] BPIR 145.   [47] Unrep (1999) 11 March, but available on Lexis.

[48] *Budget Rent A Car International Inc v Mamos Slough Ltd* (1977) 121 Sol Jo 374, CA, per Geoffrey Lane LJ.

[49] Supra, HL. See (2004) 23 CJQ 132 (A Keay).

[50] *Cayne v Global Natural Resources plc* [1984] 1 All ER 225, CA.   [51] [1999] FSR 148.

[52] In *Factortame Ltd v Secretary of State for Transport (No 2)* [1991] 1 All ER 70 at 118, HL.

[53] Supra, HL. See [2004] 23 CJQ 132 (A Keay).

[54] Supra, at 118, HL; *Fellowes & Son v Fisher* [1976] QB 122 at 139, [1975] 2 All ER 829 at 841, per Browne LJ; *Cayne v Global Natural Resources plc* [1984] 1 All ER 225, CA; *Cambridge Nutrition Ltd v BBC* [1990] 3 All ER 523, CA.

The principles are as follows:

(i)   'The governing principle is that the court should first consider whether if the plaintiff were to succeed at the trial in establishing his right to a permanent injunction he would be adequately compensated by an award of damages for the loss he would have sustained as a result of the defendant's continuing to do what was sought to be enjoined between the time of the application and the time of the trial. If damages in the measure recoverable at common law would be an adequate remedy and the defendant would be in a financial position to pay them,[55] no interlocutory injunction should normally be granted, however strong the plaintiff's claim appeared to be at that stage.'[56] This is in effect a restatement of the established rule that a claimant should not be granted an interim injunction unless he is able to show that if it was not granted, he would suffer irreparable damage,[57] that is, 'the damage must be substantial and one which could not be adequately remedied by a pecuniary payment'.[58] Illustrations of irreparable damage in the cases include *Express Newspapers Ltd v Keys*[59] where the defendant trade union proposed unlawfully to induce the claimant's employees to break their contracts by participating in a political strike. The claimant did not want money but wanted its newspaper published, and would find it difficult to prove its loss; and *Hubbard v Pitt*,[60] where the defendants were picketing the claimant's premises and there was a real prospect that if it continued it would seriously interfere with the claimant's business and that damages would be an inadequate remedy, even if the defendants could pay damages.

(ii) On the other hand, Lord Diplock continued, if damages 'would not provide an adequate remedy for the plaintiff in the event of his succeeding at the trial, the court should then consider whether, on the contrary hypothesis that the defendant were to succeed at the trial in establishing his right to do that which was sought to be enjoined, he would be adequately compensated under the plaintiff's undertaking as to damages for the loss he would have sustained by being prevented from doing so between the time of the application and the time of the trial. If damages in the measure recoverable under such an undertaking would be an adequate remedy and the plaintiff would be in a financial position to pay them, there would be no reason on this ground to refuse an

---

[55] Damages can only be an adequate remedy if the defendants will be good for the money: *Dyrlund-Smith A/S v Turberville Smith Ltd* [1998] FSR 774, CA.

[56] Applied in *Polaroid Corpn v Eastman Kodak Co* [1977] RPC 379, CA.

[57] *Johnson v Shrewsbury and Birmingham Rly Co* (1853) 3 De GM & G 914. See (1989) 68 CBR 538 (P M Perell).

[58] *Litchfield-Speer v Queen Anne's Gate Syndicate (No 2) Ltd* [1919] 1 Ch 407 at 411, per P O Lawrence J; *Pinchin v London and Blackwall Rly Co* (1854) 5 De GM & G 851.

[59] [1980] IRLR 247.

[60] [1976] QB 142, [1975] 3 All ER 1, CA. See also *A-G v Guardian Newspapers Ltd* [1987] 3 All ER 316, [1987] 1 WLR 1248, HL (the 'Spycatcher' case).

interlocutory injunction.' Accordingly an injunction was granted in *Chancellor, Masters and Scholars of Oxford University v Pergamon Press Ltd*[61] to restrain the defendants from passing off Pergamon's Dictionary of Perfect Spelling as and for one of the claimant's dictionaries by the use in the title of the word 'Oxford' in conjunction with the word 'dictionary'. The claimant would otherwise suffer very great but unascertainable damage and the defendants would be amply covered by the claimant's undertaking.

(iii) 'It is where there is doubt as to the adequacy of the respective remedies in damages available to either party or both, that the question of balance of convenience arises.' The matters that will have to be considered, and their relative weight, will vary from case to case, and have been said to include the nature of the injunction that is being sought.[62] Though the phrase 'balance of convenience' is one commonly used, Donaldson MR has referred[63] to it as 'an unfortunate expression', saying the business of the court is justice not convenience. Making a similar point May LJ observed[64] that the 'balance of the risk of doing an injustice' better describes the process involved.

(iv) 'Where other factors appear to be evenly balanced it is a counsel of prudence to take such measures as are calculated to preserve the status quo', that is, the state of affairs existing during the period immediately preceding the issue of the writ claiming the permanent injunction.[65] It will clearly cause less inconvenience to stop the defendant temporarily from doing something he has not done before, than to interrupt him in the conduct of an established enterprise.

(v) In many cases the unsuccessful party on the application for an interim injunction, if ultimately successful at the trial, will have suffered some disadvantage for which he will not be fully compensated by damages. 'The extent to which the disadvantages to each party would be incapable of being compensated in damages in the event of his succeeding at the trial is always a significant factor in assessing where the balance of convenience lies.'

(vi) 'If the extent of the uncompensatable disadvantages to each party would not differ widely, it may not be improper to take into account in tipping the balance the relative strength of each party's case as revealed by the affidavit evidence adduced on the hearing of the application. This, however, should be done only where it is apparent on the facts disclosed by evidence as to which there is no credible dispute that the strength of one party's case is

---

61 (1977) 121 Sol Jo 758, CA.

62 *Potters-Ballotini Ltd v Weston-Baker* [1977] RPC 202 at 209, CA, per Scarman LJ.

63 *Francome v Mirror Group Newspapers Ltd* [1984] 2 All ER 408, CA.

64 In *Cayne v Global Natural Resources plc*, supra, CA, echoed by Lord Jauncey in *Factortame Ltd v Secretary of State for Transport (No 2)* [1991] 1 All ER 70 at 128, HL and reaffirmed *Fleming Fabrications v Albion Cylinders Ltd* [1989] RPC 47, CA.

65 *Garden Cottage Foods Ltd v Milk Marketing Board* [1983] 2 All ER 770 at 774, 775, HL.

disproportionate to that of the other party.' This seems to mean that the relative strength of each party's case is the last factor to be taken into consideration, instead of being, as was thought in the past, the first.

In *Fellowes & Son v Fisher*[66] this last proposition was thought to cause some difficulty by both Browne LJ and Sir John Pennycuick. Thus Browne LJ observed:[67] 'I cannot see how the "balance of convenience" can be fairly or reasonably considered without taking *some* account as *a* factor of the relative strength of the parties' cases, but the House of Lords seems to have held that this is only the last resort.' And Sir John Pennycuick felt[68] there would be difficulty in disregarding the prospect of success where this is a matter within the competence of a judge, in particular in cases depending in whole or in great part on the construction of a written instrument. He was also concerned about cases where immediate judicial interference is essential, for example trespass, or the internal affairs of a company, where the court cannot do justice without to some extent considering the probable upshot of the action if it ever came to be fought out. And it has also been said that in matters involving trade restrictions, where the decision on the application, whichever way it goes, profoundly affects the rights of the parties in a way which cannot easily be undone if at the trial a different result is reached, it is necessary to consider rather more than in the usual case the strength of the plaintiff's case in law.[69]

Lord Diplock himself added a gloss to his *American Cyanamid* speech in *N W L Ltd v Woods*[70] when he observed that there was nothing in the earlier decision to suggest that in considering whether or not to grant an interim injunction the judge ought not to give full weight to all the practical realities of the situation to which the injunction will apply. He pointed out that in the *American Cyanamid* case the court was not dealing with a case in which the grant or refusal of an injunction at that stage would, in effect, dispose of the action finally in favour of whichever party was successful in the application. In such a case, where the harm that will have already been caused to the losing party by the grant or refusal of the injunction is complete and a kind for which money cannot constitute any worthwhile recompense, the degree of likelihood that the claimant would have succeeded in establishing his right to an injunction if the action had gone to trial is a factor to be brought into the balance by the judge in

---

[66] [1976] QB 122, [1975] 2 All ER 829, CA.   [67] *Fellowes v Fisher*, supra, at 138, 841, CA.

[68] Ibid, at 141, 843, 834, CA.

[69] *Athletes Foot Marketing Associates Inc v Cobra Sports Ltd* [1980] RPC 343 at 348, 349, per Walton J.

[70] [1979] 3 All ER 614 at 625, 626; *Cambridge Nutrition Ltd v BBC* [1990] 3 All ER 523, CA (injunction refused: chances of success to be taken into account in cases concerning the right to publish an article, or to transmit a broadcast, whose importance may be transitory but whose impact depends on timing, news value and topicality); *Lansing Linde Ltd v Kerr* [1991] 1 All ER 418, [1991] 1 WLR 251, CA (covenant in restraint of trade where neither party would be adequately compensated by damages: judge rightly took into account strength of claimant's claim where trial could not take place until period of restraint had almost expired); *Entec (Pollution Control) Ltd v Abacus Mouldings* [1992] FSR 332, CA (injunction refused: granting it likely to put defendants out of business: witholding it unlikely to cause claimants very substantial damage); *Douglas v Hello! Ltd* [2001] 2 All ER 289, CA, noted (2001) 60 CLJ 231 (M Elliott). See (1991) 107 LQR 196 (A A S Zuckerman).

weighing the risks that injustice may result from his deciding the application one way rather than the other.

(vii) 'In addition ... there may be many other special factors to be taken into consideration in the particular circumstances of individual cases.' There was a special factor in the *American Cyanamid* case,[71] where an interim injunction was sought for the infringement of a patent relating to a pharmaceutical product. This was that, once doctors and patients had got used to the defendant's product in the period prior to the trial, it might well be commercially impractical for the claimant to deprive the public of it by insisting on a permanent injunction at the trial, owing to the damaging effect which this would have on its goodwill in a specialized market and thus on the sale of its other pharmaceutical products.

(e) DECISIONS ON SPECIAL FACTORS

It is not yet clear how the 'special factors' principle will develop, though it is submitted that it is doubtful whether it will be used so as to emasculate the first six principles, as in effect suggested by Lord Denning MR in *Fellowe & Son v Fisher*.[72] In particular Lord Denning's view in that case that covenants in restraint of trade are in a special category has been held to be mistaken.[73]

(i) In *Bryanston Finance Ltd v de Vries (No 2)*[74] the claimant sought an interim injunction to restrain the bringing of a winding-up petition. Buckley LJ said it was 'a special factor' that the injunction sought was designed to prevent the commencement of proceedings in limine. The other two judges in the Court of Appeal reached the same result on the ground that the principles of the *American Cyanamid* case were not concerned with such a case, but only with applications seeking interim relief pending determination of the rights of the parties at the hearing of the action.

(ii) The impact of the public interest is a special factor in cases in which a public authority is seeking to enforce the law against some person and either the authority seeks an interim injunction to restrain that person from acting contrary to the law, and that person claims that no injunction should be granted on the ground that the relevant law is, for some reason, invalid, or that other person seeks an interim injunction to restrain the action of the authority

---

[71] Supra, HL. Cf *Walker v Standard Chartered Bank plc* [1992] BCLC 535, CA.

[72] [1976] QB 122 at 133, 134, [1975] 2 All ER 829 at 836, 837, CA, but see *Hubbard v Pitt* [1976] QB 142 at 185, [1975] 3 All ER 1 at 16, CA, per Stamp LJ.

[73] *Lawrence David Ltd v Ashton* [1991] 1 All ER 385, CA. But see (1989) 133 Sol Jo 232 (M Jefferson) where unreported cases to the contrary are referred to.

[74] [1976] Ch 63, [1976] 1 All ER 25, CA. See also *Dunford and Elliot Ltd v Johnson and Firth Brown Ltd* [1977] 1 Lloyd's Rep 505, CA (injunction to stop takeover bid refused, Lord Denning MR found 'special factors': Roskill and Lawton LJJ reached the same result on other grounds.

on the same ground. As a general rule the problem cannot be solved at the first stage[75] and it will be necessary to proceed to the second stage, concerned with the balance of convenience. In cases in which a party is a public authority performing duties to the public, Lord Goff, in *Factortame Ltd v Secretary of State for Transport (No 2)*[76] agreed with Brown LJ in *Smith v Inner London Education Authority*[77] that the interests of the public in general to whom those duties are owed constitute a special factor. The court should not restrain a public authority by interim injunction from enforcing an apparently authentic law unless it is satisfied, having regard to all the circumstances, that the challenge to the validity of the law is, prima facie, so firmly based as to justify so exceptional a course being taken.[78]

(iii) Prior to the *American Cyanamid* case the court would not normally restrain a defendant in a libel action who said he was going to justify,[79] nor a defendant in a copyright action who had a reasonable defence of fair dealing; nor a defendant in an action for breach of confidence who had a reasonable defence of public interest. The reason in all those cases was that the defendant, if he was right, was entitled to publish, and the law is reluctant to intervene to suppress freedom of speech.[80]

In cases where the grant of relief might affect the exercise of the right to freedom of expression under Article 10 of the European Convention for the

---

[75] See *Factortame Ltd v Secretary of State for Transport (No 2)* [1991] 1 All ER 70 at 118, 119, HL, per Lord Goff and p 600, supra. The difficulties at the first stage are that the usual undertaking in damages is not normally imposed on the Crown: see p 598, supra; there is no general right to indemnity by reason of damage suffered through invalid administrative action: see *Bourgoin SA v Ministry of Agriculture, Fisheries and Food* [1986] QB 716, [1985] 3 All ER 585, CA; an authority acting in the public interest cannot normally be protected by a remedy in damages because it will itself have suffered none.

[76] Supra, HL, applied *Belize Alliance of Conservation Non-Governmental Organisations v Department of the Environment of Belize* (2003) UKPC 63, [2004] P & CR 13.

[77] [1978] 1 All ER 411 at 422, CA. See *Express Newspapers Ltd v Keys* [1980] IRLR 247. See also *Lewis v Heffer* [1978] 3 All ER 354, [1978] 1 WLR 1061, CA. (Rules not applicable in a political context where no question of quantifying anyone's loss in terms of cash.)

[78] An interim injunction was granted in *Factortame Ltd v Secretary of State for Transport (No 2)*, supra, HL, where English legislation was held to contravene Community law. See (1991) 107 LQR 1, 4 (H W R Wade). See also *R v Secretary of State for Health, ex p Imperial Tobacco Ltd* [2000] 1 All ER 572, CA where it was held that where a party sought an injunction restraining the government from implementing a Community measure pending a challenge to its validity, the court is required to apply the principles governing interim relief to be found in the Community jurisprudence.

[79] *Bonnard v Perryman* [1891] 2 Ch 269, CA. Though there are exceptions, eg where the statement is obviously untrue and defamatory: *Al-Fayed v Observer* Ltd (1986) *Times*, 14 July, neither the defendant's motive nor the manner in which he threatens publication nor the potential damage to the claimant is normally a basis for making an exception: *Holley v Smyth* [1998] QB 726, [1998] 1 All ER 853, CA. An injunction will not be granted even in relation to allegations which cannot be proved if they are inseparable from other allegations the common sting of which the defendant intends to justify—*Khashoggi v IPC Magazines Ltd* [1986] 3 All ER 577, [1986] 1 WLR 1412, CA.

[80] *Hubbard v Vosper* [1972] 2 QB 84, [1972] 1 All ER 1023, CA. In particular an injunction will not be granted to restrain political controversy—*Kennard v Lewis* [1983] FSR 346. See per Laws J in *R v Advertising Standards Authority, ex p Vernons Organisation Ltd* [1993] 2 All ER 202, [1992] 1 WLR 1289, at 205, 1293.

Protection of Human Rights and Fundamental Freedoms[81] the Human Rights Act 1998, s 12(3) provides that an interim injunction should not be granted 'so as to restrain publication before trial unless the court is satisfied that the applicant is likely to establish that publication should not be allowed'.

In *Cream Holdings Ltd v Banerjee*[82] it was said that the intention of Parliament must be taken to be that 'likely' should have an extended meaning setting as the normal prerequisite to the grant of an injunction before trial a likelihood of success at the trial higher than the *American Cyanamid*[83] standard of 'real prospect', but permitting the court to dispense with this higher standard where particular circumstances make this necessary. The effect of the section is that the court should not make an interim restraint order unless satisfied the applicant's prospects of success at the trial are sufficiently favourable to justify such an order being made in the particular circumstances of the case. As to what degree of likelihood makes the prospects of success 'sufficiently favourable', the general approach should be that courts should be exceedingly slow to make interim restraint orders where the applicant has not satisfied the court that he will probably ('more likely than not') succeed at the trial. But in some circumstances a lesser degree of likelihood will suffice as a prerequisite, for instance where the potential adverse consequences of disclosure are particularly grave, or where a short-lived injunction is needed to enable the court to hear and give proper consideration to an application for interim relief pending the trial or any relevant appeal.

Cream Holdings Ltd v Banerjee,[84] which involved a claim for breach of confidence, was distinguished in *Greene v Associated Newspapers Ltd*,[85] where it was held that the 1998 Act had not affected the rule in *Bonnard v Perryman*[86] that, in a claim for defamation where the defendant maintains that he intends to justify the alleged libel, a claimant will not obtain an interim injunction to restrain publication unless it is clear that the plea of justification is bound to fail.

(iv) In *Hubbard v Pitt*[87] Stamp LJ said[88] that it was not necessary to consider to what extent the *American Cyanamid* case is applicable where there is no relevant conflict of evidence and no difficult question of law. Previously the claimant was regarded almost as having a right to an injunction where there was a plain and uncontested breach of a clear covenant not to do a particular thing,[89]

---

[81] Incorporated into English law by the Human Rights Act 1998. The Convention is to be found in Sch 1. See chapter 28, section 6, infra. See also *London Regional Transport v Mayor of London* [2001] EWCA Civ 1491, [2003] EMLR 66, per Sedley LJ.

[82] [2004] UKHL 44, [2004] 4 All ER 617, noted [2005] CLJ 4 (A T H Smith); [2005] CJQ 194 (P Devonshire).

[83] [1975] AC 396, [1975] 1 All ER 504, HL. See p 598 et seq, supra.   [84] Supra, HL.

[85] [2004] EWCA Civ 1462, [2005] 1 All ER 30, and in *Coys v Autocherish Ltd* [2004] EWHC 1334 (QB), [2004] EMLR 482.

[86] Supra, CA.   [87] [1976] QB 142, [1975] 3 All ER 1, CA.

[88] At 185, 16, CA. See also *Newsweek Inc v BBC* [1979] RPC 441, CA.

[89] *Hampstead and Suburban Properties Ltd v Diomedous* [1969] 1 Ch 248, [1968] 3 All ER 545, applying the rule in *Doherty v Allman* (1878) 3 App Cas 709, which undoubtedly applies to perpetual injunctions—see

or where there was an admitted trespass even though it might do no harm to the claimant.[90] This seems to have been the view of the Court of Appeal in *Office Overload Ltd v Gunn*,[91] *Patel v W H Smith (Eziot) Ltd*[92] and *Lawrence David Ltd v Ashon*,[93] since the *American Cyanamid* case. In such cases there is no serious question to be tried. Further, in the most recent cases it has been held that if it is clear that the defendant is acting unlawfully an injunction should normally be granted.[94]

(v) The approach called for by the *American Cyanamid* case has, as such, no application to the grant or refusal of freezing injunctions[95] which proceed on principles which are quite different from those applicable to other interim injunctions.[96]

(vi) Letter of credit cases are special cases within the *American Cyanamid* guidelines because of the special factors which apply in such cases, or, perhaps, they fall outside the guidelines altogether.[97]

(f) INTERIM MANDATORY INJUNCTIONS

The principles laid down in the *American Cyanamid* case are not really relevant to interim mandatory, as contrasted with prohibitory, injunctions. The Court of Appeal has approved the observations of Megarry J in *Shepherd Homes Ltd v Sandham*,[98] that at this stage the case has to be unusually strong and clear before a mandatory

infra p 619. The rule was applied post-*Cyanamid* by Nourse LJ in *A-G v Barker* [1990] 3 All ER 257, CA, though it was not referred to by the other members of the court. See *McDonald's Restaurants of Canada Ltd v West Edmonton Mall Ltd* (1994) 22 Alta LR (3rd) 402.

[90] *Patel v W H Smith (Eziot) Ltd* [1987] 2 All ER 569, CA; *Woollerton and Wilson Ltd v Richard Costain Ltd* [1970] 1 All ER 483. The suspension of the operation of the injunction in this last case, so as virtually to nullify its effect, was criticized in (1970) 33 MLR 552 (G Dworkin), and opinion on the correctness of the decision reserved by CA in *Charrington v Simons & Co Ltd* [1971] 2 All ER 588 at 592. It was not followed on this point in *John Trenberth Ltd v National Westminster Bank Ltd* (1979) 39 P & CR 104 noted [1980] Conv 308 (H Street) or in *Anchor Brewhouse Developments Ltd v Berkeley House (Docklands Developments) Ltd* [1987] 2 EGLR 173. See (1988) 138 NLJ 23 (E McKendrick); (1988) 138 NLJ 385 (H W Wilkinson).

[91] [1977] FSR 39, CA.   [92] [1987] 2 All ER 569, CA.

[93] [1991] 1 All ER 385, CA. Some other cases suggest that the court retains a larger discretion: *Texaco Ltd v Mulberry Filling Station Ltd* [1972] 1 All ER 513, [1972] 1 WLR 814; *Harlow Development Corpn v Cox Bros (Butchers) Ltd* (1975) 233 Estates Gazette 765.

[94] *Express Newspapers Ltd v Keys* [1980] IRLR 247; *Ekland v Scripglow Ltd* [1982] FSR 431 (clear non-compliance with Performers' Protection Act 1963 (repealed)). See also *Redler Grain Silos Ltd v BICC Ltd* [1982] 1 Lloyd's Rep 435, CA.

[95] See p 640 et seq, infra.

[96] *Polly Peck International plc v Nadir (No 2)* [1992] 4 All ER 769 at 786, CA, per Lord Donaldson MR. Note that where there is a proprietary claim a freezing injunction is not appropriate but an interim injunction may be granted restraining the disposal of property over which the claimant has a proprietary claim. In this case the approach prescribed by the *American Cyanamid* case should be followed: ibid, and see (1992) 108 LQR 559 (A A S Zuckerman).

[97] See *Deutsche Ruckversicherung AG v Walbrook Insurance Co Ltd* [1996] 1 All ER 791, CA.

[98] [1971] Ch 340, [1970] 3 All ER 402; *Leisure Data v Bell* [1988] FSR 367, CA; *Zockall Group Ltd v Mercury Communications Ltd* [1998] ESR 354, CA.

injunction will be granted,[99] and has said that these observations are unaffected by the *American Cyanamid* case. Thus in *De Falco v Crawley Borough Council*[100] Bridge LJ said that the principles of the *American Cyanamid* case had no relevance to a claim for a mandatory injunction ordering a local authority to provide accommodation for the plaintiffs under the Housing (Homeless Persons) Act 1977.[101]

In relation to industrial disputes, Geoffrey Lane LJ, in *Harold Stephen & Co Ltd v Post Office*,[102] observed: 'It can only be in very rare circumstances and in the most extreme circumstances that this court should interfere by way of mandatory injunction in the delicate mechanism of industrial disputes and industrial negotiations.' However it should be noted that interim prohibitory injunctions were granted in *Thomas v National Union of Mineworkers (South Wales Area)*[103] to working miners who were being unreasonably harassed, in exercise of their right to use the highway for the purpose of entering and leaving their place of work, by the presence and behaviour of pickets and demonstrators.

(g) DELAY AND ACQUIESCENCE

Delay or laches, and, *a fortiori*, acquiescence by the claimant in the infringement of his rights may disentitle him to an interim injunction,[104] particularly if the defendant has incurred expenditure in the meantime. The meaning of acquiescence has been discussed in a number of cases.[105] it involves a knowledge by the claimant of his rights infringed by the defendant,[106] and an encouragement or even merely passive inaction by the claimant on the strength of which the defendant has expended money or

---

[99] A recent clear case where a mandatory injunction was granted is *London and Manchester Assurance Co Ltd v O and H Construction Ltd* [1989] 2 EGLR 185. But even where the court is unable to feel any high degree of assurance that the claimant will establish his right, it may yet be appropriate to grant the mandatory injunction where the risk of injustice if the injunction is refused sufficiently outweighs the risk of injustice if it is granted: *Nottingham Building Society v Eurodynamics Systems plc* [1993] FSR 468; *Psychometric Services Ltd v Merant International Ltd* [2002] FSR 147. '[t]he merits threshold is a flexible one', per Lawrence Collins J in *Edwin Shirley Productions Ltd v Workspace Management Ltd* [2001] 2 EGLR 16.

[100] [1980] QB 460, [1980] 1 All ER 913, CA, applied *R v Kensington and Chelsea Royal London Borough Council, ex p Hammell* [1989] QB 518, [1989] 1 All ER 1202, CA.

[101] Now repealed and replaced by ss 58–78, Housing Act 1985.

[102] [1978] 1 All ER 939 at 944, CA, applied *Meade v London Borough of Haringey* [1979] 2 All ER 1016 at 1034, CA, per Sir Stanley Rees. See (1979) 38 CLJ 228 (John Griffiths). But the *American Cyanamid* principles should normally be applied in the ordinary way in trade union discipline and expulsion cases—*Porter v National Union of Journalists* [1980] IRLR 404, HL; see (1981) 97 LQR 214 (D Newell).

[103] [1986] Ch 20, [1985] 2 All ER 1, noted [1985] Pub L 542 (Hazel Carty). See also *Parker v Camden London Borough Council* [1986] Ch 162, [1985] 2 All ER 141, CA, discussed p 577, supra where in exceptional circumstances a mandatory order was made notwithstanding that it might give rise to an extension of an industrial dispute.

[104] *Great Western Rly Co v Oxford, Worcester and Wolverhampton Rly Co* (1853) 3 De G M & G 341; *Bovill v Crate* (1865) LR 1 Eq 388; *Isaacson v Thompson* (1871) 41 LJ Ch 101.

[105] See eg *Duke of Leeds v Earl Amherst* (1846) 2 Ph 117 and *Rochdale Canal Co v King* (1853) 16 Beav 630.

[106] *Ramsden v Dyson* (1866) LR 1 HL 129; *Wilmott v Barber* (1880) 15 Ch D 96; *Armstrong v Sheppard & Short Ltd* [1959] 2 QB 384, [1959] 2 All ER 651, CA; *Shaw v Applegate* [1978] 1 All ER 123, [1977] 1 WLR 970, CA.

altered his position in violation of the claimant's rights. The fact that the claimant has indicated that he is willing to accept the payment of a sum of money as the price of giving up his rights may well persuade the court not to grant an injunction, though it does not take away its jurisdiction to do so in a proper case,[107] and a demand for payment will not constitute acquiescence if it is shown that the defendant had statutory power to do the thing complained of.[108] If it is shown that the claimant took no steps to enforce a restrictive covenant on prior breaches, this may show acquiescence and an intent to abandon any building scheme there may be, in which case no injunction will be granted,[109] but the mere fact that the claimant has waived his right to sue for breaches in the past does not constitute acquiescence as to the future so as to prevent him from suing for some subsequent infraction, particularly if the earlier infractions were trivial in character.[110] Even acquiescence, however, may be explained away, for instance, where the claimant has been led to believe that the violation of his right would only be temporary,[111] or where he had not at the earlier time the necessary documents to establish his right,[112] or where he had been assured by the defendant that steps were being taken to prevent continued violation of his rights;[113] and if he has acquiesced in some infringement of his rights causing him only slight injury, this does not prevent him from obtaining an interim injunction if the injury is subsequently considerably increased.[114] Moreover, no equity arises if the defendant expended money with knowledge of the true legal position.[115]

(h) CLEAN HANDS[116]

'The jurisdiction to interfere is purely equitable and it must be governed by equitable principles.'[117] One of the principles is that the court will not grant equitable relief to a litigant unless he comes, as it is said, with clean hands. On this principle, as Lord Eldon observed,[118] many cases have occurred in which injunctions are applied for, and are granted or refused, not upon the ground of the right possessed by the parties, but upon the ground of their conduct and dealings before they applied to the court for the injunction to preserve and protect that right.

---

[107] *Viscountess Gort v Clark* (1868) 18 LT 343. Cf *Ainsworth v Bentley* (1866) 14 WR 630; *McKinnon Industries Ltd v Walker* (1951) 95 Sol Jo 559, PC.

[108] *Pentney v Lynn Paving Comrs* (1865) 12 LT 818.   [109] *Roper v Williams* (1822) Turn & R 18.

[110] *Kilbey v Haviland* (1871) 24 LT 353; *German v Chapman* (1877) 7 Ch D 271, CA; *Shaw v Applegate* [1978] 1 All ER 123, [1977] 1 WLR 970, CA.

[111] *Gordon v Cheltenham and Great Western Union Rly Co* (1842) 5 Beav 229.

[112] *Coles v Sims* (1854) 5 De GM & G 1.

[113] *A-G v Birmingham Borough Council* (1858) 4 K & J 528; *Innocent v North Midland Rly Co* (1839) 1 Ry & Can Cas 242.

[114] *Bankart v Houghton* (1860) 27 Beav 425.   [115] *Rennie v Young* (1858) 2 De G & J 136.

[116] The principle is more fully discussed in connection with perpetual injunctions, p 613, infra.

[117] Per Turner LJ in *Great Western Rly Co v Oxford, Worcester and Wolverhampton Rly Co* (1853) 3 De GM & G 341 at 359.

[118] *Blakemore v Glamorganshire Canal Navigation* (1832) 1 My & K 154 at 168; *Sheard v Webb* (1854) 23 LTOS 48; *Jarvis v Islington Corpn* (1909) 73 JP Jo 323.

(i) TRADE DISPUTES

The Trade Union and Labour Relations (Consolidation) Act 1992, s 221 provides that a without notice injunction shall not be granted against a defendant who would be likely to claim that his acts were in contemplation or furtherance of a trade dispute[119] without an opportunity being given to the defendant to be heard. Subsection (2) further provides that, on the hearing of an application for an interim injunction where the defendant makes such a claim, the court in exercising its discretion is to have regard to the likelihood of the defendant's establishing any of the specified matters which, under the Act, confer immunity from liability in tort.[120] This likelihood is only one of the factors to be taken into consideration by the court and different views have been expressed as to whether it is one of the elements of the balance of convenience,[121] or a separate factor. An injunction will normally be refused in cases where the defendant has shown that it is more likely than not that the defence of statutory immunity would succeed.[122]

2 PERPETUAL INJUNCTIONS

(a) GENERAL PRINCIPLES

(i) Injunctions to restrain legal wrongs

There are two important principles that have to be kept in mind. What has been called 'the very first principle of injunction law is that prima facie you do not obtain injunctions to restrain actionable wrongs, for which damages are the proper remedy'.[123] A perpetual injunction, as we have seen, is intended to relieve the claimant from the necessity of bringing a series of actions to protect his right each time it is infringed, and is, therefore, particularly appropriate where the injury is continuous, or in any case where the repetition, or in the case of a quia timet application the commission, of an injury is reasonably apprehended and the remedy of damages would be

---

[119] As to the meaning of this phrase see s 244; *Mercury Communications Ltd v Scott-Garner* [1984] Ch 37, [1984] 1 All ER 179, CA; (1983) 46 MLR 463 (B Simpson).

[120] See *Duport Steels Ltd v Sirs* [1980] 1 All ER 529, [1980] 1 WLR 142, HL; *Dimbleby & Sons Ltd v National Union of Journalists* [1984] 1 All ER 751, [1984] 1 WLR 427, HL.

[121] See *NWL Ltd v Woods* [1979] 3 All ER 614, [1979] 1 WLR 1294, HL; (1980) 96 LQR 189 (A B Clarke and J Bowers); (1980) 43 MLR 319 (Lord Wedderburn); ibid 327 (R C Simpson); (1987) 50 MLR 506 (B Simpson).

[122] Ibid; *Hadmor Productions Ltd v Hamilton* [1983] 1 AC 191, [1982] 1 All ER 1042, HL.

[123] Per Lindley LJ in *London and Blackwell Rly Co v Cross* (1886) 31 Ch D 354 at 369, CA; *Dollfus v Pickford* (1854) 2 WR 220; *Straight v Burn* (1869) 5 Ch App 163.

inadequate,[124] as is typically the case in nuisance or infringement of rights such as patents or copyrights.[125] But even if an infringement of a patent or copyright has been established, an injunction should not be granted if there is no reason to think that there will be any further infringement after the claimant's right has been established by the court.[126] The second principle is that, being an equitable remedy, the award of an injunction is discretionary. This proposition, though generally[127] true, tends to be misleading, and, even if it is recognized that the discretion is a judicial discretion to be exercised in accordance with precedent, it is easy to overestimate the discretion which the court has. From a practical point of view Lord Evershed MR's statement[128] is more helpful:

It is, I think, well settled that, if A proves that his proprietary rights are being wrongfully interfered with by B, and that B intends to continue his wrong, then A is prima facie entitled to an injunction, and he will be deprived of that remedy only if special circumstances exist, including the circumstance that damages are an adequate remedy for the wrong that he has suffered.

The existence of the discretion merely means that, to a limited extent largely dictated by precedent, the court may, indeed must, 'have regard not only to the dry strict rights of the plaintiff and defendant, but also to the surrounding circumstances, to the rights or interests of other persons which may be more or less involved'.[129] The main illustrations of special circumstances which have to be taken into account are discussed in the following subsections.[130]

(ii) Injunctions in aid of an equitable right or title

The first of the two principles just discussed has no relevance where it is sought to enforce an equitable right by means of an injunction. The question whether damages would be an adequate remedy does not arise, for the Court of Chancery originally had no power to award damages. Consequently subsection (b) below does not apply, but the other subsections are relevant.

---

[124] See *Hodgson v Duce* (1856) 28 LTOS 155, where the court took into account that the defendant was a pauper, and a mere award of damages would accordingly be a mockery of justice. In *Pride of Derby and Derbyshire Angling Association Ltd v British Celanese Ltd* [1953] Ch 149 at 181, Evershed MR pointed out that damages would be a wholly inadequate remedy for the association which had 'not been incorporated in order to fish for monthly sums'.

[125] See *Phonographic Performance Ltd v Maitra* [1998] 2 All ER 638, CA.

[126] *Proctor v Bayley* (1889) 42 Ch D 390, CA; *Coflexip SA v Stolt Comex Seaway MS Ltd* [1999] 2 All ER 593, revsd on another point [2000] IP & T 1332, CA.

[127] See, however, for an exception, chapter 28, section 1(a), infra.

[128] In *Pride of Derby and Derbyshire Angling Association Ltd v British Celanese Ltd*, supra, at 181, 197; in effect repeated in *Armstrong v Sheppard & Short Ltd* [1959] 2 QB 384 at 394, [1959] 2 All ER 651 at 655, CA.

[129] Per Kindersley VC in *Wood v Sutcliffe* (1851) 2 Sim NS 163 at 165.

[130] See also chapter 26, section 3, supra, as to the award of damages in lieu of an injunction, and *Ocular Sciences Ltd v Aspect Vision Care Ltd* [1997] RPC 289, 395 et seq.

(b) SMALL DAMAGE

When it was necessary to bring separate actions in different courts for damages and an injunction, it was held that the fact that at law only a very small or nominal sum was recovered by way of damages was not per se a sufficient ground for refusing an injunction,[131] particularly where there was the possibility of a series of actions to recover damages from time to time. In general the fact that the claimant has not suffered substantial damage does not prevent him from obtaining an injunction if he can establish an infringement of a legal right.[132] Sometimes, however, the court may regard the matter as too trivial to entitle the claimant to 'the formidable weapon of an injunction',[133] and an injunction will not necessarily be granted to restrain a trespass or a nuisance where the infringement is only temporary or occasional. Thus the court refused an injunction in *Society of Architects v Kendrick*,[134] where members of the claimant society were accustomed to use the letters MSA after their names. The claimant society sought to restrain the defendant, a non-member, from doing like-wise, but the court refused an injunction on the ground that the matter was too trivial. Again the court refused an injunction in *Behrens v Richards*[135] where it was sought to restrain members of the public from using tracks on the claimant's land situate on an unfrequented part of the coast, which use caused no damage. However in *Patel v W H Smith (Eziot) Ltd*[136] it was made clear that it is only in very exceptional circumstances that an injunction will be refused where a continuing trespass is proved or admitted. Further, in exceptional circumstances, particularly where a mandatory injunction is sought, the court may take into account the fact that an injunction would inflict serious damage on the defendant with no compensating advantage to the claimant, as in *Doherty v Allman*,[137] where the court refused an injunction to restrain ameliorating waste by a tenant under a lease with over nine hundred years left to run.

---

131 *Rochdale Canal Co v King* (1851) 2 Sim NS 78; *Wood v Sutcliffe* (1851) 2 Sim NS 163, where sums of one shilling and one farthing were referred to.

132 *Goodson v Richardson* (1874) 9 Ch App 221; *Marriott v East Grinstead Gas and Water Co* [1909] 1 Ch 70 (both cases of pipes being laid in soil under a highway, which was of no value to the owner). Cf *Armstrong v Sheppard and Short Ltd*, supra.

133 Per Buckley J in *Behrens v Richards* [1905] 2 Ch 614 at 621.

134 (1910) 26 TLR 433. Contrast *Society of Accountants and Auditors v Goodway* [1907] 1 Ch 489 (Incorporated Accountant) and *Society of Accountants in Edinburgh v Corpn of Accountants Ltd* (1893) 20 R 750 (Ct of Sess), where injunctions were granted. It seems to depend on the status of the plaintiff body.

135 Supra; *Ward v Kirkland* [1967] Ch 194, [1966] 1 All ER 609, (right to use drain to convey bath water—court refused injunction to restrain additional user of same drains for effluent from water closets).

136 [1987] 2 All ER 569, CA; *Kelsen v Imperial Tobacco Co (of Great Britain and Ireland) Ltd* [1957] 2 QB 335 (mandatory injunction granted for removal of advertising sign which constituted a trespass to claimant's airspace though no damage suffered); *Jaggard v Sawyer* [1995] 2 All ER 189, CA; *Harrow London Borough Council v Donohue* [1995] 1 EGLR 257, CA (grant of mandatory injunction for demolition of encroaching building works said to be inevitable). Contrast *Ketley v Gooden* (1996) 73 P & CR 305, CA (mandatory injunction discharged and damages awarded: *Harrow London Borough Council v Donohue* not cited); and see (1996) 140 Sol Jo 1002 (A Westwood).

137 (1878) 3 App Cas 709, HL; *Meux v Cobley* [1892] 2 Ch 253; *Sharp v Harrison* [1922] 1 Ch 502.

(c) DELAY AND ACQUIESCENCE[138]

Delay or laches has been said not to affect the claimant's right to a perpetual injunction, unless the claim itself is barred,[139] but recent cases suggest that the court may decline to interfere by injunction where the delay has been 'inordinate'.[140] Delay is, however, commonly, though not necessarily, an important factor to be taken into account in deciding whether there has been acquiescence. However, 'to justify the court in refusing to interfere at the hearing of a cause there must be a much stronger case of acquiescence than is required upon an interlocutory application, for at the hearing of a cause it is the duty of the court to decide upon the rights of the parties, and the dismissal of the bill upon the ground of acquiescence amounts to a decision that a right which has once existed is absolutely and for ever lost.'[141] The test has been said to be whether in the circumstances, it has become unconscionable for the claimant to rely upon his legal right,[142] or, in other words, whether the owner of the legal right has done something beyond mere delay to encourage the wrongdoer to believe that he does not intend to rely on his strict rights, in which belief the wrongdoer has acted to his prejudice.[143]

It should be added that it has been said it may be easier to establish a case of acquiescence where the right is equitable only,[144] but this is doubtful.[145]

(d) CLEAN HANDS

Being an equitable remedy, the principle expressed in the maxim that 'he who comes into equity must come with clean hands' applies.[146] Thus an injunction has been refused to a claimant who had wrongfully taken away partnership books,[147] and in *Telegraph Despatch and Intelligence Co v McLean*[148] a claimant in breach of an implied undertaking in a contract was held not entitled to an injunction to enforce an express undertaking therein entered into by the defendant. Again in *Litvinoff v Kent*[149] a

---

[138] As to the meaning of acquiescence, see p 608, supra.

[139] *Rochdale Canal Co v King* (1851) 2 Sim NS 78; *Savile v Kilner* (1872) 26 LT 277; *Fullwood v Fullwood* (1878) 9 Ch D 176.

[140] *H P Bulmer Ltd and Showerings Ltd v J Bollinger SA* [1977] 2 CMLR 625 at 681, CA.

[141] *Johnson v Wyatt* (1863) 2 De G J & Sm 18 at 25, per Turner LJ; *Patching v Dubbins* (1853) Kay 1.

[142] *Shaw v Applegate* [1978] 1 All ER 123, CA; *Gafford v Graham* (1998) 77 P & CR 73. CA, noted (1988) 114 LQR 555 (P Milne).

[143] *H P Bulmer Ltd v J Bollinger SA*, supra, at 682, CA, per Goff LJ.

[144] *Shaw v Applegate*, supra, CA, at 132, per Goff LJ.

[145] *Habib Bank Ltd v Habib Bank A G Zurich* [1981] 2 All ER 650 at 666, CA, per Oliver LJ; *Gafford v Graham*, supra, CA.

[146] See [1990] Conv 416 (P H Pettit) suggesting it is a last resort defence where it would be unconscionable for the claimant to have an equitable remedy. See also *Equity and Contemporary Legal Developments* (ed S Goldstein) 72 (P Jackson); *Chocosuisse Union des Fabricants Suisses de Chocolat v Cadbury Ltd* [1998] RPC 117; *Equiticorp Industries Group Ltd (In Statutory Management) v The Crown (Judgment No 47)* [1998] 2 NZLR 481 at 519–529.

[147] *Littlewood v Caldwell* (1822) 11 Price 97; *Williams v Roberts* (1850) 8 Hare 315.

[148] (1873) 8 Ch App 658; *Stiff v Cassell* (1856) 2 Jur NS 348.   [149] (1918) 34 TLR 298.

landlord had reserved a right of re-entry only for breach of the covenant in the lease to pay rent. This covenant had not been broken, but the landlord nevertheless re-entered and excluded the tenant from the demised premises. The tenant, the claimant in the proceedings, sought an injunction, but this was refused on the grounds that he had been guilty of breaches of other covenants in the lease and was using the premises for an illegal purpose.

The point has often arisen in connection with a building scheme where numerous purchasers have entered into restrictive covenants with their common vendor for each other's benefit. In such a case a claimant who has not complied with the covenants himself may be unable to enforce them against another,[150] but there is no rigid rule and an injunction may yet be obtained where the claimant's breach was only trifling, or where he has broken a much less important covenant than the one he seeks to enforce.[151] The same qualification applies to other types of case; thus in *Besant v Wood*[152] a husband was not debarred from enforcing provisions in a separation deed by reason of trifling breaches of covenant on his part. Further 'the cleanliness required is to be judged in relation to the relief that is sought'.[153] Thus in *Duchess of Argyll v Duke of Argyll*[154] the claimant was held not to be disentitled to an injunction to restrain the publication by her ex-husband of intimate confidences between husband and wife by reason of the fact that it was her subsequent immorality that was the basis for the divorce and the termination of the marriage.

The same basic idea is behind the maxim that 'he who seeks equity must do equity', though here one is looking to the future rather than the past. The equitable remedy of an injunction will not be granted to a claimant, even though his past conduct is impeccable, if he is not both able and willing to carry out any obligation he has undertaken towards the defendant.[155]

It should be added that according to *Holmes v Eastern Counties Rly Co*[156] where it would be unduly hard to refuse the claimant an injunction on the ground of his conduct, because this would leave him with no adequate remedy, the court may grant the injunction and register its disapproval of his conduct by depriving him of costs. It does not seem from the reports, however, that the courts are very ready to adopt this course.

Finally some cases which are at first sight apparently decided on the ground that the claimant has forfeited his right to an injunction by his conduct, are in fact decided on

---

[150] *Goddard v Midland Rly Co* (1891) 8 TLR 126.

[151] *Chitty v Bray* (1883) 48 LT 860; *Meredith v Wilson* (1893) 69 LT 336; *Hooper v Bromet* (1903) 89 LT 37; affd (1904) 90 LT 234, CA. In *Cantor Fitzgerald International v Bird* [2002] IRLR 867 the court refused to punish the claimant, by the refusal of equitable relief, because of his conduct in 1994.

[152] (1879) 12 Ch D 605.

[153] *Duchess of Argyll v Duke of Argyll* [1967] Ch 302 at 332, [1965] 1 All ER 611; *Grobbelaar v News Group Newspapers Ltd*, [2002] UKHL 40, [2002] 4 All ER 732; *Lewis v Nortex Pty Ltd* [2004] NSWSC 1143, [2005] 214 ALR 634.

[154] Supra. This was a motion for an interlocutory injunction, but the principle seems equally applicable to a claim for a perpetual injunction.

[155] *Measures Bros Ltd v Measures* [1910] 2 Ch 248, CA; *Re Berkeley (Applegate) Investment Consultants Ltd* [1989] Ch 32, [1988] 3 All ER 71.

[156] (1857) 3 K & J 675.

the ground that the alleged contractual right has ceased to exist either because the claimant has himself repudiated the contract or acted in such a way as to entitle the defendant to treat it as being at an end.[157]

(e) THIRD PARTIES

Again owing to the fact that it is an equitable remedy, the court in deciding whether or not an injunction should be granted may take into consideration the effect that the grant of an injunction would have on third parties.[158] Thus in *Maythorn v Palmer*[159] the defendant employee had entered into a limited and valid covenant not to enter into the employment of anyone other than the claimant. He entered into the employment of a third party who knew nothing about his undertaking to the claimant. The claimant's claim to an injunction was refused, partly on the ground of the injury this would do to the third party, who was not a party to the action.

In *Miller v Jackson*[160] a village cricket club was sued by the owner of a newly-erected house adjoining the ground where cricket had been played for some 70 years, in respect of sixes hit into his property. Lord Denning MR was in favour of allowing the appeal against the grant of an injunction on the ground that the club was liable neither in negligence nor nuisance. The other members of the court, however, thought the club guilty of both torts, but while Geoffrey Lane LJ would have dismissed the appeal (though postponing the operation of the injunction for 12 months) Cumming-Bruce LJ took the view that in the special circumstances the interests of the public required that the injunction should be discharged. 'A court of equity must seek to strike a fair balance between the right of the plaintiffs to have quiet enjoyment of their house and garden without exposure to cricket balls occasionally falling like thunderbolts from the heavens, and the opportunity of the inhabitants of the village in which they live to continue to enjoy the manly sport which constitutes a summer recreation for adults and young persons.'[161] A further statement by Lord Denning MR, that the public interest should prevail over the private interest, was said by a differently constituted Court of Appeal in *Kennaway v Thompson*[162] to run counter to the well established principles enunciated in *Shelfer v City of London Electric Lighting Co*,[163] and in *Elliott v*

---

[157] *Fechter v Montgomery* (1863) 33 Beav 22—cf *General Billposting Co Ltd v Atkinson* [1909] AC 118, HL; *Measures Bros Ltd v Measures*, supra.

[158] *Maythorn v Palmer* (1864) 11 LT 261; *Hartlepool Gas and Water Co v West Hartlepool Harbour and Rly Co* (1865) 12 LT 366; cf *PSM International plc v Whitehouse* [1992] FSR 489, CA; *Silktone Pty Ltd v Devreal Capital Pty Ltd* (1990) 21 NSWLR 317.

[159] Supra.

[160] [1977] QB 966, [1977] 3 All ER 338, CA. See (1984) 134 NLJ 183 (Judith Sharrock); (1985) 129 Sol Jo 139 and 163 (D Grant and S R Wilson).

[161] Per Cumming-Bruce LJ in *Miller v Jackson*, supra at 350, CA.

[162] [1981] QB 88, [1980] 3 All ER 329, CA; *Tetley v Chitty* [1986] 1 All ER 663. See (1981) 131 NLJ 108 (B S Markesinis and A M Tettenborn); (1982) 41 CLJ 87 (Stephen Tromans).

[163] [1895] 1 Ch 287, CA, and see p 583 et seq, supra.

London Borough of Islington[164] Lord Donaldson referred to the improbability of a situation arising in which the interests of the public would be decisive. Such a situation arose, however, in *Dennis v Ministry of Defence*[165] though the claim being against the Crown, it was for a declaration and/or damages and not an injunction.[166] The use of an airfield for training Harrier Jump Jet pilots was held to cause a nuisance by noise, but a declaration was refused on the ground of the serious public interest. However substantial compensation was awarded at the public expense.

(f) DECLARATIONS AND SUSPENSION OF INJUNCTION

(i) Claimant prima facie entitled to an immediate injunction

In some circumstances, where prima facie the claimant is entitled to an immediate injunction, the court may merely make a declaration as to the claimant's right, with liberty to apply for an injunction should this become necessary: this may be done, for instance, where there seems to be no probability that the violation of the claimant's rights will be repeated.[167] The court also took this course in *Stollmeyer v Trinidad Lake Petroleum Co Ltd*[168] where there was a clear infringement of the claimant's right, but the damage caused to the claimant was insignificant, though the grant of an injunction would seriously affect local industry. In this case the right to apply for an injunction was suspended for two years.

In other cases, for example, where it would be impossible, difficult or unduly hard on the defendant to comply with an injunction forthwith, the court may adopt the device of granting an immediate injunction, but suspending its operation for a specified time, and the defendant may even be given liberty to apply for an extension of the suspension.[169] This has frequently been done in cases against a local authority for the pollution of a stream by sewage and similar cases where immediate cessation of the nuisance would in fact be impossible,[170] or on the ground of considerations of public welfare.[171] And it has also been done where the defendant body is in the course of promoting a bill in Parliament authorizing it to do the thing complained of,[172] or

---

[164] [1991] 1 EGLR 167, CA (mandatory injunction affirmed to remove tree invading claimant's property. The other LJJ agreed with Lord Donaldson). See *Biogen Inc v Medeva plc* [1993] RPC 475 where Aldous J discussed the matter in relation to life saving drugs infringing a patent, and *Chiron Corpn v Murere Diagnostics Ltd (No 9)* [1995] FSR 318.

[165] [2003] 19 EG 118 CS, discussed [2003] Conv 526 (J Hartshorne).

[166] See Crown Proceedings Act 1947, s 21.

[167] *A-G v Birmingham, Tame and Rea District Drainage Board* [1910] 1 Ch 48, CA; affd [1912] AC 788, HL; *Race Relations Board v Applin* [1973] QB 815, [1973] 2 All ER 1190, CA (no repetition of acts complained of for 20 months).

[168] [1918] AC 485, PC.

[169] *Frost v King Edward VII Welsh etc Association* [1918] 2 Ch 180; compromised on appeal (1918) 35 TLR 138; *Pride of Derby and Derbyshire Angling Association Ltd v British Celanese Ltd* [1953] Ch 149, [1953] 1 All ER 179, CA.

[170] *A-G v Lewes Corpn* [1911] 2 Ch 495; *Phillimore v Watford RDC* [1913] 2 Ch 434.

[171] *Price's Patent Candle Co Ltd v LCC* [1908] 2 Ch 526 at 544, CA, per Cozens-Hardy MR.

[172] *A-G v South Staffordshire Waterworks Co* (1909) 25 TLR 408.

even to enable it to promote such a bill.[173] This course may also be followed where the grant of an immediate injunction coming into effect forthwith would cause difficulties with third parties.[174]

In any case where either of the above devices is adopted, the court may require the defendant, if he wishes to avoid an immediately operative injunction to undertake to pay damages from time to time as any damage is in fact suffered by the claimant.[175]

(ii) Proposed action by claimant may prima facie give a defendant right to an injunction

In exceptional circumstance the court may grant a claimant a declaration that the defendant will not be entitled to claim an injunction if the claimant carries out work that prima facie would infringe the defendant's rights. The court has jurisdiction to grant such a declaration if three conditions are satisfied, namely that the question under consideration is a real question; that the person seeking the declaration has a real interest; and that there has been proper argument.[176] These conditions were satisfied in *Greenwich Health Service Trust v London and Quadrant Housing Trust*,[177] where the grant of a negative declaration that the claimant was not exposed to possible action seeking injunctive relief was a matter of the highest utility since it was a precondition to the ability of the claimant to secure the building of a new modern NHS hospital.

---

[173] *Roberts v Gwyrfai District Council* [1899] 2 Ch 608, CA. [174] *Tubbs v Esser* (1909) 26 TLR 145.

[175] *Stollmeyer v Trinidad Lake Petroleum Co Ltd* [1918] AC 485, PC; *Stollmeyer v Petroleum Development Co Ltd* [1918] AC 498n, PC.

[176] See *Re F (mental patient: sterilisation)* [1990] 2 AC 1, sub nom *F v West Berkshire Health Authority (Mental Health Act Commission intervening)* [1989] 2 All ER 545, HL.

[177] [1998] 3 All ER 437.

28

INJUNCTIONS III— INJUNCTIONS IN PARTICULAR TYPES OF CASES

It is impossible to consider exhaustively the various circumstances which may give rise to a claim for an injunction. An injunction is commonly claimed in aid of a legal right, in which case a mere equitable owner, though he may obtain an interlocutory injunction, can only obtain a perpetual injunction by joining the legal owner in the action,[1] but it may also be granted to give effect to a purely equitable right, for instance to restrain a breach of trust,[2] equitable waste,[3] or the breach of a restrictive covenant enforceable only in equity under the doctrine of *Tulk v Moxhay*.[4] It is also available to restrain a breach of Article 86 of the EC treaty, which prohibits abuse of a dominant market position.[5] Some of the types of case in which an injunction is commonly claimed will now be considered.

1 TO RESTRAIN A BREACH OF CONTRACT

There is a close relationship between an injunction to restrain a breach of contract and a decree of specific performance. The terms of a contract may be affirmative or negative, or partly one and partly the other. Subject to the restrictions dealt with in the

---

[1] *Performing Right Society Ltd v London Theatre of Varieties Ltd* [1924] AC 1, HL. Cf *Weddell v J A Pearce & Major* [1988] Ch 26; *MCC Proceeds Inc v Lehman Bros International (Europe)* [1998] 4 All ER 675, CA.

[2] See section 8, p 638, infra.

[3] See *Standard Chartered Bank v Walker* [1992] 1 WLR 561 (injunction to restrain shareholders in the exercise of his voting rights in a very unusual situation perhaps an extension of jurisdiction in relation to waste).

[4] (1848) 2 Ph 774; *Windsor Hotel (Newquay) Ltd v Allan* [1981] JPL 274, CA. See eg Megarry and Wade, *The Law of Real Property*, 6th edn, p 1012 et seq; Cheshire and Burn, *Modern Law of Real Property*, 16th edn, p 671 et seq.

[5] *Garden Cottage Foods Ltd v Milk Marketing Board* [1984] AC 130, [1983] 2 All ER 770, HL, though on the facts the House of Lords discharged the injunction.

following chapter, specific performance is the natural remedy to enforce an affirmative term, while the injunction is appropriate to enforce a negative one. So far as jurisdiction to grant an interlocutory injunction is concerned, the general principles discussed above apply, but there are special considerations in regard to a claim for a perpetual injunction.

(a) PURELY NEGATIVE TERMS

Where it is sought to restrain by perpetual injunction the threatened breach of a purely negative contract or covenant, the court, in general, has no discretion to exercise. The classic statement on this point, though strictly only an obiter dictum, is that of Lord Cairns in *Doherty v Allman*.[6] 'If parties for valuable consideration, with their eyes open, contract that a particular thing shall not be done, all that a Court of Equity has to do is to say, by way of injunction, that which the parties have already said by way of covenant, that the thing shall not be done; and in such case the injunction does nothing more than give the sanction of the process of the Court to that which already is the contract between the parties. It is not then a question of the balance of convenience or inconvenience, or of the amount of damage or of injury—it is the specific performance, by the Court, of that negative bargain which the parties have made, with their eyes open, between themselves.' Thus in *Viscount Chelsea v Muscatt*[7] a mandatory injunction was granted requiring the tenant to reinstate the top three courses of a parapet wall taken down in clear breach of a covenant in the lease and in the face of a clear indication from the landlords that they were not prepared to consent thereto.

In these cases there is no need for the claimant to prove damage, except, it seems, in an action by a reversioner.[8] The general rule is that 'if the construction of the instrument be clear and the breach clear, then it is not a question of damage, but the mere circumstance of the breach of covenant affords sufficient ground for the court to interfere by injunction'.[9] It is no defence, therefore, to show that the claimant had not suffered any loss by reason of the breach, or even that the breach is more beneficial to him than strict performance of the contract would have been,[10] and accordingly in *Marco Productions Ltd v Pagola*,[11] where theatrical performers expressly agreed not to perform for any other person during the period of the contract, the plaintiffs were entitled to an injunction though they could not show that they would suffer greater damage by the defendants performing elsewhere than by their remaining idle. Nor can the court take into account that the matter is one of public importance, and that the

---

[6] (1878) 3 App Cas 709 at 720, HL: cited *John Trenberth Ltd v National Westminster Bank Ltd* (1979) 39 P & CR 104. See *Martin v Nutkin* (1724) 2 P Wms 266, and note *Dalgety Wine Estate Pty Ltd v Rizzon* (1979) 53 ALJR 647 at 655, per Mason J.

[7] [1990] 2 EGLR 48, CA.   [8] *Johnstone v Hall* (1856) 2 K & J 414.

[9] Per Page Wood VC in *Tipping v Eckersley* (1855) 2 K & J 264 at 270; *Wells v Attenborough* (1871) 24 LT 312; *Cooke v Gilbert* (1892) 8 TLR 382, CA.

[10] *Earl Mexborough v Bower* (1843) 7 Beav 127; *Dickinson v Grand Junction Canal Co* (1852) 15 Beav 260.

[11] [1945] KB 111, [1945] 1 All ER 155.

granting of an injunction would cause inconvenience to the public.[12] The principles as to the granting of injunctions are the same whether the injunction is sought in aid of the legal right where there is privity of contract or privity of estate,[13] or in aid of an equitable claim only, as in the case of restrictive covenants enforceable under the rule of *Tulk v Moxhay*.[14]

The principle stated by Lord Cairns must, however, be applied in the light of the surrounding circumstances and the court is not prevented from considering the effect of delay, acquiescence, or other supervening circumstances.[15] This discretionary element is of greater significance when a mandatory injunction is sought. Thus in *Sharp v Harrison*[16] a mandatory injunction was refused, where the claimant had suffered no damage, an injunction would inflict damage upon the defendant out of all proportion to the relief which the claimant ought to obtain, and the defendant was willing to give certain undertakings. Similarly, in *Wrotham Park Estate Co v Parkside Homes Ltd*[17] the judge unhesitatingly declined to grant a mandatory injunction, which would have involved the demolition of houses—'now the homes of people'—built in breach of a restrictive covenant. The claimant had suffered no financial damage from the breach, their use of the land for the benefit of which the covenant had been imposed would not be impeded, and the integrity of the restrictive covenant for the future would not be impaired by allowing the existing homes to remain. Substantial damages in lieu of an injunction were awarded.

The extent of this residual discretion must not be overrated, however, even in the case of a mandatory injunction, and dicta at first instance in *Charrington v Simons & Co Ltd*[18] and in *Shepherd Homes Ltd v Sandham*[19] to the effect that the criterion is whether a mandatory order, and if so what kind of mandatory order, will produce a fair result were treated with some reservation by the Court of Appeal in the former case[20] though this proposition seems subsequently to have met with the approval of a differently constituted Court of Appeal in *Viscount Chelsea v Muscatt*.[21] In this case

---

[12] *Lloyd v London, Chatham and Dover Rly Co* (1865) 2 De GJ & Sm 568; *Price v Bala and Festiniog Rly Co* (1884) 50 LT 787.

[13] *Spencer's Case* (1583) 5 Co Rep 16a; Law of Property Act 1925, ss 140–142.

[14] (1848) 2 Ph 774; *Lord Manners v Johnson* (1875) 1 Ch D 673; *Richards v Revitt* (1877) 7 Ch D 224. See [1996] Conv 329 (Jill Martin).

[15] *Shaw v Applegate* [1978] 1 All ER 123, [1977] 1 WLR 970, CA (damages awarded in lieu of injunction which would have operated in a mandatory fashion); *Baxter v Four Oaks Properties Ltd* [1965] Ch 816, [1965] 1 All ER 906 (damages in lieu of prohibitory injunction).

[16] [1922] 1 Ch 502. Contrast *Sutton Housing Trust v Lawrence* (1987) 55 P & CR 320, CA (wrong to refuse prohibitory injunction on ground that defendant might disobey order, and would be unlikely to be committed for contempt, or fined for lack of means).

[17] [1974] 2 All ER 321. Contrast *Pugh v Howells* (1984) 48 P & CR 298. Failure to apply for an interlocutory injunction does not necessarily disentitle the claimant to a final mandatory injunction at the trial—see *Deakins v Hookings* [1994] 1 EGLR 190 (Mayors and City of London Cty Ct).

[18] [1970] 2 All ER 257 at 261, per Buckley J; (order varied [1971] 2 All ER 588, CA).

[19] [1971] Ch 340 at 351, [1970] 3 All ER 402 at 412, per Megarry J.

[20] *Charrington v Simons & Co Ltd* [1971] 2 All ER 588, CA.

[21] [1990] 2 EGLR 48, CA (*Charrington v Simons & Co Ltd*, supra, CA, not cited).

and also in *Wakeham v Wood*[22] mandatory injunctions were awarded for breaches of restrictive covenants.

(b) CONTRACT CONTAINING BOTH AFFIRMATIVE AND NEGATIVE STIPULATIONS

In many cases a party's obligation under a contract will expressly involve both affirmative and negative stipulations. It seems that, as a general rule, the negative stipulations will be enforced by means of an injunction,[23] notwithstanding the fact that the affirmative stipulations may not be enforceable by means of a decree of specific performance. The negative stipulation to be enforceable must, however, be negative in substance as well as in form. In *Davis v Foreman*[24] there was, in a contract of personal service, a stipulation in negative form by an employer not to give notice except for misconduct or breach of agreement. It was held that this was affirmative in substance, to retain the employee in his employment, and an injunction was consequently refused. An injunction will not, moreover, be granted if it would really amount to an indirect way of compelling specific performance of an agreement where that remedy could not be obtained directly.

These matters may be illustrated[25] by reference to contracts of personal service, which cannot be enforced by a decree of specific performance. The foundation of this branch of the law is *Lumley v Wagner*[26] where the defendant had agreed to sing at the claimant's theatre during a certain period of time, and had also expressly agreed not to sing elsewhere without the claimant's written authority. The court would not grant specific performance of the affirmative stipulation, but granted an injunction to restrain the defendant from singing elsewhere than in the claimant's theatre. This decision has been consistently followed, though it is regarded as anomalous and will not be extended.[27] Further an injunction will not be granted where its effect would be to leave the defendant with the two alternatives only of remaining idle[28] or performing his contract. So in *Rely-A-Bell Burglar and Fire Alarm Co Ltd v Eisler*,[29] the court, while granting a declaration as to the claimant's legal right and awarding damages,

---

[22] [1981] 43 P & CR 40, CA, where Watkins LJ criticized *Achilli v Tovell* [1927] 2 Ch 243 in so far as it decided that in some circumstances the court has no discretion. See [1984] Conv 429 (P Polden).

[23] *Donnell v Bennett* (1883) 22 Ch D 835. In relation to charterparties see *Lauritzencool AB v Lady Navigation Inc* [2004] EWHC 2607 (Comm), [2005] 1 Lloyd's Rep 260.

[24] [1894] 3 Ch 654; *Kirchner & Co v Gruban* [1909] 1 Ch 413; *Warner Bros Pictures Inc v Nelson* [1937] 1 KB 209, [1936] 3 All ER 160.

[25] See [1991] Cambrian LR 26 (Elizabeth Macdonald); (1994) 138 Sol Jo 152 (Jillian Brown). See also, as to contracts requiring constant supervision, *Ryan v Mutual Tontine Westminster Chambers Association* [1893] 1 Ch 116, CA.

[26] (1852) 1 De GM & G 604. See (2001) 117 LQR 430 (S M Waddams).

[27] *Whitwood Chemical Co v Hardman* [1891] 2 Ch 416, CA.

[28] It was said, in *Evening Standard Co Ltd v Henderson* [1987] IRLR 64, CA, to be unclear what is meant by being idle.

[29] [1926] Ch 609; *Whitwood Chemical Co v Hardman*, supra.

refused to grant an injunction to enforce a stipulation by an employee not to enter into *any* other employment during the term of the contract.

The niceness of the distinctions that have been drawn in this context appears by comparing the *Rely-A-Bell* case with *Warner Bros Pictures Inc v Nelson*,[30] where the defendant film actress agreed not to render any services *in that capacity* for any other person during the term of the contract,[31] and the court granted an injunction. The defendant here was not confronted with the dilemma faced by the defendant in the *Rely-A-Bell Case*:[32] there were other ways in which she might earn a living, and it was irrelevant that the alternative ways might well be less remunerative. She might be tempted to perform her contract though she must not be compelled to do so. Some doubt was cast on this decision in *Warren v Mendy*[33] which has been said[34] to represent the high-water mark of the application of *Lumley v Wagner*.[35]

The above cases were considered in *Page One Records Ltd v Britton*[36] where a group of musicians known as 'The Troggs' had appointed the claimant company as their manager for five years, and had agreed not to engage any other person to act as manager or agent for them. An argument based on *Warner Bros Pictures Inc v Nelson*,[37] to the effect that The Troggs could, without employing any other manager or agent, continue as a group on their own, or seek other employment of a different nature, failed, however. Stamp J held that, as a practical matter on the evidence before him, to grant an injunction would compel The Troggs to continue to employ the claimant company as their manager and agent. 'It would', he added, 'be a bad thing to put pressure on The Troggs to continue to employ as a manager and agent in a fiduciary capacity one, who, unlike the plaintiff in those cases[38] who had merely to pay the defendant money, had duties of a personal and fiduciary nature to perform and in whom The Troggs, for reasons, good, bad or indifferent, have lost confidence and who may, for all I know, fail in its duty to them.' In *Nichols Advance Vehicle Systems Inc v De Angelis*[39] Oliver J found *Warner Bros Pictures Inc v Nelson*[40] difficult to reconcile with *Page One Records Ltd v Britton*[41] as did the Court of Appeal in *Warren v Mendy*[42] who preferred the approach of Stamp J in the latter case, both on grounds of realism and practicality and because that approach is more consistent with the earlier authorities. In *Warren v Mendy* it was said that the most significant feature of cases in which an

---

[30] [1937] 1 KB 209, [1936] 3 All ER 160. For a sideways look see (1989) 86 LSG 36 (M L Nash).

[31] The court was prepared to sever the covenants as drafted.

[32] Supra. See also *Hawthorn Football Club Ltd v Harding* [1988] VR 49.   [33] Supra, CA.

[34] Per Oliver J in *Nicholas Advance Vehicle Systems Inc v De Angelis* (21 December 1979, unreported) Ch D but cited in *Warren v Mendy*, supra, CA.

[35] Supra.

[36] [1967] 3 All ER 822. Cf *Thomas Borthwick & Sons (Australasia) Ltd v South Otago Freezing Co Ltd* [1978] 1 NZLR 538; *Dataforce Pty Ltd v Brambles Holdings Ltd* [1988] VR 771.

[37] Supra. Cf *Thomas Marshall (Exporters) Ltd v Guinle* [1979] Ch 227, [1978] 3 All ER 193.

[38] *Lumley v Wagner*, supra; *Warner Bros Pictures Inc v Nelson*, supra.

[39] Supra. See (1989) 139 NLJ 1716 (A Jennings); [1990] CLJ 28 (Hazel McLean).

[40] Supra. Cf *Thomas Marshall (Exporters) Ltd v Guinle*, supra.   [41] Supra.

[42] [1989] 3 All ER 103, [1989] 1 WLR 853, CA.

injunction had been granted before *Warner Bros Pictures Inc v Nelson*[43] was that the term of engagement was short, in none exceeding 20 weeks. Though it was impossible to lay down a rule where the line between short and long term engagements should be drawn, an injunction for two years (the period applicable in *Warren v Mendy*)[44] would practically compel performance of the contract. The other chief consideration was said to be the presence of obligations involving mutual trust and confidence, not merely because they are not mutually enforceable but because their enforcement, more especially where the servant's trust in the master may have been betrayed or his confidence in him has genuinely gone, will serve the better interests of neither party. *Warren v Mendy*[45] itself involved a contract between a boxer and his manager, and an injunction was refused. Where, as in that case, there are negative obligations in a contract for personal services inseparable from the exercise of some special skill or talent, the court ought not to enforce the performance of the negative obligations if their enforcement will effectively compel the servant to perform his positive obliga-tions under the contract. Compulsion is a question to be decided upon the facts of each case, with a realistic regard for the probable reaction of an injunction on the psychological and material, and sometimes the physical, need of the servant to main-tain the skill or talent. It was added that the assumption that has usually been made that damages will not be an adequate alternative remedy is not justified now that damages are invariably assessed by a judge or master.

An unusual feature of *Warren v Mendy*[46] was that the injunction was sought not against the servant but only against a third party who for the purpose of the proceed-ings for an interim injunction had to be taken to have induced a breach of the contract between the boxer and the manager. The court held that an injunction should usually be refused against such a third party if on the evidence its effect would be to compel performance of the contract.

Evening Standard Co Ltd v Henderson[47] suggests a way in which an employer may be able to get round the decision in *Rely-A-Bell Burglar and Fire Alarm Co Ltd v Eisler*[48] though possibly at some cost. In the *Evening Standard* case the defendant employee's contract provided that it was terminable by one year's notice on either side, and that the employee would not work for anyone else during the currency of the contract. The employee gave two months' notice only, and intended to work for a rival newspaper. An interim injunction was granted to enforce the negative restriction in the contract, on the basis of an undertaking by the employer to pay the employee his salary and other contractual benefits throughout the contractual notice period, whether he chose

[43] Supra.
[44] Supra, CA. In relation to sports cases see (1997) 17 LS 65 (P McCutcheon) who prefers the North American approach which shows a greater willingness to enforce the negative stipulation by means of an injunction.
[45] Supra, CA.   [46] Supra, CA.
[47] [1987] IRLR 64, CA. See *GFI Group Inc v Eaglestone* [1994] IRLR 119, and [1997] Denning LJ 107 (I G C Stratton).
[48] [1926] Ch 609.

to continue working for them or not. However in *Provident Financial Group plc v Hayward*[49] the Court of Appeal refused to disturb the exercise of his discretion by the first instance judge against the grant of an injunction restraining the employee from taking up employment with a rival employer during the period of his notice, notwithstanding that the employer was prepared to pay the employee his salary during that period. Here, unlike the *Evening Standard* case, the employer was not prepared to allow the employee to continue to work, but was being offered 'garden leave'. On the facts of the case there was no real prospect of serious or significant damage to the claimants from the defendant working for the rival and they should be left to their remedy in damages for the plain breach of contract.

(c) NO EXPRESS NEGATIVE STIPULATION

Where there is no express negative stipulation the question arises whether one should be implied from an affirmative stipulation which is incapable of being directly enforced by specific performance, or, which often comes to the same thing, whether what on the face of it is an affirmative stipulation is in substance a negative one and should be treated as such.

The court is slow to draw this inference.[50] Mere inconsistency of the proposed course of conduct with the positive obligation under the contract is not enough. It is necessary to point to something specific which the defendant has by implication agreed not to do.[51] Accordingly on the one hand the court will not import a negative quality into an agreement if this would in effect result in specific performance of a contract for which that remedy is not directly available. Thus so far as contracts for personal service are concerned, although the Court of Appeal has indicated[52] that it is not impossible for a negative stipulation to be implied, it is extremely difficult and no negative stipulation will be implied simply from an employee's covenant to devote all his time to his employer's business[53] or to act exclusively for his employer.[54] Again it has been held[55] that where specific performance of an agreement of a lease could not be obtained by reason of the infancy of one of the two defendants, no injunction against the granting of a lease to any other person should be decreed. Further, no injunction will be granted where it would really be ancillary to a decree of specific performance which cannot be obtained.[56]

---

[49] [1989] 3 All ER 298, CA.

[50] See *Peto v Brighton, Uckfield and Tunbridge Wells Rly Co* (1863) 1 Hem & M 468 at 486.

[51] *Bower v Bantam Investments Ltd* [1972] 3 All ER 349.

[52] *Mutual Reserve Fund Life Assurance v New York Life Assurance Co* (1896) 75 LT 528 at 530, CA, per Lindley LJ.

[53] *Whitwood Chemical Co v Hardman* [1891] 2 Ch 416, CA; *Mortimer v Beckett* [1920] 1 Ch 571. Cf *Frith v Frith* [1906] AC 254, PC.

[54] *Mutual Reserve Fund Life Assurance v New York Life Insurance Co*, supra.

[55] *Lumley v Ravenscroft* [1895] 1 QB 683, CA. See *Fothergill v Rowland* (1873) LR 17 Eq 132.

[56] *Baldwin v Society for Diffusion of Useful Knowledge* (1838) 9 Sim 393: *Phipps v Jackson* (1887) 3 TLR 387.

On the other hand, in *Metropolitan Electric Supply Co Ltd v Ginder*[57] a covenant by the defendant 'to take the whole of the electric energy required' for certain premises from the claimant was held to be in substance a covenant not to take it from anyone else; in *Manchester Ship Canal Co v Manchester Racecourse Co*[58] a contract to give 'first refusal' was held to involve a negative covenant not to part with the property without giving that first refusal, which could be enforced by injunction.

(d) DE MATTOS V GIBSON

In *De Mattos v Gibson*[59] Knight Bruce LJ laid down the principle that 'reason and justice seems to prescribe that, at least as a general rule, where a man, by gift or purchase, acquires property from another, with knowledge of a previous contract, lawfully and for valuable consideration made by him with a third person, to use and employ the property for a particular purpose in a specified manner, the acquirer shall not, to the material damage of the third person, in opposition to the contract and inconsistently with it, use and employ the property in a manner not allowable to the giver or seller.' The principle, discredited in *London County Council v Allen*[60] and *Barker v Stickney*[61] but resuscitated by the Privy Council in *Lord Strathcona Steamship Co Ltd v Dominion Coal Co*[62] was held to be invalid by Diplock J in *Port Line Ltd v Ben Line Steamers Ltd.*[63]

The authorities were reviewed by Browne-Wilkinson J at first instance in *Swiss Bank Corpn v Lloyds Bank Ltd,*[64] who came to the conclusion that this principle is good law and represents the counterpart in equity of the tort of knowing interference with contractual rights.[65] A person proposing to deal with property in such a way as to cause a breach of a contract affecting that property will be restrained by injunction from so doing if when he acquired the property he had actual knowledge of that contract. The claimant does not have to have any proprietary interest in the property: his right to have his contract performed is a sufficient interest. He must, however, establish actual, as opposed to constructive, notice of the contract by the defendant.

---

[57] [1901] 2 Ch 799; *Esso Petroleum Co Ltd v Harper's Garage (Stourport) Ltd* [1968] AC 269, [1967] 1 All ER 699, HL. Cf *Clegg v Hands* (1890) 44 Ch D 503, CA.

[58] [1901] 2 Ch 37, CA. Cf *Gardner v Coutts & Co* [1967] 3 All ER 1064 (an action for damages only), and note *Pritchard v Briggs* [1980] Ch 338, [1980] 1 All ER 294, CA.

[59] (1858) 4 De G & J 276 at 282, dist. *Mac-Jordan Construction Ltd v Brookmount Erostin Ltd (in receivership)* [1992] BCLC 350, CA. See [2003] Conv 61 (G Watt).

[60] [1914] 3 KB 642, CA.   [61] [1919] 1 KB 121, CA.   [62] [1926] AC 108, PC.

[63] [1958] 2 QB 146, [1958] 1 All ER 78. See (1958) 21 MLR 433 (G H Trietel).

[64] [1979] Ch 548, [1979] 2 All ER 853. The *De Mattos v Gibson* point was not discussed on appeal—[1982] AC 584, [1980] 2 All ER 419, CA; [1982] AC 584, [1981] 2 All ER 449, HL. See (1982) 45 MLR 241 (N Cohen-Grabelsky). See also *Binions v Evans* [1972] 2 All ER 70 at 78, CA, per Megaw LJ. *Mac-Jordan Construction Ltd v Brookmount Erostin Ltd (in receivership)*, supra, CA.

[65] See *Lumley v Gye* (1853) 2 E & B 216.

And it seems that the principle will not be used to impose on a purchaser a positive duty to perform the covenants of his predecessor.[66]

(e) DEFENCES

Finally, it may be added that the clean hands doctrine[67] applies, and a claimant may also become disentitled to an injunction by reason of his laches or acquiescence,[68] or by reason of the effect that the grant of an injunction would have on third parties.[69]

2 TO RESTRAIN LEGAL PROCEEDINGS

Before the coming into operation of the Judicature Act 1873 the Court of Chancery would restrain by injunction the prosecution of proceedings in a common law court where their continuance was inequitable, such an injunction being known as a 'common injunction' as opposed to other injunctions which were 'special'. On the fusion of the courts by the Judicature Acts, the common injunction ceased to exist, it being expressly provided[70] that no cause or proceeding at any time pending in the High Court of Justice or before the Court of Appeal should be restrained by prohibition or injunction, though every matter of equity on which an injunction against the prosecution of any such cause or proceeding might formerly have been obtained, either unconditionally or on any terms or conditions, might be relied on by way of defence thereto.

The Judicature Acts do not, however, prohibit the High Court from granting an injunction to restrain a person from instituting proceedings,[71] or continuing pending proceedings, in other courts, such as a county court,[72] or a magistrates' court.[73]

On traditional principles an anti-suit injunction restraining a party from commencing or pursuing legal proceedings in a foreign jurisdiction may be granted when the ends of justice require it. The order is, of course, directed not against the foreign court but against the parties so proceeding or threatening to proceed. It will only be

---

[66] *Law Debenture Trust Corpn plc v Ural Caspian Oil Corpn Ltd* [1993] 2 All ER 355, [1993] 1 WLR 138. See [1992] LMCLQ 448 (Alison Clarke).

[67] See chapter 27, section 2(d), p 613, supra.

[68] Lord Cairns' dictum in *Doherty v Allman* (1878) 3 App Cas 709, considered on p 619, supra does not prevent the court from considering the effect of delay, or other supervening circumstances—*Shaw v Applegate* [1978] 1 All ER 123 CA. See p 613, supra.

[69] See chapter 27, section 2(e), p 615, supra.　　　[70] Judicature Act 1873, s 4(5).

[71] *Besant v Wood* (1879) 12 Ch D 605.

[72] *Murcutt v Murcutt* [1952] P 266, [1952] 2 All ER 427. In *Johns v Chatalos* [1973] 3 All ER 410, however, the court expressly left open the question whether or not the Chancery Division has jurisdiction to grant an injunction to restrain a party from enforcing an order of a county court which is said to be a nullity.

[73] *Thames Launches Ltd v Corpn of the Trinity House of Deptford Strond* [1961] Ch 197, [1961] 1 All ER 26; *Stannard v St Giles, Camberwell Vestry* (1882) 20 Ch D 190, CA.

issued restraining a party who is amenable to the jurisdiction of the court, against whom an injunction will be an effective remedy. Since it indirectly affects a foreign court, the jurisdiction must be exercised with caution.[74] However in relation to the European Union the Court of Justice of the European Communities has recently held[75] that the courts of a contracting state are precluded by the Brussels Convention[76] from prohibiting a party to proceedings pending before it from commencing or continuing legal proceedings before a court of another contracting state, even where the party was acting in bad faith with a view to frustrating the existing proceedings.

3 TO PROTECT MEMBERSHIP OF CLUBS, TRADE UNIONS AND OTHER UNINCORPORATED BODIES

Members of unincorporated bodies can only be expelled from membership if the rules so provide and the procedure there set out is strictly complied with. The court, accordingly, can only intervene it if can be shown that the purported expulsion was not authorized by the rules,[77] or that the proceedings were irregular,[78] or not consonant with the principles of natural justice,[79] or that there was mala fides or malice in arriving at the decision.[80] If, however, a member is wrongfully expelled, he may seek a declaration that the purported expulsion is null and void, and an injunction to restrain the club, trade union, or other body from acting on the basis that he is not a member. At one time the jurisdiction of the court to grant an injunction was thought to be based purely on the member's right of property,[81] but recent decisions indicate that the jurisdiction is founded on the contractual rights of the expelled member.[82] An injunction will, however, only be granted to prevent a member's expulsion if it is necessary to protect a proprietary right of his, or to protect him in his right to earn his

---

[74] See *Donohue v Armco Inc* [2002] 1 All ER 749, HL; *American International Specialty Lines Insurance Co v Abbott Laboratories* [2002] EWHC 2714 (Comm), [2003] 1 Lloyd's Rep 267; *Sabah Shipyard (Pakistan) Ltd v Islamic Republic of Pakistan* [2002] EWCA Civ 1643, [2003] 2 Lloyd's Rep 570; *Turner v Grovit* [2002] 1 WLR 107, HL noted [2003] ICLQ 401 (Clare Ambrose). In relation to arbitration see [2005] LMCLQ 10 (P Gross).

[75] *Turner v Grovit (Case C-159/02)* [2004] All ER (EC) 485. This regrettable decision is discussed in (2004) 120 LQR 529 (A Briggs); (2004) 154 NLJ 798 (L Flannery), and see [2003] ICLQ 697 (Look Chan Ho).

[76] See Civil Jurisdiction and Judgments Act 1982, Sch 1.

[77] *Lee v Showmen's Guild of Great Britain* [1952] 2 QB 329, [1952] 1 All ER 1175, CA; *Bonsor v Musicians' Union* [1956] AC 104, [1955] 3 All ER 518, HL.

[78] *Young v Ladies' Imperial Club* [1920] 2 KB 523, CA.

[79] *Lawlor v Union of Post Office Workers* [1965] Ch 712, [1965] 1 All ER 353.

[80] *Bryne v Kinematograph Renters Society Ltd* [1958] 2 All ER 579; *Annamunthodo v Oilfields Workers' Trade Union* [1961] AC 945, [1961] 3 All ER 621, PC.

[81] *Rigby v Connol* (1880) 14 Ch D 482.

[82] *Lee v Showmen's Guild of Great Britain*, supra, CA at 341, 342, 1180, per Denning LJ; *Bonsor v Musicians' Union*, supra, per Lord Morton at 127, 524; *Bryne v Kinematograph Renters Society Ltd* [1958] 2 All ER 579.

livelihood.[83] It will not be granted to give a member the right to enter a social club, unless there are proprietary rights attached to it, because purely as a matter of contract it is too personal to be specifically enforced.[84]

4 TO RESTRAIN THE COMMISSION OR REPETITION OF A TORT[85]

Injunctions have frequently been granted to prevent a threatened or apprehended trespass to land,[86] nuisance[87] and waste, whether legal or equitable, but never, it seems, so as to stop a man being negligent.[88] Also where a person, without just cause or excuse, deliberately interferes with the trade or business of another, and does so by unlawful means.[89] An injunction has been granted to a mother against her son to restrain the commission of assaults,[90] and the court has jurisdiction in nuisance to grant an injunction retaining persistent harrassment by unwanted telephone calls.[91] Harassment has now been made a criminal offence,[92] and an actual or apprehended act of harassment within the Act may be the subject of civil proceedings in respect of which an injunction may be granted.[93] In exceptional cases the court has power to impose an exclusion zone prohibiting the defendant from coming or remaining within a specified distance of a specified property.[94]

So far as an injunction to restrain the publication of a libel is concerned, this was

---

[83] As to a right to membership when this is necessary to enable him to earn his living, see *Faramus v Film Artistes' Association* [1964] AC 925, [1964] 1 All ER 25, HL; *Nagle v Feilden* [1966] 2 QB 633, [1966] 1 All ER 689, CA noted (1966) 82 LQR 319 (A L Goodhart); (1966) 29 MLR 424 (R W Rideout).

[84] *Baird v Wells* (1890) 44 Ch D 661, CA; *Lee v Showmen's Guild of Great Britain*, supra. It follows that no injunction will lie at the suit of a member of a proprietary club.

[85] See (1992) 22 Fam Law 158 (N Fricker).

[86] *League Against Cruel Sports Ltd v Scott* [1986] QB 240, [1985] 2 All ER 489.

[87] Eg *Halsey v Esso Petroleum Co Ltd* [1961] 2 All ER 145, and see *Rugby Joint Water Board v Walters* [1967] Ch 397, [1966] 3 All ER 497 (to restrain riparian owner from abstracting water for extraordinary purposes). See (1977) 36 CLJ 294 (A I Ogus and G M Richardson).

[88] *Miller v Jackson* [1977] QB 966 [1977] 3 All ER 338 CA, per Lord Denning MR at 343.

[89] *Acrow (Automation) Ltd v Rex Chainbelt Inc* [1971] 3 All ER 1175, CA; *Esso Petroleum Co Ltd v Kingswood Motors (Addlestone) Ltd* [1974] QB 142, [1973] 3 All ER 1057. See (1972) 88 LQR 177 (P Rayner).

[90] *Egan v Egan* [1975] Ch 218, [1975] 2 All ER 167. It had been held in Australia that an injunction to restrain apprehended or threatened assaults should only be granted in exceptional circumstances—*Corvisy v Corvisy* [1982] 2 NSWLR 557.

[91] *Khorasandjian v Bush* [1993] QB 727, [1993] 3 All ER 669, CA. This decision was overruled by the House of Lords in *Hunter v Canary Wharf Ltd* [1997] AC 655, [1997] 2 All ER 426, noted (1997) 113 LQR 515 (P Cane); [1998] Conv 309 (P R Ghandhi); (1998) 61 MLR 870 (J Wightman), in so far as it held that a mere licensee could sue in nuisance: only someone with a right to the land, such as the freeholder, a tenant in possession or a licensee with exclusive possession, can sue in nuisance. Contrast *Manchester Airport plc v Dutton* [2000] 1 QB 133, sub nom *Dutton v Manchester Airport plc* [1999] 2 All ER 675, CA, noted p 216, supra.

[92] Protection from Harassment Act 1997, ss 1 and 2.   [93] Ibid, s 3.

[94] *Burris v Azadani* [1995] 4 All ER 802, [1995] 1 WLR 1372, CA.

wholly impossible prior to the Common Law Procedure Act 1854. Courts of Equity had no jurisdiction in matters of libel,[95] and courts of law had no power to issue injunctions. Such a power was conferred on the common law courts by the Common Law Procedure Act 1854, though there is no reported instance of its exercise, prior to *Saxby v Easterbrook*.[96] By the Judicature Act 1873 the High Court acquired the powers previously possessed by both common law and equity courts, and after that Act, the Chancery Division began to grant injunctions to restrain the publication of libels.[97]

It may be added that the jurisdiction to restrain the publication of a libel does not distinguish between a libel affecting trade or property and one affecting character only, and extends to an action of slander as well as to an action of libel.[98]

5 TO PROTECT COPYRIGHT, PATENT RIGHTS AND TRADE MARKS

An injunction is the appropriate remedy to restrain the infringement of any of these rights, the substantive law now being largely statutory.[99]

6 TO RESTRAIN A BREACH OF CONFIDENCE

'At the broadest level of generality it can be said that equity offers remedies where a breach of an appropriate confidence, personal or commercial, is threatened or has occurred.'[100] Various bases have been put forward.[101] In *Fraser v Evans*[102] Lord Denning MR said that the jurisdiction was 'based not so much on property or on contract, but rather on the duty to be of good faith', and in *A-G v Guardian Newspapers (No 2)*[103]

---

[95] *Prudential Assurance Co v Knott* (1875) 10 Ch App 142. [96] (1878) 3 CPD 339, DC.

[97] *Bonnard v Perryman* [1891] 2 Ch 269, CA; *White v Mellin* [1895] AC 154, HL.

[98] *Hermann Loog v Bean* (1884) 26 Ch D 306, CA.

[99] Copyright Designs and Patents Act 1988; Patents Acts 1949 and 1977; Trade Marks Act 1994.

[100] Per Lindsay J in *Douglas v Hello! Ltd (No 3)* [2003] EWHC 786 (Ch), [2003] 3 All ER 996 at [181], the beginning of a full exposition of the law of confidence. As to possible confusion with breach of fiduciary duty see (2001) 21 LS 594 (J Glover). As to the law of confidentiality as it applies to children, see (2003) 23 LS 510 (Joan Loughrey).

[101] See (1970) 86 LQR 463 (G H Jones). Lord Goff in *A-G v Guardian Newspapers (No 2)* [1990] 1 AC 109, [1988] 3 All ER 545, HL, at 288, 659 alluded to the prospect of declaring a constructive trust, but Tang Hang Wu in (2003) 23 LS 135 argues that abuse of confidence should not give rise to a proprietary right.

[102] [1969] 1 QB 349, [1969] 1 All ER 8, CA, at 361, 11. Likewise in *R v Dept of Health, ex parte Source Informatics Ltd* [2001] QB 424, [2001] 1 All ER 786, CA, Simon Brown LJ said at 796, that the 'touchstone by which to judge the scope of [the confidant's] duty and whether it has been fulfilled or breached is his conscience, no more and no less'.

[103] [1990] 1 AC 109, [1988] 3 All ER 545, HL, at 269, 649.

Lord Griffiths said it was based on 'moral principles of loyalty and fair dealing'. Whatever the basis, under the head of breach of confidence injunctions have been granted to restrain an employee or ex-employee from divulging trade secrets, whether they are in the nature of secret processes,[104] or a list of customers.[105] An injunction has been granted to restrain the improper use or disclosure of trade secrets, even though the details of the secrets were not disclosed to the court at the trial[106] but the usual procedure is for this difficulty to be dealt with by having the matter heard in private.[107] In particular, as between traders where the question most often arises, the broad principle is 'that if information be given by one trader to another in circumstances which make that information confidential then the second trader is disentitled to make use of the confidential information for purposes of trade by way of competition with the first trader'.[108] The principle is not, however, restricted to traders, and thus, for instance, a printer is not entitled to make additional copies for his own purposes of a drawing he has undertaken to reproduce,[109] a person who attends oral lectures can be restrained from publishing them for profit,[110] a spouse can be prevented from publishing confidences communicated during marriage[111] and a Cabinet Minister can be restrained from publishing information relating to discussions at Cabinet meetings.[112] Again the former client of a solicitor or accountant may be able to obtain an injunction restraining him from acting for another client if he can establish (i) that the defendant is in possession of confidential information and (ii) that the information is or may be relevant to the new matter in which the interest of the other client is or may be adverse to his own.[113]

The law was extended to the publication of unauthorized photographs of a private event in *Douglas v Hello! Ltd*[114] where the Court of Appeal stated:

Where an individual ('the owner') has at his disposal information which he has created or which is private or personal and to which he can properly deny access to third parties, and he reasonably intends to profit commercially by using or publishing that information, then a third party who is, or ought to be, aware of these matters and who has knowingly obtained

---

[104] *Morrison v Moat* (1851) 9 Hare 241; *Cranleigh Precision Engineering Ltd v Bryant* [1964] 3 All ER 289; *Lancashire Fires Ltd v S A Lyons & Co Ltd* [1996] FSR 629, CA.

[105] *Robb v Green* [1895] 2 QB 315, CA.

[106] *Amber Size and Chemical Co Ltd v Menzel* [1913] 2 Ch 239.

[107] *Mellor v Thompson* (1885) 31 Ch D 55, CA.

[108] Per Evershed MR, in *Terrapin Ltd v Builders' Supply Co (Hayes) Ltd* [1960] RPC 128 at 131, CA, based on *Saltman Engineering Co Ltd v Campbell Engineering Co Ltd* (1948) 65 RPC 203, CA. And see *Seager v Copydex Ltd* [1967] 2 All ER 415, CA.

[109] *Prince Albert v Strange* (1849) 1 Mac & G 25; *Tuck & Sons v Priester* (1887) 19 QBD 629, CA.

[110] *Abernethy v Hutchinson* (1825) 1 H & Tw 28.

[111] *Duchess of Argyll v Duke of Argyll* [1967] Ch 302, [1965] 1 All ER 611.

[112] *A-G v Jonathan Cape Ltd* [1976] QB 752, [1975] 3 All ER 484, the Crossman diaries case, though the injunction was refused as the events dealt with being 10 years old, the need for confidentiality had ceased.

[113] *Prince Jefri Bolkiah v KPMG (a firm)* [1999] 1 All ER 517, HL (injunction granted, but the possibility of an effective Chinese wall within a defendant organization was accepted); *Young v Robson Rhodes (a firm)* [1999] 3 All ER 524.

[114] [2005] EWCA Civ 595, [2005] All ER (D) 280 (May) at [118].

the information without authority, will be in breach of duty if he uses or publishes the information to the detriment of the owner.

It is not clear whether a duty of confidentiality assumed under contract carries more weight, when balanced against the right of freedom of expression, than a duty of confidentiality not buttressed by express agreement.[115] Nor is it clear what is the effect on a contractual duty of confidence when the contract in question has been wrongfully repudiated.[116]

Many of the recent cases have involved a claim for 'invasion of privacy'. The House of Lords has held that there is no general tort of invasion of privacy,[117] but the law of breach of confidence has been extended to give a remedy in some cases. In origin the confidence referred to in the phrase 'breach of confidence' was the confidence arising out of a confidential relationship. As the law has developed the need for an initial confidential relationship has been abandoned. In doing so the nature of an action for breach of confidence has changed. Now the law imposes a 'duty of confidence' whenever a person receives information he knows or ought to know is fairly and reasonably to be regarded as confidential.[118] Knowledge, actual or imputed, that information is private will normally impose on anyone publishing that information the duty to justify what, in the absence of justification, will be a wrongful invasion of privacy.[119]

The development of the law has been significantly influenced by the European Convention for the Protection of Human Rights and Fundamental Freedoms 1950 incorporated in to English law by the Human Rights Act 1998. It has recently been held[120] that the court should, as far as it can, develop the action for breach of confidence in such a manner as will give effect to both Article 8 and Article 10 rights, but giving neither of them pre-eminence. It was further said that it was not satisfactory that the court was required to shoe-horn within the cause of action of breach of confidence, claims, such as that before it, relating to the publication of unauthorized photographs of a private nature.

The courts have to carry out a balancing exercise in the context of Articles 8 and 10 of the convention. The position has been explained by Lord Hope[121] in the following terms—

The rights guaranteed by these articles are qualified rights. Article 8(1) protects the right to respect for private life, but recognition is given by art 8(2) to the protection of the rights and

---

[115] *A-G v Parry* [2002] EWHC 3201 (Ch), [2004] EMLR 13.

[116] *Campbell v Frisbee* [2002] EWCA Civ 1374, [2003] EMLR 76.

[117] *Wainwright v Home Office* [2003] UKHL 53, [2003] 4 All ER 969; *Campbell v MGN Ltd* [2004] UKHL 22, [2004] 2 All ER 995, noted (2004) 120 LQR 563 (J Morgan). See [2003] CLJ 444 (J Morgan); [2003] 66 MLR 726 (G Phillipson); [2004] SJLS 311 (Megan Richardson).

[118] See *A-G v Guardian Newspapers Ltd (No 2)* [1990] 1 AC 109, [1988] 3 All ER 545, HL, per Lord Goff at 291, 658–659; and *Campbell v MGN Ltd*, supra, HL, per Lord Nicholls at 1002, who suggests that the claim would be better referred to as misuse of private information. No claim of confidence can, however, be made in relation to matters properly described as shocking or immoral: *Maccaba v Lichtenstein* [2004] EWHC 1579, [2005] EMLR 6.

[119] *Douglas v Hello! Ltd* [2005] EWCA Civ 595, [2005] All ER (D) 280 (May).

[120] *Douglas v Hello! Ltd* [2005], supra, CA at [53].   [121] In *Campbell v MGN Ltd*, supra, HL, at 1023.

freedoms of others. Article 10(1) protects the right to freedom of expression, but art 10(2) recognizes the need to protect the rights and freedoms of others. The effect of these provisions is that the right to privacy which lies at the heart of an action for breach of confidence has to be balanced against the right of the media to impart information to the public. And the right of the media to impart information to the public has to be balanced in its turn against the respect that must be given to private life.

Lord Hope added that there is nothing new about this. This kind of balancing exercise was already part of English law,[122] but account has now to be taken of the guidance which has been given by the European Court of Human Rights on the application of these articles.

In *A-G v Guardian Newspapers Ltd*,[123] decided before the Human Rights Act 1988, an interim injunction was granted restraining newspapers from publishing information already published abroad in breach of a clear duty of confidence by a former member of the British security service. Whether a final injunction would be obtained at the trial was said to be arguable and the House of Lords affirmed that it would be a denial of justice to refuse to allow the injunction to continue until the trial. Following the trial of the action the matter returned to the House of Lords which discharged the injunction,[124] for there was no longer any secrecy attached to the contents of the book and no damage would be done to the public interest by further publication. However it was affirmed that members and former members of the Security Service have a lifelong obligation of confidence owed to the Crown. In a different context on grounds of public policy an undoubted duty of confidence has been held not to extend so as to bar disclosure to FIMBRA or the Inland Revenue of matters that it is the province of those authorities to investigate.[125]

In *Douglas v Hello Ltd*[126] a celebrity couple had given N, a magazine proprietor, exclusive rights to prevent any unauthorized photographs of their wedding, and had taken steps to prevent a competing magazine from publishing unauthorized photographs. The Court of Appeal noted that chancery judges had granted injunctions to restrain the publication of photographs taken surreptitiously in circumstances such that the photographer was to be taken to have known that the occasion was a private one and that the taking of photographs by outsiders was not permitted. In the appeal, on the facts, though it was thought likely that at the trial they would be able to establish that publication should not be allowed on confidentiality grounds, the interim injunction was discharged, an important factor being that the couple had sold the major part of their privacy rights, and damages would be an adequate remedy. In

---

[122] See *A-G v Guardian Newspapers Ltd (No 2)*, supra, HL, per Lord Goff.

[123] [1987] 3 All ER 316, HL (the *Spycatcher* case).

[124] *A-G v Guardian Newspapers Ltd (No 2)*, supra, HL. See [1989] Pub L 13 (Yvonne Cripps); [1989] 56 MLR 389 (J Michael); (1989) 105 LQR 501 (P Birks); [1989] CLP 49 (G Jones).

[125] *Re a Company's Application* [1989] Ch 477, [1989] 2 All ER 248.

[126] [2001] 2 All ER 289, CA, noted (2001) 64 MLR 767 (Nicole Moreham). See pp 605–606, supra. See also (2003) 54 NILQ 99 (R Deazley).

further proceedings,[127] however, it was said that the injunction should not have been discharged. Sufficient weight had not been given to the strength of the Douglases' claim for an injunction, and the likely level of damages which they would recover if the interim injunction was refused and, as it turned out, publication of the unauthorized photographs infringed their rights. At the trial in *Douglas v Hello! Ltd (No 3)*[128] Lindsay J held that the fact that the unauthorized photographs had been published did not prevent the claimants, having established the breach of confidence, from seeking a perpetual injunction; he would have been prepared to grant such an injunction but indicated his willingness to accept an undertaking in lieu. The intrusive nature of photography means that it may be possible to obtain an injunction to prevent the publication of photographs of activities, though an injunction to prevent a verbal description of the same activities may be refused.[129]

In *Venables v News Group Newspapers Ltd*[130] two 10-year-old boys had been convicted of murdering a two-year-old toddler and had been sentenced to be detained during Her Majesty's pleasure. At the conclusion of the trial injunctions were granted restraining publication of further information about them, based on the court's jurisdiction in relation to minors. The boys had now reached the age of 18, and there was a likelihood that the Parole Board would release them into the community before long. Permanent injunctions were now sought to protect, inter alia, information regarding changes in their physical appearances since their detention and the new identities that would probably be given to them on their release. The evidence was that there was a real and substantial risk of death or serious physical harm if they could be identified after release. The court, taking account of the potential conflict between Article 10 on the one hand and Articles 2 (right to life), 3 (prohibition of torture) and 8, held that it had jurisdiction, in exceptional circumstances, to extend the protection of confidentiality of information, even to impose restrictions on the press, where not to do so would be likely to lead to serious physical injury, or death, of the person seeking that confidentiality, and there was no other way to protect the applicants other than by seeking relief from the court. Appropriate injunctions were accordingly granted. Again in another exceptional case, *X (a woman formerly known as Mary Bell) v O'Brien*,[131] an injunction contra mundum was granted to protect the identity and whereabouts of X and her daughter Y. X had some 35 years earlier been convicted at the age of 11 of killing two children. Since her release she had been rehabilitated into society and had not reoffended.

---

[127] *Douglas v Hello! Ltd* [2005] EWCA Civ 595, [2005] All ER (D) 280 (May), CA, where it was pointed out that in the earlier decision the court did not have the benefit of the reasoning of the House of Lords in *Campbell v MGN Ltd*, supra, or the ECHR decision in *von Hannover v Germany* (24 June 2004).

[128] [2003] EWHC 786 (Ch), [2003] 3 All ER 996.

[129] *Theakston v MGN Limited* [2002] EWHC 137, [2002] EMLR 398 (the activities involved took place in a brothel); *Douglas v Hello! Ltd* [2005] EWCA Civ 595, [2005] All ER (D) 280 (May).

[130] [2001] 1 All ER 908. See [2002] CLQ 29 (Linda Clark).

[131] [2003] EWHC 1101(QB). [2003] 2 FCR 686.

Other recent cases include *A v B (a company)*[132] where the court, while taking account of the Human Rights Act 1998, set aside an interim injunction granted to the claimant, a married Premier League footballer, to prevent the first defendant newspaper publishing stories concerning his sexual relationships with two named women. Balancing the protection of the claimant's privacy against the defendant's right to freedom of expression, the freedom of the press should prevail. The House of Lords by a bare majority held that the balance swung the other way in *Campbell v MGN Ltd*.[133] This is an important case on breach of confidence, but it was a claim for damages only, it being too late to restrain publication.

It has recently been held that where the public interest justifies the publication of confidential information, there is no pre-publication obligation on the publisher to disclose to the owner of that information the material which he proposes to publish and to give the owner an opportunity to reply to it.[134]

As a general rule an injunction can be obtained not only against the original guilty party, but against any third party who knowingly obtained the confidential information in breach of confidence or in any other fraudulent manner.[135] Indeed, even if a man obtains the confidential information innocently, once he gets to know that it was originally given in confidence, he can, according to the circumstances, be restrained from breaking that confidence.[136] 'Each case will depend upon its own facts and the decision of the judge as to . . . whether the conscience of the third party is affected by the confidant's breach of duty.'[137]

The Law Commission[138] has recommended that the present action for breach of

132 [2002] EWCA Civ 337, [2002] 2 All ER 545, criticized [2002] CLJ 264 (D Howarth). The case turned on whether the information in question was properly to be regarded as confidential. Contrast *Archer v Williams* [2003] EWHC 1670 (QB), [2003] EMLR 869 (claimant not a public figure: her right to preserve her privacy outweighed the defendant's right to freedom of expression). See also *Mills v News Group Newspapers Ltd* [2001] EMLR 960; and pp 605–606, supra.

133 [2004] UKHL 22, [2004] 2 All ER 995, reversing the unanimous decision of the Court of Appeal and restoring the judgment of the first instance judge. At the time of writing there is only a newspaper report (*Times*, 25 April 2005) as a news item that David and Victoria Beckham failed to obtain an interim injunction to restrain the publication by the *News of the World* of damaging allegations relating to their private lives made by their former nanny in breach of a confidentiality clause, on the ground that the story was in the public interest. It suggests that celebrities cannot rely on a confidentiality clause if they are trying to mislead the public for commercial gain.

134 *Tillery Valley Foods Ltd v Channel Four Television Corporation* (2004) *Times*, 21 May.

135 *Morrison v Moat* (1851) 9 Hare 241; *Lord Ashburton v Pape* [1913] 2 Ch 469, CA; *Duchess of Argyll v Duke of Argyll* [1967] Ch 302, [1965] 1 All ER 611.

136 *Fraser v Evans* [1969] 1 QB 349, [1969] 1 All ER 8; *Butler v Board of Trade* [1971] Ch 680, [1970] 3 All ER 593. The above paragraph was cited and applied by Helsham CJ in *Wheatley v Bell* [1984] FSR 16 and by Seaton JA in *GEAC Canada Ltd v Prologic Computer Corpn* (1989) 35 BCLR (2d) 143.

137 Per Lord Griffiths in *A-G v Guardian Newspapers Ltd (No 2)*, supra, HL at 652; *Lord Advocate v Scotsman Publications Ltd* [1990] 1 AC 812, [1989] 2 All ER 852, HL.

138 Law Com No 110. See generally (1982) 11 AALR 273 (A M Tettenborn); (1989) 7 Otago LR 3; (1990) 14 NZULR 144 (D Laster); (1992) 12 LS 302 (G Wei). The origins are discussed in (1979) 8 AALR (R G Hammond). For an American view see (1982) 82 Col LR (A B Vickery). The defence of public interest is discussed in *Lion Laboratories Ltd v Evans* [1985] QB 526, [1984] 2 All ER 417, CA; *X v Y* [1988] 2 All ER 648; *A-G v Guardian Newspapers Ltd (No 2)*, supra, HL, and in Australia in *Sullivan v Sclanders* (2000) 77 SASR 419.

confidence should be abolished and replaced by a new statutory tort of breach of confidence.

7 TO PROTECT PUBLIC RIGHTS[139]

Although, as we have seen,[140] where a statute creates an offence, without creating a right of property, and provides a summary remedy, an individual cannot normally claim an injunction, the Attorney-General can do so if the public interest is affected,[141] unless, it would seem, the statute expressly provides that the statutory remedy is to be the only one.[142] The House of Lords, however, in *Gouriet v Union of Post Office Workers*[143] has stressed the anomalous character of the civil remedy of an injunction prohibiting conduct solely because it is criminal. The effect of an injunction in such circumstances is to add a discretionary penalty for contempt of court to the criminal penalty, which in the case of a statutory offence will have been fixed by Parliament. Further, breach of an injunction will be dealt with in the civil court by the judge alone, whereas in the criminal court the accused may be entitled to be tried by a jury. Scott J has recently[144] referred to an injunction in aid of the criminal law as a remedy of last resort, which should not be granted if other less Draconian means of securing obedience to the law are available. Long used for this purpose in cases of public nuisance the grant of an injunction has only been extended to statutory offences comparatively recently. It has been said[145] that this use of the injunction should be confined to statutes whose objects are to promote the health, the safety or the welfare of the public and to particular cases under such statutes either where the prescribed penalty for the summary offence has proved to be insufficient to deter the offender from numerous repetitions of the offence, or where the

---

[139] See generally (1979) 42 MLR 369 (D Feldman). Note also the novel case of *West Mercia Constabulary v Wagener* [1981] 3 All ER 378, [1982] 1 WLR 127, discussed (1982) 98 LQR 190 (D Feldman); *Chief Constable of Kent v V* [1983] QB 34, [1982] 3 All ER 36, CA, noted (1983) 99 LQR 1; (1983) 42 CLJ 51 (A Tettenborn); (1983) 133 NLJ 926 (D Feldman); (1983) Crim LR 723 (C P Walker); (1984) 133 NLJ 829 (Suzanne Bailey); (1989) 17 MULR 56 (J Duns). Contrast *Chief Constable of Hampshire v A Ltd* [1985] QB 132, [1984] 2 All ER 385, CA, noted (1984) 100 LQR 537 (G Samuel), and see *Chief Constable of Leicestershire v M* [1988] 3 All ER 1015; *Chief Constable of Surrey v A* (1988) *Times*, 27 October. The Criminal Justice Act 1988 now provides for restraint orders and confiscation orders. See also *A-G v Blake* [2000] 4 All ER 385, HL.

[140] Page 573, supra. But note that an individual may sue to enforce legal rights vested in the inhabitants of a parish—*Wyld v Silver* [1963] 1 QB 169, [1962] 3 All ER 309, CA.

[141] *A-G v Smith* [1958] 2 QB 173, [1958] 2 All ER 557; *A-G v Harris* [1961] 1 QB 74, [1960] 3 All ER 207, CA.

[142] *Evans v Manchester, Sheffield and Lincolnshire Rly Co* (1887) 36 Ch D 626; *Stevens v Chown* [1901] 1 Ch 894.

[143] [1978] AC 435, [1977] 3 All ER 70, HL—for a discussion of this decision in an Australian context see (1978) 5 Mon LR 133 (G A Flick); *Stoke-on-Trent City Council v B & Q (Retail) Ltd* [1984] AC 754, [1984] 2 All ER 332, HL; *Kirklees Metropolitan Borough Council v Wickes Building Supplies Ltd* [1993] AC 227, [1992] 3 All ER 717, HL.

[144] *Waverley Borough Council v Hilden* [1988] 1 All ER 807, [1988] 1 WLR 246.

[145] Per Lord Diplock in *Gouriet v Post Office Engineering Union*, supra, HL at 500, 99.

defendant's disobedience to the statutory prohibition may cause grave and irreparable harm.

Public rights are normally asserted by the Attorney-General, as representing the public. A private person is entitled to sue in respect of interference with a public right[146] if there is also interference with a private right of his, which case, however, does not depend on the existence of a public right in addition to the private one. Lord Diplock, who gave the only reasoned speech in *Lohnro Ltd v Shell Petroleum Co Ltd (No 2)*,[147] said there were two classes of exception to the general rule. The first is where on the true construction of the Act it is apparent that the obligation or prohibition was imposed for the benefit or protection of a particular class of individuals, as in the case of the Factories Acts and similar legislation.[148] The second is where the statute creates a public right (that is a right to be enjoyed by all of those of Her Majesty's subjects who wish to avail themselves of it) and a particular member of the public suffers particular, direct and substantial damage other and different from that which was common to all the rest of the public. A mere prohibition on members of the public generally from doing what it would otherwise be lawful for them to do is not enough.

The Attorney-General, however, may sue, either ex officio, or under the relator procedure. In the latter case although, as we have seen,[149] the relator is liable for the costs, and though the conduct of the proceedings is left in his hands, it is in his hands as agent for the Attorney-General, who retains control. The Attorney-General not only can, but does, scrutinize and criticize draft pleadings, and directs what interlocutory steps should be taken. He may continue relator proceedings even though the relator has died, and no compromise can be arrived at without his concurrence. It is entirely a matter for the Attorney-General to decide whether he should commence litigation or not, and that the court has no jurisdiction to control the exercise of his discretion. The only control is parliamentary.[150]

It should be added that local authorities have been given various powers to initiate proceedings without the intervention of the Attorney-General. These include, inter alia, proceedings in respect of a statutory nuisance under the Environmental Protection Act 1990[151] and more generally under the Local Government Act 1972 where the local authority considers it expedient for the promotion or protection of the interests

---

[146] But in some circumstances a prerogative remedy may be available—see (1978) 94 LQR 4 (HWRW); *R v IRC, ex p National Federation of Self-Employed and Small Business Ltd* [1980] QB 407, [1980] 2 All ER 378, CA; (1982) Cambrian LR 32 (J A Jolowicz).

[147] [1982] AC 173, [1981] 2 All ER 456, HL; *Gouriet v Post Office Engineering Union*, supra, HL, at 518, 114, per Lord Fraser of Tullybelton; *RCA Corpn v Pollard* [1983] Ch 135, [1982] 3 All ER 771, CA, discussed (1983) 133 NLJ 527 (G Mitchell); (1983) 99 LQR 182 (G Samuel); [1983] Conv 451 (H Carty); *X (minors) v Bedfordshire County Council* [1995] 2 AC 633, [1995] 3 All ER 353, HL; *Mid Kent Holdings plc v General Utilities plc* [1996] 3 All ER 132. See also (1987) 38 NILQ 118 (A M Tettenborn).

[148] *Rickless v United Artists Corpn* [1988] QB 40, [1987] 1 All ER 679, CA.   [149] See p 598, supra.

[150] *Gouriet v Post Office Engineering Union*, supra, HL. See *Imperial Tobacco Ltd v A-G* [1979] QB 555, [1979] 2 All ER 592, CA; (1978) 41 MLR 58 (T C Hartley) and [1979] Pub L 214 (P P Mercer).

[151] Section 81(5).

of the inhabitants of their area.[152] But something more than infringement of the criminal law must be shown before the assistance of civil proceedings, by way of injunction, can be invoked by a local authority.[153]

Once the matter is before the court it is for the court to decide what the result of the litigation shall be,[154] though in a case in which the Attorney-General is acting ex officio, the very fact that he has initiated proceedings, thereby showing that in his opinion the acts of the defendant warrant an injunction, will carry weight with the court.[155] In particular, where the Attorney-General establishes deliberate and still continuing breaches of the law, the court will in the exercise of its discretion normally grant an injunction, unless after hearing both sides it comes to the conclusion that the matter is too trivial to warrant it, or that an injustice would be caused by it, or that there is some other good reason for refusing to enforce the general right of the public to have its laws obeyed. The mere fact that there is no immediate injury in a narrow sense to the public is not a ground for refusing an injunction at the instance of the Attorney-General who, representing the community, has a larger and wider interest in seeing that the laws are obeyed and order maintained. Thus in a narrow sense there was no public injury, possibly even a public benefit, in, for instance, *A-G v Sharp*[156] where the defendant persistently ran omnibuses without the proper licence, and *A-G v Harris*,[157] where the defendants sold flowers from stalls erected on the pavement near a cemetery in breach of the Manchester Police Regulation Act 1844. Further, in an action by the Attorney-General the court, although retaining its discretion, ought to be slow to say that the Attorney-General should first have exhausted other remedies.[158]

Where the Attorney-General or a local authority seeks an injunction to restrain the commission of a statutory offence, the court, in deciding how it should exercise its discretion, will consider the extent to which the statutory remedies have been exhausted. In *A-G v Harris*[151] the two defendants had been prosecuted and convicted no less than 142 and 95 times respectively before proceedings were brought for an injunction, but there are exceptions to the prima facie rule that the High Court will intervene only in the case of persistent law-breaking. These include, inter alia, cases

---

[152] Section 222. See *Stoke-on-Trent City Council v B & Q (Retail) Ltd* [1984] AC 754, [1984] 2 All ER 332, HL; *Runnymede Borough Council v Ball* [1986] 1 All ER 629, CA; *Waverley Borough Council v Hilden* [1988] 1 WLR 246; (1979) 95 LQR 174 (D Feldman); [1983] JPEL 511 (E F Cousins and R Anthony).

[153] *Stoke-on-Trent City Council v B & Q (Retail) Ltd*, supra, HL; *Stoke-on-Trent City Council v B & Q plc* [1991] Ch 48, [1991] 4 All ER 221; further proceedings C-169/91 [1993] 1 All ER 481, ECJ; [1993] 2 All ER 297n, HL; *Newport Borough Council v Khan* [1991] 1 EGLR 287, CA. The exercise by the local authority of their statutory powers may be the subject of judicial review. As to the grant of an injunction under the Town and Country Planning Act 1990, s 187B in relation to breaches of planning control, see *South Bucks D C v Porter* [2003] UKHL 26, [2003] 3 All ER 1: *South Cambridgeshire D C v Persons Unknown* [2004] EWCA Civ 1280, (2004) *Times*, 11 Nov, CA and p 572, supra. See also [2004] JPEL 8 (I Loveland).

[154] *A-G v Birmingham, Tame and Rea District Drainage Board*, supra, *A-G v Harris*, supra.

[155] A local authority application under s 222 of the Local Government Act 1972 seems not to carry any special weight—see (1986) 45 CLJ 374 (S Tromans).

[156] [1931] 1 Ch 121, [1930] All ER Rep 741, CA.

[157] [1961] 1 QB 74, [1960] 3 All ER 207, CA; *A-G v Chaudry* [1971] 3 All ER 938, CA.

[158] *A-G v Bastow* [1957] 1 QB 514, [1957] 1 All ER 497.

where some permanent damage to the public interest is being done,[159] where the intervention of the court is required as a matter of urgency,[160] where the defendant is quite deliberately organizing and maintaining a system which is designed to break the law,[161] where resort to the statutory remedy would be futile[162] or where the court draws the inference that the defendant's unlawful operations will continue unless and until effectively restrained by the law and that nothing short of an injunction will be effective to restrain him.[163] In an appropriate case it may even be possible to obtain an injunction before there has been any resort to the statutory remedies at all.[164]

8 TO RESTRAIN A BREACH OF TRUST

In the exercise of its inherent jurisdiction over trustees the court will inquire what personal obligations are binding on them and in an appropriate case will enforce those obligations by the grant of an injunction.[165] Here an injunction is granted not in aid of a legal right, but to protect a purely equitable claim. Thus, for instance, in *Dance v Goldingham*[166] trustees for sale of land inserted depreciatory conditions of sale without reasonable cause. An injunction to restrain completion of the sale was issued against both the trustees and the purchaser,[167] the court holding it irrelevant that the claimant had only a small interest under the trust, that she was an infant and that the action may have been started from some other motive. More recently, in *Waller v Waller*,[168] a wife sought an injunction to restrain her husband from making or completing any sale of the matrimonial home without her consent. She and her husband were tenants in common in equity, but the legal estate was vested in the husband alone. Notwithstanding the imposition of the statutory trust for sale,[169] the husband alone entered into a contract of sale with a third party, without having appointed

---

[159] *A-G v Ashborne Recreation Ground Co* [1903] 1 Ch 101.

[160] *A-G v Chaudry*, supra, CA; *Kirklees Metropolitan Borough Council v Wickes Building Supplies Ltd* [1993] AC 227, [1992] 3 All ER 717, HL.

[161] *Stafford Borough Council v Elkenford Ltd* [1977] 2 All ER 519, CA (Sunday market: one enforcement notice under planning law and one prosecution and conviction under the Shops Act 1950); *Stoke-on-Trent City Council v B & Q (Retail) Ltd* [1984] AC 754, [1984] 2 All ER 332, HL; *Kirklees Metropolitan Borough Council v Wickes Building Supplies Ltd*, supra HL.

[162] *Runnymede Borough Council v Ball* [1986] 1 All ER 629, CA. See (1992) 142 NLJ 428 (M Beloff).

[163] *City of London Corpn v Bovis Construction Ltd* [1992] 3 All ER 697, CA; *Kirklees Metropolitan Borough Council v Wickes Building Supplies Ltd*, supra, HL.

[164] *A-G v Chaudry*, supra, CA; *Stafford Borough Council v Elkenford Ltd*, supra, CA; *Hammersmith London Borough v Magnum Automated Forecourts Ltd* [1978] 1 All ER 401, CA.

[165] *Chellaram v Chellaram* [1985] Ch 409, [1985] 1 All ER 1043.

[166] (1873) 8 Ch App 902. See generally, *Balls v Strutt* (1841) 1 Hare 146.

[167] The question whether the purchaser might have a personal right of action against the trustees was left open.

[168] [1967] 1 All ER 305.

[169] *Bull v Bull* [1955] 1 QB 234, [1955] 1 All ER 253, and see Megarry and Wade, *Law of Real Property*, 5th edn, p 438.

another trustee and without consulting his wife. The injunction was granted.[170] Other cases show that an injunction may be granted to restrain trustees from distributing the estate otherwise than in accordance with the terms of the trust instrument,[171] from introducing ministers into the pulpit who were not ministers of the Church of Scotland, in breach of the provisions of the trust,[172] or otherwise disturbing the management of a chapel by the majority of trustees,[173] from demolishing a building,[174] from mortgaging the trust property unnecessarily,[175] or from selling it to anyone at a lower price than that offered by the reversioner and without first communicating with him.[176]

9 IN MATRIMONIAL AND OTHER FAMILY MATTERS

The Family Law Act 1996, replacing and extending earlier legislation, gives the courts wide powers both in divorce and other matrimonial proceedings, and in cases where a man and a woman have been living together without being married to each other. The Act gives the courts jurisdiction to grant orders to restrain one party from forcing his or her society on another or otherwise molesting that other, and/or prohibiting him or her from entering on or coming within a specified distance of property occupied by the person seeking the order. The details of these provisions are primarily matters of family law, and are not dealt with in this work.[177]

10 IN COMPANY MATTERS

The legal capacity of a company regulated by the Companies Act 1985 is defined by the memorandum of association, and if a company attempts to do an ultra vires act, that is one beyond its legal powers, even a single shareholder has a right to resist it, notwithstanding that it may have been sanctioned by all the directors and a large majority of the shareholders, and the court will interpose on his behalf by injunction.[178] A

---

[170] The third party was not a party to the proceedings, and the injunction was granted on an undertaking by the wife to join him as a defendant, and he was given liberty to apply to discharge the injunction.

[171] *Fox v Fox* (1870) LR 11 Eq 142.   [172] *Milligan v Mitchell* (1837) 3 My & Cr 72.

[173] *Perry v Shipway* (1859) 4 De G & J 353.   [174] *Ludlow Corpn v Greenhouse* (1827) 1 Bli NS 17.

[175] *Rigall v Foster* (1853) 18 Jur 39.   [176] *Wheelwright v Walker* (1883) 23 Ch D 752.

[177] As to the balance between the freedom of the press and the protection of children see *Re S (a child)(identification: restriction on publication)* [2004] UKHL 47, [2004] 4 All ER 683; *Re X, Y (children)* [2004] EWHC 762 (Fam), [2004] EMLR 29.

[178] *Simpson v Westminster Palace Hotel Co* (1860) 8 HL Cas 712: *Mosely v Koffyfontein Mines Ltd* [1911] 1 Ch 73, CA; affd sub nom *Koffyfontein Mines Ltd v Mosely* [1911] AC 409, HL; *Parke v Daily News Ltd* [1962] Ch 927, [1962] 2 All ER 929 (principle unaffected, but decision would now be different by reason of Companies Act 1985, s 719).

mere creditor, as opposed to a shareholder, however, has no such right, and, as Lord Hatherley LC observed,[179] he cannot claim 'the interference of this court on the ground that he, having no interest in the company, except the mere fact of being a creditor, is about to be defrauded by reason of their making away with their assets'.

11 FREEZING OR MAREVA INJUNCTIONS AND SEARCH OR ANTON PILLER ORDERS[180]

In *Bank Mellat v Nikpour*[181] Donaldson LJ referred to the Mareva injunction and the Anton Piller order as the law's two 'nuclear' weapons. The object of a freezing injunction, previously called a Mareva injunction, is to freeze the defendant's assets so as to ensure that they are not spirited away before judgment leaving nothing on which the claimant's judgment can bite. It is a prohibitory injunction. By contrast the search order, previously called an Anton Piller order, is a mandatory injunction. It orders the defendant to permit the claimant to enter his, the defendant's, premises for specified purposes. It came into being to deal with situations created by infringements of patents, trade marks and copyright, and in particular with acts of so-called video piracy. It is designed to provide a quick and efficient means of recovering infringing articles and of discovering the sources from which the articles have been supplied and the persons to whom they are distributed before those concerned have had time to destroy or conceal them.

As we have seen,[182] an interim injunction—and freezing injunctions and search orders are invariably interim orders—will normally only be granted upon notice, so as to give the defendant a full opportunity to resist the claim. However it has long been accepted that in a case of urgency an interim injunction may be granted without notice, and for obvious reasons both freezing injunctions and search orders are invariably applied for without notice in the first instance, though the courts have laid down guidelines to be applied to try to ensure that the defendant is not treated unfairly. In a matter of extreme urgency it may be obtained before issue of the claim, and may even be granted over the telephone.[183]

It may be noted that a freezing injunction is often sought on its own, but a claim for a search order is almost invariably accompanied by a claim for a freezing injunction, and many of the same considerations apply to both forms of relief. There is, however,

---

[179] *Mills v Northern Rly of Buenos Ayres Co* (1870) 5 Ch App 621 at 628.

[180] See, generally, (1989) Supreme Court Journal 1 (P H Pettit); (1990) 20 UWALR 143 (Jill Martin); (1990) 20 UWALR 169 (I C F Spry); (1993) 109 LQR 432 (A A S Zuckerman); *Equity & Contemporary Legal Developments* (ed S Goldstein), 793 (P H Pettit); (1999) 62 MLR 539 (P Devonshire); (1999) 49 UTLJ 1 (R J C Deane).

[181] [1985] FSR 87, CA, at 92.   [182] Supra, p 572.

[183] See *P S Refson & Co Ltd v Saggers* [1984] 3 All ER 111. It is not the practice in the Chancery Division to grant a without notice order for more than seven days. See the *Chancery Guide*, para 1.35.

one important distinction. In both cases the defendant will be given the right to apply on short notice for the injunction to be discharged. This provides a reasonable safe-guard in the case of a freezing injunction, which can be lifted on very short notice. The defendant may have suffered some damage, but it is likely to be limited. In the case of a search order his theoretical right to apply to have the order discharged is likely to be of little, if any, value to him. He does not know the order has been made until it has been served upon him. At the same time as the order is served, he comes under an immediate obligation to consent to the entry into and search of his premises and the removal therefrom of material specified in the order. If he does not consent, he is at risk of committal to prison for contempt of court even if the reason for his refusal to consent is his intention to apply to have the order discharged. Accordingly it is right to regard a search order as an even more drastic remedy than the freezing injunction, and for the courts to act with even greater caution in granting it.

(a) THE FREEZING OR 'MAREVA' INJUNCTION

(i) Origins

In *Mareva Compania Naviera SA v International Bulkcarriers SA*[184] the Court of Appeal was following and applying its own decision given a month earlier in *Nippon Yusen Kaisha v Karageorgis*.[185] Lord Denning MR presided over both these decisions which he subsequently observed[186] set in motion 'The greatest piece of judicial law reform in my time'. Until these cases the conventional wisdom[187] was that *Lister & Co v Stubbs*[188] prevented a claimant from obtaining an injunction restraining the defend-ant from removing or disposing out of the jurisdiction property that would otherwise be available to satisfy a judgment that it was likely that the claimant would obtain against him. In the *Nippon* case[189] the court was well aware of the position, and Lord Denning, with whom the other members of the court agreed, quite deliberately enun-ciated a change in the practice. There was nothing, he said, to prohibit such an order, and it was warranted by the predecessor[190] of s 37(1) of the Supreme Court Act 1981 which empowers the High Court to grant an injunction in all cases in which it appears to the court to be just and convenient to do so. This provision, it has been held, enables the court not only to grant a freezing injunction, but also to grant any ancillary order that appears just and convenient for the purpose of ensuring that the freezing injunction is effective.[191] It may also be granted after judgment has been

---

[184] [1980] 1 All ER 213n, [1975] 2 Lloyd's Rep 509, CA.   [185] [1975] 3 All ER 282, CA.
[186] In *The Due Process of Law*, p 134. See [1999] Denning LJ 25 (J Stevens).
[187] See eg *The Siskina* [1977] 3 All ER 803, HL, per Lord Hailsham LC at 828.
[188] (1890) 45 Ch D 1, CA.   [189] Supra, CA.
[190] Section 45(1) of the Supreme Court of Judicature (Consolidation) Act 1925.
[191] *Derby & Co Ltd v Weldon (No 6)* [1990] 3 All ER 263, [1990] 1 WLR 1139, CA. See also *Camdex International Ltd v Bank of Zambia (No 2)* [1997] 1 All ER 728, CA.

entered but before execution has been successfully levied, to restrain a judgment debtor from dealing with or disposing of his assets pending execution.[192]

The juridical basis of a freezing injunction remains unclear. It is quite a different injunction from any other: it is not connected with the subject matter of the cause of action in issue in the proceedings, and it does not prevent the defendant from doing something which, if done, would be a wrong attracting a remedy. Section 37(3) of the 1981 Act, a new provision, did not, as has sometimes been said, turn the freezing injunction into a statutory remedy, but it assumed that the remedy existed, and tacitly indorsed its validity. It is, perhaps, best regarded as a special exception to the general law.[193] It has a direct effect on third parties who are notified of it and who hold assets comprised in the order.[194]

A freezing order does not entitle a party in whose favour it was granted to say that he has a property or security interest in the defendant's assets in question, even where the order fixes on a single asset and even where that asset is land.[195]

When freezing injunctions were first granted, no maximum amount was inserted. Quite soon,[196] however, it became the preferred and usual practice to make 'maximum sum' orders, that is, injunctions which only freeze the defendant's assets up to the level of the claimant's prima facie justifiable claim, leaving him free to deal with the balance. The freezing injunction has been held to be inappropriate where relatively small sums are involved.[197]

(ii) Extent of the jurisdiction

The purpose of a freezing injunction is to ensure that the orders of the court are effectively enforced, in particular that there is a fund available to meet any judgment obtained by the claimant against the defendant.[198] Prior to 1982 the effect of the decision of the House of Lords in *The Siskina*,[199] was that the court could not grant a freezing injunction unless there was in existence an action, actual or potential, claim-

---

[192] *Orwell Steel (Erection and Fabrication) Ltd v Asphalt & Tarmac (UK) Ltd* [1985] 3 All ER 747; *Hill Samuel & Co Ltd v Littaur* [1985] NLJ Rep 57. And, in aid of enforcement of a judgment against one defendant, against a co-defendant in respect of whom all causes of action had been abandoned: *Mercantile Group (Europe) AG v Aiyela* [1994] QB 366, [1994] 1 All ER 110, CA.

[193] *Mercedes-Benz AG v Leiduck* [1996] AC 284, [1995] 3 All ER 929, PC.

[194] See *Babanaft International Co SA v Bassatne* [1990] Ch 13, [1989] 1 All ER 433, CA. See also (1989) 8 CJQ 263 (Janet Dine and J MacEvoy Jnr).

[195] *Kastner v Jason* [2004] EWCA Civ 1599, [2005] 1 Lloyd's Rep 397.

[196] See *A v C* [1980] 2 All ER 347 at 351 per Robert Goff; *Z Ltd v A-Z and AA-LL* [1982] 1 All ER 556 CA, per Lord Denning MR at 565 and Kerr LJ at 575. (There is a misprint in 575, b1 where 'plaintiff' should read 'defendant'); *Charles Church Developments plc v Cronin* [1990] FSR 1.

[197] *Sions v Price* (1988) *Independent*, 19 December, CA.

[198] See *Derby & Co v Weldon (Nos 3 & 4)* [1990] Ch 65, sub nom *Derby & Co v Weldon (No 2)* [1989] 1 All ER 1002, CA, and *Derby & Co Ltd v Weldon (No 6)*, supra, CA; *C Inc plc v L* [2001] 2 All ER (Comm) 446.

[199] Supra, HL. It is available to the Securities and Investments Board—*Securities and Investments Board v Pantell SA* [1990] Ch 426, [1989] 2 All ER 673 discussed [1994] JBL 8 (D Crighton).

ing substantive relief[200] which it was within the jurisdiction of the court to grant.[201] Accordingly if a claimant had a claim against the defendant in the courts of a foreign country, but where the defendant had no assets in the foreign country, he could not obtain a freezing order freezing assets in this country with the consequence that the claimant would have no effective remedy.[202] Now, however, as a consequence of the Civil Jurisdiction and Judgments Act 1982, s 25,[203] as extended by the Civil Jurisdiction and Judgments Act 1982 (Interim Relief) Order 1997,[204] the position has been reached that the High Court has power to grant interim relief in aid of substantive proceedings of whatever kind and wherever taking place.[205] It was observed in *Fourie v Le Roux*[206] that interim relief is defined in s 25(7) as being the kind of relief which the English courts have power to grant in proceedings relating to matters within its jurisdiction. This emphasizes that where there are foreign proceedings those proceedings must have a claim the equivalent of which in England would be sufficient for the English court to accept jurisdiction for granting a freezing order.

Originally the remedy was regarded as exceptional, but it rapidly became extremely popular.[207] It will, however, only be granted where there is a good reason to apprehend that a debtor would remove assets out of the jurisdiction or otherwise dispose of them

---

[200] See *Siporex Trade SA v Comdel Commodities Ltd* [1986] 2 Lloyd's Rep 428 (injunction will be refused where declaration sought but no legal or equitable right). In *A v B* [1989] 2 Lloyd's Rep 423 a conditional freezing injunction was granted only to come into effect if, as, and when a vessel was delivered, at which point of time the plaintiffs might acquire a cause of action. This beneficial development was halted by the Court of Appeal in *Veracruz Transportation Inc v VC Shipping Co Inc* [1992] 1 Lloyd's Rep 353, noted [1992] LMCLQ 161 (P Marshall); (1992) 108 LQR 175 (L Collins); and argued to be wrongly decided by D Wilde in [1993] LMCLQ 309; and *Zucker v Tyndall Holdings plc* [1992] 1 All ER 124, [1992] 1 WLR 1127, CA, discussed (1992) 142 NLJ 1511 (R Harrison). However it has been held that where the claimant seeks a freezing injunction before accrual of a cause of action, the court may indicate that it will be willing in principle to grant the injunction once the cause of action has accrued: this happened in *Re Q's Estate* [1999] 1 All ER (Comm) 499, and the injunction was subsequently granted 25 minutes after the cause of action accrued. The requirement of a pre-existing cause of action only applies in ordinary disputes relating to the alleged violation of private rights: *Morris v Murjani* [1996] 2 All ER 384, [1996] 1 WLR 848, CA, distinguishing cases involving s 333 of the Insolvency Act 1986. See [1996] LMCLQ 268 (P Devonshire).

[201] But the mere fact that the defendant, otherwise subject to the jurisdiction of the court, is entitled to a stay does not deprive the court of the power to grant an interlocutory injunction: *Channel Tunnel Group Ltd v Balfour Beatty Construction Ltd* [1993] AC 334, [1993] 1 All ER 664, HL. See (1993) 109 LQR 342 (L Collins). It was held in *Department of Social Security v Butler* [1995] 4 All ER 193, [1995] 1 WLR 1528, CA, that there is no jurisdiction to grant a freezing injunction in relation to the duty to pay under a maintenance assessment made under the Child Support Act 1991, a duty which cannot be enforced by action in any civil court.

[202] See *Mercedes-Benz AG v Leiduck* [1996] AC 284, [1995] 3 All ER 929, PC.

[203] As amended by the Civil Jurisdiction and Judgments Act 1991, s 3, Sch 2 para 12.

[204] SI 1977/302. See (1997) 18 Co Law 188 (S Robert-Tissot).

[205] See *Crédit Suisse Fides SA v Cuoghi* [1998] QB 818, [1997] 3 All ER 724, CA; (1998) 17 CJQ 35 (D Capper). In granting interim relief a court should generally seek to avoid making orders inconsistent with those of the courts in which the primary litigation was taking place, even where the primary court had made orders of a kind that would not have been made in domestic litigation: *State of Brunei Darussalam v Bolkiah* (2000) *Times* 5 September.

[206] [2005] EWCA Civ 204, [2005] All ER (D) 111 (Mar).   [207] See *The P* [1992] 1 Lloyd's Rep 470.

to defeat a creditor's claim.[208] It cannot be used simply to improve the position of claimants in an insolvency,[209] merely to exert pressure on the defendant to settle the action, or to safeguard in advance the making of an unjustifiable payment, such as an illegal premium on the assignment of a lease.[210] And the claimant must always at least show that he has a good arguable case,[211] the ultimate test being whether, in the words of s 37(1) of the 1981 Act, 'it appears to the court to be just and convenient' to grant the injunction. In a time of rapidly growing commercial and financial sophistication the courts have adapted the remedy to meet the current wiles of those defendants who are prepared to devote as much energy to making themselves immune to the courts' orders as to resisting the making of such orders on the merits of their case. The trial judge has to exercise a discretion, with which on general principles the Court of Appeal will be reluctant to interfere.[212] Further the exercise by a judge of his discretion in one case cannot provide a precedent binding upon another court concerned with another case, save in so far as that exercise is based upon basic principles applicable in both cases.[213]

Where an injunction is sought under s 25 of the Civil Jurisdiction and Judgments Act 1982, sub-s (2) provides that the court may refuse to grant relief if, in the opinion of the court, the fact that the court has no jurisdiction apart from the section makes it inexpedient for the court to grant it. The meaning of this 'inelegant' provision was explained in *Crédit Suisse Fides Trust SA v Cuoghi*,[214] where it was observed that the English court should not be deterred from granting relief in support of proceedings taking place elsewhere by the fact that its role is only an ancillary one unless the circumstances of the particular case make the grant of relief inexpedient. The question is not whether the circumstances are exceptional or very exceptional, but whether it would be inexpedient to make the order. An order may be made even though to make such an order would be beyond the powers of the court seised of the substantive proceedings: in making an order in such a case the court would be supplementing

---

[208] *Montecchi v Shimco (UK) Ltd* [1979] 1 WLR 1180, CA; *Bakarim v Victoria P Shipping Co Ltd* [1980] 2 Lloyd's Rep 193; *Re Bank of Credit and Commerce International SA (No 9)* [1994] 3 All ER 764, CA. An injunction may be discharged or varied if there is no longer a risk that the assets will be dissipated, as may be the case where administrative receivers are appointed under a company debenture: *Capital Cameras Ltd v Harold Lines Ltd* [1991] 3 All ER 389, [1991] 1 WLR 54.

[209] *Iraqi Ministry of Defence v Arcepey Shipping Co SA, The Angel Bell* [1981] QB 65, [1980] 1 All ER 480; *K/ S A/S Admiral Shipping v Portlink Ferries Ltd* [1984] 2 Lloyd's Rep 166, CA; *Investment and Pensions Advisory Service Ltd v Gray* [1990] BCLC 38.

[210] *Z Ltd v A-Z and AA-LL* [1982] QB 558, [1982] 1 All ER 556, CA; *P C W (Underwriting Agencies) Ltd v Dixon* [1983] 2 All ER 158.

[211] *Establishment Esefka International Anstalt v Central Bank of Nigeria* [1979] 1 Lloyd's Rep 445, CA; *Ninemia Maritime Corpn v Trave Schiffahrtsgesellschaft mbH & Co KG* [1984] 1 All ER 398, [1983] 1 WLR 1412, CA.

[212] *Avant Petroleum Inc v Gatoil Overseas Inc* [1986] 2 Lloyd's Rep 236, CA; *Derby & Co Ltd v Weldon (No 2)* and *(Nos 3 & 4)*, supra, CA.

[213] *Derby & Co Ltd v Weldon (Nos 3 & 4)* supra, CA.

[214] [1997] 3 All ER 724, CA. See *Motorola Credit Corpn v Uzon (No 2)* [2003] EWCA Civ 752, [2004] 1 WLR 113.

the jurisdiction of the foreign court in accordance with Article 24 of the Lugano Convention and principles which are internationally accepted.

Where an application is made for in personam relief in ancillary proceedings, two considerations which are highly material are the place where the person sought to be enjoined is domiciled and the likely reaction of the court which is seised of the substantive dispute. Where a similar order has been applied for and refused by that court, it would generally be wrong for the English court to interfere. But where the other court lacks jurisdiction to make an effective order against a defendant because he is resident in England, it does not at all follow that it would find an order by an English court objectionable. It would obviously weigh heavily, probably conclusively, against the grant of interim relief if such a grant would obstruct or hamper the management of the case by the court seised of the substantive proceedings, or give rise to a risk of conflicting, inconsistent or overlapping orders in other courts.

(iii) Guidelines[215]

Lord Denning MR set out guidelines to be borne in mind in *Third Chandris Shipping Corpn v Unimarine SA*.[216] These have been added to and elaborated in later cases. They are:

(i) The claimant should make full and frank disclosure of all matters within his knowledge[217] which are material for the judge to know[218] and, so long as the proceedings are on a without notice basis, should bring to the attention of the court any subsequent material changes in the situation.[219] If material non-disclosure is established the court will be astute to ensure that a plaintiff who obtains a without notice injunction without full disclosure is deprived of any advantage he may have derived by the breach of duty. Thus if there has been non-disclosure of a substantial kind, the freezing injunction will normally be discharged and not immediately reimposed. 'The parties', it has been said,[220] 'should be restored to the position they were in prior to the ex parte application, that is when no freezing injunction was in force. No doubt this means that a defendant will have the opportunity of making away with his assets but that is due to the plaintiff's failure properly to make his

---

[215] For standard forms of order see CPR 25 PD-014–015.

[216] [1979] QB 645, [1979] 2 All ER 972, CA. See also *Flightwise Travel Services Ltd v Gill* (2003) *Times*, 5 December. As to the practice see *ALG Inc v Uganda Airlines Corpn* (1992) *Times*, 31 July.

[217] He will be deemed to know matters which would have been revealed if proper enquiries had been made: *Behbehani v Salem* [1989] 2 All ER 143, [1989] 1 WLR 723n, and see (1989) 139 NLJ 407 (J de B Bate).

[218] This was elaborated by Ralph Gibson LJ in *Brink's-MAT v Elcombe* [1988] 3 All ER 188, CA, where the relevant cases are referred to.

[219] *Commercial Bank of the Near East plc v A, B, C and D* [1989] 2 Lloyd's Rep 319; *W v H (Family Division: without notice orders)* [2001] 1 All ER 300. As to overlap between an advocate's individual duty to the court and the collective duty to the court of a claimant and his team of legal advisers see *Memory Corpn v Sidhu plc (No 2)* [2000] 1 WLR 1443, CA.

[220] *Ali & Fahd Shobokshi Group Ltd v Moneim* [1989] 2 All ER 404, per Mervyn Davies J at 414; *Dubai Bank Ltd v Galadari* [1990] 1 Lloyd's Rep 120, CA; *Gulf Interstate Oil Corpn v ANT Trade and Transport Ltd of Malta* [1999] 1 All ER (Comm) 97.

initial application.' But Ferris J insisted, in *Lagenes Ltd v It's At (UK) Ltd*[221] that the court retains a discretion. The court must take into account all the relevant circumstances, including the gravity of the breach of the duty of disclosure, the excuse or explanation offered and the severity and duration of the prejudice occasioned to the defendant, always bearing in mind the overreaching objective and the need for proportionality.[222] It is no answer to say that the orders improperly obtained have in fact been fruitful.[223]

(ii)   The claimant should give particulars of his claim against the defendant, stating the ground of his claim and the amount thereof, and fairly stating the points made against it by the defendant.

(iii) The claimant should normally give some grounds for believing that the defendants have assets here. There are 'no limitations put on the word "assets", from which it follows that this word includes chattels such as motor vessels,[224] jewellery, objets d'art and other valuables as well as choses in action.'[225] It may include goodwill.[226] Existence of a bank account in England is enough whether in overdraft or not.[227] It is not restricted to movable assets.[228]

The words 'his assets and/or funds' in the standard form of freezing order are not apt to cover assets and funds which belong, or are assumed to belong, beneficially to someone other than the person restrained. They are confined to assets and funds belonging to the defendant, and which are and should remain available to satisfy the claim against him. The court could, however, make an appropriately worded order to cover assets and funds which might not belong beneficially to the defendant, though such an order would be discharged or modified if it was subsequently established that the assets belonged beneficially to a third party.[229]

Assets should be identified with as much precision as is reasonably practicable.[230]

(iv)   The claimant should give some grounds for believing that there is a risk of the assets being removed from the jurisdiction, or otherwise dealt with so as to defeat the ends of justice, before the judgment or award is satisfied. The test is whether the court should conclude that the refusal of a freezing injunction would involve a real

---

[221] [1991] FSR 492.   [222] *Memory Corpn v Sidhu (No 2)* [2000] 1 WLR 1443, CA.

[223] *Manor Electronics Ltd v Dickson* [1988] RPC 618.

[224] See *Clipper Maritime Co Ltd of Monrovia v Mineralimportexport*, [1981] 3 All ER 664, [1981] 1 WLR 1262.

[225] *CBS United Kingdom Ltd v Lambert* [1982] 3 All ER 237, CA, per Lawton LJ giving the judgment of the court at 241.

[226] *Darashah v UFAC (UK) Ltd* (1982) Times, 30 March, CA.

[227] But a bank guarantee providing for payment outside the jurisdiction is not an asset here, even though it may be a chose in action whose situs under English rules of conflict of laws is in London—*Intraco Ltd v Notis Shipping Corpn* [1981] 2 Lloyd's Rep 256, CA.

[228] *Derby & Co Ltd v Weldon (No 2)*, supra, CA.

[229] *Federal Bank of the Middle East Ltd v Hadkinson* [2000] 2 All ER 395, CA.

[230] As to assets which may belong to a third party see *SCF Finance Co Ltd v Masri* [1985] 2 All ER 747, CA; *Allied Arab Bank Ltd v Hajjar* [1989] Fam Law 68, CA; *TSB Private Bank International SA v Chabra* [1992] 2 All ER 245, [1992] 1 WLR 231; *Yukong Line v Rendsburg* [2001] 2 Lloyd's Rep 113, CA. See (1999) 62 MLR 539 (P Devonshire).

risk that a judgment or award in favour of the claimant would remain unsatisfied.[231]

(v)   The claimant must, as in the case of any interim injunction, give an undertaking in damages, which, exceptionally, in this case will normally extend to the costs of third parties.[232] The claimant must disclose any material change for the worse in his financial position.[233] However, the undertaking need not always be supported by assets: a legally aided claimant may be granted an injunction even though his undertaking may be of little value.[234]

(vi)   As regards any asset to which the injunction applies but which has not been identified with precision (for example, money held in an identified bank account) the claimant may also be required to give an undertaking to pay reasonable costs incurred by any third party to whom notice of the terms of the injunction is given. This applies to the costs of ascertaining whether or not any asset to which the order applies, but which has not been identified in it, is within his possession or control.[235]

(vii) The standard form of order[236] permits the defendant to spend specified sums to meet reasonable living expenses,[237] defend himself in the action,[238] and carry out transactions in the ordinary course of business such as the payment of trade creditors,[239] which may include repayment of a loan which is unenforceable by virtue of the Consumer Credit Act 1974.[240] It may, however, be granted even where a defendant proposed to effect a bona fide transfer of assets for a price in accordance with a valuation from an independent and respectable firm of accountants.[241]

As to legal costs, where the claimant has a proprietary claim safeguards may be inserted in the order to give an ultimately successful claimant some protection from the defendant in effect paying his legal costs out of the claimant's property. Further, though the effect of the usual proviso is that it is not a breach of the order to use

[231] *Ninemia Maritime Corpn v Trave Schiffahrtsgesellschaft mbH & Co KG* [1984] 1 All ER 398, CA. For the somewhat different approach in matrimonial proceedings see *Shipman v Shipman* [1991] 1 FLR 250; *Ghoth v Ghoth* [1992] 2 All ER 920, CA, and (1991) 141 NLJ 1340 (Susan Edwards and Ann Halpern); [1995] PCB 368 (P Moor and Jacqueline Humphreys).

[232] See *Miller Brewing Co v Mersey Docks and Harbour Co* [2003] EWHC (Ch) 1606, [2004] I P & R 542, and p 596, supra.

[233] *Staines v Walsh* (2003) *Times*, 1 August.

[234] *Allen v Jambo Holdings Ltd* [1980] 2 All ER 502 [1980] 1 WLR 1252, CA. See *DPR Futures Ltd* [1989] 1 WLR 778, on undertaking by liquidator; *Belize Alliance of Conservation Non-Governmental Organisations v Department of the Environment of Belize* [2003] UKPC 53, [2004] 2 P & CR 13.

[235] *Searose Ltd v Seatrain (UK) Ltd* [1981] 1 All ER 806, [1981] 1 WLR 894.   [236] See CPR 2A-161.

[237] *TDK Tape Distributor (UK) v Videochoice Ltd* [1985] 3 All ER 345. See CPR 25 PD-014.

[238] *PCW (Underwriting Agencies) Ltd v Dixon* [1983] 2 All ER 158; *Mansour v Mansour* [1990] FCR 17, CA, where it was said that it had never been the purpose of freezing injunctions to inhibit people from taking part in litigation.

[239] *X v Y* [1990] 1 QB 220, [1989] 3 All ER 689. In *Normid Housing Association Ltd v Ralphs and Mansell (No 2)* [1989] 1 Lloyd's Rep 274, CA, the court refused to grant a freezing injunction sought with the sole purpose of preventing the defendant entering into a bona fide settlement with his insurers.

[240] *Iraqi Ministry of Defence v Arcepey Shipping Co SA, The Angel Bell* [1981] QB 65, [1980] 1 All ER 480. As to subsequent qualifications to the injunction see ibid per Robert Goff J at 71, 486; *A v C (No 2)* [1981] QB 961n, [1981] 2 All ER 126. See (1989) 86 Sol Jo 22 (T Taylor).

[241] *Customs and Excise Comrs v Anchor Foods Ltd* [1999] 3 All ER 268.

funds to pay reasonable legal expenses, it is no guarantee in advance that, if at trial the claimant is successful in establishing a proprietary claim against the defendant such that money so expended turned out to have been the claimant's, the solicitors acting for the defendant could avoid a claim of constructive trust for knowing receipt being raised against them.[242]

(viii) A claimant who succeeds in obtaining a freezing injunction is under an obligation to press on with his action as rapidly as he can so that, if he should fail to establish liability in the defendant, the disadvantage that the injunction imposes on the defendant will be lessened so far as possible.[243]

Finally, it may be noted that if the court makes an order within its jurisdiction, then a party is bound to obey it at the risk of contempt proceedings if he does not, and the subsequent discharge of the order as having been irregularly obtained does not affect the disobedient party's liability to penalties for contempt.[244]

(iv) Third parties

(a) Third party with notice of freezing injunction against defendant

Although the freezing injunction is an in personam order against the defendant, any third party who has notice of a freezing injunction which affects money or other assets of the defendant in his hands will be guilty of contempt of court if he knowingly assists in the disposal of assets, whether or not the defendant has notice of the injunction.[245] Thus as soon as a bank is given notice of a freezing injunction it should freeze the defendant's bank account, but the standard form of order does not prevent any bank from exercising any right of set off it may have in respect of any facility which it gave to the defendant before it was notified of the order.[246] As we have seen[247] where a third party is guilty of contempt the penalty imposed depends on the degree of culpability. Thus where a bank mistakenly releases assets in breach of an injunction, in some circumstances the gravity of the offence may justify sequestration of the

---

[242] *United Mizrahi Bank Ltd v Doherty* [1998] 2 All ER 230, [1998] 1 WLR 435. See [1998] NLJ Easter Appeals Supp 11 (A P Thomas).

[243] *Lloyds Bowmaker Ltd v Britannia Arrow Holdings plc* [1988] 3 All ER 178, CA; *Town and Country Building Society v Daisystar Ltd* [1989] NLJR 1563, CA; *A/S D/S Svendborg v Awada* [1999] 2 Lloyd's Rep 244 (notwithstanding delay application to discharge injunction refused: it was not a case where there had been a deliberate tactical decision by the claimants to obtain a freezing injunction and then sit on it without taking any steps in the action whatever using the freezing injunction as a weapon of attack, whereby the freezing injunction is abused).

[244] *Wardle Fabrics Ltd v G Myristis Ltd* [1984] FSR 263; *Columbia Picture Industries Inc v Robinson* [1986] 3 All ER 338, at 368. These are both cases on search orders but the same principle must apply to freezing injunctions.

[245] *Z Ltd v A-Z and AA-LL* [1982] QB 558. [1982] 1 All ER 556, CA; *Bank Mellat v Kazmi* [1989] QB 541, [1989] 1 All ER 925, CA.

[246] *Gangway Ltd v Caledonian Park Investments (Jersey) Ltd* [2001] 2 Lloyd's Rep 715. As to joint bank accounts see [1994] LMCLQ 651 (P Matthews). As to the duty of claimant's counsel and solicitors to provide a full note of the hearing to parties affected see *Interroute Telecommunications (UK) Ltd v Fashion Group Ltd* (1999) *Times*, 10 November.

[247] See p 591, supra.

bank's assets equivalent to the amount covered by the injunction.[248] Such an order would not, however, be a direct source of compensation for the claimant. It could only be used as a lever to enforce the court's original freezing order. In other circumstances there may not be such justification and the party in whose favour the injunction was made may consequently suffer loss irremediable by operation of the contempt procedure. However he may be able to succeed in negligence, for the bank owes to the party who had obtained the injunction a duty of care to prevent payments out of the frozen account.[249]

In justice to banks or other innocent third parties, the claimant comes under an obligation to indemnify them against any expenses or liabilities they are required to incur,[250] and they should be told with as much certainty as possible what they are to do or not to do. A freezing injunction is not intended to interfere with the ordinary rights and remedies of a third party in the ordinary course of its business,[251] as is well illustrated by *Galaxia Maritime SA v Mineralimportexport, The Eleftherios*[252] where Kerr LJ said it was a clear abuse of the jurisdiction to seek to prevent a ship belonging to an innocent third party, with the defendant's cargo on board, from sailing out of the jurisdiction. The rights of the innocent third party must prevail over the desire of the claimant to secure his position.

(b) Freezing injunction against third parties

If there is a claim for substantive relief by A against B (whether or not in the English court), or A has obtained a judgment against B (in the English court), then the English court can grant a freezing injunction against assets of C where it is arguable that those assets are in fact beneficially owned by B. Even where the assets of C are not, even arguably, beneficially owned by B, a freezing injunction against C may be granted in certain circumstances. The right of the claimant to such a freezing injunction is dependent upon A having a right against B, and that right itself giving rise to a right that B could exercise against C and his assets.[253]

---

[248] *Z Bank v D1* [1994] 1 Lloyd's Rep 656.

[249] *Customs and Excise Commissioners v Barclays Bank plc* [2004] EWCA Civ 1555 (Comm), [2005] 1 Lloyd's Rep 165, noted [2005] NLJ 82 (K J Tinkler); [2005] CLJ 26 (D Capper); (2005) 121 LQR 194 (P Mitchell and C Mitchell).

[250] *Searose Ltd v Seatrain (UK) Ltd* [1981] 1 All ER 806; *Clipper Maritime Co Ltd of Monrovia v Mineralimportexport* [1981] 3 All ER 664. The jurisdiction to require a cross-undertaking for the benefit of third parties is not restricted to freezing injunctions: *Allied Irish Bank v Ashford Hotels Ltd* [1997] 3 All ER 309, CA.

[251] *Oceanica Castelana Armadora SA v Mineralimportexport* [1983] 2 All ER 65. In particular the court is slow to interfere with routine banking transactions: *Lewis & Peat (Produce) Ltd v Almata Properties Ltd* [1993] 2 Bank LR 45, CA.

[252] [1982] 1 All ER 796, [1982] 1 WLR 539, CA. See also *Guinness Peat Aviation (Belgium) NV v Hispania Lineas Aereas SA* [1992] 1 Lloyd's Rep 190.

[253] *C Inc plc v L* [2001] 2 All ER (Comm) 446 (Default judgment against Mrs L, who arguably had a right to an indemnity from Mr L, which could be enforced by Mrs L or, if she would not do so, by a receiver appointed by the court). See (2002) 118 LQR 124 (P Devonshire).

(v) Whereabouts of defendant

In some of the early cases[254] it seems to have been assumed that the remedy was only available against foreign-based defendants. The Supreme Court Act 1981[255] now makes it clear that there is no distinction between English-based and foreign-based defendants.

(vi) Whereabouts of assets

The whereabouts of the assets to be subject to the order raises quite different issues, and is a fast-developing topic.[256] As a matter of English law the court has jurisdiction to grant relief against any party properly before it in relation to assets wherever situate, for the freezing jurisdiction is not a territorial jurisdiction, but depends on the unlimited jurisdiction of the court in personam against any person (whether an individual or a corporation) who under English procedure was properly made a party to proceedings pending in England.[257] However, in the ordinary case, that is a case where there is no question of extending the order beyond local assets, the practice is to require some grounds for believing the defendant has assets locally situate within the jurisdiction of the court.[258] In *Derby & Co Ltd v Weldon (Nos 3 & 4), (No 2)*[259] the Court of Appeal followed and applied three other of its recent decisions[260] and it can now be regarded as established that the court has jurisdiction to issue a freezing injunction over the defendant's assets wherever they may be. Such a worldwide injunction may be made before as well as after judgment. In the Court of Appeal Lord Donaldson MR agreed with the statement of Browne-Wilkinson VC at first instance that three requirements needed to be satisfied before taking what he referred to as 'the extreme step that is asked for in this case'.

First, he said, the special circumstances of the case must justify the exceptional order sought.

Secondly, he said, the order must be in accordance with the rationale on which a freezing injunction is based. The basic requirement is that the court should make an effective order to preserve assets against which an effective enforcement can be

---

[254] Eg *Rasu Maritime SA v Pertamina*, supra, CA; *The Agrabele* [1979] 2 Lloyd's Rep 117.

[255] Section 37(3).

[256] The possibility of an order for disclosure of assets is discussed later. See (1989) 105 LQR 262 (L Collins); (1989) 48 CLJ 199 (N H Andrews); (1990) LMCLQ 88 (A Malek and Caroline Lewis); (1991) 54 MLR 324 (D Capper).

[257] See *Derby & Co Ltd v Weldon (No 6)* [1990] 3 All ER 263, [1990] 1 WLR 1139, CA.

[258] *Third Chandris Shipping Corpn v Unimarine SA*, supra, CA; *A J Bekhor & Co Ltd v Bilton*, supra, CA; *Ashtiani v Kashi* [1987] QB 888, [1986] 2 All ER 970, CA; *Derby & Co Ltd v Weldon (Nos 3 and 4)* [1990] Ch 65, sub nom *Derby & Co Ltd v Weldon (No 2)* [1989] 1 All ER 1002, CA.

[259] Supra, CA; *Re Bank of Credit and Commerce International SA (No 9)* [1994] 3 All ER 764, CA. See (1989) 86 LSG 17/22 (I T Taylor); [1990] CJQ 12 (P Kaye); (1996) 59 MLR 460 (J A Epp); [1996] 15 CJQ 211 (D Capper).

[260] *Babanaft International Co SA v Bassatne* [1990] Ch 13, [1989] 1 All ER 433, CA; *Republic of Haiti v Duvalier* [1990] 1 QB 202, [1989] 1 All ER 456, CA; *Derby & Co Ltd v Weldon* [1990] Ch 48, [1989] 1 All ER 469, CA.

obtained eventually if the claimant is successful at the trial. In the Court of Appeal[261] Lord Donaldson MR pointed out that while the existence of *sufficient* assets within the jurisdiction is an excellent reason for confining the jurisdiction to such assets, other considerations apart the fewer the assets within the jurisdiction the greater the necessity for taking protective measures in relation to those outside it.

Thirdly, the order of the court should not conflict with the ordinary principles of international law. To deal with this the standard form[262] provides:

(1) Except as provided in paragraph (2) the terms of this order do not affect or concern anyone outside the jurisdiction of this court.
(2) The terms of this order will affect the following persons in a country or state outside the jurisdiction of this court
  (a) the Respondent or his officer or agent appointed by power of attorney
  (b) any person who
    (i) is subject to the jurisdiction of this court
    (ii) has been given written notice of this order at his residence or place of business within the jurisdiction of this court; and
    (iii) is able to prevent acts or omissions outside the jurisdiction of this court which constitute or assist in a breach of the terms of this order; and
    (iv) any other person, only to the extent that this order is declared enforceable by or is enforced by a court in that country or state.

The so-called *Baltic* proviso[263] should normally be added, namely that nothing in the order should, in respect of assets located outside England and Wales, prevent a party from complying with (i) what it reasonably believes to be its obligations, contractual or otherwise under the laws and obligations of the country or state in which those assets are situated or under the proper law of any bank account in question, or (ii) any orders of the courts of that country or state provided reasonable notice of any application for such an order has been given to the claimant's solicitors.[264]

Two further points may be made. First, a freezing injunction may relate not only to specified assets, but also to unspecified but ascertainable assets which may increase during the life of the injunction, such as all the defendant's assets within the jurisdiction.[265] Secondly, it may be noted that it was held in *Derby & Co Ltd v Weldon (No 6)*[266] that there is no reason in principle why, in an appropriate case, the court should not order the transfer of assets to a jurisdiction in which the order of the English court after the trial would be recognized, from a jurisdiction in which the

[261] *Derby & Co Ltd v Weldon (Nos 3 and 4), (No 2)*, supra CA.
[262] CPR 2A-161.
[263] From *Baltic Shipping v Translink Shipping Ltd* [1995] 1 Lloyd's Rep 673. See CPR 2A-161.
[264] *Bank of China v NBM LLC* [2002] 1 All ER 717, CA.
[265] *Cretanor Maritime Co Ltd v Irish Marine Management Ltd* [1978] 3 All ER 164.
[266] [1990] 3 All ER 263, [1990] 1 WLR 1139, CA, noted [1991] LMCLQ 26 (D Capper).

order would not be recognized and the issues would have to be relitigated, if the only connection of the latter jurisdiction with the matters in issue is financial in nature. However in considering whether to make such an order the court will proceed with great caution.

Finally, to cure the oppression potentially inherent in the worldwide enforcement of a worldwide freezing injunction the standard form of order contains undertakings not, without the leave of the court, (i) to seek to enforce the order, or seek a similar order, outside England and Wales, and (ii) to use information obtained by the order for the purpose of civil or criminal proceedings in England or Wales, or any other jurisdiction.

(vii) Disclosure of assets[267]

A v C [268] seems to have been the first reported case in which the question arose whether the court has jurisdiction to make an order for discovery in aid of a freezing injunction. In that case Goff J held that it had, and less than 10 years later Nicholls LJ was able to say, in *Derby & Co Ltd v Weldon*[269] that it was now established law that the English courts have jurisdiction to make a disclosure order in respect of assets outside England and Wales[270] both before judgment[271] and after judgment.[272] The Civil Procedure Rules[273] now provide that the court may grant an order directing a party to provide information about the location of relevant property or assets or to provide information about relevant property or assets which may be the subject of an application for a freezing injunction.[274]

(viii) Privilege against self-incrimination

The same principles apply in relation to freezing injunctions and search orders, and they are discussed in relation to the latter in respect of which the question more often arises.[275]

---

[267] See (1989) 139 NLJ 875 (P Kaye); (1998) 47 ICLQ 3 (C McLachlan).

[268] [1981] QB 956n, [1980] 2 All ER 347.

[269] [1990] Ch 48, [1989] 1 All ER 469, CA. The jurisdiction is conferred by s 37(1) of the Supreme Court Act 1981. It also appears to arise within the court's inherent jurisdiction: *Grupo Torras SA v Sheikh Fahad Mohammed Al-Sabah* [1996] 1 Lloyd's Rep 7, CA. See (1994) 144 NLJ 932 (P D Friedman).

[270] *A fortiori* they may do so in respect of assets within the jurisdiction.

[271] See *Republic of Haiti v Duvalier* [1990] 1 QB 202, [1989] 1 All ER 456, CA.

[272] *Interpool Ltd v Galani* [1988] QB 738, [1987] 2 All ER 981, CA; *Maclaine Watson & Co Ltd v ITC (No 2)*, supra, CA.

[273] CPR 25.1g. Risk of personal violence is no defence to disobedience to an order: *Coca Cola and Schweppes v Gilbey* [1996] FSR 23, CA.

[274] Cross-examination on an affidavit of assets may be ordered as an exceptional measure but should not become a routine feature: *Yukong Line Ltd v Rendsburg Investments Corpn of Liberia* [1996] 2 Lloyd's Rep 604. See also *Den Norske Bank ASA v Antonatos* [1999] QB 271, [1998] 3 All ER 74, CA; *Memory Corpn plc v Sidhu* [2000] Ch 645, [2000] 1 All ER 434.

[275] See p 657 et seq, infra.

(ix) Other orders in support of freezing injunction

The court has jurisdiction under s 37 to appoint a receiver by way of or in support of a freezing injunction,[276] and in an appropriate case it may be just and convenient to order a defendant to make a payment, or periodic payments, into a special account out of money already in his hands or coming into his hands from time to time. This may be a simpler and cheaper way of putting the money out of the reach of the defendant, though in most cases a freezing injunction can be buttressed adequately by notification of the injunction to banks and others.[277]

(b) THE SEARCH OR ANTON PILLER ORDER

(i) Origins

The search order slightly predates the freezing injunction. The first reported case is *EMI Ltd v Pandit*,[278] decided on 5 December 1974, and the first Court of Appeal decision, the one which gave its original name to the order, was *Anton Piller K G v Manufacturing Processes Ltd*,[279] decided at the end of 1975. The practice of granting search orders was approved in principle by the House of Lords in *Rank Film Distributors Ltd v Video Information Centre*.[280]

Let us consider the sort of situation which may give rise to a claim for a search order. A claimant may believe that it is essential to his case to have inspection of documents or other things in the possession of the defendant, and may have reason to fear that if the defendant is forewarned there is a grave danger that vital evidence will be destroyed, for example that papers will be burnt, or lost, or hidden, or taken beyond the jurisdiction, and thus the ends of justice will be defeated. It was established long ago in the leading case of *Entick v Carrington*[281] that no court has any power to use a search warrant to enter a man's house so as to see if there are papers or documents there which are of an incriminating nature, whether libels or infringements of copyright or anything else of the kind. In the *Anton Piller* case[282] itself Lord Denning MR said: 'None of us would wish to whittle down that principle in the slightest', and no doubt in theory that principle remained unimpaired.

The defendant served with a search order might well have regarded this as a lawyer's quibble and Lord Denning MR himself said it might seem to be a search warrant in disguise,[283] for what such an order did was to direct the defendant in personam by

---

[276] *Derby & Co Ltd v Weldon (Nos 3 and 4)* [1990] Ch 65, sub nom *Derby & Co Ltd v Weldon (No 2)* [1989] 1 All ER 1002, CA. See p 692 et seq, infra.

[277] *3 Style Ltd v Goss* (11 April 1990, unreported), CA, but available on Lexis.

[278] [1975] 1 All ER 418. See generally, (1983) 46 MLR 274 (Anne Staines); (1983) 80 LSG 467 (A Rosen); [1986] All ER Rev 225 (A A S Zuckerman). As to the position in Canada see (1996) 54 UT Fac LR 107 (P D Godin).

[279] [1976] Ch 55, [1976] 1 All ER 779, CA.   [280] [1982] AC 380, [1981] 2 All ER 76, HL.

[281] (1765) 2 Wils 275.   [282] Supra, CA.

[283] See also *Bhimji v Chatwani* [1991] 1 All ER 705, [1991] 1 WLR 989, where Scott J said that such orders 'involve the court in the hypocrisy of pretending that the entry and search are carried on because the owners of the premises have consented to it'.

what is in effect a mandatory injunction to give permission to the person serving the order and such other persons duly authorized by the claimant not exceeding a specified number, commonly four or five, forthwith to enter the defendant's premises for the purpose of inspecting and photographing and looking for and removing the things specified in the order.[284] True it is that the defendant could refuse to allow entry and inspection, but he did so at his peril. Disobedience of the order to permit entry and inspection may be a contempt of court,[285] and in the action refusal is almost certain to lead to adverse inferences being drawn against him. Most applications for a search order are made at a very early stage, but it was held in *Distributori Automatici Italia SpA v Holford General Trading Co Ltd*[286] that the court has jurisdiction to make an order after judgment for the purpose of eliciting documents which are essential to execution and which would otherwise be unjustly denied to the judgment creditor.

(ii) The Civil Procedure Act 1997

Section 7 of the above Act put the search order on a statutory footing, without any intention to limit or reduce the jurisdiction that had hitherto been exercised. The main purpose of the section was to dispense with the fiction that the entry on the premises is with the consent of the owner. It makes it clear that it is the court order which is the basis of the requirement to permit entry, not the implied consent of the owner.

The Act provides that the court may make an order[287] for the purpose of securing, in the case of any existing or proposed proceedings in the court:

(a) the preservation of evidence which is or may be relevant, or

(b) the preservation of property which is or may be the subject-matter of the proceedings or as to which any question arises or may arise in the proceedings.

The order may direct any person to permit[288] any person described in the order, or secure that any person so described is permitted:

(a) to enter premises in[289] England and Wales, and

(b) while on the premises, to take in accordance with the terms of the order any of the steps specified in the Act.

---

[284] The standard form of order set out in CPR 25 PD-016 extends to vehicles on or around the premises. The defendant is entitled to refuse access to anyone who could gain commercially from anything he might read or see on the premises.

[285] It has been held that a defendant will not be in breach until after a reasonable time for legal advice to be obtained has passed: *Bhimji v Chatwani*, supra, where the refusal of the defendants to permit entry until after the hearing of an application to discharge or vary the order heard in the afternoon of the day of service was held on the facts to be a mere technical breach of the order which did not justify committal or the imposition of any other penalty.

[286] [1985] 3 All ER 750, [1985] 1 WLR 1066.

[287] On the application of any person who is, or appears to the court to be likely to be, a party to proceedings in the court: Civil Procedure Act 1997, s 7(2).

[288] The meanings of the words 'any person' and 'permit' are considered in (1998) 17 CJQ 272 (M Dockray and Katherine R Thomas).

[289] 'Premises' includes any vehicle: ibid, s 7(8).

These steps are:

(a) to carry out a search for or inspection of anything described in the order, and

(b) to make or obtain a copy, photograph, sample or other record of anything so described.

The order may also direct the person concerned:

(a) to provide any person described in the order, or secure that any person so described is provided, with any information or article described in the order, and

(b) to allow any person described in the order, or secure that any person so described is allowed, to retain for safe keeping anything described in the order.

(iii) Pre-conditions to making order

According to Ormrod LJ in the *Anton Piller* case there are three essential pre-conditions to the making of an order. 'First, there must be an extremely strong prima facie case. Secondly, the damage, potential or actual, must be very serious for the plaintiff. Thirdly, there must be clear evidence that the defendants have in their possession incriminating documents or things, and that there is a real possibility[290] that they may destroy such material before an application inter partes can be made.' To these one may add Lord Denning MR's dictum[291] that the inspection must do no real harm to the defendant or his case. Lastly, the court will normally want to be satisfied that the plaintiff is good for any damages which might ultimately be ordered against him on the undertaking in damages that he will be called upon to give as a condition of the order.[292]

(iv) Safeguards to defendant

Guidelines have been promulgated and a standard form of order provided.[293] They provide for the order to be served by a supervising solicitor and carried out in his presence and under his supervision. The supervising solicitor should be an experienced solicitor, having some familiarity with the operation of search orders, who is not a member or employee of the firm acting for the applicant. Where the premises are likely to be occupied by an unaccompanied woman and the supervising solicitor is a man, at least one of the persons attending on the service of the order should be a woman. Where appropriate the applicant should be required to insure items removed.

---

[290] *Lock International plc v Beswick* [1989] 3 All ER 373, [1989] 1 WLR 1268. Because there is no such possibility it is inappropriate to make an order against a practising barrister—*Randolph M Fields v Watts* (1984) 129 Sol Jo 67, CA.

[291] In the *Anton Piller* case, supra, CA, at 783.

[292] *Vapormatic Co Ltd v Sparex* [1976] 1 WLR 939. But see *Allen v Jambo Holdings Ltd* [1980] 2 All ER 502, [1980] 1 WLR 1252, CA; *Belize Alliance of Conservation Non-Governmental Organisations v Department of the Environment of Belize* [2003] UKPC 53, [2004] 2 P & CR 13.

[293] See CPR 25 PD-016; *Gadget Shop Ltd v Bug.Com Ltd* [2001] FSR 383.

Entry is limited to working days between 9.30 am and 5.30 pm. The supervising solicitor must offer to explain to the person served with the order its meaning and effect fairly and in everyday language, and inform him of his right to seek legal advice, provided he does so at once.

The applicant must give the usual undertaking in damages, and an undertaking to issue a writ of summons as soon as possible. Any information or documents he obtains as a result of the order can only be used for the purposes of the proceedings.

To prevent other defendants being alerted the standard form of order provides that except for the purpose of obtaining legal advice the defendant must not directly or indirectly inform anyone of the proceedings or the contents of the order, or warn anyone that proceedings have been brought against him by the applicant, until a specified date.

As we have already seen, on a without notice application the court is concerned to see that the defendant is not treated unfairly. Just as in the case of an application for a freezing injunction the claimant should make full and frank disclosure of all matters within his knowledge which are material for the judge to know. The principles which have already been discussed in relation to freezing injunctions apply with at least equal force in applications for a search order.[294] Two additional points may be made.

First reference may be made to *Guess? Inc v Lee Seck Mon*[295] where a search order in relation to a claim for infringement of copyright had been discharged for substantial and serious non-disclosure of relevant facts by the claimant. In the Hong Kong Court of Appeal the question arose whether the judge, on a subsequent application for a fresh search order and an interim injunction, was entitled to take into account the 'yield' from the original search order. It was held that the judge had a discretion whether to exclude evidence thus obtained. However even where non-disclosure was innocent in that it was not done for improper motives, the court should not lightly allow a party to keep the benefit of it. Where non-disclosure was both serious and substantial the court should allow it only if good and compelling reasons for doing so are shown.

Secondly, in the case of an executed search order the court will not normally entertain an interim application for its discharge. Normally the only consequence of discharge is to enable the defendant to enforce the cross-undertaking in damages and that is a decision which can wait until the trial. Exceptionally, as in *Lock International plc v Beswick*[296] justice may require that the order should be discharged at an earlier point of time.

---

[294] See *Columbia Picture Industries Inc v Robinson* [1987] Ch 38, [1986] 3 All ER 338; *Lock International plc v Beswick* [1989] 3 All ER 373, [1989] 1 WLR 1268; *Intergraph Corp v Solid Systems CAD Services Ltd* [1993] FSR 617.

[295] [1987] FSR 125, applied *Naf Naf SA v Dickens (London) Ltd* [1993] FSR 424.

[296] Supra: *O'Regan v Iambic Productions Ltd* [1989] NLJR 1378.

(v) Privilege against self-incrimination

In *Rank Film Distribution Ltd v Video Information Centre*[297] the House of Lords held that a defendant would not be compelled to answer questions or disclose documents where compliance might involve self-incrimination including self-incrimination for civil contempt.[298] There is no way in which a court can compel disclosure while at the same time protecting the defendant from the consequences of self-incrimination. While there seems to be no privilege against self-incrimination in the case of offences under foreign criminal law, Morritt J in *Arab Monetary Fund v Hashim*[299] could see no reason why the possibility of self-incrimination or, indeed the incrimination of others, should not be a factor to be taken into account in deciding whether, and if so in what terms, a disclosure order should be made. The standard form of order informs the defendant of his right to refuse to disclose documents or answer questions which might incriminate him,[300] and the Civil Procedure Act 1997 expressly provides[301] that it does not affect any right of a person to refuse to do anything on the ground that to do so might expose him or his spouse to proceedings for an offence or for the recovery of a penalty.

Section 72 of the Supreme Court Act 1981 imposes an important restriction on the privilege against self-incrimination. It provides that, in proceedings to which it applies, primarily proceedings for infringement of rights pertaining to any intellectual property or for passing off, but not otherwise, a person is not to be excused from answering any question or complying with any order by reason that to do so would expose that person, or his or her spouse, to proceedings for a related offence or for the recovery of a related penalty.[302]

The withdrawal of the privilege against incrimination of self or spouse in these cases is qualified by a provision that statements or admissions made in answering questions or complying with an order shall not be admissible against the maker of the statement or admission or his spouse in proceedings for any related offence or for the recovery of any related penalty,[303] except in proceedings for perjury or contempt of court.[304]

Where s 72 does not apply the principle of the *Rank Film Distribution* case remains fully effective, which may give rise to great difficulties of proof in fraud cases. If there is a real risk of a conspiracy charge the judge will be unable to make a search order and

---

[297] [1982] AC 380, [1981] 2 All ER 76, HL, discussed (1981) 44 MLR 580 (A Stains) and (1982) 132 NLJ 471 (Philip Davis and Peter Russell).

[298] *Cobra Golf Ltd v Rata* [1998] Ch 109, [1997] 2 All ER 150.

[299] [1989] 3 All ER 466, [1989] 1 WLR 565. *Crédit Suisse Fides Trust SA v Cuoghi* [1998] QB 818, [1997] 3 All ER 724, CA; *Memory Corp plc v Sidhu* [2000] Ch 645, [2000] 1 All ER 434.

[300] See *Cobra Golf Ltd v Rata*, supra; *Den Norske Bank ASA v Antonatos* [1998] 3 All ER 74, CA.

[301] In s 7(7).

[302] As defined in s 2(5) of the Supreme Court Act 1981. Section 72 is discussed in (1982) 132 NLJ 983 (N Garnham). See *Crest Homes plc v Marks* [1987] AC 829, [1987] 2 All ER 1074, HL; *Cobra Golf Ltd v Rata*, supra. Cf the provisions in s 31 of the Theft Act 1968 in relation to offences under that Act; *Khan v Khan* [1982] 2 All ER 60, [1982] 1 WLR 513, CA.

[303] Section 72(3). See *Charles of the Ritz Group Ltd v Jory* [1986] FSR 14.   [304] Section 72(4).

in consequence vital evidence may be destroyed. This has led to judicial calls for an amendment to the legislation.[305]

Apart from the question of privilege the court will not require a defendant to reveal breaches he has committed either of an undertaking given by him or of an order made upon him in exercise of the ancillary jurisdiction to secure enforcement of a court's order, such as a freezing injunction or a search order, unless that disclosure is necessary for the actual working out or the proper operation of the court's order.[306]

(vi) Exceptional or routine?

Between 1974 and 1986 the search order had ceased to be the very rare and exceptional remedy that had been envisaged in the early cases, and such orders were according to Scott J in *Columbia Pictures Industries Inc v Robinson*[307] 'regularly applied for and granted in all divisions of the High Court'. In no previous case had the propriety of the obtaining and execution of a search order been examined otherwise than in interim proceedings.

Scott J of course accepted that search orders have become established as one of the tools of the administration of justice in civil cases with the main purpose of preserving evidence necessary for the claimant's case. He was, however, concerned with the effect that such an order, made in secrecy ex parte, may have on the defendant. It had to be realized, he said,[308] 'that a common, perhaps the usual, effect of the service and execution of an Anton Piller order is to close down the business which, on the applicants' evidence, is being carried on in violation of their rights.' If that is the intention of the applicants it is, he later stated,[309] an improper one and an abuse of the search order procedure.

He also pointed out[310] that the service and execution of a search order may well have a personal as well as a commercial effect. 'Anton Piller orders are often granted not simply in respect of business premises but in respect of the respondent's home. He is required, on pain of committal, to open the doors of his house to the plaintiff's representatives and to permit a search of the contents thereof. The plaintiffs and their representatives are at liberty to search and rummage through the personal belongings of any occupant of the house and to remove the material they consider to be covered by the terms of the order. The traumatic effect and the sense of outrage likely to be produced by an invasion of home territory in the execution of an Anton Piller order is obvious.' He asked the question:[311] 'What is to be said of the Anton Piller procedure which, on a regular and institutionalized basis, is depriving citizens of their property

---

[305] *Sociedade Nacional de Combustiveis de Angola UEE v Lundquist* [1991] 2 QB 310, [1990] 3 All ER 283, CA, noted (1990) 106 LQR 389 (A Zuckerman), (1990) 134 Sol Jo 1365 (N Padfield). *Den Norske Bank ASA v Antonatos* [1999] QB 271, [1998] 3 All ER 74, CA. See (1986) 13 Co Law 66 (Ben Strong); (1990) 106 LQR 601 (M Dockray and H Laddie). See also *At & T Istel Ltd v Tully* [1993] AC 45, [1992] 3 All ER 523, HL, noted (1994) 15 Co Law 26 (J Cotton); (1993) CLJ 42 (N H Andrews).

[306] *Bhimji v Chatwani (No 3)* [1992] 4 All ER 912.   [307] [1986] 3 All ER 338, at 369.

[308] In *Columbia Picture Industries Inc v Robinson*, supra, at 369.   [309] Ibid, at 377.

[310] Ibid, at 368, 369.   [311] Ibid, at 369.

and closing down their businesses by orders made ex parte, on applications of which they know nothing and at which they cannot be heard, by orders which they are forced, on pain of committal, to obey, even if wrongly made?'

Scott J concluded[312] that the 'decision whether or not an Anton Piller order should be granted requires a balance to be struck between the plaintiff's need that the remedies allowed by the civil law for the breach of his rights should be attainable and the requirements of justice that a defendant should not be deprived of his property without being heard.' In his view the practice of the court had swung much too far in favour of the claimants and search orders had been too readily granted and with insufficient safeguards for respondents. This view was endorsed by Hoffman J in *Lock International plc v Beswick*[313] and it has been stated[314] that the warning signals in these two cases have been heeded and that search orders are now made much more sparingly than previously.

(vii) Guidelines

Scott LJ[315] went on to lay down guidelines that should be applied bearing in mind the draconian and essentially unfair nature of the order from the point of view of the defendant. They are:

(i)   Search orders should be drawn so as to extend no further than the minimum extent necessary to achieve the purpose for which they are granted,

(ii)   a detailed record of the material taken should always be required to be made by the solicitors who execute the order before the material is removed from the defendant's premises,

(iii)   no material should be taken from the defendant's premises by the executing solicitors unless it is clearly covered by the terms of the order. The practice which had grown up whereby the defendant is procured by the executing solicitors to give consent to additional material being removed is wholly unacceptable,

(iv)   seized material the ownership of which is in dispute, such as allegedly pirated tapes, should not be retained by the plaintiff's solicitors pending trial. It should be delivered to the defendant's solicitor as soon as he is on the record subject to an undertaking for its safe custody and production, if necessary, at the trial. All documents which are removed should be immediately photocopied and returned,[316]

(v)   affidavits in support of an application for a search order ought to err on the side of excessive disclosure. In the case of the material falling into the grey area of possible relevance, the judge, not the plaintiff's solicitors, should be the judge of relevance.

It may be added that a solicitor in charge of the execution of a search order who does

---

[312] Ibid, at 371.

[313] [1989] 3 All ER 373, [1989] 1 WLR 1268. See (1990) 106 LQR 173 (L Collins).

[314] By Nicholls V-C in *Universal Thermosensors Ltd v Hibben* [1992] 3 All ER 257, [1992] 1 WLR 840.

[315] In *Columbia Picture Industries Inc v Robinson*, supra, at 371, 372; *Araghchinchi v Araghchinchi* [1997] 2 FLR 142, CA.

[316] *L T Piver SARL v S & J Perfume Co Ltd* [1987] FSR 159. As to the duty of a solicitor in relation to items obtained by him, see *Gordon v Summers* [2003] FSR 719.

not observe the exact terms of the court's order may be held to be in contempt of court.[317]

(c) EXTENSION OF FREEZING INJUNCTIONS AND SEARCH ORDERS

The Court of Appeal has been prepared to extend the jurisdiction by making further orders, even if of a novel character, if that is thought necessary for the proper protection of the claimant. In *Bayer AG v Winter*[318] the judge had granted relief in the freezing injunction and search order forms, including orders requiring the defendants to disclose all documents relating to the counterfeit insecticide with which the case was concerned, and to make an affidavit detailing all transactions relating thereto. The judge at first instance, however, refused to make further orders restraining the defendant from leaving the jurisdiction for a specified time and ordering him to deliver up his passport to the claimant. The Court of Appeal made the orders sought. It was said that if the defendant failed to provide the information ordered to be given by the first instance judge, the defendant, if within the jurisdiction, could be compelled to attend for cross examination. However, the order of the court would be frustrated if he left the jurisdiction without having done so. The further order sought would prevent this happening and any risk of hardship to the defendant was covered by his right to apply to the court for the order to be varied or discharged. Both Ralph Gibson and Fox LJJ referred to the observations of Cumming-Bruce LJ in *House of Spring Gardens Ltd v Waite*.[319]

The court has the power (and, I would add, the duty) to take such steps as are practicable upon an application of the plaintiff to procure that where an order has been made that the defendants identify their assets and disclose their whereabouts, such steps are taken as will enable the order to have effect as completely and successfully as the powers of the court can procure.

This principle was held to justify the orders made, though the restraint on leaving the country was limited to two days, since it was recognized that it was an interference with the liberty of the subject. *Bayer AG v Winter*[320] was cited in *Re J (a minor)*[321] where it was said that if the orders made in that case were available to protect a claimant's financial position, *a fortiori* they should be available to provide for the welfare and future upbringing of a ward of court.

The order in *Bayer AG v Winter* was served on the defendant on 22 December, and

---

[317] *VDU Installations Ltd v Integrated Computer Systems and Cybernetics Ltd* [1989] FSR 378.

[318] [1986] 1 All ER 733, [1986] 1 WLR 497, CA. A disclosure order contained in an injunction carries with it an obligation to do more than simply tell the truth. Accordingly a party who gave a truthful but inaccurate answer, without taking reasonable steps to investigate its truth, has been held to be in contempt of court: *Bird v Hadkinson* [1999] BPIR 653.

[319] [1985] FSR 173, CA, at 183. In this case in aid of a freezing injunction an order had been made that the defendants identify their assets and disclose their whereabouts.

[320] Supra. See *O'Neill v O'Keeffe* [2002] IR 1.

[321] [1988] 1 FLR 65; *Den Norske Bank ASA v Antonatos* [1999] QB 271, [1998] 3 All ER 74, CA.

on Christmas Eve Scott J[322] was asked for orders that the defendant be directed to attend the court at a suitable time for cross-examination, and that his liberty to leave the country be further restricted to enable the cross-examination to take place. Scott J again[323] referred to the tendency of the courts to make ex parte orders of an increasingly extensive sort and thought that the basis on which ex parte orders can properly be made requires to be very carefully examined. Though he accepted that the court has, through its in personam jurisdiction, power to subject citizens to an interrogatory process designed to enforce court orders, he found it very difficult to envisage any circumstances in which, as a matter of discretion, it would be right to make such an order as was sought in the case before him. In ringing tones reminiscent of Lord Denning he said.[324]

Star Chamber interrogatory procedure has formed no part of the judicial process in this country for several centuries. The proper function of a judge in civil litigation is to decide issues between parties. It is not, in my opinion, to preside over an interrogation.

Accordingly Scott J refused to order the defendant to submit himself to cross-examination, or to restrict his liberty to leave the country for a further period.

In another case, *Coca-Cola Co v Gilbey*,[325] a search order required the defendant, inter alia, to disclose information about the activities of a criminal organization manufacturing counterfeits of the claimant's products and the names of other individuals involved. It was accepted that there was a prima facie case for the defendant's involvement. He applied for the discharge of the disclosure part of the order on the ground of the risk of violence to him and his family if he complied with it. In the exercise of its discretion the court had no hesitation in holding that the interest of the claimant and the public in the provision of the information outweighed the interest of the defendant in avoiding any risk of violence to which the disclosure might expose him.

It may be useful to look in a little more detail at *House of Spring Gardens Ltd v Waite*.[326] A freezing injunction and a search order having been granted there was a hearing at which there was affidavit evidence in opposition to the continuance of the freezing injunction described by Vinelott J as 'almost insultingly brief and inexplicit'. He proceeded to order disclosure of the defendant's assets which was, he said, 'essential if the Mareva injunction is to be properly policed'. The claimants did not think that the affidavits sworn by the defendants in purported compliance with Vinelott J's orders were a proper compliance, and sought an order that they should be at liberty to cross-examine the defendants.

The applications came before Nourse J and the order was made by consent. The

---

[322] *Bayer AG v Winter (No 2)* [1986] 2 All ER 43, [1986] 1 WLR 540.

[323] *Bayer AG v Winter (No 2)* supra, was decided a few days after *Columbia Picture Industries Inc v Robinson*, supra.

[324] *Bayer AG v Winter (No 2)*, supra, at 46.

[325] [1995] 4 All ER 711 (the CA refused leave to appeal).

[326] Supra CA. See *Arab Monetary Fund v Hashim* [1989] 3 All ER 466, [1989] 1 WLR 565. See KCLJ 1 (1990–91) 1 (Jill Martin).

cross-examination was arranged for hearing before Scott J, who was troubled by the fact that there was no specific present issue which would call for immediate decision by him after the cross-examination. He commented: 'It is not the business of the court to "police" its orders. The business of the court is to decide issues between parties', and discharged Nourse J's order, apparently on the ground that Nourse J had not in fact had power to make an order in that form. The Court of Appeal, as already indicated, reversed this ruling and affirmed the wide power of the court to implement a lawful order by ancillary orders required for their efficacy, such as an order calling for cross-examination on an affidavit. Slade LJ, giving the leading judgment, said that the court would always take care to ensure that the defendant is not unfairly treated, and will be particularly on guard against potential oppression in a case where there is no immediate issue calling for decision. But though in general, as Scott J said, the business of the court is to decide issues between parties, in the special context of the freezing injunction there is the function of protecting the parties to the litigation in such manner as may be just and convenient pending the final resolution of the issues at the trial.

It is convenient to mention here *B v B*,[327] where Wilson J fully accepted that under s 37(1) of the Supreme Court Act 1981 there are a number of circumstances in which it is possible to restrain a party from leaving the jurisdiction and to make a consequential order for the surrender of his or her passport. The jurisdiction exists where the other party has established a right to interlocutory relief, such as a search order, which would otherwise be rendered nugatory, and, indeed, exists in principle in aid of all the court's procedures leading to the disposal of the proceedings. It can also be invoked after judgment. However it was not available in the case before the court to enable the court to restrain a judgment debtor from leaving the jurisdiction indefinitely until the debt was paid, since it was ancillary to other powers of the court and was not a free-standing enforcement procedure in its own right.

[327] [1997] 3 All ER 258, [1998] 1 WLR 329.

29

SPECIFIC PERFORMANCE

1 NATURE OF REMEDY

(a) MEANING

This equitable remedy consists of an order of the court directing a party to a contract to perform his obligations thereunder according to its terms. It has been said[1] that it 'presupposes an executory as distinct from an executed agreement, something remaining to be done, such as the execution of a deed or a conveyance, in order to put the parties in the position relative to each other in which by the preliminary agreement they were intended to be placed'. In this passage Lord Selborne was drawing a broad distinction between the class of executory agreements, such as agreements for the sale of land and marriage articles, and the principles applicable to specific performance of them on the one hand, and on the other a very different class of agreements which he described[2] as 'ordinary agreements for work and labour to be performed, hiring, and service, and things of that sort', for which specific performance is not available. The strict or proper sense of the term 'specific performance' apparently designates the first type of case where an executory agreement is to be followed by the execution of a more formal instrument. However, the term is commonly used, and will henceforward be used in this work, as including the equitable right to specific relief in respect of an intermediate class of agreements which do not call for the execution of a further instrument. The principles applicable seem to be the same.[3]

The basis of the jurisdiction to grant specific performance has always been the inadequacy of the common law remedy of damages for breach of contract. 'The court gives specific performance instead of damages, only when it can by that means do

---

[1] Per Lord Selborne LC in *Wolverhampton and Walsall Rly Co v London and North Western Rly Co* (1873) LR 16 Eq 433 at 439; approved by Lord Macnaghten in *Tailby v Official Receiver* (1888) 13 App Cas 523 at 547, HL. For a review of New Zealand law, see (1987) 6 Otago LR 420 (A Beck).

[2] Ubi supra.

[3] *Australian Hardwoods Pty Ltd v Railways Comr* [1961] 1 All ER 737, PC. But see Meagher, Gummow and Lehane, *Equity—Doctrine and Remedies*, 3rd edn, pp 495–498, Heydon, Gummow and Austin, *Cases and Materials on Equity and Trust*, 4th edn, para 3801.

more perfect and complete justice.'[4] An alternative way of putting it is to say that the question is whether it is just in all circumstances for the plaintiff to be confined to his remedy in damages.[5] Thus the common law remedy may be regarded as inadequate and specific performances may be available in an appropriate case, where only nominal damages could be recovered by an action at law,[6] though it is not clear why this should be so. Nominal damages are awarded because the claimant is regarded as having suffered no loss, and they should accordingly be regarded as adequate in principle. Specific performance may also be available where there is a continuing obligation which would necessitate a series of actions at law for damages.[7] Further, there are, on the one hand, as we shall see, many cases where specific performance is not available although damages may be obtained, and on the other hand, although originally specific performance was not granted unless the claimant had first recovered damages at law[8] it has long since been recognized that in some cases specific performance may be granted though there is no right to recover damages at law at all. Thus damages at law can only be awarded for a *breach* of contract, but a breach of contract is not absolutely essential to a claim for specific performance. Accordingly the claimant in *Marks v Lilley*[9] was held to be justified in issuing a writ for specific performance of a contract for the sale of land after the date fixed for completion had passed, although no notice had been served making time the essence of the contract, and in *Hasham v Zenab*[10] even before the date for completion had been reached. Further, it seems that the fact that an action of law will not lie,[11] or even that it is doubtful if it will,[12] may itself be a ground for granting specific performance. And specific performance may be granted where equity takes a less rigid view than the

---

[4] Per Lord Selborne LC in *Wilson v Northampton and Banbury Junction Rly Co* (1874) 9 Ch App 279 at 284; *Chinn v Collins* [1979] Ch 447, [1979] 2 All ER 529, CA; reversed without affecting this point [1981] AC 533, [1981] 1 All ER 189, HL. See, generally, Reiter and Swan, *Studies in Contract Law*, pp 123 et seq (R J Sharpe); (1987) 38 NILQ 244 (Elizabeth Macdonald); (1999) 10 KCLJ 1 (R Austen-Baker).

[5] *C N Marine Inc v Stena Line A/B (No 2)* [1982] 2 Lloyd's Rep 336 at 348, CA, per May LJ. Jones and Goodhart, *Specific Performance*, 2nd edn, p 5, say: 'Specific performance should be decreed if it is the *appropriate* remedy.'

[6] *Beswick v Beswick* [1968] AC 58, [1967] 2 All ER 1197, HL.   [7] See *Beswick v Beswick*, supra, HL.

[8] *Dodsley v Kinnersley* (1761) Amb 403.

[9] [1959] 2 All ER 647. It has now been held that failure to complete a contract for the sale of land on the date specified in the contract constitutes a breach thereof both at law and in equity, even though the time for completion was not expressed to be of the essence of the contract—*Raineri v Miles* [1981] AC 1050, [1980] 2 All ER 145, HL. See [1982] Conv 191 (M P Thompson).

[10] [1960] AC 316, PC; *Manchester Diocesan Council for Education v Commercial and General Investments Ltd* [1969] 3 All ER 1593, [1970] 1 WLR 241. Of course the decree would not order performance to take place before the date of completion. And damages 'in addition' may be awarded under Lord Cairns' Act even though no decree of specific performance is made because the contract has been completed by the date of the hearing —*Oakacre Ltd v Claire Cleaners (Holdings) Ltd* [1982] Ch 197, [1981] 3 All ER 667, where damages could not have been awarded at law because the writ was premature having been issued five days before the completion date, at which time there had been no breach of contract. See also (1960) 76 LQR 200 (R E Megarry).

[11] *Wright v Bell* (1818) 5 Price 325.

[12] *Buxton v Lister* (1746) 3 Atk 383; *Doloret v Rothschild* (1824) 1 Sim & St 590.

common law; thus in *Mortlock v Buller*[13] Lord Eldon pointed out that specific performance with compensation might be granted where some unessential misdescription would defeat an action at law.

The question has not infrequently arisen as to the effect of a clause in the contract that if the primary obligation is not performed, a specified sum of money is to be paid either by way of penalty or as liquidated damages. The answer depends upon whether on the true construction of the contract, the defendant is intended to be able to choose either to do the thing specified in the contract or, alternatively, to pay the specified sum, or whether the intention is that he is bound to do the specified thing, the money clause being added by way of security. If the first construction is the correct one, specific performance cannot be obtained for the parties have in effect agreed that damages will be an adequate remedy and thus taken away the basis of a claim for specific performance.[14] If however the second construction is the true one, the court will decide the claim for specific performance disregarding the presence of the money clause. It makes no difference for this purpose whether the sum is intended as a penalty[15] or as liquidated damages, such as the common case of forfeiture of a deposit on a sale of land.[16]

It should be noted that although a contract for the sale of land continues to exist after an order for its specific performance has been made, the rights conferred by the contract do not remain unaffected. By applying for an order of specific performance and obtaining it, the applicant puts it into the hands of the court how the contract is to be carried out. If the order for specific performance is not complied with, the claimant may either apply to the court for enforcement of the order, or may apply to the court to dissolve the order and ask the court to put an end to the contract.[17]

(b) REMEDY IN PERSONAM

In relation to specific performance equity, as always, acts in personam. The leading case is *Penn v Lord Baltimore*[18] where Lord Hardwicke LC decreed specific performance of an English agreement relating to the boundaries between Pennsylvania and Maryland, despite the inability of the court to enforce its remedy in rem. And in

---

[13] (1804) 10 Ves 292 at 306. As to a condition substantially but not exactly performed see *Davis v Hone* (1805) 2 Sch & Lef 341, esp per Lord Redesdale, at 347.

[14] *Magrane v Archbold* (1813) 1 Dow 107; *Legh v Lillie* (1860) 6 H & N 165.

[15] *Howard v Hopkyns* (1742) 2 Atk 371; *Logan v Weinholt* (1833) 7 Bli NS 1.

[16] *Crutchley v Jerningham* (1817) 2 Mer 502 at 506, per Lord Eldon. Cf cases of negative contract specifically enforced by an injunction such as *Bird v Lake* (1863) 1 Hem & M 111. See *Ranger v Great Western Rly Co* (1854) 5 HL Cas 72.

[17] *Johnson v Agnew* [1980] AC 367, [1979] 1 All ER 883, HL, and see p 706 et seq, infra.

[18] (1750) 1 Ves Sen 444. Contrast *Re Hawthorne* (1883) 23 Ch D 743, where the claim was not for specific performance, but for account. There was no contract. The question was as to the title to land in a foreign country, and the court had no jurisdiction. See also *Chellaram v Chellaram* [1985] Ch 409, [1985] 1 All ER 1043.

Richard West Partners (Inverness) Ltd v Dick[19] specific performance was decreed of a contract for the sale of land outside the jurisdiction[20] against a defendant within it.

(c) DISCRETIONARY CHARACTER

'From the very first, when specific performance was introduced it has been treated as a question of discretion whether it is better to interfere and give a remedy which the common law knows nothing at all about, or to leave the parties to their rights in a Court of Law.'[21] It is undoubted however that this discretion is not arbitrary or capricious, but is governed so far as possible by fixed rules and principles.[22] The result is that in many cases, where the parties are under no disability and there is nothing objectionable in the nature or circumstances of the contract, a decree of specific performance is as much a matter of course in equity as damages are in common law,[23] and will be ordered even though the judge may think it to be a hard case for the defendant.[24] But, as will be seen, matters which would be irrelevant at common law, such as the conduct of the claimant, may be material in a claim for specific perform-ance.[25] Further, the court may have to take into account other equitable doctrines. Thus in *Langen and Wind Ltd v Bell*[26] the purchaser brought a specific performance action for the sale of shares, under a contract whereby the purchase price could not be ascertained for about two years after the agreed date for the transfer of the shares. The court had regard to the equitable principle that an unpaid vendor is entitled to a lien on the subject matter of the sale, and refused to grant an order for specific performance except in a form which would effectively safeguard the equitable lien.

(d) DAMAGES IN ADDITION TO OR IN SUBSTITUTION FOR SPECIFIC PERFORMANCE

The same statutory provisions apply in the case of a claim for an injunction which were discussed together with the relevant cases in chapter 26, section 3, p 580, supra.

---

[19] [1969] 1 All ER 289; affd [1969] 2 Ch 424, [1969] 1 All ER 943, CA. See also *Webb v Webb* [1992] 1 All ER 17, [1991] 1 WLR 1410, further proceedings [1994] QB 696, [1994] 3 All ER 911, ECJ; *Ashurst v Pollard* [2001] Ch 595, [2001] 2 All ER 75, CA.

[20] It was actually in Scotland.

[21] Per Rigby LJ in *Re Scott and Alvarez's Contract* [1895] 2 Ch 603 at 615, CA.

[22] *White v Damon* (1802) 7 Ves 30; *Lamare v Dixon* (1873) LR 6 HL 414. See *Haywood v Cope* (1858) 25 Beav 140 at 151.

[23] *Hall v Warren* (1804) 9 Ves 605.　　　[24] *Haywood v Cope* (1858) 25 Beav 140.

[25] *Cox v Middleton* (1854) 2 Drew 209; *Lamare v Dixon* (1873) LR 6 HL 414.

[26] [1972] Ch 685, [1972] 1 All ER 296.

(e) SPECIFIC PERFORMANCE WITH COMPENSATION

This is discussed in section 2(e), p 678, infra.

(f) SPECIFIC PERFORMANCE AND FREEZING INJUNCTION

In an appropriate case a court which had made an order for specific performance could, by a separate freezing injunction, restrain the vendor from dealing with all or some part of the purchase money. In *Seven Seas Properties Ltd v Al-Essa*[27] Hoffman J said that it would be excessively formalistic to insist upon two separate orders and that they could be combined into one.

2 GROUNDS ON WHICH SPECIFIC PERFORMANCE MAY BE REFUSED

Specific performance will not, of course, be granted unless there is, in accordance with the law of contract, a concluded contract, complete and certain[28] and even such a contract will not be enforced by specific performance if it is illegal or against the policy of the law,[29] even though valid according to the law of the country where it was made.[30] Moreover, a claimant who seeks specific performance can obtain it only if there is before the court every other person entitled to join with him in enforcing the contract.[31] Assuming, however, that these matters are satisfied, there are certain classes of contract where specific performance will nevertheless not be granted and certain defences may be available. Those more commonly arising will now be discussed.

---

[27] [1989] 1 All ER 164, [1988] 1 WLR 1272.

[28] See *Waring and Gillow Ltd v Thompson* (1912) 29 TLR 154, CA; *Fountain Forestry Ltd v Edwards* [1975] Ch 1, [1974] 2 All ER 280 (administrator purported to enter into a contract for the sale of land on behalf of himself and his co-administrator, who never ratified the contract. Purchaser refused specific performance against administrator); *Sudbrook Trading Estate Ltd v Eggleton* [1981] 3 All ER 105, [1981] 3 WLR 361, CA (option to purchase at price to be fixed by valuers nominated by parties—one party refused to appoint valuer—no concluded contract), reversed [1983] 1 AC 444, [1982] 3 All ER 1, HL, on ground that there was on its true construction a complete contract for a sale at a fair and reasonable price, and the court would substitute its own machinery for the agreed machinery which had broken down.

[29] *Rees v Marquis of Bute* [1916] 2 Ch 64; *Stuart v Kingman* (1979) 90 DLR (3d) 142 (contract document understated price to defraud revenue authorities). It is not clear how heavy is the burden of proof—see *De Hoghton v Money* (1866) 2 Ch App 164. Cf *Ailion v Spiekermann* [1976] Ch 158, [1976] 1 All ER 497—specific performance decreed free of illegal premium.

[30] *Hope v Hope* (1857) 8 De GM & G 731 at 743.   [31] *Tito v Waddell (No 2)*, supra, at 325, 310.

(a) CONTRACT RELATING TO PURE PERSONALTY

In general, specific performance of a contract relating to land[32] is granted as a matter of course, but it was settled at an early date that specific performance would not as a general rule be granted of a contract relating to other forms of property, primarily on the ground that damages is an adequate remedy. Thus, for instance, specific performance will not be granted of a contract to transfer government or other stocks or shares freely available on the market,[33] or coal[34] or other merchandise.

Where, however, for some reason damages would not be an adequate remedy, specific performance may be granted. Thus it may properly be granted where there is a contract for the purchase of articles of unusual beauty, rarity and distinction, or of a chattel of peculiar value to the plaintiff.[35] Though refused on other grounds, it would have been granted in *Falcke v Gray*[36] of a contract to purchase two china jars apparently worth at least £200, and no objection seems to have been taken to the jurisdiction in *Thorn v Public Works Comrs*[37] which involved a contract for the purchase of the arch-stone, the spandrill stone, and the Bramley Fall stone contained in the old Westminster Bridge which had been pulled down. Again specific performance may be granted of a contract for the transfer of shares,[38] or other property,[39] not freely available on the market. Specific performance may also be granted in relation to goods where there is an entire contract of land and goods,[40] and the goods are of such a nature that it would damage the land to remove them, or where there is a contract for the sale of a house and chattels in it, with the furnishings in situ, if damages would not be an adequate remedy.[41]

---

[32] Including a contractual licence—see *Verrall v Great Yarmouth Borough Council* [1981] QB 202, [1980] 1 All ER 839, CA, discussed infra p 680. Contrast *Webster v Newham London Borough Council* (1980) *Times*, 22 November (damages an adequate remedy—no specific performance). See [1984] Conv 130 (J Berryman) suggesting there may be a reappraisal where, for instance, the land is being purchased as an investment and damages would be an inadequate remedy, and (1985) 17 OLR 295 (J Berryman) for an historical perspective. And in Canada it has been held that specific performance should not be granted as a matter of course absent evidence that the property is unique to the extent that its substitute would not be readily available: *Semelhago v Paramadevan* [1996] 2 SCR 415.

[33] *Cud v Rutter* (1720) 1 P Wms 570 sub nom *Cuddee v Rutter* 5 Vin Abr 538 pl 21; *Adderley v Dixon* (1824) 1 Sim & St 607; *Pooley v Budd* (1851) 14 Beav 34. For an American suggestion for extending the remedy see (1979) Yale LJ 271 (A Schwartz).

[34] *Dominion Coal Co Ltd v Dominion Iron and Steel Co Ltd* [1909] AC 293, PC.

[35] Ships seem to be readily so regarded—*Behnke v Bede Shipping Co Ltd* [1927] 1 KB 649, [1927] All ER Rep 689; *Société Des Industries Métallurgiques SA v Bronx Engineering Co Ltd* [1975] 1 Lloyd's Rep 465, CA; *C N Marine Inc v Stena Line A/B (No 2)* [1982] 2 Lloyds Rep 336, CA—but it must depend on the facts.

[36] (1859) 4 Drew 651. See also *Phillips v Lamdin* [1949] 2 KB 33, [1949] 1 All ER 770.

[37] (1863) 32 Beav 490.

[38] *Duncuft v Albrecht* (1841) 12 Sim 189; cf *Sri Lanka Omnibus Co Ltd v Perera* [1952] AC 76, PC. As to choses in action see *Cogent v Gibson* (1864) 33 Beav 557.

[39] *Sky Petroleum Ltd v V I P Petroleum Ltd* [1974] 1 All ER 954 (petroleum where no alternative source of supply). The order was in form an injunction, but in substance specific performance. Cf *Re Wait* [1927] 1 Ch 606, CA where, however, the claim to specific performance was based solely on the predecessor of s 52 of the Sale of Goods Act 1979, discussed below. See (1984) 4 LS 102 (A S Burrows).

[40] *Nutbrown v Thornton* (1804) 10 Ves 159.

[41] *Record v Bell* [1991] 4 All ER 471, [1991] 1 WLR 853.

Finally statute[42] has intervened to empower the court to grant the buyer, but not the seller, a decree of specific performance in any action for breach of contract to deliver specific or ascertained goods. 'Specific goods' means 'goods identified and agreed upon at the time a contract of sale is made' and includes an undivided share, specified as a fraction or percentage, of goods identified and agreed as aforesaid,[43] and 'ascertained' probably means identified in accordance with the agreement after the time a contract of sale is made.[44] The court will exercise its discretionary power on established equitable principles.[45] In no case does it matter whether the property has passed to the buyer or not.[46] A new part 5A added to the Sale of Goods Act 1979[47] gives the court power to order specific performance of goods which do not conform to the contract of sale. It remains to be seen whether this provision will be held to apply to ordinary goods readily available on the market.

(b) VOLUNTARY CONTRACTS

Lord Hardwick's dictum[48] that 'the court never decrees specifically without a consideration' has been consistently followed, and it makes no difference that the contract is by deed. The rule, which can be regarded as an application of the maxim that equity will not assist a volunteer,[49] applies equally to a contract to create a trust or settlement.[50] It is thought not to have been affected by the Contracts (Rights of Third Parties) Act 1999.[51]

It should be noted that if a valid option to purchase is duly exercised, there will be constituted a perfectly ordinary contract for sale and purchase to which the remedy of specific performance may be applicable in the ordinary way. It is irrelevant that the contract may have arisen in pursuance of an option granted for valuable consideration, even though that consideration may be described as a token payment or, if by deed, may in fact have been granted without any payment.[52]

---

[42] Sale of Goods Act 1979, s 52, replacing earlier legislation.

[43] Ibid, s 61(1), as amended by the Sale of Goods (Amendment) Act 1995, s 2.

[44] Per Atkin LJ in *Re Wait* [1927] 1 Ch 606 at 630, CA.

[45] *Behnke v Bede Shipping Co Ltd*, supra; *Société Des Industries Metallurgiques SA v Bronx Engineering Co Ltd*, supra, CA.

[46] *Re Wait*, supra, at 617, per Hanworth MR; *Cohen v Roche* [1927] 1 KB 169 at 180.

[47] Added by the Sale and Supply of Goods to Consumers Regulations 2002, SI 2002/3045. See (2003) 119 LQR 541 (D R Harris).

[48] In *Penn v Lord Baltimore* (1750) 1 Ves Sen 444 at 450; *Groves v Groves* (1829) 3 Y & J 163; *Dean and Westham Holdings Pty Ltd v Lloyd* [1990] 3 WAR 235.

[49] *Ford v Stuart* (1852) 15 Beav 493 at 501. See p 104, supra.

[50] *Jefferys v Jefferys* (1841) Cr & Ph 138; *Lister v Hodgson* (1867) LR 4 Eq 30.   [51] See p 108, supra.

[52] *Mountford v Scott* [1975] Ch 258, [1975] 1 All ER 198, CA. Option to purchase a house for £10,000 in consideration of payment of £1 valid. Purported withdrawal ineffective. Option exercised and specific performance granted of contract thereby created. See (1958) 74 LQR 242 (W J Mowbray) and, for an unorthodox view, (1977) 127 NLJ 806 and 897 (K Davies).

(c) CONTRACTS TO CARRY ON A BUSINESS OR ANY COMPARABLE SERIES OF ACTIVITIES

Though it is a matter for the judge's discretion, it is the settled practice of the court not to grant a decree of specific performance which would have the effect of compelling the defendant to carry on a business indefinitely, or, indeed, any comparable series of activities. The House of Lords has recently reaffirmed, in *Co-operative Insurance Society Ltd v Argyll Stores (Holdings) Ltd*,[53] that this practice should be applied in all but exceptional circumstances. The facts of the case were that the defendants had taken a 35-year lease of the anchor unit at a shopping centre, and had covenanted to use the premises as a supermarket and to keep it open for retail trade during the usual hours of business. Some 14 years into the lease the defendants, who were making a considerable loss on the operation, gave short notice that they intended to close the supermarket, and within little more than a month the shop was closed and stripped out. It would cost £1m to reinstate the premises. In allowing the appeal against the order of specific performance made by the Court of Appeal, Lord Hoffman said that the most frequent reason given for declining to order someone to carry on a business was that it would require constant supervision by the court.[54] It was the possibility of the court having to give an indefinite series of rulings to ensure the execution of the order that had been regarded as undesirable. The only means available to it to enforce its order was the quasi-criminal procedure of punishment for contempt, and the use of such a heavy-handed mechanism had undesirable consequences.

There were, he continued, other objections. If the terms of the court's order, reflecting the terms of the obligation, could not be precisely drawn, the possibility of wasteful litigation over compliance was increased. So was the oppression caused by the defendant having to do things under threat of proceedings for contempt. Further, an order requiring the defendant to carry on a business might cause injustice by allowing the claimant to enrich himself at the defendant's expense. The loss that the defendant might suffer through having to comply with the order might be far greater than that which the claimant would suffer from the contract being broken. A remedy that enabled the claimant to secure, in money terms, more than the performance due to him was unjust.

From a wider perspective, it could not be in the public interest for the courts to require someone to carry on business at a loss if there was any plausible alternative by

---

[53] [1998] AC 1, [1997] 3 All ER 297, HL, noted [1997] CLJ 488 (G Jones); (1998) 114 LQR 43 (G McMeel); [1998] Conv 396 (P Luxton); [1998] SJLS 150 (Yeo Hwee Ying); (1998) 61 MLR 421 (A Phang). See also (1999) 50 NILQ 102 (Oonagh Breen).

[54] See *Ryan v Mutual Tontine Westminster Chambers Association* [1893] 1 Ch 116, CA (contract to appoint a porter to carry out certain specified duties); *Barnes v City of London Real Property Co* [1918] 2 Ch 18 (contract to appoint a housekeeper to be in attendance during certain fixed hours); *Peto v Brighton, Uckfield and Tunbridge Wells Rly Co* (1863) 1 Hem & M 468 (contract to construct railway).

which the other party could be given compensation.[55] The cumulative effect of the various reasons for it showed that the settled practice was based on sound sense. The decision has, nevertheless, been criticized[56] as an unfortunate failure to liberalize the rules of specific performance and grant an effective remedy to a plaintiff who is clearly deserving and who is likely to be severely short-changed by a mere award of damages. It also sits ill with the idea that it should be the function of the courts to make sure, as far as possible, that contracts are performed rather than broken.

Relatively recent cases where the objection relating to supervision did not prevail include *Posner v Scott-Lewis*,[57] where the claimants sought specific performance of a covenant to employ a resident porter for certain specified purposes. In granting the order it was said that the relevant considerations were: (i) is there a sufficient definition of what has to be done in order to comply with the order of the court; (ii) will enforcing compliance involve superintendence by the court to an unacceptable degree; (iii) what are the respective prejudices or hardships that will be suffered by the parties if the order is made or not made? In *Co-operative Insurance Society v Argyll Stores (Holdings) Ltd*[58] Lord Hoffman pointed out the distinction between orders which require a defendant to carry on an activity, such as running a business over a more or less extended period of time, and orders which require him to achieve a result. In the latter type of case there is a much reduced risk of repeated applications for rulings, and this distinction explains why the courts have in appropriate circumstances ordered specific performance of building contracts and repairing covenants.

The conditions which have to be fulfilled if specific performance of a building contract is to be granted were set out by Romer LJ in *Wolverhampton Corpn v Emmons*,[59] and his statement would appear still to hold good. 'The first', he said, 'is that the building work, of which he seeks to enforce the performance, is defined by the contract; that is to say, that the particulars of the work are so far definitely ascertained that the court can sufficiently see what is the exact nature of the work of which it is asked to order the performance.'[60] The second is that the claimant has a substantial interest in having the contract performed, which is of such a nature that he cannot adequately be compensated for breach of contract by damages.[61] The third is that the defendant has by the contract obtained possession of land on which the work is contracted to be done. This last condition was criticized in *Carpenters Estates Ltd v*

---

[55] *A-G v Colchester Corpn* [1955] 2 QB 207, [1955] 2 All ER 124; *Gravesham Borough Council v British Railways Board* [1978] Ch 379, [1978] 3 All ER 853 (mandatory injunction to maintain frequency of ferry refused).

[56] [1998] Conv 23 (A Tettenborn).

[57] [1987] Ch 25, [1986] 3 All ER 513, noted (1987) 46 CLJ 21 (G Jones); *Barrow v Chappell & Co Ltd* [1976] RPC 355.

[58] Supra, HL.

[59] [1901] 1 KB 515, CA, at 525; *Rainbow Estates Ltd v Tokenhold Ltd* [1999] Ch 64, [1998] 2 All ER 860, noted [1999] CLJ 283 (S Bridge); [1998] Conv 495 (M Pawlowski and J Brown).

[60] *South Wales Rly Co v Wythes* (1854) 5 De GM & G 880, CA.

[61] If the building is to take place on the plaintiff's land, damages will normally be adequate because some other contractor can be paid to do the job and any increased price be recovered as damages.

Davies[62] and it is submitted that the formulation in that case is to be preferred, namely, that the claimant must establish that the defendant is in possession of the land on which the work is contracted to be done. The point is that the claimant cannot go on the land in order to do the work himself or through other agents.

In the two cases last mentioned in the text the conditions were fulfilled and specific performance was granted. Their facts, slightly simplified, were in *Wolverhampton Corpn v Emmons*[63] that the claimant corporation, in pursuance of a scheme of street improvement, sold and conveyed to the defendant a plot of land abutting on a street, the defendant covenanting with the corporation that he would erect buildings thereon in accordance with certain plans and specifications within a certain time. The defendant failed to erect the buildings. In the other case, *Carpenters Estates Ltd v Davies*,[64] a vendor who sold certain land to purchasers for building development, retaining other land adjoining it, failed to perform his covenant to make certain roads and lay certain mains, sewers and drains on the land retained.

In relation to a covenant to repair contained in a lease, Lord Eldon laid down[65] that a landlord cannot obtain an order for specific performance in the case of a tenant's covenant to repair. This no longer represents the law. It has recently been held[66] that a modern law of remedies requires specific performance to be available in appropriate circumstances, and that there are no constraints of principle or binding authority against the availability of the remedy. Subject to the overriding need to avoid injustice or oppression, the remedy should be available when damages are not an adequate remedy or, in the more modern formulation, when specific performance is the appropriate remedy. The court, however, should be astute to ensure that the landlord was not seeking the decree simply in order to harass the tenant. In so doing, it may take into account considerations similar to those it must take into account under the Leasehold Property (Repairs) Act 1938.[67] In practice it was said that it would be a rare case in which the remedy of specific performance would be the appropriate one.[68]

In the case of a landlords' covenant to repair it had previously been held in *Jeune v Queen's Cross Properties Ltd*[69] that an order could be made where there has been a plain breach of a covenant to repair and there is no doubt at all what is required to be done to remedy the breach. Further, in the case of a dwelling, it is now provided, by s 17 of the Landlord and Tenant Act 1985, that in the case of a breach on the part of

---

[62] [1940] Ch 160, [1940] 1 All ER 13.   [63] Supra, CA.

[64] Supra. Cf *Hounslow London Borough Council v Twickenham Garden Development Ltd* [1971] Ch 233, [1970] 3 All ER 326, and comments of Jones and Goodhart, *Specific Performance*, pp 142, 143.

[65] In *Hill v Barclay* (1810) 16 Ves 402.   [66] In *Rainbow Estates Ltd v Tokenhold Ltd*, supra.

[67] The 1938 Act imposes restrictions on the recovery of damages or forfeiture, but does not apply to decrees of specific performance.

[68] In the case of commercial leases, the landlord would normally have the right to forfeit or to enter and do the repairs at the expense of the tenant; in residential leases the landlord would normally have the right to forfeit in appropriate cases.

[69] [1974] Ch 97, [1973] 3 All ER 97.

the landlord of a repairing covenant[70] relating to any part of the premises in which the dwelling is comprised, the court may order specific performance. The statutory jurisdiction is discretionary, but may be exercised whether or not the breach relates to a part of the premises let to the tenant and notwithstanding any equitable rule restricting the scope of the remedy of specific performance.

(d) CONTRACTS FOR PERSONAL WORK OR SERVICE

'The courts, as such, have never dreamt of enforcing agreements strictly personal in their nature.'[71] Accordingly equity would not normally order specific performance of a contract of employment, whether at the instance of employer or employee, nor could the same result be achieved indirectly by means of an injunction. In addition to the ordinary contract of service, such as the employment of a valet, coachman or cook referred to in *Johnson v Shrewsbury and Birmingham Rly Co*,[72] specific performance has been refused on this ground of a contract between a company and its managing director,[73] of an agreement to compose and write reports of cases in the Court of Exchequer,[74] of an agreement to supply drawings or maps,[75] of a claim to fill the office of receiver to the Bishop of Ely,[76] of an agreement to sing at a theatre,[77] and of articles of apprenticeship.[78] The same principle applies to any contract of agency.[79] Relief was also refused in *R v Incorporated Froebel Institute, ex p L*[80] where a pupil had been suspended from a private school for alleged misconduct, including theft. In refusing to order specific performance of the contract between the school and the parents Tucker J observed that the courts are reluctant to force one body of persons into daily contact with another against the will of one of the parties. In cases such as that before the court there are difficulties inherent in the breakdown of trust and the undesirability of requiring parties to coexist in a pastoral or educational relationship.

So far as contracts of employment are concerned, the Trade Union and Labour Relations (Consolidation) Act 1992[81] provides that no court can decree specific performance so as to compel an employee to do any work, nor can the same result be achieved by means of an injunction to restrain a breach of contract. Moreover,

---

[70] *Quaere*, whether the section applies to an obligation assumed under hand only—see *Gordon v Selico Co Ltd* [1985] 2 EGLR 79. It was held in that case that, given a deed, the word 'covenant' extended to implied promises, and this seems to have been accepted on appeal [1986] 1 EGLR 71, CA.

[71] Per Jessel MR in *Rigby v Connol* (1880) 14 Ch D 482. See, generally, [1991] Cambrian LR 26 (Elizabeth Macdonald); (1994) 138 Sol Jo 152 (Jillian Brown); (1998) 27 Ind LJ 37 (D Brodie).

[72] (1853) 3 De GM & G 914 at 926.   [73] *Bainbridge v Smith* (1889) 41 Ch D 462, CA.

[74] *Clarke v Price* (1819) 2 Wils Ch 157.

[75] *Baldwin v Society for the Diffusion of Useful Knowledge* (1838) 9 Sim 393.

[76] *Pickering v Bishop of Ely* (1843) 2 Y & C Ch Cas 249.

[77] *Lumley v Wagner* (1852) 1 De GM & G 604.

[78] *Webb v England* (1860) 29 Beav 44; *De Francesco v Barnum* (1890) 45 Ch D 430.

[79] *Chinnock v Sainsbury* (1860) 3 LT 258; *Brett v East India and London Shipping Co* (1864) 2 Hem & M 404; *Morris v Delobbel-Flipo* [1892] 2 Ch 352.

[80] [1999] ELR 488.   [81] Section 236.

although in a case of unfair dismissal a tribunal may make an order for reinstatement or re-engagement, there is no provision for such an order being specifically enforced. If not complied with, however, the employer will not only have to pay compensation for unfair dismissal but an additional award of compensation may be made.[82]

The reasons commonly put forward for the above rules are partly the difficulty of supervision and partly the undesirability on grounds of public policy of compelling persons to continue personal relations with each other against their will. Fry LJ put the latter reason rather dramatically in *De Francesco v Barnum*[83] saying 'the courts are bound to be jealous, lest they should turn contracts of service into contracts of slavery'. Other factors are that damages is normally an adequate remedy, and in many cases, where an employee has been replaced, the difficulty of reinstatement. Megarry J has recently suggested,[84] however, that the reasons are 'more complex and more firmly bottomed on human nature'. He speculated on the effect of a decree of specific performance of a contract to sing. 'If a singer contracts to sing, there could no doubt be proceedings for committal, if ordered to sing, the singer remained obstinately dumb. But if instead the singer sang flat, or sharp, or too fast or too slowly, or too loudly, or too quietly . . . the threat of committal would reveal itself as a most unsatisfactory weapon; for who could say whether the imperfections of the performance were natural or self-induced? To make an order with such possibilities of evasion would be vain; and so the order will not be made.'

Nevertheless, in Megarry J's view it depends on the circumstances of the particular case, and though there is always a reluctance on the part of the court to decree specific performance of a contract for personal services, the rule is not a rigid one. *Hill v C A Parsons & Co Ltd*[85] supports the view that the courts do not regard themselves as bound by an inflexible rule. The case was actually concerned with a motion for an interim injunction, but is directly relevant as this could only be granted with a view to specific performance of the contract at the hearing. The majority[86] of the Court of Appeal granted the injunction on the ground of special circumstances, in particular that damages would not be an adequate remedy, and that a combination of the injunction and the coming into operation of the Industrial Relations Act 1971, would safeguard the claimant's position.

---

82 Employment Rights Act 1996, s 117, as amended.

83 (1890) 45 Ch D 430. See (1969) 32 MLR 532 (G de N Clark).

84 *C H Giles & Co Ltd v Morris* [1972] 1 All ER 960 at 969.

85 [1972] Ch 305, [1971] 3 All ER 1345, CA, applied *Irani v Southampton and South West Hampshire Health Authority* [1985] ICR 590, noted (1985) 14 Ind LJ 248 (Graham Smith); and see *Dietman v Brent London Borough Council* [1987] ICR 737. See (1983) 133 NLJ 68 (B W Napier); (1984) 4 LS 102 (A S Burrows); (1988) 85 LSG (5) 29 (J Hendy and J McMullen).

86 The two common law members, reversing the Chancery judge at first instance. Per Lord Denning MR at 1359. 'It is the common lawyers who now do equity!' Cf *Associated British Ports v Transport and General Workers' Union* [1989] 3 All ER 796, [1989] 1 WLR 939, CA; revsd on other grounds [1989] 3 All ER 822, [1989] 1 WLR 939, HL.

It has, however, subsequently been stressed by the Court of Appeal[87] that the facts of *Hill v C A Parsons & Co Ltd*[88] were unusual, if not unique, and it is clear that it is extremely difficult in practice to find exceptional circumstances which will take a case outside the general rule. In affirming that *Hill v C A Parsons & Co Ltd* is an exception to the long-standing general rule, the Court of Appeal in *Powell v London Borough of Brent*[89] said that the court would not by injunction—and the same must apply to specific performance—'require an employer to let a servant continue in his employment, when the employer has sought to terminate that employment and to prevent the servant carrying out his work under the contract, unless it is clear on the evidence not only that it is otherwise just to make such a requirement but also that there exists sufficient confidence[90] on the part of the employer in the servant's ability and other necessary attributes for it to be reasonable to make the order.' However in *Wadcock v London Borough of Brent*,[91] notwithstanding an affidavit by the Deputy Director of Social Services deposing to a breakdown of confidence such that it was quite unrealistic to expect the employer/employee relationship to be reestablished, the court made an order that, on undertakings by the claimant to work in accordance with proper instructions, he should be employed by the defendants pending trial. An important distinction was drawn in *Robb v Hammersmith and Fulham London Borough Council*[92] where it was accepted that if an injunction is sought to reinstate an employee dismissed in breach of contract, so that when reinstated he can actually carry out the job for which he was employed, trust and confidence are highly relevant. The all important criterion, it was said, is whether the order is workable. Accordingly loss of trust and confidence is of little relevance where the employee seeks an order which would have the effect of requiring the employer to treat him as suspended with pay until contractual disciplinary procedures have been complied with. On the facts an order should be made. Apart from these recent cases, there are also earlier decisions in which it has been held that in exceptional circumstances specific performance may

---

[87] *Chappell v Times Newspapers Ltd* [1975] 2 All ER 233, [1975] ICR 145, CA. See also *Price v Strange* [1978] Ch 337, CA, where Goff LJ expressly approved the opinion of Megarry J referred to above, though Buckley LJ said that there was no jurisdiction to grant specific performance of a contract for personal services; *Gunton v London Borough of Richmond upon Thames* [1981] Ch 448, [1980] 3 All ER 577, CA; *Regent International Hotels (UK) Ltd v Pageguide Ltd* (1985) *Times*, 13 May, CA.

[88] [1972] Ch 305, [1971] 3 All ER 1345, CA.

[89] [1988] ICR 176, CA, noted (1989) 48 CLJ (K D Ewing)—dist *Wishart v National Association of Citizens Advice Bureaux Ltd* [1990] ICR 794, CA. See also *Hughes v London Borough of Southwark* [1988] IRLR 55; (1990) 140 NLJ 1007 (A Burrows).

[90] The confidence may be comparative. In *Alexander v Standard Telephones and Cables plc* [1990] IRLR 55, noted (1992) Ind LJ 58 (Aileen McColgan) redundancies were inevitable. So far as the dismissed plaintiffs were concerned 'it cannot be said that the defendant has complete confidence in the plaintiffs, as it has less confidence that they can do the work than the other members of the workforce that have been retained'.

[91] [1990] IRLR 223.   [92] [1991] ICR 514, noted (1991) 42 NILQ 374 (Elizabeth MacDonald).

be decreed of some personal obligation, where it forms only a small part of a larger contract which is otherwise suitable for such an order.[93]

It should be added that there is a vital distinction between an order to perform a contract for services and an order to procure the execution of such a contract. The mere fact that the contract to be made is one of which the court would not order specific performance—such as the service agreement as managing director of a company in *C H Giles & Co Ltd v Morris*[94] is no ground for refusing to decree that the contract be entered into. In the last cited case the defendants were properly ordered to procure the execution of the service agreement.

(e) CONTRACTS WANTING IN MUTUALITY

(i) General rule

English judges and writers[95] commonly state and apply the general rule that specific performance will not be granted unless the remedy is mutual, that is, if by reason of personal incapacity, the nature of the contract or any other matter A cannot obtain specific performance against B, then B will not be granted specific performance against A even though, taking A's obligation by itself, this would be an appropriate remedy. The defence of mutuality may be waived.[96]

In accordance with this general rule a minor cannot obtain a decree of specific performance,[97] for specific performance cannot be decreed against him[98] and a claimant against whom specific performance should not be decreed because his obligation is to do something of a personal or a continuous nature cannot obtain specific performance even though this is prima facie appropriate to the defendant's obligation.[99] It should be observed, however, that it has been long settled that in the case of the ordinary contract for the sale and purchase of land, the vendor is as much entitled to a decree of specific performance as the purchaser, notwithstanding that the purchaser's obligation is merely to pay the purchase price. This has been explained by Lord St Leonards[100] on the ground that damages would not be an adequate remedy— 'a seller wants the exact sum agreed to be paid to him, and he wants to divest himself

---

[93] *Fortescue v Lostwithiel and Fowey Rly Co* [1894] 3 Ch 621; *Kennard v Cory Bros & Co Ltd* [1922] 2 Ch 1; *Beswick v Beswick* [1968] AC 58 at 97, [1967] 2 All ER 1197 at 1218, HL per Lord Upjohn; *C H Giles & Co Ltd v Morris* [1972] 1 All ER 960 at 969.

[94] Supra.

[95] See Ames in *Lectures On Legal History*, pp 370 et seq, (1992) 108 LQR 280 (C Harpum). See per Kekewich J in *Wylson v Dunn* (1887) 34 Ch D 569 at 576.

[96] *Price v Strange* [1977] 3 All ER 371 at 384, CA, per Goff LJ.

[97] *Flight v Bolland* (1828) 4 Russ 298. See Law Commission Working Paper No 81 on minors' contracts proposing that specific performance should be available to a minor, and against him if he has first sued the adult. However in their Report No 134 they did not recommend legislation on this point.

[98] *Lumley v Ravenscroft* [1895] 1 QB 683, CA.

[99] *Johnson v Shrewsbury and Birmingham Rly Co* (1853) 3 De GM & G 914; *Page One Records Ltd v Britton* [1967] 3 All ER 822.

[100] In *Eastern Counties Rly Co v Hawkes* (1855) 5 HL Cas 331 at 376 and see per Lord Campbell at 360.

legally of the estate, which after the contract was no longer vested in him beneficially. This is accomplished by specific performance, whereas, at law, he would be left with the estate on his hands, and would recover damages . . .'

(ii) Time when mutuality has to be shown

This was given detailed and careful consideration by the Court of Appeal in *Price v Strange*.[101] The essential facts were that the defendant orally[102] agreed to grant the claimant a new underlease at an increased rent of the maisonette in which the claimant was living in consideration of the claimant executing certain repairs to the interior and exterior of the building in which the maisonette was situated. The claimant completed the interior repairs, but was not allowed to carry out the external repairs because the defendant repudiated the agreement and had the exterior repairs done at her own expense, nevertheless accepting rent at the increased rate for some months. The claimant's specific performance action was dismissed at first instance on the ground that the remedies were not mutual at the date of the contract, since the claimant's obligation to execute the repairs could not be specifically enforced. The decision was unanimously reversed by the Court of Appeal, where Buckley LJ stated:[103]

The time at which the mutual availability of specific performance and its importance must be considered is, in my opinion, the time of judgment, and the principle to be applied can I think be stated simply as follows: the court will not compel a defendant to perform his obligations specifically if it cannot at the same time ensure that any unperformed obligations of the plaintiff will be specifically performed, unless, perhaps, damages would be an adequate remedy to the defendant for any default on the plaintiff's part.

An unusual feature of the facts in *Price v Strange*[104] was that although all the agreed repairs had been done, they had not all been done by the claimant. It was held that the claimant should nevertheless succeed, for the failure of the claimant to do the work was not due to any default of his, but to the defendant's unjustified repudiation of the contract. Nevertheless it was only equitable that specific performance should be ordered on the terms that the claimant should pay the defendant proper compensation for the work done by her.

(iii) Exceptions to the requirement of mutuality

First, it has been said that the holder of an option to purchase may be able to obtain specific performance even though the other party may have no such right against

---

[101] [1977] 3 All ER 371, CA, applied *Sutton v Sutton* [1984] Ch 184, [1984] 1 All ER 168; *E Johnson & Co (Barbados) Ltd v NSR Ltd* [1997] AC 400, [1996] 3 WLR 583, PC.

[102] It was conceded that there were sufficient acts of part performance to make the contract enforceable as the law stood before the Law of Property (Miscellaneous Provisions) Act 1989.

[103] At 392. See also per Goff LJ at 383, who accepted as valid the established rule that where the vendor has no title the purchaser can on discovering the defect repudiate the contract forthwith, the vendor losing any right to specific performance albeit he is able to make title before the date fixed for completion. This is a special right arising out of the difficulty of making title to land in England. See also (1977) 41 Conv 18 (C T Emery).

[104] Supra, CA.

him.[105] This may be explained, however, on the ground that specific performance could not be obtained prior to the exercise of the option, after which there would be mutuality.

Secondly, an exception arises in connection with the grant of specific performance with compensation,[106] a special variant of the remedy limited to cases of misdescription in a contract for the sale of land, whether the misdescription relates to the title, or the quantity or quality of the land.

In other words it is only available where the vendor is unable to convey to the purchaser property exactly corresponding to that which he has contracted to convey, and not even in the case where there has been a misstatement not incorporated in the contract but in the form of a misrepresentation inducing it.[107] When specific performance with compensation is granted the court, exceptionally, does more than simply enforce the agreement between the parties. It enforces an agreement somewhat different than that agreed upon, and compels the acceptance of compensation which the parties never agreed to give or receive. Compensation in every case means compensation to the purchaser and not to the vendor. The general position is, on the one hand, that where the vendor cannot fulfil the exact terms of the contract, but can convey to the purchaser substantially what he had contracted to get,[108] either the vendor or the purchaser may obtain a decree of specific performance with compensation. If, however, it is impossible to estimate the amount of compensation, specific performance will be refused.[109] Where, on the other hand, the vendor cannot even convey to the purchaser substantially what he contracted to get the remedies are not mutual. In such case the vendor is not entitled to specific performance at all, but the purchaser can, as a general rule,[110] elect to take all that the vendor is able to convey to him, and to have a proportionate abatement from the purchase money, provided that this is capable of computation.[111] The purchaser may, of course, alternatively rescind the contract.[112]

Lastly by s 17 of the Landlord and Tenant Act 1985 there is no need for mutuality where the tenant of a dwelling sues his landlord for breach of a repairing covenant.[113]

---

[105] *McCarthy & Stone Ltd v Julian S Hodge & Co Ltd* [1971] 2 All ER 973 at 980, per Foster J.

[106] See (1981) 40 CLJ 47 (C Harpum) and *Rutherford v Acton-Adams* [1915] AC 866 at 869, 870, PC. The contract in practice commonly contains special provisions. As to the extent of a claim for damages where even extinguishment of the purchase price would not be adequate compensation, see *Grant v Dawkins* [1973] 3 All ER 897, noted (1974) 38 Conv 45 (F R Crane); (1974) 90 LQR 299 (P H Pettit).

[107] A purchaser may have other remedies in such cases, eg rescission, or damages for deceit if the vendor has been fraudulent, or possibly damages for breach of a collateral contract. See *Rutherford v Acton-Adams*, supra, PC.

[108] As to what is meant by substantial in this context, reference should be made to Fry *Specific Performance*, 6th edn, and works on conveying such as Williams on *Vendor and Purchaser*, 4th edn, vol 1, p 723 et seq.

[109] *Westmacott & Robins* (1862) 4 De GF & J 390; *Cato v Thompson* (1882) 9 QBD 616, CA.

[110] Not, however, if innocent third parties would be prejudiced—*Thomas v Dering* (1837) 1 Keen 729. And some general defence such as those discussed below may be available.

[111] *Westmacott v Robins* (1862) 4 De GF & J 390; *Cato v Thompson* (1882) 9 QBD 616, CA.

[112] See chapter 30, section 3, infra.   [113] See p 672, supra.

(f) CONTRACTS CAPABLE OF PARTIAL PERFORMANCE ONLY[114]

Suppose that a contract contains two terms, under one of which X is obliged to do an act for which, taken by itself, specific performance would be an appropriate remedy, and under the other he is obliged to do an act say of a personal nature, for which it is not. Here the rule[115] is that a contract cannot be specifically performed in part; it must be wholly performed, or not at all. Thus in *Ogden v Fossick*[116] an agreement was entered into between Fossick and Ogden that Fossick should grant Ogden a lease of a coal wharf at a certain rent, and should be employed throughout the tenancy at a salary of £300 pa plus a commission on the coal sold at the wharf. Although the first part of the agreement was typical of the kind of matter of which specific performance is decreed, this remedy was refused on the ground that it was inseparably connected with the second part of the agreement which was clearly of the kind of which specific performance is not granted. It is an *a fortiori* case where the term sought to be enforced by specific performance is merely an ancillary or subsidiary term of a contract, the principal terms of which are unenforceable by specific performance.[117] Megarry J's observations in *C H Giles & Co Ltd v Morris*[118] suggest that the rule may be less strictly applied nowadays. The presence of a provision not by itself specifically enforceable does not in his view necessarily prevent the contract as a whole from being specifically enforced.

There is an exception or apparent exception to the traditional rule where the contract is divisible, that is, where on its true construction there is not one contract containing two or more parts, but two or more separate agreements. In such a case specific performance will lie in appropriate circumstances for breach of a separate agreement.[119] This is what happened in *Wilkinson v Clements*,[120] from which it seems that the burden of proof that the contract is divisible lies upon the person who alleges that this is so, Mellish LJ observing[121] that as a general rule all agreements must be considered as entire and indivisible. Where, however, property is sold in separate lots specific performance can normally be obtained in relation to one lot, even though it may be unobtainable in relation to the others.[122]

What has been called 'the doctrine of partial performance' may apply in a rather different situation, namely, where a person has represented that he can grant a certain property, or is entitled to a certain interest in that property, and it later appears that

---

[114] See also chapter 28, section 1 as to the enforcement by injunction of a contract of which specific performance will not be granted.

[115] See per Romilly MR in (1852) 15 Beav 493 at 501; *Merchant's Trading Co v Banner* (1871) LR 12 Eq 18 at 23.

[116] (1862) 4 De GF & J 426; *Barnes v City of London Real Property Co* [1918] 2 Ch 18.

[117] *South Wales Rly Co v Wythes* (1854) 5 De GM & G 880; *Brett v East India and London Shipping Co Ltd* (1864) 2 Hem & M 404.

[118] [1972] 1 All ER 960 at 969. Jones and Goodhart, *Specific Performance*, 2nd edn, p 58, suggest that the general rule no longer exists.

[119] *Wilkinson v Clements* (1872) 8 Ch App 96; *Odessa Tramways Co v Mendel* (1878) 8 Ch D 235, CA.

[120] Supra. [121] *Wilkinson v Clements*, supra, at 110; *Roffey v Shallcross* (1819) 4 Madd 227.

[122] *Lewin v Guest* (1826) 1 Russ 325; *Casamajor v Strode* (1834) 2 My & K 706.

there is a deficiency in his title or interest. In such case the other party can obtain an order compelling him to grant what he has got.[123]

(g) WHERE A DECREE OF SPECIFIC PERFORMANCE WOULD BE USELESS

In such cases a decree will not be granted. Thus it has been refused of an agreement to enter into a partnership at will, which could be dissolved immediately afterwards,[124] of an agreement to grant a deputation of an office which was clearly revocable,[125] and of an agreement to grant a lease for a term expired before proceedings were commenced.[126]

Somewhat similarly, a decree will not be granted if it would be substantially impossible to carry it out. Thus if X and Y are joint tenants of Blackacre and X contracts to sell Blackacre to P without the knowledge or subsequent approbation of Y, it has been held that P will be unable to obtain specific performance against X. X could not convey the legal estate as he is only one of the two trustees of land, and a transfer of X's beneficial interest would be a transfer of something substantially different from the subject-matter of the contract.[127] It has been doubted[128] whether this latter ground can be sustained in the light of *William and Glyn's Bank Ltd v Boland*.[129] Another example would be where there was a contract to grant a lease at a rent greater than that which could be lawfully recovered at the time when the contract is due to be performed.[130]

It may be added that it was held in *Verrall v Great Yarmouth Borough Council*[131] that there was no reason why the court should not order specific performance of a contractual licence of short duration, in that case two days, and the same principle must surely apply to an agreement for a lease for a short term. The court expressly disapproved earlier cases to the contrary, and further held that in an appropriate case, such as the case before it, specific performance could be ordered where a licensee's licence had been wrongfully repudiated before he entered into possession.

---

[123] *Thomas Guaranty Ltd v Campbell* [1985] QB 210, [1984] 2 All ER 585, CA; *United Bank of Kuwait plc v Sahib* [1995] 2 All ER 973; affd [1996] 3 All ER 215, CA, without discussing this point.

[124] *Hercy v Birch* (1804) 9 Ves 357.   [125] *Wheeler v Trotter* (1737) 3 Swan 174n.

[126] *Gilbey v Cossey* (1912) 106 LT 607; *McMahon v Ambrose* [1987] VR 817.

[127] *Watts v Spence* [1976] Ch 165, [1975] 2 All ER 528. And see (1977) 41 Conv 141 (Angela Sydenham); [1980] Conv 191 (P W Smith).

[128] (1981) 40 CLJ 47 (C Harpum).

[129] [1981] AC 487, [1980] 2 All ER 408, HL.

[130] See *Newman v Dorrington Developments Ltd* [1975] 3 All ER 928 where, however, the principle did not apply on the facts of the case and specific performance was granted.

[131] [1981] QB 202, [1980] 1 All ER 839, CA (attempt by local authority, after a change of control following local elections, to withdraw licence to National Front to hold annual conference in council premises).

(h) CONTRACTS TO LEND OR ADVANCE MONEY

Such contracts are not enforceable by specific performance, whether or not the loan is to be secured by mortgage. The reason is that the remedy at law is adequate—the borrower can borrow the money elsewhere, and claim at law if he is compelled to pay a higher rate of interest, and likewise the lender has a simple money demand if his money has laid idle or been invested less advantageously.[132] Exceptionally, by statute,[133] a contract with a company to take up and pay for any debentures of a company may be enforced by an order for specific performance.

Specific performance can, however, be obtained of a contract to execute a mortgage, that is of an agreement to give security, when the money has been actually advanced.[134]

It should be observed that it is quite possible for a decree of specific performance to be obtained in appropriate circumstances of a contract to make a money payment. For instance a purchaser of land is commonly compelled to pay the purchase price in a specific performance action at the instance of a vendor, where as has been seen[135] damages is not regarded as an adequate remedy, and it has been held that it makes no difference that the price is payable by instalments, or that the price is not payable to the plaintiff but to some third party.[136] Similarly the Minister of Transport can sue for specific performance of the agreement between himself and the Motor Insurers' Bureau,[137] under which the Bureau agreed that if a judgment for an injured person against a motorist was not satisfied in full within seven days, the Bureau would pay the amount of the judgment to the injured person.[138] Hitherto it has generally been thought that the courts would be unwilling to extend the limited type of case in which specific performance of a contract to make a money payment would be granted, but *Beswick & Beswick*[139] perhaps heralds a more liberal approach.

(i) A CONTRACT TO REFER TO ARBITRATION

Such a contract is not specifically enforceable.[140] It may, however, be indirectly enforced under the provisions of the Arbitration Act 1996,[141] which gives the court a discretionary power to stay an action in respect of any dispute which the parties have

---

[132] *Larios v Bonany y Gurety* (1873) LR 5 PC 346; *Western Wagon and Property Co v West* [1892] 1 Ch 271; *Loan Investment Corpn of Australasia v Bonner* [1970] NZLR 724, PC.

[133] Companies Act 1985, s 195.

[134] *Ashton v Corrigan* (1871) LR 13 Eq 76; *Hermann v Hodges* (1873) LR 16 Eq 18.

[135] See p 676, supra.

[136] *Beswick v Beswick* [1968] AC 58, [1967] 2 All ER 1197, HL. And see (1967) 30 MLR 690–693 (G H Treitel).

[137] The agreement is set out in a note to *Hardy v Motor Insurers' Bureau* [1964] 2 QB 745 at 770–775.

[138] *Gurtner v Circuit* [1968] 2 QB 587, [1968] 1 All ER 328, CA.   [139] Supra, HL. See p 110, supra.

[140] *South Wales Rly Co v Wythes* (1854) 5 De GM & G 880, CA; *Doleman & Sons v Ossett Corpn* [1912] 3 KB 257, CA.

[141] Section 9 replacing earlier legislation.

by writing agreed to refer to arbitration. If the court exercises this power the plaintiff must either give up his claim or proceed by arbitration.

Specific performance may, however, be granted of the award of the arbitrator 'because the award supposes an agreement between the parties, and contains no more than the terms of that agreement ascertained by a third person'.[142] It follows that it is enforceable on the same principles and subject to the same limitations as an ordinary contract.

(j) PARTNERSHIP AGREEMENTS

As a general rule the court will not decree specific performance of an agreement to perform and carry on a partnership,[143] for this would involve the court in constant superintendence of the partnership affairs. *A fortiori* the rule applies in the case of a partnership at will where specific performance would be useless as either party could forthwith dissolve the partnership.[144]

Exceptionally it seems that, where there has been part performance of the partnership agreement, the parties may be compelled specifically to perform a term to execute a partnership deed, incorporating any subsequent variations to the original agreement which may have been made between the partners.[145]

(k) CONTRACTS TO LEAVE PROPERTY BY WILL

In these cases, an action for damages will clearly lie against the covenantor's estate if the contract is not carried out, and the Court of Appeal had no doubt in *Synge v Synge*[146] of the power of the court, where the contract related to a defined piece of real property, to decree a conveyance of that property after the death of the covenantor against all persons claiming under him as volunteers.[147] Specific performance will not, however, be decreed where the covenantor is merely donee of a testamentary power of appointment.[148]

---

[142] Per Lord Eldon in *Wood v Griffith* (1818) 1 Swan 43 at 54.

[143] *Scott v Rayment* (1868) LR 7 Eq 112.   [144] *Hercy v Birch* (1804) 9 Ves 357.

[145] *England v Curling* (1844) 8 Beav 129; *Sichel v Mosenthal* (1862) 30 Beav 371. See Lindley and Banks on *Partnership*, 18th edn, pp 23–46.

[146] [1894] 1 QB 466, CA; *Schaefer v Schuhmann* [1972] AC 572, [1972] 1 All ER 621, PC.

[147] There seems no reason to doubt that other persons may be bound by the equitable interest and liable to specific performance according to the ordinary rules.

[148] *Re Parkin* [1892] 3 Ch 510; *Re Evered* [1910] 2 Ch 147, CA; *Re Coake* [1922] 1 Ch 292.

3 DEFENCES TO AN ACTION FOR SPECIFIC PERFORMANCE

(a) MISREPRESENTATION AND MISTAKE

As we shall see,[149] both misrepresentation and mistake[150] may be grounds for rescission, and in such cases will *a fortiori* be a defence to an action for specific performance. Both pleas have, however, a wider scope for the latter purpose. Misrepresentation, even though not sufficient to induce a court to rescind a contract, may be sufficient to defeat a claim for specific performance,[151] the point being that rescission has the drastic effect of avoiding the contract for all purposes, while refusing specific performance leaves it open to the claimant to seek other remedies, such as damages. It is commonly the wiser course to seek rescission, if this is possible, rather than to wait to raise the defence of misrepresentation if a specific performance action is brought,[152] particularly as in the latter case the burden of proof rests on the defendant to show that he repudiated the contract upon, or at least within a reasonable time after, discovery of the truth.[153]

Mistake may be a defence to a specific performance action even where there has been a mistake in a popular rather than a technical sense. This does not mean that a man can be careless in entering into a contract, and then avoid liability simply by alleging or even proving that he did so under a mistake,[154] for to allow this would open the door to perjury and fraud. If, however, he can establish that he made a bona fide mistake, and that he had a reasonable ground for the mistake, it may well be thought inequitable to grant specific performance. This is likely to be the case where the claimant has contributed to the defendant's mistake,[155] even though unintentionally.[156] Thus in *Denny v Hancock*[157] on a sale by auction the plan annexed to the particulars showed on the western side a shrubbery with an iron fence outside it, and within the fence three very large and fine elm trees. He successfully bid for the

---

[149] Chapter 30, section 3(c), infra.

[150] Mistake may also give the court jurisdiction to rectify the contract. See chapter 30, section 4, infra.

[151] *Re Banister* (1879) 12 Ch D 131 at 142, CA; *Re Terry and White's Contract* (1886) 32 Ch D 14 at 29, CA. As to the duty of a vendor to disclose defects in title of which he is aware see *Faruqi v English Real Estates Ltd* [1979] 1 WLR 963.

[152] *Fenn v Craig* (1838) 3 Y & C Ex 216 at 222; Cf *Aaron's Reefs Ltd v Twiss* [1896] AC 273 at 293, HL.

[153] *United Shoe Machinery Co of Canada v Brunet* [1909] AC 330 at 338, PC; *First National Reinsurance Co v Greenfield* [1921] 2 KB 260 at 266, DC.

[154] *Goddard v Jeffreys* (1881) 51 LJ Ch 57; *Tamplin v James* (1880) 15 Ch D 215, CA. Cf *Williams v Bulot* [1992] 2 Qd R 566 where it was held no defence to an action for specific performance that the defendant would only have been prepared to sell at a much higher price if he had known that the other contracting party was the undisclosed agent of the claimant.

[155] *Higginson v Clowes* (1808) 15 Ves 516; *Moxey v Bigwood* (1862) 4 De GF & J 351.

[156] *Baskcomb v Beckwith* (1869) LR 8 Eq 100; *Bray v Briggs* (1872) 26 LT 817.

[157] (1870) 6 Ch App 1.

property in the belief that he was buying everything up to the fence, but the real boundary was denoted by stumps largely concealed by shrubs, and the elm trees were outside it. It was held, on appeal, that the defendant's mistake was induced by the plan for which the vendors were responsible, and the vendor's specific performance action was accordingly dismissed. Further, Lord Macnaghten has said[158] that it cannot be disputed that a unilateral mistake by the defendant may be a good defence to a specific performance action even when the mistake has not been induced or contributed to by any act or omission on the part of the claimant, though most of such cases have been cases where a hardship amounting to injustice would have been inflicted upon the defendant by holding him to his bargain, and it was unreasonable to hold him to it. It has indeed been judicially suggested[159] that some of the cases have gone too far. *Malins v Freeman*[160] may perhaps be one of these cases, where specific performance was refused against a purchaser, whose agent had mistakenly bid for the wrong property, the mistake being an unreasonable one not in any way contributed to by the vendor.

The mistake has, in effect, been held to a reasonable one and specific performance refused, where it was caused by some ambiguity, even though the defendant was the author of the ambiguity.[161] One case is *Webster v Cecil*[162] where the defendant, due to an arithmetical error, offered his property to the plaintiff for £1,250, instead of £2,250. The claimant, though his previous offer of £2,200 had been refused and he must have known of the mistake, accepted the offer and brought his action for specific performance. The action was dismissed. A case may arise for refusing specific performance where through the ignorance, neglect or error of the vendor's agent, property not intended to be sold is included in the sale.[163]

(b) HARDSHIP AND WANT OF FAIRNESS

Even though there may not be fraud or other vitiating element which would support a claim for rescission, unfairness or hardship on the defendant, or oppression or sharp practice on the part of the claimant may be a sufficient reason for the court to refuse a decree of specific performance, while leaving open the possibility of a claim for damages.[164] Mere inadequacy of consideration is not however by itself a ground for refusing a decree, even though it may in fact cause considerable hardship to the

---

[158] In *Stewart v Kennedy* (1890) 15 App Cas 75 at 105, HL; *Jones v Rimmer* (1880) 14 Ch D 588, CA.

[159] *Tamplin v James*, supra, per James LJ at 221.

[160] (1836) 2 Keen 25 doubted by Kekewich J in *Van Praagh v Everidge* [1902] 2 Ch 266; reversed on another ground [1903] 1 Ch 434, CA.

[161] *Butterworth v Walker* (1864) 11 LT 436; *Wycombe Rly Co v Donnington Hospital* (1866) 1 Ch App 268; *Douglas v Baynes* [1908] AC 477, PC.

[162] (1861) 30 Beav 62. See the comment of James LJ in *Tamplin v James*, supra, at 221. See also *Deputy Comr of Taxation (NSW) v Chamberlain* (1990) 93 ALR 729.

[163] *Leslie v Tompson* (1851) 9 Hare 268; *Re Hare and O'More's Contract* [1901] 1 Ch 93.

[164] *Willan v Willan* (1810) 16 Ves 72; *Martin v Mitchell* (1820) 2 Jac & W 413. Jones and Goodhart, *Specific Performance*, 2nd edn, p 113 point out that in most of the more recent cases in which a court has refused to order specific performance on the ground of unfair conduct it has also set aside the contract.

defendant,[165] and this principle applies to a sale at a valuation. Thus specific perform-ance was granted[166] where it was admitted that the valuation appeared very high and perhaps exorbitant, in the absence of any other factor such as fraud, mistake or misconduct by the valuer, but the additional presence of any of these factors may be a defence to such a claim.[167] On the same principle it is no defence that the purpose for which the defendant entered into the contract cannot be carried out, as where he had purchased a lease and it turned out that the activities intended to be carried on there were prohibited by the lease.[168] Inadequacy of consideration may however be an important factor where combined with other circumstances,[169] and may be evidence, and in an extreme case conclusive evidence, of fraud.[170]

Questions of fairness, hardship and the like are normally to be judged as at the time when the contract was entered into,[171] and subsequent events are in general irrelevant. Exceptionally specific performance may be refused because of a change of circum-stances subsequent to the contract such that a decree of specific performance would inflict on the defendant 'a hardship amounting to injustice'.[172] This is particularly the case where the hardship is attributable to the claimant,[173] the more so if his conduct has acted as a trap for the defendant, even though unintentionally.[174] But clearly hardship which the defendant has brought upon himself is no defence.[175]

In deciding questions as to the fairness of a contract the court considers the sur-rounding circumstances—if the consideration is inadequate and there are suspicious circumstances the court may refuse a decree, though there may not be enough to enable it to set the contract aside. Relevant factors may include weakness of mind, not amounting to insanity, age, illiteracy, poverty, want of advice, and financial distress.[176] The fact that an agreement was obtained from the defendant while he was intoxicated

[165] *Kimberley v Jennings* (1836) 6 Sim 340. It is submitted that the early cases to the contrary, followed in *Falcke v Gray* (1859) 4 Drew 651, are no longer good law.

[166] *Collier v Mason* (1858) 25 Beav 200; *Weekes v Gallard* (1869) 21 LT 655.

[167] *Chichester v M'Intire* (1830) 4 Bli NS 78; *Eads v Williams* (1854) 4 De GM & G 674.

[168] *Morley v Clavering* (1860) 29 Beav 84; *Haywood v Cope* (1858) 25 Beav 140.

[169] *Cockell v Taylor* (1851) 15 Beav 103; and see *James v Morgan* (1663) 1 Lev 111, the geometric progres-sion trick where a horse was sold at a barleycorn a nail, doubling it for each nail on the horse's feet. See also *K v K* [1976] NZLR 31.

[170] *Griffith v Spratley* (1787) 1 Cox Eq Cas 383; *Stilwell v Wilkins* (1821) Jac 280.

[171] *Francis v Cowcliffe Ltd* (1976) 239 EG 977 (financial inability to complete not hardship—specific performance decreed although it was said it would inevitably result in the defendant company being wound up). See *Stewart v Ambrosina* (1975) 63 DLR (3d) 595; *Roberts v O'Neil* [1981] ILRM 403.

[172] *Patel v Ali* [1984] Ch 283, [1984] 1 All ER 978, where long delay was also a factor. See (1984) 134 NLJ 927 & 949 (Jacqueline A Priest); (1984) 100 LQR 337.

[173] *Duke of Bedford v British Museum Trustees* (1822) 2 My & K 552; *Shell UK Ltd v Lostock Garage Ltd* [1976] 1 WLR 1187 at 1202, CA, esp per Ormrod LJ.

[174] *Dowson v Solomon* (1859) 1 Drew & Sm 1.

[175] *Storer v Great Western Rly Co* (1842) 2 Y & C Ch Cas 48.

[176] *Martin v Mitchell* (1820) 2 Jac & W 413; *Stanley v Robinson* (1830) 1 Russ & M 527; *Huttges v Verner* (1975) 64 DLR (3d) 374. Contrast *Mountford v Scott* [1975] Ch 258, [1975] 1 All ER 198, CA (decree granted though defendant could not read. He was intelligent, had been given an oral explanation, and the price was adequate).

may also be a defence.[177] The question is whether in all the circumstances it would be unfair and inequitable to grant specific performance. It is not on the other hand necessary to show any intentional unfairness or misconduct on the part of the claimant.[178]

In general the court will not grant specific performance of an agreement relating to a lease if the consequence would be a forfeiture,[179] though it is, of course, otherwise if the state of affairs is due to the defendant's own acts.[180] Cases where specific performance was refused on the ground of hardship include *Wedgwood v Adams*,[181] where trustees personally undertook with the purchaser of trust property to see it freed from incumbrances, and it appeared that the purchase money would be adequate to an uncertain extent; *Denne v Light*[182] where the purchaser might have found himself with no means of access to his land: and *Hope v Walter*[183] where the court refused to 'thrust down the throat of an innocent buyer the obligation of becoming the landlord of a brothel'.

The hardship or unfairness which may cause the court to refuse a decree may be suffered by a third party[184] rather than the defendant.[185] In particular the court will not normally grant specific performance if this would necessarily involve breach of a prior contract with a third party,[186] or would require a person to do an act which he is not lawfully competent to do.[187] And an order for partial performance was refused in *Thames Guaranty Ltd v Campbell*[188] of a husband's contract to create an equitable charge, because an order, if made, would expose the wife to proceedings under s 30 of the Law of Property Act 1925[189] likely to result in an order for sale of the matrimonial home she occupied. Again there are many cases where the court has refused a decree against trustees on the ground that performance by them would constitute a breach of trust,[190] or even that it is reasonably and seriously doubtful whether it is a breach of trust.[191] If, however, an innocent breach of trust has already been committed as a

---

[177] *Cooke v Clayworth* (1811) 18 Ves 12; *Cox v Smith* (1868) 19 LT 517. Cf *Matthews v Baxter* (1873) LR 8 Exch 132. *Lightfoot v Heron* (1839) 3 Y & C Ex 586.

[178] *Mortlock v Buller* (1804) 10 Ves 292; *Huttges v Verner*, supra.

[179] *Helling v Lumley* (1858) 3 De G & J 493; *Warmington v Miller* [1973] QB 877, [1973] 2 All ER 372, CA.

[180] *Helling v Lumley*, supra.   [181] (1843) 6 Beav 600; *Watson v Marston* (1853) 4 De GM & G 230.

[182] (1857) 8 De GM & G 774 (the judgment of Knight Bruce LJ is worth reading for its entertainment value alone).

[183] [1900] 1 Ch 257 at 258, CA, per Lindley MR; *Talbot v Ford* (1842) 13 Sim 173.

[184] But not, semble, by the public—*Raphael v Thames Valley Rly Co* (1866) LR 2 Eq 37; revsd (1867) 2 Ch App 147. Aliter if it would be a fraud on the public—*Post v Marsh* (1880) 16 Ch D 395.

[185] *Thomas v Dering* (1837) 1 Keen 729; *McKewan v Sanderson* (1875) LR 20 Eq 65.

[186] *Willmott v Barber* (1880) 15 Ch D 96; *Manchester Ship Canal Co v Manchester Racecourse Co* [1901] 2 Ch 37, CA; *(Earl) Sefton v Tophams Ltd* [1965] Ch 1140, [1965] 3 All ER 1, CA. This point was not discussed on appeal sub nom *Tophams Ltd v (Earl) Sefton* [1967] 1 AC 50, [1966] 1 All ER 1039, HL.

[187] *Tolson v Sheard* (1877) 5 Ch D 19, CA; *Warmington v Miller*, supra, CA.

[188] [1985] QB 210, [1984] 2 All ER 585, CA. The husband, now bankrupt, who was co-owner with his wife, had purported to charge the whole legal and beneficial interest.

[189] This section has been repealed and replaced by s 14 of the Trusts of Land and Appointment of Trustees Act 1996.

[190] *Maw v Topham* (1854) 19 Beav 576.   [191] *Rede v Oakes* (1864) 4 De GJ & Sm 505.

result of a contract, the court may grant specific performance and compel the other party to carry out his part of the bargain.[192]

(c) RIGHTS OF THIRD PARTIES

In contracts for the sale of land problems have sometimes arisen where a purchaser has sought specific performance against a vendor who is unable to give a good title without the consent of some third person, or where he has contracted to give vacant possession and some third person is in possession. Megarry J summarized the position in *Wroth v Tyler*[193] as follows:

A vendor must do his best to obtain any necessary consent to the sale; if he has sold with vacant possession he must, if necessary, take proceedings to obtain possession from any person in possession who has no right to be there or whose right is determinable by the vendor, at all events if the vendor's right to possession is reasonably clear; but I do not think that the vendor will usually be required to embark on difficult or uncertain litigation in order to secure any requisite consent or obtain vacant possession. Where the outcome of any litigation depends on disputed facts, difficult questions of law or the exercise of a discretionary jurisdiction, then I think the court would be slow to make a decree of specific performance against the vendor which would require him to undertake such litigation.

In *Wroth v Tyler*[194] itself the judge refused to decree specific performance which would compel the defendant to take legal proceedings against his wife, who had, after the contract and without his knowledge, registered rights of occupation under the Matrimonial Homes Act 1967,[195] and with whom he was still living.

If, however, a defendant vendor has it in his power to compel a third party to convey the property in question, specific performance will be decreed against the defendant. Indeed an order may be made against the third party if it is the creature of the defendant, such as a limited company in the defendant's ownership and control.[196]

(d) CONDUCT OF THE CLAIMANT

In general, a claimant who seeks specific performance must come with clean hands, that is he must have fulfilled all conditions precedent and performed, or at least have tendered performance, of all the terms of the contract which he has been under a duty to perform, and he must, seeking equity, be prepared to do equity, that is, to perform all his future obligations under the contract.[197] It has been held that a

---

[192] *Briggs v Parsloe* [1937] 3 All ER 831.
[193] [1974] Ch 30, at 50, [1973] 1 All ER 897 at 913.
[194] Supra; *Watts v Spence* [1976] Ch 165, [1975] 2 All ER 528. On the damages award in the latter case see *Sharneyford Supplies Ltd v Edge* [1987] Ch 305, [1987] 1 All ER 588, CA.
[195] Now replaced by the Family Law Act 1996.
[196] *Jones v Lipman* [1962] 1 All ER 442, [1962] 1 WLR 832.
[197] *Australian Hardwoods Pty Ltd v Railways Comr* [1961] 1 All ER 737 at 742, PC; *Chappell v Times Newspapers Ltd* [1975] 2 All ER 233, [1975] ICR 145, CA. A defence alleging that a wife claiming specific performance did not come to equity with clean hands because of the conduct of her husband was rightly held

contractual term purporting to oust this principle cannot fetter the courts' discretion to grant or refuse specific performance after taking account of the claimant's conduct.[198]

First, it is clear that where a contract is subject to the performance of some condition precedent there can be no decree of specific performance unless and until the condition has been performed.[199] Thus specific performance has been refused of a covenant to renew a lease conditional on compliance with repairing covenants,[200] and of an agreement to take a lease of a public house conditional on the grant of a licence,[201] where the respective conditions had not been fulfilled. The condition remains capable of fulfilment, in a case between vendor and purchaser, at any time until the time fixed for completion of the contract.[202] Conditions may be express or implied, as a matter of construction of the contract,[203] and the performance of a condition precedent may be waived by the person or persons who alone benefit therefrom.[204]

Turning to the terms of the contract, the claimant must be able to show he has performed all the essential terms of the contract, express or implied, which he was under a duty to have performed by the time the writ was issued.[205] The breach of a non-essential or trivial term is not, however, necessarily fatal to a specific performance action,[206] nor is it absolutely vital to show the exact performance which would be required at law.[207] Non-performance of a term by the claimant cannot be used as a defence where the defendant has waived performance,[208] or where non-performance has been caused by the defendant's acts or defaults.[209] Moreover, if the term which has not been performed is independent and collateral to the contract sought to be enforced, even though contained in the same document, the non-performance will not prevent specific performance being obtained.[210] If there is a stipulation in the contract intended to benefit the claimant, he may waive it and obtain specific perform-

---

to be unarguable in *Boulding Group plc v Newett* (1991) *Independent*, 24 June, CA. As to the correct approach where there are alleged improprieties on both sides, see *Sang Lee Investment Co Ltd v Wing Kwai Investment Co Ltd* (1983) *Times*, 14 April, PC.

[198] *Quadrant Visual Communications Ltd v Hutchinson Telephone (UK) Ltd* [1993] BCLC 442, CA. See [1992] CLJ 263 (C Harpum).

[199] *Regent's Canal Co v Ware* (1857) 23 Beav 575; *Scott v Liverpool Corpn* (1858) 3 De G & J 334.

[200] *Bastin v Bidwell* (1881) 18 Ch D 238; *Greville v Parker* [1910] AC 335, PC.

[201] *Modlen v Snowball* (1861) 4 De GF & J 143.

[202] *Smith v Butler* [1900] 1 QB 694, CA; *Re Sandwell Park Colliery Co* [1929] 1 Ch 277; *Aberfoyle Plantations Ltd v Cheng* [1960] AC 115, [1959] 3 All ER 910, PC.

[203] *Williams v Brisco* (1882) 22 Ch D 441, CA.

[204] See *Graham v Pitkin* [1992] 2 All ER 235, [1991] 1 WLR 403, PC, discussed [1992] Conv 318 (C Harpum).

[205] *Modlen v Snowball* (1861) 4 De GF & J 143; *Tildesley v Clarkson* (1862) 30 Beav 419.

[206] *Dyster v Randall & Sons* [1926] Ch 932; cf *Oxford v Provand* (1868) LR 2 PC 135.

[207] *Davis v Hone* (1805) 2 Sch & Lef 341.   [208] *Lamare v Dixon* (1873) LR 6 HL 414.

[209] *Murrell v Goodyear* (1860) 1 De GF & J 432.

[210] *Green v Low* (1856) 22 Beav 625; *Phipps v Child* (1857) 3 Drew 709.

ance, provided the stipulation is in terms for the exclusive benefit of the claimant.[211]

Somewhat similar to what has just been discussed are the cases which show that a claimant who has repudiated his obligation under a contract, or who has done acts at variance with it, may be refused specific performance. Thus an employer who has wrongfully dismissed a servant cannot specifically enforce a term in restraint of trade contained in the service contract,[212] and a vendor who, having given possession under the contract, repossesses the property cannot obtain specific performance.[213] There is also a line of cases which show that a tenant under an agreement for a lease who is in breach of his obligations thereunder cannot compel a lease to be granted.[214] Again the act must not be merely trivial and unsubstantial,[215] and the doctrine of waiver applies.[216]

Failure to perform representations which induced the defendant to enter into the contract may also be a defence to a claim for specific performance, even though the representations were not such as would ground an action at law.[217] Further, the claimant must be ready and willing to perform all the terms of the contract which have yet to be performed by him. Thus a purchaser who has committed an available act of bankruptcy of which the vendor has notice cannot enforce the contract, because he is incapable of so paying the purchase money to the vendor as that the latter shall be certain of being able to retain it against the trustees, should bankruptcy supervene.[218] And in one case the fact that the vendor could not produce the title deeds, which had been destroyed by fire, prevented him from getting specific performance.[219]

(e) LACHES

In equity, in general, the rule has always been that time is not of the essence of the contract, that is, of the particular contractual term which has been breached,[220] and accordingly a claimant may obtain specific performance even though he has not performed the terms of the contract to be carried out by him at the time specified.[221]

---

[211] *Heron Garage Properties Ltd v Moss* [1974] 1 All ER 421 noted (1974) 33 CLJ 211 (R J Smith); *Federated Homes Ltd v Turner* (1974) 233 Estates Gazette 845, and see (1975) 39 Conv 251 (S Robinson). Cf *Scott v Bradley* [1971] Ch 850, [1971] 1 All ER 583. See also *BICC plc v Burndy Corpn* [1985] Ch 232, [1985] 1 All ER 417, CA, noted (1985) 101 LQR 146.

[212] *Measures Bros Ltd v Measures* [1910] 2 Ch 248, CA.

[213] *Knatchbull v Grueber* (1815) 1 Madd 153; affd (1817) 3 Mer 124.

[214] *Coatsworth v Johnson* (1885) 55 LJQB 220, CA; *Swain v Ayres* (1888) 21 QBD 289, CA. See (1960) 24 Conv 125 (P H Pettit); *Equity and Contemporary Legal Developments* (ed S Goldstein) 829 (C Harpum).

[215] *Parker v Taswell* (1858) 2 De G & J 559; *Besant v Wood* (1879) 12 Ch D 605.

[216] *Gregory v Wilson* (1852) 9 Hare 683.

[217] *Myers v Watson* (1851) 1 Sim NS 523; *Lamare v Dixon*, supra.

[218] *Dyster v Randall & Sons* [1926] Ch 932. Similarly as to the vendor's bankruptcy—*Lowes v Lush* (1808) 14 Ves 547.

[219] *Bryant v Busk* (1827) 4 Russ 1. But secondary evidence may suffice—*Moulton v Edmonds* (1859) 1 De GF & J 246.

[220] *British and Commonwealth Holdings plc v Quadrex Holding Inc* [1989] 3 All ER 492, at 504 per Browne-Wilkinson VC.

[221] Cf s 41 of the Law of Property Act 1925, replacing s 25(7) of the Judicature Act 1873 and note *Raineri v Miles* [1981] AC 1050, [1980] 2 All ER 145, HL, where it was held that damages may be available for failure to adhere to the original completion date.

The parties may, however, agree that time should be of the essence of the contract, in which case specific performance will not be granted if the time limit has not been observed by the claimant as to his part.[222] Likewise the circumstances of the case or the subject matter of the contract may indicate that the time for completion is of the essence, and even though not originally of the essence, time may be made of the essence by serving an appropriate notice at the proper time.[223]

Even though time is not of the essence of the contract, long delay by the claimant[224] in performing his part, or in bringing proceedings, may defeat his claim to specific performance. It has been said that the claimant must come to the court promptly, and as soon as the nature of the case will permit[225] but Megarry VC has observed[226] that specific performance should not be regarded as a prize to be awarded by equity to the zealous and denied to the indolent. In his view if it is just that the claimant should obtain a decree, it should not be withheld merely because he has been guilty of delay. Over two years' delay was held not to be a bar in that case, but in different circumstances and in earlier times three and a half years' delay was a good defence in *Eads v Williams*,[227] and less than two years in *Lord James Stuart v London and North Western Rly Co.*[228] As little as three and a half months was held to be enough in *Glasbrook v Richardson*,[229] a case concerning the sale of a colliery, said however to be 'a property of an extremely speculative character, approaching a trade' to which special considerations applied.

If the writ has been issued promptly, it seems that delay in bringing the action to trial will not normally defeat the claimant's claim to specific performance. This result will only follow if the claimant by his conduct has lulled the defendant into a belief that he is going to ask for damages only and not specific performance.[230]

Laches will not, however, defeat a claim nearly so soon, if at all, where the claimant is in possession and is the equitable owner, and the action is brought merely to clothe the claimant with the legal estate. Thus in such circumstances specific performance was decreed of an agreement for a lease after eighteen years delay in *Sharp v Milligan*,[231] and of a contract for the sale of land after ten years in *Williams v Greatrex*.[232] To have this effect the possession of the claimant must be possession under the contract.[233] It

---

[222] *Steedman v Drinkle* [1916] 1 AC 275, PC; *Union Eagle Ltd v Golden Achievement Ltd* [1997] 2 All ER 215, PC (order refused where purchaser 10 minutes late), noted (1997) 113 LQR 385 (J D Heydon); [1997] Conv 382 (M P Thompson); (1998) 61 MLR 255 (J Stevens).

[223] *Behzadi v Shaftesbury Hotels Ltd* [1992] Ch 1, [1991] 2 All ER 477, CA, noted (1991) 107 LQR 536 (P V Baker).

[224] Whether vendor or purchaser—*Rich v Gale* (1871) 24 LT 745.

[225] *Eads v Williams* (1854) 4 De GM & G 674.

[226] *Lazard Bros & Co Ltd v Fairfield Properties Co (Mayfair) Ltd* (1977) 121 Sol Jo 793.   [227] *Supra*.

[228] (1852) 1 De GM & G 721.

[229] (1874) 23 WR 51. Cf *Wroth v Tyler* [1974] Ch 30, [1973] 1 All ER 897.

[230] *Du Sautoy v Symes* [1967] Ch 1146, [1967] 1 All ER 25. As to delay in enforcing a decree once obtained, see *Easton v Brown* [1981] 3 All ER 278.

[231] (1856) 22 Beav 606; *Shepheard v Walker* (1875) LR 20 Eq 659.

[232] [1956] 3 All ER 705, CA, applying a dictum of Lord Redesdale in *Crofton v Ormsby* (1806) 2 Sch & Lef 583, who contemplated forty or fifty years delay. See *Frawley v Neill* (1999) 143 Sol Jo LB 98, CA.

[233] *Mills v Haywood* (1877) 6 Ch D 196, CA.

may well be different where the transaction which brought the proprietary interest into being is disputed.[234]

It need hardly be said that the defendant may waive, or by his conduct be deemed to have waived, the defence on the ground of laches.[235]

(f) ABSENCE OF WRITING

Section 2(1) of the Law of Property (Miscellaneous Provisions) Act 1989,[236] which provides that 'A contract for the sale or other disposition of an interest in land can only be made in writing and only by incorporating all the terms which the parties have expressly agreed in one document or, where contracts are exchanged, in each', applies just as much to a claim for specific performance as to a claim for damages. It is more stringent than s 40 of the Law of Property Act 1925 which it repeals and replaces, and is generally thought to leave no scope for the application of the doctrine of part-performance.[237]

In *Yaxley v Gotts*[238] Beldam LJ observed that it is not 'inherent in a social policy of simplifying conveyancing by requiring the certainty of a written document, that unconscionable conduct or equitable fraud should be allowed to prevail'. Section 2(5), he continued, which provides that nothing in the Act is to affect the creation or operation of resulting, implied or constructive trusts effectively excludes from the operation of the section cases in which an interest in land might equally well be claimed by relying on constructive trust or proprietary estoppel. The majority of the court[239] did not think that there was a contract in that case, but on the basis that there was, indicated that circumstances giving rise to a proprietary estoppel that might not at the same time bring about the creation of a constructive trust could be sufficient to displace the strict provisions of s 2(1), provided that they did not run contrary to the public policy underlying the Act.[240] Beldam LJ further said:[241] 'The general principle that a party cannot rely on an estoppel in the face of a statute depends upon the nature of the enactment, the purpose of the provision and the social policy behind it.' This was unanimously agreed to be an accurate statement of the law in *Shah v Shah*,[242] where the defendants were estopped from denying the validity of a deed where the witnesses had not been present when the document was signed as they should have been in order to comply with s 1(3)(i) of the 1989 Act.

---

[234] *Joyce v Joyce* [1979] 1 All ER 175, [1978] 1 WLR 1170.

[235] *Seton v Slade* (1802) 7 Ves 265; *King v Wilson* (1843) 6 Beav 124.

[236] As amended by the Trusts of Land and Appointment of Trustees Act 1996.

[237] See *Yaxley v Gotts* [2000] Ch 162, [2000] 1 All ER 711, CA, which silences the doubts expressed by Neill LJ in *Singh v Beggs* (1996) 71 P & CR 120, CA. See also *Grossman v Harper* [2001] 2 EGLR 82, CA; [2002] Conv 216 (G Griffiths). See also *Grossman v Hooper* [2001] 2 ECLR 82, CA and [2002] Conv 216 (G Griffiths).

[238] Supra, CA. See p 198, supra.   [239] Beldam and Clark LJJ.

[240] [2001] EWCA Civ 527, [2002] QB 35, [2001] 4 All ER 138; *Kinane v Mackie-Conteh* [2005] EWCA Civ 45, [2005] WTLR 345;*Cobbe v Yeomans Row Management* [2005] EWHC 266 (Ch), [2005] All ER(D) 406 Feb. See (2005) 146 PLJ 11 (Laura McDonald).

[241] In *Yaxley v Gotts*, supra, CA, at 734, 191.   [242] [2001] 4 All ER 138, CA.

30

OTHER EQUITABLE
REMEDIES

1 THE APPOINTMENT OF A RECEIVER, OR
RECEIVER AND MANAGER

(a) RECEIVERS

The jurisdiction of the Court of Chancery to appoint a receiver has been said to be one of the oldest equitable remedies.[1] It is now statutory and, like an injunction, may be granted 'in all cases in which it appears to the court to be just and convenient to do so'.[2] A receiver may be appointed on the one hand in order to preserve property which is in danger, or on the other hand to enable a person to obtain the benefit of his rights over property, or to obtain payment of his debt, where the legal remedies are inadequate. Generally, the appointment may extend over any form of property,[3] provided it is capable of assignment, but there are important restrictions, which are discussed later,[4] on the kinds of property over which a receiver by way of equitable execution may be appointed. A receiver has been described[5] as 'a person who receives rents or other income paying ascertained outgoings, but who does not . . . manage the property in the sense of buying or selling or anything of that kind'. This description is not comprehensive, for the purpose of the appointment may be simply to preserve property pending the settlement of legal proceedings, the property in the meantime bringing in no income. It is the duty of a receiver to take possession of the relevant property, and the order appointing him will usually direct any parties to the action in possession to deliver it up to him.

A person appointed receiver may be required to give security[6] for what he receives as such receiver; the appointment may be conditional upon security being given, or the receiver may be ordered to give security by a given date, with liberty to act at once,

---

[1] *Hopkins v Worcester and Birmingham Canal Proprietors* (1868) LR 6 Eq 437 at 447, per Giffard VC; *A-G v Schonfeld* [1980] 3 All ER 1 at 5, per Megarry VC.

[2] Supreme Court Act 1981, s 37(1), (2), discussed p 568 et seq, supra. See also CPR Sch 1, RSC Ord 30.

[3] Including property situated out of the jurisdiction: *C Inc plc v L* [2001] 2 All ER (Comm) 446.

[4] See p 700 et seq, infra.

[5] Per Jessel MR in *Re Manchester and Milford Rly Co* (1880) 14 Ch D 645 at 653, CA.

[6] CPR Sch 1, RSC Ord 30, r 2.

on an undertaking by the applicant to be answerable for what he receives or becomes liable to pay.

(b) MANAGERS

Where it is desired to continue a trade or business, it is not sufficient to appoint a receiver for, as we have seen, he has no authority for this purpose. Though not so old a remedy as appointing a receiver,[7] the court has, however, for many years had jurisdiction for this purpose to appoint a manager, and normally the same person is appointed and known as the receiver and manager.[8] The effect is that the management of the business is carried on by the court, through its officer, but the court will only do this for a limited period of time, for the purpose of preserving the assets.[9] 'Nothing is better settled than that this Court does not assume the management of a business or undertaking except with a view to the winding up and sale of the business or undertaking.'[10] Accordingly in the first instance a manager will not normally be appointed for longer than three months, though this may be extended from time to time if a proper case is made out.

(c) WHO MAY BE APPOINTED AS RECEIVER, OR RECEIVER AND MANAGER

Any party to the action, but not a stranger thereto,[11] may nominate a person to be appointed as receiver. In making the appointment the general principle is that the person appointed should be independent and impartial. Prima facie, therefore, the court will not appoint a party to the action,[12] or anyone who has shown a partiality for one of the parties,[13] or whose interest may conflict with his duties.[14] Again the court will not normally appoint a person who should act as a check on the receiver. Thus a trustee will not normally be appointed receiver of the trust property, for the beneficiaries should be able to rely on him to control the receiver,[15] nor will the court appoint the next friend of a minor claimant.[16] Similarly the court will not normally appoint the solicitor having the conduct of the case,[17] nor any member of the firm of solicitors acting for the claimant.[18]

---

[7] *Re Newdigate Colliery Ltd* [1912] 1 Ch 468, CA.

[8] *Re Manchester and Milford Rly Co* (1880) 14 Ch D 645 at 653, CA.

[9] *Waters v Taylor* (1808) 15 Ves 10; *Taylor v Neate* (1888) 39 Ch D 538.

[10] *Gardner v London Chatham and Dover Rly Co (No 2)* (1867) 2 Ch App 201 at 212, per Cairns LJ; *Re Andrews* [1999] 2 All ER 751, CA.

[11] *A-G v Day* (1817) 2 Madd 246.   [12] *Re Lloyd* (1879) 12 Ch D 447, CA.

[13] *Blakeway v Blakeway* (1833) 2 LJ Ch 75; *Wright v Vernon* (1855) 3 Drew 112.

[14] *Fripp v Chard Rly Co* (1853) 11 Hare 241.

[15] *Sykes v Hastings* (1805) 11 Ves 363; *Sutton v Jones* (1809) 15 Ves 584.

[16] *Stone v Wishart* (1817) 2 Madd 64, nor the son of the next friend in *Taylor v Oldham* (1822) Jac 527.

[17] *Garland v Garland* (1793) 2 Ves 137.   [18] *Re Lloyd*, supra.

694   EQUITY AND THE LAW OF TRUSTS

The court may, however, and frequently does, depart from this general principle if the parties consent, and even without their consent if a proper case is made out. Thus if a receiver is appointed on the dissolution of a partnership, a solvent partner will usually be appointed as receiver, if he has not behaved improperly,[19] in order that the partnership business may be wound up to the best advantage of all concerned.[20] Again where a company is in liquidation and the duties to be performed by the liquidator and the receiver are identical, the court will in general appoint the liquidator as receiver to avoid additional expense and to prevent conflict between them.[21] However, in *Boyle v Bettws Llantwit Colliery Co*[22] the claimants successfully applied to be appointed receivers. They were the unpaid vendors of the property of a company in voluntary liquidation. The liquidator had no funds to reopen the colliery or carry on the workings, while the claimants, who were said to be 'really the owners of the colliery',[23] were willing to provide funds for this purpose.

A minor cannot be appointed as receiver.[24] In an old case[25] the court refused to appoint a peer on the ground that parliamentary privilege would protect him from the ordinary remedies against a receiver; however, a member of the House of Commons was appointed in *Wiggin v Anderson*.[26] And where a receiver and manager is to be appointed, which will involve trading, it seems that a beneficed clergyman of the Church of England[27] is ineligible, as is a practising barrister. Moreover by statute[28] a body corporate is not qualified for appointment as receiver[29] of the property of a company, and it is an offence for an undischarged bankrupt to act as receiver or manager of a company on behalf of debenture holders,[30] save in the unlikely event of his being appointed by the court. An administrative receiver, as defined in s 29(2) of the Insolvency Act 1986, must be an individual, that is a natural person, who is qualified to act as an insolvency practitioner.

Two or more persons may be appointed as joint receivers,[31] or exceptionally as separate receivers of different parts of the assets.[32]

---

[19] *Young v Buckett* (1882) 51 LJ Ch 504.

[20] *Collins v Barker* [1893] 1 Ch 578; *Harrison-Broadley v Smith* [1964] 1 All ER 867 at 872, CA.

[21] *Re Joshua Stubbs Ltd* [1891] 1 Ch 475, CA; *British Linen Co v South American and Mexican Co* [1894] 1 Ch 108, CA.

[22] (1876) 2 Ch D 726.   [23] At 728.   [24] Co Litt 171b, 172a.

[25] *A-G v Gee* (1813) 2 Ves & B 208, but see *Re Gent* (1888) 40 Ch D 190; *Earl of Aylesford v Earl Poulett* [1892] 2 Ch 60.

[26] (1982) unrep, but referred to in Picarda *The Law relating to Receivers, Managers and Administrators*, 3rd edn p 357. See, however, *Re Armstrong* [1892] 1 QB 327.

[27] Pluralities Act 1838, s 29.

[28] Insolvency Act 1986, s 30; *Portman Building Society v Gallwey* [1955] 1 All ER 227.

[29] The disqualification apparently does not apply to appointment as manager.

[30] Insolvency Act 1986, s 31.   [31] *Duder v Amsterdamsch Trustees Kantoor* [1902] 2 Ch 132.

[32] *British Linen Co v South American and Mexican Co* [1894] 1 Ch 108, CA.

(d) SALARY AND ALLOWANCE

Unless otherwise ordered, a receiver or manager appointed by the court will be allowed proper remuneration.[33] Any remuneration allowed is payable out of the assets in the receiver's hands, but the receiver has no personal claim for his remuneration from the parties to the action, even though they all consent to his appointment.[34] A trustee who is appointed receiver will not usually be allowed remuneration,[35] though he may be in exceptional circumstances.[36] Similarly a party to an action who is appointed receiver will normally be required to act without remuneration,[37] but it seems that remuneration may be allowed in partnership cases,[38] and in any case he may be paid for any extraordinary trouble and expense beyond what his duties as receiver required, provided it was for the benefit of the estate.[39] In practice the receiver should apply to the court for directions before undertaking the exceptional work or expense, otherwise he runs the risk that additional remuneration will not be allowed. The court has no power to order that a receiver's remuneration should rank before prior securities.[40]

(e) POSITION OF RECEIVER

A receiver is an officer of the court. It is his duty to take possession of the property over which he is appointed and his possession and acts are the possession and acts of the court.[41] As Chitty J expressed it,[42] 'A receiver is not an agent for any other person, and a receiver is not a trustee. The receiver is appointed by the order of the court and is responsible to the court, and cannot obey the directions of the parties in the action.' By reason of the fact that the receiver is an officer of the court, any interference by anyone with his possession of the property he has been directed to receive is a contempt of court, even though the order appointing him is perfectly erroneous.[43] Interference may be punished by committal,[44] and restrained by the issue of an injunction.[45] Thus in *Dixon v Dixon*[46] an injunction was granted to the receiver and manager of a partnership

---

[33] CPR Sch 1, RSC Ord 30, r 3. It is normally fixed by reference to fixed scales of rates of professional charges. Exceptionally it will be assessed by a costs judge or a district judge. See *Mirror Group Newspapers v Maxwell (No 2)* [1998] 1 BCLC 638. See also *Re Andrews* [1999] 2 All ER 751, CA; *Hughes v Comrs of Customs & Excise* (2002) *Times*, 31 May, CA.

[34] *Boehm v Goodall* [1911] 1 Ch 155; *Evans v Clayhope Properties Ltd* [1988] 1 All ER 444, CA, noted [1988] Conv 363 (C P Rodgers); *Re Andrews*, supra, CA.

[35] *Pilkington v Baker* (1876) 24 WR 234.

[36] *Newport v Bury* (1857) 23 Beav 30; *Re Bignell* [1892] 1 Ch 59, CA.

[37] *Sargant v Read* (1876) 1 Ch D 600; *Taylor v Neate* (1888) 39 Ch D 538.

[38] *Davy v Scarth* [1906] 1 Ch 55.

[39] *Potts v Leighton* (1808) 15 Ves 273; *Harris v Sleep* [1897] 2 Ch 80, CA.

[40] *Choudhri v Palta* [1994] 1 BCLC 184, [1992] BCC 787, CA.

[41] *Aston v Heron* (1834) 2 My & K 390; *Re Flowers & Co* [1897] 1 QB 14, CA.

[42] In *Bacup Corpn v Smith* (1890) 44 Ch D 395 at 398. See *Re Andrews*, supra, CA.

[43] *Ames v Birkenhead Docks Trustees* (1855) 20 Beav 332.

[44] *Helmore v Smith (No 2)* (1886) 35 Ch D 449, CA.

[45] *Dixon v Dixon* [1904] 1 Ch 161.   [46] Supra.

business to restrain one of the old partners from inducing employees of the receiver to leave his employment and enter the employment of a rival business set up by the old partner, even though due notice was given to the receiver and breach of contract was neither instigated nor committed. Apart from physical interference it would be a contempt of court to institute legal proceedings to assert a right over property of which the receiver has either taken or been directed to take possession[47] without first obtaining the leave of the court, which will, however, readily be given unless it is perfectly clear that there is no foundation for the claim.[48] There will, however, be no actionable interference if the order for a receiver does not make it clear on its face that he is to be receiver over the property in dispute,[49] nor where the order is made conditional on the giving of security, and security has not yet been given.[50]

Not being an agent for anyone, a receiver is personally liable for his acts, for instance contracts entered into in carrying on a business,[51] or existing contracts adopted as his own.[52] He is, however, entitled to an indemnity out of the assets for all costs and expenses not improperly incurred,[53] including the costs of an action brought against him as receiver where the defence was for the benefit of the trust estate,[54] but, as with a claim for remuneration, he is not entitled to any personal indemnity,[55] even though he has been appointed with the consent of all parties.[56] Further by the doctrine of subrogation, the receiver's creditors will be entitled to the same rights against the property as the receiver himself.[57] Where multiple receivers have been appointed it is an issue of construction whether they can act severally as well as jointly.[58]

(f) CASES IN WHICH A RECEIVER MAY BE APPOINTED BY THE COURT

Except where the appointment is to enforce an equitable mortgage or charge, or by way of equitable execution, the general ground on which a receiver is appointed is for

---

[47] *Ames v Birkenhead Docks Trustees*, supra; *Defries v Creed* (1865) 12 LT 262.

[48] *Hawkins v Gathercole* (1852) 1 Drew 12; *Lane v Capsey* [1891] 3 Ch 411; *Brenner v Rose* [1973] 2 All ER 535. Provided such leave is obtained an action may be brought against a receiver even by the person at whose instance he was appointed—*L P Arthur (Insurance) Ltd v Sisson* [1966] 2 All ER 1003, [1966] 1 WLR 1384.

[49] *Crow v Wood* (1850) 13 Beav 271.   [50] *Edwards v Edwards* (1876) 2 Ch D 291, CA.

[51] *Burt, Boulton and Hayward v Bull* [1895] 1 QB 276, CA; *Moss Steamship Co Ltd v Whinney* [1912] AC 254, HL. Contrast *Land Rover Group Ltd v UPF(UK) Ltd (in administrative receivership)* [2002] EWHC 3183(QB), [2003] 2 BCLC 222 in relation to the effect of breach by receiver as agent of company.

[52] *Re Botibol* [1947] 1 All ER 26.

[53] *Burt, Boulton and Hayward v Bull*, supra, CA; *Strapp v Bull Sons & Co* [1895] 2 Ch 1, CA.

[54] *Re Dunn* [1904] 1 Ch 648; contrast *Walters v Woodbridge* (1878) 7 Ch D 504, CA, where the defence was merely to vindicate the receiver's character against charges of personal fraud and misconduct in his office and not to benefit the estate.

[55] *Re Bushell, ex p Izard* (1883) 23 Ch D 75, CA; *Batten v Wedgwood Coal and Iron Co* (1884) 28 Ch D 317.

[56] *Boehm v Goodall* [1911] 1 Ch 155; *Rosanove v O'Rourke* [1988] 1 Qd R 171.

[57] *Re London United Breweries Ltd* [1907] 2 Ch 511.

[58] *Gwembe Valley Development Co Ltd (in Receivership) v Koshy* (2000) *Times*, 8 February.

the protection and preservation of property for the benefit of the persons who are, or, as a result of litigation are ultimately held to be, beneficially interested.[59] It was said in *Owen v Homan*[60] that where 'the property is as it were in medio, in the enjoyment of no one, the court can hardly do wrong in taking possession. It is the common interest of all parties that the court should prevent a scramble.'

The main types of case in which a receiver may be appointed are as follows:

(i) Pending the grant of probate or letters of administration

Where the assets of a deceased person are in jeopardy a receiver may be appointed to protect the assets of the estate,[61] and similarly if a sole executor dies a receiver may be appointed pending a fresh grant being obtained.[62] If, however, probate proceedings have been started the proper procedure is to apply for an administrator pendente lite.

(ii) As against executors and trustees

The court may dispossess an executor or trustee of the trust estate by appointing a receiver if a strong case is made out.[63] Gross misconduct or personal disability on the part of the executor or trustee, such as wasting or misapplication of the assets, may justify the appointment of a receiver,[64] or even mere mismanagement without any corrupt intention.[65] Mere poverty is not a sufficient ground,[66] but insolvency is a different matter, though in this case, as in others where a receiver has been appointed in the past, it will now commonly be possible and better to deal with the matter by removal of the trustee and the appointment of a new one.[67]

(iii) In partnership cases

The court will readily appoint a receiver if it can be shown, when the application is made, that the partnership is at an end.[68] The court, however, finds itself in a difficulty if the defendant claims that the partnership is continuing. On the one hand, if a receiver is appointed, the effect is to bring to an end the partnership which one party claims to have a right to be continued; while, on the other hand, if a receiver is not appointed, it leaves the defendant at liberty to go on with the business with risk of loss and prejudice to the claimant.[69] The court tries to weigh the various factors,

---

[59] *Bertrand v Davis* (1862) 31 Beav 429.   [60] (1853) 4 HL Cas 997 at 1032.

[61] *Re Oakes* [1917] 1 Ch 230; *Re Sutcliffe* [1942] Ch 453, sub nom *Jackman v Sutcliffe* [1942] 2 All ER 296.

[62] *Re Parker* (1879) 12 Ch D 293; *Re Clark* [1910] WN 234.

[63] *Middleton v Dodswell* (1806) 13 Ves 266; *Bainbridge v Blair* (1835) 4 LJ Ch 207.

[64] *Evans v Coventry* (1854) 5 De GM & G 911; *Swale v Swale* (1856) 22 Beav 584; *Re Brooker's Estate, Brooker v Brooker* (1857) 3 Sm & G 475. For an exceptional case where the order was made ex parte, see *Clarke v Heathfield* [1985] ICR 203, CA.

[65] *Whitehead v Bennett* (1845) 6 LTOS 185.

[66] *Anon* (1806), supra; *Howard v Papera* (1815) 1 Madd 142.

[67] See chapter 15, supra. Older cases include *Re H's Estate* (1875) 1 Ch D 276; *Dickens v Harris* (1866) 14 LT 98 (sole executor remaining outside the jurisdiction).

[68] *Pini v Roncoroni* [1892] 1 Ch 633; *Taylor v Neate* (1888) 39 Ch D 538.

[69] *Madgwick v Wimble* (1843) 6 Beav 495.

but will not in general appoint a receiver unless it appears reasonably clear either that the partnership is already at an end or that the court will order a dissolution at the trial.[70] For similar reasons the court will be slow to appoint a receiver if the defendant denies the existence of the alleged partnership, though there is no rigid rule preventing it.[71]

(iv) Companies

Receivers are usually appointed under express powers in debentures or debenture trust deeds,[72] though any such appointment may be superseded by an appointment by the court.[73] An appointment may be made by the court at the instance of shareholders or the company itself where, for instance, there is no governing body, or such disputes between the directors that the management is not being carried on.[74] Debenture holders may ask the court to appoint a receiver if their security is in jeopardy,[75] even though they have reserved a power under the debenture which has not yet become exercisable.[76] The mere fact that the security is insufficient is not enough,[77] there must also be evidence that the security is in jeopardy, as, for instance, where the company is threatening to distribute all its assets among the shareholders,[78] or where it has ceased to be a going concern.[79]

(v) Mortgages

The court may appoint a receiver at the instance of a legal mortgagee when it thinks it just and convenient to do so,[80] and it may do so, if a special case is made out, even though the mortgagee has gone into possession or himself appointed a receiver under the express power which is almost invariably included in a mortgage deed.[81]

An equitable mortgagee or chargee has, however, always had a right to have a receiver appointed by the court,[82] where there has been no prior incumbrancer in possession,[83] on the ground that he was unable to take possession for himself.[84] He has this right whenever there has been a breach of any of the mortgagor's obligations, or

---

[70]   *Goodman v Whitcomb* (1820) 1 Jac & W 589; *Smith v Jeyes* (1841) 4 Beav 503.

[71]   *Floydd v Cheney* [1970] Ch 602, [1970] 1 All ER 446.   [72] See p 702, infra.

[73]   *Re Maskelyne British Typewriter Ltd* [1898] 1 Ch 133, CA; *Re Slogger Automatic Feeder Co Ltd* [1915] 1 Ch 478.

[74]   *Trade Auxiliary Co v Vickers* (1873) LR 16 Eq 303, CA; *Stanfield v Gibbon* [1925] WN 11.

[75]   *McMahon v North Kent Ironworks Co* [1891] 2 Ch 148; *Edwards v Standard Rolling Stock Syndicate* [1893] 1 Ch 574.

[76]   *McMahon v North Kent Ironworks Co,* supra.   [77]   *Re New York Taxicab Co Ltd* [1913] 1 Ch 1.

[78]   *Re Tilt Cove Copper Co Ltd* [1913] 2 Ch 588.

[79]   *Hubbuck v Helms* (1887) 56 LT 232. See also *Re London Pressed Hinge Co* [1905] 1 Ch 576; *Re Braunstein and Marjorlaine* [1914] WN 335.

[80]   *Tillett v Nixon* (1883) 25 Ch D 238; *Re Prytherch* (1889) 42 Ch D 590.

[81]   *Gloucester County Bank v Rudry Merthyr Coal Co* [1895] 1 Ch 629, CA. See p 702, post.

[82]   *Sollory v Leaver* (1869) LR 9 Eq 22; *Re Crompton & Co Ltd* [1914] 1 Ch 954 at 967.

[83]   *Berney v Sewell* (1820) 1 Jac & W 647.

[84]   The ground, however, seems doubtful as regards an equitable mortgagee. See *Barclays Bank Ltd v Bird* [1954] Ch 274, [1954] 1 All ER 449; Megarry & Wade, *Law of Real Property,* 6th edn, pp 1214, 1215.

even without this, where the security is in jeopardy.[85] Where the application is made by a subsequent incumbrancer, and the appointment is made in the usual form, expressly without prejudice to the rights of prior incumbrancers, a prior incumbrancer can take possession without leave of the court.[86] Where no reservation is made of the rights of prior incumbrancers, they are not in fact destroyed, but can only be exercised if the leave of the court is first obtained, which will not in practice be refused.[87]

(vi) Creditors

In *Cummins v Perkins*[88] Lindley MR observed that the authorities clearly showed 'that, quite independently of the Judicature Act 1873, if a plaintiff had a right to be paid out of a particular fund he could in equity obtain protection to prevent that fund from being dissipated so as to defeat his rights'. It was, he said, 'settled that a person who had a right to be paid out of a particular fund could obtain an injunction (and if an injunction, it followed on principle that he could obtain a receiver) in a proper case to protect the fund from being misapplied'.[89]

(vii) Between vendor and purchaser

In appropriate cases a receiver may be appointed both in actions for specific performance and for rescission. Thus it has been done where proceedings had been brought to set aside a sale for fraud where the court thought it hardly possible that the transaction could stand, though it was also said that this was not the usual practice.[90] More commonly it has been done in order to preserve the property, for instance, where the property is a mine and it is clearly desirable to keep it working,[91] or a farm which should clearly be kept in a state of cultivation.[92] And an unpaid vendor may be granted a receiver for the protection of his lien.[93]

(viii) Other instances

These have included cases where the owner of a chattel was suing for its return from a bailee, who claimed a lien over it;[94] pending a reference to arbitration;[95] pending litigation in a foreign court;[96] in aid of a freezing injunction;[97] where the affairs of a

---

[85] See cases cited in notes 75–78, p 698, supra. [86] *Underhay v Read* (1887) 20 QBD 209, CA.
[87] *Re Metropolitan Amalgamated Estates Ltd* [1912] 2 Ch 497. [88] [1899] 1 Ch 16 at 19, 20, CA.
[89] See also *Kearns v Leaf* (1864) 1 Hem & M 681; *Owen v Homan* (1853) 4 HL Cas 997.
[90] *Stilwell v Wilkins* (1821) Jac 280.
[91] *Boehm v Wood* (1820) 2 Jac & W 236; *Gibbs v David* (1875) LR 20 Eq 373.
[92] *Hyde v Warden* (1876) 1 Ex D 309, CA.
[93] *Munns v Isle of Wight Rly Co* (1870) 5 Ch App 414. Cf *Cook v Andrews* [1897] 1 Ch 266.
[94] *Hattan v Car Maintenance Co Ltd* [1915] 1 Ch 621, [1911–13] All ER Rep 890, where the receiver was authorized to allow the owner to use the chattel.
[95] *Law v Garrett* (1878) 8 Ch D 26, CA; *Compagnie du Senegal v Smith* (1883) 49 LT 527.
[96] *Transatlantic Co v Pietroni* (1860) John 604.
[97] *A-G v Schonfeld* [1980] 3 All ER 1, [1980] 1 WLR 1182; *International Credit and Investment Co (Overseas) Ltd v Adharn* [1998] BCC 134 (where worldwide freezing injunctions had been granted over property it was right for the court to pierce the corporate veil and appoint a receiver over the property in circumstances where there appeared to the court a real risk that the freezing orders might be breached).

charity were in a state of disarray and controversy;[98] and where a landlord has failed to comply with his repairing obligations.[99] However, a court will not appoint a receiver and manager to manage houses owned by a local authority.[100]

(ix) Appointment of a receiver under special statutory provisions

These include the Mental Health Act 1983,[101] the Insolvency Act 1986[102] and the Drug Trafficking Act 1994.[103] The circumstances in which appointments can be made under these Acts, and their effects, are outside the scope of this book.

(x) Equitable execution

Lastly, there is the rather separate case of the receiver by way of equitable execution.[104] Before the Judicature Acts the Court of Chancery would come to the aid of a judgment creditor who was unable to enforce his judgment by a common law writ of execution, by appointing a receiver over certain assets of the debtor. Despite its title, equitable execution is not really execution at all, but equitable relief which the court gives because execution at law cannot be had. 'It is not execution, but a substitute for execution.'[105] Accordingly the executors of a deceased judgment creditor, who may obtain leave to issue a writ of execution under CPR Sch 1, RSC, Ord 46, cannot under this order obtain the appointment of a receiver.[106]

Before the Judicature Acts, the Court of Chancery would only appoint a receiver where the plaintiff could show that he had exhausted his legal remedies. Since the Judicature Acts, which, as we have seen, give the court jurisdiction to appoint a receiver whenever it appears just and convenient to do so,[107] it has been unnecessary to go through the 'useless and absurd form'[108] of issuing a barren writ of execution,[109] though apart from cases within the Supreme Court Act 1981[110] it is still in general necessary to show that there is no remedy available at law. It is still not sufficient merely to show that to appoint a receiver by way of equitable execution would be a more convenient mode of obtaining satisfaction of a judgment than the usual modes

---

[98] *Derby and Co Ltd v Weldon (Nos 3 and 4)* [1990] Ch 65, sub nom *Derby & Co Ltd v Weldon (No 2)* [1989] 1 All ER 1002, CA (against a foreign company with no assets in this country).

[99] *Hart v Emelkirk Ltd* [1983] 3 All ER 15; *Daiches v Bluelake Investment Ltd* (1985) 275 Estates Gazette 462; *Clayhope Properties Ltd v Evans* [1986] 2 All ER 795, CA, and see (1985) 135 NLJ 1215 (N Madge).

[100] *Parker v Camden London Borough Council* [1986] Ch 162, [1985] 2 All ER 141, CA.

[101] Section 99. See eg *Re Oppenheim's Will Trusts* [1950] Ch 633, [1950] 2 All ER 86.

[102] Section 286. See *Dunn v Rio Properties* [2004] EWCA Civ 1043, [2004] 1 WLR 2702.

[103] Sections 26, 29. See *Re Piper* [1999] 4 All ER 437, CA.

[104] For a Canadian view, see [1988] 67 CBR 306 (E R Edinger).

[105] Per Bowen LJ in *Re Shephard* (1889) 43 Ch D 131 at 137, CA; *Levasseur v Mason and Barry Ltd* [1891] 2 QB 73, CA; *Holmes v Millage* [1893] 1 QB 551, CA.

[106] *Norburn v Norburn* [1894] 1 QB 448.   [107] See p 692, supra.

[108] Per Jessel MR in *Anglo-Italian Bank v Davies* (1878) 9 Ch D 275 at 285, CA: *Re Watkins, ex p Evans* (1879) 13 Ch D 252 at 260, CA.

[109] *Re Whiteley* (1887) 56 LT 846; *Hills v Webber* (1901) 17 TLR 513, CA.

[110] Section 37(4), discussed infra.

of execution.[111] What has to be shown is that there is some hindrance arising from the nature of the property which prevents the judgment creditor from obtaining execution at law but which the appointment of a receiver can overcome. It has not been settled whether it must be shown that execution at law is impossible, or whether it will suffice to show that it is difficult or impractical.[112]

Obvious cases for the appointment of a receiver are over an interest in a settlement of personalty,[113] even when reversionary,[114] or a legacy or share of residue under a will.[115] Other property over which a receiver by way of equitable execution has been appointed includes debts and sums of money payable to a judgment debtor and a claim to be indemnified by a third party[116] to which garnishee proceedings are not applicable,[117] rents of land outside the jurisdiction,[118] and goods in the possession of a third party, subject to that third party's lien.[119] Generally, in determining whether it is just and convenient to appoint a receiver by way of equitable execution, the court must have regard to the amount of the debt claimed, the amount likely to be obtained by the receiver, and the probable cost of his appointment.[120]

If the nature of the property is such that it could not be reached by either law or equity, an appointment will be refused.[121] Thus a receiver has been refused over a patent which was not producing any profits,[122] and a sum the payment of which to the debtor was wholly contingent and dependent on the will of another person.[123] These cases may require reconsideration in the light of *Soinco SACI v Novokuznetsk Aluminium Plant*[124] where, not following earlier decisions, it was held that the court had jurisdiction under s 37(1) of the Supreme Court Act 1981 to appoint a receiver by way of equitable execution to receive future debts as well as debts due and accruing due at the date of his appointment.

It remains to say that by s 36 of the Administration of Justice Act 1956, now repealed and replaced by s 37(4) of the Supreme Court Act 1981, which has 'made a

---

[111] *Harris v Beauchamp Bros* [1894] 1 QB 801, CA; *Holmes v Millage*, supra, CA; *Morgan v Hart* [1914] 2 KB 183, CA; *Maclaine Watson & Co Ltd v International Tin Council* [1988] Ch 1, [1987] 3 All ER 787; affd [1989] Ch 253, [1988] 3 All ER 257, CA; on appeal [1990] 2 AC 418, [1989] 3 All ER 523, HL.

[112] *Maclaine Watson & Co Ltd v International Tin Council*, supra, at first instance and in CA. See also *Bourne v Colodense Ltd* [1985] ICR 291, CA.

[113] *Oliver v Lowther* (1880) 42 LT 47; *Webb v Stenton* (1883) 11 QBD 518, CA; *Ideal Bedding Co v Holland* [1907] 2 Ch 157.

[114] *Fuggle v Bland* (1883) 11 QBD 711, DC; *Tyrrell v Painton* [1895] 1 QB 202, CA.

[115] *Re Marquis of Anglesey* [1903] 2 Ch 727.

[116] *Maclaine Watson & Co Ltd v International Tin Council*, supra, HL.

[117] *Westhead v Riley* (1883) 25 Ch D 413.

[118] *Mercantile Investment and General Trust Co v River Plate Trust Loan and Agency Co* [1892] 2 Ch 303 (though in the circumstances the court refused to make the appointment).

[119] *Levasseur v Mason and Barry Ltd* [1891] 2 QB 73, CA.   [120] CPR Sch 1, RSC, Ord 51, r 1.

[121] *Maclaine Watson & Co Ltd v International Tin Council*, supra, at first instance and in CA.

[122] *Edwards & Co v Picard*, [1909] 2 KB 903, CA.

[123] *R v Lincolnshire County Court Judge* (1887) 20 QBD 167, DC.

[124] [1998] QB 406, [1997] 3 All ER 523. As to future earnings see the Attachment of Earnings Act 1971 which is a complete code and excludes any power to appoint a receiver of future earnings.

revolutionary change in the enforcement of judgments',[125] the power of the court to appoint a receiver by way of equitable execution was extended[126] so as to operate in relation to all legal estates and interests in land, whether or not a charge has been imposed on that land under s 1 of the Charging Orders Act 1979 for the purpose of enforcing the judgment; and the power is in addition to and not in derogation of any power of any court to appoint a receiver in proceedings for enforcing such a charge. The remedy of a judgment creditor against land is accordingly either the imposition of a charge,[127] or the appointment of a receiver, or, perhaps,[128] both.[129] In practice because of the greatly increased scope of charging orders the appointment of a receiver by way of equitable execution is rarely necessary.

(g) APPOINTMENT OUT OF COURT

It is possible for a receiver to be appointed out of court, and indeed this is commonly done under mortgages and debentures, and may be done in other cases, for instance where partners by agreement appoint a receiver and manager to wind up the partnership business.[130] An express power to appoint a receiver was at one time commonly inserted in mortgage deeds, but reliance is now usually placed on the statutory power contained in the Law of Property Act 1925.[131] On the other hand, although in most cases debentures and debenture trust deeds are mortgages to which the statutory power would apply,[132] they still commonly include an express power in order to confer extended powers on the receiver. Strictly speaking, any discussion of a receiver appointed out of court is out of place in a chapter on equitable remedies, but it seems desirable to consider briefly the position of such a receiver by way of contrast and comparison.

Unlike a receiver appointed by the court, a receiver or manager appointed out of court is prima facie an agent for the person appointing him.[133] However, the statutory provisions in the case of mortgages and the usual express provisions in debentures make the receiver the agent of the mortgagor or company, as the case may be, with the object of making the mortgagor or company liable for the receiver's acts or defaults, and this is now made a statutory rule in the case of the administrative receiver of

---

[125] Per Danckwerts LJ in *Barclays Bank Ltd v Moore* [1967] 3 All ER 34, CA.

[126] But see *Re Pope* (1886) 17 QBD 743, CA.

[127] Under the Charging Orders Act 1979. See *National Westminster Bank Ltd v Stockman* [1981] 1 All ER 800, [1981] 1 WLR 67.

[128] See (1985) 82 LSG 674 (J M Dyron).

[129] As to the effect of a charging order in the event of the debtor subsequently becoming bankrupt or being wound up see *Roberts Petroleum Ltd v Bernard Kenny Ltd* [1983] 2 AC 192, [1983] 1 All ER 564, HL.

[130] *Turner v Major* (1862) 3 Giff 442. For different examples see *Knight v Bowyer* (1858) 2 De G & J 421; *Cradock v Scottish Provident Institutions* [1893] WN 146; affd [1894] WN 88, CA.

[131] Sections 101(1)(iii) and 109.

[132] Cf *Knightsbridge Estates Trust Ltd v Byrne* [1940] AC 613, [1940] 2 All ER 401, HL. Contra, *Blaker v Herts and Essex Waterworks Co* (1889) 41 Ch D 399 at 405, 306.

[133] *Knight v Bowyer* (1858) 2 De G & J 421; *Ford v Rackham* (1853) 17 Beav 485.

a company under the Insolvency Act 1986.[134] The better view is that the agency is nevertheless a real one[135] and certainly the receiver is under a duty to account to the mortgagor or company.[136] The receiver is however primarily concerned to look after the interests of the person who appointed him,[137] and he cannot in general, short of misconduct, be controlled by the court at the suit of the mortgagor or company.[138] The relationship is in fact tripartite and involves the mortgagor, the receiver and the debenture holder.[139] He is receiver for the benefit of all those interested in the property of which he is receiver.[140] He does not, however, owe a duty to the general creditors, to contributors, to officers of the company, or members.[141] A receiver appointed out of court ceases to be an agent for any person if he is superseded by a receiver appointed by the court,[142] and, on general principles of agency, his authority will be terminated by the death of the principal.[143] It is however, no longer possible for an administrative receiver to be removed from office by the appointor, thus strengthening the receiver's independence.[144] If under a debenture, a receiver is appointed as agent for the company, winding up will deprive the receiver of power to bind the company personally by acting as its agent. It will not, however, affect his powers to hold and dispose of the company's property comprised in the debenture, including

---

[134] Section 44(1). See Insolvency Act 1994, s 2; *Powdrill v Watson* [1995] 2 AC 394, [1995] 2 All ER 65, HL.

[135] *Hibernian Bank v Yourell (No 2)* [1919] 1 IR 310 at 312, per O'Connor MR; *Ratford v Northavon District Council* [1987] QB 357, [1986] 3 All ER 193, CA; Kerr on *Receivers*, 17th edn, p 341. Contra, (1977) 41 Conv 83 (P J Millett).

[136] *Smiths Ltd v Middleton* [1979] 3 All ER 842. As to the ownership of documents created during receivership, see *Gomba Holdings UK Ltd v Minories Finance Ltd* [1989] 1 All ER 261, CA. As to his duty towards guarantors see *Standard Chartered Bank Ltd v Walker* [1982] 3 All ER 938, [1982] 1 WLR 1410, CA; *American Express International Banking Corpn v Hurley* [1985] 3 All ER 564, noted [1986] JBL 154 (R M Goode) which also discuss the duty of care owed by the receiver in realizing assets. See (1982) 132 NLJ 1137 (G Mitchell); (1982) 132 NLJ 883 (H W Wilkinson).

[137] *Re B Johnson & Co (Builders) Ltd* [1955] Ch 634, [1955] 2 All ER 775, CA; *Gomba Holdings UK Ltd v Minories Finance Ltd*, supra, CA. As to the effect on the powers of the directors, see *Newhart Developments Ltd v Co-operative Commercial Bank Ltd* [1978] QB 814, [1978] 2 All ER 896, CA.

[138] *Rottenberg v Monjack* [1993] BCLC 374, where, however, it was held that where the debenture holder who had appointed the receiver had been paid in full but there was a dispute as to the receiver's remuneration, the company was entitled to an interlocutory injunction to restrain him from selling any further property, which might be unnecessary.

[139] See *Gomba Holdings UK Ltd v Minories Finance Ltd*, supra, CA, per Fox LJ at 263; *Re Leyland DAF Ltd* [1994] 1 BCLC 264.

[140] A receiver managing mortgaged property owes duties to the mortgagor and anyone else with an interest in the equity of redemption. The duties include, but are not necessarily confined to, a duty of good faith. *Medforth v Blake* [2000] Ch 86, [1999] 3 All ER 97, noted [1999] Conv 434 (Ann Kenny); (1999) 143 Sol Jo 950 (M Griffiths); (2000) 63 MLR 413 (Sandra Fisher). See *Downsview Nominees Ltd v First City Corpn Ltd* [1993] AC 295, [1993] 3 All ER 626, PC, noted [1993] Conv 401 (Ross Grantham); [1994] Co Law 28 (R Nolan); (1994) 45 NILQ 61 (M Fealy); *Raja (administratrix of the estate of Raja (deceased)) v Austin Gray (a firm)* [2002] EWCA Civ 1965, [2003] 1 EGLR 91; *Silven Properties Ltd v Royal Bank of Scotland plc* [2003] EWCA Civ 1409, [2004] 4 All ER 484.

[141] *Lathia v Dronsfield Bros Ltd* [1987] BCLC 321.

[142] *Hand v Blow* [1901] 2 Ch 721, CA; *Ratford v Northavon District Council*, supra, CA.

[143] Semble, this is not the case when the appointment is made under the statutory power by reason of the definition in the Law of Property Act 1925, s 205(1)(xvi).

[144] Insolvency Act 1986, s 45(2).

his power to use the company's name for that purpose, for such powers are given by the disposition of the company's property which it made (in equity) by the debenture itself.[145]

As we have seen a receiver appointed out of court is prima facie a mere agent, and accordingly he incurs no personal liability for acts properly done by him as receiver,[146] though he may make himself personally liable for some transaction by giving his personal promise to carry it out,[147] and may always make himself liable for breach of warranty of authority. However in the case of a receiver or manager of the property of a company, the Insolvency Act 1986[148] provides that he is to be personally liable on any contract entered into by him in the performance of his functions to the same extent as if he had been appointed by order of the court except in so far as the contract otherwise provides. And he may incur personal liability after a winding up when he ceases to be the agent of the company, and is not apparently the agent for the debenture holders.[149]

In general, there are no restrictions as to who may be appointed receiver out of court, but the statutory restrictions in relation to receivers, already discussed,[150] apply.

The statutory power provides for the payment of remuneration,[151] and the Insolvency Act 1986[152] contains provisions for remuneration where a receiver of a company is appointed for debenture holders. If there is no provision for remuneration, a receiver may be entitled to claim on a quantum meruit.[153]

2 ACCOUNT

(a) ACTIONS OF ACCOUNT[154]

At common law an action of account could be brought in certain special cases, but it was said by Alderson B[155] to be 'so inconvenient, that it has been long discontinued, and parties have gone into a court of equity in preference'[156] '—partly on account of

---

[145] *Sowman v David Samuel Trust Ltd* [1978] 1 All ER 616; *Barrows v Chief Land Registrar* (1977) *Times*, 20 October. See (1977) 41 Conv 83 (P J Millett).

[146] *Owen & Co v Cronk* [1895] 1 QB 265, CA.

[147] *Robinson Printing Co Ltd v Chic Ltd* [1905] 2 Ch 123.   [148] Section 37.

[149] *Bacal Contracting Ltd v Modern Engineering (Bristol) Ltd* [1980] 2 All ER 655.   [150] Supra, p 694.

[151] Law of Property Act 1925, s 109(6). There is no need to apply to the court unless the receiver wants more than 5%—*Marshall v Cottingham* [1982] Ch 82, [1981] 3 All ER 8.

[152] Section 58. This enables the court to interfere with the receiver's remuneration, but not his right to an indemnity for costs, retrospectively—*Re Potters Oil Ltd (No 2)* [1986] 1 All ER 890.

[153] *Prior v Bagster* (1887) 57 LT 760.   [154] See, generally, (1987) 11 Adel LR 1 (Fiona Patfield).

[155] In *Sturton v Richardson*, (1844) 13 M & W 17, at 20; Blackstone's *Commentaries*, Vol III, 164.

[156] It was resuscitated, however, by the plaintiff in *Godfrey v Saunders* (1770) 3 Wils 73, because his action in Chancery had been 'fruitlessly depending there for more than twelve years'.

the difficulty attending the process under the old writ of account, but chiefly from the advantage of compelling the party to account upon oath, according to the practice of courts of equity.'[157]

It did not follow from this that a person with a legal claim had a right to an account in equity, as he would normally have in an equitable matter, such as where a beneficiary sought an account from his trustee, or a mortgagor from a mortgagee in possession. The Court of Chancery refused to lay down definite rules as to when it would allow a bill for an account, and when it would leave the plaintiff to his action at law. The principle on which the court acted was, however, reasonably clear: jurisdiction would not be exercised where the matter could be as fully and conveniently dealt with by a court of common law.[158]

In practice, equity would normally exercise its jurisdiction in the following cases. First, where there were mutual accounts, unless these were extremely simple.[159] Secondly, where there was some confidential relationship between the parties, as between principal and agent, or between partners.[160] A principal could normally maintain an action of account against the agent by reason of the confidence reposed and the fact that the only way of ascertaining the state of the account was by the equitable procedure of discovery,[161] but the agent had no corresponding right for the facts were within his knowledge and he placed no special confidence in his principal.[162] Thirdly, where the account was so complicated that a court of law would be incompetent to examine it, a question of degree left somewhat indefinite.[163] Fourthly, Lindley LJ has said[164] that an account would be ordered where the plaintiff would have had a legal right to have money ascertained and paid to him by the defendant, if the defendant had not wrongfully prevented it from accruing. Fifthly, as regards waste, although this was normally a tort for which a remedy lay at law, an account would be ordered where an injunction was also sought, and waste had already been committed, in order to prevent the need for two actions,[165] and in any case of equitable waste, which was not recognized at common law.[166] Sixthly, an account was also ordered as incident to an injunction, but not otherwise, in cases of infringement of patent rights.[167]

The Judicature Acts[168] have now assigned actions for an account to the Chancery

---

[157] Per Lord Redesdale in *A-G v Dublin Corpn* (1827) 1 Bli NS 312 at 337, HL.

[158] *Shepard v Brown* (1862) 4 Giff 203; *Southampton Dock Co v Southampton Harbour and Pier Board* (1870) LR 11 Eq 254; (1964) 80 LQR 203 (S J Stoljar).

[159] *Phillips v Phillips* (1852) 9 Hare 471; *Fluker v Taylor* (1855) 3 Drew 183.

[160] But there is no such relationship between a banker and his customers—*Foley v Hill* (1848) 2 HL Cas 28.

[161] *Beaumont v Boultbee* (1802) 7 Ves 599; *Mackenzie v Johnson* (1819) 4 Madd 373.

[162] *Padwick v Stanley* (1852) 9 Hare 627.

[163] *Taff Vale Rly Co v Nixon* (1847) 1 HL Cas 111; *Phillips v Phillips*, supra.

[164] In *London, Chatham and Dover Rly Co v South Eastern Rly Co* [1892] 1 Ch 120 at 140, CA; affd [1893] AC 429, HL.

[165] *Jesus College v Bloom* (1745) 3 Atk 262; *Parrott v Palmer* (1834) 3 My & K 632.

[166] *Duke of Leeds v Earl of Amherst* (1846) 2 Ph 117.

[167] *Price's Patent Candle Co v Bauwen's Patent Candle Co* (1858) 4 K & J 727; *De Vitre v Betts* (1873) LR 6 HL 319; see now Patents Act 1977, s 61.

[168] Now the Supreme Court Act 1981, s 61(1) and Sch 1, para 1.

Division. Provisions as to taking accounts are contained in the Civil Procedure Rules.[169] Any party who wishes to contend:

(a) that an accounting party has received more than the amount shown by the account to have been received;

(b) that an accounting party should be treated as having received more than he has actually received;

(c) that any item in the account is erroneous in respect of amount; or

(d) that in any other respect the account is inaccurate,

must, unless the court otherwise orders, give written notice to the accounting party of his objections with appropriate details and a statement of the ground on which the contention is based.

3   RESCISSION

(a)   MEANING OF 'RESCISSION'[170]

In *Buckland v Farmer and Moody*,[171] Buckley LJ said that the word 'rescind' had no primary meaning. The sense in which it was used in a particular case must be discovered from the context. This has sometimes given rise to confusion. One should distinguish between the following:

(i) rescission in the strict sense, with which alone we are concerned. Here the contract contains an inherent cause of invalidity, for example, mistake, fraud or lack of consent, which makes it voidable at the suit of one of the parties. If and when that party declares his intention not to be bound by the contract, he is said to rescind it.

(ii) rescission in a looser sense includes one of the options which the innocent party may have where a perfectly valid contract is broken by the other party. He may, of course, affirm the contract, and sue for damages for breach of contract, or, in an appropriate case, pursue the equitable remedy of specific performance. This does not absolve the innocent party from carrying out his obligations under the contract. If, however, the breach is a serious one going to the root or substance of the contract, the innocent party may treat it as a repudiation of the contract by the other party which

---

[169] CPR 40 PD.

[170] See the valuable article in (1975) 91 LQR 337 (Michael Albery); see also (1976) 92 LQR 5 (W Gummow); (1976) 39 MLR 214 (F Dawson); (1980) 39 CLJ 58 (A J Oakley); [2000] CLJ 509 (Janet O'Sullivan); [2002] RLR 28 (Sarah Worthington). Partial rescission is not permissible, but see (2005) 121 LQR 273 (J Poole and A Keyser).

[171] [1978] 3 All ER 929; CA; *Johnson v Agnew* [1980] AC 367, [1979] 1 All ER 883, HL.

relieves him from performing his part of it, while retaining his right to sue for damages for breach of contract.[172] This may also be called 'rescission', and in this looser sense is a matter of contract law. An innocent party who thus accepts the repudiation cannot thereafter seek specific performance.

(iii) further questions have arisen where a vendor has chosen to affirm a contract for the sale of land and has obtained a decree of specific performance, with which the purchaser has failed to comply. In such case the vendor may either apply to the court for enforcement of the decree or apply for an order of the court rescinding the contract at this stage, the latter application being no mere formality. In this context, rescission means that the vendor will be permitted to retain the land on the basis that he is no longer bound to perform his part of the contract in consequence of the purchaser's repudiation of it. At the same time he is entitled to claim damages at common law for breach of contract.[173] It should be remembered that since the court is at this stage necessarily exercising its equity jurisdiction, it will act in accordance with equitable principles, and would not accede to the plaintiff's claim and make an order dissolving the decree of specific performance and terminating the contract (with recovery of damages) if to do so would be unjust, in the circumstances then existing, to the purchaser.[174]

(iv) a contract may confer on a party to it a power of 'rescission' on certain terms in certain events. There is no reason why effect should not be given to such a provision, but the meaning of the term 'rescission' in a contract is whatever the contract gives it.

(b) RESCISSION IN ITS STRICT SENSE

Where there is a right of rescission in the strict sense, the contract remains fully valid and binding unless and until the party entitled to do so repudiates it, which repudiation must normally be communicated to the other party.[175] A valid repudiation, however, terminates the contract, puts the parties in statu quo ante and restores things, as between them, to the position in which they stood before the contract was entered into. Strictly speaking rescission is the act of a party and not the act of a court: if the court makes an appropriate order this has been said to be 'merely the judicial determination of the fact that the expression by the plaintiff of his election

---

[172] *Johnson v Agnew*, supra, HL. See also *Millichamp v Jones* [1983] 1 All ER 267, [1982] 1 WLR 1422.

[173] *Johnson v Agnew* [1980] AC 367, [1979] 1 All ER 883, HL, (which also decides what is the measure of damage—see p 586, supra). See (1980) 9 Sydney LR 71 (Marion Hetherington).

[174] *Johnson v Agnew*, supra, HL, discussed (1980) 96 LQR 403 (Marion Hetherington), (1981) 97 LQR 26 (D Jackson); *G K N Distributors Ltd v Tyne Tees Fabrication Ltd* [1985] 2 EGLR 181.

[175] Exceptionally, communication is not required where election to rescind is shown by retaking goods transferred under the contract, or, at any rate in a case of fraud, where the other party has made communication impossible—*Car and Universal Finance Co Ltd v Caldwell* [1965] 1 QB 525, [1964] 1 All ER 290, CA; *Newtons of Wembley Ltd v Williams* [1965] 1 QB 560, [1964] 3 All ER 532, CA.

to rescind was justified, was effective, and put an end to the contract'.[176] It may be asked, therefore, why the matter should come before the court at all. This may happen for a variety of reasons: for instance, the other party may refuse to accept the repudiation and bring an action on the contract, to which the defence may be that the contract has been rescinded; or, the party who claims the right to rescind, perhaps knowing that his claim is not accepted by the other party, may prefer to bring an action to have the contract set aside, or, commonly, there may be some consequential question on which the decision of the court is required, as to the steps that have to be taken to arrive at the restitutio in integrum, the restoring of the parties to their original positions, which is an essential concomitant of rescission. It was because of the ancillary relief commonly sought that, originally, questions of rescission generally arose in the Court of Chancery. The accounts and inquiries that might be necessary to enable restitutio in integrum to be implemented could not usually be carried out in a court of common law.[177] Also a court of equity might be prepared to set aside a contract in circumstances which would not render it voidable at common law. But if restitutio in integrum merely required the repayment of money paid or the recovery of property transferred, and the contract was voidable at common law, the matter could be completely remedied by a common law action for money had or received,[178] or trover.[179] Actions for setting aside deeds or other written instruments are now assigned to the Chancery Division.[180]

It may be, of course, that the act relied upon as a ground for rescission will also be a ground for an independent action in tort. Thus a fraudulent misrepresentation which induces a man to enter into a contract may give him a right of action for damages at common law for the tort of deceit. If this is so it may be either, alternative or additional to rescission:[181] the party defrauded may either affirm the contract and be compensated for his loss by damages for the tort, or rescind and yet bring his action for deceit to cover any loss beyond restitutio in integrum, which, however, in many cases will be merely nominal.

[176] Per Lord Atkinson in *Abram Steamship Co Ltd v Westville Shipping Co Ltd* [1923] AC 773, 781, cited *Baird v BCE Holdings Pty Ltd* [1996] 134 Fed LR 279. See also *Aaron's Reefs Ltd v Twiss* [1896] AC 273, HL; *United Shoe Machinery Co of Canada v Brunet* [1909] AC 330, PC; *Horsler v Zorro* [1975] Ch 302, [1975] 1 All ER 584.

[177] *Erlanger v New Sombrero Phosphate Co* (1878) 3 App Cas 1218 at 1278, per Lord Blackburn. See also *Cheese v Thomas* [1994] 1 All ER 35, [1994] 1 WLR 129, CA, discussed (1994) 144 NLJ 264 (Jill Martin); [1994] LMCLQ 330 (J Mee); (1994) 110 LQR 173 (M Chen-Wishart); and *O'Sullivan v Management Agency and Music Ltd* [1985] QB 428, [1985] 3 All ER 351, CA, per Dunn LJ.

[178] *Stone v City and County Bank* (1877) 3 CPD 282, CA; *Kettlewell v Refuge Assurance Co* [1908] 1 KB 545, CA; affd [1909] AC 243, HL.

[179] *Jones v Keene* (1841) 2 Mood & R 348.   [180] Supreme Court Act 1981, s 61(1) Sch 1.

[181] *Newbigging v Adam* (1886) 34 Ch D 582 at 592, CA, per Bowen LJ; affd sub nom *Adam v Newbigging* (1888) 13 App Cas 308, HL.

(c) GROUNDS UPON WHICH RESCISSION MAY BE GRANTED

The main grounds on which a contract may be rescinded are mentioned briefly below, but for a fuller discussion the reader is referred to books on the law of contract.[182]

(i) Fraudulent misrepresentation

This rendered a contract voidable both at law and in equity.[183] For this purpose what is relevant is fraud in the common law sense, sometimes called actual fraud, which will sustain an action of deceit. A fraud is proved when it is shown that a false representation has been made knowingly, or without belief in its truth, or recklessly, careless whether it be true or false.[184] The fraudulent party need not have acted with a corrupt motive,[185] but the false statement must have been made with the intent that it should be acted on,[186] and it must actually have been acted on by the other party.[187]

(ii) Innocent misrepresentation

As such, this had no effect at common law, unless incorporated into the contract. In equity, although it might be a good defence to a specific performance action, it was, somewhat illogically, not for a long time regarded as sufficient to enable a court of equity to set the contract aside.[188] From the middle of the nineteenth century, however, the courts of equity have asserted this jurisdiction,[189] which Jessel MR explained, in *Redgrave v Hurd*,[190] either on the ground that equity would not permit a man to get a benefit from a statement made by him which has in fact been proved false, or that it would be fraudulent to allow a man to insist upon a contract obtained by the aid of his own false statement. Since the Misrepresentation Act 1967,[191] rescission has been equally available where the misrepresentation has become a term of the contract. Any misrepresentation which in fact induces a person to enter into a contract entitles him to rescind; the question whether or not it would have induced a reasonable person to enter into the contract relates only to the question of onus of proof.[192]

---

[182] Eg Cheshire, Fifoot and Furmston, *The Law of Contract*, 14th edn.

[183] But see *Halley v The Law Society* [2003] EWCA (Civ) 97, [2003] WTLR 845, noted [2004] CLJ 30 (Tang Hang Wu).

[184] *Derry v Peek* (1889) 14 App Cas 337, HL.   [185] *Polhill v Walter* (1832) 3 B & Ad 114.

[186] *Peek v Gurney* (1873) LR 6 HL 377.   [187] *Smith v Chadwick* (1884) 9 App Cas 187, HL.

[188] *Attwood v Small* (1838) 6 Cl & Fin 232; *Bartlett v Salmon* (1855) 6 De GM & G 33.

[189] *Reese River Silver Mining Co v Smith* (1869) LR 4 HL 64; *Torrance v Bolton* (1872) 8 Ch App 118; *Walker v Boyle* [1982] 1 All ER 634, [1982] 1 WLR 495.

[190] (1881) 20 Ch D 1 at 12, 13, CA.

[191] Section 1. See (1967) 30 MLR 369 (P S Atiyah and G H Treitel); (1967) 31 Conv 234 (J R Murdock).

[192] *Museprime Properties Ltd v Adhill Properties Ltd* (1990) 61 P & CR 111.

(iii) Mere silence

This does not usually amount to a representation, but it may do so if the concealment gives to the truth which is told the character of falsehood,[193] or if there is a duty to make disclosure, as is the case where the contract is one *uberrimae fidei*.[194]

(iv) Executed contracts entered into as a result of misrepresentation

If the misrepresentation was fraudulent the fact that the contract has been completed does not destroy the right of rescission. Before the Misrepresentation Act 1967 it was the law that there could be no rescission for innocent misrepresentation after completion of a contract for the sale of land,[195] or, probably, the execution of a formal lease.[196] This rule was less firmly established in other cases.[197] The Act now provides[198] that rescission may be allowed for innocent misrepresentation where the contract has been performed in the same way as where the representation is fraudulent.

(v) Constructive fraud

A contract may be rescinded in equity on the ground of constructive fraud. There has been held to be constructive fraud in cases involving taking advantage of weakness or necessity, including catching bargains with expectant heirs, breach of fiduciary duty, such as a purchase by a trustee of the trust property, and frauds on a power.[199] In particular it includes undue influence.

'Undue influence' has long been a ground on which equity might relieve a party to a transaction where it was entered into by reason of the undue influence of the other party, thus enabling a gift to be recovered or a contract to be set aside. In *Allcard v Skinner*[200] a woman was persuaded to join a religious order which involved a strict vow of poverty as a consequence of which she gave some £7,000 to the order. All but £1,671 had been spent by the order when the woman left it. Subsequently she sought to recover this money. It was held that as the gift had been made under a pressure that she could not resist she was in principle entitled to recover it in so far as it had not been disbursed with her consent for the purposes of the order. On the facts, however,

---

[193] *Oakes v Turquand* (1867) LR 2 HL 325.
[194] Principally, contracts of insurance of all kinds. See *Wales v Wadham* [1977] 2 All ER 125.
[195] *Early v Garrett* (1829) 9 B & C 928; *Wilde v Gibson* (1848) 1 HL Cas 605.
[196] *Angel v Jay* [1911] 1 KB 666, DC; *Edler v Auerbach* [1950] 1 KB 359, [1949] 2 All ER 692.
[197] *Seddon v North Eastern Salt Co Ltd* [1905] 1 Ch 326, [1904–7] All ER Rep 817; cf *Leaf v International Galleries* [1950] 2 KB 86, [1950] 1 All ER 693, CA; *Long v Lloyd* [1958] 2 All ER 402, [1958] 1 WLR 753, CA.
[198] Section 1.
[199] For the doctrine of unconscionable bargains see *Portman Building Society v Dusangh* [2000] 2 All ER (Comm) 221, CA, and cases there cited. See (2000) 21 T & ELJ 12 (M Hardwick); [2001] Conv 573 (Lara McMurtry).
[200] (1887) 36 Ch D 145, CA. This case, in the Australian context, is considered in (2003) 26 UNSWLJ 66 (Pauline Ridge).

her claim was barred by her laches and acquiescence.[201] The leading case is now *Royal Bank v Etridge (No 2)*.[202]

Whether a transaction was brought about by the exercise of undue influence is a question of fact, and in general the person who alleges undue influence must prove it. It must be affirmatively established that the donor's trust and confidence in the donee has been betrayed or abused. The principle is not confined to cases of abuse of trust and confidence. It includes other cases where a vulnerable person has been exploited. Various expressions have been used. Trust and confidence, reliance, dependence or vulnerability on the one hand and ascendency, domination or control on the other. 'None of these descriptions is perfect. None is all embracing. Each has its proper place.'[203] Moreover the fact that the donee's conduct was unimpeachable and that there was nothing sinister in it is no sufficient answer to a claim.[204] The evidence required depends on the nature of the alleged undue influence, the personality of the parties, the extent to which the transaction cannot readily be accounted for by the ordinary motives of ordinary persons in that relationship, and all the circumstances of the case.

A distinction is drawn between 'actual undue influence' and 'presumed undue influence'. Actual undue influence does not depend upon a pre-existing relationship between the two parties though it is most commonly associated with and derived from such a relationship. The party who alleges actual undue influence must prove affirmatively that he entered into the impugned transaction not of his own will but as a result of actual undue influence exerted against him.[205] He must show that the other party to the transaction, or someone who induced the transaction for his own benefit, had the capacity to influence the complainant; that the influence was exercised; that the exercise was undue; and that its exercise brought about the transaction. It is not necessary, however, to show domination. Whether actual undue influence has been exercised is a question of fact.[206]

The evidential burden may, however, shift to the defendant if the complainant can show that he placed trust and confidence in the defendant in relation to the management of his financial affairs, coupled with a transaction which calls for explanation, that is, is not readily explicable by the relationship between the parties.[207] This is

---

[201] See p 545, supra.

[202] *Royal Bank of Scotland v Etridge (No 2)* [2001] UKHL44, [2002] 2 AC 773, [2001] 4 All ER 449. The salient points in the speech of Lord Nicholls, which reflected the views of the House of Lords, were summarized in *Randall v Randall* [2004] EWHC 2258 (Ch), [2005] WTLR 119.

[203] See *Royal Bank of Scotland v Etridge (No 2)*, supra, HL, at [11]; *Macklin v Dowsett* [2004] EWCA Civ 904, unrep, 14 June 2004.

[204] *Hammond v Osborn* [2002] EWCA (Civ) 885, [2002] WTLR 1125; *Niersmans v Pesticcio* [2004] EWCA (Civ) 372, [2004] WTLR 699.

[205] See *Royal Bank of Scotland v Etridge (No 2)*, supra, HL.

[206] *Langton v Langton* [1995] 2 FLR 890; *UCB Corporate Services Ltd v Williams* [2002] EWCA Civ 555, [2003] 1 P & CR 168; *Wright v Cherrytree Finance Ltd* [2001] 2 All ER (Comm) 877.

[207] *Michael v Cansick* [2004] EWHC 1684 (Ch), [2004] WTLR 961. See *Turkey v Awadh* [2003] EWCA Civ 382, [2005] 2 FCR 7, where the transaction, curious as it might otherwise seem, was explicable by the ordinary motives of people in the position of the parties. The classification of presumed undue influence cases in *Bank*

commonly referred to as a case of 'presumed undue influence'. Once the presumption is raised it is presumed, unless and until it is rebutted, that the donee has preferred his own interests and has not behaved fairly to the donor.[208] In such a case the court interferes not on the ground that any wrongful act has in fact been committed by the donee, but on the ground of public policy and to prevent the relations which existed between the parties and the influence arising therefrom being abused. The presumption may be rebutted by proof that the gift was 'the spontaneous act of the donor acting under circumstances which enabled him to exercise an independent will and which justifies the court in holding that the gift was a free exercise of the donor's will' or, to put it more shortly, where it is proved that the gift was made by the donor 'only after full, free and informed thought about it', that is, fully informed not only of the nature of the gift but also of its effect.[209]

Moreover in the case of certain well known relationships, such as solicitor and client and trustee and beneficiary,[210] the law presumes, irrebuttably, that one party had influence over the other. In these cases the complainant need not prove he actually reposed trust and confidence in the other party; it is sufficient to prove the existence of the relationship, but even here he must show that the transaction was wrongful in that it constituted an advantage taken of the person subjected to the influence which, failing proof to the contrary, was explicable only on the basis that undue influence had been exercised to procure it.[211]

---

of *Credit and Commerce International SA v Aboody* [1990] 1 QB 923, [1992] 4 All ER 955, CA, at 953, 964 (overruled on other grounds by *CIBC Mortgages plc v Pitt* [1994] 1 AC 200, [1993] 4 All ER 417, HL) adopted in *Barclays Bank plc v O'Brien* [1994] 1 AC 180, [1993] 4 All ER 417, HL, into Class 2A where the law presumes the legal relationship between the parties to be one of trust and confidence, and Class 2B where the claimant must establish by affirmative evidence that he or she was accustomed to repose trust and confidence in the alleged wrongdoer has lost most of its significance since *Royal Bank of Scotland v Etridge (No 2)*, supra, HL, esp per Lord Clyde at [92], Lord Hobhouse at [107] and Lord Scott at [158], [161]. The presumption was not rebutted in *Goldsworthy v Brickell* [1987] Ch 378, [1987] 1 All ER 853, CA, or in *Hammond v Osborn*, supra, CA, noted [2003] LMCLQ 145 (Karen Scott); (2004) 120 LQR 34 (P Birks), where a very large gift, both in absolute and comparative terms, was not made after 'full, free and informed thought'. Contrast *Re Brocklehurst* [1978] 1 Ch 14, CA; *Chater v Mortgage Agency Services Number Two Ltd* [2003] EWCA Civ 490, [2003] HLR 61, and see *In the Estate of Bennett (decd)* [2004] EWHC 396 (Ch), [2004] WTLR 485 where the relationship did not give rise to any evidential presumption of undue influence.

208 *Wright v Hodgkinson* [2004] EWHC 3091 (Ch), [2005] WTLR 435.

209 *Randall v Randall*, supra, where it was that the two formulations have consistently been treated as expressing an identical test.

210 Also parent and child, guardian and ward, fiancé and fiancée, medical, religious and other advisers and their patients, etc, but not husband and wife. Nor does it arise on the case of an adult child and his or her elderly parent, though this may be a factor in establishing the necessary trust and confidence. As to undue influence and elderly persons generally see (2003) 23 LS 251 (Fiona R Burns). In relation to banker and customer see (1986) 65 CBR 37 (Donovan Waters).

211 See *National Westminster Bank plc v Morgan* [1985] AC 686, [1985] 1 All ER 821, HL, per Lord Scarman at 703–707, 826–829; *Allcard v Skinner*, supra, CA, per Lindley LJ at 185. In citing and applying these dicta in *Royal Bank of Scotland v Etridge (No 2)*, supra, HL, Lord Nicholls said that the label 'manifest disadvantage' which had been attached to this latter requirement had given rise to misunderstanding and should be discarded. See (2005) 121 LQR 29 (N Enonchong). See also *Jennings v Cairns* [2003] EWCA Civ 1935, [2004] WTLR 361.

One way in which a claim of undue influence may be defeated is by showing that the claimant received independent legal advice, but the involvement of a solicitor does not necessarily prevent a finding that a transaction was tainted by undue influence.[212] It is a question of fact whether the outside advice had an appropriate emancipating effect.[213] It has been said[214] that it would be sensible for a person who may be at risk of being alleged to have exercised undue influence, whether presumed or actual, to ensure that the solicitor who gives legal advice to the potential claimant is wholly unconnected with that person.

So long as the undue influence persists, a claim can be brought regardless of how much time has passed since the transaction.[215]

Many cases have come before the courts in recent years where a wife has charged her interest in the matrimonial home to a bank as security for her husband's indebtedness or the indebtedness of a company through which he carried on business. Subsequently when the bank seeks to realize its security the wife alleges that she is not bound because she has executed the charge under the undue influence of her husband. Assuming undue influence is established the wife would have no difficulty in claiming a remedy against the husband. The difficulty in these cases is that (commonly supported by her husband) she seeks to prevent a third party, the bank, which has not exercised any undue influence, from enforcing its security.

The traditional view of equity in this tripartite situation was that the wife could only succeed if the third party was privy to the conduct which led to the wife's entry into the transaction. There is no legal obligation on one party to a transaction to check whether the other party's concurrence was obtained by undue influence. The leading case of *Barclays Bank plc v O'Brien*[216] has now introduced into the law the concept that, in certain circumstances, a party to a contract may lose the benefit of his contract, entered into in good faith, if he ought to have known that the other's concurrence had been procured by the misconduct of a third party. The *O'Brien* principle, as it has been called, was recently affirmed and elaborated in *Royal Bank of Scotland v Etridge (No 2)*.[217] Though most of the cases have involved a wife becoming

---

[212] *Randall v Randall*, supra; *Vale v Armstrong* [2004] EWHC 1160 (Ch), [2004] WTLR 1471, noted (2004) 18(7) T & E 2.

[213] *Randall v Randall*, supra.

[214] Per Neuberger J in *Pesticcio v Huet* [2003] EWHC 2293 (Ch), [2003] WTLR 1327 at [106], affd sub nom *Niersmans v Pesticcio* [2004] EWCA (Civ) 37, [2004] WTLR 699 (the evidence established that the brother had the necessary degree of trust and confidence in his sister).

[215] *Humphreys v Humphreys* [2004] EWHC 2201 (Ch), [2004] WTLR 1425.

[216] Supra, HL. As to the possibility of severing from an instrument affected by undue influence the objectionable parts leaving the part uncontaminated by undue influence enforceable, see *Barclays Bank plc v Caplan* [1998] 1 FLR 532.

[217] Supra, HL, noted (2002) 118 LQR 337 (D O'Sullivan), 351 (P Watts); [2002] MLR 435 (R Bigwood); [2002] Conv 174 (M P Thompson), 456 (Georgina Andrews); (2002) 61 CLJ 29 (Mika Oldham); [2002] JBL 439 (Simone Wong); [2002] LMCLQ 231 (A Phang and H Tjio); [2002] RLR 100 (D Capper). See also *Meredith v Lackschwitz-Martin* [2002] EWHC 1462 (Ch), [2002] WTLR 1451; *A-G v R* [2003] UKPC 22, [2003] EMLR 499, noted [2003] RLR 110 (A Phang and H Tjio); [2003] LMCLQ 341 (Joan Wadsley); *Nel v Kean* [2003] EWHC 190 (QB), [2003] WTLR 501.

surety for her husband, the principle is not restricted to cases where a creditor obtains a security from a guarantor whose sexual relationship with the debtor gives rise to a heightened risk of undue influence. It applies equally where a husband stands surety for his wife, and in the case of unmarried couples, whether heterosexual or homo-sexual, where the bank is aware of the relationship. Cohabitation is not essential.[218] It has been applied where the relationship was employer and employee,[219] and is applicable in every case where the relationship between the surety and the debtor is non-commercial.[220]

In the above cases the bank (or other creditor) is, as it is said, 'put on inquiry', and in *Royal Bank of Scotland v Etridge (No 2)*[221] detailed guidance was given as to the steps that the bank should take to protect itself in these circumstances. One way is for the bank to insist that the wife attends a private meeting with a representative of the bank at which she is told of the extent of her liability as surety, warned of the risk she is running and urged to take independent advice. In practice banks are reluctant to follow this course and prefer to rely on the wife's having obtained independent advice from a solicitor. To obtain protection in this way the bank must communicate directly with the wife, informing her that for her own protection it will require written confirmation from a solicitor, acting for her, to the effect that the solicitor has fully explained to her the nature of the documents and the practical implications they will have for her. She should be told that the purpose of this requirement is that thereafter she should not be able, once she has signed the documents, to dispute that she is legally bound by them. She should be asked to nominate a solicitor (not necessarily a different solicitor from the one advising her husband) whom she is willing to instruct to advise her, separately from her husband, and act for her in giving the necessary confirmation to the bank. The bank must supply the solicitor with all the necessary financial information.

Where a mortgage is voidable for undue influence as against a husband and against a bank, a replacement mortgage would itself be voidable, at any rate if the replacement mortgage were taken out as a condition of discharging the earlier voidable mortgage, even if undue influence were not operative at the time of such replacement, and even if there were a new contract rather than a mere variation.[222]

---

218 *Massey v Midland Bank plc* [1995] 1 All ER 929, per Steyn LJ at 933, approved by Lord Nicholls in *Royal Bank of Scotland v Etridge (No 2)*, supra, HL, at [47].

219 *Credit Lyonnais Bank Nederland NV v Burch* [1997] 1 All ER 144, CA .

220 See eg *Avon Finance Co Ltd v Bridger* [1985] 2 All ER 281, CA (son and elderly parents); *National Westminster Bank plc v Amin* [2002] UKHL 9, [2002] 1 FLR 735 (English speaking son and non-English speaking parents), noted [2002] Conv 499 (M Haley).

221 Supra, HL. The guidance was said to be applicable to future transactions. In relation to past transac-tions the test applicable was said to be that set out by Lord Browne-Wilkinson in *Barclays Bank plc v O'Brien*, supra, HL, at 196–197, 629–630. See also *McGregor v Michael Taylor & Co* [2002] Lloyd's Rep 468; *UCB Corporate Services Ltd v Williams*, supra, CA; *UCB Group Ltd v Hedworth* [2003] EWCA Civ 1717, [2003] 3 FCR 737; [2001] PLJ 16 (M Pawlowski); *First National Bank plc v Achampong* [2003] EWCA Civ 487, [2004] 1 FCR 18, discussed [2003] LMCLQ 307 (N Enonchong); [2003] Conv 314 (M P Thompson).

222 *Yorkshire Bank plc v Tinsley* [2004] EWCA Civ 816, [2004] 3 All ER 463, noted [2004] Conv 399 (M P Thompson); [2005] CLJ 42 (N P Gravells).

(vi) Mistake

After a full discussion of the cases, the Court of Appeal held in *Great Peace Shipping Ltd v Tsavliris Salvage (International) Ltd*,[223] disapproving *Solle v Butcher*[224] as being unable to stand with *Bell v Lever Bros Ltd*,[225] that there is no jurisdiction to grant rescission of a contract on the ground of common mistake where that contract is valid and enforceable on ordinary principles of contract law. The court observed, however, that just as the Law Reform (Frustrated Contracts) Act 1943 was needed to temper the effect of the common law doctrine of frustration, so there is scope for legislation to give greater flexibility to the law of mistake than the common law allows.

(d) LOSS OF THE RIGHT TO RESCISSION

This may occur in various ways.

(i) Affirmation of the contract

Where a man has a right of rescission, he may elect either to rescind the contract or to affirm it. If, with full knowledge not only of the relevant facts, but also of his legal right to rescind, he, either by express words or by unequivocal acts, affirms the contract, his election has been determined for ever.[226] Although the question remains open until he elects one way or the other, lapse of time and acquiescence will furnish evidence of an election to affirm the contract, and when the lapse of time is great it would probably in practice be treated as conclusive evidence to show that he had so determined. The court will, of course, on equitable principles, take all the circumstances into account,[227] including the nature of the contract,[228] and the presence or absence of fraud.[229]

---

[223] [2002] EWCA Civ 1407, [2002] 4 All ER 689, discussed [2002] NLJ 132 (M Pawlowski); [2002] NLJ 1654 (D Dabbs); [2002] LMCLQ 449 (G McMeel); (2003) 119 LQR 177 (F M B Reynolds); (2003) 119 LQR 180 (S B Midwinter); [2003] CLJ 29 (C Hare); [2004] JBL 34 (A Chandler, J Devenney and Jill Poole); [2003] RLR 93 (J Cartwright); (2004) KCLJ 127 (J Edelman); [2003] Conv 247 (A Phang).

[224] [1950] 1 KB 671, [1949] 2 All ER 1007, CA.   [225] [1932] AC 161, HL.

[226] *Clough v London and North Western Rly Co* (1871) LR 7 Exch 26; *Peyman v Lanjani* [1985] Ch 457, [1984] 3 All ER 703, where the point is also made that if A has acted to his detriment in reliance on an *apparent* election by B, he will in most cases be able to rely on an estoppel by conduct; *Cornish v Midland Bank plc* [1985] 3 All ER 513, CA.

[227] See, generally, *Erlanger v New Sombrero Phosphate Co* (1878) 3 App Cas 1218, HL; *Senanayake v Cheng* [1966] AC 63, [1965] 3 All ER 296, PC; *Laurence v Lexcourt Holdings Ltd* [1978] 2 All ER 810. And see *William Sindall plc v Cambridgeshire County Council*, supra, CA.

[228] *Leaf v International Galleries* [1950] 2 KB 86, [1950] 1 All ER 693, CA (where a claim to rescind an executed contract for the sale of goods for innocent misrepresentation was barred by five years delay, although the plaintiff brought his action as soon as he knew the true facts); *Re Scottish Petroleum Co* (1883) 23 Ch D 413 at 434, CA (where shares are allotted in a going concern it is doubtful if repudiation in a fortnight would be soon enough).

[229] *Charter v Trevelyan* (1844) 11 Cl & Fin 714; *Spackman v Evans* (1868) LR 3 HL 171.

(ii) Restitutio in integrum

The basic rule is that rescission is not permitted unless it is possible for the contract to be rescinded in toto,[230] and the parties replaced in statu quo ante. On the one hand, this means that rescission necessarily involves the restoration of money paid or property transferred under the contract which has been avoided; where there is no independent right of action for damages, as may still be the case even after the Misrepresentation Act 1967 where rescission is decreed for innocent misrepresentation,[231] this includes a right to an indemnity against liabilities necessarily incurred or created under the contract which has been avoided, but this may well be something less than what would be recoverable in an action for damages. On the other hand, it follows that if it is not possible to restore the parties to their pre-contract position then the remedy of rescission will not lie.[232] In applying this rule the courts are primarily concerned with the restoration of the defendant to his pre-contract position and do not lay stress on the restoration of the plaintiff.[233]

The requirement of restitutio in integrum seems to have been strictly enforced at common law, but the equitable rules were, or became, more flexible. The result is that the doctrine is not applied too literally, the court fixing its eyes on the goal of doing what is practically just in the individual case, even though restitutio in integrum is impossible, and being more drastic in exercising its discretionary remedy of rescission in a case of fraud than in a case of innocent misrepresentation.[234] Fraud includes constructive fraud, in particular a transaction which has been procured by undue influence, or where one party is in breach of a fiduciary duty to another. Thus in O'Sullivan v Management Agency & Music Ltd[235] it was held that the wrongdoer must give up his profits and advantages, while at the same time being compensated for work he had actually performed under the contract. At least in relation to a transaction entered into in breach of a fiduciary relationship, the transaction 'may be set aside even though it is impossible to place the parties precisely in the position in which they were before, provided that the court can achieve practical justice between

---

[230] *Thorpe v Fasey* [1949] Ch 649, [1949] 2 All ER 393—severely criticized on other grounds in (1975) 91 LQR 337 (Michael Albery).

[231] Section 2(1) of the Misrepresentation Act 1967 did not altogether abolish the common law rule laid down in *Gilchester Properties Ltd v Gomm* [1948] 1 All ER 493. A misrepresentor may defend an action for damages by proving that 'he had reasonable ground to believe and did believe up to the time the contract was made that the facts represented were true'. Quaere, whether non-disclosure can ever constitute misrepresentation for the purposes of this section.

[232] *Clarke v Dickson* (1858) EB & E 148; *Urquhart v Macpherson* (1878) 3 App Cas 831, PC; and cases cited in the following two footnotes.

[233] *Western Bank of Scotland v Addie* (1862) LR 1 Sc & Div 145; *Spence v Crawford* [1939] 3 All ER 271, HL.

[234] *O'Sullivan v Management Agency and Music Ltd* [1985] QB 428, [1985] 3 All ER 351, CA; *De Molestian v Ponton* [2002] 1 Lloyds Rep 270. Where the victim of a fraudulent misrepresentation has lost the right of rescission because restitution in integrum is no longer possible, he could still rely on the misrepresentor's reprehensible conduct in resisting on application for specific performance, provided he has not affirmed the contract: *Geest plc v Fyffes plc* [1999] 1 All ER (Comm) 672.

[235] Supra, CA. See also *Mahoney v Purnell* [1997] 1 FLR 612; (2002) 16 Tru LI 151 (T Akkouh); (2003) 17 Tru LI 66 (V J Vann).

the parties by obliging the wrongdoer to give up his profits and advantages, while at the same time compensating him for any work that he has actually performed pursuant to the transaction'.[236] The equitable course may not be rescission at all but may be to enforce specific performance with compensation.

(iii) Rights of third parties

If an innocent third party has acquired for value an interest in property affected by the contract which would be prejudiced by rescission, the person who would otherwise have a right to rescind will be precluded from exercising it.[237] The right of rescission being, it is submitted, a mere equity, this is a correct application of the basic principle that such a right is ineffective against a subsequent purchaser for value without notice of either a legal estate or an equitable interest.[238]

(iv) Misrepresentation Act 1967

In any case of innocent misrepresentation giving rise to a right of rescission, the court may declare the contract subsisting and award damages in lieu of rescission, if of opinion that it would be equitable to do so, having regard to the nature of the misrepresentation and the loss that would be caused by it if the contract were upheld, as well as to the loss that rescission would cause the other party,[239] but according to *Government of Zanzibar v British Aerospace (Lancaster House) Ltd*[240] the court has no power to award damages if the right of rescission has been lost.

4 RECTIFICATION OF DOCUMENTS

(a) GENERAL

Where a transaction is embodied in a written instrument which, by mistake, does not express the true agreement of the parties, the remedy of rectification may be available. Where it is ordered, such alterations or amendments will be made in the written instrument as may be necessary to express the true agreement, and after such rectification 'the written agreement does not continue to exist with a parol variation; it is to be read as if it had been originally drawn in its rectified form'.[241] This may have the result of validating with retrospective effect some act which was invalidly done under the instrument in its original form.[242] It is vital to realize that it is only the written

---

[236] *O'Sullivan v Management Agency and Music Ltd,* supra CA, per Dunn LJ at 466.

[237] *Clough v London and North Western Rly Co* (1871) LR 7 Exch 26 at 35; *Oakes v Turquand* (1867) LR 2 HL 325.

[238] See chapter 1, section 5, p 20 et seq, supra.   [239] See [1987] Conv 423 (J Cartwright).

[240] [2000] 1 WLR 2333, critically noted (2001) 117 LQR 524 (D Malet).

[241] Per Sterndale MR in *Craddock Bros Ltd v Hunt* [1923] 2 Ch 136 at 151, [1923] All ER Rep 394 at 402, CA; *Johnson v Bragge* [1901] 1 Ch 28.

[242] *Malmesbury v Malmesbury* (1862) 31 Beav 407 at 418.

expression of the parties' agreement which is rectified, never the agreement itself. 'Courts of Equity do not rectify contracts; they may and do rectify instruments purporting to have been made in pursuance of the terms of contracts.'[243]

Rectification will only be granted if the court is satisfied that there is an issue, capable of being contested, between the parties (or the grantor/covenantor and the persons he intended to benefit). If there is such an issue it is irrelevant that rectification is sought or consented to by all parties, or that rectification is desired because of the fiscal consequences. But rectification cannot be granted if the rights of the parties will be unaffected and the only effect is to receive a fiscal benefit.[244]

'In order to get rectification, it is necessary to show that the parties were in complete agreement on the terms of their contract, but by an error wrote them down wrongly ... If you can predicate with certainty what their contract was, and that it is, by a common mistake, wrongly expressed in the document, then you rectify the document.'[245] It is not a bar to relief that the need for rectification arises from an error of the claimant's solicitors: and, generally speaking negligence is an irrelevant consideration.[246] The remedy is available in respect of nearly all kinds of documents, such as a conveyance of land,[247] a lease,[248] a settlement,[249] a bill of exchange,[250] a policy of life[251] or marine[252] insurance, a building contract[253] and a disentailing deed[254] but not the articles of association of a company.[255]

Prior to the Administration of Justice Act 1982 it was not available in the case of a will, but s 20 of that Act now empowers a court to order rectification of a will, if satisfied that it is so expressed that it fails to carry out the testator's intentions in consequence of either a clerical error[256] or of a failure to understand his instructions. However, in the case of a will an application for rectification cannot be made, except

---

[243] Per James VC in *Mackenzie v Coulson* (1869) LR 8 Eq 368 at 375.

[244] *Whiteside v Whiteside* [1950] Ch 65, [1949] 2 All ER 913, CA; *Sherdley v Sherdley* [1986] 2 All ER 202, CA; *Racal Group Services Ltd v Ashmore* [1995] STC 1151, CA, noted [1996] Conv 228 (I Ferrier); [1996] 146 NLJ 1589 (Sarah Lacey). See also *Martin v Nicholson* [2004] EWHC 2135 (Ch), [2005] WTLR 175.

[245] Per Denning LJ in *Frederick E Rose (London) Ltd v William H Pim Jnr & Co Ltd* [1953] 2 QB 450 at 461, [1953] 2 All ER 739 at 747, CA. See also *Olympia Sauna Shipping Co SA v Shinwa Kaiun Kaisha Ltd* [1985] 2 Lloyd's Rep 364.

[246] *Weeds v Blaney* (1977) 247 EG 211, CA.   [247] *White v White* (1872) LR 15 Eq 247.

[248] *Murray v Parker* (1854) 19 Beav 305. Cases on leases are reviewed in (1984) 270 EG 1012 (D W Williams) and (1984) 81 LSG 1577 (S Tromans).

[249] *Welman v Welman* (1880) 15 Ch D 570.   [250] *Druiff v Lord Parker* (1868) LR 5 Eq 131.

[251] *Collett v Morrison* (1851) 9 Hare 162.   [252] *Motteux v London Assurance Co* (1739) 1 Atk 545.

[253] *Simpson v Metcalf* (1854) 24 LTOS 139; *A Roberts & Co Ltd v Leicestershire County Council* [1961] Ch 555, [1961] 2 All ER 545.

[254] Notwithstanding s 47 of the Fines and Recoveries Act 1833—*Hall-Dare v Hall-Dare* (1885) 31 Ch D 251, CA; *Meeking v Meeking* [1917] 1 Ch 77.

[255] *Evans v Chapman* (1902) 86 LT 381; *Scott v Frank F Scott (London) Ltd* [1940] Ch 794, [1940] 3 All ER 508, CA.

[256] Ie an error made in the process of recording the intended words of the testator in the drafting or transcription of his will: *Wordingham v Royal Exchange Trust Co Ltd* [1992] Ch 412, [1992] 3 All ER 204; *Re Segelman (decd)* [1996] Ch 171, [1995] 3 All ER 676, noted [1996] Conv 379 (Elise Histed); *Re Bell (decd)* [2002] EWHC 1080 (Ch), [2002] WTLR 1105. See [2003] CLJ 250 (R Kerridge and A H R Brierley).

with the permission of the court, more than six months after the date on which representation with respect to the estate of the deceased was first taken out.[257]

Rectification must be kept distinct from the power of the court to correct an obvious mistake or error on the face of the instrument as a matter of construction, where this can be done without recourse to extrinsic evidence. As Amphlett LJ said in *Burchell v Clark*,[258] 'the courts of law and equity—for the rule was the same in both— where there is a manifest error in a document will put a sensible meaning on it by correcting or reading the error as corrected'. There are innumerable instances in the reports of this being done. Thus in *Re Doland*[259] a testator disposed of his residuary estate in percentages and gave two per cent to W F L. The testator further provided that if the gift of any share should fail his trustees should hold 'my residuary estate' upon trust for H C and P R C absolutely. The gift to W F L having failed it was argued that the whole of the residuary estate passed to H C and P R C. The court, however, held that the words 'such share of' must be inserted before 'my residuary estate'. The mistake may be corrected on this principle whether it involves inserting words omitted, as in the case cited, deleting words,[260] altering words, as for instance in *Wilson v Wilson*,[261] by reading Mary for John, where in a separation deed the trustees had apparently covenanted to indemnify the husband against liability for *his* debts, or re-arranging them.[262]

It must be emphasized that this constructional escape is only available where, without the aid of extrinsic evidence, both the error on the face of the document, and the intention of the parties, are manifest from the document itself.

(b) COMMON MISTAKE

A party seeking rectification must show that—

(1) the parties had a common continuing intention, whether or not an actual concluded contract, in respect of a particular matter in the instrument to be rectified;

(2) there was an outward expression of accord;

(3) the intention continued at the time of the execution of the instrument sought to be rectified;

---

[257] See (1983) 80 LSG 2589 (A Mithani); (1989) 86 LSG 26 (D A Chatterton).

[258] (1876) 2 CPD 88, 97, CA; *Key v Key* (1853) 4 De GM & G 73 at 84. See [1992] 1 MLJ cxiii (J C C Tik).

[259] [1970] Ch 267, [1969] 3 All ER 713; *Coles v Hulme* (1828) 8 B & C 568 (the accidental omission of the word 'pounds' said to be a 'moral certainty'). Contrast *East v Pantiles (Plant Hire) Ltd* (1982) 263 EG 61, CA, where the rectification claim failed on appeal.

[260] Eg deleting 'not'— *Wilson v Wilson* (1854) 5 HL Cas 40 at 67 per Lord St Leonards.

[261] Supra; *Fitch v Jones* (1855) 5 E & B 238; *Nittan (UK) Ltd v Solent Steel Fabrication Ltd* [1981] 1 Lloyd's Rep 633, CA.

[262] *Re Bacharach's Will Trusts* [1959] Ch 245, [1958] 3 All ER 618; *Schneider v Mills* [1993] 3 All ER 377.

(4) by mistake, the instrument did not reflect that common intention.[263] Contrary
to earlier decisions,[264] the rule is now settled that while it is necessary to show
that the parties were in complete agreement on the terms of their contract, it is
not necessary to find a concluded and binding contract between the parties
antecedent to the instrument which it is sought to rectify.[265] There must, however, be some outward expression of their continuing common intention in
relation to the provision in dispute.[266] Moreover that common intention must
be formulated with certainty. Accordingly claimants who pleaded two claims
for rectification in the alternative, based on inconsistent assertions of the parties' common continuing intentions, failed. They had demonstrated at the
outset that there was no certain intention which would found a claim.[267]

Where the necessary antecedent agreement is established, rectification can be granted
of a written agreement, even though that agreement is complete in itself and has been
carried out by a more formal document based upon it.[268] Nor is it a valid objection to a
claim for rectification that the contract in question is one that is required by law to be in
writing, and that the evidence of the antecedent agreement is merely oral,[269] for the
jurisdiction to order rectification is outside the scope of such provisions, and the contract when rectified will satisfy them. If a contract is rectified, the court may order
specific performance of the contract as rectified in the same action.

It is not enough to establish the existence of an antecedent agreement whose terms
differ from those of the instrument which is sought to be rectified, unless it is also
established that the instrument was intended to carry out the terms of the agreement
and not to vary them. If the evidence shows that the parties have changed their intentions and the instrument represents their altered intentions there is no case for rectification.[270] As Simonds J said in *Gilhespie v Burdis*[271] 'in order to establish [rectification], it
must be shown beyond all reasonable doubt that up till the moment of execution of
the agreement, it was the common intention of the parties that something should find

---

[263] *Grand Metropolitan plc v The William Hill Group Ltd* [1997] 1 BCLC 390; *Swainland Builders Ltd v Freehold Properties Ltd* [2002] EWCA Civ 560, [2002] 2 EGLR 71. See (2005) 150 PLJ 7 (Allyson Colby).

[264] See *Mackenzie v Coulson* (1869) LR 8 Eq 368 at 375; *W Higgins Ltd v Northampton Corpn* [1927] 1 Ch 128.

[265] *Joscelyne v Nissen* [1970] 2 QB 86, [1970] 1 All ER 1213, CA, expressly approving the judgment of Simonds J in *Crane v Hegeman-Harris Co Inc* [1939] 1 All ER 662; (affd [1939] 4 All ER 68, CA (but not on this point)). Omitted passage at first instance printed as note to *Prenn v Simmonds* [1971] 3 All ER 237 at 245, HL. See also *Rooney and McParland Ltd v Carlin* [1981] NI 138, CA.

[266] Per Denning LJ in *Frederick E Rose (London) Ltd v William H Pim Jnr & Co Ltd* [1953] 2 QB 450, [1953] 2 All ER 739, CA; *Joscelyne v Nissen*, supra, CA. The necessity for an outward expression is attacked in (1971) 87 LQR 532 (Leonard Bromley).

[267] *C H Pearce & Sons Ltd v Stonechester Ltd* (1983) Times, 17 November, dist. *Swainland Builders Ltd v Freehold Properties Ltd*, supra. It is not enough to show that there had been confusion between the parties and their solicitors as to what land should be included in the conveyance: *Cambro Contractors Ltd v John Kennelly Sales Ltd* (1994) Times, 14 April, CA.

[268] *Craddock Bros Ltd v Hunt* [1923] 2 Ch 136, [1923] All ER Rep 394, CA.

[269] *Craddock Bros Ltd v Hunt*, supra; *United States of America v Motor Trucks Ltd* [1924] AC 196, PC.

[270] *Breadalbane v Chandos* (1837) 2 My & Cr 711.   [271] (1943) 169 LT 91, 92.

a place in the agreement which is not there as expressed by the agreement'. Thus where a written agreement for a lease has been followed by a regular lease with, however, some differences in the terms, it has been held that the prima facie conclusion must be that there was a new agreement with which the lease is in conformity.[272]

Since the principle behind rectification is to make the written instrument correspond with the parties' intentions, there can be no rectification where some term is deliberately omitted or put in a particular form,[273] even though this may have been done because of a mistaken belief by the parties that the inclusion of the term would be supererogatory,[274] or (in a sub-lease) a breach of covenant contained in the head lease,[275] or illegal.[276] The documents in such a case express the parties' intentions, and it is irrelevant that they might have had different intentions if all the material facts had been present to their minds.[277] Again there was held to be no case for rectification of a contract for horse beans, though it was established that both parties were under the mistaken belief that horse beans were the same things as feveroles.[278] On similar grounds, rectification will not be granted where a person has deliberately executed a document, though under protest and threatening in due course to bring proceedings for rectification.[279] Rectification can, however, be granted notwithstanding that the clause in question is a perfectly proper one usually contained in documents of that kind,[280] and the fact that the instrument may have been drawn up by the plaintiff or his agent is not a bar to relief—even though the common mistake was engendered by the negligence of the plaintiff or his solicitors.[281]

Another question is whether rectification is possible where there is a mistake of law as opposed to a mistake of fact, that is, where the mistake is as to the legal effect and consequences of the words used. Though dicta can be found denying the possibility of rectification on this ground, it now appears to be settled that if the parties addressed their minds to, and were under a common mistake as to the legal effect of a provision in a deed, rectification may be an appropriate remedy. Thus in *Re Butlin's Settlement Trust*[282] rectification was decreed where both the settlor and his solicitor were under a misapprehension as to the effect of a clause giving power to the trustees to decide by a

---

[272] *Hills v Rowland* (1853) 4 De GM & G 430. Cf *Bold v Hutchinson* (1855) 5 De GM & G 558; *Viditz v O'Hagan* [1899] 2 Ch 569 in connection with marriage settlements.

[273] *Rake v Hooper* (1900) 83 LT 669.   [274] *Worrall v Jacob* (1817) 3 Mer 256.

[275] *City and Westminster Properties (1934) Ltd v Mudd* [1959] Ch 129, [1958] 2 All ER 733.

[276] *Lord Irnham v Child* (1781) 1 Bro CC 92.

[277] *Barrow v Barrow* (1854) 18 Beav 529; *Tucker v Bennett* (1887) 38 Ch D 1, CA; cf *Carpmael v Powis* (1846) 10 Beav 36.

[278] *Frederick E Rose (London) Ltd v William H Pim Jnr & Co Ltd* [1953] 2 QB 450, [1953] 2 All ER 739, CA.

[279] *Eaton v Bennett* (1865) 34 Beav 196.   [280] *Torre v Torre* (1853) 1 Sm & G 518.

[281] *Weeds v Blaney* (1977) 247 Estates Gazette 211, CA.

[282] [1976] Ch 251, [1976] 2 All ER 483; *Farmer v Sloan* [2004] EWHC 606 (Ch), [2005] WTLR 521 (clause added to deed by draftsman produced a document contrary to parties' true intentions—rectification granted); *Stamp Duties Comr (NSW) v Carlenka Pty Ltd* (1996–97) 41 NSWLR 329. See also *Whiteside v Whiteside* [1950] Ch 65, [1949] 2 All ER 913, CA. Contrast *Frederick E Rose (London Ltd v William H Pim Jnr & Co Ltd* cited in n 278, supra—no rectification when mistake as to material fact which led to the words used—and see (1976) 92 LQR 325.

majority. Similarly rectification is available where the parties believe that certain wording will give effect to their bargain but mistakenly overlook some other aspect of their arrangements, with the result that the wording will not in fact do so.[283] It may be added that 'if there is a written contract which accurately gives effect to the agreement or common intention of the parties, the fact that a statute, passed later, in effect provides that that intention shall be frustrated and that the instrument shall not operate according to its tenor, seems to afford no ground for rectification.'[284]

(c) UNILATERAL MISTAKE

The general rule is that there cannot be rectification if the mistake is merely unilateral.[285] Thus there could be no rectification of a separation deed although the husband and the husband's and wife's respective solicitors were under a common mistake, where the wife thought she was getting under the deed what in fact the deed, according to its terms, gave her.[286] To this general rule there are exceptions.

First, on general principles, the court can rectify an instrument where one party only is mistaken, but the other party is guilty of fraud, whether actual, or constructive or equitable. Thus in several cases[287] a marriage settlement has been rectified where the intended husband acted as the intended wife's fiduciary agent in the preparation of the settlement, and failed to inform or explain to her the inclusion therein of unusual provisions advantageous to him. The principle is not restricted to marriage settlements.[288]

Secondly, it was held in *A Roberts & Co Ltd v Leicestershire County Council*[289] that 'a party is entitled to rectification of a contract on proof that he believed a particular term to be included in the contract and that the other party concluded the contract with the omission or a variation of that term in the knowledge that the first party believed the term to be included'.[290] In that case Pennycuick J suggested[291] that possible bases for the doctrine were estoppel or fraud. More recently Buckley LJ said in the Court of Appeal, in *Thomas Bates & Son Ltd v Wyndham's (Lingerie) Ltd,*[292] that it

---

[283] *Co-operative Insurance Society Ltd v Centremoor Ltd* (1983) 268 Estates Gazette 1027, CA.

[284] Per Asquith J in *Pyke v Peters* [1943] KB 242 at 250.

[285] *Fowler v Fowler* (1859) 4 De G & J 250; *Sells v Sells* (1860) 1 Drew & Sm 42; *Earl Bradford v Earl of Romney* (1862) 30 Beav 431.

[286] *Gilhespie v Burdis* (1943) 169 LT 91; *Fowler v Scottish Equitable Insurance Co* (1858) 28 LJ Ch 225.

[287] *Clark v Girdwood* (1877) 7 Ch D 9, CA; *Lovesy v Smith* (1880) 15 Ch D 655.

[288] *Hoblyn v Hoblyn* (1889) 41 Ch D 200; *McCausland v Young* [1949] NI 49.

[289] [1961] Ch 555, [1961] 2 All ER 545; *Riverlate Properties Ltd v Paul* [1975] Ch 133, [1974] 2 All ER 656, CA; *Weeds v Blaney* (1977) 247 EG 211, CA.

[290] Per Pennycuick J in *A Roberts & Co Ltd v Leicestershire County Council*, supra, at 570, 551.

[291] *A Roberts & Co Ltd v Leicestershire County Council*, supra, at 570, 552. See (1961) 77 LQR 313 (R E Megarry).

[292] [1981] 1 All ER 1077, [1981] 1 WLR 505, CA (omission of provision in rent review clause for fixing rent in default of agreement—tenant claimed to hold either rent free or at original rent—lease rectified). Note (1982) 126 Sol Jo 251 (Paul Matthews) criticizing Buckley LJ's obiter dictum that if rectification were not available the tenant 'on construction and by a process of implication' would have to pay a fair rent.

depends on the equity of the position. Buckley LJ went on to explain that for the doctrine to apply it must be shown (i) that one party, A, erroneously believed[293] that the document sought to be rectified contained a particular term or provision, or possibly did not contain a particular term or provision which, mistakenly, it did contain,[294] (ii) that the other party, B, was aware of the omission or the inclusion and that it was due to a mistake on the part of A; (iii) that B has omitted to draw the mistake to the notice of A; (iv) that the mistake must be one calculated to benefit B. On this last point Eveleigh LJ thought it would suffice that the inaccuracy of the instrument as drafted would be detrimental to A. According to some cases it must be shown that B had actual knowledge of the existence of the relevant mistaken belief at the time when the mistaken A signed the contract.[295] Most recently it has been said to be sufficient that B had wilfully shut his eyes to the obvious, or had wilfully and recklessly failed to make such inquiries as an honest and reasonable man would make.[296] However where B, intending A to be mistaken as to the construction of the agreement, so conducts himself that he diverts A's attention from discovering the mistake by making false and misleading statements, and A in fact makes the very mistake that B intends, then notwithstanding that B does not actually know, but merely suspects that A is mistaken, and that it cannot be shown that the mistake was induced by any misrepresentation, rectification may be granted.[297] Though the court must be satisfied that it would be unconscionable to deny the remedy of rectification, it is unnecessary to show sharp practice as such on the part of B.[298]

Thirdly, in a few cases[299] of unilateral mistake the court has given the defendant the option of accepting rectification of the instrument against him or having the contract rescinded. These cases can no longer be relied on, particularly since *Riverlate Properties Ltd v Paul*,[300] which in effect decides that unilateral mistake is not a ground for rectification unless there is fraud, or the principle of *A Roberts & Co Ltd v Leicestershire County Council*[301] applies.

Fourthly, a quasi-exception appeared in *Wilson v Wilson*.[302] In that case the defendant wished to purchase a house and, his own income being insufficient to qualify him for a loan, he requested the plaintiff to join him in an application to a building society for this purpose. The plaintiff agreed to do so, and in due course the house was

---

[293] In *Coles v William Hill Organisation Ltd* [1998] 11 LS Gaz R 37 it was held sufficient that the inclusion of a break clause in a lease had been overlooked by the plaintiff's solicitors, though they had had every opportunity to check it.

[294] No rectification in *Kemp v Neptune Concrete* (1988) 57 P & CR 369, CA, where requirement that there was in fact a mistake made by the party seeking relief when executing the deed was not satisfied.

[295] See *Agip SpA v Navigazione Alta Italia SpA* [1984] 1 Lloyd's Rep 353, CA; *Irish Life Assurance Ltd v Dublin Land Securities Ltd* [1986] IR 333 (no knowledge—no sharp practice—no rectification).

[296] *Coles v William Hill Organisation Ltd*, supra.

[297] *Commission for the New Towns v Cooper (Great Britain) Ltd* [1995] Ch 259, [1995] 2 All ER 929, CA.

[298] *Coles v William Hill Organisation Ltd*, supra.

[299] *Garrard v Frankel* (1862) 30 Beav 445; *Harris v Pepperell* (1867) LR 5 Eq 1; *Bloomer v Spittle* (1872) LR 13 Eq 427; *Paget v Marshall* (1884) 28 Ch D 255.

[300] [1975] Ch 133, [1974] 2 All ER 656, CA. [301] [1961] Ch 555, [1961] 2 All ER 545.

[302] [1969] 3 All ER 945, [1969] 1 WLR 1470.

conveyed into their joint names and the conveyance expressly declared that they were beneficially interested as joint tenants. It was held on the facts that the plaintiff never made any contribution to the purchase price, and that the common intention of the plaintiff and the defendant was that the beneficial ownership should be solely vested in the defendant. It was held that the conveyance should be rectified by striking out that part of it which declared the beneficial interests, notwithstanding the fact that the vendor was not a party to the action.[303] It was pointed out by the court that the vendor would not be concerned with or affected by the part of the deed that was being rectified, and that the declaration of beneficial trusts could perfectly well have been contained in a separate document. Though superficially a unilateral mistake by the purchasers, in substance there was a common mistake by the plaintiff and defendant in that the expressed declaration of beneficial interests did not represent the terms of their agreement.

(d) VOLUNTARY SETTLEMENTS

The court has jurisdiction to rectify a voluntary settlement, not only at the instance of the settlor,[304] but even at the instance of a beneficiary who is a volunteer.[305] Rectification will not, however, be decreed against the wishes of the settlor,[306] even though it is clear that the document does not represent his intentions at the time of the execution thereof. 'No amount of evidence, however conclusive, proving that he did so intend, will at all justify the court in compelling him to introduce a clause into the deed which he does not choose to introduce now, although he might at the time have wished to have done so.'[307] However, if the settlor is dead 'and it is afterwards proved, from the instructions or otherwise, that beyond all doubt the deed was not prepared in the exact manner which he intended, then the deed may be reformed, and those particular provisions necessary to carry his intention into effect may be introduced'.[308] In the case of a voluntary settlement the burden of proof is perhaps even heavier and in particular the court is slow to act on the evidence of the settlor alone, unsupported by other evidence such as written instructions, even though the rectification sought would make the settlement more in accord with recognized precedents and may have reasonably been intended.[309] Further in *Weir v Van Tromp*[310] Byrne J, while accepting that there was jurisdiction, observed that he had not been referred to any case where

---

[303] The consequence was that the property was held on trust for the defendant who had put up the purchase price.

[304] *Re Butlin's Settlement Trust* [1976] Ch 251, [1976] 2 All ER 483.

[305] *Thompson v Whitmore* (1860) 1 John & H 268.

[306] *Broun v Kennedy* (1863) 33 Beav 133 at 147; affd (1864) 4 De GJ & Sm 217; *Lister v Hodgson* (1867) LR 4 Eq 30; *Weir v Van Tromp* (1900) 16 TLR 531.

[307] Per Romilly MR in *Lister v Hodgson*, supra, at 34.

[308] *Van der Linde v Van der Linde* [1947] Ch 306.

[309] *Rake v Hooper* (1900) 83 LT 669; *Constandinidi v Ralli* [1935] Ch 427; *Van der Linde v Van der Linde* [1947] Ch 306.

[310] (1900) 16 TLR 531.

judgment had in fact been given in favour of reforming a voluntary settlement at the instance of a volunteer.

In *Re Butlin's Settlement Trust*[311] the court had to decide whether a settlor, seeking rectification of a voluntary settlement to which trustees were parties, was required to establish that the mistake was mutual, or whether it was enough to prove that he alone made a mistake. If the settlement involved an actual bargain between the settlor and the trustees a mutual mistake would presumably be required: in other cases the judge stressed the discretionary nature of the remedy and put forward the following propositions—(i) a settlor may seek rectification by proving that the settlement does not express his true intention, or the true intention of himself and any party with whom he has bargained, such as a spouse in the case of an ante-nuptial settlement; (ii) it is not essential for him to prove that the settlement fails to express the true intention of the trustees if they have not bargained; but (iii) the court may in its discretion decline to rectify a settlement against a protesting trustee who objects to rectification, and, perhaps, would normally refuse where the objection was reasonable and the trustee had accepted office on the faith of the settlement as executed and in ignorance of the mistake. On the facts of the case (which did not involve a bargain with trustees) rectification was granted, for the only trustee to oppose rectification gave no evidence to support her opposition. Rectification was also ordered in *AMP(UK) plc v Barker*[312] in relation to amendments to a pension scheme which in terms benefited all early leavers, but where there was overwhelming evidence that the trustees and the employer intended to improve the benefits only of those leaving on account of incapacity. And, with some hesitation as to whether the high standard of proof required was satisfied, in *Martin v Nicholson*[313] where in a deed of variation of a will the upper limit of the nil rate band applicable to the estate was substituted for £200,000. But it was refused in *Tankel v Tankel*[314] where it could not be said that the settlement in question differed, by reason of some mistake, from that which the settlor intended to execute. It was not enough for the judge to consider that the proposed rectification would improve the settlement, or that if the settlor's attention had been drawn to the point he would have approved it. It may be added that in the case of a deed poll the need for a common mistake is necessarily modified and it may well be sufficient to prove a mistake on the part of the settlor.[315]

Finally it should be noted that in some cases of mistake it may be appropriate to set aside the deed rather than rectify it. This may be done where there is a voluntary transaction by which one party intends to confer a bounty on another, if the court is

---

[311] [1976] Ch 251, [1976] 2 All ER 483; *Re Frey's Settlement* [2001] WTLR 1009 (Bahamas Supreme Court).

[312] [2001] WTLR 1237.   [313] [2004] EWHC 2135 (Ch), [2005] WTLR 175.

[314] [1999] 1 FLR 676.

[315] *Wright v Goff* (1856) 22 Beav 207; *Killick v Gray* (1882) 46 LT 583. See *Pappadakis v Pappadakis* (2000) *Times*, 19 January where the court refused to rectify a purported declaration of trust in the absence of clear and convincing evidence both (a) that although it has said one thing, the party concerned intended it to say something else, and (b) of what that 'something else' was intended to be.

satisfied that the disponor did not intend the transaction to have the effect which it did. It may be a mistake of law or of fact, so long as it is as to the effect of the transaction itself and not merely as to its consequences or the advantages to be gained by entering into it.[316]

(e) EVIDENCE

The rule which applies in the construction of documents, that parol evidence is not admissible to add to, vary or subtract from a written instrument, clearly cannot apply in an action for rectification which is, of course, based on the proposition that the written instrument fails to carry out the true agreement of the parties. Evidence must necessarily be admitted of the true agreement which is allegedly not expressed in the written instrument.[317] There are many dicta to the effect that 'the burden of proof lies upon the plaintiff,[318] and that this court, upon an application to reform an executed deed, looks at the evidence in a very jealous manner'.[319] In *Joscelyne v Nissen*[320] Russell LJ, giving the judgement of the Court of Appeal, discussed what the plaintiff has to show and adopted the phrase 'convincing proof'. He expressly approved the judgment of Simonds J in *Crane v Hegeman-Harris Co Inc*,[321] who said that the jurisdiction is one 'which is to be exercised only upon convincing proof that the concluded instrument does not represent the common intention of the parties ... and [where the court] is further satisfied as to what their common intention was'.

Another way in which it has been put is that the court must be 'sure' of the mistake, and of the existence of a prior agreement or common intention, before granting the remedy.[322] Brightman LJ has, however, pointed out[323] that this does not mean that the standard of proof is other than the normal civil standard of balance of probability. 'But', he continued, 'as the alleged common intention ex hypothesi contradicts the written instrument, convincing proof is required in order to counteract the cogent evidence of the parties' intention displayed by the instrument itself. It is not ... the standard of proof which is high, so differing from the normal civil standard, but the evidential requirement needed to counteract the inherent probability that the written instrument truly represents the parties' intention because it is a document signed by the parties.'

The court has jurisdiction on the one hand to rectify a document solely on the

---

[316] *Gibbon v Mitchell* [1990] 3 All ER 338, [1990] 1 WLR 1304; *Dent v Dent* [1996] 1 All ER 659, [1996] 1 WLR 683; *Anker-Petersen v Christensen* [2002] WTLR 313, noted (2002) 38 TELTJ 10 (T Dumont); *Wolff v Wolff* [2004] EWHC 2110 (Ch), [2004] STC 1633, noted (2004) TELTJ 11 (Clarissa Vallat). See [2004] PCB 357, [2005] PCB 31, 159 (J Hilliard).

[317] See eg per Cozens-Hardy MR in *Lovell and Christmas Ltd v Wall* (1911) 104 LT 85, 88, CA.

[318] Ie the person claiming rectification.

[319] Per Romilly MR in *Wright v Goff* (1856) 22 Beav 207 at 214; *Tucker v Bennett* (1887) 38 Ch D 1, CA.

[320] [1970] 2 QB 86, [1970] 1 All ER 1213, CA.   [321] [1939] 1 All ER 662 (see n 265, p 720, supra).

[322] *Etablissements Georges et Paul Levy v Adderley Navigation Co Panama SA* [1980] 2 Lloyd's Rep 67.

[323] In *Thomas Bates & Son Ltd v Wyndham's (Lingerie) Ltd* [1981] 1 All ER 1077 at 1090, CA, discussed (1981) 131 NLJ 967 (H W Wilkinson); *Agip SpA v Navigazione Alta Italia SpA* [1984] 1 Lloyd's Rep 353, CA.

evidence afforded by a perusal of it,[324] and, on the other hand, may act purely on oral evidence,[325] and on the uncontradicted evidence of the person seeking relief.[326] It is too late to seek rectification after an agreement has been construed by the court and money paid under a judgment founded on that construction,[327] or if the contract is no longer capable of performance,[328] and rectification will not be decreed to the prejudice of a bone fide purchaser for value who has acquired an interest in the property dealt with by the instrument.[329] In accordance with familiar equitable principles a claim may be barred by laches and acquiescence.[330] It may be added that it may be more difficult to persuade the court that there has been a common mistake where the matter has been dealt with through professional advisers.[331]

5 DELIVERY UP AND CANCELLATION OF DOCUMENTS

In some circumstances a court of equity was prepared to order a void document to be delivered up for cancellation. The idea behind this remedy is that it is inequitable that the defendant should be allowed to remain in possession of an apparently valid document, with the risk to the plaintiff that an action may possibly be brought against him on the document many years later, when evidence to support his defence may have become difficult or impossible to obtain. Thus if a document is voidable, and avoided, for fraud, whether actual or constructive, delivery up can be ordered.[332] Where, however, the document is void at law, and the invalidity appears on its face so that there is no risk of a successful action being brought on it, delivery up will not be ordered.[333] Where the invalidity does not so appear, however, it has long been held that the court has jurisdiction to order delivery up,[334] though there was at one time doubt as to the position.[335]

All kinds of documents may be ordered to be delivered up, for instance negotiable

---

[324] *Banks v Ripley* [1940] Ch 719, [1940] 3 All ER 49; *Fitzgerald v Fitzgerald* [1902] 1 IR 477, CA.

[325] *Lackersteen v Lackersteen* (1860) 30 LJ Ch 5; *M'Cormack v M'Cormack* (1877) 1 LR Ir 119. But see *Re Distributors and Warehousing Ltd* [1986] BCLC 129.

[326] *Edwards v Bingham* (1879) 28 WR 89; *Hanley v Pearson* (1879) 13 Ch D 545.

[327] *Caird v Moss* (1886) 33 Ch D 22, CA.   [328] *Borrowman v Rossell* (1864) 16 CBNS 58.

[329] *Garrard v Frankel* (1862) 30 Beav 445; *Smith v Jones* [1954] 2 All ER 823; *Lyme Valley Squash Club Ltd v Newcastle under Lyme Borough Council* [1985] 2 All ER 405.

[330] *Fredensen v Rothschild* [1941] 1 All ER 430 (30 years); *Burroughs v Abbott* [1922] 1 Ch 86, [1921] All ER Rep 709 (12 years—rectification granted).

[331] *Hazell, Watson and Viney Ltd v Malvermi* [1953] 2 All ER 58.

[332] *Duncan v Worrall* (1822) 10 Price 31; *Hoare v Bremridge* (1872) 8 Ch App 22; *Brooking v Maudslay, Son and Field* (1888) 38 Ch D 636.

[333] *Gray v Mathias* (1800) 5 Ves 286; *Simpson v Lord Howden* (1837) 3 My & Cr 97.

[334] *Davis v Duke of Marlborough* (1819) 2 Swan 108 at 157; *Underhill v Horwood* (1804) 10 Ves 209.

[335] *Ryan v Mackmath* (1789) 3 Bro CC 15.

instruments,[336] forged instruments,[337] policies of insurance,[338] and documents which, as it has been said, form a cloud upon title to land.[339] The document must, however, be altogether void, and not merely void as against creditors.[340] Nor will a document be ordered to be delivered up where it is alleged that there would be a good defence to an action at law, but the document is neither void nor voidable.[341]

Delivery up and cancellation being an equitable remedy, it has been said that it will only be granted on terms which will do justice to both parties, an application of the maxim that he who seeks equity must do equity. Thus in *Lodge v National Union Investment Co Ltd*[342] where a borrower gave certain securities to the lender under a money lending contract which was illegal and void under the Moneylenders Act 1900,[343] the court was only prepared to order delivery up of the securities on the terms that the borrower should repay such of the money borrowed as was still outstanding. The Privy Council, however, has declared[344] that this case 'cannot be treated as having established any wide general principle that governs the action of courts in granting relief in moneylending cases'. It seems that where the moneylending contract is merely unenforceable[345] as opposed to illegal and void, the lender is, paradoxically, in a worse position, for in such a case the borrower can recover his securities without any terms being imposed. To impose terms would be an indirect way of enforcing a contract declared unenforceable by statute.[346]

It should be added that the Court of Appeal has held[347] on similar facts to those in *Lodge v National Union Investment Co Ltd*[348] that a declaration that the transaction is illegal and void may be made without any terms being imposed, on the ground that a declaration is not 'equitable relief' or 'true equitable relief'. This ground is not altogether convincing for a declaration has long been recognized in equity, though under the inherent jurisdiction there was only power to make a declaration as ancillary to some other remedy.[349]

Finally, it should be made clear that no attempt has been made above to set out the present law relating to moneylending contracts. This is largely contained in the Consumer Credit Act 1974, which repealed the Moneylenders Act 1927.

---

336 *Wynne v Callander* (1826) 1 Russ 293.   337 *Peake v Highfield* (1826) 1 Russ 559.

338 *Bromley v Holland* (1802) 7 Ves 3; *Kemp v Pryor* (1802) 7 Ves 237.

339 *Bromley v Holland*, supra; *Hayward v Dimsdale* (1810) 17 Ves 111.

340 *Ideal Bedding Co Ltd v Holland* [1907] 2 Ch 157.

341 *Brooking v Maudslay, Son and Field* (1888) 38 Ch D 636.

342 [1907] 1 Ch 300, [1904–7] All ER Rep 333.

343 Section 2, repealed by the Moneylenders Act 1927.

344 *Kasumu v Baba-Egbe* [1956] AC 539 at 549, [1956] 3 All ER 266 at 270, PC.

345 This was the effect of the Moneylenders Act 1927, s 6, repealed by the Consumer Credit Act 1974.

346 *Kasuma v Baba-Egbe*, supra; *Barclay v Prospect Mortgages Ltd* [1974] 2 All ER 672.

347 *Chapman v Michaelson* [1909] 1 Ch 238, CA.   348 [1907] 1 Ch 300, [1904–7] All ER Rep 333.

349 *Ferrand v Wilson* (1845) 4 Hare 344 at 385; *Clough v Ratcliffe* (1847) 1 De G & Sm 164 at 178. The only case to the contrary seems to be *Taylor v A-G* (1837) 8 Sim 413. See generally, Zamir, *The Declaratory Judgment*.

6 *NE EXEAT REGNO*

The issue of the writ *ne exeat regno* is a process whereby an equitable creditor can have the debtor arrested and made to give security if, but only if, the debtor is about to leave the realm. It is essential that the debt shall be an equitable and not a legal one. In connection with this writ the provisions of s 6 of the Debtors Act 1869 are applied by analogy. This means that four conditions have to be satisfied before the writ can be issued, namely (i) the action is one in which the defendant would formerly have been liable to arrest at law (ii) a good cause of action for at least £50 is established (iii) there is 'probable cause' for believing that the defendant is 'about to quit England' unless he is arrested, and (iv) the absence of the defendant from England will materially prejudice the plaintiff in the prosecution of his action, as opposed to the execution of any judgment he may obtain. Even if these four conditions are satisfied—and the standard of proof is high—the issue of an order is discretionary.

The law was fully reviewed by Megarry J in an unsuccessful application in *Felton v Callis*[350] and after a long period during which the writ was rarely issued, if at all, it is now clear that in appropriate cases its validity is unimpaired. In many cases the freezing injunction will sufficiently protect the claimant, but in a small number of cases the additional power in support of the freezing order may assist the cause of justice. The writ was issued in *Al Nahkel for Contracting and Trading Ltd v Lowe*[351] to prevent the defendant fleeing the jurisdiction with assets in order to frustrate a lawful claim before the court. Tudor Price J's observation in that case that the writ can issue in support of a freezing injunction gave Leggatt J some anxiety in *Allied Arab Bank Ltd v Hajjar*.[352] He agreed if the statement was intended to refer only to cases in which both remedies might properly issue, with the result that the arrest of the debtor might incidentally prevent him from breaching the freezing injunction. He disagreed if it was intended to go further and to suggest that the writ might be ordered for the purpose of enforcing the freezing injunction, for which purpose the appropriate remedy is an injunction to restrain him from leaving the jurisdiction. A freezing injunction is a remedy in aid of execution. It is not part of the prosecution of the action. Condition (iv) is therefore not satisfied if the purpose of the writ is to enforce a freezing injunction.

---

[350] [1969] 1 QB 200, [1968] 3 All ER 673; *Re B* [1997] 3 All ER 258. See (1972) 88 LQR 83 (J W Bridge).

[351] [1986] QB 235, [1986] 1 All ER 729; *Ali v Naseem* (2003) *Times*, 3 October. See (1987) 104 LQR 246 (Lesley J Anderson); (1986) 45 CLJ 189 (G Marston); (1987) 137 NLJ 584 (Lesley J Anderson).

[352] [1988] QB 787, [1987] 3 All ER 739, noted (1988) 47 CLJ 364 (N H Andrews). Point not discussed in further proceedings reported [1989] Fam Law 68, CA.

7 SETTING ASIDE A JUDGMENT OBTAINED BY FRAUD

Shortly after the Judicature Acts came into force, the Court of Appeal held, in *Flower v Lloyds*,[353] that it had no power to review its own decision on the ground of the subsequent discovery of facts indicating that its order had been obtained by fraud. It held, however, that the jurisdiction of the old Court of Chancery under which if a decree had been obtained by fraud it could be impeached by bill, had been transferred to the High Court with the effect that since the Acts a fresh action could be brought to set aside a judgment which has been obtained by fraud.

In the Australian case of *Wentworth v Rogers (No 5)*[354] Kirby J summarized the principles which govern proceedings of this kind.

First, the essence of the action is fraud. As in all actions based on fraud, particulars of the fraud claimed must be exactly given and the allegations must be established by the strict proof which such a charge requires.[355]

Secondly, it must be shown, by the party asserting that a judgment was procured by fraud, that there has been a new discovery of something material, in the sense that fresh facts have been found which, by themselves or in combination with previously known facts, would provide a reason for setting aside the judgment.[356]

Thirdly, mere suspicion of fraud, raised by fresh facts later discovered, will not be sufficient to secure relief. The claimant must establish that the new facts are so evidenced and so material that it is reasonably probable that the action will succeed.[357]

Fourthly, although perjury by the successful party or a witness or witnesses may, if later discovered, warrant the setting aside of a judgment on the ground that it was procured by fraud, and although there may be exceptional cases where such proof of perjury could suffice, without more, to warrant relief of this kind, the mere allegation or even the proof, of perjury will not normally be sufficient to attract such drastic and exceptional relief as the setting aside of a judgment. The other requirements must be fulfilled.[358]

Fifthly, it must be shown by admissible evidence that the successful party was

---

[353] (1877) 6 Ch D 297, CA.

[354] [1986] 6 NSWLR 534. See generally (1995) 14 U Tas LR 129 (G D Pont).

[355] *Jonesco v Beard* [1930] AC 298, HL.

[356] *Boswell v Coaks (No 2)* (1894) 6 R 167 per Lord Selborne at 170, 174; *Birch v Birch* [1902] P 130, 136–138; *Everett v Ribbands* [1946] 175 LT 143, 145, 146.

[357] *Birch v Birch*, supra, at 136, 139.   [358] *Everett v Ribbands*, supra, at 145, 146.

responsible for the fraud which taints the judgment under challenge. The evidence in support of the charge ought to be extrinsic.[359]

Sixthly, the burden of establishing the components necessary to warrant the drastic step of setting aside a judgment, allegedly affected by fraud or other relevant taint, lies on the party impugning the judgment. It is for that party to establish the fraud and to do so clearly.

---

[359] *Perry v Meddowcroft* (1846) 10 Beav 122 at 136–139.

31

CONVERSION AND RECONVERSION

1 THE DOCTRINE OF CONVERSION

English law has divided property into two categories, realty and personalty, which in many respects were, before the 1925 property legislation, governed by different rules, perhaps the most important difference being that on a man's death intestate, his realty passed to his heir-at-law,[1] while his personalty passed to his next-of-kin.[2] This difference has now disappeared and the law of real and personal property was assimilated in many respects by the 1925 property legislation, but the distinction between realty and personalty may still be material in some circumstances, for instance if, in his will, a testator has made separate dispositions of his real and personal property. Under the doctrine of conversion property in one category is, in certain circumstances, treated in equity as if it were in the other.

Before 1997 the most important situations were where land was held by trustees subject to a trust for sale, or personal property was subject to a trust for sale in order that the trustees might acquire land. Suppose, for instance, that a settlor conveyed realty to trustees on trust to sell it forthwith and hold the proceeds of sale on trust for X and Y in equal shares. If, after the trustees had carried out their duty and actually converted the realty to personalty X died having by his will left all his realty to R and all his personalty to P, clearly X's half share in the trust property would pass to P. Under the doctrine of conversion the result would be exactly the same even though X died before the trustees had carried out their duty.

The doctrine of conversion was partially abolished by the Trusts of Land and Appointment of Trustees Act 1996, which provides[3] that where land is held by trustees subject to a trust for sale, the land is not to be regarded as personal property; and that where personal property is subject to a trust for sale in order that the trustees may acquire land, the personal property is not to be regarded as land. The abolition applies

---

[1] Ascertained in accordance with common law rules as amended by the Inheritance Act 1833 and the Law of Property Amendment Act 1859.

[2] Ascertained in accordance with the Statute of Distribution 1670 and Administration of Intestates' Estates 1685 and the Statute of Frauds 1677.

[3] Section 3(1). The old law was considered in the 7th edn, chapter 30.

to trusts whenever they came into being, with the exception of a trust created by the will of a testator who died before 1 January 1997.[4]

2 CIRCUMSTANCES IN WHICH THE DOCTRINE OF CONVERSION CONTINUES TO APPLY[5]

Notwithstanding the side-note to s 3 of the Trusts of Land and Appointment of Trustees Act 1996, it is thought that the doctrine of conversion continues to apply in the following circumstances.

(a) UNDER AN ORDER OF THE COURT

It is clearly established as a general principle that if the court by an order directs the sale or purchase of realty, this operates as a conversion as from the date of the order.[6] The general principle may, however, be affected by statutory provisions. Thus under the Mental Health Act 1983, where the court orders the disposal of real property belonging to a patient,[7] any property representing it is to be treated as if it were real property so long as it remains part of the patient's estate,[8] and the judge, in ordering any disposal of property which apart from s 101 would result in the conversion of personal property into real property, may direct that the property representing the property disposed of shall, so long as it remains the property of the patient or forms part of his estate, be treated as if it were personal property.[9]

(b) UNDER A CONTRACT FOR THE SALE OF LAND

It is familiar law, going back at least to *Lady Foliamb's* case[10] that a contract for the sale of land causes a conversion. Vaisey J restated the law in *Hillingdon Estates Co v Stonefield Estates Ltd.*[11]

when there is a contract by A to sell land to B at a certain price, B becomes the owner in equity of the land, subject, of course, to his obligations to perform his part of the contract by paying the purchase money; but subject to that, the land is the land of B the purchaser.

---

[4] Section 3(2), (3).   [5] See (1997) 113 LQR 207 (P H Pettit).

[6] *Steed v Preece* (1874) LR 18 Eq 192: *Fauntleroy v Beebe* [1911] 2 Ch 257, CA; *Re Silva* [1929] 2 Ch 198, [1929] All ER Rep 546.

[7] Ie, a person incapable, by reason of mental disorder, of managing and administering his property and affairs—s 94 of the Mental Health Act 1983.

[8] Ibid, s 101(1).

[9] Ibid, s 101(2). *A-G v Marquis of Ailesbury* (1887) 12 App Cas 672, HL; *Re Silva*, supra. Cf *Re Searle* [1912] 2 Ch 365.

[10] (1651) cited in *Daire v Beversham* (1661) Nels 76. Cf chapter 8, section 4, supra.

[11] [1952] Ch 627 at 631, [1952] 1 All ER 853 at 856. See (1960) 24 Conv 47 (P H Pettit).

What is the position of A, the vendor? He has, it is true, the legal estate in the land, but, for many purposes, from the moment the contract is entered into he holds it as trustee for B, the purchaser. True, he has certain rights in the land remaining, but all those rights are conditioned and limited by the circumstance that they are all referable to his right to recover and receive the purchase-money. His interest in the land when he has entered into a contract for sale is not an interest in land; it is an interest in personal estate, in a sum of money.

It follows as a result of the application of the doctrine of conversion, that if the vendor has died between contract and completion, any specific devise of the property contained in a will preceding[12] the contract is revoked or adeemed,[13] and the right to receive the purchase money goes to the person entitled to the personal property. On the death of the purchaser between contract and completion, the property correspondingly passes to the person entitled to his property, though since Locke King's Acts[14] he takes it subject to the ability to pay the whole or the balance of the purchase price as the case may be.

In order for the doctrine of conversion to apply there must be a valid contract of sale, and, as Jessel MR pointed out in *Lysaght v Edwards*,[15] as regards real estate there is no valid contract unless the vendor is in a position to make title according to the contract, or the purchaser has accepted the title notwithstanding the fact that it is not a good one. Though it is commonly said[16] that there is conversion under a contract only where the contract is enforceable by specific performance, the availability of this remedy does not seem to be an altogether satisfactory criterion.[17]

The doctrine of conversion applies in the ordinary way to a contract imposed by statute,[18] and the point has arisen in connection with land taken by compulsory purchase. In such a case the notice to treat does not operate as a conversion,[19] even though the owner has stated the price which he is willing to take, if he dies before it has been accepted.[20] Again if there is agreement on the price per acre to be paid, but the quantity of land to be taken has not yet been ascertained, there is no conversion.[21] Where, however, the notice to treat has been followed by ascertainment of the price, whether by agreement or arbitration or some other procedure, there is a

---

[12] If subsequent to the contract, it is a question of construction of the will whether the disposition therein contained extends to the purchase money. See *Re Calow* [1928] Ch 710, [1928] All ER Rep 518.

[13] Strictly, it seems to be revocation by alteration of the estate, see (1957) 21 Con 152; *Andrew v Andrew* (1856) 4 WR 520.

[14] The Real Estate Charges Act 1854, 1867 and 1877 now repealed and replaced by the Administration of Estates Act 1925, s 35.

[15] (1876) 2 Ch D 499.

[16] Eg per Lord Westbury LC in *Holroyd v Marshall* (1862) 10 HL Cas 191 at 209–210; per Lord Parker in *Howard v Miller* [1915] AC 318 at 326, PC.

[17] See *Rose v Watson* (1864) 10 HL Cas 672; *Gordon Hill Trust v Segall* [1941] 2 All ER 379, CA. Some of the latent difficulties in this field are discussed in (1960) 24 Con 47.

[18] Eg Coal Act 1938—*Re Galway's Will Trusts* [1950] Ch 1, [1949] 2 All ER 419.

[19] *Haynes v Haynes* (1861) 1 Drew & Sm 426.   [20] *Re Battersea Park Acts* (1863) 32 Beav 591.

[21] *Ex p Walker* (1853) 1 Drew 508.

complete valid contract and conversion takes place in the ordinary way.[22] A somewhat analogous case is enfranchisement under the Leasehold Reform Act 1967, under which a leaseholder who satisfies certain conditions may convert his interest from leasehold, that is personalty, into freehold, that is realty. There is as yet no authority on the application of the doctrine of conversion to this situation, but it would seem on principle clearly to apply, perhaps at the point of time when the tenant as well as the landlord becomes irrevocably bound to the enfranchisement process.[23]

(c) UNDER AN OPTION TO PURCHASE

If T, having made his will devising all his realty to R and bequeathing all his personality to P, and having granted X an option to purchase Blackacre, died before X had exercised the option, one would expect, on principle, that Blackacre would pass to R, who would become entitled to the proceeds of sale if X subsequently exercised the option thereby creating a valid contract of sale. Under the rule in *Lawes v Bennett*,[24] however, the devise to R would be adeemed and the proceeds of sale would be payable to P,[25] Blackacre being treated for the purpose of devolution on death as devolving from the date of the exercise of the option as proceeds for sale and not as real estate. It would make no difference that the option was not even exercisable until after T's death.[26] Though generally castigated as an illogical anomaly in many of the subsequent cases, it is now acknowledged to be settled law, certainly as far as the Court of Appeal[27] and probably, having stood so long, in the House of Lords. It was held in *Re Sweeting*[28] to be equally applicable to a conditional contract where the condition is fulfilled or waived after the death.

It has been made clear in a series of cases[29] that conversion does not take place at the date when the option is granted, but only at the time when it is exercised. Thus in the illustration given, R would get an estate or interest defeasible by the exercise of the option, upon which event and not before conversion would take place. It follows from this that any rents and profits which accrue between the date of death and the exercise

---

[22] *Harding v Metropolitan Rly Co* (1872) 7 Ch App 154; *Watts v Watts* (1873) LR 17 Eq 217.

[23] For a full discussion see (1969) 22 Conv 43 and 141 (J Tiley).

[24] (1785) 1 Cox Eq Cas 167; *Weeding v Weeding* (1861) 1 John & H 424.

[25] Unless, perhaps, the sale was a collusive transaction between X and P to oust R.

[26] *Re Isaacs* [1894] 3 Ch 506, where the rule was applied on intestacy before 1926, as between the heir-at-law and the next-of-kin.

[27] *Re Marlay* [1915] 2 Ch 264, CA; *Re Carrington* [1932] 1 Ch 1, [1931] All ER Rep 658, CA; and see [1950] CLP 30 (O R Marshall).

[28] [1988] 1 All ER 1016. An option is neither a conditional contract nor an irrevocable offer, though it resembles each of them in certain ways. The grant of an option to purchase an interest in land falls within the provisions of s 2 of the Law of Property (Miscellaneous Provisions) Act 1989, as amended, but the exercise of the option is a unilateral act which does not: *Spiro v Glencrown Properties Ltd* [1991] Ch 537, [1991] 1 All ER 600.

[29] *Re Isaacs* [1894] 3 Ch 506; *Re Marlay*, supra; *Re Carrington*, supra.

of the option would go to R and not to P.[30] If there is conversion, it seems to make no difference that the contract is not carried through to completion.[31]

Prima facie, the rule in *Lawes v Bennett*[32] applies whether the option precedes the will, as in *Lawes v Bennett*[32] itself or whether the will precedes the option, as in *Weeding v Weeding*.[33] It may, however, be possible to argue successfully that a case falls outside the rule, where the option comes first and the will contains a specific devise of the property.[34]

This excepting principle has been applied not only where the will follows the option,[35] but also where the will was merely republished after the option by the execution of a codicil,[36] and even where the will and the option were executed on the same day, though it was uncertain which in fact came first.[37]

Owing to its anomalous character the courts will only apply the doctrine of conversion under *Lawes v Bennett*[38] in deciding claims between persons entitled respectively to the real and personal property of a deceased grantor of an option. Thus it was not applied in *Edwards v West*[39] where under the terms of a lease the landlord covenanted to insure, and the tenant had the option to purchase for a fixed sum. Before the time for exercising the option, the buildings demised were burnt down, and the landlord received the insurance money. The tenant then exercised his option to purchase, but his claim to receive the insurance money as part of his purchase failed.

Notwithstanding the general reluctance to extend the doctrine of *Lawes v Bennett*,[40] the Court of Appeal felt itself bound to apply the doctrine in *Re Carrington*,[41] where there was a specific legacy given of certain shares over which an option to purchase was granted, which was exercised after the testator's death. On the basis that the doctrine of conversion applied, it was held that the specific legacy of the shares was adeemed.

(d) PARTNERSHIP PROPERTY

Real property belonging to partners had always been regarded in equity as personalty,[42] and this was made the statutory rule by s 22 of the Partnership Act 1890, subject to the expression of a contrary intention, not only as between the partners, including the personal representatives of a deceased partner, but as between the persons entitled

---

[30] *Townley v Bedwell* (1808) 14 Ves 591; *Collingwood v Row* (1857) 26 LJ Ch 649.

[31] *Re Blake* [1917] 1 Ch 18.

[32] (1785) 1 Cox Eq Cas 167.   [33] (1861) 1 John & H 424.

[34] See *Weeding v Weeding* (1861) 1 John & H 424 per Page Wood V-C at 431.

[35] *Drant v Vause* (1842) 1 Y & C Ch Cas 580.

[36] *Emuss v Smith* (1848) 2 De G & Sm 722.   [37] *Re Pyle* [1895] 1 Ch 724.

[38] (1785) 1 Cox Eq Cas 167.

[39] (1878) 7 Ch D 858. Cf *Reynard v Arnold* (1875) 10 Ch App 386.   [40] Supra.

[41] [1932] 1 Ch 1, CA, critically noted by Professor Hanbury in (1933) 49 LQR 173, and necessarily followed in *Re Rose* [1949] Ch 78, [1948] 2 All ER 971.

[42] *A-G v Hubbuck* (1884) 13 QBD 275, CA.

to the real and personal property of a deceased partner. This section was repealed by the Trusts of Land and Appointment of Trustees Act 1996, but it is not clear whether the effect is that there is no conversion, or that the equitable rule is restored. The answer would seem to depend on whether that rule was based on contract,[43] or on an implied trust for sale.[44] Only in the latter case would s 3 of the 1996 Act apply to prevent the operation of the doctrine of conversion.

[43] *Darby v Darby* (1853) 3 Drew 495.   [44] See eg *A-G v Hubbuck* (1884) 13 QBD 275, CA.

32

SATISFACTION, ADEMPTION AND PERFORMANCE

Satisfaction was defined by Lord Romilly[1] as 'the donation of a thing with the intention that it is to be taken either wholly or in part in extinguishment of some prior claim of the donee'. This can perhaps best be made clear by giving illustrations of the types of circumstances in which questions of satisfaction may arise:

(i) A owes B £500. Subsequently A makes a will giving B a legacy of £X00. Can B claim both his debt and the legacy in full?

This type of case is discussed in section 1, p 739, infra.

(ii) A owes B £500. Subsequently A pays B £X00, without reference to the debt. Can B still claim the debt in full?

This type of case is discussed in section 2, p 744, infra.

(iii) A father covenants in his daughter's marriage settlement to pay £5,000 to the trustees thereof. He subsequently makes a will leaving the daughter a settled legacy of £X,000 and then dies without having paid any money to the trustees. Is the father's estate liable to pay both the £5,000 under the marriage settlement and also the legacy settled by the will?

This, and the following two types of case, are discussed in section 3, p 745, infra.

(iv) By his marriage settlement a father has covenanted to provide portions of £1,000 for each of the children of the marriage. His wife dies, leaving two children of the marriage, and by a settlement made on his remarriage the father, inter alia, conveys Blackacre to trustees upon trust to raise £X,000 to be settled on the children of his first marriage in equal shares. Can the children claim under both settlements?

(v) By will a father gives £5,000 to his daughter Susie. Subsequently, on Susie's marriage, he pays, or covenants to pay, £X,000 to the trustees of her marriage settlement. Can Susie claim under both the will and the settlement?

---

[1] In *Lord Chichester v Coventry* (1867) LR 2 HL 71 at 95, adopting White and Tudor's *Leading Cases in Equity*, now 9th edn, vol II, pp 326–327.

(vi) By will A gives B £2,000 to a particular purpose. Subsequently A hands over £X,000 to B for the same purpose. On A's death can B claim the legacy in full?

This type of case is discussed in section 4, p 760, infra.

(vii) A by will gives B a legacy of £700. Elsewhere in the will, or in a codicil, he gives B a legacy of £X00. Can B claim both legacies in full?

The term 'satisfaction' has been used to include all the above types of case. More strictly satisfaction is restricted to the first four types of case, as presupposing an existing legal obligation, which does not arise, of course, under the will of a living person. The next two types of case are properly described as cases of ademption, or sometimes equitable ademption to distinguish another and perhaps stricter sense of the term where a testamentary disposition fails by reason of the fact that the subject of the disposition had ceased to exist as a part of the testator's estate at the time of his death. The last type of case is purely a question of construction of the testamentary instrument or instruments as to whether the provisions are intended to be cumulative or substitutional. As such it is outside the scope of the book.[2]

In every case it is a question of the intention of the settlor or testator whether the prior claim is satisfied. Of course the intention that there is or is not to be satisfaction may appear expressly or by implication on the true construction of the instrument itself,[3] in which case the usual rule applies that parol evidence will not be admitted to contradict, add to or vary a written instrument. Where there is no such provision there is in many cases a presumption of satisfaction: if there is neither a provision contained in the instrument nor a presumption applicable, both benefits can be claimed. We must now turn to discuss the variant presumptions of satisfaction and ademption which may arise in the types of circumstances set out above.

1 SATISFACTION OF ORDINARY DEBTS BY LEGACIES

(a) THE GENERAL RULE

The presumption of satisfaction is to the effect that if a testator gives a legacy to his creditor the legacy being at least equal in amount to the debt, there is a presumption that the testator does not intend the creditor to have both his debt and the legacy, but intends the legacy to be in extinguishment of the claim of the creditor. Where the presumption applies the affect is that if the creditor-legatee wishes to have the legacy,

---

[2] Reference may be made to Jarman on *Wills*, 8th edn, vol 2, p 1101 et seq. The leading case is *Hooley v Hatton* (1773) 1 Bro CC 390 n where prima facie rules of construction to be applied are laid down.

[3] Questions of construction may arise on such a declaration. See *Cooper v Cooper* (1873) 8 Ch App 813 for a discussion of a line of authority 'in which the use of precedents has, sometimes, caused the courts of this country, first to slide into manifest error, and afterwards to follow that error under the notion that they are bound to do so' (per Lord Selborne LC at 825).

he must give up his claim to the debt. The presumption is commonly regarded as being founded on *Talbot v Duke of Shrewsbury*[4] where 'it was said by Mr Vernon and agreed to by the Master of the Rolls[5] that if one, being indebted to another in a sum of money, does by his will give him as great, or greater sum of money than the debt amounts to, without taking any notice at all of the debt, that this shall nevertheless be in satisfaction of the debt, so as he should not have both the debt and the legacy.' *Talbot v Duke of Shrewsbury*[6] is not in fact the earliest case where the presumption was applied,[7] and it appears that the statement of the general rule therein contained was a mere dictum, as the will actually directed that legacies should be taken in discharge of debts.[8] Nevertheless the existence of the rule has been consistently accepted ever since this decision, and it will prevail in the absence of other relevant circumstances.[9] Though consistently accepted, the rule had also been consistently criticized but the 'principle being established, successive judges have said they cannot alter it. But what they have done is to rely on the minutest shade of difference to escape from that false principle.'[10]

(b) DIFFERENCE BETWEEN THE LEGACY AND THE DEBT

The differences which will prevent the presumption of satisfaction from arising may be differences either of amount or in kind. It was settled at an early date that there is no presumption of satisfaction where the legacy is less in amount than the debt, not even satisfaction pro tanto.[11] Similarly if the legacy is given on a condition or a contingency,[12] or is of an uncertain amount, such as a share of residue, it is or may be less beneficial than the debt and is therefore no satisfaction, even though it in fact turns out to be more beneficial.[13]

Again, there is no satisfaction if there is some other difference between the debt and the legacy which makes the legacy less advantageous to the creditor. Thus if the legacy is by the will expressly made payable at a later date than the debt, there is no satisfaction.[14] Where there is no special provision as to the date of payment of the legacy, so that it is payable at the end of the executor's year, the cases are in conflict. According

---

[4] (1714) Prec Ch 394.   [5] Sir J Trevor.   [6] Supra.

[7] See eg *Atkinson v Webb* (1704) 2 Vern 478.

[8] See the argument of counsel in *Re Rattenbury* [1906] 1 Ch 667 at 668.

[9] Eg *Re Rattenbury* [1906] 1 Ch 667; *Re Haves* [1951] 2 All ER 928.

[10] *Hassell v Hawkins* (1859) 4 Drew 468, per Kindersley V-C at 470.

[11] *Gee v Liddell* (1866) 35 Beav 621; *Coates v Coates* [1898] 1 IR 258. Aliter in *Hammond v Smith* (1864) 33 Beav 452, where, however, the intention that the legacy should be in part payment of the debt was communicated to the debtor and not objected to by him.

[12] *Mathews v Mathews* (1755) 2 Ves Sen 635; *Tolson v Collins* (1799) 4 Ves 483; *Sanford v Irby* (1825) 4 LJOS Ch 23.

[13] *Devese v Pontet* (1785) 1 Cox Eq Cas 188; *Lady Thynne v Earl of Glengall* (1848) 2 HL Cas 131; *Re Pottruff* (1972) 27 DLR (3d) 405.

[14] *Adams v Lavender* (1824) M'Cle & Yo 41; *Re Roberts* (1902) 50 WR 469.

to *Re Horlock*,[15] where there was a debt of £300 payable within three months of death, and a legacy of £400, as to which no time of payment was fixed, there is no satisfaction in such a case, since there is a difference in the times of payment. If this is right, the effect would be virtually to abolish the rule, for the payment of legacies can never be enforced for a year after the death,[16] while debts are normally payable at once. The contrary and, it is submitted, the better view was taken in *Re Rattenbury*[17] where Swinfen Eady J pointed out that Lord Hardwicke had decided in *Clarke v Sewell*[18] that a legacy in satisfaction of a debt where no time is fixed for payment carries interest from the date of death, contrary to the normal rule. This can be regarded as preventing the legacy, by reason of the delay in payment, from being less beneficial than the debt. The same reasoning is not applicable where the 'debt' consists of an annuity, and it had been held accordingly that there was no satisfaction where the annuity under the deed was payable quarterly[19] or half-yearly,[20] while under the will the first payment would not become due until a year after the testator's death, and similarly where under the deed it was payable quarterly in advance, under the will, quarterly in arrears.[21] But there can be satisfaction of an annuity, as in *Atkinson v Littlewood*,[22] where both under the deed and under the will, the payments were to be made on the same special quarter days.

Another question which has arisen is whether a debt carrying interest, some of which is due at the date of death, is satisfied by a legacy of the capital sum. Thus in *Fitzgerald v National Bank Ltd*[23] there was a debt of £100 carrying interest at the rate of five per cent and a legacy of £100. At the date of death £3 was due on account of interest. It was argued that the legacy was accordingly less than the debt and the presumption of satisfaction did not arise. The judge, however, held that it was a case of satisfaction since the 'debt' did not include the interest due thereon and consequently was equal to the legacy. This doubtful decision was based on the ground that at the time when *Talbot v Duke of Shrewsbury*[24] was decided a debt had to be sued for in an action of debt, while interest thereon had to be sued for separately in an action of assumpsit, and that 'debt' in the rule accordingly excluded interest thereon. If rightly decided, an action would presumably lie for any arrears of interest due.[25]

Other differences which may rebut the presumption of satisfaction are that the debt

---

[15] [1895] 1 Ch 516 purporting to follow *Re Dowse* (1881) 50 LJ Ch 285, which, however, was a case of an annuity.

[16] Even if directed to be paid before, according to the generally accepted opinion. The cases do not make the point very clearly— *Benson v Maude* (1821) 6 Madd 15; *Brooke v Lewis* (1822) 6 Madd 358. There are dicta to the contrary in *Re Riddell* [1936] 2 All ER 1600 (not reported on this point in [1936] Ch 747); *Re Pollock* [1943] Ch 338, [1943] 2 All ER 443.

[17] [1906] 1 Ch 667.   [18] (1744) 3 Atk 96.   [19] *Re Stibbe* (1946) 175 LT 198.

[20] *Re Dowse* (1881) 50 LJ Ch 285.

[21] *Re Van den Bergh's Will Trusts* [1948] 1 All ER 935 (but this was said by the judge to be, in this case, a subsidiary question).

[22] (1874) LR 18 Eq 595; *Re Haves* [1951] 2 All ER 928.

[23] [1929] 1 KB 394, [1928] All ER Rep 596.   [24] (1714) Prec Ch 394.

[25] In *Fitzgerald v National Bank*, supra, the arrears had been paid before the action was heard.

is secured, while the legacy is not,[26] that the debt—an annuity—is free of taxes, while the legacy is not,[27] that the legacy is of an annuity liable to forfeiture, while the covenanted annuity is not,[28] and, possibly, that the debt is payable to one set of trustees, while the legacy is payable to a different set of trustees,[29] even though on the same trusts, or to the beneficiary.[30] In *Fairer v Park*[31] it was held that there was no satisfaction where the debt was due from the testator as trustee and the legacy was to one of the beneficiaries. The mere fact that the creditor-legatee is also appointed executor is irrelevant.[32] It should also be observed that 'it is a general rule of satisfaction that the thing to be considered as a satisfaction should be exactly of the same nature'.[33] Thus a debt cannot be satisfied by a devise of land, and an annuity cannot be satisfied by a life interest in a house and furniture.[34]

(c) DEBTS TO WHICH THE PRESUMPTION APPLIES

Since the rule is based on the presumed intention of the testator, it follows that no debt can be satisfied unless it was in existence when the will was made.[35] Again there is no satisfaction in the case of an open and running account for in as much as the testator could not be supposed to know what the balance of a running account would be, or whether he owed any money or not, he could not intend the legacy to be in satisfaction of a debt which he did not know that he owed.[36] It is not a running account, where the creditor has merely deposited moneys with the testator, who from time to time makes repayments, and there is no possibility of the testator becoming the creditor.[37] Nor will a negotiable instrument be satisfied by a legacy.[38]

It should be observed that if the debt was in existence when the will was made, the presumption of satisfaction will apply notwithstanding that the debt was subsequently paid during the testator's lifetime, at any rate where the amount of legacy exactly equals the debt. The legacy in such case will accordingly fail to take effect.[39]

If the debt is entered into by a document contemporaneous with the will, so that

---

[26] *Re Stibbe*, supra; *Hales v Darell* (1840) 3 Beav 324; cf *Re Haves* [1951] 2 All ER 928.

[27] *Atkinson v Webb* (1704) 2 Vern 478.

[28] *Re Van den Bergh's Will Trusts* [1948] 1 All ER 935.

[29] *Pinchin v Simms* (1861) 30 Beav 119; contra, semble, *Atkinson v Littlewood* (1874) LR 18 Eq 595.

[30] *Smith v Smith* (1861) 3 Giff 263; *Re Hall* [1918] 1 Ch 562.

[31] (1876) 3 Ch D 309. Cf *Tennant v Tennant* (1847) 9 LTOS 217.

[32] *Re Rattenberry* [1906] 1 Ch 667.

[33] Per Lord Hardwicke in *Barret v Beckford* (1750) 1 Ves Sen 519 at 521; *Alleyn v Alleyn* (1750) 2 Ves Sen 37.

[34] *Coates v Coates* [1898] 1 IR 258.

[35] *Thomas v Bennet* (1725) 2 P Wms 341; *Fowler v Fowler* (1735) 3 P Wms 353.

[36] *Rawlins v Powel* (1718) 1 P Wms 297; *Buckley v Buckley* (1888) 19 LR Ir 544.

[37] *Edmunds v Low* (1857) 3 K & J 318.

[38] *Carr v Eastabrooke* (1797) 3 Ves 561; *Re Roberts* (1902) 50 WR 469.

[39] *Re Fletcher* (1888) 38 Ch D 373.

both must have been present to the mind of the testator when he executed each of them, it is a strong reason against applying the presumption of satisfaction.[40]

(d) DIRECTION TO PAY DEBTS, OR TO PAY DEBTS AND LEGACIES

'It seems tolerably clear that a direction for payment either of debts and legacies,[41] or of debts simpliciter,[42] is treated as being, whether or not artificially—and I do not think it is particularly artificial—something which prima facie takes the case altogether out of the rule.'[43] It is something from which the court will readily infer an intention by the testator that the creditor shall have both his debt and the legacy. It was held in *Wathen v Smith*,[44] however, that 'debt' in this context did not include liability on a bond or covenant to pay a sum of money after the testator's death. This unsatisfactory view, however, can hardly stand in the light of subsequent authorities.[45]

(e) DEBT DUE TO A CHILD OF THE TESTATOR

It seems that where the debt is an ordinary debt,[46] the fact that the creditor-legatee is a child of the testator makes no difference to the application of the rule.[47] The same is true where the creditor-legatee is the wife of a testator.[48]

(f) ADMISSIBILITY OF EXTRINSIC EVIDENCE

As has already been seen, the presumption of satisfaction is deemed to represent the intention of the settlor, and accordingly the presumption may be rebutted, or, indeed, reinforced, by some express provision in the will or by implied expressions of intention therein contained.[49] For instance the court may infer an intention that the legacy shall be in addition to the debt from the motive expressed in the bequest of the legacy. Moreover, as has been explained, differences, even slight ones, between the debt and the legacy are construed as indication of an intention that the creditor shall have his legacy as well as his debt.[50]

---

[40] *Horlock v Wiggins* (1888) 39 Ch D 142, CA.

[41] *Chancey's Case* (1725) 1 P Wms 408; *Field v Mostin* (1778) 2 Dick 543; *Hassell v Hawkins* (1859) 4 Drew 468.

[42] *Re Huish* (1889) 43 Ch D 260; *Re Manners* [1949] Ch 613, [1949] 2 All ER 201, CA; *Re Pottruff* (1972) 27 DLR (3d) 405.

[43] *Re Manners* [1949] Ch 613 at 618, [1949] 2 All ER 201 at 204, CA per Evershed MR.

[44] (1819) 4 Madd 325.

[45] *Cole v Willard* (1858) 25 Beav 568; *Re Huish* (1889) 43 Ch D 260; *Re Stibbe* (1946) 175 LT 198; *Re Manners*, supra, CA.

[46] See section 3, p 745, post, for the rule in case of a portions debt.

[47] *Tolson v Collins* (1799) 4 Ves 483; *Edmunds v Low* (1857) 3 K & J 318.

[48] *Cole v Willard* (1858) 25 Beav 568; *Atkinson v Littlewood* (1874) LR 18 Eq 595.

[49] *Douce v Torrington* (1833) 2 My & K 600; *Glover v Hartcup* (1864) 34 Beav 74.

[50] *Charlton v West* (1861) 30 Beav 124.

As to how far extrinsic evidence is admitted, the rules are the same as in relation to other cases of satisfaction, and are discussed in section 3(j), p 759, post.

2 SATISFACTION OF A DEBT BY AN INTER VIVOS PAYMENT

(a) DEBT DUE TO A CHILD FROM ITS PARENT

In *Wood v Bryant*[51] Lord Hardwicke observed,[52] 'there are very few cases where a father will not be presumed to have paid the debt he owes to a daughter, when, in his lifetime, he gives her in marriage a greater sum than he owed her; for it is very unnatural to suppose that he would choose to leave himself a debtor to her and subject to an account.' This decision was followed in *Plunkett v Lewis*,[53] which in turn was treated by the Court of Appeal, in *Crichton v Crichton*,[54] as showing that a debt[55] owing by a parent to a child is presumed to be satisfied by the subsequent payment to him, on marriage or some other occasion, of a sum equal to or greater than the debt. There is not much authority, but the rules seem to correspond so far as possible with those applying to the type of satisfaction dealt with in the previous section. It was made clear in *Crichton v Crichton*[56] that in this sort of case there could be no satisfaction pro tanto, and that the debt must have been in existence at the time of the inter vivos advance.

(b) OTHER CASES

Although the above cases refer to payments by a parent to a child, it is doubtful in principle whether this relationship is essential: there is at least one case[57] where it was assumed there could be satisfaction between a brother and sister, though held in the circumstances that there was not. It will be remembered, as Plumer MR expressed it in *Goldsmid v Goldsmid*,[58] that 'where there is a question of satisfaction, there must be a reference to the intention. Satisfaction is a substitution of one thing for another: and the question in cases of that kind is whether the substituted thing was given for the thing proposed.' Though less likely to arise in practice, it would seem that the presumption of satisfaction should be stronger in the absence of the parent–child relationship.

---

[51] (1742) 2 Atk 521; *Chave v Farrant* (1810) 18 Ves 8.   [52] At 522.

[53] (1844) 3 Hare 316.   [54] [1896] 1 Ch 870, CA.

[55] There seems no reason to restrict it to liability for a breach of trust, which was in question in *Crichton v Crichton*, supra, itself.

[56] Supra.   [57] *Drewe v Bidgood* (1825) 2 Sim & St 424.

[58] (1818) 1 Wils Ch 140 at 149. Cf *Scrimes v Nickle* (1982) 130 DLR (3d) 698.

3 SATISFACTION OF A PORTIONS DEBT BY A LEGACY OR BY A SUBSEQUENT PORTION: ADEMPTION OF A LEGACY BY A PORTION

(a) DOUBLE PORTIONS

It will be observed that this one section deals with three different types of circumstances. This is by reason of the fact that the presumption which arises is in each case based on the leaning of the courts against double portions and consequently the rules are, in general, the same, and authorities on one type of case are authorities also on another. There are, however, some differences, which will be explained in due course, between ademption of a legacy on the one hand and the two cases of satisfaction on the other. Cottenham LC explained the matter thus in *Pym v Lockyer*.[59]

All the decisions upon questions of double portions depend upon the declared or presumed intention of the donor. The presumption of equity is against double portions, because it is not thought probable, when the object appears to be to make a provision, and that object has been affected by one instrument, that a repetition of it in a second should be intended as an addition to the first. The second provision, therefore, is presumed to be intended as a substitution for, and not as an addition to, that first given.

This presumption of ademption has been held to apply to an appointment under a special power of appointment.[60] It may also apply where the attorneys under an Enduring Power of Attorney[61] make a provision which would have given rise to the presumption if it had been made by the donor of the power, not having lost dispositive capacity.[62]

On the one hand, as regards the satisfaction of portions debts by legacies,[63] it should perhaps be made clear that if the portion has actually been paid, no question of satisfaction can arise.[64] A legacy cannot be intended as a substitution for something that has already been given. Thus if, for instance, on his son's marriage a father paid £5,000 to the trustees of his marriage settlement, a subsequent legacy to the settlement trustees would be payable in full. But if he merely covenanted to pay £5,000 to the trustees and did not pay it in his lifetime, and by a subsequent will gave them a legacy, the presumption of satisfaction would prima facie apply. On the other hand, where the will comes first, there is no reason why a legacy therein contained should not be adeemed by a covenant contained in a subsequent settlement just as much as by actual

---

[59] (1841) 5 My & Cr 29 at 34–35; *Re Vaux* [1939] Ch 465 at 481, [1938] 4 All ER 703 at 708–709, CA per Greene MR.

[60] *Re Peel's Settlement* [1911] 2 Ch 165.   [61] See p 461, supra.

[62] See *Re Cameron (decd)* [1999] 2 All ER 924, noted (1999) 8 T & ELJ 14 (A Darroch).

[63] Or subsequent portions ie where the father subsequently makes an actual payment inter vivos to or for the benefit of his child, such payment being regarded as a portion.

[64] *Taylor v Cartwright* (1872) LR 14 Eq 167.

payment.[65] It should be observed, however, that a will may contain a provision, known as hotchpot,[66] requiring a child to bring into account advancements actually made during the father's lifetime. The exact effect of such a provision depends upon the construction of the particular words used and is outside the scope of this book.[67]

Though the presumption of satisfaction and ademption have their supporters,[68] there has been considerable criticism from early times. The more common attitude of the courts is perhaps typified by the forthright statement of Bowen LJ in *Montague v Earl of Sandwich*:[69]

Whatever may be the view to be taken of the rule against double portions, it is a rule that exists; and there is nothing worse than frittering away an existing rule ... Feeling no confidence that in applying this doctrine of double portions in this particular case we are giving effect to the real intention of the testator ... I record my judgment accordingly in favour of the appeal as a sacrifice made upon the altar of authority.

(b) MEANING OF A PORTION

As appears from the above citations it is essential, in order for a presumption of satisfaction or ademption to arise, for both the relevant provisions to be gifts or advancements in the nature of portions.[70] In considering what is meant by the term 'portion', it seems permissible to refer to decisions on the hotchpot provisions on intestacy, to be found in s 47(1)(iii) of the Administration of Estates Act 1925. This subsection, now repealed by the Law Reform (Succession) Act 1995, replaced the Statute of Distribution 1670, which referred to advances 'by portion'. Jenkins LJ in *Re Hayward*,[71] after referring to the different language, stated his view that s 47(1)(iii) was, if anything, narrower than the provisions of the Statute of Distribution 1670, but that decisions on the old Act were, generally speaking, applicable to the new.

Lord Jenkins has pointed out, in two different cases, two factors which tend to confuse the matter. One is[72] 'that the word "advancement" seems to be used in two ways. First, there is the typical gift by way of advancement for establishing a child in life; the child is there spoken of as being advanced because he is forwarded in life and

---

[65] *Hopwood v Hopwood* (1859) 7 HL Cas 728; *Stevenson v Masson* (1873) LR 17 Eq 78. In *Clarke v Burgoine* (1767) 1 Dick 353, legacies were adeemed in part by a payment on marriage and in part by a covenant to make a further payment on death.

[66] As to the derivation of this word Littleton explained: 'this word is in English a pudding; for in this pudding is not commonly but one thing alone but one thing with other things together'—Coke upon Littleton 176a sect 267. And see (1962) 78 LQR at 262 (J E S Simon).

[67] See eg Jarman on *Wills*, 8th edn, vol 2, p 1156 et seq.

[68] Eg Lord Cottenham in *Lady Thynne v Earl of Glengall* (1848) 2 HL Cas 131 at 153.

[69] (1886) 32 Ch D 525 at 544, CA; *Re Lacon* [1891] 2 Ch 482, CA. See, generally, (1987) 17 UWALR 272 (N Crago), who suggests that in contemporary society the rule against double portions 'may appear as a curious anomaly without a sound theoretical basis'.

[70] *Re Lacon* [1891] 2 Ch 482 at 497, CA; *Re George's Will Trusts* [1949] Ch 154 at 159, [1948] 2 All ER 1004 at 1008.

[71] [1957] Ch 528 at 535, [1957] 2 All ER 474 at 477, CA.

[72] *Re Hayward* [1957] Ch 528 at 540, [1957] 2 All ER 474 at 480, CA.

made to stand better with the world.' This is the meaning with which we are concerned. Secondly, where for instance a legacy is adeemed by a subsequent portion 'the
word "advancement" is sometimes used . . . as being an advancement or anticipation
of the interest under the will'. It may be added that in the same case, in the court of
first instance,[73] Upjohn J referred to yet another sense of the word, namely 'whether a
sum of money paid by a parent to a child is by way of advancement or whether the
child held the money from the parent on a resulting trust. When any payment is made
by a parent to a child, there may be a presumption of advancement in that sense,[74] but
that type of advancement is not the advancement with which we are now concerned,
which is an advancement by way of portion.' Further, 'portion' is not restricted to
provision for younger children, in the sense in which it is commonly used in connection with a strict settlement.[75] The other factor was pointed out by Lord Jenkins, when
a judge of first instance, in *Re George's Will Trusts*,[76] a case of ademption. Here it was
contended:

that, having regard to its character and the circumstances in which it was made, the testator's
gift inter vivos . . . was not in the nature of a portion at all, and, alternatively that, if this gift
was in itself the nature of a portion, its character and the circumstances in which it was
made were sufficient to rebut the presumption. The question of portion or no portion being
necessarily to a great extent a question of the testator's intention, it is hardly possible to
distinguish circumstances relied on as tending to show that the gift inter vivos was not in the
nature of a portion at all from circumstances relied on as tending to rebut the presumption
on the footing that it was in itself in the nature of a portion.

According to Kay LJ[77] 'a "portion" means such a share of the father's personal
property as he intends to be a provision for that son, or . . . a substantial part of the
provision for that son'. This, however, is hardly adequate, and according to Jenkins
LJ,[78] 'the nearest approach to a definition of what is an advancement that our case law
has achieved' is contained in two short judgments[79] of Jessel MR in *Taylor v Taylor*[80] In
the first he said:[81]

I have always understood that an advancement by way of portion is something given by the
parent to establish the child in life, or to make what is called a provision for him . . . You may
make the provision by way of marriage portion on the marriage of the child. You may make
it on putting him into a profession or business in a variety of ways . . . [or by] a father giving
a large sum to a child in one payment. . . . [However] it is not every payment made to a child
which is to be regarded as an advancement, or advancement by way of portion. In every case

---

[73] [1956] 3 All ER 608 at 611.   [74] See chapter 9, section 2(d), supra.

[75] *Re Stephens* [1904] 1 Ch 322.   [76] [1949] Ch 154 at 159, [1948] 2 All ER 1004 at 1009.

[77] In *Re Lacon* [1891] 2 Ch 482 at 501, [1891–1894] All ER Rep 286 at 293, CA.

[78] In *Re Hayward* [1957] Ch 528 at 537, [1957] 2 All ER 474 at 478, CA.

[79] Alleged 'advancements by portion' under the Statute of Distribution 1670, were made by a father to two
sons: the first judgment deals with payments made to one son, the second with payments to the other.

[80] (1875) LR 20 Eq 155.

[81] At 157–158. In *Re Cameron (decd)* [1999] 2 All ER 924 Lindsay J drew attention to the word 'or' in line 2
of the passage cited above.

to which I have been referred there has either been a settlement itself, or the purpose for which the payment was made has been shewn to be that which everyone would recognize as being for establishing the child or making a provision for the child.

And in the second judgment, according to his view:

nothing was an advancement unless it were given on marriage, or to establish the child in life. Prima facie, an advancement must be made in early life; but any sum given by way of making a permanent provision for the child would come within the term establishing in life.

A legacy, including a gift of residue,[82] from a parent to a child 'is presumed to be intended to be a portion; because providing for the child is a duty which the relative situation of the parties imposes upon the parent',[83] though the principle would not apply universally, for instance to a bequest of personal chattels.[84] And, as appears from *Taylor v Taylor*,[85] a provision made on the marriage of a child is always regarded as being a portion.[86]

In *Taylor v Taylor*[87] it was held on the one hand, that sums given for the following purposes constituted advancement by way of portion for the purpose of the Statute of Distribution 1670, namely, the payment of the admission fee to one of the Inns of Court in the case of a child intended for the Bar,[88] the price, following a change of career,[89] of a commission and outfit of a child entering the army, and following yet another change of career the price of plant and machinery and other payments for the purpose of starting a child in business. On the other hand, the following were held not to be advancements by way of portion, namely, the payment of a fee to a special pleader for the same child, on the ground that this was in the nature of a payment for preliminary education,[90] the price, after becoming an officer in the army, of an outfit and passage money for him and his wife on going out to India with his regiment, and the payment of debts incurred by him in India, this being in the nature of temporary assistance. The decision on this last point was preferred by the Court of Appeal in *Re Scott*[91] to the contrary decisions in *Boyd v Boyd*[92] and *Re Blockley*.[93]

The size of the gift is a matter of importance. Referring again to Jessel MR's first judgment in *Taylor v Taylor*[94] the rule is that 'if in the absence of evidence you find a father giving a large sum to a child in one payment, there is a presumption that that is intended to start him in life or make a provision for him; but if a small sum is so given you may require evidence to show the purpose.' On the one hand, the presumption that the gift of a large sum constitutes a portion was affirmed by the Court of Appeal

---

[82] *Lady Thynne v Earl of Glengall* (1848) 2 HL Cas 131; *Montefiore v Guedalla* (1859) 1 De GF & J 93; *Stevenson v Masson* (1873) LR 17 Eq 78.

[83] *Pym v Lockyer* (1841) 5 My & Cr 29 at 35 per Lord Cottenham; *Ex p Pye* (1811) 18 Ves 140 at 151 per Lord Eldon. So held or assumed in all cases of ademption.

[84] *Re Tussaud's Estate* (1878) 9 Ch D 363 at 367, CA, per Jessel MR.

[85] (1875) LR 20 Eq 155; *Re Tussaud's Estate*, supra.   [86] *Leighton v Leighton* (1874) LR 18 Eq 458.

[87] Supra.   [88] Similarly in *Boyd v Boyd* (1867) LR 4 Eq 305 in relation to a premium to a solicitor.

[89] *Hoskins v Hoskins* (1706) Prec Ch 263; *Andrew v Andrew* (1874) 30 LT 457.

[90] Contrast *Boyd v Boyd*, supra.   [91] [1903] 1 Ch 1, CA.   [92] Supra.

[93] (1885) 29 Ch D 250.   [94] (1875) LR 20 Eq 155 at 158.

in *Re Scott*[95] and *Re Hayward*,[96] the decision in *Re Liversey's Settlement Trusts*,[97] which at first sight seems to be to the contrary, being explained in *Re Hayward*,[98] as turning upon the language of the particular document. Although the relative size of the amount of the gift compared with the size of the testator's estate is a factor to be taken into account, in order to raise a presumption of satisfaction or ademption 'it must be shown that the fund in question was sufficiently substantial in itself to be in the nature of a permanent provision without pressing too far the question of proportion.'[99] Thus in *Re Hayward*,[100] admittedly a border line case, it was held that the gifts did not constitute advancements under s 47(1)(iii) of the Administration of Estates Act 1925, although they amounted to over £500 and the value of the net estate, exclusive of the gifts, was less than £1,800. The decision in this case might have been different if the donee had been younger; he was 43 years old at the date of the gift and it will be remembered that Jessel MR in *Taylor v Taylor*[101] stated that prima facie, an advancement must be made in early life. The decision went the other way in *Hardy v Shaw*,[102] where the matter also arose under s 47(1)(iii), but where the gifts in question were substantial both absolutely and relatively to the deceased's estate. Although the donees cannot have been in early life, the prima facie rule was overridden by the size of the gifts and the fact that they could fairly be described as making a permanent provision for the donees.

On the other hand, not only is a single small gift, such as £100 to a daughter to buy a wedding outfit,[103] not a portion, but 'the court has never added up small sums in order to show that if the child claims those sums as well as the larger provision made for him by the parent, he would be taking a double portion'.[104] As regards annuities, Lord Eldon had no doubt, in *Lord Kircudbright v Lady Kircudbright*,[105] that an annuity was an advancement by way of portion under the Statute of Distribution. In *Hatfield v Minet*,[106] however, where by a separation deed a father covenanted to pay annuities to his children, it was held that so much of the annuities as were paid in the father's lifetime were not in the nature of advancements, but that the value of the annuities must be estimated as at the date of death and brought into hotchpot. And in *Watson v Watson*[107] an annual allowance of £60 was held not to be a portion.

A portion is commonly money, but may, of course, comprise securities such as stock or shares in a limited company. Setting a child up in business may involve buying the goodwill of a business for a child and giving him stock in trade, which was given as a typical instance of a portion by Jessel MR in *Taylor v Taylor*,[108] and in *Re*

---

[95] Supra.   [96] [1957] Ch 528, [1957] 2 All ER 474, CA.   [97] [1953] 2 All ER 723.

[98] Supra.   [99] Per Jenkins LJ in *Re Hayward* [1957] Ch 528 at 542, [1957] 2 All ER 474 at 482, CA.

[100] Supra.   [101] (1875) LR 20 Eq 155.   [102] [1976] Ch 82, [1975] 2 All ER 1052.

[103] *Ravenscroft v Jones* (1864) 4 De GJ & Sm 224.

[104] Per Wigram VC in *Suisse v Lowther* (1843) 2 Hare 424; *Watson v Watson* (1864) 33 Beav 574; *Re Peacock's Estate* (1872) LR 14 Eq 236.

[105] (1802) 8 Ves 51.   [106] (1878) 8 Ch D 136, CA.   [107] Supra.   [108] (1875) LR 20 Eq 155.

George's Will Trusts[109] Jenkins J had 'no doubt that a gift by a farmer to his son of live and dead stock with which to set up in business as a farmer may be in the nature of a portion, and, in the absence of circumstances tending to show the contrary, would generally be regarded as such.'

It has recently been held that there is no rule of law that the rule against double portions does not apply to land.[110]

(c) DONOR MUST BE PARENT OR IN LOCO PARENTIS

The presumptions of satisfaction and ademption only arise where both provisions in question are made by the child's parent[111] or by some other person who stands in loco parentis to him.[112] Prima facie, there is no presumption, and the child is entitled to both provisions, not only where the donor is completely unrelated, but equally where he or she, as the case may be, is the grandfather,[113] grandmother,[114] uncle,[115] or other collateral relative.[116] It used to be held that there was no presumption as between a father and an illegitimate child,[117] but in such a case there is an obvious duty to make provision for the child and doubtless the presumption would now arise without evidence,[118] and equally in the case of a mother.

If the gifts have not been made by the parent of the child, the question arises whether the donor was, at the relevant time,[119] in loco parentis to him. Whether in any case a person has put himself in loco parentis to a child has been said[120] to be 'probably one of the most difficult of legal problems to solve'. Lord Cottenham considered the question in *Powys v Mansfield*[121] saying that he readily adopted Lord Eldon's definition in *Ex p Pye*[122] and continuing:

Lord Eldon says [one in loco parentis] is a person 'meaning to put himself in loco parentis; in the situation of the person described as the lawful father of the child; but this definition

---

[109] [1949] Ch 154 at 160, [1948] 2 All ER 1004 at 1009. It was further held in this case that the fact that the gift was in a sense a forced one did not prevent the gift from being a portion.

[110] *Race v Race* [2002] EWHC 1868, [2002] WTLR 1193.

[111] Until recently it was generally thought that the presumption did not apply in the case of a mother unless it was established that she was in loco parentis to the child. However in *Re Cameron (decd)* [1999] 2 All ER 924 Lindsay J, after a careful consideration of the cases, held that so far as concerns portions both parents should nowadays be taken to be in loco parentis unless the contrary is proved.

[112] *Ex p Pye* (1811) 18 Ves 140; *Powys v Mansfield* (1837) 3 My & Cr 359; *Suisse v Lowther* (1843) 2 Hare 424; *Fowkes v Pascoe* (1875) 10 Ch App 343.

[113] *Roome v Roome* (1744) 3 Atk 181; *Re Dawson* [1919] 1 Ch 102, cf *Pym v Lockyer* (1841) 5 My & Cr 29; *Campbell v Campbell* (1866) LR 1 Eq 383.

[114] *Lyddon v Ellison* (1854) 19 Beav 565.

[115] *Brown v Peck* (1758) 1 Eden 139; *Powys v Mansfield*, supra.

[116] *Shudal v Jekyll* (1743) 2 Atk 516; *Williams v Duke of Bolton* (1768) 1 Dick 405.

[117] *Ex p Pye*, supra; *Wetherby v Dixon* (1815) 19 Ves 407.   [118] *Re Lawes* (1881) 20 Ch D 81, CA.

[119] In *Watson v Watson* (1864) 33 Beav 574, a case of ademption, this was said to be the date of the will; on principle it would seem that the relationship must exist at the date of both gifts—in practice, once established it is unlikely to determine.

[120] Per James LJ In *Fowkes v Pascoe* (1875) 10 Ch App 343 at 350.

[121] (1837) 3 My & Cr 359 at 367.   [122] (1811) 18 Ves 140.

must, I conceive, be considered as applicable to those parental offices and duties to which the subject in question has reference, namely, to the office and duty of the parent to make provision for the child.'

He went on to stress the importance of the intention of the person alleged to be in loco parentis, and the fact that one is concerned with the duty to make financial provision. Recently it has been emphasized that the matter is dependent on the circumstances of the individual case.[123]

Applying the above principles, it was held in *Powys v Mansfield*[124] that a rich unmarried uncle, whose brother had not got the means of adequately providing for his children, and who had furnished, through the father, the means of their mainten-ance and education, and negotiated the marriage settlement of a niece, to which the father was not a party, putting in the necessary money, was in loco parentis to the niece, notwithstanding the fact that she had continued to live with her father until her marriage.[125] Similarly in *Booker v Allen*[126] where the donor, a near relative, had not only contributed to the maintenance and education of the child from the time she lost her father in early infancy, but was consulted as to her place of education, was regarded by her as the person whose consent was necessary to her marriage and had expressly taken upon himself the obligation to make a provision for her in that event. The court was, perhaps, too easily persuaded that the grandfather was in loco parentis in *Campbell v Campbell*,[127] but refused to extend this status in *Fowkes v Pascoe*[128] to a woman who had made gifts to the son of her daughter-in-law, though he had lived with her for some years before his marriage, stayed with her on his visits to London, and had been given a handsome present on his marriage. It would seem to be easier, as would be expected, to establish that one is in loco parentis to another where there is a close blood relationship, whether legitimate or not.

A qualification to what has been said above arises where both portions are settled by a parent or someone in loco parentis on a child, his or her spouse, and their children. If the limitations in the settlement and the will are identical, then the presumption of satisfaction or ademption will apply not only to the interest of the child, but equally to the interests of the other beneficiaries: the effect of differences in the limitations is considered below.[129]

It may be added, in conclusion, that parol evidence is, of course, admissible to establish that the donor was in loco parentis to the child at the relevant times.[130]

---

[123] Per Danckwerts LJ giving the judgment of the Court of Appeal in *Re Paradise Motor Co Ltd* [1968] 2 All ER 625.

[124] (1837) 3 My & Cr 359; *Monck v Lord Monck* (1810) 1 Ball & B 298 (elder to younger brother).

[125] Similarly in *Pym v Lockyer* (1841) 5 My & Cr 29, where a grandfather was held to be in loco parentis to grandchildren although their father was living and had maintained them during childhood.

[126] (1831) 2 Russ & M 270.   [127] (1866) LR 1 Eq 383; cf *Lyddon v Ellison* (1854) 19 Beav 565.

[128] (1875) 10 Ch App 343.   [129] See section, 3(h), p 755, infra.

[130] *Booker v Allen* (1831) 2 Russ & M 270; *Powys v Mansfield* (1837) 3 My & Cr 359.

(d) SATISFACTION AND ADEMPTION PRO TANTO

It was at one time thought[131] that where, for instance, a father bequeathed a legacy of £10,000 to a child, and subsequently advanced him £5,000 on marriage, the legacy was wholly adeemed, the idea apparently being that the father was fully entitled to change his mind about the amount which would be an appropriate provision for the child. The matter was carefully considered by Lord Cottenham in *Pym v Lockyer*,[132] and his decision has always been regarded as establishing that ademption or satisfaction is only pro tanto, so that in the illustration given, the legacy would only be adeemed to the extent of the subsequent advance of £5,000, and the balance of £5,000 would remain payable.

It may happen that a will contains two provisions bestowing portions on a child, and the question may arise as to which of these is adeemed by a subsequent advancement. The answer is, that which the latter portion most closely resembles. Thus in *Montefiore v Guedalla*,[133] a father by his will gave an absolute pecuniary legacy to a son and also settled on him and his family a share of residue. On the son's marriage, the father transferred property to the trustees of his marriage settlement. It was held this was an ademption pro tanto of the gift of residue and not of the absolute legacy.

The value of an advancement has to be ascertained as at the time when it was made.[134]

(e) BOTH PORTIONS MUST BE PROVIDED BY, AND FOR, THE SAME PERSONS

On the first point, that both portions must be provided by the same person, the rule stated by Romilly MR[135] applies to both satisfaction and ademption, namely, that 'satisfaction can only arise where the person who makes the payment is himself the party bound to pay, or is the owner of the estate charged with the payment'. On the other point, that both portions must be provided for the same persons, equity looks to the substance of the matter,[136] and there are innumerable cases where there has been held to be ademption or satisfaction where the portions have been payable to different trustees, but the respective beneficial limitations have been substantially the same.[137] There have also been a number of cases where the question has been whether a legacy

---

[131] See eg *Ex p Pye* (1811) 18 Ves 140.

[132] (1841) 5 My & Cr 29; *Lady Thynne v Earl of Glengall* (1848) 2 HL Cas 131; *Montefiore v Guedalla* (1859) 1 De GF & J 93; *Re Pollock* (1885) 28 Ch D 552, CA.

[133] (1859) 1 De GF & J 93.

[134] *Watson v Watson* (1864) 33 Beav 574. The principles that used to be applied for deduction of estate duty would presumably now be applied in relation to inheritance tax—see *Re Beddington* [1900] 1 Ch 771; *Re Turner's Will Trusts* [1968] 1 All ER 321.

[135] *Samuel v Ward* (1856) 22 Beav 347 at 350; *Douglas v Willes* (1849) 7 Hare 318.

[136] See *Re Cameron (decd)* [1999] 2 All ER 924.

[137] Eg *Lady Thynne v Earl of Glengall*, supra; *Russell v St Aubyn* (1876) 2 Ch D 398; *Romaine v Onslow* (1876) 24 WR 899 and see section 3(h), p 755, infra.

to a daughter has been adeemed by a subsequent advancement to her husband. The cases are somewhat confused but it is submitted that on principle the better view is that expressed by Romilly MR in a case actually concerned with an express provision. He said,[138] 'Nothing turns on the fact that it was given to her husband rather than to the wife; if, in truth, the money was paid by way of marriage portion, or by the way of advancement, it falls within the provision, whoever received it.' The crux of the matter is whether the money, although paid to the husband, was paid by way of the wife's portion. Thus the same judge observed in a later case,[139] 'I do not know of any case in which it has yet been determined that the gift of a sum of money to the husband of a daughter, by her father, simpliciter, after the marriage, and not in consequence of any promise previous to the marriage taking place (which might have a very different effect), has been held to be an ademption of a legacy given to the daughter.' In this latter case[140] it was held there was no ademption of a legacy to the daughter, where some three weeks after her marriage the father gave £400 to the husband and when thanked said 'that he hoped it would do him some good'. On the other hand, there was ademption in *Nevin v Drysdale*[141] where there was a legacy of £500 to the wife, and a subsequent payment of £400 to the husband in pursuance of an ante-nuptial understanding that the wife's father would contribute towards the furnishing of the matrimonial home. The presumption was not rebutted by evidence of a promise by the father to contribute a further £600. And in what appears to be the only recent case, *Re Cameron (decd)*,[142] it was held that payment of a sum to trustees for the private education of the child of a son adeemed pro tanto the share of the son in the testatrix's residuary estate. In so deciding Lindsay J observed that the rule against double portions is entirely judge-made and is amenable to reshaping by the courts and should be reshaped to coincide with 'good sense' and the 'ordinary transactions of mankind' as they are from time to time seen to be.

It is difficult to reconcile *Cooper v Macdonald*[143] with the above principles: this case seems to be decided on the view that there can never be ademption where or in so far as the persons taking under the several instruments are different. Accordingly it was held that there was no ademption of a share of residue settled on the wife and her children by the payment under the terms of her marriage settlement of £1,000 absolutely to the husband, notwithstanding that it was expressed to be given as a marriage portion.[144]

---

[138] *M'Clure v Evans* (1861) 29 Beav 422 at 425.

[139] *Ravenscroft v Jones* (1863) 32 Beav 669 at 670–671; affd (1864) 4 De GJ & Sm 224; where one judge refused to express an opinion on this point and the other seems to have disagreed with Romilly MR.

[140] *Ravenscroft v Jones*, supra.

[141] (1867) LR 4 Eq 517; the same result in *Kirk v Eddowes* (1844) 3 Hare 509, depended on extrinsic evidence of intention.

[142] [1999] 2 All ER 924, where it was observed that there is no need for the donee either to know of the prospective gift by will or to be a party to or to know of the inter vivos gift.

[143] (1873) LR 16 Eq 258.

[144] There was, however, ademption of the share of residue as to £4,000 by the same settlement covenanted to be paid to trustees as a provision for the daughter.

(f) APPLICATION OF THE DOCTRINES TO BENEFIT STRANGERS

It is not altogether clear how far, if at all, someone not a child can claim the benefit of these presumptions. The question does not seem to have been raised prior to *Meinertzagen v Walters*,[145] where Mellish LJ stated that 'in the ordinary case of a legacy, where a legacy has been left to a child, and then a gift has been made which amounts to an ademption of that legacy, there certainly appears to be no possible way of holding it to be an ademption so as to carry out the general rule against double portions, except by holding that whoever has the residue benefits by it; because by the necessity of the case the persons who have the residue must benefit by the act of the previous legacy not being paid from any cause whatever.' Though not discussed therein, this view is supported by cases[146] where the presumption of ademption has been applied although the residuary legatee was a stranger, and to some extent by the existence of cases where it has not been considered necessary in the reports to state to whom the residue has been given.[147]

In *Meinertzagen v Walters*,[148] however, the court refused to allow a stranger to benefit where residue was given to children and a stranger, and an advancement was made to a child, the principle, according to obiter dicta in *Re Heather*,[149] and the decision at first instance in *Re Vaux*[150] being that a rule designed to produce equality[151] among children ought not to be applied so as to reduce their shares for the benefit of a stranger. Thus if a father gave his residue worth £9,000 equally between A and B, his children, and X a stranger, and subsequently advanced £2,000 to A, X would receive £3,000 only, but as between A and B, A's share of residue has been adeemed pro tanto and accordingly B would get £4,000, and A £2,000, which together with the advance he had already received would, of course, make him equal to B. Again, suppose a father having two children A and B, by his will gave a legacy of £3,000 to A and his residue equally between A and B and X, a stranger, and subsequently made an advancement of £3,000 to A, and died leaving a net estate of £15,000. In distributing the estate, the presumption of ademption would not be applied for the benefit of X, who accordingly would get one-third of the residue of £12,000 (net estate less the legacy of £3,000), namely £4,000. The net assets available for distribution would now be £11,000. As between A and B the presumption of ademption would apply, the legacy of £3,000 would be treated as adeemed by the inter vivos advancement and accordingly A and B would get £5,500. Consequently A would have had, in the result, £3,000 more than B, which was presumably the testator's intention.

---

[145] (1872) 7 Ch App 670 at 674.

[146] *Trimmer v Bayne* (1802) 7 Ves 508; *Booker v Allen* (1831) 2 Russ & M 270.

[147] *Debeze v Mann* (1789) 2 Bro CC 519; *Robinson v Whitley* (1804) 9 Ves 577.

[148] (1872) 7 Ch App 670 at 674.   [149] [1906] 2 Ch 230.

[150] [1938] Ch 581; revsd [1939] Ch 465, CA, where it was not necessary to discuss this point. See (1977) 93 LQR 65 (P H Pettit).

[151] Or proportionate division as intended by the testator.

It remains doubtful, however, whether the general statement in *Re Vaux*,[152] that in the case of ademption of a legacy the rule is not to be used to benefit a stranger, applies where the sole residuary legatee is a stranger.

(g) THE OPERATION OF THE PRESUMPTIONS

Where the presumption of ademption applies, the legatee has no option, the legacy having gone, his only choice is to take the subsequent portion. Where, however, it is the presumption of satisfaction that applies, he cannot be compelled to take the second provision offered in lieu of that to which he is legally entitled under the settlement or covenant: all he can be compelled to do is to elect or choose between them. The distinction is that in cases of ademption the first benefit is given by a will, which is a revocable instrument which the testator can alter as he pleases, and consequently when he subsequently gives benefits in circumstances which give rise to the presumption of ademption, he is readily assumed to have intended to substitute the second gift for the first, which he had the power of altering at his pleasure. The law uses the word *ademption* because the bequest contained in the will is thereby *adeemed*, that is, taken out of the will. In cases of satisfaction, however,[153] where, for instance, a father, on the marriage of a child, enters into a covenant to pay money to the trustees of the marriage settlement, he cannot unilaterally avoid or alter that covenant, and if he gives benefits by his will to the same objects, in circumstances which give rise to the presumption of satisfaction, he necessarily gives the objects of the covenant the right to elect whether they will take under the covenant, or whether they will take under the will.

It may be added that if, for example, a father covenants with the trustees of his daughter's marriage settlement to pay them a sum of money to be settled on the daughter and her children, and by his will bequeaths a legacy to the daughter absolutely, the daughter may be called upon to elect, but this cannot effect the rights of the children under the covenant.[154]

(h) REBUTTING THE PRESUMPTIONS

It need hardly be said that if the donor has, in his second provision, expressed an intention that it is to be in addition to, and not in satisfaction or ademption of, the first, his intention must be carried out. In other cases, since the presumptions are based on the presumed intention of the donor, it is always open to the donee to rebut a presumption by intrinsic or extrinsic evidence. By reason of the distinction just discussed, it is much easier to rebut the presumption in a case of satisfaction than in

---

[152] Supra, at first instance, at 589, 591.

[153] *Lord Chichester v Coventry* (1867) LR 2 HL 71 at 90–91; *Lady Thynne v Earl of Glengall* (1848) 2 HL Cas 131; *McCarogher v Whieldon* (1867) LR 3 Eq 236, criticized in (1977) 93 LQR 65 (P H Pettit), and discussed in *Re Gordon's Will Trusts* [1978] Ch 145, [1978] 2 All ER 969, CA.

[154] *Lord Chichester v Coventry*, supra.

case of ademption. It follows from this that, on the one hand, circumstances which will rebut the presumption of ademption will, *a fortiori*, rebut the presumption of satisfaction: but, on the other hand, cases which decide that certain circumstances rebut the presumption of satisfaction cannot be relied on in connection with ademption. It is now proposed to consider the effect of intrinsic evidence derived from the nature of two provisions.

(i) Differences in the limitations

Dealing first with the presumption of satisfaction, the rule is that differences between the limitations contained in the two provisions will rebut the presumption of satisfaction, unless the differences are merely slight. Unfortunately 'it is not possible to define what are to be considered as slight differences between the two provisions. Slight differences are such as, in the opinion of the judge, leave the two provisions substantially of the same nature; and every judge must decide that question for himself.'[155] It is submitted, nevertheless, that some guidance can be obtained from previous decisions. On the one hand, the differences were held to be slight, and the presumption of satisfaction not rebutted, in *Lady Thynne v Earl of Glengall*,[156] where by a marriage settlement one-third of the sum of £100,000 was paid and the remaining two-thirds covenanted to be paid to four trustees on trust for the wife (the settlor's daughter) for life, to her separate use, with remainder to the children *of the marriage* as the husband and wife should *jointly* appoint; and by the will half of the residue was given to two of the settlement trustees on trust for the wife's separate use for life with remainder for *her* children generally as *she* should by deed or will appoint.

On the other hand, the differences were held to be great enough to rebut the presumption of satisfaction in *Re Vernon*,[157] where under the daughter's marriage settlement there were successive life interests to wife and husband, with remainder to such of their issue as they jointly or the survivor of them should appoint and in default of appointment a trust for the children of the marriage; and by the will the limitations were to the wife for life, remainder to her children, but if she should die without leaving any child surviving her, to any husband she should leave surviving her for life, and then the fund to fall into residue.

Sometimes the difference alleged is that the will makes provision for one only, or some only, of the beneficiaries under the prior settlement. In such case, as Lord Romilly explained in *Lord Chichester v Coventry*,[158] 'a provision by will may satisfy one part of the covenant without satisfying the other parts of it; for instance, that if a father, on the marriage of his daughter, should settle £10,000 on her for life, remainder to the children of the marriage, a bequest of £10,000 to that daughter would satisfy her life interest in the £10,000, but would not satisfy or touch the

---

[155] Per Leach MR in *Weall v Rice* (1831) 2 Russ & M 251 at 268; *Lord Chichester v Coventry* (1867) LR 2 HL 71; *Re Tussaud's Estate* (1878) 9 Ch D 363, CA.

[156] (1848) 2 HL Cas 131; *Russell v St Aubyn* (1876) 2 Ch D 398.

[157] (1906) 95 LT 48; *Re Tussaud's Estate* (1878) 9 Ch D 363, CA.

[158] (1867) LR 2 HL 71 at 95; *Re Blundell* [1906] 2 Ch 222.

interests of her children.' Similarly a bequest to the children of the marriage, omitting the parent, could be a satisfaction of so much of the covenant as related to them, without affecting the right of the parent to claim under the covenant.

Turning to the ademption of legacies by subsequent portions, there are numerous cases where it was held that differences in the limitations did not prevent ademption, but there does not seem to be any reported case in which the presumption has been rebutted solely on this ground. Thus there was ademption in *Earl of Durham v Wharton*,[159] where by the will £10,000 was settled on a daughter for life, with remainder to such of her children as she should appoint, and in default of appointment equally, and if there should be no children, the fund was to fall into residue; and by the marriage settlement, the father agreed to give £15,000 to the intended husband expressly as the marriage portion, who agreed to secure to his wife pin money of £500 a year, a jointure of £1,200 and portions for the daughters and younger sons of the marriage; in *Powys v Mansfield*,[160] where by the will there were limited successive life interests to the wife and husband, and remainder to the wife's children; by the settlement successive life interests to husband and wife and remainder to the *younger* children of the *marriage*, and in *Stevenson v Masson*,[161] where the will gave the daughter an absolute legacy, and the settlement provided for the covenanted sum to be settled.

(ii) Gifts must be eiusdem generis

Here the cases do not draw any distinction between the presumptions of ademption and satisfaction. In *Bellasis v Uthwatt*,[162] however, Lord Hardwicke laid down that 'the thing given in satisfaction must be of the same nature, and attended with the same certainty, as the thing in lieu of which it is given, and land is not to be taken in satisfaction for money,[163] nor money for land'. This was applied in *Holmes v Holmes*,[164] where the presumption of ademption was rebutted by the difference in nature between a legacy of money and an advance of a share in a partnership. The Court of Appeal in *Re Jacques*[165] affirmed that the law laid down in these cases had not been changed, disapproving the interpretation placed by North J[166] on the earlier Court of Appeal decision in *Re Lawes*.[167] The court made clear, however, that if a thing is given by reference to its pecuniary value, then it is treated as equivalent to a gift of money. As Jessel MR observed,[168] 'where a testator gives to a child a beneficial lease or share of works, or any other thing, and says nothing about the value, he is not to be taken to be giving it in satisfaction of a pecuniary bequest; but where he does refer to the value the presumption of satisfaction may arise.'

---

[159] (1836) 10 Bli NS 526. See *Re Cameron (decd)* [1999] 2 All ER 924, discussed on p 753, supra.
[160] (1837) 3 My & Cr 359.   [161] (1873) LR 17 Eq 78. See also *Re Furness* [1901] 2 Ch 346.
[162] (1737) 1 Atk 426 at 428.
[163] *Chaplin v Chaplin* (1734) 3 P Wms 245; cf *Re Aynsley* [1915] 1 Ch 172, CA.
[164] (1783) 1 Bro CC 555; *Davys v Boucher*, supra.   [165] [1903] 1 Ch 267, CA.
[166] In *Re Vickers* (1888) 37 Ch D 525.
[167] (1881) 20 Ch D 81, CA; *Bengough v Walker* (1808) 15 Ves 507.
[168] In *Re Lawes* (1881) 20 Ch D 81 at 88, CA; *Re George's Will Trusts*, supra.

The difference between a gift of money and a gift of consols,[169] or bearer bonds,[170] is disregarded for this purpose, but if one gift is absolute, the other contingent, this difference rebuts the presumption,[171] unless the contingency is so remote that the settlor did not think it should be taken into consideration.[172] And since *Lady Thynne v Earl of Glengall*[173] it has been consistently held that there can be both ademption of and satisfaction by a gift of residue.

It has recently been held, in *Race v Race*,[174] that the test does not call for a technical approach and requires the court to look at the matter broadly. There it was held to be ademption even though one gift was a gift of money (the net proceeds of sale subject to testamentary expenses) and the other a gift of land.

(iii) Differences between the times of payment

These do not rebut the presumption of ademption or satisfaction, at any rate where the difference is only a matter of months.[175]

(iv) Direction for the payment of debts prior to ascertainment of residue contained in the will

So far as the presumption of ademption is concerned, any such direction is irrelevant, for a previous will can throw no light on the intention with which a subsequent advance was made.[176] In connection with the satisfaction of a portions debt by a subsequent will, however, a provision giving to a beneficiary under the covenant a share of residue, after payment of debts, shows an intention that the beneficiary shall first be paid what is due under the covenant, and then take in addition his share of what is left.[177] The obligation under the covenant, however, may not be a 'debt' within the provision in the will, in which case the presumption of satisfaction will not be rebutted on this ground.[178]

(i) ADEMPTION—SUBSEQUENT ADVANCEMENT FOLLOWED BY A CODICIL

If the presumption of ademption applies, a subsequent codicil has no effect. 'It is very true that a codicil republishing a will makes the will speak as from its own date for the purpose of passing after-purchased lands, but not for the purpose of reviving a legacy

---

[169] *Pym v Lockyer* (1841) 5 My & Cr 29; *Watson v Watson* (1864) 33 Beav 574.

[170] *Re Jupp* [1922] 2 Ch 359.

[171] *Bellasis v Uthwatt* (1737) 1 Atk 426 (satisfaction); *Spinks v Robins* (1742) 2 Atk 491 (ademption).

[172] *Powys v Mansfield*, supra at 374, 375, per Lord Cottenham.

[173] (1848) 2 HL Cas 131; *Cooper v MacDonald* (1873) LR 16 Eq 258; *Re Cameron (decd)* [1999] 2 All ER 924.

[174] [2002] EWHC 1868, [2002] WTLR 1193.

[175] *Davys v Boucher* (1839) 3 Y & C Ex 397; *Stevenson v Masson* (1873) LR 17 Eq 78.

[176] *Dawson v Dawson*, supra; *Cooper v Macdonald*, supra.

[177] *Lord Chichester v Coventry* (1867) LR 2 HL 71; *Smyth v Johnston* (1875) 31 LT 876.

[178] *Re Vernon* (1906) 95 LT 48.

revoked, adeemed, or satisfied. The codicil can only act upon the will as it existed at the time; and, at the time, the legacy revoked, adeemed, or satisfied formed no part of it.'[179] Contrary, however, to the further opinion of Lord Cottenham in the same case, it has been held that the codicil can be taken into account in deciding the intention with which the advancement was made.[180]

(j) THE ADMISSION OF EXTRINSIC EVIDENCE

The Court of Appeal stated clear rules in *Re Tussaud's Estate*,[181] though without a full discussion of the somewhat conflicting dicta to be found in earlier cases. First, the rules are the same whether it is a case of satisfaction or ademption. Secondly, if the second instrument contains an expression of intention as to whether there is or is not to be satisfaction, parol evidence will not be admitted to contradict it.[182] Thirdly, if there is no such expression of intention, and no presumption of satisfaction or ademption, extrinsic evidence will not be admitted to raise a plea of satisfaction or ademption.[183] Fourthly, however, if in the circumstances equity raises a presumption of satisfaction or ademption, parol evidence is admissible to rebut that presumption, and also, in such case, counter-evidence is admissible to fortify it.[184] It seems doubtful whether, as stated in *Kirk v Eddowes*,[185] the parol evidence is restricted to declarations made contemporaneously with the second provision: it seems that they are also admissible whether made before or afterwards.[186]

In any case the onus of rebutting a presumption raised by equity rests upon those who allege that in the circumstances it does not apply.[187]

The above rules must now be applied taking account of s 21 of the Administration of Justice Act 1982 which permits extrinsic evidence, including evidence of the testator's intention, to be admitted to assist in the interpretation of the will in so far as it is meaningless, ambiguous on the face of it, or shown to be ambiguous in the light of surrounding circumstances by evidence, other than evidence of the testator's intention.

---

[179] Per Lord Cottenham in *Powys v Mansfield* (1837) 3 My & Cr 359 at 376; *Montagu v Montagu* (1852) 15 Beav 565; *Hopwood v Hopwood* (1859) 7 HL Cas 728; cf *Re Warren* [1932] 1 Ch 42.

[180] *Ravenscroft v Jones* (1864) 4 De GJ & Sm 224; *Re Scott* [1903] 1 Ch 1, CA.

[181] (1878) 9 Ch D 363, CA.   [182] *Kirk v Eddowes* (1844) 3 Hare 509.

[183] *Hall v Hill* (1841) 1 Dr & War 94. Contra, *Monck v Lord Monck* (1810) 1 Ball & B 298; *Kirk v Eddowes* (1844) 3 Hare 509, in cases where the second transaction is not made by an instrument in writing; and see *Re Shields* [1912] 1 Ch 591 perhaps restricting this to cases of agreement between donor and donee.

[184] *Powys v Mansfield* (1837) 3 My & Cr 359; *Kirk v Eddowes*, supra.   [185] Supra.

[186] *Weall v Rice* (1831) 2 Russ & M 251; *Robinson v Whitley* (1804) 9 Ves 577.

[187] *Papillon v Papillon* (1841) 11 Sim 642; *Hopwood v Hopwood* (1859) 7 HL Cas 728.

4 ADEMPTION OF LEGACIES GIVEN FOR A PARTICULAR PURPOSE

The same principles as have been discussed in the preceding section apply, even though the testator is neither the parent nor stands in loco parentis to the legatee, where he 'gives a legacy for one particular purpose only, and after that applies a sum of money to the same purpose'.[188] The crux of the matter is what constitutes a particular purpose: on the one hand, it was held that there was no particular purpose and accordingly no presumption of ademption where a testator bequeathed a legacy of £200 to his wife to be paid within ten days of his death, and subsequently during his last illness, gave her a cheque for £200;[189] and where he gave a legacy to a trustee for the benefit of an infant, and subsequently a gift of the same sum to the same trustee for the same purpose[190]—in substance they were merely gifts to the infant and no particular purpose was declared.[191] On the other hand, there was held to be a particular purpose and accordingly a presumption of ademption in *Re Corbett*,[192] where there was a legacy to the trustees of the endowment fund of a hospital followed by an inter vivos gift of the same amount to the same trustees; and in *Re Jupp*,[193] where both legacy and inter vivos gift were to the trustees of a fund the income of which was to be expended in making up the aggregate income of three sisters, strangers to the testator, to a certain sum, and in meeting their extraordinary expenses incurred through illness or other causes, the balance after the death or marriage of all the sisters to be divided among the subscribers in proportion to their contributions.

This head of satisfaction or ademption was, perhaps, slightly extended by the Court of Appeal in *Re Pollock*[194] to cases where the bequest and subsequent gift are 'expressed to be made in fulfilment of some moral obligation recognized by the testator, and originating in a definite external cause, though not of a kind which (unless expressed) the law would have recognized, or would have presumed to exist'.[195] The idea behind this is said to be the same as that which lies behind the presumption against double portions, namely that as the purpose of both gifts was to fulfil one and the same antecedent obligation or duty, a double fulfilment was presumably not intended. The need for the intention to fulfil a moral obligation to be expressed in the bequest was stressed in *Re Jupp*.[196] *Re Pollock* itself is the leading case in this field, where it was held that there was a presumption of ademption pro tanto: the facts were that a legacy of £500 was given by the testatrix to a niece of her deceased husband, with the words 'according to the wish of my late beloved husband', and a

---

[188] *Roome v Roome* (1744) 3 Atk 181 at 183 per Fortescue MR; *Debeze v Mann* (1789) 2 Bro CC 519; *Re Pollock* (1885) 28 Ch D 552, CA.

[189] *Pankhurst v Howell* (1870) 6 Ch App 136.   [190] *Re Smythies* [1903] 1 Ch 259.

[191] *Re Corbett* [1903] 2 Ch 326; *Re Jupp* [1922] 2 Ch 359.   [192] Supra.   [193] Supra.

[194] (1885) 28 Ch D 552, CA.   [195] *Re Pollock*, supra at 556, CA per Selbourne LC.

[196] [1922] 2 Ch 359.

subsequent gift was described in contemporaneous entries in her diary as 'a legacy from' the niece's 'uncle John', that is, the testatrix's husband.

5 PERFORMANCE

(a) GENERALLY

Performance is closely related to satisfaction,[197] and in the older cases one finds that what would now be classified as performance is commonly referred to as satisfaction by implication. The doctrine has been much reduced in importance by the changes made in the law of intestate succession by the property legislation of 1925. The principle behind the cases has been said[198] to be that 'where a man covenants to do an act, and he does an act which may be converted to a completion of this covenant, it shall be supposed that he meant to complete it', or, in other words,[199] 'that a person is to be presumed to do that which he is bound to do; and if he has done anything, that he has done it in pursuance of his obligation'. The cases fall naturally into two groups.

(b) COVENANT TO PURCHASE AND SETTLE LAND

Where a man has covenanted to purchase and settle land[200] or to convey and settle land,[201] or to pay money to trustees to be laid out by them in the purchase of land,[202] and has failed to carry out his obligation; but has nevertheless subsequently to the covenant purchased lands, the court will, under this doctrine, presume that the purchase was made in performance or part performance of the covenant. The effect of the doctrine, and indeed many of the rules, can be seen from the leading case of *Lechmere v Lady Lechmere*:[203] it will be remembered that when this case was decided, on intestacy realty descended to the heir-at-law but personalty passed to the next-of-kin. In *Lechmere v Lady Lechmere*,[204] Lord Lechmere, by marriage articles in 1719, covenanted to lay out £30,000 within one year of the marriage in the purchase, with the consent of trustees, of freehold lands in fee simple in possession, to be settled on Lord Lechmere for life and after his death a jointure to his widow, with remainder to the sons of the marriage in tail male, and an ultimate remainder to Lord Lechmere in fee simple. At the date of the marriage Lord Lechmere was already seised of some lands in fee simple. After the marriage he purchased and contracted to purchase several estates in fee simple, but not within the year nor with the consent of the trustees: he also

---

[197] See *Scrimes v Nickle* (1982) 130 DLR (3d) 698.
[198] Per Kenyon MR in *Sowden v Sowden* (1785) 1 Cox Eq Cas 165 at 166; *Weyland v Weyland* (1742) 2 Atk 632.
[199] Per Brougham LC in *Tubbs v Broadwood* (1831) 2 Russ & M 487 at 493.
[200] *Lechmere v Lady Lechmere* (1735) Cas temp Talb 80.   [201] *Deacon v Smith* (1746) 3 Atk 323.
[202] *Sowden v Sowden* (1785) 1 Cox Eq Cas 165.   [203] Supra.   [204] Supra.

purchased some estates for lives, and some reversionary estates in fee, expectant upon lives. None of these estates was settled in accordance with the covenant. Lord Lechmere died in 1727 intestate and without issue, but leaving his widow surviving him. Under the doctrine of conversion it was held that the £30,000 ought to be treated as land and go to the heir-at-law, who was, of course, entitled to all the realty of which Lord Lechmere died seised. The heir-at-law accordingly claimed, first, all the deceased's realty, and, secondly, that £30,000 should be raised out of personalty and laid out in accordance with the articles with the result that it would pass to him under the ultimate remainder. The next of kin, while admitting the prima facie validity of the claim, argued that the estates purchased by Lord Lechmere must be taken to have been made in part performance of the covenant, and their value deducted from the £30,000 claimed by the heir-at-law. The next-of-kin's plea had a limited success. It was held that the estates of which Lord Lechmere was already in possession could not be regarded as performance of the covenant in the articles, since they were acquired before there was any obligation capable of being performed. Again the estates for lives and the reversionary estates expectant upon lives, being of a different nature from those covenanted to be settled, could not be taken in part performance. The estates in fee purchased or contracted to be purchased were, however, to be taken in part performance of the covenant, notwithstanding that they were not purchased within a year of the marriage, for time was not the essence of the matter, nor with the consent of the trustees, for this was merely to prevent unreasonable purchases and it does not matter if the purchases made are in fact reasonable.

The same presumption of performance was held to apply in *Tubbs v Broadwood*,[205] where the obligation to purchase was imposed, not by covenant or contract, but by statute.

(c) COVENANT TO LEAVE MONEY

Where a man has covenanted that he will leave, or that his executors will pay, a sum of money or a share of his personalty to another, and has then died intestate, but that other has taken a share of the personalty under the law of intestate succession, such share is presumed to be taken in performance, or part performance, of the covenant. The leading case is *Blandy v Widmore*,[206] where by marriage articles a man covenanted to leave his wife £620 on his death: he died intestate, but the wife's share on intestacy was worth more than £620. It was held that this must be taken in performance of the covenant. This was followed in *Lee v Cox and D'Aranda*,[207] and in *Garthshore v Chalie*,[208] where the cases were fully discussed by Lord Eldon. The doctrine has been

---

205 (1831) 2 Russ & M 487.
206 (1715) 1 P Wms 324, applied in *Goldsmid v Goldsmid* (1818) 1 Swan 211 to a case where by reason of the death or renunciation of the executor the estate had to be distributed according to the rules applicable to an intestacy.
207 (1747) 3 Atk 419, 1 Ves Sen 1.   208 (1804) 10 Ves 1. Cf *Re Hall* [1918] 1 Ch 562.

held to apply to a case where a father covenanted to exercise a special power of appointment by will in favour of a daughter, and failed to do so, the daughter also being one of the persons entitled in default of appointment.[209]

The fact that the direction is to pay, say, three or six months after death, while, in the administration of the estate, payment could not be claimed until a year after the death, does not matter,[210] but it is different if there is a covenant by a man to pay during his lifetime which is broken before his death. Thus in *Oliver v Brickland*,[211] a man covenanted to pay a sum of money within two years of his marriage, and if he died that his executors should pay it. He lived more than two years and died intestate. It was held that the widow's share on intestacy was not to be taken in performance of the covenant.

Finally it has been persuasively contended[212] that a presumption of performance may arise in the case of a gift by will as well as on intestacy. The obligation and the testamentary gift must, however, be identical and there will be no performance of a covenant to pay money by the gift of a legacy payable at a later date than the debt,[213] or of a legacy of specific chattels.[214]

---

[209] *Thacker v Key* (1869) LR 8 Eq 408.   [210] *Garthshore v Chalie*, supra.

[211] Cited in *Lee v Cox* and *D'Aranda*, supra incorrectly cited sub nom *Oliver v Brighouse* in the report in Ves Sen. See Ves Sen Supp 1.

[212] (1964) 38 ALJ 145. Contra, Halsbury's *Laws of England*, 4th edn (Reissue), vol 16(2) para 757.

[213] *Haynes v Mico* (1781) 1 Bro CC 129.   [214] *Devese v Pontet* (1785) 1 Cox Eq Cas 188.

33

THE EQUITABLE DOCTRINE
OF ELECTION

Election 'is a principle which the courts apply in the exercise of an equitable jurisdiction enabling them to secure a just distribution in substantial accordance with the general scheme of the instrument'.[1] More particularly, as Lord Cairns observed,[2] by this doctrine 'where a deed or will professes to make a general disposition of property for the benefit of a person named in it, such person cannot accept a benefit under the instrument without at the same time conforming to all its provisions, and renouncing every right inconsistent with them.' In other words, as Lord Redesdale said,[3] 'the general rule is, that a person cannot accept and reject the same instrument, and this is the foundation of the law of election'. Though, in general, the rules elaborating this general principle apply equally to deeds and wills, it is convenient to treat its application to each of them separately.

1 ELECTION UNDER A WILL

(a) APPLICATION OF THE DOCTRINE TO WILLS

'The ordinary principle is clear that if a testator gives property by design or by mistake which is not his to give, and gives at the same time[4] to the real owner of it other property, such real owner cannot take both.'[5] Thus if a testator by his will devises Blackacre, which in fact belongs to George, to Mary, and elsewhere in the will bequeaths George a legacy of £50,000, George will have to elect. George cannot, of course, be compelled to give up his own property, Blackacre, over which the testator

---

[1] Per Lord Haldane in *Brown v Gregson* [1920] AC 860 at 868, HL.

[2] *Codrington v Codrington* (1875) LR 7 HL 854 at 861, 862. Cf *Re Edwards* [1958] Ch 168, [1957] 2 All ER 495, CA.

[3] In *Birmingham v Kirwan* (1805) 2 Sch & Lef 444 at 450.

[4] Prima facie the two gifts must be contained in the same instrument, but two wills—*Douglas-Menzies v Umphelby* [1908] AC 224, PC—or two contemporaneous documents—*Bacon v Cosby* (1871) 4 De G & Sm 261—may be treated as one for this purpose.

[5] Per James VC in *Wollaston v King* (1869) LR 8 Eq 165.

had no disposing power. What he can be compelled to do, however, if necessary by proceedings in the courts,[6] is to elect, as it is said, to take either under the will or against it. If he elects to take under the will, he will be entitled to receive all the benefits given to him by the will, but will have to allow his own property, of which the testator wrongfully purported to dispose, to be treated as if it belonged to the testator,[7] that is in the case put he will be entitled to his legacy of £50,000, but will have to convey Blackacre to Mary. Alternatively he may elect to take against the will, which means that he insists, as he is fully entitled to, on keeping his own property. If he does this, however, the benefits which he would otherwise be able to claim under the will must be used so far as may be necessary to compensate the person who is disappointed by this insistence on keeping his own property. Thus, in the case put, if George insists on keeping Blackacre, Mary will be disappointed of her testamentary expectations. George, however, will not get his legacy of £50,000 in full. Mary will be paid out of it the value of Blackacre, and George will be able to claim only the balance. If Blackacre should be worth more than £50,000, Mary cannot get more than that sum; in such case George will clearly get nothing under the will, but will, of course, continue to hold Blackacre.

(b) LEGAL BASIS OF THE DOCTRINE[8]

In the early cases[9] the doctrine is often said to be based upon a tacit or implied condition that the person to whom the testator has given his property is only to take if he allows his property to go over to the person to whom the testator has purported to give it. This theory has rather fallen into disfavour, for, as has been pointed out, while failure to comply with an express condition would cause forfeiture of the interest granted, under the doctrine of election a person who insists on keeping his own property only has his interest under the will taken away so far as necessary to compensate the person disappointed for his disappointment.

Again it is only in a limited sense that the doctrine can be said to depend on the intent of the testator. In *Cooper v Cooper*[10] Lord Cairns said in so many words that the rule did not proceed either upon an expressed intention, or upon a conjecture of a presumed intention. In the same case Lord Hatherly said that the only relevant intent, apart from an intention to dispose of property not belonging to the testator, was the ordinary intent implied in the case of any man who makes a will that he intends that every part of it shall be effective. Effect is given to this latter intent, erroneously based

---

[6] *Douglas v Douglas* (1871) LR 12 Eq 617.

[7] It becomes subject to all the incidents to which it would have been subject if it had been the testator's property, such as his debts—*Re Williams* [1915] 1 Ch 450.

[8] See (1990) 106 LQR 487 and 572 (N Crago) and the comment in response at (1990) 106 LQR 571 (P J Millett). See also (1998) 114 LQR 621 (Elise B Histed).

[9] See eg *Noys v Mordaunt* (1706) 2 Vern 581; *Streatfield v Streatfield* (1735) Cas temp Talb 176; *Bor v Bor* (1756) 3 Bro Parl Cas 167; *Ker v Wauchope* (1819) 1 Bligh 1.

[10] (1874) LR 7 HL 53.

though it usually is on a wrong belief that property belonging to another belonged to the testator, by the doctrine of election. This theory has been applied in cases such as *Re Vardon's Trusts*[11] where the beneficial interest given to the person called upon to elect had been given on terms rendering it inalienable. This restriction was held to show a particular intention inconsistent with and capable of rebutting the general intention that every part of the will should take effect and accordingly there was no case for election.

Probably, however, it is best to adopt the view of Lord Cairns[12] that the doctrine of election 'proceeds on a rule of equity founded upon the highest principles of equity, and as to which the court does not occupy itself in finding out whether the rule was present or not present to the mind of the party making the will'. As was said more recently[13] 'it is a doctrine by which equity fastens on the conscience of the person who is put to his election and refused to allow him to take the benefit of a disposition contained in the will, the validity of which is not in question, except on certain conditions'.

(c) COMPENSATION NOT FORFEITURE

Although there was doubt expressed in some of the earliest cases on election. It was fairly soon settled that if a person elected to take against the will, he did not lose his legacy altogether, but only to the extent necessary to compensate the persons disappointed thereby for their disappointment.[14] Of course, depending on the relative values, it might be that the entire legacy would be needed for the purposes of compensation. It is, however, clear that no more compensation can be required than the value of the testator's own property given to the person called upon to elect, even though this is inadequate to compensate for the disappointment. 'The obligation [to compensate] is only to the extent of the benefit he derives: it cannot go beyond that.'[15] Jessel MR[16] has pointed out that what really happens when a person elects to take against the will is that he claims both to keep his own property and also to take the benefits under the will: equity then steps in and declares that he can only take the latter benefits subject to the obligation to make compensation.

The same principles have been applied in more complex cases. Clearly if more than one person is disappointed, the compensation, if election is made against the will, must be made to the beneficiaries in proportion to their disappointment.[17] Where, in addition, more than one person was called upon to elect, it was held in *Re Booth*[18] that

---

[11] (1885) 31 Ch D 275, CA (a case upon election under a deed).

[12] In *Cooper v Cooper* (1874) LR 7 HL 53 at 67; *Brown v Gregson* [1920] AC 860, [1920] All ER Rep 730, HL.

[13] *Re Mengel's Will Trusts* [1962] Ch 791 at 797, [1962] 2 All ER 490 at 492, per Buckley J.

[14] See eg *Rich v Cockell* (1804) 9 Ves 369; *Ker v Wauchope* (1819) 1 Bligh 1.

[15] Per Jessel MR in *Pickersgill v Rodger* (1876) 5 Ch D 163 at 174.

[16] In *Pickersgill v Rodger*, supra.   [17] *Howells v Jenkins* (1863) 1 De GJ & Sm 617.

[18] [1906] 2 Ch 321.

persons electing to take against the will were respectively bound to make compensation to other persons so electing, as well as to persons who took under the will only, for any disappointment caused by such election, the compensation being limited to the extent of the benefits received under the will by the several persons electing to take against it. It was further held that all compensation so paid to any person electing to take against the will must be included in the benefits received by him under the will.

In any case where election is made against the will, the amount of compensation which has to be paid must be ascertained as at the date of death of the testator.[19]

(d) ELECTION UNDER A POWER OF APPOINTMENT

Before going further it will be convenient to mention special powers of appointment in relation to election. Where a testator has a special power of appointment by will he can only appoint to or among a limited number or class of persons—the objects of the power—and if he fails to make a valid appointment other persons, who may or may not also be the objects of the power, will be entitled. Such other persons taking in default of appointment do not claim under the will, but under the instrument creating the power. They are in effect the owners of the property, though their interests are liable to be defeated by an exercise of the power of appointment. Accordingly, if the testator purports to appoint to persons not objects of the power, which appointment is, of course, ineffective, he can be and is regarded as wrongfully purporting to dispose of property belonging to the persons entitled in default of appointment, who will be called upon to elect if they are also given other property of the testator's own. This means that they can either elect to take under the will, by allowing the non-objects to take the property wrongfully appointed to them; or against the will, by insisting on their claims as persons entitled in default, in which case the non-objects will have to be compensated out of the gift of the testator's own property.

There will, however, be no case for election where the appointor, having made an appointment in favour of an object of the power, seeks to impose a trust or condition in favour of a non-object. As Page Wood VC explained in *Woolridge v Woolridge*,[20] 'where there is an absolute[21] appointment by will in favour of a proper object of the power, and that appointment is followed by attempts to modify the interest so appointed in a manner which the law will not allow, the court reads the will as if all the passages in which such attempts are made were swept out of it, for all intents and purposes, that is, not only so far as they attempt to regulate the quantum of interest to be enjoyed by the appointee in the settled property, but also so far as they might otherwise have been relied upon as raising a case of election.' *A fortiori* mere precatory words attached to an appointment do not raise a case of election.[22]

---

[19] *Re Hancock* [1905] 1 Ch 16.

[20] (1859) John 63 at 69; *Churchill v Churchill* (1867) LR 5 Eq 44; *Re Neave* [1938] Ch 793, [1938] 3 All ER 220. Cf *White v White* (1882) 22 Ch D 555.

[21] Cf the rule in *Lassence v Tierney* (1849) 1 Mac & G 551; *Hancock v Watson* [1902] AC 14, HL.

[22] *Blacket v Lamb* (1851) 14 Beav 482; *Langslow v Langslow* (1856) 21 Beav 552.

(e) THE ESSENTIALS OF ELECTION

The essentials of election are that there should be an intention on the part of the testator or testatrix to dispose of certain property; secondly that the property should not if fact be the testator's or testatrix's own property; and thirdly, that a benefit should be given by the will to the true owner of the property.[23] It is clear that it is wholly immaterial whether the testator thought he had power to dispose of the property over which he had in fact no such power, or whether he knowingly purported to dispose of property not his own. In nearly every case the testator in fact has made a mistake as to his power of disposition, very often by exercising a power of appointment in favour of someone not an object of the power, but the rule in regard to election applies in precisely the same way whether or not the testator knows he is purporting to dispose of the property of another.[24]

An apparent intention on the face of the will to dispose of property which in fact at the date of death does not belong to the testator will not give rise to a case for election, if the true view of the matter is that there is no real intention to make the apparent testamentary disposition. This may happen as a result of ademption. If, for example, a testator by his will devised Blackacre of which he was the owner at the date of the will to X, and subsequently in his lifetime sold and conveyed Blackacre to Y, the devise in the will to X must obviously fail. The devise is said to have been adeemed, which means that the will has to be read as if there were no gift of that property in the will at all. 'The true position in such a case is', it has been said, 'that the testamentary disposition has clean gone.'[25] Accordingly, the testator would not be regarded as manifesting any intention to devise Blackacre and no case for election could arise, even though a legacy were given to Y. The Court of Appeal, in Re Edwards,[26] held that the same principle applied where the testatrix had entered into a specifically enforceable contract relating to the property between the date of her will and the date of her death, thus bringing into play the doctrine of conversion.

In order to raise a case of election it is vital that the intention to dispose shall relate to property which does not belong to the testator. The courts are naturally slow to hold that a person has purported to dispose of property over which he has no power of disposition, and if general words are used by a testator they will prima facie be taken to refer only to property over which he has such power and thus not raise a case of election.[27] 'A man must be presumed to have intended to have devised what he actually possessed. The onus probandi lay on the parties who alleged the contrary.'[28] Questions have often been raised in cases where a testator has used words which

---

[23] Re Edwards [1958] Ch 168 at 175, [1957] 2 All ER 495 at 499, CA, per Jenkins LJ.

[24] Cooper v Cooper (1874) LR 7 HL 53; Pitman v Crum Ewing [1911] AC 217, HL; Re Harris [1909] 2 Ch 206 and see Re Brooksbank (1886) 34 Ch D 160.

[25] Re Edwards, supra at 177, 500, 501, CA, per Jenkins LJ.

[26] Supra, and see (1957) 21 Conv 152. Cf Plowden v Hyde (1852) 2 Sim NS 171.

[27] See eg Blomart v Player (1826) 2 Sim & St 597; Re Harris [1909] 2 Ch 206; Re Booker (1886) 54 LT 239.

[28] Per Turner LJ in Evans v Evans (1863) 2 New Rep 408 at 410.

would be wide enough to carry an absolute interest but where he has in fact only a limited interest: in general in such cases, the provision will be construed as referring only to the limited interest. 'It is difficult in any case to apply the doctrine of election where the testator has some interest in the estate disposed of, though it may not be entirely his own.'[29] In such a case, 'the court will lean as far as possible to a construction which would make him deal only to that to which he was entitled'.[30] Where, however, on its construction, the will must be taken to refer not only to the limited interest of the testator, but also to the interest of another, there may be a case for election: there is no rule that only a positive declaration to that effect can show the wider intention.[31] Thus in *Padbury v Clark*,[32] for instance, the testator, who was entitled only to moiety of a freehold house, devised 'all that my freehold messuage or tenement, with the garden . . . now on lease to X and in his occupation' to one and gave property of his own to the owner of the other moiety. Elsewhere in his will he devised a moiety of another property to which he was entitled in proper words. It was held that the intention to dispose of the entirety of the freehold house was clear, and accordingly the other owner of a moiety thereof was put to his election. And in *Re Mengel's Will Trusts*,[33] where the property of the testator and his wife was subject to the Danish law of community of assets, it was held that the testator, by his bequest of 'all my personal and household goods and effects' purported to dispose of the whole property in those goods, that is both his own share and the share of his wife,[34] though in the same will the disposition of residue was held to extend only to the testator's own property, in accordance with the principle that a mere general devise or bequest will not raise a case of election. Exceptionally, even a gift of residue had been held to raise a case of election where in the context, on the true construction of the will, the testator intended to refer thereby to the property of a beneficiary.[35]

It can now be regarded as settled[36] that the intention of the testator to dispose of property not his own must appear from the will itself: if on the face of it the will does not appear to attempt to dispose of another's property, extrinsic evidence directed to show that the testator regarded himself as the owner of some other's property and

---

[29] Per Lord Eldon in *Lord Rancliffe v Lady Parkyns* (1818) 6 Dow 149 at 185; *Miller v Thurgood* (1864) 33 Beav 496.

[30] *Howells v Jenkins* (1862) 2 John & H 706 at 713, per Page Wood V-C; affd (1863) 1 De GJ & Sm 617; *Re Mengel's Will Trusts* [1962] Ch 791, [1962] 2 All ER 490.

[31] *Wintour v Clifton* (1856) 8 De GM & G 641; *Usticke v Peters* (1858) 4 K & J 437.

[32] (1850) 2 Mac & G 298; *Miller v Thurgood* (1864) 33 Beav 496; *Wilkinson v Dent* (1871) 6 Ch App 339.

[33] [1962] Ch 791, [1962] 2 All ER 490.

[34] It is difficult to understand, however, how the court came to the conclusion that there was a case for election, since the wife's interest under community of assets was not given to a stranger, but to the wife herself.

[35] *Re Allen's Estate* [1945] 2 All ER 264, criticized on another point Cheshire, *Private International Law*, 13th edn, p 1005; (1945) 10 Conv 102 (J H C Morris); Dicey and Morris, *Conflict of Laws*, 13th edn, p 1046. And see *Orrell v Orrell* (1871) 6 Ch App 302.

[36] But see Jessel MR in *Pickersgill v Rodger* (1876) 5 Ch D 163 at 171 where cases subsequent to *Pulteney v Lord Darlington*, a decision of Thurlow LC cited in *Pole v Lord Somers* (1801) 6 Ves 309 at 314, and *Hinchcliffe v Hinchcliffe* (1797) 3 Ves 516 at 521, do not appear to have been cited.

must have intended to dispose of it by some general or residuary disposition will not be admitted. The early case of *Pulteney v Lord Darlington*[37] held to the contrary, but has been disapproved in numerous cases, and it is submitted that the rule set out above, as stated in subsequent cases,[38] now represents the law.

(f) GIFTS OF THE TESTATOR'S OWN PROPERTY

There can be no case for election unless the testator has given some of his own property to the person called upon to elect, out of which compensation can be made in case he elects to take against the instrument. Thus in *Bristow v Warde*[39] a father had a power of appointment over certain stock in favour of his children, who were also entitled in default of appointment. He appointed part of the stock to his children, and a part to persons not objects of the power, but gave no property of his own to his children. It was held that there was no case for election, the children being fully entitled to keep both what was appointed to them, and also what came to them in default of appointment by reason of the invalid appointment to non-objects. But in *Whistler v Webster,*[40] on similar facts, save that the children were also given legacies out of the testator's own property, the children had to elect. 'In all cases there must be some free disposable property given to the person, which can be made a compensation for what the testator takes away.'[41] Provided, however, that the testator's own property which is given is bounty, it makes no difference that it is expressly given in payment of a statute barred obligation.[42]

Even where there is a gift to the person called upon to elect of the testator's own property, there will be no case for election unless the interest given to such person will in his hands be freely available to be applied in compensating the disappointed parties. Accordingly, in *Re Gordon's Will Trusts*[43] the doctrine of election was excluded where the person it was alleged should elect was given by the testatrix a protected life interest[44] under s 33 of the Trustee Act 1925,[45] which interest he was incapable of alienating.

---

[37] Supra, followed with reluctance in *Druce v Denison* (1801) 6 Ves 385; *Guillebaud v Meares* (1829) 7 LJOS Ch 136.

[38] *Doe d Oxenden v Chichester* (1816) 4 Dow 65, HL; *Clementston v Gandy* (1836) 1 Keen 309; *Re Harris* [1909] 2 Ch 206.

[39] (1794) 2 Ves 336; *Re Fowler's Trust* (1859) 27 Beav 362; *Re Aplin's Trusts* (1865) 13 WR 1062.

[40] (1794) 2 Ves 367.   [41] *Bristow v Warde* (1794) 2 Ves 336 at 350, per Loughborough LC.

[42] *Re Fletcher's Settlement Trusts* [1936] 2 All ER 236.

[43] [1978] Ch 145, [1978] 2 All ER 969, CA, revsg the judge below whose decision was criticized in (1977) 93 LQR 65 (P H Pettit) and (1977) 41 Conv 188 (T G Watkin).

[44] The statutory trusts were in fact varied, but this did not affect the result. It may be noted that there was a case for election in respect of other unfettered gifts in the will.

[45] See p 79 et seq, supra.

(g) ALIENABILITY OF THE PROPERTY WRONGFULLY PURPORTED TO BE DISPOSED OF

Where the property of the person whom it is alleged should elect is not freely alienable, so that it would be impossible for him to elect effectively to take under the will, no case for election arises. Thus in *Re Chesham*[46] the testator purported to dispose in favour of younger brothers of heirlooms over which his eldest son had no power of disposition, and gave that son other benefits. It was held that there was no case for election and that the eldest son was accordingly entitled to enjoy the heirlooms and take the other benefits in full.

It was contended, indeed, in *Re Dicey*[47] that election only arises when the person on whom the obligation falls can, if he elects in favour of the will, secure that the relevant provisions of the will take effect precisely according to their terms. There, subject to the testatrix's life interest, the proceeds of sale of Blackacre belonged as to one half to the defendant and as to a quarter each to the plaintiff and the plaintiff's brother. The testatrix purported to devise the whole of Blackacre to the plaintiff and gave other property of her own to the defendant. Accordingly, the most that the defendant could do, by electing to take under the will, was to secure for the plaintiff an absolute beneficial interest in three quarters of the proceeds of the sale of Blackacre. The court, however, refused to hold that the obligation to elect should depend on the chance of the existence of some outstanding interest in the property, however small it might be, in a third party, which was unaffected by the question of election. The defendant, therefore, had to elect. In so deciding the court affirmed the decision in *Fytche v Fytche*[48] that if two or more persons are called on to elect each of them has not only an individual obligation but an individual right to elect and can exercise it independently of the way in which the right may be exercised by the other or others. The following illustration was given in *Re Dicey*:[49]

A testator gives Blackacre or the proceeds of its sale to A. Blackacre in fact belongs to B, C and D as joint tenants and the testator gives legacies to each of these persons. Each of them has a separate and individual right and obligation to elect for or against the will notwithstanding that the gift to A can only take full effect according to its terms if B, C and D all elect in favour of the will. In other words, a class is not exempted from the principle of election merely because each can contribute only a part of the total subject-matter of the gift which the testator has purported to effect.

The principle is exactly the same if persons are entitled successively instead of concurrently.[50]

[46] (1886) 31 Ch D 466.   [47] [1957] Ch 145, [1956] 3 All ER 696, CA.
[48] (1868) 19 LT 343; less well reported in (1868) LR 7 Eq 494; *Cooper v Cooper* (1874) LR 7 HL 53.
[49] [1957] Ch 145 at 158, [1956] 3 All ER 696 at 702; per Romer LJ, reading the judgment of CA.
[50] *Ward v Baugh* (1799) 4 Ves 623.

(h) THE RULE AGAINST PERPETUITIES

Although there has been powerful adverse criticism,[51] it can now, for practical purposes, be regarded as settled that where a testator exercises a special power of appointment in such a way that the appointment is void by reason of its offending against a rule of law such as the rule against perpetuities, there is no case for election. The persons entitled in default of appointment will be entitled to claim the property as invalidly appointed, and also to claim in full any benefits given to them by the testator out of his own property, even though they might be able to carry out the testator's wishes without any infringement of the rule. This might be possible because the perpetuity period in the case of a special power of appointment runs from the date when the power was created not from the date when it is exercised, but the limitations in a void appointment might well be good if contained in a settlement or trust set up on the testator's death by the persons who it would be claimed should elect.[52] The reason behind this rule is said to be that the court will not assist a testator to evade a rule of law founded on public policy,[53] and it has been said[54] that the will must be read as if the clause which is void for perpetuity were not there. The matter has not been before the courts since the passing of the Perpetuities and Accumulations Act 1964, which does not, however, affect the position directly though it perhaps makes the reasons given sound less convincing.

(i) CLAIM DEHORS THE WILL

In *Wollaston v King*[55] it was clearly stated that 'the rule as to election is to be applied as between a gift under a will and a claim dehors the will, and adverse to it, and is not to be applied as between one clause in a will and another clause in the same will'. There a testatrix had a special power of appointment. By her will she made an appointment of a part of the fund which was void for perpetuity and then made a general residuary appointment to three objects of the power, who were also given other benefits by the will out of the testatrix's own property. This was not a case of default of appointment, for in so far as the appointment failed, it was swept up in the general residuary appointment which accordingly applied to the whole fund. It was held, therefore, that there was no case for election: the residuary appointees took the whole fund under the residuary appointment in the will, and the other benefits also under the will.

Although the above rule was accepted in *Bate v Willats*,[56] and repeated, obiter, by

---

[51] See Gray on *Perpetuities*, 4th edn, section 541 et seq; Morris and Leach, *The Rule Against Perpetuities*, 2nd edn, p 158. The argument is that there is no difference in principle between an appointment void for remoteness, and one which is void as being an excessive exercise of the power.

[52] *Wollaston v King* (1869) LR 8 Eq 165; *Re Oliver's Settlement* [1905] 1 Ch 191; *Re Nash* [1910] 1 Ch 1, CA, overruling *Re Bradshaw* [1902] 1 Ch 436.

[53] See eg *Re Oliver's Settlement* [1905] 1 Ch 191, but see Gray, op cit.

[54] *Re Warren's Trusts* (1884) 26 Ch D 208 at 219, per Pearson J.

[55] (1869) LR 8 Eq 165 at 174.   [56] (1877) 37 LT 221.

Viscount Maugham in *Lissenden v CAV Bosch Ltd*,[57] it has met with academic criticism[58] and was not applied by Neville J in the curious case of *Re Macartney*.[59] There the testator by his will gave a sum of colonial stock to his daughter Maggie and all his shares in the Company X to his seven children including Maggie, in varying proportions. The testator held substantially all the issued share capital of the company, and that company had promoted company Y and held 90 per cent of its issued share capital. The colonial stock was in fact held by the testator in trust for company Y, so that the gift to Maggie failed. The court held that the legatees of the shares of company X could not take the benefit of their legacies without compensating Maggie in respect of her legacy of the stock, and that such compensation was a charge on their legacies in an equal amount to the value of the stock on the death of the testator. It is clear that this decision cannot stand with the above stated rule in *Wollaston v King*,[60] and it is accordingly submitted that it is wrongly decided. It is further submitted that in all cases, not only in most cases as stated in *Re Macartney*,[61] where there are two claims made under the will, the only question is one of finding the intention of the testator on the true construction of the will itself. There are other grounds on which the decision in *Re Macartney*[62] seems to be unsatisfactory. As decided, it did not give the legatees of the shares any right of election at all: they had no choice to take either under or against the will, for the court decreed that they were to take the shares charged with the payment of a sum to compensate Maggie. There was no alternative—save to refuse the legacy altogether—and it was made clear that the other benefits received from the testator were not in any way liable. Even assuming that there was a prima facie case for election, it is submitted that *Re Chesham*[63] was not and cannot be validly distinguished, for on the facts of *Re Macartney*[64] it does not seem that the legatees of the shares had the power, even if they wished, to transfer the colonial stock to Maggie. The stock belonged to company Y and a gift of the company's property to a stranger would be ultra vires the company.[65] Indeed, Neville J seems to have failed to recognize the significance of the interposition of companies X and Y between the legatees of the shares and the colonial stock. He apparently took it for granted that the legatees of the shares in company X were the beneficial owners of the stock in fact beneficially owned by company Y, but, even disregarding the further remove, shareholders in a company have long since ceased to be regarded as having any equitable interest in the assets of the company; they 'are not, in the eye of the law, part owners of the undertaking'.[66] This being so it would seem to follow that no case for election arose.

---

[57] [1940] AC 412 at 419, [1940] 1 All ER 425 at 429, HL.

[58] See Gray on *Perpetuities*, 4th edn, p 541 et seq. The main point made is that the appointees do not really claim under the will, but under the instrument creating the power.

[59] [1918] 1 Ch 300. [60] (1869) LR 8 Eq 165. [61] [1918] 1 Ch 300.

[62] Supra. [63] (1886) 31 Ch D 466 and see p 771, supra. [64] Supra.

[65] See Gower & Davies, *Principles of Modern Company Law*, 7th edn, p 130 et seq as to the present position in relation to the doctrine of ultra vires.

[66] Per Evershed MR in *Short v Treasury Comrs* [1948] 1 KB 116 at 122, [1947] 2 All ER 298 at 301, CA; affd [1948] AC 534, [1948] 2 All ER 509, HL; and see Gower, op cit, p 358.

(j) ELECTION BY THE HEIR

It is settled that a case for election arises in English law where a testator has purported or attempted to dispose of foreign land in a way not effective by the foreign law[67] and has given English land[68] or, being domiciled in England, any moveables[69] to the foreign heir who takes that land. Such heir, claiming adversely to the will, will, prima facie, be called upon to elect, not only where or in so far as the foreign law deprives the testator of any power of disposition over the property,[70] but also where the testator had a power of disposition, but his purported exercise of it is ineffective because of failure to comply with the necessary formalities.[71]

The prima facie rule that there is a case for election where a testator has disposed of foreign land in a way not effective by the foreign law, has, in accordance with the principle previously discussed,[72] no application where it would be impossible for the foreign heir, who is alleged should elect, to deal with the property which devolves on him as heir in accordance with the terms of the will. Thus it was held that there was no case for election where a testator declared trusts of his Argentine land, which were invalid by Argentine law, because his children, who took as foreign heirs and who were given other benefits by the will, could not by any act of their own render the lands subject to the trusts of the will, such trusts being invalid by the law of Argentina whether created inter vivos or by will.[73]

Before 1926 the position of the heir-at-law of English real estate caused some difficulty. The heir-at-law was abolished by the Administration of Estates Act 1925, in respect of deaths after 1925, and there do not seem to be any circumstances in which the persons entitled on intestacy can be called on to elect. The primary reason is that in relation to property passing to persons on intestacy, the testator cannot, by an ineffective disposition thereof, be said to be purporting to dispose of property not his own but belonging to the intestate successors, for the intestate successors have no beneficial interest in any of the assets, unless or until an assent or conveyance is made in their favour.[74]

This subsection should not be concluded without mentioning by way of contrast the rule that if a legacy is given upon the express condition that the heir should give up the realty, he will forfeit the legacy if he refuses to do so.[75] The distinction between

---

[67] Scottish law is foreign law for this purpose. The Scottish law of approbate and reprobate has often been said to be the same as the English doctrine of election, and Scottish cases where the testator has been made a disposition of English realty ineffective by English law may accordingly be cited as authorities also on the English doctrine—*Ker v Wauchope* (1819) 1 Bligh 1; *Pitman v Crum Ewing* [1911] AC 217, HL; *Lissenden v CAV Bosch Ltd* [1940] AC 412, [1940] 1 All ER 425, HL.

[68] Governed by the *lex situs*.   [69] Governed by the *lex domicilii*.

[70] *Haynes v Foster* [1901] 1 Ch 361; *Re Ogilvie* [1918] 1 Ch 492.

[71] *Dundas v Dundas* (1830) 2 Dow & Cl 349; *Orrell v Orrell* (1871) 6 Ch App 302; *Brown v Gregson* [1920] AC 860, [1920] All ER Rep 730, HL.

[72] See p 771, supra.   [73] *Brown v Gregson*, supra; *Hewit's Trustees v Lawson* (1891) 18 R 793.

[74] See p 38, supra.   [75] *Boughton v Boughton* (1750) 2 Ves Sen 12.

the doctrine of election and the case of an express condition was completely settled at an early date, though often criticized as anomalous.[76] The anomaly was clear enough at a time when the doctrine of election was regarded as based on an implied condition[77] but is less apparent on the view taken in more modern cases that the doctrine of election is based entirely on principles of equity, and is settled as giving rise to compensation, not forfeiture.[78]

(k) DERIVATIVE INTERESTS

Where X, the person who should have elected, dies without having done so[79] there may be two alternative sets of circumstances. On the one hand, the same person may be entitled, under X's will or on his intestacy, so far as it passes thereunder, both to the property of X of which the original testator wrongfully purported to dispose, and also to the original testator's property given beneficially to X. In such a case, that person will have the same right and duty of electing as X had during his lifetime.[80] On the other hand X's own property may go to A, and the property of the original testator given to him to B. In such a case it is sometimes said that there is a presumed election against the instrument. It is clear that X's own property passes to A unfettered, while B only takes the original testator's property after compensation has been made out of it to the persons disappointed. In fact as Jessel MR observed in *Pickersgill v Rodger*,[81] there is in such case no power of election in the ordinary sense. 'You must treat the case as if each of those two persons took his property separately, and then, as I said before, you must discover upon whose property the obligation lies to make good what is required to satisfy the disappointed legatees.'

There will, however, be no case for election where a person claims derivatively through a person who has himself elected. Thus where a married woman elected to take against a will and retain her interest in Blackacre it was held, after her death, that her husband, as tenant by the courtesy therein, could not be called upon to elect, notwithstanding that he had himself also received benefits under the will.[82] Clearly to have decided otherwise would have meant that the persons disappointed would have been claiming compensation a second time. Further, there will be no case for compensation where the derivative claim is made through someone who could not be called upon to elect, because, for instance, he was given no benefits by the will.[83]

---

[76] *Carey v Askew* (1786) 1 Cox Eq Cas 241; *Sheddon v Goodrich* (1803) 8 Ves 481; *Brodie v Barry* (1813) 2 Ves & B 127.

[77] See section 1(b), p 765, supra.   [78] See section 1(c), p 766, supra.

[79] It is submitted that the decision in *Re Carpenter* (1884) 51 LT 773 that in such a case the personal representatives have the same right and duty of electing was made per incuriam.

[80] *Cooper v Cooper* (1874) LR 7 HL 53.   [81] (1876) 5 Ch D 163 at 174.

[82] *Lady Cavan v Pulteney* (1795) 2 Ves 544; (1797) 3 Ves 384.

[83] *Grissel v Swinhoe* (1869) LR 7 Eq 291.

(1) MODE AND TIME OF ELECTION

It is clear that a person is fully entitled to ascertain the respective values of the properties involved and any other relevant information before he makes his election,[84] and it seems that the court will in general entertain an action for this purpose if necessary.[85] 'Two things', it has been stated,[86] 'are essential to constitute a settled and concluded election by any person who takes an interest under a will, which disposes of property belonging to that person. There must be, in the first place, clear proof that the person put to his election was aware of the nature and extent of his rights; and, in the second place, it must be shewn that, having that knowledge, he intended to elect.' An election made in ignorance of the relevant circumstances will not be binding.[87]

Election may either be express, or may be inferred from the circumstances, and from the acts of the person under an obligation to elect, where the two essentials set out above are satisfied. Moreover, it seems that an express election must be communicated to, or the fact of an unequivocal act have come to the knowledge of, the persons who will be affected by the election.[88] Receiving the income of or dealing with property prima facie implies an election to take it,[89] but even doing so for a long period will not necessarily raise an inference of election where it was done without full knowledge of the rights involved,[90] and 'if a party being bound to elect between two properties, not being called upon so to elect, continues in the receipt of the rents and profits of both, such receipt, affording no proof of preference, cannot be an election to take the one and reject the other'.[91]

The only disabilities which may now prevent a person from electing are minority and mental disorder. In cases of minority the court has sometimes directed that election is to be deferred until the minor attains full age,[92] but the usual practice today is for an election to be made on his behalf after any necessary inquiry as to what would be most for his benefit.[93] As regards a person incapable by reason of mental disorder of managing and administering his property and affairs, the court has similar

---

[84] *Chalmers v Storil* (1813) 2 Ves & B 222; *Pigott v Bagley* (1825) M'Cle & Yo 569.

[85] *Douglas v Douglas* (1871) LR 12 Eq 617 per Wickens V-C.

[86] Per Romilly MR in *Worthington v Wiginton* (1855) 20 Beav 67 at 74; *Spread v Morgan* (1865) 11 HL Cas 588 (election under a deed); *Wilson v Thornbury* (1875) 10 Ch App 239.

[87] *Pusey v Desbouverie* (1734) 3 P Wms 315; *Kidney v Coussmaker* (1806) 12 Ves 136.

[88] In *Re Shepherd* [1943] Ch 8, [1942] 2 All ER 584, where there was an express condition of election, it was held that there was no election, where the interest under the will was reversionary, by writing letters, announcing an intention of electing in a certain way, to trustees who were not persons interested in the election.

[89] *Giddings v Giddings* (1827) 3 Russ 241; *Dewar v Maitland* (1866) LR 2 Eq 834.

[90] *Reynard v Spence* (1841) 4 Beav 103; *Fytche v Fytche* (1868) 19 LT 343 less well reported in LR 7 Eq 494; *Re Turner* (1892) 66 LT 758.

[91] Per Lord Cottenham in *Padbury v Clark* (1850) 2 Mac & G 298 at 306; *Spread v Morgan* (1865) 11 HL Cas 588.

[92] *Boughton v Boughton* (1750) 2 Ves Sen 12.

[93] *Prole v Soady* (1859) 2 Giff 1; *Re Montagu* [1896] 1 Ch 549.

powers and an appropriate election will normally be made for him, after due inquiry as to what is for his benefit, by the Court of Protection.[94]

2 ELECTION UNDER A DEED

In general it is thought that the rules relating to election under a deed are the same as those relating to election under a will, being based on the same principle that a person cannot accept and reject the same instrument. One difference, as Lord Selborne pointed out in *Codrington v Lindsay*,[95] is that the rule in the case of wills that there must be a clear intention on the part of the testator to give that which is not his property is not applicable or appropriate in the case of deeds. A case for election may arise where X had agreed, as consideration for benefits he is to receive thereunder, to bring property into a settlement. If it turns out that for some reason the agreement to bring property into the settlement cannot be enforced, X will have to elect. He can either put his property into the settlement as agreed, when he will be entitled to the agreed benefits; or he can refuse to settle his property, in which case his interest under the settlement will be used, so far as may be required, to compensate other persons entitled under the settlement for their disappointment. Thus in *Anderson v Abbott*[96] there was a post-nuptial, that is, a voluntary, settlement under which the husband and wife covenanted to settle the after-acquired property of the wife. Some after-acquired property was in fact duly transferred to the trustees, and as to this the trust was completely constituted. After the death of the husband, the wife claimed successfully that she could not be compelled to settle her after-acquired property, although it was within the terms of the covenant. The court held, however, that if she stood on her rights and refused to do so, the other persons entitled under the settlement would be able to claim compensation out of her interest therein. Lord Selborne in *Codrington v Lindsay*,[97] after referring to numerous cases said:

in all of them the party who, claiming by a title not bound by the deeds, thereby withdrew part of the consideration for which the deeds were intended to be made, was held obliged to give up, by way of compensation, what he or she was entitled to under the deeds, or ex converso . . . was held bound, if taking the benefit of the deeds, to adopt and make good the contract forming the consideration for those benefits, as to matters by which, without such election, he would not have been bound.[98]

---

[94] See Mental Health Act 1983, Part VII, and cf *Re Earl of Sefton* [1898] 2 Ch 378, CA.

[95] (1873) 8 Ch App 578 at 587, 588; affd sub nom *Codrington v Codrington* (1875) LR 7 HL 854, HL.

[96] (1857) 23 Beav 457; *Brown v Brown* (1866) LR 2 Eq 481; *Codrington v Codrington* (1875) LR 7 HL 854.

[97] (1873) 8 Ch App 578 at 587. Cf *Halsall v Brizell* [1957] Ch 169, [1957] 1 All ER 371; *Tito v Waddell (No 2)* [1977] Ch 106 at 289 et seq, [1977] 3 All ER 129 at 280 et seq.

[98] Eg *Mosley v Ward* (1861) 29 Beav 407.

Finally it may be mentioned that the suggestion made in some early cases[99] that the rule as to deeds was different from that as to wills, involving forfeiture and not compensation, did not find favour with the courts, and later cases take it for granted that the doctrine here is also one of compensation.[100]

---

[99] See eg *Green v Green* (1816) 2 Mer 86.

[100] See eg *Codrington v Codrington*, supra; *Hamilton v Hamilton* [1892] 1 Ch 396; *Re Gordon's Will Trusts* [1978] Ch 145, [1978] 2 All ER 969, CA.

INDEX